NEW UNDERSTANDING

COMPUTER SCIENCE

For Advanced Level

Fourth Edition

Ray Bradley

Stanley Thornes Publishers Ltd

First published in 1987 by Hutchinson Education
Second and third editions published by Stanley Thornes (Publishers) Ltd in 1991 and 1995
Fourth edition published in 1999 by:
Stanley Thornes (Publishers) Ltd
Delta Place
27 Bath Road
Cheltenham
GL53 7TH
United Kingdom

00 01 02 03 / 10 9 8 7 6 5 4

A catalogue record of this book is available from the British Library

ISBN 0 7487 4046 5

Typeset by Florence Production, Stoodleigh, Devon
Printed and bound in Italy by G. Canale & C.S.p.A., Borgaro T.se, Turin

Acknowledgements

Cover image: 'Beautiful Spiral' by Philippe Wautelet.
Visit Philippe's web site at
http://www.ulg.ac.be/aerodyn/people/wautelet/default.html

The author and publishers are grateful to the following examination boards for kind permission to reproduce examination questions:
Associated Examining Board
London Examinations, A Division of Edexcel
Northern Examinations and Assessment Board
Northern Ireland Council for the Curriculum Examinations and Assessment
University of Cambridge Local Examinations Syndicate (incorporating University of Oxford Delegacy of Local Examinations)
Welsh Joint Education Committee

The authors and publishers are grateful to the following for permission to reproduce photographs and other material:
3-COM (UK) Ltd Plate 2; AEB p. 2 (1.1); Apple p. 182 (10.1b), p. 183 (10.1d); @Work p. 60 (use of Java Applet); Axon Images p. 194 (10.12); Britstock IFA (Eric Bach) p. 189 (10.6); Bull HN Information Systems p. 18 (2.9b); Compaq p. 18 (2.8); Cray Research p. 136 (Fortran subroutine); EDEXCEL Foundation p. 198 (10.14); FAST Electronic (UK) Ltd p. 202 (10.18); Eyeball Productions p. 58 (VRML language example); Fujitsu p. 19 (2.10b), p. 223 (11.9a), p. 254 (12.8), Plate 3b; Future Publishing p. 91 (6.1); Hakuto International (UK) Ltd p. 120 (7.4); Hewlett-Packard Ltd Plate 28, Plate 33, Plate 35; IBM Plate 20; Image Bank Plate 6, Plate 25 (Steve Niedorf); Images Colour Library Plate 15; Intel Corporation (UK) Ltd Plate 38; Her Majesty's Stationery Office: p. 573 (extract from Data Protection Act 1998). Reproduced with the permission of the Controller of Her Majesty's Stationery Office; Ken Musgrave Plates 43, 44 and 45; Leslie Garland Picture Library p. 219 (7.17), p. 201 (10.17a), Plate 5; Logitech p. 186 (10.3a), p. 187 (10.4b); Maltron p. 183 (10.1c); Martyn Chillmaid p. 196 (10.13a), p. 200 (10.16a), p. 201 (10.17b); Matrox (UK) Ltd Plate 27; Mikrofax p. 101 et seq. (extracts from The Buyer's Assistant – stock-control system); Microsoft p. 191 (10.8a); Minolta Co. Ltd p. 232 (11.19a); Natwest Group p. 200 (10.16b); NEC p. 213 (11.1c); Nikon UK Limited p. 203 (10.20c); PC World Business Direct: p. 203 (10.19 Intel), p. 203 (10.20a Olympus), p. 203 (10.20b Sony), p. 213 (11.1a Phillips), p. 222 (11.8a Citizen), p. 250 (12.5a Seagate), Plate 7 (Adobe), Plate 7 (Corel), Plate 21 (Psion), Plate 29 (Creative), Plates 32 and 37 (Kingston), Plate 34 (Avantis); Penman Products Ltd p. 231 (11.18b); Pictor Uniphoto p. 250 (12.5b); Precision Flight Controls Inc p. 191 (10.7abc); QCA p. 2 (1.2); Quickshot (Europe) Ltd p. 191 (10.8bc); Rex Features Plate 24 (left); Roland (UK) Ltd p. 230 (11.17b), p. 231 (11.18a); Science Photo Library: p. 130 (7.18a Jerry Mason), p. 130 (7.18b Philippe Plailly), p. 131 (7.20 Philippe Plailly), Plate 8 top (Alfred Pasieka), Plate 8 middle and bottom (Rosenfield Images Ltd), Plate 12 (Sam Ogden), Plate 18 (Steve Horrell), Plate 26 (Klaus Guildbrandsen), Plate 30 (Peter Menzel), Plate 31 (NASA); Silicon Graphics Inc p. 19 (2.11), Plate 1, Plate 3, Plate 4, Plate 9, Plate 10, Plate 13; Sony Electronics Inc Plate 13, p. 25 (3.1), p. 213 (11.1d); Sunset Laboratory Inc. Plate 16; Thrustmaster (Europe) Ltd p. 191 (10.7d); Tony Stone Images Plate 19 (Alfred Wolf); TRIP: p. 121 (7.7 H Rogers), p. 123 (7.9 S Grant), p. 182 (10.1a H Rogers), p. 185 (10.2a, 10.2b S Grant), p. 187 (10.4a H Rogers), p. 230 (11.17a H Rogers), p. 232 (11.19b H Rogers), Plate 11 (Nissan), Plate 14 (N Wilson), Plates 17 and 21 (S Grant), Plates 23 and 24 right (H Rogers); Viglen p. 17 (2.7)

Whilst every effort has been made to contact copyright holders the publishers would like to apologise if any have been overlooked.

Contents

Changes in Computer Science

The only constant in the last few years has been great change! The academic curriculum has undergone many alterations. The computers used on most computer science courses have increased in power by several orders of magnitude. The applications and operating-systems software have become much more sophisticated, and the facilities available to ordinary users have increased out of all recognition. It is interesting to note that, fortunately, much of the content of this book has not had to be changed. There are good reasons for this. **Algorithm design, problem solving, ethical issues** and **data structures,** for example, have remained the same for many years. Computer languages may come and go and fashions change. *However, the fundamental principles outlined in numerous parts of this book will still be useful for many years to come, and this is one of the reasons why computer science is useful as a subject for study in its own right at this level.* It is not simply learning a particular programming language like Java or C++, or learning how the latest systems are making revolutionary changes to our society. These topics, important in themselves, are only part of what goes into making a well-rounded computer science student. A fundamental understanding of the principles involved will prepare you well and make you very employable in the future. You will then be well placed to learn new languages and techniques that will inevitably come along later in your career.

Due to the broad nature of computer science courses *this book is still applicable not only to the **Advanced-level courses,** but very useful too for **BTEC, GNVQs, first degree courses,** which assume no prior knowledge of this subject, and **for Part 1 of the British Computer Society examinations.*** Indeed, some students may find that the 'less rigorous nature' of the Advanced-level course may help them to understand topics, which, quite rightly, are often introduced in highly mathematical ways in most university computer science departments.

The impact of the Internet

It's difficult to believe, but when the 3rd edition of this book was written in 1994, the Internet was not very popular and had not exploded into what we take for granted today. Just a few years ago the technology was such that reliable connection to the Internet was too expensive for many, or at a more affordable price, was slow and unreliable. At that time information available on the Internet was specialist and most of it not relevant to students outside of the university environment.

From just a few paragraphs of coverage in the 3rd edition, to between fifteen and twenty thousand words in the 4th edition – this is a measure of the impact that the Internet has had on computing. There is hardly a chapter in this book that does not mention the Internet in some form. In chapter 1 students are invited to use the Internet to find out the latest curriculum developments from the QCA and the examination boards. It is used as a constant reference throughout for finding up-to-date information on many topics. *For the first time in the history of education, ordinary students now have the tools to find out what's going on in their subject at all levels.* This is a little frightening for some teachers, as most students now have access to vast databases of information, often containing extensions to a subject area that their teacher may not know well, or may not know at all! This is a large challenge to education in general, and to teachers in particular. It does, however, open up a whole new world in which students are not restricted any more by their teaching staff, or the materials available at their school or college. Students can follow up many related areas, which would not usually be available from a conventional paper-based library. They therefore have a rich diversity of information, which, if used wisely, can enhance the learning experience considerably. The government has also recognised the importance of the Internet, and is striving to ensure that all pupils and students in schools and colleges will have access to it. The government is also taking steps to ensure that all school pupils will have e-mail addresses within the next few years. Indeed, it's unlikely that anyone going on to higher education would be able to study effectively without having an e-mail address or access to the Internet and local intranets. Many lecturers and teachers now routinely send out massive amounts of course information in this way.

Key features of the 4th edition

This 4th edition has been considerably enhanced to reflect many of the course requirements for the year 2000 and beyond. Specifically, public-key encryption has been included to reflect this controversial and important topic, and the social implications chapter has been brought right up to date, including a mention of schoolgirl Sarah Flannery's encryption techniques, which won her the *Irish Young Scientist of the Year* contest. The business applications chapter has been expanded to include stock-control systems, retail systems in some detail, banking and finance. It now reflects the importance of training and self-help. The scientific and graphics applications chapter now covers simulations such as forecasting the weather, hurricane prediction, and computing the effects of *El Nino*. The computer network chapters have been updated and a large new chapter has been included on the Internet. The chapters on input, output and storage techniques now reflect the latest technology, including liquid plastics for computer displays, DVD systems, DLT libraries and speech-recognition software. Recent updates to the Data Protection Act are included, and the chapter on software engineering has been considerably enhanced with black-box and white-box testing methodologies. Colour is used effectively in text and diagrams throughout and full colour is used to stunning effect in the plates at intervals through the book.

A comprehensive glossary is included and there is extensive cross-referencing. 'Concept checkpoints' and 'Hints and tips' give advice from obtaining student licences for major software packages, for example, through obtaining cost-effective computer equipment, to getting free software from magazines.

The post-16 curriculum

Like the field of computer science, the post-16 curriculum is also undergoing change which is probably the most important since the introduction of the original Advanced-level qualifications. Several bodies now regulate quality, approve changes and develop new course materials. For example, Edexcel, AQA and OCR, the Unitary Examination Authorities, are some of the awarding bodies who write the existing syllabuses and new Subject Specifications that replace them. The DfEE (a Government department) must approve any changes made. The QCA (Qualifications and Curriculum Authority) is effectively the quality assurance body. The catalyst for these changes was Dearing's 'Review of Qualifications for 16–19 year olds', which outlined the importance of 'breadth of study post 16', 'key skills development', and the 'bridging of the academic/vocational divide', whilst retaining the Advanced-level qualifications. All of these changes will have a major impact on teaching from September 2000, and these principles have contributed much to the development of the 4th edition of this book.

We now have a national qualification framework showing the relationship between the general and vocational qualifications. These are summarised in the following table.

Level	General	General Vocational	Vocational
5	Post-graduate programmes. Professional qualifications.		NVQ5
4	Undergraduate programmes, Professional qualifications.	HND	NVQ4
3	A level	Advanced GNVQ	NVQ3
2	GCSE – Grades A–C	Intermediate GNVQ	NVQ2
1	GCSE – Grades D–G	Foundation GNVQ	NVQ1

Specifically, the structural impact on the Advanced-level course post September 2000 is as follows.

- We now have **Subject Criteria** and *not* a Subject Core
- We will have **Subject Specifications** and *not* Syllabuses

- All boards will offer six equal-sized **modules**, (3 AS and 3 A level)
- Students can choose to have **staged** (January and June) or **end-of-course assessment**
- There will now also be **synoptic assessment** that provides questions across the entire range of the course programme
- **Modules** will now be **individually certified**
- There will be a fixed shelf life for modules (i.e. students can't take forever to do an Advanced-level course!)
- There will be *one opportunity* to resit modules, with the better result counting
- There will be 'signposting' of **Key Skills**, with the main key skills being:
    Application of Number
    Communication and Information Technology

The new title for AS from September 2000 is to be **Advanced Subsidiary** and this is effectively the first half of the Advanced-level course. It is a stand-alone course which counts for 50% of the A-level marks (and will count towards the corresponding UCAS tariff too). Your school or college will have to take some major decisions on how your course is run. For example, do you take some modules early so that your UCAS form looks impressive when you go for a university interview, or do you wait until the end, when a greater degree of maturity is likely to be reflected in your examination answers? *From September 2000 all Advanced-level courses will be modular in nature,* but you will still have the opportunity to take all modules at the final examination sitting.

The **modular nature** of the new courses *has been reflected in the re-organisation of the 4th edition of this book.* In general, if major topics have been split up into two chapters, the first chapter is usually applicable to the Advanced Subsidiary modules, and the second chapter is usually applicable to the A-level modules. Good examples of this are the two network chapters, 3 and 5, and the two databases chapters, 28 and 29. However, you do need to check your course requirements or Subject Specification very carefully to make sure that you know what material belongs to a particular module for your examination board.

Happy birthday!

Finally, I would like to take this opportunity of wishing the computer a belated happy 50th birthday, which occurred in 1998. If the next fifty years are as exhilarating as the previous fifty, then society is in for an exciting ride.

Ray Bradley 1999

1 How to Make the Best Use of this Book

In this chapter you'll learn about:

◆ The best way to use this book

◆ How to find up-to-date course requirement information

◆ The subject criteria for computing

◆ Key information on projects

◆ Schemes of work

◆ Materials and equipment required

◆ Applications and languages to learn

◆ Techniques to make your course interesting

◆ Revision preparation

Key Resources

To carry out this work most successfully it's best if you have:

◆ Access to the Internet

◆ Information about the computer systems you have at school or college

Concept checkpoints

◆ At the beginning of each chapter there will be some concept checkpoints which will point you to other parts of this book if you need to revise certain topics.

◆ You will need to have a very basic familiarity with the Internet.

◆ In the unlikely event that you know nothing about the Internet, then you will find the required information in chapter 4. However, you do not need to study this in detail for the purposes of this introductory chapter.

Introduction

Put the kettle on, make a cup of coffee, then spend just a few minutes reading this short chapter on how to make the best use of this book – you'll find it's well worth the effort. Indeed, it's also worth the effort to re-visit this chapter at regular intervals throughout your course to bring important features back into focus.

Keeping up to date with subject requirements

As stated in the preface to the fourth edition of this book, the Internet has literally changed the way that we now do business. For example, in the first three editions, there was a syllabus-analysis guide, with each examination board appearing in a column, and topics in the book were mapped onto a particular board. The problem with this approach was that it became outdated quickly, and many things have changed over the last couple of years in the educational world. Some examination boards have disappeared altogether, some have merged with others, and this has meant that even the exam-board names have changed almost as rapidly as the syllabuses, which are now called subject specifications! Nevertheless, the Internet has come to our rescue, and the good news is that as computer science and IT students you should be well able to make use of it.

For example, let's suppose that you are doing the AEB Computing Advanced Level course. If you wish to know exactly how the marks for your project are to be allocated to each section, then surf the Web, find the AEB site, then search the site and you could find the exact information you require. The results of this particular search at http://www.aeb.org.uk/ can be seen in figure 1.1. You should read chapter 4 if you are unfamiliar with the Internet and using a web browser. Indeed, if like the author, you were using an electronic version of this book, then clicking over the web address shown above would automatically load the browser. You would be automatically logged on to the Internet, and then onto AEB's site; assuming, of course, that your computer is set up correctly – something you will easily be able to do after reading just some of this book!

What a marvellous thing this is. Here you can see the candidate assessment sheet for the 1999 A level computing project. However, surf the net a year later, and you will see the detailed project scheme for the year 2000 instead. You can now keep up to date with all the latest information for your particular board, including the **dates of all**

> **Hint:** There is much information about computers on the web. If you find some piece of theory very difficult, then you will almost always find a forum in which you can discuss it with other students. There is also help at special sites with homework.

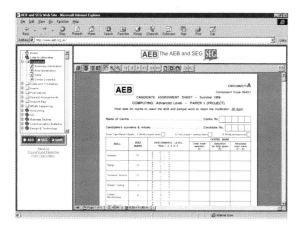

Figure 1.1

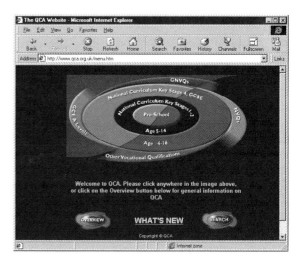

Figure 1.2

your examinations, project deadline dates, the latest news from the boards, summaries of what marks are awarded for the papers and the other information too. You can even order a copy of your subject specification on CD-ROM for just a few pounds. Unfortunately, at the time of writing, you can't get the very detailed information without paying for it, but you can **order paper copies of the subject specification** via the net, as well as **past papers** and a whole host of other useful information. Also, don't forget that your school or college should be able to provide you with the subject specification too, and this should be your first port of call for this basic information.

The 'A' and 'AS' computer science subject criteria

All advanced level computer science courses, along with other 'A' and 'AS' courses have what are called subject criteria, which is similar to the old common core. These are the *specifications* to which *all courses of study must adhere*. There is a wealth of information regarding computing 'A' level at the **Qualifications and Curriculum Authority (QCA)**. See figure 1.2.

From here you can find out how your course is meant to be organised, and what skills etc. you should expect to obtain if you study for a particular qualification; assuming, of course, that you are successful! As would be expected, to find out this information, we surf the Web! Figure 1.2 shows the page to navigate the QCA's web site, which can be found at http://www.qca.org.uk

From figure 1.2 you can see that GNVQs, NVQs and GCE A (and AS) levels are all catered for, as well as other vocational qualifications. If you choose the 'A' level option, for example, you would find the subject criteria for Advanced and Advanced Subsidiary (AS) computing. You would find out what the aims and objectives of the course are, what knowledge and understanding you are meant to have, what key skills are to be obtained

from a study of your chosen course, the assessment objectives and many other things too. Interestingly, if you hope to get a grade A in Computing at 'A' level, then you should be able to demonstrate the criteria listed below.

Criteria for a grade A

Candidates demonstrate:

- good understanding of theoretical concepts
- appropriate and accurate use of technical language
- detailed knowledge of a range of applications
- informed opinions on effects of computing on society
- the application of knowledge and understanding to unfamiliar problems
- good understanding of data types and structures and how to use them
- effective and appropriate use of a range of software
- ability to design and produce effective solutions to complex problems
- a methodical, analytical and critical approach to problem solving
- the ability to design, operate and justify appropriate testing strategies
- clear communication of design decisions and solutions to problems
- effective skills of evaluation.

The criteria for a grade C and a grade E are also available on the site. However, let's keep the target high at the beginning of your course!

The layout of the fourth edition

Although you could undertake your computer-science course by reading this book from cover to cover, by starting at page one and working your way through in a linear fashion, this is not the most productive and certainly not the most interesting way to proceed. Different parts of this book can be tackled simultaneously, and the harder chapters can be left out on first reading. Indeed, AS level candidates obviously won't have to study the entire text. Also, many schools and colleges have different teachers/lecturers who tackle different parts of the course. To help both students and staff plan their courses more effectively, the following important information about this fourth edition should be noted.

- *The whole book has been rearranged to reflect the proliferation of the AS and modular A level subject specifications. However, read the whole lot and it's obviously ideal for the non-modular courses too. Indeed, the original layout of the book was based around the very popular AEB 'A' level computing examination. The easier parts of the subject specification such as applications, the Internet, social implications, and peripherals have been put near to the front of the book, together with the chapters on networking, which reflect the increasing importance of the Internet and Intranets at the start of the 21st century.*
- *Throughout the main bulk of the book you will see that many topics are covered in two parts. For example chapter 28 is called 'A first look at databases', and chapter 29 is called 'Further databases'. Broadly speaking, chapter 28 covers the material appropriate for most AS subject specifications, and chapter 29 covers the remainder of the work for the full 'A' level. This natural split is also applicable to the chapters on networking, high-level languages, systems analysis and design, operating systems, data structures, file handling, the binary system, and, of course databases. You will, however, have to be careful, as the modular nature of some of the courses means that you can take different options, and 'A' level work for one board might appear in the 'AS' section for another. You are reminded that the 'A' and 'AS' work is of the same standard, it's just that more topics are covered for the full 'A' level. You will have to check very carefully with your teacher to determine which parts of the book are applicable to your chosen route to either AS or A level computing.*

A suggested scheme of work

Different teachers and lecturers obviously have very different ways of working, and there is no ideal way to tackle the incredibly broad spectrum of work required for computing. For example, it would be less interesting to tackle all of the work on structured analysis and design, making no reference whatsoever to actually doing things on the computer. However, successful programming on the computer requires some degree of understanding of structured analysis and design.

Therefore, you may wish to work through several chapters at the same time. Another consequence of the rearrangement of the subject specifications is that Chapter 8, for example, on real time and engineering applications, appears along with the other applications chapters. However, the work in chapter 8 is considerably harder, and does depend on knowledge of some of the later material. Therefore, you might wish to leave out chapter 8 first time round. Figure 1.3 has been devised to help you decide on possible routes through the system.

You should note that the numbers inside the small boxes on the top of each chapter refer to the chapters that should be read before this chapter is tackled. For example, look at chapter 26 in figure 1.3. The numbers on top indicate that it's best if you have read chapters 14, 19, 24 and 25 before tackling this particular chapter.

Figure 1.3 shows both the theoretical and practically based components of many computer-science courses. The important thing to notice is that the work has been split up into 6 major terms – namely Christmas, Easter and summer over a period of two years. The space allocated to the width of each term varies in proportion with the amount of work that can usually be accomplished within it. For example, the Christmas term is often nearly twice as long as the Easter term.

As you can see from figure 1.3, chapters 1 and 2 are suggested compulsory reading at the beginning of the course, but options then present themselves for going off at different tangents.

By doing this in an effective way, the course can be made more interesting, and long stretches of harder theory can be avoided – practical work, projects, visits, debates, extra reading and videos etc. can be interwoven with the more theoretical concepts to make a better, more balanced course.

The suggested scheme has particular merit because it ensures that most of the important work necessary for the major practical project has been covered before

> **Hint:** If you are doing a modular course then your first examination may be just a few months after the start of your course. You will need to identify which parts of the book are applicable to your first module. Photocopy figure 1.3, and mark the appropriate chapters with a highlighter pen.

> **Hint:** If you would like a computer but don't have much money, then consider making your own or buying an ex surplus computer from a place like the on-line Internet auctions. You can pick up brand new colour monitors for a few tens of pounds and complete computer systems for less than a couple of hundred pounds at the time of writing. They won't be cutting edge technology, but they *will* run most of the software needed for your course.

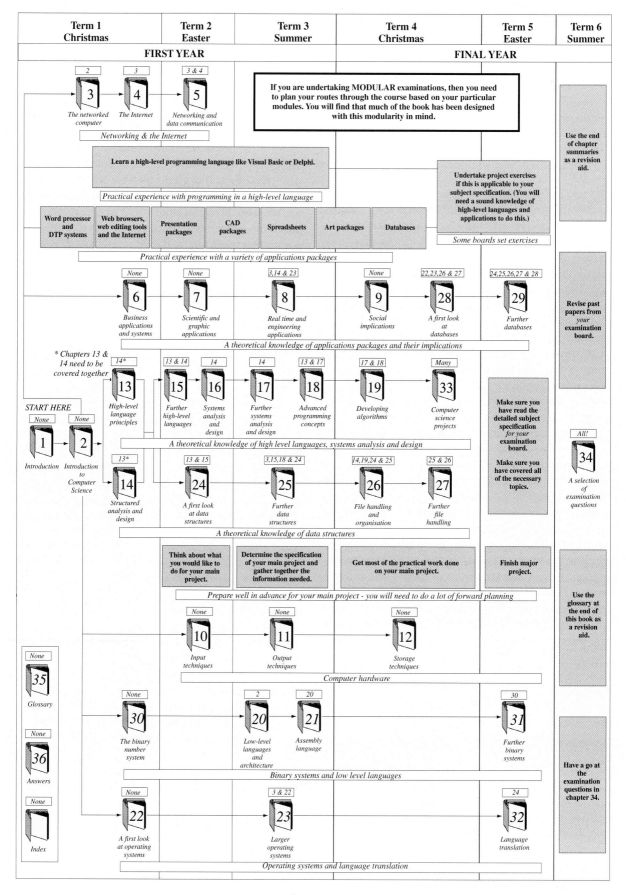

Term 1 Christmas	Term 2 Easter	Term 3 Summer	Term 4 Christmas	Term 5 Easter	Term 6 Summer

FIRST YEAR | FINAL YEAR

If you are undertaking MODULAR examinations, then you need to plan your routes through the course based on your particular modules. You will find that much of the book has been designed with this modularity in mind.

2 — 3 — 3 & 4
3 The networked computer
4 The Internet
5 Networking and data communication

Networking & the Internet

Learn a high-level programming language like Visual Basic or Delphi.

Practical experience with programming in a high-level language

Undertake project exercises if this is applicable to your subject specification. (You will need a sound knowledge of high-level languages and applications to do this.)

Some boards set exercises

| Word processor and DTP systems | Web browsers, web editing tools and the Internet | Presentation packages | CAD packages | Spreadsheets | Art packages | Databases |

Practical experience with a variety of applications packages

None | None | 3,14 & 23 | None | 22,23,26 & 27 | 24,25,26,27 & 28
6 Business applications and systems
7 Scientific and graphic applications
8 Real time and engineering applications
9 Social implications
28 A first look at databases
29 Further databases

A theoretical knowledge of applications packages and their implications

* Chapters 13 & 14 need to be covered together

14* | 13 & 14 | 14 | 14 | 13 & 17 | 17 & 18 | Many
13 High-level language principles
15 Further high-level languages
16 Systems analysis and design
17 Further systems analysis and design
18 Advanced programming concepts
19 Developing algorithms
33 Computer science projects

START HERE
None | None
1 Introduction
2 Introduction to Computer Science

A theoretical knowledge of high level languages, systems analysis and design

13* | 13 & 15 | 3,15,18 & 24 | 14,19,24 & 25 | 25 & 26
14 Structured analysis and design
24 A first look at data structures
25 Further data structures
26 File handling and organisation
27 Further file handling

A theoretical knowledge of data structures

Make sure you have read the detailed subject specification *for your* examination board.

Make sure you have covered all of the necessary topics.

All!
34 A selection of examination questions

Think about what you would like to do for your main project.

Determine the specification of your main project and gather together the information needed.

Get most of the practical work done on your main project.

Finish major project.

Prepare well in advance for your main project - you will need to do a lot of forward planning

None | None | None
10 Input techniques
11 Output techniques
12 Storage techniques

Computer hardware

None | 2 | 20 | 30
30 The binary number system
20 Low-level languages and architecture
21 Assembly language
31 Further binary systems

Binary systems and low level languages

None | 3 & 22 | 24
22 A first look at operating systems
23 Larger operating systems
32 Language translation

Operating systems and language translation

None
35 Glossary

None
36 Answers

None
Index

Use the end of chapter summaries as a revision aid.

Revise past papers from *your* examination board.

Use the glossary at the end of this book as a revision aid.

Have a go at the examination questions in chapter 34.

Figure 1.3

term 4. For example, using this scheme ensures that, by term 4, students have covered practical DTP systems and CAD packages, which are both useful for writing up their projects as they proceed. This scheme ensures that the students have covered the practical work on spreadsheets and databases, which is so often needed for their projects. Finally, the scheme ensures that students have covered the all-important high-level languages, and have also studied enough about data structures, structured analysis and systems analysis to be useful for the design and analysis parts of their project.

Timing

You should take special note that much work has been covered early on in the course (during the first year) so that class time can be spent on projects during the fourth and fifth terms. Also, and this comes as a shock to some students – there's not much time during term six for anything other than revision! Some 'A' level computer-science examinations are taken in May. This leaves only a few weeks after coming back from the Easter vacation to wrap up the whole course. There really is very little time for learning anything new or covering major topics from scratch – all learning of the theory, the practical work, exercises (if applicable) and projects must be done within the first five terms. Your timing is obviously going to be quite different if you are tackling a modular course. Examinations occur throughout the year, and you must be well briefed as to exactly what topics are expected for each module. It is usual for the 'A' and 'AS' students to be taught in the same class, or to do similar work, because several of the modules will overlap. 'A' level students will simply do more modules than the 'AS' students. Usually the 'AS' students do three modules (including the project work) and the 'A' level students do six.

Other materials required

Hint: If you have a PC at home then it's a good idea to practice learning programming and software applications in the comfort of your own home. Don't forget that Microsoft offer student licences, which enables you to purchase expensive software, like Office 2000 or Microsoft Developer's Studio for hundreds of pounds less than the list price. Your teacher will have to sign a special form to confirm that you are a bona-fide student.

Much of the practical work in the fourth edition of this book revolves around the use of the popular PC Windows platform. However, computer science covers a very broad spectrum of knowledge, and different hardware and software platforms ensure that no one book is able to cover all the work *exactly* as it is tackled on *your* particular system. Much of the software available for the Apple Mac is fortunately identical. This includes word processors, spreadsheets, databases, art packages, CAD packages and some languages. The Acorn systems are still popular in some schools, although at the time of writing Acorn has stopped production of any new models. Other companies are likely to take over the Acorn range, but the future development of software for the Acorn systems is not certain. Nevertheless, thousands of Acorn systems still exist in schools and colleges, and will do so for the foreseeable future. Therefore, some of the work in this book still uses BBC basic. Fortunately, the syntax is *very similar* for the non-visual components, and thus it's still suitable for 'A' level standard work. However, you are unlikely to get a suitable range of experience of application packages on the Acorn machines alone, and you are thus advised to get considerable experience on the PC if you possibly can.

Other source material needs to be available throughout your course. In particular, you should make sure that you have access to, and experience of, *all* of the following materials.

Applications

At the beginning of your course you should learn how to use an application like a DTP system or a top-of-the-range word processor, together with a CAD package that is able to build up diagrams suitable for inclusion in your chosen DTP or word-processor package (for example, Microsoft Word and Corel Draw). You should use packages like these at frequent intervals throughout your course so that you are literally an expert by the time that it comes to write up your major project report (usually during term 5 or during the Easter holidays if you have a suitable machine at home). Hastily-hand-written documentation is no longer acceptable, and usually

Hint: If you have little or no cash with which to buy applications and software, buy (or borrow!) a computer magazine with an appropriate CD-ROM on the cover. Complete application development environments like Delphi version 2, for example, can be had for literally the price of the magazine. These are intended to wet your appetite to buy the latest versions, but the software on these CD-ROMs is very suitable for 'A' level project work.

indicates lack of planning on the part of the student concerned. Also, if you write up the report using a word processor system as you are actually doing the project then much hassle and time is saved later, and you can cut and paste material into the main report which will save a huge amount of time.

Other packages of primary importance are spreadsheets and database systems. (Packages like Microsoft Excel and Microsoft Access are typical of what is now required.) The only way in which you can truly appreciate these packages is to *use them extensively*. It's also most important that you program databases using a suitable SQL language, and program a spreadsheet using a suitable macro language. This work should supplement your work with high-level languages.

You must make sure that you have access to all the necessary manuals and/or textbooks (or videos) available for use with these basic packages. There are few excuses (other than financial ones) these days, as literally thousands of suitable books, magazines and videos are available for all manner of computer-based applications. Don't forget that libraries often carry suitable books, and if your own library is not up to scratch then make use of a specialist technical library. There is usually one in each county, so you should ask your local librarian if you don't know where it is. Books can be borrowed from the specialist technical library via your own local library.

High-level languages

I suggest that you learn one (or preferably two if you are keen and have the time) high level language/s in depth. This must be a modern structured programming language such as the latest versions of Visual Basic, Delphi or Visual C++ may also be used if you are keen to get started on a high-powered language. It's also essential that you have some experience of using a compiler – experience of interpreted BASIC alone will not be sufficient. All versions of the languages mentioned here have compilers available for most machines. If your school or college does not have the latest visual windows-based versions of these languages, don't worry too much. The majority of the code in this book and the pseudocode, which you will be required to produce in the examinations, is not the visual version either. It's just that the latest visual versions of all these languages make project work so very much easier, assuming, of course, that you wish to do your project using a high-level language.

> **Hint:** At the time of writing, Visual Basic, Visual C++, Visual Java and lots of other goodies can be found in Microsoft's Developer Studio. Don't forget that you can get a student licence for this software, saving hundreds of pounds on the list price.

It's also an added advantage if you have access to and can play around with other high-level languages such as Fortran 90, COBOL or Prolog, for example. Without a computer to test out and run simple programs in these languages, work such as that covered in chapter 15 becomes gut-wrenchingly boring! Much time can be saved if you are presented with many pre-written procedures which carry out particular functions in different languages – it's then easy to make small modifications to these procedures which you can easily run on your own machine in a short space of time. You should never forget the famous quote that goes something like this.

Tell me and I forget – Show me and I remember – Let me do it and I understand.

There is no substitute for practical experience with different languages, even if it's only for an hour or so.

Low-level languages

BORIS – the Beginner's Optimised Reduced Instruction Set microprocessor, together with the other material in chapter 20 will teach you the rudiments of microprocessor systems. Chapter 21 on low-level languages will teach you much more, but there's no substitute for running your own assembly-language programs on the machines which you have at school or college. Without practical experience on a real machine, concepts of low-level languages are much more difficult to grasp. Make sure that you have access to an assembler and are able to run simple programs on it. The experience is well worth it and you can more readily appreciate what is going on when you come to read more advanced work on operating systems later in the course.

Using the glossary

Computer science is riddled with jargon – most of which, in my opinion, is justified. Any academically respectable science must have an extensive technical language or you can't communicate effectively. For example, can you imagine referring to 'non-volatile memory' as 'the little black boxes with funny legs sitting on the main electronic board inside the computer which do not lose the contents which have been stored inside them when the electricity to the system is switched off'?

The glossary built up in the third edition has been extensively revised and updated, and now contains well over 1,500 explanations of technical terms. Moreover, terms used within a definition, which are in the glossary, are highlighted in bold type too. Make extensive use of the glossary, especially in the early stages of your course. It will also act as a neat way to do an alternative form of revision towards the end of your course.

Using this book with different courses

Understanding Computer Science for Advanced Level has been used on a wide variety of different courses for many years, and the fourth edition of this book still reflects this wide user base. Therefore, you will have to be particularly careful in making sure that you spend most of your time on the material which is very important as far as *your* particular course is concerned, unless, of course, you're interested in expanding your knowledge in other areas of computer science as well. This can obviously be no bad thing. The key to an efficient analysis of any course is modularisation. Fortunately, computer science as a subject can be modularised easily, and this makes it particularly easy to identify various sections that are applicable. Having identified an appropriate topic, the only thing yet to be established is the depth in which to study it. This is a slightly more difficult problem, but considerable help is at hand by referring to figure 1.3, and remembering that major topics are split up into easier and harder chapters.

For example, if 'Structured Analysis and Design' forms part of your course, then looking in detail at the sub-sections of chapter 24 and 25 and your subject specification will help you to identify those parts of this topic which are relevant to you. You may find, for example, that 'JSP' or 'Decision tables' are not specifically listed in your course, in which case, don't bother to learn them if you don't want to! However, they are very useful indeed if you decide to use a high-level language for your project, irrespective of whether they are in your course or not. If you are not clear on these details, then ask your teacher or lecturer whether such topics are needed. Unfortunately, some subject specifications are so general that they are not particularly helpful in the detailed lists that they give. Even teachers and lecturers are often not too sure in one or two instances. One can gain an inkling by studying past examination papers in some considerable detail, but even this would not help if a topic were completely new. Computer Science is a very open-ended subject, and you will often find that sub-sections of topics not listed in your subject specification will help considerably when it comes to taking the final examination. There are so many different ways of tackling similar problems that knowledge of several techniques is often helpful, and you will obviously not be penalised in an examination for knowing something which is not in the course, or for tackling a particular problem in a more sophisticated or professional manner.

BTEC courses

There are such a huge variety of specialist BTEC courses that it would take up too much space to list all the details of possibilities for which this text would be useful. However, core courses, large parts of which are particularly suited to this book, include *Computer Systems*, *Communication Skills*, *Information Systems*, *Introduction to Programming* and *Quantitative Methods*.

ONC/D, HNC/D and BCS part 1

Students on BTEC ONC/OND and first year students on BTEC HNC/HND computer-related courses will also find this book useful, as will students undertaking Part 1 of the British Computer Society examinations.

First degree

Many students undertaking computer-science degree courses start the course without having undertaken an 'A' level or even a GCSE in this particular subject. Therefore, this book can act as a valuable reference to help students on first-degree courses to understand many of the unfamiliar concepts, which they will be required to assimilate, often at a lightning-fast pace. Students on degree courses may find that the slightly less rigorous approach of 'A' level will help them to understand a large number of the fundamental concepts that are being covered in their courses at great speed.

GNVQs

A large number of GNVQ courses have appeared on the curriculum of some institutions, and a number of these courses too should find that many sections of this book are appropriate. Again it would take up too much space to map out all curricular details, but the exercise would be well worth your while if you were undertaking one of these courses. Don't forget that you can use the Internet as described at the beginning of this chapter, and make use of the QCA information on GNVQs too.

Keeping up to date

You probably won't need reminding that computer science is a rapidly changing subject. There is, fortunately, a huge core of knowledge that does not change too rapidly, and large sections of this book will be useful for some considerable time to come. However, the rapid advancement in microprocessor technology leads to changes on an almost monthly basis in the new microcomputers that are built around these new processors, and the level of sophistication of the software which such systems can support. The fourth edition of this book has been completely re-written in all areas that have seen rapid advances. However, it is up to you to keep even more up to date by reading appropriate magazines, the computer press, and articles in some of the more serious daily newspapers; and, of course, by surfing the Internet.

The number of computer-based magazines on sale in the newsagents these days testifies both to the quantity and diversity of available material. Although some magazines are not suitable for gaining very much new knowledge, the vast majority of magazines will have articles which make suitable reading material for keeping right up to date. In particular, you should scan the news sections at the beginning of the magazines each month. I have found that the following magazines, newspapers and TV programmes etc. are particularly worthwhile in the context of computer science courses at advanced level.

Useful magazines

BYTE – for in-depth technical articles
Personal Computer World – PC-based technical information
Computer Shopper – gives you a good idea of the latest prices
Mac User – Mac-based technical information

Don't forget also that there are many specialist magazines catering for individual needs. For example, magazines about the Windows NT operating system or the Unix operating system to name but two.

Useful newspapers

Computer Weekly – free to schools and colleges
Network News – free to schools and colleges
The Times and the *Daily Telegraph*

Indeed, most of the broadsheets have good articles on computing and technology at some time during the week.

Useful TV programs

Horizon and *QED* – both excellent technical programmes

Obviously series like Horizon and QED etc. start and stop according to the season, but other similar programs will come on tap. Watch out for specialist programs like *Glory of the Geeks*, a recent program about the development of the Internet, which follows on from the successful *Triumph of the Nerds* series.

Useful videos

Triumph of the Nerds (BBC publications) – One of the best explanations of the growth of the microcomputer industry – this should not be missed.

There is also a wide variety of software training videos, which you can buy in computer shops or by mail order. These cover most topics under the sun from advanced programming to simple use of a database or word processor, for example.

Useful CD-ROM material

There are thousands of CD-ROM computing titles available. Many of the training videos are now more interactive through being ported over to CD-ROMs.

Useful Internet sites

These are too numerous to mention in detail, but don't forget the standard search engines at the following web addresses.

YAHOO	www.yahoo.com
AltaVista	www.altavista.digital.com
HotBot	www.hotbot.com
InfoSeek	www.infoseek.com
Lycos	www.lycos.com

Newsgroups and forums

There are thousands of specialist computer newsgroups. A special search engine called Deja.com is available to search them.

Newsgroup search engine www.dejanews.com

For example, at the time of writing, a look at Deja.com revealed the following major computer categories.

- Algorithms
- Architecture
- Archives
- Artificial Intelligence
- Buying, Selling and Trading
- Communications and Networking
- Computer Companies
- Computer Games
- Education
- General
- Graphics
- Information and Documentation
- Internet
- Jobs
- Multimedia
- Organisations
- Programming
- Real-time Computing
- Security and Encryption
- Software
- Standards
- Supercomputing and Parallel Computing
- Year 2000

As you can see, many of the newsgroup categories mirror a lot of the chapter headings of this book. Hundreds of newsgroups appear in many of these categories, and they are growing by the day. However, realise that people can, and indeed do, post anything they want to these newsgroups, therefore you will find some rubbish in with the wealth of superb quality information.

CompuServe and other forums

Don't forget that there are a huge number of forums in which you can discuss virtually all computer-related issues with like-minded individuals. However, be careful with the phone bills, especially if you don't pay them!

Digital and satellite television

The digital television channels, on satellite, cable and terrestrial TV offer a wealth of specialist programs, many of then dealing specifically with information technology and computers. You should always be on the lookout for new programmes that may be of use – do this by scanning through the TV and Radio programmes each week and consult the educational TV guides produced by the BBC and ITV (your teachers or lecturers should have seen them).

Past examination papers

Computer-science examinations at advanced level have now been going for over 30 years. Unfortunately, only the most recent papers (about the last five years) have any hope of containing many questions which are relevant to today's subject specifications. The author used to teach a lot of mathematics at 'A' level, and was always grateful for the vast bank of past-paper questions containing relevant material.

> **Hint:** Don't forget that you can often order past papers via the Internet. Most reputable companies now offer secure credit-card transactions over the net.

Getting past computer-science papers from different boards *will* enable you to increase the range of suitable questions and thus build up a sizeable bank. However, even doing this is not quite as good as it used to be – the agreed inter-board common core, now called the subject criteria, has meant that some questions on different examination papers are literally identical – that's life! Much relevant practice of the appropriate standard can be found in the many exercises throughout this book. Together with a range of past papers as described above, you should not lack suitable material.

Visits

> **Hint:** Don't forget to thank your hosts during the visit, (and after by writing a suitable letter) – even if you feel that the visit was not one of the highlights of your year.

You should try to visit one or two professional computer-based organisations. Without this experience it's possible to get into a rut where you think that computing revolves around the micros which you have at your school or college. If you can go and see a mainframe or even a supercomputer in operation, then this would be much to your advantage. You must try to ensure that you are able to get a proper look and have the systems explained properly – it's no good just looking at the box in which the computer is housed – you can easily do this from a book. Remember to build up a bank of suitable questions so that you appear to be intelligent!

Debates and discussion groups

If possible, try to get your school or college to arrange one or two talks from a computer expert in a particular field. At the author's school we have had successful visits from local-health-authority computer managers, travel agents, banking personnel, engineering companies' staff, computer animation artists and professors from universities.

Although chapter 9 deals with a good number of different social issues, you will need to do some extra reading to get different views regarding major issues affecting computing. There are suitable books in most libraries, each containing strong arguments both for and against computerisation. How about choosing a topic and then giving a presentation to the rest of your class, or even better to a larger group of students? There's nothing guaranteed to sharpen up the mind as much as presenting a case for or against some particular argument in front of an audience. If you don't do your homework then you will not look particularly impressive. How about using your DTP systems to present professional-standard OHP (acetate) sheets – they can be produced by a bubble-jet or LASER printer. (Note that different types of acetate sheets are needed for each!) How about linking up one of your computers to a projection TV or OHP system if these facilities are available to be used? Many students at the author's school make use of Microsoft's Power Point to produce lectures of the sort described here. Use all the technology at your disposal to present the most powerful arguments that you can – these visual aids also act as a prompt if you can see your pre-prepared material on the screen.

If possible arrange full-scale debates on particular subjects like 'Virtual reality', 'Do computers possess intelligence?' or 'Are computers enhancing or detracting from our children's education?'. The number of possible topics is endless. As a computer scientist you should be able to argue rationally from a position of strength, because you have considerable knowledge about computing. Much argument from non-computer scientists revolves around irrational fears and prejudices, and is based on misconceptions through lack of knowledge.

Revision

There is just one magic formula for carrying out effective revision – and that is to make sure that you have worked hard over the entire course beforehand – it's difficult to revise things that you have not learned properly in the first place! Nevertheless, even if you *are* in this unfortunate position, and there are several weeks to go before the examination, all is not lost. What effective revision will enable you to do is to build on whatever foundation you have built up for yourself, and thus ensure that your chances of getting a better grade are maximised. Specific areas in this book, which are useful for revision, are as follows.

● Use the coloured text and the end-of-chapter summaries to revise a specific area quickly. Make use of the glossary for extra revision material. Go through the glossary or end-of-chapter summaries by getting a friend to ask you the questions, or by covering up the explanations with a piece of paper and asking yourself the questions.
● Build up a revision schedule over the space of *6 to 8 weeks before the examination*. Integrate this schedule with your other subjects so that you are not overloaded. Make a list of the topics which you don't understand and get your teacher to go

over them or re-read the relevant sections of this book.
● Find out early on which are your most productive times regarding doing effective work. Do get up early if you can work well first thing in the morning, but don't stay up very late if you can't do productive work at night. Make sure that you are doing effective work by monitoring your progress – if you have spent the last half an hour staring at the wall then stop work and do something else – or do nothing.
● Make sure that you tackle entire past papers and limit yourself to the actual time, which you would have been allowed in the final examination. Get your teacher or lecturer to mark the work that you have done under these conditions – this is the only way in which you can effectively measure your actual progress regarding your performance in the final examination.
● There is no substitute for having your own subject specification in front of you. Changes from year-to-year are likely. Get a photocopy of the subject specification and tick off parts, which you have learnt, still understand, and can do.

End of chapter revision aid and summary

Cover up the right-hand column and see if you can answer the questions or define the terms on the left. They appear in the order in which they are covered in this chapter. Alternatively you may browse through the right-hand column to aid revision.

What sort of vital course information might be found on the Internet?	Vital information such as project mark sheets, subject criteria, grade descriptions and a host of other things can be found on the Internet.
From which site can the subject criteria for 'A' level computing be found?	The 'A' and 'AS' level subject criteria can be found by logging on to the site www.qca.org.uk.
How is the work for AS and A level split up in this book?	The 'AS' and 'A' level split is achieved largely by splitting major chapters into two parts. The first part reflects mainly 'AS' material, and the second part reflects mainly 'A' level material.
What sort of applications should you learn for your course?	You should learn applications such as word processors, web browsers, presentation packages, CAD packages, spreadsheets, art packages and databases if you wish to get the most from your 'A' level course.
What sort of high-level languages need to be learned?	It's best if you can become competent in a language like Visual Basic or Delphi, for example. However, if you don't have access to modern software, then the older non-visual versions of Basic and Pascal will do most of what you require.
Make a list of seven different ways in which you can keep up to date with the latest computer developments.	You can keep up to date with the latest developments by making use of specialist magazines and newspapers, by watching TV programmes and videos, by using CD-ROM based material, by searching web sites, by using the forums and communities provided by your Internet services providers, or by using the hundreds of specialist computing newsgroups available on the Internet.

2 Introduction to Computer Science

Key resources

To carry out this work most successfully it's best if you have:

- Access to modern computer magazines
- Access to the computer systems which you have at school or college
- Don't forget the **glossary** at the back of this book. It should be very helpful to explain some concepts with which you may not be familiar

Concept checkpoints

- At the beginning of each chapter there will be some concept checkpoints which will point you to other parts of the book if you need to revise certain topics.
- There are none needed in this particular chapter.

Introduction

This chapter is designed to give an introduction to the fascinating world of computer science at a simple level. It is intended to give a broad overview of many fundamental concepts and will act as a base from which the more complex ideas in other chapters can be developed. The material here is essential reading if you have not done any previous computer studies or information technology courses. It will also act as a useful reminder for those students who are starting out with a wider knowledge base. **There can be few subjects, which are taught against such a rapidly changing background. However, look on this as 'exciting and challenging' rather than 'daunting'. Prices of computer equipment have fallen, often by several orders of magnitude in just a few years. Even if the price does not drop by very much, then the performance in terms of 'processing power' and the 'speed' which you get for the same money goes up by several orders of magnitude instead! However you look at it the result is the same – the computer and its related technology have become all pervasive in the modern industrialised world.**

Those of you who are starting from scratch are advised to take time to absorb the new concepts, and to undertake the work in the exercise at the end of this chapter.

What is a computer?

A computer is basically a processor of information. What gives it such tremendous power and versatility is the fact that the information contained in it may be processed in many different forms, with text, sound, video and computer-generated graphics being just a few common examples. Add to this the fact that a computer is very fast, and can make use of the global network to communicate with other information-based systems, and you will start to appreciate just a fraction of the potential of these information-processing machines. At this early stage in your course you should appreciate the importance of what is meant by the term 'information', and realise that **information** *which can be processed* forms the basis of **knowledge** itself. It is the essentials from which modern ideas such as **intellectual capital** are formed. *These ideas are this fundamental* – a fact not often appreciated by people with little or no computer literacy.

The information rich and poor

In the future there's likely to be a tremendous gap between those people who simply make use of the computer as an effective tool in carrying out their day-to-day tasks, and those who can understand, and therefore start to mould, the future. People in the second category are able to apply their own innovative ideas to help develop new and better information technology. There will be an even larger gap between those nations that can develop high technology effectively by applying IT principles and those that cannot. Nations in the former category have been described as the 'information rich', and nations in the latter category have been described as the 'information poor'.

Many people in the so called developed countries can and do make use of computers in the normal course of their work, and one has only to look at the millions of people using **applications** such as **word processors**, **DTP** systems and **spreadsheets**, for example, to illustrate this fact. Nevertheless, *most of these people do not understand* anything at all about the systems beyond the immediate application they are using. This pays tribute to the immense advances that have been made in the last few years in making computer systems much easier to use – once they have been set up properly by people with more advanced knowledge. By undertaking an advanced course in computer science, you are already starting out on the road to a fundamental understanding of computers and information technology in general. Should you be successful in your chosen course, you will be well on the way to becoming the sort of person who is able to make a valuable contribution to the advanced technological development of IT and computing well into the 21st century.

Technical jargon

As with any technologically based subject, there is much technical jargon in computing. *Don't forget, however, that there is a glossary at the back of this book, which covers all of the important terms.* To get to grips with computer science you will have to come to terms with many new technical terms, most of which are useful. Computer scientists do have a sense of humour, and some of the jargon is a little ridiculous to say the least. Nevertheless, it's only when your technical vocabulary has increased beyond a certain point that you will start to appreciate and therefore enjoy learning more detail.

Data and information

Data is the **raw material** on which a computer operates. When some appropriate **structure** has been applied to the data then it becomes **information**. As we have seen above, information can be processed in many different forms, so a simple numerical example will help to explain. Consider, for a moment, the following numbers:

`262, 294, 330, 349, 392, 440, 494 and 523.`

It is doubtful whether too many readers would be able to guess what the above **data** represents – it is therefore an example of **raw data**, where **structure** has yet to be applied. (In fact the structure has been applied – it's just that most of us don't know what it is yet!)

Did you know that . . .

Data, without knowledge of the structure applied to it, forms the basis of many encryption techniques used for sending top secret messages. These techniques are discussed in chapter 9.

Suppose that you were told that the above numbers represent the frequencies, to the nearest Hz, of musical notes starting from 'middle C' and spanning one octave. You are then enlightened because meaning has been given to a previously meaningless set of data. **Structure** has been applied and the **data** has become **information**, as shown in the following important relationship.

Information = Data + Structure

The new **information** is now shown pictorially in figure 2.1. You should note that this is not a mathematical formula to be applied in the normal sense, but is simply a way of describing a fundamental concept in computer science. Throughout your computer-science course you will consciously and unconsciously be applying structure to extract information from given data.

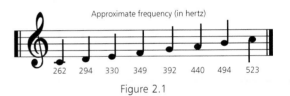

Figure 2.1

A **computer**, under the guidance of a *set of instructions* called a **program**, could be connected up to an appropriate musical instrument via a **MIDI interface** (see chapter 10), and be made to play the scale as described by the original **data**. Indeed, had the original data been an entire Beethoven symphony, then this too could be processed in a similar way.

Some basic ideas

From the previous section you have seen how **processing** needs to be applied to some **input data**, and after this **processing** has been accomplished, the **information** can then be **output** from the system. In the previous section you used your brain to carry out the appropriate thought processes, but we now look at some fundamental principles of organising machines to perform similar tasks.

The musical example in the previous section is just one specific case of an infinite variety of scenarios that could have been chosen – *translating a foreign language*, *drawing a picture*, *controlling a robot* or *sorting names into alphabetical order* would also have served the same purpose. What makes a computer so versatile is the ability to model the data such that it can represent almost anything. In the past people have become used to machines built to perform a specific purpose. For example, a typewriter can produce neat text, a musical instrument can produce a certain type of sound or an airbrush and stencils can produce a professional illustration for a magazine. However, a computer can do all of these things, *often more efficiently than the purpose-built devices* just mentioned. How then do we start to think in terms of such generality? How do we begin to organise such a general information-processing machine?

The simplest computer system

Figure 2.2 shows how the general concepts outlined above can represent the basic parts of any information-processing system. The ideas of **input**, **processing** and **output** are fundamental to all modern computer systems.

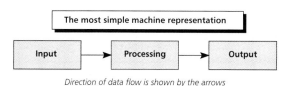

Direction of data flow is shown by the arrows

Figure 2.2

An expanded computer system

Such ideas might seem simple, and indeed they are, but they help to categorise what's happening in our general information-processing system. You will quickly realise however, that the terms are a little vague to say the least, and will need to be expanded considerably to be of any use. Figure 2.3, for example, shows the next stage up

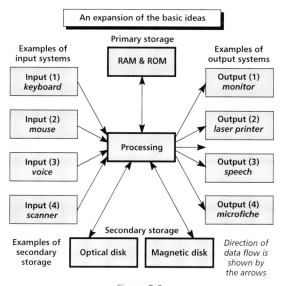

Figure 2.3

the evolutionary ladder, with the input and output sections expanded to show more detail.

The diagram also shows the addition of the vital **primary storage** or **memory**, which is needed to store the *sets of instructions* that the computer will follow. It also shows the necessary **secondary storage**, which enables the computer to *save information or get information from other sources* such as CD-ROM or floppy disk etc.

Notice that there are a wide variety of methods for getting **data** *into the computer* (the **inputs**) and getting **data** *out from the computer* (the **outputs**). In our expanded diagram only very few of the possible inputs and outputs have been shown. For example, our system has no means of communication via a telephone line or computer network, could not operate a magnetic tape machine and has no means of controlling a robot. Nevertheless, it's the ideas that are important here, and all the details mentioned are covered in great depth in other parts of this book.

We have come only a short way along the road to a generalised machine, but you should already appreciate the need to split up the system into different types of **inputs** and **outputs**. You should also appreciate that some complex **processing** is magically carried out by the **central processing unit**, where *instructions* held in the **primary storage** are followed. Finally, information can be *saved* and *loaded* from **secondary storage devices** such as **CD-ROM** and **disk**.

Hardware and software

An important distinction is made in computing between the *devices* made up from the *mechanics* and *electronics* which are used to *build the system*, and the *instructions* (the **ideas**) which are used to *control* the system. The term '**hardware**' is easy to understand – it simply means all the equipment and other devices that you can see and touch (literally) – it's *simply the computer equipment*. The sets of instructions called **programs** mentioned earlier are called **software**, and the word 'idea' is more important than might appear at first sight – you can't touch an idea – you can only appreciate the consequences of what the idea conveys. Without trying to be pedantic, *if* the **program instructions** are *written down on a piece of paper* then you are staring at **hardware**! This is because the **paper** and **ink** which have been used are both things you can touch, and are, therefore, **hardware**. However, it's the ideas and concepts *conveyed by these instructions* which is the software. Of course we would not get very far without hardware – we need a machine to control, we need manuals, **on-line** help and a whole host of other documentation which usually accompanies **software packages** and **programming languages**. About 20% of the content of this book covers hardware – the rest concentrates on software,

> **Hint:** Consider software as an intellectual idea rather than a physical thing and you won't go far wrong.

data structures, applications and implications, as well as large sections of material specifically written to help students with their studies. This ratio in favour of 'software and analysis methods' reflects modern trends in computing, and mirrors what's going on in the real world. Most often it's the software that causes the problems, and a much greater investment now goes into software analysis than was the case hitherto.

To give you some idea of the complexity of current software, Windows NT, one of the windows-based operating systems, has over 5 million different software instructions! An **operating system** is the name given to the **software** which is responsible for giving the computer its personality – *it's what makes the fast and powerful hardware much easier for us to use.* Before the advent of easy-to-use operating systems computers were very difficult machines to understand, and used only by specialists such as engineers and scientists. In less than 50 years we have progressed from computers being cumbersome, difficult to use and costly, to being a versatile tool which is accepted and used by tens of millions of people each day.

Why a digital computer?

These days everything seems to have gone **digital.** Digital Compact Disks (CDs), digital tuning on radios, digital information received by the TV to display teletext, digital controls on video recorders, digital washing machines and microwaves, and let's not forget the digital watch which decimated the traditional Swisswatch industry a couple of decades ago. At the heart of most of these devices lies a **chip** which is identical in principle to the *main chips* controlling all of our **personal computers**, but first let's see why the digital systems reign supreme.

The common thing regarding all the devices mentioned in the last paragraph is that they are controlled by **electronics**. Now electricity can be controlled in many different ways, but the easiest and quickest way of all is simply to switch the stuff on and off. This has led to a system in which the **two states – 'on'** and **'off'**, are used to represent the **data** and hence the **information**. These simple ideas happen to mirror the **binary** (two state) **system** in mathematics exactly, where a '**1**' can be used to represent '**on**' and a '**0**' can be used to represent '**off**'. This is why a *full appreciation* of the

binary system is so important to obtain a fundamental understanding of computers.

It might seem a tremendous stretch of the imagination to make the connection between these binary-digit 'ons' and 'offs', and the tremendous variety of things which a computer can do – but that's exactly what's happening in practice. To help explain this most fundamental of concepts I have invented a simple machine called **BASIL – the Binary Apparatus for Sending Intelligent Letters**. BASIL can be used to clarify how information can be sent backwards and forwards between two remote points by making use of binary – the remainder of this book will help to explain the rest of the theory of computers at advanced level!

BASIL is a machine in which eight electric-light bulbs can be independently switched 'on' or 'off' by a group of switches. If a particular bulb is *switched* '**on**' then this represents a '**1**', or if a particular bulb is *switched* '**off**' then this represents a '**0**' as shown in figure 2.4.

> **Hint:** It's very easy to build your own apparatus for sending messages. It can be done using simple light bulbs, batteries and switches. It can also be constructed using more sophisticated electronics, or programmed on the computer if you have suitable programming experience. It's great fun to set up the system!

We have thus devised a simple way of sending **data**, which, when it's *received and decoded*, becomes **information**. We would need some sort of table, part of which could be as shown in figure 2.5. If this particular table is used it would obviously be relatively simple for anyone to work out the code. The principles of **data encryption** are covered in chapter 9 for those readers who feel the need to make their data a little more secure.

You may feel that sending data in this way would be tedious in the extreme, taking a long time for even a simple request such as 'Put the coffee pot on' to be sent – and indeed you would be right. However, don't forget the fundamental point about computers mentioned at the beginning of this chapter – these machines are *very* fast.

A high-speed fibre-optic (see chapter 3) link could transmit about 100 million of these codes each second! At this rate we would be able to send the entire textual contents of Encyclopaedia Britannica in just a few

Did you know that . . .

Some of the early computers were not 'digital' but were 'analogue' in nature. These analogue computers were ideal for solving some types of mathematical equations. The output from these computers was a graph displayed on a cathode ray oscilloscope like the ones that you use in physics.

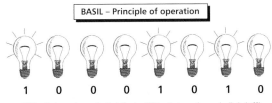

BASIL – Principle of operation

| 1 | 0 | 0 | 0 | 1 | 0 | 1 | 0 |

'1' indicates when a bulb is 'on' – '0' indicates when a bulb is 'off'
Code for this part of the message is 10001010

Figure 2.4

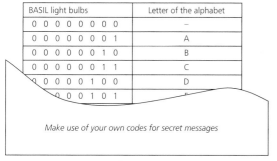

BASIL light bulbs	Letter of the alphabet
0 0 0 0 0 0 0 0	–
0 0 0 0 0 0 0 1	A
0 0 0 0 0 0 1 0	B
0 0 0 0 0 0 1 1	C
0 0 0 0 0 1 0 0	D
0 0 0 0 0 1 0 1	

Make use of your own codes for secret messages

Figure 2.5

seconds – have you just changed your mind about this method of communication? Other operations carried out inside the computer are just as impressive, but you will have to wait until later on in your course to find out more.

Did you know that . . .

Going at a speed of 100 million characters per second, two computers would be able to exchange the entire textual contents of Encyclopaedia Britannica in just a few seconds! However, the latest supercomputers can do it considerably faster than this!

Basic binary

Nearly all students seem to think that the **decimal system** is the most obvious way to count, but this is certainly *not* true. The decimal system was probably developed because we have ten fingers, so imagine that you're an alien from Alpha Centauri who only has five fingers, then, using the same arguments, it would seem more natural for this Alpha Centaurian to count in base five! Similarly, other aliens might have 20 fingers, and therefore count in base 20 and so on. Although computers don't have two fingers, you should appreciate from reading the last section that working in **binary** or **base 2** is the most natural and obvious method because of the electronics involved in the construction of the hardware. Binary is covered in some considerable detail in chapters 30 and 31, but here we will introduce the simplest principles – enough to get you going.

There are only ten characters in the decimal system and only five characters in the base five system, for example. Therefore, it stands to reason that there will only be **two characters** in the **binary system**. These could be 'true' or 'false' or perhaps 'red' or 'green', but if we wish to count, then the numbers '0' and '1' are the most convenient symbols to use.

In the base-ten system of counting we have the column headings 'units', 'hundreds', 'thousands' etc. In the base-five system, for example, the column headings 'units', 'twenty fives' and 'one hundred and twenty fives' etc. would be used. The simple rule, therefore, applic-

able to all number bases, is start with the units column, then multiply by the base you are using to generate the next column heading to the left. Therefore, applying this rule to the binary system, we would get the column headings 'units', 'twos', 'fours', 'eights' etc. We simply double the previous heading to get the next one.

When writing down numbers in different bases we can get an idea of their size by common sense, and making use of the column headings. For example, in the base ten or decimal system, the number:

Column headings	thousands	hundreds	tens	units
Decimal number	3	2	0	1

would be 3 lots of a thousand, 2 lots of a hundred, 0 lots of ten and 1 unit, giving us a number which we call three thousand two hundred and one.

In the binary system, for example, the number:

Column headings	eights	fours	twos	ones
Binary number	1	1	0	1

would be 1 lot of eight, 1 lot of four, 0 lots of 2 and 1 unit, giving us a number for which we have no name in the binary system, but which, in our decimal system would be thirteen, because eight plus four plus one is thirteen.

You can now see how groups of 1's and 0's in the binary system could represent numbers in the decimal system, and this is what happens inside a computer when arithmetic is worked out. It's all done in the binary system, then converted back into decimal to save us having to do the above conversions. Indeed, on the very early computers of the 1940s and 1950s, that's exactly what the operators had to do!

Numbers or codes?

Groups of binary digits as described in the last section do not have to represent numbers. More often than not in computing we are processing non-numerical data, so groups of binary digits have to represent other attributes such as 'letters', 'punctuation symbols', 'special characters to control different computer functions' or 'colours on the screen' for example. As long as everybody agrees as to what is being interpreted at any particular time, there should be few problems. You can liken it to the use of BASIL as described in the last section. It's very similar to the games, which you probably played when you were a child – sending secret messages to each other. You might, for example, invent a code in which the number 65, represents an 'A', the number '66' represents a 'B' and so on until the number

'90' which would represent a 'Z'. You could then transmit the codes, eight bits at a time, if you had eight switches and eight light bulbs like BASIL. At the transmitting end you would encode the message, and at the receiving end you would decode the message. Suppose for example, you wish to send the word 'HELLO', you would go through an encoding process, which involves working out which 'lights' to switch on and off. The following table shows the idea. Here we have written down the word 'HELLO', worked out the numbers using the above scheme, then worked out the binary numbers to be transmitted by using the column headings explained in the last section.

Message	Number	Binary patterns to be transmitted (Column headings)							
		128	64	32	16	8	4	2	1
H	72	0	1	0	0	1	0	0	0
E	69	0	1	0	0	0	1	0	1
L	76	0	1	0	0	1	1	0	0
L	76	0	1	0	0	1	1	0	0
O	79	0	1	0	0	1	1	1	1

When the above codes are being received, the 'person' at the receiving end must then decode the message by looking at the patterns of digits received, converting them to decimal, and finally looking up the table to find out what the original message must have been. The idea is shown in the second table.

Binary patterns received (Column headings)								Number	Message
128	64	32	16	8	4	2	1		
0	1	0	0	1	0	0	0	72	H
0	1	0	0	0	1	0	1	69	E
0	1	0	0	1	1	0	0	76	L
0	1	0	0	1	1	0	0	76	L
0	1	0	0	1	1	1	1	79	O

It's amazing just how many computer operations are performed using similar techniques to those just described. The codes used here are not made up at random, but are part of what's called the ASCII code, developed by the Americans and explained in more detail in chapter 12. Communication over the Internet or communication between the main computer and a peripheral would all be carried out using similar principles. If you have understood the simple binary techniques outlined above, then you will be able to appreciate what happens when computers and other similar devices communicate information.

Generations of computers

Inside each computer there are tiny devices called **transistors**, which carry out these lightning-speed switching operations. Today millions of these transistors can

'easily' be packed into a **silicon chip** – but this has obviously not always been the case. In the early days of electronic computers, **valves**, as shown in figure 2.6(a), were used as the switching device. They were quite large, consumed lots of energy, and thus the computers built up using these components took up the space of a very large room – they became known as the **first generation of computers**. Later on the **transistor** was invented, and this smaller and more energy-efficient device led to the **second generation of computers**. They were more powerful, consumed less energy, and took up less space than the first generation machines.

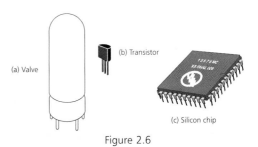

(a) Valve (b) Transistor (c) Silicon chip

Figure 2.6

A real break through came in the 1960s when several transistors were put into a single package called an **integrated circuit** or **silicon chip**. These became known as the **third generation machines** and were smaller and more powerful again. In the 1970s and 1980s it became possible to pack more and more transistors into a single silicon chip, until at the end of the 1990s, it's now possible to get well over 5,000,000 in a single-chip device. Computers making use of these latest chips are called **fourth generation computers**. **Fifth generation computers** have been on the drawing board for a number of years, but are discussed elsewhere in this book.

A modern overview of computers

In the following sections many ideas are introduced that will be covered in detail elsewhere. However, it's important to get a modern up-to-date overview of computers in general, and the hierarchy of computer systems in particular. More jargon will be thrown around in this section but it's not important to understand every detail at this stage of your course. Nevertheless, if there are one or two terms you don't understand at all, make use of the glossary at the back of the book.

From laptops to supercomputers

Until recently, computers could easily be classified into **minis**, **micros** and **mainframes** by considering their **size**, **performance** and **cost**. However, today, these definitions are not so cut and dried due to the ever-increasing pace of technology. Indeed, in a few years time some of these definitions may drop out of common usage altogether. The manufacturers are not helping by bringing out many terms such as **mini-supercomputers**, **superminis** and **micromainframes** etc. These are obviously terms used to describe the approximate position in the hierarchy to which their products belong. To understand this mass of jargon, it's still necessary to understand the older definitions of the terms minis, micros and mainframes. And a guide to the accepted use of these terms now follows.

The microcomputer

This is, quite simply, a small computer which uses one or a few microprocessors as its central processing unit(s). A microprocessor is the name given to the very complex chip, which contains most of the basic parts needed to set up a computer system using this single chip as the central processing unit. Microcomputers are usually the smaller **'desk-top models'** which range in price from a few hundred pounds to well over ten thousand pounds. A single keyboard usually accompanies a microcomputer; it usually has a printer, one or two hard disk drives, and maybe is connected to a network in a school, college or office.

Did you know that . . .

Most consumer products like the telephone, television and video recorder took 25 years to become established as standard equipment in the home. Microcomputers were invented in 1976. . . . As we come up to the start of the Millennium, almost 25 years later, this is actually coming true for the microcomputer too!

In the late 1970s the first microcomputers were 8-bit machines. (Although some less-useful 4-bit microprocessors were available earlier.) This meant that their fundamental unit of data was *eight* **binary digits**, just like the **ASCII code** example mentioned earlier. However, the 1980s saw a tremendous increase in both speed and processing power, and 16-bit and 32-bit microcomputers are now common. We have more recently also seen the introduction of the first 64-bit microprocessor which gives the effective power of a mainframe of the early 1980s! However, if you think that's impressive, in 1994, a company called MIPS brought out the new R8000 64-bit RISC chip which is claimed to have the power of a CRAY YM/P supercomputer. This particular micro can perform over '300 million double-precision floating-point operations/sec', and in 1994 sold at a very reasonable £110,000. (That *was* reasonable compared to the cost of a Cray at that time!) However, the very latest Pentiums, (called the Merced project), still under development at the time of

writing, will probably be even more powerful than the chip just described, and for raw processing power it's difficult to beat the latest Cray T3E supercomputers described in chapter 7.

It's still relatively unusual for a microcomputer that we ordinary mortals can afford to be **multi-user** (i.e. *more than one person can make use of it at the same time*). However, **multi-tasking** is now very common (i.e. the computer *carrying out several different tasks at apparently the same time)*. The very powerful microcomputers (see Plate 1) tend to be used for powerful applications such as top-of-the-range CAD that requires an enormous amount of processing power, graphics-handling ability and pots of memory such as the Silicon Graphics Workstations, for example. A typical modern microcomputer can be seen in figure 2.7.

Figure 2.7

The laptop computer

Portable power came of age towards the end of the 1980s. Indeed some of these **laptop portables** now have the same ability as some of the larger microcomputers, and in the late 1990s Intel's powerful 'Pentium Pro' processor found its way into portables too. It's now usual to have 32 or 64 megabytes of main memory, together with a medium-capacity (3 or 4 Gbyte) hard disk and coloured monitor. In addition to this, the laptop portable can have sophisticated communications facilities, made even better by the introduction of the credit-card-size PCMCIA architecture. It's now possible for any person to get important data back to the office via a network or the telephone system from anywhere in the world.

Did you know that . . .

Most computers used by ordinary people may well be portable at some time in the not-too-distant future. They may be connected to the Internet and Local Area Networks via satellite or other radio links. You will be able to access data from almost anywhere in the world – and beyond!

Most of the software that can run on a desktop micro can be run on a top-of-the-range laptop portable. It is these portables which have revolutionised the way in which many people make use of their computers. If you have a computer available wherever you are, then you are more likely to make use of it. Indeed, in many years time, most computers may be of the laptop variety, perhaps permanently linked to a network via a radio link similar to that used for portable phones, or direct via satellite. It has been estimated that the power of today's supercomputers will be available in a laptop or even a 'pocket calculator' in less than a decade. If you think that this statement is a little far fetched, just ponder for a moment on the facts mentioned earlier in this chapter. A computer which used to take up the space of a very large room, can now have the equivalent processing power on a piece of silicon 1 cm^2 in area, and a few fractions of a millimetre thick! If you're still not convinced, think for a moment about the computer, which fits inside a standard credit card! As a final example, the mathematical processing ability of my Texas TI 85 calculator far exceeds the capacity of the mainframe to which I had access when I took my degree back in 1975 – it's certainly an exciting field to be in!

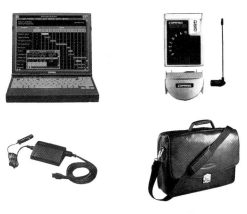

Figure 2.8

Some typical laptop equipment can be seen in figure 2.8

Remember the above facts when being asked about the social effects of microminiaturisation and computerisation. The microcomputer started off the personal computer revolution, the portable laptop computer will take it many stages further, especially when combined with mobile phone or radio-linked network technology.

The minicomputer

This is a medium-sized computer and can vary in power from a *very large and powerful* **micro** to a **small mainframe**. Indeed, because of the increasing power of minis, the mainframe market has shrunk considerably over the last few years. A minicomputer is often a floor-standing model, although some modern ones now fit onto the top of your desk – but there's not much space left for the pot of coffee! A small **minicomputer** might be able to support from ten to twenty users. It is, therefore, ideal for use within a single department within a college or university, or for use in a medium size business. However, the minicomputer market is now being taken over by powerful file servers and networks as described in chapters 3, 4 and 5.

The mini has been designed with **multi-user access** in mind, and is therefore usually easy to expand up to the maximum possible numbers of users. A schematic diagram of some typical minicomputer facilities can be seen in figure 2.9(a) and a typical minicomputer is shown in figure 2.9(b).

The ability to upgrade is the name of the game when considering minis. For example, **DEC** (the **Digital Equipment Corporation**) has a range of **VAX computers** which go from a desktop microcomputer to a powerful mainframe supporting thousands of users. This has the added advantage that, when changing from the smaller to the larger machines, you do not have to change operating systems. They all run **Ultrix**, which is DECs version of **Unix**. This makes the VAX a popular machine

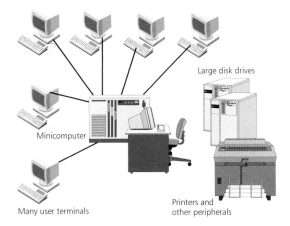

Large disk drives

Minicomputer

Many user terminals

Printers and other peripherals

Figure 2.9a

Figure 2.9b

for companies which need to expand, but don't wish to make fundamental changes to the computer systems which lie at the heart of their operations. Other major players in the market also do similar upgrade paths.

Mainframe computers

These are the *largest* of computer systems (*not necessarily the fastest or most powerful*) – they certainly won't fit on the top of your desk! It is common to have hundreds of simultaneous users on such a system. There is usually a vast amount of **RAM**, and many extra peripherals such as tape and disk machines. A schematic is shown in figure 2.10(a), and a typical mainframe, in this case a global server, is shown in figure 2.10(b). You should pay particular attention to **mainframe** and *larger computer systems* throughout your advanced level course, because many questions in examinations which revolve around these large machines will not make too much sense if you are mentally locked into the world of microcomputers.

Figure 2.11

Supercomputers

These are the **fastest and most expensive modern computer systems**. They are usually not used for normal data processing, but for *intense mathematical calculations* such as forecasting the weather, or super high-resolution graphics such as ray-traced images. Nevertheless, for very large systems such as the customs-clearance system in the port of Singapore, all the government departments are linked to a supercomputer which is then able to produce all the necessary documentation for clearance in just a few minutes, compared to several days under the older manual systems. There are also many scientific and engineering applications that require enormous processing speed and power.

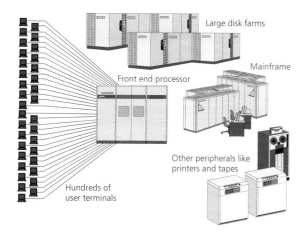

Figure 2.10a

> ### Did you know that . . .
>
> The Cray T932 series, shown in figure 2.11 is capable of 56,000 million calculations per second – not bad for a mere £10,000,000 in the late 1990s!

Some modern computing ideas

After the above whirlwind tour of different computer types, we will finish off this chapter with an equally fast whirlwind tour of some other major concepts, which are useful to appreciate at the beginning of your course.

Multi-tasking

A **single processor** may have the ability to carry out several tasks at apparently the same time. This process is called **multi-tasking**. A good demonstration of this ability can be seen on some of the most modern microcomputers when running different software packages

Figure 2.10b

in two different windows on the same screen 'simultaneously'. It's obviously not as fast as running each process individually, but is often a great help. For example, you could be writing a letter on a word processor while a database package is searching the database to produce a report. Or you can make use of the windows clipboard which enables you to transfer data between the two different packages with ease.

The virtual machine

This idea can be considered as apparently having multiple copies of the same hardware. For example, **virtual memory** makes it appear that the machine has more memory than it has actually got by making use of a disk to transfer data to and from the main memory. A **virtual peripheral** might be a printer that can serve several different people simultaneously. If you are to print out your document and another person is using the printer, then your file is automatically saved on disk until the printer is free, when it will be automatically printed out as though the printer had been free all the time. You will see the term 'virtual' crop up in many situations. For example, the **VAX machines** mentioned in the previous section mean **Virtual Address eXtension** machines. The operating system on this machine is **VMS**, which stands for **Virtual Memory System**. This gives an effective '4096 Megabytes of RAM'!

Parallel processing

It is possible for one processor to carry out several tasks as described in the multi-tasking section, but it's also possible for **several processors** to carry out a **single task**. This can range from a simple multi-processor machine that has a main microprocessor for the running of the programs, and a separate microprocessor for the handling of the peripherals, through to a powerful machine having many processors operating on the same problem in parallel. Much work has recently gone into parallel processing, as it gets over the traditional computer bottleneck of only being able to do one thing at a time. Such systems often make use of **transputers**, and some typical approaches to parallelism are covered in chapter 20.

Integration of these ideas

You will find that systems are being developed all the time, which use combinations of the **hardware** and **software techniques** mentioned above. Therefore you may see descriptions such as a '*multi-processor multi-tasking supermini running a virtual systems architecture*'!

Computer languages

Although we have seen that computers ultimately work in **binary code**, it would be tedious in the extreme if humans had to instruct them in this way too. At a fundamental level *people can instruct the computer in binary* and this is called **machine code**. However, a more convenient way of carrying out fundamental operations is to replace the binary code by *easy-to-remember instructions*, which is called **assembly language**. **Assembly language** makes use of **mnemonics** (*aids to the memory*), where MUL, for example, might be part of the instruction to MULtiply two numbers together. Both the **machine code** and **assembly language** methods of programming are known as **low-level language programming**, because they are intimately tied up with operating the machine at a very low level.

Did you know that . . .

Large computer firms fight tooth and nail to try and get their **computer languages** accepted as the industry standard. Hundreds of millions of dollars are usually at stake for the company that succeeds in outdoing its rivals.

It's fortunate that we are able to program computers in much simpler ways, and many high-level languages have been developed. These high-level languages are far removed from the detailed ways in which the machine operates, and are closer to English-like instructions and the ways in which humans like to think. Examples would be languages like **BASIC**, **Visual Basic**, **Delphi**, **Pascal**, **Prolog**, **C++**, **Java++ and FORTRAN 90**. Such languages can be split up into two major different methodologies called **imperative languages** and **declarative languages**, although others are also considered later in this book.

Imperative languages typify the type in which the programmer gives the computer a set of instructions (called imperatives) which explain exactly how to achieve a result. However, declarative languages typify giving the computer declarations in which the user has not had to state explicitly how the end result is to be achieved – all will be revealed in time!

Applications

Most of the population would either not want to or not be capable of programming computers in either high or low level languages. It's fortunate, therefore, that specialist companies write their own very complex programs to perform specific jobs such as turning the computer into a **word processor** or DTP system, for example. These programs enable non-specialist users to be able to use the computer as a tool without an understanding beyond the system that they are currently using. Such useful programs are called **applications packages** or, more simply, **applications**. There are literally thousands of different applications on the market, and more are being developed each day. As computer hardware becomes more high-speed and sophisticated, applications become more powerful and easier to use by all. Much computer literacy is obtained by being familiar with and able to use a variety of different applications packages. In your advanced level courses, it's essential that you are able to use **word processors**, **DTP systems**, **spreadsheets**, **CAD packages**, **databases**, **communications packages** and a variety of others such as **control systems** and **data loggers** if possible.

Computer control of industrial plant and other machinery is also a major area in which computers are currently employed; it varies in range from the control of robots and aircraft, to the control of oil installations in the North Sea. Such systems make heavy demands on the **operating systems**, and **real-time systems** are often employed. These real-time systems are generally those which have to respond very quickly to external events, and need very high reliability factors too.

Defining a problem

Even with a superabundance of applications and high-level languages, it's still up to individual people to use their talents and initiative to invent new ways of using computers or to improve existing methods. Complex projects have to be managed, and resources such as time and money have to be used efficiently. Much computer science is therefore devoted to organising your thoughts into ways of getting defined outcomes to problems quickly and efficiently. Many graphical techniques of problem solving, together with a huge variety of other computer-based methods are covered later on in the book. At the most fundamental level you have to write down your solution to a problem in some particular way and in computing this vital recipe for the solution to a problem is called an **algorithm**.

> **Hint:** You need to pay particular attention to the methods which allow you to define complex problems in clear and concise ways. This will pay dividends when it comes to planning and implementing your project work later on in your course.

Many different methods exist for constructing algorithms, including **flowcharts**, **pseudocode**, **structure diagrams**, **JSP diagrams** and **state-transition diagrams** to name but a few. All have advantages for particular types of problem, and by the end of your course you should be able to realise where each one would be most helpful. Some methods are reasonably obvious, such as flowcharts for example. Figure 2.12 shows a very simple

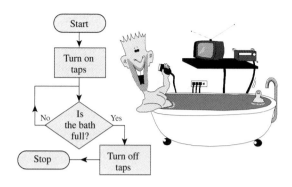

Figure 2.12

flowchart, which describes the very last part of an algorithm to turn off the taps when filling the bath.

Notice that in this particular mode of operation, a machine would spend most of its time whizzing round the loop asking if the bath is full. When it has decided that the bath is full, probably by some suitable sensor attached to an appropriate position to detect the water level, then the taps will be turned off and this particular part of the bathtub algorithm would be completed.

The future

Most people perceive computer science as being a rapidly changing subject, and in the main they are right. However, many of the basic principles don't change, it's just that the technology used does change at an amazing pace. For example, **hard disks** have been with us now for about 30 years. Their principles of operation have changed little, but what *has changed* is a *great increase* in their **speed of operation**, a *vast increase* in their **memory capacity**, *drastic reductions* in their **size**, even more *drastic reductions* in their **price** and a *huge increase* in their **reliability**. Disks with Gbyte capacity would have been regarded as a mainframe peripheral device just ten years ago. Today they are now common inside portables – tomorrow who knows? **Nanotechnology** (see chapter 7) might mean that they will fit inside a credit card!

> **Hint:** To keep up to date with the latest technology make sure that you read some of the many computer magazines published each month. They are an invaluable source for keeping up with future developments in the computer industry.

What has now revolutionised computing is the linking up of the computers via the Internet and Intranets. You are no longer regarded as a 'Nerd' if you surf the Net, and getting information from some of the millions of Web sites is now regarded as normal.

Videophone calls to anywhere in the world for the cost of a local call (see chapter 4), secure credit-card transactions and on-line banking are becoming the norm for the 'information rich' societies. With the introduction of VRML giving us 3D access to information, it's a small step to the common use of VR helmets and perhaps the whole-body suits. Put this together with the simulators which are now available at reasonable cost and the future for computer interaction should reach new heights in the next decade. Couple this with the real-time analysis of speech which is on the verge of being perfected at sensible cost, and the potential for education and training alone is truly breathtaking.

Exercise 2.1

1 **a** Into which three major divisions can a computer system be split? What benefits are achieved by doing this?

   b Which is the odd one out in the following list? (*Use the glossary if necessary.*)

   Monitor, Keyboard, Microprocessor, Compiler, Printer, Paper.

2 Explain the relationship between raw data and information.

3 Answer the following questions about the computer systems that you have at your school or college.

   a List the main types of computers used.

   b Which high-level languages are supported?

   c List ten different software packages.

   d How much RAM is available in each computer?

   e What is the name of the operating system in each type of computer?

   f If a network is used, what type is it, and how many bits/sec can it transmit?

4 Which *electronic components* are used to define each **generation** of computers?

5 Make a list of some of the important characteristics associated with each of the following types of computer: *micro, mini, mainframe, laptop.*

6 What does a parallel processing architecture mean?

7 Explain in principle how a machine as versatile as a computer may carry out all of its tasks by 'simple' manipulation of binary digits.

8 Considering the current rapid changes in technology, suggest some changes (*other than the communications one mentioned at the end of this chapter*) which you feel might lead to differences in the ways in which computers might be used in the future.

End of chapter revision aid and summary

Cover up the right-hand column and see if you can answer the questions or define the terms on the left. They appear in the order in which they are covered in this chapter. Alternatively you may browse through the right-hand column to aid revision.

What is a computer?	A computer is a processor of information.
Define information.	Information = data + structure
Into what three different basic units can a computer system be split?	A computer system can be split up into input, processing and output sections.
What is software?	The set of instructions inside a computer is called a program. Software is the name given to the programs which control the computer system.
What is hardware?	Hardware is the machines and materials like the monitors, printers and paper etc.
Describe the binary system.	The binary system is a two-state system on which digital computers operate. Any information can be encoded into binary form and manipulated electronically.
What is the basic electronic component out of which a digital computer is made?	Electronic digital computers are built up making use of tiny transistors used as switches.
What is a silicon chip?	A silicon chip is an Integrated Circuit (IC) which contains many transistors.
What is a microprocessor?	A 'complete computer' on a single chip is called a microprocessor.
What is a microcomputer?	A microcomputer is a small computer based around one or just a few microprocessors.
Define first generation computers.	The first generation of computers makes use of valves.
Define second generation computers.	The second generation of computers makes use of discrete transistors.
Define third generation computers.	The third generation of computers makes use of integrated circuits.
Define fourth generation computers.	The fourth generation of computers makes use of VLSI (Very Large Scale Integrated) circuits.
Define fifth generation computers.	The fifth generation of computers employs a different philosophy and is designed around knowledge-based machines (see chapter 9).
What is a minicomputer?	A minicomputer is a medium-sized computer allowing several users to use it via a number of terminals.
What is a mainframe computer?	A mainframe computer is a very large-scale computer often allowing hundreds of users simultaneous access – it usually has a vast array of peripheral devices too.
What is a supercomputer?	A supercomputer is the most powerful computer in terms of having the fastest available processors. It's usually used for applications such as forecasting the weather.
What is multi-tasking?	Multi-tasking enables a computer to apparently do more than one thing at the same time.

What is a virtual system?	A virtual system is one that has apparently got more memory or other resources than are actually physically present.
What is parallel processing?	Parallel processing is the ability to do more than one thing at the same time, often by utilising more than one processor in the same system.
What is an operating system?	The Operating System (OS) is a huge and complex piece of software which controls the entire operation of a computer.
Into which two main categories can computer languages be split?	Computer languages can be split up into low level and high-level languages.
What is a low-level language?	A low-level language uses machine code or assembly language which is near to what happens inside the electronics of a particular machine.
What is a high-level language?	A high-level language is nearer to the natural languages in which humans think.
What is an algorithm?	An algorithm is a sequence of instructions to solve a specific problem in a finite amount of time.

The Networked Computer

In this chapter you'll learn about:

◆ Local, metropolitan and wide-area networks

◆ Network architectures

◆ File servers and terminals

◆ Fat and thin client networks

◆ The advantages and disadvantages of using a network

◆ Bandwidth and it's associated problems

◆ Network topology

◆ FDDI, ATM and other modern technologies

Key resources

To carry out this work most successfully it's best if you have:

◆ Access to Ethernet or other similar network-based systems

◆ An account located on a file server to which you can log on

◆ Use of e-mail or other facilities such as an 'Intranet' or 'Teletext server', for example

◆ Access to the network manager at you school or college. He or she may be a teacher, or, more likely, a technician

◆ Don't forget the **glossary** at the back of this book. It should be very helpful to explain some concepts with which you may not be familiar

Concept checkpoints

◆ Basic units such as Mega and Giga etc. (see chapter 12).

◆ How codes are used to transmit messages (see chapter 2).

To understand the technology which underlies the Internet and Intranet is to understand the fundamental direction in which modern computing is heading. **Therefore, before covering the Internet in depth (see chapter 4), we take a look at the infrastructure upon which this pervasive technology is based.**

You should be in no doubt at all about the popularity of the 'information superhighway' or the 'Internet'. These terms are a 'catch all' for the marrying together of different technologies such as telephone systems, satellite systems, computer networks and multimedia. Together with an appropriate set of software and hardware facilities, stir in a large number of information providers, some bulletin-board systems and Newsgroups, and you have what's come to be known as the 'Internet', 'net', 'World Wide Web' or simply, 'the Web'. **Recent innovations such as better compression techniques, the increasing digitisation of the telephone networks and the tumbling prices of equipment needed to connect to such systems, have all proved positive factors in enabling millions of people to have access to the net.**

Today we have the remarkable ability to communicate with anybody else at any time, and in virtually any place. For example, via satellite systems we can communicate from a car travelling in a London high street to a ship sailing in the South Pacific Ocean. It's now even possible to 'surf the web' without a conventional computer. This, for example, could be done using multimedia boxes such as those produced by Sony, which can now give you web access through your TV set for about £200 pounds at the time of writing. The idea is shown in figure 3.1

Figure 3.1

Many homes now have interactive two-way communications via this vast web of networks, so let's see what technologies have championed this cause, and how these technologies have revolutionised the ways computers are used in industry and commerce today.

Computer networks

The LAN

Computer networks are categorised according to how they are organised physically, the ways in which they are used, and the distances over which they can operate. There are three main categories, although alternative names are also used. The first type of network is called a **LAN**, which stands for **Local Area Network**. As its name implies, this typifies a 'small' network operated *locally*. The term 'small' is obviously relative, as hundreds or even thousands of computers may be connected up via a LAN. The term LAN can more usefully be quoted in relation to the *length of the cabling which the network can support*. About *1.5 km* is a typical maximum length for a **LAN**, although the newer and faster LAN technologies can't usually go more than a few hundred metres without the signals being boosted by what's called a **repeater**. Each part of the LAN will usually be under the exclusive control of the educational, business or industrial establishment operating the system.

The MAN

Next in the hierarchy comes a **MAN** or **Metropolitan Area Network**. These typify the more recent **FDDI networks** where fibre optics are used, and the range of these is typically about *10 km, although 100 km is now available* – hence the term **MAN**. However, fibre is becoming more extensively used in a LAN environment, especially where very heavy usage is likely.

The WAN

Finally, **WANs** or **Wide Area Networks** make use of *public and private communication and phone lines*. These are the **national** and **international computer** and **telephone networks** provided by the telecommunications companies such as British Telecom or Mercury, and can thus reach the parts of the world that the other networks can't reach! These *global networks* are sometimes known as **LHNs** or **Long Haul Networks**, but the preferred term **WAN** is more extensively used.

Increasingly sophisticated methods of connection have become possible over the last few years, because the telephone networks are changing from the old style analogue system (see chapter 8) to the new style high-speed digital technology. WANs can make use of the standard telephone system, but, as is more likely in the case of high speed computer communications, use special dedicated lines instead. Satellite, land-based and underwater links are all increasing, and a combination of many different types of network is also common. We will now look at these networks in more detail.

Local area networks

A **LAN** refers to the connection of computers in a **local area** such as a *school, office* or *factory*. These may be in the same building, or, just as likely, involve connection of many computers in several different buildings on the same campus, or at different sites relatively close to each other. Bear in mind the maximum length of an individual network is usually limited to about 250 m, 1 km or 2 km depending on geometry and type of network. However, it's common on larger sites to have *several* **LANs** interconnected by the use of **bridges, routers, repeaters** or **hubs**. In this way, two **LANs** connected via a **bridge**, for example, will give you double the cable length.

A *very simple* **local area network** or **LAN** would probably consist of just ten or twenty computers sharing some resources, and a typical one is shown in figure 3.2

Did you know that . . .

You can surf the web using a variety of underlying technologies including conventional phone lines, computer networks, cable TVs and satellite links. Christmas 1999 saw the launch of WebTV, a non-technical service which it is hoped will help make the web more popular for people who do not have access to microcomputers, and who are likely to be less technically minded. Many more similar facilities are likely to follow.

In such a system each computer connected to the network is often referred to as a **terminal** or a **workstation** (not to be confused with the same term used to denote a high-end micro). The **file server** is usually a *high performance micro* with several large drives, often giving many Gbytes of capacity, and perhaps ten or twenty CD-ROM drives too. The **printer server** such as the one shown in figure 3.2 allows all networked machines to have access to a laser printer in this particular case. One printer server can, however, control access to many different laser printers or colour printers, and on some systems the file server takes on the task of printing. Printing jobs sent to the server would be **queued** if necessary (i.e. more than one thing needs to be printed), and the work is usually **spooled** (see chapter 23) and sent to the printer when it's free. It's also possible to have access to *other servers* such as **teletext servers**, or **proxy servers** (see chapter 4) which allow all the micros access to

> **Hint:** If possible, ask your network manager to show you how the LAN manages print spooling. Get a few students to print several jobs simultaneously, and see how the print-spooler software handles the task.

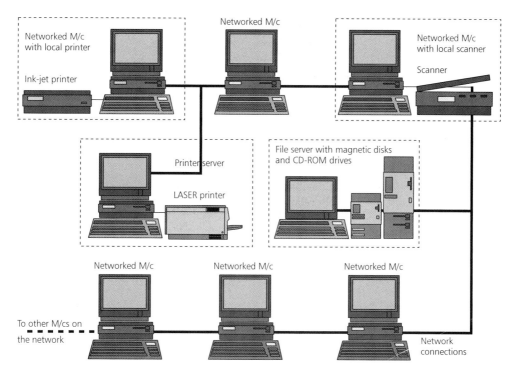

Figure 3.2

external networks via the **public telephone system** or dedicated lines. It's also very common to set up file servers containing different databases, or **internal web sites**, in which case the system running would be called an **Intranet** (see chapter 4). The microcomputer workstations can often work totally independently of the network by using their *own resources*, or use the network *instead of their own resources*, or use a *combination of both* simultaneously.

The NC or Network Computer

Managing local resources on each of the workstation's hard disks is often difficult and time consuming for the network administrator, unless he or she locks up the hard disks by using a security system like that provided by the Windows NT operating system, for example. Even then, any changes to each of the hard disks on the network must either be done locally, or by special software which updates each of the disks in turn from the file server – a mammoth undertaking, even in a relatively modest sized network such as those found in schools. Due to these administrative difficulties, it's now becoming a popular option to place some of the processing power at the server end, and have what's effectively an intelligent terminal (a simpler computer) as workstations on the LAN. These very small *diskless machines* (i.e. no floppy or hard disks!) can also prove to be a cost-cost effective option. Each NC would effectively have a large chunk of RAM (memory) allocated to it in the file-server's memory, and much of the processing is carried out using this RAM instead of

RAM held locally – even the windows-based operating system (see chapter 22) is not held on the local machine! As far as the user of an NC is concerned, they have similar functionality to a PC. However, it's obviously going to react more slowly, especially if the network is being heavily used, or if so many users are logged on to the system that the amount of RAM that can be allocated by the file server to each user is less than optimum. However, if this system is used then you may find that lack of local resource such as sound cards, graphics cards and CD-ROM etc. mean that you can't run some of the 'normal' software. Typically you would need at least 256 Mbytes of RAM in a file server for about ten users, and you would need a fairly fast network, especially if you were going to run software such as real-time video images like those from the Encarta Encyclopedia CD-ROM.

This novel NC idea is taken even further with the advent of the NC for use on the Internet, and the language Java (see later) and other developments are championing the cause of having less processing power and resources held on the local machine. There are pros and cons to each philosophy, and we will have to wait and see which ideas win in the long term. Other companies are also getting in on the act with what's called the **Network PC**. This PC *does* have a local disk and *does* have a floppy, but integrates the machine with the network and the Internet in fundamental ways not seen hitherto with stand-alone PCs. Microsoft's 'Internet Explorer 5' software and 'Windows 98' are classic cases in point. Here the Internet itself is a natural extension of the user's desktop, where the Internet is available from within almost any application. If a system such as the 'diskless workstation' mentioned above is used, then it is called a **thin client**, and the file server often does some if not all of the processing. However, if a fully blown PC with disks and all the trimmings is used, then it's called a **fat client**! Here the PC itself can deliver applications, and does most of the processing locally, with the possible exception of storing huge amounts of information. The system in which both workstations are operated is known as a **client/server architecture**.

There are many political and other commercial considerations which sometimes override the technical problems (see chapter 13), and these reflect the characters in the computer industry who constantly try to outdo each other by attempting to get their systems adopted as the norm.

Why make use of LANs?

There are lots of reasons for making use of networks as opposed to having many independent microcomputers or workstations. The networked computers can make more efficient use of common resources such as **applications software**. This saves the bother of having to store the software on many different disks for each machine – as described in the last section – a nightmare scenario for network managers.

The network gives the computers attached to it the ability to communicate with each other. For example, you can easily set up **electronic mail** systems (see later) and **bulletin boards**. You can also make use of **facsimile (FAX) systems** (i.e. scanning a document and transmitting the contents around the network or via the phone system), can carry out **distributed transaction processing** (i.e. workstations have access to and help control parts of a networked business system) and access central **databases** etc. Relatively expensive resources such as laser printers can also be shared between several people. A network of machines will usually be cheaper to operate than the equivalent number of machines each having the same facilities locally (i.e. printers, disks and software etc.). It also means that a manager can easily maintain all the software if it happens to be stored on a single centralised-distribution system. You could, if you wished, share the processing of some complex problem between several machines on the network, or even play some interactive games of the shoot-em-up variety! There are many different possibilities and no doubt many others will soon be invented. The use of the LAN in both educational and business systems is now so pervasive that *it's the norm rather than the exception to have networked computers for everyday tasks.*

Using a LAN in practice

To make use of a LAN-based network the user would usually have to **log on** to the **file server**. In some very sophisticated systems, this may mean logging onto a powerful **mini** or **mainframe** computer, but on most LANs it means logging onto a powerful PC such as an NT or Novel file server, for example. The **file server** is an appropriate name because this is the machine on which the users' **files** are usually stored, then *served out* to the users when necessary. It is also usual to store **applications** such as **web browsers**, **DTP systems**, **CD-ROM** based systems, **spreadsheets** and **databases** etc. on the same or a physically different file server to which the user has access.

> **Hint:** If possible, get your network manager or teacher to explain how the local resources are organised on your network. Where are your personal files stored and where are the software packages stored?

There would normally be a **security system** whereby each user would have 'full access' only to those parts of the file-server disks on which his or her particular files are stored. In addition to this they would probably have **public access** (i.e. **read-only access**) to **utilities** and **packages** used by everybody. Such security is normally implemented by a **password system**, and some suitable **data structure** that helps to identify which areas of the disk *belong to which user.*

In addition to making sure that the user gets access to his or her own resources, it's possible to give each user his or her own personal profile. This means that the user can customise backdrops to the desktop, customise sounds, have his or her own customised application settings (such as tool bars used in the word processor, for example) and generally create an environment typical of that which would be available to them on their home micro. All this customisation information can be stored on the file server, so when a user logs on at any machine on the LAN, these settings take effect. It takes a little longer to log on if all of this information has to be downloaded, but it's more fun, and creates an environment in which users are usually 'very happy'. The alternative is to allow them no customisation at all, to have a boring standard desktop, and restrict use of the computer to such an extent that it becomes a boring tool for unimaginative work. However, as a network administrator of a large system with very inquisitive students, I understand why many people choose the latter option – it's far easier to manage!

If you are using a Microsoft Windows NT file server, for example, each user may have a home directory allocated to him or her. Although not necessary, it may be that the home directory is the same as the user's name that is required for log on purposes. The directory, which belongs to each user is usually shared. Thus 'security permissions' are granted giving them full control (i.e. read and write access) to all of their files. These are then stored in the root or other subdirectories within their shared directory. The idea is shown in figure 3.3. Here you can see that a pupil called 'Adamson' has created many directories in which to organise his or her own work effectively. To the user it's as though they

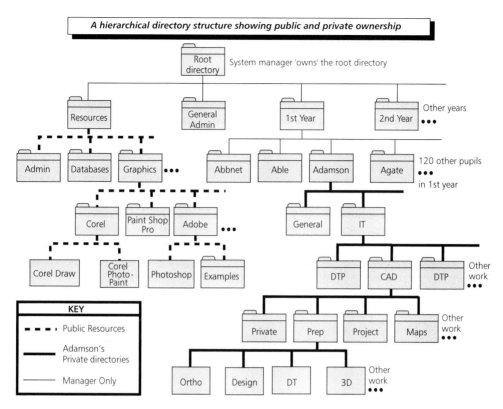

A hierarchical directory structure showing public and private ownership

Figure 3.3

have their own local disk. However, to the administrator and the file server, it's just part of the large disk on the file server. This makes it especially easy to do backups of the users' work. It would be common in a school or college, for example, to back up each user group by 'year of entry' at the end of each day.

Practical problems

Under normal conditions, once the user has logged onto the system, there would theoretically be little difference between using the local area network and operating on local (i.e. inside your own machine) hard or floppy disk drives. However, problems often occur when many machines are being heavily used *at the same time* – this is due to the mass of computer data that has to be transmitted over the same wires. There is often an appreciable delay between requesting a particular operation and getting the appropriate response. This is particularly true with powerful 32-bit or 64-bit microcomputers running complex software on networks that were never originally designed with these very powerful facilities in mind. The problems occur due to the **limited bandwidth** of the network system, and this is explained in the next section.

Problems of bandwidth

Bandwidth is a *physical limitation* of any practical communication system – it is to do with the range of frequencies which can be transmitted and received over a communications link. To understand bandwidth, it's best to start with a simple analogy. The human ear, for example, can only hear frequencies in the approximate range of 20 Hz to 20 KHz depending on age. As you get older the higher frequencies tail off. The bandwidth of the human ear is therefore said to be between 20 Hz and 20 KHz for a young healthy person. These limitations are imposed because of the unique way in which human beings are built. Other animals, such as bats, for example, have a totally different bandwidth because they are built differently. In a similar way, transmission systems such as networks have a limited bandwidth due to the ways in which *they* are built, and the *materials* such as copper cable or fibre optics etc. from which they are made.

The lower the **bandwidth** of the system, the cheaper it is to produce, but the rate at which data can be transferred is usually less. It's rather similar to a motorway in the rush hour. If too many cars are trying to get from point A to point B, then there will be traffic jams, and the traffic will take a long time to get through. However, on a computer network, the traffic would be bytes of computer data, and instead of a traffic jam occurring, the computers would keep getting signals that the network is busy. They would have to wait for a free slot before they could send more data. If many computers are trying to send and receive information at the same time, then there will be many clashes and the effective data transfer rate for each computer will be small. More expensive higher-bandwidth systems will cope better. It's rather like having many more lanes on the motorway, more cars can be sent along the lines at the same time.

An understanding of the **bandwidth limitations** of different network connections is *essential* to gain an understanding of what can be done in practice when using **LANs** and **WANs**. For example, a simple **e-mail** connection might be very satisfactory on **low-band-width links**, but **full video conferencing** (see chapter 4) would *not* work over the same link. You would need a **much-higher bandwidth** to cope with the increased amount of information in the video signal which needs to be sent very quickly (more bits/sec) if you are to use the system in real time.

Network topology

This is the name given to the ways in which the **networks** are physically *organised in terms of how they are wired together*. It is also known as **network architecture**. The name is derived mainly from the ways in which the data is distributed along the network to each of the computers connected to it.

Star networks

The **star-network** connection can be seen in figure 3.4. The central resources for the network would be located at the 'centre' of the star. (*Note that the physical wiring need not be laid out like this – it's the connections that are important.*) Each workstation would be connected to the central **computer** or **file server** by means of its own *unique* link. With a high-speed computer controlling the **central node** then *very fast* communication

with all machines would be possible. The **bandwidth** of the network is also less of a problem because data for 'one machine only' is being sent down each of the single lines. This is the system that is most often used when many workstations are connected to a mainframe computer via a front-end processor (see chapter 2).

If there were many computers then this would be an expensive option. However, it does have the advantage that security is high. This is because no workstation can interact with any other without going via the **central-node computer** (i.e. the computer at the centre of the star). With sophisticated software, security can be *very tight* indeed. However, star networks do have some disadvantages; if one of the links becomes severed then the computer that relies on that link would become permanently disconnected. With some other network topologies it would be possible to route the data such that communication would still be possible between the main computer and the workstation.

Bus and tree networks

A **bus network** is shown in figure 3.5. As you can see it has a *common cable* which, on some networks, is terminated at each end, either inside a computer or by a special box as shown in this diagram. (The size of the box is obviously exaggerated!) One or more of the stations on the network acts as the file server and controls access to the hard disks, which are used for all the common resources and users' files.

The most prolific example of a bus system is **Ethernet** *when wired up as 10base5 or 10base2*. This is a network, which, in its original form, connects using a single co-axial cable, similar to but not the same as that

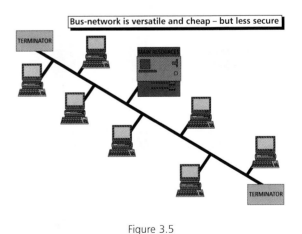

Figure 3.5

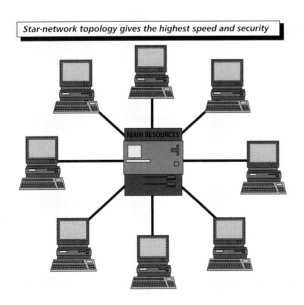

Figure 3.4

Did you know that . . .

Ethernet derives its name from the mythical 'ether' through which signals in the atmosphere were supposed to propagate according to the early scientists.

used for the aerial socket on a standard TV. Ethernet was developed jointly by Rank Xerox, the Digital Equipment Corporation (DEC) and Intel.

Ethernet is one of the main network-connection methods used for the interconnection of PCs or any other machine with an Ethernet interface card – in these days virtually all machines. **Ethernet** is *ideally suited* to the **business**, **educational** and **industrial** environments, giving satisfactory transmission rates of *10 Mbits/sec* in its original form. Ethernet is found in many universities, and has at last become cheap enough to install in most schools.

Over the years Ethernet (see **Plate 2**) has gone through several stages of metamorphosis, as faster technologies have been developed. The faster Ethernet systems now make use of a star topology, and copper or fibre-optic cabling. In this form they are wired up as 100BaseT (Fast Ethernet) and 100baseF (Fibre optics). **Fast Ethernet (100 Mbits/sec)**, for example, has now become very cheap, because the more expensive **Gbit Ethernet (1 Gbit/sec)** was launched in 1998. These ideas are shown in figure 3.6. When used in this way, the bus network is said to have a **tree-network topology**. This uses a baud rate of *100 Mbits/sec or 1 Gbit/sec*, and is thus more suited to today's higher speed interactive multimedia technology. There is also a cheaper 10 Mbit/sec version that can utilise the same cables and hubs. Fast Ethernet is a little more expensive than the original Ethernet, but the only major disadvantage is that the maximum length of cable is now cut down to 250 m before needing to be boosted.

Inside each computer you will need an **NIC** or **Network Interface Card**. This is a card that plugs into your PC and enables you to connect it to the network. You can have 10 Mbit/sec and 100 Mbit/sec versions, or even faster **Gbit Ethernet** (1 Gbit) using the higher-bandwidth links – the cost of 1 Gbyte Ethernet is coming down at the time of writing, but is mainly intended for 'beefy' file servers. Certain types of hubs also allow you to connect 10 Mbit/sec and 100 Mbit/sec machines to the same network. In this way the link to the file server could be at 100 Mbit/sec or even 1 Gbit/sec. The link to each of the workstations could also be at 100 Mbits/sec or 10 Mbit/sec, thus saving money in terms of the NICs which you would have to purchase, but giving you much better overall performance in terms of bandwidth. This information is summarised in the table below.

Ether type	Specification	Typical use
Ethernet	10 Mbit/sec.	Small office or computer room.
Fast Ethernet	100 Mbit/sec.	Large office, school or college campus.
Gbit Ethernet	1000 Mbit/sec.	Ethernet backbone on a campus.

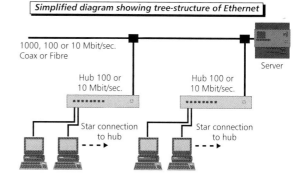

Simplified diagram showing tree-structure of Ethernet

1000, 100 or 10 Mbit/sec. Coax or Fibre

Server

Hub 100 or 10 Mbit/sec.

Hub 100 or 10 Mbit/sec.

Star connection to hub

Star connection to hub

Figure 3.6

Did you know that . . .

Any radio or copper-wire based electrical system is vulnerable to snooping via an analysis of the electromagnetic radiation emanating from the cables. The only way to get over this problem is to use fibre optics, or, more sensibly, encrypt the data before it is transmitted over the network.

The bus network is cheaper to operate than the star network because, for a large number of computers, there is often much less cable. However, bus type networks can never be totally secure as the data for one workstation must pass many others. Under normal operation this should not be a problem, but if very clever hackers are determined to illegally interrogate the packets (see chapter 5) of data as they go by, then there is little to stop them. It's much more difficult to hack a star network because you don't ever see data that is intended for other machines. If a **bus network** is being very heavily used, then, because everybody is sharing the same communications link, the response will be slow unless the **bandwidth** of the network is quite high. However, with **modern compression techniques** *it's possible to load large windows-based applications within an acceptable number of seconds*, and with a network that's not being heavily used the speed is comparable to that of a local hard disk.

The bus network is also less reliable than the star network, which is not too surprising considering that it's a cheaper alternative. If, for example, there is a fault in the network cable then all the machines will not be able to use the network. On a star network, and also to some extent on a tree network, there is a much larger redundancy built in. If one cable has a fault then it does not affect all the other workstations connected to the central node. However, the Ethernet system, when wired up using hubs as shown in figure 3.6, is much more reliable from this point of view.

Ring networks

As with the bus systems, **physical ring networks,** shown in figure 3.7, are *less secure* because data intended for a particular machine may have to pass by other machines to get to its destination. Neither the ring nor the bus network is as secure as the star network.

> **Hint:** If possible, get your network manager or teacher to show you any bridges or routers that control the interconnection of networks in your school or college. You will probably be amazed to see the amount of traffic that constantly flows across several busy network systems.

One of the first types of ring network was the **Cambridge ring**. This was developed at Cambridge University. In this network one station on the ring is the originator of a message which gets sent to the next station along the line. If the message is intended for this station, it is received, else the signal is boosted by a **repeater** and sent onto the next station. This situation continues until the correct station receives the message. A special station on the network called the **monitor** would provide power for the repeaters. This means that if an individual computer is disconnected from the network, then the messages are still sent round. However, these methods have been considerably improved, and better **token-ring** systems (see next section) have now been developed.

Token ring system

One method of sharing out the network bandwidth between all the machines is called a **token-ring** network. An electronic **token** is the name given to a *message* that contains a number of bits that are passed around a network as a packet. Each station may 'grab hold of' a token, and thereby gain control and send data along the network. When the token is released then it may be grabbed by another machine. A typical-token ring system would operate at about 4 Mbits/sec; however, the latest token rings go up to about 16 Mbits/sec. Although this sounds a little slow compared to fast Ethernet, for example, where rates of 100 Mbits/sec are now common, the method does not suffer from collisions like the Ethernet network, in which collisions happen when data transmission is attempted simultaneously by two machines.

Interconnection of LANs

Many business sites or educational campuses, for example, may have established a number of *separate* **LAN topologies**. It would be useful if these different types of networks, or even a number of networks of the same type could be **interconnected** so that *information could be shared* as if they were all joined together as one larger homogeneous network. Similar principles apply as the networks get much larger, as would be typical when considering the Internet. In this case more sophisticated interconnection devices such as **gateways** are needed to route the more complex network information to the appropriate destinations, and these techniques are covered in chapter 5.

A device called a **bridge** is one means of connection between two networks which make use of the same **logical protocols** (see chapter 5), but might use different **physical protocols** such as a ring and a bus for example. The idea is shown in figure 3.8. The **bridge** will look at the **electronic packets of information** and determine if the information needs to be passed on to the other network or not. **Intelligent bridges** are also available in which the station numbers of different machines could be used to determine which machines can have access over the bridge – this is useful for network security

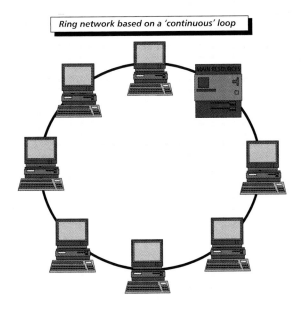

Ring network based on a 'continuous' loop

Figure 3.7

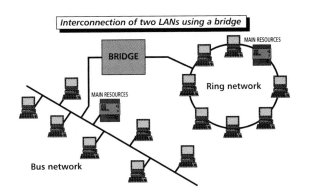

Interconnection of two LANs using a bridge

BRIDGE

MAIN RESOURCES

Ring network

MAIN RESOURCES

Bus network

Figure 3.8

purposes. The more complex the differences between the networks become, and the more sophisticated the requirements for security and routing etc. get, then the more sophisticated these interconnecting bridge devices need to be. A **router**, for example, is used on more sophisticated networks. These **routers** have the ability to connect different physically and logically organised networks. They can often work out the optimal routes, and are generally more 'aware' of the network because of the more sophisticated processing that can be carried out inside them – they can even work out the most cost-effective routes. If the networks are to be connected over long distances, then the interconnection devices often make use of **gateways**.

Types of network media

The **physical topologies** outlined in the last few sections may be implemented using a wide variety of network-transmission **media**. For example, many networks use copper cables such as coaxial (*similar to your TV-aerial lead at home*) or **twisted pair** (two copper cables literally twisted together), but others make use of fibre optics, land-based **radio** and **micro-wave** links, **satellite** links or even **infrared** and **laser** links.

WANs are *usually a combination of many of these systems*. For example, if you are making use of the **Internet** from a LAN-based workstation at college, your data might start off at a respectable rate by going along the college's '10 Mbit/sec coaxial cable Ethernet network' until it gets to the external **file server**. This may then link via a **MODEM** (see chapter 5) along a *standard* **telephone line** (ordinary thin wire) to your local Internet service provider. Depending on the type of MODEM, and how busy this particular link happens to be, your data might then have to crawl along this line at a pedestrian 2400 bit/sec! Your friendly UK-provider might then have an X-25 **packet-switched-network** link to a **mainframe** installation. Going through this part of the network, your data might travel along the higher-bandwidth cable at a rate of 64 kbit/sec. Let's say, for the sake of argument, to satisfy your request the mainframe installation might have to contact a **supercomputer**, which might have a 100 Mbit/sec **fibre-optic link** between these two monster computers. This whole scenario is shown in figure 3.9, but it's important to realise that the data transferred back to you is only as good as the performance of the weakest link at the time of transmission of the data.

The **types of media** used in practice and the **data transfer rates** that can be achieved are of *fundamental importance to the performance of the network*. For example, the college system is capable of loading applications from the file server simply because of the relatively high speed 10 Mbit/sec **Ethernet** coaxial cable. If, for the sake of argument, you tried to load the same software from the **mainframe** computer, then because of the 2400 bit/sec

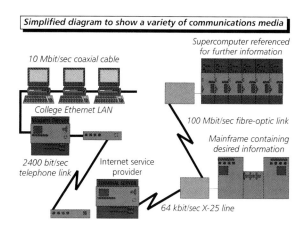

Figure 3.9

weakest link in the system at the time of connection, the software would take over 4,000 times as long to load. For example, if it takes 10 seconds to load a DTP system from the file server – it would take just over 11 hours to load it from the mainframe!

It's important to appreciate the sheer number of *different* **physical** and **logical** (see chapter 5) **topologies** over which your data has to pass, and to understand that the number of **logical** and **physical transformations** between different **protocols** that is taking place is literally staggering. Eventually your message will be decoded and activate the appropriate software at the host's computer – then it has to go through the reverse procedure to get back to your PC connected to your network back at the college – it's no small wonder that the entire system works at all!

> **Hint:** If possible, get your network manager or teacher to show you different types of Ethernet cable and cable connections. The common types are coax and twisted pair. Also, if possible, have a look at some typical fibre-optic cabling.

The **superhighway** is a network of staggering proportions, and the national and international communication network structure mind-boggling. In fact, the complexity is so great that some scientists have likened the combined international communication networks to a huge **neural network** (see chapter 9). It is said that this network could have a 'mind' of its own, and some believe that it could eventually exhibit some of the properties predicted by chaos theory – a fascinating topic to brush up on if you have a spare month or two.

Radio, laser and infrared links

A novel idea for creating a data link between two buildings can be seen in figure 3.10. Here a **laser beam** (coherent light beam) is used to transmit the data between two different sites.

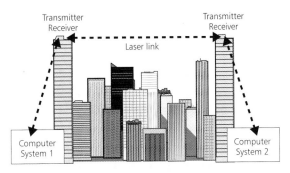

Figure 3.10

The distance between the buildings can be up to a maximum of 20km, but it is usually considerably less than this as the quality of data communications can be adversely affected by the weather. **Infrared links** are also used to link machines together *inside* the same building. This saves having to have cables underneath the floor or round the walls etc. It's rather like using the remote control with the TV. One unit controls the data sent to the others in similar ways. The same idea has also caught on for printing from portables. In this case both the portable computer and the printer would need infrared ports – simply point the portable towards the printer, and you are able to print without a cable connection between the portable and printer – magic!

Radio networks are also becoming popular and this has huge implications for both business and for educational institutions. For example, if you had a portable computer suitably equipped, and if your school ran a radio-based network, then you could use your portable computer from anywhere on the school site, provided that it was in range of the radio receiver. Imagine taking your portable from one classroom to another, or using it in the middle of the school playing fields, with access to all the benefits that you would have from a conventional permanent network connection. This is probably the way that some institutions will go when the price of such systems becomes affordable. Indeed, direct satellite links like this might be the way in which the whole planet may go when millions of people wish to connect to the Internet wherever they happen to be. Make the computer pocket sized, and you are getting very near to permanent connection from anywhere in the world, with all the implications that such a service might bring – the future does look very exciting indeed.

Fibre-optic networks

Some of the highest data-transfer rates are made possible by using **fibre optic networks** that are currently under continuous development. Also, if you make use of ordinary or coaxial cable, then these can suffer from electromagnetic interference. Fibre optic cables, being used to transmit light, do not suffer from

these problems. There has been an enormous amount of money put into the development of fibre optic networks, and recently they are becoming cheap enough to develop high-bandwidth cost-effective LANs and MANs. At the time of writing the **FDDI (Fibre Distributed-Data Interface)** system has become the standard. A single network can have a length of up to 100km, and transmit data at a rate of 100 Mbits/sec. The second version, called **FDDI II** has been developed with an even higher data transfer rate of up to 1 Gbit/sec. These systems are still a little expensive at the time of writing, and not many NICs would support or even need to support such a high bandwidth, and even if they did, the bus speed inside the PC would not be able to cope either. These 1 Gbyte and future faster systems are intended for use in places like the **Internet backbone**, and are not really intended for getting data from your PC at that rate, even if it were physically possible to do so.

> ## Did you know that . . .
>
> Just over ten years ago, the original 10Mbit/sec. Ethernet cards were far too expensive for most schools and colleges. Today, however, the high-speed 100 Mbit/sec. Ethernet cards are actually much cheaper than the original cards. Schools and colleges can now afford to install high-speed fibre links as the main backbone across their sites. This is the measure of network progress in just ten years.

These fibre optic networks are similar to the ring networks described earlier in this chapter. However, they often work on a more complex dual-ring system, which can get over problems such as an entire break in the fibre optic network! To appreciate how a network is able to do this, consider the diagram shown in figure 3.11

You can imagine the dual ring to be both carriageways of a large and busy motorway. If one of the links became severed in both directions (i.e. the same as a break in the fibre optic cable), then you could, theoretically, drive the other way round the motorway to get to the other side of the blocked link! This is exactly

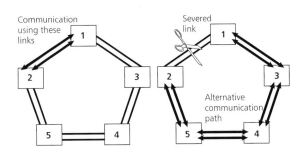

Figure 3.11

how the computer data would be routed round the two-ring fibre optic network. It would take a long time in your car (not to mention the danger!), but a very short time indeed for the light signal to travel round 100km of cable.

The UK Atomic Energy Authority at Harwell has an **FDDI network** in operation. It's fast enough to connect an IBM mainframe, some DEC VAXs and two CRAY II supercomputers! **Bridges** are used to connect this network to **Ethernet** and **token ring** systems.

The **bus**, **star** and **ring** networks mentioned earlier are some of the most common for LANs. However, other types of topology exist and these are shown in figure 3.12. The **mesh network** of figure 3.12(a) is common for long distance networks.

You can imagine each node on the network to be a computer in a different town or part of the country. Indeed, one of the earliest WANs was **ARPAnet**. This was started off by the American government's department of defence, and was called the **Advanced Research Project Agency** network. This was a **packet-switched** (see chapter 5) **mesh network** that originally linked the United States cities of Seattle, San Francisco, Los Angeles, Dallas, Houston, Atlanta, St Louis, Minneapolis, Milwaukee, Chicago, Detroit, Cleveland, Pittsburgh, Cincinnati, Boston, New York, Philadelphia and Washington. However, it's much bigger now! Even the U.K. now forms part of the former ARPAnet system, and the older ARPAnet system is the 'granddaddy' to the global **Internet** system.

If you made use of ARPAnet, then your computer was known as a **host**. This was to distinguish it from the computers at the **nodes**, which control the network and were known as **node computers**. The destination computer was also known as a host, and these names have stuck and are now internationally recognised terms. An alternative name for the **mesh network** is a **distributed network**.

A mesh network may be **fully interconnected** as shown in figure 3.12(a), or, more likely, **partially connected** as shown in figure 3.12(b). For links between cities, between military systems, and other systems where high reliability is important, fully connected mesh networks are sometimes used because there is a large amount of redundancy built in. For example, if a bomb severs the link between two computer systems, (back in the 1970s the defence department was keen to survive being nuked!) then the data can still pass between the two disconnected computers via several other paths.

Wide area networks

As can be seen from the **Internet/ARPAnet** example mentioned earlier, a wide area network is unlikely to be organised in the same way as a local area network. For a start, many different types of powerful computers would probably be interconnected by means of special land-based and satellite links. As lots of different computers are talking to each other, then a **communications protocol** (i.e. set of rules) must be established. Many details must be sorted out, and agreements must be made on how the information is to be transferred. (See **ISO OSI model** in chapter 5.)

Unlike the centralised control of the resources in a local area network, a wide area network is more likely to have **completely distributed control**. In such networks, the control lies with the computers at the individual nodes. At these **node computers** the communications protocol is established, and they efficiently control the flow of data between different computers and networks at local, national and international levels. *Very high bandwidth* **fibre optic** cables are now being installed between these links handling very high volumes of data.

Most of the operation of even the most sophisticated wide area networks is transparent to the user. Once they have logged onto the system, as with the local area networks, it is just like using a computer with its own local resources. Therefore, most of the advantages and disadvantages of LANs also apply to WANs. It's just that the phone bills are a lot bigger!

ATM

ATM stands for **Asynchronous Transfer Mode**. This type of network has been developed to try to cope with real time video and audio, as well as with the computer data being used in most other parts of this chapter. You should realise that any binary digit that gets corrupted when computer data is transmitted can have disastrous consequences. If you fail to appreciate this, then imagine that you have just won a million on the lottery, and an error in a few binary digits means that your bank account is credited with only £1,000! You now appreciate the point exactly! However, when transmitting real-time audio or video, the human brain can easily cope with quite a high error rate in the signal, probably without realising that anything is actually wrong.

The ATM method of transmitting data over computer links, mainly on WANs and more sophisticated and expensive LANs, has been developed by the telecom-

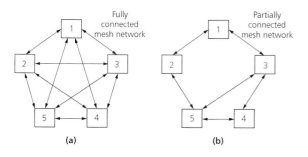

(a)   (b)

Figure 3.12

munication companies to overcome these little diffi-culties. The details of ATM would take up too much space in this book. However, the ATM networks, currently under continuous development at the time of writing, enables speech and video to be routed differ-ently from computer data. This is done so that the different requirements of 'speech and video' (constant signals where some errors are acceptable) and 'computer data' (bursts of data in which no errors are acceptable) are both catered for. The ATM network uses techniques such as multiplexing and packet switching, which are covered in chapter 5. There is also a big rival to ATM in the LAN market. Gbit Ethernet might take over from ATM as the preferred method for transmit-ting high-bandwidth information over LANs – we will have to wait and see what develops.

Networks and you!

It's important at the end of this chapter to gather together your thoughts and to apply what you have learnt to computer science in general. Many examina-tion boards now test what you know through a variety

of methods; the most important of which is the appli-cation. They will often ask what sort of hardware and software you would consider necessary to solve 'this or that problem'. Therefore, you must view networks in this particular way, especially for some of the modular examinations. Having read this chapter you are now in a position to appreciate what networks can do, and in what situations networks can be used. You can appreciate that problems can occur when the band-width of the network is not up to the job, or if Internet connections are too slow. Carry all this information with you when you consider applications in later chap-ters. You need to do more than say, 'A network may or may not be useful', you should be in a position to say that a certain type of network would be useful in a particular scenario, and back up your arguments with facts and figures. These facts should include informa-tion regarding 'data transfer rates' and the 'amount of use' that the network is likely to have.

You must, therefore, put all of the knowledge acquired in this chapter into the context of planning to solve particular problems, and this sort of methodology will be used on many occasions throughout this book.

Exercise 3.1

1 Outline some of the *main factors* that have influenced the development of computer networks over the last few years.

2 What are the main differences between a LAN and a WAN?

3 Typically, what facilities would you expect to find on a LAN set up, for example, to service a large computer room in a school?

4 Networks are becoming increasingly difficult to manage. New strategies have been developed in the hope that they will overcome these administrative difficulties. Outline the principles behind such a move.

5 What is the difference between an NC and a Network PC?

6 Lack of bandwidth is a constant problem with many networks. What is meant by the term bandwidth and why is this important?

7 Outline typical security procedures, which would usually be followed when logging on to a LAN.

8 Suggest a situation where a star network topology would be better than a bus network topology.

9 Make a list of five different network topologies.

10 Why do educational environments like schools and colleges, for example, put strains on a network system, which are *not usually* present in industry? Give at least two typical scenarios to illustrate your points.

11 Outline some typical functions which a network manager would have to undertake in order to maintain a LAN based system.

12 Why has the Ethernet network become so popular in the last few years?

13 What is the function of an NIC?

14 A college runs a large Ethernet based LAN which has 300 computers linked to it throughout several different buildings. There is a physical limit of 250m for this 100 Mbit/sec network, and this is not sufficient to reach the distances between the buildings. How is this problem solved?

15 List three typical scenarios in which a LAN would help to solve a business or scientific problem. For each of your scenarios, state *why* a LAN is an essential component of your chosen solution.

16 WANs are now part of life for millions of people. Using the Internet as an example, explain the infrastructure, which makes it possible for a user to connect their PC at home to a mainframe computer thousands of miles away.

17 A rich computer user has an FDDI II 1 Gbyte/sec link to the Internet. However, when downloading some information from his favourite site, he finds that it's actually being downloaded at 28.8 kbits/sec! Explain the likely cause of this drastic reduction in performance.

18 If you have access to a network-based system at your school or college, find out how it is organised in terms of file servers and domains etc. Find out what resources are available, the disk-drive capacity, and whether it operates on a thin or thick client basis. Your network manager should be able to help answer these types of questions.

End of chapter revision aid and summary

Cover up the right-hand column and see if you can answer the questions or define the terms on the left. They appear in the order in which they are covered in this chapter. Alternatively you may browse through the right-hand column to aid revision.

What is a network?	A network is a communication system, which allows the transfer of data between different computer systems.
What is a local area network?	Local area network – a network usually confined to one building or several buildings on the same site – under control of the local management.
What is a wide area network?	Wide area network – usually implying national or international communications making use of public communications systems.
What is a metropolitan network?	MAN is an acronym for Metropolitan Area Network – usually implies several networks working together over a wider area (perhaps up to a few hundred km). The term was coined due to the much more capable FDDI systems now in operation.
What is an LHN?	LHN is an acronym for Long Haul Network – an alternative name for a WAN.
Describe network architecture.	Network architecture is the name given to the *topological layout* of the network, and the *type of network used*.
What is the function of a file server?	A file server is a computer used to distribute files over a network system, and to help maintain the security of a network.
What is a work station or a terminal?	Computers connected to distributed-processing systems such as networks are often referred to as workstations or terminals. Microcomputers running appropriate software can act as terminals or workstations on a network.
What is a thin client?	A machine connected to a network that is unlikely to have any local hard disks for storing software. All resources, often including the operating system itself, would be downloaded from the fileserver. The file server often does much of the processing too.
What is a fat client?	A machine connected to a network that is likely to have a hard disk that can be used for application delivery and storage e.g. a normal PC connected to a network. Here the file server would do little, if any processing. The file server might still be used for application delivery.
What is client-server architecture?	The name given to the environment in which networked computers interact with the file server on the network. The clients are the

workstations and the server is the file server or ISP on the Internet, for example.

List some of the advantages of using a network.

Networks have advantages including efficient sharing of common resources and the ability to set up electronic mail, intranets and video conferencing, for example.

List some of the disadvantages of using a network.

Networks have disadvantages such as slow response time if the bandwidth is low and usage is high.

What is a distributed processing system?

A network in which the workstations carry out their own processing and help to control the resources on the network is called a distributed processing system.

What is a printer server?

A printer spooler or a printer server accepts data from any station on the network and directs it to a printer(s) connected to the spooler.

What does logging on mean?

Logging on means identifying yourself to a file server or main computer on the network so that you can gain access to a set of resources.

What are typical responsibilities for a network manager?

A network manager is the person responsible for maintaining the network – he or she would have the highest level of security possible.

Explain what is meant by bandwidth, quoting typical bandwidths for modern network systems.

The bandwidth of a network is the maximum rate at which it's possible to transmit data – e.g. Ethernet is about 10 Mbits/sec, fast Ethernet and FDDI is about 100 Mbits/sec and Gbit Ethernet and FDDI II are both 1 Gbit/sec.

What determines a particular bandwidth?

The bandwidth of a system is determined by physical attributes such as the material out of which the cables are made, and the performance of the 'interfacing electronics', for example.

What is network topology?

Network topology is the name given to the physical attributes of a network in terms of how the cables are routed etc.

What is a star network?

A star network has separate cables going from the central file server or computer to each workstation. This is the best system in terms of security and speed of operation.

What is a bus network?

A bus network has a single cable linking all computers in a 'straight line'. There is usually an appropriate terminator at each end.

What is a tree network?

A tree network is typical of Ethernet, fast Ethernet and Gbit Ethernet when hubs are used to join several workstations to the Ethernet backbone system.

What is a ring network?

A ring network has the wires at each end joined so that a complete ring of cable linking the systems together is formed.

What is meant by token ring?

The token ring network operates by sending an electronic token around the network, which must be grabbed by a machine before transmission is possible.

How might laser links be used?

Laser links can be used to connect networks together where line-of-sight communication is possible. Infrared links are used to connect up devices without cable. Typical uses would be the connection of portable computers to printers.

How might a radio link be used?

Radio links provide a very convenient method of connecting computers to a network, which is particularly suited to portables. You can use your computer on the net as long as it is in range of the radio receiver.

What is FDDI?

FDDI stands for Fibre-Distributed-Data Interface – This is a network in which signals are sent in the form of pulses of light via a fibre-optic cable. It has a very high bandwidth indeed, with 100 Mbits/sec being typical.

What is ARPAnet?

ARPAnet is an example of an extensive national and international network, which has now grown into the Internet system.

What is ATM?

ATM stands for Asynchronous Transfer Mode. It is a protocol that has been developed to try and overcome the very different requirements of speech and video, for example, from transmitting computer data. ATM is meant to optimise both systems simultaneously.

4 The Internet

Introduction

Statistics like those shown in the 'Did you know that' boxes on the next page are staggering. They are a measure of the popularity of a system which has now been in operation in one form or another for well over 20 years, but which has caught the public and business imagination during the last few years only. It's now no longer unusual to surf the net, and most schools have Internet access in one form or another – much of it being given away free by some of the Internet service providers (ISPs). It's an amazing thing, but when the third edition of the previous incarnation of this book was written in 1994, most of the public had not even heard of the Internet. This chapter, however, will take an in depth look at this most important topic, and will outline why the Internet is likely to continue to reform the way in which information is provided in the foreseeable future. Indeed, if these trends continue, then the net is likely to be the most important source of up-to-date reference material that is available. These facts, together with the net's ability to deliver 'e-mail facilities', 'real-time audio and video', 'still pictures', act as a 'telephone' or 'fax service' and 'generally entertain' are impressive. They should all make you appreciate that society is on the threshold of an evolutionary process, which is rapidly turning into an Information and Communications Technology (ICT) revolution.

The origins of the net

The first wide-area network of any significance was called ARPANET. This was set up in the 1960s (see chapter 3), and run by the American defence agency as a possible solution to communication problems in the event of a nuclear war. The academic institutions were quick to see the potential for swapping research information, and national and eventually international links were set up over the next couple of decades. The early systems were not that user friendly – you had to be a bit of a computer boffin or scientist to make use of them. You should, of course, realise that this was a long time before the general introduction of the windows-based GUI interface, and esoteric textual commands accompanied most information that had to be sent.

The linking up of these networks via national and international telephone systems continued at an amazing pace, with academic and government institutions leading the way. However, it was not until the late 1980s or early 1990s that small businesses, schools or even individuals could contemplate a 'good' connection to this very large network of networks, which *we call* the net. Back then the expense was prohibitive, with modems costing well over £1,500 for a 'fast' 9600 bit/sec model! It was also often necessary to go in via an academic institution such as a local university to get a link onto the actual network. Most schools in the late 1980s had to be content with an acoustic coupler linked to Prestel (a two-way teletext-like service) at a very low baud rate of just a few hundred bits per second.

Also, if you coughed too near to the handset of the phone, it was likely that you got scrambled data on the screen! This looked a little as if a badly received tele-text page is being displayed – you can sometimes observe this phenomenon today on the TV if the reception conditions are bad.

The net today

During the mid 1990s commercial information providers such as CompuServe (now taken over by AOL) really started to mushroom, and the cost of modems was reduced to less prohibitive prices. For example, during 1998 the cost of a very powerful computer, including a modem, was much less than the original cost of a modem in the late 1980s! Competition from other ISPs such as MSN for example, have made on-line costs more attractive, and most of the UK can now boast connection to many of these and other similar providers for the cost of a local telephone call. Indeed, if the UK telecom companies follow the lead given by the Americans and introduce free local calls, then institutions such as UK schools will be able to use the net for nothing. This is a measure of the progress achieved during the last 20 to 30 years – from a slow and complex-to-use service costing a fortune to operate, to a much faster and efficient service costing (in comparison) virtually nothing to operate.

In chapter 3 we have already investigated large networks from a theoretical point of view; therefore, in this chapter we will look mainly at the practical aspects of using the web (the world-wide-spiders-web of networks). Finally, we will take a look at the myriad of applications and industries that have been developed on the back of these basic systems.

Internet service providers

To surf the net you need access to the **Internet backbone**, (the top-level high-speed routes across the world) and a company who has expensive high-speed connections and appropriate hardware usually provides this. Many individuals have accounts, which are provided by companies like AOL, Demon, CompuServe, or Microsoft, for example. These and many other similar companies offer a service which provides you with access to their computer systems which, in turn, are connected to the Internet – they are known as **Internet service providers** or **ISPs**. ISPs are also often referred to as IAPs or **Internet Access Providers**.

Did you know that . . .
During 1993 world-wide web traffic was increasing at a rate of 300,000%. By the end of the 1990s it's predicted that over 200,000,000 people will have access to the net.

Most companies, like those mentioned above, have what are known as **POPs** (**Points Of Presence**) in many sites throughout the world, usually linked to a local telephone area. In this way you dial up a POP and get the *connection for the price of a local call*. Some ISPs have negotiated deals with the telecom companies using special numbers which act as though you have a POP in your local area – at least in terms of the price which you pay for the phone call. In this way it's possible for entire countries to have access at local-call rates. This is obviously important for cost-effective surfing, but is particularly important if you travel around the country with a portable, and thus require on-line connection from many different locations with the same ISP.

The huge numbers of ISPs are all acting in competition with each other and a variety of deals are usually available. You will need to evaluate the most cost-effective solution using criteria such as those listed below.

- Do you spend only a few hours on line each month?
- How many different e-mail accounts do you need?
- Is there browser software available for your operating system?
- Are you given any free web-site space?
- Are there ISDN connections or will you make do with a normal MODEM?
- Are there any restrictions such as access to some newsgroups?
- What level of technical support is available and when is it available? Etc.

Did you know that . . .
During 1998 there were well over 250 different ISPs serving the United Kingdom. This number is growing all the time!

Once you have decided on an ISP you can usually open an account on-line, probably using one of the freebie CD-ROMs which happen to be on the front of computer magazines or given away free at computer shows. People who don't require fast or multiple-user access 24-hours a day do not usually need expensive equipment, but make use of a standard telephone line and a MODEM (see chapter 5). Connection to the ISP using this method usually makes use of the **SLIP (Serial Line Internet Protocol)** or **PPP (Point to Point Protocol)**. Using these protocols it's easily possible to establish connection with a simple user ID and password, and it is thus ideal for the new user who can then receive their proper user ID and password at a later date via snail mail.

Most software provided by the ISPs works automatically from the Windows environment, and selects the appropriate protocols without the intervention of the user. Windows even goes so far as to autodetect the

MODEM and selects an appropriate baud rate (see chapter 5) assuming, of course, that you have Windows 95 or Windows 98 or a later version. The software also manages things such as 'what to do if the line is busy' (i.e. multiple re-dials) or 'what to do if the site you're trying to contact is busy', (i.e. should the dial-up connection stop after a set period of time?). The software can usually remember your password if you instruct it to do so, and can also store much other information. In this way it can be automatically set up to dial the numbers, then log on and supply your user ID and password with the click of a mouse. If your software does not provide these luxuries then third-party scripting software can also act as an automatic log in, providing the computer at the other end with the information that you would have had to type in manually at the keyboard.

ISDN

For those requiring faster access or for companies, who require several or even many users to access the net simultaneously, a simple MODEM-based connection won't do. Instead it's possible to have what's called an **ISDN or Integrated Services Digital Network connection**. With this type of set up you need a special connection to your house or business which can handle the **higher bandwidth** (see chapter 3). For example, ISDN2, one of the systems, which are supplied by British Telecom, consists of two twisted-pair copper cables. This combination can supply two 64 Kbps channels plus a third 16 Kbps data channel which acts as a control for the other two channels. This is quite versatile because you can use the normal phone at the same time as transferring computer data – this facility alone is often enough to please some serious surfers who work from home, and are thus often in competition with other family members for telephone access! The basic ISDN2 channel can be configured such that you can use the two 64 Kbps channels together to get a throughput of 128 Kbps. The cost of using the system varies, but it's usual to find a much higher quarterly rental, otherwise the cost of the phone calls is identical. However, don't forget that you can transfer data much faster, and therefore spend much less time on the phone – at 128 Kbps you would obviously spend about a quarter of the money on phone bills for the same data transferred via a typical 33.6 Kbps MODEM. Do look at the satellite and mains-borne connections in chapter 5 too.

You will learn from chapter 5 that the function of a MODEM is to modulate the digital signals into an analogue form ready for transmission over the normal telephone link. With an ISDN connection the line can handle the digital signals as it's designed to be able to do so. Therefore, you don't need a MODEM anymore. Instead you need what's called a **Terminal Adapter** or **TA**, also known as an **ISDN TA**. This has the function of interfacing your computer with the ISDN line. TAs

usually come in **parallel**, **serial** or **PCMCIA** (i.e. portable computer interface) types. Other devices like faxes can also be connected to appropriate ISDN links. ISDN lines have no dial tone so they sound dead when you pick up a telephone receiver! However, dial the number and the connection is made in a fraction of a second – this is quite a shock if you are used to dialling with a conventional MODEM and telephone line.

Did you know that . . .

During 1998 some of the fastest Internet backbones were being upgraded to 622 Mbps – a staggering 22,000 times the data throughput of the fastest 28.8 Kbps MODEMs typical in the late 1990s. Impressive though this may be, however, it's going to have to go a lot faster in the future if we are to keep pace with 'video on demand', 'video phones' and other 'high-bandwidth services'.

Leased lines

Some companies need to have access to the net 24 hours a day. This is ideal for universities, colleges, schools and businesses in which many different people are on line for much of the time. However, the phone bills can get astronomic, even with a fast ISDN link. Therefore, a **leased line** is a better alternative if the amount of time any institution spends on the net is great. *A leased line is a permanently open connection* – i.e. equivalent to being on line 24 hours a day. The cost of a leased line is often far greater than can be afforded by a home user, but it becomes cost effective for an educational establishment if the number of hours on the phone would be great. Indeed, compared to separate Modems from many different computers it can be a positively cost-effective option. Usually the users would operate workstations in a LAN-based environment and have access to the net via a **local server** (called a **proxy server**) which has been set up on site. The cost of the leased line varies from a few thousand pounds a year for a 64 Kbps model, to hundreds of thousands of pounds a year for a typical 60 Mbps line. Although these options sound very expensive, don't forget that you now have 24-hour access and no phone bills. You must, of course, choose a service provider which allows you 24-hour access for a sensible cost, or have a **direct Internet connection** – without these the whole leased-line exercise would be pointless.

With the above leased lines in mind, add a little extra hardware and you could actually set yourself up as an ISP, although I would not recommend this as it would be very hard work! However, in principle that's all that's necessary – a high speed leased line, the hardware to interface many users and a powerful computer to handle the front-end communications. However, as people come to expect faster and faster access methods and ISDN in the home becomes more common, then the ISPs will have to respond with even faster-access services. Anyone providing less than a 100 Mbps backbone would probably not be able to cope with the technology that an increasing number of users will eventually have.

Connecting a LAN to the Internet

How is a computer system organised so that many different people in a business can all access the net via a LAN, and what sort of things would be needed in house to be able to do this efficiently? You will also need to determine what each user on the LAN will be allowed to do. For example, can they send and receive e-mail, can they browse the net 'willy nilly' or will you control access to what's available via the LAN? Will it be a two-way process with outsiders being able to dial into your site? If so, what about security? Do you have a variety of operating systems on the LAN or do you have just Windows 98 or NT, which will be just a little easier to deal with? If you have different communication lines does your ISP provide the facilities for more than one user to use the same account at the same time?

If you try using the same ISP account via two different lines from two different computers at the same time, you will almost certainly be logged off from one of the computers! If you go to the *same* ISP account via a **proxy server**, although you can now access only one ISP in a simple system, many people can use the same account as all the requests are now routed down the same ISDN link. To the ISP it looks as though a single person with the dexterity of Superman is using the account. To the company operating the LAN, it's as though you have many 'different' accounts on the Internet all going at the same time!

A **proxy server** is simply a **file server** set up to control access to the net from your LAN. It can also control access from outside to the web sites, which have been set up internally. A proxy server, together with other equipment like routers and special software is also sometimes known as a **firewall,** because you can prevent hackers from being able to access your LAN via the Internet. Using these methods you can also connect directly to the net without going via an ISP if you have a leased line, a direct connection and an appropriate domain name (see in a moment).

To connect a LAN you will need a **domain name** and some **IP addresses.** Getting an appropriate domain name for yourself or your company is not too difficult, but your friendly ISP can usually provide a route to your **proxy server,** which in turn gets the users on the LAN connected to the net. On the WWW the domain name system actually maps the domain names onto the IP addresses. In this way users can use an alias to locate a company, rather than having to type in some horrible IP address like 183.087.209.146, for example.

As you can see, the IP address is basically four numbers separated by full stops, and this refers to the address of a computer on the Internet. It is basically an Internet address. The system is such that it is ideal for routing information to a particular computer. After the server (which is set up with the appropriate domain name) has received the information, the IP address can be used to route the information to various LANs around the site, and to various computers in an individual LAN. It is the job of the network administrator to work out the best arrangements for a particular site given the knowledge of a site's network topology. (See chapter 3.)

The simplest way to connect the Internet to a LAN is to have what's called a **router**. This is basically a piece of hardware which connects to your ISDN line at one end and has an Ethernet connection (see chapter 3) at the other end. More sophisticated routers can handle more versatile connections to a different number of LANs as the needs of your business grow.

The Intranet

The above system, although set up primarily to connect a LAN to the Internet, can also be used on an internal basis. For example, there is no reason why the people internal to the company could not surf the company's web site from within – there's not much point going out into the WWW only to be directed back into the company again! However, these facilities can be extended considerably beyond the ability to surf the company's web site, which is usually intended for outsiders.

> ### Did you know that . . .
>
> During 1998 it was estimated that over 3,000,000 computers were connected to the Internet. This number is continuing to grow at an amazing pace.

Many companies have now set up complete internal systems for their own use. If the WWW is an ideal information-gathering tool for the masses, then it's also an ideal medium when used on a smaller scale offering information, which is specific to a group of users within an organisation. All 'software which is used to surf the WWW', all the 'e-mail systems' and other 'similar facilities' could be set up on an internal-only basis. When used in this way the system is referred to as an **Intranet**. It's effectively the same as providing and managing your own web site within a company or other organisation, which might contain confidential information not intended for outsiders. It's proved so successful over the last few years that it's catching on in a big way, especially for companies who already have a heavy investment in LAN-based technologies. Information, including pictures, text, audio and video can be passed around in very efficient ways, and internal video conferencing and e-mail systems are proving to be a real bonus. The potential for things like staff training and finding information that would usually be printed in manuals is amazing. Just think of the power of a search engine set up to access internal company information – the timesaving aspects of these activities alone make the system worthwhile. All these systems and techniques will be considered later on in this chapter.

URLs

Uniform Resource Locators have been established for some considerable time. URLs effectively represent 'address information' which contains the protocol used for connection to the server, and other parts of the path name that are needed to locate the exact resource once connection has been established. The usual syntax of the URL is as follows:

```
PROTOCOL://MACHINE/DOCUMENT_PATH
```

but the full syntax of the URL is:

```
PROTOCOL://MACHINE:PORT/DOCUMENT_PATH
```

The port number is an optional element in the full syntax, and, if omitted, the default port number of 80 is used. The port number could, if necessary, refer the client to a different port on a particular server. If, for example, you set up a home page called 'my_brilliant_page' with an ISP called 'my_provider'. Assuming that you are called 'my_name', and the provider is an American commercial organisation, (this is the '.com' part), then the absolute URL for your home page could be something like:

```
http://WWW.my_provider.com/my_name/my_brill
iant_page.html
```

URLs play a pivotal role in making the Internet easy to use, and examples of URLs can be found when using HTTP, FTP and Gopher addresses. The **HTTP** or **Hyper-Text Transfer Protocol** (the example used above) will be familiar to anybody who has surfed the net using a modern browser. They will be very familiar with the URLs starting **http://www** ... used to jump to a particular site. For example, 'http://www.ft.com' would be the web site, which holds information about the Financial Times. In most modern browsers the http part can be omitted when actually typing in the address. Other types of URL such as FTP addresses are covered later. Another Uniform Resource Locator in common use is based on the **Gopher protocol**.

The next stage

So you have decided on an ISP, set up an ISDN line for faster access, and have installed the software to surf the net. What can you now expect, what facilities are available and how do you track down the information that will give your company a competitive edge? Typical uses of the net are now looked at in detail in the next few sections.

Typical ISPs

Most of the big ISPs have similar front ends (i.e. the GUI interface) and CompuServe is typical of what to expect. The ISPs upgrade the look of their GUIs at frequent intervals, and thus the sophistication seems to get better and better as each tries to outdo the others. The MSN (Microsoft Network) seems to have taken a slightly different (channel-based) route similar to that which will probably be popular when **Digital TVs** (i.e set top boxes to surf the net) really come into their own. Channels are particularly easy to use, unless you are quite experienced, in which case you might find it frustrating because it takes a little longer to get anything done.

At the time of writing CompuServe's front end is as shown in figure 4.1. It consists of graphically based **hypertext links**. These are the links (see later) that allow you to click the mouse, and then be presented with a new screen of information to which the previous link refers.

As you can see from the picture a variety of options are available including CompuServe forums and communities. This particular screen is the one which is displayed prior to log on. Pressing a button such as 'Communities' will cause CompuServe's software to activate the automatic log-on procedure which then dials the appropriate number, logs on to the service, verifies the account information, and flags if you have any e-mail. After logging on, figure 4.2 shows a typical screen displayed via Internet Explorer, the browser being used to display the pictures.

One of the advantages of choosing companies like CompuServe, AOL or MSN is the vast amount of information which is available from the provider without actually going into the net proper. In other words, you could spend hours, days or even your entire time just searching through the huge quantities of information which are provided within the ISPs vast databases.

Figure 4.3 shows what happens if you decided to choose the 'Search' option. Here you can see a variety of submenus, typical of that which is provided by most large companies. Alternatively, you can use a directory listing like Yahoo, and this is shown in figure 4.4. Here you can see one of the 'search engines' called Yahoo. There are other search engines too, and the search

Did you know that . . .

During 1998 Microsoft was taken to court in the USA for alleged abuse of their near monopoly by bundling their Internet browser software with Windows 98. The court is suggesting that Microsoft bundle the Netscape Navigator software too. Bill Gates, the head of Microsoft, compared this decision as 'Equivalent to Coca-Cola being forced to bundle 3 cans of Pepsi in every six pack sold'!

Figure 4.1

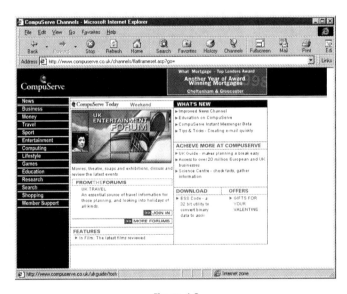

Figure 4.2

engine called Alta Vista is shown in figure 4.5. You can see that the word 'sounds' has been typed in. The Alta-Vista search engine has come up with 2,829,888 suggestions, of which the first one is shown on the page displayed! To save space only the first Web site is displayed in figure 4.5. As you can see from this simple example, you will have to be considerably more discerning in the description of your search criteria if you want to end up with a manageable set of sites from which to start your investigations! You will also have to phrase your search criterion carefully. I will never forget the technology student who wished to surf the net to find out information about a washing-line project which he was developing. He was designing a large fan to blow wind on the washing if there was no natural wind present at the time. He therefore required infor-

mation about the dynamics of propellers and information about the size and type of blade needed to produce a certain amount of wind. Needless to say, typing in 'washing line' as the search criterion revealed no suitable sites which would help him with his technology project! Phrases like 'wind tunnel' or 'propellers' would probably be more useful, with much greater ingenuity than this required for a successful search in this particular case.

Searching the web in efficient ways is an acquired art, but once you get used to the techniques it can often produce one of the most efficient information retrieval systems known to man. It is a skill which does not take too long to learn – just a few hours using typical search engines will easily be enough to make sense of the advanced search criteria available. In addition to

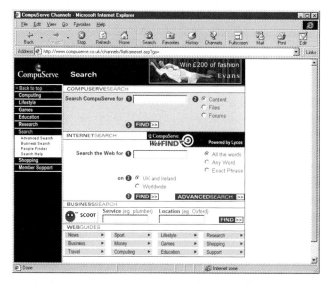

Figure 4.3

Figure 4.4

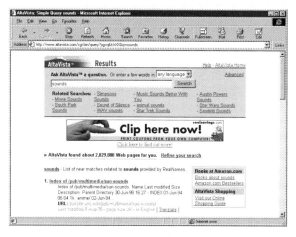

Figure 4.5

the typical Boolean and logical operators (i.e. the 'AND' and 'OR' etc.), you have the standard library-type searches which can search literally or intelligently, with words in a particular order or in any order etc.

It's identical in principle to the search methods needed when using CD-ROM based systems in public libraries or on your computer at home. Indeed, the front-end software can often be identical, and this is what makes the net so easy to use.

Other facilities, not immediately obvious from the CompuServe front end shown in figure 4.1, are the facilities to go straight to the site of interest by typing GO followed by the CompuServe name. There are also facilities to go straight to one of your favourite places or the facility to call up a

Did you know that...

In 1998, a search engine like AltaVista deals typically with over 30,000,000 successful searches each day.

recently visited site to name but a few. The possibilities are endless and more techniques become available with every new release of the software.

Searching the search engines!

In my opinion, one of the most useful additions to the web is the ability to simultaneously search many different search engines. For example, WebSeeker from ForeFront enables you to search many search engines at the same time. Figure 4.6 shows a typical screen during a live search when 'Windows NT' has been typed in as a search string.

As you can see, the search engines 'DejaNews', 'Excite', 'Galaxy' etc. all the way down to 'Your Personal Network' are being fed with the search string 'Windows NT'. Some are being searched at this very moment, some are finished and others have not quite started yet. It's as though Superman is sitting at your computer keyboard and searching the search engines at the same time. It's amazing to watch, and quite a sobering thought that usually the slowest component in a network search is the user!

After a small period of time all the searches will have been completed, and you will be invited to view the successful results, with all the identical pages on each search engine eliminated so that you do not have multiple copies of the same site in the same query. Figure 4.7 shows the results of this search, which found about 1,300 suitable sites dealing with some aspect of Windows NT.

The result of this search shown in Figure 4.7 is effectively a huge web-site page containing many HTTP links, all of which are in the correct form to be clicked on (i.e. a hypertext link) to go straight to the specific site of interest. You will be amazed at how much money you can save when you get your MODEM working flat out on many tasks simultaneously!

There is another similar piece of software called Web-Whacker from the same company, which can be programmed to visit web sites when you are not present at your computer, and download information of your choice. It's effectively an off-line browsing tool. For example, you could program WebWhacker to search for and download complete sites, or parts of sites, then view them later at your leisure without being on line. Obviously you will need a considerable amount of hard disk space if you make use of this facility very often, and are not sensible about how you schedule the process. Finally, also from ForeFront, there's WebPrinter, a utility that let's you correlate entire web sites into handy A5 size pamphlets. It also works with other applications too.

Did you know that...

During 1998 there were over 1250 different search engines available. Some search engines such as AltaVista, Yahoo, and HotBot, for example, are general, but other specialist search engines are available on topics ranging from aviation to medicine and beyond. New search engines appear on the net quite frequently.

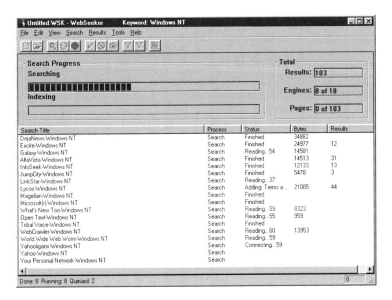

Figure 4.6

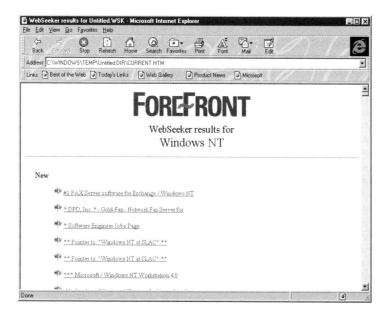

Figure 4.7

e-mail

Electronic mail systems

e-mail is the name given to the system whereby you can write a letter to someone else with a computer and Internet connection, and, assuming that you are connected via an Internet Service Provider, get your ISP to deliver the message for you. Virtually everything that can be done with normal mail can be done with e-mail too. It's also faster and cheaper than sending the same information by *snail mail* – the name usually associated with the ordinary mail service! Unfortunately, until we get transporter-beam technology, we obviously can't send parcels! – but all computer-based material in whatever form – i.e. text, code, graphics, sound and video etc. can be sent via e-mail.

Just as you have a physical address at home, so it is with e-mail. If, for example, you are subscribed to America On Line (AOL), and your name happens to be 'James Bond', then you might have an e-mail address like 'JBond@AOL.com'. All the major ISPs provide these e-mail facilities. If you are a 'home user' then there's little to choose between them. Nevertheless, business and educational users often require *many different e-mail addresses* for use with *the same account*, and therefore their choice of ISPs may be more limited. Some service providers limit you to one or just a few different e-mail address on the same account. Nevertheless, at the author's school we need over 800 e-mail accounts, and this would be typical of a medium-sized educational establishment. Large colleges and universities would require thousands of accounts, and would probably not need to go via an ISP because they might have a direct Internet connection. At the author's school we have an account with the service provider called Demon, and this provides us with the large number of unique e-mail accounts that we require. Our Demon e-mail address is subdivided into individual accounts so that they can be sorted automatically and eventually distributed around the school's LANs. In this way, the 800 individuals mentioned above can have their own e-mail ready when they log on at one of the many computers connected to our LANs. The local **mail server** will collect and distribute the e-mail automatically.

The above ideas are quite simple – if, for example, you attend a school called St Trinians, and if your name is Hilda Bloggs, then part of your e-mail address might be BloggsH@StTrinians. If St Trinians has an account with Demon, then Demon.co.uk would form the last part of the address. Therefore, the pupil called Hilda Bloggs may have an Internet e-mail address like:

`BloggsH@StTrinians.demon.co.uk`

In this way, just as at the author's school, all the mail ends up at Demon, then it's downloaded to the school as one large 'file', and finally split up locally by using 'BloggsH' and other names which form the first part of

Did you know that . . .

Many companies use their Internet connections for one reason only – that of being able to send and receive e-mail messages. The amount of money which can be saved, compared to using conventional mail, is staggering and has forced the Post Office in the UK to start thinking about e-mail facilities too.

the address. The only disadvantage of this system is that the response is not so rapid because we collect everybody's mail in one large chunk at two or three hourly intervals during the day and night. However, if you send a message from home, for example, and are a subscriber to CompuServe, and if your message is being sent to a friend who is a subscriber to AOL, then you would expect your friend to receive the e-mail within minutes or even sooner! Assuming, of course, that he was on line at the time! It's good fun to do this, then get your friend to ring you back to see how long it actually took!

The rest of the e-mail address is simple to understand too. If mail is being sent from Umbongoland, for example, to the address at St Trinians school, then the last part 'UK' would tell the sending computer where the mail would have to go – just like England, for example, might be used on a snail-mail letter. The 'Demon.Co' part of the e-mail address identifies the ISP, and is in effect Demon's domain name. This name must be unique on the Internet. The 'StTrinians' part identifies the school, and is effectively the user ID for a customer of the 'company' using Demon – this must also be unique within the province of the Demon server. You could obviously have the same name with other service providers, but not the same name if you wish to have direct Internet access.

If the pupil called Hilda Bloggs has private e-mail accounts with AOL and CompuServe, for example, and *if she decided to use the same format for the personal part of the address*, then her private e-mail addresses for these two accounts would probably be something like:

bloggsh@aol.com	**For America On Line**
or **bloggsh@compuserve.com**	**For CompuServe**

The '.com' part of the above e-mail addresses represents an American commercial organisation, just like the UK part at the end of the Demon address represents a United Kingdom address. Some others, for the sake of example, would be 'edu', an educational establishment that awards degrees, or 'org', which represents a non-profit making organisation. Node computers (see chapter 5) use these different parts of the e-mail address in the above ways to route the e-mail via the most efficient routes around the World Wide Web.

What's needed to use e-mail?

Apart from an account with the ISP (or a direct Internet connection) and the valid e-mail addresses mentioned above, you would need some software on which to compose your message. The software supplied with CompuServe is shown in Figure 4.8

Here you can see that we have all the facilities of a simple text editor – plus the ability to file the letter (i.e. keep your own copy), send the letter now, or send it later. The software also gives you cut and paste facil-

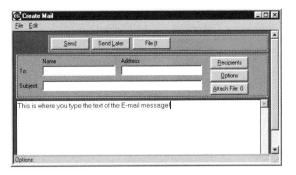

Figure 4.8

ities, the ability to save and print the documents, and other facilities you would expect from a simple text-editing system. If you click on the 'recipients' button then you could stipulate who receives the mail (one or many people), or you could call up your address book, which would fill in the personal name and the e-mail address automatically. This is useful if you write to the same person or group of people quite frequently.

Did you know that . . .

During 1998 it's estimated that over 30,000,000 people have access to the net. That's a lot of potential e-mail accounts, and a massive market for on-line commercial activities, which are now starting to take off in a very big way.

It is always polite i.e. good **netiquette** – (**Internet etiquette**) to fill in the subject when sending e-mail. Many people receive lots of e-mail each day, and will often scan the subject list before deciding whether to look at the mail (or even delete it without reading it first!). Therefore, you need to catch their attention with a short word or two in this subject box. You can, if you wish, use the 'options box' to mark the message urgent, which would then be brought to the attention of the reader very quickly. You can also set up the system such that your computer is notified with a suitable message when the person who is receiving the message has received it on their computer. This might, of course, be one of the disadvantages of using e-mail – you can no longer use the excuse that you did not receive the letter! However, if you have a home account you can always say that a member of the family must have downloaded it by mistake and not told you about it!

Turning on the style

If you use a bog-standard text editor for sending your e-mail messages, then you will probably soon realise just how basic the facilities are when compared with your favourite word processor, for example. The **bold** and *italic* styles, the different point sizes, coloured text and so forth make plain text look so boring by comparison! However, there is a good reason for this – styles like 72pt cyan-coloured text or bold underlined superscript etc. can't usually be sent via the normal e-mail channels. The reason for this is that the e-mail message often has to pass over systems which use older-style transmission protocols, and the parity bit (see chapter 5) is often not used in the same way on all systems. Also, different computer systems and even different software on the same system store the same information in a variety of different ways. As the World Wide Web consists of many different computer systems, this spells disaster for any kind of compatibility. To ensure that the message is totally compatible with all systems we must ensure that it is sent as text, or at least use only the lower 7 bits of the byte which represents the ASCII code (see chapter 12). The older systems use only the basic ASCII code, but modern word processors and other software such as art packages, for example, would probably use the complete ASCII set in an infinite variety of ways. Therefore, we need a way of encoding the attached data such that it can be sent over the entire net, even over the parts of the net where vastly different methods used in a huge variety of systems would normally scramble your message.

There is a way in which *any data* can be converted into a suitable form to be sent over the Internet. This is to develop a system whereby the more-complex codes used for specific styles or pictures etc., are converted into larger groups of bits which use only the simpler codes. These simpler codes can't be screwed up by all the different systems. For example, 'UUencode' and 'MIME' encoding are popular methods on PCs, and the 'BinHex' code is popular on Macs. Both these encoding methods would result in larger files than the original files which were being sent in native format, because a greater number of simpler strings of binary digits are being used instead of the original format.

Getting attached

One of the convenient things about the e-mail system is that you can create an **attachment** to your e-mail which could be computer data in any acceptable computer format, and this is handled by the 'attach file' button shown in figure 4.8. So you *could* use your favourite word processor, including all the colours, styles and pictures, and send this over the e-mail system without being scrambled by using UUencoding, for example. Assuming that the recipient had the appropriate word processor, which was used to create the original message, all the information in the original would be preserved. Indeed, the entire text for the book you are now reading could be sent over the Internet in this way from the author's computer to the publishers computer – however, it would be a *very* long phone call indeed using the author's 33.6 Kbps MODEM! For

example, this chapter needs about 16 MB if stored as a Microsoft Word 95 document, and therefore *this chapter alone* would take about $16 \times 1024 \times 1024 \times 8 / 33600 = 3,395$ seconds = *56 minutes*. Therefore, '30ish' similar-size chapters would take about 28 hours! In practice it would actually take longer than this because of the overheads (see chapter 5) and the inevitable 'less than optimum' performance of the system over a 28-hour period. In practice we would obviously use compression techniques as described later. However, interestingly enough, if Microsoft Word 97 is used, then very much less space is actually needed. The 16 Mb needed for this chapter is actually reduced to less than 1 Mbyte!

Did you know that . . .

It's now possible to get a digital ID from an independent certifying authority. There are various levels of ID, but it helps to verify who you are, and is most useful when doing on-line transactions, encrypting messages, or simply for verification of authenticity. Systems like this will help on-line commerce in the future.

Some software companies produce e-mail editors which can construct fancy text, such as formatting, styles and colours, etc. using HTML as the format. But unless you know that the recipient has exactly the same type or similar type of e-mail system at the other end, then there's little point in using these facilities – the message might end up as being incorrectly formatted or, worse still, be total gobbledegook! If you must send really fancy documents then use the attachments method mentioned above.

Useful e-mail facilities

There are a whole host of other useful facilities, which vary from one proprietary e-mail package to another. For example, you can send mail to a single user or send the same message to a group of users with a single button click (assuming, of course, that the group has already been created). Typical groups might be departments in an educational establishment or a business if you are dealing with an internal e-mail system on an Intranet, or a set of external e-mail addresses if you are dealing with a group outside of an individual organisation. Instead of setting up groups you may wish to send just a copy of the message to someone else, and this can be achieved by adding them to the **CC** (**Carbon Copy**) list. If you do not wish the person to whom you are sending the message to know that you are sending a copy to another party, then use the **BCC** (**Blind Carbon Copy**) option if this is available on your system!

Other facilities include an Address book in which you can easily identify colleagues and friends – this saves you having to type in their e-mail address each time you send them a letter. Therefore, you could send a message to your pal called Nick, and this might automatically get sent to BrownNEW@compuserve.com, if his name happened to have this particular e-mail address in your address book. When used in this way 'Nick' would be referred to as an **alias**.

At the bottom of most e-mail letters you may set up what's called a **signature**. This is simply a message which identifies you, which might consist of a name, title, telephone number, fax number and an address, for example. This makes the system friendlier and easily identifies you to the person who is receiving mail from you.

Other typical facilities would be indicators which tell you which messages have actually been read, or facilities for queuing messages off line. This is a useful feature which can save you money if you pay for 'on line time' by the number of minutes you are connected to your ISP. For example, you can compose a string of different e-mail messages, queue them, log on, and then get the messages sent automatically. You can also automatically download your mail from the ISP at the same time. Never compose e-mail messages while on line, unless you have a 24-hour leased line where the charge is the same whether you are using the system or not.

Mailing lists

It's possible to extend the concept of the group (i.e. the users to whom you may send e-mail messages) even further. There are tens of thousands of mailing lists, and you may, of course, subscribe to them. Any mail, which you send to the list, gets re-directed to all the people who have subscribed to the list. Similarly, any e-mail other people have supplied to the list gets redirected to you if your address is on the list. Therefore, if you are interested in 'Outer-Mongolian Snow Camels', for example, then you may well be able to subscribe to a suitable list – if one does not exist, then you could set up your own! However, you must be careful what you do here, or your mailbox could be inundated with **junk mail**.

Privacy issues

Don't forget that anything you send over an e-mail link can be subject to hacking. Worse still, your e-mail address will probably have been cached (stored) by a variety of host computers with whom you have communicated. Therefore, if you have sent e-mail to a variety of destinations, then someone, somewhere, may have a list which indicates where you have been and what your likely areas of interest are! Although unlikely to happen, unless you are being monitored for some criminal or other reason, your e-mail could be intercepted and read. It is unlikely to be read on a casual basis, as this would be virtually impossible to do, at least with any sense of purpose. However, it is possible to program

powerful computers to filter e-mail containing certain words, for example. These mail messages can then be brought to the attention of the system operator who could, for example, hand them over to the police if the force had the appropriate authority.

The only sure-fire way to get over the above problem is to use a strong-encryption program like **PGP** (see chapter 9) but this would raise suspicion even further, and probably get you deeper into trouble! Some governments in countries like France, for example, ban the use of encryption altogether, and the USA considers encryption programs to be munitions. In other words, you might be regarded as being involved in subversive military or terrorist activity if you export or import an encryption utility. Public-key encryption systems (see chapter 9) are being considered as a possible way of keeping your e-mails secret from everybody else, but governments want to have a copy of your private key so that they can decode your messages easily! The other alternative is to use weaker encryption algorithms so that anybody with a powerful computer could crack the code, but it's unlikely to be cracked by run-of-the-mill hackers. The current version of Netscape does have a secure channel feature, which will be built into future versions of its e-mail system.

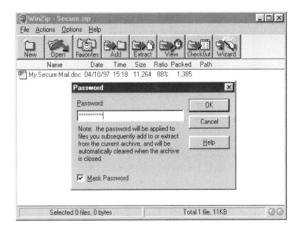

Figure 4.9

One other way to get a great deal of privacy without the need for the strong encryption algorithms described above is actually open to anybody. All you need to do is to use a compression utility like WinZip, for example – Zip the file you are sending, and then use the password-protection option as shown in figure 4.9. You could then send the file to your colleague with whom you have previously agreed a password or set of passwords that change on certain dates. **This gives you a very secure e-mail transaction, and you are unlikely to be breaking the law in most countries – but don't quote me on this!**

The security issue is one of the reasons why it's not usually a good idea to send credit-card numbers over unsecured channels. Systems are being developed for on-line commerce, but at the time of writing are still under consideration. The **SET** (**Secure Electronic Transaction**) system has been developed with the backing of Visa and MasterCard, and also includes major companies like Microsoft and IBM. If you see the SET mark on a web site then it is meant to conform to a standard, which includes authentication and identification and a safe way of actually transmitting the credit-card data. For example, NatWest on-line banking makes use of 128-bit encryption which, at the time of writing, had never been broken.

Other secure channels also exist, with user IDs, multiple passwords and pin numbers to be typed in to help in the identification process. The author has been using on-line banking systems for some time which make use of these secure (totally secure?) channels. Netscape, for example, shows that its system is secure (it's actually encrypted) by displaying a small (unbroken) key at the bottom left-hand side of the browser.

Other security problems also exist. Even on a small internal e-mail system problems of authentication arise – for example, some time ago a pupil at my school made it look as if I was sending e-mail to other pupils telling them that they had a detention! All they had to do is to manually fill in the 'from box' with my e-mail address, so it looked to the recipient as if it had come from me! Fortunately, the TCP/IP address encoded with the system identified the machine from which these e-mails were originating, and so we were able to monitor this station quite closely and find the culprit. This problem, however, is obviously very important in business – how do you know that the person who apparently sent the e-mail is really the person who sent it? The same problem obviously exists with snail mail too, but it's easier to abuse the e-mail system because people feel that it is more anonymous. Therefore, it's possible to use a **digital signature** system, which can be purchased for about 10 dollars. This ensures that the originator of the message is genuine, and has overcome the problems, which are outlined above. If you need authentication, then make use of this system.

Other useful communication facilities

Voice systems

Systems exist to send voice over the net – in real time! For example, 'CoolTalk', which is given away free with Netscape Navigator. This enables you to undertake real-time audio and data conferencing over the net. The astute readers amongst you will realise that this means that you can have a 'telephone' conversation with someone else with similar facilities over the net. The even more astute readers will realise that this means that you can have long distance phone calls for the price of a local call – yes, you can chat to your friend in Australia for the cost of a local call! However, before you get too excited and sell all your shares in British Telecom, don't forget that the recipient will also have to have a computer. They will also need to be on line when you wish to make contact! It's not quite like phoning up with the normal phone to see if they're in, but it's close, especially with the answering-machine service, which is available, which means that you could agree on a time for a long chat. CoolTalk is shown in figure 4.10

It was mentioned at the beginning of this section that CoolTalk is able to handle data as well as real-time audio. In a nutshell this means that you could, should you so wish, transmit text or even doodles in real time. Part of the CoolTalk system consists of a utility called a 'whiteboard'. If the person at the other end is also using the whiteboard utility then, as you are talking to them, you can display instructions in the form of a rough sketch as though you had a notepad placed on the desk in front of you. What you draw appears on both yours and the recipient's computer. They too can draw on the whiteboard at their end, and you can see modifications to your diagram too. The interactivity is wonderful – it brings a whole new dimension to communicating via computer. You can even capture parts of your screen and display it on the whiteboard so that your colleague can see what your computer was

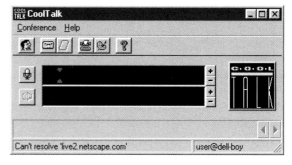

Figure 4.10

doing at the instant in which the snapshot was made. Using these methods is much easier than trying to explain diagrams or concepts over a normal phone just by making use of words.

Video conferencing

The ultimate phone at the time of writing is obviously the videophone. You could, for example, pay a telecom company several hundred pounds for a video phone, then hope that the recipient has one too, or you could make use of some appropriate software on your computer and dial up over the Internet, again for the price of a local call! Sounds too good to be true? It is actually true – but you'll need some extra equipment (such as a video camera attached to your computer) and a relatively fast Internet connection to make the best of it. We now take a brief look at the technology of sending video over the net and the technology of video conferencing.

You will be aware from reading chapter 3 that transmission of information over a communication link requires a significant bandwidth, which is measured in bps (bits per second). It's a sobering thought to work out typically how much bandwidth is required to send a suitable signal. When this is done you will realise why it's necessary to compromise on quality or use very high bandwidth digital links.

A normal (i.e. not wide screen) video signal would have 625 lines which typically makes up the picture information. (It's actually slightly less than this but we don't need to bother with this minor detail). The aspect ratio (ratio of the width to the height) is 4:3, therefore, a single picture would consist of about $625 \times (3/4 \times 625) \approx 293,000$ pixels. If this is to be displayed typically at 25 times a second, the minimum needed to prevent flicker, then you can see that we need about $293,000 \times 25 = 7,325,000$ bits/sec – and this would give us only a black and white image! This is already much higher than the fastest available Modems on a standard telephone line (55,600 bits/sec at the time of writing), and therefore we must make our first compromise – *the size of the picture must be considerably less than an entire 'TV' screen.* More sensibly, a 300×200-bit image is chosen in some of the current software packages, with 160×120 resolutions used for modes where the connection is less fast.

If we now transmit the revised 300×200 at 25 pictures/sec, then we would need $300 \times 200 \times 25 = 1,500,000$ bits/sec – still a long way ahead of a sensible bit rate given the current technology, and we still have only a black and white image. If we have an ISDN line we are not going to fare much better, and even the 10 Mbits/sec Ethernet LAN will not be able to cope if we add the extra bits for colour – we therefore have no alternative but to compress the information using a suitable code. Typically we might use the MPEG or JPEG compression methods (see later), and this might give us a compression ratio of about 10 to 1, thus making 1.5 Mbit/sec come down to a more sensible 150 Kbits/sec. However, until better compression algorithms and standards are developed, we currently accept a lower frame rate of about 10 frames/sec, and this effectively reduces the compressed rate to about 60 Kb/sec, something more acceptable, assuming, of course, that you have an ISDN line or the fastest MODEM. Nevertheless, standards are being developed all the time, and the international telecommunication companies will no doubt get the video transmission standards over the Internet to a fine art in the next few years. Until then, we will have to put up with slightly jerky reasonably small images.

Even with the limitations outlined above the videophone system is taking off in a big way. Don't forget that we are still talking about full-duplex (see chapter 5) national and international sound and colour vision communication together with real-time data like the whiteboard facility mentioned in the voice-communication system earlier – all for the price of a local phone call – no wonder it's catching on! Think of the advantages to business if you can have eyeball-to-eyeball communication with sound and whiteboards thrown in. The only disadvantage is that it's obviously not as pleasant as going on business trips, staying in first-class hotels and sampling first-class food and wine in strange and exotic lands! Nevertheless, it functions much better than an ordinary phone call, and one day might catch on as being the norm for modern communication.

The title at the beginning of this section is 'video conferencing' – so far we have talked only of a single two-way conversation. Software exists now which can enable three or more people to share the same video-conference with all the facilities outlined above. This is obviously ideal for businesses as entire meetings between people could be carried out on this basis. When several people are communicating in this way then we obviously have a **videoconference**.

Finally, we must not forget the advent of the digital TV linked to the NC (Network Computer). With direct satellite links or cable TV into the home, the higher bandwidth links hinted at earlier will be provided on a national basis. Therefore, videophones will definitely become a possibility making use of these facilities in addition to the PC facilities mention above. Also, faster Internet links are provided by the cable and satellite

Did you know that . . .

Some companies now rely on videoconferencing for some of their meetings. It's an efficient way of getting eyeball-to-eyeball communications without actually meeting in person. However, some business people are complaining that the perks of the job are being taken away. If videoconferencing is used then you have lost the stay in a 5 star hotel.

companies too – the future for more acceptable video-phone links looks very exciting indeed, and we will be very close to the communication portrayed in sci-fi movies within the next few years.

Compression techniques

We will see on numerous occasions throughout this book that compression techniques are needed to overcome limited bandwidth and storage problems. For example, in chapter 10, when flatbed scanners are being considered, it is demonstrated that many tens of Megabytes are needed to store a single-A4 colour image. Drastic reductions in the size of these images can be obtained, without too much degradation in the original image. Indeed, for transfer over the Internet and for display in Internet browsers, ordinary people would not really notice the difference, because the compression techniques are actually very good, and people have been used to seeing compressed images for several years. However, print out one of these images in a book, and you will soon realise that the picture might need to be obtained in its original form! For example, some of the images for this book were obtained from Intel's Web Site. You could view the image as a JPEG (see in a moment), but download it as a TIFF from Intel's pressroom for publication purposes. One particular JPEG image took only seconds to load, but the TIFF image took ten minutes using a 56 Kbyte/sec MODEM. People would not want to wait ten minutes for an image to appear in their web browser, but I am grateful to Intel for the ability to get publication-quality images direct from the net.

Bitmaps and JPEGS and GIFs

There are too many graphics file formats and compression utilities to consider here, so we will use just one as an example. **JPEG** is the **Joint Picture Experts Group**, a body of people, who have developed the algorithms to help cut down the size of pictorial information that will be viewed, usually on the Internet. When an image is created, either by an art package like Adobe PhotoShop or scanned in using a scanner, it is usually in **bitmap** form. This means that each dot which makes up the picture (determined by the resolution) is coded separately, using 3 bytes for 24-bit colour (see chapter 11). This takes up an enormous amount of memory, and therefore takes a long time to send over a typical Internet link. JPEG is an example of what's called 'Lossey Compression'. This means that a very large file can be drastically reduced from its original size, and still look good to a human being. It does this by using attributes of human vision to decide which things don't matter so much. For example, small colour changes can't be perceived so easily as small changes in brightness. By using this and many other techniques, JPEG compression encodes the image into a format that is much smaller than the original. For example, a 10 Mbyte file could

be compressed, using JPEG techniques, to anywhere between 200 Kbytes and 1.2 Mbytes depending on the final quality of the image. If the 200 Kbytes version is acceptable, then this will obviously load 50 times quicker than the bitmap version over the same bandwidth link.

In practice you should use the JPEG format for photographic work. It is, however, not designed for, nor is it very good at line drawings of the CAD variety. It's best to use a GIF for this purpose. Also, if you are producing images that will need to be re-scanned into the computer at some later stage, then JPEG compression is not usually satisfactory. This is because the machine that will analyse the image can see all the imperfections, which the unaided human eye can't see. There are simpler graphics formats such as a **GIF** (**Graphics Interchange Format**), but these only store 8-bits of colour information and can thus only display 256 colours. The JPEG format stores colours as 24-bit, and can, therefore, reproduce all 16 million colours. It would be silly, for example, to use JPEG compression techniques on an image containing just black and white only!

One disadvantage for developers is that you are meant to pay royalties for using the JPEG format. This has meant that other formats, such as PNG (Portable Network Graphics), are becoming popular too.

MPEG

This is a group that is called the **Moving Picture Experts Group**. As implied by the name, this compression utility is for moving pictures like video. Indeed, it is the new MPEG II standard which has made it possible to have digital TV at the end of the 1990s. The digital terrestrial TV, Sky digital and cable channels all use MPEG compression techniques. This is one reason why it's possible to fit many channels into the bandwidth, which would have been occupied, by a single analogue TV channel. MPEG compression techniques are the reason why it's now possible to have hundreds of TV channels beamed into your home, and why it's possible to watch real-time video on the Internet, albeit at limited quality at the time of writing. MPEG is also being applied to audio information.

Newsgroups

One of the fastest growing, and *the* most notorious area of the net is the UseNet Newsgroups. UseNet is a large body of users who communicate using the UUCP or the Unix to Unix Copy Protocol system. On the UseNet Newsgroups you will find topics on literally everything under the sun. However, as with other areas of the net, you have to be careful about the authenticity and breach of copyrights which goes on unabated. There are literally tens of thousands of newsgroups, and information ranges from large amounts of help for teachers of all subjects, through detailed postings on computer bugs in software, via astrophysics to terrorism, bomb making and hard-core pornography! Indeed, some of these areas are so controversial that most of the larger and more reputable ISPs will not provide the necessary links to some of these groups. It is possible to set up your computer to find such information, but don't forget that much of the material contained in some of these sites is illegal, and you could be arrested for downloading illegal information onto your computer. Don't forget also that your e-mail address can be cached by such computer systems and therefore the government and the police could, and probably do, have a list of the names and addresses of individuals who visit particular sites on a frequent basis, and, more importantly, post information onto them! You have been warned!!

On a brighter note, and concentrating on the majority of newsgroups which are well run and contain useful academic and other information both serious and less serious, you will find a wealth of hints and tips that you are unlikely to acquire elsewhere. If you download the 25,000 or more newsgroups from MSN (The Microsoft Network), for example, and if you then filter out the newsgroups that are concerned with computers, you may get the list, part of which is shown in figure 4.11. However, don't forget that new groups are formed on an almost daily basis, and your list will probably be very different if you try it yourself.

Here you can see that the list starts of with the newsgroup 'alt.folklore.computers', continues with 'alt.religion.computers' and continues through hundreds of newsgroups which have computers contained within the title. Going down the list and clicking on the group 'aol.commerce.computers.forsale' would reveal the further list shown in figure 4.12.

On the day on which this particular newsgroup was accessed, the list in figure 4.12 was available. As you can see, it is not unexpected to see a large number of companies and private individuals that are selling computers and computer-related parts. As this is the newsgroup section and literally anything goes, you will see the odd messages like the 'old coke bottle' message

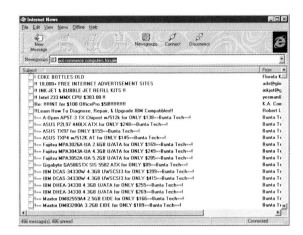

Figure 4.12

at the top. People can, and do, post anything to newsgroups, so you can expect plenty of rubbish mixed in with gems of relevant information. Suppose, for example, that you were interested in the ink-jet and bubble-jet refill kits shown on the third message down in figure 4.12, then double-clicking on that particular message on that particular day would reveal the information shown in figure 4.13.

From the above message you can see that the bubble jet refills can be obtained by e-mailing inkjet@glenfinnan.com. Often people order things like this from companies abroad, and get

Hint: If you wish to delete the secret database that some web browsers keep on their users, or if you do not wish other people to see where you have been by analysing your local machine, then IE or NS clean from Webtronix fits the bill. However, unless you make use of an alias then the web sites you have visited can still send junk mail. There is, however, no way to cover your tracks if your ISP or the police are particularly determined to investigate your network activities!

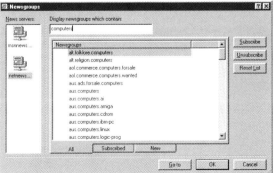

Figure 4.11

Figure 4.13

identical goods cheaper than is generally possible in Europe, especially when being ordered from the USA. Indeed, many governments are becoming concerned about the loss of tax revenue when shopping is done through such channels. You can also see that a list of other newsgroups is shown at the top of the Internet News window – all carry this same newsgroup message.

The whole point of the newsgroup network is that people can communicate with each other very effectively and very efficiently. Used properly it provides a forum for buying and selling a whole host of products, for disseminating information, and for generally getting in contact with people having similar interests all over the globe. It's a wonderful system, which has been given a bad name because the press will normally concentrate on the paedophiles and other pornographers, religious fanatics, nazi propagandists and other subversives who regularly use these methods to communicate with other like-minded individuals. Ignore these sites, and don't forget the warning about caching your e-mail address if you happen to visit some of them by 'accident'!

FTP

Yet another method of getting information from the net is called **FTP** or **File Transfer Protocol**. You will recall that e-mail was never originally intended to download computer files, but FTP was originally designed for this purpose. There are literally hundreds of sites around the net specifically set up for FTP access. In general, you will find that they require you to log on with the user name 'anonymous', and supply your 'e-mail address' as the password. Often you might be told that a file you require for your computer is available on an FTP site, and most of the major ISPs provide for easy FTP access. It does not have all the bells and whistles associated with the HTTP web browsing, but it does enable you to get an important file quickly and easily.

Many companies provide FTP access for their employees so that they can get access to the firm's files if they work from home, or are out on the road with their portable computers. The system works well, although you could obviously not gain access to these sites using 'anonymous' and your 'e-mail address'- at least I hope that you can't!

Reliability and privacy

As with all computerised systems it must be realised that the network's facilities may not always work reliably. Using e-mail or making use of the net in many other ways is not without the normal range of frustration experienced by computer users – and a few more to boot! Common frustrations include the slow connection experienced by many when the network is busy – no matter how fast your particular local connection may be, if the site you're attempting to contact is very busy indeed, then you will get a relatively slow response. Indeed this

response may occasionally be so frustratingly slow that it's best to give up and try again later. If you are connected via a LAN then your local proxy server (see earlier in this chapter) or mail server may go down. A software upgrade at the author's school actually completely trashed our mail server and it took us a day to get it back again – some upgrade! Also, you can have problems with the organisation and management of the Internet itself, which can cause simultaneous problems for millions. An unusual but classic example occurred in July 1997 when a company, which maintains the domain-name database (the equivalent to an electronic telephone directory), released a copy which contained errors. Always remember the saying – 'To err is human, to really foul things up you need a computer!'

Another avenue of concern has arisen due to the advent of **cookies**. These are small pieces of information which are stored on your hard drive, ostensibly to help to create customised web pages just for you! What a nice idea this is! For example, when you log onto your ISP and use the web, some sites might wish to set a cookie. This information could be used the next time you log on to make different information appear than would be the case if someone else's cookies were present. You could imagine a scenario that could present you with certain adverts at log on rather than others: if you have surfed the net recently and expressed an interest in searching the automobile sites, then you might get a few car adverts thrown at you! A more sinister interpretation could be that some of your surfing habits might be stored within the cookies contained on your hard drive! Indeed, if you have not looked already, you might be amazed to see what information is already cached on your hard drive in directories like 'history', 'temporary Internet directory', and various cache directories splattered all over the place. The knowledgeable parent can therefore easily see where their less knowledgeable children might have been surfing recently!

The threat of a virus infection from a cookie is also a possibility because you are allowing any site to place information on your hard disk without your permission. Most ISPs and web sites are above board, but you only need to visit one that isn't – and you may have your hard disk trashed for the privilege of visiting their site! It is for this reason that both Netscape Navigator and Microsoft's Internet Explorer have warnings, which can

Did you know that . . .

Much of the Internet came to a halt in July 1997 when a duff version of a domain-name database was released onto the net by accident. This meant that millions of e-mails could not be sent and millions of sites ending with the address '.com' could not be accessed! For several hours there was chaos on most of the net, and many businesses who relied on the net could not function during this time.

be enabled when a site you are visiting wishes to set a cookie. The only down side to this is that you're constantly responding with 'yes' or 'no' as you are surfing the net, and this gets annoying to say the least. Cookies can be deleted very easily as they are all meant to be stored in the window's cookies directory.

HTML

Although not the earliest of web developments, perhaps it's the development of **HTML** together with **JAVA** (see later) above all else which has led to the popularity and ease of use of the system today. **HTML** stands for **Hypertext Mark-up Language**, and, put simply, is the system which enables easy navigation of many parts of the net by clicking over **hypertext links** – these links can easily take you to other places on the net at the click of a mouse button.

The easiest way to understand about HTML is to develop a couple of simple web pages which are linked together locally (i.e. on a hard disk). Once this has been accomplished, it's very easy to extend the same concepts to international web servers – it's simply the path name that's different, and, of course, the web over which these links are established.

HTML is a textually based language, it therefore needs no special provision for creating the text, just a word processor or a simple text editor will do. However, life is much easier if you make use of a special purpose editor such as Microsoft's FrontPage, HotDog or Arachnophilia, for example. It's far easier to use a WYSIWYG system like FrontPage, but here we will use Arachnophilia for two reasons – (1) It emphasises the true nature of HTML, and (2) It's available as a free download from the net! It's called **CareWare** (as opposed to **shareware**). Put simply, the author, Paul Lutus, wants people to care for (or be nice to) other people, and that's payment enough for the use of his software – a nice idea, and a good HTML editor into the bargain! If you wish to download the Arachnophilia HTML Web-site designer, then you could go straight to the Internet address http://WWW.arachnoid.com/lutusp/arach.html. However, realise that these addresses, especially the last parts, may change. If you can't find the page at the above address, then use one of the search engines with 'Arachnophilia' as the key word.

HTML pages

Most students find this activity extremely satisfying, and often spend hours learning much more than we can hope to cover in just a few pages of this book. At this level, all we need to do is concentrate on the principles of HTML and on web-page design in general. The tools with which we do the job will probably change as fast as the rapidly expanding HTML language itself. Here we will make use of the Arachnophilia web page designer. The start-up

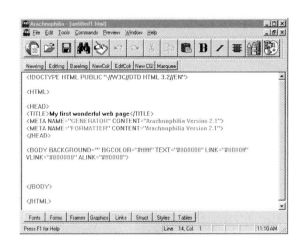

Figure 4.14

screen after choosing a new HTML page and inserting an appropriate title is shown in figure 4.14.

The structure of an HTML document

HTML documents are made up of **TAGS**, which are the parts of the document enclosed within angle braces. Notice the **<HTML>** part (i.e. the first tag) of the document – this defines the text that follows to be an HTML file – the **</HTML>** (last tag) defines the end of the HTML document. The **<HEAD>.....</HEAD>** defines the heading which, in the above case, is a title which will appear on the title bar of the window when the page is being displayed by a web browser such as **Netscape Navigator** or **Microsoft's Internet Explorer**, for example. The **<BODY>...</BODY>** defines the main body of the page, and all that is set in the above case is a default background, text and link colours etc. *Notice that the HTML tags often operate in pairs*, switching various effects on and off. Arachnophilia has also set up the colours by assigning hexadecimal values to the three primary colours 'RGB' as explained in chapter 11. For example, BGColour #FFFFFF would be FF (maximum Red), FF (maximum Blue) and FF (maximum Green) which gives a default white BackGround Colour (BGColour) because 'Red + Green + Blue' gives 'White' when using light. Some other parameters have also been set up.

> **Hint:** I would suggest that you have a go at building up some web pages. It is very easy, and you will learn a lot about programming in general and HTML or DHTML specifically. Many applications now also generate HTML code for inclusion in web sites.

Designing web pages is simply a matter of writing suitable text, setting up links, inserting graphics, animated GIFs and live video etc. You can split your pages up into frames, capture data via forms and GCI scripts (Common Gateway Interface) and a whole host of other activities.

VRML

VRML stands for **Virtual Reality Modelling Language**. It is literally capable of producing a virtual world, which you can download and explore from your browser, which supports these file types (most of the latest ones like IE4, for example, do.) Indeed, if you have Version 3.0 of Netscape Navigator, then there's a freebie, which comes with it in a subdirectory called Live3D. Many sites on the net now produce proper VRML images, and the latest version of the language and some of the models, which have been produced by various companies, are impressive. It should soon be possible to put on your VR helmet (see chapter 11) and wander around inside 3D worlds via the net. Of course people are already doing this, and you can have interactive battles with others via your VRML 3D interface.

There are obviously many spin offs from such technologies, not least in education, entertainment and general business. You really do have complete control over the image, and are therefore able to view the image from an infinite variety of viewpoints. Think of the advantages that this would provide for companies like estate agents, architects, or travel agents. However, the fidelity (realism) of such images still leaves a little to be desired. Nevertheless, such technology would have been unthinkable over a standard telephone

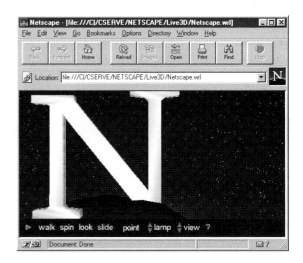

Figure 4.15

line just a few years ago, and the advent of higher bandwidth systems and faster computers can only make the realism more effective.

Part of the source code for the site in figure 4.15, created by Eyeball Productions Ltd, is shown in the following program.

> **Hint:** I would suggest that you leave this section until you are a little more familiar with programming techniques. However, it can be read as is, as long as you don't try to make much sense of the code such as that shown in the boxes on this page.

```
#VRML V1.0 ascii
Separator {
   Info {
      string "Created by Eyeball Productions,Ltd. for Paper Software, Inc."
   }
   Info {
      string "Netscape Logo is a trademark of Netscape Communications, Inc."
   }
      DEF BackgroundImage Info{
      string "Starbak2.bmp"
      }
#Setup camera
      PerspectiveCamera {
      position       0 -150 110
      orientation 1 0 0  1.57 #4.712389
      focalDistance   5
      heightAngle .5
      #farDistance 1300
      #nearDistance 1
      }
   DirectionalLight {
      direction 0 1 0  # Light shining from viewer into scene
```

Figure 4.16 (continues)

```
        intensity 1
    }
    MaterialBinding {
        value PER_FACE_INDEXED
    }
    Material {
#       ambientColor [ 0.9 0.9 0.9, ]
        diffuseColor [ 0.9 0.9 0.9, ]
#       specularColor [ 1.0 1.0 1.0, ]
    }
WWWAnchor {
name "http://home.netscape.com"
description "Netscape"
    DEF NetscapeN Separator {
        Coordinate3 {
            point [ -26.981634 -30.467356 97.903259,
                    -20.832026 -30.467356 98.528000,
                    -19.008020 -30.467356 100.063354,
```

Figure 4.16 (continued)

The above VRML language is controlling the image in real time, and responding to the menu settings and mouse clicks provided by the user. In other words, we are now making use of a browser originally intended to show simple HTML pictures and text, and using it to explore complete worlds of some complexity. Notice we are now downloading actual software, which is controlling the browser and the computer. As newer versions of the language become available, and Java (see in a moment) and complex 3D-rendering art packages come down in price, the future for the Internet and web browsing looks very exciting indeed. To create an original VRML page, you need to have access to a VRML editor such as Pioneer, for example. It's a very time-consuming business to produce convincing images, but the rewards are enormous for talented people who can master this exciting media innovation.

We have covered only a fraction of the features of HTML here, but together with object oriented languages such as JAVA (see later), web pages can simulate virtually any aspect of which the computer is capable. Indeed, with the advent of the Network Computer (NC), the language Java is essential to its entire operation.

JavaScript

Before looking at Java, it's worth mentioning JavaScript. **JavaScript** is a joint venture between Netscape and Sun Microsystems. JavaScript can be used to add functionality to your HTML web pages. It is very much easier than the full Java language, does not need to be compiled, and is designed to be able to be used by people who are composing HTML scripts as the JavaScript code is embedded inside the HTML page. As a student at this level you should appreciate that JavaScript is not a fully object-oriented language like Java, as it does not support classes or inheritance (see chapter 15).

One of the ideas behind the development of JavaScript is the need to place some of the processing power at the web-browser end rather than rely on the server. This has helped to reduce the processing bottlenecks at the server end, and therefore helps to increase the effective bandwidth of the system. For example, local JavaScript could be used to validate user input at the browser end. Without this you might send the wrong information back to be validated by the CGI script at the server end. This would involve a lot more overheads in terms of wasted transmitted information, and is just one example of why we get more efficient use of the available network bandwidth.

JavaScript, just like any other HTML language option is enclosed between appropriate tags. A new script, which forms part of an HTML script, will look something like the following.

```
<SCRIPT Language="JavaScript">
<!- Hide this from older browsers
// end hide ->
</SCRIPT>
```

This, of course, assumes that the code itself will reside on the HTML page in the space shown in the above script. It is normal to include the script between the <HEAD> and </HEAD> tags of the HTML document by convention. The code may also optionally be stored in a separate file that is stored along with the web page. This means that several web pages could share the JavaScript code in the file, and not have to have the same code repeated on every HTML page. If an external script is used then it is referenced as follows.

```
<SCRIPT Language="JavaScript" SRC=
"http://WWW.myserver.com/myscript.js">
```

The URL (Uniform Resource Locator – shown by the http://…. part as described earlier shows where the script is located. As before in this chapter, it could be placed somewhere on your local hard drive. A very simple example of a JavaScript program is shown in Figure 4.17. When set up, this script would form part of the HTML page which displays a button (lots of different buttons etc. can be defined) on which it is written – "Do NOT press this button again!" – obviously inviting any potential user to press it! You can see that when the button is defined, *if it is clicked*, by using the "onClick= WriteSomeText()>" part, then the function WriteSomeText will be called, which in turn starts a new page and prints the message "Do not press this button again!". Rather silly really, but it demonstrates a JavaScript program which causes some action which is easily understandable on a whirlwind tour of the web. I suggest that you learn some JavaScript, especially if you are into Web page design – it really is great fun.

JavaScript is an interpreted language, which works with the HTML document. The actual code is contained within the HTML document, unlike Java (see next section) where the code is downloaded from the web browser when the Java applet tags are encountered.

Java – the objected oriented programming language

Architecture independence

For many years computer scientists have had a dream – this dream is to run the same software on different platforms and architectures such as Pentium-based PCs, Power PCs, RISC PCs and a whole host of others. The language Java is the nearest that the computer world has come to this Utopian dream. Suppose, for example, that you have written the best piece of software since the invention of sliced bread. If you wanted to run it on Microsoft Windows then you would need to write one version of the software. Another version would be needed for the Mac OS, yet another one for RISC OS, another for Sun's operating system and perhaps another for DOS – it is a developer's nightmare. *If you wrote the same piece of software using Java, then you would be able to run it on all the platforms mentioned above, plus any other that supports a Java Interpreter* – that's magic. It's never been successfully achieved before. It is now achieved by compiling the source code (see chapter 21) into an *intermediate code* which is to be further interpreted on the target machine. This intermediate stage is called **Java byte code**, and it is this code which gets interpreted by the machine on which the program is eventually run.

> **Hint:** Unless you are already familiar with some programming techniques, I suggest that you leave this section until later. Come back during the later part of your 'A' level course and the codes being described here will make a lot more sense.

Java has transformed, and still is transforming what can be achieved, especially via the net and the WWW. Java has increased the interactivity of the web by several orders of magnitude, and is in no small way responsible for the recent explosion of hitherto unimagined uses of the Internet. Who would have thought, just a few years ago when the HTML language was developed to browse pages, that people could interact with web sites in ways which are taken for granted today. No longer do we have to be content with a generalised page for everyone, but pages can be tailored to the needs of individuals by clever use of **Java applets** (*a* **Java**

```
<HTML><HEAD><TITLE>Very simple JavaScript demo</TITLE>
<SCRIPT LANGUAGE="JavaScript">
<!– hide this from older browsers
function WriteSomeText () {
    document.write ("<I><P><H1>Do not press this button again!</H1></P>") ;
}
//end hide –>
</SCRIPT>
</HEAD>
<BODY>
<H1>Demonstration of very simple JavaScript</H1>
<FORM>
<P><INPUT TYPE="button"  VALUE="Do NOT press this button" onClick=WriteSomeText()>
</P></FORM>
</BODY>
</HTML>
```

Figure 4.17

program *embedded into a web page*). For example, animated sequences could be tailored to the individual responses made by the user, and the web page can do virtually anything that a program could do on the local user's machine – a very powerful but potentially dangerous option with huge security implications!

A Java applet on a web page could turn part of the web page into a full-function word processor, a spreadsheet, a calculator, an art package or any other thing that the programmer may define. This is one of the reasons why the NC is able to function – all these applications can, and indeed are written in Java. To take the analysis even further, the NC is configured to have a minimal system with no hard disk. You could, for example, log onto the network, and the operating system itself and any other applications could be downloaded when needed. This system works relatively well because not all parts of all applications are needed all of the time. With a conventional word processor, for example, all the functionality is stored locally on your hard disk, whether you make use of it or not. If you don't happen to need the thesaurus during a session then why bother to load it? Many functions of modern software are not used by the majority of users, and this is where the NC concept and Java makes sense – it is possible to download the operating system (or parts of it) and just the bits of the software which you need at the time. It's an interesting concept, and one in which the Utopian images of the 'zero maintenance' option looms large. Currently, much of the effort in maintaining PCs goes into sorting out missing files and other associated screw ups on the hard disk – if there is no hard disk, then there is less to go wrong. However, in 1997, one of my colleagues was running one of these first NC-based LANs to be installed in a school in Britain, and it took several months to get the system working properly! – I am sure that it will be better when the bugs are ironed out, but this is hardly anywhere near the theoretical zero maintenance option mentioned earlier.

Java applets

A Java applet is simply a Java program assigned to an HTML web page. As with anything else in HTML, the Java applet is placed between special HTML tags – this is so that Java-enabled browsers can run them, and non-Java browsers can ignore them. If you have a Java enabled browser then this would have a built-in Java interpreter which will automatically detect any Java Applets and run them.

There are many sites on the web which show examples of Java Applets, and Black Coffee is, at the time of writing, one of the best sources, in addition to the actual Java site, of course. It belongs to Knowledge Media Inc. and is a mine of information regarding the development of Java in general. The site can be found at the address http://www.km-cd.com, and a CD is produced containing similar information to that contained within the site. The front end to the site is shown in figure 4.18.

An example, typical of what can be accomplished with a Java Applet, is shown in figure 4.19. This is an example, developed by Jeff Marin, which shows a sketchpad, which interacts with the user in ways similar to a simple art package. The user can choose different pens, and can doodle in the window as can be seen from figure 4.19.

The HTML source document, which shows how the Java applet is handled by the browser is shown in

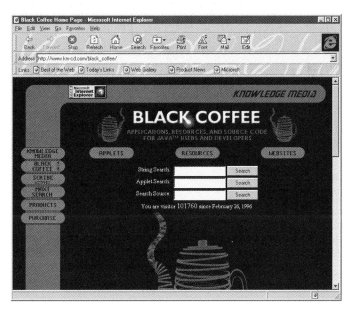

Figure 4.18

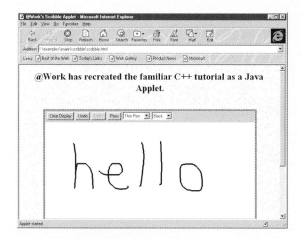

Figure 4.19

the next section. This includes the text, which would be displayed in the event that you have a browser which is not capable of running a Java applet, shown in the following section. Note the `<applet code=Scribble class width=600 height=300>` and `</applet>` parts which contain the tags mentioned above.

To get a very small taste for Java, part of the main code for the scribbling applet, produced by Jeff Marin, is shown in Figure 4.20. As you can easily see, if code like this can be run via a Java-enabled browser, then you are indeed limited only by your imagination and programming ability. In practice, when your browser is running the HTML document shown above, the <Applet> tag would be encountered, this causes a request to the web server which holds the Java class file, and this causes initialisation and starting of the Java applet at your end. If you have a Java-enabled browser then the program should run the applet according to the program instructions, part of which are shown in the following section.

The Utopian image of Java running on all machines started to crack in 1998/99. Microsoft, for example, developed Java++, which has extensions specific to their Windows operating system. Also, browsers like Microsoft's Internet Explorer can now run Visual Basic scripts, and new Active X controls further complicate the situation. At the time of writing this book, legal battles in the USA are raging as to who has the right to do what to the Java language. If companies do extend the language without the consent of others, then not all machines without the Windows operating system will be able to view the latest bells and whistles. You should always remember that the only constant in computer science is 'rapid change'!

In this chapter we have investigated just a small fraction of what is available on the World Wide Web. It's estimated that something relatively new on the web is invented every six months, so try to keep up to date by reading the computer press and computer magazines. Also, don't forget that the best way to keep up to date on the Web is simply to 'surf the Web'!

```
<HTML><HEAD>
<TITLE>@Work's Scribble Applet</TITLE>
</HEAD>
<BODY BACKGROUND="coiled.gif">
<H1><CENTER>@Work has recreated the familiar C++ tutorial as a Java
Applet.</CENTER></H1>
<BR>
<BR>
<CENTER>
<applet code=Scribble.class width=600 height=300>
<param name=Trace value="true">
<BR>If you can see this, then you don't have a Java-capable browser.
<BR>Pick up <A HREF="http://www.netscape.com/">Netscape 2.0</A> or
<A HREF="http://www.microsoft.com/">Microsoft Explorer 3.0</A>, then come back and
see our applets!
</applet>
</CENTER>
<P><A HREF="http://www.worktechs.com/index2.html"><IMG SRC="../home.gif" BORDER=0
ALIGN=MIDDLE>Return to the @Work home
page.</A></P>
<BR>
<CENTER><I>&#169  Copyright 1996 @Work Technologies</I></CENTER>
</BODY></HTML>
```

Figure 4.20 (continues)

```
// class ScribbleDocument
//
// The ScribbleDocument keeps a list of strokes which are used to recreate the
// scribble drawing. It also keeps a list of the connected views for refreshing.
import java.awt.*;
import java.util.Vector;
public class ScribbleDocument
{
                            Vector              viewList = new Vector();    //
series of strokes
                            Vector              strokeList = new Vector();  //
series of strokes
                            Vector              undoList = new Vector();
                            public void ScribbleDocument()
                            {
                            }
                            public void ClearDocument()
                            {
                                        strokeList.removeAllElements();
                                        undoList.removeAllElements();
                                        PaintAllViews();

                            }
                            // View operations
                            public void AddView( ScribbleView view )
                            {
                                        viewList.addElement( view );

                            }
                            public void RemoveView( ScribbleView view )
                            {
                                        if( view != null )
                                        {

viewList.removeElement( view );

                                        }
                                        return;

                            }
```

Figure 4.20 continued

Exercise 4.1

1 Outline both the hardware and software needed for a private individual at home to connect to the Internet making use of one of the ISPs.

2 Outline both the hardware and software needed for a small company with 100 employees to connect to the Internet via their LAN and make use of e-mail facilities.

3 What typical facilities are used when making use of e-mail? Illustrate your answer with examples making use of an e-mail system with which you are familiar.

4 Outline three advantages and three disadvantages when using e-mail compared to the conventional postal system for sending textual information.

5 What factors have to be considered when choosing an ISP for business or home use?

6 Make a list of typical features, which would usually be provided by some of the larger ISPs.

7 What is a search engine and why are they so useful when surfing the net? Outline typical features, which you would expect a standard search engine to exhibit.

8   What is meant by a URL? Explain, giving several different examples.

9   Software exists that enables us to search many search engines simultaneously. Outline the principles of such software.

10 It is now possible to 'surf the net' off line! This seems a contradiction in terms, so how is it done?

11 It is now possible to have real-time 'voice to voice' and 'video' links via the net. Outline how this might typically be achieved, listing several advantages and several disadvantages compared with the normal telephone system.

12 Videophones via the net are still in their relative infancy. What major bottlenecks need to be overcome during the first few years of the 21st century to make real-time flicker-free video a possibility?

13 Outline some of the facilities, which are available when using a typical video conferencing system. In addition to the video facilities, what other facilities might there be?

14 What are UseNet newsgroups on the Internet, and why are they so controversial?

15 There are serious privacy issues when surfing the net. Comment on this giving some typical examples of what can go wrong and why.

16 HTML has revolutionised the way in which the net is used. Give some detail as to why this is so, outlining typical facilities, which are available when using a modern HTML browser.

17 GIF files and JPEG files are often used by web site designers. Outline where each type of compression file might be most effectively used. What is meant by an animated GIF?

18 What is VRML, and what does it enable you to do when equipped with a suitable web browser? Give five different examples where VRML would be very effective.

19 When JavaScript is embedded in an HTML page, what advantages are to be had over an HTML page without this ability?

20 Comment on how languages like Java are already revolutionising the ways in which we use the web.

21 How are Java applets and ActiveX further extending what we expect from our web browsers?

22 Make a few predictions as to what might happen regarding the use of the web during the first few years of the 21st century. Outline some advantages and possible disadvantages, which might be had if the technology continues at its current pace or develops even more rapidly.

End of chapter revision aid and summary

Cover up the right-hand column and see if you can answer the questions or define the terms on the left. They appear in the order in which they are covered in this chapter. Alternatively you may browse through the right-hand column to aid revision.

From what was the Internet developed?	The Internet was developed from ARPANET, an American defence-industry project started back in the 1960s.
How long has the net been evolving?	The net (short for Internet) has been gradually evolving for about thirty years, but has reached an astounding growth rate to become mainstream in the mid to late 1990s.
What is an ISP?	ISP is short for Internet Service Provider – the name given to the companies which provide high-speed connections to the net.
What is a POP?	POP (Point Of Presence) – a local link provided by an ISP so that it's possible to link to the ISP's computer, usually for the cost of a local telephone call.
What is an IAP?	IAP (Internet Access Provider) is an alternative name for an ISP.
What is the Internet backbone?	Internet backbone – the top-level high-speed access network provided by the telecom companies and used mainly by the ISPs to route information across the world.

What is PPP?	PPP (Point to Point Protocol) – a communications protocol to link computers to an ISP via a MODEM and standard telephone line.
What is SLIP?	SLIP (Serial Line Internet Protocol) – another communications protocol to link computers to an ISP via a MODEM and standard telephone line.
What is an ISDN?	ISDN (Integrated Services Digital Network) – a faster method of connecting to your IAP, it involves a special line being connected to your computer and a special box called a 'terminal adapter' instead of using a MODEM.
What is TA?	TA (Terminal Adapter) – an alternative to a modem used for ISDN links.
What is a leased line?	Leased line – a permanently open Internet connection (i.e. you are effectively 'on line' 24h/day).
What is a proxy server?	Proxy server – a file server set up so that users of a LAN can have supervised (or unrestricted) access to the net. With this system it's possible to have many users using the same line simultaneously.
What is a domain name?	Domain name – the name given to a computer which is connected to the Internet. It also used for an Internet address.
What is an IP address?	IP address – the numbers that correspond to the Internet Protocol address for each computer. You will need one IP address for each computer on your LAN.
What is a URL?	URL (Uniform Resource Locator) – the general name given to the Internet addresses which contain both the Protocol and routing information. HTTP, FTP and Gopher help to make up types of URL.
What is HTTP?	HTTP (HyperText Transfer Protocol) – commonly used by most of the modern Internet browsers such as Internet Explorer and Netscape Navigator, for example.
What is FTP?	FTP (File Transfer Protocol) – a common system used for copying files on the Internet.
What is a Gopher?	Gopher – one type of URL.
What is a cookie?	Cookies – small items of information which can be splattered on your hard disk to help the web sites you are visiting create pages customised to your requirements and find out other information about you!
What is the TCP/IP protocol?	TCP/IP protocol – used by applications to talk to each other over LANs and the Internet. This protocol is covered in detail in chapter 5.
What is an NC?	NC (Networked Computer) – a very cost effective computer designed to operate solely on the net (LAN or Internet) – all resources are obtained from the net, and languages like Java will make this possible.
What is digital TV?	Digital TVs – some digital TVs are likely to be network ready – this means that they could have the equivalent of a Networked Computer inside.
What is a router?	Router – an interface that can connect an ISDN line to Ethernet so that you can connect LAN-based computers to the net.
What is meant by the term 'snail mail'?	Snail mail – the conventional mail system in which people put paper into envelopes, post them into funny little boxes, which are then collected by the postman, taken to the sorting office, sorted into piles, put on trucks and trains, then maybe planes . . . – you get the idea!
What is e-mail?	e-mail – electronic mail, the electronic alternative to sending messages via snail mail (the conventional post).

What is an e-mail address?	e-mail address – a unique electronic address which consists of several parts strung together to form an address which can be used to route information over the World Wide Web.
What is an attachment?	Attachment – a file which is attached to an e-mail document so that it may be sent along with the message, it will probably need encoding to be sent and received correctly.
What is a mail server?	Mail server – A file server set up so that it can distribute e-mail around a LAN when users log onto the system and load the appropriate software.
What is UU or MIME encoding?	UUENCODE, MIME and BinHex are three different methods which enable more complex information to be attached to an e-mail system designed to send only 7-bit ASCII information as plain text.
What is meant by netiquette?	Netiquette – Internet etiquette – being polite on the net.
What is plain or ASCII text?	Plain text – basic ASCII text (see chapter 12).
What is a CC?	CC – Carbon Copy for sending a copy of an e-mail message to another person.
What is a BCC?	BCC – Blind Carbon Copy – same as carbon copy except the original person to whom you sent the message does not know that someone else is also receiving it!
What is an alias?	Alias – an e-mail term used to describe a simpler address for the purposes of sending mail. For example, 'BloggsFT@demon.co.uk' might be described in your address book as 'Fred'. When Fred is typed in to the appropriate place it is replaced with the real e-mail address.
What is a mailing list?	Mailing list – a list of e-mail address such that any messages sent to this list are transferred automatically to all of the people on the list.
Outline some privacy issues on the net	Privacy issues – There is virtually no privacy on the Internet unless strong encryption such as PGP is used – however, this is a *very* contentious and politically sensitive issue.
What is UseNet?	UseNet – a large group of Internet users who connect using the UUCP instead of the TCP/IP protocol mentioned in chapter 5.
What is UUCP?	UUCP – the Unix to Unix Copy Protocol.
What is a UseNet Newsgroup?	UseNet Newsgroups – this is a method whereby anybody can post any material on any topic to like-mined individuals who log onto the system and see the messages contained in the groups. There are literally tens of thousands of newsgroups available.
What is a voice system?	Voice systems – There are many systems, which enable you to have a real-time conversation over an Internet phone with someone who has similar equipment at the other end. Using this method it's possible to have long-distance and international calls for the cost of a local call. These systems also have utilities to send sketches and screen captures etc. by using the whiteboard system.
What is a whiteboard?	Whiteboard – the system that acts like a whiteboard in a classroom – when used on the net it enables the users to send doodles to each other, or send captured screen images at the same time as having a real-time audio conversation.
What is video conferencing?	Video conferencing systems – it's possible to have either one-to-one or one-to-many video links and hence establish a national or international videoconference. However, to do more than a few real-time video calls simultaneously requires powerful equipment and high-speed links.

What is a hypertext link?	Hypertext links – links to other parts of the same site, of other parts of the net with a simple click of the mouse.
What is HTML?	HTML (Hypertext Mark-up Language) – a page-description language designed for world-wide-web browsers.
What is a browser?	Browser – a special piece of software designed for viewing an HTML document.
What is a tag?	TAG a fundamental part of an HTML document, which consist of angle braces used to enclose an HTML command e.g. is a line break.
What is an HTML link?	HTML links – the active part of a document, which can be used to link to anywhere on the WWW. A word or graphic can be clicked on to go to the web page specified in the HTML script.
Name some common web browsers	Web browsers – software such as Microsoft's Internet Explorer, Netscape's Netscape Navigator or NCSA's Mosaic, for example.
What is a GIF?	GIF (Graphics Interchange Format) – a file type developed by CompuServe for sending 256-coloured images quickly over the net. They are also useful for creating animation sequences.
What is GIF animation?	GIF animation – a sequence of GIF files played one after the other to create an illusion of a moving image. These are used extensively in web site design.
What is JPEG?	JPEG (Joint Picture Expert Group) – a file compression standard used to transmit photos and other photo-quality images over the net.
What is an HTML editor?	HTML editors – specialist software such as Microsoft's Frontpage, Ken Nesbit's WebEdit and HotDog etc. This software provides easier creation of HTML documents via conventional word-processor-like controls.
What is a CGI script?	CGI script (Common Gateway Interface script) – used to process the information gathered by HTML forms, for example. The CGI script is operated on the server, which receives the information, and is basically a link to the HTTP servers.
What is VRML?	VRML (Virtual Reality Modelling Language) – the language to turn a suitably equipped web browser into a place where you can literally explore 3D worlds on your computer.
What is JavaScript?	JavaScript – an interpreted language, which can be embedded inside HTML web pages. It adds lots more functionality and relies on local processing power.
What is Java?	Java – a fully object oriented language in its own right. It is this language, along with the development of the Internet in general which is revolutionising the way in which computers are being used for many different activities.
What is VB script?	VB script – the scripting language part of Microsoft's Visual Basic which, along with the ActiveX controls give you a tremendous amount of power provided that you have a suitably equipped browser.

5 Networking and Data Communication

Key resources

To carry out this work most successfully it's best if you have:
◆ Access to a modem
◆ Don't forget the **glossary** at the back of this book. It should be very helpful to explain some concepts with which you may not be familiar

Concept checkpoints

◆ A good knowledge of the work carried out in chapter 3.
◆ A working knowledge of the Internet (see chapter 4).

The basic principles of computer communications

The simplest type of communication system is called simplex! This would allow for the transmission of data in one direction only. However, such a system would obviously not be practical for normal communication between computers. The next stage up from simplex is called half duplex – this means the transmission of data in both directions, but only in one direction at any one time. Finally, full duplex means the simultaneous transmission of data in both directions. **These ideas are shown in figure 5.1**

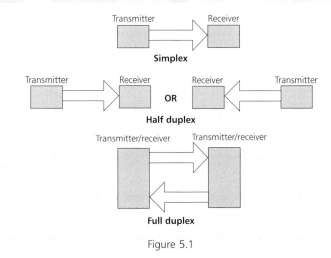

Figure 5.1

Many networks control the flow of data by having special electronic devices that switch the direction of data flow (i.e. half duplex), or control the data over full duplex links. However, if computers had been invented before the telephone system, then the world of communication systems would probably have been designed in a very different way. In fact, as the new digital lines replace the old analogue telephone systems – this is exactly what's happening. **The original telephone system was designed to transmit speech with a relatively small bandwidth (see chapter 3) of 300 Hz to 3400 Hz. Speech, unlike computer data, is an analogue signal (see chapter 8). Therefore, if computer data is to be sent over a normal telephone line, it's not surprising that some method is needed to change the computer data into the sort of electrical signals that the telephone line is expecting i.e. audio or speech. Different tones are therefore used, and this is why you can hear the data if you route it through to a suitable loudspeaker system, or simply dial up and listen to a fax line on a normal phone. (Don't do it for very long!)**

Most computer data is represented by one or more bytes. Inside the computer these binary digits would be transmitted in parallel, making use of a parallel bus system, as is explained when studying computer architecture in chapter 20. Using this extremely fast method of communication means that there is one wire for each bit. A 64-bit machine, for example, would need at least 64 parallel wires to transmit its data from one place to another. Parallel transmission is therefore *not practical* for long distance communication. (Note that under these circumstances, long distance means more than a few metres!) This parallel bus system is therefore only practical for internal computer connections or for the connection of local peripherals such as printers and scanners etc.

For cost effective communication over long distances, serial transmission must be used. This means that each byte of data would have to be changed from parallel to serial form, before being transmitted over a single wire or communication link such as a radio. Figure 5.2(a) shows a typical example where the ASCII code for the letter 'A' is in parallel form. Figure 5.2(b) shows the same data changed into serial form, ready to be transmitted over a serial link. In practice, some extra digits may be added so that checks can be done on the integrity of the data being received (see later). Synchronisation problems also have to be solved by the addition of some extra information. These problems are covered in a little more detail later on in this chapter, and when computer interfacing is studied in chapter 8.

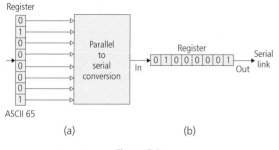

Figure 5.2

Did you know that . . .

The 'electricity', 'cable TV' and 'satellite' companies are offering faster Internet connections. Using these new systems, it's possible to connect your computer to the net at speeds of up to 10 Mbit/sec. It's usual to make use of an ADSL type system in which you can receive the data at a rate much faster than you can transmit it from your home. The future of these systems looks very exciting indeed.

Bit rates

The rate at which the data can be transmitted is measured in **Bits/sec**. However, the **bandwidth**, which measures signal changes per second, is measured in Baud. (This is after **Baudot** who did a lot of work with electronic signals.) However, because extra information as mentioned in the last paragraph may be transmitted along with the data, the actual '**information transmission rate**' may be lower than the rate at which the network is actually transmitting. This all sounds complicated, but is really quite obvious. For example, if ten bits are used to send a single byte of data, then the transmitted bit rate might be 10 bits/sec. (A little bit slow but it's only an example!) However, as only one byte of data has actually been sent, the information transmitted is only at a rate of 8 bits/sec.

Typical bit rates for transmission of data over standard telephone links are 28.8Kbit/sec, 33.6Kbit/sec and 56Kbit/sec. If you do the sums then you will realise that this is pathetically slow. It's enlightening to compare this with the fast-Ethernet LAN Baud rate of 100,000 Kbit/sec! Using the conventional telephone system *is* slow because it was originally designed for the transmission of **speech**, not computer data. We can't raise the data transfer rate due to the limited bandwidth already mentioned. However, using clever modulation techniques, such as a combination of phase and amplitude modulation, means that *it is possible to get a* **bit rate** *higher than the actual* **Baud rate**. This, together with a general improvement in compression utilities, is why we can send data at hitherto unimaginable speed, even over a conventional telephone line.

Modems

If we make use of the standard telephone system, then it's the job of a special piece of hardware called a **modem** to turn the computer data into a suitable type and level of signal ready for transmission. *Another* **modem** at the other end of the line would perform the reverse process. i.e. it would receive the audio signals, then convert them back into a suitable form (serial binary digits) to be fed back into the computer system.

These ideas are shown in figure 5.3. On sophisticated high-speed links, **modems** would not be used, as the networks are already designed to accept high-speed digital communications. The name **MODEM** comes from the words '**MODulation**' and '**DEModulation**'. These are the electronic terms for changing a signal into a form suitable for transmission (**modulation**), and then changing it back again into its original form (**demodulation**). Therefore, the transmitting modem acts as a **modulator,** and the receiving modem acts as a **demodulator**. These ideas are covered in the next section.

Similar principles apply to the transmission of data using **satellites** and **land-based microwave** or other radio **links**. The land-based microwave links are, however, limited to line-of-sight transmissions where the receiver must literally be visible from the transmitter, as was the case with the laser link shown in figure 3.10. In all of these systems the computer data must be changed into a suitable form to be transmitted

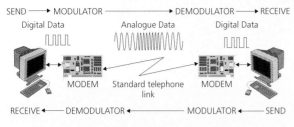

Figure 5.3

over the appropriate link. The methods of modulation that are used vary from one system to another, but some common methods will now be investigated.

The ideas of modulation

High frequency radio waves are often used to transmit signals over land-based or satellite-based microwave links. We use this radio wave as a **carrier**, which means that the radio wave will literally carry the data that is to be sent. However, it's not like riding on the back of a horse! Instead, some characteristic of the radio wave is varied in sympathy with the data to be transmitted. Consider the radio signal shown in figure 5.4(a). Here we have a high frequency sine wave. In practice the frequency would be very high – for microwave communication we are sending signals in the region 10 GHz (i.e. 10,000,000,000 cycles/sec!). As this is the wave that will carry the signal to be sent, it is called the **carrier**, or **carrier wave**.

> **Hint:** Turn up the volume on your modem and you should be able to hear frequency-modulated sounds being received and transmitted over the telephone system. Sound is used because the modem is designed for use with the telephone – a device designed to handle speech.

Let's suppose that we wish to transmit the serial binary signal as shown in figure 5.4(b) at the top of the diagram. This 'data signal' is called the **modulating**

signal, because it is being used to modulate the carrier. For the sake of argument, let's also suppose that we decide to change the **amplitude** of the **carrier** wave so that it varies in sympathy with the data in the binary signal to be transmitted. The unmodulated carrier (i.e. with no information being sent) is shown in figure 5.4(a), and the effects of the amplitude-modulation process on the carrier wave for this particular binary signal are shown in figure 5.5(b). As the **amplitude** of the carrier wave has been altered, this process is known as **amplitude modulation**.

If the **frequency** of the carrier is altered, then this would be called **frequency modulation**, or if the **phase** of the carrier were altered then this would be called **phase modulation**. The results with the same modulating signal are shown in figure 5.5. Figure 5.5(a) shows the effect of frequency modulation, and figure 5.5(b) shows the effect with phase modulation.

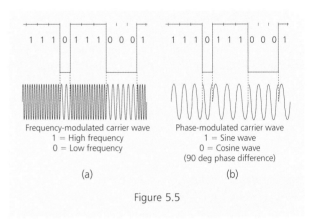

Frequency-modulated carrier wave
1 = High frequency
0 = Low frequency

Phase-modulated carrier wave
1 = Sine wave
0 = Cosine wave
(90 deg phase difference)

(a)   (b)

Figure 5.5

The above types of modulation were shown using a digital data signal. However, they work just as well, and are extensively used with analogue signals. They are the methods of modulation used everyday in TV and radio transmissions, and most readers will be familiar with the terms AM and FM on their radio sets or 'Ghetto Blasters'.

There are other methods of modulation that are particularly suited to digital signals, and some of the principles are shown in figure 5.6. These would include **pulse code modulation, pulse position modulation** and **pulse width modulation**. The most important thing to appreciate is that some characteristic of the carrier signal is altered in sympathy with the data that is being sent. At the other end of the line the process is reversed, so that the original signal can be reconstituted ready to be fed into the receiving computer.

Multiplexing

In all the data transmission systems considered so far, only one signal can be sent over a single link at its original frequency at any moment in time. Such systems, usually employing data transmission rates of up to about 10Gbits/sec, are often known as **baseband systems**. Networks such as Ethernet are, therefore,

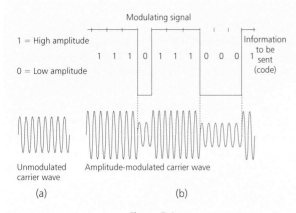

Modulating signal

1 = High amplitude

1 1 1 0 1 1 1 0 0 0 1

0 = Low amplitude

Information to be sent (code)

Unmodulated carrier wave

Amplitude-modulated carrier wave

(a)   (b)

Figure 5.4

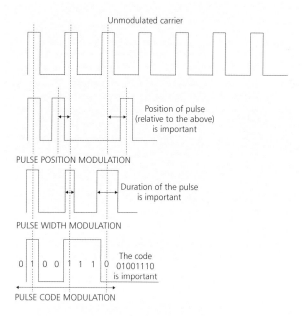

Unmodulated carrier

Position of pulse (relative to the above) is important

PULSE POSITION MODULATION

Duration of the pulse is important

PULSE WIDTH MODULATION

| 0 | 1 | 0 | 0 | 1 | 1 | 1 | 0 |

The code 01001110 is important

PULSE CODE MODULATION

Figure 5.6

examples of '**baseband**' networks, as all the bandwidth of the network is taken up by a single transmission of data from a single computer.

By making use of techniques such as **multiplexing**, it's possible to send different data down the same wire or communication link simultaneously or, apparently simultaneously. Analogue as well as digital data can often be sent. Various clever methods of getting over this single-channel limitation are now considered. The process of sending many signals together over a single line is called **multiplexing**. The basic ideas of upward multiplexing (i.e. many signals going onto one line) and downward multiplexing (getting the signals back again) can be seen in figure 5.7.

The ways in which this is actually achieved are discussed in the next few sections.

Time division multiplexing (TDM)

This is the simplest method, and is basically similar to the methods considered hitherto. In this mode the **transmission time** is split up into *tiny* **time slices**. A

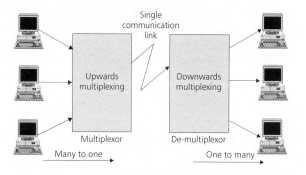

Figure 5.7

signal to be transmitted sends some data, then, after the system has given all the other signals a turn, the original signal gets another turn. The entire system continues to operate in this way.

This may sound very slow, but if the bandwidth of the system is quite high, then the turns can be taken at such a high rate that all the signals look like they are being transmitted at exactly the same time! As an example, it's possible for many people to have simultaneous conversations down the same piece of wire if time division multiplexing is used. If the rate at which the turns are taken is sufficiently high, then nobody would notice any difference. They all think that they have exclusive use of the line. Although done electronically, a mechanical system making use of switches can be seen in figure 5.8. This makes time-division multiplexing very easy to understand. Many **digital packets** (see later) of information are sent through networks in a similar way. It can therefore be seen that similar principles are used on high-speed digital communication systems.

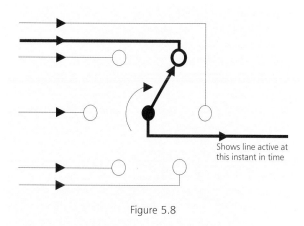

Shows line active at this instant in time

Figure 5.8

Frequency division multiplexing (FDM)

You already know that carrier waves can be used to transmit data over a link. Now it would be possible, by using a different carrier frequency, to send two or more different signals simultaneously down the same link. They would not interfere with each other because the carriers are separated by a suitably large frequency. The frequency spectrum for sending three different modulated signals over the same link in this particular way is shown in figure 5.9.

Hint: You should already be familiar with broadband networks, you make use of them all of the time. The radio, television and satellite channels are all based on broadband transmissions. They all have their own unique frequency at which they transmit the signal.

You can see that a wider bandwidth is needed to send more signals over the link. (This should relate

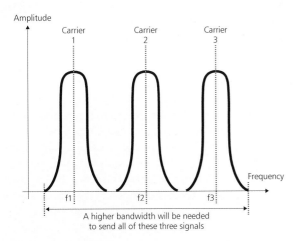

Amplitude

Carrier 1   Carrier 2   Carrier 3

Frequency

f1   f2   f3

A higher bandwidth will be needed
to send all of these three signals

Figure 5.9

quite well to common sense and to what was discussed earlier in this chapter). These are known as **broadband networks**. At the other end of the line the carrier signals are separated by using electronic filters to filter out the appropriate carrier wave. The demodulation process then extracts the original signal.

An example of a broadband network is the system developed by WANG computers. Here each machine on the network would need a special modem capable of transmitting and receiving the appropriate radio signals. The bandwidth, and hence the information transmission rates of these networks, is usually much higher than the baseband networks mentioned earlier. There is nothing strange about frequency division multiplexing. It's the same ideas that are used when you tune into some radio stations. The act of turning the tuning knob on the radio selects an appropriate carrier frequency. (The frequency at which the radio station is transmitting.) The radio set then demodulates your selected carrier wave so that you can hear the original signal (i.e. the music or speech for your selected station).

Although broadband networks are being used, the digital **ISDN networks** also offer great potential for the future, and even many radio networks are now packet switched. However, Broadband networks might come to the rescue over a conventional telephone line as described in the next section.

Megabit MODEMS

A very recent innovation is proving to be exciting for small businesses, the home and educational users. Companies like NORTEL (Northern Telecom) have developed systems to transmit at incredible megabit speeds over a conventional telephone link! Hitherto, speeds of 56 Kbps or even 128 Kbps have been cutting edge, so anything that pushes Internet access speeds up by a factor of 32 times over the conventional 33.6 Kbps at the time of writing is nothing less than revolutionary. These devices are obviously intended to

fill the gap between the expensive high-bandwidth links available to large businesses, and the small business and home markets.

The technique lies with installation of some special equipment in the local telephone exchange, and the addition of an Ethernet card (NIC see chapter 3) and a special box at the local computer. One end of the box is plugged into the Ethernet card on the PC, and the other end of the box is plugged into a conventional (*not* ISDN) telephone socket. To get maximum performance you must live within a relatively short distance (about 3 miles) from a local telephone exchange which has appropriate equipment installed, but most of the population (i.e. those living in cities, towns and large villages) will probably meet this criterion.

The system does not work at the same speed in either direction, but the PC can receive at the full 1 megabit per second, and send at a reduced 120Kbits/sec. However, remember when surfing the net, for most people the bulk of data is being received. Therefore the higher-speed is being used very effectively. The megabit modems are also known as **Digital Modem Technology** because they do not operate on the same principles as the analogue modems covered earlier in this chapter. The idea of the megabit digital modem is shown in figure 5.10. As you can see, the system can cope with

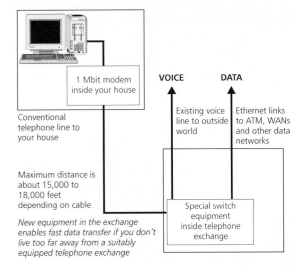

1 Mbit modem
inside your house

VOICE   DATA

Existing voice line to outside world   Ethernet links to ATM, WANs and other data networks

Conventional telephone line to your house

Maximum distance is about 15,000 to 18,000 feet depending on cable

New equipment in the exchange enables fast data transfer if you don't live too far away from a suitably equipped telephone exchange

Special switch equipment inside telephone exchange

Figure 5.10

simultaneous voice over the same link, and thus you can use the phone at the same time too.

Other recent consumer technologies

Other technologies, similar in nature to the broadband megabit modems mentioned here, involve transmission of the digital information over the power lines instead of the telephone cable. Again, special boxes need to be located near to your home, and the power-system infrastructure enables companies like NORWEB, a UK electricity provider, to connect you to the Internet at megabit speeds. If you don't mind having a small microwave satellite or land-line connection, then its also possible for consumers to connect at speeds of about 20 megabits/sec. Many cable companies are also offering similar deals. The future of the web looks tremendously exciting, and it looks like the world wide web will no longer be known as the world wide wait. Nevertheless, you can be confident that other businesses, realising the potential that these faster access speeds have to offer, will launch services like video on demand or realistic interactive virtual reality simulators. We will then be looking for faster web access again!

Improving telephone services

It's ironic, but most of the telephone systems in the western world are now digital in nature. The only part to have escaped this revolution is the antiquated connection between the telephone exchange and your home, and this is where the megabit modems mentioned in the last section come into their own. However, think how much better it would be if you had access to the faster technologies *because* you had the right cables, equipment and infrastructure coming right up to your door. You would then be in the same position as the businesses with a much faster link capability. There are various different systems, and we have already seen the **V.34 system**. This is the *standard telephone link*, capable of transmitting at up to about 56Kbps, although analogue modem technology is tortuously trying to improve this. We have also seen the **ISDN** lines which push the limits up to 128 Kbps.

Did you know that . . .

ADSL and VDSL are likely to be the ways that the telecom companies can steal business back from the increasingly sophisticated cable and satellite markets. One thing is for sure – Internet connections will be faster and cheaper in the near future.

The next stages of digital technology involve systems like SDSL, T1 and E1, and ADSL which can operate at up to 9 Mbps. **ADSL** stands for **Asymmetric Digital Subscriber Line**, and allows the transmission of video signals over ordinary telephone cables. Assuming, of course that you are near enough to the digital equipment to make use of this without degradation. The current limit for ADSL is about 1.7 miles. As with the megabit modems mentioned in the last section, the transmit and receive rates are different, with ADSL giving about 640Kbps for sending information from the host PC. If this is a little slow for your requirements, then **VDSL (Very fast high data rate Digital Subscriber Line)** will allow up to 52 Mbps receive, and 2.3 Mbps transmit. Again, assuming that you are not too far away from the digital processing equipment (less than a mile in this case!). These speeds are now approaching fast network speeds, and you effectively have a digital network connection right up to your home! If the telephone companies can supply such systems for a reasonable price, then surfing the net will operate at lightning speed. This all sounds wonderful, assuming, of course, that the Internet backbones, the service providers and Internet sites can keep up with the demand from millions of people with these high-bandwidth links.

Network switching

The next few sections on network-switching techniques are important if you are to appreciate the fundamentally different ways in which computer networks route their data compared to the simpler ways in which a standard telephone system would route its data.

Circuit switching

If the normal telephone system is used, then the method of switching between one computer and another is likely to be that of **circuit switching**. This means that a dedicated physical electrical path has to be established between the two computers for the duration of the time that this particular path is needed (until somebody puts the phone down!). This means that with **circuit switching** *the line is in use all the time* that the computers are likely to need to communicate, and can't, therefore, be used by other systems during this time. You have also seen that the normal telephone system has an inadequate bandwidth for fast computer communications, and so this method would not be used for a dedicated fast computer link, unless there is no alternative – e.g. the connection of a modem from most private houses, for example. There are also several other disadvantages to using the normal telephone system. Without extra specialist equipment, it's not possible for one computer to communicate with more than one other computer at the same time. In addition to this, the time taken to route the call on a standard telephone line is unacceptably long (i.e. to dial the number and wait for an answer!). However, tone dialling is now considerably better than the old pulse-dialling systems being phased out now in most parts of the country.

Message switching

A better solution is to make use of **message switching**. This means that a permanent higher-bandwidth line is installed between two node computers. A typical network topology would be a partially connected mesh network as shown in figure 5.11(a). It would be usual for the computer that wishes to communicate with another to set up the message with a **header** that contains the address of the destination computer. The idea is shown in figure 5.11(b).

> **Hint:** Imagine little messages being routed around the network. Each message, rather like a letter at the post office, has a destination address. Again, like the letter in the post, many different routes can be taken, according to which routes happen to be busy at the time of the journey.

The message will be sent off in an appropriate direction and, when the next computer receives it, the header information will be inspected. If it is not for the inspecting computer to deal with, then it will be transmitted again in a direction that will get the message nearer to the destination computer. In other words, the computers at each node are acting as **routers** and will pass the message on in the appropriate direction until it gets to its destination. One of the main things to realise is that these dedicated lines are only occupied for the relatively short duration of the message. They are then instantly available to deal with other traffic on the network, unlike the circuit switching method where the line is tied up for the entire duration of the computer session. The **node computers** (i.e. the computers at each node) would be powerful enough to respond in **real time** to all the messages that are being received, but you should note that not all messages are dealt with immediately, they are often buffered in a queuing system. The node computers would probably be powerful minicomputers or even a mainframe, but no doubt they will be replaced by extremely powerful micros when these become available.

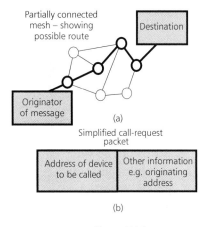

Partially connected mesh – showing possible route

Destination

Originator of message

(a)

Simplified call-request packet

| Address of device to be called | Other information e.g. originating address |

(b)

Figure 5.11

You should now be able to see the difference between **message switching** and **circuit switching**. In circuit switching, a direct link is established between the two computers for the duration of the session, and can't be used for other traffic. In message switching, the messages are routed via various node computers until they reach their final destination. There is no mechanical switching involved as the dedicated high-speed links between each node computer already exist. Message switching is therefore much more suitable than circuit switching for high-speed computer links. However, if infrequent connections making use of low bandwidth lines are all that is needed, then the 'normal phone line circuit switching method' would be a more economical option for the small user. The message-switching lines are quite expensive to rent, but there is no appreciable delay in the connection from one computer to another, except for the slight delay while the node computer decides on the appropriate route. The circuit and message switching ideas are summarised in the following table.

Method	Intended use
Circuit switching	Conventional telephone and modem connections. Exclusive use is made of a dedicated phone line for the duration of the call.
Message switching	Ideal for computer data. Communication line is only used for the time needed to send the message.

Packet switching networks

The message switching method can get slowed down if the messages to be sent are very large and other systems are queuing up to use the line. It would be far easier to manage if the size of a large message were chopped up into smaller parts. If this is done then large messages can be sent as several smaller messages. These smaller chunks are called **packets,** and the resulting system is known as a **packet switching network**. If the packets were all the same size, then this would enable efficient storage management and switching at the node computers. It would also enable other messages to be inserted into the middle of messages that were already being sent. As far as the users are concerned, they get an apparent increase in the speed of the network, but, as we have seen before in this chapter, it's simply better management of the available resources. Packet switching networks making use of the X25 protocol are now *some of the most common* means of communication between computers over WANs. The splitting up of messages into packets does introduce some extra complexity, but the processing power of the node computers is such that this added complexity is outweighed by the increased throughput of the data over the network. **JANET**, the **Joint Academic NETwork** that connects British universities, and more recently SuperJANET are examples of large packet switching networks that have been established in the UK and which are now part of the **Internet** system. An ideal connection for the packet switching network would be the higher bandwidth links. The fibre optic links that were mentioned in chapter 3 would give the best performance.

Packet switching is an important concept. It's used not only for cable and fibre optic links, but for land-based radio and satellite links too. As an example of a satellite link, consider a satellite that is geostationary over the North Atlantic. This could be used to link North America and some of Europe. The host computer sends a message up to the satellite which is some 36,000km above the Earth. The satellite then broadcasts to all the ground stations. The appropriate ground station would then pass on the messages after the header had been decoded.

Radio networks

It's interesting to note that packet switching networks have also been established by making use of radio links. Indeed, some radio communications are now undertaken using packet switching techniques, and computer communications via radio are normally packet switched.

Radio systems are now being taken very seriously indeed, and will probably lead to the idea that all computers can be connected permanently to a network. This can be done either by an infrared link near to a suitable connection point, or, more conveniently, by a radio link similar in principle to the portable-phone system. The consequences of such systems are far reaching. It will, for example, be possible to be virtually anywhere in the world and still have connections to the Internet from your portable via a suitable radio link. I have often lamented that it's not yet possible to have access to all human knowledge at any time and in any place, and this may be the first step towards this ultimate goal.

Buffering

You will appreciate from reading the last few sections that interconnection of networks with very different Baud rates needs to be carried out in practice. **Buffering** is therefore used to match the differing speeds of the various systems used in a network. It is effectively a block of memory that can hold the data to be transmitted if the line is busy, or if data has to be taken in and sent out at

different rates. The ideas are identical in principle to the buffering systems covered in the operating-systems in chapter 23. **Buffering** is also sometimes carried out at board level on the PCs, and new Ethernet interfaces have become available which assemble **Ethernet frames** (see later) at the *same time* as sending other frames.

International network standards

Before the advent of internationally agreed standards, companies were often at the mercy of the large manufacturers. Indeed, it was often not possible to get information from one system to another because each manufacturer had their own different protocols. Technical information required was often hard to get, and there was little co-operation between competing companies. It was against this unsatisfactory background that the **International Standards Organisation** (ISO) began working on a set of manufacturer-independent network communication protocols (i.e. a system to allow different networks and machines to communicate with each other). From reading chapters 3 and 4, and from the first half of this chapter, you should already appreciate the enormity of their task!

The OSI model

The **ISO OSI model** is the **International Standards Organisation Open Systems Interconnection model**. (An **open system** is simply a system that supports the OSI standards.) It is used to define the ways in which different computer networks may be connected to each other. Without standards such as this, it would be impossible to work towards the idea of a **global communications network**.

The ISO OSI model forms the basis of all the interconnections for most of the modern **packet switching networks**. These special **network protocols** are needed to make sure that the enormously complex data communications between different systems are manageable. You will soon be aware that, throughout your computer science course, the concept of **structure** is *very important* i.e. **structured programming**, **structured models** and **structure diagrams** etc. The ISO OSI model is therefore a comprehensive **structure** for **data communications**.

ISO OSI model for open systems interconnection

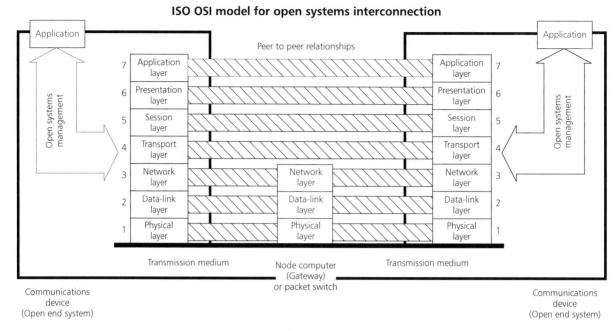

Figure 5.12

As you can imagine, trying to form a standard for the interconnection of different communication systems is no easy task. The model therefore simplifies things to some extent by breaking down this huge task into **seven different sub-tasks**. Each sub-task goes progressively from the most fundamental aspects such as where the wires are to be connected (called the **physical level**) right up to the **application layer** which gives high-level support for **applications** making use of the network. Each layer is shown in the diagram of figure 5.12. The first three layers are concerned with the details of the actual networks being used. You can imagine it to be similar to trying to route the post on a railway system. The individual letters are bundled together and then, according to where they have to go, they are joined onto different engines and sent down the most appropriate routes to arrive at their destination. However, here we must realise that this engine analogy would be compared to adding more and more complex electronic information to the binary digits that are actually being transmitted. The brief details of each layer are as follows, but if you start to get bogged down with the definition of what's happening at each layer, read the 'how it all works' paragraph on the next page first!

The physical layer

This is the specification of the electronic and mechanical connections, i.e. the nuts and bolts of which wires go where, and what types of electrical signals will be used. It's therefore the environment for the **physical** systems that carry the streams of data between different points in the network. This layer therefore provides the interface between the data and the actual **hardware**

connections such as plugs and sockets. For example, **V.24** is one of the specifications for the connection of devices to **modems**.

The link layer (data-link layer)

This layer provides for transfer of data between two devices that are connected together, perhaps on the same LAN. It allows data to be transferred in such a way that it's possible to detect any errors in the transmission, and also provides synchronisation.

The '**X25 level 2**' is an example of a common **network link layer**. This specifies how the information is to be transmitted in the form of a **frame**, e.g. bits to specify where the data is to go, and **CRCs** (see later) for **error detection.** The generalised idea of a data-link frame is shown in figure 5.13.

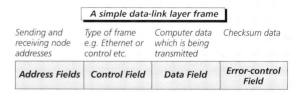

Figure 5.13

The network layer

This is the layer that gives the system the ability to be linked to other types of network so that a much larger more comprehensive network can be made up, i.e. we are now dealing with communications across networks by routing, switching and other methods of connection.

The information is now being sent in the form of a packet. The **network layer** will therefore have to deal with problems such as routing the data and making sure that the packet sizes match – this is because the different networks may have different maximum packet sizes. It must also be able to cope with different messages from one computer to many others and from many computers to a single computer by some form of sequenced delivery. The node computers in the network undertake these tasks and are known as **Interface Message Processors** or **IMPs**. The **Internet** uses **IMPs** to route data messages across some parts of the network.

A simple analogy for one type of packet routing can be thought of as working out and assembling the route by which the 'train' (network layer packet) will travel to get from the source to the destination, e.g. we might start off at Edinburgh, and, on our way to London, the network packet layer might route the information via Newcastle, Darlington, York, Doncaster, Sheffield, Leicester, Northampton and Luton. In practice there are many more sophisticated routing methods than the simple analogy described above. The '**X25 level 3**' defines one type of **network layer packet** protocol which is in common use.

The transport layer

This is a layer that is designed to match the **network layer** to the **session layer** to be covered in a moment. It will provide functions such as trying to work out the **cheapest route**, possibly by **multiplexing** the signals. It determines the optimum size for each unit that is going to be sent, and also provides some extra **error recovery** etc. It is designed to make the interfacing of the higher levels much easier to do. It is needed as the data to be transmitted may go over several different types of network each having its own characteristics. It therefore provides data communication facilities through a **standard interface**, irrespective of whether the data has come from a specific type of LAN or any other system. It effectively takes whatever is thrown at it and assembles it into a more-reliable form for the higher layers, thus ensuring a better quality and consistency of service when viewed from the top layers. The bottom three layers are effectively hardware dominated, and the top three are effectively software dominated. The transport layer is the 'piggy in the middle'.

The session layer

The **session layer** undertakes the **management of communications sessions** between two different systems. It deals with things such as synchronisation and requesting permission to send the data etc. This is the first level at which you do not have to get involved with any of the communications systems elementary methods such as network characteristics. Full-duplex communication is possible at this level. Notice how we are progressing

up the ladder from raw binary digits towards the end user of the system. i.e. the **lower four layers** are **communication-systems oriented**, and we are now progressing into the **top three layers** that are **applications oriented**. This is what the OSI model is all about.

The presentation layer

The **presentation layer** deals with how the 'information to be represented' is **presented**. It should be reasonably obvious that the way in which the individual characters and numbers etc. are stored will vary from one manufacturer to another, and from one system to another, with ASCII and EBCDIC being just two particular examples. There may even be special protocols for creating characters that represent pictures. In addition to this, different node computers might handle their **syntax** in different ways. However, the **presentation layer** will provide the appropriate **transfer** to the agreed '**transfer syntax**', i.e. the syntax that all the communication systems will understand no matter who manufactured them. For example, there might be three types of syntax involved – one for the environment that is sending the data, one for the transfer environment and a third for the environment which is going to receive the data. The presentation layer would cope with all of these types of problems. The presentation layer can also be involved in **data encryption methods** as described in chapter 9.

The application layer

This is the *highest level* of the **OSI model** and defines the interface through which the users' **applications** (or **programs**) gain access to the communications services. Such typical facilities would be **file transfer** and **message handling**, but there may also be more specific facilities offered by specialised applications. For example, **databases, viewdata systems, teleconferencing systems** and **distributed data processing systems** would all have their own **architectures** (or **structures**). The application layer will provide support such that these applications can make use of the other layers previously defined. It is this particular layer that makes it easy to write software for the global directories involved on the Internet system, for example.

How it all works

If you keep in mind the simple train analogy described at the beginning of the last section, then you should be able to appreciate what's happening at a fundamental level. If for example, you are transmitting data from one machine to another over a network, then, as you are probably aware, this data would be put into a suitable packet. Consider the data as shown in figure 5.14.

After being processed by the application layer, another 'carriage is put onto the train', containing information that has been added so that the transmitting computer's application layer can 'talk to' the receiving computer's application layer. Next, the whole packet, represented by the data and the 'application layer data header' as shown in figure 5.14, is processed by the presentation layer and this adds it's own header as shown. The process then continues until all the headers have been added to the original data, and it's transmitted over the network. The only time in which no extra data is added is when the data is sent over the physical link – don't forget that this is not a protocol as such, but is the specification of the connections and voltage levels etc. regarding the hardware.

At the receiving end, the reverse process occurs. Each header is stripped off until the original data is presented to the receiving computer after having been processed by the receiving computer's application layer, i.e. all the headers (little carriages in our trains) have been gradually removed, one by one, in reverse order until the original data is available on the recipient's computer. That's all there is to it!

TCP/IP

One of *the* most important sets of communication protocols in operation today is **TCP/IP** standard. This stands for the **Transmission Control Protocol / Internet Protocol**. This is basically a set of protocols that support connectivity between LANs and WANs, and seems to have become the *de facto* standard. These protocols have evolved from the original **ARPAnet packet-switched system** mentioned earlier in chapter 3. This system forms the primary mechanisms whereby data is sent over the global Internet network. **TCP/IP** is also embedded in the **kernel** (see chapter 22) of many operating systems.

There are many other protocols, with 'RIP', 'SAP' and 'Watchdog', being just three other examples. However, you may be wondering why they all exist if the OSI

standard was meant to be the system to which everybody conforms? The fact is that all (most in practice) these other standards *do conform* to the ISO OSI model, and the *relationships* between **OSI model** & **TCP/IP**, for example, are shown in figure 5.15.

As you can see, the **Internet Protocol (IP)** conforms to *level 3* of the **ISO/OSI model**, and **TCP** conforms to level 4. **TCP/IP** is, therefore, an example of a system of protocols that conform to the **network** and **transport layers** of the **ISO OSI model**. These protocols might sit on top of an Ethernet environment as shown in the diagram. The *Ethertype* in this diagram refers to the type of data in the field such as an **Internet packet** or a **NetWare packet**, for example, and the *Ethernet* physical layer is the 'guts' of the **Ethernet** system. What goes on the top layers depends on the operating system and applications that are being used. In practice other systems for error checking etc would also be included, but, for the sake of simplicity, these are not shown in the diagram.

Asynchronous Transfer Mode (ATM)

As described in chapter 3, one other **packet-switching** system that is gaining in popularity is **ATM** or

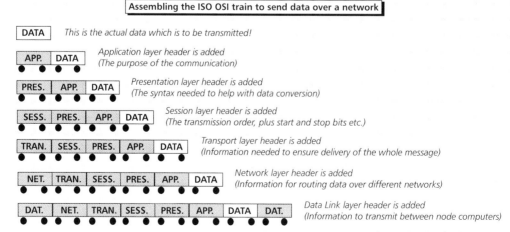

Assembling the ISO OSI train to send data over a network

| DATA | | | | | | | This is the actual data which is to be transmitted! |

APP. DATA — Application layer header is added (The purpose of the communication)

PRES. APP. DATA — Presentation layer header is added (The syntax needed to help with data conversion)

SESS. PRES. APP. DATA — Session layer header is added (The transmission order, plus start and stop bits etc.)

TRAN. SESS. PRES. APP. DATA — Transport layer header is added (Information needed to ensure delivery of the whole message)

NET. TRAN. SESS. PRES. APP. DATA — Network layer header is added (Information for routing data over different networks)

DAT. NET. TRAN. SESS. PRES. APP. DATA DAT. — Data Link layer header is added (Information to transmit between node computers)

Note that data-link information is added to both ends
Note also that the actual data sent would be much larger than is implied from the above diagram

Figure 5.14

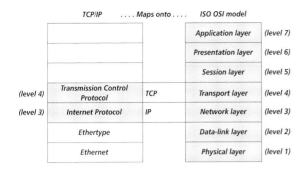

TCP/IP	.... Maps onto	ISO OSI model	
		Application layer	(level 7)
		Presentation layer	(level 6)
		Session layer	(level 5)
(level 4)	Transmission Control Protocol	TCP	Transport layer	(level 4)
(level 3)	Internet Protocol	IP	Network layer	(level 3)
	Ethertype		Data-link layer	(level 2)
	Ethernet		Physical layer	(level 1)

Figure 5.15

Asynchronous Transfer Mode. ATM is popular because it supports a very large range of different data types including **computer data**, **voice data** and **video data**, and is thus a *very flexible system* for implementing parts of the **information superhighway**. In the ATM system, packets of data are referred to as **cells**, and each ATM cell is 48-bytes of data plus 5 bytes of header information containing, for example, cell destination information to be used at the **nodes** which route the data over the networks. **Multiplexing** (see earlier) on this particular system is carried out at this cell level. Another plus for the ATM system is that it's proved to be more reliable than some of the other systems which have been used in the past, and ATM has been developed for use in LANs too. ATM, together with an appropriate optical or cable network defines the physical and data-link layers (layers 1 and 2) of the OSI model.

Errors

It has been mentioned at frequent intervals that error checking goes on around most networks. It's obviously important that the messages arrive without any errors, and while it's obviously not possible to guarantee this, it is possible to reduce the probability of error by various mechanisms that will be discussed in the next section. Errors arise from interference on the network. This is usually in the form of electrical noise, but the end result is that some bits get corrupted and binary zeros get turned into binary ones etc. or the complete message is so unrecognisable that you can't make any sense of it!

There are very sophisticated methods for **detecting** *and* **correcting** errors when transmitting data over communication links, but these often involve a large amount of extra data being sent. However, when using most networks, it's usually enough just to be able to detect that an error has occurred. If an error is detected then the packet of data can be re-transmitted. Two of the most common error checking techniques make use of **parity** and **cyclic-redundancy checks**. Both methods are explained in the next few sections. However, because most students find it unbelievable that you can receive a corrupted message, and then change it back to what it should have been, we have included a very simple example using two-dimensional parity shown in the next section. Although more sophisticated methods are used in practice, this shows how it's physically possible to correct a corrupted message – at least in theory! It's also a good way of winning a bet – your friends won't believe that you can receive the wrong message and change it to what it should have been!

Parity

Parity is a very simple method of checking the **integrity** of received data. As an example, consider the ASCII codes for the message 'A very thick fog' shown in Figure 5.16. Normal ASCII characters do not make use of the most significant bit of each byte that is being used to send the data. Figure 5.16 shows the decimal and binary codes using just seven bits each. (Don't forget that a space is also a character.)

> **Hint:** If you have a modem connected to your computer, go to the set-up procedures for the modem, and you should be able to find out if any parity bits are set. Along with some other settings, a US Robotics modem, for example, allows both odd and even parity to be switched on or off.

If these digits are transmitted using just seven bits, then there is no check that the received message is the one that was sent. We can, however, make use of the eighth bit to perform a check on the pattern of bits representing each character. When used in this way, this eighth bit is called a **parity bit**. There are two methods, but we will consider **even parity** first.

Even parity

Using this method you simply count up the number of 1's in the data to be sent and, *if even*, the **parity bit** is set at **zero**. If the number of 1's were *odd*, then the parity bit is **set** to **one**, and this, therefore, makes the number of 1's in the data to be sent even again. Therefore, after the parity bits have been added, there is always an even number of 1's in each byte of data that is being sent. The new codes for the message, including the parity bits are shown in figure 5.16 (b).

At the receiving end, a check would be made on each byte, and if there are an even number of 1's then the data is assumed to be correct. If an odd number of 1's has been received, then the data is in error.

Odd parity

The ideas are similar to even parity. The only difference is that the number of 1's in each byte is made odd by setting the appropriate value of the parity bit. The message ready to be transmitted using odd parity is shown in figure 5.16(c).

	Decimal	Binary (no parity)	Binary (even parity)	Binary (odd parity)
A	65	0 1 0 0 0 0 0 1	0 1 0 0 0 0 0 1	1 1 0 0 0 0 0 1
	32	0 0 1 0 0 0 0 0	1 0 1 0 0 0 0 0	0 0 1 0 0 0 0 0
V	86	0 1 0 1 0 1 1 0	0 1 0 1 0 1 1 0	1 1 0 1 0 1 1 0
E	69	0 1 0 0 0 1 0 1	1 1 0 0 0 1 0 1	0 1 0 0 0 1 0 1
R	82	0 1 0 1 0 0 1 0	1 1 0 1 0 0 1 0	0 1 0 1 0 0 1 0
Y	89	0 1 0 1 1 0 0 1	0 1 0 1 1 0 0 1	1 1 0 1 1 0 0 1
	32	0 0 1 0 0 0 0 0	1 0 1 0 0 0 0 0	0 0 1 0 0 0 0 0
T	84	0 1 0 1 0 1 0 0	1 1 0 1 0 1 0 0	0 1 0 1 0 1 0 0
H	72	0 1 0 0 1 0 0 0	0 1 0 0 1 0 0 0	1 1 0 0 1 0 0 0
I	73	0 1 0 0 1 0 0 1	1 1 0 0 1 0 0 1	0 1 0 0 1 0 0 1
C	67	0 1 0 0 0 0 1 1	1 1 0 0 0 0 1 1	0 1 0 0 0 0 1 1
K	75	0 1 0 0 1 0 1 1	0 1 0 0 1 0 1 1	1 1 0 0 1 0 1 1
	32	0 0 1 0 0 0 0 0	1 0 1 0 0 0 0 0	0 0 1 0 0 0 0 0
F	70	0 1 0 0 0 1 1 0	1 1 0 0 0 1 1 0	0 1 0 0 0 1 1 0
O	79	0 1 0 0 1 1 1 1	1 1 0 0 1 1 1 1	0 1 0 0 1 1 1 1
G	71	0 1 0 0 0 1 1 1	0 1 0 0 0 1 1 1	1 1 0 0 0 1 1 1
		(a)	(b)	(c)

Figure 5.16

Is parity any good?

It's not any good for sending complex packets across networks, but at a simple level, the probability of receiving the correct message must obviously be higher if parity is used. Using a single-bit parity method means that we can detect if the message received is incorrect, and demand a retransmission if this proves to be the case.

More sophisticated techniques exist to correct errors in messages, and although this highly theoretical topic can take up a whole book in itself, a simple example should convince you that this is easily possible. The main idea is to send extra redundant information along with the message, which can be used as a check on integrity and as a mechanism for the correction process. If, for example, we use two-dimensional parity, we can sometimes receive a message containing an error, then actually correct it! The ideas are shown in figure 5.17.

Even parity checks have been done on the message vertically as well as horizontally. Figure 5.17(a) shows the message with the parity bits added. Let's suppose that a bit gets changed and the message received is 'A

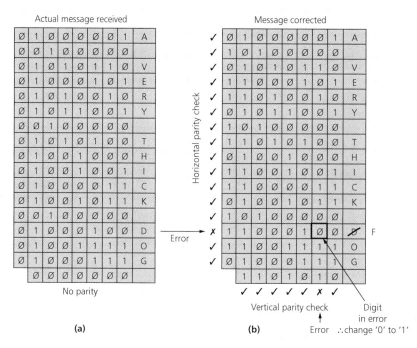

Figure 5.17

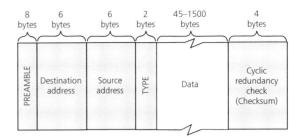

Figure 5.18

very thick dog'. Now if this message is actually received, then a dog psychiatrist might be called for! However, after the parity checks have been done, we have detected an error in the position shown in figure 5.17(b). As we are using binary code (just two states only), if a digit can be identified as being wrong, then all that has to be done is to change it! We therefore have the ability to correct a message after it has been received!

It's obvious that parity checking could not cope with multiple errors. If two digits were changed then the parity checking would not show up any errors at all. It's also unfortunate that, with modern communication systems, when errors do occur, the data is likely to become too corrupted for parity to be of any use. Most of the time the messages are transmitted and received free of errors, then, if a burst of noise occurs on the line, much of the message that was being transmitted at that time is corrupted.

There are many more sophisticated checking procedures available, but these are beyond the scope of this book. Even so, the most important thing to realise is 'if an error is detected in the received message', all that's necessary is to 're-transmit the original message', and this is what's normally done in the majority of situations. Therefore, a more efficient way of error detection is required, and this is covered in the next section.

Cyclic redundancy checks (CRC)

Often the packet of data sent around the network would have a **cyclic redundancy check** (**CRC**) carried out on the information associated with it. For example, the **CRC** information for an Ethernet packet is shown in figure 5.18.

In addition to the CRC, you can see the source and destination addresses, and the data to be sent. There is also some synchronisation information. The CRC is used as a check on the **integrity** of the data at the receiving computer. A cyclic redundancy check is a mathematical method which, when applied to the data using some suitable algorithm, provides some extra digits that can be transmitted along with the original data. When the data has been received, the same algorithm can be used to see if the digits derived are the same as the additional digits in the CRC check.

There are different CRC methods. These range from simple techniques similar to those developed for the hashing algorithms in chapter 27, to more complex ones which are designed to detect the largest possible range of likely errors that will occur when data is transmitted. Over a modern network the success rates can be in excess of 99.9999%. One of these modern methods, used for CRC checks on the X.25 lines mentioned earlier in this chapter, makes use of a standard 16-bit polynomial **generator G(x)** as follows:

$$G(x) = x^{16} + x^{12} + x^5 + 1.$$

Coding this as a sixteen-bit binary number is simple – it would be represented inside a register as 10001000000100001 (i.e. 1 lot of x^{16}, 0 lots of x^{15}, right down to 1 lot of x^0). Now you probably think that the quadratics and cubics which you cover in maths are complex enough, but the data from the **message** to be sent is fed into yet another polynomial called a **message polynomial**, **M(x)**, which for a simple 4-bit message consisting of 1011 might be:

$$1011 \rightarrow M(x) = 1x^3 + 0x^2 + 1x^1 + 1x^0 = x^3 + x + 1$$

The above polynomials are then processed in a variety of ways by multiplication and division, to end up with a **quotient polynomial Q(x)** and a **remainder polynomial R(x)**. Look at chapter 31 if you have forgotten about 'quotient' and 'remainder' from your school arithmetic days! In fact, if you're good at long division, then it's dead easy to divide polynomials and a simple example for unrelated data is as shown in Figure 5.19.

$$\begin{array}{r} x \quad + \text{ Remainder } x + 1 \\ x^2 + x \enclose{longdiv}{x^3 + x^2 + x + 1} \\ \underline{x^3 + x^2 + \qquad} \\ 0 \quad 0 \quad x + 1 \end{array}$$

$$G(x) \enclose{longdiv}{M(x)} \quad Q(x) + \text{remainder } R(x)$$

Figure 5.19

Did you know that . . .

Some hackers use characteristics of network transmission systems to help them crack codes. For example, hash functions and CRC checks obtained by sniffing packets going by on the network can be used, together with a dictionary attack, to help decode an encrypted password.

Here you can see that the answer to the polynomial division sum

$$(x^3 + x^2 + x + 1)/(x^2 + x) \text{ is } x$$
$$\text{with a remainder of } (x + 1).$$

Now in a real CRC example, the **remainder polynomial R(x)** is used to produce the **bits** for the **CRC check**. By examination of the coefficients of the remainder polynomial – 1 lot of x^1 and 1 lot of x^0 in the above arbitrary example – the CRC bits are generated and inserted into the end of the message. At the receiving end the same procedure is followed, and the CRC bit pattern is checked to see if it conforms to the bit pattern calculated at the transmitting end.

Until recently, CRC checks were not often used, as they are complex to carry out in practice. However, it's now easily possible to do all of the above mathematical manipulations totally in hardware. This includes the division of the binary numbers representing the coefficients of the polynomials. With the current processing power of microprocessors, it takes very little time indeed to carry out these mechanistic but tedious techniques. CRC checks making use of the polynomial methods generate a very compact number of bits compared to other methods. Because of the *very high* **error-detection rates** and the *very low* **overheads** in terms of extra bits transmitted with the data, **CRC checks** are *used extensively* in all modern communication systems.

Security on computer networks

One of the potential problems of extensive computer networking is that of security. **Distributed data processing** poses extra problems for security not present in stand-alone systems. There are several aspects of security to consider.

Hacking

A **hacker** is the name given to a person that breaks codes and passwords etc. to gain unauthorised entry into computer systems. Unfortunately, the challenge of breaking into systems for some people is irresistible and, therefore, the designers of network systems must take protective measures. There are also other hazards that affect the security of data, these include loss of data through interference, loss of data through viruses, and sophisticated electronic methods used to gain access to unauthorised information. The risks can be categorised as follows.

Prevention of access to buildings

Many security systems ranging from **code locks**, via **magnetic stripe cards** to combinations of both of these systems are put at the entrances to buildings housing computers which have access to the network. Also well developed are systems such as **retina scans**, **palm prints** and **voice recognition**, and these are covered in other parts of this book. However, many problems still

> **Hint:** Choose a double-word password like 'Wobbly-Belly', for example. It's much easier to remember than a single-word password, and much more difficult to crack.

have to be overcome before these other systems are in common operation, not least the one of cost. Whatever system is used it is usually linked to the main computer so that access to buildings may be monitored by the security system. Visitors to high security installations will often have to be booked into the buildings, and given special badges that they have to wear for the duration of their visit. The fact that they are physically inside the building could also be logged on the main computer system to help with security checks. At the end of a set period of time, the main computer could help to make sure that all personnel have left the high security areas.

Passwords to log on

Once into the building, a system of **password protection** would be in operation. To log onto the system each person would be allocated a **special password**. There would probably be many categories of users. These may range from ordinary employees who have to make use of the system for their day to day work, through to users who have complete control over what can be done with any information contained in the files that are accessed over the network. For a more detailed description of defining the types of users refer to the database security system in chapter 28. In addition to these passwords it may be necessary to have a **key** which will be needed to **physically unlock the system**, i.e. make sure that power is applied to the computer that is being used for access.

Location of specific workstations

There may be extra security by providing the highest levels of access from a limited number of workstations. You can imagine there to be an 'inner sanctum' into which people have had to pass to get physical access to certain terminals. The highest levels of users may only be able to access certain sensitive parts of the system from these terminals. In the most sensitive installations there would probably be closed circuit security cameras constantly monitored by security personnel. Therefore, even if some of the passwords were known, the hacker would have to gain access to an inner part of a high security building before being able to make use of them. The passwords would also need be changed at frequent intervals.

Protection of transmitted information

This might sound a little like the activities that would be carried out by 'James Bond', but it's now possible to get sensitive electronic equipment that can monitor the electromagnetic fields that are radiated from systems carrying computer data. When electrical signals travel down a cable, there is an associated electromagnetic field that radiates a weak signal, which can be picked up by using sensitive electronic-detection apparatus.

To get over these problems would involve the screening of cables so that these electromagnetic fields can't be picked up. It's interesting to note that fibre optic communications, making use of light instead of electrical signals, do not radiate these fields. LASER beams are also relatively safe. Radio transmissions however, especially via satellite, are most vulnerable to these types of hacking.

As it's virtually impossible to guarantee that these electromagnetic fields could not be picked up, one way to get over the problem is to make use of some sophisticated encryption techniques. This means that data is not sent making use of standard ASCII in the normal sense, but has some algorithm applied to the data that scrambles the signals to be transmitted. The data must then be unscrambled at the other end of the communication system. Provided the encryption codes are not known by the hacker, it would be virtually impossible to crack the codes. Indeed, it has been calculated, that by making use of some sophisticated encryption techniques, it would take a supercomputer longer than the universe has been in existence to crack some of these codes – the details of which are covered in chapter 9.

Electrical interference

One must not forget the fact that the data may not be lost through malicious interference from human beings, but from noise that might affect the signals. This could be electromagnetic interference from many sources such as cars, power stations, radio and T.V. broadcasting and electrical distribution systems etc. These can affect the integrity of the data. What is actually being received might not be that which was actually sent. These types of problems are overcome by making use of error detection systems such as CRCs and parity, and these have been explained earlier on in this chapter.

Physical damage

Finally, there is the physical security of the system. For example, data may be lost through fire, flood or any number of natural hazards. In addition to this there may be faults in the systems such as a 'disk becoming corrupted' or a 'power cut' etc. Making appropriate backup procedures and ensuring that these backups are stored in different locations to the originals can cater for all of these events.

Exercise 5.1

1 Simplex is a communication method in which signals are transmitted one way only. Name the other two fundamental methods of communication.

2 Define what is meant by the term Baud rate. Why might the information transmission Baud rate be less than the actual transmission Baud rate?

3 Explain why it is necessary to use a modem to transmit a computer signal via a standard telephone network.

4 Explain 'modulation' and 'demodulation', using 'frequency modulation' to illustrate your answer.

5 Explain the following terms:
(a) Time-division multiplexing
(b) ADSL
(c) Data encryption.

6 What is the difference between circuit switching and message switching? Why is message switching more suitable for computer communications and what has been done to overcome the problem of one computer hogging all the available bandwidth?

7 Buffering is often used to help match speed differences in some networks. Explain these terms and how these ideas work.

8 Why did the ISO have to devise a complex standard for transmission over international networks?

9 Outline the ISO/OSI model for network communication, briefly stating the function of each level of the model.

10 TCP/IP and ATM are two different network transmission protocols. Briefly outline the function of each.

11 CRCs and parity have been used in the past to help with error detection and correction. Briefly outline the concepts of each of these systems.

12 You are to set up a maximum-security network system in a government institution. Outline some of the security measures that you would take to ensure that information from the network does not fall into the wrong hands.

13 You are to devise a network system for use by the military in the jungles of Borneo. The system will be used to enable commanders back in the USA to contact their operatives in the field. The field operatives will also use the same system to pass messages. Outline, in principle, the type of network that would be most appropriate, given that some of the computers that form part of the network could be many kilometres apart. What extra measures would also need to be taken?

End of chapter revision aid and summary

Cover up the right-hand column and see if you can answer the questions or define the terms on the left. They appear in the order in which they are covered in this chapter. Alternatively you may browse through the right-hand column to aid revision.

What is simplex?	Simplex is the transmission of data in *one direction only*.
What is duplex?	Duplex is the transmission of data in *both directions* – but *only one at a time*.
What is full duplex?	Full duplex is the *simultaneous two-way transmission* of data.
In what unit is Baud measured?	The Baud rate is the number of bits/sec.
Why might the information Baud rate be less than the transmitted Baud rate?	The information Baud rate may be slightly less than the actual transmission Baud rate because of added data acting as a check on integrity, e.g. parity or CRCs.
What is serial transmission?	Serial transmission is the transmission of data along a single wire or radio link.
What is parallel transmission?	Parallel transmission is the simultaneous transmission of a number of different binary digits by separate parallel paths (e.g. by using a bus). If data is to be transmitted over a link such as the standard telephone system or radio link then it needs to be modulated.
What is modulation?	Modulation means changing the signal into a suitable form for the medium over which it is being sent.
What is demodulation?	Demodulation means extracting the original data signal from the modulated signal.
From where is the word MODEM derived?	A modem performs both the MOdulation and DEModulation functions.
What is a carrier?	A carrier is the name given to the signal which carries the data over a transmission link such as a satellite link, for example.
Name several different methods of modulation.	Different methods of modulation exist including Amplitude Modulation (AM), Frequency Modulation (FM), Phase Modulation, Pulse Position Modulation, Pulse Code Modulation and Pulse Duration Modulation.
What is multiplexing?	Multiplexing is a system whereby many signals may be transmitted over the same link. A broadband network is needed for this.

What is a broadband network?	A broadband network is one in which different frequencies can be used to transmit information simultaneously.
What is a baseband network?	A baseband network can only transmit one signal at a time.
What is Time Division Multiplexing?	TDM is Time Division Multiplexing – this system allocates each signal a slot of time.
What is Frequency Division Multiplexing?	Frequency Division Multiplexing allocates different carrier frequencies to different signals.
Compare the new digital modems with the standard analogue modems used on a conventional telephone line?	There are digital modems which make use of technology installed in the local telephone exchange or make use of the power lines to transmit digitally at speeds of up to several megabits per second. Analogue modems change the digital signals into analogue form and thus transmit at a slower Baud rate.
What is a V.34 connection?	A V.34 connection is the standard analogue phone connection!
What is an ISDN?	Integrated Services Digital Network – the first stage of replacing the analogue network with a faster all-digital link.
What is an ADSL?	Asymmetric Digital Subscriber Line – a digital link capable of a maximum 9 Mbps. Data is transmitted and received at different rates.
What is a VDSL?	The Very-high data rate Digital Subscriber Line is capable of a maximum 52 Mbps.
What is circuit switching?	Circuit switching networks are systems like the normal telephone system where a specific line is routed from A to B and is dedicated but not necessarily used all of the time (e.g. two people might be stuck for what to say but the line is still being used).
What is message switching?	Message switching is where a message may be routed by any convenient route. The line is released for the next job immediately the message has been sent.
What is packet switching?	Packet switching is where packets of information are routed from A to B by whatever route is convenient at the time. If a packet is not actually being sent at a particular moment in time, then another packet from a different computer may be sent.
What is the ISO OSI model?	The ISO OSI model is a well-structured internationally agreed communications protocol for network systems.
How many layers are there in the ISO OSI model?	The ISO OSI model contains seven different layers ranging from how applications make use of the system to how the physical wires are connected.
Name each of the layers of the ISO OSI model.	The layers of the ISO OSI model are the physical layer, the link layer, the network layer, the transport layer, the session layer, the presentation layer and the application layer.
What is TCP/IP?	TCP/IP stands for Transmission Control Protocol/Internet Protocol.
What is Transmission Control Protocol?	Transmission Control Protocol is an example of the transport layer of the ISO OSI model.
What is the Internet Protocol?	Internet Protocol is used by the Internet system and is an example of the network layer of the ISO OSI model.
What is Asynchronous Transmission Mode?	Asynchronous Transmission Mode is a reliable method of sending computer data, voice and video data over a packet-switching network.
What is parity?	Parity is a simple method of checking the integrity of received data.

What is even parity?	Even parity involves an even number of 1's in each byte.
What is odd parity?	Odd parity involves an odd number of 1's in each byte.
What is two-dimensional parity?	Two-dimensional parity can sometimes correct a corrupted message.
What is a cyclic redundancy check?	A cyclic redundancy check is one method of checking data integrity – it usually works on mathematical processing of polynomials, and is very efficient in terms of high rates of error detection and low overheads.
What is hacking?	Hacking is the unauthorised use of a computer system. It is a constant problem and password systems are usually set up to counteract this threat.
What is data encryption?	Data encryption encodes the message using secret keys. It can increase the security in sensitive systems.

6 Business Applications and Systems

Key resources

To carry out this work most successfully it's best if you have:

- Access to a modern WYSIWYG word processor and/or DTP system
- Access to a spreadsheet that supports macros and charts
- Access to some training material
- Don't forget the **glossary** at the back of this book. It should be very helpful to explain some concepts with which you may not be familiar

Concept checkpoints

- There are no concept checkpoints needed in this chapter.

Introduction to business applications

Most students will be familiar with application packages such as word processors and DTP systems etc. Nevertheless, few people make use of all the available facilities in these packages, and students are often hard put to make a sensible list of the features provided by even the most basic of word processors. Fewer still have thought about whether one particular system may better suit the needs of the user than any other, and therefore simple questions in examinations regarding these sorts of topics are sometimes answered badly. All students must make extensive use of these packages throughout their courses. It is only after you have used such systems for extended periods of time that you are able to give other people advice on the choice of their systems, and in particular what sort of facilities are ideal to solve their specific problems.

Modern computer science syllabuses require that students consider these systems in terms of the information requirements, and the ability of 'this or that package' to solve a particular problem in the context of a scenario that is dreamed up by the examiner. A receptionist in a doctor's surgery, a school secretary or a modelling-agency director would, for example, provide just some of the infinite number of suitable scenarios in which such application packages could be examined. Therefore, this chapter has two main functions – to introduce you to the typical facilities offered by common applications, and to apply these to real-life scenarios in which such facilities could be used. You should never approach these problems with attitudes like 'I've not done "modelling agencies" or "doctor's surgeries" before!' – you will be surprised at how techniques learnt in one area are applicable to many others. Bear these points in mind as you are progressing through the work covered in this and the other applications' chapters – it will help to put things in perspective.

Word processing

Always remember that most businesses exist to make money. Virtually all need to process **textual information**, and the **word processors** used in any business must therefore be able to do the required tasks quickly and efficiently. They must also integrate into the existing way of doing things without too much fuss. You must not forget the **training requirements** needed by staff to operate these systems effectively, and identify important areas in which integration with other packages and computer systems might be essential.

In recent years **desk top publishing (DTP)** and **word processing (WP)** packages have *moved very closely together*. The text-processing capabilities of DTP systems and the graphics-handling capabilities of the word processors have increased out of all recognition. Indeed, integration with other **drawing** and **art packages**, **spreadsheets** and **databases** has now meant that word processing can no longer be considered in isolation from these other packages. The linked capability from WP packages to the Internet is also of fundamental importance. This is one of the main reasons why it's of use to consider the system as a whole, and to analyse problems with regard to the users' information-processing requirements. However, before going on we will list just some of the typical facilities which you should expect from a *good* WP package. The following sections briefly outline these major features.

Professional layout

The ability to lay out text to a professional standard using any **font** that you have on your computer, and to be able to scale these **fonts** to any sensible **point size** is a basic requirement. You must be able to see on the screen exactly what is to be printed out on the printer before it is actually printed. (This is called **WYSIWYG** or What You See Is What You Get.)

Did you know that . . .

Word processors were difficult to use in the days before WYSIWYG. Special control codes such as 'CTRL G' had to be used to 'move the cursor up' or 'CTRL V' had to be used to 'move the cursor backwards'!

You should note that the term '**font**' is simply the *set of characters* that make up a type face – 'Century Gothic' or 'Courier New', for example. The size of the type face is usually measured in a unit called a **point**, of which there are **72 points to one inch**. A **style** can usually be applied to a particular font such as *italic* or **bold** etc. Therefore, the following message is printed in a font called 'Brush Script MT' at 18pt (¼ inch high) with a bold-italic style.

¼ inch high bold italic Brush Script MT

The word processor must also give control over the colour of the fonts, and be able to apply **special effects** such as ^superscript, subscript, ~~strikethrough~~, highlighting and **drop capitals** (shown at the beginning of this paragraph). The layout of the text must also be controllable at a microscopic level by the use of a technique called **kerning**. This means that individual letters or larger units of text can be moved up or down and left or right by minuscule amounts – usually down to fractions of a point size so that text may be positioned exactly as required by the user.

Formatting the text

The WP must be able to format the text in terms of **tabs**, **left**, **right** or **full justification**, **centring** and allocation of **margins**. There should be provision for **headers**, **footers** and footnotes, automatic **page numbering**, the insertion of **dates** and **times**, and should be able to define different **indents**, **numbering** and **bullets**, and the ability to alter **line spacing**. As well as being

> **Hint:** Always set up an in-house template for your own work. It saves the bother of having to redefine styles and formatting over and over again, and gives a professional look to your correspondence.

able to manually apply fonts and formatting to the selected text, the WP should enable the user to define different named styles that may be applied easily. For example, by specifying a style called 'Main Heading', you could define all attributes of the heading font and style, including its position on the page. This saves having to manually reapply all these attributes each time a 'Main Heading' needs to be created.

Most word processors allow the user to produce complex **tables** that are easily inserted into the WP document, or be able to act as a source of information for the mailing lists mentioned in the next section. Virtually any attribute of the tables in terms of the column widths and heights, borders, line widths and colours etc. should be customisable.

Whole **templates** or **master pages** should be easy to set up so that formatting and style may be defined once only, and then re-used when needed to create new documents that conform to the same styles in terms of layout. The author was supplied with a suitable template file for the book you are now reading, for example. It is highly likely that a business would have templates ready for their employees to use, simply by clicking over the appropriate document, probably delivered from a central resource via a network file server. This enables a company to utilise 'house styles' in terms of its correspondence and other stationary.

Fancy text effects

Many word processors give you the ability to add some **fancy text effects** such as this:

Nevertheless, much better effects may easily be created and imported from other **art packages** as a graphic. Indeed, the ability of most word processors to produce effects like those shown above are painfully limited compared to even the most humble of art packages. All these points underline the need for integration of such art packages with WP and DTP systems.

Saving the work in different forms

Many word processors also allow you to format text to particular requirements, and enable you to save the document in a variety of formats which are compatible with other word processors. For example, you might be able to save the document as **HTML** (for use on the Web), as plain **ASCII** text, as **RTF** (Rich Text Format) so that all styles, formatting and fonts etc. are preserved when viewed by other word processors with RTF capability. You might also wish to save in a format completely compatible with a particular version of another word processor, in which case the entire document should look perfect! These features are particularly important in offices where information might have to be shared between incompatible systems.

Editing and proofing

The WP must allow text to be edited easily. You should be able to **insert**, **delete** and **move** text anywhere in the current document, and be able to **cut** or **copy** and **paste** portions of the text into other documents. You should be able to **find** and/or **replace** text, formats, fonts and styles throughout the document. You should be able to check the **spelling** and **grammar**, preferably **in different languages**, make use of on-line **thesauri**, and be able to do **word counts** and other **statistics** such as **readability levels** in terms of the target audience, for example.

Mailing and mail merge

Mail merging is a way of managing **mailing lists** such that **standard letters** can be sent out to customers, given that all the names, addresses and other information is stored in a suitable database. This can either be from within the WP software itself (usually by means of a table), or preferably from an external database created independently of the WP. Such techniques are ideal for the production of envelope labels, the creation of customer invoices, or even to create a batch of personalised Christmas cards. Once set up, these techniques save hours of time for the people who operate such systems.

Graphics creation and handling

All word processors should have the ability to create **frames** into which **graphics** may be imported. The actual creation of the graphics is less important,

although it's very handy and highly convenient to be able to draw the odd shape or two without having to leave the WP. Different graphics file formats should be supported so that most pictures can be displayed inside these frames.

Mathematical formulae

A reasonably sophisticated level of **formulae creation** is needed, *especially* for use in educational establishments where students frequently need to type up their maths or science projects.

$$\int_G \int f(x,y)dG = \lim_{\substack{n\to\infty \\ \Delta Gi\to 0}} \sum_{i=1}^{n} m_i \Delta G_i = \lim_{\substack{n\to\infty \\ \Delta Gi\to 0}} \sum_{i=1}^{n} M_i \Delta G_i$$

The above equation, for example, would test the limits of some of the lesser word processors! Try making up the above equation if your word processor allows you to do so – it will certainly test your skill in being able to build suitable equations.

> **Hint:** The equation here was constructed using Microsoft Word. If you have access to Word, try making this equation!

Inserting other objects

It is useful to have the ability to insert objects such as **spreadsheets** or **database reports** etc. into the word processor document. These are usually related to the real-time data contained in the spreadsheet or database application, so that any print out of the document would reflect the latest data contained in the spreadsheet or database etc. Some word processors allow you to embed virtually any information from compliant applications. For example, although not normally rated among the most useful facilities, **sound** and **video clips** may also be inserted inside some word-processor documents – ideal if you wish to send the 'Dance of the Sugar Plum Fairy' in a letter to your granny! (She would obviously have to read the letter on a suitably equipped and set up computer!)

Macros and other customisation

It is usually possible to record macros. These enable you to record a set sequence of operations that can be given a suitable name. The same sequence of operations may then be applied to 'selected text' by replaying the macro. This can often save much time if you have to apply a set of the same operations frequently. Many other features of word processors can be customised in similar ways. For example, you could customise the number of tools that are available, the position of the toolbars on the screen, or add your own tools for specific purposes.

Help and wizards

Any application package these days needs to have extensive help and perhaps some on-line tutorials. Modern word processors are no exception, and most come with an abundance of help that includes searching for help on an **index**, on **key words**, or by observing standard techniques. There are normally a large number of pre-prepared templates like 'faxes', 'time sheets', 'invoices' and other common business items. These are usually set up so that it's easy to alter the names of the fictitious companies to your own, and customise every available detail. A typical example of this is actually shown in the spreadsheet section in figure 6.3 where similar ideas are covered.

Real-time voice input

During the last few years, speech-input systems have come on by leaps and bounds. Just a few years ago the thought of real-time speech input would have been in the realms of science fiction, or only possible with very specialist packages on large mainframe computers. Today, however, nothing could be further from the truth, and cost-effective real-time speech recognition is here at an affordable price. Systems like 'Dragon Dictate' by Dragon Systems, or 'Simply Speaking' by IBM represent a real break through in price and performance. There are set commands like 'Bring up Microsoft Word' for example, which, assuming the system is awake and paying attention to your voice, would cause the word processor to be loaded up. You can then put it into 'Dictate mode' and, assuming that you have had a sufficient amount of practice with the system, it will respond to your voice reasonably reliably.

Did you know that . . .

Voice recognition could one day be used as an aid to computer security. A 'specially trained computer' could recognise your voice and, together with some appropriate word input, be used to unlock certain facilities on a computer system, like your bank account details, for example.

New systems are coming out at more frequent intervals, and acceptance of speech without any pause in between is now also possible. Indeed, in the next few years the problem is not likely to be lack of suitable software, but the inability of most humans to speak the way that they write! Having used the system for some time I personally still find this hard to do, and for the moment at least will not throw away the keyboard. Nevertheless, exciting sets of possibilities are emerging with these new software packages for windows.

You should appreciate also that other software packages such as spreadsheets, databases, and indeed Windows itself, can all be controlled with packages such as these. Commands such as 'Mouse left' or 'Mouse up' will control the mouse cursor on the screen, and commands like 'Mouse double-click', for example, will cause the appropriate response to happen. It really is good fun and obviously highly appropriate for some disabled people.

Other functions

There are many other functions, too numerous to mention in such a short space, on word processors. Indeed, you have only to look in the book shops and you will find lengthy tomes, often exceeding 1000 pages, on how to use just one particular word processor – the features really are this comprehensive. In fact, some people are now starting to think that there are too many functions, leading to over-large and cumbersome applications. Although the applications are now certainly large, I personally believe that the feature list will continue to grow as software evolves. People expect their computers to do more things more quickly and easily than before. Don't forget the statement made at the beginning of this word-processing section – 'businesses are set up to make money' and this applies to software vendors too. For this reason alone, there will be many more sophisticated software packages becoming available over the next few years.

Desktop publishing systems

The best way to think of a **DTP system** is by the results that such a package can produce. For example, take the most complex glossy magazine layout that you can find in the newsagents. This is probably produced on a top-of-the-range DTP system. Try doing the same sort of thing on a **word processor** and you will see that it's well and truly beaten into the dust, both in terms of the ease with which you can accomplish the effects, and the actual layout which can finally be produced. Figure 6.1 shows a typical complex page from a DTP system.

In professional printing houses, such as the companies that make up the glossy magazines etc. it is usual to produce the **text** on a **word processor**, the **graphics** in **art packages**, and then *assemble these elements* using the **DTP** facility. Therefore, the best way to describe the difference between a DTP system and a word processor is by the facilities that each system offers. You have already seen what facilities are present in a word processor from the last few sections. The **DTP system** can, therefore, best be described as the **final page make-up software** that enables you to place text and images with great precision. It enables you to combine these basic features in ways such that any attribute of the 'position', 'colour', 'transparency' or 'page-description format' can be altered and customised ready for printing out on the 1200 dpi professional typesetting machines. Indeed, the post-production-processing capabilities of most DTP systems in terms

Figure 6.1

of setting up for colour-matching etc. is awesome. If you do not see the need for such systems, try printing out the same coloured image on a range of different printers – you will probably find that they are all slightly (or sometime quite markedly) different. This is not acceptable in the publishing industry where the final colour in an art or scientific publication is probably critical.

You will often find that modern DTP systems are a combination of software, which includes suitable word processors, art packages, page make-up packages and other suitable links to digital cameras, scanners, video cameras, Internet connections and virtually any other document or picture source you can imagine. Many of these techniques and facilities are covered in other parts of this book.

Spreadsheets

It has been said that economics is a subject which is chosen by people who think that accountancy is too exciting! Spreadsheets have a similar undeserved image in computing. Students often associate spreadsheets with adding up boring columns of numbers, and although spreadsheets are used for this, they are infinitely more versatile. A spreadsheet is now universally associated with computers, although the original idea of a spreadsheet was simply a 'piece of paper' on which people added up columns and rows of numbers to help them plan their budgets. Although the computerised spreadsheet is basically the same idea as the paper one, the facilities offered bear little relationship to the original paper concepts. To consider a spreadsheet as a simple mechanism for carrying out tedious operations which could have been done manually would be missing the point by several miles. The computerised **spreadsheet** *has literally revolutionised the way in which many businesses operate*, but in addition to this, there

are many other uses to which spreadsheets can now be put, and some of these will now be examined in more detail.

The basic ideas

Facts and figures form the basis of most company financial-management strategies. In businesses, columns of figures have been added up and manipulated for many years, and the name '**spreadsheet**' was originally used because the figures were literally *spread* out on a *sheet* of paper. Computerised spreadsheets give modern businesses the powerful ability to create vast spreadsheets without the tedium of having to manually perform any of the arithmetical or other operations. With a large spreadsheet, the computer screen acts as a window through which some of the cells (see in a moment) can be viewed. Some systems allow you to view multiple parts of the spreadsheet at the same time.

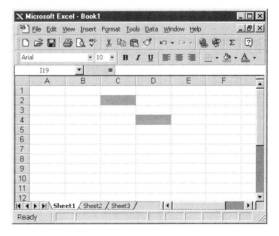

Figure 6.2

At the simplest level a spreadsheet consists of a two-dimensional arrangement of cells as shown in figure 6.2. Looking at the intersection of the row and column numbers and letters gives us the cell's reference. The cells C2 and D4 are shown highlighted in figure 6.2. However, as we shall see later, computers have also given businesses the ability to think in more than two or even three dimensions.

Normal text can be typed in almost anywhere, and is very much like using a word processor. However, the power of a spreadsheet stems from the fact that it is easily able to **manipulate formulae** based around the **cell references**. As a simple example, the number in cell C3 could be added to the number in cell C4 and the result put in cell C6. In this way, figures are worked out automatically because the computer has done the adding up for you. This does not sound too amazingly useful, until you start to think of a **large spreadsheet** having **thousands of numbers**, **hundreds of rows** and **columns**, and some **very complex interrelated data**.

Think of the cells as being interrelated by very complex mathematical functions that need to be put into some pre-determined order based on some obscure relationships. Think also of the complex date-related calculations involving leap years and the like, and you will start to appreciate just a small part of the overall problem. Change even one important number, and several thousand other numbers that may depend on the one just altered can be automatically updated.

Spreadsheet functions

The **range of functions** available on most spreadsheets are limited only by your imagination and programming ability. Standard mathematical functions such as '*trig*', '*statistical*', '*matrix*', '*complex*', '*logs*', '*ints*' and '*mods*' etc. are all available. **Financial functions** such as '*future values of investments*' and '*net present value of cash flow*' are available too. **Statistical functions** such as '*mean*', '*mode*' and '*standard deviation*', and **date functions** help sort out data based on dates. A whole host of **database functions**, **time functions**, and *many others* too numerous to mention are to be found in most spreadsheet applications. Indeed, you can invent your own functions and **macros** (see in a moment), and many spreadsheets are now providing a language like **BASIC** as the macro language for the development of user-constructed or third party routines. For example, Microsoft's Excel 97 spreadsheet has Visual BASIC as it's macro language. This means the users can write BASIC programs that can then be used to control the spreadsheet. Virtually anything that can be done via BASIC can therefore be used to control the sheet. This makes programming the spreadsheet for simulations much easier (see chapter 18), as new esoteric macro languages no longer have to be learned from scratch.

It's absolutely essential that you are familiar with a spreadsheet, as **it's literally one of the most important computer-based applications,** and one of the most interesting pieces of software once you have mastered the basics.

Why all the fuss about spreadsheets?

A **sophisticated spreadsheet** can be built up to represent **very complex relationships between a huge number of variables**. Doing the same thing by hand could literally take many hundreds of hours. However, with a computerised spreadsheet modelling the problem, the variables could be altered and the spreadsheet would automatically re-calculate all the implications for you.

Editing functions

It's easily possible to do a large range of editing comparable in sophistication to some word-processing systems. You can mark blocks of cells so that they may be moved, copied and deleted etc. In addition to this, there are commands to insert and delete rows, put individual cells in rows or columns, and virtually every other manipulation of the data within the sheet that you can think of. Many spreadsheets even allow you to draw shapes like boxes and arrows etc. and this makes for marvellous professional printouts direct from the sheet. It's easily possible to produce professional presentations, and a good example of such a layout is shown in figure 6.3, where Microsoft's Excel spreadsheet is used to display a custom set up sheet for a company invoice. It does not look like it has been produced by a spreadsheet at all!

> **Hint:** The output from a spreadsheet does not have to be boring. Take a look at figure 6.3 to see what can be accomplished with a little bit of creative imagination.
> Spreadsheets like Excel enable you to produce sophisticated output of which this is just one example.

Macro functions

Macros give you the ability to make up your own sophisticated procedures by using a combination of many of the functions described above. It's usual to be able to save the **macro** (**list of commands**) on disk, so that specifying the name of the macro can carry out the effects simply. In addition to being able to write complex macros in a high-level language like Microsoft's Visual BASIC for Applications (VBA), for example, there is often a record-macro facility. This puts the computer into a mode where data entered from the keyboard and movements with the mouse etc. are recorded so that complex or tedious combinations of events only have to be repeated once. Next time the macro is called, the computer can be instructed to process the new data in ways identical to those shown previously.

> ## Did you know that . . .
>
> The spreadsheet is a marvellous vehicle for advanced computer science projects. When coupled with macros and extensions like VBA, for example, the sky is the limit. It's easily equivalent to a complex programming project if you choose the right sort of ideas. Simulations are particularly exciting.

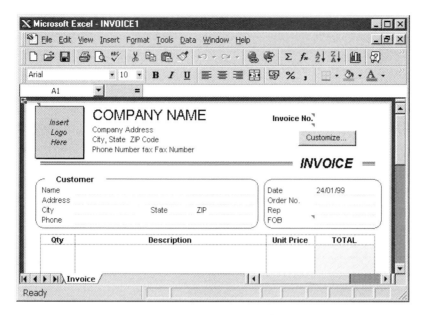

Figure 6.3

It's sometimes tremendous fun to look at the computer automatically working through a macro, and this is one of the easiest ways to impress non-specialists in the office, at school or at college. Some teachers, for example, who know little about spreadsheets, seldom fail to be impressed when they see this package picking names and examination data off a disk, putting the names and data into alphabetical order, and printing out a list on the printer. They are even more impressed when the sheet goes on to automatically work out the examination statistics, re-ordering the names to produce another list in descending numerical order and assigning grades depending on the marks awarded. Finally, the system can be used to pass the data over to a DTP system ready for the teacher to produce their reports. Indeed, you can even get the system to produce the reports for you – but that would be giving away too many trade secrets!

'What if' questions

Ordinary data, mathematical and other relationships can be changed very easily with a spreadsheet. At the touch of a button you could ask yourself, 'What if we increase the price of our goods and sell less?', 'What if we reduce the price of our goods and sell many more?', 'What will be the likely effect of each of these strategies on our profits?' After the analysis has been performed by a spreadsheet, you can make use of the charting section of the sheet, or export the data into a separate presentation graphics package (see later). With a well-set-up spreadsheet, you can test out a hypothesis, generate the graphics and fax the results through to another country within minutes – that's the power of these new spreadsheets and other integrated systems.

Charts and mapping data

All spreadsheets allow for the creation of a variety of charts. From 2D and 3D histograms, via pie charts and scattergrams to linear and polynomial regression (line and curves of best fit), the number of graphical facilities is usually quite comprehensive. Some of the chart options in Excel are shown in figure 6.4

Demographic data (study of the population) such as that used by geographers can often be analysed more

Figure 6.4

Did you know that . . .

Some specialist charting packages offer hundreds more charts than are available from most spreadsheet packages.

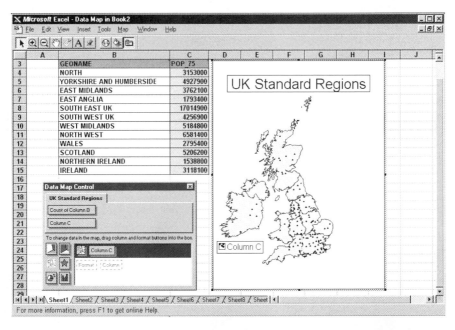

Figure 6.5

effectively by visually making the links between the data and the maps to which the data refers. For example, figure 6.5 shows part of a spreadsheet, which has been set up with a simple map of the UK.

Column B contains the geographic names of the places which relate to the areas on the map, like 'South East' or 'East Midlands', for example. Column C contains the population statistics for these areas in 1975, and the UK Standard Regions map contains dots which reflect the population densities of these areas which are derived from the numbers in column C. The window at the bottom left of figure 6.4 allows for the mapped data to be customised in particular ways. Techniques such as these are very useful indeed to display sales and other economic data on a regional basis. If there are not enough maps or if the detail is insufficient, then a company called MapInfo based in New York will provide hundreds of others. You could even construct your own maps if you had the time or the inclination.

Integrated spreadsheets

Most spreadsheets can now easily **integrate** with **word processors** and **databases**, and indeed some spreadsheets have word processors and database functions built in. However, as we have seen elsewhere in this book, such packages are called **integrated software packages**. It's most unlikely that the facilities offered by such an integrated package would equal those of the separate specialist packages – this is why it's so important to ensure that the spreadsheet that you use can **import data** from other packages such as databases and word processors. Microsoft Works is an example of an integrated package.

Beyond the second dimension

Some spreadsheets now have the facility for **three dimensions or more**. These are called **multi-dimensional spreadsheets**, but large spreadsheets in many different dimensions obviously take up pots of memory and require a powerful computer if the results are to be obtained by the end of the coffee break! Lotus, for example, manufactures a system called 'Improv', and although this is not a spreadsheet in the strictest sense, it can model data in 12 dimensions. Some modern spreadsheets now also have the ability to refer to a particular cell by name instead of by row and column. This is particularly useful if multiple spreadsheets are being used at the same time. Such spreadsheets are known as **relational spreadsheets**, and many such separate sheets could, of course, model any number of separate dimensions. You could even simulate multi-dimensions on different parts of the same sheet.

Other uses of a spreadsheet

It was mentioned near the beginning of this section that spreadsheets are very versatile, and by having a high-level language such as BASIC as the macro language you should appreciate this point only too well. Spreadsheets are not just limited to financial and business data; anything at all, which can be expressed **algorithmically** (see chapter 19) can be programmed into a spreadsheet. This means that scientific and engineering simulations as well as business simulations can be carried out with ease. Spreadsheets can be most useful in mathematics for helping to visualise and analyse number patterns, they are useful for modelling simulations based on random numbers of the type shown

Figure 6.6

with relative ease. Disparate **video clips**, **MPEG movies**, **JPG or PNG still images**, **WMF clip art images**, **HTML documents**, **DTP documents** and **sound** etc., will do little or nothing for the all-important company image or training package *unless* they can be seamlessly moulded together. If, for example, you start to 'play around' with the transfer of images from one system to another, then you'll find out what a mess the computer-data industry is in with regard to the *transfer* of seemingly-innocuous files – and *these problems occur even on the same hardware platform*! Don't forget that video, audio and other pictorial data take up pots of memory, so they often have to be **compressed** if large numbers of images and sound are to fit on a single CD-ROM drive or magnetic disk. If you then go on to the next stage and expect your computer to get data from *and* also control the **CD-ROM drives**, **video-cassette recorders**, **video cameras** and **scanners** etc. which are connected to it, then you are entering a proverbial mine field. In addition to this, you will need a powerful computer with a healthy chunk of RAM (preferably 256 Mbytes or more) and a large hard disk (more than 21 Gbyte) if you are intending to master your own CD-ROMs from video, audio and computer-data sources. Fortunately, as these sort of specifications are becoming the norm, most people can now dabble in the production of CD-ROM based material. It's ideal for the production of in-house training materials, and some companies are making thousands off the back of such demand for interactive computer-based training in business. The only down side is that it takes a huge amount of time to produce a successful CD-ROM, hence the expense of such systems.

Moving-image standards

Many hardware systems are now supporting most of these multiple standards and are currently being relatively successful in this awkward role. The **MPEG** standard is one of the emerging stars in the 1990s. It is an **ISO standard** designed for moving images. MPEG stands for the **Moving Picture Experts Group,** and is a

system recognised for being extremely good at **compression** *and* **storage** of video and animation material. Indeed, it is the basis for the digital TV standards, which were in production by the end of 1998.

Unlike conventional compression utilities, MPEG, or more specifically MPEG II in its latest incarnation, uses the information in the frame (video clip) at the beginning of a 'sequence of clips' as a reference. It then uses this reference frame, together with a vastly reduced amount of information in the next few frames which describe *only those parts of the video picture that actually move*. For example, if you are looking at a moving-video sequence in which the background remains static, but in which an object or person is moving in the foreground, then only enough information to generate the moving bits is sent in the next few frames. Now the original video frame can't remain a reference for too long (unless it's a very boring video!), therefore, another reference frame must be sent, and the next few frames in the sequence are referenced to this new one – and so it goes on. The system does not give a perfect image if most of the information in the scene is moving rapidly, and this manifests itself as an image with softer (slightly fuzzy) edges. However, MPEG are constantly working on problems like this and are rapidly finding solutions.

The above makes MPEG sound easy, but you try developing the algorithms to do it! Using this incredibly-complex technique, a massive amount of compression can take place, and it is this which enables us to fit a full-length movie onto just one or two CD-ROMs – about 74 minutes of Full-Motion Video (**FMV**) of VHS quality per disc. It's also this system which enables us to send full-motion video down an analogue phone line designed in the Middle Ages! One advantage of the **MPEG** standard is that it can cope with *real-time encoding* and *decoding*. This means that the computer system is fast enough to be able to extract the data from a CD-ROM, decode it and display it to get real-time video images and stereo sound on the monitor or TV set – an amazing technological feat. It's also fast enough (just) to encode moving-computer images in **real time** (see chapter 8) and store them onto **recordable CD-R**. You will learn from chapter 12 that Philips have been producing different coloured 'books' as standards for CD-ROMs – the latest CDs encoded with MPEG conform to what is known as the white-book standard. There are also many other formats such as **VideoCD**, **AV-I**, **PhotoCD**, **CD-Audio**, (for sound) and **CD-i** etc. – and these do not include some of the computer-games console formats.

Still-image standards

Still images and 'ordinary' computer graphics have their own set of standards too. **TIFF**, for example, stands for **Tagged Image File Format**, and is one of the standard ways to store and exchange bitmapped-graphics files across different platforms. The popular TIFF format was originally designed with scanning in mind. **GIF**, the **Graphics Interchange Format** (not the washing up liquid!) was developed for compressing graphics, when making use of the on-line network services such as those found on the **Internet** (remember the threat to CD-ROMs from the networks?). However, the **PNG** (**Portable Network Graphics**) format is currently gaining in popularity, largely due to the better compression ratios and the fact that no royalties have to be paid when making use of these algorithms! **JPEG**, the **Joint Photographic Experts Group** is another compression format for graphics files, which is extremely popular because it allows you to control the compression ratio and hence the quality of the image. For example, 20:1 is good quality and 100:1 is particularly awful, but good if you just want an initial thumbnail sketch before deciding to download an image on the Internet.

In addition to all these standards you have the **PCX** format which is a popular graphics-file format for bitmapped images stored on the PC, and like TIFF, was also developed for handling scanned images. The PCX format is useful because most DTP systems accept it. **EPS**, or **Encapsulated PostScript** format is also useful to transfer graphics images between applications, because, like **Postscript** (see chapter 11) itself, the resolution of the graphics depends simply on the printing device. There are many other formats, such as **PIC**, **PICT** and **PICT2** (Apple's graphic-file format), **RLE** and **TGA** etc. – this only goes to outline what was echoed in the previous section – it makes multimedia systems extremely complex to implement in practice.

Authoring tools for CAL

CAL, or **Computer Aided Learning** is the production of computer-based materials for individuals or groups who wish to learn making use of the computer. Full multimedia facilities make this an interesting way to learn, but ingenuity and great imagination is needed on the part of the designers of such systems if they are to be successful. Much has changed in the last few years regarding these systems – we have gone from 'rote learning of material presented in boring ways', to the 'use of materials which would not be out of place in a full-length feature film'.

Just a few years ago, the production of material for CD-ROM based training would have needed a specialist video and computing studio costing many tens of thousands of pounds. Today, nothing could be further from the truth. Many ordinary users now have the technology to produce their own multimedia productions including video, audio, 2D and 3D animations, and, of course, text and hypertext links. When they have finished producing their masterpiece, they can then master their own CD-ROM using the CD writers which are now available at reasonable cost. They can then master an individual CD for about 50p. It does, however, still take masses of creative enthusiasm and skill to produce really professional results. Also, most people would not have the vast amount of time needed, nor have the inclination to produce material, the likes of which can be obtained from professional companies using video studios of the sort described in chapter 10. The advent of HTML, DHTML, XML, ActiveX, VbScript, Java and JavaScript, together with suitable Web browsers like Netscape Navigator or Internet Explorer have in no small way helped to change this situation. *Multimedia production and training material can now be made available via the Web, Intranets or CD-ROM.* Also, presentation packages like Microsoft PowerPoint now have enough power to produce CAL packages too. The Web has already been covered in great detail in chapter 4, and so we will take a quick look at some of the alternative ways to produce a CAL package using the PowerPoint example quoted above.

PowerPoint

Specifically designed for the production of material to be used in presentations, this versatile package nevertheless is useful for the production of training material. Indeed, some teachers at school use it all the time for this purpose. It's a better alternative to the OHP because it is more dynamic, interactive, and customisable. You can also go off at tangents by following hypertext links to other slides, can play sounds, video clips, or create dynamic links to other packages such as spreadsheets and databases. A typical start up screen for a new presentation is shown in figure 6.7.

Here you can see that the user of the system is invited to add text to a title, drop some clipart into the box (for a logo perhaps), and then add some text in the third frame.

At a simple level, an ordinary user could create a professional presentation, or teachers could make up some interactive notes that would be useful in a lesson or for individual learning. Indeed, this is a good method if a pupil is absent from a particular lesson. He or she can use the presentation created by the teacher, and run through the lesson on the computer in his or her own time. However, don't forget that it would take the teacher many hours to learn how to use the package and create suitable material for a half-hour lesson.

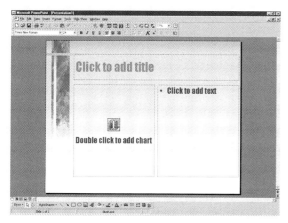

Figure 6.7

It was stated at the beginning of this section that Web browsers and HTML etc. could have been used to create an identical CAL package. Indeed, PowerPoint itself could save the entire presentation in HTML format for publication on the Internet or an Intranet. This is now a measure of the interactivity of these presentation packages, and also underlines the importance of networks and the Web as an information dissemination tool for CAL.

> **Hint:** Don't choose a multimedia-training application for your 'A' or 'AS' level project. They are great fun to do, but need a huge amount of time spent on them if they are to be successful. If you are unconvinced, allow about 18 months to produce a good training package or guide to your school, for example!

Just as JavaScript enables interaction with Web pages, Visual Basic can be embedded into a Powerpoint presentation via VBA (Visual Basic for Applications). This enables you to insert a powerful degree of interactivity into your presentation, and customise the lesson to the individual by the use of VbScript. It would, for example, be possible to build up a lesson in which the students logged in with a password, ran the demonstration, answered questions whose responses were monitored by the VbScripts, and the results were then exported to a database like Microsoft's Access. Some of the options for writing a Visual Basic script inside a PowerPoint demonstration can be seen in figure 6.8.

Here you can see that the Visual Basic Editor has been loaded, after activating the appropriate tool from the PowerPoint toolbox. This is the window, into which your VBA script can now be written. Figure 6.8 shows the VB editor, and the window (shown within the VB editor) is now ready to accept some code for this particular module. When the appropriate button has been created on the PowerPoint demonstration, then the Visual Basic code can be called up and executed from within PowerPoint. In this way it's possible to create highly interactive pages or slides, which are ideal for Computer Aided Learning.

Business systems

This section deals not with specific application packages like **word processors** and **spreadsheets** etc., but with overall solutions to problems specific to the business community. The work covered here is necessarily of a general nature, and is not intended to be an exercise in the design of computer systems. At this stage of your course you have probably not got the experience even to start thinking about designing these systems yourself. This knowledge will start to come about after you have read the chapter on '**structured analysis and design**', the two chapters on '**systems analysis and design**' and the chapters on '**networking**'. You will also need the experience that is gained by reading the '**databases**', '**file handling**' and '**peripherals**' chapters. *The intention here is to introduce you to typical computer systems that are implemented to solve common business problems.* The knowledge gained here will be invaluable for an appreciation of how larger systems operate in the real world, and for answering typical examination questions which frequently come up on these topics.

Why use computers at all?

It's important to realise, in general terms, why computers are so useful in large or small business environments. Typically the **huge volume of work** would often be impossible without the use of automation. Even if it were possible to employ thousands of people to do the same tasks, the **correlation of all the information in a given time frame** would probably be impossible. A startling example of this would be forecasting the weather, which is actually considered in chapter 7. It would be possible to get hundreds of thousands of people to perform the complex calculations necessary to predict what tomorrow's weather is likely to be, but it might take this number of people about a month to correlate the answers to this question!

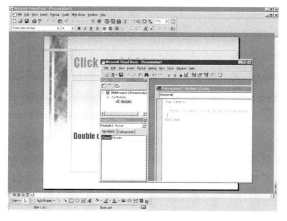

Figure 6.8

Many of the tasks undertaken are **repetitive** in nature; such repetition, incredibly boring for humans, is ideal for solution by a machine. Humans also get tired and, under these conditions, often make mistakes. The computer, however, provides much more **consistency**, and has the ability to perform many checks, which makes the system inherently more **accurate** in its transactions. The computerised systems also have the ability to **cross-reference data**, and are able to make use of huge centrally stored databases of information very efficiently. The alternative manual systems would require an enormous number of clerks to handle the data which would have to be unnecessarily duplicated in many filing cabinets at different locations. Assuming that the systems are installed and operated properly, one can easily appreciate that this constitutes a very **cost-effective** option compared with the manual alternatives.

There are, however, problems associated with the implementation of such systems, and it's not hard to guess that increased **unemployment** would be a consequence from reading the last couple of paragraphs. There are quite a number of related problems that should be considered in addition to the implementation of the actual system. Bear this in mind as you progress through the following sections.

Stock control and warehousing

Unless you have actually worked in a large company or studied one in detail, it's quite difficult to appreciate the sheer enormity of the paperwork task. This is just one of the many reasons why computer systems have come to the rescue in virtually every business of any significant size. These systems are also applicable to smaller companies, and the modular software systems being considered here are just as applicable to a single-user-one-man business as they are to a multi-national company or government departments like the Inland Revenue, for example. The only difference is the scale of the operation, and therefore the added complexity that enormous scale would bring in terms of demographic considerations, sharing of database information, complex networks and security. Here we are going to consider some of the problems and solutions regarding stock-control and warehousing.

The best way of sorting out such complex systems is to split them up into modules. For example, most businesses will need to be *supplied with goods* from other companies, and so we would need a module that deals with these **suppliers**. Having established that this is a sensible module, we can deal with the details of the supplier's module such as 'supplier names and addresses' or 'bank account details' etc. later. Proceeding in this way, typical modules for a business might be as shown in figure 6.9.

Hint: The only way to appreciate what's going on in the business world is to get out there and have a look. Talk to people who operate the systems, and find out what it's really like. Get your teacher to organise a visit if possible or, if not, try to organise one yourself via parents, friends or relatives.

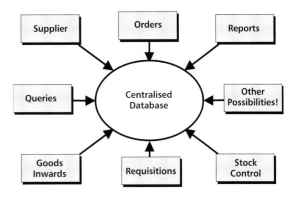

Figure 6.9

Just in case you are not familiar with typical business terms, the boxes outlined in figure 6.9 are explained in further detail as follows:

Suppliers	Companies that supply goods to the business.
Orders	Details of orders to be dealt with by the business.
Reports	For extracting specific statistics about any aspect of the business.
Goods Inwards	Details of goods received by the business.
Requisitions	Allow for the input of purchase requests.
Stock control	An inventory for the management of stock.
Query systems	Enables people to query any data item in the system.
Other possibilities!	There are many other systems such as specialised printed stationary.

You will find that the modular approach taken above is very common when dealing with computer systems. It is useful not only to split the problem up into more manageable tasks, but also to offer businesses the opportunity to purchase only those parts of the systems that are applicable to them. In this way a price may be quoted for the product which depends not only on the number of users and the scale of operations, but also on which facilities they have purchased. It also means that the software companies producing such systems can upgrade them more easily, or add a specific customised module for special situations. We now look at the above systems in a little more detail.

Supplier's module

This software module should contain details about the suppliers to your company. A typical example from MikroFax 'The Buyers Assistant' is shown in figure 6.10. As you can see from the screen shot, familiar icons such as the binoculars (find) are used to guide the business user through the act of searching for a particular company.

A particular supplier could be found by typing in their name or by identifying them from a unique supplier number. Things to note here are the sort of facilities available. For example:

Supplier code	Company	Address
Telephone	Fax	
Supplier rating	Contact names	Contact telephone
Contact e-mail	Commodity	Contract number

Most of the above information is obvious, but supplier rating indicates the category into which a particular supplier belongs, for example, 'Primary', 'Preferred', 'Alternative' or 'Unsuitable'. 'Commodity Supplied' would be a list which typically shows the category into which this particular supplier belongs – 'Software support', 'Catering' or 'Financial services' might be typical, depending on your company. These categories really depend on how you wish to split up the internal finances of your company, particularly in terms of departments and budget allocations etc.

Extra information, not shown on the above screen, but available by clicking on the 'More info' button would be:

Account number	Payment terms	VAT reg. no.
Bank acc. no.	Sort code	Rating assessed date
Rating review date		

There is also a notepad facility (to jot down free-form notes), links to the supplier's statistics, and to call up the supplier record in a more detailed form than is possible from the record-card layout shown here. The supplier record and statistics are in a form that can be printed out and analysed easily. Statistics can include vendor performance analysis, which includes statistics like 'delivery times' and 'payment dates'.

Other vital information available from the database would be a delivery point code. This is used by suppliers to ascertain exactly where deliveries are to be made, and special instructions like 'Not after 6pm and not at weekends', or 'If not in the key is under the doormat!'

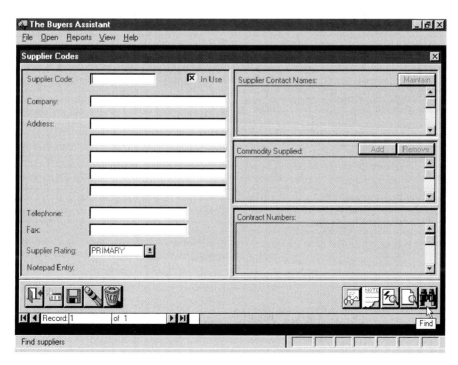

Figure 6.10

Taking stock

It is worthwhile pausing at this point. Assume that you had not read the last couple of pages, and were asked to make a list of what information you think should have been included in the suppliers' file? Most students would have suggested 'name and address', a few astute students would probably suggest 'telephone, fax and e-mail', but how many would have made suggestions regarding 'late payments', 'good or bad delivery times', 'alternative supplier' or 'delivery point code' information? Indeed, we have only just started to scratch the surface of this particular module, which also includes a large number of cross-referenced information to other parts of the database to ensure things like 'unique order numbers', 'unique contract numbers', 'item codes' and 'commodity codes' . . . the list is almost endless.

Software such as this enables the supply of goods to be run efficiently. It enables companies to purchase 'off-the-shelf-Windows-compatible systems' that integrate with other Windows-compatible software such as word processors and spreadsheets etc. Never underestimate the power that pre-written specialist software can provide to a business. It can be operated very easily with little knowledge needed to get the system up and running. It is certainly much easier than writing your own software using systems like Access or Visual Basic, for example.

Stock control module

This is the module that enables you to keep track of the goods that you have in stock. As before, in a large company this could be a massively complex problem. Even in a medium-sized factory, for example, there are many items of information that are needed to process this part of the business efficiently. Try making a list of requirements before going on any further! The actual details will depend very much on the sort of industry which you choose – food, for example, would have to include shelf life.

Typical things to consider would be ways to **issue** and **return** items of stock. You will need a system to **report** on the state of the stock at any particular instant in time. You must be able to **edit** stock items if any details are incorrect. If stock is issued then to whom is it given, and what **documentation** needs to accompany this transaction? For example, in an engineering production factory you might have to issue £10,000 worth of stock items to a particular employee – he or she will probably have to sign a piece of paper to

> **Hint:** Simplifications of the systems being considered here are ideal for 'A' and 'AS' level projects. All the ingredients are here for a comprehensive system's analysis (see chapter 16) and highly successful projects can result. Ideal vehicles for systems development would include a database like Microsoft's Access or Visual Basic, for example.

confirm that they are now responsible for these items. This piece of paper will need to be designed, and contain vital information like the **date**, details of 'goods received', 'item codes', **'name of the person who issued the goods'**, **'name of the person who received the goods'**, **'quantity issued'** and a **'unique number'** describing this particular **transaction**.

If the person in charge of the stores is to issue a component then he or she will need to know exactly where that component is located. Imagine a huge warehouse with tens of thousands of different bins and you will start to appreciate that **location** and **bin number** are important items of information. If one or more items are taken from stock then how many are left? The **quantity in stock** is also a vital data item. Do we need to order more after this transaction has taken place, you will need a **minimum stock quantity** which can be used to automatically trigger the ordering of new components if this number is reduced below the minimum required.

If stock has to be returned for any reason, then a similar reverse-transaction process would need to be undertaken, updating the database information accordingly.

Special statistics and reports will need to be compiled from the database specifically regarding the state of the stock. For example, you might want to **track the movement** of a particular item. This could be vital in the aircraft industry, for example, where a bad batch of components might lead to a possible 'life or death situation'. You might want to **list all items of a particular type** in stock, list what **stock items move quickly**, or what **stock items move very slowly**. Statistics like these are often of fundamental importance in the retail trade. Even weather statistics might need to be fed into the stock control computers in a supermarket, for example, so that more salad and ice creams are ordered in advance if there is about to be a heat wave. Important **date** information could be useful in the food industry where you could easily have a print out of all items in stock which will run out by a due date. Armed with this information you could decide whether to put a particular item on special offer to clear the stock before it is outdated.

You could have individual statistics such as **'which items are out of stock'**, **'which items are below the recommended level'**, or **'amend any attribute of stock'**. The last item is ideal if incorrect data has been entered into the system.

Part of the 'Inventory control' module for the Microfax Buyers Assistant is shown in figure 6.11.

Here you can see that 25 Compaq computers are in stock, and other information relating to this particular item.

Don't forget also the awesome task of stocktaking – that time of the year when you manually count up all of the goods in stock to see how the numbers on the computer relate to the actual amount on the shelves. The stock-control software must therefore allow for adjustments to be made to the system, and comments to be entered such as 'Quad Pentium 500 MHz'

Amend Stock Details For Item Code :1

Item Code: 1   STOCK ITEM

Description   Compaq Computer 486/33 550Mb Hard drive.
Fitted with 32 bit Network interface card and super VGA colour low
radiation screen.
CD-ROM drive and multi media support software

Stock Item   ☒

Stock Location   MFAX1

Bin Number   MFAX3

Enter the re-order quantity in the unit of
measurement (Each, Box, Kilogram,
Metre, etc.)

Unit   Each

Re-order Quantity   2

Lead Time (Days)   0

The quantities below are a sub-set of the unit
of measurement. Enter the amounts in pack
size units (per one, per pen, etc.)

Pack Size   5

Current Stock Level   25

Minimum Stock Level

Re-order Level   6

Maximum Issue Quantity   1

Record: 1   of 1

Figure 6.11

computer was crushed by a forklift truck which was moving stock in the warehouse! You would therefore have to decrement the stock total by one so that the accountants are happy.

Goods inwards module

When items are delivered to a company the people who receive these items, check them and book them into the stores are called the 'Goods inwards department'. They will need to produce suitable documentation for the company, and link into the computer system so that stock that is on site can be located and used quickly if necessary. Don't forget that some of the goods may arrive in a damaged state, and so some or all of an order might have to be returned to the company that supplied the goods. If the goods are in an excellent condition then the software should allow for the production of a 'goods received note'. If some goods are damaged then the software should automatically cope with all of the implications such as 'goods returned notes', 'flagging' that we have only received a partially completed order, and enter the appropriate statistics into the database for further analysis. For example, if this particular supplier or delivery firm is in the habit of delivering damaged goods, then this company might be removed from the 'primary or secondary' to 'unsuitable' status in the supplier's module mentioned at the beginning of the section.

A typical rejection screen is shown in figure 6.12. Again this is from the MikroFax 'The Buyers Assistant' software.

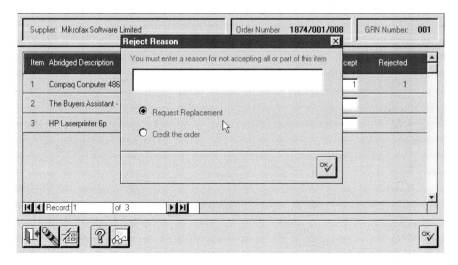

Figure 6.12

Here you can see that the software has detected that the complete order has not been accepted by the goods inwards department, and is prompting for a reason for rejection. Typical things to be put in here might be 'goods damaged in transit' or 'goods failed inspection test' etc. The replacements request and credit for the damaged goods are also automatically handled by this sort of system.

Reports (utility) module

From reading the previous few sections you will appreciate that there is an infinite number of reports which could be produced, depending on the type of company and on the whims of the management. For example, you could do a complete report on who owes you money, or who owes you overdue money; how much money your company owes to its suppliers; how the above statistics will affect the balance sheets in the next 30 days, etc. Indeed, information like this is vital to the survival of the company, and constitutes part of the overall management strategy for the company. You can see that the stock-control software, far from just maintaining a boring list of what you have in stock, forms a vital string in the bow of managers whose job it is to maximise the profits.

For example, figure 6.13 shows the top 20% of suppliers in terms of order value. This has been produced using the MikroFax Buyers Assistant.

Summing up

As you can see from the last few very brief sections, there is much more to stock control and purchasing systems than meets the eye. This critical software can form a central part of the financial analysis of a business, and can provide vital information in forms that are compatible for use with other Windows based systems. Software such as this is also ideal for people who are setting up in business and have little knowledge about the organisation of software to deal with purchasing and stock control.

As with all applications these days there needs to be extensive on-line help, and some of the screen shots shown in the last few sections were taken making use of the interactive help demonstrations provided by Mikrofax. It was downloaded from their Web site at http://www.mikrofax.com, and used with their permission.

Retailing, POS and EFTPOS systems

This section will concentrate on the general nature and use of computer systems in the retail trade. You should note that details of the equipment such as **barcode readers** etc. are covered in chapter 10 when the hardware is considered. You should note also that most of the **POS** (**Point of Sale**) and **EFTPOS** (**Electronic Funds Transfer at the Point of Sale**) systems considered here can be totally integrated with the 'stock control' and 'warehousing' systems considered in the last section. In practice it's unlikely that the front-end of a retail outlet would be considered in isolation from the stock control or warehousing requirements. We are considering the problems separately to compartmentalise the knowledge into more manageable chunks, and this reflects the design of these systems that are inevitably modular in nature.

Supplier Code Expenditure Analysis

Expenditure for the top 20% between 01/01/07 and 31/07/07, group by Order Value

Code	Company Name	Number of Orders	% of Total	Value	% To
ACE	ACE REFRIGERATION	7	1.38%	489,400.02	29.9
KOP	KOPCKE TRADING	45	8.88%	292,601.92	17.9
EDW	EDWARDS OF ABERDEEN	22	4.34%	105,166.90	6.4
WWM	WILSON WATSON MC VINNIE	33	6.51%	61,233.96	3.7
BERK	BERKLEY TRADING LTD	5	0.99%	42,161.67	2.5
NORT	NORTH OFFSHORE LIMITED	4	0.79%	40,120.00	2.4
COLI	COLIN MAC LEOD	15	2.96%	38,295.80	2.3
PEGS	PEGS AGENCIES	17	3.35%	36,184.03	2.2
BVV	BUKKVIDEKI VENDEGLATO RT	3	0.59%	32,930.46	2.0
SCOTT	SCOTT HAIG & CO LIMITED	4	0.79%	29,203.74	1.7
MOFF	E & R MOFFAT	8	1.58%	27,307.80	1.6
OSP	OSPREY FOODS INTERNATIONAL LTDS	1	0.20%	24,441.00	1.5
CANON	CANON (SCOTLAND) BUSINESS MACHI	3	0.59%	23,880.00	1.4
FERG	FERGUSON SHAW	3	0.59%	21,671.92	1.3
QUI	QUICK STOP GROUP	2	0.39%	20,540.05	1.2
ALI	ALLIED GARMENTS SERVICES	20	3.94%	20,410.13	1.2
AUT	AUTCBAR	18	3.55%	19,357.98	1.1
SDA	STRATHCLYDE DOMESTIC & APL.	3	0.59%	17,604.88	1.0
OCE	OCEAN TRADING LIMITED	2	0.39%	16,623.57	1.0
CLAR	CLAREMONT BUSINESS EQUIPMENT	2	0.39%	14,701.50	0.9
LOCK	LOCKHART	10	1.97%	14,525.26	0.8
INV	INVERCLYDE LAND ROVER	8	1.58%	12,328.00	0.7

Figure 6.13

The restaurant and pub trade

As always, it's useful to consider a specific example, then you should be able to transfer the general skills you will learn to other similar systems. Here we could have chosen a 'supermarket', a 'sports store' or 'spares for automotive parts'. All these and many of the other retail trades have much in common – often using identical hardware with different software modules selected. The food and drinks trade is a good example to choose because most students will have been to a restaurant, and one or two may even have been in a pub!

Introduction

Unless you have actually managed or worked in a large and busy restaurant, you will probably not appreciate the complexities inherent in any computer system designed to manage it. For example, many people in the restaurant will order lots of different types of food during the course of a meal. The orders for food will come into the kitchen at random intervals, and the chef will have to prepare the food. It may be that different tables have ordered the same or similar food, which all needs to be prepared in the fastest possible time. Therefore, the chef might have to prepare five steaks, not necessarily for the same table. It's often difficult for him or her to look ahead at all the pieces of paper that would be brought in by the waiters and waitresses, and make sure that the food is prepared in the most efficient order. It would be convenient if the computer system installed in the restaurant presents information to the chef in ways different to those that would be presented to the front-of-house staff. This is exactly the sort of problem that a good retail-ordering system in a restaurant would have to solve, and is just one tiny example of the sort of ways in which these systems can help.

Typical requirements

As can be seen from the above example, the person serving the table takes the order, but the information needs to be presented in different ways to different staff. For example, the chef needs to know what food to prepare, and special instructions, if necessary, for the preparation of particular foods. The steak might need to be 'rare', 'medium rare', 'medium', 'medium well' or 'well done', for example. The bartender will need to know which drinks to prepare, and special instructions for the drinks. For example, you could have a 'Vodka Martini – shaken, not stirred', or 'Vodka Martini – stirred, not shaken'. It could be a 'double' or a 'single', or again a customer might have his or her own 'special requirements' such as a dash of 'Angostura bitters'. In general, such systems would allow for a basic menu (both in terms of food and drink), and then add modifiers such as the attributes ('medium rare' or 'with ice and lemon' etc.) described in this section.

A networked system

It would be less efficient for the person who has taken the order to rush into the kitchen with assorted pieces of paper, then rush over to the bar and give the bartender the drink order. The waiter or waitress would also have to work out the price of the meal as the meal is progressing, and also try to satisfy the needs of other customers who may be waiting.

With the above scenario in mind, the waiter or waitress could enter the order into one of the main terminals at the counter, then the chef's printout would appear in the kitchen, and the bartender's printout would appear from the printer at the bar. All the modifiers mentioned above would be present, complete with the table number for which the food or drink is destined. Perhaps the time at which the order was placed could be printed out too. As the order has been entered into the main system, the prices are automatically calculated, and the stock used can be debited from the main stock control database as described in the section on 'stock control and warehousing' earlier in this chapter.

These ideas are identical in principle to the networked computer systems covered in chapters 3 and 5, here we are describing just one specific example which could be used in the restaurant trade as shown in figure 6.14.

Notice how standard equipment and network solutions can be used in a variety of scenarios. Here the central database would probably be stored on the file server in the office where a small network of PCs has been set up for administrative tasks, including stock

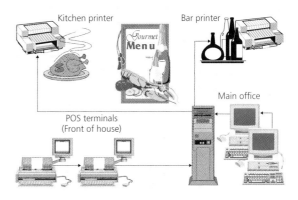

Figure 6.14

control, goods inwards and ordering etc. Requests from the waitresses and waiters can be entered in to the POS terminals, processed by the POS software resident on the file server and the appropriate print outs are spooled to the kitchen or bar printers. When the meal is finished the bill can be printed out on the local printers attached to the POS terminals, and payment methods (such as debit or credit cards (see later in this section) can be handled by this system too. You may already be surprised how all the work that you have covered on networks is applicable to most of the retail trade.

The food and drinks orders

It would take longer if the waiter or waitress had to write down exactly what is needed, and it's usual to have codes assigned to the food or drink. For example, 'Fillet of Steak in a Stilton Sauce' might have a code of '33', if the steak was to be medium rare this code might be modified to '331'. It is unlikely that the front-of-house staff would wish to memorise these codes, so programmable keys are often used on the POS terminal. These keys can either have a special keyboard overlay (like the **concept keyboard** described in chapter 10), or be programmed on screen. The concept keyboard idea is ideal for establishments like fast-food outlets where the customer is ordering the food in front of the POS terminal (e.g. McDonalds) but not as suitable for table service, where the POS terminal is some distance away. The solution here would be to have a special note pad which prompted the staff, or, a special electronic organiser which could take the order and then be plugged into the POS terminal or radio linked directly to the POS terminal. Now that would be a high-tech restaurant!

Other variations

As you will see when you come to carry out your own system's analysis later on in the course (chapters 16 and 17), it's most important that you don't unduly restrict operations in any way. For example, if three people order a meal at the same table, are you assuming that one person is paying for all three, or should the bill be split two or even three ways? The wonderful computer system would look very stupid if it could not cope with such scenarios. Therefore, the software must be able to split up the bill in a variety of ways, done either at the time of ordering, or at any time up to and including the payment of the bill.

Methods of payment

Many POS systems will be able to deal with a variety of different payment methods, either manual or electronic. For example, cash, cheques, debit cards (e.g. Switch) or credit cards (Visa, MasterCard, Amex etc.) are usually catered for. If credit or debit cards can be handled, then the terminal is usually called an EFTPOS (Electronic Funds Transfer at the Point of Sale) terminal. If such a

system is used then an additional telephone link is required for authorisation of payment by the debit card or credit card, and this system is covered from the bank's point of view in the next section. There may also be a facility for accepting own-brand cards such as the loyalty cards used by the large supermarkets. It's even possible for large restaurant chains to have their own customer cards, and discounts for pensioners before certain times in the evenings or a staff-discount card may all have to be catered for.

As mentioned in the last section, a single bill might be split up into three or four parts, with each part being paid in a different way. One customer might decide to use cash, another a credit card, yet another a debit card, and finally one who is a pensioner using a debit card, and therefore happens to be eligible for an age discount because they are eating before 7 o'clock in the evening! This degree of sophistication would not be easily possible without the types of computer systems now installed in large stores and restaurant chains.

> **Hint:** Don't forget, in addition to the payment and ordering systems being considered here, the restaurant trade will also make use of the stock-control systems, word processors and spreadsheets mentioned earlier. A business system like the one being developed should not be considered in isolation from other typical requirements.

Figure 6.15

The above cartoon will be only too familiar to the busy waiter and waitress – the computer systems installed in the restaurant must be able to cope in these demanding situations.

Special requirements

Many retail systems will need a considerable degree of customisation. For example, staff discounts, or pre-paid cards such as those found in the canteens on university campuses. This is where the student will purchase 'credits' that may be used in the staff canteen as 'cash on a card'. A magnetic stripe card can be charged up with cash by placing it into a special machine.

Other specials might be charging meals to a particular room in a hotel, or the 'happy hour' in a public house where drinks might be half price between the hours of 7.00pm and 8.00pm. A common request in a pub is 'same again please' when ordering drinks. It's nice if the computer systems can handle such requests without having to re-enter all the data regarding a complex round of drinks.

If the system is connected to a database then it's very easy to analyse the trends in terms of sales, time of sales, most popular items, use of special discounts or special offers, use of particular credit or debit cards, profits made on particular lines, or total profits etc. The actual list is endless, and is limited only by the customisability of the software, the available hardware and the staff who set up the systems.

WAN considerations

If you have a large chain of restaurants or other businesses then it's useful to be able to correlate statistics such as those described above into the larger picture. It's easily possible to have a centralised office which is linked via the public utilities so that each file server, can be linked up to the file server at head office. In this way the company can set up a centralised ordering and delivery system, with all the advantages that large scale would bring, especially in terms of purchasing power. Chains like Pizza Hut, for example, can order large quantities of the same food at discounted prices, and then have the goods delivered to individual restaurants.

Banking and finance

The banking systems would not be able to survive for long without the use of computers. Indeed, unemployment could probably be solved at a stroke, *if* all of the computers were removed from the banking system and replaced by people. However, the resulting system would not be particularly useful in today's high-speed-cost-conscious world – instead of paying virtually nothing to clear a cheque in 3 days, it might cost ten pounds to clear a cheque within a few weeks! Therefore, banking without the use of computers is now unthinkable.

Banking is made up of a large number of interrelated systems. For example, word processors are extensively used for correspondence, databases (see chapter 28) are used to keep customer details, and networks are used in the same ways as in all large-scale office and multi-national companies. Therefore, in this section we will concentrate only on those areas of banking which are very specific to the needs of the larger financial institutions. The cash-machine networks, the clearing system (cheques), credit-card authorisation, and the movement

of large amounts of money with the consequent security implications are particularly good cases in point.

ATM systems

There can be few more positive signs of automation in banking than the '**hole in the wall**' cash machines or **ATMs** (**Automated Teller Machines**) as they are also known. The original machines were used to dispense cash, but the more modern machines have a variety of other services designed for banking and the retail trade. For example, some modern ATMs can do the following:

- Cash withdrawals
- Credit card advances
- Balance enquiries
- Print out the transaction if required
- Electronic bill paying
- Cash deposits
- Arrangement of financial facilities such as loans
- Dispensing of goods such as stamps, coupons and phone cards
- Airline and event tickets handling
- On-screen advertising
- Special displays and systems to help with access for disabled persons.

Some modern systems have full colour screens, often with either vandal-proof keyboards or touch screens, and can be located both inside and outside of businesses for maximum convenience. Whole business infrastructures have been built up on the back of this cash-machine network. The Link system, for example, was developed as a means of letting the participating banks and building societies in the UK share data regarding accounts held by the customers in the different institutions. In this way a customer of NatWest, for example, could withdraw cash from an Abbey National or Bristol and West cash machine. Indeed, I must confess to being unable to remember the last time I actually withdrew cash over the counter at the bank! It was certainly many years ago! The convenience of the ATM has meant that this technology has permeated into the psyche of the people, and is obviously here to stay. Unless, of course, cash gets superseded in the next decade or two, and even then, these machines will probably be used to charge up the smart cards (see chapter 9) which might be used as a cash alternative.

From the banks point of view this vast network of tens of thousands of machines will alleviate the need for

Did you know that . . .

The Link system had over £1,000,000,000 drawn from their system in October of 1997. This was the first time that the magic billion-pound-per-month figure had been passed and is an indication of the success of these systems over the last few years.

doing much paper work regarding all the transaction processing and paper pushing which used to be carried out manually. For example, the cash just withdrawn at the local branch would have to be accounted for and debited from the local branch account. The person who has withdrawn the cash needs to be identified, both in terms of his or her bank, the branch number and the account number. The money must then be debited from their account, and paid into an account belonging to the bank from which the cash is withdrawn. If it is a Visa or MasterCard transaction, then the computers dealing with this particular account must be notified so that the appropriate debit appears on the monthly statement – and this will happen tens of millions of times each day! Some systems will have live links to these computers, and others will create a database which will then be used to create a file which might be sent to the other banks or Visa and MasterCard on a daily basis. This file is useful not only from the point of view of transferring the actual cash, but for transferring data so that the appropriate fees may be paid by each of the institutions operating the systems.

Networks again!

Network technology pervades most areas of computing these days, and ATM machines are no exception. Most of the large banking systems have leased lines (see chapter 4), but some of the ATMs in the smaller retail outlets do have the option for a standard telephone socket with a dial-up connection. This saves the cost of paying for a leased line if the numbers of transactions are small compared to a large bank in a busy high street.

The network can also be used to diagnose faults on the system remotely. This means that a computer can interrogate the ATM from the comfort of an office far away. Such a system is useful to generate messages regarding 'low on cash' or 'system fault', in which case bank staff could be dispatched to fill up the machine, or an engineer could be sent to repair it. If it is a software fault then it might be possible to restart the machine from a remote location. It is also possible to remotely update modern ATMs with the latest software. In this way a system's engineer could update all the ATMs in a particular network by issuing some commands from a centralised system. Indeed, some of the most modern ATMs fully integrate with the Windows environment, so that conventional computers and software may carry out all statistical analysis. There is no reason, for example, why a shop can't lease an ATM, and then integrate it into their computer system to provide banking services for their customers. It's a powerful incentive to buy something in the shop if there is very easy access to cash or similar facilities.

The software which controls such networks usually has many extra value-added services such as monitoring of statistics regarding the use of the machines (useful when deciding where to site extra ATM machines).

Physical security

Security on ATMs is of the utmost concern. Clever design and attention to detail are obvious key points here. For example, hole-in-the-wall cash machines are usually filled up from the rear, thereby making robbery from the outside of an institution less likely. The physical system is built to international security-safe requirements, and multiple sensors are placed at salient points throughout the system. If an attempted 'break in' is detected, then this can be logged both locally and via the network, and local alarms could be set off if desired. It is also possible to fit time locks so that unauthorised opening outside business hours is not permitted. Small video cameras are also being put onto the modern ATM machines. These are activated during a transaction so that a mug-shot of the person withdrawing the cash is taken! Nice touches like the retraction of uncollected banks notes after a set period of time shows that security has usually been thought about in some detail. It is also possible to have a UPS system (Uninterruptible Power Supply) so that transactions can be completed, even in the event of a power failure.

Software security

The data transmitted both from and to the ATM machine would probably be encrypted (see chapter 9). If the ATM is going to be used to deal with credit card transactions then there must be a secure network link to the credit-card companies' computers for authorisation purposes. For example, it's possible for a request for withdrawal to be encrypted and routed to head office where the main card database is held. Software at head office (or even in the bank or shop behind the ATM) can translate the request, interrogate the database, and then provide both positive and negative transaction processing (see next section).

EFT systems

If you have studied the retail end of the system (see earlier in the chapter) then you will realise that the banks and credit card companies have to verify all the credit and debit-card transactions which are requested by the retail trade. One method involves a vast network in which a front-end processor (see chapter 2) is used to route communications handling both ATM and EFT transactions. It can link to either your own host network, to a bank's host network or to a number of internationally recognised financial networks. It is in this way that Visa, MasterCard and Amex, for example, can be used on

Hint: Look at chapter 9 to see how the EFT and ATM machines can be abused by unscrupulous criminals if people are careless in the way in which they operate these systems.

an international basis. In this way transactions can be monitored on behalf of a particular business, bank, or financial institution, or may be authorised by one of the financial networks mentioned above. Such systems are based on the open-systems technology covered in chapter 5 where networks are covered in great detail.

The Visa, MasterCard and Amex systems all have their own network world wide, and often operate on a negative-file-transaction process. This means that the system debits whatever transactions are made but few, if any, extra checks are made. It's also possible to have a positive authorisation system where you must contact the computer that holds the details of the cardholder, and positively verifies the transaction. The software that controls the front-end processors can be configured to route the request to different places depending on a variety of scenarios. For example, it can act as an inter-bank network switch, and automatically route the request through to the issuing bank's computers for authorisation. Retailers can also phone up numbers for a manual check if they do not operate a full EFT system and the amount of the transaction exceeds their limit for an unauthorised check.

The reliability of these network systems must be high, and the packet-switch (see chapter 5) nature of these systems means that multiple routing is possible in the event of a fault. Although the systems can never be 100% reliable, at least it's possible to get around 'down time' for maintenance schedules and failures in parts of the networks. The inter-bank financial networks above all use encryption for the transmission of the data, and are therefore less likely to be hacked than normal transactions over the Internet.

Related industries

The number of related industries which have built up on the back of EFT is impressive. Consider for example, the supply of equipment for handling EFT. You have ATM machines, the front-end switches on the networks, receipt printers, magnetic stripe readers, magnetic stripe encoders (the machines which put the data onto the cards) and passbook printers for banks to name but a few. We also need smart card manufacturers, lamination machines that laminate the cards, embossing machines that emboss the numbers on the cards, and guillotine machines that cut the cards to shape. Hot-stamping machines for fixing the holograms, and the magnetic stripe press, which puts the magnetic stripes onto the credit cards also exist. It is a multi-billion dollar industry which is gradually taking over the running of financial transaction processing.

The importance of training

You should never underestimate the importance of training in the business community. After complex computer systems have been installed, and after the team of software and hardware engineers have ironed out most of the bugs, it's up to the users of the system to get on with the job. There are many levels of training, from 'self help' present in modern programs, to formal courses run at educational institutions. The appropriateness of the training depends on the 'experience and level of the personal to be trained', the 'number of personnel to be trained' and the 'budget' and 'time available' for training. All too frequently the last two items are woefully inadequate.

Self help

Millions of people each year are put in the position of being given a new piece of software which they have never used before and being told to just 'get on with it!' Educational establishments are particularly bad at this, with teachers and administrative staff in schools often coming bottom of the list for training by several orders of magnitude! The same is true of many small companies, and secretaries are often presented with a new 'word processor', for example, and are expected to start straight away on tackling a busy and important schedule. Needless to say this is not the most efficient way to proceed, but thankfully the help systems which now accompany most software packages are very useful indeed. They often have animated demonstrations to get all but the most advanced tasks sorted out relatively painlessly. Some of the latest help files from Microsoft's Office 97 suite of programs are shown in figure 6.16.

Here 'Power Pup' comes to the aid of those who don't know how to do this or that. If you want more adventurous help then other options such as a 'bouncy ball with a face on it' or 'Einstein' might be to your taste – never let it be said that getting help is boring! Self help can range from simple requests like 'How do I insert a bullet point' to expert help that is available such as 'Visual Basic Books on line' or 'Visual C++ books on line' for example, in which entire libraries of examples are available. Figure 6.17 shows the on-line help for Visual Basic 5.0. It is actually showing the screen that explains the syntax of an 'IF' statement. Such help systems are so comprehensive that it's often possible to learn complete languages such as Visual Basic or C++ just by reading the help files and working your way through the examples.

Integrated help systems are now becoming so useful and friendly to use that it's increasingly likely that

Did you know that . . .

Many thousands of hours are lost each working day through inefficient use of computer systems. Many people have only rudimentary skills and could operate much more effectively if they knew how to operate the computer at a more sophisticated level. A typical example would be carrying out the same task many times without a knowledge of macros.

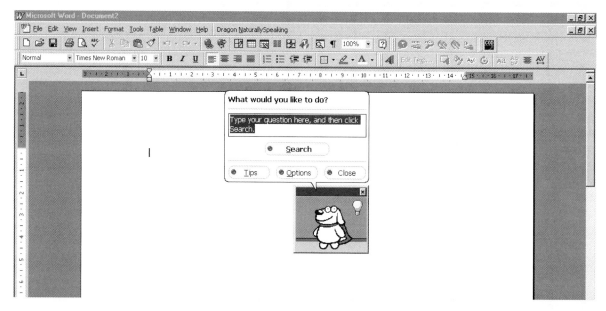

Figure 6.16

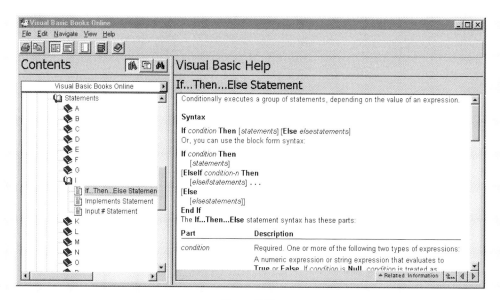

Figure 6.17

fewer printed training manuals accompany the system. The on-line help offers advantages because it is easy to search for the information more quickly, and hypertext links point you to related topics very easily. It's very similar indeed to using an HTML web browser, and indeed some help systems are written for use with standard web browsers such as Internet Explorer or Netscape Navigator.

Never forget the role that is played by the Internet in help with training. Special sites are often devoted to helping with problems, especially those of a more technical nature. I have personally surfed the net thousands of times looking for specialist help either from the Microsoft Knowledge base, specialist sites for particular hardware or software items, specialist forums in ISPs like CompuServe and AOL, or specialist UseNet newsgroups. All theses sources, plus a huge range of CD-ROMS and textbooks from shops provide an enormous amount of help for those with enough technical knowledge to be able to use these systems.

Such self-help in the modern systems is an absolute boon for teachers, as they will inevitably tell a student to use the help files if they can't answer a particular question! The only problem with the on-line help is that students in particular are often too lazy to use it, preferring the solution to be explained by a teacher or fellow pupil.

The on-line help files won't solve all of your problems, especially if you have not understood some of the concepts or don't know the sort of things to look for. It can often be a frustrating search if you type in a slightly different word, or if you forget that much of the spelling is likely to be American. For example, type in the word 'Colour' might reveal no help at all on some 'Art packages' Type in the word 'Color' and you are presented with a plethora of suitable help. Don't forget when searching the Internet that similar problems may apply.

Formal training

Most companies and educational establishments worth their salt will provide some formal degree of training. In fact this should be considered as a vital part of the implementation of a new system as described in chapter 16. This is an efficient method of instruction with larger numbers of personnel to be trained, as the trainer does not have to go through the same processes over and over again. Whole businesses have been developed on the back of the boom in computer training, ranging from simple courses on word processors through to advanced programming courses in most languages.

Formal training can range from in-house training accomplished by the computer staff in an institution like a school or college, to external training sessions provided by colleges or other specialist companies. Such courses would range from day, through residential to courses lasting several months or more. However, the short intense courses that last a day or two are more the norm, and costs vary from under a hundred pounds to several thousand pounds depending on the complexity and duration of the course. *If you are in charge of implementing new business systems then the cost of training should be included as an integral part of the IT solution to a problem.*

Even after you have been on a formal course, it often takes some considerable time for all the new concepts to sink in. Also, the 'self help' systems mentioned earlier should really be backed up by occasional formal courses.

Exercise 6.1

1   Computers now form an essential part of modern business strategy. Outline, in general terms, why this is so, giving examples for each of the points you have chosen.

2   Computers have had some negative effects on business. State, with reasons, a couple of examples where this has actually happened.

3   Word processors have become part of everyday life in the office community. Make a list of twenty typical things that a word processor is able to do efficiently.

4   It is often difficult to tell the difference between some of the modern word processors and DTP systems. Outline the reasons for this and state typical tasks for which each of these systems is most appropriate.

5   Make a list of advantages that having text in an electronic form has over having the same text in conventional form.

6   Word processors have become integrated into complex office suites. What advantages would this have over a stand-alone word processor?

7   Explain the following terms when applied to a word processor:

- Mail merge
- Macros
- Template or master page.

8   Describe the function of a typical spreadsheet. Why has this software package revolutionised many of the financial planning and processing which goes on in business?

9   Make a list of twenty typical processes that could be carried out by a modern spreadsheet.

10 Give some examples of how a spreadsheet might exchange some data with a word processor and a database.

11 Describe how a typical multimedia authoring system package is able to help out with the production of a training package for military training.

12 Why is there such a plethora of different graphics standards for the PC and other computer platforms? How is it possible to use a combination of graphics standards in a single package?

13 A small company has purchased some software to help with 'stock control'. List six typical modules which are likely to appear in such a business system.

14 Outline the major functions of the following modules in a stock control package:

- Supplier
- Goods inwards
- Reports.

15 You are in the process of specifying categories for the database in a new 'stock control' module for a supermarket. Make a list of some of the items that you feel should be included in this module.

16 It's important that any specialist business software integrates with existing or proposed systems in the current office environment. Bearing this in mind, make a list of some of the ways in which a 'stock control' system might integrate with word processors and spreadsheets.

17 Outline some of the typical requirements that would need to be taken into consideration when installing a POS or EFTPOS system into a high-street clothes shop having 12 branches nationally.

18 Outline the importance of a network system to an EFTPOS system installed in a large department store.

19 Some retail outlets are now starting to install ATM machines in store. Outline some of the things that can be accomplished with an in-house ATM machine.

20 List some of the security features that have to be taken into account when an ATM machine is used to dispense cash to the general public 24 hours a day.

21 Training is important for all the business community. There are many ways in which employees can learn about computers and new computer systems. Outline some of the ways giving the advantages and disadvantages that such training would incur.

End of chapter revision aid and summary

Cover up the right-hand column and see if you can answer the questions or define the terms on the left. They appear in the order in which they are covered in this chapter. Alternatively you may browse through the right-hand column to aid revision.

Briefly describe a modern word processor.	A modern word processor is a software package designed for the manipulation of text-based documents. Modern WP systems also handle graphics layouts with relative ease.
What is point size?	Point size is a measurement of the size of typeface (or width of a line). There are 72 points to an inch.
What is WYSIWYG?	What You See Is What You Get – the print out should look identical to the screen layout.
What is a font or typeface?	A font or typeface is a set of characters such as 'Times New Roman'. Italic, bold or underlining etc. can be applied to a particular typeface.
What is a style?	A style is the name given to a set of characteristics which can be applied to text in a word processor. For example, a 'heading' or a 'footer' style might be applied.
What is formatting with regard to text?	Formatting is laying out the text by using styles and justification etc.
What is meant by justification?	Justification is the lining up of text either left, centrally, right or fully justified (no ragged margins on either side).
What are headers and footers?	Headers and footers are the text at the very top and very bottom of the page – they usually contain the page numbers etc.
What is ASCII, RTF and HTML when applied to a word processor?	ASCII, RTF and HTML are just some of the forms in which WP output may be saved. They are ASCII – plain text see chapter 12, RTF – Rich Text Format or text with styles and HTML for Web pages etc.

What is editing?	Editing is the ability to insert, delete, move and copy text etc. using a word processor.
What is a mail merge?	A mail merge is the automatic processing of information such as 'names and addresses' and the ability to combine this with standard text, to produce multiple copies of similar documents or address labels etc.
Briefly describe the graphics-handling capability of a typical WP.	Graphics handling capability is the ability of a WP to insert graphics into frames and display the composite document on the screen. Some WPs also offer limited graphics-creation facilities.
What's an equation editor or layout tool when considering a WP?	An equation editor or layout tool enables a WP to handle a complex mathematical formula and integrate it with the text so that scientific documents may be produced with ease.
Comment on a modern WP's ability to produce textual effects.	Modern WPs can produce fancy textual effects such as curved text or drop shadow etc. This can often be accomplished in an art package and then imported as a graphic into the WP system.
What sort of objects might be inserted into a typical word processor system?	Objects such as spreadsheets, charts and media clips etc. might be able to be imported into the WP system.
What is a macro when considering a word processor?	A macro is used to record a set sequence of operations and get the WP to carry out the same sequence at a later time by replaying the recorded macro commands.
Comment on real-time speech input?	Systems now exist so that WPs and other software packages can accept real-time speech input via a microphone.
List some advantages of having documents in electronic form.	An advantage of having a document in electronic format is that it may be transmitted over the Internet as e-mail, and shared with other packages such as spreadsheets and databases etc.
What is a DTP system?	A DTP system is primarily designed for the production of professional documentation and the layout of such documentation ready for the printers.
What is a spreadsheet?	A spreadsheet is a layout of columns and rows, which form cells, into which text or formulae may by typed. Business scenarios, particularly accounting, can be modelled using this package.
Comment on the common functions available on a spreadsheet.	Many hundreds of mathematical and other functions are available in a typical spreadsheet including financial functions, statistical functions and programming, for example.
What is a macro language with regard to a spreadsheet?	Most spreadsheets have powerful macro languages, which enable you to program the sheet to perform many customised functions.
What is a 'What if' scenario?	The spreadsheet gives businesses the ability to model scenarios such as, 'What if I halve the price of a product? – What would be the effect on our profits?' etc.
Comment on the type of chart that it's possible to obtain with a spreadsheet.	Spreadsheets often have the ability to graph the data in numerous ways, making use of a variety of charts such as histograms, pie charts and scatter charts etc.
Comment on the demographic capability of some spreadsheets.	Some spreadsheets give geographers and others the ability to map demographic data directly onto charts such as the UK or Europe, for example.
What is CD-ROM recordable?	CD-ROM Recordable is the system for recording your own material on a CD-ROM disk.

What is CAL?	Computer Aided Learning and Computer Aided Instruction – the use of (usually) interactive multimedia systems to help with the production of training materials.
What is MPEG?	MPEG (Moving Picture Experts Group) – standard for compression of moving images.
What is JPEG?	JPEG (Joint Photographic Experts Group) – standard for compression of still images.
Name several different types of graphics file formats.	There are many graphics standards such as GIF, TIFF, PNG and PIC etc. for different platforms.
Why do businesses make use of computer systems?	Business make use of computer systems because they save them time and money. Many businesses make use of stock control systems which typically contain modules like 'stock control', 'goods inwards', 'reporting', 'supplier', 'orders', 'queries' and 'requisitions'.
What is a typical 'stock control' module?	'Stock control' module – used for keeping tabs on what's in stock by maintaining an inventory of the items in stock.
What is a typical 'goods inwards' module?	'Goods inwards' module – used for monitoring the activity and quality of the goods arriving at a business.
What is a typical 'requisitions' module?	'Requisitions' module – allows for the processing of requests such as items requisitioned by an employee, for example.
What is a typical 'query systems' module?	'Query systems' module – queries items in stock such as 'where it's located' or 'how much it cost' etc.
What is a typical 'suppliers' module?	'Suppliers' module – database of all the suppliers including details like 'contact names' etc.
What is a typical 'orders' module?	'Orders' module – details of all the orders processed by the business.
What is a typical 'reports' module?	'Reports' module – for printing reports on a variety of scenarios like, 'who's not paid the bill!'.
What is POS?	Point Of Sale (POS) – the name given to electronic tills and the like, usually linked to computer systems and networks. POS systems are usually linked to complex software which helps to manage the day-to-day running of businesses such as restaurants, supermarkets and department stores etc.
What is EFTPOS?	Electronic Funds Transfer at the Point Of Sale (EFTPOS) – electronic transfer of cash such as debit and credit cards, for example.
What is an ATM?	Automated Teller Machine (ATM) – a hole-in-the-wall cash machine, but modern systems can do much more than simply dispense cash.
What is EFT?	Electronic Funds Transfer (EFT) – the name given to the transfer of money by electronic means such as credit or debit cards, or for inter-banking use.

7 Scientific and Graphic Applications

Key resources

To carry out this work most successfully it's best if you have:

◆ Access to a good CAD package
◆ Access to CNC software would be useful
◆ Access to a good pixel-based art package
◆ Access to a good object-oriented (vector based) art package
◆ Access to some computer simulation software
◆ Made a visit to a suitable manufacturing and/or graphics production company
◆ Access to some computer games!

Concept checkpoints

◆ You need to understand the difference between mainframes and micros (see chapter 2).
◆ Have an appreciation of how fast processors affect the performance of computer systems (see chapter 2).
◆ You may want to leave some of the last part of this chapter for a later reading.

Introduction

This second major-applications chapter concentrates on the engineering, scientific, artistic and simulation applications of computers. The business applications and systems considered in the last chapter have probably got a higher profile in the public's mind due mainly to contact that people have with word processors, spreadsheets, databases, and the like. However in the fields of engineering and science, computers have had just as great an impact for an even longer period of time. Don't forget that it was in these fields that computers were first used, and their use has been continuing at an unabated pace ever since. From Computer Aided Tomography (the CAT scan) used in medicine to generate three-dimensional images of the internal organs of the body, to simulation of the entire structure of the known universe, scientific and technical applications will no doubt continue to grow at an ever increasing pace.

Computer Aided Design

Computer Aided Design, or CAD for short, used to be taken to mean the production of technical drawings for use by engineers and architects etc. However, as we shall see later in this chapter, it is now *very much* more than this. Nevertheless, CAD has its roots in the production of technical drawings, and it is to this important subsection of CAD that we will turn to start our journey through the powerful and wonderful design facilities that are now available to engineers in the modern industrial world.

Technical drawings

Firstly, it's important to realise the difference between the type of drawings required by a graphic designer or artist, for example, and the type of drawings required by an engineer or an architect. Most of the time a **graphic designer** or **artist** might be engaged in the *production of drawings of the sort shown in figure 7.1(a)*. However, an **engineer** is more likely to be involved in the *production of a totally different type of drawing similar to that shown in figure 7.1(b)*.

Figure 7.1(a) shows an artistic-interpretation of a car, and is the sort of diagram that gives an excellent overall impression of what the finished artefact might look like. However, we would not expect to be able to manufacture the car from such a diagram. To do this more technical operation, thousands of diagrams of the sort shown in figure 7.1(b) would be required. Such diagrams show the *exact physical dimensions*, and the *details of where holes are to be drilled*, and *the material* out of which the component is to be made etc.

Object-oriented techniques

In general, the type of **artistic diagram** shown in figure 7.1(a) is typically based on a **pixel-based art package**. However, the type of diagram shown in figure 7.1(b) is based on a **precise mathematical description of the picture**, in which each **object** (such as the lines and circles etc.) is represented, not by a group of pixels (dots on the screen), but by the **mathematical equation of the object itself**. This later method, ideal for technical and engineering-type diagrams is called an **object-oriented** or **vector diagram** (vector graphic), and the package that produced it is called an **object-oriented or vector-based CAD package**.

Astute readers will notice that the last paragraph started off with the words 'in general'! In computing, progress continues at an unabated pace, and diagrams of the type shown in figure 7.1(a) can indeed now be done by advanced object-oriented packages. Powerful systems now have the ability to render surfaces to make them appear to be shiny metal, wood, plastic, leather, woven material or indeed anything under the sun. Therefore, it's becoming increasingly difficult to tell just by looking at the end result which type of package has been used for the production of a particular diagram. Even competent home based art and CAD packages can now render surfaces with surprising accuracy and detail, which used to be possible only on the professional systems. With the increasing use of 24-bit or 32-bit colour (see chapter 11), very high resolutions and solids-rendering techniques, it's also getting impossible to tell the difference between computerised output and professional air-brushing techniques. Computer graphics is now a mature technology, and what can be achieved is quite astonishing.

There is a *world of difference* between what can be accomplished with an image produced on a **pixel-based art package**, and the same image produced on an **object-oriented CAD package**. With a pixel-based art package, for example, zooming into a section of the diagram will reveal larger and larger pixels, as shown in figure 7.2(a). However, zoom into an object-oriented diagram, and you can observe more detail – the idea is shown in figure 7.2(b).

In this section, from this point onwards, we will concentrate entirely on object-oriented CAD techniques, and investigate the tremendous potential for complete integration of the design and manufacturing processes so frequently used in the engineering and design industries.

Being able to zoom into the diagram to obtain more detail is particularly useful, because an engineer can build up infinitely complex diagrams that would be too

Figure 7.1a

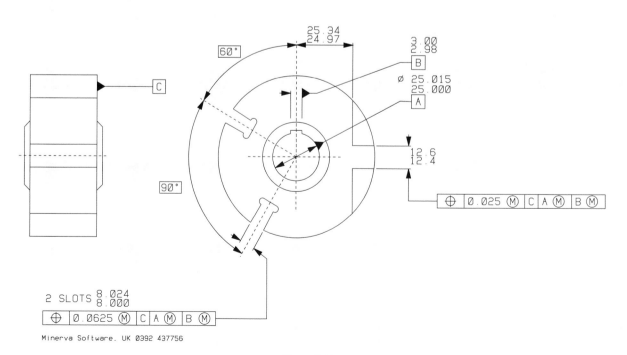

Minerva Software, UK 0392 437756

Figure 7.1b

Did you know that . . .

When powerful CAD packages are linked to simulations and CAM, it's possible to completely simulate an engineering artefact without ever having to build a prototype. This sort of technique is now used extensively in the aircraft industry, where entire planes can be designed and tested inside powerful computer systems. When the first model is finally made, there is a very good chance indeed that it will be able to fly without incident.

detailed to commit to a single sheet of paper. A good example here would be the city maps used by the services and utilities departments of large city corporations. For example, it's possible to have the water, electricity, gas, telephones, cable TV and the like all mapped out in different colours on the same diagram for a city the size of Birmingham. The engineer may then call up a utility such as the 'sewage system', and zoom into a particular street to see how the storm-drain system is connected to a particular house. The equivalent system without using an object-oriented CAD package would be to make use of tens of thousands of diagrams in which each street and house in the city would all be mapped out on different pieces of paper. Any alterations to such a major system would need many diagrams to be altered – with an object-oriented CAD package, one change carried out in a few minutes would instantly update all information. This means that any zoomed-in image is automatically updated too.

There are many **other advantages** to **object-oriented CAD** which are not too obvious unless you have made extensive use of such systems. For example, if you have put all the dimensions onto a diagram, then suddenly decide to reposition a critical part in relation to others, the computer can automatically recalculate the dimension. By the time you have moved the object, the new-position dimensions are correct! Try doing this manually, and you would probably spend a few hours cursing whoever decided to move the object!

As all the objects are defined mathematically, this gives us **the ability to perform mathematical operations on the objects**. For example, if we wish to calculate the area or volume of an object – then this is no problem. Similarly if we know the volume of material and the price/(unit volume), then the CAD package can calculate the materials cost of the component being manufactured – it could then be linked directly to a **database system** which holds information regarding suppliers of the appropriate materials. As all the data regarding every attribute of the component is held in the CAD package, data can be sent to **CNC machines** (see later) or automatically used to give instructions to the robots to manufacture the product. Object-oriented CAD systems are already this powerful, and it's even possible to carry out these operations in the technology departments of many colleges and some schools – in fact, manufacturing industry has been doing just this for very many years.

Object-oriented CAD packages are ideally suited to processing complex pictures with little memory used

Figure 7.2a

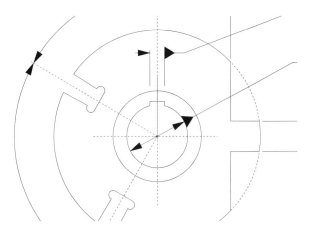

Figure 7.2b

for storing the actual picture. However, there are disadvantages in that a **lot of mathematical processing** has to be undertaken to re-draw the picture from a different view. This is why powerful workstations or powerful microcomputers are needed to perform these operations effectively. Try designing a complex aircraft part on your Pentium II 500MHz machine and you will be struggling a little! Try doing the same thing on a machine with two or three DEC Alpha 21164 chips (see later) inside it, and there will be few problems.

CAD facilities

In the next few sections we briefly list just a few of the features that are common on many CAD packages. You should note that it takes hundreds of hours to learn how to use these packages to the full, and the instruction manuals, often several thousand pages long, bear witness to the complexity and versatility of such systems.

A creative design tool

Engineers and designers make extensive use of drawings to visualise their ideas. It is often tedious and time consuming to hand draw different ideas to see if they would work. By making use of a CAD package, it's usually possible to check out an idea more quickly. You can get the computer to check out the dimensions to see if it is physically possible to manufacture the artefact. You are also more likely to experiment if changes can be made at the flick of a switch. This aids the creative process and usually means that people are more likely to experiment until near perfection is reached.

On some of the CAD systems it's possible to interface the computer to a machine that actually manufactures a 3D physical model of the design in the computer! Making use of special soft plastic materials, which are scanned by powerful LASER beams, the actual model is produced automatically. After much processing, the 3D model can be extracted from the machine. This gives the engineer or artist a much better idea of what the component or model looks like. It is very much quicker than manufacturing a prototype by hand, which would usually involve many sculptors, craftsmen and craftswomen in hundreds of hours of work.

Accuracy

It should be obvious that the **CAD software** and computer, together with the **associated peripherals** such as **plotters** or **LASER printers**, can produce *more accurate drawings* than by using a hand drafting method (i.e. making use of a ruler and pencil). Often the output from CAD packages might produce minuscule photomasks for silicon chip production with lines of less than 1 micron (millionth of an inch).

Editing

If you have ever attempted any really complicated technical drawing, then you will readily appreciate an application that allows you to make many changes without leaving marks on the paper where you have been continually rubbing out. Even so, you would be even more impressed with the other, more advanced facilities. Powerful editing features are usually provided which enable you to change one or more parts of the drawing.

Libraries of parts

When an architect designs a house they are usually making use of an extensive range of parts such as 'windows' and 'doors' etc. Most of these parts are standard, and it would seem a waste of time to have to draw them all from scratch. Most CAD packages allow the use of extra **libraries**. With an architect's library loaded, this would enable the designer of a house to position the appropriate components in place on the drawing of a building. The same ideas are also used for electronic components in the electronics industry, bushes and shrubs for garden designers, materials designs for fashion designers and many others.

Repetitive tasks

There is often the need to draw many **similar shapes** or parts on a diagram. For example, you may be drawing a diagram that represents 100 pigeonholes that will be used as a storage system. You could also instruct the CAD system to automatically insert numbers 1 to 100 in the appropriate place in each pigeonhole. Indeed, you would use the same type of system to generate 100 pigeonholes in the first place. Processes such as these are unbelievably tedious if carried out by hand.

Integration with other systems

Suppose that you're producing a mechanical drawing of an engine. It's obvious that this consists of many different parts. Indeed there would almost certainly be many people working on different parts of the engine at the same time, and CAD makes an ideal base from which to join together all of their work.

It's usually a requirement to have a parts list generated. This is simply a list of parts that go into making a particular component such as an engine. Each of these parts would probably have a number that is used to uniquely identify it. Many of the parts would be brought in from other factories to be assembled at the factory that is making the engine. Each part would therefore have to be ordered, and the part-number information which is used in the CAD package can be sent off to a **database** (see chapter 28) that deals with the ordering of the components required. Indeed, it is often the case that the components required could also be linked to the stock-control systems undertaken in the last chapter.

Each part would have an associated cost, and this information (gained from the part number) can be used to generate statistics from a financial package. Even the ordering can be done automatically. If the stock-control system decides that stocks of certain part numbers are running low, then the goods can be ordered automatically from the warehouse. Any paperwork needed can then be produced from the database and printed out making use of a report facility.

Indeed some high-tech companies now operate a totally integrated system as described above. They do not carry much stock, and order the components as and when necessary. This saves much money because you don't have expensive warehouse systems tied up in storing a vast stock. If the suppliers are geared up with the same sort of systems, then, by using networks for the interconnection, the computer in the manufacturing company can order direct from the computer in the supplier's company.

Such extensive systems are in use today. The **CAD package** contains much of the information that is needed to start off the incredible chain of events that go into the manufacture of some complex products. If all these processes were carried out by hand, then you would need an army of people to perform the same tasks. The time between the perceived need for a component and it's actual ordering would often take days or weeks. By making use of extensive computerisation, this is often reduced to minutes. Managers are also in the position of having instant analysis about the state of any job being done within the company.

Parametric CAD packages

Some **CAD packages** allow you to define relationships **parametrically**. This means that special parameters are used which show the relationship between one part of the diagram and another. Oak Computers have created one example of a parametric CAD package, and a typical example is shown in figure 7.3. Here a two-cylinder internal combustion engine is simulated.

> **Hint:** If you have a parametric CAD package then it might be able to aid you with some maths or physics homework. Loci or projectile paths, for example, can often be programmed with ease and diagrams of the paths taken printed out.

All the geometric relationships between the moving parts have been previously defined making use of the parametric CAD software. When such relationships have been established, and when the diagrams have been drawn in the appropriate place, an amazing relationship then exists – you have the ability to generate different positions of the mechanism by specifying different angles and linear positions etc. i.e. by *varying* the **parameters**. If you create several appropriate pictures,

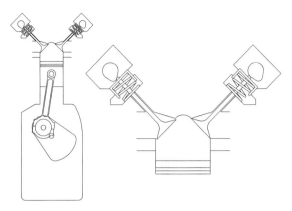

Figure 7.3

you can build up a movie of the mechanical linkage. Yes, it really moves! Indeed, with enough time and practice, complete **animation sequences** can be generated. This gives you the powerful ability to visualise moving parts on the computer screen before they are actually built. It is also a great aid in educational institutions where mechanics and physics are taught.

The user interface

The **human machine interface** or **HCI** is of particular importance when considering applications (**see Plate 3**). Just as the mouse has revolutionised the **WIMP environment**, so the **puck** and **graphics tablet** (see chapter 10) makes data entry into a CAD package much simpler. A typical **CAD package template** for use on a **digitiser tablet** is shown in figure 7.4. It is the template that provides a custom-programmable menu system.

Placing the cursor on the puck over the appropriate position on the template and pressing one of the buttons can choose various settings. The buttons are similar to a mouse, but, due to the construction of the graphics tablet, the cross-hair cursor keeps its relative position even if the puck is removed completely from the tablet and then replaced. Some superb effects are now possible making use of sophisticated CAD processes (see **Plate 4**). Examples of wireframe, light shading and texture can be seen in figure 7.5.

Micro, mini or mainframe?

Most of the facilities shown above are available on **powerful microcomputer systems**. However, some very advanced facilities, such as the **3D laser modelling systems** mentioned earlier, could only be achieved by using powerful **mini** or **mainframe computers**. Such facilities would include the ability to multitask with very complex drawings (i.e. carry out more than one task at the same time). This is useful if you wish to display several drawings on the screen at the same time, either on one or a number of monitors connected to the same computer! This may sound extravagant, but is often useful if you wish to edit a drawing whilst looking at part of another, as is often the case in the aircraft industry, for example. They also offer advantages in terms of **great speed**, especially when complex 3D modelling is required. However, the popularity of CAD packages has really taken off with the advent of powerful micros, and what can easily be done in the home today was state of the art in industry just ten years ago.

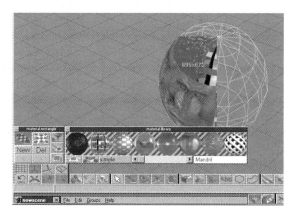

Figure 7.5

Figure 7.4

Disadvantages of CAD

CAD was never designed for the initial doodles that help to form concepts in people's minds. It can't replace the ease of use and convenience of a pencil and paper for the early stages. It was also not designed for a simple one-off diagram, and the following scenario is only too typical.

Sometimes students are so impressed with CAD that they go overboard in using it to do things that can often be done better in other ways. This is, unfortunately, a particular problem with students at school and college. They will often spend a long time learning about a particular CAD package merely to include some fancy diagrams in their project reports. Often it is done in a hurry because the reports are due to be handed in, and mistakes are therefore made. This leads to a high degree of frustration and discontent with the application being used. Another student may have produced an acceptably neat diagram in five minutes by making use of a much simpler diagramming tool! The obvious solution to this particular problem is to use a simpler CAD package and leave enough time to do the diagrams properly. (See chapter 33 on writing up your projects.)

Top-of-the-range CAD packages usually take hundreds of hours to learn to use properly. They need a large investment both in terms of hardware and time. It would be silly not to make extensive use of the system after such training and commitment.

Computer aided manufacture (CAM)

Computer Aided Manufacturing, or **CAM** as it is known, is the entire process of getting computers to aid many or all of the stages in a production process. Using a variety of Numerically Controlled (NC) machine tools, or Computer Numerical Control (CNC) and robots these complex manufacturing operations can be accomplished (see later).

Typical machines used in the manufacturing industry would be: **lathes** (see **Plate 5**) – to turn materials into components such as those shown in figure 7.6(a); **milling machines** – to produce components like those shown in figure 7.6(b); **drilling machines** – to drill the holes; and a whole host of other more specialist equipment. For example, there might be a specialist robot that inserts the electronic components into a printed circuit board, and this is shown in the detailed example that follows.

> **Hint:** It does not take very long to master CNC software, which produces suitable code for the CNC machines. However, beware of using the CNC machines themselves. You will need expert help, and they can take a long time to set up for a one-off project. They are also dangerous if not used safely. Make sure that you enlist the help of a teacher or technician before attempting to manufacture anything.

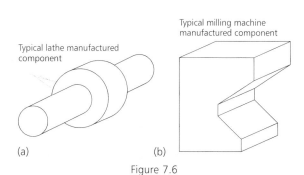

Typical lathe manufactured component

Typical milling machine manufactured component

(a) (b)

Figure 7.6

Traditionally, skilled operators controlled these mechanical machines. These people would carefully wind the knobs and dials on the machines so that the right amount of metal was cut off, or the right size drill was inserted into the machine so that the appropriate hole could be drilled in the component. Although a great deal of skill was needed to operate these machines, the processes were essentially 'many simple steps performed one after the other'. This is especially true for the repetitive tasks on the production line when thousands of the same type of object were to be manufactured in the same batch.

As long ago as the 1950s, it was realised that groups of numbers could be used to give the machines instructions. It was identical in principle to machine code (see chapter 20) used for computers. In the early days, paper tape (a long reel of paper with holes punched into it) was used to control these machines, but now they are more likely to have special computers **embedded** into the system. (See chapter 8 for an explanation of **embedded systems**.) The name '**numerical control**' is, therefore, derived from the fact that **machine-code type numbers** are used to **control the machines**. Instead of the operators winding the knobs, electric motors would replace them and be controlled by making use of special computer interfaces (see chapter 8). **A typical CNC machine is shown in figure 7.7.**

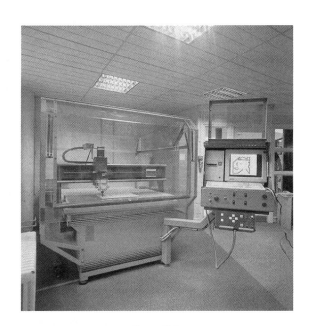

Figure 7.7

These machines may be used in stand-alone mode, or, more usefully, be integrated with other computer systems to produce what is known as **CAD/CAM**. (See in a moment.) If a machine is used by itself, then a special language is needed. This is similar to the way assembly languages and high level languages (see chapter 2) have been developed to make machine code programs easier to write on computers. Special

languages like **APT** (**Automatic Programmed Tools**) and **COMPACT II** would be used on the machines to help the operators more easily describe what is necessary to manufacture and assemble the components. (This gives a whole new meaning to assembly language!)

It is also possible to get a CAD package to produce an output called a Gerba file or G-code direct to a CNC machine. In this way a CAD package could produce a suitable drawing, and then the code to drive the CNC machine could be generated by the CAD package. The numbers would then be saved on to disk, and the floppy disk could be taken down to the CNC machine in the workshops, which could then be used to control the machine as if the data had been entered manually.

CAD/CAM techniques

It's a natural consequence of computerisation that, if the **data** for a component's manufacture exists in a **CAD package**, and if the machine that produces or assembles the components can be controlled by **machine code**, then all you have to do is to *translate the numbers from one system to the other*, and then you have an **integrated design and manufacturing base**.

In some factories it's literally possible for the designer to produce all the information which can control an automatic factory. A typical example can be found in the electronics industry, where here it can be taken several stages further (see **Plate 6**). Figure 7.8 shows a diagram of some of the typical processes that might be involved.

Did you know that . . .

One of the reasons why computers are becoming less expensive is the large-scale use of automated production. Entire motherboards can be built up by facilities of the sort being described in the PCB section. Once set up, these facilities can churn out many thousands of boards with the minimum of labour. The alternative is to use very cheap human labour, which is socially unacceptable in today's modern society.

The initial concepts

The designers of a system would be given a specification for some particular electronic process. They would then apply their knowledge to designing an appropriate circuit. Note that for very advanced systems, an **expert system** (see chapter 9) may be used to help or even completely carry out this initial design process.

Computer aided design of circuit

The designer converts his or her designs into an electronic circuit and, with the aid of a computer, draws the circuit. The next stage might be to get a special **electronic circuit analysis program** to run tests on the

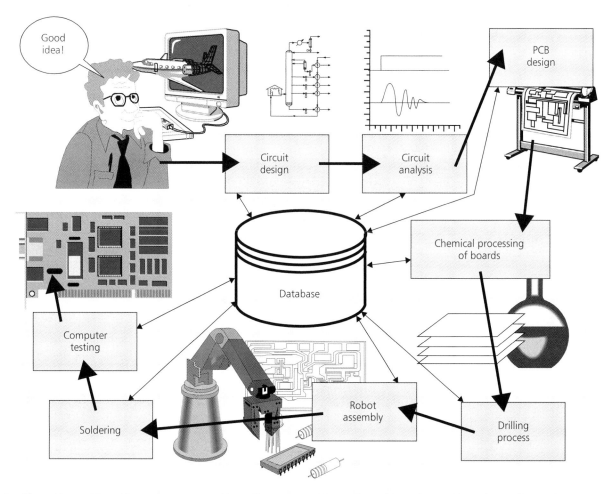

Figure 7.8

circuit to see if it performs to specification. It's possible, by holding theoretical models inside the computer of each component used in the circuit, to *predict exactly what effect the overall design will have before any prototypes have yet been built.* Such techniques are extensively used in the aircraft industry, where planes now take to the air on computer simulation alone. It's no longer necessary to build up an expensive mechanical mock up to see if the beast will fly, but I don't think that I would volunteer for the inaugural flight!

Computer aided design of PCB

Information about each component (e.g. its physical size, what legs of the chips have to be connected where, etc.) is already held in the computer system. As the electrical connections are already known from the circuit diagram, then it's a relatively easy matter to get a different computer package to design the **printed circuit board (PCB) layout.** Sophisticated systems can now cope with many layers of copper track used to connect up all the chips. Get your teacher to show you a modern printed circuit board if you have not seen one before, you will then appreciate what's happening in great detail

– you have only to look at the motherboard inside your PC to see an example of a complex PCB.

Production of the artwork

Artwork for the production run of the **PCBs** is produced by getting the PCB design system to plot out the appropriate pattern. This can then be fed into the machines so that the physical boards containing the copper tracks are produced.

A **numerically controlled drilling machine** can get data from the **PCB layout** so that all the appropriate holes to put the wires through are drilled in each board.

Computer-controlled drilling

A special **robot**, see figure 7.9, is next used to place the appropriate components onto the PCB. The components are then ready to be soldered onto the board by the next process.

Hint: If you can arrange a visit to see CNC and robots in operation, then it's well worth the effort. Companies like Ford Motors arrange tours for schools. It puts this section into perspective if you can see the sheer scale of the operation.

Plate 1
Part of the range of Silicon Graphics workstations and servers. These are the sort of machines used in university research, government science-based institutions and other high-end applications

Plate 2 ▶
A range of modern Ethernet hubs. Notice the size of this equipment compared to a standard 3.5 in floppy disk which appears to the left of the hub.

◀ **Plate 3**
Powerful workstations like those shown, built by Silicon Graphics, are needed to drive the most complex CAD packages and simulations. This machine is driving two monitors simultaneously

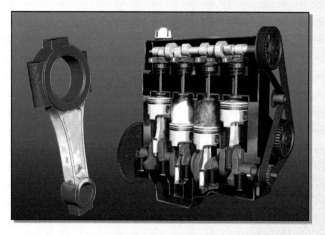

▲ **Plate 4**
A computer-generated image of an internal combustion engine. Notice how colour and texture are used to help analyse and visualise complex problems

▲ **Plate 5**
A computer-controlled lathe being used to turn out steel components. CNC machines like this have been used extensively in industry for several decades

◄ **Plate 6**
A robot inserting a chip into a complex circuit board of the type that you have inside your computer. This requires the robot to move very precisely or the chip will not fit exactly into the appropriate holes on the board

▲ **Plate 7**
Packages such are those shown have revolutionised the image creation and manipulation industry. The features in most of these art-based application packages are staggering and the quality of the final image is very professional. If you're using these packages, however, make sure that you have a fast computer with lots of memory or you will get a slow response when producing very complex images

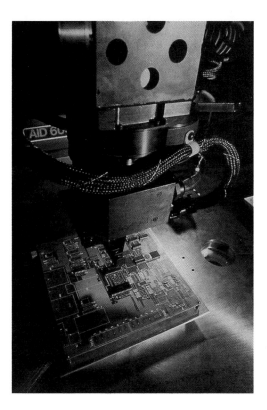

Figure 7.9

Flow soldering

This stage involves all the components being soldered onto the board by automatically passing the board over a flow solder bath – it's a lot quicker and far more effective than soldering each component by hand.

Computerised testing

A **numerically controlled testing machine** can now be used to perform hundreds of measurements on the completed system to ensure that the original specification is met. Again, this would be a very tedious and time-consuming process if carried out by hand, and the skill level of the technicians required to manually perform this operation would be very great.

Other links to the CAD/CAM process

There are other spin-offs which may not be immediately obvious from reading the above. For example, a components and parts list could be automatically generated from the initial design on the computer. This list could be used, together with the potential orders, to automatically generate the computerised lists for the parts required. This could then be tied up with the stock control systems. There is no reason why a **database system** similar to that described in chapter 28 could not be used as the *main hub of the organisation* of which these

CAD/CAM methods form a part. A natural extension to this would then be the extensive use of national and international networks to connect the company with its subsidiaries and component suppliers.

From reading this section you should now have a good appreciation of how CAD and CAM systems can be used at every stage of the manufacturing process. Indeed, the use of these systems is the only viable economic option in the industrialised world where skilled labour costs a great deal of money. As always, the unskilled worker comes off worse, and such consequences are covered in detail when social implications are covered in chapter 9.

Pixel-based art packages

These software packages are primarily *ideal* for **graphic designers** and **artists** who have to create images for inclusion in magazines, graphics images for inclusion in video productions such as those seen in the TV-adds, or for retouching photographic input etc. They should be *compared and contrasted* with the **object-oriented CAD packages** (see earlier) used by engineers to produce industrial designs for machinery and architectural plans etc. considered in the last section. However, it should not be forgotten that many modern packages such as Corel Draw 8, for example, integrate the two systems admirably.

If you wish to familiarise yourself with the theory of the production of **bit-mapped images**, this is covered when **graphics displays** are studied in chapter 11, and a typical bitmapped image (from Photodesk by Spacetech running on Acorn's RISC PC) is shown in figure 7.10. In this chapter we will concentrate on typical facilities offered by these impressive image-manipulation programs, some of which offer conversion between the different graphics-image standards mentioned in the multimedia section of chapter 6.

Did you know that . . .

Some art packages today are so good that it's very difficult to tell the difference between a real photo and the output produced from one of these systems. People can now easily touch up photos by scanning them in, and altering them with packages such as Microsoft's 'Picture it'. Superb quality printouts are also easily possible on bubble-jet printers, especially if high-quality glossy paper is used.

There are an enormous variety of packages for the PC and Apple Mac, which is obviously most famous for its deserved reputation in the graphic design field. Nevertheless, the most recent packages on the PC such as Micrografx Picture Publisher, Adobe's Photoshop or Letraset's Fractal Design Painter are equally impressive. Most art packages, especially those with 24-bit colour

Figure 7.10

capability (see chapter 11) on all platforms now provide an enormous range of features for the professional user. Most microcomputer-based packages offer very similar facilities (see **Plate 7**), and just a fraction of the more common ones are outlined in the next few paragraphs.

Basic drawing facilities

A range of **colours** may be chosen, then applied to the screen by making use of a selection of tools such as **pencils**, **paintbrushes**, **rollers**, **spray cans**, **air brushes** and other assorted facilities. The ways of choosing from a palette of 16,777,216 colours are now getting quite ingenious, but 256-colour images can be satisfactory for run-of-the-mill work, even at modest resolutions.

Shapes

A range of **basic shapes** such as **squares**, **triangles**, **ellipses**, **circles**, **polygons**, **sectors** and **segments** etc. are usually available, plus the ability to design your own '**pen**', '**crayon**', '**charcoal**', '**brush**' and '**air-brush**' shapes. You can also create various shaped **masks**, such that you can literally use the computer-generated air-brushes in ways identical to those that you would use in a manual airbrushing environment. The secret of a good airbrushing technique is actually in clever design and use of the masks – it's a very skilled operation, even with a computer art package to help out.

Editing facilities

It's usually possible to **zoom** in and edit the picture on a pixel-by-pixel basis. Individual pixels can be placed

exactly. It's also usual to have facilities such as '**magic wands**' where you can paint certain coloured areas without affecting other colours, or a variety of ways of **distorting** images into a diversity of amazing user-defined shapes. There are also facilities to **wash** areas of the screen – an effect that would normally be produced by dipping a paintbrush in water and then gently rubbing it over an area to create a washed-out effect or blend two or more adjacent colours. It's also possible to **fade** the paintbrush as the stroke is lightened, just like the real thing, although a pressure-sensitive graphics pad (see chapter 10) would be needed to carry out this operation effectively.

Bit-map effects

There are usually a large number of special bit-map effects such as '**blending**', '**extrusion**', '**contours**' and '**lenses**', 2D effects such as '**swirls**' and 3D effects such as '**emboss**' and '**perspective**', for example. A variety of other effects are also usually available such as '**blurring the image**' or '**increasing the sharpness**' etc.

Cut and paste

The ability to cut and paste all or parts of the image, often in conjunction with a variety of masking techniques can lead to a variety of interesting scenarios, including the creation of multiple images with ease. The author remembers creating a video cover for his school in which an unfortunately-positioned video camera had to be edited out of the shot, and replaced with curtain material of the exact texture and colour to that which was next to the camera in the original picture. The adjacent curtains were cut out (a section copied) and carefully pasted so that the video camera was obscured. It then looked like the curtains were pulled across the entire area. A feat that took just a few minutes using a computer-art package.

More advanced facilities

The list of specialised features is now too enormous to mention. Letraset's Fractal Design painter package even allows you to use a brush style so that you can paint in the appropriate style of the grand masters like Van Gogh and some others. However, I don't think that my version of the Mona Lisa will end up hanging anywhere other than on the wall of the 'Loo Gallery' in my house!

Internet connectivity

In common with many modern packages, there are often links built into the menu structure of the program that could automatically launch a browser, log onto the **Internet** and connect you to the appropriate **web page** designed by the manufacturer of the package. This is often a convenient way of finding out the latest information, downloading the latest bug fixes, or locating appropriate **UseNet newsgroups** which relate exactly to the topic of interest – i.e. the particular art package you are using.

Who will make use of these packages?

In general, most fine artists have not been completely won over just yet, but many are now interested in computer-generated art as an alternative medium that can now be seriously explored. The professional artistic community can no longer ignore the latest full-featured packages, and computer art has now become accepted and common place. Even so, most artists tend to *like* working with paint brushes and canvas, and, just like the poet who feels that they are in more intimate contact with their work when they are actually applying the ink to the paper, it is unlikely that all artists will make use of a micro. What a boring world it would be if they did!

Autostereograms

Computers are finding much use in graphic art such as advertising and animation of cartoon films etc. and there are obviously some things which are virtually impossible to do in art without a computer – with the 3D **autostereograms** being a good case in point. Can *you* read the **hidden message** in figure 7.11?

There can be few people in the country who have not encountered these images, and there are several ways of successfully viewing the image, two of which are as follows.

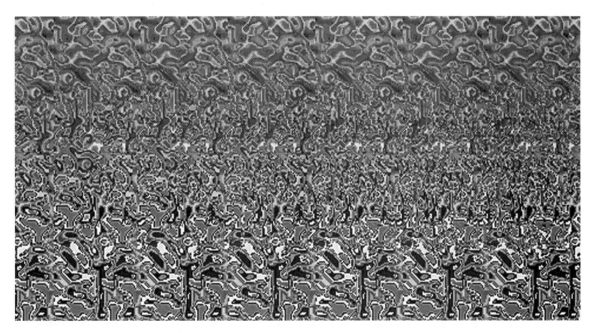

Figure 7.11

(1) Stick a piece of glass over the image, look into the glass and focus, not on the image itself, but on the reflection of your face in the glass, which is actually behind the image – you should see parts of the image start to produce a stunning 3D effect.

(2) Stick your nose on the page just in front of the image, but don't focus on the image. Gradually move the image away from your eyes while still not focusing on the actual image – you should eventually see a 3D image, in which case stop moving your nose.

If you have defective sight in one eye, then you unfortunately will not be able to see the image. Also, some people find it difficult if not impossible to do, and think that those who can actually see a 3D image are pulling their leg!

The people who really benefit from these packages are the *majority* of the population who find it difficult to produce a professional quality image. Even moderately good packages allow people to experiment with ideas. **Art packages** give you *infinite flexibility*, and you can rub out your artwork thousands of times without leaving a mark or rubbing a hole in the paper. However, put one of these art packages in the hands of a talented and computer-literate artist, and the results can be absolutely stunning. It's not true what some people say about computer art packages taking the creativity out of the production of artwork. It just gives very talented people another dimension in which to operate.

3D art packages

Just a few years ago the thought of modelling in 3D would have been beyond the realms of the ordinary PC. Today, nothing could be further from the truth. Packages such as Corel's CorelDream 3D, Caligari's TrueSpace or MicroGrafix's Simply 3D give you the ability to render very realistic images at a fraction of the cost of professional systems. A typical screen shot from CorelDream 3D, shown in figure 7.12 shows just a fraction of what's possible using this software.

The basic techniques involve creating wire-frame images in 3D i.e. *real* 3D images which can be viewed from any standpoint. After choosing 'colours', 'backdrops' and 'lighting conditions' etc., render the image by means of ray tracing (see next section) with an appropriate material such as metal, wood or plastic etc. The basic shapes can be constructed in similar ways to those in a conventional 2D art package, therefore, a chair, for example, would be built up from components such as

> **Hint:** If you are designing the set for a theatre, and wish to know how the lighting will affect parts of your set, you can use one of these 3D packages to construct the set, and experiment with different lighting conditions. Some packages allow the use of coloured lights, and are therefore ideal for this purpose.

the 'seat', 'arms', 'back' and 'legs' etc. The added complexity arises from having to consider the depth and hence the 3D shape of the object. For example, the chair leg might be the same shape viewed from both sides, or it might be curved in one dimension but straight in the other. You will also have to determine the material out of which the leg is to be made, and this is done by applying effects such as wood grain to the surface of the object that you have just constructed. In addition you will have to provide lighting so that the object can be seen, determine the degree of reflection off the surface (whether it is shiny or matt etc.), and whether the object is viewed in a dark or light room.

These packages really are a lot of fun to use. You are literally put in the same position as a lighting and scenic director on a stage set. You can choose what background you will have, but no background exists in figure 7.12 so that you can see the 3D grid from which the object is created. You can also choose how many lights you wish to use, where the lights are placed, and how bright each light is. Don't forget that the light will cast shadows onto the background just like the light in a real stage set. Indeed, using these packages you are literally creating your own virtual 3D worlds. For example, the bicycle shown in figure 7.12 could be copied, it's colour changed, then both bicycles could then be placed in a garage together with a car and lots of tools such as those found in a workshop. If you consider the scene to be made up of real 3D objects just like in real life, then you won't go far wrong in your concept of this fascinating technology.

Some of the best computer images are made possible by making use of wire frame and rendering (see **Plate 8**). It has long been the goal of computer scientists to generate mathematically created images that look as if they are real. Indeed, over the last few years, the techniques have been getting better and better. However, the actual method of producing these images is *anything but* art.

High-end 3D packages

Very high-end 3D art packages (see **Plates 9** and **10**) are used to create the images which you see in movies like 'Star Trek', 'Star Wars' and 'Toy Story', for example. The same principles apply as shown in the last section, but the packages usually work in 16 million colours with very high resolutions, and are required to produce a large number of images in a

> **Hint:** If you are lucky enough to be able to arrange a visit to a film company which does special effects, then it will be well worth the effort. If you ever visit EPCOT in Florida, these facilities are on show.

sensible amount of time. Therefore, machines like Sun Workstations are used for these operations, usually in

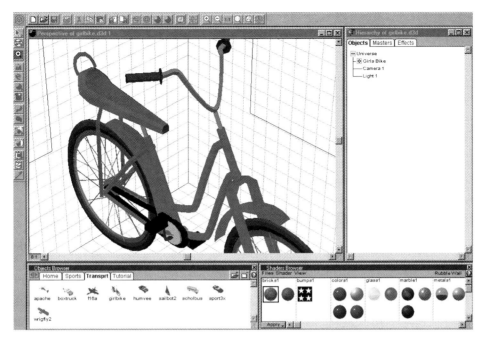

Figure 7.12

rooms where a dozen of these machines are used by an army of programmers and artists. These machines are very expensive and collectively a studio set up to do these effects would need to spend millions of pounds. However, the cost-effectiveness of these systems is such that it is well worth the money, often costing millions of pounds less than the equivalent stage sets built up using models. Indeed billions of mathematical calculations are often necessary and, even on a **64-bit microcomputer**, it may take several hours to do enough calculations to generate a few images. Powerful **mainframes** can produce stunning images in a fraction of this time, as their processing ability is many orders of magnitude higher. Indeed, the **Cray supercomputers** (see later) have generated some of the best graphics seen on computers to date, and **mainframes** or **supercomputers** *are still useful* for generation of a sufficient quantity of high-quality ray-traced images to produce a long movie.

Ray tracing

Hint: You really should have a go with some of the 3D ray-tracing packages. Rendering your own creations is extremely satisfying, and it's good fun changing the materials out of which your object is made. You may even produce a work of art that's worth hanging on your bedroom wall!

Ray tracing is based on a method which involves the **physics of optics** (**light**). Rays of light are shone onto a mathematically generated scene, and the **shadows, reflections** and **refractions** etc. that would occur in real life are painstakingly worked out point by point.

The ideas are based on **rays of light (photons**

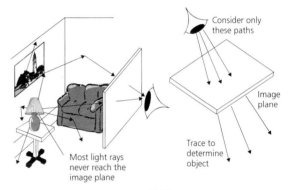

Figure 7.13

being emitted from a light source and then, by complex or simple paths, finding their way to the viewer's eye. The idea is shown in figure 7.13.

It would be impossible, even for a supercomputer, to calculate all possible light paths. Even so, this would not be necessary as few of the light paths would hit the viewer's eye anyway. Therefore, a technique known as **backward ray tracing** is used. This is where the rays are traced backwards from the viewer's eye to determine the objects from which the photons might have emerged. The idea is also shown in figure 7.13. Even with this massive reduction in calculations, it still takes a huge amount of computing power.

The techniques for generating ray-traced images are now well established. However, computer scientists often ask themselves if the images they have created look real enough. Almost all of the time the answer is no, and therefore they have to ask what is different between the mathematical images that they have created, and the real objects which they are trying to simulate. Various techniques such as texture have now been added to increase the realism of these pictures. It's relatively easy to generate textures such as metallic objects (even with all the reflections) and matt objects and materials such as cloth, but it's still very difficult to generate all the subtle skin tones of a human being. However, it is being worked upon and will, I am sure, be simulated with great realism in the next few years. Couple this with the use of these images in a VR system, (see chapter 11) and the human imagination may reach hitherto unknown areas.

Morphing

Another computer-art based technique, which would be virtually impossible without a computer, is that of **morphing**. Morphing got its name from the term metamorphosis which means changing from one thing into another. There are now a large number of morphing packages available, but they have yet to be included in most standard computer art packages – no doubt they will be one day. One package called **Morpheus** by Oregan Developments for Acorn's RISC PC has a demonstration created by Henning Hansen, in which a picture of a girl, shown on the left of figure 7.14, is

turned into the picture of a Tiger, shown in the right of figure 7.14. Just one of the intermediate stages is shown in the middle of figure 7.14.

To carry out morphing with a suitable package is quite simple. It revolves around importing two suitable bitmapped images for the start and end frames, then making use of a grid which is placed over the images as shown in figure 7.15.

The grid has to be altered from the default shape in figure 7.15 so that salient points on the start grid can be mapped to salient points on the end grid. As you can see from the example shown in figure 7.16, the points around the eyes, ears and nose are very important in this particular transformation. Points at the intersection of the grid on the first image are mapped to the new positions of these same intersections on the final grid. It's up to the user of the package to interpret creatively the start and end positions of the grid to get the best effects.

> **Hint:** If you have a couple of suitable subjects for morphing, then they could make a fabulous introduction to a business presentation. For example, you could save the animated clips as a movie, and play them back in real time during the opening of a special presentation sequence.

 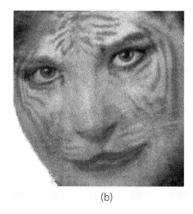 

| (a) | (b) | (c) |

Figure 7.14

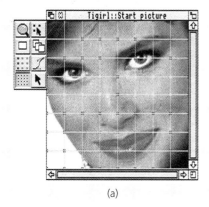 

| (a) | (b) |

Figure 7.15

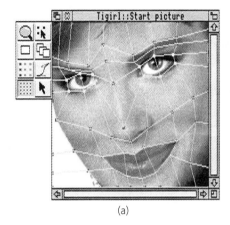
(a)

(b)

Figure 7.16

Wonderful fun can be had with **morphing packages**. Any image, created from a **computer**, **video camera**, **video cassette recorder**, images pulled off of **bulletin boards** or loaded from **CD-ROM** etc. can all be used as the source files, and converted into a suitable form for the morphing application by an art package. The TV and film advertising companies have taken to morphing in a big way.

Industrial robotics

Industrial robotics as a science is a far cry from the *sci-fi images* portrayed in books and some of the popular press, which unfortunately tend to have views more akin to the robot cartoons as shown on TV! The early application of industrial robots stems from an extension of the numerically controlled machine tools still found in operation today. As we have seen in this chapter, these **CNC** (or **Computer Numerical Control**) machines are devices such as drills, milling machines and lathes etc. and these can be observed carrying out automated processes in many modern industrialised plants. It was the automobile industry, where these automation processes were proceeding at an unprecedented pace, that acted as a spur for the development of these specialised robots. They were often seen manufacturing a particular part of a car component, helping with the work on the assembly line or spraying paint onto the cars. Parts also had to be moved from one process to another, and a mechanical arm similar to that shown in figure 7.17 was ideal for this purpose. You should note at this stage that the detailed interfacing of these robotic devices is considered in chapter 8 where computer-control systems are looked at in much more detail – in this chapter we are concerned more with the effects and use of this particular scientific application of computers.

Interestingly enough, the distribution of robots throughout the world is far from uniform. For example, in the mid 1990s, Japan has somewhere in the region of just over half a million robots working in industry, but the USA, the next-largest user of robotics, has only about 100,000 – just 20% of the number being used in Japan! The UK comes a long way behind Germany and some other industrialised countries, with the 'car' and 'electronics' industries leading the way. These trends tend to reflect political and other issues in addition to reasons of a more technical nature. For example, in the Far East, where some workers tend to have jobs for life, robots, even the non-human looking ones, are

Figure 7.17

Did you know that . . .

In 1998, the University of Tokyo displayed a robot, which is capable of walking like a human being. It has two legs, complete with joints not dissimilar to the knees and ankles etc. If you push the robot backwards or forwards then it counteracts this movement to prevent being pushed over, just like a human being would. It is also the first robot, which could actually walk up and down the stairs successfully. Not surprisingly, in 1998, it still needed a mainframe to control all these highly complex operations.

Figure 7.18a

Figure 7.18b

viewed as having their own personalities and being a 'friendly help' in the work place. In the industrialised West, they are often viewed as a threat to job security.

At present, **robots** tend to be able to do **very specific tasks** *very well* (see **Plate 11**). For example, a robot such as that shown in figure 7.18(a) represents the heavy high-power end of the market. It has been designed specifically for lifting huge weights – a task that hitherto would have needed a human in conjunction with a crane. At the other end of the spectrum, personal robots such as that shown in figure 7.18(b) have appeared on the market. This is more like the image that the public has of a robot, but unfortunately, the technology to implement all the expectations from such a 'human-looking' machine are far from a sufficient stage of development (see **Plate 12**). Nevertheless, researchers in Japan are actively working on domestic robot technology, which will literally be able to do the cleaning around the house. Tokyo University has also developed a robot which can walk up the stairs unaided – an amazing feat of balancing technology. However, don't hold your breath waiting, they are unlikely to be ready for retail purchase in the next few years. In between the heavy and light end of the market are a wide variety of applications. These include remote-controlled robots such as those used to deal with terrorist bomb threats, automatic vehicles such as those found moving stores from one part of a factory to another, medical applications such as artificial limbs, robots able to perform hip replacements, educational robots and many others.

Robot technology revealed

At the heart of most of these **robotics-based systems** is usually one or more dedicated **microprocessor-based** **computer control systems** as explained in great detail in chapter 8, but for the purposes of this chapter, the main sub-systems of a robot can be thought of as follows:

- Systems of movement
- Sensors
- Control systems
- Interfacing.

Systems of movement

Most **robot arms** have associated with them what are called **degrees of freedom**. This is simply the name given to each **axis of movement**. One common system uses six degrees of freedom (ways of moving) as shown in figure 7.19. The movements of each axis may be controlled by **electric motors**, **hydraulics** (oil-based systems), or **pneumatics** (air-based systems). Whichever system of movement is used, the movements can be initiated by sending the correct digital information from the command computer to the interfacing electronic systems.

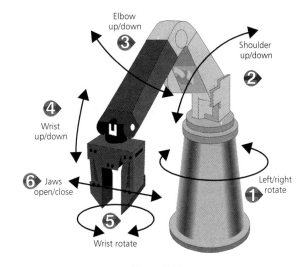

Figure 7.19

Robots may operate in what is called **open loop mode** or, more likely, **closed loop mode** (see chapter 8 section on **feedback**). This is simply the way in which the **feedback systems** that control the system of movements operate. If, for example, the robot is working in open loop mode, then no check is made on the actual position of its arms. Let's suppose that the computer instructs the robot's wrist to move to the 3D-coordinate (234, 076, 512), then it will assume that after the execution of this command and a suitable time delay the wrist will take up this new position – irrespective of what actually happens, e.g. something may be in the way and the arm could be physically obstructed. When in **closed loop mode**, a system of **feedback** *is* used. This involves **sensors** (see in a moment) being placed at strategic points on the robot, which then feed back electrical signals to the computer which indicate the exact position of the robot. These signals are usually compared with the desired position and the computer takes action, until the desired and actual positions of the robot are the same, otherwise an error condition is **flagged** indicating that it's not possible to obey this particular command. Other sensors can also stop the robot if they detect that something is wrong such as an object being in the way. This is the technique that is used, for example, when robots move goods around on the factory floor. Feedback sensors would sense if the robot has bumped into anything and, if a collision is detected, the systems will be shut down and an alarm may ring.

Sensors

Much of what a robot can do depends not only on its ability to move efficiently, but also on its ability to sense the environment. Sensors may range from a simple microswitch that can be activated if the robot bumps into something, to complex sound and vision analysis undertaken in conjunction with powerful mainframe computers. Many different types of sensors are covered in chapter 8, but here we will take a very brief look at some of the ways in which a robot can simulate the human senses. You must also not forget that robots fitted with appropriate sensors can have more than the five (six?) human senses, because quantities such as *magnetism*, *radiation* and many others can be sensed by appropriate electronic devices.

Touch

There are electrical components called **strain gauges** which can respond to small changes in pressure – actually they respond to bending, and hence to a change in shape, but the result is nevertheless the same. The resistance of a strain gauge changes when pressure is applied to it. This 'resistance change' can be converted into an analogue voltage and fed via an **A to D converter** (see chapter 8) before being analysed by a digital computer. Sensitivities of these systems are such that

Figure 7.20

they may deal with weights of just a few grams or many tonnes.

If the robot has many sensors such as those described above, then it can perform quite delicate operations without damaging fragile components – it's possible, for example, for a robot to pick up an egg without cracking it. Indeed one of the more amusing applications of robotics is the automatic sheep-shearing machine developed at the University of Western Australia. Touch sensors prevent the sheep from having too close a shave! – this remarkable device is shown in figure 7.20.

Sight

The ability to see is one of the greatest assets possessed by a human being, and although it is relatively easy to make a **robot see** (i.e. connect a **video camera** to it), it

---

Did you know that . . .

It is not surprising that much of the work in robotics is derived from mimicking nature. There are many feedback mechanisms in the human body, similar to those described here for robots. Man learns much from nature. The coming together of technology and biology to form biotechnology will ensure that this continues to be so.

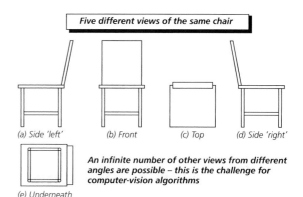

Five different views of the same chair

(a) Side 'left'   (b) Front   (c) Top   (d) Side 'right'

(e) Underneath

An infinite number of other views from different angles are possible – this is the challenge for computer-vision algorithms

Figure 7.21

is the **analysis of the complex images** produced that is *the* major stumbling block. **A simple example will demonstrate just some of the problems involved.** Let's assume that the robot observes a simple 'chair' as shown by the first view in figure 7.21(a).

Programming the computer to recognise the image in figure 7.21(a) is reasonably simple. It should be well within your grasp, for example. However, even the *same chair* can present an infinite variety of different shapes to the camera! Different possibilities are shown in figures 7.21(b) to 7.21(e). There are, however, an infinite number of different viewing positions – add to this the fact that an infinite number of different backgrounds are also possible, and you should now start to see the enormity of the task facing the image-analysis software.

At present it *is* possible for **mainframe computers** to do simple versions of such image analysis, but it will be some time before enough computing power and speed can be packed into a micro, even when more efficient algorithms become available. The 64-bit micros now available would be a minimum requirement, and even these would have to be paralleled up with other processors to perform the complex analysis. Therefore at present, we must be content with a different perception of what is meant by 'robot vision', and be content with the robot detecting movement, colour and easy shapes or shapes from familiar angles, i.e. simple pattern recognition compared to human visual analysis. Nevertheless, these pattern-recognition robots have been developed with some success, and are able to sort out different-shaped objects on a production line – and **neural-network technology** (see chapter 9) is also bearing fruit.

It does not need too much of an advance for pattern recognition software to have very many commercial applications. Reading typed or hand-written text, the ability to analyse weather patterns from satellite pictures, analysis of radar and sonar patterns in the military, or detection of cancerous cells under a microscope are but a few of the good examples of commercially-lucrative markets which are being used now.

Speech

Speech can be divided into two sections. First, the **production of speech** and, second, the infinitely more complex task of **interpreting human speech** to initiate some desired course of action. More information on computer speech can be found in the input and output peripherals chapters 10 and 11, and in chapter 6 which describes how modern speech input to computer applications is coming of age.

Speech production

Speech production can itself be divided into subsections, according to whether the human voice has been recorded in any form for the computer to use, or

whether a speech sound has been generated by using digital patterns within the computer. The first method involves digitising a **pre-recorded human voice**, and storing the sound as a digital pattern within the computer. Using this method the vocabulary is limited to the number of pre-recorded words. The second method is more flexible, and relies on what are called **phonemes**. This is simply the name given to all the sounds that go to make up a particular language. Any word can be built up by joining the phonemes together. However, the speech does sound slightly unusual if this method is used, and much progress still needs to be made if we are to get away from the awful sounding and obviously artificial machine-generated voice.

Another problem with computer speech is the way in which the words are used – without the natural feeling that would be put into them when spoken by a human. The robot's speech tends to be a little monotonous – the feelings of frustration, excitement and nervousness, for example, all add to our experience of what speech ought to be like in different situations.

Speech recognition

Speech recognition suffers from similar (but far easier to solve) problems to those of robot vision. The problems here are the endless **variety of sounds** that can be produced by different people even when speaking the same word. Also, *the same word spoken by the same person may not sound the same* – for example, they may have a cold. However, these variations do not present an insurmountable problem, and much work has gone into computer analysis of the spoken word with a reasonable degree of success.

> **Hint:** Very good speech-recognition packages can now be purchased for just a few tens of pounds. Look at these systems in the business applications chapter.

Most systems have to 'learn' the words that may be said before being used in earnest. This usually involves the people who are going to speak to the system sitting down with the computer and speaking the words into the machine. Each word is usually spoken several times and a mathematical model of each word is then stored inside the computer's memory.

When the computer is ready to be used, after the word has been spoken, it will compare the mathematical analysis of the spoken word with the models that it has inside its memory. When the best match has been found (determined by the closest correlation), then the computer will choose the word that it 'thinks' you have said.

There are major problems still to be overcome – for example, there are many words that sound very similar. For instance dog, fog and log etc. will be very difficult to distinguish using these techniques – these problems will obviously not be solved until they can be combined with powerful real-time context-sensitive grammatical analysis of the spoken word – at the present rate of progress this is not too far off! Indeed, great progress has been made in this area and context sensitive speech analysis systems are now available with an acceptable speed of operation for some applications, and experts in using such a system can often achieve near-normal speech speeds.

Smell

Smell, in a limited sense, *is* being used by robots in industry today. These applications are usually connected with the detection of gas leaks, and indeed robots are boldly going where no robot has gone before, in an attempt to sniff out leaks in hostile environments. Special sensors are all that are needed, but **real-time chemical analysis**, needed for more advanced smell-type systems is not yet possible. Nevertheless, chemical analysis by smell is being applied with great effect in some applications.

Taste

There are four basic types of taste – namely **sweet**, **sour**, **salt** and **acidity**. Sensors for some of these are easier to deal with, but, a technique currently under development, uses what are called biosensors. At Imperial College London, a course has been given by bio-technologists that introduced the ideas that computers can taste and smell. Indeed, this is not so far fetched as it may seem. For example, salt can be measured by electrical conductivity, and acidity can be easily measured using a pH meter. In several years time we may see robots developed to give their opinion of the Beaujolais nouveau, and computers *are* already being used to determine the quality of various Champagnes.

Other sensing devices

There are many other sensing devices which can be connected to robots to detect heat, magnetic fields, radiation, ionisation etc. When the technology has been developed over the next few decades, the robots will be able to detect many more changes in their environments than an unaided human can.

Control systems

At the heart of any robot system is the computer which is used to control it, and the specialised interfaces that are used to connect the robot with the ports on the computer. However, these important concepts are covered separately in chapter 8 when computer control is considered in detail.

Nano technology

No section on robots would be complete without a brief mention of **nano technology**. Nano technology derives its name from the fact that devices are built up on a **nano-meter scale i.e. 1×10^{-9} m**! Unbelievable though it may sound, small devices, including motors and gears have been designed and developed at this very small scale. This opens up possibilities for sending robots inside restricted areas such as the human body. For example, imagine a robot which is able to move along inside your veins and cut away the cholesterol! Such robots are indeed being developed, although there are many problems, most noticeably, and not surprisingly, with the materials. For example, in 1994, the nano-technology gear wheels were so small that they wore out in a matter of seconds!

If and when advances in nano technology can be made, then much invasive surgery may become a thing of the past – computer controlled robots might be able to be injected into the blood stream and carry out various operations. Other applications for this technology are also just as astounding.

Computer simulations

It's unlikely that many students of advanced computing have reached this level without dabbling in the odd computer simulation or game. However, games have much more in common with computer simulation software than you might think – the only real difference being that establishments like the military, the Met Office and large companies have more to spend on their toys than most of us do at home (see Plates 13 and 14)! A classic example would be Microsoft's Flight Simulator 98. This realistic flight-simulation program is good enough for initial pilot training, but obviously can't be compared with a real flight simulator, like those made by the Redifussion company for Jumbo Jets, which retail for tens of millions of pounds.

Simulations fall into several categories. The first is hardware and software pretending to be something else, like the aircraft simulator and computer games mentioned above. The second category is actual simulations run to predict the behaviour of a particular thing being studied, e.g. forecasting the weather at the Met Office, where lucky scientists have some of the fastest computers in the world to play with. Therefore, it is to this scientific application which we now turn to get a true taste of high-end computer power.

Forecasting the weather

It is one of the functions of the Met Office at Bracknell to gather appropriate information to enable them to forecast the weather and, more recently, to enable them to predict possible changes in the global climate. Over the years, as the computer systems have become more powerful and general meteorological knowledge has grown, it's been possible to increase the accuracy of these forecasts by some considerable margins. Regular customers like the military, local authorities and media companies like the BBC, rely heavily on the Met to provide information relatively quickly and with the best possible accuracy achievable given today's technology. This magnificent achievement can easily be appreciated if you are able to understand just some of the processes that have to be carried out to generate the forecast. We now take a brief look at some of the computer-science features that help the Met Office and other similar institutions to undertake this gargantuan task.

Gathering information

Much observational information such as temperature and humidity etc. is deduced from satellite readings by monitoring the infrared, visible and microwave radiation emitted from the surface of the sea and at various points in the atmosphere from sea level to high altitudes. This information, gathered from satellites such as NOAA (the National Oceanic and Atmospheric Administration) is then used, together with other information from more conventional weather stations, weather balloons and aircraft, to provide billions of readings which cover the entire globe. These readings can then be sent to the Met Office computer systems via computer networks. Indeed, over the last few years the Met Office at Bracknell has been developing its own high-speed computer networks, which link it to other players in the global meteorological market. Bracknell now forms an integral part of both the European and global telecommunication systems for very-high speed transfer of meteorological data over dedicated computer networks.

The mathematical models

There is a huge amount of physics behind predicting the weather, and topics such as 'gravity wave drag', 'convective cloud and precipitation' and 'surface and sub-surface processes' give a clue to the enormous scientific complexity underlying the **Unified Model** which has been developed over the years. The **Unified Model** is a *very* **complex numerical model**, which means that vast numbers of complex interrelated equations are used to model both the physical and dynamic aspects of the weather. When these models are run by the supercomputer systems housed in the Met Office, they can predict what the short-term weather is likely to be with a resolution of just a few kilometres. At the other end of

the scale the Unified Model can predict what the global weather is likely to be up to about one month ahead.

If you are studying 'A' level mathematics or its equivalent, you will probably undertake some simple numerical analysis of your own. For example, finding the roots of an equation by making use of the Newton-Raphson method, perhaps with a spreadsheet or a programming language like BASIC. Let's suppose that you wanted the roots of your equation to ten decimal places – it might take your powerful Pentium processor a long time to find them, especially if the algorithms which you have written for the task are not the most efficient. Now multiply the complexity of what you are attempting to do in your maths courses by a factor of several billion, and you will have just a small inkling of the task that the Met Office routinely does in just a few hours!

One of the methods used in the Unified Model is that of finite differences (see the Fortran 90 code in the next section). This is a scheme whereby geographical areas are split up into smaller parts, and the calculation of a particular parameter is obtained by observing and processing the parameters of adjacent data points (i.e. the points to the north, south, east and west). In this way pictures can gradually be built up as the evaluation of the equations progresses. At the edge of the chosen area the model will have to interact with other areas which are undergoing a similar analysis, and it's this exchange of data which makes the system a lot more complex to manage. However, the globe is obviously far too big an area to be processed in one go, even by the latest generation of supercomputers.

The computer systems

Both hardware and software play an important role in the construction of such a complex numerical model used in the simulation of atmospheric conditions. The hardware has improved considerably over the years, and at the time of writing the Met Office is changing over to the Cray T3E supercomputer briefly covered in the next section. The **Unified Model** was originally programmed using **Fortran 77**, but is being ported over to **Fortan 90** to make extra use of the new facilities of this language such as support for parallel processing (see chapter 20).

> ### Did you know that . . .
>
> In 1959 the original Met Office computer system could do just 3,000 calculations per second. Compare this with the 400,000,000,000 calculations that their 1998 computer system can do!

> ### Did you know that . . .
>
> In 1959 the amount of main memory in the Met Office computer was just 1k! Compare this with a typical micro, which you may have at home, which probably has at least 128,000 times the memory capacity of the original Met Office computer!

As stated in the last section, it would take a powerful Pentium processor several minutes or more to work out the answers to just one typical equation. Clearly then, the processor at the Met Office must be a little more powerful. Indeed, the **latest Cray T3E massively parallel supercomputer** installed in 1997 contains between **600 and 700 powerful Dec 21164 Alpha (RISC) processors** all able to operate in co-operation with each other. This has a *theoretical* peak performance of about **400 Gflops**, which means that it's able to carry out **400,000,000,000 floating point calculations** (see chapter 31) per second. Due to limitations of memory access speeds and inter-processor co-operation, the actual throughput is less than this limit, but this is impressive none the less. To further enable you to understand this massive processing power, an individual Dec Alpha 21164 RISC chip is capable of carrying out 600 million calculations per second. And this is just one processor, which could easily run the most expensive workstations capable of carrying out the complex CAD/CAM work described earlier in this chapter. However, should you need something a little faster, try **the 2.5 Tflop Cray T3E 1200 series super-computer.**

The Cray T3E is a scalable-shared-memory multi-processor computer. Although the shared-memory system (as opposed to the dedicated memory systems making using of the vector processor – see chapter 20) is less efficient, the overall system performance is much more cost effective from the Met Office's point of view. This is very evident when compared to the older super-computers that did not operate on the massive parallel processing principle.

The Cray T3E provides shared memory for up to a maximum of 2048 processors in the shape of a 3D torus. Part of this system can be visualised as a large molecular structure as shown in figure 7.22(a). Each of the theoretical maximum of 2048 processors forms what's called a **node** in the system. *Each node* consists of a **Dec Alpha 21164 processor, a system control chip**, from **64MB to 2GB of local memory**, and a **network router** which provides a raw bandwidth of 600MB/sec in each direction – wow! Each of the possible 2048 nodes can be visualised diagrammatically as shown in figure 7.22(b).

You may be surprised to find that the control logic goes only at 75 MHz, compared with similar systems going at 66 MHz in your PC, and the Dec Alpha processor is going between 300 MHz and 400 MHz compared to the 400 MHz Pentium Pro in top-of-the-range PCs. However, this is where the comparison ends! The bus bandwidth is very much larger. The Pentium is a 32-bit processor and the Alpha is a 64-bit processor (this can process twice as much data for the same clock rate), and the Alpha has a 128-bit internal data bus. However, the real difference in speed stems from the fact that there are so many processors all going at the same time, and from the architecture and software capabilities of such systems in general.

The memory transfer rate between the control chip, the local RAM and the Dec Alpha chip is 1.2GB/sec. The Met Office has between 600 and 700 of these nodes as stated in the initial specification for the Bracknell-based T3E.

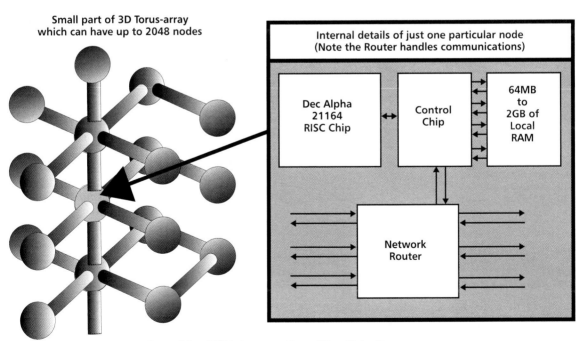

Small part of 3D Torus-array which can have up to 2048 nodes

Internal details of just one particular node
(Note the Router handles communications)

Dec Alpha 21164 RISC Chip

Control Chip

64MB to 2GB of Local RAM

Network Router

Part of Cray T3E interconnection of Dec Alpha Processors

(a)

(b)

Figure 7.22

```
COURTESY OF CRAY RESEARCH LTD
SUBROUTINE FDTD(CAEX,CBEX,CAEY,CBEY,CAEZ,CBEZ,EX,EY,EZ,HX,HY,HZ
REAL CAEX, CBEX, CAEY, CBEY, CAEZ, CBEZ
REAL EX(129,129,128), EY(129,129,128), EZ(129,129,128)
REAL HX(129,129,128), HY(129,129,128), HZ(129,129,128)
        DO J   2, 127
                DO I = 2, 127
                    DO K = 2, 127
                            EX(K,I,J) =   CAEX-(EX(K,I,J) +
&                           CBEX-(HZ(K,I,J) -   HZ(K,I,J-1) +
&                           HY(K,I,J) -   HY(K-1,I,J)))
                            EY(K,I,J) =   CAEY-(EY(K,I,J) +
&                           CBEY-(HX(K-1,I,J)   - HX(K,I,J) +
&                           HZ(K,I-1,J)   - HZ(K,I,J)))
                            EZ(K,I,J) =   CAEZ-(EZ(K,I,J) +
&                           CBEZ-(HX(K,I,J-1)   - HX(K,I,J) +
&                           HY(K,I,J) -   HY(K,I-1,J)))
                    END DO
                END DO
        END   DO
RETURN
END
```

Figure 7.23

Special routines written in **Fortran 90** (see chapter 13) can set the sizes of arrays to be calculated to the exact internal architectures of the system by carefully dimensioning the arrays (see chapter 24) to match the exact size of the system's various cache (see chapter 12) elements.

The Fortran 90-program segment in figure 7.23 shows typically how a small part of a finite-difference application might be coded.

> **Hint:** You should be able to work out how many calculations are needed in the small section of the program shown here. If you can't work it out now, wait until you have read chapter 12, then try again.

Try running the above program on your top-of-the-range Pentium machine at home! This is, of course, assuming that you have enough time to set up the data in the arrays, that your computer has enough memory to hold this data, and you have enough time to wait while it is doing it (see **Plate 15**).

Hurricane forecasting

It is fortunate that we don't get too many hurricanes in the UK. However, in countries less fortunate from this point of view, like the USA, similar Cray Super-computers are constantly predicting the progress of hurricanes around the globe. For example, the Geophysical Fluid Dynamics Laboratory at Princeton, New Jersey, also has a Cray T3E supercomputer on which they predict the paths of hurricanes. Large hurricanes, often containing up to a million cubic miles of the atmosphere present the forecasters with an overwhelming amount of data. Only the best of the current range of super-computers are able to analyse this mass of data in a sensible amount of time.

If you are wondering why hundreds of millions of pounds are spent on such a complex analysis procedure, it's estimated that in some parts of the USA it costs $640,000 dollars per square mile to evacuate the citizens, and hurricanes can affect hundreds of square miles of territory. If the path of a hurricane can be predicted more accurately, then smaller areas need to be evacuated, with consequent massive savings in cost. Viewed in this light, the millions of pounds spent on the huge computer systems seem money well spent.

El Nino

Few students won't have heard of El Nino, the phenomenon which starts in the Pacific Ocean but which seems to affect the whole world. 'El Nino' is Spanish for 'The Child', and was so named because the early fishermen of the South Pacific noticed that the El Nino effect often arrived around Christmas time, thus corresponding with the birthday of Christ.

Many millions of pounds have been poured into investigating this effect, and, thanks largely to complex mathematical models and powerful supercomputers, the phenomenon is now starting to be understood. One of the key elements in the analysis of this effect is the use of supercomputers to analyse sea-surface temperatures around the globe, especially in the South Pacific Ocean. The National Oceanic and Atmospheric

Administration (NOAA) has established a research institute, which is dedicated to providing early warnings of the effects of El Nino. In 1997 El Nino produced droughts in Africa, Australia and Indonesia, as well as drastically affecting the fish populations in the South Pacific.

Supercomputers around the world are starting to correlate information using various models set up in different parts of the world. Hence, hurricane forecasters in the USA will use some of the results from the El Nino project's computers to feed into their own numerical models. This will enable them to predict the effects of hurricanes more accurately.

As you can see from the above, computer simulations can provide the vital information needed to produce the desired predictions in climatic changes. Being forewarned of potential catastrophes can help to save many lives and much money.

Computer games

This is a topic with which many users of computers will be familiar! As the graphical and sound processing ability of computers becomes even greater, and the interactivity over the Internet becomes easier and faster, this means that it's now possible to play interactive games with friends or even with people who you never see. These games, usually of the shoot-em-up variety enable people or teams of people to interact strategically with each other and 'blast the hell' out of the opposition. It's great fun, but can be addictive, and the phone bills can get astronomic if you are playing on line for a few hours at a time.

Did you know that . . .

In 1997, a quarter of the profits made by the massive Sony Corporation were derived from the Play Station, a computer-games console.

The thousands of games available pays testament to the success of this industry, and the amount of hardware which can be added onto the computer for greater realism is now quite remarkable. Force feedback joysticks, flight yokes, racing car cabins, whole fighter-aircraft cockpits, virtual reality helmets, body suits and data gloves have all been used with great effect in the computer gaming industry. Dedicated embedded microprocessor systems of the Sega and Nintendo variety, along with the specialist arcade machines all have a part to play in computer gaming. The arcade machines usually have the upper hand with regard to realism and speed, followed by the dedicated microprocessor systems. However, the PCs don't lag far behind, and arcade games of today are usually the PC games of tomorrow.

To get a PC to respond in real time on the latest games front usually requires the fastest domestic processors such as the Pentium III 550 MHz or more, a graphics card with about 12 Mbytes of RAM, and about 128 Mbytes of RAM. Even so, a specification such as this, common in the late 1990s will be far superseded in the next few years. When this happens, the realism of games will approach even greater heights, and the ingenuity of the games programmers will be pushed to new limits.

Did you know that . . .

One of Liverpool Football club's goalkeepers let in three goals during a particular match. He blamed his poor performance on a hard night of computer gaming!

To find out what's happening on the game front, one has only to look at the latest batch of CD-ROMs on the magazines which specialise in PC games. Also, there are many sites on the Internet which are dedicated to computer games, and Internet newsgroups too numerous to mention.

You are expected to know about computer games, and their impact on society. There's no better way to find out than to play a few. However, be careful when installing some of the games. They do have a reputation for altering important settings on the computers, and this is why they are rarely allowed in a complex network environment in a school or college.

Exercise 7.1

1   Outline the difference between a pixel-based art package and an object-oriented CAD package.

2   Make a list of five different features that you would expect to find in a typical CAD package.

3   Make a list of five features that you would expect to find in a pixel-based art package.

4   When would it be more prudent to use a pencil and paper instead of a CAD package?

5   Outline the advantages that CAD/CAM techniques have over manual production methods. Many parts of the world still don't make use of CAD/CAM techniques. Why might it be more efficient for these countries to carry on as they are?

6   What is CNC and why have these machines become more popular in industry?

7   By using the game of chess, outline the difference between a robot with feedback and a robot without feedback moving pieces on a standard chessboard. What sensors might be useful in helping the robot with feedback to move the pieces more effectively?

8   What is meant by ray tracing and rendering?

9   Briefly outline some problems which might arise in getting a computer system to carry out the following human-type activities:

    a   Hearing

    b   Seeing

    c   Smelling

    d   Touching

    d   Tasting.

10 Why are very powerful computers needed to forecast the weather?

11 Choose one of the latest computer games and comment on its playability, its addictiveness, and the need for powerful hardware systems.

End of chapter revision aid and summary

Cover up the right-hand column and see if you can answer the questions or define the terms on the left. They appear in the order in which they are covered in this chapter. Alternatively you may browse through the right-hand column to aid revision.

What is CAD?	CAD is the acronym for Computer Aided Design. It is the use of computers to help with the design stages of a product. The object-oriented or vector-based packages are used for technical drawings and engineering, and the pixel-based art packages are used for helping with graphic art.
What is an object-oriented package?	Object-oriented package – one in which the objects (parts of the drawing) are represented by mathematical equations.
What is a pixel-based package?	Pixel-based package – one in which parts of the drawing are made up from tiny dots called pixels.
Name some advantages of CAD over hand-drafted drawings.	Advantages of CAD – the ability to edit very easily, to make use of library drawings, to communicate the drawing electronically over the net, to merge existing pictures, to use clip art etc.
Why is fast hardware needed for a good CAD package?	CAD is a mathematically intensive program, and therefore fast processors are needed to accomplish the tasks in a sensible amount of time.
What is a parametric CAD package?	Parametric CAD package – one in which parameters, such as lengths and angles etc. can be varied as the program is being run. It's useful for technical animations of the sort needed by engineers.

What is CNC?	Computer Numeric Control – the control of machines from codes generated by a special computer program.
Why are CAD and CAM usually integrated?	Integration of CAD and CAM – enables the designs from the CAD packages to generate the data needed to operate the machines in the factory and help with the ordering and pricing of goods etc.
What are the advantages of CAM?	Advantages of CAM – cheap automated production for large volumes. Also, it can do repetitive work, 24 hours a day, and the quality control is excellent.
Name some advantages of 3D CAD.	Advantages of 3D CAD – some packages are able to render objects under different lighting conditions. You can thus simulate realistic looking 3D images with surface textures and other added realism.
Outline some of the basic tools which you would expect to be available in a pixel-based art package.	A pixel-based art package should have access to a large range of brushes and pens, the shape and type of which are customisable. There should be a huge range of fill effects, ways to choose one of the 16.7 million colours available, and the ability to mask off parts of the image to name just a few.
Outline one or two of the advanced tools you might expect in a pixel-based art package.	Some of the more advanced facilities available on a pixel-based art package could be tools to distort the image into a variety of shapes, both 2D and 3D. The ability to generate autostereograms, or special effects which can be applied with a camera lens such as 'swirls' and 'star bursts', for example.
Briefly describe some of the 3D effects which might be used in the movie industry.	High-end 3D art packages are now finding their way into the movie production business. By using techniques such as wire-frame construction and surface rendering, it's possible to create your own characters, aliens, robots, or special effects, without having to build up the models and video them. Such effects can be seen in films such as Toy Story and Titanic.
What is morphing?	Morphing – the use of a computer program to gradually change one image into another such that it looks like an actual metamorphosis is taking place.
What is industrial robotics?	Industrial robotics is the use of specialised robots in the manufacture of goods or for working in dangerous environments etc.
What sensors are available to robots?	All the human senses are available to robots, plus many others defined by the available sensors.
What is a transducer?	Transducer – a device for changing some physical quantity such as light, heat or sound, for example, into an electrical signal which can be processed ready for input to a computer system.
What is a simulation?	Simulation – a computer pretending to be something else, or mathematically modelling events such as the weather, for example.
What types of computers are required to model the weather?	A powerful computer such as a Cray supercomputer and some highly complex mathematical models such as the Unified Model are used by the Met Office.
Comment on the hardware needed to play the latest computer games.	Top of the range PCs are needed to play the latest games if a quick response time is needed. As games get more sophisticated, lots of memory and a powerful graphics card are necessary requirements.

8 Real-time and Engineering Applications

Key resources

To carry out this work most successfully it's best if you have:

- Access to an interface box for your computer
- A range of input and output sensors which can be connected to your computer interface
- Control software for the interface
- Don't forget the **glossary** at the back of this book. It should be very helpful to explain some concepts with which you may not be familiar

Concept checkpoints

- The role played by the operating system (see chapter 22).
- Concepts of data transmission (see chapter 3).
- Electrical signals representing binary digits (see chapter 2).
- Flowcharts (see chapter 14).
- Have a simple awareness of sensors and other transducers used in physics and engineering (e.g. bulbs and motors etc.).

Introduction

Control is a vast area of computing. It ranges in size from the small microprocessors embedded inside modern electronic equipment such as video recorders, via control of complex lighting rigs such as those found in some theatres, to the control of entire industrial plants such as those found in the chemical industry. **In fact, a computer can in turn control virtually any process that can be controlled by a machine. This is due to the enormous variety of sensors available which convert physical quantities into electrical signals, and the huge variety of control equipment and actuators such as relays and valves etc., which can be used to switch external devices on and off, or cause things to move.** In these systems it is the computer or microprocessor which acts as the decision-making element under the guidance of a set of instructions or program which controls the process. There is much to be considered here in terms of the sensors, feedback systems and interfaces, but one should not forget the important role played by the operating systems (see chapter 22) when computers are used in control. Real-time operating systems will therefore be considered in detail later in this chapter.

Some basic ideas

We start by considering the humble micro as a vehicle for our first examples. The concepts of control are very similar irrespective of whether a microprocessor, microcomputer, mini or a mainframe is controlling the process.

To **interface** with the outside world, wires (or fibre-optics, radio or infrared connections etc.) must be brought out from the computer system to connect to an external device. One can easily appreciate this concept by reflecting on the fact that printers or keyboards, for example, are devices, which are external to the main parts of a computer system. However, here we are thinking more in terms of devices such as **motors** and **solenoid valves** which could be used to switch the flow of a fluid on or off, **light bulbs**, **magnetic door locks** or **heating elements** etc. All these are examples of output devices, as the computer is controlling what happens to them. For example, is the motor going round or not? If it's rotating then is it going backwards or forwards? Is the heater element switched on or off? Is the door open or closed? More correctly, these devices are referred to as **transducers**, or more specifically **output transducers**.

Transducers

A **transducer** is the name given to any device that *converts energy from one form into another*. Therefore, a motor is an example of an output transducer, which converts electrical energy into rotary motion. A light bulb would be an example of an output transducer, which converts electrical energy into light.

Input transducers are equally important, for without them the computer system would have no idea of what is actually going on. These input transducers are the 'eyes' and 'ears' of the computer system, and typical examples would be **heat sensors** which convert temperature into an electrical signal, or **alternators** and **generators** which convert rotary motion into electrical signals.

Interfacing

Signals from the **input transducers** *must be converted into a form* that the **computer** can understand. Similarly, **signals from the computer** *must be converted into a form* suitable for driving (operating) any particular **output transducer**. Occasionally the signals coming from or going into the computer are compatible with the transducers, but most often it is necessary to have extra electronic circuits which perform the necessary conversions. These **electronic circuits** are called **interfaces**.

Some interfaces, such as those necessary to drive printers, for example, are usually incorporated into the main computer system itself, as most people require a printer on their system. One typical standard for printers is the centronics parallel port, but most computers also have other ports (see in a moment), such as the RS 232 or RS 423 serial ports, which can be used to interface many devices such as MODEMS and Data Loggers, for example. However, if we wish to drive any trans-

ducer or receive any signal from a variety of sensors, then a special interface of a more-general nature is usually needed (see later).

You should already appreciate that signals inside the computer are in **binary form** – where a 'zero' represents a signal being 'off' and a 'one' represents a signal being 'on'. Many computers work with 5V representing 'on' and 0V representing 'off'. Therefore, if you were to connect a voltmeter between two appropriate points at the back of your computer, you could observe whether a signal is 'on' or 'off' by measuring the voltage between the appropriate output pin and the GND (Ground or Earth) line inside the computer. These simple ideas are shown in figure 8.1(a), and form the basis of many control system principles.

Did you know that . . .

You could use the printer port on the computer, via a suitable interface, to control robots and other devices. All you need to do is map out the ASCII codes to make sure that the pins on the printer port are in the right state to switch things on and off. The author had to do this once when he ran out of lines to control a robot, which poured out drinks!

You will need special software to control whether a particular pin is on (high) or off (low), and this software aspect of interfacing will be considered later on in this

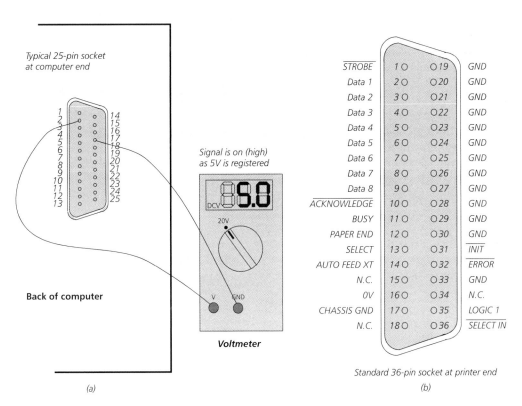

Figure 8.1

chapter. For the moment we will assume that we can simply switch the appropriate signals on and off at will.

Computer ports

A **port** is the name given to the place on the periphery of the computer system where you can extract signals from the computer or put signals into the computer. Consider, for a moment, the centronics parallel port mentioned above. In practice, all you will probably see at the back of your computer is a 25-pin socket into which you could put a plug from the device being controlled (i.e. it's the place where you would plug in a standard printer). Inside this socket are tiny pins, which represent the places where the signals come into or go out from the computer system. Observant students will probably notice that the plug, which goes into the printer itself, is usually bigger – on most systems it has 36 pins! Obviously, most parallel printer ports at the back of microcomputers do not use the full compliment of facilities that are available at the printer end. All the pins at the printer end are shown in figure 8.1(b).

Thirty-six pins are quite a lot, but fortunately, for our purposes, many of them can be ignored. However, the thing to note is that there are 8 data lines available on pins 2 to 9 inclusive, and a convenient means for connecting the other end (0V or GND) of the signal or signals. In fact these 8 data lines correspond to an 8-bit data bus along which the ASCII characters, for example, could be sent to the printer. Being a specialist printer interface, control signals such as 'select' on pin 13, for example, tell the computer that the printer is on-line and ready to go.

At the computer end, the eight data lines are available at pins 2 to 9 inclusive, and pins 17 to 25 provide the 0V or GND connections. If your computer has this interface then inside the computer special electronics generate the appropriate signals, and inside the printer appropriate electronics receive the signals. Therefore, to control a standard printer involves connecting up an appropriate lead making sure that the connections go to the correct places at each end. The manufacturers of the computer and printer systems have already done all the hard work of interfacing for you at both ends. Inside your computer it would be the job of a special piece of **software** called a **printer driver** to drive the appropriate printer when it is connected to your computer system. However, *there is no reason why you could not use these outputs to control devices other than printers if you so wished* – assuming that you have the appropriate interface electronics connected between the centronics port and your own devices.

The whole point of going through the above scenario is to show you that most computer's are already acting as control systems. Therefore, it's a simple and logical extension to consider other interfaces which operate on very similar principles, but do a very different range of jobs.

Other types of interface

External disk drives, audio inputs and outputs, video inputs and outputs and a variety of other devices all need to be plugged into computer systems for various purposes. Therefore, a variety of special interfaces has been designed to cope with the variety of different specifications. For example, **SCSI** (Small Computer-Systems Interface), **SCSI 2**, **IDE** (Integrated Drive Electronics), **IDE II** and **USB** (Universal Serial Bus) interfaces are typical of the types of port needed to connect many devices such as disk drives and CD ROMs to your computer system. However, special **general-purpose interfaces** designed to enable the **user** to interface almost any device to the computer are also available. After dealing with serial and parallel communications, *it is these general-purpose types of interface that will be considered for the rest of this chapter.*

Expansion slots and user ports

Most **special** and **general-purpose interfaces** enable external devices to be connected to the **address bus**, **data bus** and **control bus** of the **CPU** (see chapter 20). Indeed, most modern microcomputer systems enable extra boards (special electronic circuits) called **expansion cards** to be plugged into the system. These electronic circuit boards provide the connections to the appropriate buses inside the computer, *and* provide suitable sockets into which a variety of different external devices can be plugged. The principles are similar to that of the centronics printer interface considered earlier, and many different standards of interface have been designed since the centronics printer port was devised over a couple of decades ago.

Serial and parallel data transmission

As computers become more powerful there is a need to transmit data at ever increasing rates. Therefore, the number of pins on many modern interfaces is considerably in excess of the 36-pin centronics example considered above. 16, 32 and even 64-bit data buses are now common on some types of interface, enabling more data to be sent in parallel at the same time. You should note

Did you know that . . .

As processors get faster and faster, the bottleneck in the computer system is the bus. Most ordinary bus systems at the time of writing transfer data using a 33 MHz-clock rate. If faster speeds are needed, then new motherboards need to be developed, which can cope with the added throughput of data. In mid 1998, these new motherboards with faster bus speeds started to be developed for the mass market and now include 66 and 100 MHz versions.

that the difference between different bus systems *is not trivial* – indeed, it can make or break an entire computer system. If your particular computer system does *not* support a bus system that becomes popular, then most of the wonderful new devices being developed will not be able to be used with your particular micro, a potentially disastrous situation for some computer manufacturers.

Before going on to consider computer control in more detail, it's important to understand the fundamental differences between transmitting data in serial and parallel mode.

If more than one binary digit can be sent *simultaneously* (as was the case with the centronics printer port), then data is said to be sent in **parallel**. The printer port covered earlier can send up to 8 bits in parallel because it has 8 different and independent data lines available at the output. Some of the more-powerful interfaces mentioned in the last section can send 16, 32 or 64 bits in parallel because they have up to 64 data lines available. Up to 128 data lines are not unheard of when considering powerful processors, and more will definitely be used in the future.

It is not always practical to send so many bits at the same time, not least because of the expense involved in needing so many wires simultaneously connected between the computer and the device that the computer is controlling or monitoring. Therefore, an alternative and cheaper method is to send the binary digits, one bit at a time, over a single wire from the source to the destination. This is called **serial transmission of data** and is ideal for long distances, or where single fibre-optic, infrared or radio signals are used. **Parallel data transmission** is used almost exclusively *inside the computer* because of the bus systems, but **serial data transmission** is normally used when the distance between the transmitter and receiver is *greater than a few metres*, or if transmission media such as a standard telephone line is required. From reading the above you should not jump to the conclusion that serial data transmission is always slow – when fibre optics are used, the data transfer rate can be 1000 Mbits/sec – far faster than conventional parallel transmission of data in some practical systems.

Timing and synchronisation

Whenever data is transmitted or received by a computer system it's of paramount importance to get the two devices in **synchronisation** with each other or vital data could be lost or corrupted. Inside the computer this is no problem as the **clock signals** can keep everything in step. (See BORIS in chapter 20.) Even when outside the computer, in the case of the centronics printer port mentioned earlier, the printer itself can signal the computer that it is ready to receive data. If the printer were not switched on, indicated by no signal on the appropriate pin, then it would be silly for the computer to send the data down the wires to the printer or the data would be lost.

From reading the above you should appreciate that some serial links will need extra control lines, and therefore, even when the data itself is sent along just one line, you will often find that several lines are used in the actual connection of a serial port. In fact, the full RS-232 serial standard contains 25 pins!

There are often times when separate wires can send no synchronising information at all, and you are down to a single wire or radio signal, for example. In this case it is necessary to carefully control the **rate** at which the binary digits are sent, and to add some extra information to alert the receiving device that some data is about to arrive. The *rate at which the data is being sent* is the bit rate, and is a measure of the data transmission rate in **bits/sec**. Therefore, if all the bits being sent represent data, then 56,000 Baud would be 7,000 bytes/sec of data being transmitted. This is typical of the figures quoted for serial devices such as Modems, which transmit their information down a telephone wire. Sometimes the data is sent and received at different rates, as is the case with some Internet connections, for example.

Not all bits being sent necessarily represent data. Extra bit patterns called **control bits** are often sent to indicate the **start** *and* **stop points** in a typical group of bits of data. Figure 8.2 shows a typical case in which extra information is sent to help control synchronisation between the serial transmitting and receiving devices.

Note that the start bit is used to 'wake up' the receiving device. In practice this bit would be used to synchronise the clock inside the receiver. The Baud rate at the receiver has been set up to be exactly the same rate as the Baud rate at the transmitter. Therefore, the next 8 bits are clocked into the system and read at exactly the right moments in time so that the levels for each bit are correctly interpreted. After the data has been clocked in at the receiver, the stop bit is used to signify the end of this byte of data. (Note that the **start bit** changed the 'no data transmission' level of the line from *high to low*, but the **stop bit** has ensured that the level *goes back high again* before the next start bit can arrive.) This level then remains high until the next start bit is received which indicates that the next byte of data is whizzing down the line. If the Baud rate of the transmitter and receiver are not set up to be the same, then this method of transmission will obviously fail as all the bits will arrive at the wrong times and be misinterpreted. Many readers will probably be familiar with this situation if you have made extensive use of modems, and garbage is produced when the Baud rates are incorrectly set.

The standard outlined in figure 8.2 is one of those defined in the RS 232 system, and in this case has transmitted the letter 'A' with no parity, one start bit and one stop bit. You will appreciate that if this system is used, then the actual data transfer rate (i.e. bytes/sec) is less than the transmission rate because of the extra

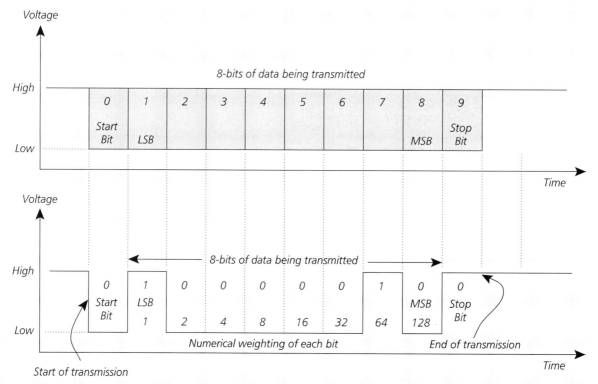

Figure 8.2

Byte of data being sent is 01000001 binary = 65 decimal = ASCII code for 'A'

bits used for the start and stop bits. Therefore, if the transmission rate were set to 56,000 Baud, only 5,600 bytes/sec of data (ASCII code in this case) is actually sent, and not the 7,000 bytes/sec of data that might be incorrectly implied by reading the specification of the system!

Analogue and digital signals

The signals considered so far have all been **digital** – i.e. 'on' or 'off', 'high' or 'low' or '1' or '0'. Nevertheless, many signals, which need to be monitored, are of a very different nature. **Temperature**, **humidity** and **pressure**, for example, are *all* **continuously variable** or **analogue** in nature. A signal, which can vary continuously between two values, is called an **analogue signal**, and a typical example is shown on the left of figure 8.3.

It's currently *impossible* for a computer to deal directly with analogue signals and therefore a **special interface** called an **analogue-to-digital converter (A to D converter)** is required to change the continuously variable analogue signal into a digital form which can be interpreted by the computer (see **Plate 16**). This analogue-to-digital conversion process must take place if the analogue signal is to be transmitted along the communication path and data bus before being stored in the memory of the computer.

Figure 8.3 shows the simple principles of analogue-to-digital conversion. Consider the analogue signal

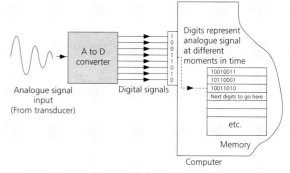

Figure 8.3

shown at the left-hand-side of the diagram. The level (magnitude) of this analogue signal is being measured (sampled) at frequent intervals (see in a moment), converted into an appropriate digital value by the A to D converter, then stored in the computer's memory ready for processing – all this is supposed to be happening in real time.

The **input signal range** needs to be *split up* into a number of *discrete levels*. This process is called **digitisation** or **quantisation**. The number of discrete levels determines the level of **resolution** with which the original analogue signal can be faithfully reproduced or analysed. The idea is shown in figure 8.4(a). With an 8-bit A to D converter, for example, 256 different levels (2^8) are possible. However, with a 16-bit A to D (2^{16}) we can get 65,536 different levels. Although it is

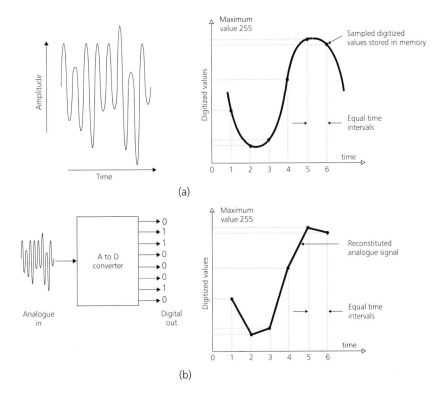

Figure 8.4

possible to get more levels than this, the cost of the 'A to D converter' circuit becomes prohibitively high. If we try to reconstruct the original analogue signal from the stored data, then the result would be as shown in figure 8.4(b). This is not as bad as it looks, because we need not assume that straight lines join the points. On audio systems, for example, the straight-line graph would naturally be smoothed out by the electronics. We could also use other techniques to make the reproduction more like the original if this is regarded as being important in a particular application.

Did you know that . . .

If you own a CD player, you may have been listening to the output from a D to A converter for some time. The digital signals from the audio CD need to be converted into analogue form. This is so that they can be fed into the electronic amplifier which drives the signals to the loudspeakers.

The next thing of importance to note is the **frequency** with which **samples** of the analogue input signal are taken. If this rate is too slow then important events, which might happen to the analogue input signal, could be lost. On the other hand, if this rate is too high, then storing unnecessary bit patterns that give us no extra information will waste much memory. (See compression techniques in a moment.) **Nyquist** developed a system, which states that *the sampling rate must be at least twice as high as the highest frequency component in the signal being investigated.* Therefore, if the input signal varied at a maximum rate of 10KHz, or had important harmonics at this frequency, then a sampling rate of 20,000 samples per second would need to be made.

The audio frequency spectrum for good hi-fi systems is generally regarded to be between 10Hz and 20KHz. It's not surprising, therefore, to find that the A to D converters used inside audio compact disk systems sample at a rate of just above 40KHz – about twice the maximum important frequency in the audio spectrum.

It should be realised that huge amounts of memory can be eaten up when sampling high frequency analogue signals. If, for example, a 16-bit A to D is used, and if the sampling rate is set to 40KHz, then $40\,000 \times 16 \times 60 \times 3 = 115\,200\,000$ bits or 14.4 Mbytes of memory would be needed to store a 3 minute piece of music!

Compression techniques

From reading the above you should be able to appreciate the problems associated with A to D conversion techniques. However, there are methods for reducing this huge memory overhead, which have been used very successfully indeed to compress the huge amount of data generated into more manageable proportions. Consider the signal shown in figure 8.5.

Let's assume that we're going to change this analogue signal into digital values using A to D techniques, and

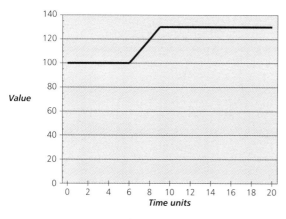

Figure 8.5

the sampling frequency can be determined from the arbitrary time slots shown on the horizontal axis. Now if a sample is taken at each time slot and converted into an 8-bit binary number, then the data shown in figure 8.6 would be generated.

Time slot	Data (Decimal)	Data (Binary)
0.00	100.00	01100100
1.00	100.00	01100100
2.00	100.00	01100100
3.00	100.00	01100100
4.00	100.00	01100100
5.00	100.00	01100100
6.00	100.00	01100100
7.00	110.00	01101110
8.00	120.00	01111000
9.00	130.00	10000010
10.00	130.00	10000010
11.00	130.00	10000010
12.00	130.00	10000010
13.00	130.00	10000010
14.00	130.00	10000010
15.00	130.00	10000010
16.00	130.00	10000010
17.00	130.00	10000010
18.00	130.00	10000010
19.00	130.00	10000010
20.00	130.00	10000010

Figure 8.6

From the list we can see that the 21 readings (0 to 20) are encoded as $21 \times 8 = 168$ bits. Let's now use a different approach. We only need to send data if a change occurs. Therefore, once some specific data has been sent, the receiving end need only be notified if the data has changed. If we were to store this data in RAM or on disk, then an extra number, usually associated with the number of digits that have stayed the same, is stored along with the data. Therefore, 100,500 might be the decimal representation for storing the 'value of 100' 500 times. We have therefore used a much

more efficient storage technique. You will be surprised how similar many readings can be, especially from data logging and monitoring systems mentioned in this chapter.

There are other devices called **D to A converters** which take a digital output from the computer, then convert these digital values into an appropriate analogue voltage. D to A converters are often necessary to control the speed of a d.c. motor, for example, by varying the **magnitude** (an analogue value) of the voltage placed across the motor terminals. D to A converters are necessary to drive a range of **output sensors** (**actuators**) including audio (loudspeakers), varying the light intensity of many types of lamp, and accurate positioning using conventional servo-mechanism control systems.

When a D to A converter has been used it should be understood that, as with A to D converters, the number of bits used determines the resolution of the system. For example, if an 8-bit D to A is used to control the brightness of a bulb, then only 256 different levels of brightness would actually be available. Whether this is important or not depends upon the application. If we are using this to dim lights in a theatre, for example, then working through all values from 255 (representing) full brightness, to 0 (representing off) would convince most people that the brightness of the lamp is being faded very gradually in a smooth way. This is just one of the many reasons why computers are so useful in controlling the light and sound for professional theatre productions.

Sensors (input transducers)

Many quantities which may be measured are **analogue** in nature, and just a small selection of typical sensors which are available might include the following.

Resistance	Voltage	Current	Temperature
Pressure	pH	Light intensity	Sound intensity
Colour	Humidity	Time	Rotational speed
Radiation	Capacitance	Inductance	Magnetic-field strength
Strain	Wind speed	ECG monitor	EEG monitor

Each of these transducers converts the appropriate quantity into an **analogue voltage** which can then be fed into an **A to D converter** so that the **digital values** may in turn be fed into a computer system as shown in figure 8.4.

A study of the physical principles of many of the above transducers is not required by most computer-science courses. However, we will need to know about the range of the output voltage from a particular transducer, and then translate these numbers into appropriate digital values which could then be used to control the display on a computer monitor, or produce an appropriate data file on disk, for example.

An example

Take the case of a typical temperature sensor. This would probably contain an electronic component that is sensitive to temperature, such as a thermistor. Now the resistance of the thermistor changes with temperature, and we will assume for simplicity that extra electronics have been added which ensure that this resistance change produces a linear voltage between defined levels. (A simple chip is available to do this.) Let's assume that '0 volts represents 0 degrees Celsius' and '2.55 volts represents 100 degrees Celsius'. (Unlikely, I know – but it makes the maths easier!) Let's also assume that we have an 8-bit A to D converter. We therefore have 256 different outputs from our A to D, which represent the voltages between 0 and 2.55 inclusive. Therefore, a '00000000 out from the A to D' means a temperature of '0 °C', and '11111111 out from the A to D' means a temperature of '100 °C'. Anything in-between will be represented to the nearest level. Therefore, a reading of 00001111 would represent:

Temperature = 15 / 255 which is approximately 5.9 °C.

Note that we can't quote temperatures between 5.9 °C and 5.5 °C (the nearest output corresponding to 14/255), not because our temperature sensor is not capable of representing this temperature, but because our 8-bit A to D has not got the appropriate **resolution.**

Hint: Don't assume that something is more accurate just because it's digital. It depends solely on how many bits are used to represent the values being encoded. (See chapter 31 where this issue is covered in more detail.)

Note also that it would be silly to quote 5.89 and 5.49 for the temperatures stated above. It is not possible to justify two decimal places with the resolution possible from an 8-bit A to D converter. One final point worthy of note is that **accuracy** is another thing entirely, and this depends upon the accuracy of the original temperature transducer and interfacing electronics (which is making the output linear). See chapter 31 for the definition of the difference between the terms resolution and accuracy.

You will recall that we are using a chip to remove the possible non-linearity of the temperature-sensing device. We could, however, easily get rid of any non-linearity by accepting whatever readings we get from the A to D converter, and then having a look-up table inside the computer which converts the values received into actual temperatures. Indeed, it is the ability of the computer to do this that often makes computerised interfaces considerably cheaper and easier to develop than their pure-electronic counterparts. Any 'bodges' to the readings that are necessary can be catered for in the software!

Transducer control

It is very easy to say that a digital signal can switch an electric motor on and off, but I hope that few students would dream of connecting a d.c. motor across the output terminals of a typical port at the back of any computer! Although the computer *is* supplying the signal to switch on the motor, it obviously can't supply the required current (and hence power) needed by the motor. Therefore, an external power supply (or battery) needs to be used. We effectively use some electronics to interface the low-power output from the computer to the higher-power motor as shown in figure 8.7(a).

Hint: It's far easier than you might think to control devices like motors and bulbs from the computer system. If you have a suitable interface unit, get your teacher to demonstrate how you could control various devices such as motors and bulbs. Some good projects can be done in this area too.

You should note that the system diagram shown in figure 8.7(a) is easy to draw and understand. It is this type of diagram that will be used in preference to the more-practical diagram shown in figure 8.7(b). However, if you wish to actually connect up a system and make it work, then you will have to get used to wiring up the arrangement in a similar way to the practical wiring layout.

Most microcomputer ports designed to enable the user to extract signals from the system are capable of outputting a current of a few mA at about 5 V. However, make use of a transducer driver and you will probably have the capacity to drive transducers such as motors up to 0.5 A or even up to 1 or 2 A if you have a beefy unit. Don't forget to follow the manufacturer's instructions carefully, or if you are building your own, *then make sure that you know what you are doing!*

Feedback

We have seen how signals can be fed into a computer system and stored in the computer's memory, and have also seen how to monitor signals, via an A to D converter if necessary. We can achieve a more-comprehensive control system if we combine *both* the **monitoring** *and* **control functions.** For example, the temperature of a chamber or room could be monitored, and a heater switched on if it is too cold, or a motor-driven fan switched on if it is too hot. It is the role of the computer, or more-specifically the software which controls the computer, to act as the decision-making element in the system.

The system described above makes use of an important control concept called **feedback.** The fan or the heater being controlled by the computer alters the temperature, which, in turn is being monitored by the computer system, which again affects what is happening at the output. The idea is shown in figure 8.8.

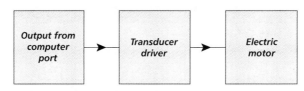

(a) Systems diagram showing the simple concepts

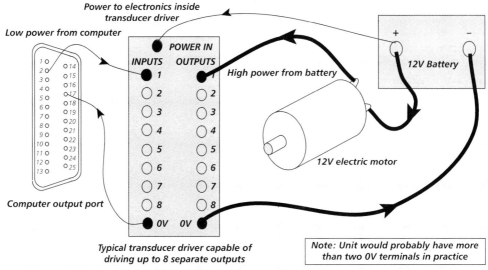

Note: Unit would probably have more than two 0V terminals in practice

Typical transducer driver capable of
driving up to 8 separate outputs

(b) Practical implementation of the system

Figure 8.7

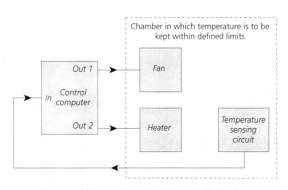

(a) Simple computer-control system with feedback

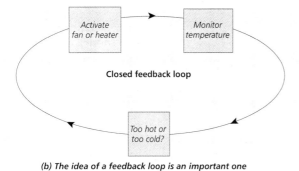

(b) The idea of a feedback loop is an important one

Figure 8.8

Notice how the fan or heater modifies the temperature, which is itself monitored to modify the behaviour of the fan or heater, which in turn modifies the temperature

Did you know that . . .

Biological feedback can be used as a mechanism for controlling machines. It's possible, for example, to wire up some electrodes to the brain, and via a machine which monitors the EEG activity, control various machine-based activities via 'thought'. At a rudimentary level we are simply controlling the α and β waves, but one day it might be more like the fictional thought-controlled aircraft called Fire Fox. This appeared in a film starring Clint Eastwood.

etc. Any system, which modifies its behaviour in this way, makes up what is called a **closed loop system** and employs **feedback**. Feedback means that information about what is happening to a particular process is **monitored**, **fed back** to the computer and can then be used to *modify the behaviour* of the system being monitored.

There are many instances of feedback systems in real life. For example, incubators in hospitals, some traffic-light systems, and ABS (Anti-lock Braking Systems) on some cars. In an incubator system, temperature and a whole host of other quantities are measured and acted upon. In the traffic-light system the number of cars passing over sensors are monitored to modify the behaviour of the lights. In the ABS system, whether or not the wheels are locked is monitored and, if they are starting to lock, a pumping-action on the brakes is initiated which automatically helps to stop the wheels locking and the car skidding, and thus makes the car easier to control. There are also many natural examples of feedback. Take the temperature-control system in the human body, for example. If we get too cold we shiver, or if we get too hot we sweat. We don't have to think about doing this; it happens automatically because of the biological feedback mechanisms inside our bodies.

The decision-making element

Although many types of control system can be accomplished by wiring together a few electronic components, *making use of a microprocessor or using a computer gives us the ability to solve more-complex problems in ways which are extremely cost effective*. Also, the behaviour of the systems can be modified more easily as software changes are inevitably easier than rebuilding parts of the electronic circuits. Most modern installations of any complexity make use of programmable systems as the decision-making element within the complete control system environment.

Embedded systems

Some systems, such as the control systems found in washing machines, microwave ovens and video recorders, for example, have purpose-designed microprocessor chips which, together with other chips perform all the necessary control functions. The detailed functions of these devices are usually programmed by the manufacturer and can't be altered by the users of the system. These are examples of what are commonly referred to as **embedded microprocessor systems**. You should also note that these systems are a major source of the millenium bug.

Although it is possible to rip out the existing control system from your washing machine, connect up your computer and operate the machine in this way, it would be a waste of money. It would be ludicrous to have a VDU, full QWERTY keyboard, disk drives and printer performing such a limited range of functions! However, the idea is not so silly as would appear at first sight. For example, in industry, computers are connected up to electronic devices such as video recorders, to help find faults in the system, or to monitor the progress of certain parts of the video machine during the development and manufacture of new models. Automatic testing and generation of statistics about the systems being monitored are commonly gathered making use of these computerised methods.

Stepper motor systems

The motors considered so far have been **d.c. motors** in which the *speed* is usually *proportional to the magnitude of the voltage* placed across the terminals. If **speed**

control is required on these systems, then **D to A converters** would normally be employed to give the necessary alteration in voltage amplitude required to match any given speed. Complex **feedback mechanisms** (see later) would also be needed if we are to have any idea of the positional information of the output shaft of the motor, and extra equipment is needed if the direction of the motor is to be reversed.

A very different system of *speed, direction* and *positional control* is obtainable by making use of what are called **stepper motors**. Indeed, these devices are *so appropriate* for computer control, they could almost have been invented with the computer in mind. The ideas on which a stepper motor is based are simple, and the ease with which they can be controlled from a computer is extremely convenient to say the least.

Did you know that . . .

Stepper motors were actually invented over 25 years ago, way before anyone thought about connecting them up to a digital computer or an embedded microprocessor system. In those days separate digital electronic circuits controlled these motors.

The principles of the inside of a stepper motor are demonstrated in figure 8.9. In practice more poles (the bits that stick out from the stator) would be present, but this diagram illustrates the principles well. A series of coils of wire (not shown on the main diagram but one is shown in the top left-hand corner) are wrapped round certain poles of the stator which produce patterns of north and south poles. The arrangement on the left shows one particular pattern, and the rotor (the bit that goes round in the middle) takes up a stable position held solid by the magnetic-field pattern. Next a different pattern is produced by another coil wrapped round a different set of poles, and this produces a different magnetic pattern as shown in the second part of the diagram. Being unstable in the old position, the rotor now moves round to the new position. This is a new stable state, and the motor has stepped round, in this case by about 45 degrees. If we made a different pattern the motor could be made to step round another 45 degrees – eventually the rotor would get to a position in which the original pattern would move the rotor a further 45 degrees. If the appropriate pattern repetition is carried out fast enough then the motor would appear to go round continuously. Typical stepper motors would have steps of about 1.8 degrees depending on price – the more expensive motors have smaller steps.

You should note that the magnetic pattern chosen was such that the motor would move round in a clockwise direction. A different pattern would cause it to move anticlockwise. Therefore, the signals that drive the motor determine the direction, the geometry of the

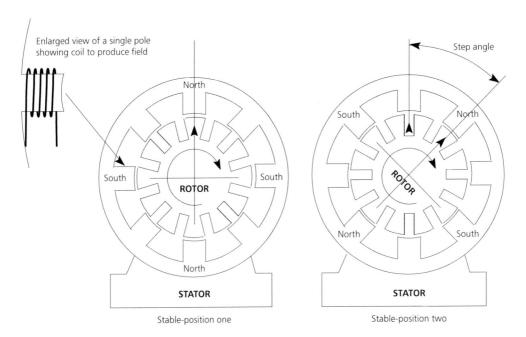

Figure 8.9

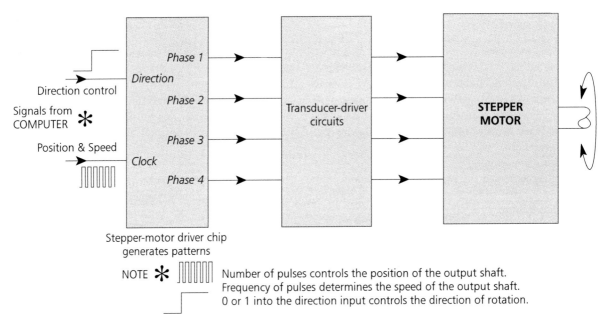

NOTE ✳ Number of pulses controls the position of the output shaft.
Frequency of pulses determines the speed of the output shaft.
0 or 1 into the direction input controls the direction of rotation.

Figure 8.10

motor determines the step angle (it's also possible to drive the motor in different ways to get what's called half steps), and the rate at which the patterns are changed determines the speed.

A typical motor would have four sets of coils, which are wound around different poles, and each set of coils is usually referred to as a different phase. It's convenient to use a proprietary chip, which generates these patterns for you, and the idea for a four-phase stepper motor is shown in figure 8.10. As can be seen from this diagram, control of position, direction and speed of the motor can all be obtained from just two binary signals.

If motors with small step angles are employed then very small amounts of rotation can be programmed, making these motors ideal for use inside peripheral devices such as **plotters**, **disk drives** and **printers** etc. They are also ideal for robotics, and indeed anywhere where speed, position and direction need to be controlled from a computer or from an embedded system.

It should be noted that *very accurate positional* information is possible **without the use of feedback**. However, this assumes that the motor does not stall, and is actually doing what it's told! It may be, for example, that the inertia of the motor and the mechanical system to which it is connected keeps the shaft rotating after the pulses have been removed. Therefore, the practical use of stepper motors is a little more complex than might appear from reading the last section. Nevertheless, they have revolutionised the computer industry, enabling more complex and sophisticated control systems to be built with relative ease. Larger versions of these motors are very expensive, and therefore these output devices are usually found in precision control systems, with the original d.c. motors and feedback systems being used to move much larger loads like trains or the Jodrell Bank telescope, for example.

Having seen some of the many devices that it's possible to 'simultaneously' connect to a computer, you may be under the impression that an enormous number of different bus systems are needed. However, you will see from the computer-architecture chapter (chapter 20) that different devices are all connected to the same computer bus. It does not matter if we are dealing with getting data from a CD-ROM drive or controlling a stepper motor, the same data bus will probably be used for each device, apparently simultaneously.

Tri-state buffers

To understand how this is carried out in practice is relatively straight forward, and involves the use of a

Did you know that . . .

Computer control of the sort being considered in this chapter has decimated parts of the electronics industry. Several years ago, specialist circuits were made up to perform a variety of functions. Today, however, embedded microprocessor systems can be programmed to perform the same functions, often more cheaply than the original purpose-built circuits. This is due to the mass-production of millions of similar programmable systems.

chip called a tri-state buffer. You will encounter the term **buffer** on many occasions, but in this context, the buffer is referring to *carrying out some form of isolation so that the signals in one part of the circuit do not affect the signals in others.* Consider the data-bus system shown in figure 8.11.

We can see from figure 8.11 that two stepper motors are connected 'simultaneously' to the computer system, but the principles we are discussing can be applied to any number of input or output devices connected at the same time. Data on the bus is usually intended for one device only, and so it has to be routed through the 'computer highways' so that it ends up in the right place. If data is placed on the data-bus or address-bus system then it 'instantly' appears at all points on the

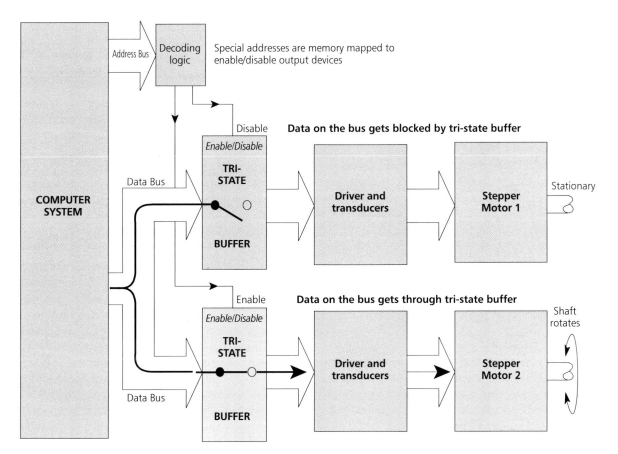

Figure 8.11

bus. It's then possible, for example, to open a 'gate' to let the signals through or close the 'gate' so that the signals can't get through. If many of these gates are attached between the computer's bus and the peripheral devices, then only one gate need be opened at any one time, thus routing the data from and to the correct place.

Circuits, which perform this 'gate' function, are called **tri-state buffers** – this is because, unlike most digital chips inside the computer, these chips can have **three stable states**. The inputs and outputs on the tri-states can be either a '1' or a '0' just like any of the other circuits, but if the chip is disabled then it goes into what's called a **high-impedance state**. This can be thought of as being equivalent to little switches inside these devices being opened and closed – one switch would be necessary for each line on the bus, but only a single switch is shown in figure 8.11 for the sake of simplicity.

Some tri-state chips are unidirectional, as shown in figure 8.11 when driving the stepper motors, but others are bi-directional, thus allowing data to be controlled in either direction. Of course, these bi-directional chips would have a 'control input' with a binary digit controlling the direction. We can see that these ideas are virtually identical in principle to those used when multiplexing is considered earlier. Indeed, the arrangement in figure 8.11 could be used as a multiplexer circuit to drive two stepper motors at the same time. The data for each motor would be switched very fast between one motor and the other, the tri-states making sure that the right data gets to the right place. Of course, this assumes that the software driving the system is capable of responding fast enough to drive the two motors simultaneously.

Control software

It's the job of the **software** *inside* the **computer** or **embedded-microprocessor system** to form the **decision-making element** of the control system. There is nothing difficult about this – the majority of readers of this book should be able to write suitable software after reading the appropriate chapters in this book. This assumes, of course, that you have an appropriate high-level or low level language, which can be used to monitor signals from, or output signals going to a suitable port on the computer.

Let's take the case of the temperature-control system outlined in Fig 8.8. A typical flowchart for this particular system might be as shown in figure 8.12. From the flowchart you can see that most of the time is spent going round loops and checking for certain conditions. If it's too cold then the heater will be switched on, or if it's too hot then the fan will be switched on. If the temperature is OK, then both the fan and the heater are switched off. Note that it does not matter if you switch off a device

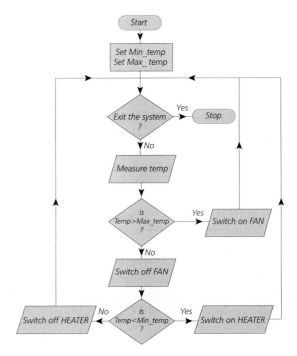

Figure 8.12

that is already switched off – this means that the output pin from the appropriate port remains 'off' or 'low' when this operation is carried out. It also does not matter if you switch a device on which is already on.

Hint: Flowcharts are covered in detail in chapter 14. However, you should be able to follow the ideas shown in figure 8.12 by applying common sense.

There may be some conditions under which the control system can't cope. For example, if the chamber being monitored gets damaged, then it might not be possible for the heater to heat up the chamber to a sufficient temperature, even if the heater is on all the time. Under these conditions it would be possible to activate an alarm if the temperature does not reach a desired level in a set period of time. An alarm can easily be connected to a third output from a suitable port of the computer.

Most control systems, no matter how complex, are variations on the simple themes described above. Feedback is constantly being monitored to provide the necessary data for the control system to be able to make decisions. Alarms can be activated or systems shut down if continuation with a particular process would be unsafe. Real-time clocks (usually the one set up inside the computer system) can be used in conjunction with the data to provide further analysis. Statistics may be produced such as a graph of temperature against time at five-minute intervals throughout the night if this was thought to be necessary. Salient points at which the fan or heater was brought into play could be plotted on the graph too. You are limited by your imagination only.

Real-time systems

Real-time systems must generate some sort of response (this may be action such as 'switching on a heater or a fan', for example) in relation to what's happening to some external event (such as the rise or fall of temperature, for example). Most of the real-time systems in operation today must act quickly, or extremely quickly, but this is *not* necessarily so for a system to be classified as 'real time' (see in a moment).

From reading the above paragraph you can easily see that real-time systems are of obvious importance in control. It is in this type of environment that a response is required from the controlling computer, often under the most stringent of time constraints. A typical example of the most stringent of real-time control-system constraints would be an embedded microprocessor system required to guide an anti-missile missile to its target. If a surface-to-air missile is launched from a ship, for example, sometimes only a few seconds are available for the missile just launched to lock onto, track and destroy the incoming target. The author knows of an ex Marine, who used to be a chaplain at Tonbridge school, who owes his life to a real time system such as the one being described. It is obviously no fun sitting in a frigate thinking that you have about twenty seconds to live before an incoming missile is about to strike. The microprocessors embedded into the anti-missile defence systems must act as quickly as possible on all the information being received from its sensors, (the input transducers) make the appropriate decisions (guided by the software) and activate the appropriate guidance systems (the output transducers).

The designers of such systems must ensure that the best communication systems are available and that none of the vital incoming data is missed or misinterpreted – you get no second chance in some of these life-threatening situations. A *large* amount of redundancy is usually built into this type of embedded system, both in terms of processing power and duplication – sometimes triple-fail-safe systems ensure that reliability is extremely good. Often embedded systems costing tens of thousands of pounds or more do absolutely nothing for most of their life – but when a missile containing the system is launched, all hell breaks loose and the system bursts into action for a few seconds – and then it's blown to pieces! Nevertheless,

> **Hint:** You should be able to get a good idea of a real-time system if you have access to a computer interface of the sort being described here. Try setting up the computer to count how many times a signal goes high or low at one of the inputs. If you use a signal generator to simulate the 'ons and offs', you will quickly realise how soon your software will fail to count properly as the frequency of the input signal is raised!

hopefully the missile has done its job, a ship has been saved from sinking, tens of millions of pounds of equipment has been saved, but, most important of all, several hundred lives may have been saved too.

You will probably be pleased to know that real-time systems aren't only used in life-threatening situations. For example, when considering industrial and scientific instrumentation, it may be necessary to continuously monitor some readings and shut down a process if the safeties of the plant or personnel are compromised, or if the specification for the product being manufactured is not within tightly controlled limits. Therefore, for this particular system, although not necessarily lightning fast, the readings must be taken at appropriate intervals, or the system has failed to perform to specification, and some damage or loss of money may result.

Real time or not real time?

There have been many arguments in the computer world as to what actually constitutes a real time system. An airline booking system, for example, might be able to respond within a few seconds, as it is the wish of the Airline Company to make sure that booking a flight is not a lengthy and time-consuming process. In this case nothing drastic will happen if the response takes a few seconds longer, but it is obviously not performing to specification if a longer-than-acceptable delay should happen. Very long delays when booking airline tickets are not practical, and so this type of system is correctly referred to as real time. However, if this sort of argument is pursued to the limit, then a system which took 6 months to respond – *as long as this is acceptable in terms of the response time*, must be a real time system! This may be so, but it would usually defeat the object of what is intended when real-time systems are used in the modern world.

Most people today agree that real-time systems are, in general, ones in which the response must be very quick, but it's now becoming common to include parameters like reliability, and special requirements such as the *recovery* from possible fault conditions. Having worked through the rudiments of control systems you will appreciate that failure to respond quickly or reliably in many situations could literally result in a catastrophe. Failure of the control system in a nuclear power plant, for example, would be unacceptable. Just like the missile system considered earlier, double or triple redundancy is often built into these systems, with fail-safe devices acting as a backup in the event of a total failure of the computer system which is in control.

There can be no totally-safe system which is 100% reliable, but reliability factors of 1 failure in every 100,000,000 landings, for example, might be typical of acceptable figures for the computerised control systems on large civilian aircraft such as Jumbo Jets, or for those systems employed in air-traffic control systems. *Real time systems therefore encompass most of the conventional requirements of ordinary systems, but with added design requirements with regard to time constraints and reliability being dictated by the events being controlled.*

Real time operating systems

When you read chapters 22 and 23 you will be well aware of the pivotal role played by the operating system inside a computer. From reading the first part of this chapter you will also be aware of the fact that synchronising and reacting to **real-time events** which are happening in the outside world is the essence of a real-time system. Therefore, the designers of real-time computer systems have one of the most difficult tasks to date in terms of time-critical and reliable software and hardware design.

You will learn from chapter 22 that conventional operating systems make use of interrupts to sort out priorities and get things done in the most efficient way. Although the same techniques can be used in real-time systems, it may be that conventional software or hardware restraints prevent the system from responding in real time. For example, is the data bus wide enough to get the required amount of data from point A to point B in an acceptable time given the current clock rate inside the computer? If not, then either a new bus system needs to be designed or the clock rate needs to be increased. If the clock rate is increased then different and more expensive electronics are needed for the system. Is the memory fast enough? Is the communication of data from the sensors to the computer at an acceptable Baud rate? Also, and most importantly, given the constraints of the hardware just mentioned, are the software routines in the operating system capable of operating at a speed sufficient to process the data in time?

After reading the above one might be tempted to give up and go and do anything other than be a real-time-systems engineer. However, remember that most computer systems have been designed as a compromise on cost, speed, reliability and convenience of use. Although we obviously can't say that money is no object, most people would agree that the enormous defence budgets in the West have financed the most sophisticated of computer systems, and the speediest of critical or real-time systems. No longer should we be content with building a general-purpose computer for less than a thousand pounds, which will appeal to the business and personal computer market. Most real time systems of the sort being discussed in this chapter have large budgets for their implementation. In this case the designers of such systems can afford to make use of the fastest hardware available if this is necessary.

When writing real-time operating systems the advantage usually comes from the fact that you are designing the system to accomplish one purpose only – that of getting a very specific and specialised job done in a time which is acceptably quick. An operating system that is purpose designed for one application only will perform its job very quickly indeed. For less time-critical applications off-the-shelf real-time operating systems can be purchased, as this is less hassle than attempting to write one from scratch.

It is often the case that most of the unacceptable delays are created because of the complex and time-consuming processing that must be undertaken during the decision-making part of the system. The software being run on a real-time system is often working through many lines of code, and much effort is usually put into cutting down the number of lines of code, and performing the same functions in the most time-efficient way.

In addition to responding to interrupts in the ways described in chapter 22, real time systems must process interrupts within a specified time scale, irrespective of the number of other interrupts which may actually be happening at a particular moment in time. If this were not the case then valuable input data may be lost altogether. As with most operating systems, higher-priority interrupts may cause an interrupt to occur while the computer is mid way through processing one or more other interrupts. The use of very fast buffers is often incorporated into the system so that interrupts awaiting service can be processed with the maximum speed. Also, critical parts of the program which process the interrupts are often kept in high-speed cache memory. The code must also be written such that there are very few routines that must be completed before an interrupt can be serviced. If there are any non-re-entrant routines of this sort, then they should be kept as short as possible.

There are several **real-time high-level languages** available, of which **ADA** (see chapter 13) is the most notable. This language was developed by the American military for real-time control purposes of the sort considered in this chapter.

The performance of many real-time systems can obviously be enhanced with parallel processing making use of several independent microprocessor systems (see chapter 20). Nevertheless, it is still often necessary to wait for the results from one processor before another can start on a new task that requires this information. Simple algorithms for parallel processing are covered in chapter 20.

Many **embedded systems** don't have an operating system at all, but are written directly in the low-level language of the particular processor being used. Although extremely tedious to write, these programs obviously offer the highest speed advantage for specialised systems. Also, for simple embedded systems such as those found in washing machines and video recorders, an operating system is totally unnecessary, with simple machine-code (or washing-machine code!)

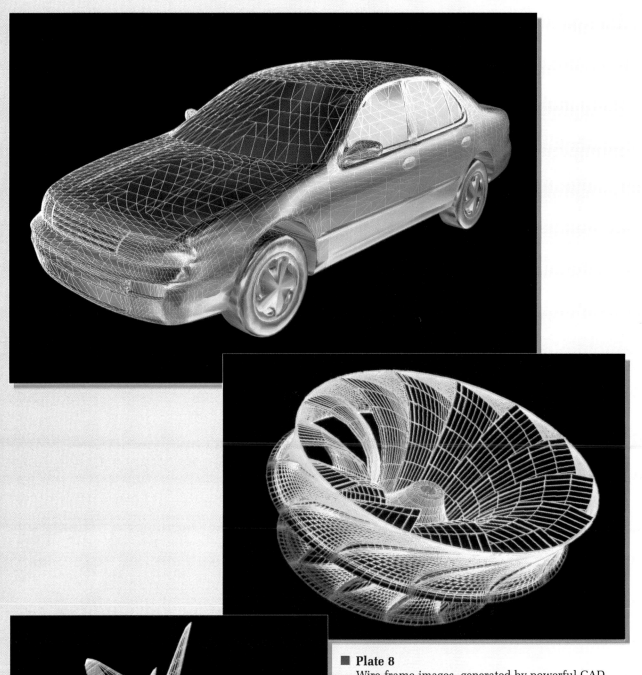

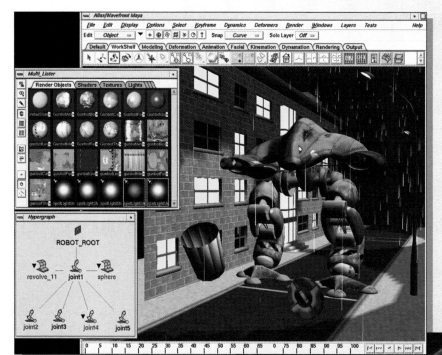

Plate 9
This is the sort of package that can be used on a Silicon Graphics workstation to generate animation of the kind used in the film industry. The generation and rendering of images like the one shown would take a very long time indeed using more conventional technology

Plate 10 ▶
For some time, cartoon characters like these have been produced using powerful Silicon Graphics workstations. These computers have the power to generate and render the images quickly enough for the production of feature-length movies

routines controlling simple functions such as monitoring and controlling transducers.

Industrial control systems

Many industries make extensive use of computerisation to monitor and control various production processes. From the control of large chemical complexes to the control of a small CNC milling machine in a school or college, computer control of previously manual processes is now common. It's the computer's ability to be able to monitor what's happening 24 hours a day, seven days a week, and the precision with which it is possible to work which has lead to the demise of these often boring and tedious chores being carried out by manually-operated machines. The overriding factor is, of course, an economic one. If it were more cost effective to use manual labour in the industrialised world then computers would not have been introduced in the great profusion that we find today. There is also the safety aspect to consider, and the fact that most people today would not, in most cases, want to spend all of their time watching dials and taking down readings at frequent intervals.

Computers also have the edge when it comes to speed and efficiency. It would be impossible, for example, for a person to take readings at a rate of 1,000 per second – this is, of course, no problem for a computerised system. It would be tedious in the extreme for a person to take readings at half-hourly intervals for a period of six months – again, for a computerised system, this is not a problem. Computers don't get tired or bored, and can go on for years without deviating from the task that they have been set. This is not to say that computers never go wrong – far from it. We have to make sure that the systems fail-safe when we consider the design of any process that was previously carried out by human beings.

Before going into further detail regarding a particular system, it's worth making a few observations about the many factors which may have to be taken into consideration when designing computerised control systems. All of the principles being investigated here are applicable to a wide variety of computer-control scenarios. Anything from monitoring the stresses and strains caused by the traffic going over a bridge – to looking after babies in intensive care units can be considered in similar ways.

Control systems analysis

Modern systems-analysis techniques are extensively covered elsewhere in this book, and the majority of the advice and methods outlined elsewhere apply here too. However, to cut a long story short, we will list some of the main points to be considered when control systems in particular are being designed.

The purpose of the system

Some detailed objectives will be required and may include areas such as 'an increase in the level of safety' for some particular process, or an 'increase in efficiency', for example. This might be expressed as a consequent increase in production or a reduction in costs, the ability to work 24 hours a day seven days a week, or the ability to monitor and control environmentally dangerous places. The extraction and production of statistics regarding a particular process or plant, for example, is also usually important. These objectives *must* be defined carefully or there can be no measure of the degree of success or failure of the project. *Quantitative and measurable parameters for each system are essential.*

Inputs and outputs

If a specific project is being undertaken, from an analysis of the quantitative objectives you should be able to determine what inputs and outputs are required. For example, in a SCBU (Special Care Baby Unit), we might be measuring heart rate, blood pressure, temperature, oxygen content of the blood and a whole host of other important parameters. Parameters like these effectively define what input transducers would be necessary for the particular project. However, in practice we need to be much more specific than this. For example, if we are monitoring temperature in the SCBU, over what range should this temperature be monitored? What resolution is necessary? What about the accuracy? A better specification might be 25C to 45C with a resolution of 0.1 degree and no deviation beyond $\pm$ 0.25% over this critical range.

What outputs are necessary? How should these outputs be presented? What form of display would best be suited to the conditions under which the system is to be used? Do we make use of a standard computer screen, or would an oscilloscope screen, LED or LCD screen (see chapter 11) be more appropriate? A computer screen might be appropriate for a permanent set up, but a small LCD screen would probably be more appropriate for a portable SCBU device, which may be used on the move in an ambulance.

Do we need hard copy of what's been happening to the system? If so, over what time period do we need to have continuous readings available, and how frequently should these readings be taken? Should readings only be taken when an abnormal situation occurs? Is a standard printer acceptable or would a small thermal printer be ideal if the equipment were to be portable? If hard copy is not required, how should the output on the screen be presented – in the form of a graph, as a table of values, or some other more-specialised form of output such as a simulated control panel? Some alternative ideas for the representation of temperature in a SCBU are shown in figure 8.13. The

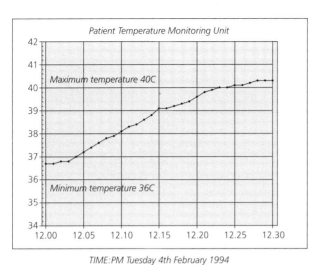

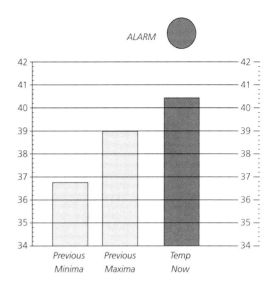

TIME:PM Tuesday 4th February 1994

Figure 8.13

first diagram shows an historical record of the patient's temperature for a half-hour period. The second diagram shows the previous maximum and minimum temperature, perhaps over the last hour, and the actual temperature now. In both cases it can be seen that the desired maximum temperature has been exceeded, and in the second case an alarm has also been automatically sounded. There are a whole variety of alternative representations, each having their strengths and weaknesses. For example, from the first graph it's possible to determine the rate of rise in temperature if this is important. The second graph shows that an alarm has been activated. This might also make a sound until attention has been given to the unit controlling the device, in which case the system can then be reset.

Is the standard QWERTY computer keyboard the most appropriate form of input for the person who is controlling the system? It's likely that a concept keyboard (see chapter 10) with a special overlay would be more appropriate in many cases. Indeed, special keyboards are usually an essential part of most modern control systems. If no specialist keyboard is used then extensive use is sometimes made of the soft keys or function keys on a standard keyboard.

The human computer interface (HCI)

If a first-class systems analysis has taken place then we should have considered a *range* of possible output presentations and input possibilities for the system making full use of our knowledge of **Human-Computer Interaction** (HCI) (also called the **Human-Computer Interface**). It should be ergonomically sound and the presentation of the data should be in a form which can be easily understood and digested, given the level of technical competence of the people who will be operating the system. One must always bear in mind that

people who are not computer experts will operate most of the systems. Also, if we are dealing with systems such as the SCBU mentioned above. A quick glance at the system's output for a fraction of a second might be all that can be managed before some life-saving techniques have to be carried out under conditions of great emotional and physical stress.

Did you know that . . .

Xerox developed the famous 'Windows and mouse HCI' at the Palo Alto Research lab. The Xerox executives at the time did not see the potential, so it was left to Apple to commercialise the system, which has since been taken up by Microsoft and other companies. Xerox did not receive a penny for this development. The rest is history!

There is a whole science (art!) devoted to **human computer interaction**. For many years psychologists have been studying how humans react to the information presented to them by the computer in many different forms, and how it is best for humans to put information into the computer. Indeed, it was through the 'psychology of HCI' that interfaces like **windows** were developed. As far as the control systems being considered in this chapter are concerned, we are interested mainly in the clarity of information regarding its interpretation by the people who operate the control-systems. For example, an analogue display is usually best for an instant idea of the magnitude of a signal compared to its maximum allowable level, and a digital display is usually best for taking a specific reading. The development of pointing devices like the mouse, the use of touch-sensitive screens, speech input and output, and more recently hardware like the data glove are giving us new perspectives on how we can relate to computer systems in ways which increase productivity, creativity and safety. All of these devices and many others too are considered in the chapters on input and output systems covered elsewhere in this book.

Humans are not noted for their vigilance and concentration, especially when looking at information which is not changing for extended periods of time. Also, it may not be physically possible or even desirable to monitor the many different systems simultaneously. Therefore, parameters could be set which can activate some sort of alarm system if a maximum or minimum value is exceeded, as was the case in the temperature examples given earlier. Use could be made of colour to alert personnel to changing situations. For example, if a temperature reading is well within limits then no action need be taken. However, if a temperature is getting dangerously close to activation of an alarm, then the display or a light on the control panel might change from green to amber to alert the personnel to a situation in which close and attentive human intervention is highly desirable. One must also not fail to recognise the consequence of replacing people with automatic control processes. Some people have some justification in feeling undervalued if all they are doing is watching a machine carrying out the processes that they used to do themselves. This process has come to be known as **de-skilling**.

Activation of alarm systems may actually lead to confusion if too many alarms are going off at the same time. When controlling large and complex processes such as those found in a nuclear power station or a sheet-steel rolling mill, for example, one fault in one part of the system can, and often does, lead to lots of faults in many other parts of the system. If the original fault is not identified and corrected quickly, often within a few seconds of it occurring, then great confusion can result. This confusion can be compounded if operators misinterpret what's happening and this, in turn, can compound the confusion again! It's fortunate that scenarios like this don't happen too often, but the underlying message is that when things do go wrong, if the principles of HCI have not been properly considered and applied, then the humans trying to deal with the situation will often not be able to cope efficiently. One must also not forget the compounding effects that a fault in the control system could have. A faulty indicator or sensor, for example, could lead to the wrong action being taken. This is why the reliability of safety-critical plant must be as high as is cost-effectively possible.

Automatic monitoring

If the process being monitored or controlled is completely automatic, as might be the case with an industrial-control monitoring station, for example, then automatic shutdown of the process in the event of some particular parameter being exceeded might be the most appropriate course of action. For remote control and data logging situations such as the types used to constantly monitor weather parameters, an automatic phone call could be made alerting the on-duty operator so that appropriate remedial action can be taken as soon as is thought necessary.

Remote interrogation of systems via a phone line or network might be extremely useful for systems such as the weather stations or pollution-monitoring systems. Data could be changed into an appropriate form before being sent over the telephone to a computer, which may be some distance from the logging or control station. In this way data from many remote stations may be automatically logged and correlated.

Signal conditioning

Are the signals being monitored in an appropriate form to be fed into the computer system? Will any 'A to D' or 'D to A converters' be necessary? If the analogue signals are too small then electronic amplifiers will be needed to boost the signals to acceptable values for the A to D converters to handle. Are any analogue signals too large? Special attenuation circuits might be necessary to reduce the amplitude of these signals to a sensible value that can be handled by the A to D converter circuits. Are the signals available in parallel or serial form? If they are in the wrong form then either serial-to-parallel or parallel-to-serial conversion may be needed. If there are too many signals to plug into the computer at the same time then some form of multiplexing might be necessary (see earlier). In practice, for systems like the SCBU mentioned above, many specialist interfaces would need to be designed for both the input and output systems.

Software for the system

Are we going to use a microcomputer, minicomputer or an embedded microprocessor system? The software available for each might be very different indeed. For large control systems there will probably be a combination of many of these smaller systems, perhaps communicating with each other via a suitable network. For embedded systems, it's likely that the software is developed and tested on a separate computer-based system, then compiled into the appropriate machine code, and finally blown into a suitable ROM-based memory chip ready to be plugged into the final controlling or monitoring device.

Exercise 8.1

1   What is a transducer and how is it used in a computer control system?

2   Interfacing is an important concept in computing. Explain what is meant by an interface giving some typical examples.

3   What is the purpose of a port on the back of a computer?

4   Make a list of five different input transducers and five different output transducers stating whether each deals with analogue or digital electrical signals.

5   Explain the main difference between serial and parallel transmission of data in computer systems. Under what conditions is either system ideal?

6   When using serial data transmission synchronisation between the transmitting and receiving devices is essential. Explain how this is achieved in practice.

7   Explain the difference between analogue and digital signals giving an example of each.

8   Explain the principle of Digital to Analogue (D to A) conversion with reference to a 12-bit D to A converter. Your answer should include why resolution is important and you should calculate the number of different levels available from the analogue output of this particular 12-bit D to A.

9   Feedback is particularly important when the safety of computer control of an industrialised plant is being considered. Explain what is meant by the term feedback and why it is so important from a safety point of view.

10 What is the difference between an embedded control system and a computer-controlled system. Give some examples of each and outline some advantages and disadvantages of each method of control.

11 Stepper motors are ideal for control via a computer system. What is a stepper motor? Compare and contrast this motor with computer control using conventional d.c. motors.

12 Explain why tri-state buffers are needed inside most computer systems. Give an example of how tri-state buffers could be used to handle data going to a printer, and going to and coming from a disk drive.

13 Most control systems work in real time. Give an example of a real time system and explain why it is more difficult to design these systems than conventionally based computer systems.

14 Real time control systems often have to react extremely quickly to outside events. Outline a typical scenario in which this is the case and state what other factors need to be considered besides speed of operation.

15 What is meant by HCI and why is the science of HCI so important to the design of computerised control systems?

16 Design a computerised control system to make the perfect cup of coffee. You may assume that you have coffee, water, milk and sugar dispensers operated by valves. A water heater, appropriate fluid-flow measuring devices, and a set of six mugs on a carousel, which is controlled by a motor. State any assumptions that you may have to make.

End of chapter revision aid and summary

Cover up the right-hand column and see if you can answer the questions or define the terms on the left. They appear in the order in which they are covered in this chapter. Alternatively you may browse through the right-hand column to aid revision.

What is a computer control system?	A computer control system may range in size from embedded systems to the control of entire industrial processes involving a mini or mainframe computer. Control systems usually have input and output transducers which must be correctly interfaced with the computer.
What is an interface?	An interface converts the signals into a form which the computer system can handle, or changes computer signals into a form, which can operate the transducers.
What is an input transducer?	Input transducers convert physical quantities such as light or temperature into an electrical signal.
What is an output transducer?	Output transducers convert electrical signals into other forms of energy such as rotary or linear motion, heat, light or sound etc.
Under what conditions is a serial or parallel interface ideal?	Serial interfaces are ideal for communication over long distances. Parallel interfaces are ideal for internal computer communications (e.g. the bus system) or over distances up to a few metres.
What is a port?	A port is the name given to the part of the interface to a computer in which the signals come into or go out from the computer.
What is a general purpose interface?	General-purpose interfaces, often called user ports or special-purpose expansion cards enable the bus systems inside the computer to be interfaced to the outside world.
Why is the bus system important?	Bus systems are important when considering the connection of external devices. Compatibility versus increasing performance is often a problem.
What are the two types of electronic signal?	Two types of signal are common – analogue and digital.
What is an analogue signal?	An analogue signal is one, which is continuously variable between two limits.
Why is an A to D converter needed?	Computers deal with digital signals, and circuits called analogue to digital (A to D) converters are needed to change the analogue signals into digital form.
How does an A to D work?	A to D converters work by sampling the analogue signals at frequent intervals to produce a digital value for each sample.
List some of the typical sensors, which are available.	Many different sensors are available which can convert quantities like pH, light intensity, radiation, pressure or velocity etc. into appropriate electrical signals.
What is a feedback signal?	Signals, which are fed back into the computer system to provide information for the computer such that it can make effective decisions, are called feedback signals.
What is a closed loop system?	A system which both monitors and controls functions and acts upon the information received such that more effective control is exercised is called a closed-loop feedback system.
What is an embedded microprocessor system?	A microprocessor used in a control system is called an embedded microprocessor system. Embedded microprocessor systems are typically found in devices ranging from washing machines to guided missiles.

What is a stepper motor?

A stepper motor is ideal for computer control because position, speed and direction can all be controlled from digital signals. Stepper motors are used in disk drives, plotters, printers and many other peripheral devices.

Is control software different to 'ordinary' software?

The control software inside an embedded system or computer-controlled system is similar in principle to all other software.

Comment on the response time in a control system.

Response in real time is often important in control systems if damage or a disaster is to be averted.

What is 'real time'?

Real time is taken to mean that the response from the system is fast enough to deal with the information coming in, process it, then give a suitable response before a set deadline. This is usually taken to mean a very fast response, but real time does not have to be fast on some systems.

List some attributes of a real time system.

A real time system often has a high reliability factor built in, and much redundancy is often incorporated to ensure that reliability is as high as is cost-effectively possible.

Name some real-time languages.

Some languages are designed for real time operation. ADA and CORAL are typical examples.

⑨ Social Implications

Key Resources

To carry out this work most successfully it is best if you have:

◆ Access to modern computer magazines and newspapers

◆ A good grasp of contemporary computer issues which can only be accumulated by reading the press

◆ Don't forget the **glossary** at the back of this book. It should be very helpful to explain some concepts with which you may not be familiar

Concept checkpoints

◆ A good appreciation of the social consequences can come only with a considerable knowledge of computer systems in general.

◆ You may wish to re-read this chapter when you are further through your computer science course.

◆ You may also wish to omit the cryptography section on first reading.

The social implications of computers should not be considered in isolation from the rest of this book. Indeed, it is only by understanding a considerable proportion of the work at this level that you are in a position to argue rationally at the correct intellectual standard about these implications. **There are some topics on which the majority of the populace consider themselves to be experts, and social implications of computers is, unfortunately, one of them. Irrational fears which are based on ignorance, misconceptions which are usually perpetuated in science-fiction movies, and sensationalised exaggeration in the popular press go a long way to reinforce these jaundiced views. As computer science students you are expected to be able to transcend this morass, and to apply rational arguments based on current technological fact and likely possible future scenarios. You will get few marks in an examination if you follow the herd mentality and write bland statements such as 'computers seem to be taking over the world' or 'big brother is watching you', for example.**

A balanced point of view

It is essential to be able to perceive both sides of an argument and produce plausible presentations in either case. Few things in computing are wholly good or bad, and misuse of technology designed for other purposes usually provides you with the converse of any particular assertion. **Typical social implications are considered in this chapter, but it is also essential to keep up to date by reading appropriate newspapers, technical magazines, by listening to the radio and watching suitable TV programmes (see chapter 1) if your arguments are to have the added thrust of topicality. I would suggest that you choose a few controversial topics, and prepare an argument for and against in each case. You've already got a large arsenal of possibilities – with artificial intelligence, neural networks, virtual reality, expert systems, robotics and global networks to name but a few. If your teacher agrees, then this sort of classroom activity can be highly enlightening, and help to prepare you for examination questions on this topic.**

Computer crime

Computer crime has only recently been taken very seriously. Surprisingly, in the late 1990s, most police officers in the UK still have no formal training in the use of computers, or in the ways in which today's high-tech criminals are using computers. However, the government is, at last, slowly starting to address this particular problem, and there is a special computer crime unit at New Scotland Yard. The statement at the beginning of this paragraph may amaze you. However, until recently, most computer criminals were regarded as little more than misguided and curious boffins who hacked into systems to satisfy their intellectual curiosity. Unfortunately, some teachers at school still accept this childish-prank mentality when students attempt to hack into their systems too.

Nevertheless, hundreds of millions of pounds lost each year to computer fraud in the commercial world have rapidly changed these ill-advised perceptions. There are many aspects to computer crime, with theft of money or information, infection with viruses, destruction of stored information and fraud to name but a few. In the next few sections we will briefly investigate some of the main areas, but information regarding actual cases can easily be obtained by searching the CD-ROM and Internet databases of newspapers such as *The Times* and *Sunday Times*, for example.

Financial gain

Although most commercial computer fraud involves financial gain, here we are referring specifically to fraud involving the mishandling of money on the computer system itself. How this might be done in practice depends upon the access that a particular individual has got to a computer system. For example, bank employees who are programmers may have the ability to alter figures on their own or somebody else's account. Don't forget that it is these programmers who write the error detection and correction routines, which would flag such errors when financial checks are performed automatically by the system! One would be stupid to attempt to transfer large sums of money in this way, but a famous example involved a programmer who rounded down interest payments due to customers to the nearest penny, then transferred the odd fractions of a pence to one of his own accounts. A fraction of a penny does not sound very much, and the customers would obviously not complain if they are 0.5 pence short, for example, on the interest paid by the bank, especially if this trivial amount is part of a larger payment involving hundreds or even thousands of pounds. Nevertheless, over a few years, and with millions of customers involved, the amount grew into tens of thousands of pounds – and nobody is ever going to complain!

The hole-in-the-wall gang

It's not difficult to gain access to machines which can program magnetic stripes on cards, as many companies and academic institutions now produce their own identity-card systems for in-house use. If you know the encoding methods used by a particular bank (some employees obviously do), then all that is needed is an account number and a PIN number to gain illegal access to an account via an ATM machine. Criminals have

Did you know that . . .

More money is lost each year from hole-in-the-wall Automatic Teller Machines (ATMs) than through the archetypal bank robbery hold ups!

been known to observe other people entering their PIN numbers, then to pick up a carelessly discarded receipt on which an account number may be present. Armed with this information the criminal can then use the portable machine to code the account number, a fictitious daily credit allowance and PIN number into the magnetic stripe of a newly created illegal ATM card. He or she can then take this card to a variety of machines and remove the cash, taking particular care not to let other people see him or her using an obviously blank card on which a magnetic stripe has been encoded. To other members of the public this individual is going about his or her normal business. Unfortunately, it is then up to the customers to pay the bill as the bank rightly thinks that it is their card that has been used. As far as the bank is concerned phantom withdrawals don't take place. In this particular case it is true – the bank is right in thinking that a customer's card and PIN have been divulged, and the customers are right in thinking that they have not used their cards or told anybody about their pin numbers. That will teach people not to drop litter after they have used the ATM machine! It should also teach them to make sure that nobody else is close enough to look over their shoulder during any transactions which they may be undertaking – you have been warned.

Management embarrassment

Commercial organisations such as banks and insurance companies are often reticent about publicising computer fraud. Just think of the panic that would ensue if a particular bank admitted that one million pounds a week, for example, is being lost through computer system fraud! Apart from being made a laughing stock, the negative publicity would probably cause more financial loss through legitimate customers withdrawing their money, as these customers would perceive it to be unsafe if left in this particular system. No company wants to admit that their computer system has inadequate security.

Forged documentation

DTP systems are good – in fact they're so good that together with a decent LASER printer it is getting difficult to tell the difference between real documentation and a forgery. Many pupils at school now have access to high-quality image creation systems, and it would be an unusual school in which some of the pupils have not, at some time in the past, attempted to forge documentation such as birth certificates or other ID cards. This is serious in itself, but when one considers the potential for creating false examination certificates, false receipts for the tax man or false tickets and passes etc, then one is into

> **Hint:** Don't forge documentation on your systems at school or college. It is not worth it and you may get caught!

very serious criminal activities which involve major fraud if carried out on a large scale. Colour LASER printers with the ability to print on different coloured card add to the authenticity of documentation. With many hundreds of different fonts (see chapter 6) currently available it's becoming possible to recreate exact duplicates of almost any desired documentation. The only things left which are still outside the range of all but the most determined criminals are holographic inserts, or in the case of forging money – metal stripes inside the paper and getting special paper which passes the UV reflection test.

Computer viruses

Computer viruses are now commonplace, or so the viral-protection ads would have us believe! Unfortunately, viruses are becoming more common, and at the time of writing, there are now thousands of computer viruses in the UK. Many different viruses are unfortunately obtainable from questionable bulletin boards over the Internet (see chapter 4), and some joker has even produced a CD-ROM to distribute thousands of different strains of all types of virus! However, I suppose this could be used to check your system's virus protection software! Prudent companies must obviously take serious measures to protect themselves against this potentially disastrous threat. A **computer virus** is an **illegal program**, which usually *propagates itself* and *modifies* or *destroys* other programs. At best it can cause annoying messages to be displayed on the screen, and at worst it can ruin a business through massive losses of essential data. There are hundreds of known computer viruses, with some of the most common having names like Michaelangelo, the Trojan horse and the Worm, for example.

Did you know that . . .

A major viral infection could bring a business to its knees. Make sure you take appropriate precautions.

The Michaelangelo virus is a particular example of one type of virus called a logic bomb or a **time bomb**. This is a disastrous virus, which usually wipes data off of your hard disk on some predetermined date. This is often Friday 13th, or March 6th in this particular case which happens to be the great artist's birthday.

The Trojan horse is an example of a virus which appears to do something legitimate but at the same time actually does something illegal. For example, whilst generating some data for transfer to a disk, an illegal copy of the data can be made and placed in an unauthorised place. This illegal copy could then be used at a later date for blackmail or other extortion purposes. The Worm is an example of a virus that replicates itself and takes over computer memory. Therefore, software

that would normally run with no problems at all on a particular computer eventually won't be able to run properly because of lack of memory due to multiple infections of the same virus. Viruses usually propagate themselves by attaching to and causing modification of a boot file (see chapter 22) used when the computer starts up, and others append themselves onto memory-resident modules by intercepting and diverting pointers via the virus to the original location for the module.

Typical viral infection symptoms

Many viruses cause error messages to be generated, which apparently come from the operating system. Therefore, users spend some time trying to rectify errors, which don't actually exist! Others link to applications, which then cause these applications to fail to run on certain days (a non-destructive but equally annoying variation on the Michaelangelo virus theme). One particular virus on the Acorn Archimedes computer called DataDQM causes the screen to judder by increasing amounts on Thursdays!

Some viruses display nasty messages on the screen. For example, after sixteen infections of the CeBit virus you get the message 'From the Devil, The lord of Darkness'. A virus will often load itself into an illegal area of memory and thus cause the computer to crash because routines normally resident at this point in the memory map (see chapter 22) may not be there. Others might do something as simple as change an ASCII code from one value to another, thus causing errors in certain documents or, even worse, in the source code of some of your programs or applications. Some viruses attempt to protect themselves in particularly nasty ways. For example, if you attempt to delete some types of virus you can actually activate a logic bomb or time bomb effect, thus causing more damage than the original manifestation.

Some software pirates also provide an unwelcome extra bonus, obtained by purchasing or obtaining software, which has been ripped off by them. One such system allows you to start up the software and use it in the normal way for a period of time, then it displays the message 'Software piracy is theft – your system is DOOMED'. It then proceeds to format your hard disk – I suppose that is some sort of rough justice for the person who received the pirated software in the first place!

Practice safe hex!

There are some measures you can take to prevent being infected by a virus. Work only on stand-alone computers (i.e. no network or Internet connections). Don't share data with any of your colleagues or friends. Don't use public domain software or shareware, and buy only legal original copies of software from bona fide suppliers. If you do all of this then your hexadecimal data on your disks will probably be safe from infection by a virus!

Unfortunately, in the real world, people do have to share data, illegal or pirated software is used, shared databases are often accessed over local and international networks, and workers with malicious attitudes do deliberately infect systems with viruses. Therefore, there will always be a need for virus protection software.

The cost of a viral infection

It's difficult to put precise figures on the cost of being infected by a computer virus, but conservative estimates put the total cost in the region of tens of millions of pounds each year. The real cost of data loss could be astronomic, and lead to the eventual collapse of a company if insufficient backup procedures are in place. Even if no physical damage is actually done, it's extremely time consuming to remove viruses from a computer system, especially if the viral infection is via a network. For example, a single Worm virus sent out on the Internet system infected about 6,000 different computer systems – the cost of removing the virus from this number of computers is obviously not trivial. From reading the section on typical viral-infection symptoms you will be aware that a variety of different infection methods exist, making it difficult to track down by following set patterns. Random names for the same virus, random positions in memory and boot files, and random effects after a random number of infections all conspire to make sure that removing a virus is an extremely tedious, time consuming and costly business. Don't forget that the level of technical expertise to remove a virus from an infected computer is very great – and people with this level of technical expertise don't come cheap. You also have the added cost of diverting these people from their normal day to day operations.

Besides removing the virus one must obviously include the cost of loss of time and business opportunities while the system is down, or while users are unable to run copies of essential software. For example, word processors, databases, spreadsheets and the like may not be able to be used in a company until a Worm has been removed from the system, thus releasing sufficient memory for the software to be able to run.

Anti-virus software

It's obviously far more efficient not to get infected with a virus in the first place, and many viral-detection and viral-killer programs are available on a variety of different platforms. Once a particular virus is known about then software can be written to detect and therefore remove it from the system. It's usual to get frequent updates of any inoculation software so that your system is protected against the latest known viruses. Most viral protection schemes are indeed excellent, and millions of pounds have probably been saved by the appropriate use of viral-protection software. Nevertheless, no viral detection and protection scheme can guarantee protection and is therefore not a substitute for rigorous and efficient procedures to re-establish data in the event of a viral or any other type of disaster.

Software piracy

Software piracy is an enormous problem. It has been estimated that it costs the computer industry in excess of one billion pounds each year through loss of royalties, and loss of profit to bona fide shops and distribution warehouses. Complete black-market industries have grown up around pirated software, especially in countries like Russia, the Middle East and Far East where pirated software is blatantly on display in market stalls together with photocopied versions of the original manuals! Software, which usually costs several thousand dollars, is on sale for about ten dollars!

> **Hint:** If an institution like a school or college gets software for a special educational price, then a condition of acceptance might be that a nominated company could arrive to audit software installed on the school system. They can swoop at any time without notice, and insist on payment for software that is not properly licensed, or take legal proceedings!

Software theft is now so widespread that it's not economically possible to prosecute all but the most blatant offenders. As can be seen from reading the above it's even becoming acceptable in many parts of the world. Nevertheless, this huge loss of income does have a deleterious effect on everyone, as the software companies do not receive the full revenue, some of which could be ploughed back into an increased development strategy for even better software. Internationally it's difficult to get all countries to stop such practices as software piracy forms a significant proportion of the local economy in some areas! In the industrialised world customs and excise officers are hard pushed to enforce the law, and in many other countries officials turn a blind eye. Along with other counterfeited goods like clothes and perfumery, pirated software is going to be a major problem for some considerable time to come.

It's the end users who eventually suffer – there's obviously no guarantee with pirated software, no after sales service, no technical support, no bug fixes from the company and no upgrade paths to the next version. However, in my opinion, the software, distribution chain and shops are not totally blame free – when identical software is on sale in the USA for half of the price in the UK, one starts to ask oneself who is making all the profits? Good deals are usually also available for educational establishments. However, major producers of network software and applications, for example, require tens of thousands of pounds for the pleasure of a few hundred pupils being able to learn how to use their software. Most schools are unable to afford such high prices to run multiple copies of business-standard software legally. This has been addressed to a large extent in the last few years, but the cheap educational and student license packs often don't provide for an upgrade path to the later versions of the new software.

Security measures

We have already seen how billions of pounds can be lost each year through various types of computer misuse. It is not surprising, therefore, to find that enhanced security measures are needed at almost every stage of the proceedings from the guard at the factory gate through to the screening of employees before granting them a position with the company. These increased security measures help to prevent considerable financial loss, but ever-tighter security measures make increasing intrusions into the private and confidential side of people's lives – this is why we are considering this particular aspect in the social-implications chapter.

Possible security breaches can be split up into two different aspects – physical security of the buildings and plant, and software security to prevent illegal access over a network, or to prevent illegal access to the systems once potential criminals are inside the building. We will concentrate first on the physical-security aspect.

Most establishments are not quite at the stage of the retina-scan security systems as portrayed in films about high-tech military systems, but fingerprint (see Plate 17), palm-print and voice recognition systems are now available for ordinary PCs at only a few hundred pounds each. Few systems employ these as standard procedure in the late 90s, but it's now very likely that smart cards (see Plates 18 and 19) or preferably smart keys are employed to gain access to even modest security sites like academic institutions or small businesses, for example. One such system is manufactured by EMOS, and a general idea can be obtained by looking at the system in figure 9.1.

The diagram shows a possible system, part of which is actually installed in some schools and colleges throughout the UK. It's easily possible to extend the systems to make them exactly as shown, or even to extend them considerably further.

As far as the security of the computer systems is concerned, assuming that an intruder has got into the grounds, the smart-key operated doors deter them from entering buildings during out-of-school hours. The beauty of the smart key or smart card system is that it's still possible to let staff or students enter any building

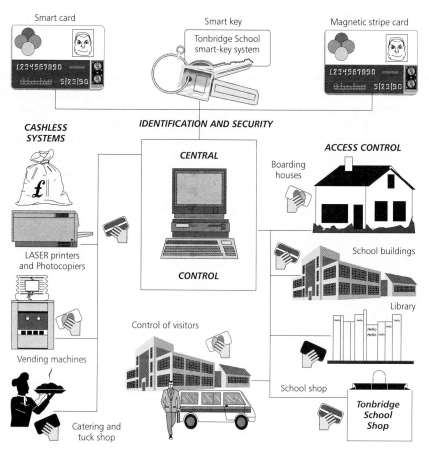

Figure 9.1

at any time of the day or night according to their programmable security status. For example, students might have access to their own boarding house, the library and perhaps the main computer room until 10pm. The same smart cards or keys can be used to purchase goods from the school shop, food from the catering establishments, drinks from the vending machines or to loan books from the library. They can be used either on a debit or credit basis, with a cash top up machine being housed in the Porter's lodge. This means that students could insert their card into a special machine, insert a couple of ten-pound notes, for example, and then get electronic credit on their cards for use with the school photocopiers, LASER printers and vending machines.

Big Brother might be watching you!

Coming back to the system security for the moment, it is possible to log what happens where and when, but implementation of such a system in a school context is neither desirable nor necessary. In a higher-security environment it would be possible to build up a complete dossier of staff and students' movements according to entry and exit points, including dates and times. It would be possible to extend the system to registration at the beginning and end of the day, and to increase the system security still further; PIN numbers in addition to the smart-key system could also be used. At Cambridge University they have gone a little further – voluntarily, of course – enabling students to know the exact whereabouts of computing staff at certain times during the day. A monitor on the wall shows where the duty staffs are located inside the computing building, because of the electronic tags worn by staff during these particular times.

Such systems are of obvious importance in industry, especially when one considers the enormous amounts of money lost through pilfering and fraud. Nevertheless, physical security is not enough. The very workers who are issued with the smart cards and PIN numbers commit some crimes! Therefore, extra system security might be needed in addition to the above physical security.

System security

Let's assume that an intruder has got past the security guard, gained access to the building by kidnapping one of the employees and using their finger prints! They have also obtained the smart card and PIN number, got in through some locked doors and gained access to a terminal connected to the main system. (It would have been far easier to get to this stage by using a modem and phone line!) What extra measures can now be taken to prevent further unauthorised access to the precious computer system?

Firstly, a bona fide user must log onto the system using an appropriate **user name** and the all-important **password**. The network-control software should monitor

and make a note of *all attempts* to log on. *If* a **user** has tried several times to log on and failed, then the system should lock out that particular terminal or modem link and raise the alarm. If a genuine user has forgotten their password, they should see the computer manager as soon as possible and get it reallocated. Such inconvenience is necessary as special software can easily be written which tries thousands of different passwords in a relatively short space of time. Any high-security system which lets a user log on after many different password attempts have been tried is useless in the extreme.

Passwords

Passwords should be relatively long so that they are unlikely to be stumbled upon quickly by chance or intelligent guesswork. For example, if all 128 ordinary ASCII codes may be used in a 20-character password, then 128^{20} or 1.38×10^{42} password combinations are possible – that's a lot of guessing! Even at a rate of one million guesses each second,

> **Hint:** Always use a combination of words if possible, separated by unusual characters. For example, the password **'ten:green:bottles'** is easy to remember but more difficult to crack.

it would take 4.4×10^{28} years to cover all the possibilities – and this is assuming that the software does not lock you out for repeated unsuccessful attempts at access. Unfortunately, the guessing of most passwords is a little easier than would be implied from the above. For example, all characters are not equally likely. Words like table, rabbit, ghost or antidisestablishmentarianism, for example, would all be more likely than '!j*&', '^$jbz@' or '((*jg%'. This has led to a password attack mechanism known as a **dictionary assault**, in which standard words or phrases can be tried instead of random guesses.

It's far more likely that some inside knowledge might be used to guess the actual password much more quickly than this. Some idiots, for example, use their telephone number, bank-account number, car registration number or their girlfriend's name. This is suicidal – you must always ensure that passwords bear no resemblance whatsoever to any information relating to your personal life or a particular project on which you are working. Institutions should have a policy of frequent password changes, and make sure that appropriate passwords are changed each time an employee with access to the system leaves or is sacked.

Let's now suppose that the appropriate password has been guessed – what other measures can now be taken? There are just a few other options now available, with further password protection of the sort described in the database-security section in chapter 28 being the most obvious. Even if you have successfully logged onto the system, you should not have access to all data, unless you have gained access at the highest level of security – that of the system manager or DBA (see chapter 28).

Cryptography

One highly successful method of security is that of applying the science of **cryptography** or **data encryption**. Even after gaining access to the building, breaking through the password security, successfully logging on at the computer terminal and negotiating your way to the source of the data – if you cannot actually make sense of what you are looking at then the whole criminal exercise has been pointless. Cryptography is a study of the techniques for keeping data secret, and the simple ideas behind it are shown in figure 9.2.

Did you know that . . .

Sending secret messages in code has been used for many hundreds of years. From the wheel used by Julius Caesar, through the Great Wars and the Enigma machines, to the present PGP and public-key encryption systems, people have always had a need to keep vital information a secret.

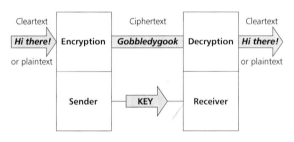

Figure 9.2

The system shows how a **cleartext** or **plaintext** message 'Hi there!' could be transmitted over a communication link as 'gobbledygook' called **ciphertext**, then re-established as **cleartext** at the receiving end by making use of the all-important **key**. Without having access to the key, deciphering the text is very difficult or almost impossible if strong encryption is used (see later). The link does not have to be a communication link, but could be the interface through which the encrypted data held on disk can be viewed i.e. without the right software package and key the data can't be decoded because it's not in straight ASCII or EBCDIC form etc. Most computer-science students will probably

Did you know that . . .

16 year-old Sarah Flannery developed a new encryption algorithm which won the 1998 Irish Young Scientist of the Year Contest. Her revolutionary method involves chopping up the messages and storing them in arrays, giving a system that is very hard to break but very easy and fast to use.

be aware that it's possible to type out any file on disk as ASCII data and make some sense of the contents – if the data is encrypted then this is not possible.

One particularly simple method of encryption makes use of a substitution table in which letters of the alphabet, for example, are replaced with others. A simple combination for one type of key is shown in the following table of figure 9.3.

Letter	Replace	Letter	Replace	Letter	Replace
A	M	J	F	S	C
B	V	K	I	T	S
C	O	L	B	U	D
D	P	M	A	V	J
E	Y	N	Z	W	E
F	G	O	X	X	K
G	R	P	Q	Y	N
H	L	Q	W	Z	U
I	H	R	T		

Figure 9.3

Therefore, the message HI THERE would be encrypted as follows.

H→L, I→H, T→S, H→L, E→Y, R→T, E→Y

HI THERE →→→→→→ LH SLYTY

Unfortunately, assuming the language is English, for example, then known frequencies of occurrence of certain letters together with well-known combinations of other letters can help the bad guys decipher this text reasonably easily. Criminals would employ people known as cryptoanalysts to try and break the codes. Governments do this too when trying to analyse international secret communications such as hot lines between different nations! The most famous code-breaker to date is probably the **Colossus** computer and **Enigma** machine, used to decipher Hitler's messages to his generals during the second world war. If you're interested in code cracking and the history of computing in particular, then a reconstruction of Colossus can be seen in the Museum of Computing at Bletchley Park near Milton Keynes in Buckinghamshire.

A more-complex method than that shown above would be needed if a secure link is to be maintained, or if highly sensitive data is to be stored safely on disk. One such method is to supply a **repeating key** and use the positions of the letters in the key and the clear text to determine the position of a letter in the final alphabet. For example, using the repeating key ABCD-ABCDABC . . . etc, and applying it to the message HI THERE, we get the following.

```
A B   C   D   A   B   C   D      Repeating KEY
H I       T   H   E   R   E      Cleartext (Message)
I K   C   X   I   G   U   I      Ciphertext
```

H→I because H (the 8th letter in the alphabet), is added to A (the first part of the repeating key which is the 1st letter in the alphabet) to get I (the 8th plus the 1st which gives us the 9th letter in the alphabet). Similarly, B goes to K because we get (B) the 2nd plus (I) the 9th to give us K the 11th. Modulo 26 (see chapter 18) is used so that we wrap round to the beginning of the alphabet if necessary. The longer the repeating key the more secure the message. If the repeating key is as long as the message itself, then this would be extremely secure indeed, as the cryptoanalyst has no alternative but to try all possible combinations to try and decipher the message – an impossible task for messages of reasonable lengths.

Various arithmetical methods have also been developed, and are more convenient in practice because a long key does not have to be used to decipher the message. The positions of the letters in the alphabet or the ASCII code can be used to change the letters into numbers, and then an arithmetical algorithm can be applied to generate a new series of numbers representing the ciphertext. At the deciphering end an arithmetical method can be used to get back the original numbers, which can then be used to decode the message in the normal way. Such methods are used in the banking system where Electronic Funds Transfer (EFT) takes place on a routine basis.

Strong and weak encryption

It's important to realise that cryptography can make or break entire governments. In some Western countries like France, for example, its use is illegal, and in the USA it is considered to be the same as munitions. This means that you are not allowed to export it without severe restrictions. Strong encryption means that it's virtually impossible to crack, even with the power of supercomputers working for hundreds of years. Weak encryption means that most people would not have the power to crack the message, except for government institutions like the CIA or GCHQ, for example. There are arguments in favour of weak and strong encryption, and most governments would rather that weak encryption is used so that police and the secret services can spy on their own citizens if necessary. If strong encryption is used then governments are unlikely to be able to crack the codes, and the fight against terrorism, international drug trafficking and other illegal activities is severely curtailed. However, in the early 1990s, Phil Zimmermann released a strong encryption algorithm called **PGP (Pretty Good Privacy)** onto the Internet, and now all people with an Internet connection have access to this program. It now seems a little ridiculous to say that its use is illegal in some countries, because the people who use it in anger will probably not be deterred at all by statements such as this. The governments have already lost the battle to stop strong encryption becoming a tool of the masses due to global communication networks. Also, the increasing speed of computer systems means that the weaker encryption algorithms of yesterday can easily be cracked in a sensible amount of time by the faster computers of today and tomorrow. This would obviously put the secure Internet communications and e-mail at risk.

A possible compromise is to use a system where strong encryption is allowed, but people give their keys to a government agency so that they can easily unlock the messages if they wish! On the one hand this sounds terrible, but on the other hand it would allow companies to use strong encryption to send secure communications so that competitors and other rivals would not be able to decrypt the messages. It would also give all individuals the power to send secure communications. However, they have this power now if they use PGP!

Public key cryptography

One of the problems which had plagued cryptographers for years is that of getting the encryption key to the person to whom you will send the message. It does not matter how strong your encryption algorithms happen to be, if the person who is eavesdropping intercepts the original message in which you tell your partner how the cryptographic system will operate. An ingenious method to get over this problem was invented by Whittfield Diffie and Martin Hellman. This method involved two keys called a **public key** and a **private key**. The **public key** can be used by anyone to **send an encrypted message**, *but the only individual who can decode it is the one that has the private key*. Therefore, all that anyone wishing to send an encrypted message has to do is to use the public key to encode it. It does not matter that the eavesdropper has the public key too, because this can only be used to encrypt the message. Therefore, if the eavesdropper happens to intercept the original message in which the encryption key is sent it does not matter. The only thing that the eavesdropper could do is to send an encrypted message back to the person from whom they are trying to steal the information.

The actual mathematical methods on which these methods are based are very complex. Before Diffie and Hellman invented the public-key-cryptography method, most systems relied on mathematical symmetry whereby things were decrypted by using the inverse process of the encryption method. This means that when decrypting the message it was usual to do the opposite thing to the algorithm that created it. This is why intercepting the original encryption method could easily be used to deduce the decipher method. The mathematical methods used by Diffie and Hellman do not rely on mathematical symmetry, but on very complex asymmetrical methods, which are virtually impossible to deduce from the method of encryption. Therefore, you could easily send someone the information on how to encrypt the

Hint: You can easily find Phil Zimmermann's PGP software on the Internet. However, do make sure that it's not illegal to use it in your country. At the time of writing its use is legal in the UK. Also, it's not illegal to import the source code from the USA!

message without giving away the secrets as to how to decrypt it. In this way the public-key-encryption method was born, and these gentlemen, along with Phil Zimmermann who invented PGP, are ensured a place in the history of secure electronic transactions.

It's the people that count

As you can see from the above, any security measures are only as good as the honesty and integrity of the people who run the system. The most complex of ciphers, impossible to crack with the fastest super-computers would prove no problem to a 10-year old if the key sequence were known. As can be seen from the previous few sections, there are plenty of unsuitable employment opportunities for computer criminals – and this leads us nicely into the debate about computers and their effect on employment.

Computers, employment and privacy

You will need to appreciate the effects of computerisation in more general terms. As computer science students you will be expected to produce balanced arguments as to whether the introduction of computers and information technology has had a beneficial or detrimental effect on employment in general. It depends on your perspectives, on the part of the world in which you live, on the work which you do and on your perception of progress.

Few, if any, workers remain unaffected in some way or other by the introduction of information technology. IT has permeated into helping with decision making at the highest levels of management, in helping to increase office efficiency by several orders of magnitude, and with the automation of manual processes on the shop floor. There will be many people who have had their jobs replaced by automated systems, and many more previously sacrosanct job descriptions will probably fall prey to increasingly sophisticated technology. We will now look in a little more detail at some of the effects caused by this rapidly increasing evolutionary trend.

IT in the office environment

Historically, offices have been undergoing transformations for a great many years. Twenty years ago, for example, masses of personnel were employed in what was called the typing pool – literally hundreds of girls used to pound away on mechanical typewriters, making carbon-copy duplicates for the filing cabinets, and re-typing anything that needed re-drafting. Electronic typewriters, and increasingly sophisticated word processors in some industries, especially those which make use of large chunks of standard text such as the

legal professions, have now made a single employee as productive as about 10 to 15 old-style employees with their mechanical machines. Therefore, for each person employed in a new-style office, about ten jobs have been lost, ten salaries have been saved and the productivity output has remained very similar – an obvious and necessary increase in efficiency for any profit-motivated company. Work carried out by many people in the typing pool can now be handled by a handful of trained word-processor operatives.

Extensive national and international networks, together with modem links now give us the option of not going into the office at all. Office workers can receive and edit their work via the network or normal post, and send their completed work down the network back to the central office – which may literally be hundreds or thousands of miles from their home. Such arrangements are obviously ideal for mothers with children, for example, as the hours worked may be tailored to suit the needs of the child. If, for example, the child wakes at some ungodly hour, thus ensuring that the mother is awake half the night, then some work could be done during this period of insomnia – if the mother wishes to sleep through the next morning then this is no problem. There is also a significant saving on the fares or petrol needed for transportation to the conventional office, and the consequent saving in pollution of the environment because less travelling needs to be done. There are also numerous advantages for the company too – less office space is needed (if any at all!), therefore, there are savings on initial building costs, building taxes, insurance and heating.

There are, however, some obvious disadvantages from a human point of view. For example, people have lives to live and have needs in which human interaction plays a very important role. Society revolves not just around the work which people do at the office, but around the social interactions which people experience at work with their colleagues. People meet other people at the office, and a large part of their social life is organised around people they encounter at the office. Social interaction with other people would be drastically cut if people worked at home in ways which are now possible because of this new technology. The introduction of new technology will continue unabated. This is obvious because of the increased efficiency and reductions in cost, but we will also have to look at the social consequences of the ways in which the technology is currently being employed if people are to have meaningful lives and remain mentally healthy.

It may be that people will go to the office, not because they have to, but because they want to. Video conferencing is now possible, and is used extensively in multinational companies. However, most people still like to do important business by having eyeball-to-eyeball contact with their potential customers. Compromises will probably be made, not for technological but for sociological reasons. Nevertheless, is it up to companies to pay for the sociological and emotional needs of their employees? Should it be the responsibility of a company to provide an office, not to get work done in the most efficient manner, but to provide a meeting place for the people they employ? Perhaps happy employees do better work than miserable ones who might be lonely if they do extensive work at home – perhaps there are some employees who like to work at home? There are many issues to be resolved here, and what's absolutely clear is that no one has currently got all the right answers.

My best friend's a robot!

Factory workers are not exempt from the above office-automation arguments. Increasingly sophisticated robots have been introduced over the last couple of decades and are currently undertaking boring and repetitive tasks that used to be carried out by an army of people. No matter how dull some people may view jobs such as loading or unloading a conveyor belt, putting the same type of parts together hundreds of times during the day, or pushing the same monotonous sequence of buttons, for example, this to the people who undertook these tasks, was a job. It gave them some purpose in life, and during tea breaks, lunch breaks and after work in the factory club or pub they met with other people who did the same type of job. It was a better alternative for them than being unemployed. More importantly, the jobs were often of an unskilled nature and therefore needed little training or qualifications.

Present day robots are extremely good at doing repetitive tasks over long periods of time. They don't get bored or tired, don't need tea breaks and can work 24 hours a day, seven days a week. However, some tasks, no matter how simple they may appear to us, are still not susceptible to solution by modern robotics and computer technology. For example, recognition of 'duff' chocolates on a confectionery production line is still undertaken by humans who sit down all day watching the chocolates go by and manually pick out the mishapes. This boring and repetitive task (unless you're a chocoholic!) is still not possible automatically because there is no efficient algorithm to determine subtle differences in the shape of a chocolate. (See chapter 7.) One must not forget that we are indeed a long way off having robots like R2D2 in Star Wars or Data in Star Trek, for example. The industrial robots employed today are not

humanoid, they are for specific tasks only, and are not usually good if things start to go wrong or part of the production line breaks down. The present generation of technology must go through many more stages of metamorphosis before we begin to approach human recognition capabilities.

Your perspective of technological progress will probably depend on the part of the world in which you live. In the industrialised West, for example, we make use of robots because they are cheaper and more efficient than employing people to do the same work. It is also becoming increasingly socially unacceptable to expect anybody to spend 8 to 10 hours a day on mindless tasks. However, in parts of the third world, where social security payments and the National Health Service do not exist, many people will literally do anything for a very small wage indeed. Just 30p per day is not unheard of for a 12-hour shift in a factory – the alternative is starvation or crime. If there are thousands of people who are prepared to do menial tasks for a pittance – then who needs robots – it's much more profitable for the company to employ child labour instead, for example. Goods made in these sorts of situations are on sale throughout much of the industrialised world – part of the software piracy problems mentioned earlier in this chapter and many other types of counterfeit goods are produced in these sort of factories.

You should also realise that robots are capable of doing much more than mediocre tasks. For example, a human brain surgeon working with a scalpel is capable of removing about 98% of most brain tumours – a robot currently being developed is reported to be able to remove 99.9% of the tumour. One leading surgeon has been quoted as saying that at some time in the future it will be regarded as barbaric if one human takes a knife to perform surgery on another – most surgery will be carried out by robots under the guidance of computers. With information about the inside of a body from various scans computers can build up 3D images of organs in incredible detail, remote-controlled robots can make use of this information to perform better corrective surgery in a much less intrusive fashion.

Retraining opportunities

There are literally hundreds of categories besides factory workers and office staff where we could easily have organised convincing arguments as to why jobs are becoming automated. If these people are not to be sacked, then the only sensible alternative is to retrain them so that they can be usefully employed elsewhere. If these opportunities are not available within an organisation then government-run training schemes, if they exist, should be used to make sure that vital human resources are not wasted. One must not lose sight of the fact that many new jobs are created by the introduction of new technology, but these jobs tend to be of a higher skill level than the previously manual tasks which many of the workers would probably have undertaken. The opportunities for small businesses and individual companies have grown tremendously since the introduction of the personal computer. Individuals now have technology available at a sensible cost to run their own typesetting or publishing businesses, for example. Many individual companies now act as service industries developing software and hardware products for the ever-increasing arsenal of PC related goods.

Privacy

More information has been stored about individuals in the last decade or so than in all of previous history put together. A couple of decades ago, assuming you did not have a criminal record, the only available information was to be found on birth certificates, marriage certificates, driving licences, death certificates and the like. Correlation of this information was either difficult or impossible, as the computer systems of the day could not communicate with each other. Today nothing could be further from the truth – each time an individual takes out an insurance policy, applies for a financial loan, opens a bank account, receives a new credit card or, in some cases, applies for a new job, the information super highway is put into top gear. Information on some of these systems is quite revealing – for example, financial status, medical details, criminal prosecutions, current salaries, tax details, financial transactions including dates and times, and many others too numerous to mention.

The role played by the computer

Let's suppose that all of the above information were to be stored in tens of thousands of filing cabinets. Let's also suppose that these manual filing systems are to be processed by an army of tens of thousands of people with similar intentions to the role played by the KGB before the break up of the Soviet Union. If this were all true then this massive amount of activity would pale into insignificance compared with the data processing ability of today's networked computer systems. It is only legislation such as the Data Protection Act (see chapter 28) which is hopefully preventing unscrupulous people and organisations from building up comprehensive dossiers on people's private lives. Already many companies make extensive use of some of these computer systems to filter out potential customers by profiling for

receipt of mail shots. For example, if your income is above £70,000 per annum, if you are in the 40 to 60 year age group, and if you go on holiday regularly, then these criteria might be used by a company to send you details about particular world cruises on their liners, for example. This is far more effective advertising than targeting the population at random, many of whom would not be able to afford the services which the company has to offer.

From reading the above you may be starting to think that George Orwell's vision of the future is a little nearer than anticipated. However, there are tremendous advantages also. For example, if you are applying for a loan then a computer check can be made quickly and a suitable loan granted almost instantly. Credit transfer such as salaries being paid into bank accounts or clearance of cheques within days would not be possible without extensive computerised networks, but correlation of seemingly irrelevant information by bona fide organisations can have unexpected and useful spin offs to society. For example, on 19th May 1994, Robert Black, the serial child killer was sentenced to ten life sentences. He was convicted on the basis of the evidence created by the use he had made of a credit card to buy petrol in various BP garages. The dates and times of the transactions, held on BP's main computer at head office confirmed that he was in all the areas at the times in which the children were murdered over a number of years. A very powerful use of seemingly harmless information stored on just one of the thousands of different computer systems throughout the UK.

Computers in education, training and the home

Powerful interactive multimedia systems are now a reality. The potential for education and training is inevitably enormous, especially now these systems have become available on high-powered machines at a sensible cost. Complete customised training sessions can be developed making use of multimedia packages. It is now possible to place a person in front of a machine and put them through a complete interactive training schedule with few, if any, training personnel

Did you know that . . .

Individual learning through computers used to be regarded as second rate. Recently, more sophisticated technology, coupled with high-quality learning experiences, and automatic marking and reporting is starting to take off. If things continue at the same pace then computer assisted learning will become much more prominent at home and at school. Pupils get individual attention and can progress at very rapid rates.

needed. Menu-driven systems let the user explore various avenues, tests of material just learned can steer the machine through appropriate diagnostic areas, real-time audio, video, and eventually VR systems (see chapter 6) will add to the realism of the training experience. If you think that this might sound a little far fetched, in Germany they are already training surgeons with the help of VR techniques – student surgeons don their VR helmets, and weald a scalpel in their data-gloved hand. It's very effective training – they're even getting to the stage of simulating virtual blood spurting out of the virtual body when the virtual cut has been made.

The power of these multimedia systems should not be underestimated. In the computer industry, for example, equivalent high-standards of training carried out by professionals within a normal classroom environment often costs a couple of hundred pounds per person per day. If a company invests several thousand pounds in a multimedia system, then the cost can often be recouped within a few weeks. Indeed, training packages, based on multimedia interactive demonstrations could actually make money for the company in the longer term.

The consequence for the educational use of cyberspace is mind boggling. For example, what's the point of talking to astronaut trainees about what it must be like to walk on the moon when pupils can don their VR helmets, put on their VR suits and physically and emotionally experience what it's like to virtually walk on the moon? Imagine you're there. Turn your head and look back at the far away Earth – experience this for too long on your own and you will probably start to feel incredibly isolated – perhaps this particular emotion would not have been experienced if one was trying to convey these images by the spoken word.

If we take these developments further then one can begin to appreciate that they could and probably will have an impact on education itself. Imagine a scenario in which information about virtually any topic is almost instantly available to any depth that is required by the user of the system. What skills should the students at school now possess? Perhaps the recall of facts will play a less prominent role than at present. The ability to manipulate data to extract the required information so that appropriate conclusions can be drawn might become paramount. If such a scenario is to exist in the future then, as in the past, we will probably have to redefine what is meant by education – these ideas could be as fundamental as this. Some teachers may throw their hands up in horror at the thought of what is being implied here, but we have only to look back at history to see that such fundamental changes have happened in the past. From the invention of language itself, the availability of books in quantities large enough for everybody to use, the invention of television or the introduction of microcomputers and video recorders have all played their part. The political, moral and philosophical directions taken by entire nations can be influenced by the use of such technologies – one has only to see the effect that satellite systems have had on the population of India. Visit some of the poorest areas, and you might see a shack with no sewage system, no windows or doors, and the people with only just enough food to survive – but you will probably notice the satellite dish on the roof feeding a TV signal into their home.

Multimedia and VR packages are obviously not the be all and end all of students' educational experience, and high-quality packages are obviously time consuming and expensive to develop. The potential market for such systems has to be huge if they are to be successful, and this has obvious implications for getting to a situation in which too many people have exactly the same experience. This may not be good from an educational perspective, even if a particular experience is excellent from an individual's point of view. Just think of the potential for indoctrination! There is obviously a need for a balanced approach involving the use of high technology where it can be shown to be useful, but using conventional human interaction where this is most appropriate. There is a minefield of opposing philosophies here, and arguments will no doubt rage for many years to come. However, if we do not address the problems which are posed by the introduction of these new technologies, or if opposition is based purely on a Luddite philosophy, then we will be doing the next generation of children a grave disservice.

Artificial intelligence (AI)

In determining whether or not a machine can think (see later) we are usually walking on thin ice, and expect to get much flak from the non-scientists and philosophers. An excellent example of this type of philosophy is called Tesler's law, which defines artificial intelligence in a way which ensures that machines will never be able to think – no matter what properties they might eventually exhibit. Tesler's law states:

> *'Artificial intelligence is that which machines cannot do.'*

However, I think that this law might be more usefully modified to read:

> *'Artificial intelligence is that which machines are not very good at – YET!'*

If we are to investigate whether a machine can exhibit intelligence, then we must first agree on a set of conditions about what is meant when intelligence is exhibited, and this is obviously not easy, and perhaps even impossible. It might be argued that activities such as learning, inference, understanding natural language, visual perception etc. are all things that would obviously require intelligence if carried out by a human being. However, here we will concentrate on the scientific application of AI.

Master chef?

In the past we have all been used to the idea that it is people who are in control, and most adults have grown up with the idea that machines are simply an extension of man's muscle – but not an extension of his thought processes, i.e. it's the people who do the thinking and it's they who control the machines. However, consider the interesting example of the preparation of a gourmet meal. If a chef creates a masterpiece of culinary delight by putting in just the right ingredients, and then cooking the dish to perfection, we would obviously not say that the oven or the cooking utensils etc. have created the dish! It was obviously the intelligence, skill and manual dexterity of the chef. But the chef was probably following a precise set of instructions that were laid down by the person who originally created the recipe. Suppose now that a robot does the cooking, and uses suitable microprocessor-controlled equipment. If the results have turned out just the same, what has exhibited the intelligence, skill and manual dexterity this time? The machine? Surely not! It must have been the original creator of the recipe! Do we therefore give no credit to the chef as we obviously did in the first part of this example? In the second case it was definitely a machine that has done the cooking. If cooking requires any intelligence at all, then the machine must possess at least enough of it to do this particular task, or we must conclude that the cooking requires no intelligence. Perhaps we are back to Tesler's law, which implies that people need intelligence to do particular tasks, but machines carrying out identical tasks have no intelligence.

Artificial learning

AI is concentrating on one of the most exciting areas of software development. In the past it was usual to supply the computer with a predetermined task, and then program it with a set of specific instructions on how that task is to be performed. Imagine instead, that the computer can be programmed in such a way that

it can learn and reason. If it is now given a specific task, then the system constructs the algorithm whereby this particular task can be accomplished.

Does the above example mean that the computer is going through a set of thought processes? In a limited sense this must obviously be true, for the computer must analyse the task such that it decides on one set of actions rather than another in a totally logical and non-random way. It must decide on the possible outcome if it instigates a certain set of actions. If it did not know the outcome of such actions, then it must learn by performing these actions and analysing the result. In this way, the computer is learning in a very similar way to that in which a child learns. Indeed, some of the research is getting so sophisticated that the computer models are actually helping us to understand the way in which children learn. Once this is understood, better ways of teaching may be devised.

A typical example of the way in which computers can learn from experience is the way in which some chess programs get better the more games that are played. It is literally a case of remembering things like, 'If I make that mistake again then the consequences will be that I will lose. Therefore, if there is an alternative, I will make that move, if not, I will concede the game and analyse any previous moves that caused me to get into this situation.' This is learning by experience in the true sense of the word. The physical processes that are going on inside the machine and the human may be entirely different, but they are both achieving exactly the same end result.

In 1990, a computer chess program beat Anatoli Karpov. This was the first time that a machine had beaten a grand master. Computers do have an advantage over humans in that they have an infinitely larger memory capacity, and the ability to correlate related facts in seconds, i.e. no such bad luck as the 'I've got it on the tip of my tongue but can't quite remember what it was' syndrome. It is possible that computers will eventually exceed man in what we currently think of as intelligence and logical thought, but this is indeed a long way off, and some people think that it may never be achieved.

As advanced students you should be very open minded about the whole issue, and realise that today's computers and algorithms are indeed a long way from achieving anything like the thought processes that can be achieved by human beings. However, you should also realise that much progress has been made, and appreciate that human beings have taken several million years to evolve into what they are today – computers have been evolving for just over 50 years – a sobering thought! Although you may be polarised one way or the other on philosophical or religious grounds, don't forget that the frontiers of science are being continually pushed forward, and many things which in the past have been thought of as totally impossible have become probable.

> ### Did you know that . . .
>
> In 1997, Big Blue, an IBM manufactured computer, beat the world chess champion Grand Master Gary Kasparov, over an extended series of matches, and therefore won the tournament. The microprocessor inside Big Blue was a P2SC superchip which, at the end of 1998, is now being replaced by the Power3 processor (see Plate 20) which contains even more power in its 15-million-transistor configuration.

Neural networks

These are *nothing to do with actual computer networks* but are related to the way in which the human brain can be mimicked by a machine. It must be realised that, at the time of writing, the current technology for this is only in its infancy. There is no way that in the immediate future we are likely to equal the parallel processing power of the human brain, and this is just one of the reasons why **AI** is held back from achieving its true potential. However, the ideas are great fun and some university degree courses are now offering biological cells as one of the options in their computer science degrees. This theory is indeed taken very seriously, and has already had tremendous spin-offs in the field of artificial intelligence, especially with learning to recognise visual images. It is likely that this theory may provide a possible solution to the problems discussed when dealing with robot vision systems in chapter 8.

To understand the principles involved with neural networks it's probably best to start off by considering a *simple model* of a neuron inside the **human brain**. A simplified form is shown in figure 9.4.

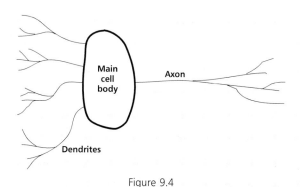

Figure 9.4

The basic logic device inside the human brain can be considered to be the neuron as shown in figure 9.4. The inputs to this basic logic element are via the **dendrites**, i.e. it is the dendrites that carry the input logic signals to the main cell body. A typical **neuron** inside the human brain might have an average of **1000 dendrites** feeding in signals. (Most students think that a 12-input AND gate is a lot!) The outputs from the system are obtained from one or more axons. It's most important to realise that we are no longer dealing with electronic logic which is described by Boolean algebra, but are dealing with organic material that works on threshold logic levels, i.e. if the inputs together make up a large enough signal, then the system might give an output. It is, therefore, more like an analogue system than a digital one. However, as we shall see in a moment, it's possible to simulate neurons on a digital computer. (Isn't it possible to simulate almost everything?)

To make life even more complex, there are **two types** of **neural connections**. These are called **excitatory** and **inhibitory connections**. An excitatory connection is one which tells a neuron to fire a signal if the threshold level described above is exceeded. An inhibitory connection would, therefore, be prevented from firing if the input threshold is exceeded. Inside the human brain, these neurons would be interconnected by what are called synapses.

The above sounds tremendously complex, but, in practice, it is really quite simple. Basic electronic circuits called summing amplifiers can be used to directly simulate the situations described above. Also, via algebraic relations we can simulate these neurons on a digital computer. For example,

Output = 1 if (Sum of the inputs) > Threshold level

Output = 0 otherwise

It's *easily possible* to **model an individual neuron** using more elegant relationships than the simple one shown above, but these ideas are enough to get you going at an elementary level. Indeed, you may be surprised to learn that even simple neural networks simulated on standard micros using just a few hundred neurons can start to exhibit pattern-recognition and other capabilities. However, what is impossible, using present day technology, is to approach anywhere near the number of parallel connections in the human brain – the brain has many billions of neurons such as those described above.

Faced with such a daunting task you might think that pursuing neural networks is a waste of time, but nothing could be further from the truth. Using digital simulations with a more realistic number of neurons, it's been possible to make some outstanding discoveries. Interestingly enough, in the past few years, neural networks have had a reasonable degree of successes in helping out in unexpected ways. For example, it's possible to teach a neural network the difference between a busy underground-station platform and an empty one, or teach it to tell the difference between a traffic jam and free-running traffic. These examples are just two typical ones in a vast application area of image analysis. It is important because the computer can be taught not to recognise a particular image, but to be able to recognise a trend such as empty or busy, for example. This information can then be fed back to the main system and the machines, which are controlling the traffic, may take appropriate action.

> **Hint:** Don't try to view computers as mimicking human beings. They may be able to function in better ways than human beings, but they need not necessarily do or act in the same ways as people to be regarded as intelligent. Constant comparisons with humans cloud the issues.

Consequences of neural nets

A neural network starts off by being connected up in a random fashion. Then, by stimulating the inputs and then monitoring what the outputs are (i.e. by using some appropriate feedback paths), it's possible to model the network such that the outputs will eventually generate the required results. Each output is associated with one or more of the possible set of inputs.

If the above sounds a little vague, then a specific example will make it easier to understand. For example, you could stimulate the system with a particular visual image, via some appropriate interfaces such as a matrix of tiny light-sensing cells. This will set up a complex pattern of paths through the network based on the threshold logic levels that you have assigned to the various neurons, i.e. we might be trying to simulate an electronic retina. Every time you present this particular visual image to the system, you wish to get the same, or very similar, associated outputs. Varying numbers of visual images can be presented to the system, and, via feedback paths, the threshold logic levels can be automatically programmed to get the desired result. In this way the system can literally learn to recognise a number of different visual images.

Even better is the ability of a neural network to recognise partial visual images and be able to associate these with previously stored visual images. This means that a neural network, just like a human being, can recognise an object if it is partially covered. For example, you would be able to recognise that the object, which you are observing, is a foot, even if you were presented with just the toes. You are doing this by comparing similar previous visual experiences with the one you are currently looking at, i.e. you are using your past experience to interpret the new stimuli.

Another outstanding feature of neural networks is their **tolerance to faults**. If, for example, several of the connections get completely destroyed, then the network still functions perfectly, or, at least, relatively well. This is the ultimate in parallel distributed processing. Compare this to the current electronic circuits, most of which would collapse completely if there is the slightest fault inside a chip. A single-bit fault within 128 Mbytes of RAM, for example, would cause faults to occur, even though only $1/(128 \times 1024*1024)$ – or just 0.000000007% of the total memory is actually affected.

This neural-network advantage should not be too surprising, as it's a network that has been modelled on the human brain, and people loose thousands of brain cells every day! Therefore, neural networks have a tremendous potential for the future. They can be constructed by the new micro-miniaturisation techniques called wafer scale integration, or, just as likely, make use of genetically engineered protein which has been specially grown for the purpose. If this were done, then we would literally see the start of living material form-

ing part of a computer system. These processes are also called organic molecular electronics and **biocomputers**.

In addition to the hardware mentioned above, a language such as **Prolog** (see chapter 13) allows for a high degree of parallel processing. Combine this with the fifth generation of computers and heuristic programming (see in a moment) and you have a very exciting, but perhaps turbulent future ahead.

Expert systems

These are applications which, over the past few years, have developed into amazingly useful and commercially successful systems. An alternative name for an **expert system** is a **knowledge-based system**, for reasons soon to become obvious. Such systems are best described by means of an example.

Consider the problem of diagnosing a particular illness that a patient may have in hospital. After tests have been carried out on the patient, the results are analysed and, together with the experience of the doctors, a probable diagnosis is made. Now the processes that have gone on are simply the gathering of facts, using one's experience of previous similar cases, and, together with a mountain of text-book knowledge, the doctors come up with the likely cause of the illness. Indeed, before a final conclusion is made, further tests and analysis may be necessary to follow one particular train of thought. The processes that have just been described can be broken down into sorting through a mass of relevant (and irrelevant) data, until the results and symptoms fit most closely to the diagnosis - a task that's ideally suited to a computer.

The reason why such systems are called **expert systems** is an obvious one. It is usual for a **team of experts** such as 'doctors' and 'surgeons' etc. to feed their knowledge into the computer so that the computer will eventually be able to diagnose the illnesses better than the individuals who provided their knowledge. This is not really surprising, as the computer can sift through the facts very much faster than humans, and is less likely to forget some obscure point that may occur if an illness is very rare indeed. The new term that has recently been used for this process is called **mind mining**! Some people may think that this is sinister, but it is simply having the 'knowledge of a team of specialists' together with a 'very large medical library' that can be searched in seconds rather that in hours or days. Such systems have been in operation for some time with outstanding results. If a patient were lying on their deathbed because no one could diagnose their disease quickly enough, a computerised system would certainly be a great help and get my vote.

One other area where expert systems have had remarkable success is in the oil and mineral exploration industry. Details of probable deposits can be fed into the computer, and, together with information from satellite pictures and drilling holes etc, can be processed by the expert system. After the computer has analysed many potential sites, it then comes up with the site where the greatest probability of finding the resources occurs. Models have proved very reliable in the past, and have indeed pointed out finds in places geologists did not think particularly likely. An example of such a system is called Prospector, and was developed at Stanford University.

Expert systems - the next generation

The expert systems available at the moment are primitive in comparison to those which are predicted when fifth generation technology becomes a reality in the 21st century. It has long been realised that knowledge and its application to computers is not something that can be compartmentalised very easily or based on a set of formal rules. (At least not for a very long time until very sophisticated theories might be developed.) Therefore, heuristic programming has become a common technique when dealing with knowledge engineering, i.e. the process of getting an expert's knowledge into a computer system.

A heuristic approach means to develop a set of 'rules of thumb', i.e. things that have proved useful in the past, based on previous experience. These rough rules will probably be continuously modified and moulded in the light of new experience, and, in this way, the answers that you get from these systems will get nearer and nearer to those that the human expert would give. It's interesting to note that, many years ago, the science fiction writer Arthur C Clarke, wrote about a computer called HAL in the film 2001. HAL is shorthand for Heuristic ALgorithm!

The expert systems available now are examples of specialised knowledge; they are obviously useless if they are asked questions outside their sphere of influence. For example, the medical expert system would not be able to determine that the reason a car might have stopped was because it had run out of petrol! Generalised systems are being developed in a limited way that enable people to have 'conversations' with the computer. However, with the current state of the art, it does not take long before you realise that you are talking to a machine rather than another human being, and the following section makes interesting reading regarding this age-old problem.

The Turing test

Alan Turing (a prominent mathematician) developed a simple test to determine if a computer possessed intelligence. It runs along the following lines:

A computer and a person are placed behind a screen so that a second person can't see either of them. Let's call the person in front of the screen, A, the person behind the screen, B and the computer behind the

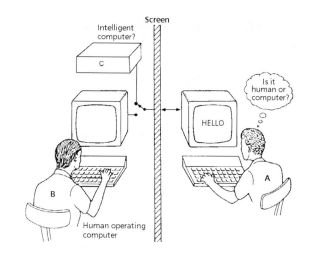

Figure 9.5

screen C as shown in figure 9.5. It is the task of A to ask any question of either the computer or the person behind the screen. However, there is the twist – either the computer or the person behind the screen can lie! It is the job of A to determine which is the computer.

Although this test was developed a long time ago (1950) it is a test which has still not been passed by the latest generation of machines, although some systems are reasonably convincing until you realise what they are doing. The BBC program Tomorrow's World ran a similar competition via the Internet in 1998. In this competition many people were convinced that the computer at the other end was human, even though the majority still guessed correctly. The famous Eliza program is a good example of this phenomenon. Eliza is a system developed by Joseph Weizenbaum, which mimics the conversation that could be had with a psychotherapist. (No insult is intended to budding psychotherapists here). The following is a typical extract:

ELIZA	Hi I'm Eliza do you have a problem?
PERSON	I am feeling worried.
ELIZA	Did you come to see me because you were feeling worried?
PERSON	Yes I did. I thought that you might be able to help me.
ELIZA	Why do you think that I can help you?
PERSON	I just need someone to talk to.
ELIZA	Now you have me to talk to.
PERSON	I think that the whole of my life is just crushing down on top of me.

One of the tricks in the above extract is that the computer locks onto key words in each sentence, and makes a reasonable response which it is hoped will be sensible in the context currently being used. If you study the material in chapter 32, then you will appreciate that there are plenty of problems in getting the computer to understand formal programming languages. Getting the computer to analyse a natural language, such as English, is very much more difficult due to the context sensitivity of such an environment. Perhaps the neural networks described earlier might change this state of affairs in the next few years when pattern recognition in speech might be possible, in the same way that pattern recognition systems for images are starting to be solved.

The thinking machine?

Computers have already proved their worth in a huge variety of situations ranging from undertaking boring and repetitive tasks to the simulation and modelling of many different physical and theoretical scenarios. However, philosophical arguments have raged for a number of years, and will probably continue to do so for a good deal longer, regarding the possibility of building computers which are able to think for themselves. Much of the argument revolves around the issues relating to the fact that all the computers invented so far, and those yet to be invented are based around the algorithmic approach to solving problems. From reading this book you will all be aware of the fact that an algorithm is a step-by-step sequence of instructions to solve a particular problem, and you will all realise how computers can achieve spectacular results at lightning speed by the application of suitable algorithmic methods. It was a brilliant mathematician called Turing who first proposed the idea of an idealised algorithmic machine, which can be used to solve any computable problem in the form of an algorithm. Indeed, if you study computer science at degree level, you will cover details of these abstract machines when you cover the theory of automata. However, the long and short of all this theory is based on our current levels of understanding: all machines built out of any physical devices such as mechanical bits and bobs, electronics or light, for example, must all obey the consequences imposed by this theoretical model of the Turing machine. That is, all computers solve their problems by following a linear sequence of events. Very large sequences of events may be cleverly disguised in terms of recursive algorithms (see chapter 18), or may be considerably speeded up by splitting up the problems into many parallel sequences (see chapter 20). However, following algorithms is essentially all that the current computers and computers in the foreseeable future can do.

Algorithms and religion

Learning, for example, can be simulated on algorithmic machines by the use of neural networks (see earlier), and pattern-recognition capabilities are getting surprisingly realistic. But what about the more human characteristics such as insight, confidence and a greater awareness to experience emotionally moving events such as music or dance, for example? Our perception of these, and other emotions such as anger or love can't possibly be programmed into an algorithmic-based computer – or can they? On the one hand there is the powerful materialist philosophy which states that we are all just made out of different physical materials. All these materials interact within the laws of nature. We have not yet begun to understand very much about the interaction between the sensors our bodies use to perceive what's happening to us, and the relaying of this information to our brains. When these signals reach our brains, they are then processed to produce other signals relating in some way to such useful outcomes as emotion, and eventually to perceptions of understanding. At the other end of the spectrum there are the religious beliefs of people who argue that the mind and the body are indeed separate, and that the spiritual part of us is what makes us different from machines. A less-rational but nevertheless equally powerful argument based on convictions of people who know that such theories can't be disproved scientifically on the current basis of our knowledge.

The materialist philosophy is an argument based on scientific rationale, and assumes that if we were able to simulate the exact working of the brain in all its intimate detail (a feat that might be possible within the next few generations), we would get to a stage when this simulation will be no different from the real thing, because it would be the real thing! Such a system would behave as though it had all the characteristics of a human because it had got all the physical characteristics of a human brain. Nevertheless, Roger Penrose, a professor of mathematics at Oxford University provides us with an alternative argument as to why computers won't ever be able to think. This is because of a strong argument that some problems, which can easily be solved by children, for example, are not computable by algorithmic means. Penrose feels that any problem which can't be expressed algorithmically can never be solved by a computer, and further goes on to argue that much of human intuition is based on solving problems that are not based on algorithmic methods.

At one stage the brain can be considered to be a complex interconnection of neurons and synapses as explained earlier. It is entirely possible to simulate this complex network in the form of an algorithmic computer, and this is what happens in a neural network, whether it is simulated electronically or in software. Biologists have also found a further sub-structure deep within the brain, far below that of the neural networks, and this sub-structure seems to operate on quantum-mechanical phenomena. This network too is entirely computable and therefore reproducible on an algorithmic machine. However, Penrose believes that there is an as yet undetermined interaction between this quantum-mechanical level and the classical level of the operation of the neurons that is not computable. Because of this he believes that it's impossible to simulate the brain on an algorithmic based machine – Q.E.D so to speak. However, if this quantum mechanical level and the classical level of the brain physically exist, then perhaps one day it may be possible to build a different type of computer such that the same interaction takes place because of the actual presence of the other two systems – who knows? Professor Minosky, at Cambridge University, is one of the current experts developing nanotechnology systems (see chapter 7). He believes that one-day it may be possible to develop machines with intelligence.

What is exciting is that people will go on trying to achieve what is perhaps impossible – this, at least, is what history tells us if we are to put faith in human nature. For if we do not go on trying to understand our universe in greater and greater depth, and if we do not go on building better machines then there would be nothing more left to achieve in these important and major areas of human endeavour. Many humans need to move forward on the scientific and technological frontier. If it's possible to build a thinking machine at some time in the distant future, then with insight and ability for original thought, coupled together with an algorithmic logical processing capability – we would indeed have built up a formidable device. I am not sure whether it would be used for the good of humanity or otherwise or, as is the case with all previous human achievements, for both!

Exercise 9.1

1   If you have a suitable database, such as the Internet or the CD-ROM version of *The Times* newspapers, find and extract some suitable articles on criminal activities regarding the use of computers.

2   The Internet is a vast international communication network of networks in which people linked to computer systems can have conversations in real time or via e-mail, or download virtually any type of information. Write a short essay in which you outline a number of points, both for and against the proliferation of such networks.

3   Bulletin boards and Newsgroups have been set up internationally for the distribution of illegal material. For example, pornographic images, pirated versions of software, information about how to make bombs and a whole host of other politically sensitive or racially motivated material is available to anyone who dials into one of these systems.

   a   Suggest ways in which such systems can be controlled.

   b   Is it possible to monitor people's access to such systems without compromising their human rights?

   c   Should some newsgroups be banned?

   d   Would the banning of these newsgroups solve the social problems posed here?

4   It's possible that, at some stage in the future, virtual reality systems will be so effective that some people may be in danger of being unable to tell the difference between real life and life within their virtual worlds. Such a state of mind is potentially dangerous to say the least.

   a   Comment on the technical possibilities of this scenario occurring.

   b   VR will probably be a force for both good and evil – explain.

   c   How could VR help scientists to understand more about the real world?

   d   Suggest some uses for VR within the context of the educational environment.

   e   Couch potatoes (i.e. people who stay indoors and watch TV) might be able to exercise in a virtual world. What other interfaces to the computer would be needed to make this scenario a reality?

5   Some people think that machine intelligence will never be able to approach that of a human brain. Others think that, given time, this may be possible.

   a   What factors are in favour of either argument?

   b   If it were possible, suggest some uses for such a device.

   c   Suppose it is possible, what are the potential dangers?

6   Explain how it's possible to protect computer data from physical damage, theft, and misuse. What techniques are currently available which prevent unauthorised access to computer systems?

7   A Worm virus is suspected of infecting a computer. What are the symptoms and how

would it be possible to eradicate the virus? What should be done in the future to increase the level of protection? Are your protection methods foolproof?

8 A Michaelangelo virus has been detected on your system. You do not have the technical knowledge to eradicate it and no viral-killer software is available – what sensible precaution can be taken?

9 Data encryption is vitally important in the modern world. Discuss whether weak or strong encryption algorithms should be used, outlining the potential dangers and advantages of each.

10 Explain the principles of public-key encryption techniques. Why does it not matter if an eavesdropper gets hold of the key which is used to transmit an encrypted message, if public-key encryption is being used?

End of chapter revision aid and summary

Cover up the right-hand column and see if you can answer the questions or define the terms on the left. They appear in the order in which they are covered in this chapter. Alternatively you may browse through the right-hand column to aid revision.

As computer science students what should you be able to do regarding the social implications of computers?	You should be able to argue rationally on many different social issues backed up by sound reasoning making use of your technical knowledge of computer systems.
Into what sections might computer crime be split?	Computer crime may be split up into many crimes involving financial gain, forged documentation, injection of viruses and deliberate destruction of data.
With regard to privacy, what extra problems are posed by computer systems?	Interconnectivity of computer systems enable seemingly harmless information to be collected together to build up comprehensive dossiers on people's private lives.
What legislation is available in the UK?	Legislation such as the Data Protection Act 1998 and Computer Misuse Act 1990 are intended to curb misuse of data.
What is a computer virus?	A computer virus is a program that infiltrates a computer system and replicates itself with the intention of causing damage or inconvenience.
How might your computer best avoid catching a virus?	Practice safe hex to avoid being infected with a virus: this means don't share data with other people, purchase illegal software or download information from the Internet.
Why is it not possible to guarantee that your computer won't catch a virus?	People must share data with others, will download things from the Internet, and new viruses, not covered by their protection software are being developed all the time.
Have computer viruses got the potential to be financially disastrous?	The cost of large systems being affected by a virus is often enormous. It can run into millions of pounds if a large number of computers are infected.
Why is it difficult to stop software piracy?	Software piracy is an increasing problem which is difficult to irradicate, as it's often tolerated in certain parts of the world.
What two fundamental types of security are essential?	Security measures on computer systems involve both physical security and software-protection schemes.
What is physical security?	Physical security involves smart card and keys etc., palm print and fingerprint scans, physical locks with PIN numbers, and conventional burglar alarms.
What is software or system security?	Software security involves things like passwords, and cryptography.

What is cleartext?	Cleartext or plaintext is the input to a cryptographic system.
What is ciphertext?	Ciphertext is the encrypted text, which, without a suitable key, is gobbledygook.
What makes a cryptographic message difficult to decipher?	Cryptographic techniques involving long repeating key sequences are almost impossible to decipher.
What is weak encryption?	Weak encryption is encryption which could be cracked by a person with enough computer power to do so.
What is strong encryption?	Strong encryption is virtually impossible to crack irrespective of computer power.
What is PGP?	PGP is Phil Zimmerman's strong encryption algorithm called Pretty Good Privacy.
What is public-key encryption?	Public key encryption is a method of being able to receive secret messages without having to give your private key to the person who is sending the message. A public key is used instead, to which anybody can have access. Only your private key will decrypt the message encoded with your public key.
What is a public key?	A public key is that which you give to your colleagues to encrypt messages which they send to you.
What is a private key?	A private key is that which you use to decrypt a message which has been encrypted using your public key.
What is the limiting factor of most security systems in practice?	Any security system is only as good as the integrity of the people who operate it.
In what ways have computers affected the office and factory environments?	Computers have had an enormous impact on office and factory environments in terms of methods of working and employment.
Do computers pose a threat to individual privacy?	Computers pose many extra threats to privacy of the individual if misused.
How might education change in the future due to increasing computerisation?	Education and training will probably undergo major changes in the future due to increasingly sophisticated technology being available.
Can a computer think?	The thinking computer has not yet been built – it may yet prove impossible to build given our current level of understanding.
Will computers ever be able to do any intellectual activities better than a human being?	Many religious and philosophical problems revolve around the development of a computer which eventually might be able to do as well if not better than a human being.

10 Input Techniques

In this chapter you'll learn about:

- Many different input devices such as mice, keyboards, scanners and digital cameras etc.
- The different characteristics of each of these devices, including current performance and price
- The different applications for which these input devices are most applicable

Key resources

To carry out this work most successfully it's best if you have:

- Access to a wide variety of different input peripherals
- Access to software which makes use of a wide variety of input peripherals such as joysticks, graphics tablets and bar codes etc.

Concept checkpoints

- Have an appreciation of WIMPS and GUIs.

Introduction

The variety of computer-input devices currently available is remarkable. From the humble keyboard in its many different forms, to pen-based input on PDAs or HPCs (Personal Digital Assistants or Handheld Personal Computers) and from the remarkable digital cameras which are now transforming photographic input, to the increasingly reliable form of voice recognition systems now available at low cost – man's ingenuity for coming up with new ways for data entry into a computer system never ceases to amaze.

Students at this level are required to have a thorough knowledge of the implications of input devices for computer systems, and be able to make reasoned choices from the vast range available. They are not usually required to remember any of the technical details of operation, with the exception of relative speeds and costs where these are appropriate to the solution of a problem. **However, as with later chapters on output devices and storage devices, in the author's opinion, it is desirable to understand a few technical details at a simple level. Without this knowledge, a device like the mouse, for example, becomes just a magic box, and students may use an inappropriate input device due to lack of technical knowledge regarding its performance. For example, a hand-held scanner is most unlikely to be appropriate for inputting high-quality photos – due to its lack of resolution and consistency of scanning. Students are also usually very curious to know how things work, even if it's only at a relatively simple level. Therefore, some technical details are included in this chapter – mainly to satisfy insatiable curiosity about how these ingenious modern devices function, and to overcome the problems mentioned above.**

Although this chapter will concentrate on computer-input devices or computer-input peripherals from a hardware perspective, you should not forget the part played by a formidable array of software, and this aspect is extensively covered in the system-software and other software and application-based chapters.

Peripherals

A computer **peripheral** is the name given to equipment on the periphery of the computer system. Devices such as **disk drives**, **VDUs**, **printers** and **keyboards** are therefore examples of peripherals. In this chapter we will concentrate almost exclusively on *input peripherals*, with the other peripherals such as printers and disk drives etc. being considered in chapters 11 and 12.

The word **peripheral** was easier to interpret in the early computer systems. Indeed, all peripherals *were* on the **periphery** of the system and housed in separately identifiable boxes, with the **main processor** boards housed in a separate box too. With **mainframes** and many

minis, as can be seen from figure 2.10(b), this *is* still usually the case, but with micros the term can't be so literally applied. For example, some tower systems might house a **hard disk**, **floppy disk**, **CD-ROM drive** and a **tape streamer** in the same box that houses the main processor. Most portable computers now have integral liquid-crystal-display screens, and some have **printers**, **faxes** and **modems** housed in a box with a footprint no larger than an A4 piece of paper! Nevertheless, the word peripheral *is still the correct term to use* when talking about computing devices other than the main processor board, its associated electronics and main memory.

The keyboard

This has been *the* standard input device for a great number of years, and will certainly be around in one form or another in the foreseeable future. The standard computer keyboard is similar in layout to that of the old typewriter keyboard, and is based on the QWERTY design (look at the keys along the top row). Computer keyboards usually have extra keys called **soft keys** or **function keys**, **control keys**, **escape keys** and some **other special-purpose keys**. In addition it's also usual to have a numeric keypad incorporated for fast entry of numeric data. The QWERTY layout is *not* the most efficient in terms of speed of typing or ergonomics (see in a moment). In fact, it's a popular myth that it was actually designed to slow down typists so that the mechanical arms operating the keys on the old-style typewriters were less likely to jam, but modern touch-typing methods came just a little later than the QWERTY layout.

Ergonomic keyboards

The key (pun intended!) method of data entry for many years has been to make use of a standard keyboard, but this has unfortunately led to health problems in recent years, namely **repetitive strain injury** or **RSI**. This mainly affects **data-entry operatives** who use the keyboard for prolonged periods. It does not usually affect computer programmers (and authors!) who normally spend half of their time making coffee and wondering what to do next – instead of typing in data at a frantic rate as would be the case for a typical secretary or data-entry clerk.

Government legislation is currently limiting the amount of time that can be spent at the keyboard (and VDU, see chapter 11) without a break, but more **ergonomic designs** of keyboard have been manufactured to help get over these health problems. Figure 10.1(a) shows a Microsoft Natural Ergonomic keyboard. It still has the standard QWERTY layout, but has a large resting area for the palms of the hands. Note also that the V-shape leads to a more natural position for the hands. The **Adjustable Keyboard** for the Apple Mac is shown in figure 10.1(b). Although it may look like somebody has dropped the keyboard on the floor and shattered it into several pieces, people who have used these types of keyboard for extended periods don't want to go back to the conventional system. Indeed, yours truly, the author, was originally sceptical about the use of these ergonomic keyboards. A few years ago, before I could type properly, I found them very difficult indeed to use. However, now that I can type quite fast with the proper fingers, and have been using a natural keyboard for a couple of years, I too would never want go back to the conventional keyboard – the new systems really are much more comfortable.

Did you know that . . .

One legend has it that the original layout of the QWERTY keyboard was designed to slow down the typist. This was so that the mechanical keys did not jam up inside the mechanical typewriter!

Alternatives to the keyboard?

A more-radical design is the **Maltron keyboard** shown in Figure 10.1(c). This is ergonomically very good and supports much higher typing speeds for suitably trained operatives. It unfortunately does not use the standard

Figure 10.1(a) and (b)

to get an **infrared mouse**. This device is identical in principle to the species just described, but the wire link is replaced by an infrared beam, and works rather like the remote-control unit, which accompanies a TV. So now we now have mice without tails!

Mice with no balls!

One disadvantage of the modern mouse is that it picks up biscuit crumbs, human hair, dust, bits of pickled onions and the like from the mouse mat, which makes the rollers inside the mouse slip. A recent development makes use of a beam, which is transmitted to and reflected back from a special mat or the top of the table. Movement can be detected without the need for a rotating ball, and hence the system is more reliable if used under these conditions.

The track ball

Large track balls are currently available as stand alone devices, and are often used in place of a mouse, especially on CAD systems where very small movements of a typical mouse are needed to perform intricate operations on a drawing. The track ball is a device on which the ball, which serves the same function as the ball on the mouse, is placed on top of the device so that it can be rotated with the palm of the hand, finger or thumb. The track ball is sometimes incorporated on top of a 'mouse' that does not have to be moved around the desk. A typical incarnation of this device is shown in figure 10.4(a), and when used in this mode, the thumb usually controls the ball and two or three fingers control the buttons. One of the advantages of a large conventional track ball is that is takes up very little desk space, and performs the same operations that can be done with the mouse due to the addition of extra buttons on the device. A mouse with a wheel is shown in figure 10.4(b).

Figure 10.4 (b)

| The track ball | | |
Cost	Data entry speed	Other considerations
A typical track ball would cost about £35. It is usual to have a few buttons on the device, which simulate the clicking of a mouse button. Luxury track balls integrated with mouse-type controls are more expensive.	Depends on the human operator; it is typically similar to that of a standard mouse.	This is an ideal device to be used where space on the desk is very limited, or on portables where it's difficult to use a mouse on your lap! Some people actually prefer the trackball to the mouse, but the peripheral is more expensive than a basic mouse. It's often possible to make very precise movements with this input device, especially if the ball is very large.

Figure 10.4 (a)

Touch pads and nipples

These are the alternatives to mice and track balls which are usually to be found on portable computers, although stand-alone touch pads can be purchased for your desk top computer too. A touch pad is a small touch-sensitive pad over which the operator moves his or her finger, and this movement translates into movements of the cursor on the screen – it therefore enables you to use your finger as a pointing device. **Touch pads on portable computers tend to be quite small, but the stand-alone desktop versions can be very much larger.**

Yet another method for simulating the movement of a mouse is the 'nipple' or button which can often be

The touch pad

Cost	Data entry speed	Other considerations
A typical stand-alone touch pad would cost about £75	Depending on the human operator, it is typically similar to that of a standard mouse. However, the data entry rate on portables is slightly lower because the buttons to simulate clicking of the mouse are often not so conveniently located.	These devices are ideal for controlling 'mouse type' operations on portable computers. Larger desk top touch pads are available, and these are an alternative to the track ball system where little desk space is available to move a mouse.

found protruding from the centre of a portable computer keyboard. The button is very like a small joystick in that it can be moved in all directions to simulate the up/down left/right movements that are available with the conventional mouse. Very small movements indeed are all it takes to shoot the cursor from one side of the screen to the other, and therefore it takes a little getting used to. However, if you take a few hours to master this method it becomes quite efficient, and some people actually prefer it to the original mouse.

Pen-input methods

The Apple Newton, shown in figure 10.1(d) is an example of a small hand-held computer, which makes use of **pen-based-input** techniques. Although these techniques have been available on several larger computers for a number of years, the Apple Newton was the first computer that could *analyse hand-writing as it is written* (i.e. in real time) *and cope with joined-up writing*. Previous versions of this technology such as the Amstrad **Personal Digital Assistant (PDA)** required that single letters representing words were written one letter to a box – which made for a very unnatural form of input. In fact the term Personal Digital Assistant or PDA is now being commonly used for organiser-type computers with pen-based-input

Did you know that . . .

PDAs such as the Sharp Zaurus (also called the 5800) use the pen in several modes of operation according to the software being run on the PDA. Not only can you write or draw with the pen, you can also use it to point and click on the screen, to choose operations similar to those being carried out on a conventional computer using the mouse.

technology, fax and Internet capability and the rest of the gismos which usually accompany these machines (see **Plate 21**).

Other companies, such as Pen Power, for example, are producing systems, which can recognise 19,500 different Chinese characters with reasonable accuracy. Other languages such as Japanese and Korean are being added too – this is a measure of the power that pen-based input methods have achieved over the last few years and is nothing short of remarkable.

There are several techniques available to detect the position of the pen, but most revolve around the use of a modified **LCD screen** (see chapter 11). Pressure applied with the pen on this special screen causes different currents to flow depending on the x and y positions of the pen. Some computers need special pens which generate electromagnetic fields, but others, including the Apple Newton, have displays that do not require special pens – the tip of your finger would produce shapes on the screen if you happen to loose the **pen (stylus)** provided. By monitoring the currents produced by the action of the pen, the processor can work out where the pen is in relation to an origin on the screen.

The next stage can be compared to drawing with a **pixel-based** art package (see chapter 7) using a pen and graphics tablet. As the pen is moved across the screen, tiny **pixels**, which correspond most closely with the position the pen has touched, have their colour changed. On a monochrome screen this might correspond to black pixels on a green background. As the pen is moved then more pixels are turned on as shown in figure 10.5.

The real-time analysis of handwriting can be disconcerting, and the Newton has a user-controlled variable time delay, which prevents your handwriting from being instantly turned into typed text. If desired you can wait until the end of the message and then ask the computer to perform the analysis.

A specialised windows environment (e.g. Windows CE or Psion's Epoc) causes different effects to happen according to the icons or words on menus underneath the pen. For example, if it is put into a letter-writing mode, then the computer will mirror the pen's actions

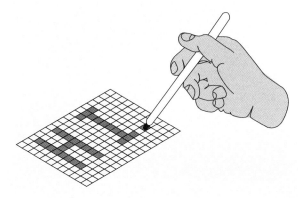

Figure 10.5

in exactly the same way as the magic pads did which you probably all used when you were children (i.e. the type of pad where you could draw a picture, then make it disappear so that another may be drawn in its place). If the pen is then raised and placed over a special area, this might, for example, instruct the computer to interpret what has just been written and change it into a typeface of the desired **font** (see chapter 6). If the text has been successfully interpreted (see in a moment) then the screen will look as if the message had been typed in instead of hand written – and all without a keyboard – magic!

Obviously some text will not be recognised correctly, and as the analysis is performed, systems will usually make an intelligent guess from an internal spell-check dictionary. The user can then point with the pen to replace a word or, if it is not in the dictionary, you have the option of adding it. Errors may be corrected by a variety of methods. For example, if a cross is drawn over an existing word, then special software inside the computer could interpret this as meaning that the word is to be deleted. The system learns as it goes along and so the recognition process gets better with time.

Pictures (or any scrawl) can be saved 'as is' by instructing the machine to save the image in bit-mapped mode rather than as ASCII codes with an appropriate font. In this way you could save your actual handwriting, although this does seem to be defeating the object of the exercise somewhat – this mode is really intended for doodles.

Utilities for tidying up shapes etc. make useful additions to what these organisers and communicators can do. For example, if you make a bad attempt at drawing a circle you can instruct the PDA to make your scrawl into a perfect circle. In this way drawings compiled on

the screen can be made to look quite professional. The potential for new and innovative ideas on these special breed of machines over the next few years would seem to be tremendous.

The graphics tablet

Pen-based input is not confined to the PDAs described in the last section – professional engineers and artists often make use of pen-based input techniques as a more natural input mechanism compared to the mouse (see Plate 22). A graphics tablet would normally be used for these specialist purposes and a typical one is shown in figure 10.6. The graphics tablet is very similar in operation to the special screens described in the PDA section, but the drawing obviously comes out on the computer screen instead of on the tablet over which the stylus is writing (unless you use a biro instead of the stylus by mistake!). Software which accompanies the graphics tablet, usually in combination with the **art** or **CAD software** being used on the machine at the time, determines the range of facilities which will be available. For example, on some models the hardware and software is able to detect 120 different pressure levels with the stylus, and this can be mapped into 120 different thicknesses of line – from thin if little pressure is applied to very thick if lots of pressure is applied. A typical resolution for a graphics tablet is about 1/100th inch, which is easily enough to cope with the minutest movement of the human hand.

Figure 10.6

Pen-based input methods		
Cost	Data entry speed	Other considerations
Typically the pen-based input method for desktop computers would be sold in conjunction with the graphics pad mentioned in the next section. The combined cost would usually be a few hundred pounds.	Depends on the human operator and on the use to which the pen is being put i.e. fast for menu selection but much slower for hand writing recognition.	This device can be used to draw pictures or input hand-written text. It is not limited to a particular language, and some companies have now developed a system that copes with most Chinese characters too.

An alternative input device called a **puck** usually accompanies most graphics tablets when used for CAD, but the **pen-based** methods described in the last section are also just as popular. We have already considered pen-based techniques in the last section, so here we will concentrate on the puck. This device has buttons

The graphics tablet and puck (can be used as a pen-based alternative)

Cost	Data entry speed	Other considerations
Typically a pen or puck based graphics tablet is available for a few hundred pounds. The cost really depends on the size, with A5, A4 and A3 sized tablets being common.	Depends on the human operator – the puck is ideal for menu selections and CAD, the pen-based alternative is ideal for artists.	This device can be used to draw pictures for art, do very accurate input for CAD, or help with the analysis of hand-written input. Electronic signatures can be inputted with this device, and with the spread of security on the Internet this feature alone might be useful for the installation of an A5 pad on some computer systems – such methods are already being used for credit-card signature verification.

somewhat similar to a mouse, and a window through which cross hairs can be viewed. Unlike a mouse, if the puck is picked up and moved to a different position on the tablet, the cursor will move to a different position on the screen. This is because the puck does not rely on a rolling-ball mechanism, but the graphics tablet itself detects its position. In this way the tablet mirrors the screen much more closely, and the artist or engineer can think of the tablet as the piece of paper on which he or she is working.

The concept keyboard

Concept keyboards bear little resemblance to the standard QWERTY keyboards described earlier (see **Plate 23**). The idea is similar to the graphics tablet shown in Figure 10.6. Indeed, *most* **graphics tablets** can be used as **concept keyboards**. A special overlay relevant to a particular application is placed on top of the pressure-sensitive pad. A typical overlay might be for a CAD package such as Autocad, and contain a vast array of useful menu selections. If you press your finger on top of the appropriate part of the pad, the sensors inside the pad will translate the co-ordinates to the computer and thus appropriate actions may be taken which relate to the item on the menu, which has just been pressed. The stylus can also be used to prevent the tip of your finger from wearing out!

Games accessories

Lots of specialist devices now exist for helping to play computer games or interacting with the computer in interesting ways. For example, if you fly a typical flight simulator, then, although it's possible to control the simulation from the keyboard or with a joystick, it's much more fun if you have a console, which is called a **flight yoke**. As can be seen from figure 10.7(a), this consists of conventional flight yoke for control of the aileron and elevator controls, and the professional version also contains controls for flaps and landing gear. If you want even more realism then add some **pedals**, shown in figure 10.7(b), which enable you to control the rudder and toe brake with your feet. You have only to add a VR helmet (see chapter 11) and you are realistically inserted into the flight-simulator world. You can also **get steering wheels** and dashboard simulators for car-racing games. If you really want to go the whole hog, then the **cockpit** complete with many real and simulated inputs and outputs can be purchased. This is shown in figure 10.7 (c).

In essence, all of these controls connect to your computer via the joystick ports or other COM ports, and simulate the pressing of buttons on the keyboard or movements of the mouse.

Flight yokes, driving consoles and pedals etc.

Cost	Data entry speed	Other considerations
A cheap flight-simulator yoke or steering-wheel/dash-board combination would typically cost about £100. Expensive flight simulator cockpits can cost in excess of a few thousand pounds.	Depends on human operator. These devices enable humans to integrate with the computer using both hands and feet for added realism.	These devices, although primarily designed for games and fun, act as serious training devices in their professional incarnations. For example, the company BMW has developed a driving simulator, which might actually feature in driving tests of the future.

Joysticks

This input device has now been around in one form or another for a considerable number of years. However, the latest devices, as can be seen from figure 10.8, bear little resemblance to the original models. The joystick, as all the games fanatics will know, is a device which stands on the desk, grabbed hold of by the hand, and is intended to simulate the movement of a stick similar to those found in aircraft. The addition of a few extra buttons usually replicates the 'fire button' so that you

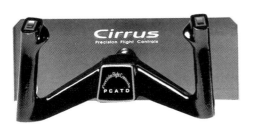

(a)

(b)

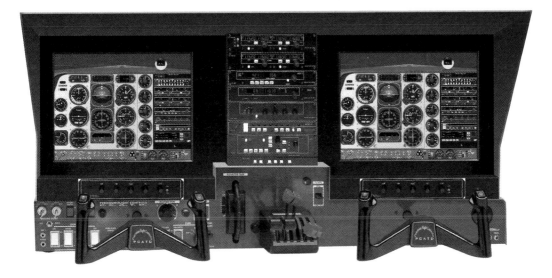

(c)

Figure 10.7

can blast away the enemy without taking your hands off the stick. Indeed, the Microsoft Joystick shown in figure 10.8 is a two-handed job with extra buttons for added armour and missile control!

It's obviously great fun to play computer games with a joystick and the added realism means that the enjoyment from the game is greatly enhanced. However,

don't underestimate the usefulness of a joystick from a professional point of view. For example, when undertaking virtual reality simulations such as walking

Figure 10.8

Joysticks		
Cost	Data entry speed	Other considerations
A cheap joystick costs about £10, but better quality or more sophisticated force-feedback joysticks can cost up to £100 or more.	Depends on human operator. These devices enable a natural form of integration with a variety of environments and are ideal for games and other simulations.	Primarily used for games, but better quality joysticks are essential for professional simulations such as VR. Also very useful in control of robots and other similar situations.

Did you know that . . .

One of the latest joystick innovations is the force-feedback joystick from Microsoft. Although very expensive at the time of writing, it's excellent in the games and flight-simulation environments, where the movement and vibration of the stick is controlled by the computer. If, for example, you were about to stall an aeroplane in flight, then the stick would start to vibrate violently. It certainly is much more realistic!

through a 3D building or for robotics control etc. the joystick is an essential tool for smooth and efficient operation.

Bar codes

Most people will be familiar with **bar codes** since they appear on products ranging from tins of baked beans to library books. A typical bar code displayed on a product is shown in figure 10.9(a).

Did you know that . . .

Some graphics software packages now enable you to make up your own bar codes. The Corel Suite, for example, comes with a utility called a 'bar-code wizard', which enables you to make 18 different types of bar codes – easily enough for the most discerning of 'barcodeophiles'! All you have to do is to type in the numeric information, then specify the size etc.

As can be seen from figure 10.9(a) a bar code consists of varying thickness vertical lines that represent **a unique code** for the product. There are several different types of bar code in circulation, but the European Article Number (EAN 8) shown in figure 10.9(a) is the most common for food and other goods in the UK. The Universal Product Code (UPC A) shown in figure 10.9(b) is the most common for items of grocery and other goods in the USA. However, there are many other types of barcodes now in use, and the number of types grows with the passing years.

In both the EAN and UPC systems there are three different widths of bars and each character is represented using two bars and two spaces. Several different devices called **bar code readers, bar code scanners**, or **optical wands** can be moved over the surface of the bar code and the data is recorded in the computer or a portable hand-held device. The device can be moved in either direction in the case of a wand, or even upside down in the case of the scanner!

Although you would not be asked to quote such detailed information in an examination, it is infuriating not to be able to decode the bars on the side of the cans and so the principle of the EAN system will now be explained.

Did you know that . . .

Although it will be sometime yet, the barcode is under threat from a new technology, which involves placing a radiosensitive tag onto items like cans of beans. Using this system you drive your loaded trolley through the checkout, and a radio signal will pick up all the information from the tags. It will even pick up items, which might happen to be in the shopper's pocket! Using this method, all items in the trolley are scanned 'simultaneously'. However, it's a little too expensive at present.

The system appears a little complex at first sight. However, this is necessary due to the fact that the system has to be operated under quite arduous conditions as the optical wand is often passed over the bar code in either direction, and at many different and inconsistent speeds. If the code is not instantly recognised by the reading device then an error signal must

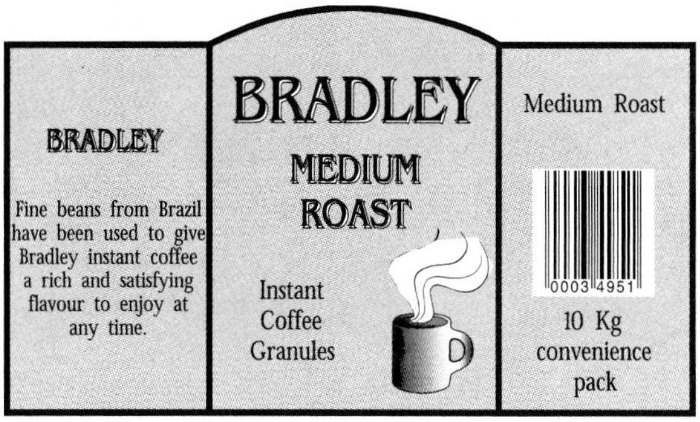

Figure 10.9(a)

Figure 10.9b

Figure 10.10(a)

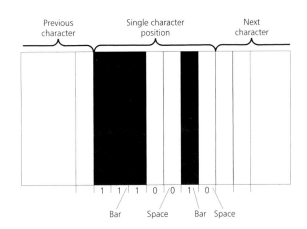

Figure 10.10(b)

EAN Code sets			
Number	Set A	Set B	Set C
0	0 0 0 1 1 0 1	0 1 0 0 1 1 1	1 1 1 0 0 1 0
1	0 0 1 1 0 0 1	0 1 1 0 0 1 1	1 1 0 0 1 1 0
2	0 0 1 0 0 1 1	0 0 1 1 0 1 1	1 1 0 1 1 0 0
3	0 1 1 1 1 0 1	0 1 0 0 0 0 1	1 0 0 0 0 1 0
4	0 1 0 0 0 1 1	0 0 1 1 1 0 1	1 0 1 1 1 0 0
5	0 1 1 0 0 0 1	0 1 1 1 0 0 1	1 0 0 1 1 1 0
6	0 1 0 1 1 1 1	0 0 0 0 1 0 1	1 0 1 0 0 0 0
7	0 1 1 1 0 1 1	0 0 1 0 0 0 1	1 0 0 0 1 0 0
8	0 1 1 0 1 1 1	0 0 0 1 0 0 1	1 0 0 1 0 0 0
9	0 0 0 1 0 1 1	0 0 1 0 1 1 1	1 1 1 0 1 0 0

Figure 10.10(c)

EAN Code sets for left-hand side of barcode						
First	Combinations of sets shown in Fig 11.10(c)					
	A	A	A	A	A	A
	A	A	B	A	B	B
	A	A	B	B	A	B
	A	A	B	B	B	A
	A	B	A	A	B	B
	A	B	B	A	A	B
	A	B	B	B	A	A
	A	B	A	B	A	B
	A	B	A	B	B	A
	A	B	B	A	B	A

Figure 10.10(d)

be generated so that the operator attempts to read the bar code again.

The EAN 13 consists of 12 codes grouped together as two lots of six, separated by a centre pattern and guard bits at each end. The arrangement of F.A.T. Petfood's code for F.A.T. Cat Food is shown in figure 10.10(a).

The bar code is split up into 15 regions plus an initial number not coded in bars that represents the country of origin. Two bars and two spaces represent each character, and each character position is split up into seven segments. A typical seven-segment two-space-two-bar code character is shown in figure 10.10(b). If this is decoded assuming that white is '0' and black is '1' then we obtain the code 1 1 1 0 0 1 0 which could represent 0. The reason that it could represent zero is that there are three types of coding system called set A, B and C. To decode the bar code properly you need to know which set of codes is being used. The codes, which represent the second set of six digits (i.e. the numbers at the right-hand side of figure 10.10(a)), are always coded using the C set. The codes for each set A, B and C are shown in figure 10.10(c).

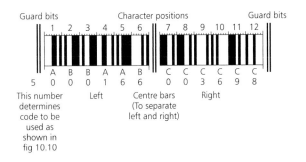

Figure 10.11

The arrangement for the six digits on the left is more complex, and depends on the number at the beginning of the bar code. Set A, or a combination of set A and set B is used to code this first sequence of six digits. The combinations are shown in figure 10.10(d).

As an example of decoding a bar code, consider the cat food bar code shown in figure 10.10(a). A larger version is shown in figure 10.11. The first number at the left-hand side is 5. Hence we use the ABBAAB system for decoding the first six digits as indicated in figure 10.10(d).

The first digit uses the A set and is 0001101 i.e. 0

For convenience the decoding process is set out in tabular form below:

Digit number	Set used	Binary representation	Number
Guard bit			
1	A	0001101	0
2	B	0100111	0
3	B	0100111	0
4	A	0011001	1
5	A	0101111	6
6	B	0000101	6
Centre pattern			
7	C	1110010	0
8	C	1110010	0
9	C	1000010	3
10	C	1010000	6
11	C	1110100	9
12	C	1001000	8
Guard bit			

Using the above figures together with the 5 at the beginning we get:

5   000166   003698

Fortunately the numbers are usually written at the bottom of the bar code, as it would not be easy for a human operator to go through the above process!

Such systems are used in supermarkets to perform a variety of functions such as looking up the details and price of a product so that this can automatically be fed back to a checkout terminal printer, i.e. the customer would get a detailed itemised account such as the one shown in figure 10.12.

In some supermarkets an optical wand is not necessary as the product can be put into an automatic **laser scanning mechanism.** In fact in this case the customer can simply place the items on the conveyor belt and the machine will automatically scan the goods and produce the bill.

Both types of system (laser and optical wand) would be linked to the store computer (the checkout is effectively a computer terminal) and could therefore be used to take control of stock levels automatically and re-order when necessary. Such a computer terminal is known as a **point of sale (POS) terminal** (see chapter 6).

There are also a great deal of 'behind the scenes' operations that could go on as a result of bar codes being used in the retail trade. Not only can they help to give up-to-date information regarding stock levels, and therefore help with purchasing, but they can also be used to help maintain a huge database (see chapter 28) for an entire chain of stores. The business can then extract statistics such as which are the best selling

lines nationwide, which goods sell best in a particular area, or which goods are not selling as well as they should. It can even go one stage further and have automatic links with the companies that manufacture the cans, and the companies that produce the labels. Such systems can easily be put into operation with the introduction of the new **FDDI national and international networks** mentioned in chapter 3.

In addition to the bar codes, the current generation of POS terminals can deduct money directly from people's bank accounts. Methods using 'switch' cards are common, but some systems go one better so that the actual transaction appears on one's monthly bank statement. These systems are generally known as **EFTPOS** or **Electronic Funds Transfer at the Point Of Sale**.

At the other end of the price scale, users with home micros can now purchase inexpensive bar code readers together with software than can produce bar codes on a printer. These are also useful in education for demonstrations to students, computerising the school library system, or even to produce a system of stock control in the school shop.

```
            SAINSBURY'S
             BRIDGEMEAD
        ASHWORTH ROAD SWINDON
          WILTSHIRE  SN5 7YH
      TELEPHONE NO. 01793 420046
                              £
* KITCHEN TOWELS            1.32
EXTRA REWARD POINTS
*    25 POINTS *
* ORANGE JCE 1L             2.39
S/PARSNIP SOUP              1.29
* WOTSITS X6                0.93
SOFT ROLLS X6              0.59
DIET BIO YOGURT            1.29
GRANARY BREAD             0.55
JS TORTELLONI              1.69
CHKN MASALA               2.99
ORANGES
      4 @ £0.19            0.76
BANANAS
  0.83 lb @ £0.49/lb       0.41
BRAEBURN APPLES
  1.21 lb @ £0.69/lb       0.83

     15 ITEMS PURCHASED
     BALANCE DUE           15.04


  1 REWARD VCHR
------CASHBACK------       40.00
DEBIT CARD                 55.04
     675960214033442515  01 08/00


***********************************
```

Figure 10.12

Bar code systems

Cost	Data entry speed	Other considerations
The cost of an optical wand is about £50, but a better quality bar-code scanner would be a couple of hundred pounds. Obviously the EFTPOS terminals are several thousands of pounds.	Assuming that the bar code can be read immediately, the input speed depends on the human operator. Typically, a trained bar-code operative could read about 60 bar codes/minute, all other things being equal.	These machines have now become the norm in the retail industry, in libraries, schools, and many other institutions where ID cards or similar systems exist. The cost of the bar code reader is very much less than was the case just a few years ago, and much software now exists to enable you to enter data into virtually any application that exists on your personal computer.

OCR systems and scanners

The distinction between **machine-readable** and **non-machine-readable** documents is becoming *less* distinct with the advent of some **OCR** (optical character recognition) systems. One type of **OCR** system which is becoming a common option on **flat-bed scanners** (see next section) is the ability to read a page of pre-typed text into the computer in a form which can be understood, i.e. *not* simply a **bit-mapped image** (see chapter 7) but in a form where the scanned characters are replaced by **ASCII codes** in the computer's memory – which means that the text may be processed as though it had been manually typed in on a word processor. The ability to be able to do this is obviously a tremendous advantage because of the phenomenal amount of data already available in pre-printed form. Without this sort of system the user has no option but to get a typist to re-type the entire text into the computer system manually – a daunting task if the text to be entered is vast.

Did you know that . . .

In 1995, when a previous edition of this book was being written, a typical A4 scanner cost over £1,000. In 1998, a similar scanner could be obtained for about £75!

The modern systems employ a two-stage process, where the text to be input is first scanned as a bit map. When this bit map image has been grabbed, the OCR software then scans the image making use of pattern-recognition software, which attempts to turn the printed word into the codes that the computer can understand. After this second-stage process has been undertaken, you will usually be prompted to sort out anything that has been misunderstood, either by manually changing any mistakes or, more usefully, by getting the computer to do it for you by using its internal spell checking dictionary.

The modern OCR software systems are becoming impressive, and even systems which are given away free with inexpensive scanners (see next section) would be worth paying quite a bit of money for if you have tens of thousands of words to scan in. Systems like OmniPage or TextBridge professional versions represent the state of the art. These systems will not only attempt to get the text into the computer, but will try to match the nearest available font. They will keep the point size approximately right, will cope with multiple columns (a real pain without this facility), and will also input pictures at the same time if you wish!

We have, at last, got the ability to change documents into computer readable format, even if they are not perfectly laid out or are mixed in with many other objects such as would be encountered within a typical newspaper. The progress in the last few years has been remarkable. This is even more so when you consider that the price of a typical scanner, needed to scan in the text in the first place, has come down from thousands of pounds to less than a hundred pounds. A cheap A4 flatbed model capable of scanning at 300 dpi in 16 million colours now costs about £75.

Did you know that . . .

Not so long ago it was quite unusual to have a fax machine in the home. Today, with the advent of cost-effective computer scanners, it's quite common to have a fax machine, scanner and OCR machine, plus a colour and black and white photocopier – all in the same device. All this technology costs much less than the original purpose-built fax machine (see Plate 28)!

Scanners

The ability to scan a document (e.g. the OCR mentioned in the last section) or a picture into a computer is now taken for granted. However, the types, quality and cost of these scanning devices vary tremendously from small **hand-held scanners** costing about £50, via A4 scanners, which cost between £100 and £800 depending on quality, to much larger scanners for professional quality work. It is also becoming the norm to be able to buy printers, which include a scanning facility such as the HP Office Jet Pro 1175C. If you have both a printer and a scanner in the same device, then you also have a photocopier! Fax machines too are being thrown in for good measure. However, the cost starts to rocket once

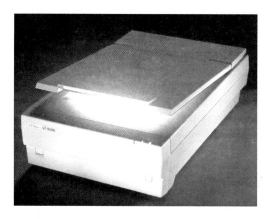

(a)

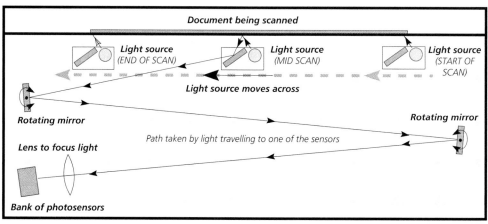

(b)

Side view of flat-bed scanner showing just a single light path

Figure 10.13

you get to A3 and beyond, because these machines are only used in specialist markets.

A typical scanner is a **flat-bed scanner** capable of working with an A4 document as shown in figure 10.13(a), and the principle on which all these scanners operate is shown in figure 10.13(b). Most of these devices (with the exception of the hand-held scanners) are used rather like a photocopier, where the picture or document to be scanned is placed face down onto a glass surface and covered by a lid.

A powerful light inside the scanner is used as a source to reflect light from the image on the document that is being scanned. This thin tube of light slowly traverses the image, and thus a beam of light the width of the page is diverted onto a bank of photocells by a system of rotating mirrors, which is similar in principle to those shown in figure 10.13(b). These mirrors rotate so that the light beam is correctly directed at the bank of photocells, irrespective of the many different positions of the light source passing under the document during the scan. A lens then ensures that a sharp image is presented to the photocell bank. For simplicity only a single beam of light representing a single pixel at a particular instant in time has been shown in this diagram. You should appreciate that you are looking at

the scanner from the side, and have taken a slice through the device to have a look inside it. Therefore, the eventual path taken by this particular beam of light would represent a vertical stripe of pixels from the top to the bottom of the page being scanned.

First let's consider a **grey-scale image** (i.e. **shades of grey from black to white**). Different levels of light will be reflected from different parts of the picture depending on whether they are white (lots of light being reflected), black (little or no light being reflected), or somewhere in-between. Therefore, each photocell in the bank will experience a signal from the reflected light whose strength depends upon the amount of light being reflected. These light levels are obviously **analogue** in nature (see chapter 8), and therefore some sort of A to D conversion must be made so that binary signals may be sent to the computer system's memory. It is common to construct these black and white (monochrome) images considered here as being represented by 256 grey scales, thus requiring an 8-bit (2^8) A to D converter chip.

A typical scanner might have 300-dpi (dots per inch) resolution, which means that 300 photocells per linear inch in the photocell bank would be needed. Therefore, if we were to scan an A4 page which has a width of about 8¼ inches, then 300×8.25 or just under 2500 different photocells would be needed to produce the necessary 2500 pixels across an A4 page. Therefore, each square inch on the page is split up into about 90,000 squares if this typical resolution is being used. If a 256-grey scale is used, then one byte of memory would be needed to store each pixel. An A4 page is about 11.25 inches long and 8.25 inches wide, therefore, about $11.75 \times 8.25 \times 90,000$ bytes would be needed to store a 256-grey level A4 page. This works out at just over 8Mbytes of memory.

If a **colour scan** is needed then the above process must be repeated 3 times in principle (although the latest scanners offer a single-pass facility) – *once* using a **red filte**r, a *second time* using a **green filter** and a *third time* using a **blue filter**. This produces three monochromatic images which, when combined, produce a coloured image in the ways described in chapter 12 when monitors or VDUs are being considered. An A4 coloured image would thus need about 24Mbytes if 24-bit colour is used (see chapter 12) – and this is only at 300dpi! Good though this is, professional quality publications require higher resolutions so that no difference can be seen between a scanned image and an original photograph. If 600 dpi is used, for example, then over 100 Mbytes would be needed for this single very-high-quality A4 coloured image! However, compression techniques can often be used to reduce this final figure to something more realistic (see chapter 4).

The special machines that manipulate and process these high-quality images are therefore quite expensive. For example, a company in Tunbridge Wells, which helps to produce the luxury-liner brochures for companies like P&O, produce the brochures on machines with about 11Gbytes of RAM. These are obviously specialist machines running special software.

From the above you can easily see that without much thought, the scanning of images would take up an enormous amount of memory. Therefore, for all but the most affluent of computer users, we must restrict the amount of memory used when working with scanned images. The only sensible way to get over this problem is to use **compression techniques** such as **JPEG**, which are explained in chapter 4. At the author's school we insist that any scan is carried out as a 100 dpi JPEG image, and this cuts down the enormous amount of memory needed for a typical image from a few Mbytes to a few hundred Kbytes. Anybody with very large scanned images won't be able to save them onto their network files because we limit the amount of space, which is available, by using a program called Quota Manager. Without this little facility the pupils would soon fill many Gbytes of space on the NT file server, and the whole system would collapse within weeks – simply because of pupils saving large scanned images to disk!

Other forms of OCR

Optical character recognition (OCR) is *not* solely to do with the conversion of typewritten documents into computer-based text via a scanner. Similar techniques have been used in the mainframe computer environment for many years. These ideas are used extensively in service industries such as banking, gas, electricity, water supply and mail order companies, for example. These companies might choose to produce an invoice on a computer, which is then sent out to the customer. When the customer pays the bill, the same invoice is fed into a machine, which can read special characters on it that might represent the customer's account number, for example. In this way the cashier who is carrying out the transaction does not have to type in any details regarding the customer, the machine which has scanned the invoice, and translated the customer-account number into a form which the machine can understand has automatically read it. When a document, such as the invoice quoted in the above example, has been used in this way, it is called a **turnaround document**. This is because the document (called the source document) was originally produced by the computer, and has now been **turned around** and *fed back* into the computer at some later date.

The electricity supply companies are, however, going one stage better – it is now possible to electronically read special meters via the mains cables to the house. Although the water and gas companies obviously can't do this, it's possible to link up all utilities via the telephone systems so that special water or gas meters could also be read. This obviously presupposes that each house has a telephone system. Nevertheless, it could be possible for data to be transmitted via satellite systems to each house, and a small transmitter could relay back the meter readings – this is not crystal ball

Flat-bed scanners and OCR

Cost	Data entry speed	Other considerations
These machines vary from under £100 to about £800 for an A4 model depending on the quality. Larger A3 models are more expensive, with A2 models being for the specialist markets only.	Scanning of pictures depends on the quality of resolution required. Scanning of text takes about one minute for a typical page of text, much faster on the more expensive models.	These machines have made it possible for the majority of people to scan in images and perform OCR of text. Although the cheaper models are quite slow at OCR, the up-market models usually have a paper-feeder mechanism and so you can have several cups of coffee while the computer is scanning in a few hundred pages automatically.

gazing – computers linked to **radio networks** (see chapter 5) are available now.

Characters on documentation can also be used to collate different documents into some sort of order, or be used to update files automatically as they are read from the OCR peripheral machine. High-speed machines are capable of reading several thousand characters per second, and are thus capable of handling huge quantities of documents per day. Cheques are handled by the clearing banks using methods (see later) which are very similar in principle.

OCR techniques

Cost	Data entry speed	Other considerations
The larger machines capable of reading in many thousands of documents quite quickly are relatively expensive costing many thousands of pounds	Several hundred documents per minute may be read by the larger machines	These machines are gradually being superseded by the ability of many retail outlets to automatically read documents locally (i.e. from the shop) and transmit the information over a network to the mini or mainframe computer system.

Mark sense reader

Most students are only too familiar with this method of optical input – it's the method by which multiple-choice examination questions are automatically marked by computer. However, there are many other uses for this type of system such as patients ordering their food from a hospital bed, or waiters placing an order in your

Mark sense readers

Cost	Data entry speed	Other considerations
The cost of these machines varies from a few hundred pounds for small machine capable of reading examination marks for an individual school, for example, to thousands of pounds for machines which can read documents at high speed into a mini or mainframe environment.	Depends on the cost of the machine. The smaller machines for use in school could handle a few pages per minute, whereas the larger machines would handle tens of pages per second.	These machines should not be confused with conventional scanners, which can perform OCR of documents at a few pages per minute. The larger machines mentioned here are capable of inputting hundreds of thousands of candidates for examinations, and are used extensively for gathering statistical information for companies which typically carry out opinion polls or for the national census, for example.

favourite restaurant. Part of a typical multiple-choice answer form is shown in figure 10.14. An HB pencil is used to make a mark on a specific area of the paper. When the document is fed through the mark-sense reader at a later stage, the light being reflected from the pencil marks is at a different level from the light being reflected from a space where there is no pencil mark. This gives the computer the ability to determine the appropriate responses.

OCR machines typically read examination-type documents at speeds of a few hundred documents per minute. This means that it takes much less than 1/100th of a second to read in your examination responses, which you have probably sweated over for about an hour. Further food for thought is that it would take a mainframe considerably less than 1/100th of a second to mark your entire paper – then you have to wait months for the results, but that's life!

Key-to-store, key-to-disk, key-to-tape

These methods are applicable to very large companies where huge amounts of data have to be processed before being analysed by a mini or mainframe computer. The ideas are shown in figure 10.15(a) The need for such systems arises from having to convert the data from large numbers of **source documents** into machine readable format. Key-to-disk, key-to-tape, key-to-floppy and key-to-cassette systems are all available, but companies

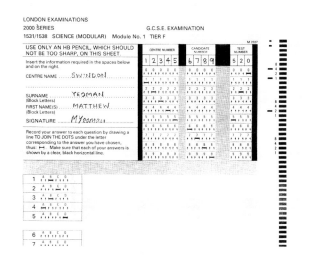

Figure 10.14

Hint: You will see these key-to-store machines only in large data-processing companies, which deal with huge volumes of batch production each day. Due to the cost effectiveness of on-line operations, they are becoming less popular as a general input method.

are now more sensibly making use of the vastly improved OCR technology mentioned in other sections in this chapter. Other techniques such as networked workstations and file servers are also taking over this role.

It is important to be able to prepare data for **batch entry** into large computer systems because it would be inefficient to tie up a high-speed computer CPU with such a slow task. Batch entry methods are those where the data to be entered is **off-line** as opposed to **direct entry methods** where the data is entered from a terminal **on-line**. **'On-line'** means 'under the control of the computer' and 'off-line' means under the control of some other device such as a key-to-disk encoder. The data is therefore transferred on to the magnetic medium ready for high-speed entry into the computer system at some later stage. Many large systems have multistation key-to-disk systems where, it is possible to have many operators typing data on to the key-to-disk system simultaneously. On such systems a minicomputer might be employed to supervise and control the entire operation including verifying the data before being entered into the main system. The principle of such a system is shown in figure 10.15(b).

Verification of data is checking data to see if any errors such as words being mistyped have occurred. Such a process involves a different operator typing in the same data again. The machine then checks the data in memory with that currently being entered.

Another important concept is **data validation.** This is where the data is checked to see if it is sensible in

the context for which it is intended, e.g. a source document might contain the age of a person as being 361 years. If this is 'correctly' typed in and verified then it would get past the checks. However, the data validation process could be set to a sensible age limit that would detect such an error. Similar validation checks could be made to ensure that letters are not typed in when numbers are expected etc.

Hint: Students often confuse the terms 'verification' and 'validation'. Don't forget that validation checks the validity in some context, and you may need to verify if something is exactly as it should be.

Key-to-store systems (key to disk, key to tape and key to cassette)

Cost	Data entry speed	Other considerations
These are specialist machines used in the context of huge data entry tasks where many people would sit down purely for the purpose of getting data onto disks or tape etc. Being specialist machines they are therefore expensive.	Depends on the speed of the operator, but typically the same as for typing, which on average is just under a few hundred words per minute.	These machines are still used in large data processing companies, but will quickly be super-seded by the rapidly reducing costs of networked computers, where operatives can have their own workstations and key the data directly into a suitable database held on a file server.

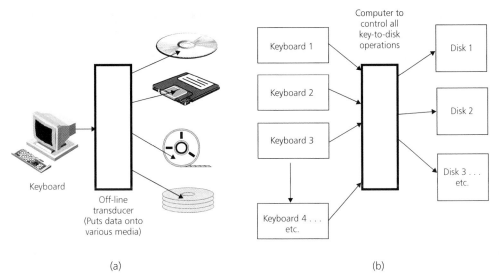

(a)   (b)

Figure 10.15 (a) and (b)

Figure 10.16 (a)

Magnetic ink character recognition (MICR)

One of the best examples of MICR is the line of characters that appears at the bottom of bank cheques (see figure 10.16(a)). The special characters form the numbers which represent the cheque number, branch number (sort code), and customer account number. These characters are designed to be read by humans but also by a special machine called an **MICR reader**, hence the slightly weird shape of the numbers. A picture of a typical MICR reader is shown in figure 10.16(b).

Figure 10.16(b)

Special ink is used that can be magnetised by passing the characters through a magnetic field before the cheque is read by the **MICR** reading head inside the machine. The system of characters is known as the **E13B** font and only 14 different characters are available. These are the characters 0 to 9 and four special symbols. There are no alphabetic characters available. The advantage of the MICR process for banks is that enormous numbers of cheques may be cleared quickly and the system is capable of reading the characters even if the numbers on the cheques have been folded. The banks put on further MICR information representing the amount of the cheque after the cheque has been cashed, to aid the

processes which are carried out at a later stage. Without such machines, the major clearing banks would not be able to maintain a system of clearing all cheques within just three days.

MICR		
Cost	Data entry speed	Other considerations
The cost of these machines is quite high because they are used in a very specialist market for the clearing banks and the like.	Depends on the machine but thousands of cheques can be processed in minutes.	Although these machines have been around for a long time, they will be with us until society decides not to make use of cheques anymore, and this will probably be a considerable number of years yet. A very reliable and fast method of data entry for banking purposes.

Did you know that . . .

MICR is one of the oldest and most established of the character-recognition methods. It dates back to the very earliest of methods for getting information from bank cheques into a computer, and is still used, almost unmodified, in today's modern banking environment. Until recently, people had to read the amount on the cheque and encode the information by hand, but Courtesy Amount Recognition (CAR) is now automating this last operation of cheque processing that used to be carried out by humans.

Electronic funds transfer (EFT)

There are very few large banks without EFT machines sitting outside. These machines are generally known as **cash terminals, teller machines, automatic cash**

Figure 10.17 (a) and (b)

dispenser machines, or financial transaction terminals. A typical terminal is shown in figure 10.17(a) and a typical cash card complete with magnetic strip is shown in figure 10.17(b).

These machines act as a 24-hour banking service which offers facilities to customers such as withdrawals and deposits. The customer has to insert a plastic card with data such as account number and credit limit (the maximum amount that can be withdrawn each day) magnetically encoded on to it. A **personal identification number (PIN)**, which acts as a password, must then be typed in. After the password has been typed in and accepted by the computer the customer may choose from a range of services consisting typically of balance enquiry, statement request, withdrawal and, in some cases, deposits.

In fact the cash machine outside the bank is only a very small part of the complete EFT system now in operation. Much more grandiose schemes are being developed here and in the USA. Instead of an encoded magnetic strip or stripe it is now possible to incorporate a microchip inside the card. Much information could be stored inside this chip and updated each time it is plugged into the EFT machine. Cards that incorporate microchips are known as **smart cards** and have become more widespread in the late 1990s. The computers inside the latest version of these smart cards can be programmed to self-destruct if the wrong password is entered too many times! EFT facilities are not limited to cash dispenser machines. Businesses are using EFT to transfer money electronically from one business to another.

As well as smart cards it is possible to get smart keys, i.e. door keys with microchips inside them. Such keys can form the basis of security systems in industry and some high-tech hotels (see chapter 9). Information regarding who has entered what door and when can be logged by the computer system, which is linked to all the doors. If the system were used in conjunction with a

Did you know that . . .

Smart cards are now so cheap that you can use them in projects at school or college. For less than a couple of hundred pounds, you can buy a machine that programs the cards. You could then use a smart-card reader to transfer the program into a device like a small robot, for example. 14-year old pupils use this in their technology lessons at the author's school.

digital keypad at the point of entry, then a password (which can be changed at any time by the central computer system) as well as a key would be needed to gain entry and a very secure system is therefore established.

Video input

Having a video signal connected to a computer system is not new but the variety of things that can now be done with this signal is getting pretty exciting. With a suitable interface it is now easy to plug in a standard video signal from a camcorder or a TV receiver, and then display the picture within a window on the computer's screen.

The **graphic (resulting video picture)** can usually be displayed in real time (i.e. as a moving image), or you can capture a still at exactly the right moment in time. The resultant **graphic** can then, for example, be imported into an **art package** for further processing, be used as an image in a **DTP** frame, saved as a **still photo** on an **optical disk** or sent via the telephone line to a colleague who is far away. Being digitised, the image is then in a computer-data format – which may obviously be processed in any way that you wish.

A whole new industry has been built up around processing video images on the computer, and a powerful computer with the appropriate hardware attached can now act as a professional editing suite for making excellent-quality videos at a fraction of the cost of using more-conventional equipment. A typical system from Fast is shown in figure 10.18.

Video recorders can be remote controlled by the computer, do assemble and insert edits, colour correction, time-base correction and a variety of other useful processing can be carried out. Video processors and special effects units for producing wipes and fades can now be replaced with a suitable computer system. Titles and other graphics can be superimposed onto any video image, and colour-separation overlay (CSO) can easily be achieved. Making use of the CSO technique it is possible, for example, to create effects which make it look like Superman is flying over New York, when in actual fact, he is lying down on a blue background. A moving video image of New York has been used as a backdrop for his image, which is actually superimposed. Most people are already aware that powerful computers can produce stunning surrealistic images, which, when coupled with real-time video control, will produce a whole new arsenal for the next generation of professional and amateur film makers.

Non-linear editing

A more-recent development for video processing is called **non-linear editing**. Traditionally one or two video recorders are used as the source to provide material that is to be recorded in sequence onto a third video recorder. However, it's now possible to store a couple of hour's video on large optical CD-ROM drives, and edit the lot in one go. The computer stores all the instructions necessary for the entire video production, and then goes through the process of putting the whole thing in the correct sequence onto a single video recorder. The amount spent on computer kit is probably saved by having to have fewer video recorders and effects processors etc. A very powerful PC-type computer can do it all.

Video communications

Video input makes it possible to turn your PC into a **videophone**, and some companies (including IBM and BT) are now manufacturing the technology to do exactly this (see **Plate 24**).

A video camera placed on top of the screen relays your image to the person at the other end of the phone via the **modem** (see chapter 5) in your computer, and a similar arrangement transmits the recipient's image back to your computer. The audio signals are obviously sent by microphone. Figure 10.19 shows this system in operation. Technology such as this obviously has much to offer the commercial market, especially in the field of **video conferencing** (see **Plates 24** and **25**). Companies can set up meetings with 'eyeball-to-eyeball' communication between people who are not in the same room, building, or even the same country – and all because the computer can handle **video input**. However, much use has to be made of compression techniques (see chapter 4) if acceptable non-jittery video images are to be transmitted over a standard telephone line in real time.

Figure 10.18

over the last few years. Initially the professionals laughed at these cameras because of the poor quality image compared to film. However, even this has been overcome to some extent, especially if you are still prepared to pay thousands of pounds for the appropriate camera. A typical digital camera which most of us can afford is shown in figure 10.20(a) with a more expensive version in figure 10.20(b). A very high quality camera at the time of writing is shown in figure 10.20(c).

Did you know that . . .

Companies like estate agents are now turning their attention to the digital camera. This has a very fast turnaround time and is something which is particularly useful when the housing market is buoyant. However, the wide-angle versions of these cameras, so necessary for estate agent's work, are still more expensive than conventional techniques at the time of writing.

Figure 10.19

The digital camera

This revolutionary camera technology does not store the image on film, but stores the picture image in a bank of memory inside the camera, or on a special memory card that may be plugged into the camera for extra storage. The pictures can then be downloaded into the computer at a later date and stored on disk, where the post-production process is limited only by your imagination, hardware and software available.

Hint: If your school has a digital camera, this may be useful for some of your project work. For example, a project which involves some robotics may be instantly photographed and downloaded into your project documentation.

These cameras have made very significant technological advances in the last few years and typically have come down in price so that the average person is now able to think about owning one. From thousands of pounds to as little as £150 has been the drop in price

These cameras make it possible to capture an image and have printouts within minutes. As a bonus these cameras are also able to show you instantly the picture you have just taken, so there's no more disappointments such as not realising that you had your finger over the lens! Most reasonably priced cameras now come with a range of facilities including zoom and flash, and the more advanced cameras have facilities for manual focus and macros etc.

The amount of storage that you have and the resolution with which you wish to take the picture determines exactly how many pictures you can take without downloading the images into your computer first. Typically the cheaper cameras would have resolutions of 640×480, but more expensive models would have 1024×768 or 1280×960 for good quality shots. Typically you would be able to take about 60 low-resolution shots or 36 medium resolution shots with a mid-range camera at the time of writing. The professional cameras allow images of 4500×3648 in 16

Figure 10.20 (a), (b) and (c)

million colours, but I would not like to have to buy the hard disks or CD-ROMs to store many of these exceptional quality images – work it out – it's about 50 Mbytes/image if no compression is used! And the top quality cameras allow you to set white balance, colour calibration and exposure settings etc.

Don't forget the enormously important role that the software that usually accompanies some of these cameras performs. It is no exaggeration to say that virtually any attribute of the original image can be changed, with the possible exception of trying to correct an original image which was out of focus.

Digital cameras

Cost	Data entry speed	Other considerations
The cost of these machines varies from a few hundred pounds for cameras intended for schools and the home, through to a few thousand pounds for professional use to about £10,000 for photographic studio standard work.	Comparable to that of normal cameras but much faster to get the actual image processed because there is no film processing to do.	These cameras have really come into their own in the last few years. They are ideal for businesses such as estate agents or for the police who need to process an image quickly in order to get information out quickly, compared to the use of film techniques. With high-quality glossy paper photographic quality is easily possible and software for post-production processing is impressive. These are also ideal for the production of images for Internet sites.

Speech input

To a human, speech is a deceptively simple means of communication, but to a machine it's extremely complicated due to the vast variety inherent in human speech. Not only are there different ways of saying exactly the same thing, there are different languages, different dialects within the same language, different sounds within each dialect, and even the same people can sound quite different on different days because they might have a cold, for example. Such a system is obviously going to be fraught with difficulty, unless we can find some common characteristic on which to perform some sort of analysis.

One method is to undertake an analysis of the speech by breaking up the sound into what are called **phonemes**.

Using this method one can analyse (and produce) acceptable speech by stringing together the many basic sounds which can be made by humans using their vocal chords. However, even when this method is perfected, there are usually problems relating to the actual spelling of the text, especially in a language like English, for example, in which the spelling of a word sometimes bears little relationship to how it sounds.

> **Hint:** If you have the patience to train a speech recognition system for many hours, then you too may be able to dictate into your computer at near-typing speeds. As each new generation of speech recognition gets better, the Utopian dream of being able to speak to the computer becomes ever closer.

It's also important to understand the principles that will be covered in later chapters on computer languages. It is mentioned that natural languages, such as English, for example, are context sensitive. Therefore, words like 'there' and 'their', which sound exactly the same phonetically, will have to be interpreted in different ways by the computer. Humans use the context-sensitive nature of language without thought, and it is this which enables us to understand a foreigner, for example, trying to speak English. Due to the large amount of redundancy contained within a language like English, we are able to get the gist of what someone is trying to say. Therefore, if a computer is to correctly interpret what's being said, then it too must cope with context sensitivity, in addition to the huge number of problems outlined above.

Even if we can correctly interpret the sound in a context sensitive way, we have the additional human problems of making false starts, uttering words which we then instantly alter, and speaking against a background of noise such as traffic, a radio or other people chatting. Our brains automatically filter out what we don't want to hear, and we use facial expression and other body language to help rectify our far from faultless modes of conversation.

After reading the above one might be tempted to throw ones hands in the air and give up. However, tremendous progress has been made, and many different research projects are going on around the world. Computer models of the human vocal and auditory systems have been simulated on powerful computers, mathematicians are frantically working on sound analysis and pattern recognition, and computer scientists are developing algorithms that are getting more successful. The next section shows what can be achieved by a state-of-the-art package at a very reasonable cost.

Practical speech recognition

During 1997, speech recognition became available at very low cost indeed. For example, the Dragon Dictate system from Dragon Systems and the Simply Speaking system from IBM are both excellent systems which can now deliver amazing results if you are patient and are prepared to put in the practice. Here we will use the excellent Dragon Dictate system as an example of how speech recognition may be integrated into the Windows environment.

The most important thing to realise is that there are several modes of operation. There is not sufficient space to go into much detail here. However, after activating the software, and going through a typical voice-training session for the first time so that the system can get used to your voice, you could issue the command [Wake up], and the software will now pay attention to your voice!

Next, issue a command like [Mouse grid], for example, and a grid will appear on the screen as shown in figure 10.21.

In figure 10.21 you can see that a numbered grid has appeared. Speak one of the numbers like, 1, for example, and the mouse pointer would move to the middle of grid space number one, where a finer grid with a similar numbering system would be presented. Other commands such as [Mouse Right], [Mouse Up] or [Mouse Left] etc. would enable you to fine-tune the position of the mouse until it is exactly over the icon of your choice. Finally, speak a command like [Mouse Double Click], and, assuming that you happened to be over a folder icon, then the folder would be opened up – and all done by the power of speech – magic.

There are many useful commands, such as [Bring Up Microsoft Excel], or [Bring Up Microsoft Word], for example. These commands, assuming that you are in command mode, would cause the spreadsheet or the word processor to be loaded. Assuming, for example, that you have loaded Microsoft Word, then you could issue the command [Dictate Mode], and away you go! This mode is, actually, the most difficult to operate well, due to the vast increase in the vocabulary compared to command mode. There are other commands such as [Scratch That], which will scratch a previous word if you have got it wrong, and commands like [New Line] or [New Paragraph] etc. help with the formatting.

If you are in dictate mode, for example, then after issuing the words [Command Mode] will ensure that your commands are not interpreted as dictation. Furthermore, you can issue a command like [Menu Pick View], which if you were in Microsoft Word, for example, would cause the View menu to appear at the top of the screen. Speak some of the words in the menu like 'Zoom' for example, and the zoom sub menu will be displayed, where you can also issue commands like '75%' or 'Page width' etc. and when you are finished you can say OK, and the screen will be altered accordingly. It really is very good indeed, and well worth the £40 cost, which includes the headphones and microphone combination, and an interface box which plugs into the back of your computer.

Currently Dragon systems are working on an updated version which will cope with continuous speech with an 80,000 word vocabulary at speeds of up to 200 words per minute – easily fast enough to keep up with the most demanding chatterbox! When, (not if), these systems work, as usual we will be limited only by the person's ability to speak or think more quickly. A few years ago, if such a system had existed it would have cost many thousands of pounds – the affordable price is a measure of the progress which speech recognition systems have made in the last few years. Dragon Dictate also does a professional version, and this has even more powerful facilities, but is obviously very much more expensive. The future looks very exciting indeed, and I look forward to the next five years with eager anticipation.

Speech

Cost	Data entry speed	Other considerations
Excellent cost-effective speech systems now exist for about £40. Professional versions are also available for a few hundred pounds or less.	Depends on the human operator, but a trained operator can dictate into the computer at speeds in excess of 90 words per minute. The keyboard is, at last, becoming threatened for the first time.	This input medium is ideal for hands-free operation, and is thus suitable for industries where this is a requirement. It is also ideal for disabled people who are able to talk to their computer.

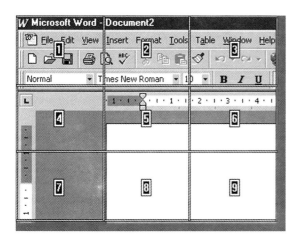

Figure 10.21

Sound input

Sound from a *variety of sources* (e.g. microphone, DAT, CD etc.) can now be stored and processed with ease making use of today's modern microcomputers.

Sound input

Cost	Data entry speed	Other considerations
The cost depends on the facilities available, but typically a sound card, some software and a micro-phone are all that are need. If you want to do recording then a better quality soundcard, and a computer with a recordable CD would be ideal.	Real time – it's as simple as that!	These systems have also come of age in the last few years. It is now usual to find a computer in the theatre for sound effects, and to find computers increas-ingly used in record-ing studios, especially in conjunction with high-quality DAT machines. The post-production facilities in some of the software is extremely impressive, with some software being able to alter any attribute of the audio quality of the recording that you care to define.

A special **digitiser board** is necessary to convert the **analogue signals** (see chapter 8) which represent the sound, into **digital signals**, which the computer can understand. The device, which carries out these con-versions, is called an A-to-D converter. If 16-bit A to D converters are used, then, assuming the sampling rate is sufficient (see chapter 8), CD-quality sound will be input ready for processing.

Sound sampling

Sound input (**sound sampling**) takes up pots of memory, with 40Kbytes/second of memory being typical. At this rate it would take nearly 8Mbytes to store a 3-minute pop song. However, computers are rarely used simply to replace a tape recorder – the advantage comes with the computer's ability to processes the sound in an infinite number of ways. For example, an old scratchy record could be digitised, and then all the scratches (repre-sented by very sharp peaks on the sound graph) could be removed. The digitised information can then be recorded on a CD ready for mastering a new batch of scratch-free recordings.

Computers with fast A to Ds attached can act as spec-trum analysers for the recorded sound thus replacing very expensive specialist equipment. This allows engi-neers to obtain a frequency spectrum of the sound which could help them to design better acoustics for buildings, for example.

Sound effects

In the theatre the computer has become part of the stan-dard kit for producing sound effects, digitised sound effects can be precisely queued, or a quadraphonic sound stage can be controlled giving the audience the illusion that aircraft are buzzing round the theatre, for example. Effects such as these are difficult to control by manual means.

MIDI

MIDI is a special standard, which was originally devel-oped to link electronic keyboards (of the **musical** variety!) together. **MIDI** stands for **Musical Instrument Digital Interface**. As is the case with most things electronic, the addition of a computer can consider-ably enhance functionality, and much special software for controlling these key-boards from the computer has been developed.

> **Hint:** If you are a musician, why not make use of the software which translates what you are playing into a musical score? It beats writing it out by hand!

MIDI is being considered here because it is a special form of computer input. Musicians are able to play on these MIDI-equipped electronic keyboards (or any other device connected up to the MIDI interface such as a guitar or clarinet, for example) and the music being played appears on the screen. The system is not without its problems, the biggest of which is that most musi-cians are not robots (but some robots are musicians!) and therefore what appears on the screen might not be

MIDI

Cost	Data entry speed	Other considerations
The cost varies according to the facilities and quality of the keyboard, software and other equip-ment, but typically a good MIDI keyboard would be a few hundred to a few thousand pounds.	Real time – i.e. the same speed as playing a musical instrument when recording.	Whole recording industries are built up around this technology. Note that it is not the same as recording the sound, you are recording the electronic patterns of the notes, and can thus change the instruments and do very fancy things like this later on. You can also overlay many tracks to make a single musician sound like an entire orchestra!

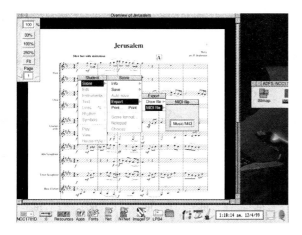

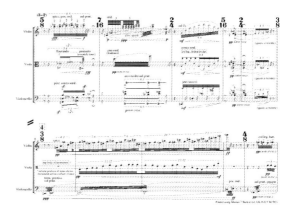

Figure 10.22

quite that which was intended. However, bum notes can be edited out, and any other attribute of the system may be changed too.

With a suitable system such as Sibelius that is shown in Figure 10.22, professional standards of music capture and consequent printing is easily possible.

Virtual reality input

Virtual reality or VR provides the current state-of-the-art in computer input. Appropriate hardware devices like the data glove shown in figure 10.23 could enable a user to interact with his or her virtual environment by pointing a finger or operating a virtual control panel. For example, the image of an imaginary control panel can be projected into the user's eyes via a helmet that is worn on his or her head (see chapter 11). The human hand wearing the data glove could produce a virtual hand in the computer's memory, which is also projected into the eyes of the user. By moving the real hand the virtual hand can mirror the operations, and be used to operate a virtual control on the virtual panel. People at NASA have already programmed such systems to play virtual musical instruments or to pick up virtual tools and do virtual work.

The data glove

The data glove may contain fibre-optic cables, some LEDs and a special tracking mechanism which is able to determine the position of the glove within a specified 3-D Cartesian co-ordinate system (usually a room).

For simplicity the body of the glove on the hand has not been shown, and the fibre-optic sensors are only one per finger. However, the principles are all here – the amount of light being detected from the

LED (detector not shown) via the fibre-optic link depends upon the degree of bending of the finger joint. Therefore, this system can detect if a finger is straight (pointing) or bent – it can also detect the degree of bending. If multiple fibre-optic and LED arrangements were put on each finger, then more-sophisticated movements could obviously be detected. A separate system called a **Polhemus** (part of which is shown at the top of the hand), relays positional information regarding the hand (or VR helmet – see chapter 11) back to a system which is completely separate from the fibre-optic network inside the glove. The data glove has found many practical uses, and one system that has been developed translates sign language for the deaf into script on the computer – now that's computer input!

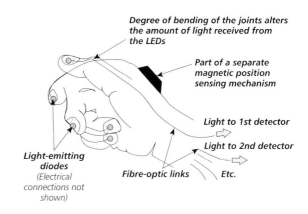

Figure 10.23

Current conventions dictate that certain movements of the hand will cause the software controlling the virtual environment to react in a particular way. For example, point with the index finger of one hand (you could have a data glove on each!) and you might move within the virtual world in the direction in which you have just pointed. This sort of technology has been used as an interface to control robots in hostile environments. For example, with the appropriate output devices, it would be possible to get a mechanical hand to mirror the action of a virtual hand, which in turn is being controlled by a real hand inside the data glove. The mechanical hand could belong to a robot that is defusing a bomb! Being telepresent in this situation is a far safer experience than being actually present.

Did you know that . . .

Many Internet sites now make use of VRML, the virtual-reality modelling language (see chapter 4). Very soon it will be possible to surf the net by making use of a VR helmet (see chapter 11) and a data glove. You can imagine going round a virtual supermarket and actually picking up the goods to put into the trolley by using your own hand.

The data glove is probably the most commonly known example of VR (see **Plate 26**) input, but whole-body suits have been wired up in similar ways to enable humans to react with machines in ever more sophisticated ways. With the vast increase in microprocessor power over the next ten years VR systems will become more sophisticated and realistic. For example, trans-

ducers (see chapter 8) already exist to apply pressure so that the user experiences *g* force, and hence torque or the feeling of picking up some weight within the virtual world, and heat pumps are being used to give feelings of hot and cold – the mind boggles. People have already started working on brain-wave monitors and limited success with these systems has meant that people can 'think about' turning machines on and off – and it actually happens. It is reasonably trivial to get a trained person to control brain-wave activity in simple ways, monitor this activity via EEG electrodes placed on the scalp, and get the person to 'think' about activating a machine. This is a far cry from the film *Fire Fox* in which Clint Eastwood stole a thought-controlled Russian fighter plane – but who knows what we can expect in the future?

Smells

This is currently an underdeveloped form of input, but is rapidly gaining popularity in industry with the development of new software techniques. In the second edition of this book it was predicted that computers would probably be giving their opinions on the Beaujolais Nouveau! Although we are not quite at this stage yet, 1994 saw the development of computers which can sort out different varieties of champagne by 'sniffing' the contents of the glass. The system operates using the principles of **neural networks** (see chapter 9), coupled with appropriate input transducers (see chapter 8), and provides a very reliable means of sorting out fake champagne from the real thing. The system has been praised by leading wine-tasting experts and should open up whole new avenues in the fight against forgery in industries like food, drink and perfumery. You may also like to link this little gem of knowledge with that of smelly-vision described in chapter 11 where smells are generated as a computer output.

Other forms of input

There are literally hundreds of other more-specialist ways of entering data into a computer system, for example, **light levels**, **pollution levels**, **currents** and **voltages**, **pH measurements** and the like can *all* be **monitored automatically** and **logged** by using a suitable range of *input transducers*. However, this area of computing is so vast that it is considered in a separate chapter on computer control. All the necessary input techniques for physical quantities such as those just described are covered in chapter 8.

VR input		
Cost	**Data entry speed**	**Other considerations**
The cost of these devices varies. At the time of writing this is still a specialist field, but no doubt data gloves and the like will be on sale in the high street in a few years time at a reasonable cost.	Real time – depends on the movements of the body. Most systems can cope rather well with very rapid bodily movements.	These devices, in conjunction with the VR helmet covered in chapter 11 have revolutionised the ways in which human beings can interact with the computer. We are still in the early stages of development, and much computer processing power is needed to be able to cope with these VR devices.

Exercise 10.1

1 Choose one or more appropriate methods of data entry for the following situations or applications – in each case fully justify your answers:

  a Marking multiple-choice examination scripts

  b CAD

  c Cyberspace – virtual reality

  d Retail outlet

  e Production of CD-ROM based texts from existing books

  f Getting quality coloured images into a DTP system

  g Production of sheet music from a music keyboard.

2 Why have ergonomic keyboards recently increased in popularity?

3 Explain a typical use for OCR with turnaround documentation.

4 Explain how a concept keyboard might be appropriately used in a children's nursery.

5 What is EFTPOS, where is it used, and what advantage does it have over conventional methods of transferring funds?

6 Write brief notes on the following topics:

  a Different types of computer keyboards

  b Using the mouse and track-ball as a computer input device

  c The graphics tablet as a computer-based input medium for artists

  d Computers as alternatives to video-editing equipment

  e Getting a computer to give its opinion on the Beaujolais Nouveau.

7 When perfected, voice input will obviously lead to the demise of the keyboard! Make up two convincing arguments – one for and one against this idea.

8 PDAs are beginning to change the face of sub-notebook computer design. Find out about recently developed PDA systems and comment on some likely possible future scenarios for this particular technology.

9 Bar codes, magnetic stripe cards and smart cards can all be used as a means of gaining access to a secure building. Comment on which system would be the most effective, stating reasons for your answers. Name three other measures, which could be taken which would enhance security still further when used in combination with your chosen system.

10 Comment on the likely differences in computer-input techniques regarding office PCs and mainframe computer installations.

11 When a document is scanned it might be in what's called bit-mapped image form. What is meant by this statement and what would have to be done to the text to get it into a form which could be understood by the computer?

12 A systems analyst has been asked to suggest ways of getting computer input from severely disabled people with very limited movement capacity. For example, a 'nod of the head' or 'the movement of a big toe' etc. Suggest several ways in which this particular type of computer input may be transferred into a system whereby the disabled person could make use of a specialised word processor.

End of chapter revision aid and summary

Cover up the right-hand column and see if you can answer the questions or define the terms on the left. They appear in the order in which they are covered in this chapter. Alternatively you may browse through the right-hand column to aid revision.

What is a peripheral and why is the term still used?	An input, output or secondary-storage device is called a computer peripheral. Input peripherals are devices for getting data into a computer system. The term peripheral is still appropriate even though in modern micros many of these peripheral devices are likely to be housed in the same unit as the main processor.
What layout would you find on a standard British or American keyboard?	The standard QWERTY keyboard is still the most common manual data-input device, but new forms of ergonomic keyboards are helping to reduce RSI.
What is RSI?	RSI – Repetitive Strain Injury, caused by long uninterrupted use of the keyboard.
What is the purpose of non-standard keyboards?	Non-QWERTY keyboards are available and useful for special purposes, but are unlikely to supersede standard and ergonomic keyboards in the foreseeable future.
What is a touch screen?	Touch screens enable users to point at the screen with their finger, usually at an icon or word. With appropriate software loaded this causes some action to take place.
What is a light pen?	Light pens enable users to draw pictures on the screen by using an appropriate pen connected to the computer. This can also act as a pointer-input device.
What is a mouse?	The mouse is currently the most popular pointing device for input on desktop micros, but is also becoming standard equipment due to extensive use of windows.
What is a WIMP?	WIMPs (Windows Icons Menu Pointer) are now the most-common forms of GUI (Graphical User Interface).
What is a track ball?	Track balls are commonly becoming an alternative to the mouse for input, especially for portables where they are built into the keyboard.
What is a joystick?	Joysticks are a common form of computer input, especially with computer games and software such as flight-simulators where they are often integrated into a control panel called a yoke (i.e. with some of the flight controls built in). The force-feedback joystick is the latest innovation.
Comment on pen-based input methods.	Pen-input methods are a common input technique on PDAs (Personal Digital Assistants), and provide an alternative to the keyboard for entry of small amounts of data. It is now possible to input joined-up handwriting using these techniques.
What is a graphics tablet?	Graphics tablets are used in conjunction with a stylus or puck to input graphical information. They are ideal for art or CAD applications.
What is a concept keyboard?	Concept keyboards are useful for specialist-data input ranging from primary schools to complex CAD packages.
Comment on OCR from a batch-processing perspective.	OCR (1) (Optical Character Recognition) is used extensively in batched-based turnaround documentation. It enables characters (usually in human-readable form) to be input into the computer system. Used for fast data input.
Comment on OCR from a single-user perspective.	OCR (2) (Optical Character Recognition) is used to enter pre-typed or neatly-hand-written documents into the computer. A bit-mapped image is

usually produced by a scanner, which then gets interpreted by comparison with known patterns. Some current systems are often slow and unreliable.

What is a mark-sense reader?

Mark-sense readers are devices designed to read marks usually made with an HB-pencil. A common example is the multiple-choice-exam script marking system.

What is a bar code?

Bar codes are now commonly found on all types of consumer goods, food and books etc. They can be easily read by bar-code readers (optical wands) or LASER scanners as found at many supermarket EFTPOS (Electronic Funds Transfer at the Point Of Sale) terminals.

What is MICR?

MICR (Magnetic Ink Character Recognition) uses the E13B font found at the bottom of bank cheques. It is used by the bank's clearing-house system.

What is EFT?

EFT stands for Electronic Funds Transfer and refers to teller machines, cash terminals, hole-in-the-wall machines etc., which accept credit, smart and cheque cards for obtaining cash and other transactions.

What is a scanner?

Scanners are the devices that convert images (and text) into bit-mapped images so that the picture or text can be loaded into a computer system in bit-mapped form.

What is a hand-held scanner?

Hand-held scanners are lower quality scanners with more limited resolutions and smaller scanning areas.

What is a flat-bed scanner?

Flat-bed scanners vary in size from small A5 to A3 models or larger. The large high-resolution 24-bit colour scanners are more expensive and much memory is needed to store the image produced from the scanner.

How might video input be used?

Video input is a means of digitising a video signal from a camcorder or VTR so that it may be processed by a computer system. Input for art packages and DTP images are common using this method, but video phones, powerful editing suites and video processors for the film industry are now available at a reasonable cost.

How is video editing achieved on a computer?

Video editing is now possible using a computer system instead of a vast array of more-specialist electronic equipment. Real-time video editing needs a powerful machine with a large hard disk.

Comment on the current state of voice-input technology.

Voice input is still a long way from the ideal, but is becoming quite reasonable if properly trained. It won't be long before large vocabulary systems are in common use at a reasonable price.

What is MIDI?

MIDI input from a suitably equipped musical instrument or keyboard can be used to input data about music into a computer. The music may then be printed out on a printer or used to play any suitably-equipped keyboard.

What is a data glove?

A data glove is a device worn on the hand with connections to a computer system. With appropriate software loaded, movements of the hand may be translated into actions in a virtual world.

How might VR be used for computer input?

Virtual reality (VR) systems may use special input devices such as the data glove.

11 Output Techniques

In this chapter you'll learn about:

- The enormous range of standard output peripherals, such as monitors, printers and COM
- More unusual output peripherals such as VR helmets
- When it's most appropriate to use each type of output peripheral
- The price and performance of current output peripheral devices

Key Resources

To carry out this work most successfully it's best if you have:

- Access to a range of current output peripheral devices such as a dot-matrix printer, laser printer and ink-jet printer
- Access to various types of monitors found on desktop and portable computers
- Access, if possible, to systems such as voice input and MIDI

Concept Checkpoints

- Understand the binary number system as outlined in chapter 2.

Introduction

The extraction of data in whatever form from a computer system is of obvious fundamental importance, and this chapter is therefore devoted to these essential output peripheral devices. As with the computer-input-devices chapter, students undertaking computer science courses should be fully aware of the hardware from a performance and usefulness point of view, but are not usually expected to remember any of the technical details. Nevertheless, some technical details are included here as understanding a few of these helps considerably. For example, an understanding of bit-mapped graphics, which is required in most syllabuses, is enhanced considerably with a little knowledge of raster displays. Students are also usually curious, and many interesting modern developments would remain a complete mystery if no technical details were included at all. Most students wish to know at a simple level how colour LCD displays on the latest portable work, for example. Therefore, this chapter goes slightly beyond the conventional syllabuses by giving simple and clear answers to the sort of hardware questions most often asked by the students in the classroom at this level.

Computer monitors

Some time ago the only output peripheral on a computer system was a printer, which had upper-case only characters! Next came low-resolution computer screens and the versatile dot-matrix printers and plotters – but in the last ten to twenty years the variety of output devices has become vast, ranging from **COM** via **voice** *and* **bubble jets** to **photo-CD ROMs** to name but a few. Today the computer screen is probably *the* most-common form of output, and is used on all but a very few of the current computer systems. The computer screen is more correctly called a **monitor**, but the term **VDU (Visual Display Unit)** and **monitor** are interchangeable. The term **computer display** is also sometimes used. Being the most prolific form of output, monitors will therefore be considered first in this chapter.

Basic principles

Gone are the times when you simply went out and asked for a computer monitor! Do you need TTL RGB, analogue RGB, hi-res, low-res, colour or monochrome? Do you need CGA, EGA, (nobody in their right mind would want these types anymore!) – or perhaps you might need VGA, SVGA, UVGA, multi-sync, non-multisync, low radiation, touch-sensitive – the list of features is enormous. **Figure 11.1** shows some high-quality modern monitors, but let's look at the basics first, and get to the bottom of the details concerning the ever-growing complexity and terminology associated with computer monitors.

(a)　　　　　　　(b)　　　　　　　(c)　　　　　　　(d)

Figure 11.1

The LCD screens found in portables will be covered shortly, but most **monitors** for **desk-top microcomputers**, **mainframes** and **minis** are based around a **CRT** (**Cathode Ray Tube**) similar to that found in your TV sets. However, this is where the similarity ends. Most people don't sit just a few inches away from their TVs, thus lower-quality tubes can be used when it comes to domestic sets. Due to this short-viewing distance and the fact that very small text (compared to the screen size) must be easily readable, computer monitors tend to have a much-higher quality screen than a conventional TV. (This is just one of the reasons why you can buy a good-quality large television for just a few hundred pounds, whereas a good large monitor (i.e. 25 or 30 inch, for example, costs a few thousand pounds.) In practice this means that the tiny dots which make up the picture on the screen are much closer together. You will thus see adverts, which say that a monitor has a 0.25 mm dot pitch, for example, which refers to the distance between the dots. The smaller distances represent the better quality monitors.

Raster scanning

The early computer screens were low-resolution-text-only monochrome (i.e. white on black or black on amber etc.) models. However, the ideas are still very similar, where a single electron beam scans from the top to the bottom of the screen as shown in figure 11.2. Each time the electron beam passes a point on the screen this causes the phosphor dots on the screen to glow for a short period of time. By turning the beam on and off very quickly as the picture is scanned, an illusion of a picture (or text) can be made to appear on the screen. This method, whereby dots are generated line by line on the screen, is known as a **raster scan**. Notice that in figure 11.2 the electron beam starts off at the top left-hand side, then scans across the screen line by line. The beam is very quickly returned to the left-hand side at the end of each line, and this is known as the 'flyback period' – the picture is thus blanked off during flyback. Similarly, when the beam reaches the bottom of the screen, another flyback period and blanking gets it back to the start at the top left-hand side again. Figure 11.2 shows what is called a non-interlaced raster scan. This mode of operation is common in computer monitors, but interlaced raster scanning where the screen is constructed as two separate parts called fields is also available, and is the system used in many domestic TV sets.

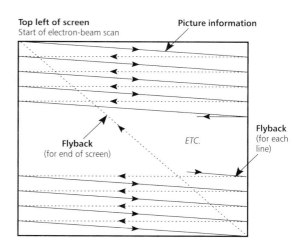

Figure 11.2

Did you know that . . .

When the author started teaching computer science, back in 1976, most computers did not have a monitor! There was no screen on which to view the results of your efforts, and all output, even things like the cursor for the operating-system prompt was printed out on a mechanical typewriter called a teletype.

TTL colour monitors

The next generation of monitors to be introduced were **colour**, and are based on the fact that most colours (when using light) can be made up by a mixture of just **three primary colours** namely **red**, **green** and **blue**

Hint: If you still have an old BBC computer, you will probably find that the monitor is TTL. If you manage to connect this to your new PC, you will only get a very few colours displayed.

(hence the term **RGB monitor**). Artists should note that colour mixing making use of light is *not the same* as with paints. Figure 11.3(a) shows a Venn diagram, which represents the three **primary colours**, together with the other combinations, which can be obtained by having the primary colours switched completely on or off. As *three* primary colours are used, colour monitors need *three electron guns* inside them, and each gun illuminates the red, green or blue phosphors on the screen. (This is why colour monitors are so much more expensive than monochrome ones.) A clever arrangement of dots 'in groups of threes' (called triads), similar in idea to the Venn diagram, creates an illusion of a single colour. As each triad of dots is so close together, at normal viewing distances you can't distinguish between them – hence you are fooled into thinking you are seeing a single colour. Other systems making use of stripes instead of dots are also available.

The early colour monitors had simple electronics inside them based on a system called TTL (Transistor-Transitor Logic) logic. This meant that the guns could only be switched completely on or off, and hence a choice of just 8 colours were available. (Poetic licence enables us to call black and white colours.) These systems were typical of what was then available on computers such as the old BBC micro. Figure 11.3(b) shows a truth table in which the colours and corresponding bits needed to control the colour are mapped out. It can be seen that just 3 bits are needed for the colour information which controls each triad of dots

on the screen. Each bit is used to control one of the three electron guns.

Eight colours are not over exciting, and ingenious interweaving methods gave the illusion of more. However, the more-expensive **analogue RGB** monitors allowed many more colours than this.

Analogue colour monitors

Analogue monitors were the next step up this evolutionary scale, and this monitor technology allowed the electron guns (and hence the intensity of the R, G and B components) to be infinitely variable. This is great as far as the monitor is concerned, but unfortunately the system can mop up pots of computer memory. For example, if we allowed just two bits per R, G and B component, then 2^6 or 64 colours would be possible, but we would need 6 bits per pixel instead of the original 3 for the eight-colour mode. Note that a **pixel** is the name given to a **picture element,** and refers to the smallest **logical element** used for building up a picture in a particular graphics mode. For example, if you have a 640 × 480 graphics mode, then you have exactly this many (307,200) pixels. There does not necessarily have to be any relationship between the number of triads-of-dots on the actual screen, although you could obviously not display more pixels than the screen has triads, even if your computer was capable of doing so. A pixel is therefore a logical rather than a physical unit, although if there is a one-to-one correspondence between pixels and triads in a particular mode, then a single pixel would represent a single triad on that particular colour monitor, and the logical and physical units would be the same.

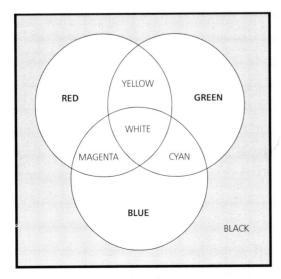

(a)

COLOUR	THREE GUNS		
	R	G	B
BLACK	0	0	0
BLUE	0	0	1
GREEN	0	1	0
CYAN	0	1	1
RED	1	0	0
MAGENTA	1	0	1
YELLOW	1	1	0
WHITE	1	1	1

(b)

Figure 11.3

24-bit colour graphics

Today 256 colour modes are common for 'normal' computer work, but over 16,777,216 colours is not unusual, especially if you have a good graphics card with about 12 Mb of memory or more on board. This number is convenient because it is derived from assigning 1 byte to each of the colours R, G and B. Therefore, we have 24 bits assigned to the colours leading to the often-used term **24-bit colour graphics**. You should appreciate that with 24 bits available, 2^{24} or 16,777,216 colours are now possible. This is easily enough for *photo-realism* and the most demanding *professional film and video graphics*. It has therefore become the standard on many top-of-the-range machines, and is also available too on micros, which pride themselves on their graphics capability such as the Apple Mac, and the Pentium-based PCs, for example. You may also hear the term **32-bit** CMYK (see later) graphics, but this does *not* apply to the addition of any further colours. It refers to conventional 24-bit colour *plus* a control for the black (key) level used on printer systems which is explained later on in this chapter.

Returning to the memory problem, if 24 bits are assigned to each graphic element, and assuming that you are driving a high-resolution display of say 1200×1600, then you will need an astonishing $1200 \times 1600 \times 24 = 46$ Mbits or 5.76 Mbytes just for a single coloured image! Don't forget also that this says nothing of the processing power needed to alter it! Although the memory for such graphics is usually built into a special board called a **graphics card**, it was not until recently (late 1997) that RAM became cheap enough for this to be considered as a possibility. In the late 1990s 16 Mbytes of ordinary RAM (see chapter 12) is now available for under £25 – an amazing reduction in the last couple of years, considering that 4 Mbytes of RAM was over £100 just a few years earlier! Although video RAM is more expensive than ordinary RAM (it needs to be as fast as possible) it's now not unusual to have 12 Mbytes or more of VRAM (Graphics RAM) on board a **graphics card** (see next section), and this allows you to have even higher resolutions. No doubt by the time the next edition of this book is written, 32 Mbytes of graphics memory might be the norm! However, there's not much point getting much better than this because the human eye is not capable of resolving more colours or greater resolutions on normal-size monitors, you would need 25 inch or 30 inch monitors to appreciate these higher-resolution modes.

Graphics cards

Graphics cards and different types of monitor cause a dilemma for software writers – do you stick with the older systems, or go for the more-modern ones with the consequence that your software no longer works on the older machines? To help get over some of these problems, in 1987 the **VGA standard** (640×480) was introduced by IBM, which used to be the base standard, but which has been superseded several times by **Super VGA** (800×600), **Ultimate VGA** or sometimes XGA (1024×768) and others. Indeed, as manufacturers constantly try to outdo each other, very little consistency of standards now exist, especially between the older and newer machines. Graphics and monitor standards are a very messy area of computing, and one, which causes constant problems with compatibility. Upgrades sometimes involve both a change of monitor (if you don't happen to have a modern multi-synch monitor) and a graphics card – this can obviously be quite expensive, but this is the trend that has been adopted, or else progress could not be made.

> **Hint:** You should always try to get the best graphics card that you can afford. This drastically affects the performance of your computer system. A 3D graphics card with 16 Mbytes of VRAM is good at the time of writing.

As can be seen from the above analysis, graphics processing is an intensive activity in modern PCs, and *extra processing power* has been put onto the **graphics cards** or **display adapters** (see **Plate 27**). Over the last few years these cards have been developed from elementary devices which supported just a few colours and low resolutions, to the **3D high-resolution graphics cards** of today. However, because of the different and rapidly progressing standards, it is only the advent of reasonably priced multi-sync monitors that has made all of this possible.

The older graphics-display standards required that the main microprocessor inside the computer did most of the work (i.e. translation of the commands into the actual display properties to make the image appear on the monitor). However, later graphics cards have **graphic accelerator chips** which can take a graphic command from the system, then do all the 'donkey work'. Some of the later MMX processors may take over some of the graphics work too.

The latest 3D cards are ideal for the 3D animation, which is now common in computer games, although these cards will obviously be good at doing conventional 2D animation too. Finally, it is important to realise that due to the plethora of different graphics cards and operating systems, it's most important that you have the appropriate piece of **software** called **a graphics-card driver** for your system. If you do not have the proper driver installed then your system may not work at all, or, if it does, will work with a greatly reduced set of features.

Multiscan monitors

It's essential that the picture is presented to the user at a rate which is fast enough to prevent flicker. If the picture is presented at about 35 times/sec then the flicker would be terrible – 50 Hz or 50 times/sec is acceptable, and faster rates are preferable. Without working out the maths, if you wanted a graphics mode of say 800 × 600 at a refresh rate of 56 Hz, then the monitor must be capable of a 35.2 KHz horizontal scan rate (frequency at which the lines are drawn). However, for a higher-resolution mode, say 1024 × 768, then, if interlacing is not used, a rate of 48.7 KHz is necessary.

Different modes and refresh rates imply different scanning frequencies for the raster scan mechanism, and multisync or multiscan monitors (unlike domestic TV sets) can cope with these different scanning frequencies. **Multiscan** or **multisync** monitors are now common for medium and high-resolution graphics work, but you get what you pay for. The higher-scanning-frequency monitors, capable of getting the highest resolutions are more expensive than the slower scanning monitors, and this is just one of the reasons why you can no longer use the TV as a computer monitor. However, this is exactly what WebTV, the system for surfing the net using a conventional TV does! After reading through this section you can see that the number of colours and the resolution will be quite low.

Health issues and energy saving

All monitors emit radiation, with most of it fortunately coming out the back of the monitor. More modern monitors are of the **low-radiation type**, and this, hopefully, will reduce any perceived risks from prolonged periods of sitting in front of these monitors. It is still unclear as to whether there is a potential problem from electromagnetic radiation coming from sources like computer monitors, and studies are currently underway to determine the facts. It will be some time yet before we know for sure.

Did you know that . . .
More radiation comes out of the back of the monitor than the front. If you wish to be absolutely safe, make sure that you don't design a computer-room layout where people are placed very close indeed to the back of a monitor. A few feet away is not really a problem at all.

Monitors use a relatively large amount of energy compared to other components in a computer system, and both hardware and software solutions now exist to help reduce these energy overheads. Some of the latest energy-star-compliant monitors work alongside the operating systems like Windows NT and Windows 98, for example, and allow the user to configure the amount

of time for which 'inactivity on the computer' would result in the monitor automatically switching itself into a low-power mode. Any movement of the mouse or pressing a button on the keyboard will usually bring the monitor back to its normal state within a couple of seconds.

In addition to the energy-saving aspects mentioned above, **screen savers** are often used so that an image does not get burnt into the screen by having the same image displayed on the monitor for extended periods of time. A screen saver is simply a piece of software, which is activated only when the computer has not been used for a set period of time determined by the operating system settings. Indeed, a whole industry has grown up around the production of amusing screen savers.

Basic computer monitors		
Cost	Data entry speed	Other considerations
Between £80 and £150 for a basic 14in multisync monitor.	N/A – as long as the screen is refreshed fast enough so that no detectable flicker is evident.	Monochrome monitors are no longer easily available, and low-resolution 14in colour monitors are now only about £80.
Large multisync monitors vary from less than a couple of hundred pounds for a 15in model to well over £1000 pounds for the larger 25in and above.	N/A – as long as the screen is refreshed fast enough so that no detectable flicker is evident.	With a modern PC it's essential to have a good multisync monitor capable of displaying the modes required for the applications which you intend to use. 800 × 600 is adequate for conventional word processing but higher resolutions are required for CAD and art work.

Graphical display methods

All the methods considered so far in the monitor section have made use of **raster displays** (i.e. generating the dots line by line), and the most-common method for displaying graphics on these types of monitors is known as **bit mapping**.

1 bit/pixel monochrome

For simplicity let's start with a monochrome display in just two intensities – on and off. Let's also suppose, for the sake of argument, that there are 200 vertical lines (dots) and 640 horizontal dots. (Far less than this will actually be shown in the diagrams!) We require on-off information regarding $200 \times 640 = 128,000$ pixels. If we make use of 128,000 bits of memory, where each location might be 1 if a pixel is to be on, or a 0 if the pixel is to be off, then these 128,000 bits in memory contain a bit map of what should be happening on the screen. By *continually referencing* each **bit** in the **map** at the appropriate time, the electron beam in the raster-scanning mechanism can be switched on or off. By storing the appropriate map in memory (**Video RAM**) then the corresponding picture or text is displayed on the screen. See figure 11.4.

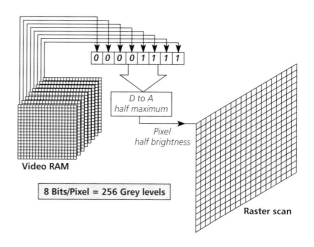

Figure 11.5

8 bits/pixel monochrome

Next let's choose a 256 grey-level 'monochrome' screen. It is convenient to assign one byte of memory to each pixel in this case because a byte is all that is necessary to describe 256 levels of grey from black (00000000 – min) to white (11111111 – max).

An analogue monitor would obviously be needed here and the digital values stored in the memory map are used to control the intensity of the gun via a D to A converter (see chapter 8) on the graphics board. Although bytes are being used here the system is obviously still the same and is therefore still called a bit-mapped system. The idea is shown in figure 11.5.

We can easily introduce colour by assigning, in effect, three different bit maps of the type described for the 256 grey-scale display. One map would be for Red, one for Green and one for Blue (RGB). Consider the 24-bit graphics described earlier. Each red byte would control the red gun, each green byte would control the green gun, and each blue byte would control the blue gun in ways identical to the way in which the 256-grey level bit-map controlled the display in the previous section.

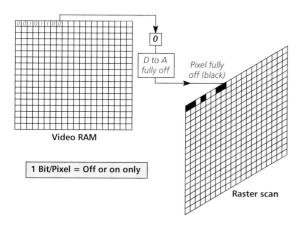

Figure 11.4

Character graphics

At this point it is worth contrasting this with a system that is called memory mapping or **character graphics**. Under this alternative system the extended ASCII codes for each character are held in memory, one character per byte. These codes are then sent to the graphics display or special monitor not as a bit-mapped image but as the ASCII code. Hardware inside the monitor then converts these codes into the appropriate characters to be displayed on the screen. This idea is similar to the character graphics generator inside a normal TV set if **teletext** is being used. The codes being received are received by the set and a special teletext chip inside the TV generates the appropriate raster-scan patterns. Teletext is an example of character-based graphics generation.

Vector graphic displays

Most graphics computers make use of **bit-mapped images** described in the last few sections. However, some specialist systems make use of what's called **vector graphics**. In this system, a **line (vector)** is drawn directly on the screen by the electron beam. You can imagine it to be rather like the plotter output (see later), but the vector would obviously have to be refreshed at a fast rate or the line would disappear. It's unlikely that the computer would be able to cope with the constant and demanding refreshing on this type of screen, and so a buffer is used to continually drive the display electronics.

The picture is usually based on a system of co-ordinates and characters are generated by special electronics inside the display. As with many computer images, most of the picture is probably static, and so the processor only has to pass that part of the image which has changed since the previous picture was drawn over to the display electronics.

Computer graphics cards and display modes

Cost	Resolution	Other considerations
A bottom of the range graphics card can be obtained for about £20.	800 × 600 and 1024 × 768 modes. 256 colours easily supported with 2 Mbyte VRAM.	This base model is easily enough for basic home PC use, but faster graphics cards are desirable for very high-speed interactive games.
Good graphics cards cost over £100, and have either 8 Mbytes or 12 Mbytes of VRAM	All 'sensible modes' supported in up to 16 million colours.	Useful for high-speed games, art packages and CAD for the non-specialist user. Also useful for photo retouching on a home microcomputer.
Extremely powerful graphics such as real-time 3D rendering would require processing power beyond the abilities of all but the most powerful PCs. These workstations would be very expensive.	These top-of-the-range workstations, which are powered by DEC and Sun specialist chips, sometimes use resolutions of up to 4500 × 3648 in 16 million colours.	At the moment this is a very expensive and specialist market. But who knows – just a few years ago, the 1024 × 768 16 million-colour mode, common on many of the new home microcomputers was considered specialist too!

Other display technologies

LCD displays

The amount of energy needed for a raster CRT display is very significant, and far in excess of that which could be supplied from the batteries in a portable computer. You may think that the few hours battery life on a typical portable is not long, but hang a CRT on the end and the battery would probably last a few minutes!

Backlit LCD displays

The term **LCD** stands for **liquid crystal display** and is based on a development of a technology that has been used in small calculators for a number of years. A liquid crystal is one in which the molecules can be in a state which is part liquid (freely moving about) and part crystal (fixed). This state exists at just a few degrees above the melting point of some special materials. By using an electrostatic field it is possible to make the rod-shaped molecules line up with each other, and this modifies the optical properties of the material from the original state. Figure 11.6(a) shows how the rod-shaped molecules in the material may be twisted by increasing the action of the electrostatic field (charge).

The whole secret of this display method lies in the following facts about polarised light (light shining in one plane only). The light will either pass through the crystals if the plane of polarisation is chosen correctly and the crystals are not twisted, or will be attenuated (cut down or cut out completely) if the degree of twist of the molecules is sufficient. Therefore, little or no light will be let through from the fluorescent panel behind the display if the plane of polarisation is at right angles to the light. The LCD display is made from a huge

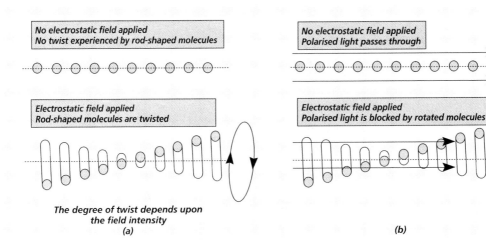

The degree of twist depends upon
the field intensity
(a)

(b)

Figure 11.6

matrix of these crystals – all of which are individually controllable by applying the appropriate degree of charge. Figure 11.6(b) shows how polarised light may be attenuated by the liquid crystals. However, you should note that the method just described assumes a backlit display. Cheaper portables often rely on the properties of reflected light, which gives an inferior display which can't be used in bad lighting conditions. In these types of display ambient light is reflected off a reflector which occupies the same position as the backlit plane in the backlit display.

Colour LCD displays

LCD colour displays operate on the same backlit principles, but with three coloured filters for each pixel placed at strategic points on the screen producing the red, green and blue components. By increasing the degree of twist on the R, G and B components, and by making sure that the dots are very close together (see CRT displays) it is possible to fool the human eye into thinking that it is seeing a single dot of some composite colour. For example, figure 11.7 shows how 'bright yellow' would be produced by attenuating all of the blue, but none of the red and green light.

Did you know that . . .

Although very expensive indeed at the time of writing, large 28 in LCD screens of only a few cm deep are now available. These large monitors weigh in at a fraction of the many pounds of the equivalent size CRT monitor. A 28 in conventional monitor would require two people to lift it. The equivalent LCD monitor could be picked up with one hand.

Figure 11.7 is obviously not to scale, and in practice the R, G and B components of the light would be minuscule compared to that shown in the actual diagram. However, it illustrates the principles quite well.

LCD displays consume minute amounts of power compared with the CRT displays and are therefore ideal for

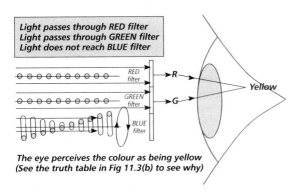

Light passes through RED filter
Light passes through GREEN filter
Light does not reach BLUE filter

The eye perceives the colour as being yellow
(See the truth table in Fig 11.3(b) to see why)

Figure 11.7

use in portable computers. However, compared with the CRT, the response times of the screen are relatively slow, with 50ms or 100ms being typical. This is why cheap portable screens often can't react to the speed at which the mouse is moving, or leave a 'comet tail' in the wake of the mouse pointer.

Hint: When buying a portable computer, you're far better off with an active display if you can afford it. You will find that it's less stressful to use in the long term, and gives a much clearer display. Also, go for the largest LCD display that you can afford.

We have seen above how the liquid crystal state is quite temperature sensitive, and therefore LCD screens will not tolerate large changes in temperature, with especially spectacular results in the cold. (Don't stick your portable in the fridge – use someone else's!)

There are several technologies available and you will often come across the **terms 'passive displays'** and **'active displays'**. Active displays are best as more charge controllers (transistors) are used inside the display (one for each pixel) and the colours are therefore much brighter. However, they are considerably more expensive than the passive displays used in the cheaper portables. You may also come across the term supertwist when looking through technical literature on portable computers. This is referring simply to the technique of rotating the molecules through 270° instead of 90°, which provides for a display with greater clarity. Double supertwisted displays where the interaction of two supertwist molecules give an even better display are also on the market, and no doubt other developments will enhance the displays for portables even further.

The future of LCD displays

Liquid crystal technology has developed at an amazing pace in the last few years, and manufacturers have now developed 20-inch colour displays for desk-top PCs – just a couple of inches thick! If the price of these new large LCD displays can be reduced significantly, then these energy-saving larger displays should become more prevalent. Other innovations include the **FLCD** (The Ferroelectric Liquid Crystal Display), which does not need refreshing and will therefore consume even less power. This could be important for the laptop market as battery-supply time is still currently a major concern.

Light emitting plastic displays

This technology is so new that at the time of writing there is little information available. However, it looks like it could revolutionise the entire concept of computer and video displays. **Light emitting plastic** (or **LEP**) displays are cheap (compared to the CRT and LCD competitors), very flat (about 2 mm), and surprisingly, flexible. This means that these displays could be wrapped around a curved surface, for example. How about moulding this screen onto the face of a manikin, then getting facial expressions to appear as if by magic. As is indicated by the name, LEP emit their own light, and are therefore likely to be more akin to the expensive active LCD displays. Moreover, it would appear that these displays could be very large indeed, perhaps one day covering an entire wall. You could imagine that great works of art or tranquil scenes could be projected from your wall with a thickness little more than that of a piece of wallpaper! The potential for large cheap screens is enormous, and if these technologies can be manufactured in volume, the entire monitor industry could be turned on its head. Don't forget also that the monitor is currently one of the most expensive components in any portable or desk top computer system.

Touch-sensitive screens

The technology of this type of monitor has nothing to do with the internal guts of the system (i.e. CRT or LCD), but is usually carried out as an add-on to an existing monitor. What makes a touch-sensitive screen different is the addition of a matrix of infrared beams which criss-cross the front of the screen at right angles. If a finger is pointed at the screen then some of these infrared beams will be broken – some in the vertical and others in the horizontal direction. This interception of the beams can be converted into a co-ordinate and thus the system can easily determine the position of the finger on the screen. (These devices have been covered in the computer-input techniques chapter on page 10).

It should be relatively obvious that a special program is usually used in conjunction with the pointer information from the infra-red display which together enable the user of the touch-sensitive screen to point a finger at the screen and cause some pre-determined action to happen.

Projection TV output

A projection TV takes an RGB signal from the computer, and via a complex system of electronics and optical lenses projects an image of the computer screen onto a much-larger cinema-type screen. The most expensive projection TVs are now capable of quite high-resolution modes (800×600 or 1024×768) with screen sizes of several square metres. They are ideal for use in lecture theatres when audiences of several hundred people have to watch the computer screen simultaneously. On a more modest scale, a normal OHP (Over Head Projector) as found in most classrooms, can be turned into a projection system for a computer by placing a special LCD device on top of the projector where the transparency would normally be placed.

Although not anywhere near as sophisticated as the projection TV in terms of resolution or colours available, an acceptable medium resolution display for a group of 50 to 60 people can be satisfactorily carried out by making use of this technology.

Monitors and their uses

Most displays today are usually colour, but it must not be forgotten that monochrome displays are still useful in many circumstances. For example, if you are writing COBOL programs for a large bank, then you are unlikely to need a colour display, as most of the work that you do is based around text. Word processors and some DTP systems for newspaper production need only monochrome monitors too. However, it must now be said that the days of the monochrome monitor are numbered, simply through lack of demand. Many of them will still be around for a large number of years to come, but anyone requiring a monochrome monitor in the future will probably have to simulate the situation on a colour monitor!

Modern CAD packages demand the highest resolution monitors, and the art packages used by the film and advertising industry demand 24-bit colour graphics on top of this too. Therefore, the most expensive top-of-the-range monitors are found in this sort of industry. Most microcomputers now have colour monitors as standard, as the consumer obviously expects many colours on the current generation machines. (How else would you be able to enjoy the games during the coffee break?)

For portables, LCD displays are the only current monitor technology with power consumption low enough to be driven from batteries. However, portables for use outside the office present special problems, especially as the LCD screens are sensitive to temperature. LCD displays are essential in the sub-notebook and PDA (see chapter 10) range of miniature computers, and have been modified slightly to accommodate the increasingly popular pen input.

Smelly vision

Although still in its infancy, some centres are now successfully experimenting with the production of smells in association with computer-generated graphics and video. For example, the Museum of Perfumery at Bourton on the Water in Gloucestershire, England, has a demonstration which shows an image of an orange while at the same time spraying orange-smelling chemicals into the room. The most difficult problem to solve is obviously completely dispensing with the smell before another is needed. When smelly vision is used in conjunction with computer-generated graphics, sounds and lights, you obviously have the potential for a spectacular advertising launch of virtually any product. The link to virtual-reality systems is an obvious one too.

LCD and projection TV display technologies

Cost	Data output speed	Other considerations
Mostly used on portables, so the cost of a standard LCD screen is usually academic. However, on some portables you do have the option of changing the screen.	N/A – as long as the screen is refreshed fast enough so that no detectable flicker is evident.	The active-matrix technologies provide better displays than the passive LCD screens but are more expensive.
Large desk-top LCDs are now available but they are, at the time of writing, extremely expensive compared to the equivalent size CRT displays	N/A – as long as the screen is refreshed fast enough so that no detectable flicker is evident.	Often the viewing angle from an LCD display is not as great as that from a conventional CRT display. However, they use very much less energy, and the depth of the device is just a few inches for a 21 in display, compared to about 18 in for a conventional 21 in CRT display. If desktop space is at a premium, then this could be the answer.
LCD projection systems for OHPs (Over Head Projectors) are now available at a sensible cost of a few hundred to a couple of thousand pounds depending on the model.	N/A – as long as the screen is refreshed fast enough so that no detectable flicker is evident.	Ideal for schools and for companies who go round doing displays in lecture theatres. These portable devices are far easier to carry around than their big brothers mentioned at the end of this table. Resolutions and colours on the early models were not as good as the later incarnations.
LEP or Light Emitting Plastic displays are likely to be very cheap, but have yet to be commercially developed at the time of writing.	Unknown at the time of writing but believed to be fast enough for excellent computer graphics.	Very large screens may be possible. Screens can be wrapped around irregular shapes giving novel display possibilities. Could revolutionise the future of monitor technology, and might be a force to be reckoned with after the year 2000.
Projection TV systems have come down in price by leaps and bounds over the last couple of years. They do, however, still cost a few thousand pounds for a good-quality 1024×768 model.	N/A – as long as the screen is refreshed fast enough so that no detectable flicker is evident.	The resolutions are limited to about 800×600 for sensible prices at the time or writing. These projection TVs, especially if used in conjunction with a reflective screen, will provide large displays (6–12 ft across is typical) so that a few hundred people can view the screen simultaneously. Great for universities, colleges and school lecture theatres.

Hard copy

Printers

After computer monitors, the printer is probably the next most common form of output, and the output from any printer is known as **hard copy**. Printing technology in the last few years has made very significant progress, and what used to be regarded as acceptable just a few years ago is now only suitable for **draft copy**. The all-important company image is paramount in today's competitive environment, and the plummeting costs of hardware have enabled us to set our limits *very* much higher.

During the 1980s the dot matrix printers ruled supreme, but LASER printers and bubble-jet printers have now pushed them out as the main contenders for the most-common form of output from microcomputers. Nevertheless, the dot-matrix printer is still very common, especially for invoice production in shops and businesses, and is still much cheaper than LASER printer technology. Dot matrix printers have therefore not yet been confined to the ever-growing heap of computer technology that has rapidly become out of date.

Dot matrix printers

Dot matrix printers, or indeed any printer that prints just '*one character*' *at a time* are known as **serial**

printers. (This term should be compared with the terms '**line printers**' and '**page printers**' considered elsewhere in this chapter.)

Dot matrix printers work by firing a matrix of tiny pins, usually arranged in rows, through a ribbon similar to that found in a typewriter. The older dot matrix printers had just 9 pins, but 24 pins are now the most common number available. **Figure** 11.8(a) shows a typical modern dot matrix printer, and for the sake of simplicity, the mechanism for a 9-pin dot matrix printer is shown in figure 11.8(b).

> ## Did you know that . . .
>
> The dot matrix printer was the first computer-based printer to move away from the character-based technology of previous printers. Indeed, this earlier technology, based on pressing ink-soaked characters onto the paper, had existed since the invention of the printing process in the 15th century. Therefore, dot matrix printers were literally a revolution in their time, and will still have a large part to play for many years to come.

The tiny pins are fired by activation of electromagnets which force the pins to make an impact on the paper through the ribbon, thereby making a tiny dot on the paper. The mechanism containing the pins is called the print head. As the head is moved across the page the pins are fired in the desired combination to produce the correct effects. Figure 11.8(c) shows how

the letters 'RJB' would be produced with just 9 pins. Notice that not all-9 pins are used for capitals, two pins are reserved for the descenders, which form the parts of the letters below the line (as with a 'g' or a 'p', for example).

Dot matrix printers are much more versatile than older printing techniques such as those found in typewriters and daisy-wheel printers. The hard copy, being made up of lots of tiny dots, can give a tremendous range and number of styles and different sized letters, or effects such as **bold**, <u>underlined</u>, *italic*, double height or condensed modes of text are easily possible by altering the pattern of dots. However, it is the ability of the dot matrix printer to produce **graphics images** which has really put this printing technology in an enviable position in the cheap-printer market. A typical speed for a dot matrix printer is a few hundred characters per second, although speeds of 1,000 cps or more are possible on the more expensive models.

> **Hint:** You can purchase dot matrix printers very cheaply now. However, don't expect the quality of output which you can get from an ink-jet printer. If you don't need high-quality colour or laser-like output, then the dot matrix is very cost effective indeed, but don't forget also that noise may be a problem.

There are two distinct modes of operation when it comes to printing characters on a dot matrix printer. They can either be printed

Figure 11.8(a)

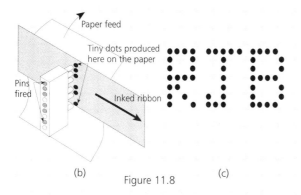

(b)   (c)

Figure 11.8

Dot Matrix printers		
Cost	**Data output speed**	**Other considerations**
Low cost dot matrix printers are available for less than £75.	Depends on print quality, but draft mode can be up to several hundred characters per second.	Although some might think that this technology is outdated, it is one of the few technologies which supports continuous-feed stationary, and is cheap enough to install on shop tills for the production of invoices.
Fast dot matrix printers are now just a few hundred pounds.	Depends on quality, but fast printers can exceed about 1000 characters per second.	Higher-quality dot matrix printers have been largely super-seded by low cost laser technology, but fast dot matrix printers are still used in the batch produc-tion of invoices on pre-printed stationary.

as a graphic, which obviously gives you an infinite variety of styles, but this is painfully slow – taking up to a few minutes to print a single A4 page of text in a high-resolution graphics mode (300 or 600 dots per inch). The second mode of operation is to pass ASCII characters (see chapter 12) down to the printer and get the character generators inside the printer to generate the appropriate patterns of dots. This is a much faster mode of operation, but with a limited number of styles dictated by the printer. Control codes are usually sent to the printer to change styles or put the printer in *italics* or <u>underlined</u> mode etc. It is often possible to purchase a font card, which plugs into the printer to enhance the range of text styles that are available. The method used to print standard fonts on most dot matrix printers is called bit-mapped fonts, and this is described in detail later on in this chapter.

The biggest disadvantage of the 9-pin first generation of dot matrix printers is their poor quality of output compared to conventional typewriters, and the amount of noise that these printers make. However, the advent of 24-pin technology and using techniques such as double strike has largely got over the quality problem. When special techniques such as these are used to produce better quality output, the resultant hard copy is often known as **NLQ** or **Near Letter Quality**. Letter quality refers to the quality obtained from daisy wheel and conventional typewriters. Some of the modern dot matrix printers are now considerably quieter than the previous generations, and acoustic hoods can be purchased to cut down the noise even further. However, 24-pin printers are extensively used in offices for the production of invoices and other communications where good quality is important but the highest quality is not of paramount importance.

Line printers

The **line printer** has been around for many years, although improvements in performance and a reduction in size have characterised later models. A typical line printer is shown in figure 11.9(a). The line printer is the printing device that is most common with large mainframe computer installations, where vast amounts of computer printout are required at high speed. As the name implies, text is printed 'one line at a time'. One type of print mechanism consists of many hammers and a **drum.** The characters are embossed on the edge of the drum as shown in figure 11.9(b). In fact this type of line printer is often referred to as a **drum printer** or **barrel printer.**

The drum (barrel) revolves at high speed so that each character can be presented underneath the hammer in a fraction of a second. The carbon paper is then passed between the drum and the hammers as shown in the diagram. An example is the best way to understand the mechanism of printing. Suppose the text 'A LEVEL COMPUTER SCIENCE' is to be printed on a line printer. The whole line of text would be produced within one revolution of the drum. Let us assume for convenience, that the As appear under the hammer first. The net result would be: A i.e. an 'A' in the appropriate first position of the text. There are no Bs in the text to be printed, so no hammers are activated while this letter is under them. However, when the Cs are encountered, the text printed **will** be modified to one A with three Cs. The principle is shown in figure 11.10.

Many line printers have alternative print mechanisms to the drum such as **chain** or **band.** These mechanisms are shown in figure 11.11(a) and figure 11.11(b) respectively.

The chain mechanism simply revolves as shown in the diagram and hammers strike the paper through ribbon when the appropriate character is under them. To speed up the printer's operation several sets of characters are printed around the chain. In this way the letters are presented to the hammers several times during a single revolution of the entire chain. This type of line printer is also known as a **chain printer**.

On both systems (chain and drum) 132 hammers are usually employed giving the full 132-width printout. With the drum-type line printer over 2000 lines per minute are possible.

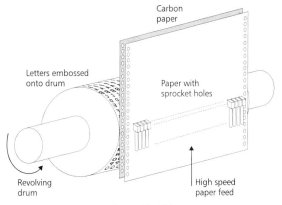

Figure 11.9(a)

Figure 11.9(b)

Text produced within one revolution
of the printer drum:

```
                                                          Letter currently
                                                          under the hammer

A                                                                      A
A               C                     C       C                        C
A     E   E     C           E         C   E   C E                      E
A     E   E     C           E         C I E   C E                      I
A   L E   E L   C           E         C I E   C E                      L
A   L E   E L   C   M       E         C I E   C E                      M
A   L E   E L   C   M       E         C I E N C E                      N
A   L E   E L   C O M       E         C I E N C E                      O
A   L E   E L   C O M P     E         C I E N C E                      P
A   L E   E L   C O M P     E R       C I E N C E                      R
A   L E   E L   C O M P     E R   S C I E N C E                        S
A   L E   E L   C O M P   T E R   S C I E N C E                        T
A   L E   E L   C O M P U T E R   S C I E N C E                        U
A   L E V E L   C O M P U T E R   S C I E N C E                        V
```

Figure 11.10

The band-type printer whose mechanism is shown in figure 11.11(b) utilises either a steel or polyurethane band with the characters embossed on it. This type of printer has the added advantage that it is possible to change **character fonts**, i.e. the style of the characters that are embossed on the band.

Line printers		
Cost	**Data output speed**	**Other considerations**
Typical machines cost a few thousand pounds.	Very fast for large batch production, typically 2000 lines per minute or more is possible.	Ideal for large batch production such as printing water or electricity bills for tens of thousands of customers.

Laser printers (black and white)

This is the current 'darling' of printers, and is rapidly becoming the norm in many office and educational environments, due to its excellent standard of print quality, high reliability, virtually silent running and rapidly-reducing cost.

LASER-printing technology is based around 'standard' photocopying machines. The basic principle of operation is shown in figure 11.12. Indeed, the only difference between a standard small photocopier and a LASER printer is that the LASER printer has been modified to accept input from a computer rather than a sheet of paper placed inside a typical photo-copier.

As can be seen from figure 11.12, a LASER beam is modulated (switched on and off or changed in intensity) by the computer, whilst at the same time a multi-sided mirror is rotated to distribute the beam of light in a line across the specially coated drum. The

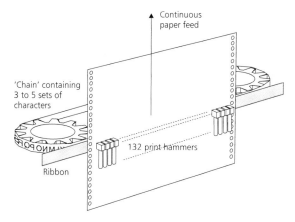

Figure 11.11(a)

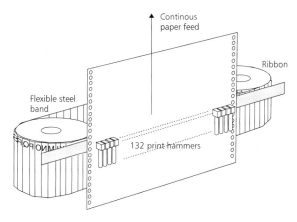

Figure 11.11(b)

Even the cheapest LASER printers have a resolution of about 300 dpi (dots per inch) and 600 dpi is now standard. Although some LASER printers can produce up to 1200 dpi, 800 is around the limit that can be seen with the naked human eye (i.e. without the aid of a magnifying glass or microscope). 1200 dpi is used for professional typesetting, but 300 or 600 dpi easily matches the letter quality required for the typical office, which is one of the reasons why these machines have become so popular.

It is the LASER printer, which has been the leading light (pun intended) in the long strive towards desktop publishing (DTP – see chapter 6). Without the quality and reliability of the LASER printer you would have to send the disk away to be printed by the professionals – a costly and time-consuming operation.

LASER printers are classed as **page printers** because they compile and print *one page at a time*. (Nevertheless you will realise that the image is produced one line at a time or even one dot at a time inside the machine – a little knowledge is a dangerous thing!) Typical LASER printer speeds are between 8 and 24 pages per minute, although increases in this speed as the technology progresses will be inevitable.

LASER printers are obviously quite memory hungry. The image, being made up of lots of tiny dots, has to be stored somewhere before it can be printed. For example, a typical A4-size piece of paper is about 11¾ × 8¼ inches, giving a total area of about 97 in². If we are working at 600 dpi then we would need 600 × 600 = 360,000 dots for each square inch on the page. An A4 600 dpi document would therefore require about 4 Mbytes to store the image if no special techniques are being used. An A3 LASER printer would obviously require over 8 Mbytes to store an image of twice these A4 dimensions, although compression techniques can reduce this figure considerably.

drum is coated with organic chemicals such that it becomes conductive when illuminated by light.

The corona wire shown in figure 11.12 is typically carrying several kV (ouch!) which charges up the drum as the surface passes by this highly charged wire. In the regions of the drum, which are not illuminated by the light, the chemicals do not become conductive and therefore this part of the drum retains its charge. However, where the light has struck an area of the drum, the chemicals become conductive and therefore these parts loose their charge. After one line of dots have been drawn then the drum contains one line of an image made up of charged parts where the light has not struck and uncharged parts where the light has struck the drum. As the drum rotates the next line of dots is produced in the same fashion.

As the drum rotates the charged parts of the drum (representing black) attract black powder called **toner** from the **toner cartridge**, but the parts of the drum which are not charged (representing white) do not attract any toner. In this way the toner is attracted only to those areas (group of dots) which represent the black part of the image.

The next part of the operation is to get the toner off the drum and onto the paper. Giving the paper a higher charge than the drum so that the charged particles of toner are attracted to the paper does this. This mechanism is not shown on the diagram.

Finally, the paper is heat treated so that the toner is fixed and does not fall off the paper when the paper looses its charge. Again, for reasons of clarity, this heating process is not shown in the diagram of figure 11.12.

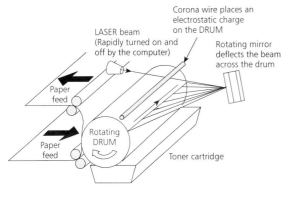

Figure 11.12

Laser printers (black and white)		
Cost	Data output speed	Other considerations
Typical machines cost from a few hundred to several thousand pounds depending on speed, quality and paper handling. Typically, quality may range from 300 dpi to 1200 dpi.	Low speed printers about 6 pages per minute – higher speed printers up to about 24 pages per minute or more.	Ideal for the home, office or school, these machines are the current workhorses of the PC industry. Extensive paper handling facilities are available, and laser printers can vary in size up to A3 and beyond.

As with dot-matrix printers, most LASER printers print text as a graphic, but some others, by sending appropriate codes to the printer using a special page-description language, give you some other useful options. There are two basic systems in operation for the production of text, namely bit-mapped and outline fonts. We will cover bit-mapped fonts first as this is the easier of the two systems to understand.

Bit-mapped fonts

We have already seen how **bit mapping** has been used to great effect in computer monitors. The principles here for **bit-mapped fonts** are identical. Each character to be formed is made up by considering it to consist of a matrix of tiny squares in which a **bit** (represented by one square) is either **on** or **off**. The idea is shown in figure 11.13.

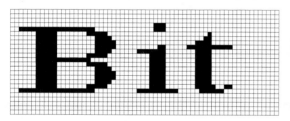

Figure 11.13

Figure 11.13 shows the word 'Bit' written in the Times font at 36pt blown up on a grid so that you can see how each character is formed as a map of bits which relate to the grid. A single bit controls each square and the state of each bit determines whether or not the pixel is on or off.

A **map** *needs to be held for* **each font and font size** that will be supported by the printer. In this way ASCII codes can then be sent to the printer which represent style and font size, followed by the codes which represent the letters themselves. For example, after the appropriate control-code sequence representing style etc., the codes 42 hex, 69 hex and 74 hex would be sent representing 'B', 'i' and 't' respectively. As a limited number of maps are available this method of producing fonts is limited. A typical printer making use of bit-mapped fonts would probably have about ten different fonts each of which may have about 6 different point sizes. However, much text is now produced by doing a graphics dump of the entire page, treating each piece of text as a graphic.

Outline fonts

A more versatile method of text production is to make use of what are called **outline fonts** or **true-type fonts**. Instead of using bit-mapped images, mathematical relationships define the attributes of these particular fonts. It's *identical in principle* to the difference between **pixel**

(**bit mapped**) **art packages** and **object-oriented CAD packages** (see chapter 7).

Page description languages

Outline fonts are versatile because large numbers of bit-mapped images do not have to be held in memory to obtain a large numbers of font sizes. The instructions or mathematical definitions describing the outline of each type of font can be sent to the printer by means of a **page description language** such as PostScript or HP PCL (Hewlett-Packard Printer Command Language). However, more recently it's been possible to drive the LASER-printing mechanism directly by using a **video signal** to drive the LASER beam rather like the electron beam in a CRT display (see earlier).

As each character in a *particular* font is **mathematically similar** to the *same character* in many different point sizes (different sizes of character), then all that is needed is the font outline definition together with information relating to its increase or decrease in size. Being similar, all angles etc. will be the same, and only lengths will increase or decrease in proportion to the size of the letter. The idea is shown in figure 11.14. Assuming that the original text is the original size, then an increase from 72pt to 300pt gives an enlargement of about 416%. Note, however, that the shape of the font is identical, with all the angles governing the serifs (little feet at the bottom) being the same, and the radii of the 'B' being relative to the height.

Note that whichever mechanism is being used to define the fonts, the medium on which the final characters are presented *must be* a **bit-mapped image** made up of dots, due to the mechanical characteristics of the LASER printer, dot-matrix printer or CRT screen. Nevertheless, outline fonts are the ones most commonly used because of their versatility, and anti-aliasing (little grey areas) is often used to make a more pleasing appearance (apparently less jagged edges as far as the human eye is concerned) when being presented on a CRT screen or printer.

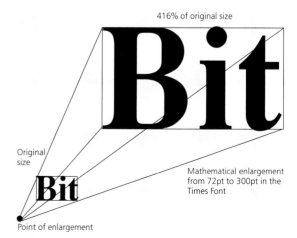

416% of original size

Original size

Mathematical enlargement from 72pt to 300pt in the Times Font

Point of enlargement

Figure 11.14

With outline fonts the language which describes each character is of paramount importance. A language such as PostScript is usually contained in a ROM within the LASER printer itself, or the computer will directly translate the outline fonts into the language, which the printer understands.

It's enlightening to consider a typical PostScript file, which would be necessary to print 'The cat sat on the mat'. The following extract is just the last 20 lines of the 284 lines, which are needed to do the job on an Acorn RISC PC driving a PostScript LASER printer. You can see the actual text just a few lines from the bottom of the end of the file in Figure 11.15!

Page description languages contain mind-bogglingly tedious and complex sets of commands, but enable the production of superb fonts to the highest standards. They include descriptions of the fonts to be used, margins on the page and lines or other shapes that may need to be drawn. Languages such as PostScript are complete languages in their own right, and if you are mad enough you can write your own PostScript commands to make your printer perform amazing feats not supported by your DTP systems.

Producing a coloured image on paper

Producing a **coloured image on paper** is *very different* indeed from the methods used to produce a coloured image on a computer monitor, for example. As we have seen earlier in this chapter, a computer monitor uses what's called the primary additive colours – namely red, green and blue. This is because when light representing each of these colours is added, the eye perceives almost any other colour if the RGB components are mixed in the right proportions. However, when looking at a picture on a piece of paper, a very different mechanism is in operation. Light does not emanate from the paper! – here we view the picture by a reflection of ordinary (assume daylight is ordinary) light from the page. The material on the page absorbs parts of the white light (i.e. it subtracts parts of the daylight coming in), and the eye perceives whatever colours are reflected after the others have been absorbed (subtracted). Making use of these facts, printers have developed a model (called the **CMY model**) based on the three **subtractive primary colours** called **cyan**, **magenta** and **yellow**.

Using cyan, magenta and yellow inks or toner it's possible to create other colours. For example, cyan and yellow make green, all three make black, or none at all makes white (assuming that you are printing on white paper!). In addition to these base colours, by using clever combinations of masses of dots printed close together, an optical illusion can be created in which the eye is fooled into thinking that it is observing a continuous colour of a different hue. For example, a less-saturated red could be made up from red dots with an increased amount of white space in between. The effect would make the eye perceive that the colour is pink.

Although in theory black is produced by the addition of all three 'inks', in practice it is found that a 'better black' is produced by having a black ink or toner just like that which would be present in a black-and-white printer. Therefore, a new colour model called **CMYK** (**cyan**, **magenta**, **yellow**, and **key** (black)) has been developed for the best results. It is this CMYK model that's used for many modern LASER, thermal and ink-jet printing devices. The CMYK model is used as the basis for 32-bit colour graphics – 3 bytes for colour and 1 for the key.

```
EndPage
%%Page: 2 2
%%PageBoundingBox: 23 28 572 814
231 7990 0 100 60 110 StartPage
-0.5 0 MT 64 (RAM::RamDisk0.$.TextStory    17:51:08 27-Sep-1993    Page 2) SS
1 0 MT 0 ( locktolinespace off;) SS
2 0 MT 0 ( ruleaboveoffset 0pt;) SS
3 0 MT 0 ( rulecontrol 6;) SS
4 0 MT 0 ( vertrulewidth 1pt;) SS
5 0 MT 0 ( ruleleftmargin 57.5pt;) SS
6 0 MT 0 ( rulerightmargin 467.7pt;) SS
7 0 MT 0 ( shortcut 459;) SS
8 0 MT 0 ( tabs vertrule 56.7pt,vertrule 155.9pt,170.1pt,vertrule
   255.1pt,269.3pt,vertrule 354.3pt,36) SS
9 0 MT 1 (|) SS 0 (8.5pt,vertrule 467.7pt}The cat sat on the mat) SS
EndPage
%%Trailer
end
%%Pages: 2
```

Figure 11.15

Colour laser printers

If you've understood how a black-and-white LASER printer works, and you've understood the principles of the CMYK subtractive colour printing process, then you could probably explain the principle of a colour LASER without reading further! A colour LASER is identical in principle to a black-and-white LASER, but the paper is processed four times – *once* with **cyan toner**, a *second time* with **magenta toner**, a *third time* with **yellow toner** and a *final time* with **black toner**.

It's important to appreciate how the coloured image is produced, and how this relates to the memory requirements of the printer. It's different to what happens on the screen because pastel shades and lighter shades of grey are not made up by turning down the intensity of an electron gun as is the case with a monitor, but in printing dots further apart to get more white space in-between. For example, if a light grey is required, then black dots are simply printed further apart. If a coloured image is required then cyan, magenta and yellow dots are printed with appropriate spacing in-between. This means that it's only necessary to have a single bit (not a byte) for each colour toner controlling each dot on the page. This means that far less memory is needed than would be the case for producing the equivalent coloured image on the screen. This is important because LASER printers have to store an entire page before printing it out, unless you drive the drum directly with a video signal, as is done from some of the Acorn range of computers, for example. A numerical example is carried out in the exercise at the end of this chapter.

It's possible to feed the paper backwards and forwards four times, but a serial arrangement with four separate electrostatic systems, four separate toner cartridges and four separate toner-removal systems could process the same paper serially but making one pass only. Needless to say, with four times the guts of a standard black-and-

Laser printers (colour)		
Cost	**Data output speed**	**Other considerations**
Typical machines cost from about £1000 pounds to tens of thousands of pounds depending on size, speed and quality. Typically, quality may range from 300 dpi to 1200 dpi.	Typically up to 12 pages per minute, these machines are not as fast as their black and white counterparts.	A little too expensive for general home use, but now to be found in some schools, and many colleges and universities. With the appropriate quality paper the output is literally publication or photographic quality.

white LASER, the price of a colour LASER is about three or four times higher than that of a standard LASER printer. Even so, drastic cost reductions have meant that less than £5,000 is now required for a typical 300dpi A3 colour LASER in the late 1990s. Even so, this is not cheap, and ordinary mortals have to make do with less expensive technology such as that found in bubble-jet colour printers.

Ink and bubble-jet printers

Ink-jet printers have evolved with several variations on a theme, namely **liquid ink-jet**, **phase-change ink-jet**, and **continuous flow ink-jet** technologies, to name but a few, which are in current production. Each of these technologies will now be covered very briefly. Some ink-jet printers make use of liquid-inkjet technology – this makes use of the fact that tiny droplets of ink can be squirted onto the page under the application of an appropriate electrical signal. This squeezing process can either be carried out by the application of heat (expansion of the ink) or pressure (caused by a piezo-electric crystal), and these simple ideas can be seen in figure 11.16. These printers are also known as bubble-jet printers.

The first method (figure 11.16(a))shows a system in which the ink is heated up very quickly by a coil or resistor. Just a few msec or less quickly vaporises a small quantity of ink and a bubble forms, thus forcing a droplet of ink out from the nozzle. The capillary action makes sure that the ink does not come out of the nozzle under normal circumstances. The second method (figure 11.16(b))is very similar in principle, and shows a 'piezo crystal' in its deformed state ejecting a droplet of ink from a similar nozzle. When no voltage is applied to the piezo crystal no extra pressure is applied to the ink and again capillary action keeps the ink in the tube – the smaller reservoir next to the piezo crystal fills up again when the voltage to the crystal has been removed.

Phase-change ink jet technology relies on the fact that some inks change phase from a solid to a liquid when heated up and melted. The ink then solidifies again when cooled down as it reaches the paper, and is then further processed by being pressed onto the paper by cold-fusing rollers.

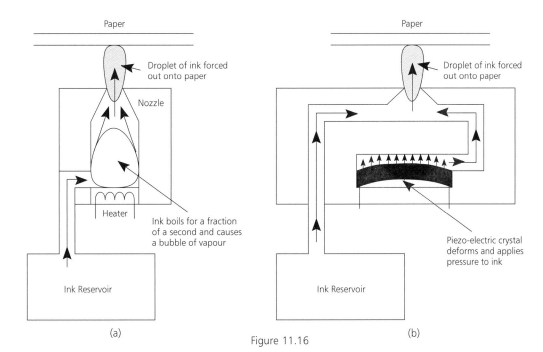

Figure 11.16

Continuous-flow technology continually squirts ink from the nozzle whether it's needed or not! To save it splatting out all over the page the ink is charged up electrostatically and then diverted back into a reservoir or allowed to be sprayed onto the page according to the magnitude of a voltage on deflection plates through which this squirt of ink is passing. It operates rather like the deflection of an electron beam in a raster scan computer monitor – however, the stream of ink is being deflected instead of the electron beam.

You may be wondering why there is such as plethora of different mechanisms and methods regarding non-LASER colour printing technology. The main reason is that manufacturers are constantly trying to find smaller, cheaper and faster ways to produce colour printers. Indeed, they have been very successful over the last couple of years. Reasonable quality colour printers are now available for just a couple of hundred pounds – something which would have been unthinkable just two or three years ago, and it's all due to these new and varied methods of shooting ink out of a nozzle!

One of the problems with some bubble-jet printers is that if ordinary paper is used then the ink either goes into globules on the paper or soaks through and spreads out. Some of the technologies are able to use ordinary paper but others need special paper to get the best results. The use of special paper makes printing with some of these technologies more expensive per sheet than with ordinary paper. A couple of other methods exist for colour-printing technology, but you already know enough to appreciate the modern range of colour output peripheral devices.

Bubble Jet printers (colour)		
Cost	**Data output speed**	**Other considerations**
Virtually all bubble jet printers are now colour. They are intended for the home market, and are thus priced from about £100 to over a thousand pounds for an A3 model.	Slower than laser printers, typically 4 pages per minute or less, although these speeds will obviously improve with time.	There is a speed/cost trade off between laser and bubble jet technologies. With some of the top-of-the-range bubble jets it's difficult to tell the difference from a laser output, especially if glossy paper has been used. The printer cartridges are also more expensive than laser toner on a £/page basis.
We have recently seen the introduction of very cost effective combinations of fax, scanner, photocopier and printer all in the same box.	Identical to the standard bubble-jet technology. The photocopier would be relatively slow compared to a stand-alone dedicated machine, but who's complaining!	Ideal cost effective machine for the small office and for use in the home environment. Together with a powerful PC and a MODEM, this represents a state of the art electronic office in the late 1990s.

Additions to printer technology

One of the trends towards the end of the 1990s is to integrate fax, photocopier, scanner and bubble jet printer in one package. For example the HP OfficeJet pro 1175C is a black and white or colour photocopier, printer, flatbed scanner and OCR facilities, all in the same box (see **Plate 28**). Other companies, including Hewlett Packard, have now made these devices even smaller, and included a fax machine too – all for a few hundred pounds. This is a feat that would have been unthinkable just three or four years ago, when a photocopier, fax machine, colour printer and scanner would together have cost well over £20,000 – a marvellous achievement.

Further output devices

Graphics output devices

Plotters are machines that are widely used to produce graphics output, as they can automatically draw pictures. They range in complexity and price from single-colour, single-pen plotters capable of drawing very slowly on A4 sheets of paper, to very large (the size of a small room) multicolour high speed systems, capable of producing top quality graphics at very high speeds. Most plotters work on the principle of a mechanical arm arrangement that holds a pen, which can be moved across the page. The paper can be positioned on a flat bed (flat-bed plotters), or arranged so that it revolves around or passes over a drum (drum plotters). The pen mechanism moves in both the X and Y directions on the flat bed type plotters, but needs only to move in the Y direction on the drum-type plotters, as the movement of the paper over the drum causes the X movement. Both types of plotter cause effective movement of the pen in both the X and Y directions, and are therefore known as X–Y plotters. A flat bed X–Y plotter is shown in figure 11.17(a) and a drum-type X–Y plotter is shown in figure 11.17(b).

The major advantages of the graphics output produced on plotters over the graphics produced on devices such as dot matrix printers are:

1. Continuous lines not made up from dots. Only the pen limits the thickness.
2. Hundreds of colours possible, limited only by the ink, but only a few at a time.

Did you know that . . .

Large laser printers are starting to eat into the plotter market. Plotters are still used extensively in CAD, particularly for architecture. They remain the only current cost-effective way of printing out drawings larger than A3.

It is therefore possible to produce diagrams of perfect quality that would previously have been drawn by highly qualified draughtsmen. What is more, the copy can be produced accurately and at very high speed. Speeds of over 100 cm per second are possible on large, high quality flat bed plotters.

Plotters are usually divided into two categories – **digital** and **incremental**. In a digital system the plotter requires information regarding the exact X-Y co-ordinates of the pen, such as move to position 12026,10973. However, in the incremental system the plotter is supplied with relative co-ordinates, such as move 300 positions to the left of the current position.

In most high quality systems an arrangement is made for more than one pen to be used without having to stop the plotter and change the colour. This is achieved by such methods as a carousel of about eight pens, which can be rotated so that the desired colour pen is automatically placed in the drawing position. If more colours than the maximum are desired then another pass over the plotting area will have to be made after the appropriate pens have been inserted into the carousel.

 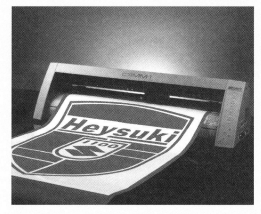

Figure 11.17 (a) and (b)

Plotters (flat-bed, drum and turtle)

Cost	Data output speed	Other considerations
Varies from a few hundred pounds for an A3 desktop model to many thousands of pounds for a specialist very large plotter.	Depends on the pens and the plotter, but typically several feet/second if drawing in a straight line!	Used mainly by architects and engineers working on CAD projects, although chip designers and electronic engineers would proof PCB designs (i.e. the design of the motherboard inside your computer, for example) on large plotters. Drum plotters are useful where space is at a premium.
Turtle-type plotters are very cheap.	Slow compared to the other plotters	Ideally suited for output from programs like LOGO, the really cheap plotters (about £50) are ideal as a mechanism for helping children to control a robot to draw shapes on pieces of paper.

Inexpensive graph plotters costing several hundred pounds or less are also available for connection to microcomputer systems. Although quite slow in comparison with the expensive machines, and usually being limited to A3 paper or less, the quality of output is very good indeed.

Another type of plotter that is often used with microcomputers is the turtle. A typical plotter of this type is shown in figure 11.18(a). It is a device that can hold one or more pens that move around under the control of the computer. It is usually attached to the computer by means of an umbilical cord. High quality printing is possible and the device is not limited to standard size pieces of paper.

Although primarily designed for pictures, plotters can produce any shape (e.g. text of any style). In fact many plotters have their own character generator chips so that standard sizes of text may be plotted simply by sending the appropriate ASCII code to the plotter. However, used in this mode, the plotter is obviously very slow compared with the standard printing devices for producing text.

As any style of text may be printed it is also possible to produce text that looks like handwriting. Signatures (actually produced with a pen) are also possible! Typical outputs from X–Y plotters are shown in figure 11.18(b).

Photographic computer output (microfilm and microfiche)

It is possible to store a massive amount of information if it is drastically reduced in size before being printed on a suitable medium. Both text and graphics can be condensed in size so that large amounts of output are obtained within a very small area.

Computer output on microfilm (COM) is a technique of reducing documents in size and photographically printing them so that they can be conveniently read at a later stage by someone with telescopic eyeballs, or, more conveniently, by a special machine!

A typical COM recorder is shown in figure 11.19(a) and a typical COM reader is shown in figure 11.19(b). The COM process is ideally suited to taking large amounts of information stored on a computer, and printing it out in a form that is convenient to store in a limited amount of space. Such systems are ideal for use in places such as libraries. As it is also possible to store pictures, the system is also widely used to store data that would normally be found in a typical book. The system is even being used to store criminals' fingerprints for police record systems.

Figure 11.18 (a) and (b)

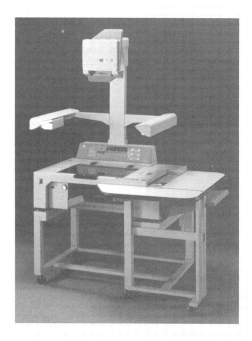 

Figure 11.19 (a) and (b)

There are two systems, which are in common use: **microfilm** and **microfiche.** Microfilm is simply a roll of 16mm film and microfiche is a rectangular photographic card on which many frames (pages of information) can be stored. Microfiche is derived from the French word *fiche*, which means file or card. The popularity of microfiche has increased tremendously as the space taken up by a filing cabinet of microfiche documents is equivalent to hundreds of filing cabinets for storing the same data in normal printed form. Typically 80 pages can be stored on a single card, however, more recently 270 sheets of information per card has become the norm. There is also the new **ultrafiche** system that can cope with 1000 pages per card!

One possible way of running a COM system is for the data requiring printing to be displayed on a special VDU screen and then photographed. It is possible to photograph a screen at a time passing the film serially through the machine, or to use a special machine adapted for the microfiche format. Either way the system is very fast. It is possible to photograph over 120 000 characters per second using high-speed cameras.

The film produced is sometimes processed in the same machine or else sent to a separate processing machine. Having got the first copy it is easily possible to run off thousands of other copies by making use of film duplicators.

The data to be printed out on **microform** (the collective term for microfilm or microfiche) is often first stored on a magnetic medium such as disk or tape. The disk or tape can then be fed into the recording machine off-line. It is also possible on alternative systems for the computer to feed the information directly (i.e. on-line) into the recorder.

Most systems used to read microfiche documents are based on manual methods of data retrieval, i.e. the operator first finds the appropriate microfiche and places it into the COM reader. After the correct card has been placed into the machine the operator then places the reading head over the appropriate part of the microfiche and the frame is displayed on the COM reader screen.

Other systems are now becoming available that can automatically retrieve and display information on microfiche. Each microfiche (and frame) is given a unique number which, when typed into the computer controlling the COM reader, initiates a search and display program. However, this system is several orders of magnitude more expensive than the manually operated

COM (Computer Output on Microform) and associated technologies

Cost	Data output speed	Other considerations
These are specialist machines for use by large manufacturers – they are therefore expensive costing many thousands of pounds.	Depends on the amount of money paid for the machine. Typically over 120,000 characters per second can be photographed ready to produce the sheets.	Used mainly by companies producing microfiche etc. for libraries and companies like car manufacturers. The actual machines, which are used to read the output, are quite cheap, costing only a few hundred pounds or less.

COM reader is. As more companies are now using COM techniques to store and retrieve information, the techniques are becoming more cost effective compared with other means of mass storage of hard copy. It is now actually less expensive to use microfiche techniques than to use ordinary paper! Add to this the considerable reduction in weight together with the reduced postal charges to send data through the post and you will realise why COM techniques are becoming very popular.

Sound cards

Computer sound is now a fundamental form of output which is common on most modern machines. In the last few years we have come a long way – from the pathetically small speaker which issues a beep when your computer is starting up, to quadraphonic 32-bit wave-table Dolby 500W megablaster with base sub-woofers! Wow – that sounds impressive – and it literally is. Computers can sound as good as the best hi-fi systems with a suitable set of kit.

No multimedia computer is complete without a sound card, amplifier and speakers (see Plate 29). It is usual to have the amplifier built into the speakers, and have 'headphone' and 'speaker outputs' from the sound card itself. In this way you can either use the speakers provided with the computer, upgrade to better speakers, or really annoy the neighbours by playing Doom through your Hi-fi.

The company called Creative Labs really set the standard for sound cards, and most cards are now usually SoundBlaster compatible. This, however, means that they are compatible with the earlier versions of Creative Labs offerings, and will work with most Windows software.

As with the graphics cards mentioned earlier, manufacturers try to outdo each other, and incorporate extra features or more realistic sounds into their cards. CD quality sound is now expected and delivered, and the array of software which usually accompanies your sound card is quite impressive, consisting of CD players, 'tape' recorders, MIDI players, speech synthesis, orchestral musical instrument simulators, games and a whole host of others too numerous to mention.

It is the job of the sound card to take the digital information produced by the computer in whatever system, and change it into an analogue form ready to be amplified by the audio amplifier before being played through the speakers. The digital processing that goes on at the computer end can be very sophisticated indeed, and we have already seen some of the options when considering sound as an input device in chapter 10.

Sound is now such an integral part of the computer scene that it is taken for granted, but like graphics cards, because of the rapidly changing and developing technology, keeping up to date by making sure that things are compatible with older computers can sometimes be a nightmare.

Types of sound

Storing good-quality digital sound takes up pots of memory. For example, 44,100 samples/sec is normal CD quality, and up to 96,000 samples/sec is the highest quality on the new **DVD** (**Digital Versatile Disc** – formerly known as the Digital videodisk) medium. Let's pause here for a moment – 96,000 samples a second means that a 3 minute piece of music would take up $3 \times 60 \times 96,000$ = just over 16Mbytes! Superb quality sound takes up one hell of a lot of space on a disc – hence why DVD is used. A maximum of 4.3 Gbytes or just over 13 hours of music could be stored on this latest double-sided optical medium (see chapter 12) – larger capacity DVD disks are being developed at the time of writing!

If you are to store sound on other media such as hard disks or floppies, or even send the sound over the Internet where the bandwidth is relatively limited (see chapter 3), then the sound must be sampled at considerably less frequent intervals. Also, it is usual for some form of compression techniques (see chapter 4) like an 'audio version of MPEG' to be used. Indeed, because MPEG was originally designed for video, and most videos have some audio accompaniment, the MPEG standard also includes a specification for sound. For example, 64Kb/sec is typical for sound being downloaded from the Internet.

WAV files and the PC

Most people who use a PC will be familiar with WAV files. These are digitally-recorded audio sounds which make up the noises when you start up windows, close down windows, make a mistake, or generally wish to mess around with some sound in your programming projects. There are many application programs on the market which allow you to record sound from a standard microphone plugged into your sound card, and even windows has a default sound recorder and other associated devices such as volume controls and

Sound cards

Cost	Data output speed	Other considerations
These vary from about £15 for a basic card to nearly £200 for an all-singing all dancing top of the range model	N/A – send it out too fast and you won't be able to hear it!	Don't forget that you will also need headphones or an amplifier and speaker if you are to be able to hear anything. Typically many utilities would accompany the sound card which can help turn your computer into a multimedia mine of information.

Figure 11.20

recording controls etc. All in all, you can have a virtual stereo system, complete with 'tape recorder' (WAV file), 'CD player' (real CD audio), MIDI (see next section) and a 'mixer' which acts as a control centre. The author's current virtual hi-fi is shown in figure 11.20.

If you have access to similar systems to the above, and your computer is plugged into a suitably impressive hi-fi, then give a demonstration to a friend who is not too computer literate. Next you make the hi-fi controls disappear, thus proving the whole control amplifiers, mixers, tape recorder and CD controls were all really virtual – most people are usually very impressed indeed. And this demonstrates how far we have come with sound-output technology over the last few years. Nevertheless, astute readers will realise that real amps and speakers are needed to actually hear the final result!

MIDI

Although MIDI has already been covered because it is also a form of computer input (see chapter 10), it is worth mentioning it in the computer-output section too, because it is so impressive. It is, for example, possible to use it to compose a complete orchestral symphony. Assigning notes to instruments, which can be played back using the computer's internal synthesisers does this. These are usually supplied with your advanced sound card, or, even more impressively, you can play the sounds through a variety of MIDI (**Musical Instrument Digital Interface**) keyboards and other instruments connected to your computer via a suitable MIDI interface. Impressive professional recording sessions can be undertaken making use of this technology.

Obviously everybody has to agree the special codes for each instrument, and the MIDI standard defines these quantities in terms of the instruments used and the notes. For example, program number 41 is a violin, and program number 14 is a xylophone. A MIDI value of 77 would give an F (frequency of 1396.91 Hz) or a MIDI value of 90 would give an F# or a G-flat with a frequency of 2959.95 Hz. These values are usually not presented in this scientific way, but the user would probably be presented with a standard keyboard on the screen over which he or she could click the mouse, or, even better, play the notes straight in on a standard keyboard.

The quality of the MIDI system depends on how good a synthesiser you have in your computer or the quality of the MIDI keyboard connected to your system. If you have a £50,000 MIDI-equipped grand piano attached to your computer, then you will literally get concert-hall quality. If you have an inexpensive MIDI compatible keyboard the sound will be less good even though the same MIDI data has been sent from your computer interface.

VR helmets

VR (Virtual Reality) helmets are devices worn over the head which project images into the eyes by using small computer screens extremely close to the eyes. It is, therefore, basically a **head-mounted CRT display** (see **Plates 30** and **31**). There is, in fact, a big difference between displaying a picture on a normal screen, and displaying a picture close to the eyes. NASA found that if the field of vision was increased such that the angle of the extreme edges of the visual field is greater than about 60 degrees, then people began to feel as if they

Did you know that . . .

Cost effective VR helmets, which are more than toys, have yet to be developed. Companies are developing these devices with the home market in mind, but it will be some time before VR helmets are part of the everyday use of computers. You will also need new computers that are more powerful than the current generation to produce effective real-time output.

VR helmets

Cost	Data output speed	Other considerations
Low cost domestic versions are available for a few hundred pounds, but this is still a specialist market.	Computers that most people can afford are not yet fast enough to update a VR helmet with good resolution in real time. Military versions are under constant development.	Ideal form of output for personal simulators, the training possibilities and other activities such as arcade games, simulations and even viewing properties by being telepresent are only limited by your budget and imagination.

were part of the picture. They feel as if they are being projected inside the virtual world portrayed by the computer-generated image. The nearest thing we can get to this effect without an actual VR helmet is to visit a theme park such as Futuroscope at Poitiers in France, where enormous screens project images such that it feels like you are actually part of the action. There is also one in the Trocadero in London.

Although great for arcade games, there are many more serious uses of the head-mounted display. For example, after a CAT scan (Computer-Aided Tomography), a three dimensional picture of a human body can be built up. Instead of trying to view this through the two-dimensional medium of a conventional computer monitor, a surgeon can put on his or her VR helmet and feel as if they are walking around inside the patient. They could move their head and see views of some cancerous tumour, for example, from different angles. In combination with the data glove (see chapter 10),

surgeons can interact with the computer generated images, perhaps by grabbing hold of a virtual organ and moving it out of the way.

VR helmets are also of educational value on training courses. Imagine a garage mechanic who has not seen some particular process before. He or she could put on a single-eyed version of a head-mounted display, and look at a video of what to do in one eye, whilst actually carrying out the process using the other eye to observe what they are doing. The possibilities are endless, and both the surgeon and garage mechanic examples are not figments of my imagination, but are actually being carried out in practice.

Exercise 11.1

1 Outline the *important differences* between computer monitors and standard domestic TV sets. Why are there so many different types of computer monitor, and why are the good ones relatively expensive?

2 What does the statement '24-bit colour graphics' mean?

3 A *bit map* of the screen can be associated with the **Video RAM** used inside the computer. Explain the principles behind the operation of this system.

4 Compare and contrast CRT and LCD computer monitors making sure that you cover the advantages and disadvantages of each system.

5 What is a touch-sensitive screen and where might the use of one be advantageous?

6 Printing technology has changed drastically over the last few years. Briefly outline major

developments from the typewriter through to the latest colour LASER printers.

7 What's the difference between a **bit-mapped font** and an **outline font**?

8 Why are **line printers** still popular on mainframe computers?

9 Explain how the **CMYK model** is used to produce a colour print?

10 How much *memory* would be needed inside a colour LASER printer if an **A5 24-bit colour image** were to be output at 300dpi with *no compression*?

11 How do you think that the computer's ability to print high quality documentation has changed the face of the printing industry?

12 Is it likely that LASER printers will eventually take over the role of plotters? Explain your answer.

13 Why is **microform** and **microfiche** still popular?

14 Outline likely *main output peripherals* for use in the following situations:

   a   A firm of high-quality architects

   b   The producer of a glossy magazine

   c   A school secretary

   d   A library information system

   e   An EFTPOS terminal.

15 Explain the need for **compression** *with regard to the output of images* on a **printer**. What advantages would the same techniques have if applied to sending information over a network or telephone system?

16 Devise and discuss *suitable* forms of **computer output** for use with people who have the following disabilities:

   a   Blind

   b   Blind *and* deaf.

End of chapter revision aid and summary

Cover up the right-hand column and see if you can answer the questions or define the terms on the left. They appear in the order in which they are covered in this chapter. Alternatively you may browse through the right-hand column to aid revision.

What is an output peripheral?	An output peripheral is used to *display output* from a computer system.
What is the most common form of output peripheral?	A computer screen, VDU or monitor is the most common form of output peripheral. VDU stands for Visual Display Unit.
Why are computer monitors more expensive that the equivalent TV?	Computer monitors need to be high quality *due to the short viewing distance*.
What is a multisync monitor?	Multisync monitors are needed to display the highest resolutions without flicker.
What is a CRT?	Most desktop monitors are based on CRT (Cathode Ray Tube) displays.
What is a TTL colour monitor?	TTL colour monitors are capable of displaying *eight colours only*.
What is an analogue monitor?	Analogue monitors are needed to display a *vast range of different colours*.
What is a raster scan?	Most CRT displays are based on the raster scan system, the method of scrolling an electron beam from the top to the bottom to draw a picture on the screen.
How many electron guns does a CRT colour monitor usually have?	Colour monitors have *three electron guns* called R,G and B, representing the colours red, green and blue respectively.
What is a pixel?	A pixel is a logical picture element, usually representing the *smallest element* (dot) which makes up a picture.
What is 24-bit colour graphics?	24-bit colour graphics can represent *16,777,216 different colours*.
What is a bit-mapped display?	Bit-mapped displays map Video RAM onto the monitor display screen, the number of pixels determines the resolution and the number of bits/pixel determines the grey scales or number of colours.
What is a character-based graphics display?	Character graphics use character generators inside the display to change ASCII code into suitable characters in a similar way to the teletext displays.
What are vector graphics displays?	Vector graphics are an alternative to bit-mapped-raster-display images – vectors are drawn directly onto the CRT screen.

What is an LCD display?	LCD (Liquid Crystal Displays) are most common in portables but are breaking into the large monitor markets, especially for projection TVs.
What is the difference between an active and a passive LCD display?	LCD displays may be passive or active, with the more-expensive active displays giving the brightest results.
What is an LEP display?	LEP stands for Light Emitting Plastic. A new and cheap way of providing a screen format which can be very large and moulded into a variety of shapes.
What is a touch-sensitive screen?	Touch-sensitive screens are 'normal' screens with the addition of a range of sensors to detect a 'finger' position when pointed at the screen.
What is a projection TV?	Projection TVs project computer and other images onto very large screens.
What is an OHP output device?	OHP output devices allow computer screens to be projected with the use of an overhead projector as found in many classrooms.
What is hard copy?	Hard copy is the term used for the computer output from printers.
What is a serial printer?	Serial printers print just one character at a time.
What is a dot-matrix printer?	Dot matrix printers print characters made up from a matrix of tiny dots, usually 24 pins firing through an inked ribbon.
What is now the most common form of printer for business and industry?	LASER printers have become the standard for most high-quality output in business and industry, but some ink-jet printers, especially at the cheap end of the market seriously challenge them.
Comment on the dpi available from a typical laser printer?	LASER printers are usually 300dpi, but 600 is common and 1200 dpi is also available.
What is a bit-mapped font?	Bit-mapped fonts map the shape of each font onto a matrix of dots suitable for the printer.
What is an outline font?	Outline fonts *mathematically define* the font's shape, but obviously have to be converted to a bit map when the characters are finally printed.
What is a page description language?	Page description languages such as Postscript define each and every attribute of the layout on the printed page.
What is a page printer?	LASER printers are an example of page printers because they print a page at a time.
What are line printers?	Line printers print a line of characters at a time. They are used mainly in a mainframe environment.
What are impact printers?	Impact printers make use of hammers or pins being fired – they tend to make a lot of noise.
What are non-impact printers?	Non-impact printers such as LASERS or bubble jet are virtually silent in operation.
What is the CYMK colour model?	Coloured images are produced on paper using the CMYK model. This should be contrasted with the RGB model used for computer monitors.
Are ink jet and bubble jet printers examples of non-impact printers?	Ink-jet and bubble jet printers makes use of various technologies. They are examples of serial non-impact printers.
What is COM?	Photographic output from the computer is called COM or Computer Output on Microfilm.
What is microfiche?	Microfiche is used extensively to store vast amounts of textual and pictorial information which can be read without a computer using a microfiche reader.

What is voice output?

Voice output is relatively common in specialised situations where a pre-set vocabulary is acceptable. For example, phone banking.

Comment on computer generated smells!

Computer generated smells are still in their infancy, but are finding their way into advertising and product launches etc.

What are sound cards?

Sound cards are the cards which form part of the kit in a multimedia computer. They convert digital information into the analogue form needed by the amplifiers and speakers.

What is a VR helmet?

Virtual reality helmets project an image which makes the user of the system feel that they have been projected into the picture.

12 Storage Techniques

Key Resources

To carry out this work most successfully it's best if you have:

◆ Access to a range of computers with different types of storage devices attached like hard disk, tape and DAT, for example

◆ Access to a system that can restore data from tape back ups

◆ Access to a variety of secondary storage media such as floppy disks, DAT, QIC, CD recordable and flopticals, for example

Concept Checkpoints

◆ Be familiar with how binary digits may be used to represent information.

◆ Understand the terms 'bits' and 'bytes'.

Introduction

Computer storage techniques have made tremendous progress in recent years, and this chapter covers the principles of all major storage media from SRAM via VRAM, EDORAM to Zip drives, RAID, DVD and tape streaming. As with the chapters on computer input and output techniques, students are expected to have a complete understanding of what is available and where these devices may be used most appropriately, but on many courses you are not expected to understand any great technical detail. However, some detail has been included at a simple level. This enables a better understanding of these devices, and answers the questions most commonly asked in the classroom. It is indeed necessary to satisfy the understandable curiosity of most readers who have progressed to this level.

The computer's memory organisation may be split up into two main parts – primary storage techniques such as the semiconductor memory chips found inside the computer, and secondary storage techniques such as the disks and tapes connected as peripherals. This chapter is, therefore, also split into these two sections.

Primary storage techniques

The most important requirement of main memory is **speed of operation**. This is because it is this type of memory which holds the **immediate instructions** used in the microprocessor's **fetch-decode-execute cycle** (see chapter 20). As the speed of the **microprocessors** increases dramatically, *memory speed limitations have become a major problem* in the restriction of the overall performance of modern computer systems, and faster memory, including speeding up access to the memory chips, is an ongoing and challenging technical requirement. An alternative name for **primary** or **main storage** is **Immediate Access Store (IAS)**.

It's amazing, but the limitation of the speed of light is becoming a significant factor in limiting computer design. Within the current realms of scientific understanding, electrical signals can't travel faster than light, which is about 300,000,000 m/sec. Let's suppose, for the sake of argument, that an electrical signal, travelling at the speed of light, has to travel along a piece of cable just 1 metre long. The time taken for the signal to get from one end to the other would be:

$$1/300,000,000 = 3.3 \times 10^{-9} \text{ sec or } 3.3 \text{ nsec.}$$

Although this is reasonably quick by any standards, this unfortunately would mean that a very fast processor would have to wait for this information while it was travelling along the wire! For example, the latest Cray T3E 900 supercomputer can execute 80,000,000,000 instructions per second, which means it could carry out between 200 and 300 instructions in this short space of time! Therefore, we have to make sure that the signal paths between main memory and the processor are considerably shorter than the one metre described above, and this is why some of the fastest computers such as the Cray are designed very carefully.

It is indeed fortunate that the actual distances involved in the CPUs are considerably less than one metre. Nevertheless, the above illustrates the point that current technologies are approaching some awkward theoretical limits – apart from the clever design modifications covered later in this chapter, the only current way known to increase the speed of operation is to reduce the distance that the signals have to travel. This is one of the reasons why chips are becoming smaller and just one of the reasons why the primary cache memory (see later) located inside the microprocessor chip itself is considerably faster than memory external to the processor chip.

Semiconductor memories are based around materials which have an electrical conductivity roughly half way between that of a **conductor** and an **insulator** – hence the name semiconductor. By doping these semiconductor materials with other materials, and by making use of precise manufacturing methods, it's possible to build up a device called a **transistor**, which forms the basis of the units inside these chips. Each transistor acts as a switch (or as a store for charge) which can either be on or off. It is the state of each transistor (or group of transistors) which represents the **state of a binary digit inside the computer**. Indeed, any physical device, which can be in one of two states, may represent a memory cell, and man is constantly striving for new technologies, which will give a better memory performance.

There are several different technologies available and some under development (see **nano technology** in chapter 7), but in the late 1990s **semiconductor chips** are still the *main devices* used for high-speed main memory inside a computer (see **Plate 32**). This is because they are *relatively cheap* to make (compared with other technologies), have a *relatively high capacity* (in terms of the number of bits that can be fitted into a single chip), and are *easy to integrate* into electronic computer systems.

Principles of main memory

Fortunately, all main memory devices can be viewed as a *matrix* of tiny **cells**, the state of which represents a binary digit (on or off). The term memory cell is therefore used to represent the smallest physical unit of any memory device, and is effectively a one-bit store. However, even with one bit, we can see the need to have a control line attached to this simple device which enables the computer to read the contents of the cell (find out what digit is located inside) or write a number to the cell (put a new number inside). The idea is shown in figure 12.1(a).

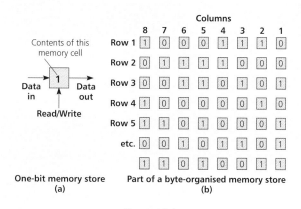

Figure 12.1

One bit of memory is not quite sufficient for today's modern computers, and so groups of cells are arranged in various ways to build up a sensible-size storage unit. The most common method is to build up **rows** and **columns** of **cells** as shown in figure 12.1(b). This shows a simple arrangement of what would be termed an 8-bit memory chip, because each row (called an address) is made up of 8 cells into which 8 binary digits or 1 byte of information could be stored. If there happened to be 1024 rows in which 8 bits could be stored, then the chip which is organised in this particular way would be called a 1024 × 8-bit memory chip. However, as it can also store 8 lots of 1024 bits then it can also be referred to as an 8k-bit chip. (See the following couple of sections and the table below if some of these units seem strange to you.)

Bits, bytes and nibbles

Memory chips are categorised both by their **capacity** (e.g. 8k bits) and by their **internal organisation** (e.g. 1024 × 8-bits). Therefore, we could have 256k, 1M or 16M-bit capacity chips for example, but the internal organisation could be **bit** (**1 binary digit**), **nibble** (**half a byte or 4 bits**), **byte** (or **8 bits** such as that shown in figure 12.1(b)), or **word** (**2 byte**) orientated. Often-used word definitions would be – **1 word = 2 bytes**, **double word = 4 bytes** and a **quad word** would be **8 bytes** or **64 bits**. Figure 11.5 shows Video RAM organised for

256-grey-level graphics using memory arranged internally as 1 bit.

It is worth remembering at this stage that the terms k (kilo), M (Mega), G (Giga) and T (Tera) do not have precisely the same meanings as used in other branches of science, but refer in computing to the **nearest binary multiple**. Therefore, 1 Kbyte of memory is actually 1024 bytes, giving us 24 bytes more than you might think from the words actually being used. Although this is not too impressive, think for a moment about having 1 Gbyte of memory. This is sometimes referred to as 1,000 Mbyte, but actually means 1024 × 1024 × 1024 = 1,073,741,824 bytes which is actually well over 74 million bytes more – a number not to be sneezed at!

Multipliers

As computers get faster, and memory gets larger, the standard units such as Kbytes and Mbytes etc. are far too small. With this borne in mind, the table shown in figure 12.2 may be helpful in extending your knowledge of multiples, which will hopefully last you for some considerable time. Many Tbytes of secondary storage in the form of disk farms (see later) are now common on larger computer systems, and even if one considers the humble micro – we now have **tape streamers** and **DVDs** which store about **20 Gbytes**. Notice that new terms have been added to this table which were not commonly available a couple of years ago. These are Zettabytes and Yottabytes – two extra large multiples with which you can now impress your friends – numbers even larger than the amount of money made by Microsoft!

Notice that in the table **smaller letters** are used to denote **multiples < 1**, and **CAPITALS** are used to denote **multiples > 1**.

How main memory is utilised

It is fortunate that most of the decoding necessary to extract information from a semiconductor memory chip is carried out electronically inside the chip itself. From an external point of view, the computer supplies the chip with a number called an **address**. This refers to the **address** (number) in memory lane at which a particular bit or group of bits reside depending on internal memory organisation. In figure 12.1(b), for example, if **address 3 (being row 3)** is being considered, then, if a read operation were carried out, the number revealed would be 00110101 – corresponding to the group of binary digits which make up the byte of information living in row 3.

The **address** is supplied to the memory chip along the **address bus**, and the **data** being put into or taken out of the memory chip is supplied or received along the **data bus** (see chapter 20). The microprocessor would determine whether a **read** or **write** operation is to be carried out by the state of one of the lines going to the memory chip.

Not all memory is organised in the same way internally, or makes use of the same number of bits. However, from a software programmer's point of view, all that is necessary is to read data from or write data to the memory by specifying an address, and knowing how the memory is organised in terms of bytes.

The processor, depending on how many lines are available on the address bus, can address different amounts of memory. With just 8 bits available, only 2^8 or 256 bytes of memory would be possible. Even on the most humble of microprocessor chips used in computer systems, 16 bits is common for the address bus giving 2^{16} or 65,536 bytes (64 Kbytes) as the maximum main

Large and small multipliers					
Name	Letter	Derivation	Muliplier	Words *(to impress your friends)*	Exact numbers used in computer science
atto	a		1×10^{-18}		0. 000 000 000 000 000 001
femto	f		1×10^{-15}		0. 000 000 000 000 001
pico	p		1×10^{-12}		0. 000 000 000 001
nano	n		1×10^{-9}		0. 000 000 001
micro	μ		1×10^{-6}		0. 000 001
milli	m		1×10^{-3}		0. 001
Kilo	K	1024^1	1×10^{3}	Thousand	1 024
Mega	M	1024^2	1×10^{6}	Million	1 048 576
Giga	G	1024^3	1×10^{9}	Billion	1 073 741 824
Tera	T	1024^4	1×10^{12}	Trillion	1 099 511 627 776
Peta	P	1024^5	1×10^{15}	Quadrillion	1 125 899 906 843 624
Exa	E	1024^6	1×10^{18}	Quintillion	1 152 921 504 607 870 976
Zetta	Z	1024^7	1×10^{21}	Sextillion	1 180 591 620 718 458 979 424
Yotta	Y	1024^8	1×10^{24}	Septillion	1 208 925 819 615 701 892 530 176

Figure 12.2

memory size. This is why the early micros were usually limited to 64 Kbytes of main memory.

On the 32-bit micros, 2^{32} gives us 4096 Mbytes or 4 Gbytes of main memory. A few years ago this used to be enough for even the most dedicated animation and video fanatic, and some processors therefore included only a 24-bit address bus, which gives a main memory of 2^{24} or 16 Mbytes. If you have an older machine and attempted to upgrade your RAM in the last year or two, then these numbers should start ringing bells as to why your machine might be limited to a maximum of 16 Mbytes of main memory. However, 4 Gbytes of RAM is more than sufficient for the home micro, even at the end of the 1990s.

The Pentium and Pentium II chips, for example, have 64-bits available, and *if* all 64 bits available were used on the address bus then a staggering 2^{64} or 1.8×1019 bytes of main memory would then be possible. However, you are often limited by other considerations such as the operating system – Windows 95, for example, could address a maximum of 4 Gbytes of RAM. It would be unrealistic to have all 64-bits available and addressable, not just because of the enormous size, but because of the cost. At mid 1990s prices, an extra 4 Mbytes of RAM cost about £150 – but by the late 1990s, 16 Mbytes of RAM could be had for only £15! If we actually desired 1.8×10^{19} bytes of RAM, then, even at late 1990s prices, this would cost us a cool £1,000,000,000,000 less bulk quantity discount of course! However, these minor irritations of cost can be overcome to some extent by the use of **virtual memory** as described in the operating-system chapter 22. When virtual memory is used, very large and fast hard disks act as an extension to RAM, hence the need for these larger processor-addressing ranges.

Moving data along the bus

The size of data bus is important too, as this affects the speed at which a quantity of data may be shifted around inside the computer. The early micros had just 8 bits available, thus a single byte could be moved around at any moment in time. However, micros with a 16-bit data bus can move twice as much data in the same time, as two bytes can travel along the wider data bus simultaneously. Similarly a processor with a 32-bit wide address bus can move data at 4 times the rate of an 8-bit-data-bus processor. Some of the latest chips have internal 256-bit data buses!

Access times

The access time of a memory chip is particularly important, because it affects the speed at which the processor can be allowed to go. The **access time** is simply the time taken for the electronics inside the memory chip to access the required cells, usually via some sort of electronic address decoding, and then place the data on the data bus ready to be transmitted to the CPU. In practice the time taken to get data from a memory chip and put data into the chip is often the same, but if not, then the 'read access' and 'write access' times would be quoted separately.

Types of semiconductor memory

A typical **static RAM** (see in a moment) memory chip would probably have an access time of about 70 nsec, thus enabling data to be extracted from it at a rate of about 14,000,000 words/sec. (Don't forget that a word refers to how many bits can be extracted from the chip at the same time, but see the definition of bits, nibbles and bytes etc. as described earlier.) If you need the speed but have not got the required word length, then this is where one-bit internally-organised chips come into their own, simply line up 64 of these 1-bit chips in parallel, and you have a **quad-word** or **64-bit word** available in <70 nsec – magic.

RAM

First let's consider **RAM**. This is an acronym for **Random Access Memory**, which means that *the time taken to access the data does not depend on the location at which it is stored*. Random access in this context should be contrasted with the **serial-access** mechanisms on a tape, for example, where the amount of time taken to read the data *does* depend on its position on the storage medium.

Dynamic RAM

There are two major types of **read/write RAM** called **static RAM** (see next section) and **dynamic RAM**. Dynamic RAM (or DRAM) is made up from transistors which store the state of a binary digit as a charge built up on a transistor, rather similar to the charge that would be stored on a capacitor. This method is the most popular because of its ease of manufacture and hence its cost effectiveness. However, it is more complex to operate than static RAM, because the stored charge leaks away very quickly and gets lost if it is not topped up at frequent intervals, which currently means every few milliseconds! This means that extra electronics have to be put into the system to carry out these operations, but this is hardly of any consequence to the users of such systems. What is of consequence is that due to this topping up cycle, the speed of access for dynamic RAM is slower than the speeds with which one can access static RAM. Dynamic RAM is currently about 60 or 70nsec – this being typical in the late 90s.

Recently **EDO RAM (Extended Data Out Random Access Memory)** has been developed, and is actually more popular and hence cheaper than the slower conventional RAM. By eliminating the need to wait for the next conventional read cycle, it is possible to speed up dynamic RAM even further. At the time of writing, the fastest EDO dynamic RAM speeds are about 40nsec. This is a considerable improvement over the typical 70nsec time mentioned earlier.

Static RAM

Static RAM (or SRAM) is more expensive to produce, as more transistors are needed for the storage of each byte. However, static RAM does not have to be topped up, as the data is stored by monitoring the state of a transistor being used as a switch, rather than a charge-storing mechanism as is the case with dynamic RAM. In the operating systems' chapter you will see that **static RAM** *is ideal for* **cache memory** (see next section) – which often increases the performance of computer systems by several orders of magnitude. The technology inside a static RAM chip is a little different – instead of being stored as a leaky charge, the transistors are permanently switched into an 'on' or an 'off' state, and thus do not need constant attention in terms of topping them up. However, it is still too expensive to have Mbytes of the faster static RAM as the mainstay of most microcomputers. Static RAM too would loose its contents if the power were to be turned off as explained in the next section.

Volatile memory

Both **SRAM** and **DRAM** are **volatile**. This means that if the power were removed from the system then all the binary data stored in the memory chips would be lost. This should be compared to the **non-volatile** nature of magnetic or optical storage media such as disks, which retain the data for a considerable period of time, usually measured in tens of years.

> **Hint:** Always consider using a UPS if loss of data stored in volatile memory is a problem for your particular application.

The use of **Uninterruptible Power Supplies** or **UPS** can overcome the problems of volatile memory. These are effectively batteries connected to the computer system which are constantly charged up from the mains under normal operation, but come into their own and provide the necessary power when a mains failure occurs. It's possible to have relatively cheap battery backup which would allow you to save the data in the event of a failure of power, or relatively expensive uninterruptible power supplies which effectively means having your own power station hooked up to your micro, mini or mainframe. Obviously the more expensive systems are used in places like hospitals where emergency generators would automatically cut in if a mains failure were detected. A big battery is usually needed to provide the power between the generators coming on line and the actual failure of the mains, but on small microcomputer systems, this time can simply be a matter of a few minutes while the computer is automatically powered down in a controlled way.

Cache memory

Caching is a useful technique if you have a really powerful microprocessor chip, which can go at a speed *considerably in excess of the ability of the memory chips to supply the processor with data from conventional dynamic RAM.* The solution is to place **faster static RAM** *in-between* the **processor** and the **dynamic RAM**. In this way the data can be processed as quickly as possible by the processor, which gets the immediate data from the faster static

> **Hint:** New variations on RAM technology will always appear with great frequency, as manufacturers try to squeeze more out of their systems. Concentrate mainly on the principles of RAM, not on all the possible variations.

RAM. When the data has been processed, it can be taken out of the fast static RAM and put back into the dynamic RAM, while new data is being put into the fast static RAM ready for the next processor operation. The trick is, however, to know exactly what ought to be put into the cache! – a tricky task, and one which is not always accomplished efficiently (see chapter 23 for an explanation).

At the time of writing, even fast static RAM chips need about 15 nsec or 20 nsec to read or write data. If you think about it, this is still slow, compared to a 500 MHz Pentium III, for example, which could theoretically read/write data at a rate of 2 nsec. Nevertheless, static RAM is fast compared to the typical 70 nsec read/write times of dynamic RAM, and this is why it is used. Some adverts might quote **Synchronous Burst SRAM or Pipelined Burst RAM**, for example, which cut down on addressing overheads by a variety of methods. Manufacturers are always coming up with new techniques, which enable data to be read from or written to the primary store in a computer system at speeds which can keep up with speeds of modern processors. Today, many of the microprocessor chips will have some RAM actually built inside the processor itself in an attempt to speed things up even further. If the cache is inside the processor itself then it's termed **primary** cache, or, if its outside the processor on the motherboard then it's termed **secondary cache**. On some motherboards using special memory chips can expand the secondary cache.

Other RAM technologies

The need for increases in speed due to the tortuous requirements of applications like real-time video, for example, has spawned a whole new breed of RAM innovations. For example, **Burst EDO**, **Synchronous DRAM**, **Enhanced RAM**, **VRAM** and **WRAM** to name but a few! You would not be expected to remember most of these names, but you will see them in computer adverts. **VRAM**, or **Video RAM**, for example, has *two different ways* in which the data can get *into* and *out of* the chip. Thus you can avoid any waiting that would normally be the case with a conventional read/write cycle. **WRAM**, on the other hand, are simply custom designed sets of memory chips to map modes like 1024 × 768, for example, to directly control the video driver board inside the PC – hence the name **Windows Random Access Memory**. As the bus speeds on PCs (see chapter 20) have gone up from 66 MHz and 75 MHz to the new 83 MHz an 100 MHz versions, then technologies like **SDRAM**, for example, have come into their own.

No doubt another dozen technologies will be invented before the next edition of this book!

ROM

Some programs, such as those parts of the **operating system** (see chapter 22) which start up the machine *must not be lost* even when the power to the system has been removed for extended periods of time. A special chip called a **ROM (Read Only Memory)** is ideal for this purpose, as it is non-volatile. However, its contents have to be programmed by the manufacturer of the chips and they can't be changed. Brave operating system designers often commit their operating systems to a ROM chip as this saves having to load the operating system from disk each time the machine is switched on. However, as you will appreciate by reading chapter 22, no operating system is ever bug free, and this means that software patches (bug fixes) would have to be loaded from disk until a new version of the operating system is available on ROM.

ROM-based operating systems are ideal for **portable computers** such as **PDAs** or **HPCs** etc. as the amount of power saved by not having to load the operating system from disk is considerable. It is also very convenient on desktop versions too, especially if the operating system

RAM		
Cost	Read/write speed	Other considerations
Dynamic RAM – prices have tumbled in the last few years – currently about £50 for 64 Mbytes of EDORAM.	Ordinary RAM can read data in about 60 or 70 nsec. SDRAM (Synchronous DRAM) is between 4 nsec and 60 nsec.	RAM is still slow compared to the speeds at which some modern microprocessors can operate. Dynamic RAM needs refreshing frequently, but is still the most cost-effective primary storage medium.
Static RAM	Fastest chips currently about 10 nsec at the time of writing	Does not need to be refreshed, much more expensive than conventional RAM or EDORAM – but, like dynamic RAM it is still a volatile storage medium.
Secondary cache RAM	About 10 or 20 nsec at the time of writing.	Fast SRAM chips are used here. RAM used to supplement the fast memory for the processor on the motherboard.
Primary cache RAM	Fastest speed currently possible – depends on processor innards.	RAM inside the microprocessor chip itself. The speed advantages would be encompassed in the performance of the processor.
VRAM	It is the same as for static RAM, but performance is better due to dual input and output mechanisms.	Video RAM used to improve performance of graphics cards and the like by allowing two paths, which enable data to be written to and read from the chips at the same time.
WRAM	Same as for static RAM	Windows RAM mapped onto specific screen modes in operating systems like Windows.
Synchronous burst RAM, Pipelined burst RAM, Synchronous RAM etc.	Better performance due to small modifications in techniques of reading and writing data.	New technologies are in constant development in the struggle to extract the last ounce of performance from these vital memory chips.

is working well. Operating systems are also quite large, and the saving in RAM by having the operating system in ROM is also of considerable benefit.

Languages too are sometimes committed to ROM, especially BASIC in some of the educational micro-computers. However, any software could be stored in this way and the term used to denote the fact that the **software** is *permanently and unalterably embedded in the ROM* chip is called **firmware**. This is to distinguish from the terms **hardware** and **software** which have been defined elsewhere in this book. A rather cheeky term is to refer to the people who operate the computers as **liveware**!

One philosophical point to bear in mind here is that ROM is also RAM! This is because the definition of RAM refers to 'access times' to retrieve any data and not to it's volatility or otherwise. ROM is random access too. Nevertheless, people have lived with this definition for years, and the only people to suffer are the students trying to understand the system!

One final point about ROM is that it's used not only in computers, but is extensively used in **embedded microprocessors** and **control systems** such as those found in a variety of equipment from cruise missiles to the controls of domestic microwave ovens. These aspects of ROM are covered in the chapter on computer control systems (see chapter 8).

PROM

It's a bit of a pain having to get the manufacturers to program the chips for you, especially if you are ordering less than a few thousands chips, as the price per chip becomes prohibitive. Therefore, developers wanted a way to test out read-only chips without having to manufacture fully blown ROMs. The answer to their prayers was the **PROM** or **Programmable Read Only Memory**. A special machine can be used to program the ROM, and this is a considerably cheaper option than getting the chip manufacturers to build up a special mask – which is a necessary and expensive stage during the programming of a ROM at the chip factory. Once the PROM has been programmed, it behaves in an identical way to the ROM. However, unlike the ROM where a mask is produced, PROMs are not suitable for mass-production methods – it would be far too slow for hundreds of thousands of identical chips.

EPROM

Although **PROM**s are better suited to development work, if a mistake is made then the chips have to be thrown away. A better method for development would be to have a system where the contents could be erased and the chip could be re-programmed from scratch if necessary. This is indeed what can be done when using an **EPROM** or **Erasable Programmable Read Only Memory**. A very cost-effective machine can program

the system, usually under the control of a standard microcomputer. However, if the contents are to be erased then UV (ultra-violet light) is shone through a special window in the top of the chip, and after a few minutes the contents are erased. Because daylight contains UV radiation, after programming an EPROM the window must be covered up or the data could be erased in a relatively short space of time.

EPROMs are not as permanent as ROMs or PROMS, and the data would be lost after a number of years even if the window were covered up. About ten years is the current norm, and this is obviously not usually a problem, as the computer designed to take the EPROM has probably been superseded by the

> **Hint:** Unlike RAM, the different types of ROM are worth considering in detail, because each performs a very different function. Different applications use different types of ROM from EEPROM to FLASH ROM. You should know where each would best be applied.

next fifteen generations of machines. Nevertheless, if permanent data storage were required, then an EPROM would not be man enough for the job.

RAM, ROM and EPROM, when plumbed into the architecture of a computer system behave as if they are all RAM (which they are!). The only difference being that you can't alter the contents of the ROMs under the control of the computer. It is usual to have a memory map of the system, which shows how the memory is allocated to the operating system software and user programs. Memory maps are extensively covered in the operating systems chapter 22.

EEPROM

Instead of using UV light to erase data, as is the case with an EPROM, the **EEPROM** chip, which stands for **Electrically Erasable Programmable Read Only Memory** chip, can have it's data erased with higher voltages than would normally be present in a normal circuit. A special machine into which the EERPOM chip may be plugged does this.

Flash ROM

This is nothing to do with the look of the chips! You may recall that an **EEPROM** can be erased by the use of higher voltages – well **flash memory** can be erased with much lower voltages, and then reprogrammed again while still inside the computer or other electronic device! *This might not sound too revolutionary but it actually is.* Imagine the scenario – for the first time a user is able to program his or her own ROM chip without even having to take it out of the computer – this is totally revolutionary. For example, the author automatically upgraded his US Robotics MODEM to cope with the new 56 Kbit/sec standard. He did this by

ROM		
Cost	Speed at which data can be read	Other considerations
ROM	Ordinary ROM is about the same speed as SRAM and can read data in about 10 to 50 nsec.	ROM is used to store permanent information such as part of the operating system stored in the ROM BIOS, for example.
PROM	For speed of each type see below.	Enables you to program a ROM with a special machine.
EPROM	45 nsec to 90 nsec.	Can erase as well as program the data into the ROM chip.
EEPROM	45 nsec to 200 nsec	More convenient erasure mechanism based on electric signals instead of UV radiation.
Flash ROM	45 nsec to 120 nsec.	Can erase and program the chip with much lower voltages, therefore, ideal to program in situ.

logging on to the US robotics web site, then downloading a program, which reprogrammed the Flash ROM inside the MODEM. This is an effective upgrade, almost identical to putting a new chip inside the MODEM, without even taking it apart or even moving the box. This is the power of the Flash ROM – a very flash idea with numerous applications regarding embedded microprocessor technology.

Disk cache

The general rule regarding RAM is that you usually don't have quite enough – if you have 32 Mbytes then you can bet that the application that you are using requires 64 Mbytes! To get over this problem, you can instruct your computer to assume that it has got more RAM than it actually has, by continuing the RAM onto disk. In other words, disk space is used to supplement the available RAM, which you have inside your computer's primary store. Disk space is much cheaper than primary store in terms of the cost/byte, and thus this is a marvellous way to extend your RAM to many Gbytes if you wish!

Unfortunately there is a catch to supplementing your RAM with disk space, and this is speed of operation. You will recall that RAM can read or write at speeds determined by a few nsec. Well, disk access is, unfortunately, a few msec, *and is thus a million times slower than fast RAM*. Nevertheless, this is a good idea, as it does enable you to run some software or run many application software tasks simultaneously, which would otherwise not be possible.

If you rely *too much* on caching in this way, then may find that you accidentally fall asleep while you are waiting for your disk drive to stop whirring! There is no real substitute for an adequate amount of RAM, but, even so, disk caching is used on virtually all machines, as it does improve system performance if used in appropriate ways.

ASCII code

The need to communicate information from one computer system to another is of paramount importance. Therefore, a common code used on all systems is needed if any sense is to be made of the masses of binary digits inside a computer's main memory. The **ASCII code** was developed for this purpose, and is an acronym for the **American Standard Code for Information Interchange**. Being a code for communications as well as data representation, the ASCII code is made up not just of letters of the alphabet and numbers etc., but of simple **communications protocols** such as ACK (acknowledge) and ENQ (enquiry) for example. Figure 12.3 shows the ASCII character set and is an invaluable reference for trying to decode the contents of memory or disks by hand. (Nevertheless, most sane people would probably make use of a memory or disk-sector editor, which does the decoding automatically!)

Extended ASCII

In the early computer systems the ASCII code consisted of just 128 characters as shown at the top of figure 12.3. This is because the 8th bit was used for parity checking (see chapter 5). However, when being used inside computers, parity was not really necessary and the top bit in the byte was wasted. It was a good idea to make use of this top bit, thus releasing a further 128 characters giving a total of 256 overall. This has led to what is now known as the **Extended ASCII** character set.

ASCII data in memory

The early micros using just 8-bits for the data bus and memory organisation had a very tidy relationship with the ASCII code. Each address in memory stored just a single character. However, as the address bus grew larger, memory became organised in 16-bit and 32-bit

Basic ASCII character codes for IBM and compatibles (all codes 0 to 127 are shown)

000 Null	001 SOH	002 STX	003 ETX	004 EOT	005 ENQ	006 ACK	007 BEL	008 BS	009 HT
010 LF	011 VT	012 FF	013 CR	014 SO	015 SI	016 DLE	017 DC1	018 DC2	019 DC3
020 DC4	021 NAK	022 SYN	023 ETB	024 CAN	025 EM	026 SUB	027 ESC	028 FS	029 GS
030 RS	031 US	032 SP	033 !	034 "	035 #	036 $	037 %	038 &	039 '
040 (	041)	042 *	043 +	044 ,	045 -	046 .	047 /	048 0	049 1
050 2	051 3	052 4	053 5	054 6	055 7	056 8	057 9	058 :	059 ;
060 <	061 =	062 >	063 ?	064 @	065 A	066 B	067 C	068 D	069 E
070 F	071 G	072 H	073 I	074 J	075 K	076 L	077 M	078 N	079 O
080 P	081 Q	082 R	083 S	084 T	085 U	086 V	087 W	088 X	089 Y
090 Z	091 [	092 \	093]	094 ^	095 _	096 '	097 a	098 b	099 c
100 d	101 e	102 f	103 g	104 h	105 i	106 j	107 k	108 l	109 m
110 n	111 o	112 p	113 q	114 r	115 s	116 t	117 u	118 v	119 w
120 x	121 y	122 z	123 {	124		125 }	126 ~	127 ■		

Extended ASCII character codes for IBM and compatibles (only codes 128 to 169 are shown)

								128 Ç	129 ü
130 é	131 â	132 ä	133 à	134 å	135 ç	136 ê	137 ë	138 è	139 ï
140 î	141 ì	142 Ä	143 Å	144 É	145 æ	146 Æ	147 ô	148 ö	149 ò
150 û	151 ù	152 ÿ	153 Ô	154 Û	155 ¢	156 £	157 ¥	158 fi	159 fl
160 ó	161 í	162 ó	163 ú	164 ñ	165 Ñ	166 ª	167 º	168 ¿	169 ⌐

Figure 12.3

chunks. This means that more than a single byte can now be stored in an individual memory location, with 4 bytes being possible on a 32-bit system or 8 bytes on a 64-bit system etc. However, the memory addresses are often byte-oriented, even in multiple-byte systems, and the habit of referring to the memory in byte-sized chunks has remained to this day in most microcomputer-based machines. On large mainframes and minis the situation is often different.

Secondary storage techniques

Although speed is still a very important criterion, the main objectives when dealing with secondary storage are **data integrity** and **mass storage capability,** coupled with **low cost. Auxiliary** or **backing store** are *alternative names* for **secondary storage**. Magnetic media such as **disks** and **tapes** have ruled supreme for the last twenty years, but are now being seriously challenged by the new writable **optical** and **magneto-optical** technologies. However, we will deal with magnetic technologies first, as these will still be around for some considerable time to come.

Direct and sequential access

Secondary storage techniques can be split into two broad categories. The first relates to **direct-access** storage techniques. This refers to the ability to go to the data you wish to access *without* having to read through all previous data. The second is **sequential-**access storage techniques where all previous data has to be gone through in sequence until you get to the item of interest. The most common form of sequential-access media is obviously magnetic tape. It's important to distinguish between direct and sequential-access devices, as the characteristics of each device give rise to very different methods of data processing, as can be seen from handling the **data structures** called **files** which are covered in chapter 26. However, we will start off by looking at **direct-access data peripherals**.

Floppy disks

These are the smallest of magnetic disks and have become the norm for use on microcomputer systems when data has to be transferred from one system to another. Floppy disks used to be the norm for software distribution, but CD-ROMs are now so cheap and have such vastly superior storage capability that these are invariably used instead. Also, with the popularity of the Internet, much software is now available direct from the net, requiring no storage media whatsoever for the actual transfer of data! However, floppies are still

Did you know that . . .

The original 8in floppy disks were single sided and stored only 40 Kbytes of data! However, this was magic compared to the alternatives at the time. These were cassette-based systems and paper tape, both of which were extremely slow and error prone. The modern floppy is also under threat from the latest floptical drives and high-capacity disks in excess of 1 Gbyte.

extremely useful, especially when used in conjunction with **compression utilities** such as **WinZip**, for example (see chapter 4). Typically up to 15 or 20Mbytes of data could be stored on a 1.4 Mbyte floppy after compression, but *it really depends on the original material that is being compressed*. WinZip also allows multiple-disk spanning, which means that if you run out of disk space on the first floppy, you simply insert a second and so on. In this way it is easily possible, if a little tedious, to transfer very large files from one computer system to another – you just need a removal van to help you carry all the floppy disks!

The early floppy disks were 8in or 5¼ in devices, and stored a relatively low volume of data. The latest 3½ in disks have now gone through several stages of metamorphosis to get to the current state of 1.44 Mbytes or up to 2.88 Mbytes depending on the type of drive. However, the latest small floptical drives (see later) can now store over 1 Gbyte!

The earlier floppy disks were single sided, but today's versions are double sided, meaning that two head assemblies are needed – one for the top surface and one for the bottom surface of the disk. Nevertheless, the principles of data storage on these magnetic disks are essentially the same, with the disk surface having to be formatted into tracks and sectors (see later).

A typical 3½ in disk is shown in figure 12.4, and the write-protect tab prevents data from being accidentally overwritten by inadvertent use of the disk. Floppy disks rotate at about 300 r.p.m. and, unlike the hard disks in the next section, the read/write heads are in constant contact with the surface of the disk whenever data is being written to or read from the disk. Hence a floppy disk will only revolve in the drive during a read or write operation. The geometry of **heads**, **sectors** and **tracks** etc. is explained in the next section when hard disks are being considered, because the principles of both are very similar.

Speed of operation

When data is stored on the disk it must be in a form such that a computer can identify where the data is, and be able to retrieve it quickly. Obviously, being a mechanical system, the longest retrieval time would be governed by a single rotation of the disk such that the desired data is underneath the head. With a rotational speed of 300 r.p.m., (5 revs/sec) then 1/5th sec or about 200 msec would be the worst time needed to find the data, assuming that the head could move in and out to the appropriate part of the disk in time. The average time (called rotational latency) is obviously half this, and this is what is inevitably used to determine the final figure in the sales literature. Not forgetting that the actual disk does not rotate until requested to do so, the actual time would obviously be a combination of the following: **rotational latency**, **the seek time** (moving

the head to the data), the **settling time** (the head getting its act together) and the **read/write time** (the time taken for the data transfer to take place). This is typically just over **250 msec**. The data transfer rate is about **500 Kbits/sec** for a typical **high density 1.44 Mbyte disk**. Needless to say, *this is slow* compared to the more-expensive forms of secondary storage.

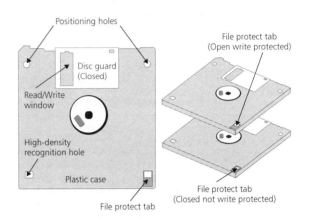

Figure 12.4

Disk formatting

If a computer is to be able to find the data stored on the magnetic surface of a floppy, then some sort of recognisable pattern to the stored data is needed. This pattern is made up of concentric circles called **tracks**, and typically a floppy would have 40 tracks on each side. Each track is further divided up into a number of smaller parts called sectors, and setting up these vital patterns for mapping the data onto a floppy is called **formatting**. This is explained in more detail when large-disk systems are being considered later.

High density & extra high density disks

Most floppy disks have a total of 80 tracks, with a density of about 96 tracks per linear inch of the surface (going from the outside to the middle). The amount of data, which can be stored on a typical disk, has increased over the years. For example, if you double the rate at which the data is written to the disk for a given disk speed, then you have doubled the amount of data that can be stored on that disk. However, the area on the surface of the disk, which represents a binary digit, has halved, and therefore the surface of the disk needs to be of a higher quality. There are different density disks available. You may still hear of the '**double density**' (**360 Kbyte**) and '**quad density**' (**720 Kbyte**) formats, but the most common is the '**high density**' (**1.44 Mbyte**) format. The '**extra high density**' or '**super high density**' disks (**2.88 Mbyte**) format is

Floppy Discs

Cost	Data transfer rate and data access times	Other considerations
High-density disk drives are now available for less than £20. Good quality high density and extra-high density floppy disks are about 20p each.	About 500 Kbits/sec. Seek time is just over 250 msec.	This media is rapidly becoming inadequate for general-purpose storage because of its limited size. It will be around for sometime yet, however, because you can still transfer things easily, and compression techniques like WinZip are extending its life for a little longer.
Iomega Zip – Parallel, IDE and SCSI versions are available ranging from about £100 to £150. Discs are about £5 each at the time or writing.	Read write speeds limited by type of interface (e.g. parallel much slower than SCSI). Access time of about 25 msec, media can be read at about 1.4 Mbyte/sec maximum, irrespective of interface.	Capacity of 100 Mbytes for the Zip and 1 Gbyte for the Jaz. Not compatible with ordinary floppy drives – the actual size of the disk is different. Don't forget that the drive takes about 3 seconds to get up to speed if it is not rotating when you request a read or a write.
Laser Servo LS-120 disks cost about £6.50 at the time of writing.	Average data transfer rate is 655 Kbits/sec.	Totally compatible with the current 1.44 Mbyte floppy described at the beginning of this table.

available too, but other much higher capacity disks are being developed using new technologies.

Zip drives

During 1996 a company called Iomega introduced the **100 Mbyte Zip drive**. This is a low cost system, which is remarkably cheap and popular in the late 1990s. These disks, being mechanically more robust rotate at **2968 revs/min**, or about 49.5 rev/sec, but take 3 sec to get up to speed because, unlike hard disk drives, they don't rotate all the time that the drive is switched on. Average access time is about **26 msec**. The maximum rate at which the data can be read from a Zip drive is **1.4 Mbyte/sec**, although in practice, expect less than this. There are a variety of interfaces which drastically affect the performance (and price) too. These disks are available connected to the **parallel (printer port)**, the **IDE bus** and the fastest of all is the **SCSI bus**. The parallel port method is a particularly cheap option.

Laser Servo drives

The Laser Servo LS-120 disk drives from NEC, for example, are able to store 120 Mbytes, but, more usefully, *are totally compatible with the existing 1.44 Mbyte floppy format*. The speed of reading from these disks is faster than normal floppies. The rotational speed is **720 rev/min** or 12 rev/sec, giving a worst case seek time of 83 msec. Therefore the average seek time is just over **40 msec**, being over twice as fast as a normal floppy. Unlike normal floppies, these 120 Mbyte disks have a different number of sectors/track (see later).

SyQuest and DynaMo drives

Other manufacturers have been offering similar drives for a number of years. The formats have changed somewhat, being reflected in physically smaller drives holding more and more information. Don't forget that most of these drives are incompatible with one another, and as technology changes, the drives which used to be in fashion change to something else within the space of a few years.

Hard drive technology

Hard-disk drives have revolutionised the microcomputer industry since they first appeared in the early 1980s, but the modern disks bear only a faint resemblance to the original Winchester designs. The magnetic surface of the disk is no longer floppy (as was the case with floppy disks), but is now contained on a rigid disk, or more likely a stack of rigid disks called **platters** as shown in figure 12.5.

Did you know that . . .

In 1982 a 10 Mbyte hard disk drive cost about £1,500 – giving a cost of **£150 per Mbyte** at 1982 prices! In 1999 a 4 Gbyte disk cost about £100 – giving a storage cost of 1p per Mbyte! And this is by no means the end of the story .

The mechanics of **hard disks** are much more precise than the mechanics inside the humble floppy – hence the extra expense. The surface of the disk drive is housed in a hermetically sealed unit (which keeps out all the dust, grit, tomato sauce, biscuit crumbs and

Figure 12.5 (a) and (b)

smoke particles etc.). This enables the tracks to be much closer together, and the oxide coating is replaced with a more reliable thin-film magnetic media, thus a higher recording density can be used.

The disk rotates continually (even when data is not being written to or read from the disk), and the read/write heads float on the surface of the disk due to the **Bernoulli effect**. This is not an illness, but the lift caused by the aerodynamic effect of the rotational speed and the very close proximity of the head to the surface of the disk – typically just 5 millionths of an inch for a modern SCSI II specification! A parking area is usually provided for the heads when no read/write activity is taking place. The rotational speed of the early hard disks was typically 10 times that of a floppy, and was thus about 3000 r.p.m., but the latest disks rotate at 5,400 or even 7,200 r.p.m., thus improving performance considerably.

The early small hard disks had very modest capacities of about 5 Mbytes, but today's hard disks have several Gbytes capacity, even on the most basic of microcomputer systems. Depending on the type (IDE or SCSI etc.) the larger hard disks for microcomputers now exceed 26 Gbytes, and you can have quite a number of these drives attached to the system, especially for file servers in LAN environments. You must, however, not forget the importance that the **operating system** and other factors such as the **BIOS** play in determining the largest size disk that you can address. For example, the **16-bit FAT** (see chapter 22) system used on **DOS** and the *first version* of **Windows95** limits the maximum size of disk to **2 Gbyte**. Therefore, putting a 10 Gbyte drive in this system without partitioning (see later) would prove to be a fruitless exercise. Later versions of Windows95 (OSR2 and beyond) and WindowsNT do not impose this limit. The 32-bit FAT system allows up to a maximum of just over 2 Tbytes. IBM estimates that by the end of the year 2000, 100 Gbyte disks will be available for microcomputers – roll on – I can't wait!

The physical size of these hard drives has been reduced considerably from 14 in in their original form, to the current generation of 5.25 in, 3.5 in, 2.5 in and 1.75 in diameter discs. Many of these disks can be fitted into portables, depending on their height. If a modern disk is thicker than its counterparts, it usually has more platters. At the time of writing, IBM have some 1 in drives in their labs at the Almaden Research centre, and in 1998 have currently achieved an astonishing storage density of 11.6 Gbits on one square inch of disk surface. This means that 1,450 average novels could fit onto a single inch of the surface of a disk!

Access speeds for the current generation of hard disks are a little less than **10 msec**, and **data-transfer rates** depend on the type of system being used. For example, the **original SCSI** specification is **5 Mbyte/sec**, but **SCSI II** can transfer **20 Mbyte/sec** and **Ultra Fast SCSI III** goes at **40 Mbyte/sec**.

Did you know that . . .

The increase in the speed of operation and memory capacity of the hard drive has been impressive. In the early 1980s, a typical hard drive for a microcomputer would have had a capacity of about 10 Mbytes. The data transfer rate would have been in the order of about 10 Kbytes/sec. Today, on a micro which you have at home, the ultra fast SCSI III specification can transfer 40 Mbyte/sec. and has a capacity in excess of 26 Gbytes. The latest drives cost very much less than the original 10 Mbyte drives!

How is the data arranged on the disk?

A modern disk, as shown in figure 12.6, would have **several thousand tracks** (measured from inside to out) placed on the **recordable surface** (called a **platter**), but only the inner and outermost tracks have been shown

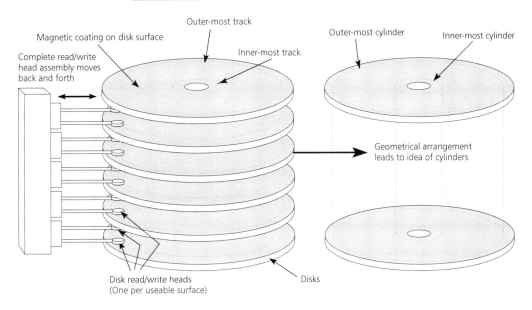

Disk-pack arrangement showing how a cylinder is generated

Complete read/write head assembly moves back and forth

Magnetic coating on disk surface

Outer-most track

Inner-most track

Outer-most cylinder

Inner-most cylinder

Geometrical arrangement leads to idea of cylinders

Disk read/write heads (One per useable surface)

Disks

Figure 12.6

in the diagram for the purposes of clarity. The diagram shows a typical disk assembly in which 6 **platters** (disks), for example, are used to create 12 surfaces onto which data could be recorded, although only ten heads are used in figure 12.6.

It's most important to note that *the entire head assembly moves in and out, thus causing all the heads to move in and out at the same time.* This naturally leads to a fundamental data storage idea associated with disks which is called a **cylinder**. For the case of the **six pack** (nothing to do with beer, unfortunately!) shown in figure 12.6, there would be **about 2000 cylinders**, where *each cylinder* consists of **10 tracks**, because there are ten heads. Figure 12.7 shows a single useable surface of a disk as viewed from the top. The tracks shown contain a number of sectors, depending on the hard disk geometry and construction, and the number of sectors per track might be 120 on a typical SCSI drive. The **sectors** making up each track are separated by small gaps as shown in the right-hand side of the diagram.

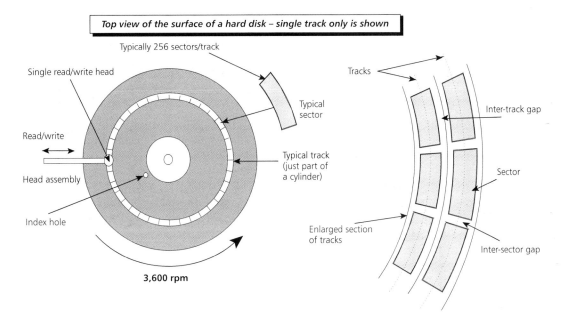

Top view of the surface of a hard disk – single track only is shown

Typically 256 sectors/track

Single read/write head

Read/write

Head assembly

Index hole

Typical sector

Typical track (just part of a cylinder)

Tracks

Inter-track gap

Sector

Enlarged section of tracks

Inter-sector gap

3,600 rpm

Figure 12.7

The number of tracks, sectors and bytes per sector can now easily be mapped to storage capability. Let's take a very simple floppy disk example first. On a humble 360 Kbyte double-density floppy, we would have **2 sides** of the disk (top and bottom), giving a crude **cylinder** with **40 tracks** per side. Finally, the **9 sectors** per track, typical for this disk, would give us:

2 (sides) × 40 tracks × 9 sectors/track × 512 bytes/sector = 368,640 bytes

Now 368,640/1024 = 360, thus we have our **360 Kbyte disk**.

Astute readers will look at the above simple calculations, and then attempt to predict what number of tracks and sectors etc. would be needed for a drive with several Gbytes. In fact, the technology required to get these orders of magnitude in such a small space is literally miraculous. For example, the Segate ST32430NC **Fast SCSI II** hard drive has **3,892 cylinders**, **116 sectors/track**, and **9 heads** which gives us: 3892 cylinders × 9 heads × 116 sectors/track × 512 bytes/sector = 2,080,382,976 bytes which is about **2 Gbytes**. The seek time on this particular drive is about 10msec and the data transfer rate is about 10 Mbyte/sec. Faster Ultra-Wide SCSII specifications would allow data to be transferred from similar disks at about 20 Mbytes/sec, and SCSI III gives about 40 Mbytes/sec.

Alternative arrangements of tracks

The **concentric-circular-track** arrangement as outlined above is the *most* obvious, but a **single spiral track system** is an alternative method that's used in **optical drives** (see later). The concentric-track arrangement is used on *all* **hard** and **floppy-disk formats**, and so any data that is stored on the disk can be directly accessed by knowing the address of the track (track number) and the address of the sector (sub-division of a track as shown in figure 12.7). If the arrangement has multiple surfaces, then a cylinder number, surface number and sector number arrangement is used instead – as track-number alone would *not* be enough to uniquely identify any specific data on a multi-platter system.

As most magnetic disks are **constant speed drives**, astute readers would have noticed that the track length on the outside of a disk is considerably longer then the track length on the inside of the disk, but there are the same number of sectors in a track. As with floppies, the packing density of the data is therefore varied so that the innermost tracks have the bytes packed much more densely than the outer tracks. This is indeed wasteful of space on the outer edges, but it makes the system considerably simpler to operate because each sector, regardless of its position on the disk, is always under the head for the same length of time. Hence the data transfer rate is constant regardless of the sector's position. As the disk rotates with constant speed the

data transfer rates at the outer edges would be much greater if this variable-packing-density system were not used. Indeed, on CD-ROMS, the data packing density *is* the same and the rotational speed of the CD is varied to compensate.

To get more packing density, some modern disk systems do make use of a **variable speed drive** in which the number of sectors on the larger outer tracks are more than the number of sectors on the smaller inner tracks. The number of bytes per sector is still the same, but the speed of the drive is slowed when reading the outer tracks so as to present a constant linear velocity to the head as it is passed over each sector regardless of where the sector is on the disk.

While the disk is whizzing round it's obvious that some form of **identification** is needed to instruct the computer where the **beginning of a track** or **cylinder** is – we need to know where sector zero begins on each track, for example. Sometimes, an index hole, as shown in figure 12.7 is used, together with an electronic optical-detection system, which shines a light through the hole. This physical marking of the boundary in this way is called a **hard sector**. In other systems, the operations are carried out by the software which electronically puts an ID onto the surface of the disk – if this later method is used it is called **soft sectoring**. These ID numbers are put onto the disk by the program, which carries out the **formatting** (see next paragraph).

The *process* of setting up the disk such that the **tracks**, **sectors** and **IDs** etc. are ready to be used is called **formatting**. It is also the job of the formatting program to map out any damaged areas of the disk's surface that may be found during this setting up process. After being formatted the disk will contain its **cylinder** (if appropriate) or **track** numbers, **sector** numbers and **control data** (see in a moment) which helps the system to be able to **read** and **write** files on the disk.

Extra control data is usually recorded onto the surface of the disk which is used only by the disk-drive-interface controller, and refers to the ways in which the formatting of the tracks and sectors etc. is mapped onto the system. For example, the number of 'sectors per track' and the number of 'bytes per sector' etc. This information, together with the track and sector numbers mentioned above, enables the operating-system software to be able to locate data items on the disk randomly – being able to do this opens up many extra possibilities for file handling over and above those available for serially-based systems (see chapter 26).

The *minimum amount of data* that can be **read from** or **written to** a **disk** at any one time is a **sector**. Even if just a single byte of data were to be altered, the complete sector containing that data would need to be rewritten. This is because there are CRCs (see chapter 5) made on the data to ensure its integrity. Sometimes small amounts of information, such as **logical records** (see chapter 27) which have a number of bytes much smaller than the physical-sector size being used on the disk, need to be stored. In this case, **blocking** (in ways identical to that of tape) helps to make sure that less physical space is wasted on the disk.

Larger chunks of data, much larger for example than a single sector on disk, need to be 'glued' together to form a larger unit which is called a **cluster** (see next section). Therefore, to store a file of data as a cluster, we would have to know about which tracks and sectors etc. are allocated to the files. A map of this information can be stored on the disk along with all the other data, and this is usually referred to as a File Allocation Table or FAT in the MSDOS system, for example. To cut a long story short, the ideas are very similar to the **linked-list data structures** covered in chapter 14. The file allocation table helps us to form the hierarchical directory structure shown in figure 27.2. The FAT is covered in more detail in the operating-system chapter 22. Newer systems such as **NTFS** (New Technology File System) are much more powerful that the FAT system, and able to cope with very much larger disk drives.

Clusters

A cluster is simply the minimum amount of space allocated by the operating system when it stores a file. For example, on a 3.5 in 1.44 Mbyte formatted floppy, there would be two disk sectors per cluster. Therefore, we have a minimum space of 2×512 or 1024 bytes taken up by the file whether it needs it or not! If you are unfortunate enough to need to store just one byte of data on this floppy, for example, then 1023 bytes of your precious floppy disk space are completely wasted, ignoring any overheads such as CRCs etc.

The above arguments are true for hard disks too, where typically 32 sectors/cluster are used on drives having sizes from 512 Mbyte to 1 Gbyte, 64 sectors/cluster on drive sizes from 1 Gbyte to 2 Gbytes, and 128 sectors/cluster on 2 Gbyte to 4 Gbyte drives, for example. This is why it's often a good idea to partition larger drives so that they appear to the computer as a number of smaller drives. Can you imagine 1 byte being stored on a large disk using 128 sectors/cluster – 65,535 bytes of storage space would remain unused.

Partitioning

This helps to match the size of the drive with the capabilities of the operating system. For example, you could run a low-level formatting program (like FDISK) so that the computer can recognise the disk. Also, as mentioned in the last section, you can optimise your drive so that less space is wasted on the larger drives.

Programs like 'Partition Magic', for example, allow you to partition your drive while you still have data on it. It's enlightening to run the software, partition your drive, and then see that you have a couple of hundred Megabytes of reclaimed space due to the more efficient cluster sizes which have been used. You can also partition disks in systems like WindowsNT, such that different physical disks can be joined together to form one larger logical drive. This is particularly useful on large file servers where hundreds of people may have their work on the system.

Disk caching

Providing some **dedicated RAM** for **disk caching** can significantly improve the apparent disk performance. With the clever allocation of some of the disk image in RAM, read or write operations regarding the disk could actually be undertaken at RAM read/write access speeds, if the required data happened to be in the disk cache RAM at the time! However, don't forget that any on-board disk cache will still be limited by the speed at which your host adapter (i.e. the hardware and software which interfaces the disk to the machine) can be driven. Therefore, the disk read/write times are, in practice, considerably less than would be obtained from primary storage, but considerably in excess of that which would be obtained from the same disk without the use of a cache system.

How does the disk know which parts to load into the cache? The simple answer is that is doesn't! At the beginning, all data read from the disk would be put into the cache, but this would soon fill up, then the system has a dilemma – what to remove and what to keep. There are two basic disk cache systems called LRU (**Least Recently Used**) and LFU (**Least Frequently Used**) which, as their names imply, get rid of things which have not been used recently or very often – which is the best system is a subject of philosophical debate.

Disk array systems and RAID

Hard disks will eventually crash. Therefore, even if you are careful, you will lose Gbytes of precious data on your hard disk sooner or later – hopefully later! Good backup procedures will usually mean that you have not actually lost your data, but there is an inconvenient period during which you have to replace the duff hard disk with a new one, and replace the data, perhaps via a network link or a tape streamer. It would be nice if the system could be made to carry on regardless (well almost) during a hard-disk crash, and often a second drive with a mirror-image of the original can be switched over immediately in the event of such an unfortunate occurrence. Such a system is

> **Hint:** From an administrator's point of view, the ability to be able to swap disks or to change drives without having to switch the computer off is a great advantage. If you are in charge of a large network, there is very little time indeed when users are not making use of the file servers.

known as a **drive array**, and the acronym **RAID** has been coined which stands for **Redundant Array of Inexpensive Drives**! This is because, when used in this particular configuration, there is no advantage to having the second drive (i.e. it's effectively redundant) until a catastrophe occurs. RAID systems are usually accompanied by software which give you the option of using them automatically in the event of a drive failure as described above, or using the two (or more) drives as a file-server configuration on a network. RAID systems for network file-server and drive-failure fail-safe applications typically have total storage capacity in excess of 100 Gbytes. No doubt we will see Tbyte systems in the very near future. On some of the latest file servers its possible to **hot link** (or **hot plug**) these hard drives. This means that you can physically plug and unplug new high-capacity hard drives without switching the computer on and off.

Terabyte disk farms

On mainframe computers and in organisations where large storage requirements are standard, the trend is to put a large number of large-capacity discs into a large cabinet and call it a **disk farm**. This mass of on-line storage can most easily be thought about if you consider it as a large array of discs, similar to that shown in the cabinet of figure 12.8

Figure 12.8

Here you can see Fujitsu's F6497KC array disk system with each capable of storing about 715 Gbytes. This particular technology delivers a system called RAID5, which is amazing, when it comes to disaster recovery – the system can keep going even in a disaster such as a hard disk crash. This is the sort of reliability that companies like a major airline need 24 hours a day, 7 days a week, 52 weeks of the year, and this system certainly delivers it. These systems are now used in preference to the older large disk systems on mainframe computers, which used to resemble a top-loading washing machine. Indeed, they were actually nicknamed the washing machine because of the noise which they made when rotating!

Compressed drives

A technique used to pack even more data onto a drive is compression. For example, compressing the C drive on my computer at home would give a considerable space saving and the uncompressed settings are shown in figure 12.9. Whether this is a good or bad idea really depends on how reliable you want the system to be, and how long you wish to wait to retrieve the data from the disk. Obviously compression is superb for storing more data, but it does take longer to carry out disk-based operations. Nevertheless, these techniques are becoming more reliable with later and better operating system versions. Much faster computers and drives also overcome these disadvantages, and therefore compression will almost certainly become the norm.

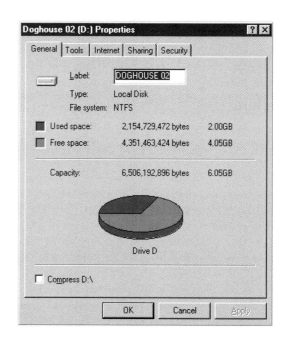

Figure 12.9

Disk cartridges

Sometimes you will get just a *single* **disk platter** inside a suitable container that fits into the disk machine. Obviously the top and bottom surfaces *are* the only ones available and are therefore used for recording data in this case. These particular disks are called **disk cartridges**, and are available on both large and small systems.

The drive technologies

There are a few disk drive technologies in current operation. The **IDE or Integrated Drive Electronics** and **EIDE** (**Enhanced IDE**) is usually at the cheaper and smaller end of the disk-drive market. The much faster and more expensive **SCSI** (**Small Computer Systems Interface**) comes in several incarnations, **SCSI**, **SCSI II**, and **SCSI**

III with an **Ultra SCSI** high-speed mode. Good though this might sound we are rapidly approaching a time when computer systems are outgrowing even the fast Ultra SCSI 40 Mbytes/sec transfer rates! Another example is the Iomega **Jaz drive,** which effectively gives you a **1 Gbyte removable disk** similar to the disk cartridges above, but which looks more like a floppy.

Other, more recent technologies, such as Firewire (100 Mbit/sec and faster) and FC-AL (Fibre Channel – Arbitrated Loop) are now being incorporated on some motherboards in 1998. There is also the USB (Universal Serial Bus) and SSA (Serial Storage Architecture). We will have to wait until the early 2000s to see which, if any, of the above systems outdo SCSI. For example, if you hook up four Ultra Wide SCSI III adapters to a typical file server, then you would have a typical data transfer rate of 160 Mbytes/sec on a system which is still compatible with the existing hardware.

Optical drives

Drastic price reductions in the last few years have made CD-ROM drives common. With many tens of thousands of CD-ROM titles available during the late 1990s, (there is even a CD-ROM of CD-ROMs!) the CD-ROM drives and magneto-optical drives (see later) look set to dominate the computer industry for some considerable time. It's not hard to see why – low cost, superior quality, robustness and greater storage capacity, plus the ability to store conventional audio and video images as well,

all conspire to make these secondary-storage devices the serious multimedia (audio + video + computer data) contenders for the foreseeable future.

Although the mechanism for reading data from a CD-ROM drive is very different from reading data from a magnetic disk, the track is still split up into sectors. The word track here is correct because, unlike conventional magnetic disk drives, a *single track* **spirals** from the outside of the CD to the inside. The *speed* of the CD-ROM drive is *varied* to compensate for the different rates at which the head would be moving past each sector, and thus each sector can have the same packing density. This should be compared with the methods used for most conventional magnetic disks, where the speed of the drive is kept constant but the packing density varies (see earlier).

A conventional CD has the equivalent of about 600 tracks per linear inch of disk surface (from the outside to the middle – don't forget that it's actually a single track!), and at current recording densities this single spiral track can store about 650 Mbytes, which is equivalent to several hundred thousand pages of textual information. A typical CD-ROM disk is about 12 cm in diameter and made out of a polycarbonate material onto which a fine coating of aluminium has been deposited. A **LASER** beam (**Light Amplification by the Stimulated Emission of Radiation**), is used to detect the presence or absence of pits, which have been burned into this surface at the writing stage by a more-powerful LASER used by the manufacturer. However, you can record your own CDs too,

Hard disk drives

Cost	Data processing speeds	Other considerations
A typical 8 Gbyte IDE drive costs about £120 at the time of writing	Varies depending on other factors.	Not many IDE drives are available any more.
EIDE drives are relatively cheap and compares to IDE pricing.	Typically 13 Mbytes/sec maximum with the right controllers.	EIDE drives currently have a maximum of about 8 Gbytes. Electronic controls are integrated into the drive.
Iomega Jaz – drives cost about £200, disks cost about £40.	SCSI interface, transfer rate of about 6.6 Mbyte/sec.	You have, in effect, an infinite amount of storage if you buy enough disks and don't mind changing the drives like a floppy.
SCSI and its derivatives allow much larger drives >30 Gbyte is currently typical of a large drive for a micro.	SCSI – 5 Mbyte/sec – SCSI II – 10 Mbytes/sec – SCSI III 20 Mbytes/sec Ultra Wide SCSI – 40 Mbytes/sec.	Highest current performance – threatened by other technologies within the next few years. Need a SCSI interface if you have not got one already.
Terabyte Disk Farms	Up to (and beyond) the Tbyte limit. Some systems are now available with several Tbytes of store	Suitable for mainframe, supercomputer and large database environments such as those required for the military or large airline-booking systems.
Firewire and FC-AL etc.	Not actual drives yet, but rather the interfaces on which new drives could be based.	The need to break the current Ultra-SCSI limit of 40 Mbytes/sec is being pushed by some of these technologies.

as shown in the next section. **Mini-format** (8 cm) **CDs** have been developed too, and these are currently being put into some portable computers.

Data transfer rates depend on the speed of rotation of the disk. The original transfer rate for a single-speed drive (i.e. going at the same speed as the audio CDs in your hi-fi), would be 150 Kbytes/sec. Therefore, the latest multiple-speed CD-ROMs are simply multiples of this figure. Typically an **8x CD-ROM** drive would deliver **1.2 Mbytes/sec**, or a **48x CD-ROM** would deliver **7.2 Mbytes/sec**. However, much current software is not written to exploit these faster drives. Note that even the faster speed CD-ROMs are pedestrian compared to the faster SCSI disk drives, for example, shown a little earlier.

Reading data from a CD-ROM

To read data from the surface of a disk requires revolving the disk and reflecting a LASER beam off of the surface as shown in figure 12.10. Figure 12.10 is obviously a simplified diagram as any physicist carefully checking the optical paths taken by the LASER beam will be able to tell! However, it does illustrate, in principle, exactly what's going on. LASER light, produced by a LASER diode is reflected off the reflective material on the underside of the CD-ROM disk. When the *original* CD master was being recorded (i.e. *not* the system shown in figure 12.8) a LASER beam is switched on and off very rapidly by the electronics which is acting as a modulator. If the LASER beam is on – it burns away the surface and what's called a pit is produced (as viewed from the top), or if the LASER is switched off – then no pit is produced, and this is called land! Therefore, the surface of the disk is made up of a single spiral track of **land**s and **pit**s which represent the binary digits being recorded, a protective layer is then used to coat the disk.

A lower-power LASER in the CD-ROM machine on your computer at home then shines LASER light at the land and pits *from the underside of the disk* as the track on the disk is being moved over the detector. If **land is encountered**, then the system causes the beam to be focused onto a light detector, which in turn can produce a suitable electrical signal. If, however, a pit is encountered by the same beam at some later stage (as shown on the *right* in figure 12.10), then the geometry and polarisation characteristics of the materials and reflectors being used cause the beam to scatter, instead of being focused as before. Therefore, **in the case of a pit**, *the detector picks up no reflected light*, and hence no electrical signal is produced. In this way the lands and pits represented by the constantly changing patterns on the underside of the CD are turned into binary digits.

Some students at this stage may well be attempting to guess whether a land or a pit represents a binary one or a zero – in fact it's neither! Even worse – it's the length of the pits, which are important, and a **binary**

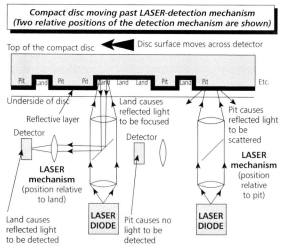

Figure 12.10

one is actually represented by a *transition* **from a land to a pit** OR the *transition* **from a pit to a land**. (That's not a typing error!) The actual coding methods employed are quite complex (this is an understatement!) due to the error checking routines that are built in to increase reliability, but needless to say groups of binary digits can be extracted from the system once the data has been decoded.

A typical CD can store about 650 Mbytes of information, but due to the complex encoding methods mentioned earlier, not all of this space is available for user data. Although this sounds like a lot of data-storage capacity – it's relatively small when you consider the vast number of moving coloured images of the sort needed to display a 2 or 3 hour video movie, for example. IBM are currently developing a system using a much more expensive **blue laser light** compared to conventional cheap **red laser light** as is used at the moment. The wavelength of blue laser light is about half of that for red, and thus an area about one quarter of that needed for the red laser light is actually used. This means that four times the quantity of data can be stored on a blue-laser CD-ROM drive. In fact IBM have actually increased this to five times normal making use of some additional techniques. This means that a massive 3 Gbytes of data may be stored on later generations of CD-ROM drives making use of blue laser light. Even so, the **HDCD** (**High Density Compact Disk**) is also under development, and this, *using conventional red laser* with better mechanisms, has produced a much higher storage density of 3.7 Gbytes, and conforms to the Gold book standard (see next section). HDCD and blue lasers may be able to push this limit much further to well over 20 Gbytes.

CD-Recordable (CD-R) and CD-E

These devices are, at last, affordable for use by some ordinary people. Indeed, the prices have now come

Hint: There are so many CD-ROM standards that you have to be very careful when recording your own. At our school we store disk-image backups on CD-ROM. However, what works perfectly in one system might not work well with another. We had to experiment for some considerable time to get it working perfectly.

down so much that it is a very cost effective storage medium, especially as an archive or for data that will not change at all. However, one disadvantage of this system is that the data to be written to the CD must be done so in one chunk without any interruptions! Each session (i.e. chunk of data) that you wish to add to the CD will require overheads of about 13Mbytes. You therefore need to think carefully when using this particular medium as it should obviously not be used in the same way as a conventional disk. Typical access time for this medium is about 20 msec, and data transfer rates obviously depend on the speed, and whether you are reading from or writing to the CD-Recordable disk. Typical systems might allow you to write to the disk at quad speed but read from the disk at 24x speed, for example.

The maximum amount of data that can be recorded onto CD-R depends on which of the five current modes of operation you are using. The block sizes, (usually measured in minutes to reflect the fact that CDs were originally used for audio recording), are 18 min, 21 min, 63 min and 74 min. For the largest block sizes you would get between 600 Mbytes and 700 Mbytes of information onto the CD-R disk.

There is yet another system called CD-E or Compact Disc Erasable. This system enables you to write many times to a CD (see Plate 33), but it can't be read back on a conventional CD-Player. However, it can be read back on a different machine of the same type as that which did the recording.

Multiple CD standards

How do you decide between **CD**, **CD-DA**, **Photo CD**, **CD-I**, **CD-R** or **CD-ROM-XA** etc? – all are variations on how data can be stored and/or used on a compact disc! A brief explanation of each now follows, but no doubt other standards will appear in the future. Originally, Philips, Sony and Microsoft all agreed on what's called the **High-Sierra** standard for CDs, and this was further split up into a number of **coloured books** all dealing with different standards. Some examples now follow.

CD or CD-DA

This is an easy one – the original **CD** (**Compact Disc**) is a 4¾-inch disk developed by Philips during the early 1980s. Although designed originally for audio, other information such as text is stored on this type of disk. (If it were not you would not be able to get a clever CD player to display the title of your favourite album!)

You will also see the term **CD-DA** that refers to **Compact Disc Digital Audio**, an alternative name to distinguish the conventional audio-based CDs from the variety of CDs such as those listed below. CD-DAs can store just over 72 minutes of audio sound track for hi-fi reproduction. This standard is known as the **Red book** of the High Sierra standard.

CD-ROM

CD-ROM is the technology developed specifically for use by computers. A special standard defined by the International Standards Organisation called ISO 9660 shows how data is to be stored on this type of disk, and is a standard, which has been generally accepted by many different manufacturers. This is the basic format used by the majority of CDs, which distribute information in forms such as encyclopaedias and databases etc. The current standard for CD-ROMs is known as the **Yellow book**.

CDI

CD-I stands for **Compact Disc Interactive**. It is designed to enable text, audio and video to be processed and displayed on a normal TV screen. It has it's own embedded-microprocessor system inside the CD-I box, which includes a special operating system. The current standard for CD-I is known as the **Green book**.

Photo CD

Photo CD is yet another system, developed by Kodak, which supports the transfer of photos or slides etc. onto CD. This is a stunning way to view your photographs if you have a high-res monitor, and also allows you to transfer the images to disk, and hence to process them in any way that you wish. Indeed, this is one way of storing personalised photos for inclusion in DTP systems. Some systems, which read conventional CD-ROMs, are Photo-CD compatible.

CD-ROM-XA

The **CD-ROM-XA** has been designed to take advantage of the **Memory eXtended Architecture** of the **PC**. It enables text, audio and video to be used simultaneously. This is an *extension* of the **Yellow-book** standard.

CD-R

This stands for **Compact Disc Recorder**, and enables the user to **Record on CD-ROM**. This allows the user to master a CD-ROM or create backups for large amounts of data. The formats of recording vary, and can use many of the techniques listed above.

MPC

Special **Multimedia CDs** – called **MPCs** (**Multimedia Personal Computer**) are now available, this is not referring to a CD standard as such, but to the type of computer needed to run the system. These run on **PCs** which have been upgraded to multimedia standard.

CD-ROM stacks

It is becoming more popular to use CD-ROMs like 'Encarta' or 'Britannica', for example, over a network. There are so many CD-ROMs now available that it is convenient to leave many CDs in a large stack controlled by its own file server (see Plate 34). Systems are now available which can serve and control access to hundreds of CD-ROMs simultaneously, and even modest systems to be found in many schools have access to about a dozen CD-ROMs from a suitably equipped file server.

DVD

Digital Versatile Disk (or **Digital Video Disk**) is a recent innovation, originally intended for the recording of video data from the latest generation of video cameras. However, the recording devices for these DVDs are a little too expensive for all but the most well heeled computer or video enthusiasts. During the late 1990s these systems were being launched, and movies and games are becoming available. However, even if you have a digital video camera, digital TV and a DVD player, a set up that would cost you the best part of £4,000 you would still need a lot more money than this to actually record the data onto the DVD disk.

At the time of writing a double sided DVD can store a maximum of about 17 Gbytes of data – compare this to the current 660 Mbyte CD-ROM, and you can see why people are getting a little excited. In the future, when the price inevitably comes down, it may be that the DVD will replace the conventional CD-ROM. This is especially so as a DVD player can read conventional CD-ROMs too!

Recording your own data will have to wait just a little longer, and users requiring to record masses of video-type data would do well to consider the CD-R format described above, where machines which can do the recording can be obtained for a few hundred pounds.

CD-ROM drives

Cost	Data transfer rates and storage	Other considerations
Original CD-ROM now superseded by higher speed drives. 32× drives are about £50.	150 Kbytes/sec for a single speed drive. Multiples of this thereafter. Storage about 650 Mbytes.	Very few single or double speed drives exist any more. 6× or 8× was a base entry model in late 1998. 1999 saw the 32× and 48×.
Higher speed drives are not much more expensive, it really depends on whether they are SCSI or IDE.	24× speed would give 3.6 Mbytes/sec. Storage 650 Mbytes.	Don't forget that not all software will allow you to exploit the speed of the fastest CD-ROMs.
CD-Recordable – typical drive cost a few hundred pounds, typical CDs cost about 70p for 650 Mbyte versions.	Typically 4× write and faster (i.e. 10×) reads. Storage 650 Mbytes.	Large overheads (about 13 Mbytes) are used for each write session, and the whole lot has to be done without interruption. However, very cheap storage medium costing only 0.5p per Mbyte.
CD-E (Erasable) – discs are more expensive than the write-once types described above. Typically £10.	These may be written to many times. They are, therefore, useful for development purposes.	These discs can't be read by a conventional CD-ROM drive. Therefore, they can't be shared so easily.
CD stack systems – costs vary with number of CDs, but a typical purpose-built CD server with about 15 CDs would be about £800.	Transfer rate depends on speed, storage in multiples of 650 Mbytes. Typically 13 Tbytes for a 20 CD-ROM stack.	If you simply want to add CDs to an existing file server, it's cheaper to build your own system! Many people trying to access the same CD over a network can be a little slow, so you need high-speed CD-ROM drives to make it tolerable!
DVDs	Transfer rate – 4.7 Mbyte/sec. Storage between 4.7 Gbytes and 17 Gbytes depending on standard.	Very expensive for recording at the time of writing, but material like videos and games are becoming available. May well replace conventional CD-ROM eventually.

Magneto Optical (MO) disks

As the unlucky ones amongst you who have placed your disks on top of hi-fi speakers will know only too well – the data on ordinary floppies and removable hard disks can be destroyed by external magnetic fields at room temperature. However, special alloys may be used in which the crystals contained inside the alloy can be altered by a magnetic field *only if* they are heated up to a suitable temperature. In this case you have a system which is far less susceptible to external magnetic fields.

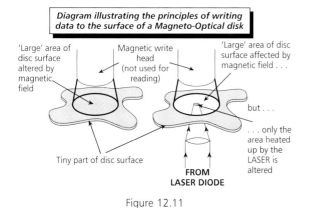

Figure 12.11

Now if a LASER beam is used to produce the required heating effect then a very small area, represented by the tiny dot of LASER light on the disk surface, can be altered by a conventional magnetic head as shown in figure 12.11. This area is far smaller than the area, which would have been affected by the same magnetic head on a conventionally based ferrite magnetic disk surface. As the area affected is much smaller, a greater packing density can be achieved if this method of altering the crystals is used. Indeed, several hundred Megabytes can be fitted onto a conventional-sized 3½ inch disk, compared to just a few Megabytes using the ferrite-based technologies described in the last few sections.

The crystals on the surface of this type of disk would normally be distributed at random. However, when a LASER beam heats up a local part of the disk past the critical temperature (known as the Curie point), then the crystals can be lined up easily if they are placed in a suitable field produced by a conventional magnetic head. When the local area of the disk is cooled then the crystals in the altered area remain in alignment, and can thus be used to represent a bit of information. Different alignment directions are used to represent a binary 1 or 0.

To read back the data from this disk a LASER beam of less intensity (otherwise the data will be destroyed!) is reflected from the surface of the disk . Where no data is stored, the light will be reflected at random because the crystals in the special alloy are randomly distributed. Where a LASER beam and magnetic head has previously altered the surface of the disk, a special light-detecting sensor can pick up the light, which is reflected from the aligned crystals. Polarisation is used to determine the difference between a binary 1 and 0.

These devices are called **Magneto-Optical drives** or **MO drives,** because **optical** (LASER beams and light sensor) and **magnetic** (the magnetic write head) methods have been used to produce the data patterns on the surface of the disk. Purely optical methods (a LASER beam reflected from the disk and picked up by a light sensor) are used to read the data.

The speed of writing and reading data on a typical Magneto-Optical drive at the time of writing is not quite up to the speed of the faster magnetic drives. However, it is comparable to magnetic drives being in the order of about 50 msec. Due to the more complex cycle of reading and writing, the data transfer rate is considerably slower than the fastest magnetic drives, especially on the write part of the cycle. The storage capacity is comparable to the medium sized magnetic drives, and drives of a few Gbytes are obtainable.

Floptical drives

Magneto-optical drives tend to be of the *removable disk-cartridge* type, although much smaller versions,

Magneto-Optical drives		
Cost	**Data transfer rates and storage**	**Other considerations**
About £400 for a 640 Mbyte SCSI version. This medium costs about £20 for a 600 Mbyte disk. 2.6 Gbyte disks are about £60 at the time of writing.	Typically seek times are about 50 msec, and so can't compete head on with conventional IDE and SCSI technology. Data transfer rates are about 5 Mbytes/sec. Largest capacity drives are about 2.6 Gbytes.	These drives have not been able to be developed sufficiently to replace the magnetic drive as the main secondary-storage medium, but they will certainly give tape and CD-R a run for its money when being considered as a backup medium. However, head crashes are impossible with this type of drive!
Worm drives	4 Mbyte/sec	Highly suitable for backing up data that will never have to be changed. This is only really applicable to specialist applications, perhaps for a legal recording device, for example.

comparable in size with the 3¼ floppies (and in almost identical containers) are called **floptical disks**. These disks revolve at about 720 r.p.m. and have a data transfer rate of only about 166 Kbytes/sec.

Worms

This is nothing to do with the species of underground animal – **WORM** is an acronym for **Write Once Read Many** times and refers to the write-once CD drives. Standard CD-ROMS are obviously read-only devices, but one type of CD is manufactured in which a gold reflective layer is placed under opaque dye. A special drive is needed which carries out the actual recording by making use of slightly higher-powered LASERS, *but get it right first time – as you can't alter the disk once its been written to*! These systems are obviously ideal for long-term backups of important data, which are never likely to change. Various formats are supported, and the cost-effective nature in terms of cost per byte of data storage is second to none. Indeed, if you can't change the data once it has been recorded, then this must be a contender for most secure backup storage medium of the decade!

Serial and sequential access techniques

Serial and sequential-access storage techniques are *not* dead. They are still used *extensively* for **batch processing** on **mainframes** and **minis**, (see chapter 23), and are also used *extensively* for **backup purposes** on **microcomputers**. Also, as can be seen when carrying out the work with files covered in chapter 26, many techniques developed from tape-based machines are often used today on *direct-access media*. We will, therefore, first take a look at the large tape machines as used on some mainframe computer systems.

Basic principles of magnetic tape

The basic *principles* of recording data onto magnetic tape are quite simple, but the incredible recording densities now available using modern recording techniques on the latest tape machines make the mechanics and electronics of these devices anything but simple. You can easily visualise the simple principles involved from considering a single **recording head** as shown in figure 12.12.

This head is acting as an electromagnet to induce lines of flux (magnetic lines of force) into the magnetic coating on the tape. The resultant patterns on the surface of the tape consist of particles (e.g. chrome dioxide or metal etc.) whose arrangements are lined up one way or another within this magnetic material which is attached to a plastic, metallic or other suitable backing material. As the tape passes by the magnetic recording

head, tiny patterns of magnetism are left in the surface of the tape. These bear a relationship to the electrical signals, which were passing through the head at the time, and these in turn bear a relationship to the original **binary data** being **written** onto the tape. We have said 'bear a relationship' here because the actual data-encoding methods are not so trivial, and a knowledge of these methods is beyond what is needed at this level.

When the tape is being **read**, the tape passes under the head and the flux patterns previously recorded onto the tape induce tiny voltages into the reading head which in turn induces a current into the coil. Depending on the encoding methods used, the characteristics of this current can be analysed and the original patterns of flux deduced. This can in turn be decoded to give the original binary data recorded onto the tape. To give you some idea of the precision here – making use of more-sophisticated methods than would be implied from reading the above section, it's now possible to record several hundred thousand bits/cm^2 on tape, giving a recording density of about 6,250 bytes/linear inch of tape. Tape speeds are in the order of 200 inches/sec, and 3,600 feet of tape is typical of what can be fitted onto a single reel.

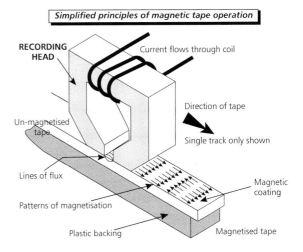

Figure 12.12

From reading the above paragraph and looking at a typical machine, the first thing to realise is that these reel-to-reel machines are built like battleships! They are

Did you know that . . .

People seem to be fascinated with the large tape drives on mainframe computers. If films ever depict large computer systems, they always seem to have a shot of the large tape machines in operation. The cost/byte of tape storage is still very favourable compared to large disk drives, and this is especially true if the data is not needed quickly. Therefore, tape drives will still be used for batch operations for some years to come, although the DLT formats are now taking over in the mainframe environment.

EBCDIC code as used on a 9-track IBM reel-to-reel magnetic tape unit

	EBCDIC Code			EBCDIC Code			EBCDIC Code	
	Zone	Digit		Zone	Digit		Zone	Digit
A	1 1 0 0	0 0 0 1	J	1 1 0 1	0 0 0 1		1 1 1 0	0 0 0 1
B	1 1 0 0	0 0 1 0	K	1 1 0 1	0 0 1 0	S	1 1 1 0	0 0 1 0
C	1 1 0 0	0 0 1 1	L	1 1 0 1	0 0 1 1	T	1 1 1 0	0 0 1 1
D	1 1 0 0	0 1 0 0	M	1 1 0 1	0 1 0 0	U	1 1 1 0	0 1 0 0
E	1 1 0 0	0 1 0 1	N	1 1 0 1	0 1 0 1	V	1 1 1 0	0 1 0 1
F	1 1 0 0	0 1 1 0	O	1 1 0 1	0 1 1 0	W	1 1 1 0	0 1 1 0
G	1 1 0 0	0 1 1 1	P	1 1 0 1	0 1 1 1	X	1 1 1 0	0 1 1 1
H	1 1 0 0	1 0 0 0	Q	1 1 0 1	1 0 0 0	Y	1 1 1 0	1 0 0 0
I	1 1 0 0	1 0 0 1	R	1 1 0 1	1 0 0 1	Z	1 1 1 0	1 0 0 1

Figure 12.13

incredibly reliable, and have data transfer rates and storage capacities, which are impressive, even by today's standards. Couple this with the relatively low cost per byte of storage compared with most other systems, and you can begin to appreciate that these tape systems will still be around well into the 21st century.

As with most hardware devices, there are a number of totally incompatible systems around, but ½-inch tape with 9 tracks is one popular system used on some mainframes. One head/track will be needed as *all 9 tracks are recorded simultaneously*. This means that if a character is to be written to tape, then it is written across the tape making use of all 9 heads.

EBCDIC

The **EBCDIC** code (**Extended Binary Coded Decimal Interchange Code**) is one of the codes used for IBM tapes, and indeed some other IBM peripheral units too. You will meet the **BCD code** when you read chapter 30, and so if you extend these ideas a little you get EBCDIC! EBCDIC is a code, which makes use of zones and digits in ways similar to those used on the old punched cards. Part of the EBCDIC code for upper case letters only is shown in the table of figure 12.13.

As shown in chapter 30, **BCD** numbers are encoded so that they can represent decimal digits very simply. In the above table, 4-bit binary numbers are coded so that they represent characters very easily. **Characters A to I** are *coded* with a **zone number of 12** (1100) *and* with **binary digits from 1 to 9**. Therefore 'E' is represented by 12 and 5, or the code 1100 0101, for example. The letters J to R are coded using zone number 13 and binary numbers 1 to 9, and finally the letters S to Z are coded using zone 14 and binary numbers 2 to 9.

Applying these principles to the actual layout showing just a very small part of the tape would result in the EBCDIC bit patterns shown in figure 12.14 – the string of characters '**BEEFBURGER**' is used for the data assuming the following.

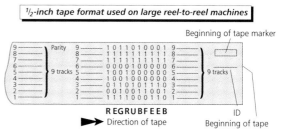

½-inch tape format used on large reel-to-reel machines

In practice information would be stored in blocks as shown in figure 12.15

Figure 12.14

(1) Track 9 is used for parity (see chapter 5) and even parity has been set.
(2) Track 1 represents the LSB of the EBCDIC digit data.
(3) Track 8 represents the MSB of the EBCDIC zone data.

As the direction of tape is usually from left to right, then the word BEEFBURGER appears to us to be the wrong way round! Nevertheless, you should be able to appreciate how the EBCDIC patterns are now represented on the tape.

Although the above illustrates the coding principles quite well, in practice it would not be efficient to code the data in one continuous stream as implied by the above scenario. It is rare for tapes to whiz from one end to the other. They are more likely to be used to read in some data, then wait until the next part is needed, then move along again – when you see a mainframe computer operating a tape, they seem to be constantly stopping and starting – it certainly makes them look more impressive!

When a tape stops, there will need to be a **gap** in which *no data has been recorded*. (You can't read data under the head if the tape's not moving, it would be like trying to expect some music from your cassette in pause mode!) Now **data processing** usually involves writing **records** to **files** (see chapter 26), and therefore it would seem to make sense if a single record were the unit of data in which to write to the tape in one go. However,

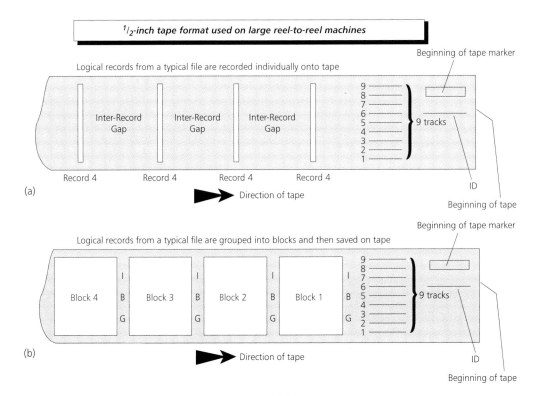

¹/₂-inch tape format used on large reel-to-reel machines

Logical records from a typical file are recorded individually onto tape

Inter-Record Gap   Inter-Record Gap   Inter-Record Gap

9 tracks

Record 4   Record 4   Record 4   Record 4

(a)

Direction of tape

Beginning of tape marker

ID

Beginning of tape

Logical records from a typical file are grouped into blocks and then saved on tape

Block 4   B I G   Block 3   B I G   Block 2   B I G   Block 1   B I G

9 tracks

(b)

Direction of tape

Beginning of tape marker

ID

Beginning of tape

Figure 12.15

given the current packing densities of 6250 bytes/inch, and given that a typical gap in which a high-performance machine would be able to stop is about 0.25 inch, recording some typical records just one at a time would result in the situation shown in the diagram of figure 12.15(a). Consider a simple calculation – for a typical name, address and telephone-number record consisting of about 100 characters, the amount of tape taken up would be 100/6250 = 0.016 in. So we have 0.016 inch records with 0.25 inch gaps! Clearly this would waste most of the space on the tape.

It would be far better to group a whole series of records into a block, such that the ratio of the used tape to unused tape is more sensible. If we bunch many logical records from the file together so that they form a **physical record** for the tape machine which is called a **block**, then the blocks may be saved on tape as shown in Figure 12.15(b). The resultant gaps in-between the blocks are known as **inter-block gaps** or **IBG**s.

Buffers

Secondary storage devices, such as disks or tapes, are usually interfaced to the operating-system software by using areas of memory called **buffers**. This means that the larger chunks of data that we have called blocks can match the available buffer size, so that efficient transfer between the tape and computer can take place. Each block shown in figure 12.15 represents a physical record on the tape machine, and all data within a particular file would be stored in this way. However, extra

header information would usually be required at the beginning of the tape for tape identification purposes, and, as is very likely, if more than one file is to be stored on a particular tape, then **file header information,** which identifies the file, will be needed too.

The actual tape drive mechanisms for this type of machine are impressive, and the idea is shown in figure 12.16. Can you imagine moving at a speed of just over 180 km/hour, then slamming on the brakes and stopping within a space of ¼ of an inch! No seat belt would save you here – it's equivalent to driving into a solid brick wall.

You can now start to see why these tape machines are so impressive. To stop the machine so quickly

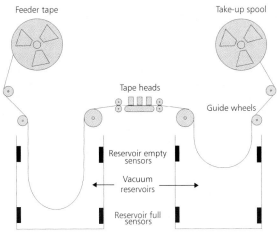

Feeder tape   Take-up spool

Tape heads

Guide wheels

Reservoir empty sensors

Vacuum reservoirs

Reservoir full sensors

Figure 12.16

without shredding the tape to bits, use is made of a reservoir system into which the tape spews out while one end is held at a dead stop. Infrared or optical detection mechanisms detect when more tape needs to be wound on or slack needs to be taken up. In this way there is virtually no tension on the tape as it is moved backwards and forwards.

What about the future of tape?

Companies still use the reel tape systems outlined in the last few pages, and you have only to surf the Internet to order your 7 in or 13 in reels of tape. However, in the modern mainframe environment, the large 9-track machines have now given way to equally huge DLT (see later) devices. Rather ironically, the very fast DLT tapes borrow much from the original reel-to-reel systems featured here, which are of course digital linear devices! This is because the data *is* recorded onto the tape while the tape head moves past in a *linear* fashion. (Other tape devices move the head in a helical fashion – see later in this chapter.) Therefore, the most modern peripherals like a DLT library are similar in priciple to the reel-to-reel systems featured here. It's just that the new DLT formats are tape cartridges, which are obviuisly easier to handle than the older reel-to-reel systems (see Plates 35 and 36).

As an example of a large modern tape system, the P3000 series high-availability (HA) **DLT library** from ATL products, supports up to 16 Digital Linear Tape drives and 326 cartridges for a native data transfer rate of 288 Gigabytes per hour, and a native capacity of 11.4 Terabytes! Up to five P3000 modules can be connected to form a single library system with up to 80 DLT drives and 1,630 cartridges for a native transfer rate of 1.44 Terabytes per hour, and a native capacity of 57 Terabytes. Now that's what I call performance in the mainframe tape environment, and this is why tapes will still be around for many years to come. You should compare these systems with the **Terabyte disk farms** mentioned elsewhere in this chapter.

You will see from the next few sections, there are many different tape formats. Indeed there are so many that specialised companies have now been set up to help convert between them. It's now possible, for example, to convert from anything like the 9 track tapes outlined on the last few pages to DLT, QIC, Travan, the Iomega 10 Gbyte QIC-EX (Extended tape formats) or even to transfer the tape data to conventional hard drives or Iomega's Zip and Jaz systems.

QIC tape streamers

A large tape machine of the sort described above would look silly sitting next to your micro. Indeed, even if you could afford one, the machine probably wouldn't fit through your bedroom door! Therefore, smaller tape formats and physically very much smaller machines exist

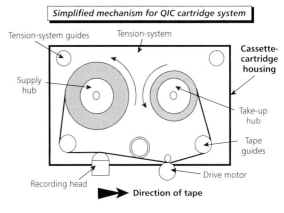

Figure 12.17

for microcomputers. A typical tape-streamer machine makes use of a cartridge tape where tiny reels of tape are mounted inside a cartridge housing as can be seen in figure 12.17. As the tape is ¼ inch wide, these systems have become known as **QICs** or **Quarter Inch Cartridges**. Typically, QIC systems enable you to back up from a few hundred Mbytes to over 2 Gbytes depending on the cartridge number and manufacturer.

These smaller machines based around a micro would also be used in very different ways. The large tape machines on mainframes are extensively used for **batch processing** (see chapter 22), but the smaller tape machines on micros are used almost exclusively for the purposes of **backup**. Because of this backup role, these tape machines are also known as **tape streamers**. SCSI tape streamers are currently available in versions which enable you to back up to 10 or 20 Gbytes of data, but tape technology is now advancing rapidly and these figures will probably be exceeded soon!

The requirement for speed is not so important here, the tape is not being used as a data-processing system, and speeds of only about 15 in/sec are typical on fast high-quality machines. Recording densities at the high-end of the range would be about 200 bytes/inch. Different standards of tape systems exist, but usually a maximum of 32 tracks is fitted onto a ¼ inch tape! Instead of whizzing through the tape reading all 32 tracks simultaneously, these small cassette machines

Did you know that . . .

The increase in capacity and decrease in size of the tape cartridges never ceases to amaze. In the last five years, the capacity of cassette-tape backup systems has increased from about 100 Mbytes/tape to over 20 Gbytes/tape. Some of the 20 Gbyte tape systems are about a quarter of the physical size of the older systems, are a fraction of the weight, and are much faster too. It obviously goes without saying that they are cheaper than the original cassettes (see Plate 37).

read just a single track at a time. The tape moves backwards and forwards so that different tracks can be read next time the heads pass by.

You should note that there are no inter-block gaps of the sort that were available on the large tape machines. Indeed, even if there were it would do no good because the tape streamer drive is not sophisticated enough to stop in time anyway! Therefore, what usually happens is that a massive amount of data (in micro terms) is recorded in a single session. It is usual to leave a tape streamer going over night as several hours of recording time might be needed to back up your hard disk. It is also usual for the **hierarchical directory structure** (see chapter 24) of the hard disk to be recorded *along with the data* on the tape. This is so that sense can be made of the data on the tape when backed-up files may need to be recovered – it's a tedious and slow process, but much less tedious *and* cheaper than losing all the data on your hard disk as the result of a crash.

DAT and video

DAT, or **Digital Audio Tape**, and ordinary **VCR** (**Video Cassette Recorder**) tapes are also used for **file-backup** purposes.

DAT uses a recording system similar to that of video in that a group of rotating heads, as shown in figure 12.18, produce tracks across the tape rather than longitudinally.

It does all this by ditching the linear-track recording systems encountered earlier, and replacing it with a helical track system. (In fact this is where the videotape name VHS comes from – Vertical Helical Scan.) You will recall that the larger tape machines go at a great speed of knots – if the DAT or video cartridge went at the same speed your favourite movies would only last a few

minutes! The vast increase in speed comes from the fact that the heads themselves rotate very quickly across the tape, and thus the speed between the tape and the head is as though the head was stationary and the tape moving by quickly – a very clever but extremely complex system. **4 mm DAT tape media**, which can store up to **26 Gbytes** is now available for only a few tens of pounds!

DAT is now very reliable, as are top-quality VCRs, but ordinary videotapes, not being designed for computer data, can be a little unreliable because of drop out. This means that some metallic particles on the coating of the tape might be missing. Use expensive professional-quality tapes and there should not be a problem. Some systems which do make use of ordinary VCRs for backup, record the data five or six times over to try and get over any potential drop-out problems. With DAT cartridges able to store up to about 26 Gbytes, and the price of DAT machines and tape streamers becoming more cost effective, these should be used in preference to VCRs for backup.

Digital linear tape

Although most tape formats are obviously digital, and all of them (with the exception of the VHS systems described earlier are linear), this **DLT** system, (ported over from the Unix systems to the PCs), travels past the head at a rate of about 3 metres per second. It is thus a system, which is intended to backup corporate network file servers etc. At the time of writing, the cost of a typical **35 Gbyte** system was just under £10,000 which, in computing terms, means that they will be a few hundred pounds in a few years if the system becomes more popular. Current transfer speeds for such a system are about **300 Mbytes/min**, but do look at the larger DLT systems designed for use on mainframes. These were mentioned earlier in this chapter.

Other secondary storage devices

To complete our tour of available methods for storing data we will look at a couple of other systems which, although less well known, do have a role to play in specialist applications.

Bubble memory

Bubble memory is available as memory on a chip, but instead of making use of silicon, it makes use of a thin coating of magnetic material on a garnet crystal. This device was to be an alternative to some of the semiconductor and disk-based systems considered earlier in this chapter, but is now only used in niche markets because it has been ousted by extremely impressive developments in all the other technologies. One big advantage of bubble memory (besides the small size of a chip) is that it is **non-volatile**. Access times are not as good as DRAM and this has probably led to the

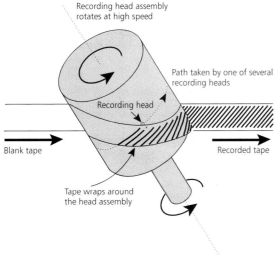

Recording head assembly
rotates at high speed

Path taken by one of several
recording heads

Recording head

Blank tape

Recorded tape

Tape wraps around
the head assembly

Figure 12.18

Serial access storage devices

Cost	Data transfer rates and storage	Other considerations
Large tape drives on mainframes are very expensive.	288 Gbytes/hour. Many Terabytes of storage for large DLT libraries.	These drives are ideal for holding vast amounts of data, which is used in the batch-processing environment.
Tape drives are usually categorised into QIC, DLT or 4 mm DAT etc. Each manufacturer has proprietary systems in operation. Typically the drives are a few hundred pounds for the larger models, and tapes vary from a few pounds to a few tens of pounds each depending on capacity.	DAT is several Mbytes/minute if an SCSI interface is used. The largest tape drives hold about 26 Gbytes of data. Larger stack systems multiply the capacity by the number of tapes in the stack. QIC tapes currently hold about 16 Gbytes compressed or 8 Gbytes uncompressed. The speed of transfer depends on the drive interface. DLT tapes currently store about 35 Gbytes with a 300 Mbyte/sec-transfer rate.	Tape drives on PCs are primarily used for backup purposes. As hard drives have become larger and cheaper, the tape drives have had to increase their capacity to stay in contention. A disadvantage of the DLT system is that it takes about 90 seconds to load the tape from start, due to the fact that alignment has to be undertaken when the tape is put into the drive.
Other cheaper alternatives are available which are driven from the floppy or parallel ports for less than £100.	The transfer rates of these systems are much slower, being typically a few Mbytes/min.	These systems are ideal for an overnight backup of the hard drive on a home micro, but are too slow for effective use in industry or education, where a SCSI DAT tape is more appropriate.

downfall of this device. A typical access time for bubble memory is about 4msec, and typically about 125 Kbytes can be stored on a single chip. It is, therefore, ideal for **embedded systems** (see chapter 8) of the sort found in applications by the military.

Plated wire store

This is a derivation from the old core store which used to be inside some of the older computers when the author was in his nappies. It is a form of magnetic storage whereby the data is stored on a thin film coated on the surface of a wire. Now you may feel that the author has lost his marbles in even mentioning such a system that the majority of people have not even heard of! However, as with the bubble memory mentioned above, it is actually quite popular in embedded systems

used in aircraft in-flight (black-box) recorders, spacecraft and satellites. This type of memory is not as susceptible to harm like that which would be experienced by an aircraft crash, for example. Access times vary, but 250 nsec is typical. These devices are useful because they are extremely robust, consume zero power when not being used, and are, therefore, non-volatile.

There have been several reasons for going into some detail regarding a huge variety of storage techniques – you are now well aware of the huge variety of different devices, and you are also aware of the vast differences in the current performance which is available from such systems. This knowledge, together with a knowledge of the other two hardware chapters on input and output devices, can be used to good effect when making decisions regarding what form of hardware is most appropriate in given data-storage situations.

Exercise 12.1

1 Describe 3 ideal characteristics of **primary storage**.

2 Explain the concepts behind **primary storage**, commenting on the importance of *memory capacity, word length and access times*. Make specific reference to the width of the address bus and data bus in your explanation.

3 Why should **primary storage** have *very fast* access times?

4 **RAM** and **ROM** is now included in most systems – explain typical uses for each. Are there any systems in which RAM only or ROM only would be used?

5 Some memory is **volatile**. What does this statement mean? What can be done to overcome this problem?

6 What is **SRAM** and where is it most frequently used?

7 What is a **memory map** and why are memory maps used?

8 What is an EPROM and in what situation is it most frequently used?

9 What is **ASCII** and why was it developed?

10 What is **auxiliary** or **secondary** storage?

11 Categorise secondary storage into its two main modes of operation.

12 Outline some of the typical problems that might be encountered when data needs to be moved from one computer system to another.

13 Why are the data-storage capacities of hard disks and floppy disks of the same physical size so different?

14 What limits the amount of data that can be stored on a hard disk, and what limits the computer's ability to quickly access the data stored on a typical disk?

15 **Optical disks** are proving to be a versatile storage medium for software distribution – what has made them so popular and versatile?

16 What are the current *limitations* of a typical CD-ROM drive? What is being done to overcome these limitations?

17 Why are there so many different standards of CD-ROM system?

18 Magnetic disk is currently the *fastest* available backing store. Given this fact, why is it necessary to have **disk-cache** memory?

19 Tapes were one of the first secondary storage media for computers. Why are they still necessary as part of a modern computer system?

20 Why are **buffers** often used when interfacing disk drives and tapes to computers? Explain the difference between **physical** and **logical records** in your answer.

21 Tapes on micros and mainframes tend to be used for very different purposes. Outline the major uses of tapes when using these different systems.

End of chapter revision aid and summary

Cover up the right-hand column and see if you can answer the questions or define the terms on the left. They appear in the order in which they are covered in this chapter. Alternatively you may browse through the right-hand column to aid revision.

What is primary storage?	Primary storage relates to the main memory inside a computer. On modern computers this usually refers to semiconductor-memory chips.
What is immediate access storage?	Immediate Access Storage (IAS) is an alternative name for primary storage.
What is secondary storage?	Secondary storage refers to storage making use of peripherals such as disks and tape etc.
What is auxiliary or backing storage?	Auxiliary or backing store are alternative names for secondary storage.
What is the most important aspect of primary storage?	The most important requirement for primary storage is speed of access.
What are the main devices used for the construction of primary storage?	Semiconductor memory chips are electronic devices made from materials which have a conductivity roughly half way between that of an insulator and a conductor.
How do we view main memory from a conceptual point of view?	Main memory can be thought of as being made up of a lot of tiny pigeonholes into which binary digits may be stored.

How is memory organised?	Memory can be organised in bits, bytes or words (multiple bytes), but the size of the main memory is usually specified in bytes, irrespective of the physical organisation.
In what units is memory measured?	The size of memory (primary and secondary) is usually specified in Kbytes or Mbytes, but Gbytes and Tbytes are now becoming increasingly common. Other useful multiples are to be found in the table in this chapter.
What is a Kilobyte?	KB means Kilobytes or 1,024 actual bytes.
What are Mbytes, Gbytes, Tbytes, Zbytes and Ybytes?	MB means Megabytes $1,024 \times 1,024$ or 1,048,576 actual bytes. Gbytes are $(1,024)^3$, Tbytes are $(1,024)^4$ ZBytes are $(1,024)^5$ and YBytes are $(1,024)^6$
What is an address?	An address is a unique number, which relates to a 'single' pigeonhole, which holds one or more binary digits (usually 8) in memory.
What is the address bus?	The address bus is the parallel group of wires along which the binary codes, which represent the address travel.
What is the data bus?	The data bus is the parallel group of wires along which the binary code representing the data travels.
What is the control bus?	The control bus is the parallel group of wires along which the binary codes representing control information such as read/write to memory can travel.
What is the access time?	The access time is the time taken for data to be written to or read from memory.
What does RAM stand for?	RAM stands for Random Access Memory; the access time does not depend on the position within the memory which holds the data.
Name the two fundamental types of RAM.	There are two types of RAM – static and dynamic.
What is DRAM?	DRAM stands for Dynamic Random Access Memory. It is the most common type of semiconductor memory used in today's computer systems. Unfortunately, because data is stored as charge, the contents need topping up at very frequent intervals which is called refreshing the memory. DRAM is the cheapest primary-storage system.
What is SRAM?	SRAM stands for Static RAM – a system which does not have to be refreshed – it is faster that DRAM, but more expensive. It is often used as cache memory.
What is synchronous burst RAM?	Synchronous burst RAM and pipelined burst RAM are ways of speeding up current RAM technologies by a small amount.
What does volatile mean?	Volatile is the term used to describe the fact that the contents of memory will be lost if the power to the system is removed. DRAM and SRAM are both volatile. ROM, PROM and EPROM are all non-volatile.
What is a UPS?	Uninterruptible Power Supplies (UPS) can overcome some of the difficulties associated with volatile RAM.
What is EDORAM?	Extended Data Out RAM – slightly faster than ordinary RAM – currently the most common form of RAM
What is video RAM?	Video RAM – fast RAM used for on-board video-card processing
What is Windows RAM?	Windows RAM – not a new technology but a way of utilising the RAM more efficiently in a windows environment.

How might SRAM be used to speed up a computer?	SRAM can be placed on the mother board to act as a faster interface to the processor. 1 Mbyte of cache would be typical. It is now also typical to have even faster access cache memory inside the processor chip itself.
What is cache memory?	Cache memory is the fast memory used to hold the most-frequently-needed instructions being used by the processor.
What is ROM?	ROM stands for Read Only Memory. Data is programmed by the manufacturer of the chip and can't be altered by the user of the computer.
Are PROM and EPROM examples of RAM?	ROM is still an example of random access because access time does not depend on storage position! Therefore, PROM and EPROM are also examples of Random Access Memory! However, the generally accepted use of the term is that they are not.
Suggest a typical use for a ROM.	ROM is usually used to hold operating systems, programming languages or for general programs when using embedded microprocessor systems.
What is a PROM?	PROM stands for Programmable Read Only Memory. A special machine can be used to program this chip – it is cheaper than ROM for lower quantities.
What is an EPROM?	EPROM stands for Erasable Programmable Read Only Memory. This device can act as a ROM, but can be programmed and erased by the user using a special machine and UV light respectively.
What is an EEROM?	Electrically Erasable Read Only Memory – more convenient form of PROM
What are the advantages of EEROM?	EEROM can be programmed in situ inside a computer or a device like a MODEM.
What is a memory map?	Memory maps map out how ROM and RAM etc. are to be used in a system.
What is ASCII?	ASCII stands for the American Standard Code for Information Interchange. This is one of the international standards for exchanging mainly textual information.
What is extended ASCII?	Extended ASCII uses the top bit normally reserved for parity, and thus produces 128 additional codes.
What are the most important characteristics of secondary store?	The most important aspects of secondary storage are data integrity and mass storage capability.
What are the two main types of secondary storage?	Direct access and serial access characterise two different types of secondary-storage techniques
What is a direct access storage medium?	Direct access refers to devices such as disks where data can be accessed directly, without having to read any other stored data.
What is a serial access storage medium?	Serial access refers to devices such as tape where direct access is not possible.
What is a floppy disk?	Floppy disks make use of a magnetic surface on which the data is stored in the form of tracks and sectors. The disk inside the case is literally floppy.
What is a track?	Track (floppy disk) – a set of concentric circular paths going across the surface of the disk. These tracks (and sectors) form the basis of a pattern, which uniquely defines how the data can be stored on the disk.
What is a sector?	Sector – Each track of a magnetic disk is split up into a uniform number of smaller parts called sectors.

What is formatting?	Formatting is the name given to the initialisation process (initialisation of the track and sector pattern plus control data) of preparing a disk ready to receive stored data.
What is a high-density disk?	High-density disks such as double-density or quad-density increase the amount of data that can be stored on a disk. However, the quality of the magnetic material used on the surface of the disk needs to be higher.
What is a hard disk?	A hard disk is the name given to a disk which is hermetically sealed and not floppy! It is currently the main secondary storage medium. The *speed of data transfer* and the *storage density* of hard disks are much higher that those of floppy disks.
What is a RAID system?	RAID is an acronym for Reduced Array of Inexpensive Drives. It is an array (two or more) of different drives intended for extra data security or file-server applications.
What is a disk pack?	Disk packs refer to the removable packs used in the large drives and mainframes. Disk packs are often multiple-platter devices, but are now largely superseded by disk farms.
What is a disk farm?	Disk farms are large (often much greater than a few Tbytes) arrays of disks held in a single cabinet and used for mass secondary storage in the fileserver, mainframe, supercomputer and large database environment.
What is a cylinder?	A cylinder is the unit of storage obtained from a consideration of the natural cylinder shape generated by the heads on multiple-surface drives. Hard disks have the data on the disk addressed in terms of cylinders, surface number and sector.
What is a disk cartridge?	Disk cartridges (1) are single-disk versions of large disk packs on a mainframe. Disk cartridges (2) are the names given to the removable hard disks on micros.
What is blocking?	The sector is the smallest unit of data that can be written to or read from a disk. Blocking (disks) is used to make storage of data on a disk more efficient.
What is a cluster?	A cluster is the name given to several sectors.
What is a FAT?	A FAT is a File Allocation Table – it is stored on disk and holds an 'information map' of where each file has been allocated space on the disk. The FAT is an example of MSDOS control information, which is stored on a disk at the time of formatting. 16-bit and 32-bit FATs are available.
What is an optical drive?	An optical drive is the name given to CD-based systems in which the data is read by a beam of light called a LASER.
What do the letters LASER stand for?	LASER – Light Amplification by the Stimulated Emission of Radiation.
What are lands and pits?	Lands and pits are the different levels on the surface of a CD after the LASER has burned the data in.
What is a CD?	CD – Compact Disc. The 12cm polycarbonate disk used for storing audio and other types of information such as computer data and video.
What is a magneto-optical drive?	Magneto-optical drives are disk drives which operate on both magnetic and optical principles. Data is written to the disk by means of a magnetic head and a LASER, and read back from the disk by a LASER in a similar way to that of a CD.

What is a WORM?

WORMs are Write Once Read Many times drives. They are special CDs, which can be written to once only by means of a special recorder machine available to users.

List a variety of different CD-ROM standards.

There is a large variety of CD-ROM standards including CD, CD-DA, Photo CD, CD-I, CD-R and CD-ROM-XA.

What is a DVD?

Digital Versatile Disk or (Digital Video Disk) – a later standard of compact disk in which a double-sided disk can store a maximum of about 17Gbytes of audio, video and computer data.

What is a disk cache system?

Disk cache systems make use of RAM as a mirror image of some parts of the disk. It helps to give an apparent vast increase in disk-access speeds.

Outline some different types of magnetic tape formats.

Magnetic tape is used in a variety of formats, the most expensive of which can be found on mainframe computers being used for batch processing. Typical formats would be QIC, DAT and DLT.

What is EBCDIC?

The EBCDIC code is a popular alternative to ASCII and is used on IBM tapes and other machines. EBCDIC is an acronym for Extended Binary Decimal Interchange Code.

What are blocked logical records?

Logical records to be stored on tape are blocked for increased data-storage capacity and efficiency.

What is an IBG?

IBGs are the Inter-Block-Gaps between blocks on a tape.

What is a blocking factor?

The blocking factor is the number of logical records per block.

What is a buffer?

A buffer is an area of memory used as an efficient interface to convert blocks to logical records and back again.

What is a QIC?

QIC – Quarter Inch Cartridge. A 20 to 32-track system depending on type.

What is DAT?

DAT – Digital Audio Tape is also used extensively for backup of disk. Smaller tape formats such as QICs and DAT are extensively used on micros for backup purposes.

What is DLT?

DLT is Digital Linear Tape. This is simply digits being recorded linearly on tape, rather like the reel-to-reel digital format. Devices range from large to humungous!

What is a DLT library?

This is the tape equivalent of the Terabyte disk farm. Many Terabytes of data can be accessed from a large number of DLT tape drives housed in the same unit.

What is bubble memory?

Bubble memory – non-volatile memory used in embedded applications.

What is plated wire store?

Plated wire store – non-volatile memory which is not as susceptible to radiation – it is therefore used by the military, in aircraft, in satellites and space ships.

13 High-level-language Principles

Key resources

To carry out this work most successfully it's best if you have:

- Access to a suitable high-level language such as Pascal or Basic, for example
- Access to several high-level languages so that you can compare and contrast the methodologies
- Access to a visual programming language such as Visual Basic or Delphi, so that you can appreciate modern programming development environments

Concept Checkpoints

- This work is intimately tied up with the work in chapter 14. If you wish to write programs of any complexity, then you will need to read both chapters first.
- You may find it easier to read this chapter after you have gained some practical programming experience with a high-level language.

Introduction

What a fabulous contribution high-level languages have made in the field of computing. Without them we would still be programming computers with low level languages like the machine code and assembly languages covered in chapters 20 and 21. Without high-level languages, the development of the computer would literally be decades behind the current levels of performance. **It is indeed to the last few decades that we must look, if we are to understand how current practices in the late 1990s have evolved and how these practices look well set to take us into the 21st century. But first, let's see why these high-level languages are so very important.**

When humans solve a problem we normally operate in a very different way to the way in which a machine would operate to solve the same kind of problem. It is difficult and unnatural for most people to have to specify how their problems are to be solved in the often-tedious machine-code forms. The further we can get away from the binary digits and registers used in the computer's architecture the better it will be, especially if the path taken gets us closer to the way in which humans prefer to think. Such human-oriented methods might include mathematics, logic, English-like statements, or indeed any method that enables us to communicate concisely and elegantly with the computer without having to 'speak' to the computer in its own primitive low-level language. **(Don't forget that the computer's language may be primitive – but what you can achieve with it is not!)**

Human or machine oriented?

A **high-level language** is, therefore, a *more convenient way for humans to communicate sets of instructions to the computer.* High-level languages are often said to be **problem specific** rather than **machine-specific** languages. However, you must remember that the computer still operates by manipulation of binary digits, and therefore these high-level languages must eventually be **translated** into a form that the machine will be able to understand. A high-level language must be able to be expressed in both **human-readable** *and* **machine-readable** format. This important translation process is covered in detail in chapter 32. Unlike the machine code and assembly languages, which depend very much on particular machine architectures, high-level languages are *meant to be* **portable**. This means that they can be used on different computers with different architectures, but total portability is rarely achieved in practice.

Natural or formal languages

The term **language** is used in *exactly the same way* as it is in French, German or Spanish, for example. However, due to current limitations of computer hardware and software, computer languages are much more restrictive. **Human languages** such as English and French belong to a class of **context-sensitive languages** or **natural languages**. This is because the **meaning** (**semantics**) of these languages depend upon the context being used, and not just the **legal arrangement** (**syntax**) of the words. For example, the sentence,

'If fat Fred wins this race I'll eat my hat!'

does not literally mean that the person concerned will eat his or her hat. It has to be taken in the context of an expression that is often used to give an opinion that, in this particular example, in the eyes of the speaker, poor-old Fred has not got very much hope of winning the race. **Computer languages** are **context free**, which *means that they are easier to analyse by machine.* Each line of a program (**set of instructions**) must be **precisely defined** so that it is **unambiguous** – we are still a very long way indeed from being able to talk to a computer system which will allow for all the idiosyncrasies in our context-sensitive languages. **Context-free languages** (i.e. computer-type languages) are also known as **formal languages**.

Software engineering

Over the last few decades computer-based languages have undergone many transformations. No longer are they simply methods for conveniently communicating with the computer – the best high-level languages have now become part of a whole new **design philosophy** which embraces what is called **software engineering**. This methodology not only considers how software should be used to solve problems, but the wider and equally important aspects of **analysis**, **debugging**, **testing** and **documentation**. It is no longer enough in professional systems to simply present the user with a program that works. Not only do the users of our systems deserve and expect continuing support over the years, but also the systems themselves have now become so complex that there is no sensible alternative strategy currently available.

High-level-language development

It's interesting, enlightening and important to realise that the long path of high-level-language development has been neither straight nor smooth. Political decisions, monetary considerations and circumstance have had just as great an impact on development as advances in methodology! Take the language 'C', for example. Although a superb language in its own right, it has proved to be very popular because it was intimately connected with **Unix** – which was, and still is, one of the most powerful operating-system platforms. Many

languages have come and gone because they were not accepted in tightly controlled hardware and operating system environments. You should also realise that people are quite naturally reluctant to re-learn methods just because a different language comes along. This is one of the main reasons why COBOL has reigned supreme for such a very-long time – the enormous investment in programs already written and the number of programmers that have been appropriately trained must be astounding. There must be very compelling reasons indeed for the professionals to start again with a new language. It is also important to realise that languages pass through **stages of evolution**. Most languages, which have stood the test of time, have probably been re-defined (usually by adding new and better features) at least several times.

> ## Did you know that . . .
>
> The development of languages is most often intimately tied up with political and business considerations, in addition to all the technical reasons outlined in this chapter. Sometimes good languages and systems will fail simply because rival companies and language developers have more financial clout. Also, there is a great inertia as people are reluctant to change systems and methods too often, especially if something is working well.

High-level languages started to be developed in the mid-to-late 1950s when **FORTRAN** and **COBOL** were introduced on **mainframe** computers. (Most of the high-level languages mentioned in this chapter will be looked at briefly in chapter 15.) It is indeed a tribute to both of these languages that they are still thriving today, unlike hundreds of other languages of much-later origin which have quietly passed away into oblivion. **COBOL** is still *the* data processing language and **FORTRAN 90** is still widely used for engineering and scientific purposes. ALGOL was also an important language developed in the 1950s because so many of the more modern languages such as **C** and **C++**, for example, are developed from it.

During the 1960s computer technology continued to grow at an amazing pace, and high-level-language development tried to emulate the same lightning-fast progress. Computer scientists of the time had a dream that an all-purpose language could be developed which encompassed all the desirable attributes of COBOL, FORTRAN and ALGOL. But this was never to be; it was far too complex a project for the available level of knowledge and the technology of the time. Also, spurred on by the enormous profits that were being made by the developers of the successful languages, many other special-purpose languages were developed during this decade. One of the several languages to survive this 1960s chaotic-development phase is **BASIC**, which in its latest incarnation is still popular, mainly in a non-professional capacity. However, **VisualBasic**, has changed the landscape considerably over the last few years, and *is* used extensively by professional programmers. Indeed, it is now one of the most prolific development environments.

Did you know that . . .

The development of computer language takes place at a much slower pace than the development of computer hardware. Every six months some new hardware technique seems to take us to a new level of performance. However, some languages, developed in the 1950s and 1960s, are still with us today. Even so, new language developments are taking place, with Visual Basic, Visual C++, Delphi and Java being notable examples.

The 1970s saw a swing in the opposite direction. Complexity was out of the window, and consistency and common platforms were of paramount importance. Pascal is an example of one of the better-structured languages to emerge in the 1970s, and is still going strong today where it has often been used as a teaching language alternative to BASIC. C and **FORTH** were also developed in the 70s, with 'C' often being referred to as a middle-level language because of the comprehensive low-level-language support available from within it.

The 1980s saw a consolidation of the better methods of the 1970s, and the continuing emergence of fundamentally different methodologies. A better version of **LISP** made this language more predominant than it was in previous versions, and the logical language **Prolog** was developed further. **Object-oriented language methods** were becoming increasingly attractive and this has led to the development of C++ (a different language to C although most of C is a subset of C++) which is currently the most popular programming language **for systems development**. I strongly recommend that all students should have a go at C++ at some stage during their advanced courses – C++ is extremely easy to use for doing basic things, and objects themselves are easily within the scope of competent programmers at this level.

In 1995 **Java** was developed, and this has produced more controversy than most other languages, as it's possible to use it independent of platform, assuming that all the companies keep to an agreed standard! However, this philosophy threatens the established players in the Windows market, and it is in this area where the controversy lies. Another innovation was the major new release of COBOL in 1997 called – wait for it! – COBOL97. This is not bad for a language that was first developed back in the late 1950s.

What's going to happen in the next millennium is obviously impossible to tell, but it looks like the object-oriented methods are helping to solve many of the current problems with complex systems programming. Therefore, until something better comes along, consolidation of this methodology with the best of the rest seems the most-likely scenario.

Generations of languages

Software, like hardware, can be classified into **generations** according to major changes in methodology. Nevertheless, not too many people applied (or even knew of!) these terms until SQLs (Structured Query Languages, see chapter 28) and the like were commonly called 4GLs or fourth-generation languages. The natural question to ask is 'What on earth were the previous three?' Unfortunately, not everybody agrees on all of these definitions! Nevertheless, it is now more-generally accepted that the following levels of abstraction apply.

Low-level languages like **assembly language** and **machine code** are the **first-generation languages**. (A bit of an insult to the latest assemblers! – *C'est la vie*.)

The **second-generation languages** are the **unstructured** high-level languages like the *early versions* of *FORTRAN* and *BASIC*. (Some definitions include assembly language as second generation with high-level languages being the third.)

The **third-generation languages** are the **structured** high-level languages like the current versions of *Pascal* and *C*. (Some definitions include all high-level languages as third generation.)

The **fourth-generation languages** are languages with the all-powerful commands like the **SQLs** considered in chapter 28, or the languages that *accompany* spreadsheets and a whole host of other **applications**. Commands such as 'SORT' are a lot easier than writing your own sort procedures using third-generation languages. However, most 4GLs are very specific in the tasks that they can easily perform.

Fifth-generation languages are languages like **Prolog** (see chapter 15) which are often regarded as *very-high-level languages*, but **expert systems** (see chapter 9), often written in Prolog, also belong to this class of language definition.

The terms 4GLs and the fifth-generation-languages are a little bit fuzzy to apply as many people in authority often refer to some of these languages as 'so-called 4GLs' etc. The situation is also not helped by manufacturers making wild claims making use of these terms – perhaps it will all be sorted out by the fifth edition of this book!

Although the labels for each generation of language might be slightly fuzzy, *what is important* is to realise that languages have gone through a slow metamorphosis starting with **machine code.** This metamorphosis then proceeds through **assembly language** and all the different versions of the **high-level languages,** to arrive at today's extremely powerful **object-oriented languages** and other equally successful methodologies (see in a moment).

Different language classes

Over the last few decades hundreds of different high-level languages have been developed, but fortunately it is possible to *categorise* these different high-level languages by consideration of the *main organising principles* used by the designers of the language. The posh term for these basic organising principles is a '**paradigm**'. There are four different paradigms considered in this book, and the ideas behind them are outlined in the next few sections.

Imperative languages

BASIC, FORTRAN, COBOL and Pascal for example, and indeed most conventional high-level languages are examples of what are called **imperative languages** or **procedural languages**. Make a special note of the fact that an 'imperative', for the purpose of computer languages, refers to an 'expression of command' – so imperative languages typify those languages in which *sequences of commands* (called **imperatives** or **procedures**) are given. Imperative languages typify telling a computer '**how to do something**' rather than telling the computer '**what to do**'. With an imperative language the programmer writes a 'sequence of instructions' which are obediently carried out by the computer. Conventional programming is based to a large extent on imperative languages, but this has led to some unfortunate restrictions which are now being overcome by the use of different organising principles (paradigms).

Declarative languages

Prolog, for example, (**P**rogramming in **log**ic) typifies a very different approach (a totally different **paradigm**) and this is just one of the reasons why it's sometimes called a fifth-generation language or a very-high-level language. When programming using Prolog, problems are expressed in terms of **structured objects** and the **relationships** between them. For example, we could type in the following two 'facts'

```
male (ray_bradley) . . . . .
owns (ray_bradley, ferrari) . . . . .
```

which means that Ray Bradley is a male and owns a Ferrari (I should be so lucky – well, at least I'm male!).

> **Hint:** If you have access to the Prolog language, try a few similar examples to get the idea of declarative languages.

Sets of statements (or clauses as they are known in Prolog) like those given above can be used to describe relationships. Prolog can then answer questions (or queries) about the relationships that have just been defined. For example, typing the query

```
? male (ray_bradley) . . . . .
```

asks the question 'Is Ray Bradley male?' – and pressing return on the keyboard would cause Prolog to answer (hopefully!)

```
yes
```

Notice that we have written *no loops or selection procedures*, and we have written *no code, which tells the computer how to handle the input*. All that is needed are sets of **clauses declaring** the properties of the problem, then we are ready to run the program. For this reason languages which operate in this way are called **declarative languages**. Declarative languages typify the '**what to do**' rather then the 'how to do it' method, and although the above example is extremely simple, it does show how programs may be written in this alternative way. Further examples of Prolog can be found in chapter 15 on high-level languages.

Object-oriented languages

An increasingly important strategy (**paradigm**) is the use of **object-oriented languages**. C++, for example, makes extensive use of **objects** (see chapter 15), which can be used to great effect in minimising mistakes in extremely complex systems. An object is really a single unit, which encapsulates both functions and data. Although this does not sound too revolutionary to the uninitiated at this stage, a sizeable chunk of chapter 15 is devoted to the language C++, where these vitally important principles are explained in some detail.

Functional languages

Functional languages or **applicative languages** as they are sometimes known make use of the final **paradigm** (organising principle) to be considered in this book. (There are other paradigms and no doubt more will be invented in the future.) LISP is an example of a functional language and this type of organising principle involves parameters that are passed to functions from expressions which are being evaluated, and then these values are returned from the functions to the calling expression. Functional programming languages owe much to the ideas of functions borrowed from mathematics, and examples of functional programming making use of LISP can be found in chapter 15.

General principles of high-level languages

From reading the above you are probably thinking that most languages contain elements of some or all the fundamental paradigms mentioned – and indeed this would be true. For example, **functional programming** from the **applicative languages** is also used in today's **declarative languages** as in Prolog. However, the categorisation in the previous few sections has taken place by considering the *overriding organising principles* on which a particular language is based.

As languages evolve, facilities are added to them which include elements of most of the four basic language classes outlined above – this is indeed the whole point of language evolution – the best of one type of language is often built into another type. You can also obviously simulate any organising principle in almost any language, but this is not the same as having these structures available to you at the most fundamental levels. Bear these important facts in mind as you progress through a tour of all the languages mentioned in this introductory section.

Recall that the *main purpose* of a high-level language is to enable humans to communicate their ideas to the computer in **human-readable form**, and be a vehicle for turning these ideas into codes in a **machine-readable form**. High-level languages do this by creating **abstract concepts**, which can eventually be turned into **machine code** programs. These abstract concepts are usually built up from the basic character set, and expressed in terms of special reserved words (or keywords), constants and special symbols etc. (all of these terms are explained very shortly). The words (or tokens) used to make up the language are used later by the compiler when the time comes to process the language instructions during the parse phase (see chapter 32). It is in this way that the code gets turned into machine-readable form.

High-level language constructs

The basic 'bricks' from which a high-level language is built are known as the **high-level language constructs**. In the next few sections, when dealing with high-level language constructs, **Pascal** will be used for many of the examples. Pascal has been chosen because it is still one of the most popular and highly respected structured teaching languages used in many universities, colleges and schools, and is a language which has most of the desired attributes for modern programming methods. However, in practice you would use the visual version of Pascal like Delphi, for example. Other languages such as C++ and BASIC, for example, will also be used when special points need to be made. When reading the next few sections you should also note that computer-related text will be `shown like this`, i.e. using the monospaced Courier font.

The syntax and semantics

The **syntax** (*i.e. the rules and regulations (or grammar) governing the* **layout** *and* **keywords** *etc.*) of different high-level languages differs from one language to another, because different **keywords** and **paradigms** (see earlier) have been chosen by the designers of the language. Nevertheless, high-level languages should *not* be so strange that conventional programmers would have difficulty in understanding what is going on. Therefore, whenever a new language is designed the designers usually pay attention to current standards and methods. This is called 'conformity', and is one of the desirable attributes of all high-level languages (see chapter 15).

In addition to the **syntax,** we must obviously be able to understand what is meant by routines written in different languages, or else we would not be able to use them to effectively convey our ideas to the computer. The **meaning**, which we attach to the statements and the 'way in which they are used' in the language, is called the **semantics**.

The character set

All high-level languages need **characters** such as **letters of the alphabet**, **digits** and other **special symbols** etc. which help to form **the higher-level** concepts that may be expressed by using the language. (All these terms are explained in the next few sections.) A typical character set for the Pascal language is as follows:

```
letters = { a b...y z   A B...Y Z }
digits = {0 1... 9}
special symbols = {+ – * / := . , ; : =
<> < <= >= > ( ) [ ] (* *) ^ ..}
other symbols = {@ & # $ ! ... plus
other ASCII characters not in special
symbols}
```

Normally, any character available from your keyboard may be used, but often symbols have a special purpose in a high-level language. The special symbols used by Pascal are shown in the special-symbols set above.

Reserved or keywords

Reserved words (**keywords**) are examples of **identifiers** (see below) which are used as labels by the language to represent words like 'if', '**function**' or '**else**' etc. Different high-level languages have *different sets* of **reserved words**, but fortunately (remember **conformity?**) many of these are both similar in **syntax** and in the effects which they produce. This is one of the most important reasons for having a general overview of high-level languages – the programmer is not allowed to use reserved words in any other context. A simple version of Pascal, for example, might have the following set of reserved words:

and	array	begin	case
const	div	do	downto
else	end	file	for
function	goto	if	in

```
label      mod        nil        not
of         or         packed     procedure
program    record     repeat     set
then       to         type       until
var        while      with
```

As language definitions are improved with later versions, extra reserved words are usually added to the set of reserved words. You should look at the latest version of Delphi as an example.

Identifiers

An **identifier** is a string of one or more characters which *uniquely* identifies a data item or element of a program. Examples would be **constants**, **variables**, **functions** and **procedures**, **arrays**, and **records** etc. Other identifiers *can't usually clash* with **keywords**, because the meaning of the language would then be ambiguous. However, BBC BASIC, for example, allows the use of identifiers with 'keyword names' as long as lower-case letters are used e.g. print would not be confused with PRINT. The standard Pascal identifiers for one simple version of Pascal are as follows:

```
abs        arctan     boolean    char       chr
cos        dispose    eof        eoln       exp
false      get        input      integer    ln
maxint     new        odd        ord        output
pack       page       pred       put        read
readln     real       reset      rewrite    round
sin        sqr        sqrt       succ       text
true       trunc      unpack     write      writeln
```

> **Hint:** If you have a Pascal compiler, then try out as many of these techniques as possible.

It should be noted that the Pascal standard identifiers in the above list are simply placed in alphabetical order. They are usually further subdivided into 'constants', 'files', 'functions', 'procedures' and 'types' according to the use to which they are put. For example, the 'functions sub division' would be:

```
abs(x)    arctan(x)  chr(x)    cos(x)    eof(x)
eoln(x)   exp(x)     ln(x)     odd(x)    odd(x)
ord(x)    pred(x)    round(x)  sin(x)    sqr(x)
sqrt(x)   succ(x)    trunc(x)
```

Functions

Although most of these are **functions** in the *mathematical* sense, (sin(x), for example), the term **function** should be considered *more generally than this*. In computing read the term **function** as something that *calls up the right subprogram during the compilation stage* (see chapter 32). **Functions** such as **eof(x)**, for example,

which determine if an 'end of file' has been detected, make a little more sense when viewed in this light.

User-defined identifiers

The user may make up their own identifiers as long as the names do not clash with any **standard identifiers** or **reserved words** in the previous lists, and follow the set of rules (**syntax**) which has been laid down (see in a moment). Examples of user-defined identifiers (constants or variables in this case) might be:

balance_of_account
foregroundcolour
perimeter

(Note some earlier versions of Pascal do not allow the use of the underscore _ character. balance_of_ account would not be allowed.)

We obviously can't go round making wild guesses as to what may or may not be valid identifiers in a particular high-level language. It is therefore fortunate that the complete **syntax** (the grammatical rules for combining the elements we are now considering) for **Pascal** can be expressed efficiently in terms of what are called **syntax diagrams**. These diagrams are simple to use and an example for a Pascal identifier is shown in figure 13.1.

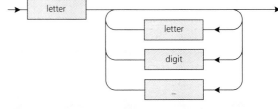

Pascal syntax diagram for an IDENTIFIER

Figure 13.1

> ## Did you know that . . .
>
> The definition of language syntax is a highly complex topic. Syntax definition can also be achieved through BNF and EBNF methods, and this is covered in detail in chapter 32.

By following the arrows, legal identifiers can be built up. You can see instantly, for example, that the identifier

```
1stnumber
```

would be illegal in Pascal as it starts with a digit – this is not allowed. By using the syntax diagram you can see that all identifiers must start with a letter, so

```
Firstnumber, Area_of_circle and
   monkeynuts
```

would all be legal. Syntax diagrams, together with the BNF or extended BNF languages for syntax definition (see chapter 32) convey what is and what is not legal in a particular high-level language. Syntax diagrams will be used extensively where they help illustrate principles throughout this chapter.

Returning to valid identifiers for a brief moment, programmers must often beware of using very long identifier names, as many compilers, (see chapter 32), although allowing the use of long variable names (as with Pascal), might only pay attention to the first eight characters, for example. If you are unfortunate enough to have a version of a high-level-language compiler which does this, then

```
statement_1, statement_2 and
   statement_3
```

would all be the same! This adds to the fun of programming – especially if you like whiling away hours of your valuable time debugging esoteric errors.

Variables

A **variable** is simply the name given to an **identifier** chosen by the user (obviously not clashing with any reserved words or standard identifiers) whose *value is allowed to vary* (change) during the execution of a program. In Pascal, variables must be declared at the beginning of the program by the use of the reserved word 'var', and a simple variable declaration (which also states the 'type' of the variables) is shown in the following Pascal example.

```
var average : integer;
    compare : boolean;
```

The syntax diagram for a variable is not shown in this introductory session on variables. Many types of variable are usually expressed in terms of other terminology such as 'field identifiers' and 'expressions', which would also have to be defined. The resulting syntax diagrams would get too large to be useful in helping to understand what is going on at this early stage.

Constants

Constants represent things that don't vary such as '46.3', which represents a **numeric constant**, or 'The cat sat on the mat' which represents a **string constant**. *When used in this way,* constants are also called **literals**, because they are *represented by their literal value – i.e. a value that is used to define itself!* However, an identifier whose value is not allowed to change (i.e. a constant identifier) can also represent a constant during the execution of a program. The syntax diagram for a Pascal constant is shown in figure 13.2.

Making use of this diagram, and after reading about 'strings' you should be able to see that

+46.3   45   −123   and   Porkpies

are all valid constants.

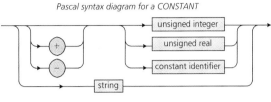

Pascal syntax diagram for a CONSTANT

Figure 13.2

Constants have to be declared too at the beginning of a Pascal program, and a typical Pascal constant declaration example using (you've probably guessed it!) the reserved word 'const' is as follows:

```
const maxnumber = 10;
      teststring = 'Testing 123';
```

Strings

A string is quite literally a **string of characters**. However, the compiler (see chapter 32) must have a way of knowing when a string ends, as spaces are usually allowed to make up part of the string. Most high-level languages therefore have what are called **delimiters** at the ends of the string, and the syntax diagram for a Pascal string is shown in figure 13.3.

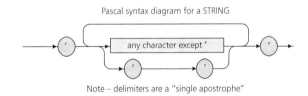

Pascal syntax diagram for a STRING

Note – delimiters are a "single apostrophe"

Figure 13.3

From this syntax diagram you can see that Pascal allows the use of a delimiter within the string only if it is followed immediately by another delimiter character. If you want to use Pascal to print out 'I don't like soggy cabbage' for example, then you would use the statement

```
writeln('I don''t like soggy cabbage')
```

Note the two apostrophes next to each other in-between the 'n' and 't' of 'don't'.

BASIC is unusual in that strings are explicitly indicated by the use of a dollar sign ($) on the end of the variable name, and do not have to be declared (i.e. explicitly stated either at the beginning or at some point throughout the program).

On the other hand, C++ for example, treats a string as 'arrays' of type 'char' (char being exactly the same as the numeric data type called 'char' described in the table a little later), i.e. C++ treats a string as a one-dimensional array of characters (which is what it is!). In C++ we can set up a string as follows:

```
char My_string[ ] = "This is what is
  inside the string"
```

In most versions of BASIC strings are limited to 255 characters, but in C++ and some versions of Pascal they can be much larger than this.

Precedence Level	Operators
1 (Highest)	( )
2	not
3	* / div mod and
4	+ - or
5 (Lowest)	= <> <= > >= in

Figure 13.4

Statements

A **statement** in a high-level language is simply a descriptive phrase that generates one or more machine-code instructions. (Sometimes it's just a single line of program code but it's often more.) Statements are *further classified* according to what they do, and the examples show different statements in Pascal, together with the statement types assigned to them.

> **Hint:** Note that a statement like 'x = x + y' would seem to be algebraic nonsense. This is why some languages, like Pascal, for example, use ':=' instead of '=' for the assignment operator to emphasise this point.

```
total := x + y + z;
```

This is called an assignment statement because the assignment operator ':=' is used to assign the value of variables x+y+z to the variable called total. Another example is

```
if number > 999 then writeln('The
  number just typed in is too big')
```

This is called a conditional statement (also known as an 'if then' statement), because the code after the 'then' part is executed only if the given condition (in this case number > 999) is true.

There are lots more examples that could be covered but different statement types will be looked at in detail within the section on basic structures covered later in this chapter.

Expressions

Programming languages often distinguish between **statements** and **expressions**. For example, 'x+y+z' is an **arithmetic expression**, but, as we have seen in the last section, when included with an assignment operator, the line of code becomes a **statement**. In Pascal, for example, you can have 'arithmetic', 'Boolean', 'integer' and 'real' expressions.

When using **arithmetic expressions** the order of precedence is of paramount importance. For example, x+y/z should be worked out by first dividing y by z,

and then adding the result to x. The levels of precedence are used by the compiler (see chapter 32) so that expressions may be worked out with the minimum use of brackets. In Pascal, the levels of precedence correspond with those in normal arithmetic and are summarised in figure 13.4.

Data types

Different data types are of fundamental importance because they describe the nature of the data. For example, the integer and floating point numbers to be considered in chapter 31 are examples of just two different data types. Data types are important because they add to the **readability** of the program and make **maintenance much easier** (i.e. if the program needs to be altered at some later stage either by the original programmer or, more usually, by someone else). If a program is easier to maintain and read then it is also likely to be more reliable. With well-defined data types both the programmer and the compiler (see chapter 32) can determine much more easily exactly what is going on within a program.

One of the many criteria by which a programming language may be judged (see chapter 15) is in the number of data types that are supported. Some of the older languages, which have not gone through many stages of development, have relatively few data types. However, one of the reasons why languages like C++ and Pascal are so popular is because of the large variety of data types that are supported. Data types may range from the simple integer numbers available in most languages, via the complex-number types (real and imaginary numbers – see chapter 18) available in FORTRAN, to the advanced objects available in C++.

Numeric data types

Most modern high-level languages (**BASIC** is one of the exceptions) require that the programmer **declare** the **data types** – either at the beginning of, or at various points throughout the program. This is so that the compiler can *make sure that the correct variable types are being properly used*. Suppose, for example, that a programmer wishes to declare that he or she is going to use three numeric variables called x, y and z, of which x and y are integers and z is a floating-point number. In C++, for example, this would be done by the following two statements

```
int x,y;
float z;
```

Hint: Different numeric data types may lead to problems when writing particular programs. In chapter 31, these problems are considered in some detail when errors, due to different data-storage techniques, are covered.

We are making a small diversion into the C++ language here because the range of numeric data types available is considerable. They are summarised in figure 13.5. Staying with the idea of numeric data types in the C++ language for a moment, as can be seen from the table, there are seven different keywords used, and this gives an enormous variation in precision and range (see chapter 31).

There are also variations of the above such as 'unsigned char', for example, which gives a range of 0 to 255 instead of -128 to +127. As you can see from figure 13.5, this range of numeric data types should prove to be adequate for most purposes. Compare the above range with that which is available in a simple version of the BASIC language – you can see just one of the reasons why C++ is a more-professional choice of language.

C++ numeric data types		
	Range	
Name	From	to
char	–128	127
int	–32,768	32,767
short	–32,768	32,767
long	–2,147,483,648	2,147,483,647
float	3.4×10^{-38}	3.4×10^{38}
double	1.7×10^{-308}	1.7×10^{308}
long double	3.4×10^{-4932}	1.1×10^{4932}

Figure 13.5

In Pascal, variables also have to be declared, normally at the beginning of the program or in the procedure declaration (although pointer-data types are an exception to this general rule – see chapter 24). If we wish to achieve the same result in Pascal as we did with our integer and real numbers declarations in C++, then we would use the alternative statements making use of the reserved word 'var' as follows:

```
var x, y: integer;
var z: real;
```

The syntax diagrams shown in figure 13.6 define unsigned integer and real number data types in Pascal.

You should be able to work out from the above syntax diagrams that the following are valid unsigned-number formats in Pascal.

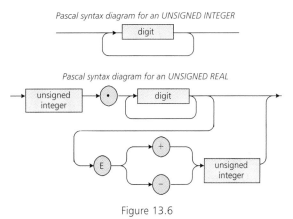

Pascal syntax diagram for an UNSIGNED INTEGER

Pascal syntax diagram for an UNSIGNED REAL

Figure 13.6

178 (unsigned integer)
12.653 (unsigned real)
6.4E-23 (unsigned real)

Other data types

Much of the power of any high-level language stems from the *number* of **data types** that it can handle. We have just seen some numeric data types, but other types exist too. For example, Pascal has 'array', 'boolean', 'char', 'enumerated', 'file', 'integer', 'pointer', 'real', 'record', 'set', and 'subrange' data types. More recent versions of Turbo Pascal and object-oriented Pascal are now available, in which this range is extended further.

Some languages, like C++, for example, enable users to *define their own* data types. This leads to more efficient programming as the user is not constantly trying to bend the problem to be solved because they are making use of the limited range of data types that some other languages allow. For example, try coding the multiple-linked-list and tree data structures (see chapter 25) using Pascal, and you will find the job relatively simple. However, try using some versions of BASIC, and due to the lack of suitable data types, you will find the job considerably more difficult, though by no means impossible. The Pascal data-type categories are shown in figure 13.7.

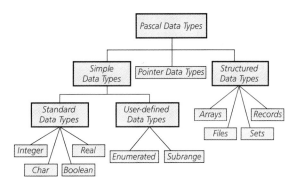

Figure 13.7

Exercise 13.1

1 Explain the 'significance of' and the 'need for' high-level languages in computing.

2 Why is there a need for so many different types of high-level language, and what is the difference between the following high-level language types?

a **Imperative** (or procedural) languages

b **Declarative** languages

c **Functional** languages

d **Object-oriented** languages

3 Why is the concept of 'software engineering' so important in modern computing?

4 To which generation of language do the following belong?

a **Pascal** and *structured* **BASIC**

b 68000 **assembly language**

c **Fortran 90** and **COBOL 97**

d **Prolog**

e *Non-structured* **BASIC**

f A spreadsheet-programming language

5 Define the following terms in the context of a high-level language giving five legal examples of each in a high-level language of your choice.

a Variable

b Identifier

c Reserved word

d Built-in mathematical function

6 a What is a syntax diagram?

b Why are syntax diagrams useful for high-level language definitions?

c Name an alternative method of language definition.

7 What is meant by a **data type** in a high-level language and why is it useful to have strictly-defined data types?

8 In a language of your choice briefly describe the syntax of the following statements:

a for loop

b while loop

c repeat-until loop.

9 In a high-level language of your choice make a complete list of the data types available to you, and make another list (similar to that shown on page 279) of the name and range of the numeric data types available in the same language.

10 Compare and contrast the use of the following data types:

a Boolean

b Integer

c Real

d String.

Further high-level language features

Other simple data types

The 'Char' (string), 'integer' and 'real-number' data types already considered earlier in this chapter are examples of what Pascal refers to as simple data types. Other data types consisting of multiple data items such as 'arrays' and 'files' are called structured data types and are considered later. In the remainder of this section we will complete our lightning-quick tour of Pascal's remaining simple data types.

Boolean data types

Boolean data types represent values that can *only be* true or false. In Pascal, true is encoded as 1 and false is encoded as 0. Boolean variables are most often combined with the Boolean operators such as AND, OR and NOT to form Boolean expressions (or Boolean conditions) which take on true or false values. For example, suppose that an integer variable called x has a value of '99', then (x > 10) would be true! Similarly, (x < 10) OR (x = 10) would be false, as the components (x < 10) and (x = 10) are both false. It's interesting to note that C++ has no Boolean data type, with the integer values 0 and 1 being used instead. These Boolean conditions are an essential part of the control and selection structures considered later in this chapter, and are therefore an essential part of structured programming techniques.

Enumerated data types

As far as computing is concerned, '**enumerate**' means to *go through a list*. It is not surprising, therefore, to find that **enumerated data types** consist of **lists of data** items. The classic examples make use of 'days of the week', or 'months of the year' etc., but any values (words) may be inserted in the list.

In Pascal, we can define an enumerated data type (using the reserved word type) which represents 'abbreviated months of the year' as follows:

```
type months =
  (jan,feb,mar,apr,may,jun,jul,aug,sep,
  oct,nov,dec);
```

The brackets and commas used for separation indicate to the **compiler** (see chapter 32) that this is an enumerated data type. Here it is only possible for the values 'jan' or 'feb' etc. to be associated with the variable called 'months'. Any value not in the list will cause an error. Numbers are assigned with the data items, and in the above example, 0 would be assigned to 'jan', 1 to 'feb' and so on up to 11 for 'dec'.

> **Hint:** Making good use of the range of data types provided by a language can lead to well structured and easier to understand programs.

Take good note of the fact that even though we have different items in the list this is still a simple data structure because the data items can't be altered during the execution of the program. To add another item to the list would require re-editing and re-compiling the source code (see chapter 32).

Being an ordered list we can use Boolean expressions on enumerated data types. For example,

```
jan < feb would be     true
```

leads to very efficient coding of problems involving, for example, chronological order.

Sub range data types

A **subrange data type** is simply referring to a sub range (i.e. part) of the original range in an enumerated data type. Using the months example again for the enumerated data type, if we have the following program:

```
type months =
  (jan,feb,mar,apr,may,jun,jul,aug,sep,
  oct,nov,dec);
      summer = jun..aug
      autumn = sep..nov
```

then summer (being defined as jun, jul and aug) and autumn (being defined as sep, oct and nov) are examples of subrange data types.

Structured data types

All the data types considered so far, as can be seen from figure 13.7, belong to the **simple-data-type category**. However, there are also **structured data types** such as '**arrays**', and '**files**' etc., which can have multiple data items that are related to one another in terms of the definition of the **structure** being used. Pascal has four structured data types and these are briefly considered in the next few sections.

Arrays

Fundamental concepts of this important data type are covered in detail in the **data-structures** chapter. However, an array called 'fred' consisting of a one-dimensional set of 100 real numbers may be declared in Pascal by use of the following syntax:

```
var fred :array [1..100] of real;
```

Multi-dimensional arrays are also no problem in Pascal, and a three-dimensional array called 'bert' consisting of a 10 by 10 by 10 matrix of integer numbers can be set up with the following syntax:

```
var bert :array [1..10, 1..10, 1..10]
  of integer;
```

The only restriction here, as in most high-level languages, is that the array elements must always consist of the same data type, and you are obviously limited by the amount of available RAM. For example, suppose a three-dimensional array containing 100 numbers in each dimension were to be set up where each entry in the array is a real number. Assuming that a real number is stored making use of 4 bytes of memory (see chapter 31 where the storage of numbers is considered), then you would need 4 Mbytes of RAM to store this item of data!

Subscripted variables

Reference to any element in an array is usually accomplished by means of a **subscripted variable**. For example, to set the 9th element of 'one-dimensional fred' mentioned above to 3.16 we would use

```
fred[9] := 3.16;
```

To print the last element of three-dimensional bert we could use

```
writeln('The last value of bert is ' ,
  bert[10,10,10]);
```

The part in brackets, which is tacked onto the variable name, is known as a subscript – hence the variable is known as a subscripted variable.

Set data types

Pascal allows you to define sets in the normal mathematical sense (i.e. a group of objects belonging to the same set). A set can relate to any user-defined objects – from 'days of the week' via 'letters of the alphabet' to 'colours of the rainbow'. For example, when defining a set of upper-case letters we could make use of the reserved words 'var' and 'type' in the following way.

```
type letters = set of char;
var upper_case : letters;
```

The set definition itself, together with the definition of a set of vowels and the generation of a set of consonants takes place in the short program that follows. Note that the sets do not have to be ordered (i.e. in the order a..z as defined in the above case).

```
type letters = set of char;
var upper_case,vowels,consonants :
  letters;

begin
   upper_case := ['A'..'Z'];
   vowels := ['A','E','I','O','U'];
   consonants := upper_case - vowels;
end.
```

As the upper-case consonants are simply the upper-case letters minus the vowels, we have used the operation of set difference ((-) in Pascal) to generate a set with upper case consonants as the elements within it. Note that the operations of union (+), intersection (*) and set difference (-) (all these set operations having the same meaning as in elementary mathematics) can be used to operate on the sets.

Record data types

Records are looked at in more detail in chapters 26 and 27 when file handling is covered. However, suppose we want to set up a list (i.e. an array) containing 500 customer-account records. Let's also suppose that we want the 'customer number', 'name' and 'balance' to be stored as fields (see chapter 26) within each record. The following code makes use of the reserved words 'type', 'var' and 'record'.

```
type account = record
       number : integer;
       name : char;
       balance : real
     end;
var customer : array [1..500] of
  account;
```

This would be one possible way of setting up the system. Here customer[10] would be the record belonging to the 10th customer, or 'customer[20].name' (note the dot) refers to the 'name field' (i.e. the actual name) of the 20th customer.

You may be wondering where the syntax diagrams have gone, but the appropriate syntax diagrams have got a little too large to be included here. If you have got access to a Pascal compiler then you can consult the manual if you are interested, or look up the help file in the Delphi system. The syntax diagram for 'type' would not help too much at this stage to further explain the concept of a record structure.

An important point can now be made which is especially poignant if you are used to programming in some elementary versions of BASIC. Notice how much easier it is to handle records when appropriate data types are available from within the language. Record handling can be done in most elementary versions of BASIC by the use of 'pointers' and 'string functions', but it's messy compared to having dedicated structures like those found in Pascal or COBOL for example.

File data types

Files (also covered in chapters 26 and 27) are essential to any language and are obviously intimately connected with the record data types described in the last section. A file may be defined in Pascal using the following syntax:

```
var file_name : file of type
```

If we use the same structure as for the record in the previous section then

```
type account = record
       number : integer;
       name : char;
       balance : real
     end;
var customer : file of account;
```

would be one possible way of setting up a file, consisting of 'N records' each having the field structure outlined above. The number N here would depend on the disk capacity of the system and does not have to be specified. Note that the array set up in the last section is usually held in memory, and the file types here are usually held on disk.

Pointer data types

Lists and pointers are slightly more complex, but are extensively covered in chapters 24 and 25. The Pascal pointer data type may be used to set up linked lists, circular lists, queues and trees etc. with relative ease. Unlike arrays and sets, pointer data types, like files, do not consist of fixed lists, but may be expanded given the limitation of available memory (or disk space in the case of most files). In this context files and pointers are

Plate 14 ▶
This is the ultimate in flight simulation technology. Pilots can receive up-to-date training for large, modern passenger and military aircraft. Simulators such as these cost millions of pounds but this expense is preferable to the risks involved in training using real aircraft

▼ **Plate 15**
Forecasting the weather is a complex process. Real-time colour displays help this scientist to track the path of inclement weather over the south west of England

Plate 16 ▶
To get analogue signals to go into or come out of a computer you need a special interface board, like the one shown here from Sunset Laboratories. This is typical of a system that would be used by professional engineers and scientists to develop computer systems for laboratory work, for example

called **dynamic data structures**, whereas **arrays** and **sets**, for example, are examples of **static data structures**. A dynamic data structure may have its size altered during the execution of a program, but static data structures can't be altered under the same program-execution conditions.

Consider the simple linked list shown in figure 13.8. This shows six sales personnel with the names and addresses shown at each node (see chapter 25). In practice much more information than name and address would probably be stored. However, as far as programming with pointers is concerned, each element in the list consists essentially of two important pieces of information represented by variables. Firstly, there is the 'pointer variable' which points to the next element in the list, and secondly, the 'referenced variable', the variable which is being pointed at.

Note, however, that the referenced variable may be a structured type containing lots of different information. (For example, it contains a 'pointer', 'name' and 'address' in this particular case.)

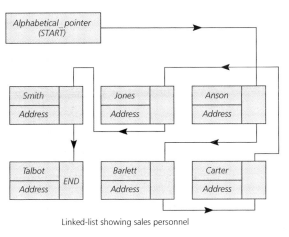

Linked-list showing sales personnel

Figure 13.8

In Pascal, dynamic variables are treated in a slightly different way to static variables, and have to be declared in those parts of the programs that alter them. This is because these variables can be created and destroyed (by inserting and removing items from linked lists) dynamically, unlike static variables which exist throughout the duration of the program, and use the conventional declaration methods outlined much earlier. The standard identifier called 'new' can be used to create a new 'referenced variable as' follows:

```
new(alpha_pointer)
```

Any pointer name will do, but alpha_pointer has been used to correspond with the link list in figure 13.8. The variable type will also have to be declared and for this particular example, this can be accomplished by using:

```
type alpha_ptr = ^sales
```

You can see the use of this pointer-data-type definition in the part of a Pascal program shown in figure 13.9. Note that (*comments are like this in Pascal*) and for simplicity an array has been used to hold the information. Note also that the structure is assumed to have been created.

Creation of the structures in the first place is not difficult, and the pointers can be utilised by making use of pointer variables in statements like the following:

```
sales_ptr^.name       := 'Bert Bloggs'
sales_ptr^.address    := 'Disneyland'
```

i.e. 'sales_ptr ^ .name' refers to the 'name field' in the record currently pointed to by the pointer.

When inserting and deleting items from a list then these pointer variables are also most useful, as pointers can be swapped or moved around the list with great ease. You are pointed (pun intended!) in the direction of the file handling chapter (see chapters 26 and 29) to investigate this fascinating topic further.

Basic language structures

All **imperative or procedural languages** (see earlier) are made up of fundamental structures which are implemented in each language by certain statements or groups of statements. The most-common structures will now be investigated and typical **flowcharts**, **Nassi-Schneiderman structure diagrams** and **pseudo-code (high-level-language-like instructions)** representations will be given where this is helpful to explain the concepts involved. *All these ideas like 'flowcharts' and 'structure diagrams' etc. can be found in chapter 14 when structured analysis and design techniques are covered.*

Linear structure

This is the simplest of structures and some might argue that this is no structure at all – but if there were no structure at all, then the statements could go in any order, and this is obviously not so! A linear structure is the simplest type of structure and a trivial example where five statements are executed to find the average of three typed-in numbers is shown in figure 13.10.

> **Hint:** This section is applicable to many computer languages, and an understanding of the work here will help to make you a proficient computer programmer.

Control structures

In most high-level languages you can't get very far without making some sort of decision, or repeating

```
type field = array[1..30] of char;
     alpha_ptr = ^sales;     (*pointer to object of type sales*)
     sales = record          (*sales record data type defined*)
         name : field;
         address  : field;
     .     (*other data could easily go in here*)
     .
     .
         next : alpha_ptr    (*store next pointer with data*)
     end;
var  sales_ptr : alpha_ptr ;(*sales_ptr declared as data-type
                                        pointer*)

procedure read_data(var dummy : field);
    begin
        .
        (*code in here to read the data*)
        .

    end;
begin (*Main part of program to read the data*)
    new(sales_ptr) (*New referenced variable called sales_ptr*)

    with sales_ptr^ do  (*Use of pointer in loop*)
        read_data(name);      (*Call read_data procedure to get name*)
        read_data(address);
        .            (*other data could easily be read here*)
        .            (* checks for EOF too*)
    end.
```

Figure 13.9

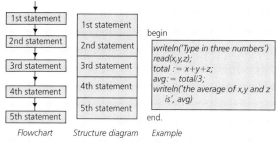

Flowchart   Structure diagram   Example

Figure 13.10

linear sequences many times. For example, you may require that a temperature is constantly monitored (see chapter 8) until a condition arises in which the temperature becomes too high – in which case control needs to be passed to that part of the program which may shut down the process or switch on a fan. These powerful control structures will now be considered.

Conditional statements

Decision making in many high-level languages can be made by using the 'if then conditional statements'. Sim-ple **Boolean conditions** (see earlier) are normally used as a basis on which to make the decisions. For example,

$$temp < 50$$

and

$$(x < 40) \text{ or } (y <> 10)$$

would be typical of the statements used in the decision-making process. If the expression or condition is true, then control is diverted to one part of the program, whereas if the condition is false, then control is diverted to another. A typical example is shown in figure 13.11.

You see from figure 13.11 that the layout of this conditional statement is quite flexible (there are other variations too). Note also the assignment-statement parts of the above can, if necessary, be replaced by multiple line statements or other structures. If this is the case then the layout on the left is preferable, but for simple conditions the layout on the right is

> **Hint:** The diagrams used in this chapter should be relatively easy to understand. However, they are covered, together with many other suitable diagrammatic methods, when structured analysis is covered in chapter 14.

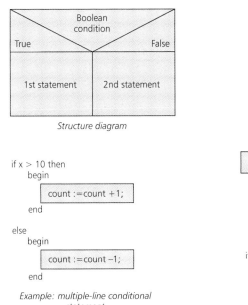

Structure diagram

```
if x > 10 then
    begin
        count :=count + 1;
    end
else
    begin
        count :=count – 1;
    end
```

Example: multiple-line conditional statement

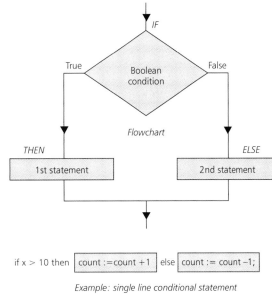

Flowchart

if x > 10 then | count :=count + 1 | else | count := count –1;

Example: single line conditional statement

Figure 13.11

all that is usually necessary. It should also be noted that, in this example, x would be called the control variable as it is used to control the loop.

Nested if-then statements

Most high-level languages, including Pascal, allow the use of **nested if-then statements**, and we will use a simple example to illustrate these techniques. In the days when the author took his exams, you failed if you got less than 40%, 40% to 59% gave you a pass, 60% to 79% gave you a credit, and 80% or more gave you a distinction. The following code, making use of nested-if-then statements, would analyse the marks (exam_mark) and print the appropriate grade on the computer's monitor.

```
if exam_mark >= 40 then
    if exam_mark >= 60 then
        if exam_mark >= 80 then
            writeln('Distinction')
        else writeln('Merit')
    else writeln('Pass')
else writeln('Fail');
```

A **case statement** is often more convenient when constants are used for the test condition. For example, if a program was written in which the user types in a number representing 'days of the week', then making use of the convention that 'Monday = 1', 'Tuesday = 2'... 'Sunday = 7', then, assuming that a variable called 'day' had already been typed in and checked for range, a case statement can be used instead of a huge row of if-then-else statements as follows:

```
case day of
    1 : writeln('Monday');
    2 : writeln('Tuesday');
    3 : writeln('Wednesday');
    4 : writeln('Thursday');
    5 : writeln('Friday');
    6 : writeln('Saturday');
    7 : writeln('Sunday');
end;
```

It is a pity that standard Pascal does not allow the use of ranges (as well as constants) for the case labels at the beginning of each line. However, other languages, such as Modula-2, do not have this restriction.

From reading the above you may be thinking that the case statement is very restrictive and not able to cope with the examination-results type of example considered earlier. However, an extension of the case statement using multiple case labels (conditions) together with some clever programming will show you that this is not so. Consider the following:

```
test = exam_mark div 10;
case test of
0,1,2,3 : writeln('fail');
4,5 : writeln('Pass');
6,7 : writeln('credit');
8,9,10 : writeln('Distinction');
end;
```

Making use of the 'exam_mark div 10' part of the first line – this takes the integer examination mark and puts the variable 'test' equal to an integer value which is the result of dividing the exam_mark by 10. Therefore, for

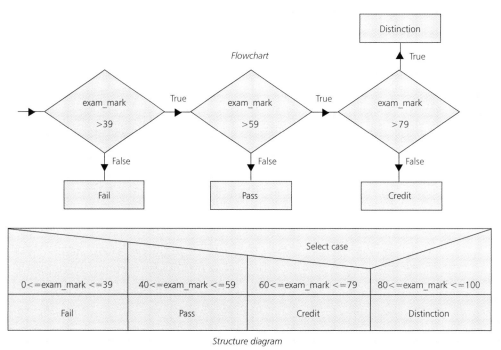

Flowchart

Structure diagram

Figure 13.12

any marks between 0 and 39, test would yield just 0,1,2 or 3, as indicated by the multiple conditions at the beginning of the first part of the case structure. Marks between 40 and 59 after exam_mark div 10 would yield 4 or 5 etc.

The structure diagram and flowchart representation for the examination-mark problem is shown in figure 13.12. It is obviously necessary to keep the nested-if-then-else structures, as more complex conditions and tests making use of different variables are possible. Nevertheless, if the case structure can be used efficiently, it's usually easier to read and understand the final code.

The 'dreaded' goto

The **goto statement** is a statement which might be more usefully described as an 'out-of-control statement' rather than a control statement! Ever since the late 1960s the goto statement (or **unconditional branch statement**) has been considered awful programming style – as misused it often leads to **spaghetti code**. This is not some unique pasta recipe, but refers to the control statements getting so tangled up with each other that it resembles a plate of spaghetti.

One of my favourite examples is a BASIC program written by one of my 14-year-old students way back in the late 1970s (see

> **Hint:** There are few reasons to make use of the 'goto' statement in modern programming. Avoid it if you possibly can, it makes your programs easier to understand by other people.

figure 13.13). (He was not one of the brightest in the set.) The code obviously does not work – but you ought to be able to get the program working for him – shouldn't you? It's worth spending ten minutes of your time if you are not convinced that 'gotos' can be easily misused.

Assuming that you have some idea of what the program is meant to do (and that's not totally obvious from the lack of comments and zero documentation), you will probably find it almost impossible to debug. It would be far easier to start again from scratch. Professional programmers can't afford to make a mess of the work they do, especially if other people have to work with them in a team. This is why structured programming (and more-recently object-oriented programming – see chapter 15) is so very important, and the 'goto' should only be used (if at all) with extreme care.

Some high-level languages have abolished the goto altogether, but in others it can still have its uses, most notably in BASIC and FORTRAN. Nevertheless, the arguments over whether it should go or stay are not over yet. It is probably best to sit on the fence and have the opinion that it should be used very sparingly, and only in essential situations where the clarity or efficiency of the program is improved.

In Pascal, the goto statement takes on the following form:

```
goto label
```

where label is a number which has a maximum of 4-digits. The label is used by placing it in front of the statement, which represents the destination for the jump. Therefore

```
 10 PRINT"What number do you want        220 Y = Y -50
    converted to Roman Numerals?"        230 IF Y < 10 THEN 270
 20 INPUT Y                              240 PRINT"X"
 30 IF Y < 1000 THEN 80                  250 Y = Y - 10
 40 PRINT "M"                            260 GOTO 230
 50 Y = Y - 1000                         270 IF Y < 9 THEN 300
 60 GOTO 30                              280 PRINT"IX"
 70 IF Y < 9000 THEN 1000                290 Y = Y - 9
 80 PRINT"CM"                            300 IF Y < 5 THEN 330
 90 Y = Y - 900                          310 PRINT"V"
100 IF Y > 500 THEN 130                  320 Y = Y - 5
110 PRINT"D"                             330 IF Y < 4 THEN 360
120 Y = Y - 500                          340 PRINT"IV"
130 IF Y < 1000 THEN 200                 350 IF Y < 4 THEN 360
140 Y = Y - 100                          360 IF Y = 0 THEN 400
150 PRINT"C"                             370 PRINT"I"
160 GOTO 130                             380 Y = Y - 1
170 IF Y < 90 THEN 200                   390 GOTO 350
180 Y = Y - 90                           400 PRINT"IS THE ROMAN NUMERAL
190 PRINT"XC"                            EQUIVALENT TO ";X
200 IF Y < 50 THEN 230                   410 END
210 PRINT"L"
```

Figure 13.13

```
goto 999
 .
 .
999: Statement to be executed after the
     goto-999 unconditional jump
```

When making use of these labels during programming, the label must be declared in a label declaration at the beginning of the program (see later).

Repetition structures

One of the reasons why computers are so good at what they do is their ability to **repeat** *sequences* many times. This is also commonly known as **iteration**. Certain fundamental repetition structures are common to most high-level languages, and these will now be considered. It should be noted that the syntax of different high-level languages varies more widely to some extent when considering these structures, but the same ideas (semantics) are used by all.

While loops

The **while loop**, also known as a **do-while loop**, or **do loop**, checks a **Boolean condition** *before* carrying out any of the statements that would be executed if the condition is true. It should therefore be noted that if 'while loops' are used, the statements may *never be executed* if the Boolean expression is false. Compare this with the repeat-until loops in the next section.

As with most structures, the statements shown in the grey boxes in the example of figure 13.14 could also be other structures too, and, as we have seen before, count would be called the control variable.

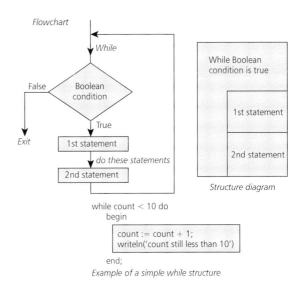

Flowchart

While

Boolean condition

False

True

Exit

1st statement

2nd statement

do these statements

while count < 10 do
  begin
    count := count + 1;
    writeln('count still less than 10')
  end;

Example of a simple while structure

While Boolean condition is true

1st statement

2nd statement

Structure diagram

Figure 13.14

Repeat loop

The **repeat loop**, also known as the **repeat-until loop** has the structure shown in figure 13.15. It should be noted that the Boolean condition is not examined until the loop has been gone through once, therefore, with repeat loops, *the statements are always executed at least once*, even if the condition is such that the loop is terminated immediately.

> **Hint:** Computers are in their element when doing repetitive tasks. Make efficient use of these methods and you will find that your programs are usually shorter and more efficient. A thorough understanding of these structures is essential.

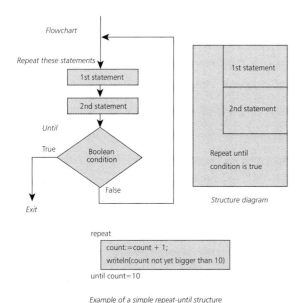

Flowchart

Repeat these statements

1st statement

2nd statement

Until

True

Boolean condition

False

Exit

Structure diagram

1st statement

2nd statement

Repeat until condition is true

```
repeat
    count:=count + 1;
    writeln(count not yet bigger than 10)
until count=10
```

Example of a simple repeat-until structure

Figure 13.15

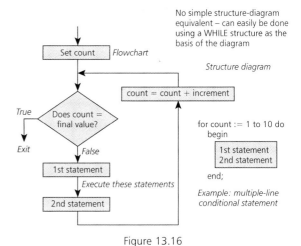

No simple structure-diagram equivalent – can easily be done using a WHILE structure as the basis of the diagram

Set count   *Flowchart*

Structure diagram

count = count + increment

True

Does count = final value?

Exit   False

1st statement

Execute these statements

2nd statement

```
for count := 1 to 10 do
    begin
        1st statement
        2nd statement
    end;
```

Example: multiple-line conditional statement

Figure 13.16

For loops

The **for loop,** or **for-to-next loop** as it is sometimes known, appears in many high-level languages. It is often compiled (see chapter 32) more easily than the **repeat** or **while** loops mentioned above, because of the close relationship between the control variables used and registers in the machine. (An increment, test and branch is all that is necessary to implement this loop in common machine code operations – see chapter 20.) This type of loop therefore often executes more quickly in some languages.

With this loop the number of repetitions is fixed, and controlled by a variable, which is incremented from 'some minimum' to 'some maximum' in 'integer' or 'non-integer' steps. Decrements from 'some maximum' to 'some minimum' are also easily possible. An example of this type of loop is shown in figure 13.16. As with the 'repeat' and 'while loops', 'for loops' may also be nested.

Between them, **'for-to'**, **'repeat-until'** and **'while-do loops'** cope with most of the situations needed for good structured programming techniques, and indeed the **repeat until** and **while-do** loops can often be interchanged, for example,

repeat loop statements until condition_red

has exactly the same effect as

while (not condition_red) do loop statements.

You should note that it is *very bad practice* (that will often cause an error) to jump into the middle of one of these loop structures from outside the loop, but it is usually *acceptable* to exit from within a loop structure.

The bad habit just mentioned can easily be accomplished by the use of a 'GOTO' or an 'if-then statement', but many languages do provide exit or break statements which allow legal jumps out of the loop from arbitrary points within. Nevertheless, if you can code your algorithms without doing this, then the code is usually a lot easier to read.

Pascal allows you to jump out of a loop but will not allow you to jump into a loop, unless you are jumping to some other part of the same loop from within.

We have already seen the use of the nested-if-then-else loops, and many other loop types can also be nested. However, you must obey the rules of loops which, simply stated, require that each loop (or structure) is completely embedded within another with no overlapping. Examples of these simple rules are shown in figure 13.17.

Examples of nested-loop structures

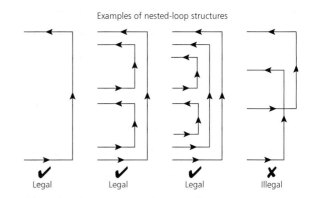

Legal   Legal   Legal   Illegal

Figure 13.17

Functions and procedures

You are probably well aware of the need to split up larger problems into smaller more-manageable chunks which perform specific tasks (see chapter 14) and you should also be aware of the need to make use of set-routines many times, if necessary, during the execution of a program. The next few sections concentrate on how a typical high-level language enables the programmer to carry out these essential modularisation principles.

One of the main concepts of **structured programming** revolves around breaking up the tasks to be solved into much-smaller subtasks, and therefore the ideas of **functions** and **procedures (or subprograms)** are of fundamental importance. Both functions and procedures can be **called by name**, and this adds to the readability of the overall program. They also prevent the same code being written more than once if it is needed in many different parts of the program. We can thus often shorten the program considerably if these two techniques are used extensively. Other important techniques of programming such as **recursion** are covered in chapter 18.

> **Hint:** If you wish your programming to be as efficient as possible, then it's essential that you make extensive use of functions and procedures. It also helps the all-important modularisation of your programs.

A 'function' is often similar in nature to a 'procedure', but you should understand the important differences between them. These differences stem not only from the uses to which these different techniques are normally put, but also from fundamental differences in their operation. A **function** is used in a *similar way* to the **built-in functions** that are available from within the definition of a language, whereas a procedure (see next section) is most often used like a completely self-contained program, which performs a specific subtask.

Functions

The end result of a function is that the **function identifier (name)** has a **value assigned to it** *after* the function has been executed. This is *not* the same as what happens when a procedure or subprogram is executed.

The built-in functions that are supplied with a programming language might be functions like 'square roots', 'logs' and the trigonometric functions such as 'sin', 'cos' and 'tan'. Many Pascal built-in functions have been defined earlier. However, there is no built-in function for working out the hypotenuse (longest side) of a right-angled triangle, for example. Therefore, using Pascal, we will invent one ourselves and call it hypot. As no function definition for hypot exists from within the language itself, we must obviously define hypot in detail ourselves, and this can be done as follows:

```
function hypot (var side1, side2 :
real) : real;
```

```
begin
   hypot :=
sqrt(sqr(side1)+sqr(side2))
end;
```

In the above function, two parameters (i.e. the variables called side1 and side2 which represent the other two sides of the triangle) are real numbers passed over to the function from the calling routine. The value returned from the function (hypot), which has been assigned its value by the maths expression contained within the assignment statement, is also real. We can call such a function from within an expression as follows.

```
longest := hypot(x,y);
```

If you are using Standard Pascal then it is worth noting that only single simple data types (see earlier) may be returned from a function.

Functions and factorials

The classic example of a function call is to calculate factorials, but before we start on this example, just a brief reminder of what is meant by a factorial. A **factorial** is denoted in mathematics by an '!' (exclamation mark) and has the following definition:

$n! = n \times (n-1) \times (n-2) \times \dots \times 3 \times 2 \times 1$ and $0! = 1$ by definition.

For example, $6! = 6 \times 5 \times 4 \times 3 \times 2 \times 1 = 720$

If, as in the following function definition, there are variables which are used within the function (in addition to the parameters that are passed to it) then these variables must be declared at the beginning of the function, thus using similar methods to those with which we declared variables at the beginning of the programs.

```
function factorial (n: integer) :
integer;
   var count,product : integer;
   begin
     if (n = 0) or (n = 1) then
product := 1
        else
        begin
          count := 2;
          product := 1;
          repeat
             product := product *
count;
             count := count + 1;
          until count = n+1
        end;
     factorial := product
   end;
begin
   x := factorial(10); (*calls the
```

```
above function*)
    writeln(x);
end.
```

You should compare and contrast this function definition with the **recursive definition** of factorials in chapter 18. Both functions and procedures **may be called from within themselves**, and this powerful technique is known as **recursion**.

Scope of variables and constants

The above factorial function looks innocent enough but illustrates a common problem in many high-level languages, especially if different people are working on different aspects of the program. We have introduced two extra variables within the function called 'count' and 'product'. Now in some languages, (Pascal is not one of them) the entire program would be messed up if 'product' or 'count' happens to be used in other parts too. Mistakes of this nature where variables interact can be a 'pig' to track down, and so the concept of the 'scope of variables' has been introduced.

The **scope of a variable** means *that area of the program which recognises it and therefore has access to it*. If, as in the Pascal example above, the variables have been defined from *within* a **function**, then they are called **local variables** as they are *only accessible from within* the **function** or **procedure** in which they have been defined. However, there may obviously be a need for a variable to be accessed both from within a procedure and from other parts of the program (including other functions and procedures). In this case the variables scope is said to be **global**. In Pascal, global variables are those defined in the variable declaration part of the data description section at the beginning of the program (see the Pascal program-structure diagram in the next section).

It should be noted that although the term variable has been used above, the concept of scope also applies to constants. Therefore, we talk of 'global' and 'local constants' in the same way as 'global' and 'local variables'. It should be obvious that the same name can be used for many different variables and constants if they are defined locally.

Problems with one programmer inadvertently messing up other programmer's data and variables have been addressed in much more sophisticated ways when the alternative paradigm (methodology) of object-oriented programming is used. These techniques are extensively used in C++ and are explained in detail in chapter 15.

Procedures

Only trivial programs are usually written without recourse to **procedures**, and the main body of many highly complex programs often consists only of a few statements and calls to procedures! Each procedure is known by a different name, which hopefully relates to the task which that particular procedure undertakes.

A **procedure** is usually **called** by stating its **name**, and although not essential, it is often necessary to **pass parameters** to the procedure from the calling routine. These **parameters** are simply the names given to the values (information) *being passed* to (or obtained from – see in a moment) a procedure. After being called, control is passed to the procedure and the statements contained within the procedure are executed (which could include calls to other procedures or functions). When the procedure is finished, control is **returned** to the statement *after the one* from which the procedure was called. Don't forget that both procedures and functions can be called recursively (i.e. from within themselves – see chapter 18).

In Pascal a procedure definition takes on the following form:

```
procedure tempconvert (var cent :
real);
var fah :real;
   begin
      fah := (9*cent/5)+32;
      writeln(cent, 'centigrade is the
same as ',fah, 'fahrenheit');
   end;
```

To call the above simple procedure (which takes a centigrade temperature, converts it to fahrenheit and then prints out the answer with a message) we could make use of the following procedure call:

```
tempconvert(reading)
```

which, if reading = 50, for example, would result in

```
50 centigrade is the same as 122
   fahrenheit
```

being displayed on the computer's monitor after the procedure had been executed. Therefore, the original variable 'reading' has had its value passed over to the variable 'cent' which is then used to calculate the variable 'fah' used to print out the information from within the procedure.

Hint: Make sure that you understand the difference between passing by value and passing by reference. It may help you to sort out some of the problems which occur when using procedure calls.

Sometimes it's useful to use two distinctly different methods of passing parameters (the values given to the variables) between the procedure and the calling routing. These two methods are now explained in the next couple of sections.

Passing by value

It's usually good practice to define *all variables used within a procedure* as being **local**, then they won't inadvertently get mixed up with any other variable that might happen to have the same name in other procedures or elsewhere in the program. Remembering that a 'parameter' is just a 'value given to a variable'. If we use a parameter-passing routine in which the 'original variable' used to pass the parameter is *not altered, then only it's value has been passed*, and this method is therefore called **passing by value**, i.e. the procedure can only modify a 'copy of the original variable', *not* the 'original variable itself'. The address at which the original variable is stored has *not been referenced*, and the original variable can't therefore be altered by the action of this procedure call.

Passing by reference

An alternative to **passing by value** would be to let the variables inside the procedure be allowed to **reference** and therefore alter the actual variable that passed it. Thus the variable used to pass the value *has been referenced and irrevocably altered*, and this method is called **passing by reference**. Note this time that it's *not* 'just a simple copy of the parameter which has been made', but the 'actual address' at which the original variable lives has been **referenced**, and the original variable has thus been permanently altered by the action of this procedure call.

Overall program structure

We have seen how structures operate within a language, but most high-level programming languages must themselves adhere to a strict overall structure. (BASIC is one of the exceptions, though structured BASIC can be well written if you apply similar self-imposed rules.) Pascal's structure, for example, consists of a program header, label declarations, data descriptions, procedures and functions, and then the main block of the program which may consist of many sub blocks. The overall structure for a Pascal program is shown in figure 13.18.

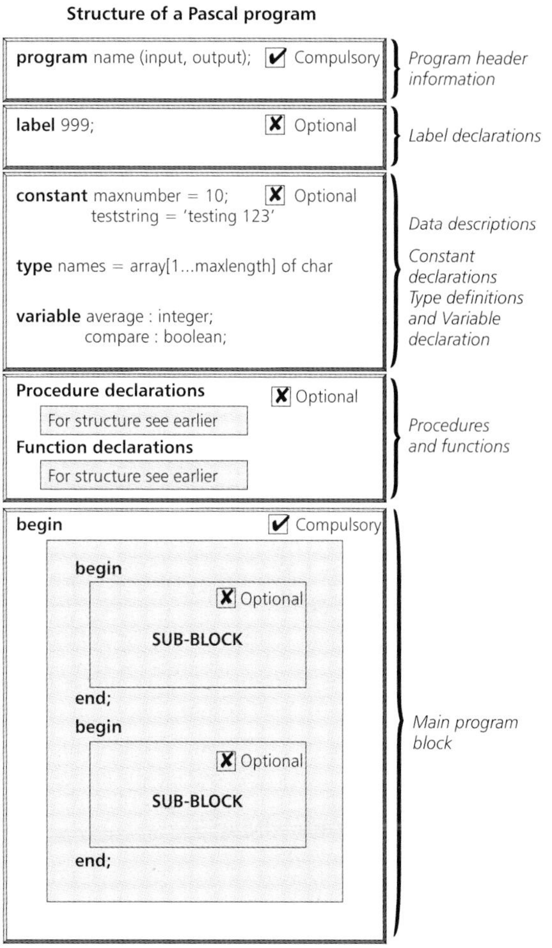

In chapter 15 on high-level-language examples, other structures are considered in detail, most notably COBOL.

We have indeed come a long way from the days when programs were a simple linear sequence of instructions with a few simple loop structures. The structured programming techniques outlined in this chapter have been developed with several decades of hindsight, and represent the best in current structured program techniques. However, this chapter has concentrated on one main **paradigm**, that of **imperative languages**. You should refer to the software-examples in chapter 15 to look at some of the alternative paradigms such as 'object-oriented programming', 'functional programming' and

'declarative programming'. Nevertheless, do not forget that as languages develop there are large overlaps. For example, even though C++ is an object-oriented language, most of the Pascal features outlined in this chapter are also available in C++. Therefore, the different methodologies are not mutually exclusive, but enhance each other to a great extent.

Visual programming methodologies

At this level you should learn about language structure so that concepts are easily developed and questions may be answered in examinations with relative ease. For example, you could easily demonstrate how parameters might be passed to a procedure, how recursion or iteration might help to solve problems, or how loop structures might be used to control the flow inside a program. However well written and implemented, these examination-type solutions would not look too impressive now that people are used to all the bells and whistles associated with even the simplest of programs that are now sold in the shops. The common GUI interface has now meant that most programs for the consumer market need to be

Structure of a Pascal program

Figure 13.18

Hint: All the programming methodologies covered in this chapter apply to visual programming too. The syntax will obviously vary from language to language, but most students are usually happy to do their projects using languages like Visual Basic, Visual C++, Visual Java or Delphi, for example. As a teacher, I would encourage you to take this route, but you still need to learn all the structures and ideas covered in this chapter, not least for the examinations!

written with a windows-based front end in mind. It's no longer acceptable to provide solutions to problems that look like they were designed ten years ago! This has led to language developers such as Microsoft and Borland developing Visual front ends to common languages such as BASIC, C++, and Pascal. These developments have been called Visual BASIC, Visual C++, and Delphi (the name given to Borland's Visual version of Pascal).

Although it's possible to program in a windows environment from scratch, it's far easier to use a custom-built development interface. This allows you to create the standard windows components such as scroll bars, buttons, title bars etc. without having to consider the horrendous code and numbers of parameters that would be needed to simulate these operations. It should also be realised that any program in the windows environment is designed to multitask with others. This means that the visual program which you have written must cooperate with the many other programs running at the same time. Don't forget that the other programs are written by other people, and could be running in the background or minimised etc. Therefore, if your program suddenly has the input focus because somebody else's program has been minimised, then part or all of the window for your program might need to be redrawn so that you can carry on with what you were doing. These are very complex operations, which are intimately tied up with the operating system. Only professional programmers used to dabble in such a complex programming environment, but the visual front ends mentioned earlier allow you to program in these environments very easily by using tools similar to those shown in figure 13.19. Here you can see the visual-development environment for Microsoft's Visual BASIC professional Version 5.

Here you can see a screen shot showing one of the projects, which I get the Year 10 GCSE students to develop. As you can see from this statement, use of such an environment is possible with 14 or 15-year-old students in a very controlled way. It really is very easy to place 'command buttons', 'frames', 'combo boxes', 'images' and 'drive-list boxes' and so on, i.e. all the components necessary to develop professional-looking front ends. The hard part is knowing how to write good programs, and you are already well on the way to an understanding of typical program structures from

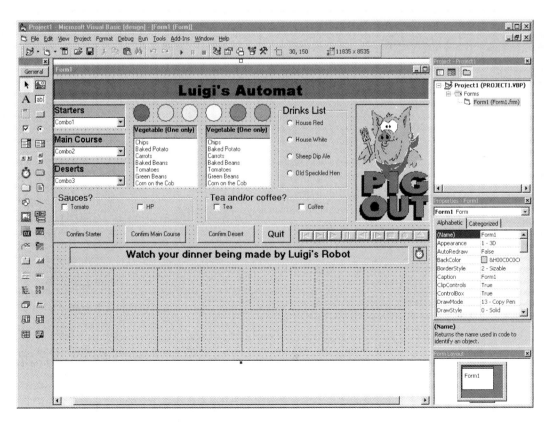

Figure 13.19

reading this chapter. The very hard part is being able to get to grips with the enormous increase in specialist syntax, which accompanies such a versatile visual environment. Also, with the addition of controls like 'Active X' these environments are developing all the time, and being good at and keeping up with such developments takes a considerable investment in time, usually far more than is available to most students of computer science. However, all these development environments are ideal for advanced level computer science projects, and certainly makes for a more professional and exciting project environment than the conventional programming techniques alone.

Finally, notice how it would be very difficult to simulate such environments under examination conditions. This is why you will be stuck with writing programs in conventional ways for examination purposes in the foreseeable future – at least until examinations are taken from a computer terminal, and perhaps this may not be too far away!

Exercise 13.2

1 What is meant by the term **enumerated data type**?

2 Using a high-level language of your own choice, explain how **subscripted variables** are used to access the elements within a two-dimensional array.

3 Explain how the **pointer data type** helps to implement structures such as linked lists and trees. (These structures are covered in chapter 14.)

4 What does a conditional jump or branch in a high-level language mean?

5 Compare and contrast the use of the 'repeat until' and the 'while do' loop structures.

6 Outline the *basic rules* that apply to **loop structures**.

7 Why is the 'goto statement' often outlawed and when is it 'safe' to make use of it?

8 Compare and contrast the use of **nested if-then structures** and the **case structure**.

9 What are the main differences between a **function** and a **procedure**?

10 In a high-level language of your choice write some code to work out the area of any circle making use of a function call.

11 In a high-level language of your choice, show how a procedure might be used to input and work out the average of a list of five integer numbers.

12 Explain what is meant by the scope of a variable making sure to use the terms local and global variables in your explanation.

13 Explain what 'passing by value and passing by reference' means when programming making use of procedures.

14 Why is it best to have a strict program structure such as that shown in the Pascal example on page 291?

15 The development of visual programming environments has made GUI based programming considerably easier. What features of these GUI-based systems enable this to be the case.

End of chapter revision aid and summary

Cover up the right-hand column and see if you can answer the questions or define the terms on the left. They appear in the order in which they are covered in this chapter. Alternatively you may browse through the right-hand column to aid revision.

What is a high-level language?	A high-level language is a convenient method of instructing the computer in a way that is in both human readable and machine-readable form. It is a problem-specific rather than a machine-specific language.
What is a formal language?	A high-level language is an example of a formal language, whereas most human languages such as English are examples of natural languages. Natural languages are context sensitive, formal languages are not.
What is syntax?	Syntax is the grammatical rules that govern the layout and use of a language.
What is semantics?	Semantics is the meaning that is applied to a language.
What is software engineering?	Software engineering is the methodology, which embraces the documentation, maintenance, debugging, testing and analysis etc. when using computer languages or other applications to solve problems.
What is a first-generation language?	First-generation languages are assemblers.
What is a second-generation language?	Second-generation languages are the unstructured high-level languages.
What is a third-generation language?	Third-generation languages are the structured high-level languages.
What is a fourth-generation language?	Fourth-generation languages are the SQLs and the like.
What is a fifth-generation language?	Fifth-generation languages are the very-high-level languages like Prolog, and this term also refers to the languages used to drive expert systems.
What is an imperative language?	Languages can be classified into different main paradigms or methodologies. Imperative languages or procedural languages typify the 'how to do it' way of programming.
What is a declarative language?	Declarative languages typify the 'what to do' way of programming.
What is a functional language?	Functional languages have parameters that are passed to functions from expressions which are being evaluated, and then these values are returned from the functions to the calling expression.
What is an object-oriented language?	Object-oriented languages are based on objects, which represent single units which encapsulate both functions and data.
What is a reserved word?	Reserved words represent identifiers used by the language such as 'if' or 'then'.
What is an identifier?	An identifier is a name, often chosen by the programmer to identify variables or special functions, files or procedures etc. It can't usually clash with keywords.
What is a keyword?	Keywords are reserved words which represent some language construct such as PRINT or IF or COS etc. They can't be used as identifiers.
What is a syntax diagram?	Syntax diagrams are often helpful when defining the syntax of a language. This pictorial method makes it easy to see if you are conforming to the syntax rules.

What is a variable?	A variable is the name given to an identifier chosen by the programmer, which represents some value, that can vary during the execution of a program.
What is a constant?	A constant is the name given to an identifier, which is not allowed to change its value. A constant is also called a literal.
What is a string?	A string is literally a string of characters (usually bound by delimiters).
What is a statement?	A statement is a descriptive phrase in a high-level language, which generates one or more machine-code instructions.
What is the 'order of precedence'?	The order of precedence determines the order in which arithmetic expressions will be evaluated.
What is a numeric data type?	Numeric data types are integer and real, for example.
What is a Boolean data type?	A Boolean data type can only have a true or false value.
What is an enumerated data type?	An enumerated data type is one that contains a list of data items.
What is a sub-range data type?	A sub-range data type is a sub-set of an enumerated data type.
What is a structured data type?	Structured data types such as files, for example, can have their contents dynamically altered during the execution of a program.
What is an array?	An array is a data structure consisting of one or more dimensions. A one-dimensional array is a linear list of data items, and a two-dimensional array consists of rows and columns of data. Multi-dimensional arrays are possible in many languages.
What is a subscripted variable?	An array is usually referenced by a subscripted variable.
What is a set data type?	Set data types are fixed lists of data items and relate to the idea of sets in maths.
What is a record data type?	Record data types mirror the record structure in a file, but can be set up in other structures like arrays.
What is a file data type?	File data types are files stored in main memory or, more usually, on disk. They make use of record data type substructures.
What is a pointer data type?	Pointer data types are the dynamic data types used to implement the pointer systems in linked lists, queues and trees etc.
To what does the basic structure of a language refer?	Basic structures within a program refer to linear, control and the repetition structures that are available.
What is a linear structure?	A linear structure is one in which one statement is executed after another in some pre-defined order.
What is a control structure?	A control structure is one in which control can be passed to different parts of the program.
What is a conditional statement?	A conditional statement is the if-then-else type statement.
What is a case statement?	A case statement can test for a multitude of conditions.
What is a repetition structure?	A repetition structure is one of the 'while', 'repeat' or 'for' structures.
What is a while structure?	A while structure executes statements only while a condition is true. If the condition is never true no statements can ever be executed.

What is a repeat structure?	A repeat structure will repeat a set of instructions until a condition is false. If the condition is always false the statements will be executed.
What is a for loop?	A for loop is used to execute a number of statements controlled by a counter with the control variable controlling the count.
What is a function?	A function is a sub-program which is usually called from within an expression, and whose name acts as an identifier which represents the value returned.
What is a procedure?	A procedure is a completely self-contained subprogram, which may be called from the main program.
What is parameter passing?	Parameter passing means passing values to or getting values back from a procedure.
What is passing by value?	Passing by value means the value of the variable used to pass the parameter to the procedure is not altered.
What is passing by reference?	Passing by reference means referring to the variable used to pass the parameter and thus the value of the variable used to pass the parameter does get altered.
Explain the term 'program structure'.	Many high-level languages require that a strict program structure be adhered to. For example, headers, label declarations, data description, procedure and function definitions and the main body of the program are typical in Pascal.

14 Structured Analysis and Design

Key resources

To carry out this work most successfully it's best if you have:

◆ No special resources are needed for this chapter

Concept Checkpoints

◆ It's essential that you are familiar with the basic programming structures as outlined in chapter 13.

◆ Specifically the ideas of sequence, iteration and selection are particularly important.

◆ You will need some experience of programming in a high-level language like Pascal, Delphi, Visual Basic, or ordinary Basic, for example.

Introduction

The first part of this chapter is concerned with the all-important initial stages of structured algorithm design. We will not be too concerned with specialist algorithms as are covered in the chapters on sorting and searching for example, nor specifically in making use of any particular high-level language constructs as are considered in chapters 13 and 15. Here we will concentrate on the basic techniques of how to convey your ideas to other people – and even to yourself if necessary. (It often is!) We will be looking specifically at some of the common diagrammatic and pseudocode methods used to help solve problems and convey important ideas in a structured way. However, a detailed discussion of the high-level-language constructs covered in chapters 13 and 15 is almost inseparable from the diagrammatic methods used in this chapter. Where necessary, we will illustrate the solution to some of the problems by making use of pseudocode (a made-up computer-like language) or a typical high level language. It should also be well understood that solving problems on modern computer systems does not necessarily mean writing programs in the conventional sense. It could also mean making use of SQLs as defined in chapter 13, or other similar software packages and applications in which 4GLs and the like play a major part. However, even when these modern and sophisticated tools are used, understanding how to solve problems and convey ideas by whatever means is still of fundamental importance, both in real life and in computer science examinations!

Algorithms

It's most important to realise that the methods we will use at the beginning of this chapter are equivalent to just a few important pieces in an infinitely more complex jigsaw of events that go into making a satisfactory and complete software development environment. This environment is described by the art of **software engineering**, which embraces many aspects of development including the **analysis**, **debugging**, **documentation** and **testing** of complete systems. We will also cover the applications of these principles in practice when dealing with the detailed systems- analysis examples covered in chapter 16, but first let's see what's meant by an algorithm.

A useful **algorithm** is a *step-by-step process* or *sequence of instructions* that can be used to **solve a problem** in a *finite* amount of time.

There's not much point in designing an algorithm that would take an infinite amount of time! For example, a simple algorithm to solve the Towers-of-Hanoi problem is given in chapter 18 where the important concept of **recursion** is covered in detail. Nevertheless, even a supercomputer working at speeds of 100 million moves/sec would take about 6,000 years to perform this particular task! The philosophers among you should also note that some problems are *not* **computable** – this means that no matter how simple some problems may appear to be to us, they have no solution based on the **algorithmic** (step-by-step) approach of computers, no matter how powerful the computer is likely to be! This fascinating area, developed mainly by a brilliant mathematician called Alan Turing, has long been used as the basis for arguments as to whether computers will ever be able to think. These ideas are discussed in more detail in chapter 9. We will now concentrate on computable problems, which can be solved in a sensible amount of time by today's **algorithmic computer technology**.

Basic flowcharts

The flowchart is one of the most basic **algorithmic constructs** (methods for representing algorithms). It has been around for many years and is *still useful* as a precise method of explanation in some circumstances. For example, basic flowcharts are still used in many explanations of Microsoft's **C++ constructs** (this is one of the most-recent object-oriented languages) and as you have probably seen in chapter 13, basic flowcharts also prove to be extremely effective when explaining the Pascal-language constructs. Even so, *the* main use of flowcharts today is in **systems flowcharts** as described in chapter 16. The use of structure diagrams and pseudocode have now superseded many of the more-basic uses to which flowcharts were put in the past. Over-use of basic-flowchart techniques should be avoided, as the resulting charts can become unwieldy and counter-productive.

Flowcharts in this basic form are therefore not adequate for all but the most basic documentation (such as the language construct explanations mentioned in chapter 17) and are inadequate for professional use when describing complex systems. Nevertheless, the basic flowchart symbols form an important subset of the popular **systems-flowchart symbols**, and deserve separate consideration.

> **Hint:** Flowcharts are ideal for a pictorial way to describe certain structures and some programming methodologies. However, they are not useful for the overall solution to a complex problem, and this is why so many other methods are considered in this chapter.

Systems and program flowcharts

There are **several different forms of flowcharts** with correspondingly different symbols and uses. We will start by looking at what are commonly called program flowcharts, because they were originally used to chart

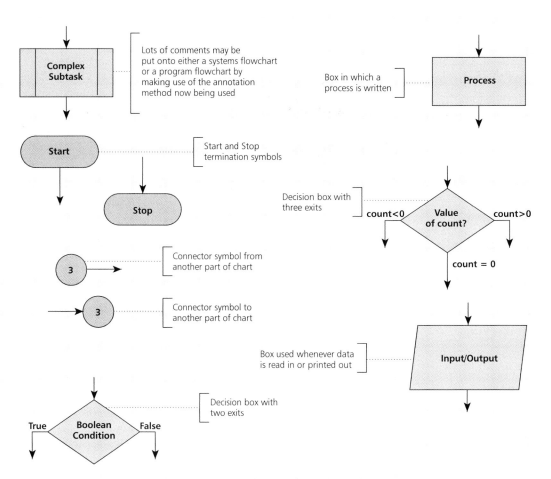

Figure 14.1

the detailed workings of programs. The basic shapes used in program flowcharts are shown in figure 14.1. Program flowcharts produce far too much detail when a problem becomes large and complex, and the overall structure of the problem is often lost in the mountain of interconnected boxes. They also do not cope easily with systems concepts such as the interrelation of a mass of different types of equipment and processes.

To get over many of the problems just described, systems flowcharts were developed. Figure 14.2 shows how a typical small part of a systems flowchart (on the left) relates to the more-detailed program flowchart (on the right), via an intermediate flowchart which contains a complex-subtask box (shown at the bottom). This is a particularly simple example, and in practice a single box on a systems flowchart can often correspond to many more boxes on a program flowchart.

A simple program flowchart example

A simple program-flowchart example is shown in figure 14.3. This particular flowchart shows one method of sorting names into ascending order. Take notice of this method as it will be used as an example to compare different techniques of picturing the same problem. Notice the correct use of the box shapes, but note also that inputting names, for example, is generally a more-complex task, perhaps involving validation (see chapter 17) and perhaps making sure that the correct number of names have been entered. Therefore, although data is being input, it is not shown as a trapezium-shape box, but as a 'more-complex task' involving detail not shown on this flowchart for purposes of clarity. Other routines in the chart have had similar treatment in terms of the shapes of boxes to represent the processes.

Flowcharts of this nature are often taught in elementary mathematics classes, but you should work carefully through the chart if you have not used them before, or have forgotten exactly what to do.

Obtaining the final solution

You should note that any useful method should lead naturally on to the next stage in the development of the solution to the problem. In the case of the name-sorting flowchart shown above, the next stage would probably be to write the code making use of a typical high-level language such as Pascal or BASIC. A quick look at the flowchart does not really help very much – does it? A longer look at the flowchart might suggest how the repeat-until or while-do structures covered in chapter 13 map onto this sort of diagram, and it is obviously possible to stare long enough at the flowchart and come up with a sensible structure – but this defeats the point. If a diagram is intended to help with the solution to a problem then it's going to have to contribute much more help than is available from a program flowchart as shown on the next page.

Structure diagrams

As with flowcharts, the basic ideas of one type of structure diagram developed by **Nassi and Schneidermann** have already been introduced in chapter 13. If we were to use these ideas instead of the program flowchart, then the structure diagram for the name-sorting problem could be represented as shown in figure 14.4. Let's pose the same question again – if the next stage in the solution to the name-sorting problem were to

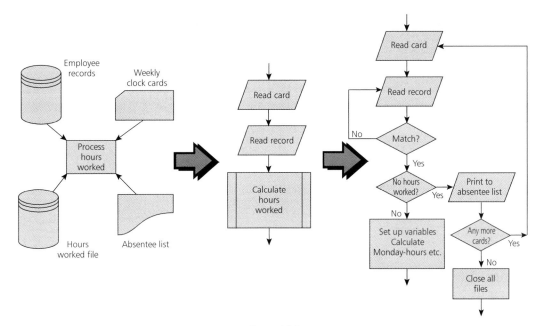

Figure 14.2

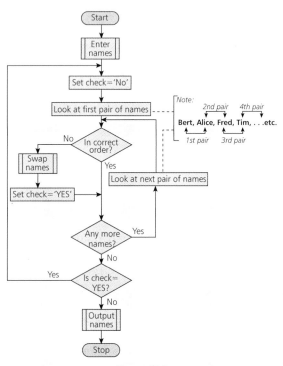

Figure 14.3

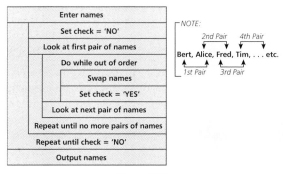

Figure 14.4

write the high-level language code, how long would it take to do this by looking at the structure diagram?

As you can see – the structure of the program instantly jumps out without too much thought. Any complex subtask can then be given similar treatment. Don't forget that in professional circles time is money, and any method that can be used to get to the final goal more quickly has an obvious advantage. However, these diagrams too can become unwieldy if not used with care, but look at the latest Nassi-Schneidermann editing software for windows shown in chapter 17.

Pseudocode

If one of the main goals is to produce code in a suitable high-level language or 4GL, then one might reasonably ask the question – why not do this straight away? Indeed, this is the idea of **pseudocode**. One might also ask – what

is the point of flowcharts if pseudocode can get straight to the heart of the matter? When considering examples such as the simple name-sorting techniques just described, then there is not much advantage in using pictorial methods, if (and this is sometimes a BIG if), you can visualise what the

> **Hint:** Pseudocode is a popular examination solution because it gives an acceptable structure, and allows the student to construct solutions based on the types of language with which he or she is most familiar. It's also a good method in its own right.

code will be straight away. Although this seems obvious today, you must remember that structures such as 'while' and 'case' etc. were not available to the early programmers using second-generation unstructured high-level languages. It was in this sort of development environment that the program flowchart was first extensively used. With the advent of **third-generation high-level languages, pseudocode** (or **direct coding** in a language such as **Pascal** or **C++** etc.) has become a much more feasible proposition for professional programmers. These languages are now so much more sophisticated than the old languages, that given a suitable number of comments, the program becomes **self-documenting** as far as other professional programmers are concerned. Indeed you may recall that readability is one of the desirable attributes of a language – you can now start to see why.

Some typical pseudocode for the name-sorting problem is given below:

(Note pairs of names are as defined in last two sections)

```
Enter names
repeat
    set check = 'NO'
    Look at first pair of names
    repeat
        while names out of order do
        begin
          swap names
        set check = 'YES'
        end
        Look at next pair of names
    until no more pairs of names
until check = 'NO'
output names Procedure definitions for
            name swapping could go here
```

Note that the **level of indentation** is of *paramount importance* as it gives a **visual indication of the scope of the loops**. It is easy, for example, to see where the inner repeat-until loop is in relation to the outer repeat-until loop. Note also that while the code is Pascal-like, it has not got the correct syntax for Pascal. (Whoever heard of 'Enter names' as being a valid command except, perhaps, in a 4GL.) It is, therefore, **pseudo-Pascal** or **pseudocode**. Indeed, code can be pseudo anything as long as you make use of acceptable loop structures, a logical layout and/or English-like terms. You should pay much attention to writing pseudocode as it is becoming an increasingly important part of examination questions at this level. The obvious advantage of using pseudocode is that the next stage of development is to translate it into an actual language such a Pascal, or BASIC for example, using the exact syntax of the language. This is often trivial compared to trying to do the same thing from diagrams.

Multiple-decision boxes

As program constructs became more sophisticated (for example the introduction of the case structure as shown in chapter 13) it soon became obvious that the basic program flowcharts just described lacked the ability to cope easily with many situations. For example, multiple decisions were particularly clumsy as many decision boxes often had to be drawn. To get over the maximum-of-two-exits problem (or three if just one box is used) the alternative forms of decision box shown in figure 14.5 can be used. Figure 14.5(a) shows a multiple-decision box for the examination-mark case structure considered on page 285, and figure 14.5(b) shows a similar alternative for the 'days of the week' case construct shown on page 285.

Design structure diagrams

In the search for different and more informative pictorial methods of communicating algorithms, alternative flowcharts called **design structure diagrams** provide yet another approach. Figure 14.6 shows the name-sorting algorithm again, but this time developed using the BS6224 (British Standard) design structure diagram. Arrows are not normally necessary in this type of diagram as the structure is arranged such that the flow is exactly as if you were reading a book, i.e. from top to bottom and from left to right.

Design-structure decisions

The name-swapping algorithm just considered, consisted only of while and for structures, and therefore did not demonstrate the ability of design-structure diagrams to handle multiple decisions – because of this a simple example making use of the BS6244 system is shown in figure 14.7. Note that an important role is played by the small diamond shapes in this particular type of diagram – if the condition being evaluated is true then the flow is from left to right, or if the condition being evaluated is false then the flow is from top to bottom. The examination-mark case structure on page 285 is used again for demonstration purposes.

Top down design approach

We have now analysed the name-sorting problem using four different methods – namely **program flowcharts**, **Nassi-Schneiderman structured diagrams**, **pseudocode** and **design structure diagrams**. You can probably now appreciate why pseudocode is so popular! However, each method has its advantages and disadvantages, and you need to do an appreciable amount of work with each method to appreciate the finer points. Nevertheless, even pseudocode becomes unwieldy and often difficult to develop in many cases, and a method called Jackson-Structured Programming (JSP see later) is used extensively in many professional circles to help develop programs by making use of the top-down approach to solving algorithms.

This method of designing systems starts off with the ideas at the highest level, and then progressively works

> **Hint:** The top-down approach is an ideal way to describe how you intend to start solving a complex problem. Use it extensively in the systems analysis phase of your project.

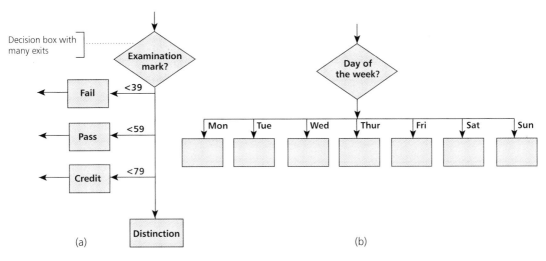

(a)   (b)

Figure 14.5

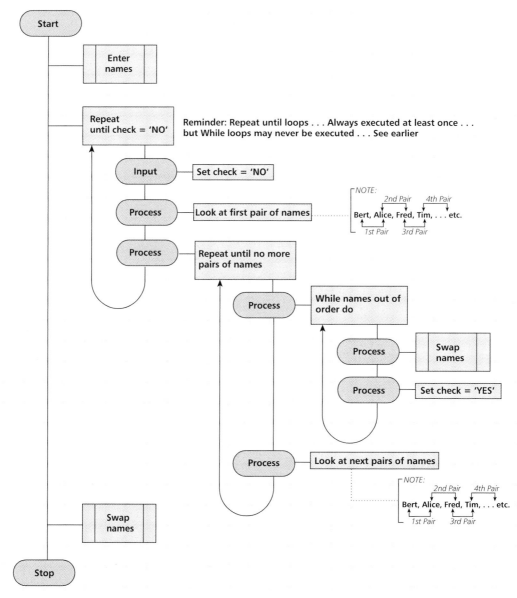

Figure 14.6

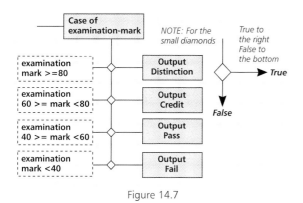

Figure 14.7

down to the **lowest level of detail**. This method of analysing a problem revolves around **hierarchical data structures** as described in the next section. Many systems can be described in terms of a hierarchical

(family-tree type) data structure and a typical example is shown in figure 14.8.

Starting at the top, you can see the highest-level idea is the production of a sales report. The next level in the hierarchy involves data initialisation and generation of the main report headings (notice how we work from left to right along the same level). However, when you arrive at the individual-report-body box, this has a sub level, which must be executed, before going on to write the cumulative totals. Indeed, for the most-likely scenario of many sales-people records, the bottom level of this structure chart would be repeatedly executed until there were no more records (we will see how to modify such diagrams for these loops very shortly). Next, control would pass to the write cumulative total box. We are then at the end of the second level – and so we return to the top level and the problem has been executed.

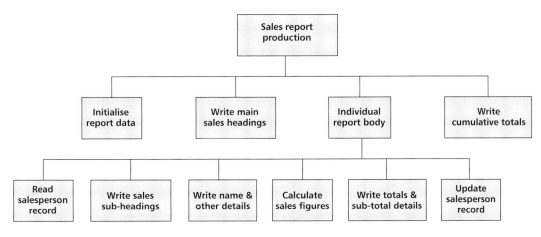

Figure 14.8

The visual advantage of this type of structure diagram is obvious, and is ideal for implementation by the JSP methods to be covered shortly. Notice how easy it is to produce pseudocode from this type of chart as the levels of hierarchy mirror the levels of indentation of the loop structures.

Assuming that many records will be read from a file, some typical pseudocode to match this top-down structure could be as follows:

```
open files and initialise report data
write main sales headings
repeat
    read sales-person record
    write sales-person sub-headings
    write name and other personal
                            details
    calc. sales figures
    write analysis of figures
    write analysis to record
until end of file
write cumulative totals
```

From the above structure diagram or by using the above pseudocode, a high-level or 4GL language program could easily be constructed.

Bottom-up design approach

The bottom-up approach to systems design *starts with* the lowest levels of detail and *works up to* the highest level of the idea. The top-down approach to developing algorithms and systems seems so obvious that the bottom-up approach is *often neglected*. The normal reaction of students who have used the top-down-design approach is to ask 'How on Earth can anyone work up from the bottom without knowing what they are working towards?' This seems an understandable attitude until the techniques of bottom-up design are more fully explained. From a programming perspective, bottom-up design is equivalent to writing modules or procedures first. This technique is often used when **prototyping** a module before joining it on to the main system. You can then glue the whole system together like bricks, which go to make up a wall – but starting from the bottom. Viewed in this light the bottom-up approach seems eminently sensible, although you still obviously need to know what you're trying to work towards. The bottom-up approach does not mean having no plans!

On a more common-sense tack – if you know that certain facilities are not available, then you will have to write them irrespective of the overall grand plan. For example, if you are dealing with a high-level language that does not provide facilities for manipulation of a particular data structure (such as complex numbers or matrices) then you will need to write typical procedures to carry out these elementary tasks.

In fact, the bottom-up approach is often used by default, as a method of working out parts of the problem, while you are trying to work out what should be happening on the whole problem! Although this often happens in practice, especially with students at school – it can hardly be put forward as a whole-hearted endorsement of the bottom-up philosophy.

Of course the major problem that a bottom-up approach can generate is in the fitting together of all the pieces into the final jigsaw puzzle – at least with the top-down approach you can ensure that all the pieces fit together at the grand-design stage. Indeed, this used to be such a large problem that the bottom-up approach was not really a viable alternative other than for writing procedures.

In chapter 13, where different programming methodologies are considered, you will recall that one of the

> **Hint:** Prototyping should form an important part of your project strategy. When prototyping, the bottom-up method of problem analysis is ideal. Why not impress the moderators by adding this to the arsenal of techniques which you have already used in your project?

major headaches with the development of complex systems was to do with the unintentional interaction between modules of programs. These modules often interacted with each other in unexpected and very subtle ways, especially if one module, which affected many others, had to be modified. It was this type of scenario that suggested doom for the bottom-up approach to algorithmic design.

With the more-recent introduction of **object-oriented programming** (see chapter 15), bottom-up approaches (or variations on this theme) have been revived. You may recall that these objects are not easily messed-up by other programmers' code. One can develop an enormous number of routines based around objects that could be built up into more comprehensive objects. These could then be built up into useful procedures, that could then be combined into useful utilities, which could in turn be joined onto other utilities – to make up useful programs that . . . you get the idea!!!

A well-balanced viewpoint

You must not forget that the top-down and bottom-up approaches are *not* mutually exclusive. It is not a case of belonging to one camp or the other, but of using combinations of sensible techniques, which are appropriate for the problems in hand.

Exercise 14.1

1   Making use of program flowcharts, solve the following problems. Make sure that suitable annotation is used if clarification of method is needed.

   (a) Read a temperature in fahrenheit and convert it into centigrade making use of the formula C = 5(F–32)/9. The process is halted when –999 has been entered.

   (b) Determine the largest and smallest numbers from a list of ten numbers, then automatically output the two answers.

   (c) Read in an unspecified number of examination marks where pupils are allowed to score between 0 and 100 inclusive. Make sure that any data outside this range is ignored, and an appropriate message printed out. Work out the average examination mark for the correct number of valid examination scores, and make sure that your program does not crash if no marks are entered.

   (d) Read an unspecified quantity of positive and negative numbers whose range is checked to be between –500 and +500 inclusive. The data is to be terminated by –999. Output how many positive, negative and zero numbers there are in the list.

   (e) Create a basic four-function calculator. The user should enter an operator (+, –, / or *), followed by the two numbers to be used in the calculation using the convention that the top number or first number in the calculation should be entered first. After checking for a valid operator and performing the correct calculation, the correct answer should be output. The calculations should terminate when a '$' is entered.

2   Making use of Nassi-Schneidermann structure diagrams, solve the problems in question (1) again.

3   Write pseudocode algorithms to solve the problems in question (1). Make use of the Nassi-Schneidermann diagrams in (2) if you have answered this question.

4   Convert the pseudocode algorithms of question (3) into code in a high-level language of your choice. Execute the code and get the programs working.

5   Compare and contrast the top-down and bottom-up approaches to solving problems giving convincing examples of where each method would be best suited to the solution of a particular problem.

6   Why have object-oriented programming techniques contributed to the resurgence of the bottom-up approach to algorithmic design?

Other structured analysis and design techniques

Jackson structured programming

This methodology was invented by the famous Michael Jackson. Not the pop singer of course, but the famous computer programmer, when writing his book Principles of Program Design. It is a method, which is ideally suited to problems that can be expressed as **hierarchical data structures**, such as those described by the **top-down-approach**. As this includes most of business data processing, you can see why this particular method is so popular with students and professionals alike.

Sequence

JSP makes use of **top-down structure diagrams** to give an indication of the **sequence of operations** to be carried out. The levels on the structure diagram are important because some operations are made up of a sequence of others. Therefore, in figure 14.9(a), for example, P is made up of the sequences Q, R and S, and in turn S is made up of the sequence T and U. Notice that although this diagram is equivalent to the linear sequence PQRSTU, structure has been implied from the hierarchy of the diagram, and may, for example, imply different procedures representing each box.

Iteration (loops)

The **notation for a loop** or **iteration** is an '*' (asterisk or star) which is normally written in the top right-hand side of the box which represents the iteration (loop structure). We obviously need to know what conditions are in force. On JSP diagrams this condition would normally be referenced by a number, which in turn refers to the actual condition written down in what is called a condition list. This saves the JSP diagram from becoming cluttered up. The idea is shown in figure 14.9(b). In this diagram W is repeated until the 'end of file' is reached.

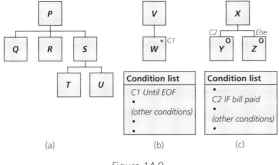

(a)   (b)   (c)

Figure 14.9

Selection

A **selection structure** is indicated on a **JSP diagram** in a similar way to an **iteration**, but this time we may need **more than one box,** and the symbol for selection is different and is indicated by a small 'o'. Figure 14.9(c) shows a selection structure whereby Y is executed if the condition is true else Z is executed. Of course any number of boxes could be used with the different conditions terminated by an 'else'.

When using JSP techniques you must ensure that **all the children in the diagram are of the same type**. In other words, when using JSP diagrams, and when considering any element in the structure as a parent (i.e. an element with sub-structures) the parent should not have children where the brothers and sisters are mixtures of sequences, iterations and selection structures. (Note that we are using parents, children, brothers and sisters etc. as used in the tree-structure diagrams shown in chapter 25.) This is not such a restrictive practice as might appear at first sight, as dummy boxes with a suitable comment (see figure 14.10) can easily be inserted to help obey these rules which are designed to make coding the structure easier. This is explained in the next section.

An example using JSP

As a very simple example, let's suppose that we wish to work out some statistics on an unspecified quantity of people's ages to the nearest year typed in by the user. Let the **rogue value** (i.e. the terminating number which is not part of the data) be –999. Let's also suppose that the following statistics are required:

The mean (or average) age
The maximum age
The minimum age

A typical JSP diagram for this example is shown in figure 14.10. Note that we could have added further detail like how the variables are set up or how the statistics are output, but these are trivial and have been left out for the sake of clarity – they have been included in the pseudocode that follows shortly. Notice that we have stuck to the rule that all components must only have children who are of the same type – we had to introduce the process-data box and the determine-max-and-min box to conform to these requirements in this particular JSP structure. Note also that the selection boxes at the bottom of the structure have no else part, therefore the simpler version shown in this diagram is acceptable. (There's not much point in drawing an empty box for the do-nothing situation if the condition C2 or C3 is not true.)

There is very much more to **JSP** than is indicated in the brief description here, but this will enable you to make use of these useful structure diagrams in your projects as part of suitable documentation if necessary.

The real beauty of JSP lies in the next stage. It really is a doddle to derive the pseudocode (or most high-level language code) directly from the structure diagram, and the following part of a Pascal program demonstrates this wonderful correspondence between the structure diagram and the final code. JSP really is to be recommended.

```pascal
program statistics(input,output);
var
age, sum, min, max, number : integer;
average : real;
data : boolean;
begin
  sum := 0;
  max := 0;
  min := 500;
  data := false;
  repeat
    write('Enter age ');
```

```pascal
    readln (age);
    if age<>-999 then
        begin
          if (age < min) then min :=
                                   age;
          if (age > max) then max :=
                                   age;
          sum := sum + age;
          number := number + 1;
        end;
      else
        begin
          data := true;
        end;
  until data = true;
  average := sum/number;
  writeln('The average age is  ',
                          average);
  writeln('The maximum age is ', max);
  writeln('The minimum age is ', min);
end.
```

Although **hierarchical data structures** (either **top-down** or **bottom-up**) may seem like the best thing since the invention of sliced bread, they do have their limitations in terms of *lack of information* when formulating some problems. For example, does anything go on in parallel with anything else? How much information will be transferred between one database and another? However, other methods, developed by Gane and Sarson start to address these problems, and are considered in more detail a little later in this chapter.

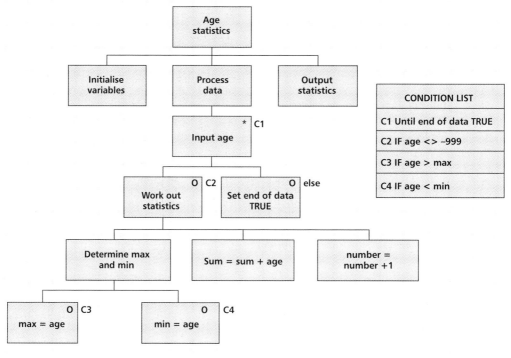

Figure 14.10

HIPO charts

A **HIPO chart** (Hierarchical Input Processing Output) is an IBM structured chart technique which helps analysts to visualise the **overall plan of a project** rather than the detailed coding. The HIPO chart *emphasises the relationships* between the elements of a system. It's the same idea as the normal hierarchical chart, but with extra information regarding the function of each module or program. A simplified example of a HIPO diagram is shown in figure 14.11.

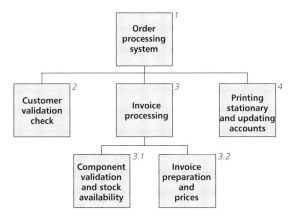

1   Controls all processing and calls the customer validation, invoice processing and delivery note printing system.

2   Receives customer number, performs validation check and checks credit worthiness of customer. Returns flag to main processing routine.

3   Accepts component numbers as input and calls routines to validate component, access prices and keep a running total of cost and availability of stock.

3.1   Validates component number, accesses and updates stock file, generates message if component is not available.

3.2   Produces invoice on screen, accepts data and messages from validation routines, accesses price files and updates the invoice on screen.

4   Prints out delivery notes for stores and updates accounts using invoice information.

Figure 14.11

As can be seen from figure 14.11, the HIPO chart is useful for asking questions like 'What does each module do?' and 'What are the inputs and outputs?' On more-comprehensive HIPOs we could obviously include more information, and go to a much-greater depth of detail. It is often more convenient to make use of a HIPO chart than to write down the same information in a long sequence of text.

Keeping the software writing on schedule is important in the business world. We have already seen how structured methods reduce the time spent on coding the software, and later in this chapter we shall see how the structured approach helps with the testing too.

Data flow analysis

The hierarchical data structure diagrams, good as they are for showing relationships between software modules and with helping to code programs, can't show many of the data interactions which are going on in many real-life systems. For example, how do we analyse how data gets transferred between different departments in a factory when computers, pieces of paper, people, and perhaps specialist machines such as CNC lathes and robots (see chapter 8) are involved? How do we cope with a telephone call from New York in our system diagram? How do we include a human messenger as part of the shop-floor flow of data in the factory?

Data flow diagrams

Fortunately there is another useful tool in our 'structured-analysis toolbox' in the form of a **data-flow diagram** or **DFD** as it is sometimes known. These methods were developed by Gane and Sarson, and initially used extensively by the McDonnell-Douglas Corporation. Other companies also developed similar methods. The **data flow diagram** can be a representation of a **physical system** such as 'specific people' or 'machines', or it can represent the **logical data flow**, which is a device-independent diagram drawn without any reference to the physical characteristics of the system. However, both types of diagram make use of the same four basic symbols, which are as follows.

Data flow symbol

The first symbol is a simple arrow as shown in figure 14.12(a). This simple data-flow symbol shows the direction of the flow of data from any source to any destination in whatever form. Therefore, there is no distinction between documents or telephones or disks or any other media.

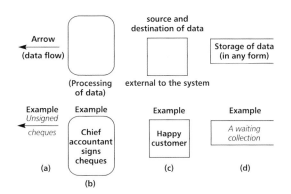

Figure 14.12

Process symbol

The Gane and Sarson symbol for processing is shown in figure 14.12(b). We could not care less about the physical device that is actually carrying out the process, so this can represent anything from a person undertaking a process to an automatic stock validation procedure carried out by a computer.

Source or destination symbols

The symbol shown in figure 14.12(c) shows any source or destination, which is outside of the system. For example, if a stock-control system is being considered, then the storekeeper could be drawn making use of this symbol. Other examples might be incoming mail or a department in a factory that makes use of the system.

Data store symbol

This symbol, shown in figure 14.12(d) represents the storage of data in whatever form. So it could be anything from a computerised CD-ROM drive to a pile of paper.

The above symbols are obviously so general that the names, which accompany them, must be very descriptive of the actual processes that are taking place. Nevertheless, the terminology of these diagrams is so simple that they can be of great use in explaining the system to experts and non-experts alike.

Data flow example

The best way to get an understanding of data-flow diagrams is to make use of them. Therefore, we will develop a data-flow diagram using a simple example.

Suppose that we wish to analyse what happens in an office where Sue, the accounts clerk, processes requests for the payment of expenses in a company.

A typical scenario would be that an employee brings along a filled-in expenses sheet, then Sue verifies the signature, transfers the information into the computer system, and makes sure that a particular budget is not over spent. If successful, then a cheque must be raised, signed by the chief accountant, then put in a tray ready for collection via Sue. How do we show these typical transactions on a data-flow diagram?

> **Hint:** Pay attention to these data flow examples. This methodology could help you to describe the solutions to some parts of your projects, which are very difficult indeed to do by other methods.

A good start to many of these problems is to mirror the actual physical situation, which is going on in the office as shown in figure 14.13. The very process of doing this often helps the analyst (and the people in the office) to understand exactly what is going on. Indeed, it is only after doing such an analysis that people often see a better way of carrying out a process that they have been doing without much thought for years.

The first stage in the process is obviously the request from the employee, and so the employee, being a source of data (in this case bringing the expenses form), is shown in a source box. Next the arrow from the employee must show the flow of data (in this case the expense form) ready to be picked up by Sue. Hence

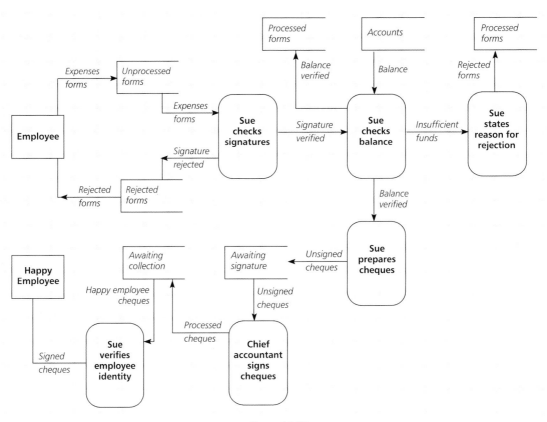

Figure 14.13

we need a data-flow arrow, going from the employee to Sue's 'in tray', with expenses form written on the arrow.

Now Sue's 'in tray' is a data store, and so a data storage symbol with unprocessed forms written on it has been used for this purpose. You can see that it's pretty obvious what's happening. This diagram is intended for non-specialists. When some sort of processing takes place, such as Sue checking the signature (i.e. the fact that the expenses form has actually been signed, and countersigned by an appropriate person), then this takes place in the appropriate shaped box too.

You should have little difficulty in following the logic of a data-flow diagram, but there are certain checks that you can do to try to ensure that the system is correct. For example, does each data-flow arrow have a name associated with it? Do all processing components have both inputs and output? Have all the data store components been used?

There are many more sophisticated uses of the data flow diagrams but an understanding of the sort displayed in figure 14.13 is all that is necessary at this level. They are really useful for describing parts of your projects that the other diagrams can't reach.

State transition diagrams

It is often convenient for us to consider a physical or logical object as being in one of a number of different states. For example, if we are considering a physical object such as a burglar alarm, then an event could activate this object such that it changes state. The states of a physical object such as a burglar alarm just described could be 'disarmed', 'armed but not activated', and 'armed and activated'. An event such as a burglar entering the premises could cause the alarm to change from 'armed but not activated' to 'armed and activated'. Another event, such as pressing the reset button could cause the state of the alarm to be changed to 'disarmed'.

Figure 14.14 shows what's often referred to as a **state-transition diagram**. This particular example shows what can happen with our simple burglar alarm system.

Note that we have three buttons which, when pushed, cause events *a*, *b* or *r* to happen as defined in figure 14.14. We have allowed any button to be pushed from any state. For example, if the alarm is in the disarmed state, then pressing reset (*r*) or the burglar entering the house (*b*) would not cause the state of the alarm to change. By following with your finger on the diagram you can predict which state transitions will occur when any event happens.

The state-transition diagram in figure 14.14 referred to physical objects, which represented the state of an alarm. However, state transition diagrams are not limited to physical objects. Software states (logical states) can be represented too. For example, when a program or job is being run by an operating system (see chapter 23), the program may be in a ready state (i.e. waiting to have some CPU time), or it might be in a running state (making use of the CPU). Events such as a time-out interrupt might flag the end of the CPU time slice, and this event may cause the state of the program to change from 'running' back to the 'ready state' (waiting to be run). Another typical scenario is that a program under the control of an operating system might be waiting for input or output. In this case it will have to be locked out of the cycle which gives it its time slice until the peripheral activity has taken place.

A state transition example

Figure 14.15 shows a typical state of affairs (pun intended!) for the OS problem.

Each of the three states of a program is shown within the 'circles', and the state-transition arrows show each event, viewed from an operating system (OS) perspective. The dispatcher is part of the operating system software which has the job of dispatching (shown by event *d*) the program so that the CPU may run it. If the program is going to hog the CPU for a long time then an interrupt will cause it to time out (shown by

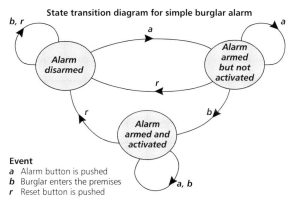

State transition diagram for simple burglar alarm

Event
a Alarm button is pushed
b Burglar enters the premises
r Reset button is pushed

Figure 14.14

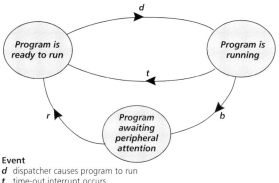

State transition diagram for operating system processes

Event
d dispatcher causes program to run
t time-out interrupt occurs
b program blocked from running
r program is reactivated

Figure 14.15

event *t*). If a peripheral request is made during the execution of a program then the running of the program is blocked by the operating system (shown by event *b*). Finally, when the peripheral request has been serviced the program is ready to be reactivated (shown by *r*). This means that it is ready for a further stint of CPU time when the dispatcher is able to get round to this particular program again.

State transition diagrams are extensively used in theoretical courses on computer science, where mathematical models of computation using the algorithmic approach of computers is considered in detail. These diagrams help to cope with the basics of helping to understand about Turing machines, and thus form a fundamental part of computer science theory. Besides helping with highly advanced theoretical computer science or helping to program a burglar alarm, state-transition diagrams are helpful in developing pattern-recognition algorithms too. For example, suppose we were to design a find-text algorithm for a word processor. Let's also suppose for the sake of argument that we wish to search for the string 'abba'. Now we can go along the text rejecting all characters until an 'a' occurs – let's suppose that this state is represented by Q1 as shown in figure 14.16. Now we either get a

'b' occurring, in which case we go to the next successful state which we will call Q2, or we don't get a 'b' occurring, in which case we go back to an unsuccessful state which we will call Q0. Unless, of course, it was another 'a', in which case we remain at state Q1.

This diagram would considerably help towards writing some code that could find the string 'abba'. State-transition diagrams often clarify quite complex situations in which the states of processes or objects are continually in a state of change. State-transition diagrams are also useful in black-box and white-box testing (see chapter 17).

Decision tables

This is a tabular arrangement of **conditions** and **actions** arranged as a matrix of rows and columns. There are alternative systems, but the most common type of decision table is shown in figure 14.17. The table can be considered as being divided up into **four main quadrants** as shown in figure 14.17(a). In the *top left quadrant* we list the **conditions** or **questions** which are to be involved in the decision-making process, and in the *bottom left quadrant* we list the **actions** that can be taken. Considering the top right quadrant, we put Yes or No in the boxes depending on which conditions are applying in a particular column. In this we are building up rules which are given the numbers 1, 2, 3, etc., where each rule is determined by the vertical column underneath each of the numbers in the top-right-hand quadrant. Finally, in the bottom right-hand quadrant we list the **actions selected** or the results, which relate to the rules indicated in the columns above.

> **Hint:** Decision tables offer a unique way to describe problems, which are difficult to tackle in other ways. Make use of them in your projects if it is appropriate to do so.

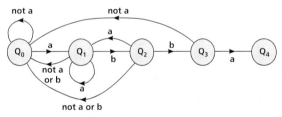

not a   not a
               a
Q₀ a Q₁   Q₂ b Q₃ a Q₄
    not a   b
    or b

    a
not a or b

Q₀ Unsuccessful search so far
Q₁ A single 'a' has been found that could belong to the sequence abba
Q₂ An 'ab' has been found that could belong to the sequence abba
Q₃ An 'abb' has been found that could belong to the sequence abba
Q₄ We have found the sequence abba

Figure 14.16

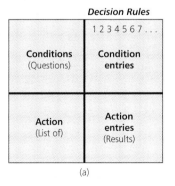

Decision Rules

	1 2 3 4 5 6 7 . . .
Conditions (Questions)	**Condition entries**
Action (List of)	**Action entries** (Results)

(a)

Conditions	1	2	3	4	5	6
Date is numeric.	N	Y	Y	Y	Y	Y
$1 <= month <= 12$	–	N	Y	Y	Y	Y
$1 <= day <= 31$	–	–	N	Y	Y	Y
month = 9, 4, 6 or 11	–	–	–	Y	–	–
day = 31	–	–	–	Y	–	–
leap year	–	–	–	–	Y	N
month = 2	–	–	–	–	Y	Y
day > 28	–	–	–	–	–	Y
day > 29	–	–	–	–	Y	–
Actions						
Reject date	X	X	X	X	X	X

(b)

Figure 14.17

You should note that when considering the conditions selected by rule number in the top right-hand quadrant, Y and N represent Yes and No respectively, and a '–' means that the condition is not appropriate. However, when considering the actions selected in the bottom right-hand quadrant, an X is used to denote that a particular action has been chosen.

Let's suppose that we wish to validate (see chapter 17) a date in the form dd/mm/yyyy. This is a classic case where a decision table is ideal for making a tabulated list of the conditions and actions. If, like the author, you can't remember how many days are in each month, then you will probably resort to the well-known rhyme:

> Thirty days has September
> April, June and November.
> All the rest have 31,
> excepting February which has but 28 days clear,
> and 29 in each leap year.

So, putting the above algorithm into action, we can derive the decision table shown in figure 14.17(b). To gain an understanding of how the table works, you need to see how the conditions have lead to the production of the rules.

First let's consider rule number 1 which is shown vertically in column (1) in the top right-hand side of the table. Looking at the first condition, if the date is not in numeric form, as indicated by the N (e.g. 6th June 1999 might have been entered) then we do not accept the date irrespective of any other condition that may be met. Therefore, if we have already rejected the date on this criterion alone, (as shown by the X in the action-entries section) then none of the other conditions need apply, as is indicated by the '–' entries for the remainder of rule 1.

Now for rule 2, we are assuming that the date is in the correct numeric form, as indicated by the Y entry in the second column. We must therefore take into account the next condition, namely 'Is the month between 1 and 12 inclusive?' If it is not, then the month is invalid, we can reject the date (as shown with the X entry at the bottom of column 2) and any further conditions are irrelevant.

For rule 3, if the date is numeric and the month is OK, but the day is outside the range 0 to 31 inclusive, then these conditions are sufficient to reject the date. The process continues in this way until all possible conditions, which could be used to reject the date, are accounted for. The rest of the table is constructed by continuing in this way.

Linked decision tables

It's often convenient to link several decision tables when solving more-complex problems. When linking tables the action that may be taken may often refer to another table. For example, we could have a list of actions which include 'Do table 1' or 'Do table 2' etc.

Used in this context the decision tables become part of a larger structured diagram with pointers between the tables.

A linked decision table example

To illustrate this idea let's consider a simple business in which there are two types of customer. Those with an account who can have credit, and those without accounts who must pay cash. Let's also suppose that discount is available to credit (*account holding*) customers at the following rates.

		Goods	< £100.......	5% discount
£100	≤	Goods	< £1000.....	10% discount
£1000	≤	Goods.	....	15% discount

Now suppose that the *cash-paying* customer gets a slightly higher rate of discount as follows:

		Goods	< £100.......	10% discount
£100	≤	Goods	< £1000.....	15% discount
£1000	≤	Goods	....	20% discount

Figure 14.18 shows how the tables may be linked, and how they can form part of a more-comprehensive decision-table diagram. By linking tables in this way, the size of each table can be more easily controlled.

Decision trees

Decision trees form another tool in our arsenal of structured-analysis techniques. They are identical to the trees, which are used in elementary mathematics to calculate probabilities and are extremely easy to use. We can use the customer status and discount-information data in the previous section to analyse the problem again, but this time making use of a decision tree.

As can be seen from figure 14.19, working from the root we can easily see which decisions must be made first. We must decide which condition satisfies any particular situation and then follow the appropriate branch of the tree. Eventually, after all the appropriate conditions have been fulfilled, we will end up at the leaf of the tree where the action to be taken is encountered.

You must not forget that **time** is also a valuable resource, which must be managed effectively if we are to make sure that complex projects are completed on time. All the analysis techniques considered so far have not included the time factor, but the **Gantt charts** and **PERT charts** considered in the next section will redress this balance.

Gantt charts

A **Gantt chart** is similar in nature to the specialist calendar charts which display the whole year on a horizontal month-by-month basis. However, instead of an arbitrary year, the actual project-activity time from

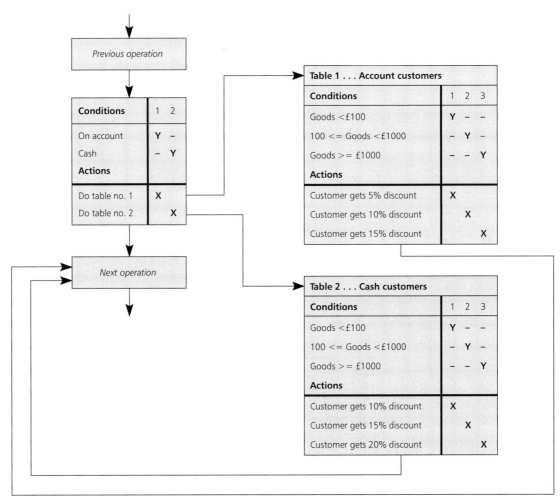

Figure 14.18

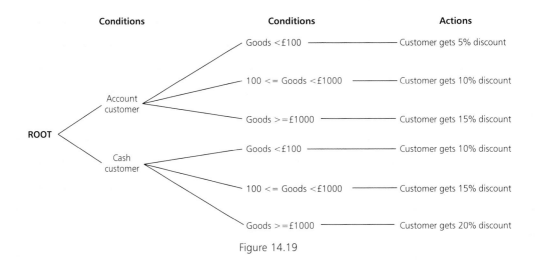

Figure 14.19

conception to completion is expressed at the top of the chart, usually in weeks. A typical example is shown in figure 14.20. The information shown here relates to the overall project structure, but other Gantt charts may be used for sub-sections of the project.

Although designed specifically for larger projects, I would advise you to make use of a Gantt chart in your own project. You will probably find that you have not got the experience to map out the exact times which will be needed, but you *have* already got the project activities mapped out in detail if you have bothered to do a structured analysis of your project! You can get your lecturer or teacher to help you with the likely project times – you'll be amazed at how much help this will give.

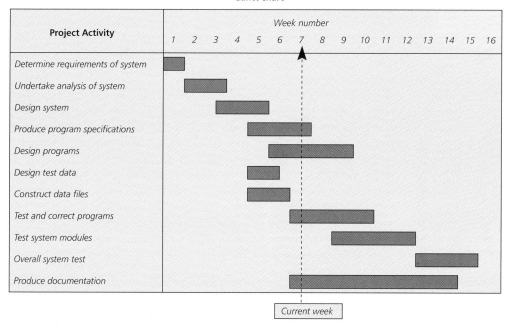

Figure 14.20

The biggest advantage of producing a **Gantt chart** is that it shows if you are *on schedule*. If one part of the project is taking considerably longer than expected, then you will obviously have to do something drastic or revise the time taken to do the rest of the project activities. This is a sobering thought as the deadline for handing in the project approaches. In industry and business, other activities like employees' holidays etc. can also be included on the chart.

> **Hint:** Use Gantt charts in your project if possible. You will be surprised at how it can concentrate the mind, especially with respect to that time when deadlines are approaching!

Although ideal for planning the simpler projects, a **Gantt chart** is *not sufficient* for an **analysis of the dynamic nature of many large projects**. For example, what happens if an expected utility is not ready? If other project activities depend on this particular piece of software, then these other activities will be delayed too. On complex projects a delay in one critical activity might result in an unacceptable extension to the project time, and usually results in the all-too-familiar over-budget scenario. As large projects often run into millions of pounds or more, this is an unacceptable state of affairs. The critical activities need to be identified and appropriate action such as putting more members of the programming team on these activities might be necessary if the overall project is not to go over the scheduled time and budget.

Pert charts

PERT (**Program** (or **Project**) **Evaluation** and **Review Technique**) **charts** have been popular for managing large projects ever since the US navy made use of this system way back in the 1950s when the Polaris Submarine project was being managed. The idea is that a project can be spilt up into activities and events.

One of the *problems* with the **top-down approach** considered earlier is that although it breaks up the project into smaller and more-manageable sections, there are no facilities to check if the overall progress of the project is being efficiently managed. Project managers are often required to ask questions like 'What shall we do next?' or 'Can this be done at the same time as that?' or 'We can't get on with X because Y has

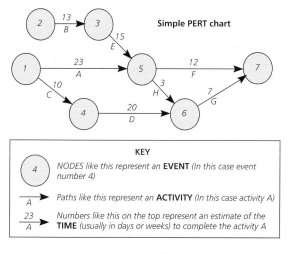

Figure 14.21

happened...therefore, what shall we do?' The Gantt or hierarchical charts don't give a visual indication of the interdependence of modules within a project.

Event timing

Consider figure 14.21, this shows a very small PERT chart, but the main ideas are embodied in this simple diagram. Here you can see that the project has been divided up into 7 events and 8 activities. Let's concentrate on event 5 in this system, and let's suppose that this event represents 'Completion of the testing modules'. Now we can see from the diagram that event 5 can't be completed until activities A and E have been done. Activity A might be 'Construct data files' which will take an estimated 23 days work, for example, and activity E might be 'Design the test data' which will take an estimated 15 days. (This assumes that the units of time on the chart are in days.)

> **Hint:** Pert charts are probably too tedious to implement without the specialist software. You don't need to use them on projects, but they are invaluable on large industrial projects, which need to be completed on schedule.

Obviously more-complex PERT charts than this would be needed for most projects, but one of the main advantages of using a PERT chart is in the ability to calculate the **critical path**, i.e. **the path which effectively dictates the completion time of the project.** If we analyse the PERT chart shown in figure 14.22, then we can see that the path 2 – 3 – 5 – 7, which takes an estimated time of 13+15+12 = 40 days dictates the time that the project will take, assuming that everything goes to schedule. However, everything does not normally run to schedule, and this is where the PERT chart comes into its own. Suppose that activity C is delayed and takes 15 days. The new critical path now becomes 1 – 4 – 6 – 7 which will take an estimated 42 days with the revised time for activity C.

If you are wondering how tedious it would be to manually recalculate these critical paths on a large project, then you need not worry because **PERT computer programs** have been doing this for years. They form an established part of project management and are an extremely effective tool both in the software industry and elsewhere.

Earliest starting times

An added dimension to the PERT chart which helps tremendously with effective project management is 'How early may we be able to start an event or how long may an event be delayed without endangering the overall project schedule?' This too can be worked out automatically by computer, but figure 14.22 shows a modified version of figure 14.21 in which this new information has been added.

To fill in the extra 'time information' you proceed along the following lines:

Events 1 and 2 can be started instantly, it does not depend on anything that has gone before; therefore, the earliest and latest event times are trivial and are both equal to zero.

Concentrate next on the top numbers only. Let's choose event 3, as it is one of the next in the chain. Now there is only one previous event (event 2) and so we simply add 13 (the time taken for activity B) to the zero already established in event 2 to get the next time of 13 which is written in the *top* of event 3. (*Don't forget it's top numbers only for the moment!*) Event 4 can be filled in by using an identical method.

Concentrate now on event 5, but again, top numbers only. There are two scenarios:

(1) Activity E   Preceding time 13   Event E time 15
    Total time 28

or (2) Activity A   Preceding time 0   Event A time 23
    Total time 23

Therefore, the earliest event time for event 5 must be 28, the largest of these two numbers, *because the 2 – 3 – 5 path will be the critical factor here* for the earliest start time if we are waiting to complete event 5. Proceed in the above manner until all the top numbers have been filled in. Note that the number in the top-right hand side of the final box denotes the minimum amount of time needed to complete the whole project.

Latest start times avoiding delays

Next let's concentrate on the *bottom numbers only*, namely, 'How late can we start an event without delaying the project-completion time?'

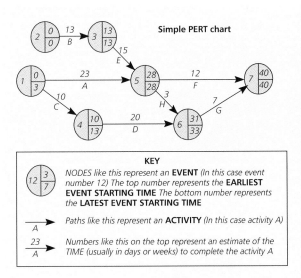

Figure 14.22

◀ Plate 17
A fingerprint security system for use when extracting cash from the machine makes this particular ATM more secure than most

▼ Plate 18
Silicon chips go into smart cards such as those used by Vodafone. Information may be read from the card by an appropriate machine and then other information may be stored back on the card after it has been used. The chip contains an in-built microprocessor, which contains a central processing unit that can store, secure and act on the information

◀ Plate 19
Inside a factory that is probably far cleaner than the world's cleanest operating theatre, this machine is manufacturing the very small chips that go inside smart cards, such as the one shown in Plate 18

Plate 20 ◼

Close-ups of the IBM POWER3 microprocessor and the inside of the POWER3 64-bit PowerPC processor die at CA level. With 15 million transistors and the ability to perform up to two billion operations per second, the chip powers the latest IBM RS/6000 SP supercomputer, also known as Deep Blue

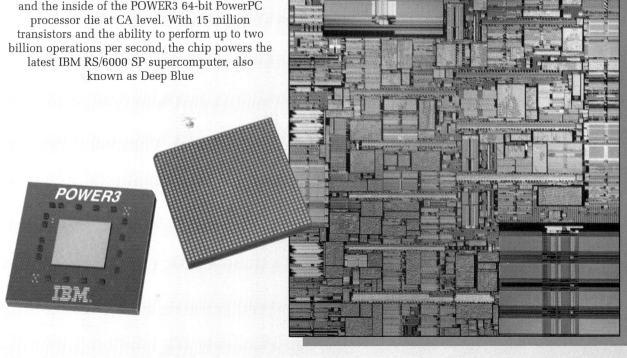

◀ Plate 21

The Psion series 3 PDA is one of the most successful organisers to be launched. It features a range of applications, such as word processor, spreadsheet, database, time manager and digital recorder

For this we start at the end of the PERT chart. If the project is to be completed without delay then 40, being the minimum necessary amount of time must be entered into the bottom box on the last event (event number 7).

Working backwards to event number 6, for example, 7 days would be needed to get from event 6 to event 7, therefore, event 6 must start 7 days before the 40-day deadline at the latest. Therefore, the number 33 must be written in this box.

To determine what the latest starting time would be for event 5, for example, use the following scenario:

(1) Activity F   Succeeding time 40 Event F time 12
    Latest time = 28
or (2) Activity H   Succeeding time 33 Event H time 3
    Latest time = 30

This time we must choose the smallest time being 28 days, as this represents the latest time at which we can start this activity without delaying the project.

All the calculated values for these times are shown in figure 14.22. Even with this simple PERT chart a project manager can start to see the flexibility which may be inherent in some activities. For example, Activity 4 could be started on day 10, or delayed until day 13, but activity 5 must be started on day 28, or the project will be delayed. The *critical path is given by events 2 – 3 – 5 – 7*, and any activities on this particular path can't be delayed.

Exercise 14.2

1   Explain why Jackson Structured Programming (JSP) techniques are particularly useful for the production of the source code for many common types of algorithm.

2   Show, making use of suitable **diagrams**, how 'sequence', 'selection' and 'iteration' (loops) are implemented making use of JSP techniques.

3   Use a JSP diagram to develop an algorithm to read in an unknown quantity of names and examination marks terminated by 'dummy', –99. The names are to be sorted into categories of pass (mark > 40%) and fail (mark < 40%). The algorithm is to produce a list of names of the students who have passed, a separate list of names of the students who have failed – both lists being in order of descending marks. You may assume that a utility exists to sort the names and marks into descending order.

4   Why is a HIPO chart sometimes more useful than a conventional hierarchical diagram?

5   Construct a typical data-flow analysis diagram for handing in your assignments to be marked by your tutor or teacher. You should allow for marks to be entered into a register and for terrible work to be returned to be re-marked if necessary. You should also allow for a list to be made of students who have not handed in their work!

6   List two or three different types of problem in which a state-transition diagram could help with

the solution. Use a state-transition diagram to show how a security-lock system can be used to control entry to a computer centre. Use a unique 4-digit code of your choice, and the system should activate an alarm if more than 3 incorrect digits are entered without some form of corrective action taking place. You may assume that a reset button is available if you think that this is necessary.

7   The following decision tree shows the delivery charges made by a furniture-manufacturing company. Show the same information making use of a decision table.

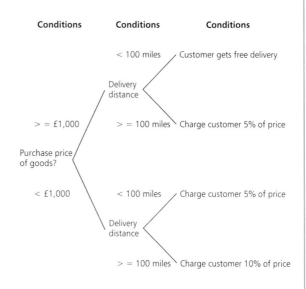

8 What is meant by a Gantt chart and why are they extensively used in project management? Why are Gantt charts less useful for showing the dynamic nature of some projects?

9 What characteristics of project management are best analysed by making use of a PERT chart? Using a simple example explain what is meant by critical-path analysis (CPA).

End of chapter revision aid and summary

Cover up the right-hand column and see if you can answer the questions or define the terms on the left. They appear in the order in which they are covered in this chapter. Alternatively you may browse through the right-hand column to aid revision.

What is software engineering?

Software engineering is the name given to the analysis, debugging, testing and documentation of a system.

What is an algorithm?

An algorithm is a step-by-step sequence of instructions to solve a particular problem. An algorithm may be expressed in many ways including English-like statements or many different forms of diagram.

What is a basic flowchart?

Basic flowcharts or program flowcharts are useful to describe relatively simple algorithms in a pictorial way, making use of termination symbols, processing symbols, input/output symbols, decision symbols and connection symbols. Complex systems can be described by making use of systems flowcharts. Flowcharts should be annotated (with added comments) where possible.

What is a structure diagram?

Structure diagrams are a useful and often better alternative to the flowchart because they mirror the structured programming constructs more closely.

What is pseudocode?

Pseudocode is useful for describing algorithms in a structured way. It makes use of English-like statements which mirror modern structured high-level languages.

What is the top-down approach?

The top-down approach to project design means splitting up complex problems into easier and easier subtasks until each subtask is of manageable proportions.

What is the bottom-up approach?

The bottom-up approach to project design involves using pre-written routines and procedures, which can be used to construct a more comprehensive system.

What is Jackson structured programming?

Jackson Structured Programming (JSP) techniques take hierarchical diagrams a stage further by including the concepts of sequence, iteration (loops) and selection. It is often very easy to produce pseudocode from JSP or structure diagrams, but not so easy from flowcharts.

What is a HIPO chart?

A HIPO chart is a structure diagram specifically to emphasise the relationships between the elements of a system but with added annotation.

What is a data-flow chart?

A data-flow diagram makes use of data-flow symbols, process symbols, source or destination symbols and data-store symbols. It is ideal for showing how data moves around in virtually any environment.

What is a state-transition diagram?

A state-transition diagram is useful for representing physical or logical objects, which can be in a variety of states. An event causes the state of an object to change.

What is a decision table?

A decision table consists of conditions and actions, condition entries and action entries. Numbered rules are derived which give the conditions under which appropriate action is taken. Linked decision tables often help to reduce the size of a decision table to make its use more manageable.

What is a decision tree?

A decision tree is a tree structure consisting of conditions, which must be executed to arrive at an appropriate action.

What is a Gantt chart?

A Gantt chart is a static time-management chart useful for visualisation of an overall project.

What is PERT?

A PERT (Project Evaluation and Review Technique) chart is a dynamic time and resource management chart, which enables time-critical paths to be calculated.

15 Further High-level Languages

In this chapter you'll learn about:

◆ Many of the different high-level languages which are in current use

◆ Simple programming in many different high-level languages

◆ Basic principles of object-oriented programming

◆ How a particular language might be evaluated against others

Key resources

To carry out this work most successfully it's best if you have:

◆ Access to a wide range of high level languages such as Pascal, Cobol, Fortran, Basic and C++

◆ Access to other languages such as Prolog and LISP could also be useful

Concept checkpoints

◆ It essential that you have a good working knowledge of the material covered in chapters 13 and 14.

◆ To complete a tiny part of the work in this section involves a knowledge of a few concepts in later chapters (specifically chapter 24). You should return to this work if your are unhappy first time round.

Introduction

Having read through chapters 13 and 14 you should now be well placed to appreciate the evolution and development of high-level languages in a more general context. You should appreciate the need for structure, the need for efficient analysis and coding, the need for self-documentation, and the need for the many other desirable facilities that go into making up modern high-level languages. You have already seen that high-level languages belong to different classes such as imperative, declarative and object-oriented, and should also be aware of the differences between the generations of languages. As systems become ever more complex, the need to strive for absolute correctness is now one of the most fundamental and demanding problems that need to be solved by computer scientists. Unfortunately, at the moment, we are a long way from being able to achieve this for very complex programs, either theoretically or in practice. Finally, you should now also be wise enough to appreciate that it's neither possible nor desirable at present to develop a single computer language. If we did, this language would have to be able to cope with the huge variety of different problems, ranging, for example, from control of a chemical plant to dealing with the accounts for millions of customers who belong to a large clearing bank.

All the above introductory work has already been covered elsewhere, so we will now concentrate on looking at particular examples of different high-level languages, and see how they have evolved over the years to get to the current state of play at the beginning of the 21st century. Major languages such as Pascal, Fortran 90, COBOL97 and C++, for example, are considered in some detail, but other, less prominent but nonetheless important languages are covered more briefly.

Student activities

Throughout this chapter you will find a range of student activities relating to the different languages being considered. They have been designed to be simple enough to be carried out within a very short space of time. If your school or college has a compiler for any of these languages then you should use it, if possible, to carry out the suggested activities. Brief answers for each activity using the language concerned can be found in the answer section at the back of the book.

Fortran 90

Fortran stands for Formula Translation, (or Formula Translator). It is *the* mathematical and scientific programming language. The Fortran language is to mathematics, engineering and science, what the COBOL language is to the 'business' or 'data-processing community'. A huge variety of mathematical and scientific applications and utilities written in Fortran have been built up over many years, and *it is probably this above all else that makes the language so convenient* for use by both engineers and scientists. Fortran has most of the built-in facilities and functions to solve their type of problems in ways that are efficient and relatively easy for scientists and engineers to understand. It's still the preferred scientific language used for number crunching in the latest generation of supercomputers, especially when used for simulations like forecasting the weather.

The Fortran language was one of the *first* high-level languages to be developed way back in 1954. Being over 40 years old, it has gone through several incarnations, the most recent of which is called **Fortran 90**. As its name implies, this new version is intended to be a language for the 1990s, unlike the older versions such as Fortran 77 or Fortran IV, for example. Many new and powerful facilities have been included giving Fortran 90 a hitherto unheard of ability to process non-numerical information in powerful ways too. It has retained all the advanced mathematical-processing abilities of the older versions, but has been considerably enhanced in the areas in which Fortran was originally lacking. However, Fortran 90's advanced mathematical features are already being extended! For example, direct use of the **parallel-processing architectures** as described in chapter 20 is an attractive proposition for any mathematically intensive language. Work is currently going on in this area where it has proved to be ideal for complex matrix manipulations which Fortran handles with ease. However, until all computers can handle parallel processing, then this feature would considerably reduce the portability of Fortran programs if they were written in this way, unless a mechanism exists for switching between the two modes.

One of the *outstanding features of Fortran* has been its **portability**. Fortran avoided differences in graphics and operating systems etc. by *not* providing any sophisticated input/output facilities in this particular area. (That's one way of doing it!) Third-party vendors tended to produce input/output/graphics interfaces to Fortran programs for their particular machines. Therefore, if you wanted to produce a stunning display with 3D graphics to impress your friends, Fortran would do all the analysis and number crunching, and then pass the data over to routines which control the graphics display – quite a clever idea really.

Did you know that . . .

Fortran 90 is the language used by the Met Office for the millions of mathematical calculations necessary for forecasting parts of the weather. Vast arrays hold the data to be processed by the Fortran programs, and a typical example, solved by a computer capable of 400,000,000,000 instructions per second, can be seen in chapter 7.

Fortran handles complex numbers with ease. (Not hard numbers! – but numbers with real and imaginary parts as used in the Mandelbrot set shown in chapter 18.) Fortran also has a vast array (excuse the pun) of MATRIX functions for manipulating matrices including 'addition', 'subtraction', 'multiplication', 'inverse', 'determinants' and 'transpose' etc. We could program all of these functions from any other competent language, but it's far easier and very much faster if the language supports them in the first place – this is one of the reasons why Fortran has reined supreme in this field. Indeed, the three-dimensional wire-frame image manipulation capabilities making use of transformation geometry can easily be implemented using Fortran – and together with a Vector display of the type described in chapter 11, scientists and engineers are easily able to move complex 3D-wire-frame images around the screen in real time.

Simplified structure of a FORTRAN 90 program

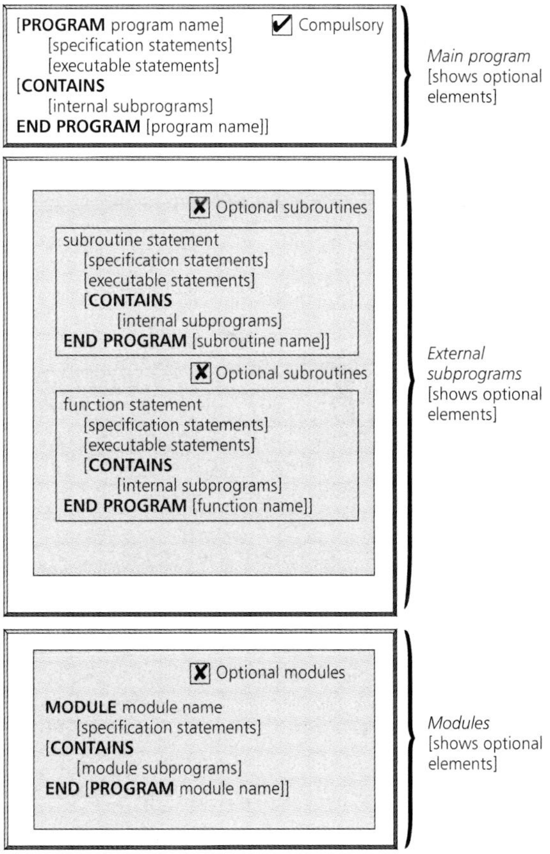

Figure 15.1

In fact wire-frame images and transformation geometry make a challenging project at this level – assuming of course that you don't mind learning the fascinating topic of transformation geometry itself, which is not too difficult and can be found in modern 'A' level or equivalent mathematics texts. If you don't have a Fortran compiler, you can write all the matrix-manipulation commands from scratch in a language like BASIC, for example. However, you will probably have to compile the source code and use a very fast machine, especially if you wish to be able to manipulate a complex image without having time to make three cups of coffee before it's finished drawing the next scene.

Fortran 90 program structure

Figure 15.1 shows the **structure** of a *typical* **Fortran 90** program. Note that the square braces [ ] show which elements are optional (most are!). As can be seen from the diagram, only the Main-program module is compulsory, and even here it's only compulsory to have the keywords END PROGRAM! However, without many of these optional elements the resulting Fortran program would be very trivial indeed (see the example in a moment). Most of the pre-written programs available to engineers and scientists would be more complex than this, and many run into tens of thousands of lines of code. There is a huge investment in Fortran both in terms of time and money – and this is one of the reasons why Fortran has remarkable staying power.

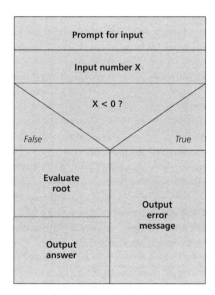

A very simple FORTRAN program

```
PROGRAM Square_Root
REAL::x,ans
WRITE (*,*) "Input a positive number:"
READ (*,*) x
Sign: IF x < 0 THEN
    WRITE(*,*) "Can't do negative
numbers"
    ELSE Sign:
      ans = SQRT(x)
      WRITE (*,*)"The square root of:
                      ", x, "is", ans
    END IF Sign
END PROGRAM Square_Root
```

Figure 15.2

A very simple Fortran program for working out the square root of a positive number, together with a trap to eliminate the possibility of entering negative numbers could be designed from the Nassi-Schneiderman structure diagram in figure 15.2.

The above program should be reasonably easy to understand for computer-science students, with the only weird part being (*,*) which is instructing the Fortran compiler to use the *current* **output** unit and the *default* **conventions** for input/output. Notice also that the **IF construct** has been used *rather* than a simple IF statement. In Fortran 90 a **construct name** (**Sign:** in the above example) is used in a way which I think makes the IF-THEN-ELSE parts far easier to understand, especially if you have many nested loops. The other parts of the program consist only of a few **executable statements** such as WRITE, READ and one to work out the answer.

Fortran 90 variable types

Fortran 90 supports the following variable types.

I – Integer   R – Real   Z – Complex   C – Character
S – Character string   L – Logical

Complex variables are *particularly useful* in **engineering** and **science**, *as they model many things in the real world*. If complex variables had been used in the above square-root program, then negative numbers could have been typed in too. With slight modifications to the program, if –2, for example, had been typed in, then the program could be

> **Hint:** If you are totally unfamiliar with complex numbers and wish to find out more, have a look at the Mandelbrot programming exercise in chapter 18 which makes extensive use of these ideas.

made to respond with the two different answers for the square root of –2, which would be (0 , 1.41421356) and (0 , –1.41421356). This is just one way of representing the numbers (0 + i1.41421356) and (0 – i1.41421356), which, if you are an 'A' level or higher-standard mathematician, you will realise that when either of these two complex numbers are multiplied together the result would be –2. We did say that Fortran was mathematical!

Fortran 90 has a very powerful set of over 100 intrinsic procedures which are available to the programmer and which act like functions. To get just a little of the flavour, a small subset has been chosen and is shown in the following list.

Name	Brief explanation
CONJ(Z)	The *CONJ*ugate of a complex number.
CLOG(X)	*LOG* of a Complex number X.
DCOS(X)	*COS*ine of X in Double-precision.
DOTPRODUCT	*Dot-product* of two vectors.

    (Vector_A,Vector_B)
MATMUL(Matrix_A,Matrix_B)   Multiply two *matrices* together.

TRANSPOSE(Matrix)   Work out the *transpose* of a matrix

Fortran 90 is indeed the tops for mathematical work, and the number of array-related functions is enormous. However, it's ironic to note that all the above functions – and many others – are now available on my Texas TI-85 cal-

> **Hint:** Don't worry if you have no Fortran90 compiler, these activities can be done on older versions of Fortran too.

culator! Indeed, my TI-85 calculator can easily solve simultaneous equations in 10 unknowns by using matrix methods – a feat, which needed a mainframe when I was a student! It's amazing what embedded microprocessor systems can now do. (See chapter 8.)

Student activities – FORTRAN 90

You will find that all of these examples can be done using the older FORTRAN 77 compilers.

(1) Write a program to input a series of positive integer numbers and work out the average. Use a rogue value of –999.

(2) Write a program to multiply two 3 × 3 matrices together and output the answer. Use real numbers only.

COBOL

COBOL (COmmon Business Oriented Language) is the *workhorse* of the **business and data processing world**. A group in the USA called CODASYL (the COnference, being made up of representatives from government agencies, computer manufacturers, universities and other interested parties on DAta SYstems Languages) originally designed the language. Work was finally completed in about 1960 and COBOL compilers have been produced in one form or another ever since. COBOL has become *the* standard business language and *is ideally suited for data processing where large volumes of business-type data and files have to be handled efficiently.* However, the **mathematical processing capability** is *strictly limited* to the more mundane arithmetic processes that are used in accounting.

COBOL structure

The language is made up of many English-like statements, which were originally used so that non-specialist computer users would have some idea of what was going on. This verbose language is therefore effectively *self documenting.* The English-like analogy was taken

Simplified structure of a COBAL program

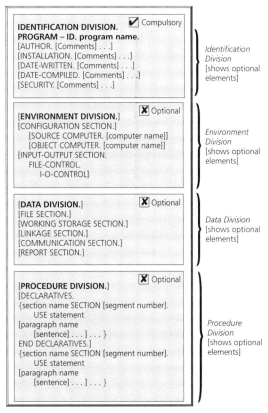

Figure 15.3

several stages further, such that statements were referred to as sentences and many sentences were grouped together to form a paragraph.

Figure 15.3 shows the simplified structure of a COBOL program. As you can see it consists of four main divisions called the **identification**, **environment**, **data** and **procedure divisions** respectively. The functions of each of the four divisions, together with some tongue-in-cheek examples, are explained in the following sections. These examples will gradually build up into part of a COBOL program, which deals with a garden-gnome computer file-handling system for the famous 'Fothergill, Sprogitt & Greendish' chain of garden centres.

Identification division

This first section of a COBOL program **identifies the program** and contains *just* **one paragraph** that is called the **program-ID**. It *must* specify the **name of the**

Did you know that . . .

Some students might consider writing Cobol programs to be unexciting. However, in 1999, if you are based in the City of London, Cobol programmers and analysts can earn somewhere between one and two thousand pounds a week.

program, but may *optionally* be used to specify the author of the program, it's intended purpose, and any other information which can be added as comments if required. An identification division for our garden-gnome example might be as follows. Note that an asterisk (*) denotes the start of a comment in COBOL.

```
IDENTIFICATION DIVISION.
PROGRAM-ID.    GardenGnomes.
AUTHOR.        FotherGill and Greendish
DATE-WRITTEN.  16/12/98
DATE-COMPILED. 16/12/98
SECURITY.      Top secret!
*Program to interrogate garden gnome
                                    file
```

Environment division

The second part of a COBOL program contains the **environment division**. It consists of *two sections* called the **configuration** and **input-output** sections. Together these specify the *type of computer* on which the program is to be compiled and run, and the *peripherals* that will be required such as the **input** and **output units**. An optimistic environment division for the garden-gnome program might be as follows.

```
ENVIRONMENT DIVISION.
CONFIGURATION SECTION.
SOURCE-COMPUTER.
    CRAY T3E 1200
OBJECT-COMPUTER.
    CRAY T3E 1200
```

Data division

The third part is the **data division** and *describes the data* used by the program. For example, the **variables** to be used, a *detailed description* of the **files** and the *organisation* of the **storage requirements**. This is a little more involved and will therefore be treated in more detail in the example that follows.

Procedure division

The final part of the program is the procedure division. This is basically the main guts of the program, and will therefore not be considered any further in this introduction, but an example follows later on in this section, and other examples of COBOL programs can be found in chapter 27 on file-handling.

A simple COBOL example

It's interesting to look at just one or two of the file-definition features in a simple COBOL program, and we will continue to use the 'garden gnomes' as an example. Although the following might appear verbose, compare it with the very primitive file handling facilities usually

Did you know that . . .

In 1998/99, as the millennium draws to a close, Cobol programmers are in great demand to reprogram older systems to overcome the millennium bug (see chapter 28). Old Cobol programmers were being dragged out of retirement to try to cope with the enormous volume of work.

Fothergill, Sproggit and Greendish – famous garden-gnomes catalogue

Cat. number	Name of gnome	Description			Stock quantity			Price
		Head	Body	Beard	Max.	Min.	Actual	
DLF 1	David	Brown	Red	Black	150	50	98	22.50
JIP 1	Jared	Black	Blue	Brown	300	100	276	25.00
KJD 1	Kevin	Red	Grey	Grey	250	75	43	15.60

Figure 15.4

available within simple versions of BASIC, for example. When dealing with the **data structures** in chapters 24 and 25, or the **files and file-handling** sections in chapters 26 and 27, for example, it is *far easier to implement all of these techniques* by using a language such as COBOL.

One nice thing about COBOL is that it mirrors very closely what would naturally be done by using common sense – after all, it is intended to be an English-like language. Let's assume that we have a manual-cataloguing system up and running in the garden centre where the garden gnomes are catalogued in a book as shown in figure 15.4. Notice that hair colour (head), body colour and beard colour, along with the names, stock description, quantities and price are all present.

We will assume that the manual stock-catalogue layout shown in figure 15.4 will be mirrored exactly on the computer system using COBOL. Now file handling (see chapters 26 and 27 for more detailed analysis) is COBOL's forte, and the relationships between the data are very efficiently described by making use of different levels.

The stock catalogue itself would represent the file. (In practice there would be other files such as customers, suppliers and accounts, for example.) Notice that a typical stock-catalogue entry (one for each gnome) naturally splits up into 5 major categories, namely, 'Cat. Number', 'Name', 'Description', 'Quantities' and 'Price'. Each entry for a single gnome represents a record, and the five major categories represent different fields within a record. Notice also that the 'description' and 'stock quantities' contain sub-fields, namely, 'head', 'body' and 'beard' belonging to the description, and 'max.', 'min.' and 'actual' belonging to the stock quantities. COBOL allows us to code this data structure very efficiently for the file as follows.

```
DATA DIVISION.
FILE SELECTION.
FD GNOME-STOCK_FILE
     LABEL RECORDS OMITTED
     DATA RECORD is GNOME
01   GNOME.
     02   CAT-NUMBER.
     02   NAME-OF-GNOME.
     02   DESCRIPTION.
          03   HEAD.
          03   BODY.
          03   BEARD.
     02   STOCK-QUANTITIES.
          03   MAX.
          03   MIN.
          03   ACTUAL.
     02   PRICE.
```

The **different levels** are assigned a number, with **01** being assigned to the **record** gnome (i.e. for each entry in the original catalogue). **02** is assigned to the **fields**, and **03** is assigned to the **sub-fields**. (You can go up to level 49!)

A COBOL compiler would now be able to deduce the structure, but does *not* yet know the type of data, which is contained within each field or sub-field. In COBOL *there are three different types of field*, namely **numeric**, **alphabetic** and **alphanumeric** (plus a variation on these fields which we will *not* use here). Each field is described in COBOL by what's called a **picture**. A picture is a simple concept – an alphanumeric field, for example, is described to the compiler by using the word PICTURE followed by a letter X, followed by the maximum number (within brackets) of alphanumeric characters which will appear within the field. Therefore, if we are describing the 4-character-catalogue-entry system for the garden gnomes, where entries consist of three letters followed by a single digit, (e.g. KJD1 or JIP1), then this would be described as PICTURE X(4).

Alphabetic fields are described by the word PICTURE and the letter A, and numeric fields are very slightly different again – they are described by the word PICTURE, and then a number of 9s are used to represent digits in an integer-numeric field. Other variations of this theme are possible, but we will limit ourselves to the garden-centre example here.

Figure 15.5 shows the maximum number of characters for each field and sub-field within the stock-file catalogue, together with the field-data description explained above.

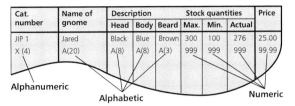

Data needed for the COBOL-PICTURE definitions in the Gnome file

Cat. number	Name of gnome	Description			Stock quantities			Price
		Head	Body	Beard	Max.	Min.	Actual	
JIP 1	Jared	Black	Blue	Brown	300	100	276	25.00
X (4)	A(20)	A(8)	A(8)	A(3)	999	999	999	99.99

Alphanumeric   Alphabetic   Numeric

Figure 15.5

Using the information in figure 15.5, together with the file structure already built up in the DATA DIVISION, the COBOL garden-gnome program now looks something like the following.

```
DATA DIVISION.
FILE SELECTION.
FD GNOME-STOCK_FILE
     LABEL RECORDS OMITTED
     DATA RECORD is GNOME
01   GNOME.
     02   CAT-NUMBER      PICTURE X(4).
     02   NAME-OF-GNOME   PICTURE A(20).
     02   DESCRIPTION.
          03   HEAD       PICTURE A(8).
          03   BODY       PICTURE A(8).
          03   BEARD      PICTURE A(3).
     02   STOCK-QUANTITIES.
          03   MAX        PICTURE 999.
          03   MIN        PICTURE 999.
          03   ACTUAL     PICTURE 999.
     02   PRICE           PICTURE 99V99.
```

(Note that the 'V' in the last definition shows the position of the decimal point.)

Notice how easy it is to describe data structures for business-type problems. Have a look at the ways in which a simple version of BASIC at school or college handles files. There is no comparison with the ease with which the files can be described, and with the self-documenting aspects of looking at programs such as the one shown above – COBOL wins hands down, as of course it should!

A complete COBOL example

COBOL contains all of the structures necessary to be regarded as a good structured language, and COBOL's

```
A very-simple COBOL program
  IDENTIFICATIOIN DIVISION.
  PROGRAM-ID.              VATMAN
  AUTHOR.                  BRUCE WAYNE.
  DATE-WRITTEN             16/12/98.
  DATE-COMPILED            16/12/98.
  SECURITY.                TOP SECRET!.
  *Program to calculate VAT-inclusive price
  *
  ENVIRONMENT DIVISION.
  CONFIGURATION SECTION.
  SOURCE-COMPUTER.
  CRAY Y-MP/832.
  OBJECT-COMPUTER.
  CRAY Y-MP/832.
  *
  DATA DIVISION.
  WORKING-STORAGE SECTION
  01   PRICE-IN      PICTURE 99999V99.
  01   VAT-RATE      PICTURE 99V9.
  01   PRICE-OUT     PICTURE 99999V99.
  *
  PROCEDURE DIVISION.
  VAT-CALCULATION-SECTION.
  ACCEPT PRICE-IN.
  ACCEPT VAT-RATE.
  MULTIPLY VAT-RATE BY PRICE-IN GIVING PRICE-OUT.
  DISPLAY "The cost of " PRICE-IN "and VAT @" VAT-RATE "% is" PRICE-OUT.
  STOP RUN.
```

Figure 15.6

input output facilities are very impressive. As COBOL is intended for business use, a very simple program to add VAT at 17.5% to a number and print it out is shown in figure 15.6.

That's all there is to multiplying two numbers together – well, we did say COBOL is verbose! To be fair, much of the above is optional, but COBOL is superb for business data processing, and an example like the above gives you little indication of COBOL's true power. As with the other programs in the section, the overall structure should be simple to understand. The only extra part, which needs a little explanation, is the WORKING-STORAGE section, which describes data that is not associated with files. The level number 01 has been used here, but in older COBOL compilers the number 77 is often used.

COBOL keywords

COBOL is a verbose language and has about 400 keywords (at the last count). Can you imagine trying to remember all of these! To keep with the style in which this chapter is written, and to get a flavour of COBOL, a small subset of keywords is shown in the following list.

Name	Brief explanation
DELETE	Removes a record from a direct-access file.
INDEXED	Indicates an index associated with a table.
OCCURS	Helps to define a table – like the decision tables, for example, shown in chapter 14.
OPEN	Prepares a file for opening.
PAGE	Helps to make sure that the printout starts on the next page.
PERFORM	Perform specified paragraph the number of times indicated.
SEARCH	Helps to implement a table look up.
USING	Helps to indicate an external file that is to be sorted.

Student activities – COBOL 97

You will find that all of these examples can be done using the older COBOL compilers.

(1) Write a program to input a price from the keyboard, then work out and print out the VAT inclusive price by adding VAT at 17.5%.

(2) Write a program to work out the 'compound interest' on a 'sum of money' for a 'specified number of years'. Both the years and the interest rate are to be entered from the keyboard.

Other language examples

Pascal

Pascal was developed by Nicholas Wirth at Zurich in Switzerland in 1968, and was completed and operational by 1971. The roots for Pascal were therefore laid down much later than FORTRAN and COBOL, for example. The name **Pascal** *is in honour of* the famous French mathematician **Blaise Pascal** who died in 1662. He developed one of the earliest calculating machines which was the first to use the concepts of 'input', 'output' and 'processing' (see chapter 2). Pascal is derived from the **ALGOL language,** which was also popular in the 1960s, but Pascal itself has evolved into languages such as **Ada**, **Modula-2** and **Modula-3**. The latest versions of Pascal have been developed into visual programming environments (see chapter 13) such as **Delphi**. As you can see – the relationship between many high-level languages is highly incestuous! It's also enlightening to note that languages themselves are usually quite stable, with variations on a theme lasting for tens of years – a fact not common in other areas of computing.

Pascal is a general-purpose easy-to-use programming language which has been *widely adopted by academic institutions* for teaching students structured-programming techniques. One reason for this is that Pascal was originally designed for teaching and for expressing algorithms in an efficient structured way. Pascal has already been extensively used throughout the rest of the book, and is the main language used when the principles of high-level languages are discussed in chapter 13. Therefore, *you have already studied Pascal* in much-greater depth than could ever be achieved by just a few pages in this chapter. Pascal or Pascal-like pseudo-code is also used extensively in other chapters on data structures. Also, don't forget that some of the latest versions of Pascal are now object oriented, and these are worth having a look at too.

Pascal program structure

The detailed-program structure for Pascal can be seen in figure 13.18. Notice that Pascal, just like COBOL, for example, forces you to declare variables used at the beginning of the program. Compare this with the simpler versions of languages like BASIC, for example, where variables do *not* have to be declared. Without variable declarations anyone reading the program has a more difficult job to work out what is happening. If variable declarations are forced onto the programmer in this way, then the programs become more readable and self-documenting. Due to the constraints placed on the programmer in this way, it is actually quite difficult to write a badly structured Pascal program.

There have been several versions of Pascal since the standard version was introduced in 1971. One of the versions, with added features in the 'string handling', 'files' and 'graphics' areas is UCSD Pascal (University of California in San Diego). **Turbo Pascal** for the IBM platform is also quite popular.

As students should be more familiar with Pascal than most of the other languages considered in this section, the student activity, which now follows, is a little more difficult than the simpler activities for the other languages.

Student activities – Pascal

You will find that all of these examples can be done using the older Pascal compilers.

(1) Write a program to sort 20 numbers into descending order using any method that you wish. (See chapter 19 if you get stuck.)

(2) Write a program to calculate factorials which includes an output indicating the time, in centiseconds, taken by the computer to complete the task. (See chapter 13 if you get stuck.)

ALGOL

ALGOL, the ALGOrithmic Language, started to be developed by a committee in 1958 for scientific, mathematical and engineering purposes. The name ALGOL derives from the fact that this language expressed programs in terms of algorithms. (Don't they all!) The first version was called ALGOL 58, but a better version, commissioned in 1962 came to be known as ALGOL 60. We are not going to study ALGOL in detail here, but simply *mention it because of its tremendous historical importance*. ALGOL **was the spur behind the development of languages like Pascal, Ada and Modula-2**, and another *spin off* from ALGOL in 1972 was the language C, and hence the C++ and Visual C++ languages of today – covered in detail in a larger section later.

ALGOL was *the first* highly structured programming language, and must, therefore, feature in any overview of high-level language development. It was the first language to introduce the ideas of block structure, was the first to introduce procedures with parameter passing (see chapter 13) *and* local variables, it was also the first to introduce recursion (see chapter 18). ALGOL was the first language to introduce the BNF (Backus-Naur Form) method for describing syntax. The BNF system is covered in detail in chapter 32, but you may have seen it used to describe the syntax of high-level languages, SQLs, other 4GLs and macro languages in your computing manuals. For example, the **Pascal 'if statement'** may be described, using BNF, as follows.

```
<if-statement> ::= if <condition> then
<statement> [else <statement>]
```

You may have noticed that the **square braces [ ]**, shown in the above definition, have already been used in this chapter to denote **optional elements** – you have already been using some BNF definitions without realising it! Of course, in the above if-statement definition, the terms <condition> and <statement> would have to be defined using BNF too – but we will not concentrate on this aspect here.

Algol 68 was later developed as a more-powerful language, but, unusually in a high-level language development context, was not simply an extension of Algol 60.

There are still Algol compilers in use today, but the language never became popular in it's own right.

BASIC

BASIC – or **Beginner's All-purpose Symbolic Instruction Code** has also been through many stages of metamorphosis. J.G. Kemeny and T. Kurtz at Dartmouth College in the U.S.A originally designed BASIC in the 1960s. It specifically enables non-specialist students to learn how to program the computer in simpler ways compared to the high-level-language heavyweights like COBOL, ALGOL and FORTRAN, which were the only sensible alternatives around at the time. The *early versions* of **BASIC** were designed specifically for use in a **time-sharing environment** (see chapter 23). In those days there were no micros, so students learnt to program by using teletype terminals (there were no VDUs either!) connected to a mainframe.

The BASIC language is usually **interpreted** rather than **compiled** (see chapter 32). This means that students did *not* have to learn how to create source code in a text editor. They also did *not* have to compile the source code to create the object code, did *not* have to link the object code with any library files, and finally did *not* have to run their programs via a separate process. Students could simply type in the code and get an 'immediate' response from the computer. More importantly, an 'instant' response to any errors made by the students was the order of the day, together with the ability to 'instantly' correct the error and try again. This created a revolutionary jump in the user-friendliness of learning to program for the first time, and was known as **conversational mode** for obvious reasons.

The early **BASIC had its critics**, and has probably been *the* most **controversial language** in the history of high-level languages to date. Computer-science students today find this criticism difficult to understand, but it was entirely justified when considering the early versions of the language. The early versions of BASIC were about as unstructured as you could get, and forced most programmers into extremely bad habits. (See the spaghetti code example in chapter 13.)

More-recent versions of BASIC have redressed the balance somewhat, but **it is still possible to write bad programs**, *because* **BASIC does not impose any structure** on the part of the programmer. Unfortunately it's possible to write bad programs in *any language*. It's up to the programmer to write the programs in a structured way if he or she so desires to do – unfortunately, some students don't desire to do. However, with good discipline, and an excellent version of BASIC like BBC BASIC for Acorn's RISC PC range of machines, or Microsoft's Visual BASIC on the PCs, it's possible to write programs with excellent structure. As to variable declarations, BASIC still does not insist, but comments can be used in appropriate places to get over this particular objection.

Did you know that . . .

It's much more exciting to program Basic from the Window's environment using development systems like Microsoft's Visual Basic, for example. These techniques can be seen in chapter 13.

One of the other problems with BASIC is its portability (or *lack of*). Different versions like QBASIC, or Microsoft's Visual BASIC, for example, are very different in some of the syntax, especially when it comes to things like graphics and sound. Therefore, professional programmers who have to make sure that their systems work on *multiple-platform machines* have not chosen BASIC. If you are writing for a single platform such as the PC, then this will not matter, and is one of the reasons why Visual BASIC has become a powerful developer's environment. The simpler versions of BASIC are grossly inadequate when undertaking operations on files and many other data structures. Nevertheless, BASIC is popular in educational institutions like schools, and some very sophisticated and elegant programs can be written using this language.

Student activities – BASIC

You will find that all of these examples can be done using any BASIC interpreter or compiler.

(1) Write a program, which analyses a sentence of characters, then prints out the number of vowels and consonants.

(2) Write a program, which puts 200 red squares on the screen in a grid being made up of 20 squares across and 10 squares down. The number of graphics units used for each square and the distance between the squares should be appropriate to the screen mode being used.

Object-oriented programming

C++

In this section we will spend a little longer investigating the importance of the language C++, and look in more general terms at the important concept of object-oriented programming.

> **Hint:** To program well in C++ takes a huge effort. However, it's worth it if you have the time. It gives you a great insight into modern methodology, is very powerful, and helps you to learn a modern language like Java too.

There have been several important high-level-language-development stages, but object-oriented programming (OOP) is probably the most important and most recent after the structured programming development techniques of the late 1970s and 1980s. After reading chapter 13 you should already know that structured programming techniques were introduced to make programs more comprehensible, and thus more easy to modify and develop. However, as systems have become ever more complex, even structured programming techniques are cracking under the strain, especially in the complex **systems programming** environment. *Don't* get the wrong idea – structured programming is still very important and is here to stay – it's just that *more* is needed. Structured programming techniques *are still an essential part of object-oriented programming*, but in addition to these more-conventional techniques, there are some powerful new concepts to be added to your arsenal of ideas. Bjarne Stroustrup developed C++ at Bell Laboratories in the 1980s. The programming language C++ has been developed with object-oriented programming in mind, and it's the "++" part, which differentiates it from C, for example, which is a well-structured language that does *not* support these object-oriented techniques. Although C++ is not the first (**Smalltalk** came before C++) or the only object-oriented programming language, it will be used to illustrate these concepts. It is by far the most popular language for **systems** and **application programming**, and looks well set to serve as a main systems-programming language into the 21st century.

Although **C++** is a superset of **C** (or C is a subset of C++), there are some important differences in the emphasis which is put on certain techniques, or the ways in which programming different structures is carried out. Things that might be frowned upon or uncommon in C are common in C++ and vice versa. Therefore, if you are hoping to learn C, then don't bother – go straight ahead and learn C++. However, if you have already learnt C, then apart from having to undo some of your preconceptions, you should be well able to go straight to the heart of object-oriented programming without having to learn all the relevant syntax of C++ before proceeding.

What makes OOP different?

Object-Oriented Programming (OOP) provides *all* of the usual programming structures (including, unfortunately, the dreaded goto!) which are available in most advanced 3GL programming languages, but in addition to this, **other fundamental concepts** have also been introduced. One of *the* most fundamental ideas addresses the problem of programmers inadvertently messing up things that they shouldn't. Consider, for example, a team of programmers working on a large project (typically 50,000 lines of code or more). Suppose also that some members of the team, that deals with the 'input and output'

> **Hint:** Some of the OOP concepts might seem strange at first sight. However, if you have access to a C++ compiler, it's worth having a go to build up a few of the basic ideas. Once you have done a few hours of successful C++ programming, these concepts fall into place more easily.

(I/O) parts of the project, have written a wonderful routine. Now it may have taken six months to perfect this large and complex routine, and after extensive testing no known bugs exist within the system.

Let's now suppose that someone alters the specification (they always do!) such that different data needs to be handled in addition to the original spec. A typical conventional-language-based scenario would be to tinker with the existing code so that it can accommodate the revised specification – but this often has unforeseen effects, especially in large and complex systems. The simplest of alterations to a small part of the code might cause very subtle changes and unforeseen actions to occur within other parts of the program. If this happens, then the complete module of the original program, which used to work is now totally messed up, with the consequent need to modify it yet again, and go through all of the testing a second time. It would be far better if the original tried-and-tested code could be used in the new system *without alteration*, or, better still, the language specification be designed so that this is no longer a big problem. This is the essence of object-oriented programming.

The above scenario is not only typical, *on complex systems it's almost inevitable!* Although it is possible to use conventional languages such that the above effects are minimised, all too often projects are late due to these sort of reasons. Object-oriented languages are designed to get over these problems by the creation of **self-contained structures** called **objects**, which can interact with other objects. This makes it very difficult to inadvertently mess up things that are already working well, and C++ does this by using a variety of techniques such as **data encapsulation** and **inheritance** etc. which are explained in the next few sections.

Classes and objects

Fundamental to C++ are the ideas of **classes** and **objects**. Although **classes** and **objects** can be regarded as theoretical concepts which relate to the most abstract of **data structures**, in practice it is best to start considering them as relating to some physical classes and objects found in the real world. This gets over the mystic of these new principles and is useful because these programming concepts can and indeed often do relate to the real-world objects and classes.

A **class** can be thought of in the same way as its normal use in English. For example, the 'teachers in your school or college' or the 'food served in a local restaurant' would represent different types of class, with each class being characterised in some particular way, and in these examples, very obvious ways. **Objects** are simply **members of classes** – for example, each teacher in your college is an object, because they are members of the class which we have just defined as 'teachers in your college'. Stilton cheese might be an object of the 'food served in a local restaurant' class. One of the advantages of using classes in this way is that data structures can mirror the real world more closely than is possible with procedurally based languages. However, choosing your classes and objects is not always so obvious, at least until you have built up some experience with OOP methods.

A **class** is defined by certain characteristics, which are exhibited by objects belonging to that class. However, each object of a particular class may and often does exhibit other characteristics. For example, each teacher in your college will probably belong to many different classes such as 'the family', 'the malt whisky association' or 'the local tiddlywinks club' for example, and exhibiting these extra characteristics does not mean that they are no longer 'teachers at your college'. These ideas are shown in a more general form in figure 15.7. Here, to be a member of the base class means exhibiting three special characteristics that we have arbitrarily called 1, 2 and 3. However, we have also shown two different derived classes. Note that each derived class,

being derived from the base class, exhibits, in addition to any other that may be present, the three characteristics of the base class we called 1, 2 and 3. One advantage of these characteristics is that they can be used to mirror the real world quite closely. If, for example, the base class were to be a definition of automobiles, then 'BMW', 'Citroen' and 'Mercedes' could be examples of objects which belong to the base class.

Inheritance

We have just seen that the original class is called the **base class**, and any classes derived from the original in this way are called **derived classes.** This leads to an important concept in **OOP** called **inheritance**. You can easily see from figure 15.7 that derived classes have inherited all the characteristics associated with the base class, and have added some new characteristics of their own. You will recall that an important idea associated with OOP was that existing structures can be used without modification to achieve different outcomes. **Inheritance** *is* one of the methods used in OOP whereby suitable work already completed can be added to by the derived class inheriting the characteristics of the base class with additional characteristics added.

Public and private

It is a natural reaction for those new to OOP to think that all the above could be achieved in conventional programming by clever use of procedures or subroutines – but this would be missing the point. In C++, for example, special **data structures** called **classes** together with the idea of **public** and **private** data associated with each class provide the necessary mechanisms whereby programmers are forced into using this powerful idea of inheritance. By using such mechanisms and all the associated data structures it is very difficult to accidentally alter the code so that previously tested routines are messed up. Programmers hell-bent on breaking the rules could obviously destroy any formalised mechanism – but in C++ this is difficult to do accidentally. Even with the most carefully structured conventional programs, it is very easy if not inevitable to accidentally create chaos on very large systems.

Data encapsulation

Another important feature of OOP is **data encapsulation**, which means that the **objects** contain **both data and functions**, unlike more-conventional programming techniques which deal with the data and the functions which may operate on the data entirely separately. In OOP the data itself is as important as the functions which operate on the data. With conventional programming techniques, although data can be global or local (see chapter 13), most data can be accessed and

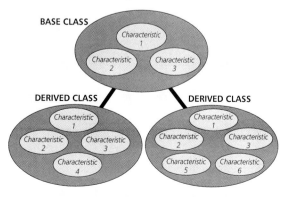

Figure 15.7

modified with relative ease. In OOP, data can typically be accessed only through the object which was designed to operate on that particular data. You access the data by what's called a **member function** of the object containing the data. In this way each object has total control over its own data, and it's therefore less likely that other routines or modifications will inadvertently alter the private data.

These ideas are far more fundamental than would appear at first sight. In a conventional procedurally based language, the whole analysis of a problem is of paramount importance, and usually involves carrying out sequences of operations using functions. For example, read a string from the disk, test to see if it contains a sub-string, if a particular sub-string is found then branch to a particular procedure to process it and re-save the data to disk. Little or no attention has been paid to the data itself, and making use of these older methods means that data plays a subservient role to the procedures that operate on it.

Data has a much-more important role in object-oriented programming. Here vital data that may have to be accessed from many different parts of the program forms part of the object which controls the data (see the real-life analogy in a moment). In conventional programming if the data is altered in any way, then *all routines* which need to have access to the data will have to be altered too. With the concept of **data encapsulation**, if the data is altered in any way, then only the object that controls the data and gives access to it needs to be altered. Therefore, modifications and alterations can be done much more quickly and efficiently. Moreover, all members of the programming team do not even have to know that this part of the program has been altered, because they are simply asking this routine to supply them with the appropriate information, not manipulating it themselves.

One other point worthy of note is that when objects are used in OOP they retain any variables used throughout the duration of the program. This may not sound revolutionary, but compare this to the use of procedures or sub-routines in a conventional language, where local variables are lost once the procedure or sub-routine has been executed. Making a variable global would obviously get over this problem, but this would make it's easier to screw up these variables inadvertently from other procedures. You can see that OOP scores well in this area too.

As can be seen from the above, C++ is bringing programming into the systems world in the conventional sense. This means that parts of the program can be considered as a black box, which responds to your request for information and passes back the appropriate information without the need to understand what is going on inside. System methods have helped in many walks of life such as electronic systems or biological systems – they are now helping programming through the use of OOP systems.

A C++ example

Although it is not appropriate to go into much detail here, I strongly recommend that you spend some time playing around with C++ if you have access to a suitable compiler. The ideas expressed above will then become more obvious, and you will gain a tremendous insight into the ways in which systems and applications are being programmed in the foreseeable future. An example of an extremely simple C++ class definition now follows. Note that // denotes the start of a single-line comment in C++.

```
#include <iostream.h>
class electronic_component //Electronic component object
{
private:
 int man_number;         //Manufacturer's component number
 int ss_number;          //School stock component number
 float cost;             //Cost of component
public:
     man_number = m_num;
     ss_number = ss_num;
     cost = c;
     void setup_part(int m-num, int ss_num, float c)
       {                    //Setup-data definition
       }
     void display_part( )//Display-data-on-screen definition
       {
             cout << "\n Manufacturers number " << man_number;
             cout << "\n Radio Spares code " <<rs_component_number;
             cout << "\n Cost of component " << cost;
```

Figure 15.8 (continues on next page)

```
}
};
        void main( )
        {
        int dummy;
        electronic_component component1;
                            //Define object called component1
                            //which belongs to the class
                            //electronic component
        component1.setup_part(1234, 1735, 1.23);
                            //Set up data
        component1.display_part( );
                            //Display data
        cout << " \n Please type in an integer number to terminate ";
        cout << "\n"        //Enter an integer number to clear
        cin >> dummy;       //the display and return

        }
```

Figure 15.8 continued

The above function can be thought of as part of a simple electronic-component-stock-control system which allows the user to set up the special stock numbers which describe the electronic components, or look at a particular component number on screen. The routine is so simple that all items in stock would have to be typed in and held in memory! Nevertheless, this simple example shows some important concepts in C++ and OOP in particular.

The above code shows how a class called 'electronic_component' is set up. It consists of just three characteristics, namely 'manufacturers number', 'school stock component number' and 'cost'. The main part of the program (as with normal C) consists of the code at the end after 'void main ( )'. This function defines an object called component1 (i.e. a component with this name) which is of the class electronic_component. The data declaration at the beginning of the main function can be compared with simpler data declarations such as '**int part1**' – which declares to the C++ compiler that you wish to make use of an integer variable called part1. One of the most-powerful features of C++ classes is that *you can define your own data types*, then make use of them in any way that you wish. Most languages give you a range of data types such as 'integer', 'floating point', 'string', 'complex' etc. but the C++ object-oriented programming language lets you define your own – with all the benefits that this flexibility is likely to bring.

Let's suppose, for the sake of argument, that you wanted to **add together two complex numbers** (numbers with real and imaginary parts as used, for example, in defining the Mandelbrot set (see chapter 18)). Unlike Fortran, many languages, including C++, do not support variables of type complex. Now it's possible to get round this restriction making use of a number of techniques such as defining a complex (in

the number sense!) procedure to add the real and imaginary parts, passing over parameters to them, and receiving data back from them. You could, for example, use something like the following in BASIC.

```
complex_add(x,y)
```

However, it would be far easier if, after defining a suitable data type, you could use the normal arithmetic operators in expressions like:

```
complex_z = complex_x + complex_y
```

The C++ language enables you to do exactly this. You are limited only by your imagination and programming expertise in the number of data types that can be dreamt up. Defining sophisticated and specialised data types often leads to enormous simplification in the readability and structure of the program.

Data hiding and member functions

The private and public parts of the above class definition ensure that private data or functions if necessary are **hidden** from *normal* view. (The term *normal* here means accessible from outside the class.) This helps to prevent inadvertent tampering with data or misuse of functions via other routines, which should not accidentally alter the data or make use of these functions. All the public functions in the above class definition are accessible from outside the class. This concept of **data hiding** is another important concept in object-oriented programming. Only **member functions**, i.e. functions which are a member of a particular class, can have access to the private data or functions within their own class.

A real-life analogy

It is interesting to see how the principles of OOP mirror real life to some extent, and the 'teacher objects' considered earlier will act as an example. We could, for example, consider the base class of 'teachers'. However, for the purposes of this example, let's consider our teachers to be subject specialists such as 'geographers' or 'physicists'. Therefore, taking our OOP analogy further, we could create classes of 'Geography teachers', 'Physics teachers', and 'Maths teachers' etc. We will now look at a typical interaction between the objects of different classes.

> **Hint:** When programming in C++, it's great fun to make up some real life examples. You could, for example, make up some objects, which mirror your interests. These might be anything from animals to different types of computer.

If we were to model a school by conventional programming techniques, this would probably mean storing all the data on students such that each object (teacher) has global access. This means that each teacher, regardless of subject would access any data via their own routines. Maths teachers, for example, would have access to geography data and could accidentally alter it. However, taking the OOP approach, and applying the principle of **data encapsulation** described earlier, we now have the following scenario. If a maths teacher, perhaps also being the tutor of a particular pupil, wishes to know how his or her student is doing in geography. He will ask the geography teacher, who will then access his or her own files and interpret the data in a way that the maths teacher can understand. Note that the maths teacher has not had access to any of the geography teacher's data – it is the geography teacher who has scrummaged in the data structures, messed around with their own functions and data and extracted the required result. It does not matter that the maths teacher did not know where to find the geography data, or how to access it, all that was necessary was to ask the appropriate geography teacher who did all of the necessary processing. In object oriented programming the ideas are similar with access to private data being controlled in a similar way to our teacher example just considered.

Now all the teachers in the school keep their own 'data functions' and 'data' in whatever form is necessary. Therefore, other teachers can only gain access to this data by asking the right person. Using these simple ideas you should now begin to appreciate one of the main principles in object-oriented programming methodology.

Disadvantages of OOP

Although OOP is *the* current way forward in the foreseeable future, there are some disadvantages. Some of the main ones are increased program size. (This is one of the reasons why some of the new operating systems are very large indeed!) If a program is larger then it may take longer to execute than similar functions carried out making use of conventional programming techniques. However, with computers becoming ever faster and more complex, and with pots of RAM now becoming the norm at a sensible cost, these are small prices to pay considering the considerably reduced development time and increased reliability of the software.

> ## Student activities – C++
>
> You will find that all these examples can be done using any C++ compiler.
>
> 1 Write a program, which accepts a number, then displays the square root of that number on the screen.
>
> 2 Write a program to enter a character, followed by a number representing the number of times the character just entered is to be repeated on the same line. Your program should then print out the required number of characters.

Further language examples

Prolog stands for **Pro**gramming in **Log**ic, or '*Programmation Logique*' as they say in France at the University of Marseilles where Monsieur Colmerauer and his team originally developed the language back in the 1970s. Along with **LISP** (see next section), these currently represent *the* two languages which are most popular for **Artificial Intelligence** or **AI** (see chapter 9) applications. You may recall that Prolog belongs to a set of languages that have been labelled **fifth-generation** languages. Put simply, this means that it is yet a stage further removed from what's happening inside the guts of the computer at the most fundamental machine level. Prolog was developed from a branch of mathematics called first-order predicate calculus, and LISP was developed from Lambda calculus, a special sub-set of the more general predicate calculus. The mathematics of predicate calculus deals with **symbolic logic** – the sort of language in which propositions are made and inferences are proved to be true or false – it's probably the language in which 'Spock' thinks on the Starship Enterprise!

Prolog *is a declarative language*, which means that we no longer have to concentrate too much on the detail of **how to** solve problems. Instead we concentrate more on the **descriptive side** of defining *relationships*, then asking appropriate questions – Prolog is then expected to figure out the response to these questions by an analysis of the database which is automatically built up by the relationships which the programmer has just defined. However, for most Prolog programs there will be *some* **imperative** or **procedural** elements – we are still some way off being able to use totally declarative languages with no reliance on procedurally based ideas which are common in all other languages.

The above ideas are typical of the type of thinking that lies behind knowledge-based systems or expert systems (see chapter 9). This is because the programmer can be concerned more with the knowledge held in the database rather than specifically thinking up the algorithms which will be used to extract subsets of this knowledge. Therefore, if a medical database, for example, is built up making use of Prolog, then Prolog's facilities are ideal for enabling the programmer (and hence the end users of the system) to extract medical facts based on complex relationships describing the possible symptoms of an illness.

Prolog is wonderfully simple for expressing hierarchical and list-type data structures. For example, consider a tree structure for parts of a typical car as shown in figure 15.9.

> **Hint:** Some other simple Prolog examples can be seen on page 274.

These ideas are identical to those associated with a family tree – so consider, just for a moment, the parent called 'Bodywork' and the four children called 'Doors', 'Wings', 'Bonnet' and 'Boot'. In Prolog this structure could be represented as follows:

```
Bodywork(doors, wings, bonnet, boot)
                         . . . . . .
```

These ideas can easily be extended so that the entire structure could be coded, and for figure 15.7, this can be accomplished with the following line of Prolog.

```
Bodywork(doors(hinges, handle, window,
    winding_mechanism( toothed_quadrant,
        parallel_arms, winding_handle)),
                    wings, bonnet, boot)
                         . . . . . .
```

The above can be regarded as a simple 'bodywork database' for a car – it's a database because that's how Prolog treats this data structure – and it's simple because we don't have the space to build up a database of the complexity needed to mirror all the parts in a real car. As you will have guessed, there are much more sophisticated ways of defining the structure of the car database than typing out an incredibly long line as implied above, but this is best left to a more detailed study of Prolog if you have a suitable compiler. Micro-Prolog is available for most computers including Acorn's Archimedes, the IBM PC, its clones and the Apple Mac ranges.

You will probably be amazed to realise just how much data in real life can be massaged to mirror the natural structure of trees, and a good Prolog programmer would probably be able to change just about any given data into the form of a list or a tree structure. Anything from books in a library via the timetable at your school or college to the information contained in a sporting almanac could all be encoded in Prolog as a set of complex tree structures. It is this which enables Prolog to act as a **knowledge-based system** in which the base of knowledge could be organised facts about almost any topic under the sun. The ability of Prolog to interact with the structure (database) and to do efficient searches based on complex criteria makes this declarative language a joy to use compared to programming the same functions in a procedural language such as BASIC, for example. With appropriate procedures to hide the end user from the complexities of predicate calculus, user-friendly knowledge-based systems can be established relatively easily – it's worth a try if you have the time.

It would take up far too much space to look into too many languages in the above detail, so snippets from other languages will now be covered in the next few sections. You are obviously not required to remember too much detail, but reading the following will add to your knowledge of the development of languages, and will allow you to impress the examiners with your knowledge of languages in general.

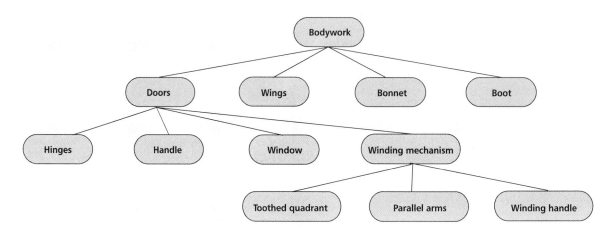

Figure 15.9

Ada

Ada is derived from **Pascal**, but has a considerable number of enhancements. The final version, sponsored by the U.S. Department of Defense, and developed in conjunction with industry and academic institutions, was presented in 1980. Interestingly enough, it was not until the development of Ada that computer scientists and other academics did very much work on the development of what makes one computer language good compared to another. These complex questions are answered subjectively to some extent in the very last section of this chapter. Ada is a very modern high-level language compared to some of the others in this chapter, and *is named in honour of* **Ada Augusta Byron**, the **Countess of Lovelace** (known as Lady Lovelace, and daughter of the poet Lord Byron), who did much pioneering work in the 1800s. Lady Lovelace is considered to be the first computer programmer, and designed programs for Charles Babbage's mechanical computers.

Ada was originally designed for **systems programming** (i.e. developing things like applications etc.), and had the unique advantage of combining **real-time** (see chapter 8) and **structured programming**. It was also ideal for programming **embedded systems** (see chapter 8) – hence the interest from the Department of Defense for real-time-missile-control applications and the like. Being able to handle events in real time, Ada also has applications in handling **concurrent events** – i.e. it's useful in modern **parallel-processing** applications. Nevertheless, Ada has become more of a general-purpose language than was originally intended, and, perhaps reassuringly, is now being used to program embedded systems in vending machines, cars and other non-military applications.

LISP

LISP, along with **Prolog** (see earlier) represents the cutting edge for programming **AI** (**Artificial Intelligence**) systems. However, the original version of LISP was the first of these languages to be developed way back in the late 1950s (that's not a misprint!) at MIT – the Massachusetts Institute of Technology in the USA – not bad for a fifth-generation language to be developed back in the 1950s! Unfortunately, the machines of the day were not good at running LISP programs, and it was not until the advent of greater processing power that LISP programming became generally available. LISP is ideal for defining and manipulating data structures such as those found in lists and trees in chapters 24 and 25 – indeed, this is where LISP gets its name – LISP stands for LISt Processing. Consider a list data structure with **nodes** (see chapter 25) in the form of a **binary tree** as shown in figure 15.10.

The concept of a **pointer** (see chapter 24) is an important one in **LISP**, and the left-hand and right-hand pointers are used to good effect in the **binary tree** of

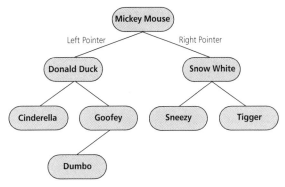

Figure 15.10

figure 15.10. In chapter 19 a system of 'sorting' names into alphabetical order is given by using a simple rule to insert the data into a **binary tree**, and using an **inorder traversal** mechanism to read back the data. Building up such data structures using languages such as BASIC, for example, is a little tedious. However, using LISP, both definition and manipulation of data structures in the form of trees and lists are simple. Making use of LISP we could print out the Walt-Disney characters in alphabetical order as shown in the next couple of sections.

First we need to define a *set of* **functions** which will make up the **node data**. In this context a **node** consists of just *three items* – a **data item** like 'Mickey Mouse', for example, along with the **left** and **right-hand pointers** which, in LISP, are curiously known as CAR and CDR respectively. CAR is a LISP function, which finds the beginning of a LIST and originally was an acronym for Content of Address Register. CDR is a LISP function, which finds the end of a LIST, and this was an acronym for Contents of Decrement Register. (We did say that LISP was developed back in the 1950s – this old-style terminology has remained to this day.) The following code consists of four **defined functions** called build_node, left_subtree, right_subtree and node_data.

```
(defun build_node (data left right)
    (list left data right))
(defun left_subtree (tree)
      (car tree))

(defun right_subtree (tree)
    (caddr tree))

(defun data (tree)
    (cadr tree))
```

To print out the data in alphabetical order the following function can be used.

```
(defun print_binary_tree (tree)  (cond
  ((null tree) nil)
```

```
(t (print_tree (left_subtree (tree))
       (print (data tree))
       (print_tree (right-subtree
                          tree)))))
```

Although quite simple once you get used to it, you can see why an alternative acronym for LISP has been thought up – Lots of Infuriating Spurious Parentheses!

Java

No section on high level languages would be complete without mention of **Java**. Java was developed from the

> **Hint:** Don't confuse the language Java with JavaScript. Java is a fully blown object-oriented language in it's own right. JavaScript is a Java-like language used to run Java programs on web pages (see chapter 4 for more information).

C++ language by Sun Microsystems, and has revolutionised what's possible over the Internet, as well as being a language in its own right, with the goal of platform independence in mind. As Java is intimately connected with applications for the WWW, it is covered at the end of the chapter on the Internet (see chapter 4).

A final overview

Much has been covered in this chapter, many languages have been briefly introduced, and together with the work covered in chapters 13 and 14, students should now have a good idea of the spectrum of high-level language development. In this final section we will try to bring these ideas together so that you are able to formulate a strategy in your own mind regarding arguments for and against language developments which have taken place and still are taking place at an incredible pace. Indeed, at the time of writing, multi-million dollar law suites are raging over the development of languages like Java and other platform independent systems, so much so that they made headline news in 1997 and 1998 – and the wars go on!

Why so many languages?

As you have seen from the beginning of this chapter, the 1960s were the boom years for software development – all future strategies were developed from the base languages developed during this period. Before the advent of the micro, bigger and better was the order of the day, and the mainframe and mini hardware manufacturers got rich on their increasingly lucrative share of the markets. Software developers tried to jump on the same bandwagon – all trying to strive for the ultimate language which would replace all other languages. PL/1 was probably the only serious contender for this

Utopian title, but the compilers were so big and clumsy, were so full of bugs, and the language was so difficult to learn that computer scientists have given up trying to develop an all-things-to-all-men language for the foreseeable future.

Criteria for language evaluation

We are, therefore, left with a variety of languages, each suitable for specific purposes, of which a general-purpose language is only yet another specific example! Don't forget that general-purpose does not mean that the language can do everything. Therefore, we have developed languages which are good at scientific and engineering applications such as Fortran, are good at data processing such as COBOL, are good teaching languages such as Pascal, or are good system's programming languages such as C++, for example.

How then, do we evaluate the effectiveness of one language compared to another? How do we decide which language to use? How do we decide which language would be the most efficient for a particular job? All these questions and many others of a similar nature need answering – unfortunately, these questions are complex ones. Much computer science beyond this level answers these types of questions in considerable detail, and during the development of Ada, for example, a wealth of suitable evaluation material was produced. However, this is beyond the scope of this book, and here we will concentrate on just a few general points.

It's relatively easy to generate some suitable criteria, which can be used for direct comparisons, but far less easy to be totally objective about how these criteria can be applied in practice. For example, Input and Output facilities would be an obvious candidate – but, as we have seen in this chapter, some languages, such as Fortran 90, for example, have third-party software, which considerably improves this area. It's rather like having a brilliant spreadsheet with no graphics capability – bolt on a graphics application and the combination might be 'dynamite', completely nullifying the initially justified criticism. However, if difficulties like this are put to one side, and ignoring some of the subjective opinions which are bound to be present in our simple-analysis techniques, then the list shown in Figure 15.11 would make a reasonable starting point. It is not in any particular order or preference.

An example using Pascal

Suppose we wish to undertake a *brief and informal evaluation* of the **Standard Pascal language**, i.e. not **Delphi** or **Turbo Pascal** (see chapter 13), both of which would do very much better in some important areas. We could work through the following list, perhaps awarding stars on a scale of 1 to 5 (with 5 representing excellent, against each criterion).

Some generally accepted criteria for language evaluation and comparison

Is the language well structured?
In terms of *modularity*.
In terms of the *data types* supported.
In terms of *control structures* supported.

Is it complex or relatively easy to use and understand?
In terms of being *powerful*.
In terms of *expressiveness*.
In terms of *comprehensibility*.

Is it self documenting?
Variable declarations etc.
Is documentation sufficient to reduce maintenance problems?

Are good run-time diagnostics available?
Debuggers – how easy is it to debug programs?

Are the input and output facilities good?

Is there a good base of pre-written utilities or library functions?
Mammoth *FORTRAN and COBOL libraries*.
Huge C and *C++ libraries* etc.

Are compilers available over a wide range of hardware and software platforms?
For, *PCs, Power PCs, Apple Macs, DECs, Suns* etc.
Different *Mainframe* and Mini computers.
Unix, Windows, MSDOS, Windows NT, *System 7 RISC-OS* etc.

Is the transferability (portability) good?
Do major modifications have to be made when going across platforms?

Speed of execution?
Fast or snail's pace? – use appropriate *benchmarks*.

Is it good for teaching purposes?
Is good structure *imposed* on the students?

Can it cope with real time systems?

Can it cope with parallel processing?
Using *real parallel processors*?
Or simple multi-tasking?

Is the language general purpose or designed for a specific purpose?
Artificial intelligence
Data processing
General purpose
Scientific, engineering or maths applications
Systems programming
Text processing etc.

Figure 15.11

Is the language well structured?

Modularity: ★★★★
Well block structured e.g. headings, compulsory declarations, data descriptions, procedures with local and global variables, functions, supports recursion, main body for program.

Data types: ★★★
Loses marks on lack of proper support for strings. Pascal supports Arrays, but does not support variable-length Arrays. Boolean, Char, Enumerated, File, Integer, Pointer, Real, Record, Set and Subrange data types etc. are all supported, and later versions including UCSD Pascal do support random-access files (see chapter 27).

Control structures: ★★★★
Most of the structures needed such as 'conditionals', 'if-then' and 'nested if-then', 'case', 'goto', 'while', 'repeat', 'for' etc. However, some non-uniformity exists because 'while' and 'if' statements require 'begin-and-end' pairs, but 'repeat' statements do not.

Powerful: ★★★★
Powerful is a relatively subjective judgement, it depends on what you are trying to do. Different users will have different perceptions of the power of a language depending on the subset of instructions, which they use most frequently. Overall, Pascal is regarded as being quite powerful, with the exception of its limited file-handling techniques. However, more objective judgements are discussed in the benchmark section at the end of this chapter.

Expressiveness: ★★★★
Expressiveness can be interpreted as fitness for the purpose for which it was intended – in terms of allowing programmers to express themselves in ways that are appropriate to the job in hand. For example, when adding the numbers B to A and putting the result back in A, then Pascal would use the following syntax.

A := A + B

The ':=' part is better than a plain '=' because 'A = A + B' is algebraic nonsense as far as most students are concerned, therefore, the ':=' sign could remind the student of this fact. Indeed when Boolean operators are used '=' is used instead because this has a more literal meaning. Compare these differences with the syntax from a language like BASIC, for example, which is far less expressive in this particular respect at least.

Comprehensibility: ★★★★★
In terms of comprehensibility Pascal scores very well indeed. The block-structured nature of the language combined with the fact that it was originally designed to enable students to be able to understand the teaching of algorithms more effectively, makes this a relatively simple language to learn and use.

> **Hint:** Don't worry if you are not able to produce similar criteria for a particular language. To do this properly you would need to be an expert in a particular language, and have used it for several years. Even the experts would argue over which language might be better than any other for a variety of reasons.

Self documenting: ★★★★★
For a language to be successful it should communicate its meaning to other users as well as the programmers. The problems of maintenance and extension are far more easily solved if a programming language, together with suitable comments is self-documenting. The structure and comprehensibility of Pascal, together with comments fulfils this requirement quite well.

Good run-time diagnostics: ★★★★★
This depends to a large extent on the compiler that accompanies the language. Most Pascal compilers have good run-time diagnostics, which include trace routines that display helpful messages.

Input-Output facilities: ★★★
Input output facilities are not brilliant compared to some of the other first-class high-level languages such as COBOL.

Good base of utilities: ★★★
Pascal suffers a little from not having a vast arsenal of library utilities like those that accompany Fortran or C++, for example.

Compilers range of platforms: ★★★★★
All popular machines have Pascal compilers, therefore Pascal covers a huge range of platforms. Also, the code generated by Pascal compilers is usually efficient in terms of being relatively short and fast to execute.

Transferability and portability: ★★★★★
Transferability is excellent. As with all languages, apart from operating system specific commands making use of Windows, for example, most Pascal programs will run on all platforms. Several extensions to Pascal exist, but most people now have the latest versions, which include all the extensions to the original versions. Pascal also goes further than many languages in making some of its features machine independent.

Speed of execution: ★★★★★
This is probably the most subjective topic, as execution speed obviously depends on what your computer has got under the bonnet. There is little data available regarding the speed of particular languages, and therefore most people rely on various benchmarks as explained in the next section.

Good for teaching: ★★★★
This language was designed with teaching in mind – you won't get much better. However, in some people's opinion Pascal is regarded as being over simplified, and this often leads to unnecessary complications when trying to program more advanced features which other more-complex languages would naturally support.

Real time?: ★
Few languages have been designed to cope with the demands of a real-time system. However, you should note from chapter 8 that real time, in the true sense of the term, does *not necessarily* mean a very-fast response. Nevertheless, it is in the context of responding to fast events that this rating has been given.

Parallel processing: ★★★★
A version of Pascal called Concurrent Pascal is available in which code can be split up for solution by machines which are capable of carrying out this facility. Making sure that code written for parallel machines works with a single-processor machine increases portability.

General or specific?: ★★★★
You can't easily give a tick rating one way or the other based on this criterion – it is usually just one or the other! However, Pascal is quite versatile and therefore scores reasonably well in this area too.

In the final section of this chapter we will take a brief look at more objective ways of evaluating actual performance parameters for a particular language or system.

Benchmarks

A **benchmark** is simply a well defined task which people have dreamt up to get the computer to perform standard operations, then measure either the speed or some other important parameter. Assuming that the hardware on which the language is being run is identical, then languages could be compared by writing various algorithms in identical ways (if possible) in different languages. Obviously different benchmarks would be needed for testing different aspects of the language, and speed of execution would also depend on other factors such as the compiler used, and the hardware configuration on which the software is being run.

Typical benchmarks might involve testing how long it takes to go round various loop structures, working out mathematical algorithms like calculation of factorials, a measurement of the precision with which numbers might be stored, and the time taken to manipulate various well-defined data structures.

You will no doubt come across benchmark terms like **Dhrystone**s, **Whetstones**, **Khornerstones** (and maybe even Blarney Stones!). The computer press is also inventing new benchmarks on a fairly rapid basis to cope with the ever-increasing demands of speeds of modern computer systems. Basically, Whetstones are tests for 'floating point operations' (see chapter 31). Dhrystones are tests for determining the number of times particular programs with a mix of instructions (based on string handling instead of floating point) may be run each second. Finally, Khornerstones are a measure of CPU input/output capability – they are also based on floating point capability and were originally designed to test Unix workstations.

As you can easily imagine, it's not as practical as it might sound to compare languages on this basis as lots of people have different hardware, different compilers, and use the same language for very different purposes.

Exercise 15.1

1   Most languages can be used to express the solution to a problem as an algorithm. Why, therefore, does it matter in practice which language is used?

2   FORTRAN 90 is particularly suited to mathematical, scientific and engineering problems. There are obvious technical reasons for this, but other factors play an important part too – outline the technical, historical and practical reasons why FORTRAN 90 often reigns supreme in these areas.

3   Many languages such as Concurrent Pascal, Fortran 90 and Ada, for example, support true parallel processing. What does true parallel processing mean and why might this compromise the portability of these languages in the short term?

4   Languages such as C++ are inherently suited to parallel processing. Why is this?

5   Write a BASIC program, which simulates the tossing of two coins 100 times, making use of the computer's random-number generator utility. Print out a table which indicates the number of head-and-tail combinations at the end of the simulation.

6   Write a BASIC program, which acts as a spell checker for single-word data entered by a user. Your maximum dictionary size should be no more than 10 words!

7   Write a FORTRAN program to analyse the distance travelled from the Earth by a stone thrown vertically into the air. A printout is to be arranged which gives the stone's distance from the ground at 0.1-sec intervals until the stone returns to Earth. You may assume that $g = -9.81$ m/sec^2, that the initial velocity (U) of the stone is 3 m/sec, and it is thrown from a height of 10m. The formula governing the motion of the stone is $S = Ut + \frac{1}{2}gt^2$ where t is the time in seconds, and S is the height above the ground in metres.

8   Write a Pascal program which generates the first 25 numbers in the Fibbonacci sequence 1,1,2,3,5,8 etc. (i.e. the next number is the sum of the previous two).

9   Write a Pascal program to convert a date typed into the computer in the form dd,mm,yyyy into the form Day, Month and Year. i.e. 16,12,1951 would get converted to 16th December 1951. You should do a simple validation on the date if possible. If you have time do a more complex validation (i.e. don't allow 31,4,1991), but don't include any leap-year validation unless you are a masochist.

10   Choose a high-level language (other than Pascal) with which you have some familiarity. Carry out a subjective analysis of the language based on the criteria show at the end of this chapter.

End of chapter revision aid and summary

Cover up the right-hand column and see if you can answer the questions or define the terms on the left. They appear in the order in which they are covered in this chapter. Alternatively you may browse through the right-hand column to aid revision.

Why is it unlikely that any single high-level language would satisfy all language requirements?

No single language is able to cope with the huge range of modern-day requirements – specialist and general-purpose languages have therefore been developed. A general-purpose language is not one that is designed to solve all problems, but one which has been designed to solve a wide variety of problems with varying degrees of success.

Why are there so many high-level languages?

Hundreds of high-level languages have been developed but relatively few have stood the test of time – some of the best have now been going in one form or another for over forty years.

What is Fortran 90?

FORTRAN 90 is a language primarily based around helping to solve numerical problems in mathematics, science and engineering. FORTRAN stands for FORmula TRANslator or Formula Translation.

What is COBOL97?

COBOL97 is now taking over from COBOL 85 (and COBOL II), the previous incarnations of COBOL. It is the primary language for data processing in the business community. COBOL is an acronym for COmmon Business Oriented Language.

What is Pascal?

Pascal is a well-structured general-purpose teaching language and is named in honour of the mathematician Blaise Pascal who invented an early type of calculator. Later versions of visually-oriented Pascal are called Delphi.

What is Algol?

ALGOL stands for ALGOrithmic Language, and was one of the first block-structured languages to be developed. Algol is still used today but is also the root from which other languages such as Ada and Pascal, for example, have been developed.

What is BASIC?

BASIC stands for Beginner's All-purpose Symbolic Instruction Code. It was originally developed as a simple unstructured teaching language, but is more respectable and powerful in its latest incarnations, especially Microsoft's Visual Basic.

What is C++?

C++ is an example of a different programming methodology called object oriented programming. It has become the de-facto standard for modern systems programming. (If you're wondering why it's called C – it was the language to be developed after A and B!)

What is Prolog?

Prolog stands for PROgramming in LOGic. It is a fifth-generation declarative language developed from 1st-order predicate calculus and is used extensively for AI applications.

What is Ada?

Ada is a language named in honour of Lady Augusta Byron who is regarded as the first computer programmer. This relatively modern language is ideal for real-time and embedded systems, and is used extensively by the military.

What is LISP?

LISP stands for LISt Processing. Along with Prolog this language is extensively used in AI applications.

Can we measure language effectiveness?

The effectiveness and efficiency of a language can be subjectively evaluated by suitable criteria, and objectively evaluated by using suitable benchmarks. Suitable criteria for subjective evaluation would be – Is the language well Structured? Is it complex or relatively easy to use and understand? Is it self-documenting? Are good run-time diagnostics available? Are the Input and Output facilities good? Is there a good base of pre-written utilities or library functions? Are compilers available over a wide range of hardware and software platforms? Is the transferability (portability) good? Speed of execution? Is it good for teaching purposes? Can it cope with real time systems? Can it cope with parallel processing? Is the language general purpose or designed for a specific purpose?

What is a benchmark?

A benchmark is a task dreamed up to test some specific aspect of a computer. An example would be speed of floating point arithmetic.

16 Systems Analysis and Design

Key resources

To carry out this work most successfully it's best if you have:

- Access to several other students so that you can work as a team
- Access to a school or college library
- Access to the chief librarian
- A visit to a computerised library system

Concept checkpoints

- It's essential to have read chapter 14 on structured analysis and design.
- Have an appreciation of programming concepts as outlined in chapters 13 and 15.

Introduction

This chapter is essential reading – not only because of its paramount importance in developing your overall understanding of systems in general – but also because it contains vital material which you should read before starting any serious work on computer-science-based projects. **It covers the art of developing systems – either by using a range of application packages and utilities – including the use of 4GLs, SQLs and macro languages, or by writing your own software in either high-level or low level languages.** This chapter enhances and extends the material covered in chapter 14 where structured analysis and design techniques were first encountered. It assumes that you have already gained a detailed knowledge of structured-programming techniques, and are familiar with Gantt charts, PERT charts and a whole range of other structure-diagram principles. It will also assume that you have a general knowledge of the facilities that are available in typical languages such as Visual BASIC, Pascal, Delphi or C++ etc. – these high-level language principles are covered in chapters 13 and 15. If you apply the techniques learnt in this chapter to your project work, you will increase the likelihood of a successful project, and thus maximise your chances of getting a good grade.

What is a system

Throughout this book you will encounter many different types of system – for example, microcomputer systems, electronic systems, control systems or information systems. In this chapter we will look at systems in a much broader context – indeed, entire organisations can be regarded as a system. In business and industry computers are used to help control, model, inform, analyse, and act upon all types of information from the shop floor to the boardroom. We therefore take a macro view of systems in this chapter – which can model anything from small companies via large institutions to multinational organisations. However, these grandiose views will often be tempered with sound advice applicable to computer-science-based projects at this level. This is often the only opportunity which students have of demonstrating their systems analysis and design knowledge in detail, and is why the mark schemes for projects reflect this importance.

Systems analysis methods

Systems analysis and systems design have changed considerably over the last few years. This has been necessary for a variety of reasons, not least of which is that computer systems have now become so complex, that new methods are needed to make these projects more manageable, especially during the software-development phase. The tools available to help deal with both system-design and system-management problems have considerably improved, and the tools to help debug complex systems are now much more sophisticated. In fact, the testing, debugging, documentation and customer-support phases have all assumed much greater prominence in the new order of things. Systems analysis and design is also intimately tied up with what's become known as software engineering. **Software engineering** is the term now often used to denote a whole cycle of software development – being made up of the **analysis**, **testing**, **debugging** and **documentation** phases, and this is considered in more detail later in this chapter and in chapter 17.

Systems analysis and design deals with the problems of helping us to understand how to analyse and design general solutions to major projects in an effective way. It helps us to understand how to apply computer techniques to the solution of problems if possible. It helps us to manage teams of people who are working on the same project, and to nurture the project through the testing, debugging and documentation phases until the final implementation phase has been achieved. However, even this is not the end – *customers expect continued support for expensive products*. It's part of the job of **systems analysts** and **software engineers** to ensure that the software and hardware can change to meet the ever-growing needs of the customer as time progresses. Systems analysis and design is all this – and much more!

Did you know that . . .

It's essential to have set methodologies for large projects involving many people working on the same task. Even with these methods, some projects still go overtime. The new air traffic control system in Southampton is a classic example. At the time of writing 21,000 errors in the computer software have been corrected, but government committees are arguing as to whether the software will ever be able to work. The project is already several years over-due, and the Americans abandoned a similar air-traffic control system a few years earlier! It's nice to know that the experts can't get it right all the time either.

The classical methods developed for analysis and design involve a set of rules to follow, which are known as the '**system life cycle**'. These 'rules' are now open to much-greater flexibility (see in a moment). However, they still form a suitable starting point for getting a general idea of how major projects can be approached. A typical system life cycle, together with some examples of the sort of activities which take place at each stage of the cycle, is shown in the following list.

(1) Detailed definition of the problem
Without a detailed definition of the problem we are trying to solve, people are often unsure of what it is they are trying to achieve.

(2) A feasibility study
A preliminary investigation is essential to determine whether a project is technically and economically feasible. Some projects may not be suitable for computer solution – it's best to realise this before a great deal of work has been started!

(3) Collecting information about the proposed system
Assuming that the project is feasible, much information needs to be collected – the system's requirements can then be determined in more detail, and more detailed estimates of the likely costs are undertaken.

(4) Analysis
An analysis of the problems using techniques such as the top-down approach, and making use of other structured methods now follows.

(5) Design of the system
Detailed design and coding (if necessary) of all the subsections of the project, followed by extensive testing and debugging.

(6) Implementation and evaluation
Installing and testing the overall system, further 'debugging and testing in situ' until it all works as expected. Staff training takes place during this phase.

(7) Maintenance
Making sure that the system continues to function correctly, and correcting bugs that may come to light after extensive use in the field.

Sound project advice!

Too rigorous an interpretation of some of these rules has led to certain problems and this was reflected quite clearly in the ways in which many computer-science projects at this level have been tackled in the past. For example, after the detailed specification was developed this was often set in a tablet of stone. The success of the entire project was then measured in relation to this original spec.

> **Hint:** Try to apply the methods learnt in this chapter to your project work. You will get more marks for working through the sort of methods shown here in a systematic way.

In the real world things are very different. Customers' needs change as projects are being developed, and good ideas, often evident only after considerable work has been done on a project, are used to *modify the original specification* if this proves to be more efficient, cost effective or of great benefit to all concerned. This more-flexible approach has proved to be effective, especially in a modern and constantly changing computing environment. Unfortunately, pupils at school or college could easily abuse such a system – unscrupulous students might think that they can modify virtually any aspect of their specification if they find some parts of their project to be too difficult, tedious or uninteresting. Nevertheless, putting laziness and lack of motivation aside for one moment – it is far more efficient to **make agreed modifications** to specifications whose outcome results in an overall improvement to the system. Modern techniques now reflect this philosophy.

Some of the basic techniques have already been started in chapter 14. Even so, you must remember that the *whole point* of **structured programming**, and the use of **structure diagrams** and the like, is to provide a methodical way of working which will *keep errors to a minimum*, and hopefully work towards the elimination of errors altogether (a thankless and virtually impossible task). Having worked through the structured-analysis sections of chapter 14, you often get some students who are impressed with the methods discussed, but then go back to their old habits of trying to develop algorithms inside their heads! For students working on their own this is often possible – but it's not desirable.

The very nature of the majority of work tackled on computer-science courses, is, of necessity, quite simple compared to the standards of project tackled in industry. You should note that this is not intended to be a derisory comment, but is a statement of fact. It is only when you have spent hours each day for months or even years working on systems with a team of other programmers that you can begin to understand the need for **good documentation**, **communication**, **consistency** and **style**. You *must* view the **software-engineering approach** used in this chapter with the above ideas and comments borne in mind, or it may all seem such a pointless exercise. At the other end of the spectrum are those students who meticulously apply what they have learnt to a comprehensive analysis of their projects. This professional approach has often resulted in near-perfect and in some cases absolutely perfect (100%) grades being awarded to these students for the project component of their advanced level courses. You would do well to bear these facts in mind.

Alternative approaches

Other philosophies exist too – **prototyping**, for example, is one of these alternative approaches. Sometimes it's very difficult to specify exactly what's required. This might sound a little strange, but customers often don't know what they want until someone shows them something to get their minds on the right track. This is not too surprising as many customers are *not* computing experts. One problem with the classic system-life-cycle approach is that it takes a long time to get anything tangible from the system that the customer can actually look at, and towards which they can make some valid contributions. Therefore, if prototyping is used, some front ends can be 'knocked up' quickly and dummy files written to act as a simple simulation of what the real system might be like. If the customer can then see something concrete in front of them, they

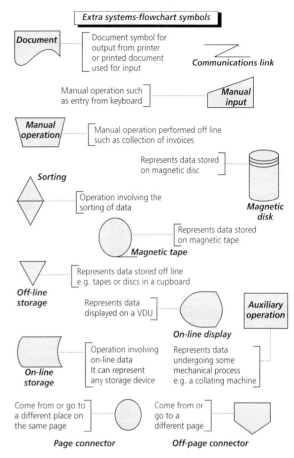

Figure 16.1

can start making good suggestions, which means that the systems can be further developed and refined. Prototyping can help the experts too – it's not only computer-illiterate people who don't know what they want! Prototyping can also be used on sub-problems.

Systems flowchart symbols

Before starting on a large systems-analysis example, you will need to add some further flowchart symbols to your 'flowchart-symbol toolbox'.

You have already studied a range of **flowchart symbols** shown in chapter 14, and the extra **systems-flowchart symbols** shown in figure 16.1 can be used in addition to the basic symbols. You can buy special templates in the shops which help you to draw the appropriate shapes in your notes, or you can set up a library in your CAD package (if none exists already) or word processor, which you can then use to draw the diagrams for your project write up.

A simple example

These symbols are very easy to use, and make certain types of process easy to understand. Let's suppose that we wish to describe pictorially the process whereby

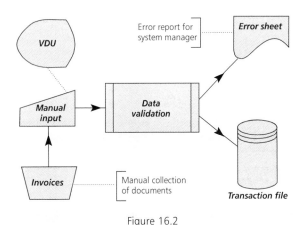

Figure 16.2

data is manually entered at the keyboard from a document, validated (see chapter 28), and then saved to disk if no errors are found, but a report generated if errors during this 'validation process' happen to occur. A systems flowchart for these operations could be as shown in figure 16.2.

The users of the systems often enhance the standard symbols used for systems diagrams, and the increase in flexibility mentioned earlier can certainly be applied to these diagrams too. Users will often invent extra notation *if* this helps to make the processes clear. For example, if a smoke sensor forms part of the diagram, then why not draw a picture of a smoke sensor? The output from the device can still be shown to activate whatever procedure by an appropriate arrow, and a picture of this device will make the diagrams easier to understand. In a similar way, networks of microcomputer terminals are often shown with 3D-images of real computers. In short, if you can make the concepts clearer by the addition of a few other symbols then it's often a good idea to do this. The advent of clip-art libraries has made this far easier to do than has been the case in the past.

The computerisation of Corpus Crumbly College Library

Systems analysis and design are most easily covered by considering an example which should be familiar to most students – that of computerising a school, college or university library. This example has been chosen because the ideas being discussed, and the aims trying to be achieved should not be alien to any student. You should all have experienced using a library, but most of you have probably not analysed the possible computerisation of such a large system in detail, or considered the repercussions that it could have on the organisation of an entire educational establishment! We will now consider such a computerised library, and use it to dis-

cuss systems principles in some considerable detail. But first let's look at some background information.

A complete systems-analysis example

Corpus Crumbly, a large, long established and very traditional college has a fine library with a massive collection of just over 350,000 books, many of which can be lent out to the students and staff at the college. The library has had a fine reputation for several hundred years, but has recently lost much credibility due to antiquated methods and organisation. A manual booking system involving filling in hand written cards and placing them (preferably in the right place!) within a cardboard index inside a shoe box is currently being used. Recent losses of books have been at an unacceptably high level, and books and periodicals are often mislaid due to the ineffective system of borrowing and returns. The system of searching for books in the library using a manual card index is also a slow and tedious process and students and staff spend many unproductive hours searching for information. The old librarian, who 'knew where most things could be found' has, unfortunately, passed away. Some prominent academics have abandoned the library altogether in favour of the easier-to-use library systems elsewhere, and this has been a blow to the pride of the college.

> **Hint:** Don't treat this section as learning about a library. There are literally hundreds of different examples that could have been chosen from estate agents to doctor's surgeries, for example. It is the analysis methods, which are all important. These are general methods which can be applied almost anywhere.

A new librarian has just been appointed who wishes to drag Corpus Crumbly into the 21st century. She intends to do this by introducing new technologies into all aspects of the library in which it can be shown to have proven benefit to both the staff and students. Some academic staff are sceptical of any new technology, and see the introduction of computers into the library as an unacceptable intrusion into a seat of learning which has served the students well for the last 400 years! Nevertheless, the new principal of the college is embarrassed by the way in which the Corpus Crumbly library is run compared to other similar colleges, most of which have already gone some way to installing new technology. You are to be placed in the role of **systems analyst** who has been charged with the task of upgrading the library and steering the project through to a successful conclusion – best of luck – you will need it!

Student activities

At frequent intervals during this library-computerisation example **you will be asked to stop and think about various points** *before* **going on to read the next section.**

If you take time out to do this you will gain a lot from the experience and start to realise the thought processes needed for good systems analysis. It's very useful practice for your projects too, as it mirrors the correct procedures.

The **classical system life cycle** will be used as the basis for investigation of this problem, so we will start to define the **information requirements** of the system.

Definition of the problem

This is obviously computerisation of the library – however, there's a little more to it than this! What do we mean by computerisation of the library? Part of the problem involved 'loss of books', therefore, efficient **security** and **booking systems** are obviously of paramount importance. If you are to use a computer for borrowing and returns, then you will need **a database of the books contained within the library** – a massive and expensive undertaking. Most modern books have **bar codes** on them, but Corpus Crumbly will obviously have many books which are too old for this form of coding – the staff would rightly object to having a bar code stuck onto an original work! Don't forget also that there are *other resources* in the library besides books – **periodicals**, **newspapers**, articles written by academic staff, specialist college literature produced in house and also **videos, CDs** and **cassettes** etc. What about the links between the main library and the smaller departmentally based libraries throughout the college? Collectively these departmentally based libraries account for a further 80,000 books and other resources such as videos etc.

> **Hint:** When doing your own analysis of whatever project you chose, make sure that you talk to the people who will operate the system. Instead of having few ideas for your project, you will probably be inundated with good ideas.

There will be supplementary considerations, which are of obvious importance when new technologies are introduced, and 'spin offs' in other directions may become apparent. For example, if a **security system** for access to the library is needed to prevent theft, are *there other security systems* already based around the college – if so, should we make use of the *same* **keys** or **card-entry systems** etc? Does the catering department have a **card** or **key system** for purchasing food? If so, could the *same cards or keys* be used in the library to pay fines or operate the proposed new **photocopiers** or **LASER printers**? We have only mentioned security and booking so far – yet you have already seen that possible interaction between the library and other systems within Corpus Crumbly may be used to advantage. *Take note about how the introduction of new technology may affect things, which at first sight would not have been apparent* – how many students would have guessed a possible link between the library and catering depart-

ments? This is one of the reasons why an organisation such as the educational institution being considered here needs to consider its systems in the wider perspective mentioned earlier. This is systems analysis at its innovative best – the art of the possible versus economic, political and other considerations.

There are many other library-specific considerations too. For example, much vital information can be found by making use of CD-ROM-based systems. This includes *Books in Print*, British Library bibliographies, and a whole host of other material from newspapers and encyclopaedias to information on global exploration. Much other information can also be gained by integrating links to the **Internet**. What about all of the administration which is carried out by the librarians? This includes: 'ordering of new books and periodicals', 'dissemination of information to the college', 'stock taking', 'fines', 'lists of people with books on loan', 'blacklisted people not allowed to use the system' and 'who's got a particular book' etc? What about connection to external databases for further information? There is already an extensive computer-based network around the college – it would seem sensible if students could interrogate the library-system databases from anywhere within the college at any time of the day or night, providing that the student has access to a suitable terminal and has the necessary authority. What about interrogation of the system from home via a modem? This facility would be extremely useful for any holiday work carried out by the students. The list of useful facilities will probably grow with continuing new developments and ideas, and should always be subject to an open-ended review from time to time. You will recall that good systems analysis should allow for systems to grow, as customers' needs change, and you have now seen some relevant examples.

Student activities – 1
Start to work on the problem

You now appreciate the problem.

(1) How would you go about starting to tackle the problem of computerising the Corpus Crumbly Library?

(2) Write down some major points which you think are important at this early stage.

(3) Do you think that the problem is technically and economically feasible?

(4) Who do you think needs to be consulted?

Feasibility study

A fully blown feasibility study is a little less important here than would be the case in industry or commerce when different major projects are being considered. For example, it's obvious that the system is feasible as many other libraries throughout the country have already computerised similar systems. Off-the-shelf library systems such as **BookShelf** or **Alice**, for example, might provide most, if not all, of the system's requirements. Such systems are already extensively used within many schools, colleges and universities. Systems analysts should not have their eyes closed to existing practice within other institutions.

In industry similar arguments apply. For example, *the application of standard packages such as databases spreadsheets and the use of network systems may solve many systems' problems.* However, some projects are often of a more open-ended nature, they may involve computerisation of systems which has not been done before, or involve projects in which there is little relevant experience. *In these cases it's essential to have an extensive feasibility study undertaken or much money and time could be wasted.* A team of experts who have proven experience in a particular field would carry out such detailed analysis. For example, it might be 'control of a chemical plant', 'analysis of a financial institution' or the 'setting up of a large medical-system database for the NHS'. In industry and commerce many projects are often undertaken simultaneously, so other constraints such as prioritisation of projects need to be considered. Projects are usually prioritised by considering the likely results relating to which projects are the most feasible, and which projects will bring in the largest economic benefits most quickly to the company.

As far as the library example being considered here is concerned, *we will assume* that the requirements are both **technically** and **economically feasible**.

Collecting information

To help draw up a broad set of objectives many members of staff and students need to be consulted. This is usually done by interview, perhaps by filling in some questionnaires, and the formation of one or more committees would usually be used to investigate major areas of concern. Unlike the competitive industrial and commercial markets, librarians are usually only too pleased to show others what they have achieved, and *visits to other libraries would therefore be an invaluable source of extra information.* The following areas would probably make a good starting point.

(1) General objectives.
(2) The database.
(3) The librarians' perspective.
(4) The academic departments' perspective.
(5) Students' perspective.
(6) Security.

Overseeing all of the areas above would be the overriding consideration of cost. Can the college afford to implement the system in one go or is a phased implementation more likely? If the implementation is to be

phased, what are the priorities? We will now consider each of the above areas in more detail.

General objectives

After some detailed consultation with interested parties, and observation of similar systems in practice, general objectives can be developed. The following is typical of what the users of the new system at Corpus Crumbly might expect to gain after successful implementation.

> **Hint:** You would be well advised to try to write down some objectives for your own project work. If you can't think of many, then perhaps you should choose a different project!

(a) **A greatly improved service** – information ought to be instantly available regarding what resources such as books, periodicals and videos etc. can be borrowed, who has which resource, and reservations should be handled with greater efficiency. This information is to be extended to include all departmentally based resources throughout the college.

(b) **Real-time system** – when a book or other resource is returned it should be instantly available to be borrowed again, unlike the old manual system where delays of up to a day or even longer used to be the norm.

(c) **On-line interaction** – students should have access to information 24-hours a day from any suitable terminal on campus, or via a modem from outside the college. Information from other sources such as CD-ROM and the Internet should be available via the networks and telephone system if possible.

(d) **Better stock security** – The system should be able to have total control over all aspects of the issuing of books and other resources. It should exclude blacklisted borrowers, be able to manage the fines system, and be able to provide accounting facilities and statistics regarding many different aspects of the use, abuse and financial management of the system.

(e) **Better physical security** – The system should provide a warning if books or other resources are about to be stolen from the library. It should only allow access to staff and students with appropriate authority at specified times of the day and night, and at specified days and weeks during the year.

(f) **Time saving** – The computer system should carry out mundane routines automatically. This will release staff so that they can spend more time helping the students and staff at Corpus Crumbly.

(g) **A more-polished image** – The image of the college should be considerably enhanced by the increased efficiency of the library.

You should now start to see the enormity of the task ahead. You will also realise that we will only be able to summarise major categories during the rest of this chapter. However, such a system has all the impact of a real system because it *is* a real system. Nothing of major importance has been left out, and the above list indicates what are typical requirements for a large and modern library. However, specific libraries might require further additions, for example, specialist materials for disabled people, music CDs, geological collections etc. – the list is limited only by the needs of the local community, finance, and the imagination of the people who design the systems – i.e. you!

At all stages you must be aware of the economic implications of what you are proposing, be aware of the technical feasibility of the proposals too, and be aware of the potential resistance from users who might undermine what you are trying to do! Don't forget that there are influential academic staff who don't want computers in the library. It does not matter that they don't understand enough to be able to appreciate the benefits of the system! It's your job to convince them of the benefits or at least neutralise their opposition if this is possible – *politics plays a large part in the development of many systems* – a point well worth noting.

Student activities – 3
The main database

Concentrate on the Information that will need to be held in the main database.

(1) What information might be needed regarding the resources such as books, videos and CDs etc. held by the library?

(2) What information might be needed regarding the borrowers? Don't forget to cater for a variety of different students and staff.

The database

Besides security, this is *the* most fundamental area. The success or failure of the system will be judged by the efficiency with which this database of books and other resources is implemented and maintained, and by the ease with which users of the system will be able to gain the considerable benefits proposed.

A **relational database** (see chapter 29) will probably be the most efficient way to implement such a system, as mundane tasks such as 'borrowing a book' will affect both the 'borrowers' and 'book' (resources) files. Typically there would be a requirement for a *library catalogue of all the resources* which we will call the **resource file** – we have not called it the book file because resources other than books are to be included within it too.

Resource file

This *is essentially the* **cataloguing information**, i.e. the detailed information about each resource held on the library catalogue. Typical information for individual catalogue fields (not necessarily in any order of importance) might be as follows.

Field	Remarks
Title	
Author(s)	
Edition	
Series	
Accession number	Number relating to multiple-copies of the same resource.
Resource status	Reference, available, on loan, requested etc.
Subject	Science, Engineering etc.
Level	GCSE, 'A' Level, undergraduate, postgraduate etc.
Key words	Key words relating to subject content
Media	Book, CD-ROM, Disk, Internet site, map, slide, video etc.
Remarks	Free-flowing text field for notes of any description
Dewey classification	Number system used to help categorise books
Location	Corpus Crumbly or departmental positional information
ISBN	International Standard Book Number
Bar-code number	
Library number	Special Corpus Crumbly reference number.
Date	Acquisition date.

Borrowers' file

This information will relate to the students and staff at the college, and their relationship with the Corpus Crumbly library.

Field	Remarks
Staff/Student no.	Unique Corpus-Crumbly ID for the college
Name	

Field	Remarks
Address	Several fields may be required
Post code	Might need alternatives for students who live abroad
Telephone number	
Borrower category	Several different **staff** and **student** categories
Date of registration	
Department	Main department to which staff or student belongs
Sub. Dept 1	Subsidiary department for use of departmental libraries
Sub. Dept 2	
Sub. Dept 3	
Books on loan	Links to books on loan
Borrower's Status	Blacklisted, owing fines etc.
Balance	Amount owed by the borrower to the library
Requested 1	A field to enable users to remotely request resources
Requested 2	
Requested 3	
Requested 4	
Requested 5	
Remarks	Free-flowing text field for notes of any description

Other information

There is a whole host of other potentially useful information. For example, a file of book publishers with links to the database. Much other information is covered in the relevant sections where the library is considered from the perspectives of different staff and student users of the system.

It's essential that some sort of simplified manual-backup for booking and returns is set up as it's inevitable that the computer will go down at some stage. *The main and departmental libraries must continue to perform a basic function under these unusual conditions.*

Besides the cost of developing the database or purchasing a proprietary database, there is the cost of the enormous task of entering information regarding several hundred thousand books. Typically companies will charge between 25p and 50p for entering data regarding a single book. The cost of this data-entry marathon alone will therefore be in excess of one hundred thousand pounds! If secretarial staff were to undertake this operation, then allowing a few minutes for the entry

> **Hint:** Always return to the main objectives at frequent intervals throughout your project to make sure that you are still on the right track. It's easy to drift away from or even forget original ideas when you are buried in working out the detail.

of a single book. The operation would take about $(350,000 + 80,000) \times 3$ minutes which is about 21,500 hours, or about 10 person years! – assuming that one person were to enter the data 8 hours a day, five days a week with no holidays. There is also a possibility of downloading information on modern books from existing CD-ROM databases. This method could save thousands of pounds.

> ### Student activities 4 – The librarian's perspective
> Concentrate on the view of the systems from the point of view of the librarian and the other assistant librarians who will run the system.
> (1) Make a list of the day-to-day tasks that the system will need to be able to perform.
> (2) Make a list of the specific administrative functions.
> (3) Are there any other useful functions, which can be performed?

The librarian's perspective

All the main functions performed by the librarians need to be listed so that the system will be able to cope with them. Some of the functions (not shown in any particular order of importance) could be as follows.

On a day-to-day basis the librarian will probably need to:

(a) Enquire about a borrower by name or number.
(b) Issue books and other resources to students and staff.
(c) Generate stamp dates automatically.
(d) Accept books and other resources back into the library.
(e) Be able to make reservations.
(f) Search the database on all fields using many different filters.
(g) Modify any of the borrower's details.
(h) Add new borrowers or delete old ones.
(i) Modify any of the catalogue resource records.
(j) Create new catalogue entries.
(k) Access the borrower's account records (for fines and other charges).
(l) Print out details from a variety of queries.
(m) Control the security system (i.e. reset the alarm if it goes off).

> **Hint:** Always consider the end users of your project. This is why it's important to have different users' perspectives on what's being designed. Don't forget that you are not usually doing the project for yourself, but for the people who will be using it for years to come.

(n) Produce standard letters to be sent to students and staff.

Specific administrative tasks might include:

(a) Statistics regarding overdue books and other resources.
(b) Financial information regarding the library.
(c) Ordering of new books.
(d) Books taken out for repair.
(e) Help with stocktaking.
(f) Save standard queries for future use.
(g) Print out reservations.
(h) Labelling of new books.
(i) Dealing with requests from/to other libraries.
(j) Automatic ordering of periodicals and other resources.
(k) Automatic accounting and billing procedures.
(l) Helping with circulation of material to relevant staff and students.

Extra useful functions might include:

(a) Statistics regarding readers' borrowing habits.
(b) A notice-board system for disseminating library information.
(c) Integration of the software with standard packages such as spreadsheets, word processors and databases etc.

The above lists are not exhaustive, and no doubt many other functions may be dreamt up – you will recall that a major objective of the system is continued development – there are bound to be many good ideas not listed above, and technical innovations yet to be invented. The system should be flexible enough to cope with the constant updates likely to happen over the next few years. One of the points of the earlier exercises, where information was gathered from a variety of staff and students, would be to collect a selection of good ideas which might enhance the system if they are both technically and economically feasible.

Student activities – 5
The academic departments

Consider the use of the library from the point of view of a typical academic department.

(1) List typical features that may be required by each department.
(2) What extra technical problems might there be?
(3) Are any political problems likely?
(4) What advantages might there be for these departments
(5) Are there any disadvantages?

The academic departments

Each academic department within Corpus Crumbly will have its own perspective of the main library, and the relationship between it and the main library. Corpus Crumbly has the following academic departments.

Biology	Business studies	Chemistry
Classics	Computing & IT	Divinity
Drama	Economics	Electronics
English	French	Geography
German	History	Japanese
Mathematics	Music	PE
Physics	Politics	Spanish
Technology		

Most have their own libraries which are run with varying degrees of efficiency from 'manual booking systems' to the 'haven't got a clue about what books we have or where they are' syndrome!

There are several camps within the school regarding grouping of departments, but the technical departments are particularly keen on the '**Key Word**' searches that could be set up in the main database. For example, type in 'nano technology', and books or periodicals in either the main library or any departmental library in which this fascinating topic is listed should be flagged – i.e. brought to the attention of the user who is searching the database. However, most heads of department don't relish the idea of typing in thousands of key words – a potential area of friction, which will have to be borne in mind! It's possible to get CR-ROMs containing huge volumes of information regarding books in print, and it might be possible to find a system in which someone else has already done the 'donkey work'. However, there is no substitute for extending the key-word systems to add local flavour, and if the task can be accomplished over a period of years then the benefits will be enormous.

The facilities needed by the departmental libraries are identical in most respects to the facilities required by the main library; however, a few other specials might come to light:

(a) Extra length borrowing periods for students within a department.
(b) Very-long borrowing periods for staff within the department.

These requirements might be able to be linked to the main database by using the borrower category and departmental information held in the borrowers' file.

Potential problems

Most departments will probably relish the idea of having someone else look after their library. However, access to the books and other resources is a potential problem because they are housed in physically-different locations around the campus, and in rooms which may be locked at times when the main library is open. Staff are naturally reluctant to have an open-access policy at all times, and it's likely that books will have to be reserved if the departmental library is closed.

Some staff will probably feel threatened by the intro-duction of the new technology. Eventually the manual methods of searching will be removed, and this may put off some staff from using the system. Staff training and a sympathetic approach will be needed. Never-theless, the many perceived advantages of the new system must not be held back to cater for a few educa-tional dinosaurs.

Student activities – 6
A student's perspective

This is the easiest option for students to answer. What do they want from the main and academic department libraries?

(1) List the features which would be useful from a typical student's perspective. (Be realistic!)

(2) What advantages would there be for the students?

(3) Are there any disadvantages of the new system?

A student's perspective

All the features covered hitherto will obviously bene-fit the students, but extra benefits could include the following:

(a) Unlimited access to appropriate library details via the computer network.
(b) Access to library information 24 hours per day.
(c) Far easier searching for information.
(d) E-mail can be used to communicate with the librarian.
(e) E-mail can be used to flag students when books are available.
(f) CD-ROM, Internet and external-database searches will add to the considerable arsenal of available methods of research.

Some students may also feel threatened by the system, and much information and publicity will need to be undertaken if the transition from the manual system to the automatic system is to be a smooth one. *The whole point of computerisation should not be to alienate the students, but to provide the mechanisms whereby the library can become a more productive environment for both work and pleasure.* The success of this system would hopefully be measured in terms of a very signifi-cant increase in productive and pleasurable student and staff activity when using the library.

Student activities – 7 Security

You must consider the physical security of the resources from the point of view of both buildings and day-to-day pilfering.

(1) What systems might be useful for the physical security of the buildings such as the main library and departmental libraries?

(2) What could be done to overcome the pilfering problems?

(3) Are there are any disadvantages of the new system?

Security

The physical security of the building is important as the library is open for long hours, and at present any member of the public can walk into the building when the library is open. With the old system it's difficult to distinguish pilfering by students or staff from pilfering by members of the public.

Some sort of door where entry and exit is controlled either by a swipe card, a smart card or a smart key (see chapter 9) would be useful. Access would then be granted only to those students and staff with an appro-priate pass. This pass could be the same one used for all financial and security transactions within Corpus Crumbly College. This is to include access to the acad-emic department libraries too.

A smart key or card system could be programmed such that entry by appropriate personnel is controlled by the system. For example, academic staff might have a smart key which gives them access to their particular departmental library at any time of the day or night, 365 days a year. (They're a dedicated lot at Corpus Crumbly!) However, students may only gain access to libraries during term time at specific times of the day or evening. Different types of student may have different privileges, which may change according to their age and status.

Disadvantages

The smart key could also be the same device used to book resources from any of the libraries, and to pay for fines if necessary. (Cash can be credited on the microchips inside these keys.) If a student is blacklisted then his or her key is nullified as far as the main library is concerned. The students could also be prevented from entering other installations within the campus including selected departmental libraries.

The smart key system offers many advantages, but some students and staff may feel that big brother is watching over them. To some extent this is true – the whole point of this system is to control access! However, students and staff must be reassured that the information-gathering potential of such a system is not

o be misused. You should refer to the Data Protection
Act of 1998 at the end of chapter 28 for further details.
It's possible to create a reasonably detailed account of
the whereabouts of particular students including the
times that they enter and leave particular buildings.
Although it's technically possible to do this – it's not
what the system has been designed to do. Students and
staff will need reassurance that no software exists to
perform interrogations of this sinister kind.

Costs

Typical smart-key systems cost in excess of one thousand pounds per door for entry and exit. Typical smart
keys cost about ten pounds each, and all students and
staff in the college will need to be issued with one.

The specialist security system for tagging books such
that alarms are activated if books are being removed
that have not been borrowed officially (i.e. stolen!) costs
about £20,000 per system.

Initial conclusions

That's the end of the information-gathering stage. We
have been reasonably brief compared to the detailed
information and opinion gathering which would have to
be undertaken in practice,
especially in terms of
detailed costing. How-
ever, as you can see, computerisation of the library
system is not a trivial matter. Readers of this book
should now be well aware
of what happens during
the information-gathering
stages of a typical system
life cycle. You should
ensure that the shorter
problems that you tackle
with your computer-science projects are done with
equal thoroughness.

It is at this stage that the potential advantages and
disadvantages of the system become clear. For example,
**are the benefits to be gained from such a system suffi-
cient to make the cost of the system acceptable?** *This
is probably the last stage at which we can sensibly withdraw from the project* without incurring any significant
expense of developing software, purchasing hardware,
and setting up the database. However, don't forget that
there has already been a considerable sum spent on the
systems-analyst's fees!

The final decisions will obviously be financial. It is
the job of the systems analyst to declare all the pros
and cons of the system in an objective way, so that the
managers of Corpus Crumbly can weigh up the potential benefits versus the cost of the system. Don't forget
that such a complex system can be phased over a

> **Hint:** Notice how much
> work has been put into
> the system before any
> programs have been
> written on the computer!
> It's very tempting for
> students who are
> starting their projects to
> write code before much
> analysis has taken place.
> Resist this temptation,
> you will get a better
> project in the end.

number of years, and this would probably be the most
likely scenario in practice.

Analysis of the problem

We will assume that the go ahead has been given, or
we won't have anything to analyse! Having seen what
is needed, we now have to analyse the best ways of
solving the problem. **We need to split up the problem
into major subsections**, produce some sort of schedule,
and start to plan for the transition from the manual to
the automatic system.

> ### Student activities – 8
> ### Analysis of the problem
> You must now split up the problems into major
> subsections so that a team of people can be
> assigned to different tasks.
> (1) What structured analysis methods would be
>   most useful here?
> (2) How would you manage the time aspects of
>   the project?
> (3) Suggest a set of suitable modular activities for
>   computerisation of the Corpus Crumbly Library.

How on earth do we estimate the time that will be
needed for this project? Past experience is probably the
best yardstick to use, but what happens if the project
has never been done before? Let's suppose, just for
the sake of argument, that the library system being
considered here had *not* been done before – the only
alternative is to break up the system into smaller parts
(already needed for modularity), then analyse the time
that would be necessary for each part. This is more
useful than may appear at first sight. **For example, if
we are to set up a relational database which deals with
just under half a million records for the resources file,
where each record has just under twenty fields** – then
this sort of activity is *not* unique. It does not matter if
we are setting up a library database or a database
dealing with 'Outer-Mongolian snow rabbits' – people
have set up databases of this size before – how long
did it take to do? – the library system will probably
take a similar amount of time.

With most projects tackled in industry and commerce
there is a project deadline – usually yesterday! Systems
analysts will have to estimate the resources that will
be needed to complete the project by the due date –
and point out any unrealistic project deadlines to the
management. It is also the job of the systems analyst
to make sure that agreed deadlines are actually met.

Unfortunately, software products are notoriously difficult to plan and predict. We always assume that things
will go to plan, and when they don't – panic sets in and
corners often tend to be cut. Most readers will be well
aware of the media hype which accompanies major

releases of new packages and operating systems – most readers will also be aware of the fact that many systems don't appear by the due date, and often contain quite serious bugs when they finally do come out! It's against this sort of background that **software-engineering techniques** (see chapter 17) are being developed which help refine our solutions to these potentially disastrous problems.

Coming back to our library systems, we will therefore concentrate on modularisation and scheduling, before getting down to the 'nitty gritty' of analysis in more detail.

Mapping out progress

Let's suppose that the project deadline to implement the entire Corpus Crumbly system has been set at twelve months. (This is not unrealistic.) The Gantt chart shown in figure 16.3 might reflect a potential solution to some of the problems. This chart shows only the most brief of details, but gives an idea of the relationship and scheduling between different parts of the project. The marker shows some arbitrary point three months into the project, and, as can be seen from the chart, by this time the resource database has been completely designed and is still undergoing tests, but the borrowers' database has been designed and tested. The librarians' utilities are about to be designed, tested and added to the existing software.

> **Hint:** It's at this stage that you can attempt to map out the likely jobs to be done in your projects. Indeed, if you split up the problem into a number of suitable tasks, together with realistic times to solve them, you are more likely to finish your project without the usual panic at the end.

Notice that a further three weeks at the beginning of the project is allowed to develop more-general ideas further. It should also be noticed that in this particular project there is considerable flexibility about when activities take place. For example, the physical security system is almost a separate issue, and does not relate to any software functions on the system at all. This activity could, therefore, be started at any time so long as the system was installed and tested before much staff training had been undertaken. There are other parts of the project which are more critical. For example, the librarian's utilities such as new-book labelling routines or fines calculation etc. can't be undertaken until all the basic database software is up and running.

If some parts of the system, such as the main database or data entry routines were late, then this would probably delay the 'Grand Opening Champagne Party'. However, if other more minor parts of the system were delayed, such as the MODEM link, for example, then this would *not* delay the most important parts of the system. **Software** such as **PERT charts** (see chapter 14) could be used to identify if certain parts of the project were getting to the stage of delaying the overall

schedule. Extra person-power could then be put onto these critical parts of the project if finances allowed.

More detailed analysis

The Gantt chart shown in figure 16.3 can, if desired, be further subdivided. If too much detail is shown on the main chart then overall project impressions get lost in a sea of horizontal bars which become meaningless. Similarly, if we undertook a top-down-approach diagram for the whole project it would become unacceptably cumbersome. The Gantt chart has split the project up into an acceptable number of major subdivisions; therefore, individual top-down-approach diagrams can be used for each part of the project.

There is neither the space in this chapter (there's probably not space in the whole book!) nor the time to cover the design of such a system in detail. Therefore, we will concentrate on just one part of the project as an example of the sort of techniques that can be used.

The borrower's database

This is one of the major parts of the project around which many other modules will be based. The biggest part of the project would be the main catalogue-index database, but this would be too large for a quick example, therefore the borrower's database will be used instead, and even this will be subdivided and only partially undertaken.

There are several phases to be considered in the design of this relational database, but here we will not go into the pros and cons of different database types as this is already covered in chapters 28 and 29 where database design is considered in more detail. Here we are concerned only with the design of the user interface, including any validation and security aspects, the relationships with the main catalogue database, and the types of end-user administrative functions which need to be carried out by reference to the borrower's database. We now look at these aspects in a little more detail, using the field information for the borrower's file given earlier in this chapter as a guide for each section that follows.

Staff/Student number facility

The staff and student numbers are unique to Corpus Crumbly College, but these numbers will not necessarily be known to the students – if they were it's obvious that some students would tell their number to others. Therefore, it's proposed that the number be encoded inside a **smart key**, which can be used with a special reading device. The idea is identical in principle to ATMs (hole-in-the-wall machines outside banks) and cards, but smart keys are more reliable and robust than swipe cards. It is possible to supplement possession of a key with a PIN number, and this would

Corpus-Crumbly library system progress chart

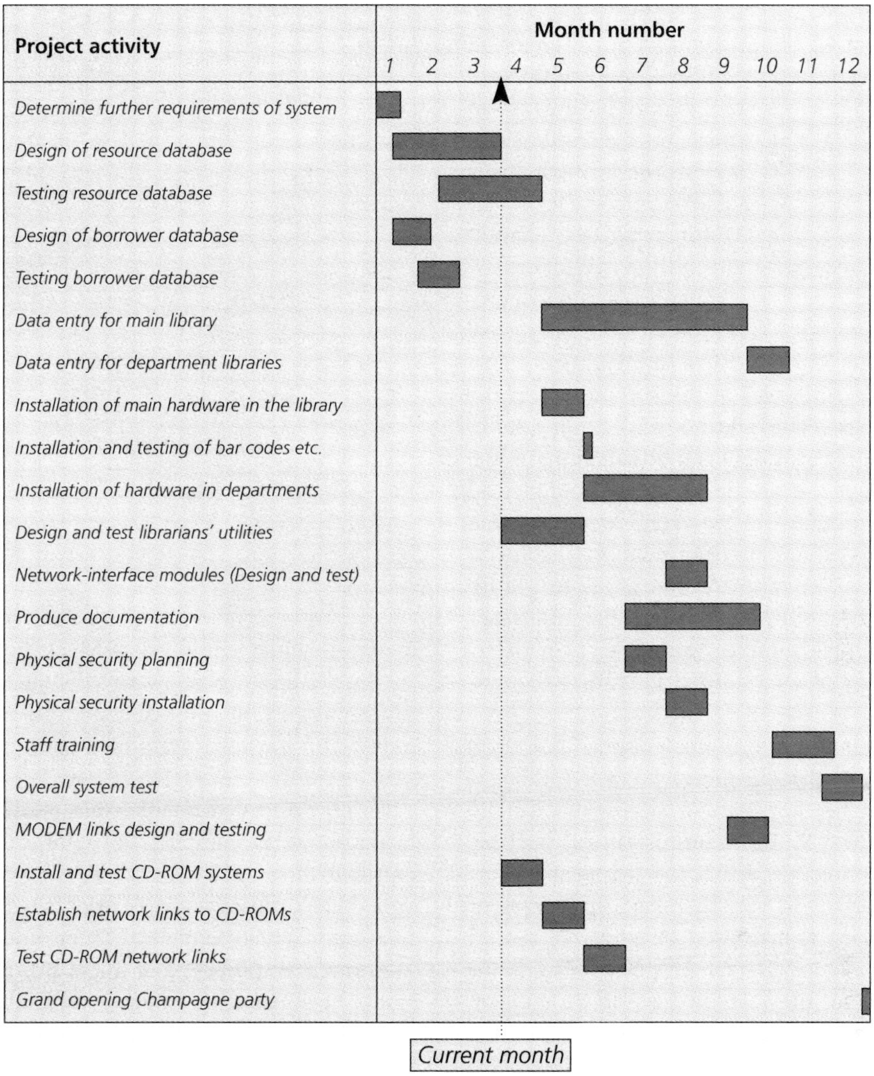

Project activity	Month number
	1 2 3 4 5 6 7 8 9 10 11 12
Determine further requirements of system	
Design of resource database	
Testing resource database	
Design of borrower database	
Testing borrower database	
Data entry for main library	
Data entry for department libraries	
Installation of main hardware in the library	
Installation and testing of bar codes etc.	
Installation of hardware in departments	
Design and test librarians' utilities	
Network-interface modules (Design and test)	
Produce documentation	
Physical security planning	
Physical security installation	
Staff training	
Overall system test	
MODEM links design and testing	
Install and test CD-ROM systems	
Establish network links to CD-ROMs	
Test CD-ROM network links	
Grand opening Champagne party	

Current month

Figure 16.3

give even-greater security. The smart keys will be used to carry out cash transactions in other parts of the college, because the chips inside are charged up by special dispensing machines in the college which accept £10 notes. They also allow students to gain access to private quarters. *It's therefore less likely that students will lend their keys to their friends and tell them their PIN numbers!*

A machine in the library will be needed into which the smart key can be placed, and the student will have to type in a PIN number. If the PIN number is verified by the system as being correct, then the holder will be assumed to be the owner of the key. However, a photo of each student and member of staff could easily be incorporated into the database as a final security check, and this could be displayed on the librarian's screen as resources are being booked out.

The main requirements for this part of the borrowers' database will therefore be as follows.

(a) An interface to the smart-key reader.
(b) An interface with the PIN number numeric key pad.
(c) Calling up the student or staff photo on screen.
(d) Automatic verification of the PIN number in relation to the key number.

Some problems

You may not think that standard information of this sort would cause any problems – but this is not so! Extensive computerisation of administration within Corpus Crumbly means *that this information already exists on other databases throughout the college.* There needs to be much thought put in to avoid possible duplication of existing information in the library system. For example, can we establish links with these other databases? The advantage of the current administrative system is that it is already being efficiently kept up to date by the administrative staff. It would seem to make little sense to get the librarians to update the same information in a different set of files – this would lead to potential sources of extra errors, and be a tedious chore, which is totally unnecessary.

Multitasking (see chapter 23) within WIMP environments is now commonplace, therefore, it would be a relatively easy solution to separate the general administrative information such as the addresses of the students from the main library database. The 'address' and 'other admin. information' regarding a student can be called up on the screen if needed from the 'admin. database', and viewed within a different window on the same screen, or even in the same window if a composite relational database (having different views of the same data) is set up (see figure 28.2). It should be realised that 'Address', 'Post code', 'Telephone number' and 'Date of registration' would not normally be needed for run-of-the-mill transactions.

It may be possible to hot-link (make use of hot keys) the two systems so that a single key press is all that is needed to call up the appropriate administrative file when needed. However, the administration database might contain information which the management do not wish the librarians to see, therefore, some sort of access level security system (see chapter 28) would need to be implemented if this proposal were to be acceptable. Therefore, time would have to be allowed for modifications to the administrative database to be carried out. You will see the advantage of planning a campus-wide computer system at the same time, but this is rarely possible in practice.

Borrower category

There will probably be different categories of borrower with 'students' and 'staff' being an obvious starting point. However, different types of student may need to be considered, with undergraduates and post-graduates being treated differently, and thus each category might have different departmental and main-library privileges. For example, a 1st-year undergraduate biologist might be able to borrow 10 books from the main library because he or she is an undergraduate, but might also be able to borrow 15 books from the biology-department library because he or she is a biologist.

These different categories can be generated automatically from the administrative department's computer as these files will store course details for each student. For example, a full-time first-year honours biology student might be registered with a course code of BIO1FTH.

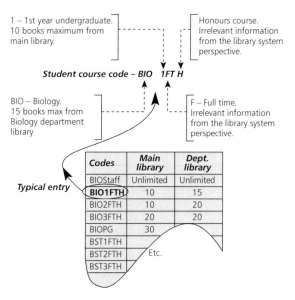

Figure 16.4

A simple table could then be set up on the library system's computer showing the relationship between course codes and privileges derived from these course codes. The start of a simplified table is shown in figure 16.4.

Tabular information like that shown above may be as simple or as complex as required. For example, all staff may have unlimited access and borrowing capacity from the main library. Particular staff members of departments may have unlimited access to their own departmental library, but more-limited access or no access at all to other departmental libraries. If all first year undergraduates have a 10-book (or 10-resource) capacity with respect to the main library, then only the year digit from the course-code string would need to be analysed and the table would be considerably simpler. If different courses allow different resources to be borrowed from different departments, then additional entries will be necessary. Also, a tabular arrangement would allow groups of students on certain combined-honours courses to book out resources from other relevant departments. For example, people on an Electronic Engineering and Physics course might be able to borrow books from the electronics, physics and mathematics department libraries.

A more-complex tabular arrangement than shown in figure 16.4 would be necessary for varied booking arrangements, but would be ideal for solution by relational-database methods (see chapter 29). An administrative utility would therefore need to be programmed which would analyse all the course codes for students, and automatically update the library-database files with the appropriate information. This program would probably be run just before the beginning of each academic year.

Department

This field can be filled in automatically by analysis of the course codes held for the staff and pupils. It would probably belong to the same utility that derives the borrower's limits for each student from the same course codes mentioned in the last section.

Subsidiary departments

These fields enable additional borrowing limits for combined-honours courses which involve several different departments. The course codes for these courses would be indicated in some way in an enlarged version of the table shown in figure 16.4.

Books on loan

This information does not need to be typed in, but should obviously be available to the librarian or student when browsing through the borrowers' file. The Corpus-Crumbly identification number can be used as a flag to extract the information from the main catalogue index if this is required either on the screen or on a printer.

Borrower's status

This is an important field because it will be used as a flag to help determine the privileges on the system. For example, if a borrower has been blacklisted, then there will be no privileges at all, even though the borrower's limits for this particular student may not have been exceeded. The borrowers' status field will need to be accessed by the main catalogue system whenever a resource is requested.

Balance

This field can be used to store information regarding fines, or costs for books lost etc. – it will have to be accessible by the administration department for the purposes of billing students who have left or been expelled!

Requested resource fields

These additional fields enable a student to request up to five additional resources (subject to their individual maxima not being exceeded) from any terminal within the campus, or via a modem from outside the campus. This system is particularly useful when the library is closed. If the resources are available and the relevant conditions have been satisfied, then the librarian will physically reserve the appropriate resource at the beginning of the day on which the main library is next open. If a resource is available and has been requested, then a flag should be set in the main catalogue index file to indicate that this resource has now been reserved. This flag will lock out other students from trying to book the same resource from a remote terminal while the library is still closed. The status field in the main catalogue index is intended for this purpose.

Remarks

This is simply a free-flowing textual field into which the librarian may add comments. It may also be possible to store recent e-mail communications here, or hot link (use a hot key) to a separate e-mail system.

Password protection

As can be seen from the above, there will be several different types and categories of users who should be allowed access to different parts of the system. For example, a student should have access to his own borrower's record. However, he or she should not be able to change the status of any field except the five requested-resource fields. Indeed, it is not necessary for students to be able to see all of the fields in their borrower's file if this is thought undesirable. The librarian, for example, might wish to keep the remarks field private. (However, the student may have a legal right to see it if they wish because of the data protection act! (see chapter 28)). No student should be able to see anybody else's borrower's record.

The librarians should have complete authority to alter any data or any field within the library database, but it should be remembered that only the DBMS administrator (i.e. the DBA) (see chapter 28) should have the authority to alter any of the structure within the database. Administrative staff will need authority to read and update the fields which contain financial information, and all students will need to have read-only access to the cataloguing files.

Finally, it may be that Corpus Crumbly gives outsiders special permission to use the system as a reference library, in which case these individuals would have restricted access to the system facilities, with no booking or other privileges. Multiple-level password protection of this kind has already been covered in the database section in chapter 28, and will therefore not be repeated here.

Further detailed analysis

Some sort of visualisation of the interaction between the different elements of the borrowers' database is now needed. A suitable diagram is shown in figure 16.5. The detail shown in this diagram contains no extra information than was presented in the previous few pages, but it does allow us to collect our thoughts and appreciate the tasks ahead more easily. For example, it reminds us that critical data is shared between several databases, and relational updates will therefore be needed. It

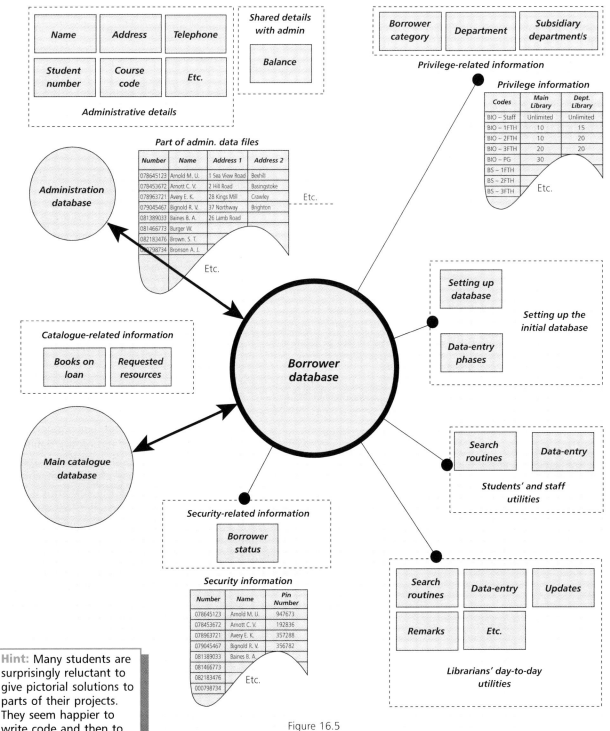

Figure 16.5

has also gathered together routines, which may be considered as belonging to certain categories, for example, 'admin.' or 'security'.

There is neither the time nor the space to consider the design of the complete borrowers' database in detail, therefore, we will take just one area to show what might typically happen in the next stage of development. We have, at last, started to reach the stage where small parts of the system can be developed in detail. You would do well to pay attention to the amount of detailed thought that has gone into this project *before* any coding has actually taken place – apply similar principles to your own project work. However, this does not stop you from prototyping some parts of the system, especially the user interfaces and menu systems etc.

The course-code utility

Let's now concentrate on the utility (module) which extracts the course-code information from the administrative department's database, and builds up the information given in the privilege table. There will probably be a need for a couple of options here – first a complete update of all students' details at the beginning of an academic year, and secondly a need to update an individual student without referring to all the rest. This is necessary if a student joins Corpus Crumbly mid-term. In essence, the module will need to carry out the following processes for each student.

(a) Accept student name/s as an input (from keyboard or file).
(b) Extract student number and course code from the admin. database.
(b) Examine course code and extract relevant information.
(c) Match up to privilege statistics.
(d) Build up entry in privilege table in borrowers' database.

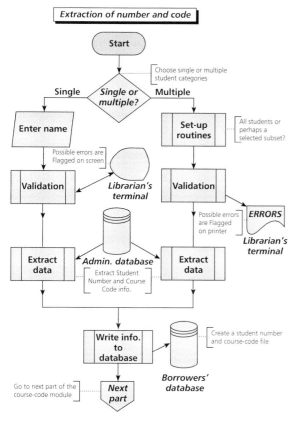

Figure 16.6

Extraction of number/code

To determine if a whole batch of students is to be processed, or if we simply wish to process a single student, then some sort of menu choice will be needed. Either way, we don't want to tie up the admin. department's computer for long, and so a file of student numbers and course codes could be saved on the library computer's disk, and then the utility can use this as the source of information.

Figure 16.6 shows a systems' flowchart for the first part of this module. If we are using the multiple-student utility, then at the end of this routine we end up with a file of student number and course code information. Errors – such as the possibility of a name not existing etc. can be echoed on screen or printed out if several names are generated from longer lists of students being processed at the same time.

The borrowers' database software now has a file of information containing the course code for each student who has access to the library. Note that not all the detail has been shown on this particular flowchart. For example, to get access to the admin database, the librarian would have to log on and go through some password procedures. **We are now into a reasonable depth of analysis, but much more detail needs to be obtained before coding or database design can take place.**

Also, in practice, there would have to be a very broad agreement between all the people that are writing the different routines as to the exact formats of the shared data. This is considered in chapter 28 when data dictionaries are discussed.

The privilege statistics

Information needs to be held in the system regarding the policies of different departments, and the policy of the main library regarding the number of books that can be leant out to different categories of students and staff. Corpus Crumbly has no agreed blanket policy, therefore, each department's information can be found by using a look-up table. A file can be set up matching the course code with the privilege level for each library. The systems analyst has suggested a more-uniform booking policy to simplify this stage of the proceedings, but traditionalists at the college will not have their lending policies dictated by a computer system! Therefore, we are stuck with an *ad hoc* system, which will have to be implemented by the computer. Each department has specified the maximum allowed number of books from a departmental library for students undertaking particular courses, and this could, in principle, be stored in a look-up table as shown in figure 16.7.

The table should be self-explanatory. From the part of the table that can be seen, it has been shown that a second-year biology student is able to borrow the following: five books from the main library (the standard second-year undergraduate ration), ten books from

Department	Codes	Year	Main Library	Departmental Libraries				
				BIO	BUS	CHE	CLA	Etc . . .
Biology	BIO1	1	5	5	0	5	0	
	BIO2	2	5	10	0	5	0	
	BIO3	3	10	15	2	10	0	
	BIOP	PG	30	30	5	10	2	
	BIOS	Staff	UL	UL	5	10	5	
Business Studies	BST1	1	5	0	5	5	5	
	BST2	2	5	0	5	5	5	
	BST3	3	10	0	10	10	10	
	BSTP	PG	30	2	20	5	0	
	BSTS	Staff	UL	5	UL	5	5	
Chemistry	CHE1	1	5	5	0	5	0	

Book allocation

UL = Unlimited
PG = Post Grad.

Figure 16.7

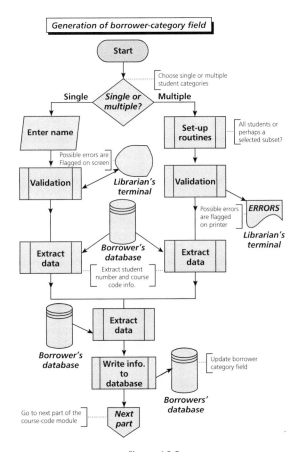

Figure 16.8

the biology-department library, and due to an arrangement with chemistry, he or she is able to borrow five books from the chemistry department library too.

Simplifications could be made to this look up table if analysed in certain ways, and it has been left to the reader to suggests some possible simplifications, not forgetting that some staff still refuse to accept a coherent booking-out policy for all libraries within Corpus Crumbly. Next we need to provide a routine which produces the above table. However, this is not shown in this brief analysis.

Coding

The next stage would be to provide a routine which reads the student number, looks up the course code, matches it within the above table and then produces the relevant information for the borrower-category field. Don't forget that it is this field that contains the information regarding the maximum number of resources that can be booked out by each student or member of staff from each library within Corpus Crumbly. There are 22 academic departmental libraries plus the main library, therefore, 23 different items of information could be stored within this field. It may be that a 46 character field could be used where each of two subsequent characters from the beginning of the field represent the 'numeric' information contained in a single row of the look-up table. The routine for constructing this field for all the students could therefore be as shown in figure 16.8.

Hint: You have, at last, arrived at the coding section. This is what students seem to enjoy the most. However, I hope that even the most sceptical student can now see how futile it would be, given the library problem outlined at the beginning of this chapter, to sit down at the computer and start writing code with little or no previous analysis!

Notice that some of the routines are starting to look similar. *Take a brief glance at the diagrams and you would think that they are the same! This should be seized upon in practice so that procedures within modules might be able to be called up and used elsewhere.* After the above has been carried out we now have the borrower privileges automatically sorted out from reading a file from the administrative-department's computer.

Summing up

We have only looked at a small part of the library system. Much co-ordination needs to be put into making sure that each person in the team is pulling in the same direction, and frequent meetings are needed if misunderstandings are to be kept to a minimum. However, the next stage would be to go further into detail of the solution to the problem.

You should note that coding does not necessarily mean jumping into a high-level language of your choice, but could be a combination of any coding methods involving SQLs, 4GLs or other suitable methods. In this particular case, where relational-database software would probably be used, writing code by using an SQL-type language (see chapter 28) would almost certainly be the way to solve the Corpus-Crumbly library problems. Nevertheless, reading the systems' flowcharts gives us an instant idea of what we are trying to achieve in a reasonable degree of detail.

Assuming that the database structure had already been created, then queries and saving of new information based on the queries can easily be established.

Exercise 16.1

1   What is meant by **the classic system life cycle**, and why has it been necessary to modify our view of this model with the hindsight of years of systems experience?

2   Why has **prototyping** become important in the context of systems design?

3   Why are program flowcharts insufficient for describing systems? What flowcharts are used instead?

4   Draw a systems flowchart representing possible solutions to the following problems (a macro view should be taken of each system – i.e. not too much detail).

(a) Logging and control of entry to a building by use of a swipe card and pin.

(b) Checking to see if students are present by using a computerised registration system (i.e. an electronic book for your lecturer/teacher!). Assume that it's linked by radio to the school's centralised database.

(c) Booking theatre tickets at a computerised box office.

(d) Helping to manage the arrivals, collation and distribution of newspapers and periodicals which arrive at a local newsagent each day. Your system should help with the lists needed by the delivery boys and girls.

5   Establish a set of suitable objectives that you think might be important if attempting a systems analysis of the following problems.

(a) A small general-practice surgery (i.e. medical doctors).

(b) Creating a database of software for a school running multi-platform machines over a network.

(c) Controlling the central heating system for a large building, which is split up into zones for the purpose of heating.

(d) Creation of a notice-board system of the sort which displays the 'flight-arrivals and departures' at Heathrow. Your system should be designed for a school or college where the principle and other teachers can broadcast notices and pictures to all parts of the campus.

6   For the systems outlined in question **5**, outline possible disadvantages the introduction of such a system might have in the short term.

7   In each of the systems outlined in question **5** discuss possible security problems and outline your plans for overcoming them.

8   For the systems outlined in question **5**, discuss whether you would use an application package, or write your own software. Give reasons for your justification.

9   For the systems outlined in question **5**, discuss how you would proceed to test some salient part of the system.

10 Briefly describe what aids are available to systems analysts and programmers developing systems of the sort described in question **5**. You might want to refer to chapter 17 to get more ideas here.

End of chapter revision aid and summary

Cover up the right-hand column and see if you can answer the questions or define the terms on the left. They appear in the order in which they are covered in this chapter. Alternatively you may browse through the right-hand column to aid revision.

What is a system?	A system can be regarded from a systems analysis point of view as being anything involving a collection of people, organisations, hardware and software etc. which has been assembled for a particular purpose.
What is systems analysis?	Systems analysis involves a detailed study of a proposed or existing system to determine the information requirements of the system.
What is systems design?	Systems design involves designing a system, which will meet a particular specification in terms of hardware and software, personnel etc.
What is the system life cycle?	The system life cycle is one method of providing a set of rules, which if followed provide an effective systems-analysis framework. However, it's not the only method, with prototyping being one alternative strategy. The system life cycle is usually made up of a detailed definition of the problem, a feasibility study, collecting information, analysis, design, implementation, evaluation and maintenance.
What is a feasibility study?	A feasibility study is a check to see if the problem is economically and technically feasible for solution by computer. The analysis and design phases make use of a variety of structured analysis and design principles.
What is prototyping?	Prototyping involves making a mock-up of parts or all of the system so that better methods of implementation may be found. Prototyping and the system life cycle can complement each other if applied and used sensibly.
What are systems flowchart symbols?	Systems flowchart symbols help express systems ideas in the form of a flowchart. It is an extension of the normal flowchart repertoire.

17 Further Systems Analysis and Design

Key resources

To carry out this work most successfully it's best if you have:

- Access to a range of software debugging tools such as trace routines and debuggers
- A small selection of simple programs which don't work, then this can provide your fellow students with much debugging practice!
- Access to some modern CASE-development environments would also be useful

Concept checkpoints

- It's essential that you have read chapter 16 on systems analysis and design.
- You should have read and understood the structures of programs covered in chapter 15.

Introduction

Having covered a detailed systems analysis example in chapter 16, we will now concentrate on some of the more general methods and tools available to help the design team reach their objectives regarding getting specified systems developed, tested and working.

Testing

The testing of programs and systems is *immensely important* because more businesses and virtually the whole of industry are increasingly putting their trust in computer-based systems. In chapter 16 we have seen a reasonably detailed systems analysis involving splitting up a major problem until just before the detailed coding and testing phases were necessary. We will now *concentrate on* individual software modules (single procedures or groups of procedures), detailed data validation and verification techniques, and the techniques necessary to ensure that these modules play an effective and constructive part in more comprehensive programs that are then ready to be used in larger systems. You are again reminded that this sort of testing can also be applied to 4GLs and other application-based command and control languages.

The bottom-up approach to testing

As well as helping to understand problems at the design stages, modularisation also helps with testing, and it is to the smallest modules that we must look to begin our testing-and-evaluation cycle. Unlike the analysis of the system in the first place, the bottom-up approach *is* the most successful when testing a system. If the bottom-up approach is used then individual modules can be tested for syntax and logical errors (i.e. errors in the logic of the program) *without the extra hassle* of having to interact with other modules in the system too. Another advantage of modularisation gained by the use of the bottom-up approach is that several areas of the project may be developed concurrently (i.e. at the same time). This is especially useful if modules will never interact with each other.

When completely tested, new modules are added to old ones, and any errors generated are most likely to be due to the interaction of the latest module with the rest. Indeed, while developing the modules themselves it's often a good idea to cut them down to the smallest operational units possible (i.e. the smallest chunk of code that does anything useful) and get this single piece of code working. You can then build up from this single working unit by adding more code and then re-testing. As for the modules, any new errors in the progressively larger code are most likely to be located in the code that has just been added.

Although the above might all sound a little tedious (especially if a **compiler** rather than an **interpreter** is being used), it is worthwhile contemplating the empirical formula

**Debugging time =
programmer time × (number of lines)²**

Thus, to ensure **minimum debugging time** – *keep the number of lines in each separate module to a minimum,* as the time taken to debug the code is generally proportional to the square of the number of lines of code. The constant of proportionality called **programmer's time** depends upon how good a programmer is. A whiz-kid programmer, for example, would have a much shorter value for programmer's time than the average programmer. If you are still not convinced of the need for modularity and testing of very small sections of code, think about the software-engineering philosophy, which is intended to be most useful in larger systems. Then think about what a large software system actually means – for example, Microsoft's Windows NT operating system has over 5 million lines of code! Think about developing a system of this complexity and there should be no arguments against any of these methods which help to keep the bugs to the absolute minimum. Even with this philosophy you are no doubt very conscious indeed that there are usually many bugs in the release of a new operating system. Remember, however, that there are other factors like political and economic issues, which usually mean that systems have to be rolled off the production line before they are truly ready.

Testing individual modules

Devising a successful test strategy for any module involves making sure that *each* **condition** or **option** is fully tested. There are a number of things to be considered in detail. First the *program itself* needs testing to ensure that the **syntax** is correct. These **syntax errors** are obviously detected by the compiler during the **compilation** stage, but it is not unknown to have errors in the compiler itself! Don't forget that few items of code are perfect, and this includes compilers. For example, it's possible to get a 'syntax error' in a complex line of code where none exists! If this is the case, then you have no alternative but to restructure a small part of the code so that the compiler is 'happy', and inform the compiler software writers that a bug exists in their code. Finally, even though a program may be syntactically correct, the **logic** must also be extensively tested. It is likely that the programmer may have 'sent control to the wrong part of the program' or 'a wrong termination condition for a loop' has slipped through, for example.

Debugging tools

Testing the logic of a program involves *running* the program (with **dummy data** if necessary) and checking

to see that the expected specifications are met. If, for example, the wrong output is produced, then the programmer must **debug** (*find and correct the bugs or errors*) the system, often by making use of **special utilities** such as **debuggers** or **debugging tools** which are designed for this purpose.

A **debugger** is a **special piece of software**, which is run along with the program being tested. A typical scenario would be to put a **break (or halt)** in the program at a salient point that needs investigation. A **string of statistics** regarding the **status of the program** at the particular point where program execution is halted can easily be produced. Typical statistics might be a list of the names and values of all the constants and variables currently being used by the program.

> **Hint:** Never forget to document the testing phases of your project. It is often the case that suitable testing and debugging has been done, but no record of it can be found in the project report. If you don't say how you did it, then no marks are awarded for this component.

Often **debuggers** are *built into* the **compiler software**. For example, in Microsoft's Visual C++ object-oriented programming language there are debugging facilities already built in. A special debug option must be included in the program during the compilation phase, which in turn makes use of a special library file, which helps with the actual debugging.

A common option in many **debugging utilities** is the inclusion of a trace routine. **This traces the progress** of the program giving a suitable indication as to 'where the program is' at any moment in time during the execution phase. For example, in the C++ compiler quoted above, it is possible to get the debugger to print out a list of messages chosen by the user and inserted in the source code by using the keyword TRACE. The C++ compiler is quite clever in that it keeps two versions of the source code – one for debugging purposes and the other for the release version of your program. In this way you don't have to edit out all of the trace statements before the final release of your masterpiece.

Trace routines are ideal for tracking down bugs like getting stuck in **endless** (or **infinite**) **loops**. For example, if, during the execution of a program, the message:

```
Starting statistical analysis section
```

is put on the screen, and if after the fifth cup of coffee it is still there, then it's worth investigating the logic of your procedure which is calculating these statistics.

Another example from Microsoft's C++ compiler is the use of an ASSERT macro. Termination of the program can be caused after an assertion (such as whether **a Boolean variable** is **true** or **false**) is made. However, these are but two examples of the huge variety of **diagnostics** available to professional programmers using C++.

Students are well advised to make extensive use of these debugging techniques when carrying out their own project work. Even if you are using just a simple version of BASIC, there are usually trace options available. Even if there are not, there is nothing to stop you halting the program using the HALT command, printing out messages, listing the variables or halting the program at any time during interpretation of the program. Part of many project write ups involves testing what you have done, and *marks are often thrown away because this phase is badly carried out and documented*. It's all too easy to say 'It seems to work', but this will not get you very many marks in the evaluation section.

On very complex systems it would normally be the job of a different team of programmers to write all the testing and debugging procedures. For reasons stated at the beginning of this section, testing and debugging is taken extremely seriously in the software industry, and often involves more effort than is involved in writing the original software! Indeed, when large systems have been shipped to the customer, then 90% of programming effort goes into **maintenance**. This means the software is updated at some later stage to iron out bugs that have come to light, or to change the system slightly in terms of the changing needs of the business.

Testing your claims!

It's most important that any claims made in the literature promoting your software be verified. For example, if you have just written a module, which should sort up to 10,000 names into alphabetical order – then check that it does exactly that! However, see the CASE method at the end of this chapter.

Testing the processed data

It's important to realise that you *can have* a **program** which is *entirely correct* but which is *unacceptable* because it does not ensure the **integrity** (**correctness**) of the **data** being processed. There's not much point in having a perfect working program that does its job badly – and this aspect is considered in the next section.

Data validation

If your module accepts or produces data then it should be **checked for limits** and/or **range** if necessary. For example, when typing in a person's age, '473 years old' is an unlikely entry. Similarly a £6,000,000 water bill is an unlikely output for a domestic customer. There may be a limited range of integer numbers such as the number of tickets booked in a theatre – it would be silly to allow a booking of 350 seats for the same performance in a 250-seat theatre. Don't forget also that a blank entry (i.e. simply pressing the return key) may be unacceptable input and cause problems with your software if it is allowed to go into the system unchecked.

Data validation is the process of getting the computer to check to see if the data is **valid** *(sensible in the context in which it is being used)*. As can be seen from the above paragraph, this also includes checks for completeness (i.e. has all relevant data been entered). It is particularly easy to validate data when using specialised database languages, as special facilities are often available. If data were not valid then the input would not be accepted by the system.

> **Hint:** You will throw marks down the drain on your project if you do not apply validation techniques where possible. This is especially true with programming and database projects.

Other checks are implicitly carried out by the **data types** (see chapter 13) being used. For example, if a **number** is expected then a **string** would be rejected. If an **integer numeric data type** is being used then a **real number** would be rejected.

Other methods of checking data integrity such as **checksums, hashing** and **CRCs** etc. are more concerned with checking the integrity of a **batch of data,** and are therefore covered in other parts of this book. However, similar methods can be applied to the entry of simple data such as account numbers, for example, and these are considered a little later in this chapter.

It's essential to use data validation techniques wherever possible, even though this makes the coding considerably more complex. Indeed, on professional projects, the data validation and other checking procedures are often the most complex parts of the program. Nevertheless, if computer systems are to gain the respect of business and industry, then this important aspect should not be overlooked.

Data verification

Data validation, important though it is, *can't detect all errors*. In sensitive areas such as the military or top-security databases, **verification** is also often used. **Verification** is a means of checking to see if the data being entered is likely to be correct. For example, has 'Mr Clarke' been entered instead of 'Mr Clark'? There's no way that a computer can tell if Clarke should have an 'e' on the end or not, unless Mr Clark gets it right in the first place! It would be

> **Hint:** It's unlikely that you will have the resources to verify very much data on your project. It's a technique which is really only suitable for sensitive data, the military and large institutions. Nevertheless, you could do some if you wished**.**

impossible, for example, to validate a new name and address. (Although it would easily be possible to verify an existing address being entered for security purposes, as the data being entered could be compared to a list of suitable names and addresses already held by the computer system.)

The practice of carrying out **data verification** is really quite simple – if, for example, it's essential that names be spelt exactly as they appear on a sheet of paper, then *independent entry* by **two different operators** can produce two independent files. These duplicate files are then compared, and any difference between the files can be used to flag an error. One operator can check to see who has entered the wrong data, and rectify the situation before the incorrect data is used in the system. With *two different people* entering the *same data* the **integrity** (correctness) of the data is considerably increased – but the system is obviously not infallible.

Clerical errors such as transcription errors (i.e. errors in copying (transcribing) the data from a sheet of paper into the computer, for example) can be reduced to a minimum if data verification is used. However, this is often too expensive for day-to-day activities – the wages bill, for example, would be doubled! Alternative methods of automatically detecting errors during the data entry phase have therefore been developed, and some common methods are covered in the next section.

Check digits

Masses of numeric data being entered by a tired operator poses horrendous problems for the designers of the input routines. It is common for long numbers to be entered with an incorrect digit, and even more common for two digits to be transposed. (64154701 being entered as 64154071, for example) However, it's possible to reduce the possibility of these all-to-frequent transcription errors by making use of what are called check digits as shown in the following example.

Example using modulo 11

Suppose, for example, we are dealing with a system in which the integrity of the customer bank account number is important. Let's also suppose that we want to generate an 8-figure number such that it could be quickly and automatically checked for integrity on input to the system. Instead of assigning random or sequential account numbers, the following standard method could be used:

Hint: Few students apply the principles in this section to their projects. This is a pity, as techniques such as these would impress your teachers and moderators if used sensibly under the right conditions.

```
Let the first seven
    numbers be        6   4   1   5   4   7   0
Assign a weighting    8   7   6   5   4   3   2
(Digits 2 to 9 only – start at two
          from right to left – use digits again if needed.)
Multiply number
    by weighting     48  28   6  25  16  21   0
```

Add numbers in
```
    previous row     48 + 28 + 6 +25 + 16 +21 +0 = 144
```
Do a modulo 11 division (see chapter 18)
144/11 = 13 remainder 1

The check digit 1 should now be added to the number so that the valid account number becomes:

```
6   4   1   5   4   7   0   1
```

Now, when this number is entered into the system, the same check is performed on the first 7 digits. Therefore, suppose the number was incorrectly entered as:

```
6   4   1   5   4   0   7   1
```

Carrying out the check-digit algorithm as above:

```
6    4    1    5    4    0    7   (1)
8    7    6    5    4    3    2
48 + 28 + 6 + 25 + 16 + 0 + 14 = 137
```

Modulo eleven check = 137/11 = 12 remainder 5 which is the wrong check digit.

Therefore 64154073 is an invalid number.

Techniques like this, although obviously not foolproof, drastically increase the chances of the detection of transcription errors at the most crucial stage – that of being input into the computer system.

The dreaded bugs

Unless programs are trivial, then **no system or program can ever be guaranteed to be error free**. It's just that the user has not yet come up with the exact sequence of operations necessary to make the program crash. It is not unusual for programs to perform error free for months or even years, and then crash because of an unforeseen set of circumstances – the **millennium bug** is a classic example of this, costing an estimated $4,000,000,000 to put right. Worse than this, it is *not currently possible* to prove that programs are correct. Mathematics is not yet advanced enough to be able to determine the correctness of complex systems, nor are our computers fast enough yet to go through every conceivable path in a complex system. All you can do is to follow a sensible strategy that will keep errors to a minimum, and this is covered at the end of the chapter.

Alpha and beta testing

The worst people to test software are the people who wrote it! This is because they know how it should be used, and are therefore less likely to do unexpected things with it. It's usual to get reasonably tolerant people to help with the first stages of testing 'in house', and this is known as **alpha** (the first stage) **testing**. After successful alpha testing some trusted customers are often given the opportunity to try out the software, knowing that it might (will!) contain some bugs – this is called **beta testing**. The **Internet** has given many millions of people the opportunity to do beta testing for nothing! You are often able to **download** a modern piece of software to try it out in 'real life' situations. This is usually a good idea, because it enables the manufactures to get feedback on the 'software under test' by using it with a huge variety of other hardware and software, both old and new. It's obvious that many people will simply download the software for personal use, and not bother to provide any feedback, but the amount of feedback from serious users far outweighs this disadvantage.

After successful beta testing has been carried out, the software is released, usually with a version number of 1.0. However, sometimes, even after extensive beta testing, there are still major bugs in the systems – the author thinks that version 1.0 released to the customers should be called Gamma testing! After many different versions, when software is almost bug free – that's the time to release a completely new version and start the process all over again!

> **Hint:** It's essential that you get other students to test your project under real conditions. If you are the only person doing the testing, you're unlikely to find all the different ways that the project might be misused.

Documentation

There's not much point in having a fancy 'error-free and completely working program' if it is not accompanied by appropriate documentation. *Without a detailed technical specification and supporting documentation* to show how the program was developed, then the program is probably *not in a position* to be **maintained effectively** by other people. As time progresses and the needs of the system change, without the ability to be maintained properly the software will become outdated and useless. It has been estimated that well over 90% of programming activity in industry is put into updating existing software, and billions of pounds are being spent each year on **software maintenance**. With this borne in mind, suitable documentation to accompany programs is of paramount importance.

> **Hint:** You should realise that the documentation, which accompanies your project work, forms the basis of most of the marks which are awarded. This is all the moderator usually sees!

What constitutes suitable documentation? This all-important question obviously depends upon the system we are documenting. For example, the documentation accompanying a project written in typical third-generation (3GL) language (see chapter 13) would be vastly different from the documentation which is needed for a user manual. The following section lists typical subsections for common 3GL scenarios.

Program documentation

This documentation is designed to allow a professional programmer to modify the program at some later stage. It's absolutely essential that some form of documentation accompanies the source code in the form of suitable comments. Without suitable comments effective software maintenance becomes very difficult, if not impossible, to achieve. You must never forget that software maintenance is just as important as all the other stages in the cycle of the development of systems. (See CASE at the end of this chapter.)

The following is typical of **internal documentation** (documentation inherent in the structure of a program) which should provide sufficient information for effective maintenance of a procedure or sub-routine in a typical 3GL. **You should pay particular attention to this section. You would do well to mirror this philosophy in any programming project which you undertake, or when you need to modify programs that you are thinking of handing in for your project work!**

A statement of purpose

It's essential that the *purpose* of any sub-routine or procedure be *explicitly stated* at the beginning of the code. For example, in the language 'C' (and still available in 'C ++'), comments at the start of a procedure might take on the following form:

```
/* The purpose of this procedure is to
accept data representing the 4 coloured
bands on a resistor, validate these
entries, reject them if necessary, then
calculate the tolerance and ideal
resistance values ready to be used by
the plotting routine.
*/
```

Remember that **the compiler ignores comments**, and therefore they don't contribute any extra object code or require any extra execution time.

Use meaningful variable names

Most 3GLs provide suitable means of using more descriptive variable names. Gone are the days when 'I', 'V' or 'R', for example, would do for variable names. It might be far better to use 'Current_mA', 'Voltage_V' and 'Resistance_kohms' if this is more appropriate. In this particular example you have dramatically increased the information content by making it obvious what the variables represent, and have included the units of measurement too.

```
*/ Inputs:    Band_1    Colour representing first digit
              Band_2    Colour representing second digit
              Band_3    Colour representing multiplier
              Band_4    Colour representing tolerance

   Outputs:   Not_valid          Boolean flag set true if data is invalid
              Resistor_value     Number representing the resistance value
              Tolerance          Number representing tolerance limits
*/
```

Figure 17.1

In addition to the use of meaningful variable names, it is also useful to include a **list of the variables** *in the appropriate part of the code* (in addition to any declarations imposed by the syntax of the language). In the resistor example quoted above, a suitable variable list might be as shown in figure 17.1.

From the above you can see that four 'unvalidated variables' representing colour are input to this procedure and two 'validated numeric values' are calculated which are to be used by another part of the program. A third variable acting as a flag will terminate the routine if necessary.

> **Hint:** Make sure that any code you write contains a suitable number of comments. Don't write too many comments or it will look ridiculous. However, much of the technical documentation can be achieved by writing suitable comments on the pseudo-code or source code.

Any other sub-routines or procedures, which may be referenced (only subordinate routines need be considered), should also be listed. In the above case we might need to make a reference to the procedure which plots the picture of the resistor along with its values if this is called from within the routine currently being considered.

Additional information

In professional circles it is usually necessary to add the author's name and the date on which the final code was completed. In addition to this a catalogue of modifications to the system might also be necessary. A typical entry for our resistor example might be:

```
/*  Author:  Mike Rofarad
    Date:       16/12/98

    Modifications      Author Milli Amp
    Date: 17/04/99    (Version 1.1)
       Tolerance validation routines now
       include 20% (No band 4) Resistors.
       Author Mike Rofarad
    Date: 30/05/99    (Version 1.2)
       Program modified to include 5-band
    resistor types.
*/
```

You would be well advised to use similar techniques in your projects.

Don't go overboard

You must *not* put too much documentation into your program or else it will obscure the overall logic, thus cancelling out the effectiveness of the structured approach. As a guide don't comment on every single line of code, but put larger comments at the beginning of procedures or parts of the program which carry out specific tasks. If professional programmers know what routines are meant to accomplish, then they should be able to follow the logic of standard language structures.

Other aids to readability

Don't forget to make extensive use of indents to emphasise the structure of the program. However, when the program is being maintained it is often very difficult to manually modify these indents and it's all to easy to get mixed up, especially if the program is a complex one. On more-sophisticated systems automatic indenting attempts to get over these problems.

Further systems help

In this chapter we have concentrated on documentation from a programming perspective. In chapter 6 we have also seen an enormous number of diagrammatic methods for helping with the structured approach to systems and programming design. However, there are currently a large number of software packages in existence which help significantly with drawing, maintaining and analysing these diagrams. These are commonly known as **diagramming tools**, and the group of software to which they belong is collectively known as **CASE**.

CASE

CASE, or **Computer Aided Software Engineering**, is now well established but still relatively new compared to the more-established technologies such as CAD and CAM, or, more recently CIM (Computer Integrated Manufacturing). However, to the software developer, CASE is just as exciting and has huge implications for the future of software development. CASE consists of many different software development tools. Just like CAD and CIM, CASE is aiming towards a totally integrated project-support environment for software development engineering. CASE tools can be found in areas as diverse as analysis and design of systems, testing, maintenance, programming, prototyping, business systems, planning and many others.

Modern testing methodology

It's extremely difficult, if not impossible to guarantee that any system of some complexity works correctly under all conditions. Nevertheless, modern CASE methods are now helping with this important aspect of software development too, and this section looks at some of the modern testing methods, and how computers can help with the development of projects. These methods have now started to appear in 'A' level computer science syllabuses, and will help considerably with your project work too. Some of the software development systems (see at the end of this section) may actually be able to help you design your whole project, including generation and testing of the actual code from computer-generated structure diagrams in languages like Visual Basic, C++ or Java, for example.

Black-box and white-box testing methods

As you are no doubt aware, it would take a supercomputer longer than the Universe has been in existence to do an exhaustive test on systems as complex as Microsoft's Windows NT 5.0, for example. (This will probably be called Windows 2000 by the time you are reading this book.) These systems contain many millions of lines of code, and it's impossible to debug the system entirely with 100% certainty. *Indeed, it is impossible to debug much simpler systems with 100% certainty, and this is one of the things that you should appreciate at the start of this section on testing.* For example, if you had a *very* simple module into which just 65,536 pairs of integer numbers are input, then, assuming you wanted to test this program under *all* possible conditions, $65,536 \times 65,536 = 4,294,967,296$ individual tests would need to be carried out! And this is only for one small module, which handles positive integer numbers only, over a very restricted range. Therefore, we can't concentrate our efforts on such **exhaustive testing**, but will have to concentrate on ensuring the highest possible success given our current knowledge of computer science.

The methods about to be considered, if applied properly to modules in your own programs, will ensure a greater degree of success of your overall project design. There are two distinct testing methods, called **black-box** and **white-box** testing. Both methods have been borrowed from the electronics industry, where they have been used with some considerable degree of success over the years. White-box testing has been particularly useful when applied to testing of microprocessor chip technology, such as the design of the gates inside the Pentium II, for example. As you can see, these testing methods are cutting edge, and are applied to the latest operating systems and processor design stages. If they are good enough for the professionals, then they deserve much consideration at 'A' level too.

Black-box testing

This methodology has been around for some considerable time, and is the simpler of the two methods. A black-box is simply a box, into which a system, or in our case a software module, can be put. All inputs to the system are shown on the left, and the output from the system is shown on the right. For example, in chapter 18 we design an algorithm to find the square root of a positive number using what's called the bisection method. The black-box representation for this particular system is extremely simple. There is just one input (the positive number called N), and one output (the square root called x3). The black-box diagram is shown in figure 17.2.

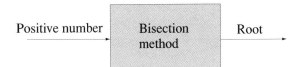

Black-box diagram for bisection method

Figure 17.2

The Nassi-Schneidermann structure diagram for this system is shown again in figure 17.3 for your convenience, along with the code for the square root module that we will develop in chapter 18. Here we are going to test this software module using both black-box and white-box techniques (see next section). You should note that the black-box techniques do not rely on any knowledge of the structure of the program – hence the name black box (i.e. you need not care too much about what is actually inside). You should compare this with the white-box techniques where an intimate knowledge of the structure is absolutely essential.

We already know that we can't test this routine for all possible input values, because it would take too long.

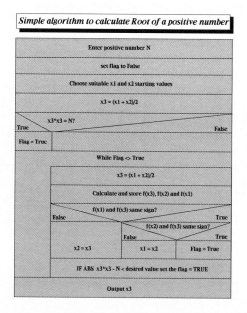

```
INPUT N
 flag = FALSE
 x1 = 1 : x2 = N
 x3 = (x1+x2)/2
 IF x3*x3 = N THEN flag = TRUE
 WHILE flag <> TRUE
    x3=(x1+x2)/2
    fx1=x1*x1-N:fx2=x2*x2-N:fx3=x3*x3-N
    IF((fx1>0) AND (fx3>0)) OR ((fx1<0) AND (fx3<0))THEN
      IF ((fx2>0) AND (fx3>0)) OR ((fx2<0) AND
                                      (fx3<0))THEN
           flag = TRUE
      ELSE
          x1=x3
      ENDIF
    ELSE
      x2=x3
    ENDIF
    PRINT "Guess so far is";x3
    IF ABS(x3*x3-N) < 0.001 THEN flag = TRUE
  ENDWHILE
PRINT "Answer is ";x3
```

Figure 17.3

Therefore, we have to choose a representative set of input values. If we choose wisely, then we can be reasonably confident other values will work too. We should, for example, consider the **maximum** and **minimum** values that it's possible to present to the system. The minimum is obviously 0 (the lowest possible positive number) but the maximum, as stated when dealing with languages on page 279, depends on the compiler being used for the language in which the program is being written. Therefore, the range of the inputs and outputs for this particular algorithm will be:

$$0 \leqslant N \leqslant \text{Maximum floating point number}$$
$$0 \leqslant x3 \leqslant \text{Maximum floating point number}$$

Anything outside of this range will obviously be outside of the specification of the program. You should take special note of this. If, for example, the maximum floating point number for a particular compiler happens to be 2×10^{60}, then it's not much point trying to find the root of 3×10^{60} in your program. It will not work because you have gone beyond the physical limitations of the system you are using. This is one of the points of testing, and is one reason *why the* **specification of** *the system ought to be written down very precisely*. This is so that the designers and users of the system both know the limitations. Bear this in mind when you are attempting to test algorithms in your own projects. You will loose marks if you assume that it will work under all conditions.

Finally, in your project, it's necessary to build up a table showing all the values, which you have used for the black-box testing, and the reason why you have chosen the numbers. For our simple system mentioned above, a suitable starting table might be as follows:

Condition number	Value	Comments
1	0	Smallest possible value of input N
2	Maximum float point	Largest possible value of N determined by the system compiler.

The above test cases obviously assume that we put no negative numbers into the system. To make sure that this is so, a simple routine would have to be added to the beginning of the code shown above. Next we need to see if there are any important numbers in-between these limits that might cause problems. For example, the nature of square roots means that the root of 1 is just 1, roots of larger numbers get bigger, and roots of smaller numbers (less than one) get much smaller. Therefore, it might be prudent to test for inputs of '1', '<1' and '>1'. Therefore, our modified table now becomes:

Condition number	Value	Comments
1	0	Smallest possible value of input N
2	Maximum float point	Largest possible value of N determined by the system compiler.
3	1	Test to see if the answer is 1 (or as near to it as is described by the accuracy required).
4	0.001	Number less than 1 to test for smaller roots.
5	1000	Number greater than 1 to test for larger roots.

As you can see, we have tested for the extremes, and tested for some salient points in between too. The next important part is to document the test procedure, and this can be done by constructing another table, similar to the above, but instead of the comments we have the actual results of the test produced by the computer during run time. The results of this table will depend on the language you use, the computer on which you run the system, and on the compiler being used for the language. It is therefore not shown here, but you are well advised to include this in your projects if you wish to get maximum marks on testing procedures.

In practice the black box would probably have more than one input, and therefore the number of tests would also have to include salient points for the extra variables in each case. Nevertheless, this is the essence of black-box testing. If there is more than one output, then we can have a separate black box for each. Therefore to carry out a black-box test on a software module, we do the following:

- *Make sure that the specification for the module is well written.*
- *Make sure that the limitations of the system are well understood.*
- *Determine the inputs and outputs for the software module.*
- *Draw a black box labelling the inputs and output.*
- *Determine salient values for any variables such as maximum and minimum, for example.*
- *Draw up a table showing the conditions under which the tests have been carried out.*
- *Provide documentary evidence that the tests have actually been carried out.*
- *If any mistakes are found, and the code is altered, you must start all the tests again!*

Don't forget that the above black-box testing will not *guarantee* that the system or module will work. However, it's a reasonable assumption that it does work, and is the best that you can do using black-box testing methods alone.

White-box testing

Again we will use the above square-root algorithm as an example. White-box testing tries to ensure that all possible paths through an algorithm are tested. It does this by using the structure of the source code under test to construct a **flowgraph** (very similar to the **state-transition diagrams** covered in chapter 14) to generate a visual indication of the paths that could be taken. These graphs are also called **digraphs or directed graphs**. This name is derived from a horrendously complex branch of mathematics known as graph theory, but don't worry too much, we will use them in a very simple way here. We must, therefore, first look at the production of a flowgraph, as this will be needed to carry out the white-box testing of the system. The simplest possible flowgraph, applicable to *any system*, is to have just one entry point and one exit point as shown in figure 17.4.

As you can see from this diagram we have two **nodes** (the letters in the circles), one for the entry point

Figure 17.4

X, and one for the exit point Y. Each node is connected by an **arc**, and the **arrow** shows the *direction of flow* from X to Y – hence the terminology 'flowgraph'. The arc represents the flow of the program between the entry point X and the exit point Y, and thus will represent the code, which could consist of other subprograms and procedures. However, don't try to do too much manually – special software will make these operations less of a chore, if you're lucky enough to possess it.

To generate a suitable flowgraph for our system, we must look at the code for the bisection method – this is shown at the beginning of the black-box testing section. We need to split up the code into identifiable parts, each part with a specific function, *but each part having only one entry and one exit point.* For example, breaking up our code using these criteria, we input a number (N) and then set up a flag and a couple of other variables. Next we have a condition which tests

to see if the answer is correct. (This would only occur if N happened to be 1, hence the importance of putting N=1 as a condition when we undertook the black-box testing in the last section.) Next we have a large WHILE loop. (Don't worry about what's inside this loop yet, we will tackle this when we take a look at the flowgraph in more detail in a moment.) Finally, we print out the answer. The code, shown in figure 17.5, has been split up to emphasise the points we have just made.

Therefore, for our bisection-method code, the new flowgraph, based on the above analysis, is shown in figure 17.6.

Figure 17.6

The next stage in the production of the flowgraph is to determine if any of the arcs in the above flowgraph need further analysis. For example, the arc between A and B represents that part of the program which inputs data and sets up some variables. It represents a simple linear sequence of just four instructions – the flow of

```
                          ENTRY POINT A
INPUT N                                              ARC — FLOW FROM A to B
flag = FALSE
x1 = 1 : x2 = N
x3 = (x1+x2)/2
                              B
IF x3*x3 = N THEN flag = TRUE                         ARC — FLOW FROM B to C
                              C
  WHILE flag <> TRUE                                 ARC — FLOW FROM C to D
      x3=(x1+x2)/2
      fx1=x1*x1-N:fx2=x2*x2-N:fx3=x3*x3-N
      IF((fx1>0) AND (fx3>0)) OR ((fx1<0) AND (fx3<0))THEN
        IF ((fx2>0) AND (fx3>0)) OR ((fx2<0) AND (fx3<0))THEN flag = TRUE
        ELSE
             x1=x3
        ENDIF
      ELSE
        x2=x3
      ENDIF
      PRINT "Guess so far is";x3
      IF ABS(x3*x3-N) < 0.001 THEN flag = TRUE
  ENDWHILE
                              D
PRINT "Answer is ";x3                                ARC — FLOW FROM D to E
                          EXIT POINT E
```

Figure 17.5

control through here will move on from one statement to the next, and this arc therefore needs no further flow analysis. The arc between points D and E needs no further analysis either for the same reason. However, the arc between points C and D will obviously need further analysis and the arc between B and C will need a little extra analysis too.

To help understand the next stage in constructing our flowgraph, let's take the arc between B and C, i.e. the arc that represents the single statement:

```
IF x3*x3 = N THEN flag = TRUE
```

There are two possibilities here. Either the condition (x3*x3 = N) is true, in which case the flag is set equal to 'TRUE' and we exit, else it's not, in which case nothing happens and we exit from this statement. Therefore, between the entry and exit points (B and C) for this particular code, there are *two* possible paths. The original single arc between B and C shown in figure 17.6 now needs to be replaced with two arcs, representing the two possible routes through this particular part of the code. The new situation, showing the next stage of the flowgraph is shown in figure 17.7.

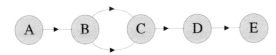

Figure 17.7

If we had any multi-line if-then statements, more arcs could be added. For example, if we had an if-then-else-endif statement, as we will see in just a moment, three arcs would be needed. For a case statement (see chapter 13), the number of arcs can also be increased to match – it's a simple idea.

We now need to investigate the more complex arc from C to D in figure 17.6. Here we can see that a loop has been used. In this particular case the 'while loop' has been chosen, but the techniques could easily apply to other loops with little modification. Consider the general flowgraph form for a loop, shown in figure 17.8.

As can be seen from figure 17.8, when implementing a loop structure using a flowgraph, there are two possible paths again. Either it goes around the loop or it does not, based on some test condition on entry to the loop. Consider the arc between points C and D in figure 17.5. While the flag is set true we go round the loop, or, if the flag is set to false, we don't go round the loop anymore. Don't forget that if N = 1, then we don't go round the loop at all, but follow the arc straight from C to D, executing no code. The modified flowgraph showing the large 'while loop' now becomes as shown in figure 17.9.

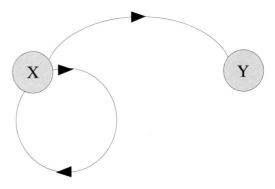

Figure 17.8

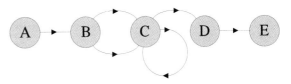

Figure 17.9

The next stage is to do further analysis on the while loop in the above diagram. We can see from an analysis of the code in figure 17.10 that there are several sections, containing either a simple linear sequence of instructions, or some if-then-else statements, to which we already know the flowgraph structure. Therefore, we already know how to represent this loop with a suitable flowgraph. See if you can get an idea of the general structure before having a look at the next diagram.

The analysis goes along the following lines (see figure 17.10). The while loop is split up, using the techniques demonstrated earlier, into the following subsections. Remember that each part can have only one exit and one entry point.

The first thing to note is that we have C at the bottom and not D. This might seem unusual at first sight, but don't forget that we are considering that loop which is going round and round. In other words, the above structure in the flowgraph will replace the 'big round loop' in figure 17.9 which goes from C to C. We already have the other arc between C and D, which represents the get-out condition, i.e. when the flag has been set to true.

We have thus split up the while loop into four parts, two of which (the arc from C to F and the arc from G to H) will need further analysis. Replacing just the loop in figure 17.9 with our four-part split, we end up with the flowgraph shown in figure 17.11.

From an analysis of the 'while end-while' routine, we can see that arc C to F is only a simple linear sequence of instructions and needs no further analysis. Arc G to H is also a simple linear sequence of instructions. Arc H to C is a simple if-then statement, therefore this arc can be replaced by *two* other arcs, because of

```
                                             C
WHILE flag <> TRUE
    x3=(x1+x2)/2
    fx1=x1*x1-N:fx2=x2*x2-N:fx3=x3*x3-N         ARC — FLOW FROM C to F

                                             F
    IF((fx1>0) AND (fx3>0)) OR ((fx1<0) AND (fx3<0))THEN ARC — FLOW FROM F to G
      IF ((fx2>0) AND (fx3>0)) OR ((fx2<0) AND (fx3<0))THEN flag = TRUE
      ELSE
          x1=x3
      ENDIF
    ELSE
      x2=x3
    ENDIF

                                             G
    PRINT "Guess so far is";x3                 ARC — FLOW FROM G to H
                                             H
    IF ABS(x3*x3-N) < 0.001 THEN flag = TRUE   ARC — FLOW FROM H to D
ENDWHILE

                                             C
```

Figure 17.10

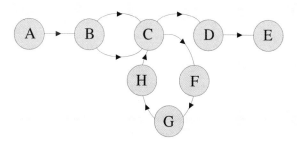

Figure 17.11

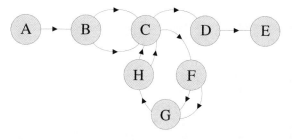

Figure 17.12

the two possibilities being true or false. Arc F to G consists of a more complex if-then else statement, in which one of the loops is nested. Therefore, for the moment, we will draw this as *two* normal loops, one of which will need further analysis. The second loop will be replaced by the necessary structure for the second if-then-else statement in the next version of the diagram shown in figure 17.12. Let's not do too many stages at once!

Now consider the final part of the code. At the moment we are representing the if-then-else structure between nodes F and G with just two arcs. However, one of these arcs contains a nested loop structure, as shown in the breakdown of the code in figure 17.13.

Therefore this nested-loop structure needs to be replaced by two nodes called I and J, linked by two arcs, as shown earlier in this section. Therefore, one of the arcs between F and G in figure 17.12, is replaced by this combination, and our final flowgraph is shown in figure 17.14.

The actual white-box tests

The whole point of white-box testing is to ensure that all feasible paths through a software module are executed when the system is being tested. To carry this out we make use of the flowgraph, which we have just created.

Interestingly enough, the number of different paths that can be taken through a flowgraph can be obtained by counting up how many separate regions there are. (This is not strictly true, but any undergraduate mathematicians who are good at graph theory will realise that it's near enough.) This is identical in principle to colouring in separate regions on a map in a geography lesson. The number of regions for the bisection method flowgraph is shown in figure 17.15.

Therefore, in our bisection-method code, there are 6 distinct paths that can be taken. To indicate the difference between the first two obvious paths,

Path 1	A–B$_1$–C–D–E
Path 2	A–B$_2$–C–D–E

F

```
IF((fx1>0) AND (fx3>0)) OR ((fx1<0) AND (fx3<0))THEN        ARC — FLOW FROM G to H
```

I

```
   IF ((fx2>0) AND (fx3>0)) OR ((fx2<0) AND (fx3<0))THEN flag = TRUE
   ELSE
        x1=x3
   ENDIF
```

J

```
ELSE
   x2=x3
ENDIF
```

G

Figure 17.13

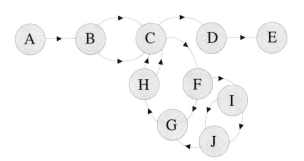

Figure 17.14

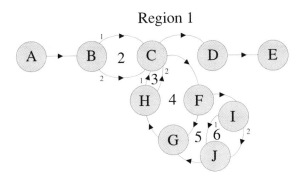

Figure 17.15

Path 5	A–B$_2$–C–F–G–H$_1$
Path 6	A–B$_2$–C–F–G–H$_2$
Path 7	A–B$_1$–C–F–I$_1$–J–G–H$_1$
Path 8	A–B$_1$–C–F–I$_1$–J–G–H$_2$
Path 9	A–B$_2$–C–F–I$_1$–J–G–H$_1$
Path 10	A–B$_2$–C–F–I$_1$–J–G–H$_2$
Path 11	A–B$_1$–C–F–I$_2$–J–G–H$_1$
Path 12	A–B$_1$–C–F–I$_2$–J–G–H$_2$

However, consider for a moment, what happens when we have tried the first two paths A–B$_1$–C and A–B$_2$–C. It is not necessary to try these two combinations again, with all subsequent passes through the program. This would be a waste of time as this path has already been tested under all possible circumstances. Therefore, on subsequent passes, we can use A–B$_x$–C to help identify that, as they have already been done once for the first two paths, they need not be considered again – it does not matter which of these two paths are taken.

Proceeding with this argument, we can now alter the possible paths to the following:

Path 1	A–B$_1$–C–D–E
Path 2	A–B$_2$–C–D–E
Path 3	A–B$_x$–C–F–G–H$_1$
Path 4	A–B$_x$–C–F–G–H$_2$
Path 5	A–B$_x$–C–F–G–H$_1$
Path 6	A–B$_x$–C–F–G–H$_2$
Path 7	A–B$_x$–C–F–I$_1$–J–G–H$_1$
Path 8	A–B$_x$–C–F–I$_1$–J–G–H$_2$
Path 9	A–B$_x$–C–F–I$_1$–J–G–H$_1$
Path 10	A–B$_x$–C–F–I$_1$–J–G–H$_2$
Path 11	A–B$_x$–C–F–I$_2$–J–G–H$_1$
Path 12	A–B$_x$–C–F–I$_2$–J–G–H$_2$

We can see straight away, that paths 3 and 5, for example, are identical, for the purposes of testing the program. Therefore we can eliminate path 5. We can also eliminate path 6, because this would be identical to path 4. Also, path 9 can be eliminated (same as path 7) and path 10 can be eliminated because it is the same as path 8.

a subscript notation is used in which the subscript corresponds to the labelling of the arcs in figure 17.15. Therefore Path 1 takes the upper arc from B to C, and Path 2 takes the lower arc from B to C. This notation has also been used between the nodes H and C and nodes I and J.

Looking at the flowchart you will probably think that there are many more than just six paths through the program. For example, we could list the following paths.

Path 1	A–B$_1$–C–D–E
Path 2	A–B$_2$–C–D–E
Path 3	A–B$_1$–C–F–G–H$_1$
Path 4	A–B$_1$–C–F–G–H$_2$

Path 1	A–B$_1$–C–D–E
Path 2	A–B$_2$–C–D–E
Path 3	A–B$_x$–C–F–G–H$_1$
Path 4	A–B$_x$–C–F–G–H$_2$
Path 7	A–B$_x$–C–F–I$_1$–J–G–H$_1$
Path 8	A–B$_x$–C–F–I$_1$–J–G–H$_2$
Path 11	A–B$_x$–C–F–I$_2$–J–G–H$_1$
Path 12	A–B$_x$–C–F–I$_2$–J–G–H$_2$

Using the same argument again, Once we have tried the paths G–H$_1$ and G–H$_2$, we can replace this path with G–H$_x$ in subsequent analysis. Therefore, the paths now become:

Path 1	A–B$_1$–C–D–E
Path 2	A–B$_2$–C–D–E
Path 3	A–B$_x$–C–F–G–H$_1$
Path 4	A–B$_x$–C–F–G–H$_2$
Path 7	A–B$_x$–C–F–I$_1$–J–G–H$_x$
Path 8	A–B$_x$–C–F–I$_1$–J–G–H$_x$
Path 11	A–B$_x$–C–F–I$_2$–J–G–H$_x$
Path 12	A–B$_x$–C–F–I$_2$–J–G–H$_x$

This now means that we can eliminate path 8 because it's the same as path 7, and path 12 because it's the same as path 11. The list of paths to check now becomes:

Path 1	A–B$_1$–C–D–E
Path 2	A–B$_2$–C–D–E
Path 3	A–B$_x$–C–F–G–H$_1$
Path 4	A–B$_x$–C–F–G–H$_2$
Path 7	A–B$_x$–C–F–I$_1$–J–G–H$_x$
Path 11	A–B$_x$–C–F–I$_2$–J–G–H$_x$

This gives us the six paths, which were predicted, by the flowgraph regions! Magic.

The next stage in the white-box testing process is to go through all the above paths using black-box testing methods. That is, the programmer should make sure that suitable variables are chosen, and listed in the tables, which will ensure that each of the above paths gets executed. However, not all the paths may be feasible due to constraints on the program. For example, some conditions may never happen in practice. Nevertheless, white-box techniques represent a big step forward in making sure that your code is tested as much as is possible. It also helps you to document the testing sections of your project precisely. You can now see why more effort goes into testing systems than the effort expended on writing the systems in the first place! It's fortunate that many of these methods can be automated with appropriate CASE tools, and we now take a brief look at some of these in the last part of this section.

Some modern development tools

At the beginning of the section on black-box and white-box testing a Nassi-Schneidermann diagram was used as the basis to generate the code for the software. However, software can be constructed *directly* from diagrams of this type. With appropriate software we can also use the computer to generate the structure diagram itself. For example, a company called Blue River Software GmbH has developed the project-development software called X32 and this is shown in figure 17.16.

Here you can see a typical environment in which a C or C++ program has been developed for changing a binary number into a decimal number. Notice the Nassi-Schneidermann structure construction tools along the right-hand side of the window. The program also

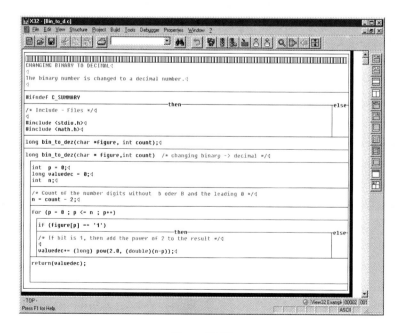

Figure 17.16

puts the structure of the C or C++ program into the boxes as you choose the layout. When you come to compile the project you can choose a variety of external compilers, and compilation wizards take you through the appropriate stages. This particular software also contains powerful **project report generators**, which help with the **documentation** phases of your project too. For example, much of the structure, code, comments and lots of other things too numerous to mention here can be exported as RTF (Rich Text Format) to a word processor. This is, of course, in addition to much other help that you would get with these systems including debugging utilities etc.

The V32 software from Blue River GmbH is shown in figure 17.17. This particular example shows the complete development environment for a heating-control system. On screen you can see several different aspects of the project, including the Nassi-Schneidermann structure diagram containing some code, a state diagram, a data transformation diagram and a context diagram, for example. This software development tool will help with all stages of the system life cycle (see chapter 16), and its modular functionality is summarised as follows.

The analysis and specification module
- helps with data-transformation diagrams
- state-transition diagrams
- entity-relationship diagrams (see chapter 29).

The code generation module
- helps to generate code for C, C++
- transferring the code and structure from the Nassi-Schneidermann structure diagrams.

The implementation module
- contains all the functionality of the X32 module.

The re-engineering module
- converts existing source code into Nassi-Schneidermann structure diagrams.
- These changes are instantly reflected in the specification graphs.

The documentation module
- prints out specification graphs
- implements structure diagrams
- constructs reports files, complete with diagrams
- exports RTF format.

The integrated user interface is shown in figure 17.17.

The case for CASE

We have looked at many different methods of analysis and design. For each method considered there are appropriate software tools to aid the design process. For

example, **PERT, 4GLs, editors, compilers** and other **utilities** are but a few of the many software packages currently available to help develop software-based projects. The following list contains just some of the major categories where specialised software development programs already exist. Many others are beyond the scope of a book at this level.

Category	Examples
Analysis and design tools	Data flow analysis
Project management tools	Scheduling (PERT)
Programming tools	4GLs, Application generators
Tools to help with testing and debugging	Data generation programs
Documentation tools	DTP systems, CAD
Prototyping tools	Modelling and simulation

The next stage currently under development is to integrate all the above (and very much more) into the *same environment*, similar to that found in a modern database management system (DBMS – see chapter 28). In this way software development engineers will have a complete set of tools which will help them to develop a project from initial conception, via specification, development, testing, documentation and maintenance. Indeed, it is hoped that the powerful simulation software will be able to carry out checks on the design and analysis phase before any code has actually been developed. It is also hoped that the necessary code will not be produced by hand, but be automatically developed *and tested* by the system. The degree of automation pointed to by these new systems is of breathtaking proportions, and already there are code generators that can produce the code for major chunks of large projects. Many of these methodologies are based on the object-oriented approach considered in detail in chapter 15.

As with all complex systems there are usually some disadvantages, and as stated in chapter 15, OOP (Object-Oriented Programming) suffers from the fact that much-larger programs are produced by this method than would have been the case if hand-optimised code had been used. Nevertheless, with machines becoming faster and memory becoming more plentiful, this disadvantage is usually of little consequence compared to the much-greater degree of automation and the faster development time. Couple this with the fact that fewer staff are needed and less expensive mistakes are made, and you have a winner until something better comes along. Don't forget that software development is an evolutionary process, and CASE is just the latest in this

> **Hint:** As software becomes more complex to analyse, CASE methods are helping to overcome potential problems. If you have any suitable software at school, you should try and incorporate it into the analysis and testing of your projects.

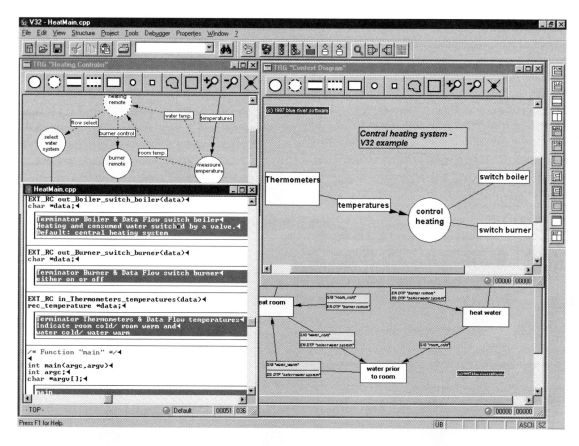

Figure 17.17

evolutionary cycle that has been going on for about 50 years.

You can see from the above that we have only just touched on the future potential of software engineering. You should see that it's not just about writing programs, but is about the development of a new and extremely complex environment that will be necessary if the enormous complexity of tomorrow's software is to be developed in a sensible period of time. It is likely that those companies, which do not fully embrace the software-engineering ethos, will not be able to produce complex code in a cost-effective manner or in a sensible time scale. In addition you should also see why the term software engineering has been used – a whole new branch of computer science has been produced which embraces many methodologies from previously unconnected branches. Keep a lookout for development of Computer Aided Software Engineering; it will bring a whole new meaning to the term CASE study!

Exercise 17.1

1   **Data verification** and **validation** are both useful when trying to ensure **integrity of data**. Briefly explain what is meant by the terms in bold type.

2   Why is it likely to take less time to complete a project if small modular parts of the project are tested independently?

3   Debugging software can be a tricky business. Outline some of the standard methods, which are available to programmers when attempting to find bugs in the software of complex systems.

4   Test data forms an important part of any project design strategy. Using the following as specific examples, outline some suitable test data in each case.

(a) Dates

(b) Numerical data representing money

(c) Numerical data representing the age of a person

(d) Data representing car-registration numbers in the UK.

5 The maintenance phase of a project is just as important as the time during which the project is developed. Outline some of the activities that might go on during a typical maintenance phase of the following:

(a) Six months after a new project has been commissioned

(b) After three years of successful running.

6 Outline some of the major features which are to be considered in the following documentation:

(a) User documentation

(b) Technical documentation.

7 What is program documentation. Give some typical entries using an example of your own choice.

8 Outline how CASE is helping with the development of more efficient projects. How does it enable us to complete projects more effectively?

9 Briefly outline the difference between black-box and white-box testing methods.

End of chapter revision aid and summary

Cover up the right-hand column and see if you can answer the questions or define the terms on the left. They appear in the order in which they are covered in this chapter. Alternatively you may browse through the right-hand column to aid revision.

What is software engineering?	Software engineering is a systematic approach to the design of software involving analysis, testing, debugging and documentation of software.
What is a debugger?	A debugger is a special utility, which helps to test software by providing statistics regarding the state of the software (i.e. variables etc.) at various stages of development.
What is a trace routine?	Trace routines are often built into debugging software. A trace routine helps to establish what's happening as a program sequences through its instructions.
What are diagnostics?	Diagnostics is the general name for debugging tools and many other utilities, which help to find and correct bugs in the system.
What is a bug?	A bug is a mistake in the system or program (or an undocumented feature if it does anything remotely useful!).
What is maintenance?	Maintenance is the name given to the phase of correcting bugs or updating the software after it has been released.
What is test data?	Test data should be such that the limits claimed by the specification are achieved in practice. As many different conditions should be tested as is possible. (See white-box and black-box testing.)
What does integrity of data mean?	It's essential that the integrity of data (correctness) within a system has been thoroughly tested.
What is data validation?	Data validation checks to see if the range of data is sensible for it's intended purpose.
What is a checksum?	Checksums, hashing and CRCs etc. can be used to check the integrity of batches of data.
What is data verification?	Data verification checks to see if the data is likely to be correct by using an alternative source of reference. Verification is often the only means of checking original transcription errors.
What is a check digit?	Check digits are often useful for reducing the likelihood of mistyping things like account numbers etc. Modulo arithmetic is often used as a means of providing the check digit.

What is alpha testing?	Alpha testing is in-house testing, preferably by people who did not write the original software.
What is beta testing?	Beta testing is testing of software by a few customers before the software is put on general release.
What is documentation?	Documentation is an essential feature of software engineering. Without adequate documentation software will cease to be useful over a period of time. Both technical and user documentation are necessary.
What is technical documentation?	Technical documentation helps future analysts and programmers to modify or update the system.
What is user documentation?	User documentation is effectively the instruction manual for the users.
What is program documentation?	Program documentation is that part of the technical documentation which describes how the programs operate. It includes comments, lists of variables, author's name, date of last modifications etc.
What is CIM?	CIM is an acronym for Computer Integrated Manufacture.
What is black-box testing?	Black-box testing splits the system into modules, each having one or more inputs and one output. A table is produced showing the value of important variables and how to relate the extremes of range or select salient points in between.
What is white-box testing?	During white-box testing, a complete analysis of the program module is undertaken, and a flowgraph produced from the structure. The paths through the system are deduced, and black-box testing is applied to each of these parts.
What is a flowgraph?	A flowgraph is a directed graph showing the path through a program structure. It consists of nodes and arcs, and the number of paths can be obtained by counting up the regions in the flowgraph.
What is CASE?	CASE stands for Computer-Aided Software Engineering. CASE involves the use of specialist software packages specifically designed to help systems analysts and software engineers to do their job more efficiently. CASE systems are becoming more integrated, and systems which will help out with the development of the entire system life cycle should be with us in the near future.

18 Advanced Programming Concepts

In this chapter you'll learn about:

- The techniques of iteration and recursion
- The concept of fractals
- How to apply the techniques of iteration and fractals to a variety of problems from solving mathematical equations to producing stunning art effects like the Mandelbrot set
- How to apply recursion to get the computer to solve more complex problems

Key resources

To carry out this work most successfully it's best if you have:

- Access to a high-level programming language like Basic, Visual Basic, Pascal or Delphi
- Access to a colour printer so that you can print out the results of your artistic efforts

Concept Checkpoints

- It's essential that you are a relatively competent programmer if you are to carry out the work in this chapter successfully. You should therefore be happy with the concepts outlined in chapters 13 to 17.
- You will have to recall some of your mathematics to carry out the work in this chapter. However, all the relevant maths is explained in some detail.

Introduction

Part of the art of programming involves a detailed knowledge of a range of standard techniques, which will enable you to use the computer as an efficient analysis tool. The power of these techniques exploits the fact that a computer can be used to create simple and elegant solutions to certain types of complex problems. **Some of these techniques are a little difficult to understand on first reading, but it is well worth spending a few hours wrestling with this type of problem to understand what's involved. Your patience and concentration will be amply rewarded if you can eventually understand enough to program making use of these powerful techniques.**

You may have wondered how computers are used to produce stunning graphics such as those found in the Mandelbrot set (see later), the beautiful landscape patterns that are produced by fractals, or even in coping with the unpredictability of chaos theory. You will find that buried inside such computer simulations are algorithms using the concepts of iteration and recursion.

Student activities

At frequent intervals during this chapter you will be asked to stop and think about various points before going on to read the next section. You will be given a set of practical questions, which ask you to perform activities that check that you have understood what you are reading. Carrying out these activities will enable you to get appropriate practice in developing algorithms, and is thus very useful practice for your examinations and projects too. It will take a little longer than usual to work through this chapter, but it is well worth the effort.

Iteration

Iteration is easy to understand – it means **repeating**. Iteration is easily carried out on a computer, because computers are in their element when things can be repeated over and over again. We have seen, for example, how software gives us ample scope for looping (repeating) in the form of FOR-TO-NEXT, REPEAT-UNTIL and DO-WHILE loops, and so it is these sort of structures that are needed to perform this most-basic of computer operations. The *art of problem solving* making use of iteration lies with **establishing patterns** within certain problems (often the most difficult bit!), *expressing these patterns as* **algorithms**, and then *coding* them using a **suitable language**. Although there are thousands of different examples that could be chosen to cover these techniques, one or two common examples will illustrate the sort of processes, which, if you can master them, will considerably improve your programming skills.

A simple example

Iteration forms a large part of computer modelling because programmers may use the computer to solve problems in ways that would be most inefficient if carried out manually. It may not matter too much if the computer takes hours or even days to produce a result – the alternative of making such calculations by hand would be unthinkable. *To widen your linguistic horizons, in this chapter, use will be made of typical BASIC-language pseudocode, but programming making use of any other high-level or macro language such as those found in a spreadsheet for example, would be just as effective.*

Square roots

Let's suppose that we wish to find the square root of a number N, by making use of an iterative method. (I know that you can push the button on your calculator, or type in a single line in BASIC and get the answer, but how do you think the calculator is working it out? This is just a simple example which is used to demonstrate an iterative method.) Other examples giving you extra practice can be found in the exercise at the end of this chapter.

The bisection method

This is an example of a very simple iterative method borrowed from numerical analysis in mathematics. It is one method for *finding the root of an equation*, and we will use it to find the positive square root of a positive number. We will illustrate the principle with a concrete example, then develop an algorithm suitable for computer solution. The concrete-example stage mentioned here is more important than you might think – for most people it's necessary to work through a method manually in order to understand fully how to develop a suitable algorithm.

Suppose we want to find the square root of 2, another way of specifying the same problem is to find the positive root of the equation $x^2 = 2$. (Don't forget that a quadratic equation of this sort would have two roots, as +1.414.. and –1.414.. are both square roots of 2, but we will concentrate only on the positive answer – finding the negative root is obviously trivial!)

> **Hint:** Don't worry about the maths here. This is not a maths lesson, it's simply an example to illustrate some iteration. Some simple numerical analysis from mathematics does this rather well.

The method is easier to understand if we rewrite this equation as $f(x) = x^2 - 2 = 0$.

If we draw a graph of $x^2 - 2 = 0$, then it would be as shown in figure 18.1(a). Now let's just concentrate on the positive root, as shown in figure 18.1(b).

By common sense, we can see that an intelligent couple of first guesses would be 'x = 1' and 'x = 2'. The first guess '1' is too small, and '2' is too big. Therefore, the actual root lies somewhere in-between 1 and 2.

We need to develop a mechanistic way to arrive at the above obvious conclusion, for less obvious numbers. (Try finding the root of 187256 in your head if you're not convinced.) Now you will see from figure 18.1(a) that a clever way to see if a guess is too small or too big is to plug in the value of our guess into f(x) and examine the sign of the result. Guesses too small will produce f(x) negative (below the x-axis), and guesses too large will produce f(x) positive (above the x-axis). Don't forget that our ideal answer, the exact root of 2, is where the graph actually crosses the axis.

For example, 1st guess will give $f(1) = 1^2 - 2 = -1$
(Negative sign)

and   2nd guess will give $f(2) = 2^2 - 2 = +2$
(Positive sign)

Next we make a guess exactly half way between our previous two best guesses (hence the name **bisection**

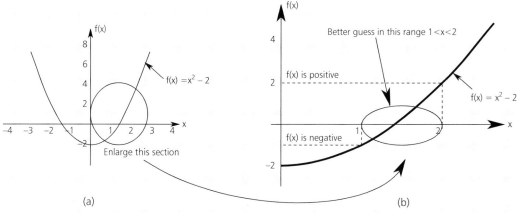

(a)   (b)

Figure 18.1

method). We carry out the above test again to see if the next guess would be between 1 and 1.5 (in which case we guess 1.25), or between 1.5 and 2 (in which case we guess 1.75). We then carry on with the same processes and tests until we get *near enough* to the answer.

Before developing this method any further, let's just concentrate on the overall principles we are trying to establish. Here we have developed a method which can be applied again and again so that we get nearer and nearer to the solution to the problem. This is the whole idea behind iterative modelling – such techniques are ideal for solution by computer programming.

The following table shows the above bisection method to finding the root of 2 applied manually (i.e. by using a calculator and writing down the intermediate stages).

Starting values		Next approximation (guess)
$x_1 = 1.0$	$x_2 = 2$	$x_3 = 1.5$
$x_1 = 1.0$	$x_2 = 1.5$	$x_3 = 1.25$
$x_1 = 1.5$	$x_2 = 1.25$	$x_3 = 1.375$
$x_1 = 1.5$	$x_2 = 1.375$	$x_3 = 1.4375$
$x_1 = 1.375$	$x_2 = 1.4375$	$x_3 = 1.40625$
$x_1 = 1.4375$	$x_2 = 1.40625$	$x_3 = 1.421875$
$x_1 = 1.40625$	$x_2 = 1.421875$	$x_3 = 1.4140625$

We could go on forever, but that would be irrational (mathematical joke!). We therefore need to decide when to stop, and it's usual to decide on a particular number of decimal places at which you would reach the required precision. You would usually go on until no changes take place in the decimal place in which you are interested, therefore, if we wish to know 'root 2' to '3 decimal places', for example, the above method would need to be taken a little further.

Hint: Don't cheat when undertaking these student activities, even if it takes you a long time to work through the examples. It will give you a lot of suitable programming and debugging experience.

Student Activity 1

An algorithm using the bisection method to find square roots
You have now seen the detailed principles of the bisection method. Build up a suitable structure diagram showing this method of solution, which must include the following:

(1) It allows the user to enter a positive number

(2) It terminates the iterative procedure after a suitable period.

(3) Test your algorithm manually using 'root 2' as an example.

A possible structure diagram for the above method is shown in figure 18.2.

Note that this is not the only solution, and some readers may find a more elegant one. Nevertheless, it is typical of what might be required to answer an examination-type question, or to solve a small section of your project work.

Student Activity 2

An algorithm using the bisection method to find square roots.
Using the algorithm described in the last section, or making use of your own algorithm, write some suitable code in a high-level language of your choice, and test the code by getting a computer to print out values of x until the iterative procedure is halted.

As Pascal is used extensively in other parts of this book, we will make a change by using BBC BASIC for the Acorn RISC PC machines. The program could be made more elegant, and better starting values could be found, but this is left up to the reader to develop. Also, if the numbers get very large, then the BASIC compiler can't do integer arithmetic with enough precision to cope with parts of the tests. Nevertheless, keep the numbers to less than 100 million and the method works quite well!

Don't forget that the whole point of this exercise is to demonstrate an iterative procedure in which a loop is executed a number of times until some condition is met. Although the bisection method usually converges on the answer reasonably quickly, it illustrates very well how a relatively small amount of code can be used to solve a problem in a way which would be extremely tedious without the use of programmable devices such as calculators or computers. (See figure 18.3.) This example has illustrated just one particular method, but there is a whole branch of mathematics and computer science called **numerical analysis** – this relates to using the computer in these sort of ways to solve problems which are often quite difficult to solve using conventional analytical techniques. Modern calculators these days work out the solutions to many different forms of equations by using different numerical methods.

Fractals

As a complete change from the above root-solving problem, we will now take a look at producing some patterns making use of **iteration** and **fractal** techniques. **Fractal geometry** has been described as the 'Geometry of Nature' – this is an apt definition because it's possible to describe intricate shapes such as **trees**, **clouds**, **mountains** and **valleys** etc. in ways that bear an uncanny resemblance to the real thing. Indeed, if you were not told that some of these objects had been

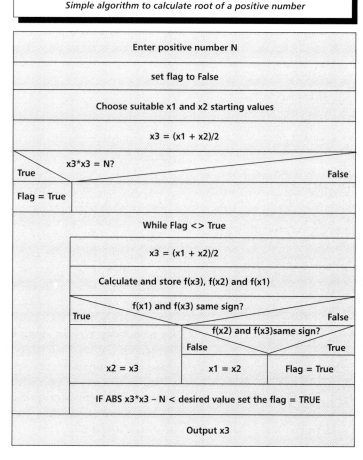

Simple algorithm to calculate root of a positive number

Figure 18.2

```
INPUT N
flag = FALSE
x1 = 1 : x2 = N
x3 = (x1+x2)/2
IF x3*x3 = N THEN flag = TRUE
WHILE flag <> TRUE
  x3=(x1+x2)/2
  fx1=x1*x1-N:fx2=x2*x2-N:fx3=x3*x3-N
  IF((fx1>0) AND (fx3>0)) OR ((fx1<0) AND (fx3<0)) THEN
          IF ((fx2>0) AND (fx3>0)) OR ((fx2<0) AND (fx3<0))THEN
            flag = TRUE
          ELSE
            x1=x3
          ENDIF
  ELSE
       x2=x3
  ENDIF
  PRINT "Guess so far is";x3
  IF ABS(x3*x3-N) < 0.001 THEN flag = TRUE
ENDWHILE
PRINT "Answer is ";x3
```

Figure 18.3

created mathematically, you would probably think that
you were looking at real pictures created by an artist or
photographer. The basic concepts of fractal geometry
were developed around the 1920s when a French mathematician called Julia proposed some extensions to what
mathematicians call measure theory. However, it was
not until the application of these techniques through
the use of computers that much general excitement
was generated. In 1982, **Benoit Mandelbrot**, a mathematician working for IBM Research at Yale University,
discovered that incredibly beautiful patterns could be
produced from relatively simple **iterative rules**. It is
to this fascinating topic which we now turn to illustrate the processes of iteration still further. You may
have to spend just a few minutes learning a little extra
mathematics, but the effort is well worth it for the
satisfaction of creating your own worlds on the screen
of the computer.

Complex numbers

First we will need to take a very brief look at what's
meant by a **complex number** – an unfortunate choice of
word, as the basic ideas are really quite simple. **Complex**
numbers are *numbers with two parts* – an **imaginary part**
and a **real part**. Imaginary is also an unfortunate term as
real problems can be solved making use of these imaginary numbers. Complex numbers can be represented on
a *special graph* called a **complex plane** or **Argand dia-**
gram, in which the real parts are plotted horizontally on
the *x*-axis, and the imaginary parts are plotted vertically
on the *y*-axis. The real part of the number is written
normally and the imaginary part of the number is pre-
fixed by using the letter 'i' (i for imaginary). Therefore, a
typical number might be written as (2 + i3), and this is
represented by the dot shown in figure 18.4(a). As far as
computing is concerned, we can view this particular
complex number as a vector (2,3), and this is why the
vector (2,3) has also been shown in this diagram.

At this stage you may well be wondering about the
difference between a co-ordinate like (x,y), for example,
and a complex number like (x + iy). As far as the plotting of the co-ordinate is concerned there is no
difference – a property that we will soon be using with
remarkable effect. Nevertheless, there must be something mysterious about these complex numbers, and
their unique properties come from the way in which 'i'
is defined. Now i can be thought of as an *operator*
which, when applied to a vector using multiplication,
turns the vector through 90° anticlockwise. Therefore, if
we start off with the real number +1, for example,
shown by the complex number (1 + i0) or the vector
(1,0) in figure 18.4(b), then after multiplying this by i,
the original horizontal vector rotates by 90° and ends
up facing upwards. The resultant new vector (0,1) now
represents the complex number (0 + i1).

Next consider what happens if we multiply the
complex number (0 + i) by i again – this operation
moves the upwards-facing vector by a further 90° until
it now faces left – the complex number for this new
position is given by (–1 +i0). Now the imaginary part
(the coefficient of i) of this latest complex number is
zero, and therefore this represents the ordinary number
–1 in the 'real world'.

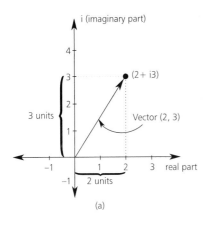

(a)

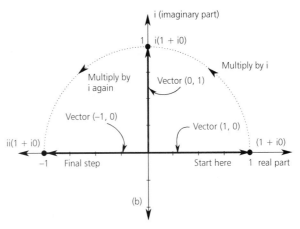

(b)

Figure 18.4

Now here comes the exciting part – we started off with +1, we then multiplied by i to get i, and then multiplied i by i again to get –1. This means that $i^2 = -1$. So what, I hear you ask? Well, if $i^2 = -1$, this means that $i = (\sqrt{-1})$ – a magical number which had eluded mathematicians for centuries. To be able to get a number which, when multiplied by itself produces a negative number was revolutionary – you are reminded that there is no ordinary number, positive or negative which has this remarkable property.

As far as we are concerned, for the purposes of the arithmetical work covered in this section, **complex numbers** *may be treated like* **ordinary numbers**, *except for the fact that* **when i^2 is encountered, it should be replaced by –1**. For example, if we want to multiply (2 +i3) by (1 + i2), then this can be done by multiplying the brackets out using the usual rules of algebra as follows,

$$(2 + i3)(1 + i2) = 2 + i4 + i3 + i^2 6 = 2 + i7 - 6$$
$$= -4 + i7 \quad \text{(Don't forget } i^2 = -1\text{)}$$

hence the answer to this particular multiplication problem is –4 + i7.

The only other thing that we need to know is how to work out the magnitude of a complex number. Now the magnitude is given simply by the **magnitude** *of the* **vector** that represents it. Therefore, the magnitude of (2 + i3), for example, will be given by the length of the hypotenuse of the right-angled triangle whose other lengths are the horizontal and vertical dimensions given by

> **Hint:** This is not meant to be a maths lesson. However, if you want to generate some spectacular computer graphics, you will have to know a little mathematics.

2 and 3 in figure 18.4(a). A simple application of Phythagoras is all that is needed. If, for example, we let Z represent a more general complex number (x + iy), then the magnitude of Z is represented by

$$|Z| = \sqrt{(x^2 + y^2)}$$

There is very much more to the theory of complex numbers, but we have already learnt all we need to know for the purposes of our iterative algorithm. Having covered the relevant details, we can now start to get down to the business of producing some interesting patterns by using iteration.

The Mandelbrot set (in this case for a squared function) is governed by the following equation,

$$Z_n \rightarrow Z_{n-1}^2 + \lambda$$

where Z and λ are both complex numbers.

Now the **iterative nature** of this problem should pose no difficulty whatsoever for computer-science students – it's identical in principle to the techniques covered when dealing with roots in the last section. For example,

choose a suitable value of Z (say Z_1) and a suitable λ (see in a moment)

put Z_1 in the formula $Z_2 \rightarrow Z_1 + \lambda$ which gives the new value for Z_2

put Z_2 in the formula $Z_3 \rightarrow Z_2 + \lambda$ which gives the new value for Z_3

put Z_3 etc.

Apart from the special case of no change, in general, there are two types of behaviour exhibited by the above iterative processes – either the value of Z_n approaches

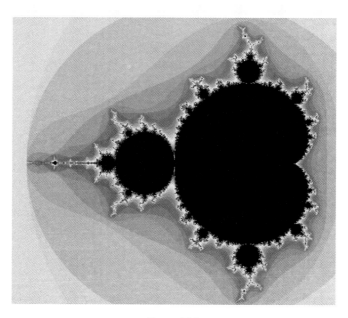

Figure 18.5

infinity, or the value of Z_n approaches some constant. If the value tends towards infinity then it is said to diverge, but if it tends towards a constant then it is said to converge. Any point that converges to a particular value belongs to the Mandelbrot set, but any point that diverges to infinity lies outside of the Mandelbrot set. The enormous fascination with this topic lies not with looking at the numbers within the set itself, but with an exploration of the boundary between the two sets. We look in detail at the patterns produced on the edge of the Mandelbrot set, which gives rise to intricate patterns of literally infinite detail – *you* will soon be writing an algorithm to generate the patterns shown in figure 18.5. Colour is really needed to appreciate the beauty of these images – see Plates 39–42.

Did you know that . . .

Examples of the Mandelbrot set and Julia sets can be seen in Plates 39–42.

The *boundary* of the **Mandelbrot set** is an example of a **fractal**. Other common examples are **Julia sets** and **Sierpinski triangles**. Because fractals literally contain infinitely complex amounts of detail, they can be used to describe the infinitely complex characteristics of many shapes such as plants and trees found in nature.

In its most basic form, the Mandelbrot set can be investigated by starting off with a value of $Z_1 = 0 + i0$, then putting this value into the above equation with a suitable value of λ (see in a moment). We then stop the process according to the rules outlined in the next paragraph, then start the whole process again from scratch using different values of λ. It is these values of λ which give the co-ordinates of the points to plot.

Now the clever part comes by a consideration of what's happening to Z for different vales of λ as these iterations proceed. If the value of Z_n converges we plot the points in black, but if the value of Z_n diverges, we colour the original points by considering how slowly or how quickly Z_n approaches infinity. If it does not take too many iterations for $|Z_n|$ to become large then it's rapidly increasing, or if it takes yonks for $|Z_n|$ to get to a large value then it is slowly increasing, and is therefore plotted in a different colour. In practice all we have to do is to count the number of iterations, test for some arbitrary magnitudes – and assign colours accordingly.

Development of the iterative algorithm

You are going to develop this algorithm in several parts. The suggestions inside the boxes will guide you through in relatively short and easy stages. Try not to look at the section of text after each box until you have attempted the work first!

Student Activity 3

An algorithm to multiply the complex numbers
You have now seen how complex numbers may be multiplied together. Using a suitable high-level language, write an algorithm that performs the following:

(1) Sets up Z = x + iy, and λ = p + iq

(2) Uses the function $Z \rightarrow Z^2 + \lambda$ to compute the next value of Z.

(3) Puts the whole lot inside a loop to investigate whether or not |Z| converges or diverges using p = –2 and q = 2.

The following procedure works out multiplication of complex numbers. What we have to do is simple – if we let Z = x + iy, and let λ = p + iq, then the new Z will be

$Z \rightarrow Z^2 + \lambda = (x + iy)(x + iy) + p + iq$
(Put in the values of Z and λ)
$\rightarrow x^2 + 2ixy + i^2y^2 + p + iq$
(Multiplying out the brackets)
$\rightarrow x^2 + 2ixy - y^2 + p + iq$
(Don't forget that $i^2 = -1$)
$\rightarrow (x^2 - y^2 + p) + i(2xy + q)$
(Collect real and imaginary parts)

This gives us the real '$(x^2 - y^2 + p)$' and imaginary '$(2xy + q)$' parts of the new Z which then become the new values of x and y respectively. This will then be used to calculate the next value of Z. Don't forget that λ, and hence the values of p and q will remain the same until a *new value* of λ is chosen for the next set of iterations.

A suitable algorithm, again using BBC BASIC V, is as follows

```
x = 0:y = 0
INPUT"Please type in p followed by
  q",p,q
FOR count = 1 TO 10
    X = x^2 - y^2 + p
    Y = 2*x*y + q
    MagZ = SQR(x^2 + y^2)
    PRINT x,y,MagZ
    x = X:y = Y
NEXT count
```

Running the above program with p =–2 and q = 2, you will probably find that |Z| gets too big for the computer to handle after about 5 iterations! Therefore, in the final program we will have to test for |Z| becoming large very rapidly, and stop the arithmetical processes before it has time to generate a run-time error on the computer.

The complex plane

In the above example you were given p and q in a rather arbitrary fashion. However, typical values for p and q

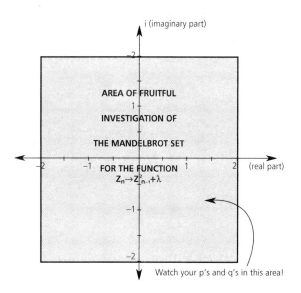

Figure 18.6

which lie between −2 and +2 give a good picture to investigate. Therefore, if we are to colour these points using the arguments stated in the last section, then the complex plane shown in figure 18.6 needs investigation.

The resolution chosen is up to you, and depends upon the graphics capability of your system, but high resolutions would be needed if great detail is to be seen. Nevertheless, you can get the iterative algorithms working with far less resolution, and this is what I would suggest doing during the initial-development phases. Techniques such as simplifying the underlying number of iterations necessary so that algorithms may be developed more quickly should be remembered when you are undertaking your project work. One strategy for the Mandelbrot problem would be to sweep values of p from −2 to +2 in suitable steps, and then repeat this procedure for each value of q from −2 to +2, again using suitable steps. Now this could represent a huge amount of calculation. For example, if we take 500 steps from −2 to +2 in each direction, then this means that we go through 250,000 tests for convergence and divergence. Each test, will possibly take up to about 50 iterations, giving typically over 12½ million calculations. Unless you have a fast computer, there will be plenty of time for coffee while you are waiting for the results.

The last thing to do before you develop the algorithm to cycle through the p's and q's in the above area is to suggest a suitable colour scheme. You will recall that the time taken to 'whiz off or escape to infinity' is used to determine a suitable colour for a chosen starting point. Now suppose that you choose a 16-colour mode, black has already been reserved for the convergent numbers, therefore, this leaves us with 15 colours for the rest of the diagram.

As a measure of speed of escape to infinity, we can simply count the number of iterations needed to get past some particular value. Therefore, we can assign 15

different values on the way to infinity.

One common colour-assignment technique is to count the number of iterations (times round the loop calculating new values of p and q), and assign a colour accordingly. For example, if you were in a 64-colour graphics mode then once round the loop could be assigned colour one, twice round the loop colour two and so on until 64 times round the loop would get colour 64. Don't forget that each time round the loop we must check for the magnitude of the complex number becoming too large, in which case we exit with the value to determine the colour. Also, don't forget that some values might change very slowly, in which case it's best to limit the number of times round the loop. Applying this method in a 16-million colour mode could be a little time consuming!

Before going any further carry out the following graphics-preparation activity in student activity 4.

Student Activity 4

Graphics preparation for the Mandelbrot algorithm
Choose a suitable graphics mode on your computer with a suitable resolution and number of colours. I would suggest just 16 colours at first. In a high-level language of your choice write the following:

(1) Map out the complex plane onto your screen graphics area (i.e. actual values of p and q need to fill up most of the screen).

(2) Vary the values of p and q from −2 to +2, and plot dots to verify that this is happening.

(3) Assign a different colour to any area of the screen based on values of p and q. (You can choose any criteria you wish.)

Using a 16-colour mode on Acorn's RISC PC with a horizontal resolution of 1600 and a vertical resolution of 1200, and assigning just two different colours according to p being less than or greater than 0, we get the following code.

```
MODE 102
FOR p = −2 TO +2 STEP 0.01
  FOR q = −2 TO +2 STEP 0.01
    IF q>0 THEN GCOL 0,2 ELSE GCOL 0,4
    PLOT 69,(p+2)*200,(q+2)*200
  NEXT q
NEXT p
```

Whatever code you have produced should fill up a large portion of the screen with dots, preferably so close together that you can't easily see them. Portions of the screen should be assigned different colours according to your chosen criteria, which in the above case is very simple indeed.

It's important to note that the origin of the complex plane used to view the Mandelbrot set is in the middle

Hint: Try to develop your projects in simple stages as we are doing here, and document the work as you go. You will be amazed at the extra work that's involved if you try to document a complex algorithm six months after you have finished working with it.

of the picture, but the origin of your graphics screen is likely to be the bottom-left-hand-side or top of the VDU. Therefore, although appropriate values of p and q must be used in the mathematical analysis, 2 has been added to each to map the complex plane so that it moves along two and up two and can be viewed on the screen. Next we have to multiply the co-ordinates by some large value (200 in the above program) so that the area of the plot is large enough to be seen in the screen.

algorithm to evaluate new values of x and y for the complex number Z, and use the colouring algorithm based on how many iterations (loop counts) are needed for Z to whiz off to infinity. Best of luck – don't forget that much of the initial thought has already been done, and don't cheat by looking at the answers first.

A suitable algorithm is shown in figure 18.7.

A program written in BBC BASIC, based on the pseudocode algorithm shown in figure 18.7 is as follows:

```
MODE 40
MagZ=0
x = 0:y = 0
FOR p = -2 TO +2 STEP 0.01
   FOR q = -2 TO +2 STEP 0.01
      Loop=1
      WHILE ABS(MagZ) < 100 AND Loop <64
         X = x^2 - y^2 + p
         Y =   2*x*y + q
         MagZ = SQR(x^2+y^2)
         x = X:y = Y
         Loop = Loop + 1
      ENDWHILE
      GCOL Loop
      PLOT 69,(p+2)*200,(q+2)*200
      x = 0:y=0:MagZ=0
   NEXT q
NEXT p
PRINT "DONE"
```

Student Activity 5

The final Mandelbrot algorithm

(1) Produce a structure diagram for the complete Mandelbrot plot. Use p and q from –2 to +2 in steps of 0.01, and 64 different colour-assignment tests. Test for the magnitude of Z getting bigger than 1E5, and stop the iterative procedure if this is true.

(2) Code the above algorithm using any suitable high-level language. Decrease the step size during the development stages if necessary for debugging.

(3) Enjoy the patterns on your computer screen!

The above code is a very basic shell. There is room for considerable improvement, and adding routines to investigate interesting parts of the complex plane are common extras. Similarly, there is no provision to save the picture, which could have taken some time to complete. It is left to the reader to develop the algorithms further if desired. Hours of practice with your programming skills will be amply rewarded.

You are now ready to program your Mandelbrot algorithm. You need to use the graphics program you developed in the last section to sweep out the appropriate area of the screen. The complex-number-multiplication

```
Initialise variables
FOR p = -2 TO +2 STEP size
   FOR q = -2 TO +2 STEP size
      Initialise iteration count
      WHILE Absolute value(Magnitude of Z) < Max AND iteration count <64
         X = x^2 - y^2 + p
         Y =   2*x*y + q
         Magnitude of Z = Square root of(x^2+y^2)
         Set new values of x and y using old X and Y
         increment iteration count
      ENDWHILE
      Choose suitable graphics colour based on iteration count number
      PLOT point at graphics position with appropriate scale factor
      Reset the variables x and y to zero
   NEXT q
NEXT p
```

Figure 18.7

Recursion

Recursion is a vitally important topic as it represents part of the ultimate dream of being able to produce lots of results with the minimum of coding. By the continued repetition of the same group of instructions, one can produce staggering graphics effects or work out mathematical equations, which would involve long and tedious coding by other methods. These are just two of the many hundreds of possible applications of recursion. Others can be found in the chapter on data structures, and in the chapter on algorithms.

Recursion and factorials

As an example, consider working out 'factorial 10', or, as mathematicians put it, '10!'.

Now 10! is defined as

$$10 \times 9 \times 8 \times 7 \times 6 \times 5 \times 4 \times 3 \times 2 \times 1 = 3,628,800$$

Similarly N! would be defined as

$$N \times (N - 1) \times (N - 2) \times (N - 3) \times \ldots \times 3 \times 2 \times 1$$

You will also need to remember that 0! and 1! are both defined as 1.

Suppose that we had to construct an algorithm to evaluate a factorial. We could proceed in several different ways:

1. Write down the function explicitly!

No one who still retains 'all their marbles' would code the algorithm in this way, as it would involve longer and longer expressions for larger and larger factorials! This method will therefore not be considered.

2. It does not take much imagination to see that a simple loop would be more efficient and could be accomplished by using pseudocode as follows:

```
Assign value to N
Set up initial conditions
  count := 2
  product := 1
Test for special case
  IF N = 0 OR N = 1 THEN
    factorial(N) = 1 in which case we
  STOP
  ELSE
    REPEAT
      product := product x count
      count := count + 1
    UNTIL count = N + 1
factorial(N) = product
```

Whenever the above routine is needed we could insert the above loop into the algorithm to evaluate a factorial. The method could also be tidied up a little by using a defined function (see chapter 13), and passing over the appropriate parameters to the routine.

3. This time we will apply a **recursive definition** to the problem of evaluating a factorial. Consider the following:

```
DEFINE MODULE factorial(N)
  IF N = 0 OR N 1 THEN
    factorial = 1
  ELSE
    factorial = N x factorial (N — 1)
END MODULE
```

The above is all the code that is required. The reason is that the module calls itself at line five. **A recursive routine** is therefore 'one that calls itself'. Consider an example using the above code to work out 4!

Modular code being executed	Comments
MODULE factorial (4) Routine working out $4 \times$ factorial (3)	Module entered with N = 4
MODULE factorial (3) Routine working out $4 \times 3 \times$ factorial (2)	Module entered with N = 3
MODULE factorial (2) Routine working out $4 \times 3 \times 2 \times$ factorial (1)	Module entered with N = 2
MODULE factorial (1) Routine working out $4 \times 3 \times 2 \times 1$	Module entered with N = 1
$4 \times 3 \times 2 \times 1 = 24$	Answer returned is 24.

You can see from the above that the routine begins by working out $4 \times$ factorial (3). However, 'factorial (3)' is then worked out by the routine calling itself. Therefore, when factorial (3) is worked out, the routine is then working on $4 \times 3 \times$ 'factorial (2)'. The routine then calls itself to work out factorial (2) etc.

A **Pascal function** (i.e part of a Pascal program) can be used in a similar way to the above as follows:

```
FUNCTION factorial (N: INTEGER):
  INTEGER;
BEGIN
  IF N = 1 OR N = 0 THEN
    BEGIN
      factorial := 1
    END;
  ELSE
    BEGIN
      factorial := N * factorial(N—1)
    END;
END;
```

The above FUNCTION may be combined with other parts to form a Pascal program as shown in figure 18.8.

```
PROGRAM factorial (input, output);
  VAR number: INTEGER;
  FUNCTION factorial (N: INTEGER): INTEGER;
    BEGIN
    IF N = 1 OR N = 0 THEN
      BEGIN
        factorial := 1
      END;
    ELSE
      BEGIN
        factorial := N * factorial (N−1)
      END;
  END;

BEGIN (* work out factorial*)
  WRITELN('Input number to be used for the factorial calculation');
  READLN(number);
  WRITELN('Original number', number, 'factorial', number, 'is', factorial
  (number));
END.
```

Figure 18.8

Example using recursion

One of the classic examples of recursion is the development of an algorithm to solve the Towers of Hanoi problem. The problem is illustrated using the apparatus shown in figure 18.9.

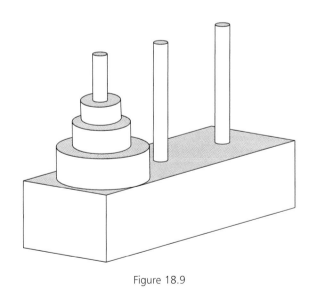

Figure 18.9

There are three vertical poles over which discs with holes in the centre are placed. Initially the discs are placed such that the largest one is on the bottom, progressively leading up to the narrowest one on the top of the pile. The object of the game is to transfer the discs, one at a time, onto another pole to end up

in the same order. The difficulty obviously arises from the rules of the game which are as follows:

● Only one disc can be moved at any time.
● After each move, all discs must be on the poles (you can't hide one in your pocket!)
● No disc may be placed on top of another disc, which is smaller than itself.

It is essential when dealing with recursive algorithms to be able to visualise how the overall problem can be split up into sub-problems. These sub-problems may then be solved by the application of the same algorithm again and again, but obviously with different parameters being passed on every time the original algorithm is recursively called, just like the factorials problem covered in the last section. Firstly, it is obvious that no matter how many discs are involved, the problem must ultimately be broken down into the movement of just one single disc. Therefore, there must be a routine that carries out this simple move, and the routine to do this is as follows:

```
Move (source, destination)
```

The source will be the pole from which to get the disc, and the destination will be the pole which is to accommodate the disc. Now it is also obvious that the source and destination will change, according to which disc is to be moved and when. Therefore, we need some method of constantly swapping over the source and destination throughout the algorithm. Although the problem seems to be very complicated, it is an excellent example of how recursion can provide the solution quite simply, and very elegantly, with only a few lines of code! Consider the following:

Let's assume that the left-hand pole is to be the 'source pole' i.e. the pole on which the pile of discs is originally placed, and the 'middle pole' is to be the 'destination pole' for the final pile of discs. Given this information, it is obvious that the right-hand pole can be regarded as a temporary store for the discs until they are needed. First we will assume that we have just three discs on the pile. The classic solution to the above problem is simple, and consists of just three stages:

> **Hint:** You will probably be amazed at how long it may take you to get to grips with this problem. I suggest that you will need many hours with some physical disks in front of you trying to convince yourself that you understand how the computer will carry out the task. However, it's worth it, you will certainly understand the concept of recursion by the end of this exercise.

1. Move the top two discs from the left-hand pole to the right-hand pole, making use of the poles as a temporary store when necessary.
2. Move the remaining disc on the left-hand pole to the middle pole.
3. Move the two discs on the right-hand pole back on the middle pole, making use of the poles as a temporary store when necessary.

The above algorithm should be quite obvious. The only way you can get the biggest disc from the bottom of the pile on the left-hand side to the bottom of the pile on the middle pole is to make sure that the rest of the discs are not in the way of this move i.e. they form a pile on the right hand side!

This is, in fact, part (1) of the above algorithm. Part (2) is simply the disc that remains on the original pole being transferred on to the final pole. The final part (3) transfers the other discs back on top of the bottom disc on the middle pole.

Suppose now that we started with four discs. This time, we would have to remove the top three discs from the left to the right for part (1) of the algorithm etc. If we had N discs, then we would have to move (N − 1) discs from the left to the middle for part (1) etc. We can therefore generalise the three major steps as an algorithm for N discs (moving the pile from the left to the middle) as follows:

1. **Move (N − 1) discs from the left-hand pole to the right-hand pole using poles for temporary stores where necessary.**
2. **Move the remaining disc from the left-hand pole to the middle pole.**
3. **Move the (N − 1) discs from the right-hand pole to the middle pole using the poles as a temporary store when necessary.**

What the above algorithm does is to split up the problem into simpler sub-problems. These sub-problems are almost identical in nature to the main problem. For example, with four discs, the problem involves moving a pile of three discs. With three discs, the problem involves moving a pile of two discs etc.

To understand how the parameters such as 'source' and 'destination' need to be swapped is a little more difficult (this is an understatement!). We will, therefore, manually work through an example using just three discs, and the above algorithm as a skeleton:

Let C = Largest disc   Let B = Medium disc
   Let A = Smallest disc

Let 1 = left-hand pole   Let 2 = middle pole
   Let 3 = right-hand pole

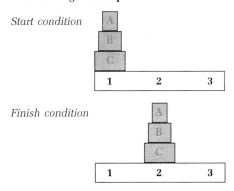

We will now manually carry out the operations based on the algorithms that we have just developed. Each stage is carefully documented in the following table. Work through it with care, and note that the level of indentation in table 18.1 is vitally important. The ideas are simple, but very tedious to do manually – this is why we are programming a computer to do it! If, for example, we wish to move 3 discs from pole 1 to pole 2, then we must solve a sub problem, first by moving 2 discs from pole 1 to pole 3, so that they are out of the way and we can accomplish our original intended move. However, to transfer two discs from pole 1 to pole 3, we must solve a further sub problem, which involves transferring 1 disc from pole 1 to pole 2 etc. This is the way to work through table 18.1, which shows the positions of the discs at any one time in the right-hand columns.

Assuming that you have not gone completely gaga by working through the above problem, we can identify the patterns and start to code the problem in the following recursive way.

1. **Identify the number of discs to be moved (supplied by the user).**
2. **IF N = 1, THEN move the disc from the source to the destination.**
3. **IF N > 1 THEN**
   (a) Call routine to move (N − 1) discs (supply N, source, temp, dest).
   (b) Move 1 disc from source to destination.
   (c) Call routine to move (N − 1) discs (supply N, source, temp, dest).

Table 18.1   Working to transfer 3 discs from pole 1 to pole 2.

Comments	Positions of the discs
Start condition	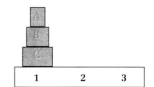
Note that N = number of discs to transfer, source = pole from which the discs are to be moved dest = pole to which the discs must be moved, temp = temporary store used to hold discs temporarily.	
(Set N = 3, source = 1, dest = 2 and temp = 3)	(Variables are initialised for the problem)
To transfer 3 discs from pole 1 to pole 2....	**(Main problem to be solved)**
(Set N = 2, source = 1, dest = 3 and temp = 2)	*(dest and temp swapped)*
To transfer 2 discs from pole 1 to pole 3....	**(Sub problem number 1 to be solved)**
(Set N = 1, source = 1, dest = 2 and temp = 3)	*(dest and temp swapped)*
To transfer 1 disc from pole 1 to pole 2....	**(Sub problem number 2 to be solved)**
Move 1 disc from pole 1 to pole 2	(Sub problem number 2 solved) 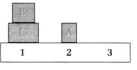
(source = 1, dest =3 and temp = 2)	*(dest and temp swapped)*
Move 1 disc from pole 1 to pole 3	(Sub problem number 1, part 1, solved) 
(source = 2, dest =3 and temp = 1)	*(source and temp swapped)*
Move 1 disc from pole 2 to pole 3	(Sub problem number 1, part 2, solved) 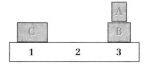
(source =1, dest = 2, temp = 3)	*(source, dest and temp all changed back to what they were when 1st part of problem was called)*
Move 1 disc from pole 1 to pole 2	(1st part of main problem solved) 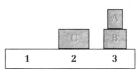
(Set N = 2, source = 3, dest = 2, temp = 1)	*(source and temp swapped)*
To transfer 2 discs from pole 3 to pole 2....	**(Sub problem number 1 to be solved)**
(Set N =1, source = 3, dest = 1, temp = 2)	*(dest and temp swapped)*
To transfer 1 disc from pole 3 to pole 1....	**(Sub problem number 2 to be solved)**
Move 1 disc from pole 3 to pole 1	(Sub problem number 2 solved) 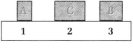
(source = 3, dest = 2, temp = 1)	*(dest and temp swapped)*
Move 1 disc from pole 3 to pole 2	(2nd part of main problem solved)
(Set source = 1, dest = 2 and temp = 3)	*(source and temp swapped)*
Move 1 disc from pole 1 to pole 2	(3rd part of main problem solved)
The entire problem has been solved!	

> **Hint:** It's essential that you develop the code using a high-level language of your choice. Don't just rely on the dry run. Write the code and get it working on the computer. It's the only way to fully understand how this problem is solved.

'N', 'source', 'temp' and 'dest' can be supplied (in the correct order) so that the routines which make the actual move know the current poles that are acting as the 'source', 'temporary-store' and 'destination' respectively. Let's build up the program by considering the following Pascal-like pseudocode which defines a procedure called 'Transfer'.

```
PROCEDURE Transfer (N, source, dest,
   temp : integer)
   IF N = 1 THEN
      BEGIN
      Move (source, dest)
   END;
   ELSE
      BEGIN
         Transfer (N − 1, source, temp,
dest)
         Move (source, dest)
         Transfer (N − 1, temp, dest,
source)
      END;
END;
```

To make the procedure easy to use, the source, temporary-store and destination will be assigned integer numerical values of 1, 2 and 3 respectively, which would represent the pole positions as follows:

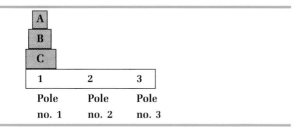

1	2	3
Pole	Pole	Pole
no. 1	no. 2	no. 3

N.B. When the routine is called again, parameters are swapped to accommodate the different poles that act as a 'source', 'destination' and 'temporary-store' throughout the problem. This is of fundamental importance in understanding this recursion algorithm, and indeed to recursion in general. It is carefully explained in the dry run that follows.

Dry run

The routine shown in table 18.2 is not long. It looks quite long because of the many comments to explain each stage carefully. The user will supply the parameters N = 3, source = 1, destination = 2 and therefore, temporary-store = 3. After you have programmed the computer to solve the problem, it should be a lot easier

to understand. Indeed, you could progam your own animated sequence showing the rings moving.

Look carefully at how the parameters are passed between the procedures. The swapping mentioned above is accomplished by swapping the variables when the procedure calls itself. This can easily be seen when line 8, for example, is encountered in the table which follows. Here you can see that the value of N is decremented by 1, the source is not altered, but dest and temp are swapped, simply because of the order in which the parameters are passed over to the next procedure call.

Note also how the parameters must be restored to their original conditions when a procedure has finished. For example, when line 12 is encountered, this means that the last call to this procedure is ended. Now supposing, as is the case being considered here, this particular procedure was called from line 8. We must return to line 9, the line that would have been executed after the procedure has finished, with all the parameters replaced with the values that were present before the procedure was called. It is by this mechanism that the values of N, source, dest and temp get set back to their original values, usually accomplished inside the computer by means of a stack (see chapter 24).

We will start off the **dry run** (manually working through the system) calling the procedure named 'transfer' with the parameters that have been used in the previous examples. You should be able to see why the lines are executed in this order by following through the algorithm (obeying the instructions) and moving to the next line with your finger. The levels of recursion shown in the last column remind you where you are.

If you worked your way through table 18.2 and understood it, then you should have a deep insight into recursion, and a terrible headache! It is remarkable how much work can be carried out with such a small amount of code. We used only three discs, but you can do several more if you program the computer to do it. All you have to do is change from N = 3 to N = 5 or 6, for example.

The final program is quite simple. All it needs is a routine to print out the moves as it goes along. The following routine simply prints out the 'source' and 'destination' of each move. However, you should be capable of programming some good graphics to make the output attractive on your machine.

If you have found the above difficult or even impossible to follow, then code the procedures given, and include a method for printing out the values of N, source, dest and temp as you go along. Finally, look at the numbers printed out by the computer – that's what the author did to generate the numbers in table 18.2!

The final routine, showing a Pascal program, which includes some very simple output, is shown in figure 18.11.

The monks of Hanoi devised the original problem. In fact they had a total of 64 discs on their model! Indeed, they believed that by the time the problem

```
1.   PROCEDURE Transfer (N, source, dest, temp : integer)
2.     IF N = 1 THEN
3.       BEGIN
4.         Move (source, dest)
5.       END
6.     ELSE
7.       BEGIN
8.         Transfer (N − 1, source, temp, dest)
9.         Move (source, dest)
10.        Transfer (N − 1, temp, dest, source)
11.      END
12.  END;
```

Figure 18.10

Table 18.2 Dry run showing how the above recursive algorithm is executed line by line for 3 discs

Line numbers being executed	Parameters passed during procedure calls				Action taken	Level of recursion
	N	source	dest	temp		
1	3	1	2	3	Procedure called with starting parameters for the problem.	1
2	3	1	2	3	N<>1. Therefore, go to line 7.	1
7	3	1	2	3	Begin the else condition as N<>1.	1
8	2	1	3	2	N altered, dest and temp swapped by passing parameters.	2
1	2	1	3	2	Procedure is called with new parameters.	2
2	2	1	3	2	N<>1. Therefore, go to line 7.	2
7	2	1	3	2	Begin the 'else' condition as N<>1.	2
8	1	1	2	3	N altered, dest and temp swapped by passing parameters.	3
1	1	1	2	3	Procedure is called with new parameters.	3
2	1	1	2	3	N=1. Therefore, go to line 3.	3
3	1	1	2	3	Begin the 'if' condition as N=1.	3
4	1	1	2	3	Move block A from pole 1 to pole 2.	3
5	1	1	2	3	End the 'if' condition.	3
6	1	1	2	3	Don't execute 'else' condition.	3
12	2	1	3	2	The third call to the procedure is ended – therefore, go back to line 9, because the third procedure was called from line 8. (*Parameters are restored to line 7 above.*)	2
9	2	1	3	2	Move block B from pole 1 to pole 3.	2
10	1	2	3	1	N altered, source and temp swapped.	3
1	1	2	3	1	Procedure is called with new parameters.	3
2	1	2	3	1	N=1. Therefore, go to line 3.	3
3	1	2	3	1	Begin the 'if' condition and N=1.	3
4	1	2	3	1	Move block A from pole 2 to pole 3.	3
5	1	2	3	1	End the 'if' condition.	3
6	1	2	3	1	Don't execute the 'else' condition.	3
12	2	1	3	2	The third call to the procedure is ended – therefore, go back to line 11, because the third procedure was called from line 10. (*Parameters are restored to line 9.*)	2
11	1	1	3	2	End the 'else' condition.	2

Table 18.2 continued

Line numbers being executed	N	source	dest	temp	Action taken	Level of recursion
12	3	1	2	3	The second call to the procedure is ended – therefore, go back to line 9, because the 2nd procedure was called from line 8. (*Parameters are restored to line 1.*)	1
9	3	1	2	3	Move block C from pole 1 to pole 2.	1
10	2	3	2	1	N altered, source and temp swapped.	2
1	2	3	2	1	Procedure is called with new parameters.	2
2	2	3	2	1	N<>1. Therefore, go to line 7.	2
7	2	3	2	1	Begin the else condition as N<>1.	2
8	1	3	1	2	N altered, dest and temp swapped.	3
1	1	3	1	2	Procedure is called with new parameters.	3
2	1	3	1	2	N=1. Therefore go to line 3.	3
3	1	3	1	2	Begin the 'if' condition as N=1.	3
4	1	3	1	2	Move block A from pole 3 to pole 1.	3
5	1	3	1	2	End the 'if' condition.	3
6	1	3	1	2	Don't execute the 'else' condition.	3
12	2	3	2	1	The third call to the procedure is ended – therefore, go back to line 9, because the third procedure was called from line 8. (*Parameters are restored to last line 7.*)	2
9	2	3	2	1	Move block B from pole 3 to pole 2.	2
10	1	1	2	3	N altered, source and temp swapped.	3
1	1	1	2	3	Procedure is called with new parameters.	3
2	1	1	2	3	N=1. Therefore, go to line 3.	3
3	1	1	2	3	Begin the 'if' condition.	3
4	1	1	2	3	Move block A from pole 1 to pole 2. (Problem solved!!)	3
5	1	1	2	3	End the 'if' condition.	3
6	1	1	2	3	Don't execute the 'else' condition.	3
12	2	1	2	3	The third call to the procedure is ended – therefore, go back to line 11, because the third procedure was called from line 10. (*Parameters are restored to last line 9.*)	2
11	2	3	2	1	End the 'else' condition.	2
12	3	1	2	3	The 2nd call to the procedure is ended – therefore, go back to line 11, because the 2nd procedure was called from line 10. (*Parameters are restored to the condition for 1st call.*)	1
11	3	1	2	3	End the 'else' condition.	1
12	**3**	**1**	**2**	**3**	**The 1st call to the procedure is ended – therefore, jump out of the procedure and back to the calling routine.**	**0**

Hint: Once you have the routine working, add some timing functions to see how long it takes for 3 disks. Then gradually increase the number of disks and see what happens. You could have a competition between different students to see who can do it most quickly!

was solved the end of the world would have arrived. However, I should not worry too much about this because it has been calculated that even if the monks worked out the perfect algorithm, and moved one disc every second, then it would take over 600,000 million years to complete the solution!

You could now develop an algorithm to solve the Towers of Hanoi problem using a computer, but first, think carefully about how long it would take the computer to solve the problem!

Suppose that we could make 100,000,000 moves every second (a very fast computer):

```
PROGRAM recursion-example (input,output); VAR N : integer;
PROCEDURE Transfer(N, source, dest, temp : integer)
PROCEDURE Move (source, dest : integer);
(* This simple procedure writes out to the screen the moves made by the computer
BEGIN
  Writeln ('Move disc from', source, 'to', dest);
  END;
  IF N = 1
    THEN
        BEGIN
        Move (source, dest)
        END;
    ELSE
      BEGIN
        Transfer (N − 1, source, temp, dest)
        Move (source, destination)
        Transfer (N − 1, temp, dest, source)
      END;
END;
BEGIN
  * This is the main calling routine
  WRITE ('Please enter the number of discs.);
  READLN (N)
  WRITE ('Please enter the source pole.);
  READLN (source)
  WRITE ('Please enter the destination pole.);
  READLN (destination)
  IF source = 1 AND dest = 2 THEN temp = 3
  IF source = 2 AND dest = 3 THEN temp = 1 ELSE  temp = 2
  Transfer (N, source, dest, temp)
END.
```

Figure 18.11

Moving at one disc per
  second   = 600 000 000 000 years
Moving at 100 000 000
  discs per second   = 600 000 000 000 / 100 000 000
                        = 6000 years!

I suggest that you limit the number of discs to a little less than 64 if you wish to try out the program and see it completed within your lifetime!

Monte Carlo methods

This is nothing to do with the famous car races at Monte Carlo! It is the name given to a technique which can be used for finding areas under a graph by making use of **random numbers**, or in fact **pseudo random numbers**, that are generated inside a computer. Consider the graph of $y = x^2$ shown in figure 18.12. Suppose we wish to find the area under this graph between the limits $x = 1$ and $x = 2$. Consider the rectangle shown in figure 18.12. We can see that 'values of x range' from 1 to 2, and 'values of y range' from 0 to 4.

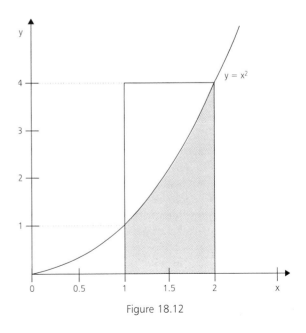

Figure 18.12

If we 'zap' (excuse this highly technical term!) this area with random co-ordinates then some of them will lie in the grey shaded area we wish to calculate, and some will lie above the shaded area in the remainder of the rectangle. If we choose many random co-ordinates, then the proportion of them lying in the shaded area will give this shaded area as a proportion of the entire rectangle.

It is relatively easy to calculate the area of a rectangle (even without a computer) and so the following formula can make an approximation to the shaded area:

$$\text{Area} = \text{Area of rectangle} \times \frac{\text{Number of random co-ordinates in shaded area}}{\text{Total number of random co-ordinates}}$$

It is easy to determine if a random co-ordinate is in the shaded area by checking to see if the y value is less than or greater than x^2. If it is in the shaded area then it is called a hit, or if it is not in the shaded area then it is called a miss.

To sum up, the procedure for the above example is as follows:

(1) Generate a random number x between 1 and 2.
(2) Generate a random number y between 0 and 4.
(3) Calculate the corresponding value of y, from $y = x^2$ for this particular function.
(4) Check to see if $y < x^2$. If it is then a hit is obtained or if not then a miss.
(5) At the end of the required number of random numbers work out:

$$\text{Area} = \text{Area of rectangle} \times \frac{\text{Hits}}{\text{Misses} + \text{Hits}}$$

Generation of pseudo random

We can see from the above that it is necessary to have a source of random numbers inside the computer. The theory of generating good random numbers is long and complex, but it is relatively easy to generate what are called **pseudo random numbers**. In *fact these are numbers with a pattern*, i.e. the numbers *will* repeat themselves over and over again. On most computers you can set the seed (see next section) of pseudo random numbers to go through exactly the same cycle each time the program is run. A statement like 'randomise', for example, is usually used if you wish the numbers to be different each time the program is run. This is very useful for checking to see if statistical simulations etc. are working properly. Imagine trying to track down a bug in your program when the data keeps changing! Therefore, a **pseudo random number** is one in which the cycle of numbers repeats itself. The trick is to make this cycle so long that no one actually notices! In practice this means making the cycle length extremely long compared with the number of random numbers that is likely to be encountered in any one application.

We will start off by using some techniques to generate a short cycle length, and then go on to more sophisticated methods reproducing very long cycle lengths.

There are many simple methods of generating random numbers, but all of them suffer from various faults eventually. For example, it may be a small cycle length, or it may be that the procedure being used is fine until a certain number happens to come up, and then the procedure breaks down. An example of a simple procedure is called the mid-product method that is shown in the next section.

Mid-product method

This method involves multiplying two numbers (called **seeds**) together, and then taking a specified number of digits out of the middle of the product. (Hence the name mid-product.) Finally, the set of digits extracted from the middle of the product is used in conjunction with the second seed to produce the second pseudo random number. The process is then repeated as shown in the following example.

Example

Starting with the seeds 1833 and 9899, and using the middle four digits of the product, we can generate 6 pseudo random numbers as follows.

Seed 1	Seed 2	Product	Pseudo random number
1833	9899	18(1448)67	1448
9899	1448	14(3337)52	3337
1448	3337	04(8319)76	8319
3337	8319	27(7605)03	7605
8319	7605	63(2659)95	2659
7605	2659	20(2216)95	2216
		etc.	

It would appear from the above that a satisfactory sequence of 4-digit random numbers is being obtained. Try writing a program starting with different seeds, and get it to print out many random numbers. You will find that for some choice of seeds the cycle length is short, and if you are unlucky enough to hit on 0000 as your four middle digits then the system collapses because all the random numbers from this one on will be 0000. Hardly a random sequence!

There are other simple methods but all pale into insignificance compared with the following types of methods using modulo arithmetic. One such method is as follows.

The linear congruential method

First a resumé on **modulo arithmetic** for those who may not be familiar with the term. Modulo arithmetic is

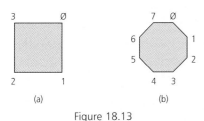

Figure 18.13

often known simply as 'clock arithmetic' because when you start to learn about it at primary school a clock is often used to explain the system. Consider the 'square clock' shown in figure 18.13(a).

There are four numbers in modulo 4, namely 0, 1, 2 and 3. You count by moving round the clock in a clockwise direction, i.e. 0, 1, 2, 3, 0, 1, 2, 3, 0, 1, etc. That is all there is to the principle of modulo arithmetic! As another example, consider modulo 8, as shown in figure 18.8(b). Here we can count as 0, 1, 2, 3, 4, 5, 6, 7, 0, 1, 2, 3, etc. To perform arithmetic is simple. Consider the following:

What is 2 + 3 in modulo 4?

Start counting round the modulo 4 clock and you will find that 2 + 3 = 1.

Did you know that . . .

Ernie, the Premium Bond machine, stands for the Electronic Random Number Indicator Equipment. There is no known electronic (hardware or software) method of generating a completely random number. This is, perhaps, why the National Lottery chose a mechanical system with different machines and different sets of balls each week.

It would not be convenient if we had to draw clocks every time, and it is relatively simple to deduce what the answer is going to be once the principle is well understood. Suppose, for example, that we want to find (2 + 3) mod 4. It is basically the remainder after division of the original number by 4. Hence:

2 + 3 = 5. Now 5/4 = 1 remainder 1.
Therefore 2 + 3 = 1 mod 4

or in modulo 9, 8 + 4 = 12. Now 12/9 = 1 remainder 3. Therefore 8 + 4 = 3 mod 9.

The linear congruence formula is expressed as follows:

$$R_{n+1} = (aR_n + i) \bmod m$$

The formula states that the pseudo random number R_{n+1}, can be obtained from the previous pseudo random number R_n, by multiplying it by a (a multiplier), and adding i (an increment), in modulo m. It is most important that sensible values of m, a and i are chosen. If not the sequence produced can be far from the best possible. The principles of choosing these numbers are beyond the scope of this book, but it does not stop you being able to use the above formula.

We have seen from the modulo arithmetic above that there are four possible remainders in modulo 4 (i.e. 0, 1, 2 and 3) and eight in modulo 8 etc. Hence if we choose modulo m (as in the above formula) then there will be m possible remainders. This effectively defines the maximum length of the cycle. We will, therefore, have to choose a large value for m. It is convenient when trying to generate random numbers to choose m to be '2 to the power of an integer', as this significantly reduces the processing time. As m must be as big as possible, the power of two is often chosen to be the maximum number that the computer's word length can hold (i.e. this would be $2^8 - 1 = 255$ for an 8-bit micro). The cycle length would obviously be more in practice. 256 is not large enough, but using multiple bytes can extend this. However, to make sure that this maximum cycle is achieved, the values of a and i must be chosen with the following restrictions borne in mind:

All of a, i, and the starting value R_n must be less than the modulo m.

Also a, i, and the starting value R_n must be greater than or equal to 0.

The maximum cycle length occurs when a lies between $\sqrt{m}$ and $(m - \sqrt{m})$.

A full treatment of the above can be found in one of the seven volumes by Donald Knuth called *The Art of Computer Programming, Vol 2 Semi-numerical algorithms*.

Example

Generate 10 random numbers using the linear congruential method with a 'starting value of 8029', a 'value of a = 37', a 'value of i = 19' and using 'modulo 65535' (16-bit word length).

n	R_n	$aR_n + i$	$R_{n+1} = (aR_n + i) \bmod 65535$
1	8029	297092	34952
2	34952	1293243	48078
3	48078	1778905	09460
4	9460	350039	22364
5	22364	827487	41067
6	41067	1519498	12193
7	12193	451160	57950
8	57950	2144169	47049
9	47049	1740832	36922
10	36922		

Computer queuing simulations

After ploughing through random number generation, let's see how it can be put to good use!

There are many occasions when computers can be used for simulating the likely outcome for decisions that can be made in a business. For example, suppose that it is proposed to build a new petrol pump forecourt. It is essential that customers are not kept waiting for too long before being able to use the pumps. Similarly, it would be bad policy to install many expensive pumps if they are never going to be used at anywhere near full capacity. It is possible to use a computer to simulate the situation that is likely to occur at the pumps if a different number of pumps are installed. One of the major advantages of such a system is that parameters such as 'number of pumps', 'customers arriving per minute' and 'number of cashiers' etc. can all be altered to see the likely outcome on the queue, hence the name **queuing theory**.

Statistics and probability play an important role in queuing theory. For example, it is most unlikely that the number of customers arriving each minute will be a rectangular distribution, i.e. it is unlikely that 0, 1, 2, 3 etc. customers per minute will arrive with equal probability. In this example let us assume the following distribution:

Table 1

Number of customers arriving per minute.	0	1	2	3	4	5	6
Probability		0.10	0.23	0.30	0.20	0.10	0.05	0.02

Notice how all the probabilities add up to 1.

Did you know that . . .

Queuing theory plays a large part in developing new supermarkets, petrol stations, theme parks and the like. It can also be used to model biological and other scientific experiments, which are based on statistical probability. Some parts of genetic engineering are particularly good examples. Some of these techniques can make some stunning projects, especially if you have an interest in the particular area being studied.

During the computer simulation we will make use of a pseudo random number generator (see earlier) which can generate random numbers in the range 0 to 1 inclusive, and then use it to generate appropriate scaled numbers. When a number is generated, we will compare it with the above table to determine the nearest match. This will then set up the number of customers arriving during that minute of the simulation.

Next it's important to realise that not all the customers are served in exactly the same amount of time. Let's also suppose that (based on previous experience of similar systems), a customer will be served according to the following distribution:

Table 2

Customer service time at the pumps in minutes	1	2	3	4	5
Probability	0.30	0.25	0.2	0.15	0.10

Finally, there is the time taken to pay for the petrol

and the buying of sweets etc. in the garage forecourt shop. For this we will use the following distribution:

Table 3

Customer service time at the kiosk to the nearest minute	1	2	3	4
Probability	0.60	0.30	0.07	0.03

It is also found that if a customer has to wait too long before being able to get to the pumps, then he or she will go away and not buy any petrol at all. Let's suppose that the probabilities of the customer going away is given as follows:

Table 4

Number of cars in queue for the pumps	0	1	2	3	4	5	>5
Probability	0.0	0.1	0.2	0.4	0.7	0.9	1.0

i.e. a 'one in 10 chance' of the customer leaving if there is one car waiting in the queue etc.

Let's consider simulating the situation for one hour, but having a printout of the state of the pumps, queues, etc. every minute. The variables may be defined as follows:

time	a variable that is incremented every 'minute', which controls the entire simulation
pumps	the number of pumps available in the simulation
cashiers	the number of cashiers available to take the money
new_cust	the number of customers arriving in one minute (from Table 1)
cust_pumps	the number of customers at the pumps
cust_kiosk	the number of customers at the kiosk
cust_waiting	the number of customers waiting in queue
cust_left	the number of customers who have left without being served
cust_pump_time	time taken for customers to use the pump (number between 1 and 5 given in Table 2)
cust_kiosk_time	time taken for customers to be served at kiosk (number between 1 and 4 from Table 3)
prob_leave	the probability of a customer leaving given the number in the waiting queue (Table 4)

We will assume that the forecourt is initially empty, and that all the variables reflect this at time = 0 minutes. At time = 0, we will generate a random number that simulates the number of customers entering the garage, based on the distribution given in Table 1. To generate

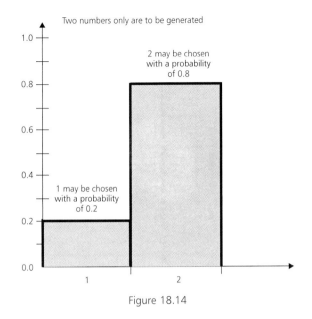

Figure 18.14

The flowchart assumes that the time taken for the computer to execute the required simple calculations is negligible, and therefore all processes that are time-dependent are checked with great rapidity. By the time the algorithm has worked through to the 'has time incremented by box one', the time will either not have incremented by one, or will be very shortly after the actual increment. An extra point that is not clear from this initial flowchart is the fact that each new customer will have new variables uniquely assigned.

That is, for the first customer to arrive at the pumps the variable

cust_pump_time(1) must be generated using the distribution of Table 1.

Similarly, when 'customer two' enters the kiosk then

cust_kiosk_time(2) will have to be generated from Table 3 etc.

We can see that when a customer has been served at the kiosk then his or her variable may be returned to the system for future use, i.e. if customer five has been served, then the variables associated with this customer are no longer needed and can be reassigned when necessary to a new customer.

We therefore literally use a queuing system where the variables can be held in an array:

new_cust(1), new_cust(2), new_cust(3) etc.

The size of the array will have to be estimated, and indeed during early simulations may cause the system to crash if its dimensions are exceeded!

The flowchart given in figure 18.15 is only really a start to point you in the right direction. For example, we have assumed that the customer service time at the kiosk can be taken from the distribution shown in Table 3. However, it might be more realistic to assume that in addition to the above information, it would be desirable to introduce a factor that increased this time as a function of the length of the kiosk queue. Also, many readers may not agree with the approach that deals with assigning the probabilities to see if a customer leaves or not before the queue has effectively moved to the pumps. However, this is one of the problems with modelling real life situations. Many simulations usually have to be carried out, often testing them against real data obtained in practice, to see if the accuracy of the results obtained is satisfactory. If not, and the discrepancy is too large, then the reasons will have to be established and the parameters changed accordingly until satisfactory results have been obtained. Only when this process has been carried out can the simulation be used to good effect to produce results that may be relied upon for the analysis of future trends.

It is a relatively simple matter to develop the basic algorithm further so that it may be perfected and the appropriate high level language code written. However,

a random number for a given probability distribution is simple, and an example is shown in figure 18.14.

Now the numbers will all be equally likely in the range 0 to 1 inclusive. We can, therefore, generate a number in this range and modify it to the above range using the following.

LET random_number	generates random number in
= RND(1)	range (0,1)
IF random_number < 0.2	generate number 1 with
THEN number = 1	probability of 0.2
IF random_number > 0.2	generate number 2 with
THEN number = 2	probability of 0.8
IF random_number = 0.2	generate another random
THEN do again	number.

As you can see, generating the distributions is simple. We will, therefore, assume that procedures have already been written that will return the appropriate numbers and times etc. So on the increment of each time slice the following number will automatically be generated:

| new_customers: | The number of new customers entering the garage in the current minute. |

Similarly, when a customer arrives at the pumps or the kiosk:

| cust_pump time: | The time taken for each customer to serve himself or herself at the pump |
| and cust_kiosk time: | Time taken for customer to be served at the kiosk. will automatically be generated. |

A typical scenario can be seen in the program flowchart of figure 18.15.

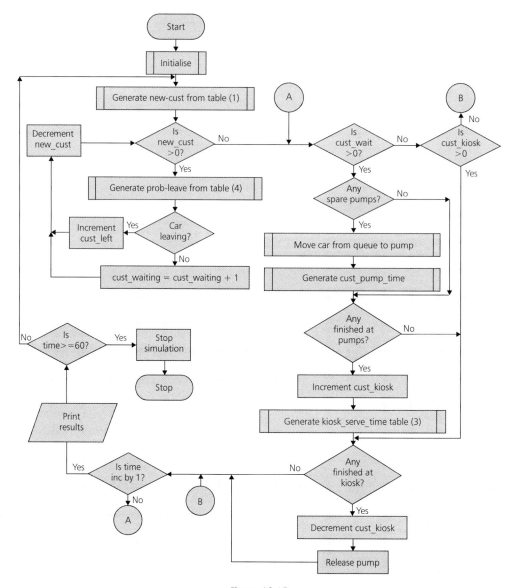

Figure 18.15

even this simple example gives you a good idea of how a simulation is tackled, and is considerably more complex than most examples you would find in an A-level examination. Perhaps it is a good idea for a project. It is also fun to make some sort of graphic demonstration so that the users are presented with an animated picture on the screen of what is going on. Also, it is possible to 'fiddle' the simulation so that it is not carried out in real time. This is obviously essential for many applications, but for the car and garage, it simply gives you a good deal of fun watching the screen operate at super high speed!

Exercise 18.1

1. An **iterative modelling technique** states that if x_n is an approximation to the square root of a number N, then a better approximation x_{n+1} may be found by using the formula

$$x_{n+1} = \frac{1}{2}\left(x_n + \frac{N}{x_n}\right)$$

   Write a program in a high level language of your choice to evaluate $\sqrt{5}$ to five decimal places. (Note that $\sqrt{5} = 2.23606798$.)

2. An approximation to π may be found by using a **Monte Carlo method**. A clue is to draw an inscribed circle (one that just touches each side of the four sides) inside a square, and use the ratio of the points that fall inside the circle to those that fall inside the square to derive a value for π. Write a program in a high-level language of your choice to estimate π by this method. How accurate can you get?

3. With thought it is possible to code many different algorithms making use of **recursive** or **iterative** procedures. Outline some of the advantages or disadvantages of each approach.

4. Making use of a **recursive** function, and using pseudocode or a high-level language of your choice, write a program to input an integer, then print out *all integers* less than this number down to 1, e.g. *if 3 is input then 3, 2 and 1 are printed*.

5. Making use of a **recursive** function, and using pseudocode or a high-level language of your choice, write a program to sum all the integers up to a maximum of n, where n is typed in by the user, e.g. *if n=5 then sum = 1+2+3+4+5 = 15 etc.*

6. Making use of a **recursive** function, and using pseudocode or a high-level language of your choice, write a program to input a string of characters and then print them out in reverse order, e.g. *'kit cat' would become 'tac tik'*.

7. You are to **simulate** customers arriving at Barry Ramsden's Fish-and-Chip Shop, and work out the possible state of the queue at one-minute intervals over a 2-hour period. The following two tables show the number of arrivals at any given minute, and the probability of serving a given number of customers in a given amount of time.
   The number of customers arriving each minute is as follows.

Cust/min	0	1	2	3	4	5
Probability	0.20	0.25	0.25	0.15	0.10	0.05

   With a full staff, the chippy can serve the following number of customers in any given one-minute period.

Cust. Serv	1	2	3	4	5
Probability	0.35	0.25	0.20	0.15	0.05

   Barry Ramsden never wants more than six people in the queue at any one time. Does he have a sufficient number of staff?

8. Explain how a computer might be used to generate **pseudo random numbers**. Why is it not possible to generate completely random numbers?

End of chapter revision aid and summary

Cover up the right-hand column and see if you can answer the questions or define the terms on the left. They appear in the order in which they are covered in this chapter. Alternatively you may browse through the right-hand column to aid revision.

What is iteration?	Iteration is the technique of repeating things by looping. Iteration may be carried out by making use of REPEAT-UNTIL, DO-WHILE and FOR-TO-NEXT constructs, for example.
Why is iteration used?	Complex problems can often be solved using a minimum amount of code and iterative techniques. Many examples of iteration can be drawn from numerical analysis, computer modelling and simulation, fractals and autostereograms, for example.
What is recursion?	Recursion is a technique where appropriate code may be arranged to call itself. This means that many steps may be coded where each step makes use of a result from the previous step.
What is a recursive procedure?	A recursive procedure is one that calls itself. Recursive procedures are elegant and efficient in terms of code, but often take up more memory than iterative techniques.
What is a dry run?	A dry run is when you manually work through some code or an algorithm to see if it will work properly.
What is a Monte Carlo method?	Monte-Carlo methods generate an approximate solution to a problem by making use of pseudo-random numbers.
What is a pseudo random number?	Pseudo random numbers are sequences of numbers where the sequence is incredibly long such that to all intents and purposes they appear random. The linear congruential and mid-product methods can be used to generate pseudo random numbers.
What is queuing theory?	A simulation using pseudo random numbers to simulate queues is called queuing theory.
Why are random numbers used in computing?	Random numbers are often used to control queuing and other types of computer simulations.

19 Developing Algorithms

In this chapter you'll learn about:

- Different ways of sorting lists into order
- Different ways of searching for an item of data in a list or a file
- Developing real algorithms for various sort methods
- Developing real algorithms for various search methods

Key resources

To carry out this work most successfully it's best if you have:

- Access to a modern programming language like Basic, Visual Basic, Pascal or Delphi, for example
- Numbers written on pieces of paper to simulate the data being used in the sort and search routines

Concept checkpoints

- It's essential that you are a competent programmer before attempting much of the work in this chapter.
- You will need to understand all the work covered in chapters 13 and 17.
- To undertake the work on the quick sort and binary search, you will also need knowledge of the advanced programming techniques covered in chapter 18.
- You may prefer not to cover all the work in this chapter at the same time.

Introduction

Much data processing is concerned with sorting and searching data. Sorting data requires putting the 'raw data' into some predetermined order. It could be alphabetical if the data is a set of words, or it might be ascending or descending numerical order if the data is numbers. Searching simply means 'finding a specific item of data from a list' of data.

The techniques used for these processes depend very much on the way in which the data is stored, and on particular aspects of the hardware. For example, is the data in main memory? Is it on disk or on tape? Can all the data fit into main memory at the same time? Factors such as these, together with considerations such as 'speed' and 'efficiency' with respect to the 'length of time taken' and 'amount of memory used', all play a part in deciding the most efficient sort or search algorithms to use.

There are very many sort and search algorithms, so at this level all we can do in a book of this size is to look at the more commonly used methods.

Sorting

When working through the following algorithms you will find it most useful to write down the numbers *on separate pieces of paper* and move them around as the algorithms proceed. In this way the author has found that students' understanding of the different sorting techniques is considerably improved. Try this method and see – you won't be disappointed.

To aid in a comparison of the methods, the following list of numbers will be used in *all* the **algorithms**. The efficiency of the algorithms can then be more easily compared and understood.

The list of numbers to be used in *all* the search-algorithm methods

N(1)	N(2)	N(3)	N(4)	N(5)	N(6)	N(7)	N(8)	N(9)	N(10)	N(11)	N(12)
27	48	13	50	39	77	82	91	65	19	70	66
		Lower elements						Upper elements			

Throughout the following sections we will talk about the elements in the above list, i.e. N(3) or N(7), for example. We will also talk about **lower elements** and **upper elements**. Suppose, for the sake of argument, we consider 'number 77' in the above list. All the elements **before** 77 (i.e. 27, 48, 13, 50 and 39) are called the 'lower elements'. Similarly all the elements **above** 77 would be called the 'upper elements' as shown in the above table.

Insertion sort

This is the simplest sort algorithm and so it will be covered first. It basically revolves around starting with a very small list containing just two numbers, and inserting the last number in the right place. We then consider the next number in the list, this number then gets put into the right place, and the list gets longer and longer until the last number in the list has been considered. After this process the list is sorted. A typical algorithm, *using the numbers in the above table*, is shown on the right.

1. Start with the second number (**48** in the original list). (*If you don't start with the second number there would be nothing in the lower elements to compare it with!*)
2. Compare the above number with *all* the lower elements and **insert** the number in the right place.
3. **Repeat** the above two stages, but moving to the third, fourth, and fifth number etc., **until** the last number has been considered in stage (1).

Using the above algorithm, the list is sorted into **ascending** order as shown in table 19.1.

Table 19.1 Sorting numbers using the INSERTION-SORT algorithm

												Comments
27	48	13	50	39	77	82	91	65	19	70	66	**Original list** (Start with the second number in the list.)
27	48	13	50	39	77	82	91	65	19	70	66	48 compared with 27 (the lower elements), no changes necessary.
27	48	13	50	39	77	82	91	65	19	70	66	13 compared with 27 and 48. Number 13 inserted at beginning of list.
13	27	48	50	39	77	82	91	65	19	70	66	50 compared with 13, 27 and 50. No changes necessary.
13	27	48	50	39	77	82	91	65	19	70	66	39 compared with lower elements, number 39 inserted in correct place.
13	27	39	48	50	77	82	91	65	19	70	66	77 compared with lower elements . . . no changes necessary.
13	27	39	48	50	77	82	91	65	19	70	66	82 compared with lower elements . . . no changes necessary.
13	27	39	48	50	77	82	91	65	19	70	66	91 compared with lower elements . . . no changes necessary.
13	27	39	48	50	77	82	91	65	19	70	66	65 compared with lower elements, number 65 inserted in correct place.
13	27	39	48	50	65	77	82	91	19	70	66	19 compared with lower elements, number 19 inserted in correct place.
13	19	27	39	48	50	65	77	82	91	70	66	70 compared with lower elements, number 70 inserted in correct place.
13	19	27	39	48	50	65	70	77	82	91	66	66 compared with lower elements, number 66 inserted in correct place.
13	19	27	39	48	50	65	66	70	77	82	91	Last number already considered.
13	**19**	**27**	**39**	**48**	**50**	**65**	**70**	**77**	**82**	**82**	**91**	**Numbers are now sorted in the correct order.**

We now analyse the above table in more detail to produce a **pseudocode solution** (and finally some real **Pascal code**) for the **insertion-sort** problem, but first let's introduce some extra terminology.

Let **current_position** be a pointer to the number (initially set to **N(2)**) being used for comparison purposes. Let **pointer_position** be a pointer to the numbers that are being compared with the 'current_position number' in the above list.

Did you know that . . .

Even if a specific sort algorithm does not appear in your syllabus, it's amazingly good practice for your programming skills and general algorithm development. The experience gained in this and the other programming chapters should put you well on the route to becoming a competent programmer in your chosen high-level language.

The argument will go along the following lines:

SET UP the current_position and pointer_position pointers.

REPEAT

  REPEAT

    Compare all the elements in the list below the current_pointer position

  UNTIL

    N(pointer_position) > N(current_position)

    (In which case we INSERT and MOVE the elements as shown in the tables in the examples given on the previous page.)

OR

N(pointer_position) = N(current_position)

(In which case no inserts or moves will be necessary.)

  INCREMENT the current_position

  RESET the pointer_position

UNTIL the current_position is at the maximum position in the list.

Using Pascal, and assuming the numbers are stored in an array called N, we get the following (figure 19.1) from the above description of the problem:

```
current_position:= 1;
REPEAT
  current_position := current_position + 1; (* Set up pointers *)
  pointer_position := 1;
  WHILE pointer_position <= current_position DO
    BEGIN
      IF N[pointer_position] > N[current_position] THEN
                                    (* Insert necessary ? *)
        BEGIN
          temp := N[current_position];    (* Insert and move routine *)
          FOR count := current_position DOWNTO pointer_position + 1 DO
            BEGIN
              N[count] := N[count − 1]
            END;
          N[pointer_position] := temp;
        END;
      pointer_position := pointer_position + 1; (*Move pointer*)
    END;
UNTIL current_position = maximum;
```

Figure 19.1

A working version would obviously have to include declaring the variables, reading in the data and printing out the sorted list. A complete working version using the above Pascal code is shown in figure 19.2:

```
PROGRAM insert sort (INPUT, OUTPUT);
VAR current_position, pointer_position, maximum, temp, count: INTEGER;
N: ARRAY [0..12] OF INTEGER;
BEGIN
 maximum := 12;
 FOR count := 1 TO maximum DO      (* Get numbers to be sorted *)
   BEGIN
     WRITELN('Please type in number', count);
     READLN(N[count]);
   END;
 WRITELN('Original list of numbers is');
 FOR count := 1 TO maximum DO      (* Print out numbers to be sorted *)
   BEGIN
     WRITELN(N[count]);
   END;

 current_position := 1;               (* Start insertion sort routine *)
 REPEAT
```

Figure 19.2 (continues)

```
      current_position := current_position + 1;   (*Set up pointers*)
      pointer_position := 1;
      WHILE pointer_position <= current_position DO
        BEGIN
          IF N[pointer_position] > N[current_position] THEN
                                      (* Insert necessary? *)
            BEGIN
              temp := N[current_position]; (*Insert and move routine*)
              FOR count := current_position DOWNTO pointer_position + 1 DO
                BEGIN
                  N[count] := N[count − 1]
                END;
              N[pointer_position] := temp;
            END;
          pointer_position := pointer_position + 1   (* Move pointer *)
        END;
    UNTIL current_position = maximum;

    WRITELN('Sorted list');
    FOR count := 1 TO maximum DO     (* Print out sorted numbers *)
      BEGIN
        WRITELN (N[count])
      END;
  END.
```

Figure 19.2 (continued)

Bubble sort

Another popular sort method is called the **bubble sort**. The name derives from the fact that the sorted item **floats** to the top of the list like a bubble in water.

Again we will use the twelve numbers N(1), N(2) ... N(12) as before:

N(1)	N(2)	N(3)	N(4)	N(5)	N(6)	N(7)	N(8)	N(9)	N(10)	N(11)	N(12)
27	48	13	50	39	77	82	91	65	19	70	66

The algorithm for the bubble sort is as follows:

1. Start with the first pair of numbers in the list and compare, i.e. compare N(1) with N(2).
2. If N(1) > N(2) then **swap**, i.e. N(1) becomes N(2) and N(2) becomes N(1). If a swap was necessary then make a note of it (i.e. set a **flag**).
3. Go on to the next pair of numbers and repeat stages (1) and (2) until the last pair of numbers in the list have been compared.
4. If a swap (1 or more) took place (i.e. the flag set up in (2) is set), then reset the flag and repeat the entire procedure. If no swaps took place then END.

In the case where swaps were necessary it is useful to indicate that this has happened by using what is called a **flag**. This is simply an indication that at least one swap has taken place. This is useful in the following algorithm because 'if the flag has been set' then swaps were necessary, and 'the routine must be entered again'. The flag must obviously be reset (NOT SET) at the beginning of every pass, and this is shown in the tables in the following examples.

The above algorithm when applied to our set of numbers produces the results shown in table 19.2:

Table 19.2 Sorting numbers using the BUBBLE-SORT algorithm

												Comments	Flag
(FIRST PASS)													(NOT SET)
27	48	13	50	39	77	82	91	65	19	70	66	27 compared with 48, no swap is necessary, don't alter flag	NOT SET
27	48	13	50	39	77	82	91	65	19	70	66	48 compared with 13, swap necessary, flag is set.	SET
27	13	48	50	39	77	82	91	65	19	70	66	48 compared with 50, no swap necessary don't alter flag.	SET

Table 19.2 continued
Sorting numbers using the BUBBLE-SORT algorithm

(FIRST PASS)												Comments	Flag (NOT SET)
27	13	48	50	39	77	82	91	65	19	70	66	50 compared with 39, swap necessary, flag is set.	SET
27	13	48	39	50	77	82	91	65	19	70	66	50 compared with 77, no swap necessary, don't alter flag.	SET
27	13	48	39	50	77	82	91	65	19	70	66	77 compared with 82, no swap necessary, don't alter flag.	SET
27	13	48	39	50	77	82	91	65	19	70	66	82 compared with 91, no swap necessary, don't alter flag.	SET
27	13	48	39	50	77	82	91	65	19	70	66	91 compared with 65, swap necessary, flag is set.	SET
27	13	48	39	50	77	82	65	91	19	70	66	91 compared with 19, swap necessary, flag is set.	SET
27	13	48	39	50	77	82	65	19	91	70	66	91 compared with 70, swap necessary, flag is set.	SET
27	13	48	39	50	77	82	65	19	70	91	66	91 compared with 66, swap necessary, flag is set.	SET
27	13	48	39	50	77	82	65	19	70	66	91	Last two numbers have been compared.	SET
												SWAPS were necessary, therefore another pass is needed.	
												RESET the flag.	NOT SET

Sorting numbers using the BUBBLE-SORT algorithm

(SECOND PASS)												Comments	Flag (NOT SET)
27	13	48	39	50	77	82	65	19	70	66	91	27 compared with 13, swap is necessary, flag is set.	SET
13	27	48	39	50	77	82	65	19	70	66	91	27 compared with 48, swap is necessary, flag is set.	SET
13	27	48	39	50	77	82	65	19	70	66	91	48 compared with 39, swap is necessary, flag is set.	SET

The above processes continue in the same way until the end of the second pass

After the second pass the numbers become:

13 27 39 48 50 77 65 19 70 66 82 91

Swaps were necessary so a third pass is needed.

After the third pass we get:

13 27 39 48 50 65 19 70 66 77 82 91

We proceed with as many passes as necessary until no swaps are recorded. In which case the list of numbers would be:

13 19 27 39 48 50 65 66 70 77 82 91

Notice that all the lower value elements are **floating** to the left and all the higher value elements are **floating** to the right. Hence the name **bubble sort**.

The pseudocode algorithm for the bubble sort would therefore be as follows:

REPEAT
    RESET flag to zero.
    COMPARE all pairs of numbers and swap if necessary.
    IF a swap occurred set a flag,
UNTIL flag is not set.

> **Hint:** To understand the techniques here it really is essential to program the algorithms using a high-level language of your choice. Working with bits of paper is all very well, but programming the computer is much more satisfying in the end.

The main Pascal code to achieve the above is shown, together with the input and output procedures for our 12 numbers in figure 19.3.

Shell sort

One of the problems encountered with previous sort methods is that the numbers being compared may only move a small distance, and therefore usually require a greater number of movements to get to their desired destination. Donald Shell proposed a method that enables numbers to be moved by much larger distances initially, thus getting over this problem to a large extent. Shell's method is most easily illustrated by means of an example.

As before, we will assume that the numbers are stored as N(1), N(2), N(3), N(4), ... N(max). In this example, as in the previous ones in this chapter, we will use the same set of numbers to illustrate the sorting method,

i.e. we will use the twelve numbers 27, 48, 13, 50, 39, 77, 82, 91, 65, 19, 70 and 66.

There will be several passes through the data, and the number of passes will depend on how many data items are present. Larger lists of numbers will require more passes. The passes are often arranged by choosing a number whose value is the nearest integer to 'max/2',

```
PROGRAM bubble (INPUT, OUTPUT);
   VAR temp, count, flag, maximum, pointer: INTEGER;
   N: ARRAY [0..12] OF INTEGER;
   BEGIN
      maximum := 12
      FOR count: = 1 TO maximum DO
        BEGIN
          WRITELN('Please type in number', count);
          READLN(N[count]);
        END;
      WRITELN('The original list of numbers is');
      FOR count := 1 TO maximum DO
        BEGIN
          WRITELN([count]);
        END;
      REPEAT                              (*Main routine*)
        flag := 0;
        FOR pointer := 1 TO maximum — 1 DO
          BEGIN
            WHILE N[pointer]>N[pointer + 1] DO
            BEGIN
              temp := N[pointer + 1];
              N[pointer + 1] :=N[pointer];
              N[pointer] := temp;
              flag :=1;
            END;
          END;
      UNTIL flag = 0;
      WRITELN('Sorted list');
      FOR count := 1 TO maximum DO
        BEGIN
          WRITELN (N[count])
        END;
   END;
END.
```

Figure 19.3

where 'max' is the number of elements in the array N. In the above case, we have 12 numbers, and so the number to be used will be 'max/2' which gives '12/2' or 6. We call this number **d**, as it represents '**the distance between elements**' which form subsets of the data. To illustrate the idea, consider carrying out this process on our twelve numbers.

The first pass

The first subsets of data are formed using d as shown in the table.

We have, therefore, formed **6 subsets of data**, with each subset containing just two elements. If there had been 16 numbers in the original list, there would have been 8 subsets of two elements each, or if we had 100 numbers, there would have been 50 two-element subsets so formed. For an odd number of elements, 11, for

Subsets of data derived using d = 6	Explanation (assuming a value of d = 6)
N(1) goes with N(7)	N(1) is grouped with N(1 + d) or N(7)
N(2) goes with N(8)	N(2) is grouped with N(2 + d) or N(8)
N(3) goes with N(9)	etc.
N(4) goes with N(10)	
N(5) goes with N(11)	
and finally,	
N(6) goes with N(12)	

example, d = 5 and hence 6 subsets would be formed N(1), N(6), being the first, N(2), N(7) being the second up to and including the final subset of N(6), N(11).

Hint: The Shell sort should be faster than the bubble sort and the insertion sorts considered previously. When you have encoded each of the algorithms, see if it's true for your code. Do you need more numbers to be sorted for this difference to be apparent?

Each subset in the above list is sorted separately. On the first pass this is obviously not a difficult operation as there are only two elements in each list! Therefore, a simple insertion sort will suffice, which in this case boils down to comparing and swapping if necessary.

If we now consider our original set of numbers:

Original set of numbers used for the Shell sort

N(1)	N(2)	N(3)	N(4)	N(5)	N(6)	N(7)	N(8)	N(9)	N(10)	N(11)	N(12)
27	48	13	50	39	77	82	91	65	19	70	66

Sorting out the numbers in each subset as described above, after the first pass, we end up with the following new set of numbers:

Numbers output from the first pass

N(1)	N(2)	N(3)	N(4)	N(5)	N(6)	N(7)	N(8)	N(9)	N(10)	N(11)	N(12)
27	48	13	19	39	66	82	91	65	50	70	77

Although all the subsets have been sorted, we only notice a change with two sets of numbers, as all the others were already in the correct order! N(4) has been swapped with N(10), and N(6) has been swapped with N(12).

The second pass

We next make d the nearest integer value to 'max/4'. For our twelve numbers, d = 3.

The second set of subsets now formed is, therefore, as follows:

Subsets of data derived using d = 3	Explanation (assuming a value of d = 3)
N(1) goes with N(4), N(7) and N(10)	N(1) is grouped with N(1 + d), N(1 + 2d), N(1 + 3d)
N(2) goes with N(5), N(8) and N(11)	N(2) is grouped with N(2 + d), N(2 + 2d), N(2 + 3d)
N(3) goes with N(6), N(9) and N(12)	N(3) is grouped with N(3 + d), N(3 + 2d), N(3 + 3d)

Each subset is now sorted separately, using an insertion sort, for example. Not forgetting that _we are now starting off with the numbers obtained from the output of the first pass_, this process carried out on the data obtained from the first pass is shown in the next table.

After sorting each subset, the result from the second pass would be:

Numbers output from the second pass

N(1)	N(2)	N(3)	N(4)	N(5)	N(6)	N(7)	N(8)	N(9)	N(10)	N(11)	N(12)
19	39	13	27	48	65	50	70	66	82	91	77

The third pass

We now make d the nearest integer value of max/8. For our twelve numbers d = 1.

In fact, the Shell sort process will always end up eventually with d having a value of 1. As d = 1, we are now sorting the whole set of data! Now I hear you ask, 'What's the point of sorting the whole set of data, when we could have done this in the first place?' Well, the whole point is that the previous operations have made the file relatively well ordered, whereas if we had done a straight insertion sort, for example, on the original set of data, then more comparisons would have been needed (assuming the data did not start off in the unlikely event of being well ordered). The final data, after an insertion sort is obviously:

Numbers output after the final insertion sort is applied

N(1)	N(2)	N(3)	N(4)	N(5)	N(6)	N(7)	N(8)	N(9)	N(10)	N(11)	N(12)
13	19	27	39	48	50	65	66	70	77	82	91

Unbelievable as it might seem, if you plug the twelve original numbers into an insertion sort then 22 swaps are necessary. Going through the Shell sort, using the same data and using the _same insertion sort techniques_ at all the appropriate stages requires only 14. You can imagine the savings on very much larger sets of data! In fact, even better results can be obtained by choosing different values of d. However, an analysis of techniques such as these is beyond the requirements of most courses at this level.

An efficient algorithm now needs to be found to sort all sets of data simultaneously, or the program will become large and unwieldy for larger lists of numbers! We can also use the amazing fact that, while sorting, if we encounter a pair of elements in the proper order, then we may stop the sorting process and go on to the next. This is a major time saver and is one of the reasons why the Shell technique wins on speed even though the 'same' insertion sort technique has to be applied to the whole set of data set during the last pass. For interested readers, it was Gale and Karp who established this fact, which you can demonstrate for yourselves by working through the methods in conjunction with the Shell-sort algorithm shown below. As before in this chapter, numbers written down on pieces of paper help a great deal with understanding of these algorithms.

The loop structure in the algorithm ensures that the data is processed using the appropriate subsets as shown on the previous pages. Two variables, i and j are used for this purpose. On the first pass, i has values ranging from 7 to 12, and j has values ranging from 1 to 6. Hence, you can see how the elements N(1) and N(7), N(2) and N(8) etc. up to N(6) and N(12) are sorted in pairs.

On the second pass, we effectively have 3 sets of data, each with 4 elements. However, each data set is being sorted 'simultaneously' by using an insertion-sort technique. Carefully work through the algorithm and you should see how i and j vary to control comparisons in each subset of numbers. For example, N(1) and N(4) from the first subset are compared and swapped if necessary, then N(2) and N(5) from the second subset up to N(3) and (N6) from the third. Next we work round again to compare N(4) with N(7), the second pair from the first subset, then N(5) and N(8) etc. Note that if no swaps are necessary then we go on comparing the next pair in a subset

using the above method. However, if swaps are necessary, then we have to compare the element with the lower elements in the list as happens in a normal insertion sort. Don't forget as stated above, when we encounter a pair that is in the correct order, we may go on to the next pair in the next subset. This is continued until d = 1, when the entire list is treated as a normal insertion sort, again with the proviso that we may stop and go on to the next elements if we encounter a pair that are already in the correct order. The part of the algorithm which moves us on to the next pair of elements, sets j = 0 if no swap is necessary, thus getting out of the current sorting process.

The main pseudocode for the Shell-sort algorithm is shown in figure 19.4.

```
BEGIN
  maximum := 12            (*Set up for the 12 numbers in the example*)
  d := maximum DIV 2       (*Set up initial distance d=6 in our case*)
  WHILE d > 0 DO
    BEGIN
      FOR i := d+1 TO      maximum DO
        BEGIN
          j := i-d
          WHILE j > 0 DO
            BEGIN
              IF N(j) > N(j+d) THEN
                BEGIN
                  SWAP( N(j), N(j+d)
                  j := j-d
                  (*Produces correct value of j for comparison with lower
                  elements, or j value to jump out of WHILE loop*)
                END;
              ELSE
                BEGIN
                  j :=0
                  (*Stop sorting if two elements found in correct order*)
                END;
            END;
        END;
      d := d DIV 2          (*Set up d for next pass*)
    END;
END;
PROCEDURE SWAP ( N(j), N(j+d)
BEGIN
  temp N(j)
  N(j)N(j+d)
  N(j+d):= temp
END.
```

Figure 19.4

Quick sort (partition sort)

This is another sort routine that is based on exchanging data. However, as its name implies, it is very quick for long lists of numbers (see later) compared with the other methods so far considered, although looking at the fol-

lowing algorithms it seems anything but quick! – This is simply because it takes longer to explain what's going on.

The method works by first splitting up the list into **two sublists,** and then quick sorting each sublist. Finally, each sublist is split up into two separate sublists and quick sorted again!

The quick-sort algorithm is demonstrated using our standard numbers as follows.

(1) Split the list up into two sublists

To do this proceed as follows:

> **Hint:** It's essential that you understand the techniques of recursion before attempting to work through this algorithm. These techniques are covered in detail in chapter 18.

Set up **two pointers** (one at each end of the list), called '**left pointer**' (as shown by →) and '**right pointer**' (as shown by ←) in the following table. (The arrows indicate the direction in which the left and right pointers will move.)

27	48	13	50	39	77	82	91	65	19	70	66
→ left pointer						right pointer ←					

Let there be a **reference number** denoted by **X**, and let the number be put in brackets to emphasise this. Also, let the reference number be the first number in the list, i.e.

(27)	48	13	50	39	77	82	91	65	19	70	**66**
X→									←		

Now **compare the two numbers indicated by the pointers** and swap if necessary:

Here 27 is being compared with 66. No swap is necessary as 27 < 66, and 27 is therefore in the right place (assuming, of course that we are sorting the numbers into ascending order).

(27)	48	13	50	39	77	82	91	65	19	70	66
X→									←		

Next move the pointer *not associated with X* towards X one place, as shown in the following table.

(27)	48	13	50	39	77	82	91	65	19	70	66
X→								←			

Compare the above two numbers: 27 < 70 **therefore no swap**.

Move the pointer *not associated with X* towards X one place, i.e.

(27)	48	13	50	39	77	82	91	65	19	70	66
X→								←			

Compare the two numbers: 27 > 19 therefore **a swap is necessary**.

19	48	13	50	39	77	82	91	65	(27)	70	66
→								X←			

Note that the **reference number** above (shown in brackets) **has now been moved due to the swap**.

Move the pointer *not associated with X* towards X one place, i.e.

19	48	13	50	39	77	82	91	65	(27)	70	66
	→								X←		

The above processes are repeated until the pointers coincide.

Each stage of this process is shown in table 19.3, together with suitable comments. For continuity the table has been started using the last entry shown in the table above.

Table 19.3 (continues)
The rest of the intermediate results of splitting up into two sublists

												Comments
19	48	13	50	39	77	82	91	65	(27)	70	66	Compare
	→								X←			
19	(27)	13	50	39	77	82	91	65	48	70	66	Swap
	X→								←			
19	(27)	13	50	39	77	82	91	65	48	70	66	Compare
	X→							←				Move pointer
19	(27)	13	50	39	77	82	91	65	48	70	66	Compare
	X→						←					Move pointer
19	(27)	13	50	39	77	82	91	65	48	70	66	Compare
	X→					←						Move pointer
19	(27)	13	50	39	77	82	91	65	48	70	66	Compare
	X→				←							Move pointer
19	(27)	13	50	39	77	82	91	65	48	70	66	Compare
	X→			←								Move pointer

Table 19.3 (continued)
The rest of the intermediate results of splitting up into two sublists   Comments

												Comments
19	(27)	13	50	39	77	82	91	65	48	70	66	Compare
	X→		←									Move pointer
19	(27)	13	50	39	77	82	91	65	48	70	66	Compare
	X→	←										
19	13	(27)	50	39	77	82	91	65	48	70	66	Swap
	→	X←										
19	13	(27)	50	39	77	82	91	65	48	70	66	Move pointer
		X⇄										Pointers coincide
19	13	27	50	39	77	82	91	65	48	70	66	
Left sublist	X		Right sublist									Sublists created

At the last stage in the above procedure **the pointers have coincided**. The sublists are represented by the elements on each side of the reference number **X**.

Note that the reference number itself is in the correct final position for the sorted list.

The above statement is confirmed by noting the very important points that:

(a) **All elements in the right-hand sublist are > 27.**
(b) **All elements in the left-hand sublist are < 27.**

This means that each sublist can be treated independently of the others, and will enable us to call the *same algorithm* **recursively** (see chapter 18).

Before going on to stage two, let's consider the routine to carry out the above operation while it is still fresh in our minds. The following Pascal-like pseudocode performs the above operation of splitting the list into two sublists.

First some terminology:

We will store our list of numbers to be sorted in an **array** called N, and refer to the individual numbers by subscripts i.e. N_1, N_2 to $N_{maximum}$

Let N[left_pointer] refer to the number in the list being pointed to by the left_pointer, and let N[right_pointer] be the number in the list referred to by the right_pointer.

Let reference number (X in the above case) be represented by ref_number.

Let 'left' be the left_hand end of the list, and let 'right' be the right_hand end of the list (i.e. left would be 1 and right would be maximum initially).

```
BEGIN
  left_pointer  := left;
  right_pointer :=  right;
  REPEAT
    IF N[left_pointer] >
                        N[right_pointer]
                        THEN
          BEGIN
          Swap over numbers and reference
                        number;
          END;
      ELSE
        BEGIN
          Adjust pointers;
        END;
  UNTIL left_pointer = right_pointer;
END.
```

A complete Pascal procedure called '**splitup**' will be used in the final routine. It is developed from the above pseudocode and is shown in figure 19.5.

The above procedure produces a list with the left_pointer, right_pointer and ref_number coinciding. The left sublist (if there is one) is to the left of the reference number, and the right sublist (again if there is one) is to the right of the reference number.

Carrying on with the original method . . .

(2) Quick sorting each sublist

Repeat the above procedure for each sublist. In practice we would now store one of the sublists so that it can be sorted later. Therefore, store the left sublist and sort the right sublist as shown in the following table.

Table 19.4 (continues)
Part (1) of the second part of the algorithm – SORTING THE RIGHT SUBLIST Comments

Left sublist			Right sublist									Comments
19	13	27	50	39	77	82	91	65	48	70	66	Start conditions
STORED												
			(50)	39	77	82	91	65	48	70	66	Compare
			X→								←	Move pointer
			(50)	39	77	82	91	65	48	70	66	Compare
			X→							←		Move pointer

```
PROCEDURE splitup(VAR left, right, left_pointer, right_pointer, ref_number :INTEGER);
  BEGIN
    left_pointer  := left;
    right_pointer := right;
    REPEAT
      IF N[Left_pointer] > N[right_pointer] THEN
        BEGIN                           (* Swap numbers and ref_number *)
          IF ref_number = left_pointer THEN
            ref_number := right_pointer
          ELSE
            ref_number := left_pointer;
            temp := N[left_pointer]
            N[left_pointer] := N[right_pointer];
            N[right_pointer] := temp;
        END
      ELSE
        BEGIN                           (* If no swap move pointers *)
          IF left_pointer = ref_number THEN
            BEGIN
              right_pointer := right_pointer - 1;
            END
          ELSE
            BEGIN
              left_pointer := left_pointer + 1;
            END;
        END;
    UNTIL left_pointer = right_pointer;
  END.
```

Figure 19.5

Table 19.4 (continued) Part (1) of the second part of the algorithm										Comments
Left sublist	**Right sublist**									
	(50)	39	77	82	91	65	48	70	66	Compare
	X→						←			Swap
	48	39	77	82	91	65	(50)	70	66	Compare
	→						X←			Move pointer
	48	39	77	82	91	65	(50)	70	66	Compare
		→					X←			Move pointer
	48	39	77	82	91	65	(50)	70	66	Compare
			→				X←			Swap
	48	39	(50)	82	91	65	77	70	66	Compare
		X→					←			Move pointer
	48	39	(50)	82	91	65	77	70	66	Compare
		X→				←				Move pointer
	48	39	(50)	82	91	65	77	70	66	Compare
		X→			←					Move pointer
	48	39	(50)	82	91	65	77	70	66	Compare
		X→	←							Move pointer
	48	39	(50)	82	91	65	77	70	66	
		X⇄								Pointers coincide
	48	39	50	82	91	65	77	70	66	
Left sublist	**Right sublist**									**Sublists created**

Note that the sublists are independently positioned so that no elements need be taken out of any separate sublist to be put into another. This enables us to treat each sublist as an independent unit, and to determine its position in relation to the other sublists.

At present, after the processes above have been carried out, the state of the original list is therefore as shown in the following table:

We now have three sublists, with two of the original numbers in the right position	Comments
19 13 27 48 39 50 82 91 65 77 70 66	
Sublist OK Sublist OK Sublist (1) (2) (3)	Sublists created

(3) The final stages . . .

Each sublist must be processed in this way until *all* the sublists contain just a single number, in which case the entire list is sorted.

The principle of a **stack** (see chapter 24) may be used to help carry out the above operations. Using this principle we push information regarding a sublist onto the stack and pop it off again when the sorting algorithm needs to be called. All that is necessary is to keep a count of the number of elements in each list, and the number of lists on the stack. The 'number of elements in each list' together with information about 'the position of the list' can be achieved by storing left-hand and right-hand pointers for each sublist. These are the pointers referred to as 'left' and 'right' in the original procedure.

All that is necessary is to write a routine that controls the stack, and ensure that the right parameters are passed over to the main routine to split up the list into two sublists. The following is a summary of the state of the pointers and the list *after* the **splitup** routine has finished with it:

Left sublist	X	Right sublist
left	left_pointer	right
	right_pointer	
	ref_number	

If the left-hand sublist contains more than one element then it should be stored, and the following condition checks to see if two or more elements are present in the left-hand sublist.

```
IF (ref_number - 1) - left >= 1 THEN
    store the left_hand sublist.
```

The right-hand list is then processed in the same way until the right-hand list contains only one element. Therefore, it is processed all the time that the following condition is true:

```
IF ((right) - (ref_number + 1)) >= 1
    THEN
        process right-hand sublist using
        the splitup procedure.
```

Once the right-hand list has been fully processed we pop a list off the stack (see chapter 24) and process this new list.

To control the stack we shall use a variable called 'stack'. If stack = 0 then the stack is empty.

The stack will be used to store two variables **left_pointer(stack)** and **right_pointer(stack)**, where 'stack' is a number that indicates the 'number of lists on the stack', i.e.

left_pointer(1) → points to the left-hand element of the first list on the stack and

right_pointer(1)→ points to the right-hand element of the first list pushed on to the stack.

left_pointer(1) and **right_pointer(1)** would be the parameters to be **pushed onto** and **popped off of** the stack, and are the *same parameters* called '**left**' and '**right**' that are needed by the splitup routine, i.e.

```
left := left_pointer[stack];
right := right_pointer[stack];
```

is needed on entry to the splitup routine.

The complete stack-management routine would also have to take into account the fact that there may not be any elements in the left-hand or right-hand sublists.

For example, if there were no elements or only one element in the right-hand sublist, then we simply pass the left-hand sublist over to the splitup routine.

If there were no elements or only one element in the left-hand and right-hand sublists, then we would have to retrieve a list from the stack (if it was not empty) and process that list.

The pseudocode shown in figure 19.6 forms the main routine, which also controls the stack.

```
REPEAT
  BEGIN
    set flag to zero (* flag used as a test to bypass some of the following routines *)
    IF (right sublist contains one element or less)AND(left sublist contains more
                                                    than one element) THEN
    BEGIN
      set up left sublist pointers to be passed on to splitup procedure
      set up reference number
      set flag to one
    END;
    IF (flag is zero) AND (left sublist contains one element or less) AND (right
              sublist contains one element or less) AND (the stack is not empty) THEN
    BEGIN
      pop a list off the stack to be passed over to the splitup procedure
      decrement stack pointers
      set up reference number
      set flag to one
    END;
    IF (flag is zero) AND (left sublist contains more than one element) THEN
    BEGIN
      store the left sublist on the stack
      increment stack pointers
      set flag to one
    END;
    IF (flag is zero) AND (there is more than one element in the right sublist) THEN
    BEGIN
      set up right sublist to be passed over to the splitup procedure
      set reference number to left
      set flag to one
    END;
  END
UNTIL (flag is zero) AND (stack is empty)
```

Figure 19.6

A Pascal routine, based on the pseudocode in figure 19.6, is shown in figure 19.7.

```
REPEAT
  flag := 0;
                                    (*Main testing and control*)
  IF (right-(ref_number + 1) <= 1) AND ((ref_number—1) — left > 1) THEN
    BEGIN                           (* Set up left-hand sublist for splitup *)
      right := ref_number — 1;
      ref_number := left;
      flag :=  1;
    END;
  IF (flag = 0) AND (right — (ref_number + 1) <= 1) AND ((ref_number—1)-left <= 1) AND
                                                    (stack > 0) THEN

    BEGIN
      left := left_pointer[stack];      (* Retrieve list from stack *)
      right := right_pointer[stack];    (* and set up list for splitup *)
      stack := stack — 1;
      ref_number := left;
      flag := 1;
    END;
  IF (flag = 0) AND ((ref_number — 1) — left >= 1) THEN
```

Figure 19.7 (continues)

```
      BEGIN
        stack := stack + 1;                    (* Store left-hand sublist on stack *)
        left_pointer[stack]          left;
        right_pointer[stack] right;
      END;
    IF (flag = 0) AND (right — (ref_number + 1) >= 1) THEN
      BEGIN
        left := ref_number + 1;              (*  Set right-hand list for splitup *)
        ref_number := left;
        flag := 1;
      END;
    splitup(left, right, left_pointer, right_pointer, ref_number);
  UNTIL (flag = 0) AND (stack = 0);
```

Figure 19.7 (continued)

A complete Pascal program now follows in figure 19.8. This enables the user to type in our original 12 numbers and, after processing the numbers using 'splitup' and the 'main control routine' above, prints out the 12 numbers in ascending order.

```
PROGRAM quick (INPUT,OUTPUT);
VAR left, right, left_pointer, right_pointer, ref_number, maximum, count, temp,
                                                      stack, flag: INTEGER;
N: ARRAY[0..50] OF INTEGER;
left_pointer: ARRAY[0..50] OF INTEGER;
right_pointer: ARRAY[0..50] OF INTEGER;

PROCEDURE splitup(VAR left, right, left_pointer, right_pointer, ref_number: INTEGER);
  BEGIN                         (* THIS IS THE splitup PROCEDURE DEFINED ON PAGE 411 *)
    left_pointer  := left;
    right_pointer := right;
    REPEAT
      IF N[left_pointerl > N[right_pointerl THEN
        BEGIN
          IF ref_number = left_pointer THEN
            ref_number := right_pointer
          ELSE
            ref_number := left_pointer;
            temp := N[left_pointer];
            N[left_pointer] := N[right_pointer];
            N[right_pointer] := temp;
        END;
      ELSE
        BEGIN
          IF left_pointer = ref_number THEN
            BEGIN
              right_pointer := right_pointer — 1;
            END;
            ELSE
            BEGIN
              left_pointer := left_pointer + 1;
            END;
        END;
    UNTIL left_pointer = right_pointer;
  END;
```

Figure 19.8 (continues)

```
BEGIN
  maximum  := 50;
  FOR count := 1 TO maximum DO          (* Routine to enter the numbers *)
    BEGIN
      WRITELN('Please type in number', count);
      READLN(N[count]);
    END;
  WRITELN('Original list of numbers is');
  FOR count := 1 TO maximum DO          (* Confirm numbers just entered by printing
                                                            them out *)

    BEGIN
      WRITELN(N[count])
    END;
stack := 0;                            (* set up initial conditions *)
flag := 0;                             (* and split up first list *)
left := 1;
right := maximum;
ref_number := 1;
splitup(left, right, left_pointer, right_pointer, ref_number);

REPEAT
  flag := 0;                             (*Main testing and control*)
  IF (right-(ref_number + 1) <= 1)AND((ref_number - 1) - left > 1) THEN
                                      (* Set up left_hand sublist for splitup *)
    BEGIN
      right := ref_number - 1;
      ref_number := left;
      flag :=1
    END;
  IF (flag = 0)AND(right - (ref_number + 1) <= 1)AND((ref_number - 1) - left <=
                                              1)AND(stack > 0) THEN
    BEGIN
      left := left_pointer[stack];     (* Retrieve list from stack *)
      right := right_pointer[stack];   (* and set up list for splitup *)
      stack := stack - 1;
      ref_number := left;
      flag := 1;
    END;
  IF (flag    0) AND ((ref_number - 1) - left >= 1) THEN
    BEGIN
      stack := stack + 1;               (* Store left-hand sublist on stack *)
      left_pointer[stack] := left;
      right_pointer[stack] := right;
    END;
  IF (flag = 0) AND (right - (ref_number + 1) >= 1) THEN
    BEGIN
      left := ref_number + 1;           (* Set right-hand list for splitup *)
      ref_number := left;
      flag:= 1;
    END;
  splitup(left, right, left_pointer, right_pointer, ref_number);
UNTIL (flag = 0) AND (stack = 0);

WRITELN('Sorted list');                 (* flag = 0; hence list sorted *)
FOR count := 1 TO maximum DO
  BEGIN
```

Figure 19.8 (continues)

```
        WRITELN(N[count]);
    END;
END.
```

Figure 19.8 (continued)

In practice, better methods of using reference numbers that are placed at random (or better still the median) in the list, produce even faster results. However, these techniques are beyond the scope of computer science at this level.

If you run the various sorting routines that we have covered, then for the 12 numbers used in our examples, you would notice that the quick sort is not appreciably quicker! However, the larger the number of elements in the list the faster quick sort becomes in comparison to most other methods. In practice one must consider when the extra work of forming another sublist outweighs the sorting of that sublist by some other technique.

As an example, it can be shown that for a bubble sort:

$$\text{run time} \propto N \uparrow 2$$

or, for a **quick sort**: $\text{run time} \propto N \log_2 (N)$

If the value of N is large then quick sort is very fast compared with other techniques. Also the initial arrangement of the data drastically affects the time taken. In fact the worst case for the quick sort is data that is already sorted in the correct order!

Tree sort (tournament sort)

There are several different types of **tree sort** techniques but the **tournament sort**, making use of a **binary tree** (see chapter 25), is a popular choice. The name tournament sort derives from the fact that the system is exactly the same as in a knockout tournament for a game such as tennis. As an example, consider the players:

Players in a Tennis Tournament					
Bill	Dave	Carol	Emma	George	Fred

Did you know that . . .

The binary tree structure being demonstrated in the tournament sort is used in many different areas of computer science. In this book, it's used for converting between infix and reverse Polish notation in chapter 32 and for searching an ordered structure very quickly in chapter 25.

Let's assume, for the sake of convenience, that 'if the initial letter of a player's name appears alphabetically before that of his or her opponent', then 'the player will beat the opponent'!

In the first round of the competition, Bill will play Dave, Carol will play Emma and George will play Fred.

The winner of each match goes on to the next level in the binary tree as follows:

Results of the first-round playoffs					
Bill		Carol		Fred	
Bill	Dave	Carol	Emma	George	Fred

There are now an odd number of players, and so we will apply the rule that the player in the right-hand side of the tree will play the winner from the other match. This is unfair, I know, but the algorithm will work irrespective of who is seeded, and we are not playing real games of tennis anyway! Therefore Bill will play Carol and Fred will sit out the semi-final. The situation is now as follows:

Results of the second-round playoffs (semi-finals)					
Bill				Fred	
Bill		Carol		Fred	
Bill	Dave	Carol	Emma	George	Fred

Finally, Bill plays Fred and Bill therefore becomes 'champion' of the tournament.

Results of the finals					
Bill					
Bill				Fred	
Bill		Carol		Fred	
Bill	Dave	Carol	Emma	George	Fred

Bill is now at the **root node** and has therefore been placed at the head of the list. Hence Bill can now be removed from the root node and placed at the head of an alphabetical list. Note that Bill would appear at the root node irrespective of who had played whom or who had been seeded.

After Bill is removed from the root node a dummy (Z in our case which is equivalent to ZZZZZZZ as far as the comparison of names in the tournament is concerned) is placed in the tree.

The binary tree now becomes:

Replacing 'Bill' (the root node information) with Z					
Z					
Z				Fred	
Z		Carol		Fred	
Z	Dave	Carol	Emma	George	Fred

The tournament is now replayed with the following final result:

Carol now wins the final					
Carol					
Carol				Fred	
Dave		Carol		Fred	
Z	Dave	Carol	Emma	George	Fred

Notice that Carol is now at the root node, and therefore is removed and placed after Bill in the list.

The sorted list now contains **Bill, Carol**.

The next phase after Carol is removed would be:

Carol (the root node information) is replaced with Z					
Z					
Z				Fred	
Dave		Emma		Fred	
Z	Dave	Z	Emma	George	Fred

The tournament would be replayed with the following result:

Dave now wins the final					
Dave					
Dave				Fred	
Dave		Emma		Fred	
Z	Dave	Z	Emma	George	Fred

The sorted list then becomes: **Bill, Carol, Dave**.

Replacing Dave with Z's and replaying we get:

Emma now wins the final					
Emma					
Emma				Fred	
Z		Emma		Fred	
Z	Z	Z	Emma	George	Fred

We proceed in the above way until the whole tree consists of Zs, in which case the list produced is sorted. More efficient ways of minimising the need to compare Z with Z can obviously be developed.

There are many more algorithms for sorting data into order. However, many examples together with programs to implement them have been given in the first half of this chapter. As a lot of pages have been dedicated to the practical sorting routines, it is left to the reader to develop an algorithm and code for the tree sort should it be desired!

During the first part of this chapter we have considered methods that are ideal for **internal sorting**, i.e. sorting using the computer's main store. Other methods

Exercise 19.1

1 Explain why it is often necessary to sort the data in a computer file.

2 (a) Describe in detail an algorithm for sorting integers into ascending order.

(b) Write a routine making use of pseudocode to execute your algorithm.

(c) Test your algorithm by making use of the following data

5, 9, 7, 3, 0, 5, 2, 1, 1, 8, 4, 1 0.

3 Explain briefly the principles of the following sort routines:

(a) Insertion sort

(b) Bubble sort

(c) Shell sort

(d) Quick sort.

4 By making use of a suitable algorithm based on a bubble sort technique, show how the following data would be manipulated into its final ascending order:

7, 3, 9, 1

5 What type of data would be best to test sort algorithms?

6 How would you carry out sorting of data files too large to fit into the computer's main memory? Illustrate your answer by means of a diagram.

7 On many occasions, the length of time taken to sort data into order depends on the initial ordering of the data. Making use of the following sets of data, and sorting into descending order, comment on the effectiveness of three different sort algorithms of your choice.

(a) 2, 5, 3, 1, 4, 8, 6, 9, 0, 5

(b) 0, 1, 2, 3, 4, 5, 5, 6, 8, 9

(c) 9, 8, 6, 5, 5, 4, 3, 2,1, 0

making use of backing store are called **external sorting** techniques. These will be covered in the chapter on files and file handling.

Search techniques

The second major topic in this chapter is that of **searching**, i.e. searching through lists of data until one or more items of data that match some specified criteria can be found. In most practical systems we will probably be searching for some item of information that is contained in a **key field** within a file (see chapter 26). The enquiry will probably want the other data associated with this key field to be processed also. However, *during the following algorithms we will assume that only one item of information is associated with any search.* The techniques of coping with the other information associated with the key field are already well established in other parts of this book. Also, it is likely that the information to be searched will be contained on media such as disks or tape. The techniques to deal with this type of application will be dealt with in the chapters on files and file handling.

In the solutions given to the following search techniques we will simply search through a list of numbers contained in the computer's main memory. The compilation of these lists is unimportant and therefore the list of numbers will be stored in an array called N. Hence the items in the array will be referred to as N[1], N[2], N[3], etc.

Search techniques are compared by considering the average number of comparisons that must be made to get to the desired item of data. This is referred to as the **search length**. If, for a certain list of data, an average of 250 comparisons must be made before an item of data is located, the search length would be given as 250. Another often-quoted parameter would be the **search time.** This is simply the average time taken to search for a given item of data. Obviously, this would be intimately connected with the search length and the hardware being used. However, the search length will just be a function of the algorithm that is being used. We will now consider just a couple of the more common algorithms.

The linear search

The simplest search technique would obviously be to examine each element in a list one by one until the desired element has been found! This is the method where the list is sequentially examined until the information required is obtained. Not much thought needed for this one!

The following pseudocode should be quite obvious:

```
BEGIN
  READ required search criteria
  count := 1
```

```
  flag := 0
  WHILE there is more data in the list
  to be read DO
    BEGIN
      READ element in list
      IF criteria satisfied THEN
        BEGIN
          WRITE information
          set flag
          increment count
        END;
    END;
END.
IF flag is not set THEN WRITE no match
  found in the list
```

The following Pascal program enables the user to find how many integer numbers of a particular size occur in a list of 20. The main algorithm is shown, and the other code is to enable the user to type in 20 numbers for test purposes. In the chapter on files and file handling these numbers will be stored on disk.

```
PROGRAM linear search (INPUTOUTPUT);
VAR count, test, flag : INTEGER;
N: ARRAY [0..20] OF INTEGER;
BEGIN
  FOR count := 1 TO 20 DO
  BEGIN
    WRITELN('type in number', count);
    READLN(N[count]);
  END;
  WRITELN('Please type in the search
                        criteria');
  READLN(test);
  count := 1;
  flag := 0;

  WHILE count < 21 DO
    BEGIN
    IF test = N[count] THEN
      BEGIN
        WRITELN('criteria matched');
        WRITELN(N[count]);
        flag := 1;
      END;
    count := count + 1;
    END;
  IF flag = 0 THEN WRITELN('Sorry, no
  match found');
END.
```

The **linear** or **sequential search** is certainly not very efficient. If the item of data to be found is at the end of the list, then all previous items must be read and checked before the item that matches the search criteria is found. No structure was applied to the data in this simple case.

The search length can easily be worked out by considering the following argument.

If, for example, there were only three data items in the list, then it could take one, two, or three, comparisons to find the required item of interest. Therefore, the *average search length* would be given by:

Average search length = $(1 + 2 + 3)/3 = 2$

Hence, if there were N data items in the list, the average search length would be:

Average search length $= (1 + 2 + 3 + 4 + \ldots\ldots + N)/N$

Using arithmetic progressions it can easily be shown that:

as $1 + 2 + 3 + 4 \ldots\ldots + N = N(N + 1)/2$ then,

for the linear search, the average search length $= N(N + 1)/2N = (N + 1)/2$

If the data has already been sorted (see beginning of this chapter) then much faster techniques for searching can be used.

Structured search techniques

The following methods rely on the data being sorted before it is searched. The techniques of adding and deleting data to such ordered lists and trees is covered in chapters 24 and 25. Here we will just concentrate on searching the specified data structures.

The binary search

This is more efficient than the linear search, *but requires the data to be in order*. The idea is very simple

and is as follows.

First compare our search criteria with the middle (the median) number in the list, or one number away from this middle number if there is an even number of numbers. Consider the following ordered list:

Original ordered list of numbers used to demonstrate the binary-search techniques

2	3	4	7	12	18	(23)	29	31	37	38	49	53

Left-hand list   Right-hand list

The binary-search algorithm can be described by the following pseudocode:

```
IF we compare the desired number with 23 (the
middle number in the list) THEN:
        If successful, a match occurs – we have
completed the search and we STOP
    ELSE
        IF the desired number is less than the middle
number THEN
            search the left-hand list
    ELSE
            search the right-hand list.
    END
```

The techniques used to search the left-hand and right-hand list can also be a binary search. Hence the algorithm will call itself **recursively** (see chapter 18).

As an example of a binary search, consider finding the number 3 in the above list. The ideas are carried out in table 19.5.

Table 19.5
Table showing how the 'number 3' can be found by application of the binary search algorithm

1	2	3	4	5	6	7	8	9	10	11	12	13	Index
													Comments
2	3	4	7	12	18	23	29	31	37	38	49	53	Original numbers
2	3	4	7	12	18	(23)	29	31	37	38	49	53	INT((1 +13)/2) = Position 7 (number 23)
2	3	4	7	12	18	(23)	29	31	37	38	49	53	3<23 ∴ left-hand list is chosen
Left-hand list							Right-hand list						
2	3	4	(7)	12	18	23	29	31	37	38	49	53	INT((1 + 6)/2) = Position 4 (number 7)
2	3	4	(7)	12	18	23	29	31	37	38	49	53	3<7 ∴ left-hand list is chosen
Left-hand list			R-H list										
2	3	4	7	12	18	23	29	31	37	38	49	53	INT((1 + 3)/2) = Position 2 (number 3)
2	(3)	4	7	12	18	23	29	31	37	38	49	53	
	(3)												Number 3 has been found

Search has been stopped

Note that only three comparisons were needed in the case in table 19.5.

If we assume that the original list is simply 'integer numbers' in an array called N, then we can set up

pointers to indicate the left- and right-hand numbers of each list.

The pseudocode algorithm can therefore be developed as shown in figure 19.9.

```
maximum := number of elements in the array. (*Set up initial conditions*)
left :=1
right  maximum
middle := INTEGER((left + right)/2)
READ search criteria
PROCEDURE split (left, right, test)         (*Perform binary split*)
   WHILE (flag is not set)AND(middle >= 1)AND(middle <= max) DO
     BEGIN
        middle := INTEGER((left + right)/2)
        IF N(middle) = search criteria THEN
          BEGIN
            print out the search criteria
            set flag
          END PROGRAM
        ELSE
          BEGIN
            IF search criteria > N[middle] THEN
              BEGIN
                left := middle + 1
              END;
            ELSE
              BEGIN
                right := middle − 1
              END;
          END;
        END;
     END;
   split (left, right, test)      (*Binary-split is called recursively*)
END;
```

Figure 19.9

A complete Pascal program to perform a search on twenty numbers using the binary split now follows. The main algorithm is shown, and the twenty numbers to search must be typed in order. If not, one of the sort procedures shown at the beginning of this chapter will have to be used.

```
PROGRAM binary-search (INPUT, OUTPUT);
VAR right, left, maximum, middle, test, flag, count: INTEGER; 15: ARRAY [0..201 OF
INTEGER; PROCEDURE split-up (VAR left, right, test: INTEGER);
BEGIN
   WHILE (flag = 0) AND (middle > 1) AND (middle < maximum) DO
     BEGIN
        middle   TRUNC((left + right)/2);
        IF test N[middle]THEN
          BEGIN
            WRITELN('match found', N[middle]);
            flag := 1;
          END.
        ELSE
          BEGIN
            IF test = N[middle]THEN
              BEGIN
                left := middle + 1;
              END;
            ELSE
```

Figure 19.10 (continues)

```
            BEGIN
               right := middle - 1;
            END;
         END;
      END;
      split_up(left, right, test);
    END;
END;

BEGIN
  maximum := 10;
  left := 1;
  right      := maximum;
  flag := 0;
  middle := TRUNC((left + right)/2);

  FOR count := 1 TO maximum DO
    BEGIN
      WRITELN('Please type in number', count);
      READLN(N[count]);
    END;
  WRITELN('Please type in search number');
  READLN(test);
  split-up(left, right, test);
  IF flag = 0 THEN
    BEGIN
      WRITELN('Sorry, no match found in the list');
    END;
END.
```

Figure 19.10 (continued)

The binary search is obviously much more efficient than the linear search, although it should be remembered that the data to be searched must be in order.

To get an idea of the *maximum search length* for a **binary search** consider the following. Suppose we wish to find the number 3 in the following lists by applying the binary search algorithms already well established:

1 (3)
Two elements would require just one comparison
1 3 (5) 6 1 (3)
Four elements would require just two comparisons.
1 3 5 6 (8) 9 12 19 1 3 (5) 6 1 (3)
Eight elements would require three comparisons.
1 3 5 6 8 9 12 19 (23) 26 27 35 37 39 40 41
1 3 5 6 (8) 9 12 19
1 3 (5) 6
1 (3)

Sixteen elements would require four comparisons etc.

The above, together with the next few results are summarised in the table:

Table showing the max. number of comparisons needed in a binary search

Number of elements in the list	Maximum number of comparisons
2	1
4	2
8	3
16	4
32	5

This suggests a logarithmic relationship. If we use logs to base two then:

$$\log_2(2) = 1$$
$$\log_2(4) = 2$$
$$\log_2(8) = 3$$
$$\log_2(16) = 4 \text{ etc.}$$

Therefore, in general, **for N elements** we require a **maximum of $\log_2(N)$** comparisons.

Hence for a binary search, MAXIMUM SEARCH LENGTH = $\log_2(N)$.

Exercise 19.2

1   A linear or sequential search involves examination of each element within an array. This can be very slow if the desired elements are near the end of a long list. A better method is to make use of a binary search. This involves storing the data in order as a binary tree. Show how it is possible to search and find any element in a list of 1000 by examining at most only ten of the elements.

2   Devise a search algorithm based on the binary search principle in question (1). Develop a pseudocode algorithm and hence develop a program using a language of your choice.

End of chapter revision aid and summary

Cover up the right-hand column and see if you can answer the questions or define the terms on the left. They appear in the order in which they are covered in this chapter. Alternatively you may browse through the right-hand column to aid revision.

What is searching and sorting.

Searching is finding an item of data in a list and sorting is putting the data in some pre-determined order. Sorting and searching are fundamental data-processing operations. There are various sorting methods including the insertion sort, bubble sort, Shell sort, quick sort and tournament sort and various search methods including the linear and binary search.

Describe an insertion sort algorithm.

The insertion sort splits the list to be sorted into lower and upper elements and a special number, starting at the second element. The special number (pivotal position) is compared with all the lower elements and numbers are inserted into the right place. The pivotal position is then moved one place right and the whole process is repeated until the pivotal position becomes the last number.

Describe a bubble sort algorithm.

The bubble sort starts with the first pair of numbers in the list, they are compared and swapped if necessary. If a swap is necessary this fact is flagged. The next pair of numbers are then compared and the process is repeated until the last pair of numbers in the list is compared. If swaps were necessary the whole process is repeated.

Describe the Shell sort algorithm.

The Shell sort method chooses a number, which is nearest to max/2 where max is the max number of numbers in the list. This number represents a distance d between elements which are to be compared. On the first pass the pairs of numbers produced in each set are compared and swapped if necessary. The second pass assigns a value of distance d = max/4. Therefore, we end up with a larger number of subsets, which are sorted separately. The third pass makes d = max/8, etc. We continue until d = 1, in which case the whole list is sorted.

Describe the quick-sort algorithm.

The quick-sort algorithm splits up a list into two sublists, pointers are used and move to indicate pairs of data to be compared and swapped. If a swap is needed then a reference number is moved towards the other pointer. This process is repeated until the two pointers coincide. After the above process the two sublists are independent and will no longer interact with each other. They can therefore be sorted separately and the algorithm can be called recursively.

Describe a tree sort.

The tree sort can be thought of as a sort of tennis tournament (hence the alternative name). 'Players' can play each other and a binary tree is built up until the 'winner' becomes the root of the tree, in which case they are removed, placed at the head of the list and the data is replaced with a dummy Z (assuming the data is to be sorted in ascending order). The process is then repeated with Zs being used instead of the name of the 'player' who has been removed. When Zs appear all through the final tree the list is sorted.

What is searching?

Searching involves scanning a list until data matching the specified criteria has been found.

What is a linear search?

The linear search is simply examining each element in the list until the appropriate one is found.

What is a binary search?

The binary search relies on the fact that the data is sorted before it is searched. The middle or median number in the list is examined and if the criteria is 'less than that being examined' the left-hand sub-list is searched, again by using a binary search.

20 Low-level Languages and Architecture

Key resources

To carry out this work most successfully it's best if you have:

◆ Access to a computerised microprocessor simulation package

◆ Access to a microprocessor trainer so that you can physically see the items of hardware involved

◆ Access to some microprocessor chips. Some old 486s or early Pentiums would be ideal, but some of the very old Z80s or 6502s would be enlightening too

Concept checkpoints

◆ An appreciation of the basic binary system as covered in chapter 2.

Basic principles

Most people should be aware of the fact that what goes on inside a computer is a very complex process. For example, one moment your computer might be acting as a desktop publishing system. Next it could change to operating a spreadsheet which might be involved in some mathematical modelling. You might then use the computer to log on to an external database via a MODEM, or you might use the computer to look at some photos which have been stored on a CD-ROM system. The same machine controlling extra pieces of hardware attached to it has performed all these very different tasks.

At the heart of most computer systems is a complex chip called a microprocessor. **You've probably seen the adverts on the 'tele' which claim that a machine has an Intel processor inside, for example. This is referring to a particular manufacturer who happens to be a large player in the microprocessor-manufacturing business.** The purpose of this chapter is to take a simple look at how a microprocessor inside a typical computer can perform many different activities like those described in the last paragraph.

The computer program

Put simply, a **computer program** is a *set of instructions*, which tell the computer what to do. This set of instructions, or program, would normally be stored in the computer's main **memory**. It is the job of the **microprocessor** which is controlling the computer to **fetch** a single program instruction from the memory, decide what to do (by **decoding** this instruction), and then carry out any action which might be needed – called **execution** of this instruction. It is the sole task of the microprocessor inside the computer to carry out this **fetch-decode-execute** cycle over and over again operating on different instructions from memory – it does nothing more, nothing less. Often the fetch-decode-execute cycle is shortened to the fetch-execute cycle, because one clock pulse (see in a moment) is used to fetch and decode the instruction, and the next clock cycle is used to execute the instruction.

You will also hear the term **CPU** used in connection with the **microprocessor**. The term **CPU** stands for **Central Processing Unit** and is referring to the *unit inside the computer which actually carries out the fetching, decoding and executing of the instructions*. However, during your computer science course you will also use the term CPU in a much-broader context – on larger computers, for example, the CPU is often used to refer to the **main processing unit** which houses one or more processors and the memory associated with the system.

The electronic clock

The **microprocessor** does *not* have a mind of its own (although if you try to program one you may not be so sure!), therefore, there *must* be something that tells it what to do. You will recall from reading the last paragraph that it is the sole function of a microprocessor to fetch, decode and execute the instructions in memory. This being a very repetitive task, it's therefore not surprising that something very repetitive is needed to get the microprocessor to carry out these actions. This *repetitive control signal* is derived from an **electronic clock** and these simple ideas are shown in Figure 20.1. The other parts of this diagram will be explained in just a moment.

Notice that the **clock** is an electronic system which produces a **train of binary pulses** which are represented by the pattern **01010101** . . . etc. Each 0 – to – 1 – to – 0 transition is called a clock pulse, and represents one cycle of the square wave shown in figure 20.1. One pulse is usually needed to **fetch** an instruction from memory – it is then **decoded** automatically by the electronics inside the microprocessor chip – then the next clock pulse *might* cause the instruction to be **executed**. The word might is important here, because in real-life systems, some instructions are too big to fit inside a single memory location – therefore another clock pulse might be needed to load the next part of the instruction into the microprocessor before it can be executed.

The **speed** (*same as frequency*) of the clock is measured in **Hz** (or *cycles per second*). Therefore, you may see statements such as 'a Pentium III – 750 MHz

processor' in an advert. This would mean that Intel's Pentium III microprocessor is being clocked at a rate of 750,000,000 times per second. In turn this means that this particular processor is being told to do different things 750 million times a second – as you can see, microprocessors don't hang around!

The *actual process* being carried out by a *single* microprocessor-program instruction would be **extremely simple**, and typically might be a check to see if a number is 'too big' or 'too small', for example. However, do a few million instructions each second, and we end up with some impressive processing power which has the ability to achieve things like the applications mentioned at the beginning of this chapter.

Computer memory

The concept of computer memory is a simple one – it's just many pigeonholes into which we can store binary data. The idea is shown in Figure 20.2(a).

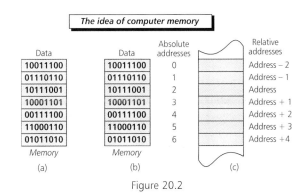

The idea of computer memory

Data	Data	Absolute addresses		Relative addresses
10011100	10011100	0		Address – 2
01110110	01110110	1		Address – 1
10111001	10111001	2		Address
10001101	10001101	3		Address + 1
00111100	00111100	4		Address + 2
11000110	11000110	5		Address + 3
01011010	01011010	6		Address +4
Memory	*Memory*			
(a)	(b)		(c)	

Figure 20.2

Here we have shown only seven pigeon holes, each able to store just **one byte (8-bits)** of data. The **data** *itself* may represent **instructions, numbers, ASCII characters** (see chapter 12) **or a whole host of different codes** which are limited only by your imagination. If we need to refer to one of these numbers inside the memory, then we will need to know exactly where this number lives in 'memory lane'. Therefore, each number is given a unique **address**. If we use the decimal system for the sake of simplicity, and if we start at address zero and take it from the top, then we can see that the number 10111001 lives at address number 2, as shown in Figure 20.2(b).

In practice millions of pigeonholes would be the norm, and in this book we will often make reference to computer memory as shown in Figure 20.2(c). Here the numbers have been replaced by words, which symbolise

> **Hint:** Computer memory has been covered from a hardware point of view in chapter 12. It might be worth looking back at this section to remind yourself how modern memory is organised in a typical computer system.

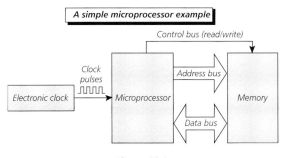

Figure 20.1

Did you know that . . .

If a computer has a fast processor, it does not necessarily mean that the computer is actually faster. It depends on the type of processor and the number of bits – a 64-bit or 128-bit processor, for example. The speed of the computer also depends, amongst other things, on the number of processors present. A beefy supercomputer, for example, might clock each processor at only 75MHz, but have 2048 different 128-bit processors!

the actual numbers – often the absolute number representing the address itself is of secondary importance.

Data and address busses

If we need to **read** a number from memory (*copy* the number from memory into the microprocessor) or **write** a number to memory (get the microprocessor to *put* the number into memory) then two obvious extra systems are needed. The first is a system of wires along which the **data** (numbers in memory) can travel. This is called the **data bus** and is shown in Figure 20.1. Next we need to tell the memory which address is to be used – therefore, a second group of parallel wires called the **address bus** is needed to carry this information. This is also shown in Figure 20.1. Instead of drawing lots of individual parallel wires, large arrows are used instead. You should note that the 'address bus' is a one-way-only bus – because the microprocessor needs only to instruct the memory as to which address is to be used. However, notice that the **data bus** is *two way* – this is because the data can travel both 'into' and 'out from' the memory and microprocessor system. It depends on whether we are reading or writing the data.

You are probably wondering how the data knows which way to go! This is the function of the final connection, which forms part of the **control bus**. This particular wire carries the signal to tell the memory whether a **read** or **write** operation is taking place. (In practice a '1' might mean read and a '0' might mean write.)

RAM and ROM

One big problem with most of the electronic memories used to store users' programs is that the contents of the memory chips disappear *if* the power to the computer is switched off! These types of memory are known as **RAM**, which stands for **Random Access Memory**, though the name is *not* because of this particular property. When you switch on your computer, a program called an operating system (see chapter 22) needs to be resident in memory, or it will not be able to make sense of what you type in at the keyboard or display on the screen, for example. Part of this program, called the **BIOS**, is stored in an alternative type of memory called **ROM**. (**Read Only Memory**) which does not loose its data when switched off. We can only read the data from this type of memory – we can't change it (write to it). Both types of memory are needed in most computer systems.

Other input/output

It would be a very boring computer if it were set up just like the diagram shown in Figure 20.1. For example, we have no keyboard from which to type in some data, we have no VDU (monitor or screen) on which we can see the results of our efforts, and we have no printer to produce any hard copy. A few

embedded systems have little more than this (see chapter 8), but most microcomputers and other computer systems need a whole host of extra hardware connected to them to enable these systems to act in useful ways described earlier in this chapter.

You should already appreciate the concept that *data* can be transferred between the **memory** and the **microprocessor** making use of the **data bus** – it's therefore a simple extension to connect *any device* to the *same* **data bus** and transfer this data in the same way too. Indeed this *is* what is done. The only difference between putting data out to memory or putting it out to a disk, for example, is the fact that the **address** used for the *destination* of the data is *different* and hence the data going along the bus is routed to a different place.

Each device is **mapped** onto the system so that it acts *as if it were memory*. As far as the microprocessor is concerned, it is simply sending out the data in the same way – the fact that it is being sent to a disk drive instead of a memory location is irrelevant. The hardware inside the disk drive, together with the programs that control the disk make sure that the data ends up in the correct physical place. A more-general concept for our computer system would, therefore, look more like the diagram shown in Figure 20.3.

To keep the diagram as simple as possible, several devices have been lumped together in the same box. In practice the disk, tape and CD-ROM system, for example, would be in different boxes. However, the principles of these systems are identical.

Memory maps

From the last section we saw how different hardware devices might be **mapped** as though they were different areas of memory. In fact we need to **map** out *all* the areas of memory that are to be used for specific purposes. If this is not done then writing to the wrong area of memory may inadvertently cause chaos. For example, if you intended to print a file, then it would have to be directed to that area of memory that controls the printer. If you sent it to that area of memory which controlled the VDU graphics instead, then the computer screen would probably go gaga as it tried to make sense of the ASCII characters meant for the printer. This is

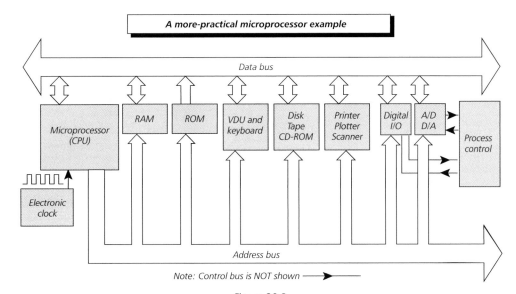

Figure 20.3

typical of the sort of thing which may happen when we get a computer crash – one of the programs is doing something that it should not do.

A very simple memory map is shown in Figure 20.4. Notice that some of the memory is allocated to **ROM** which contains a **BIOS** (see chapter 22) program – this means that the computer will be able to do a useful set of things when you switch it on. Other chunks of memory are allocated to the rest of the operating system. This would usually be loaded in from disk when the computer is started up. In practice this operating-system memory would be the place where systems like MSDOS or Windows, for example, would live. There is a little space too for some user programs!

Did you know that . . .

The memory map of a particular operating system (see chapter 22) will probably change when a different version of the operating system is released. If, as is likely, some software writers have not obeyed the rules of what goes where (given by the old memory map), then their old software may not run on the new system. This is just one of the reasons why badly written software may not work when operating systems change.

More comprehensive memory maps are shown in chapter 22 when operating systems are considered in detail.

How does it all work?

The key to a simple understanding of the above system lies in an appreciation of how a very-simple microprocessor would execute an extremely simple program

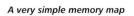

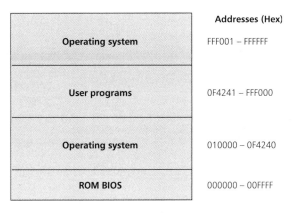

	Addresses (Hex)
Operating system	FFF001 – FFFFFF
User programs	0F4241 – FFF000
Operating system	010000 – 0F4240
ROM BIOS	000000 – 00FFFF

Figure 20.4

held in the computer's memory. We therefore present **BORIS** – a microprocessor invented for the purpose of this chapter. Real microprocessors are covered in chapter 21, but BORIS is not to be insulted – he contains *all* the necessary elements to carry out his task of running our simple program. By the way – **BORIS** stands for **Beginner's Optimised Reduced Instruction Set** microprocessor. In fact, the instruction set is so reduced that there are only three instructions – called **LOAD**, **ADD** and **STORE**!

> **Hint:** If you are good at graphics programming using a system like Microsoft's Visual Basic, for example, then building up a teaching aid like BORIS could provide the basis for a good project. It would be even better if it were combined with good animated visuals and a few simple pseudo assembly language instructions for the students to play with.

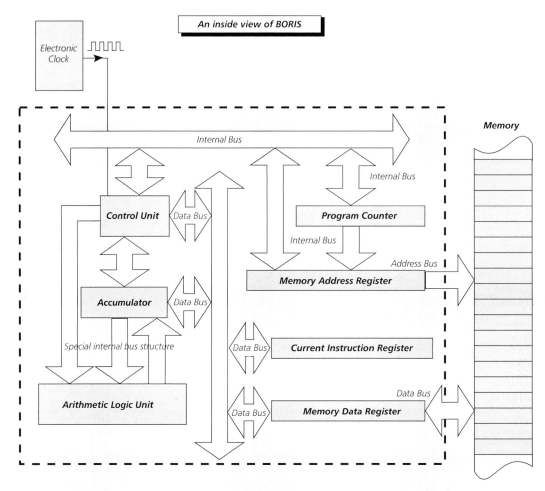

Figure 20.5

BORIS has a few electronic-storage locations inside him called **registers**. These are the places where **binary digits** can be *stored* and *manipulated* – the general layout is shown in Figure 20.5. If you imagine each of the bus lines inside BORIS to be similar to railway lines, and the binary digits which travel along these lines to be equivalent to the trains, then the registers are equivalent to the stations in which the trains are allowed to stop.

Before proceeding further we need to know what functions are performed by each of the registers inside BORIS. They are therefore explained in the following sections.

The accumulator

The **accumulator** is used to **accumulate** *results* – hence its name. It is *the* place where the *answers* from many operations are **stored temporarily** *before* being put out to the computer's memory, for example. As with most microprocessors, the accumulator plays a vital role in what's going on for most of the time.

The arithmetic logic unit (ALU)

The **arithmetic logic unit** or **ALU** as it is often known is the 'brains' of the outfit. The ALU is able to do simple arithmetic on numbers and put the answer into the accumulator.

The control unit

The **control unit** is literally *in control*. It acts under the direction of the clock, and sorts out all the **internal paths** needed inside the microprocessor to make sure that data *gets from* the right place and *goes to* the right place. It instructs the ALU which arithmetical or logical operation is to be performed, and carries out other operations like 'deciding which part of the fetch-decode-execute cycle' BORIS is in. If you imagine that the clock is like a metronome going tick-tock tick-tock etc., then the control unit is equivalent to the conductor in the orchestra. He or she will make sure that all the different sections of the microprocessor are in time with each other. If this does not happen, then the whole thing would get out of synchronisation and fail to operate properly. Some of the internal connections from the control unit to other parts of BORIS have not been shown – it would make the drawing look like a spider's web. Nevertheless, let's come back to our railway analogy for just a moment. If the data, address and control busses are equivalent to railway lines, then the control unit would be equivalent to the person who is operating all the points and making sure that they open and close at the right moments in time. The whole network must all be run to a strict timetable – which is dictated by the clock.

The program counter

The **program counter** (PC), or **sequence control register** as it is sometimes known, determines the **sequence** in which the **program instructions** are to be executed. In our simple microprocessor circuit, this will be just one after the other. Therefore, we would set up the PC to point to the appropriate part of memory where the beginning of the program can be found (hence the address-bus connection). After the first instruction has been loaded, increment the PC by 1 so that the next instruction to be fetched from memory can be accessed very easily.

It was **von Neumann** who first proposed the idea of **having a program in memory**, and then each program instruction being **fetched and executed in sequence**. All operations, even inside the most complex of microprocessors, still rely on this basic fetch-decode-execute cycle being continually repeated at great speed. Chapter 21 will deal with the added complexity of diverting control to other parts of the program, or to different programs held in memory, and towards the end of this chapter we will look at more-recent ideas which are designed to speed up the process. However, BORIS is a simple beast and has no need of such sophistication.

The current instruction register

This **current instruction register** (CIR) is a place for the **current instruction** (i.e. the instruction which has just been fetched from memory) to live. The binary digits representing the most-recently-fetched instruction are held here so that the instruction decoder in the control unit can decode them. It's most important to realise that as far as the microprocessor is concerned, data (numbers and letters etc.) and instructions all look the same. It's up to the programmer to make sure that appropriate instructions are put at appropriate places in the memory. If data intended for other purposes gets interpreted as an instruction by the microprocessor, then the computer will go gaga because it's attempting to carry out actions based on meaningless patterns of binary data. If mistakes occur in the program then these problems will occur.

The memory data register

The contents of the **memory data register** (MDR) holds the **data** that was either **read from** or **written to** the main memory – the *last time* that this read/write operation

was carried out. You will recall from reading the above that data and instructions all look similar. In fact, the codes used by some instructions are bound to be identical to the codes used for some of the data. However, if the instructions are being interpreted correctly, then instructions will be transferred to the CIR register whereas ordinary data would not.

The memory address register

The **memory address register** (MAR) holds the **address** of the data (or instruction) currently being accessed. It's used to alter the address bus without changing the PC.

A simple program

BORIS is going to **execute** (*carry out*) the simple program which now follows. Comments have been added to help clarify what's going on.

LOAD	A, [10]	;Load the Accumulator with the no. from memory loc. 10
ADD	A, [11]	;Add no. from memory loc. 11 and put result in the Acc.
STORE	A, [12]	;Store the Accumulator in memory location 12

This program will **LOAD**, into the Accumulator register, the number contained inside memory location 10, **ADD** this to the number contained in memory location 11 – then **STORE** the result from the Accumulator into memory location 12. Let's suppose, for the sake of argument, that the number 3 lives in memory location 10, and that the number 2 lives in memory location 11. Being an intelligent student, you've already worked out that the answer is going to be 5 – however, let's see how BORIS would go about achieving the same result.

First the **program** itself *would have to be stored somewhere in memory*, preferably not in memory locations 10, 11 or 12, as these have already been used up by storing the data (the numbers to be added) and reserving a place for the answer. For the sake of argument we will assume that the program will be put into memory starting at Address 100. Being three lines long, and assuming that the code for each instruction will fit into a single memory location (in most real systems it may not), we end up with the important parts of our memory map as shown in figure 20.6(a) and (b).

> **Hint:** If you want to do some real assembly language examples, then read chapter 21 on low-level languages. Assembly language is not all that difficult once you get the hang of it. It really shows you how a particular processor operates and the speed with which you can execute the programs is second to none. Try it and see. Some students really get hooked and start to work out long prime numbers or evaluate pi to 10,000 decimal places!

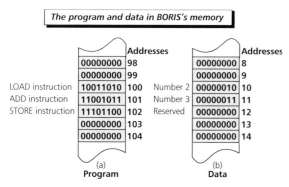

The program and data in BORIS's memory

	Addresses			Addresses
00000000	98		00000000	8
00000000	99		00000000	9
LOAD instruction 10011010	100	Number 2	00000010	10
ADD instruction 11001011	101	Number 3	00000011	11
STORE instruction 11101100	102	Reserved	00000000	12
00000000	103		00000000	13
00000000	104		00000000	14

(a)   (b)
Program   **Data**

Note: 10011010 is the machine code for LOAD the number from memory location [10]
10011010 11001011 is the machine code for ADD the number from memory location [11]
11101100 is the machine code for STORE the result in memory location [12]

Figure 20.6

We have assumed that the contents of all irrelevant memory locations have been set to zero – but in practice the contents of these memory locations are of no consequence with regard to this particular program.

You will observe that the numbers to be added are contained in memory locations 10 and 11, and are stored using pure binary. However, each program instruction needs a code too. This is usually assigned by the microprocessor manufacturer, and we have tongue-in-cheek assumed that the codes will be as in Figure 20.6. The name given to the code for the instructions when used in this form is called **machine code**.

There is usually some sort of logic to the codes used to represent the instructions, and the BORIS language works along the lines shown in figure 20.7. As can be seen from the diagram, a unique code is assigned to each operation, together with a means of identifying the source or destination of the data. In each particular case the memory location is contained in the same byte as the code – in practice, more than one byte would be

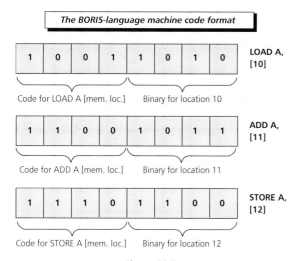

The BORIS-language machine code format

| 1 | 0 | 0 | 1 | 1 | 0 | 1 | 0 | LOAD A, [10] |

Code for LOAD A [mem. loc.]   Binary for location 10

| 1 | 1 | 0 | 0 | 1 | 0 | 1 | 1 | ADD A, [11] |

Code for ADD A [mem. loc.]   Binary for location 11

| 1 | 1 | 1 | 0 | 1 | 1 | 0 | 0 | STORE A, [12] |

Code for STORE A [mem. loc.]   Binary for location 12

Figure 20.7

needed for a greater range of instructions and a sensible addressing range.

Executing the program

If the program, which is resident in memory beginning at location 100, is to be executed, then the first stage is to make sure that the **program counter (PC)** is set to 100. The idea is shown in Figure 20.8(a). You should note that all registers hold binary numbers; therefore, the binary representation for each number is used.

Next the **memory address register (MAR)** is set up to contain the binary code for 100, obtained from the contents of the PC – this is so that the address bus can be used to access the correct location in memory, and is shown in Figure 20.8(b).

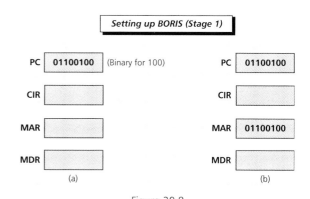

Setting up BORIS (Stage 1)

PC	01100100	(Binary for 100)	PC	01100100
CIR			CIR	
MAR			MAR	01100100
MDR			MDR	

(a)   (b)

Figure 20.8

The fetch phase for the 1st instruction

The **data** from memory location 100 is now **fetched** and loaded into the **CIR** via the **MDR**. You will recall that BORIS can't tell the difference between data and program instructions – it's all data to him. The only reason why the pattern 10011010 gets put into the CIR is that BORIS must assume that the first thing encountered in a program will be an instruction – so it's fetched from the memory and interpreted as such. Figure 20.9(a) shows that the data representing this instruction ends up in the current instruction register.

The next *vital* step is that the **PC is incremented by 1 to 101** (or the binary pattern representing this decimal number). This needs to be done so that the next instruction to be fetched from memory will be got from the right place.

The 1st instruction is decoded

The next phase involves **decoding** this instruction. This is done automatically by the instruction-decoder electronics inside BORIS's control unit. The idea can be thought of as shown in Figure 20.10.

The control unit decodes this particular instruction and finds out that this machine code means 'the

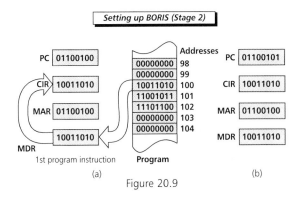

Figure 20.9

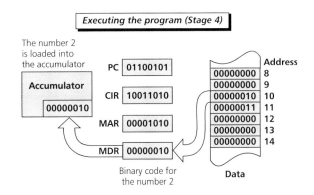

Figure 20.11

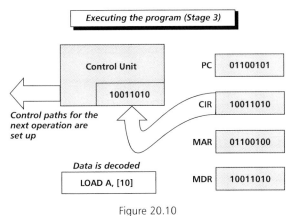

Figure 20.10

be further from the truth – in practice the above operations would take place in just a fraction of a millionth of a second on a slow microprocessor – food for thought – we said that BORIS is not to be insulted!

The fetch phase for the 2nd instruction

We now go through very similar processes again. If you have understood what's been going on, you should now find that the processes become easier to understand.

Don't forget that the **PC** has *already been incremented*, therefore the **MAR** is set to 101 (the contents of the PC) and the data from memory location 101 is loaded into the **CIR** via the **MDR** as shown in Figure 20.12(a). As before, after an instruction has been fetched, we automatically **increment the PC**. This action is shown in Figure 20.12(b).

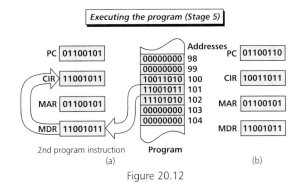

Figure 20.12

contents of memory location 10 must be loaded into the accumulator'; therefore, the MAR has to be set up to point to this new memory location. Don't forget that we have made an analogy between the control unit and the signal-box operator on a railway. Therefore, the control unit has now set up all the paths (by opening and closing the electronic points) within BORIS so that 'what is being requested by this instruction' can actually be carried out.

Execution of the 1st instruction

Hint: If this whole process seems very slow, don't forget that a modern microprocessor could carry out such operations at speeds in excess of 500 million instructions per second. It has taken two pages of this book to explain how this single operation has been fetched, decoded and executed. Working at this rate, the microprocessor could work through the 750 pages of this book in just ¾ of 1 millionth of a second!

Figure 20.11 shows the result of the execution phase of the first instruction. Eureka! We have, at last, carried out enough of these basic operations to load just one number into the accumulator! We have, therefore, **fetched**, **decoded** and **executed** the first instruction. Only another two to go – and we will have managed to add two numbers together and store the result. Now BORIS might appear to be slow – but nothing could

The 2nd instruction is decoded

The second instruction is now **decoded** as shown in Figure 20.13, and found to be an ADD instruction. After further decoding, the electronic paths are set up so the number already in the accumulator has the number contained in memory location 11 added to it. The result is then stored back in the accumulator – lots of work for the control unit to do here – many levers would have to be pulled in the right sequence to make sure that the binary trains don't go down the wrong track!

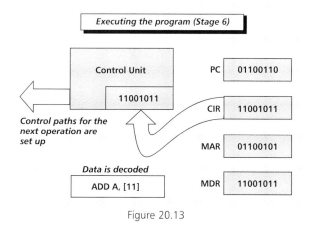

Figure 20.13

Execution of the 2ⁿᵈ instruction

To carry out these operations the control unit instructs the ALU that an 'ADD operation' is to take place. This is indicated by the part of the internal control bus shown as a single connection between the control unit and ALU in Figure 20.14. Now the numbers to be added are contained in memory location 11 and the accumulator. Therefore, as shown in the diagram, the first number from the accumulator gets transferred to a register inside the ALU. Next the MAR is set to the binary pattern for 11, and the number from memory location 11 is transferred into the accumulator, where it is then combined, by addition, with the first number already in the ALU register. This produces the sum, which is then about to be put back into the Accumulator, thus overwriting

the old contents of the Accumulator with the answer. In Figure 20.14 the overwriting part of this operation has not been shown.

On first reading, operations like these might appear to be quite complex, but they do give a very good indication of what is actually going on inside a typical microprocessor. Binary digits are constantly being got from memory, manipulated in registers inside the microprocessor, then the results put back out to memory again. In practice there would be a lot more registers than are present inside BORIS, but the principles are very similar.

If you have fully understood all the above, then you should now be capable of working out what happens when the final instruction is fetched, decoded, and then executed. See if you can actually do this by trying to predict what will happen before reading the final section.

The fetch phase for the 3ʳᵈ instruction

We are nearly there! The **MAR** is now set to the contents of the **PC**, and the data from memory location 102 is **fetched**. As before, the **PC** contents are incremented by 1, ready for the next instruction! These stages are shown in Figure 20.15.

The 3ʳᵈ instruction is decoded

The final instruction is decoded, and requires that the current contents of the accumulator be stored in memory location 12. This is shown in Figure 20.16.

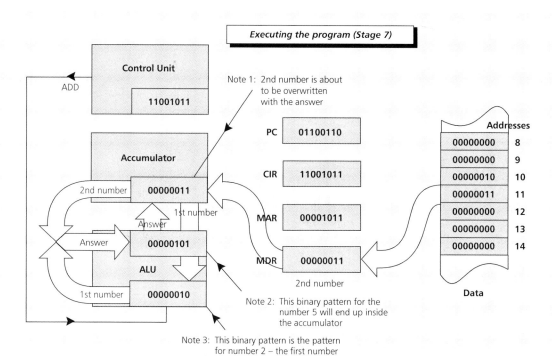

Figure 20.14

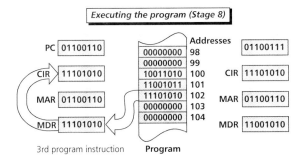

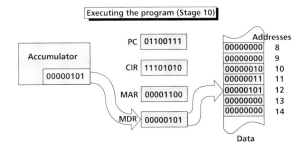

Figure 20.15

Figure 20.17

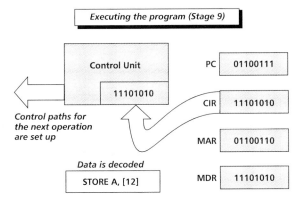

Figure 20.16

Execution of the 3rd instruction

After being executed, the result of the addition (binary for the number 5), is stored in memory location 12. This is shown in figure 20.17. We have, at last carried out all the operations necessary to work out 2 + 3! – but wait, this is not the end of the story.

As stated before, a microprocessor does not have a mind of its own. Therefore, it can't just go to sleep. You will recall that a microprocessor has just one purpose in life – to fetch, decode and execute instructions just like the ones we have been carrying out. The PC has already been set up – so let's go – BORIS will fetch the next piece of data from memory location 103, attempt to decode it, then attempt to execute it – what happens next could be literally anything. The machine which is being controlled by BORIS would certainly crash as BORIS runs through all of the memory desperately trying to do what he 'thinks' is carrying out running the program.

In practice, any program run in this way would need an instruction, which **returns control** back to what BORIS was doing before his program counter was set to 100 and he started to run this particular program.

In a real computer the microprocessor is constantly running programs, even when the machine appears to be doing absolutely nothing. Don't forget that if there is a picture on the screen then the computer is doing something. If, when you type in a character at the keyboard it appears on the screen, then the computer must be monitoring activity at the keyboard when a key has been pressed. The computer must also go through a complex program to find out what character was actually typed, then instruct the electronics controlling the video display to put the pattern which represents this particular character on the screen in the right colour etc.

It's important to understand that microprocessors are usually carrying out millions of operations each second – even if this means looping round some program while waiting for something else to happen. The only time that a microprocessor will cease to fetch, decode and execute instructions is when the clock is switched off. This usually happens only when the machine itself is actually switched off.

At switch on, the microprocessor will reset all the circuits, and then execute a program (called booting see chapter 22) which loads the operating system (see chapter 22) and gets the computer into a usable state. Normal activities such as 'loading an application from disk', for example, can then be carried out. If the application just loaded happens to be a DTP system as described at the beginning of this chapter, then the microprocessor would jump to the beginning of the DTP-system program, which is now resident in memory. It would fetch and decode the first of the hundreds of thousands of instructions which make the computer act as a DTP system – that's how it's done – and all with a few binary digits – a magnificent human achievement.

Reading chapter 21 will explain how more-complex programs may be carried out, but a fundamental understanding of the last few sections will take the mystery

Hint: Even if you don't have to learn about the fetch-decode-execute cycle for your syllabus, it's enlightening to go through this section. When armed with this vital information, the microprocessor is no longer just an unfathomable box which controls the computer. You have at last understood the essence of modern computer systems. This is an achievement in its own right and one that puts all of the other work in this book into context.

out of computers. If you have fully understood the concepts explained in this chapter, then you are already well on the way to an appreciation of the fascinating and high-speed life of a microprocessor-controlled machine. Von Neumann could not have appreciated where his work would lead – I suggest you propose a toast to him the next time you go out for a drink!

Exercise 20.1

1 Explain the meaning of the following terms:
   (a) Microprocessor
   (b) Fetch-decode-execute cycle
   (c) CPU
   (d) ALU
   (e) Program counter
   (f) Register
   (g) Bus
   (h) Memory.

2 A microcomputer is clocked at 750 MHz. What is the function of this clock and what type of signal is output from it?

3 Memory forms an integral part of any computer system. In what form is the data stored in memory?

4 There are *three* main different types of bus system external to the CPU. What is the name and purpose of each type of bus?

5 Many different devices such as disk drives, keyboards and printers etc. are simultaneously connected to a system. Briefly explain how it is possible to control many different devices in this way.

6 What is meant by a memory map and why is it necessary to have a detailed memory map for all computer systems?

7 Explain the function of the following sub-systems inside a typical microprocessor:
   (a) Control unit
   (b) Accumulator
   (c) Memory data register
   (d) CIR
   (e) Internal bus
   (f) Memory address register.

8 How is it possible for groups of binary digits to represent operations such as ADD, SUBTRACT or MULTIPLY etc? What is the name given to groups of binary digits when used in this way?

9 How does the microprocessor 'know' the difference between a machine code instruction and ordinary data?

10 A typical microprocessor has the following instruction set:

LOAD, STORE, ADD, SUBTRACT, DIVIDE, MULTIPLY

Using these instructions as a guide, carefully explain the typical processes that a microprocessor executing some machine code would need to carry out for the computer to work out the cumulative total of five numbers held in consecutive memory locations. State any assumptions that you need to make.

Other architecture systems

BORIS (see earlier) should have given you a fundamental understanding of what basic microprocessors are all about. He has done his job well, but he is slightly outclassed by today's more modern microprocessor architectures! In the remainder of this chapter we will bring you right up to date to include the most modern architectures which are poised to take us into the 21st century. We will not be able to study these systems in the detail with which BORIS was covered, but this is not necessary. It's only the principles of these more-complex architectures that need to be studied if you are to gain an appreciation of the trends, which appear to be moulding future developments.

The von Neumann bottleneck

You may recall that it was a Hungarian-born American called **von Neumann** who first proposed that **program instructions** be *stored* in **memory**, then *single* instructions be **fetched**, **decoded** and **executed** in the ways described at the beginning of this chapter. The performance of systems based on these simple ideas is impressive, but there is a fundamental queuing mentality, which is built up due to the physical constraints imposed by the system. The only way to increase the speed of the processing is to speed up the clock rate, or increase the width of the data bus. Both of these techniques have been tried with stunning success, but even greater efficiency may be achieved by having a fundamental rethink regarding the ways in which things are carried out at microprocessor level. The limitation of being able to do just one thing at a time in sequence has come to be known as the **von Neumann bottleneck**. Ways had to be found of getting over this linear nature of processing – ways had to be found of doing more than one thing at the same time, and this is called **parallel processing**.

Single-pipeline processors

One method suggested to improve the situation was that of using what's called a **pipeline architecture**. The name pipeline architecture is appropriate because several things are in the 'pipeline' (metaphorically speaking) at the same time. It's a simple idea – if you were working on three different projects simultaneously, then you would have three projects in the pipeline! In a similar way, a specially designed microprocessor could fetch one instruction, while another was being decoded, while

> **Hint:** It is only the simplest of modern microprocessors which now use the single-pipeline architecture. However, don't forget that millions of simple microprocessors are still needed in control equipment such as washing machines, digital TVs and many other consumer goods. The sophisticated microprocessors are usually used in modern microcomputer systems.

yet another was being executed. The idea can be visualised as shown in figure 20.18.

Notice that by the end of the third cycle, a conventional non-pipelined architecture would have fetched, decoded and executed just one instruction. However, if we make use of a pipeline that has the capacity to do three different parts of the cycle at once, we see that by the end of the third cycle the first instruction has been fetched, decoded and executed, the second instruction has been fetched and decoded, and the third instruction has been fetched.

We could obviously make the pipeline 'longer' and therefore process even more data. However, there is a problem – if the next instruction in the queue is *not* the one that is required, then the whole system goes to pot – you have to flush the pipeline, and start again with the instruction which *is* actually required. This is usually as a consequence of a jump instruction – something which most microprocessors are doing all the time. Therefore, although this method does increase the throughput, there are problems due to the nature of most programs. However, part of the art of getting computers to do many different things at the same time is in organising the program structure so that these

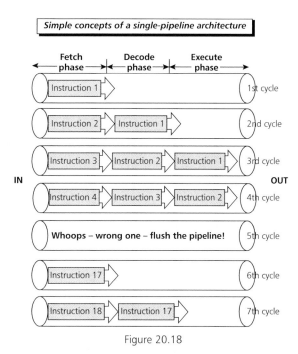

Figure 20.18

problems arise less often, and simple techniques of parallel processing are covered later on in this chapter.

Multiple-pipeline architecture

If a single pipeline architecture, as shown in figure 20.18 increases the rate at which instructions can be processed, then *more than one* **pipeline** architecture working in parallel could be much better still. *If the instructions being carried out in parallel are not connected* in any way (i.e. the result from one instruction being executed may be needed by the next, for example), then execution will take place at a much-faster rate. Some sort of check for instruction dependence would therefore be needed before putting these different instructions into the pipelines.

Array processor architecture

An **array processor** can act on **data structures** called **arrays** (see chapter 24). In practice this means that an **array of processors** can perform *identical operations* on many different items of data simultaneously, usually under the control of another processor. The term **vector processor** is also often used instead of the term array processor. However, as the mathematicians amongst you will realise, a 'vector' is simply another name for a 'one-dimensional array' – a little knowledge is a wonderful thing!

Multiprocessor architectures

Hitherto we have concentrated mainly on improving the performance of a *single* processor, but there are other lucrative lines of thought which enable *different processors* to work together as a team. Although many systems do make use of **multiple processors** in this conventional sense, you should note also that each processor does not necessarily have to be housed inside a different chip. Many processors can be built inside the same chip if required, and work is going on in the research labs to get hundreds or even thousands of processors inside the same chip! However, it should be reasonably obvious that if this latter method is being employed, then the complexity of each of the processors is relatively simple compared to the latest generation of powerful microprocessors. Silicon technology is nowhere near good enough to get several thousand of these beasts onto a single chip – yet!

Did you know that . . .

The array processor architectures are popular in supercomputers which do intense mathematical calculations like forecasting the weather. However here, too, the combination of many different microprocessors in parallel is replacing the conventional array-processor architectures.

When using multiprocessor architectures we get added complications due to the nature of the possibilities which have now opened up. For example, with a pipeline architecture, the code executed on a particular processor did not have to be modified from the basic type of code which would work on a conventional architecture of the BORIS (see earlier) variety. However, with a multiprocessor-architecture system, we have the possibility that completely different parts of the program can be executed simultaneously. If the original code has been written such that the program can only be executed in a linear fashion (most conventional programs in the past have been), then the multiprocessor architecture will not be used with great efficiency under these particular circumstances.

The greatest efficiency from true parallel processing using a multiprocessor architecture comes only when the original code has been written with this sort of scenario in mind. Much code can be rewritten in this way, and some of the very latest windows-based operating systems software and some applications software are starting to take advantage of new multiprocessor possibilities. Indeed, mainframes and communication systems have been doing this for some time, and the very powerful micros are taking this route too.

There are several different philosophies – a common one used on many micros is that of having a few different processors share the same memory, but common too on mainframes and supercomputers is having totally independent systems with shared-message-passing capability. This latter option is also typical of the **front-end-processor systems**, which help to organise the complex communications between the many possible users of a mainframe system and the mainframe **CPU**.

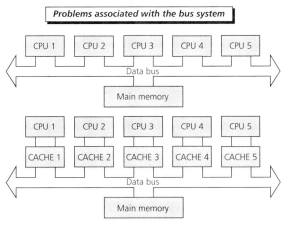

Figure 20.19

The top half of figure 20.19 shows a simple multiprocessor architecture with shared memory. It's easy to appreciate how such a system works because, apart from the scheduling of the processors which is handled by the operating system (see chapter 23), each CPU works in identical ways to those in a single-processor system.

Massively parallel architectures

At the end of the 1990s it's currently fashionable to build **supercomputers** by connecting together many powerful microprocessors in what's called a **massively-parallel processing** system. A typical example of this is the Cray T3E computer, whose massively parallel architecture is described in chapter 7. This particular machine has over 2048 Dec Alpha processors connected in parallel, each with six lines of communication to other processors in the system.

Bandwidth and the bus systems

What perhaps is not immediately obvious is the 'strain' imposed on the bus systems when being shared between many CPUs. *Any* **communication system** making use of physical wires, radio waves or fibre-optic links etc. will have physical limitations imposed on it by it's physical construction – i.e. the materials out of which it is made, and the electronics which is controlling it, for example. This is not a difficult concept to understand – your body has physical limitations imposed on it because of the way in which it is made. Your hearing, for example, can't pick up frequencies which are no problem for a dog or a bat – because they are built differently.

The **physical limitations** imposed on a typical bus system are measured in terms of the number of **bits/sec** that can be *transmitted along the bus* and is called its **bandwidth**. A bus system for a micro, for example, might be quoted as having a bandwidth of 50 Mbits per second. Now if each processor demands data at a rate of 10 Mbytes per second, then you have a problem. The CPUs are demanding $5 \times 10 = 50$ Mbytes/sec – which is eight times faster (1 byte is 8 bits) than this particular bus is able to handle, due to it's maximum-bandwidth limitation.

This problem can be reduced to some extent by transferring data from main memory into a fast **cache memory** (see chapter 12) – one for *each* **microprocessor**. In this way, many transfers of data between cache and CPU don't use the main bus at all. – until data needs to be moved from main memory to cache or vice versa. In this case this may not affect the other four CPUs which are hopefully using their own cache at this particular moment in time. However, if too many processors are added to the system, all sharing the same memory, then beyond a certain break-even point the processing ability of the system will actually go down!

Another way of increasing the bandwidth of a bus system is to increase the bus width. This is now being done in the most modern microprocessor-based systems, with 32 bit and 64 bit data busses now becoming the norm, and no doubt 128-bit data busses will be with us in the near future. As software becomes ever more demanding, and as the variety of plug-in boards such as real-time video processors, real-time sound processors and ever faster CD-ROM-based systems become common place, perhaps only multiple-processor architectures will be able to keep pace. The bus structures of such systems will also have to expand accordingly. Readers who are interested in investigating the detailed relationship between the bus systems and main memory should refer to chapter 12.

Multiple bus systems

Instead of building up a 128-bit bus to increase the bandwidth, two 64-bit busses, for example, might actually be better. Although this may not make too much sense at first sight, the better performance of the two separate 64-bit bus systems is due to the fact that in the 128-bit system, only a single bus can be used at any one time. If another processor wishes to get access to the bus, then it must wait until the current processor has finished using it. With the dual 64-bit bus system, two processors may access the bus simultaneously. Obviously extra memory management hardware would be needed so that the processor may switch between one bus system and the other according to which bus is not in use at the time. Figure 20.20 shows a four-processor triple-bus system, and includes connections to other bus systems via an intelligent communications controller.

As you can see from this diagram, multiprocessor-multibus systems with appropriate management hardware (and software) can be arranged to provide very significant increases in bandwidth and hence overall speed. However, such systems are currently quite expensive, and a system of the complexity shown in figure 20.20 would be found only in mini or mainframe computers, or in top-of-the-range workstations. Nevertheless, with the current price/performance characteristics being achieved, this probably means that such a system may be available inside a pocket calculator before the next edition of this book!

Other aids to increased speed

Data flow architectures

The natural conclusion to be drawn from parallel processing architectures is that problems may often be solved more efficiently *if* we split them up into smaller problems that can be solved in parallel. If we are to achieve this greater efficiency, then different approaches to the solution of problems present themselves. **Data flow architectures** are just one example of such techniques, and a simple example will be used to illustrate the thinking behind this type of processing. These ideas are similar in nature to the ideas involved when critical-path analysis is covered in chapter 14.

Example

Imagine working out the cost of decorating a living room having dimensions of length (l), width (w) and height (h). The walls are to be painted with paint costing 20p per square metre, and the ceiling is to be painted with paint costing 15p per square metre. Assuming that there are no doors or windows, the cost of the paint job will be:

$$Wall\ area = \frac{(2 \times h \times w) + (2 \times h \times l)}{100}$$

and $Ceiling\ area = l \times w$

Conventional sequential programs to solve the problem making use of a single processor might go along the following lines.

```
Begin
    W_Cost = 20 :Wall cost/m²
    C_Cost = 15 :Ceiling cost/m²
    Input(l,w,h)
    W_Area = (2*h*w) + (2*h*l)
```

Did you know that . . .

Some languages, like Fortran 90 and concurrent Pascal, for example, have been designed with multiple processors and parallel processing in mind. These languages have built in facilities to optimise the use of parallel processing.

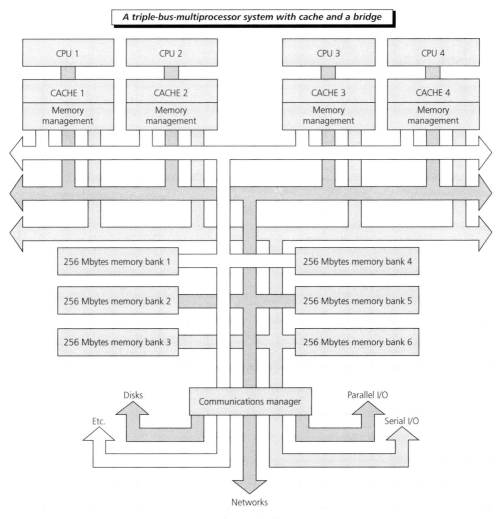

Figure 20.20

```
    C_Area = l*w
    Pence = W_Area * W_Cost + C_Area *
                                  C_Cost
    Cost = Pence/100
End
```

Now consider a **data flow** graph for the above problem. This is shown in Figure 20.21.

Notice from the above analysis of the problem that we have immediately split it up into three sub-problems – which consist of working out Temp_1, Temp_2 (temporary storage) and the ceiling area. **All three of these processes can be worked out simultaneously as the data for each part (l, w and h) is already available.** Separate processors can, therefore, work out these three operations at the same time.

You can see from the above how the data flow architecture gets its name – a data flow computation (such as W_Area = Temp_1 + Temp_2) can be carried out according to the data availability and resources (i.e. are there enough processors to carry out the required tasks?). The processors would actually be **dynamically**

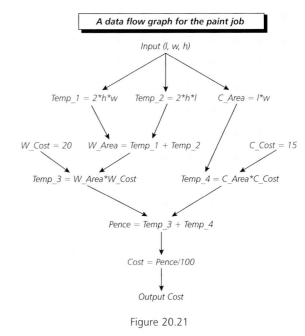

Figure 20.21

allocated – i.e. allocated as and when necessary. As you can see, this is a radical departure from the conventional architecture of the von-Neumann variety. Processors of this type are still under development, and work will probably go on for a considerable number of years to develop more powerful techniques.

There are five basic-flow nodes, which help to show the data-flow model at this level, and these are shown in figure 20.22.

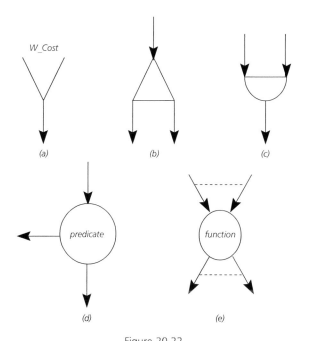

(a)   *(b)*   *(c)*

(d)   *(e)*

Figure 20.22

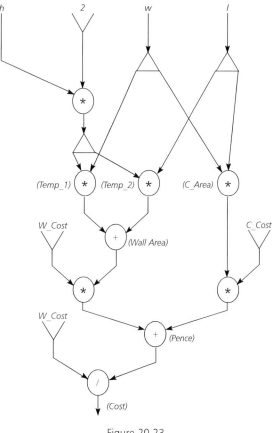

Figure 20.23

called a **predicate**. Finally, figure 20.22(e) shows a function node.

The 'decorating the room' problem is shown as a **data-flow** graph at **operation level** making use of these new symbols in figure 20.23.

There are other parallel-processing architectures under development, but a detailed analysis of them is beyond the scope of this book. However, one other architecture called a **neural network** is covered in chapter 9. This radically different approach is often used in **AI** (**artificial intelligence**) and pattern-recognition systems.

Figure 20.22(a) shows a **constant generator**, with W_Cost (wall cost) from the previous example. Figure 20.22(b) shows a **copy node**. This shows that the data generated by the previous node is copied directly to the next node or nodes. Figure 20.22(c) shows a **merge node**, where the first data to arrive is simply passed on. Figure 20.22(d) shows a **gate node**, where this input is passed on only if a condition is matched. This condition is usually expressed as a Boolean value and is

Exercise 20.2

1   What is meant by parallel processing and why is this exciting development leading to faster computers?

2   **Pipeline architectures** are currently used to increase the effective rate at which a microprocessor can fetch and execute instructions. Explain the principles of **pipelining** and show how this leads to an increased throughput under ideal conditions.

3   What problems are encountered when using **multiprocessor systems** when *compared to* conventional single-processor **architectures**?

4   Explain what is meant by the term **bandwidth** when applied to the bus systems inside computers. In what **units** is bandwidth normally measured?

5   Multiprocessor bus systems often have a bus structure with a lower bandwidth than would be needed for optimum continuous use by all of the processors. What *extra hardware* can be added to ensure that this apparently inefficient system can work well? How does this achieve its aim?

6   Name two ways of *increasing* the **bandwidth** capacity of a data bus.

7   Explain how problems may be split up for solution by using multiprocessor architectures. If the same problems are coded using conventional techniques, why might the performance of these parallel systems not be so impressive?

8   An advert regarding a particular microprocessor contains the following:

   (a) 256 k code cache

   (b) 256 k data cache

   (c) 128-bit bus

   (d) Superscalar dual-pipeline architecture

   (e) Inbuilt floating-point accelerator

   (f) 700MHz processor

   (g) Processing speeds of 1000 MIPS

   Write a paragraph about each of the above stating what is meant by this particular part of the advert, and how the use of such techniques makes this particular chip a powerful microprocessor in the late 1990s.

End of chapter revision aid and summary

Cover up the right-hand column and see if you can answer the questions or define the terms on the left They appear in the order in which they are covered in this chapter. Alternatively you may browse through the right-hand column to aid revision.

What is the device at the heart of a modern computer system?	The main device at the heart of a modern computer is called a microprocessor chip.
What is the CPU?	The term CPU (central processing unit) is an alternative to the term microprocessor in a simple microcomputer, but the CPU is also the term used for a much-larger processing unit on mainframe or mini computers.
What hardware components are needed for a simple microprocessor system?	A very simple microprocessor system would consist of a clock, the microprocessor itself, and some memory to store the program.
What function does the clock provide?	The clock provides the signals to instruct the microprocessor to go through the fetch-decode-execute or fetch-execute cycle.
In what units is the clock rate measured?	The clock rate is measured in Hz (cycles per second) – this dictates the speed at which the microprocessor is able to operate.
Where is the program stored?	The program, which controls the microprocessor, is stored in memory.
In what form is data stored in memory?	Memory chips store data as binary digits.

How is the data extracted from memory?	To get data into or out from the memory the data bus is used. The control bus is used to set the chip to a 'read' or 'write' operation.
What's used to carry the memory address?	To instruct the memory which location is to be used in the transfer of data, the address bus is used.
What is a bus?	A bus is simply the name given to a parallel group of wires, which are used to carry data. A large arrow is often used to represent these wires on a diagram.
How many ways can data travel along the address bus and data bus?	The address bus is one-way only, whereas the data bus is two way.
What is the name of the third bus?	A third bus, called the control bus, is used to carry the control signals such as the Read/Write line needed by the memory chip.
Name the two basic memory types.	Two types of memory are needed in most computer systems – RAM and ROM.
What is ROM?	ROM stands for Read Only Memory and is used to contain software such as the BIOS part of the operating system, for example.
What is RAM?	RAM can be used to store the user's programs after the computer has been switched on.
Is RAM volatile?	RAM is volatile – this means that the contents are lost when the power is removed.
Is ROM volatile?	ROM does not lose its contents when the power is removed – it is non-volatile.
What other devices are mapped onto the system as if they were memory?	Other devices such as disks, CD-ROM drives, printers, VDUs and keyboards etc. are mapped into the system as if they were memory. As far as the microprocessor is concerned these devices are identical to memory.
What is a memory map?	A memory map of the system is needed if we are to avoid inadvertently putting data where it does not belong.
What is a register?	A microprocessor contains special electronic circuits called registers, which are used as a temporary store in which to manipulate binary data.
What is the accumulator?	The accumulator is one of the main registers used to accumulate temporary results from various operations carried out by the microprocessor.
What is the control unit?	The control unit acts as an electronic manager which makes sure that all the data paths are set up at the correct moments in time.
What is the arithmetic logic unit?	The arithmetic logic unit (ALU) performs arithmetic and other operations on binary numbers, and puts the answer in the accumulator.
What is the program counter?	The program counter (PC) keeps track of the address of the next memory location from which the next byte of data is to be loaded (assuming that data is transferred in byte-sized chunks).
What is the current instruction register?	The current instruction register (CIR) keeps the binary pattern of the current instruction so that it can be analysed and decoded.
What is the memory data register?	The memory data register (MDR) keeps the binary pattern of the last data taken out of or put into memory.
What is the memory address register?	The memory address register (MAR) contains the address of the most recent memory access.

What does a microprocessor do at a fundamental level?	Data from memory is fetched, decoded and executed by the microprocessor. This is the sole function of the microprocessor – it can do nothing else.
What is special about the first part of the code fetched by a microprocessor?	The first byte of data in a program is assumed to be an instruction – if it's not, then the computer will probably go out of control and the program will produce unpredictable results.
How is the first instruction interpreted correctly?	It is up to the programmer of the system to make sure that the instructions are interpreted correctly. A single mistake is enough to cause a simple computer to crash.
Name some typical microprocessor instructions.	Microprocessors have very simple instructions like LOAD, ADD and STORE. The fact that they can carry out these simple operations at incredible speed gives computers their great power and versatility.
What is parallel processing?	Parallel processing is the ability of a computer system to undertake more than one task simultaneously.
What is needed to carry out parallel processing?	Using multiprocessors or special single-processor systems, such as pipeline and array processors, a system can carry out parallel processing.
What is a pipeline processor?	A pipeline processor is a system, which employs the simultaneous fetching, decoding and executing of different instructions.
What is an array processor?	An array processor can act on different elements in an array data structure simultaneously. It is also called a vector processor.
What is a multiprocessor system?	A multiprocessor system is one in which more than one main processor is used. Multiprocessor systems often use cache memory to reduce the activity on the main bus systems.
What is meant by bandwidth?	The bandwidth of a bus is its limitation in terms of the maximum number of bits/sec, which can be transmitted along the bus.
Why are multiple bus systems used?	Multiple-bus systems are used in high-end systems to increase the effective bandwidth of the bus.
What extra devices might be present in some microprocessor systems?	Extra devices such as maths co-processors, I/O co-processors and network co-processors increase the efficiency of specialised parts of the overall system.
What is data-flow architecture?	Data flow architectures are useful for splitting up problems such that parallel processors can solve them.

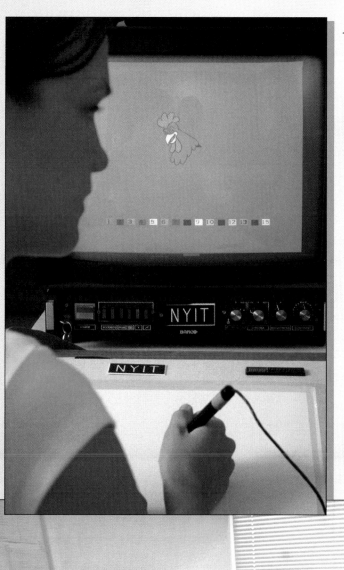

◀ **Plate 22**
A cartoonist drawing onto the computer using a graphics tablet. This is considered to be a more natural form of computer input for artists than the mouse

▼ **Plate 23**
The concept keyboard has many different uses. Here a technician is making use of a concept keyboard to help control the Burgon oil field in Kuwait

▲ Plate 24 ▲
The Relate 2000 videophone system (left) is a miracle of
technology that enables users to transmit and receive video
images over a conventional phone line. Compare this
system with videoconferencing using a computer (right)

Plate 25 ▶
An office in which the computers are
equipped with desk-top video and are
being used to communicate via
windows and the Internet. Other
information besides coloured video
images can be sent simultaneously

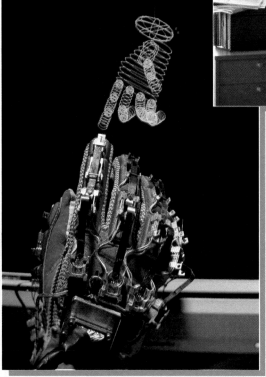

◀ Plate 26
A complex data glove. Note the
mass of sensors that detect the
position of the fingers inside the
glove and the computer-generated
virtual hand in the background
which mimics the movements
made by the wearer of the glove

21 Assembly Language

Key resources

To carry out this work most successfully it's best if you have:

◆ Access to an assembler for your computer system

Concept checkpoints

◆ It's essential that you have read and understood the work in the first half of chapter 20.

◆ Some of the more complex sections in this chapter require a knowledge of the work covered in chapter 30. You may want to tackle this work on a second reading.

Introduction

One of the most fascinating things about computers is that no matter how complex they become, or how much apparent intelligence they may exhibit, everything inside them eventually gets boiled down to binary digits. The principles of how to control these ingeniously designed machines at this most basic level are now covered.

From reading chapter 20 on 'Low level languages and machine architecture' you should already be able to appreciate how a microprocessor can be used to cycle through a sequence of simple instructions called a program. From reading chapter 2 you should also appreciate how the binary system can be used as code to represent data in different forms. Binary is considered in much more detail in chapters 30 and 31.

A low-level language is the language of a particular processor. It is the code for a particular machine (computer), and is therefore given the name machine code. In this chapter we will, therefore, deal with the binary codes (called machine code) used by microprocessors to carry out operations at machine-architecture level.

To prevent insanity on the part of the people who program at this low level, different mnemonics (aids to the memory) are used to represent the different binary patterns for each machine-code instruction. When using mnemonics instead of the pure machine code, this method of programming is called assembly language programming. Few people these days program directly in machine code, as assembly language achieves almost identical results with less effort and far less frustration.

Although a few parts of this section might be heavy going for some students, it is this work which will enable you to understand the computer at a most fundamental level. It is knowledge of this chapter, which overcomes the view, held by the general public that a computer is a strange box that they can sometimes use, but never completely understand. It has been said, 'Any sufficiently-advanced technology is indistinguishable from magic.' This chapter will enable you to look beyond what's happening on the outside of the computer, and help you to gain an insight into the fascinating micro world happening at incredible speed inside modern microprocessor-controlled systems. It's also not only the key to understanding modern computers, but the key to understanding embedded systems (see chapter 8) such as those found in video recorders, the ABS systems on cars, robot-controlled production lines in automated factories and many other control applications.

Introduction to microprocessors

To appreciate the importance of programming in a low-level language we need to look in a little more detail at some real-life microprocessor examples. It is only by doing this that you will gain an appreciation of why things are the way they are, and gain an insight into what's likely to be happening in the future.

Since the 1970s chip manufacturers have been coming up with ever more complex **microprocessors** as the technology to build these devices gets more sophisticated. Most manufacturers are obviously in competition with each other, so they try to make sure that their particular family of microprocessors becomes the most popular. Intel, for example, produce a range of microprocessors which are the current standard inside most IBM PCs and PC compatibles, and Motorola produce a series of microprocessors which are used at the heart of the Apple Mac. Other companies, such as ARM Ltd (now also owned by Intel), produce RISC processors, which are successful in Acorn's machines.

The obvious major problem with the above situation is that *all of these microprocessors are totally incompatible with each other*. **Low-level-language** software written for one type of processor will *not* work with another. **High-level language** software is not supposed to have this problem because of portability (see chapter 15), but in practice there are *many* problems, mainly due to the **operating systems** (see chapter 22) used by each type of machine. For example, the windows-based operating systems on the three main families of machine mentioned above all behave in very different ways. The term **platform** is often used when referring to a particular series of microprocessor hardware or operating system software. Therefore, you may hear terms like the Intel platform or a Unix (another popular operating system) platform.

Powerful emulation facilities

As each microprocessor becomes more powerful, other possibilities exist to overcome these incompatibility problems. Some computer manufacturers are at last getting together to develop **multi-platform machines** which will enable the *same hardware* to run *software originally designed for other machines*. For example, IBM, Apple and Motorola have developed the Power PC and Power Mac, which are in direct competition with Intel's Pentium, but with the advantage of being able to run IBM compatible and Apple Mac software on the same machine. Obviously the 'Holy Grail' of microprocessor technology would be to develop a system which is so powerful that it could emulate any other machine, but billions of dollars are at stake, and this Utopian image is unlikely to exist in the near future.

Future compatibility?

Each individual family of microprocessor attempts to be downwards compatible with the *same* family of microprocessors that has gone before. **For** example, Intel's range of processors at the time of writing consists

of the 8086/88, 80186, 80286, 80386, 80486 and different versions of the Pentium (80586). Any low-level software, which runs on the earlier processors, is supposed to run on all versions of the later processors. Unfortunately, it is this highly laudable aim which is proving to be the thorn in the flesh of many future developments. For example, if the latest microprocessor is to be compatible with the original microprocessor in the family, then the latest version of the microprocessor will probably have to do some things in ways that may not make the best use of the current technology. This is one of the reasons why the design of such processors is becoming increasingly complex. Nevertheless, the alternative would be to instruct tens of millions of people with the earlier computer systems that they must now throw them away because the latest computers won't run the software – they would have to start again from scratch. This is not a situation that would be acceptable in many business environments, especially when one considers the enormous task of transferring the company data over to the new system when the old ones are working perfectly adequately on their current tasks.

Did you know that . . .

It takes many millions of pounds to develop a new microprocessor system. As the processors themselves get more powerful, new factories sometimes have to be built to provide the technology to make the innards of these chips smaller and smaller. It is a very high-risk business, but the financial rewards are enormous (see Plate 38).

For the immediate future we are therefore stuck with a range of different types of microprocessors and operating systems, which make compatibility between different machines a nightmare. It is therefore fortunate for us that *every microprocessor does have much in common with others* in terms of the fundamental ways in which these devices can be programmed. If this were not the case then low-level-language programmers would have to learn how to program again from scratch each time they encountered a different platform! It is to this common base of knowledge that we must now turn for the rest of the chapter, and we will now look at the basic principles of machine code and assembly-language programming.

The common features

Each microprocessor has an **internal architecture** that is unique, but fortunately *all* have *common principles* which can be used to understand microprocessor systems in general. For example, each microprocessor has what's called an **instruction set**. This is simply the set of instructions, which can be understood by a particular microprocessor chip. These instructions may include some complex ones as is the case with **CISC processors**, or the instructions might be kept as simple as possible to speed up execution time, as is the case with **RISC processors**.

Basic principles

The set of instructions for each microprocessor will be different, but there are many subsets, which are common to all. For example, a logical AND will carry out the same function within different microprocessors, even though the actual machine code is almost certainly different for each machine. Therefore, we can study these common subsets and principles to gain an understanding of how modern microprocessors may be programmed, using specific examples to illustrate these more general concepts.

Instruction sets and mnemonics

Each instruction in the set is usually given a name that acts as a mnemonic. Some mnemonics, taken from a typical set are shown in the following table.

Menmonic	Function performed	M/c code
MOV	Move data	100010...
AND	Logical AND	001000...
ARPL	Adjust Requested Privilege Level	01100011...
XCHG	Exchange	1000011...

Each **mnemonic** which represents the **assembly language** (and hence the machine code) **instruction** is literally an **aid to the memory** – the function carried out by each instruction relates to the mnemonic. The start of the machine code (binary 1s and 0s) is also shown in the last column of the table. These **codes** are chosen by the manufacturer for this particular chip to represent these particular instructions. These **binary** (or, more conveniently – **hex**) numbers are called **Operation Codes** or **Op Codes** for short. Each instruction has a unique Op Code. All the Op Codes are not shown for each of the above instructions because the final few digits of the code often relate to the context in which a particular instruction is being used.

Most programming at **low level** involves tasks like 'getting data from memory' in binary form, and 'manipulating the data' in various ways before using it to control hardware connected to the microprocessor chip. Therefore, *the microprocessor is able to perform basic operations on the binary data.* For example, these might be arithmetical operations such as those carried out in chapter 30, logical operations such as 'AND' and 'OR' (see later), or checking to see if a number

has become too big or too small for the system to use. Checking special bits called flags does this (see later).

Internal registers

Inside each microprocessor chip there are special *electronic circuits* called **registers**, which act as a **temporary storage** for the data which is currently being processed. In general, the more modern microprocessor chips have greater quantities of larger-size registers

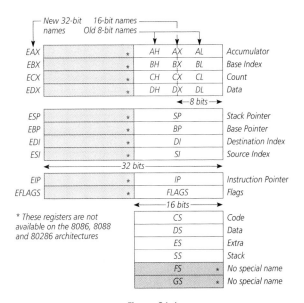

Figure 21.1

than the early versions, but the principles are the same. The Intel 80x86 range of chips, for example, operate on the register model or register set shown in figure 21.1

At first sight, register sets like these may appear to be a little daunting for the beginner. However, think for a moment about the role played by the register set. Quite simply it's just a lot of different places into which binary digits can be placed temporarily ready for processing, or a lot of places to store the results after the binary digits have been processed. Viewed in this light the principles are extremely simple – in fact, laying out the registers in an orderly manner as shown in this diagram simplifies things tremendously, because we now have a *mental model* of the registers for this particular range of microprocessor chips.

All the chip manufacturers provide diagrams similar to the above which helps programmers to appreciate the functions which each register can perform. If you look at a few different register-set diagrams you will soon start to see that concepts such as **accumulators**, **flags**, **stack pointers** and **program counters** (called an **instruction pointer** in the above diagram) etc. are common to *most* microprocessor chips.

General-purpose register sets

Many modern 32-bit and 64-bit microprocessors have more general-purpose register sets. For example, the ARM series used in Acorn's machines have fifteen general-purpose registers plus a program counter. The Motorola 68000 chips have general-purpose data and address registers with a program counter, stack pointer and a condition-code register. Although apparently very different from the more-specialised nature of the Intel chip register set, assembly language programming principles are similar on all of these different devices.

There are usually other registers inside most microprocessors, but they are often invisible to the programmer. These registers help the microprocessor with its internal organisation and will therefore not be considered in a chapter that is concerned mainly with assembly-language programming.

Notice that when the Intel range of chips is considered, downward compatibility has been maintained with the older chips in the series by keeping the old registers as parts of the new ones. The new chips still have an accumulator – it's just that it can now hold more bits than the old accumulator could. Indeed, apart from some special-purpose registers, 'size of registers' is one of the main differences between the older microprocessors and the new. Radically different architectures (see chapter 20) can also make an enormous difference to the processing speeds, but the *principles* of **assembly-language programming** are common on most modern microprocessor systems, be it RISC, CISC, 64-bit or 16-bit. In fact, the early 8-bit micros are generally more difficult to program because of the lack of many of the basic facilities now taken for granted on the more-modern chips.

Memory size and bus systems

In addition to the internal microprocessor architecture, an important feature of modern microprocessor design is the amount of **memory** that can be **addressed** by the processor, and the amount of **data** that can be moved along the **bus system** *at the same time*. The first practical microprocessors for use in computer systems were of the 8-bit variety (the earlier 4-bit micros were so limited that they were not a practical proposition). Then came the 16-bit, and currently we have the 32-bit and 64-bit

microprocessors. No doubt 128-bit and 256-bit microprocessors will be with us at some time in the future.

The **external address bus** size (see chapter 12) determines the amount of **physical memory** which a processor can address. A processor with a 32-bit address bus, for example, will be able to address $2^{32} = 4$ Gbytes (4,294,967,296 bytes) of RAM. Compare this with the older 16-bit address bus which could only manage $2^{16} = 64$ Kbytes (65,536 bytes) of RAM. The current generation of Pentium and PowerPC microprocessor chips have a 64-bit external address bus, and the top-of-the-range MPC620 chip has a 64-bit data bus too.

The **external data bus** is equally important as its size relates to the number of bytes that can be sent along it simultaneously, and therefore to the speed with which the data can be transferred from memory to the processor and back again. If a 32-bit data bus is used then data can be transferred 4 bytes at a time. If the accumulator inside the microprocessor is 32 bits wide, then these four bytes of data may be processed at the same time if this is desirable and sensible in the context of what the data represents.

The word **external** is important here as this refers to the connections coming out of or going into the chip. The **internal address busses** and **data busses** *inside* the microprocessors are often of larger size to facilitate super-fast data transfer speeds. For example, the Motorola MP601 PowerPC chip has internal data-bus widths ranging from 32 bits to 256 bits wide.

Memory organisation

As can be seen from the chapter on storage (see chapter 12), memory can be organised in a variety of ways. With an 8-bit data bus one had little alternative but to set up the memory in byte-sized chunks. However, with the advent of the larger data-bus systems as described above, we can now organise memory such that each location is bigger – 16 or 32 bits, for example. This refers to the **word length** for a particular microprocessor system. Even so, memory is still usually quoted in bytes, irrespective of the physical organisation and bus structure. One reason for this is that it's easier to compare memory size if everything is quoted in bytes – it also sounds good in the sales literature as larger numbers are encountered and the public apparently get more memory for their bucks – 64 Mbytes sounds better than 32 MWords of memory!

Basic assembly-language principles

Before looking at basic concepts such as 'modes of addressing' and 'splitting up the instruction set into suitable subsets', we need to look at a typical format for an assembly-language instruction.

Instruction formats

You will recall that the *whole point of* assembly language *is to give the microprocessor instructions to perform manipulations on groups of binary digits.* Suppose, therefore, for the sake of argument, we wish to **MOVE** the 16 bits of data contained in the **Base-indeX** register (the **BX** register) in figure 21.1, into the **accumulator** (the AX register). To carry out this particular move is simple.

    MOV AX, BX

Did you know that . . .

Companies such as AMD, Cyrix and IBM are now breaking into the Pentium-dominated PC market. There's also still ample opportunity to develop microprocessors for other applications, namely network computers, Internet TVs and a whole range of domestic and office equipment, for example.

In this particular instruction the source of the data (contained in the BX register) is MOVED (copied actually!) into the destination which is the AX register. If only it was as simple as this – well it is actually, in principle! In fact, the more general form of an assembly language instruction has *four parts* and is expressed as follows:

Label Field	Op Code	Operand/s	Comments
	(Mnemonic)	(Address field)	

Therefore, if we were to put a label at the front of our example instruction and then add a comment, the simple **MOV AX, BX** instruction might look something like

    START: MOV   AX, BX ;This is a comment

The **label field** is *optional*, and is used only for identification purposes or as a place to which program execution may jump, for example. The **comments** are also *optional*, and are totally ignored when the code is **assembled** – changed into machine code ready to be run on the computer (see later). In fact only the **Op Code**, **which is represented here by the mnemonic**, is compulsory but *most* instructions have some **operands** in the **address field**.

To get the flavour of some typical instructions, several different ones are contained in the following short extract from a real 80x86 assembly-language program.

    PUSH   AX
    MOV   AX, WORD PTR a1[2]
    XOR   AX, a2
    POP   AX
    PUSHF

No matter which microprocessor is used, we can split up the instruction set into basic subsets, with most microprocessors having very similar types of instruction subsets. The 80x86 family of microprocessors being considered here, for example, has subsets consisting of **data transfer**, **arithmetic operations**, **bit manipulation**, **string operations**, **program transfer** and **processor control** instructions. Some of these types of instruction will be looked at in detail, but first it's important to understand another concept fundamental to all assembly language programming – that of different addressing modes.

Modes of addressing

Different addressing modes are not difficult to understand – they refer simply to the *different ways in which the microprocessor is allowed to calculate and process the addresses* which represent the source and/or destination for the data. These concepts should become obvious after reading the following few sections.

Register addressing

We have just seen one mode of addressing demonstrated when the contents of the BX register were transferred to the accumulator (the AX register). On the Intel 80 × 86 range of microprocessors, this type of addressing is called **register addressing** because the data is transferred from a *source register* to a *destination register*. The idea using this specific example with 32-bit registers is shown in figure 21.2. Well – that's register addressing done! It's not possible to transfer any register to any other, but further information like this can be found in an appropriate assembly-language guide if you need to go into this amount of detail.

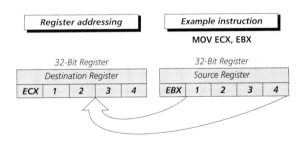

Figure 21.2

Immediate addressing

Immediate addressing is also simple. It refers to the situation where the *data* to be used is stored **immediately** after the **Op Code** for the instruction, i.e. the **operand field** *actually contains the data to be transferred.* Consider the MOV instruction again. If, for example, the hex number 1234H is to be stored in the 16-bit accumulator (AX), then 1234H follows immediately after the 'MOV AX,' part of the instruction. Therefore, as shown in figure 21.3, we end up with the immediate-addressing-mode instruction MOV AX, 1234H. Note that

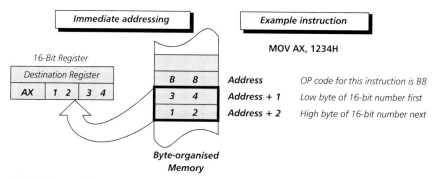

NOTE: 80 × 86 needs Low byte (AL) followed by High byte (AH)

Figure 21.3

> **Hint:** If you intend to write your own assembly language programs, then it's essential that you get to grips with all the different addressing modes which are available. Once you are over this initial hurdle, the task of writing assembly language programs becomes simpler.

two bytes are needed in memory to store 16-bits as shown in the diagram.

If you looked up the actual Op Code for 'MOV AX', you would find that it's 'B8', therefore, 'B83412' is shown for this particular example in the memory locations shown in figure 21.3. Note that the 80 × 86 microprocessor requires that the order of the bytes be swapped from what might seem to be the most logical order. You will find that most microprocessors have some little quirks of this sort! Assembly language programmers just have to get used to them. After execution of this particular instruction the data which immediately follows the Op Code is transferred into the (AX) accumulator. This method is ideal for getting constant numbers into the accumulator very quickly, and with a minimum amount of memory taken up by the Op Code itself. In chapter 8, when real-time operating systems are being considered, you will see that speed and efficiency of programming are often critical.

Direct addressing

This mode of addressing refers **directly** to a **memory address** and is able to transfer data between this memory location and a register. **Direct addressing** is also often called **memory addressing**. The idea is shown in figure 21.4.

Here the 16-bit number contained *inside the memory locations called 'Address'* is transferred **directly** from the **memory** into the accumulator. Note that we have made use of a **symbolic address** here in the example instruction that is given the name 'Address'. We could have specified the exact address (using hex numbers) of the memory location if we wished, but it is usually very bad practice to do so as we will see later. Note also that the Op Code does not have to be anywhere near the actual address in this case. Therefore, this particular mode of addressing allows you to store data away from the guts of the program details. However, the Op Code for this particular instruction is much longer than that of the immediate-mode-addressing instruction (look it up in an assembly-language manual if you are interested) and would therefore take up more memory. This might be important if you were trying to fit a very small program into an embedded system (see chapter 8), for example.

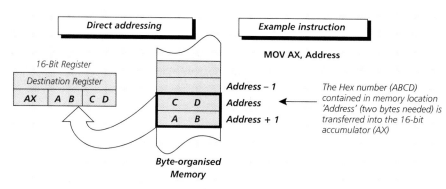

Figure 21.4

You should now start to begin to appreciate the need for different types of addressing modes – some impose restrictions but are more efficient in terms of storage and speed, and others enable you to access data in different ways. In the next section you will begin to see the power and versatility of different addressing modes.

Indirect addressing

This is the first addressing mode to make use of another register to help specify from where the data is to be transferred. In the 80 × 86 microprocessor, there are several registers which can be used for this purpose, but we will illustrate this type of addressing by making use of the **BX** (**base index**) register as shown in figure 21.5. Used in this way, this mode of addressing is called **register indirect addressing**. Here the content of the BX register is a number called 'Address'. The number inside the BX register is used to *point* to the memory location 'Address' from which the data can be found and loaded into the accumulator.

Budding 80 × 86 programmers should note that the DS (data segment) register would also be involved in this calculation. However, it has not been used in this example because it obscures the simplicity of this addressing mode. It does not matter in practice how many registers might be involved in the actual calculation, as long as you know which ones they are and take this into account. You will recall that all microprocessors are very different, and this is just another example of the type of difference, which ensures that all machine code is unique.

Indexed addressing

Indexed addressing is where a number, usually held inside an index register, is used in combination with an existing address to determine the final address to be accessed. This sounds a mouthful but is really very simple too. The idea is shown in figure 21.6. The number in the BX register is added to the number in the DI register to produce the actual address that contains the number to be put in the CX register. This method is ideal for accessing numbers stored in an array. The base-index register can be used for the **row address** and the destination index register can be used for the **column address**, for example. The idea is shown in figure 21.7. For simplicity, only a single dimensional array is shown. Two-dimensional arrays can be built up by altering the value of the base-index register to point at the memory location in which the next column of numbers would start. As before, 80 × 86 programmers should note that the DS register would also be used in practice for the calculation of the final address.

Notice how we are just starting to build up useful methods for accessing different **data structures** (see chapter 24). Using assembly-language instructions, other structures such as **queues**, **stacks** and different types of **trees**, for example, may also be built up in similar ways.

Other addressing modes

The **addressing modes** mentioned above are the *most common*. Indeed, most other addressing modes, if they exist on a particular processor, are combinations of the basic addressing modes covered on the last few pages. Any new and powerful processor will probably have a few unique modes of addressing – for example, on the 32-bit 80 × 86 range of processors there is a scaled-index-addressing mode. These new modes usually mean that the low-level language programmer will be able to do things more simply than would have been the case with the older microprocessors. Indeed, on the new processors, much can now be achieved by more-powerful addressing modes, which hitherto would have needed many lines of assembly language programming to achieve similar results.

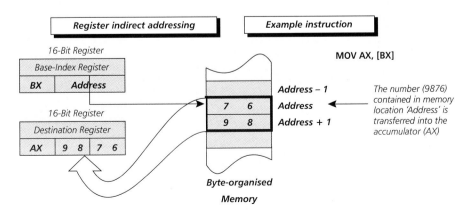

NOTE: *In practice the Data Segment register would also alter the address when using the 80 × 86 machine. It has been left out for the sake of simplicity.*

Figure 21.5

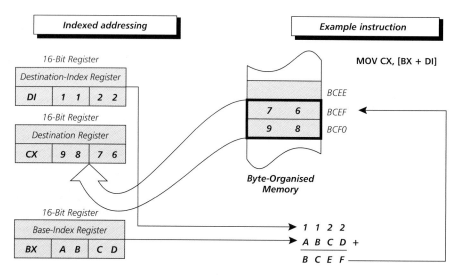

The number in the Base-Index register is combined with the number in the Destination-Index register to provide the Address of the number to be loaded into the CX register.

NOTE:
In practice the Data Segment register would also alter the address when using the 80 × 86 machine. It has been left out for the sake of simplicity.

Figure 21.6

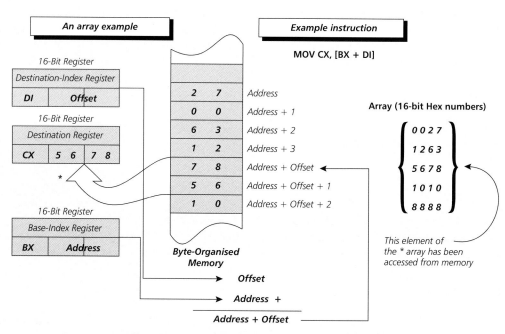

(**NOTE:** *Principles only here – 80 × 86 programmers, read the notes in the text regarding the DS register*)

Figure 21.7

In practice, some microprocessors have several different modes of operation. This often modifies the actual addressing modes by the further addition of offsets etc. We have not introduced these added complications when considering the simple modes of addressing in this chapter. For the purposes of computer science at advanced or equivalent level – an understanding of the basic addressing modes outlined in this section is all that is necessary. Any other useful addressing modes for particular processors can be learnt and used in your practical work if needed.

Other important registers

As can be seen from figure 21.1, inside a microprocessor there are usually some special registers dedicated to particular tasks which help the low-level-language programmer considerably. For example, it is possible to alert the program when certain conditions arise such as an **overflow** or a **carry** etc. (see chapter 31). Each condition may be **flagged** by the processor, either by *setting* (making the digit = 1) or *resetting* (making the digit = 0) different digits *within this register*. A special register used for this purpose is usually called a **flag register** or a **status register**. Part of the 32-bit flag register for the 80386 and 80486 processors is shown in figure 21.8.

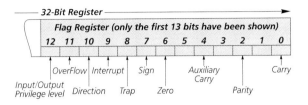

Figure 21.8

Different assembly-language instructions can be used to check the condition of the flag register, and other instructions may be used to set or reset some of the flags. If, for example, the carry flag has been set because of the result from some particular arithmetic operation, then

CLC   ;This clears the Carry flag

is the assembly language instruction (with a comment thrown in for free) that would reset bit 0 of the flag register.

Basic assembly-language instructions

Assembly language programming often involves carrying out operations like those described in the last sections, and then sending control to different routines depending on the results of the various flags. We will now take a more-detailed look at some typical assembly-language-instruction subsets, and look at some typical operations, which can be carried out by each of the subsets.

Arithmetical operations

Typical operations are obviously **addition, subtraction, multiplication** and **division**. However, as you will see from chapters 30 and 31, operations of this sort are not necessarily trivial. Typical instructions for the 80×86-microprocessor set would be as follows.

ADD AL, BL	;Add BL to AL and store result in AL
SUB AX, SP	;Subtract SP from AX and store result in AX
MUL BL	;AL is multiplied by BL and the result stored in AX (Note: AX is double the width of AL & BL).
DIV CX	;The DX-AX register pair is divided by CX with the quotient being placed in AX and the remainder being placed in DX

The above simple subset is just a fraction of the available ADD, SUB, MUL and DIV commands. The complexity of the operation depends on what is being done – for example, when dividing two numbers there will probably be an integer answer and a remainder. When multiplying two numbers the register length needed for the result is much larger than the register lengths that hold the original numbers. Other factors, including the base used, coding methods, and whether 8, 16 or 32-bit numbers are needed further complicate the issues. Besides being able to do arithmetic on decimal, binary, and hex numbers, modern microprocessors often allow you to do arithmetic in BCD (see chapter 30) too.

Logical operations

The logical operations include **AND, OR, NOT** and **XOR** etc. These instructions operate in what's called **bitwise mode**. This means that each bit of a register is matched against the equivalent bit in another register when the operation is being carried out. For example, consider the AND operation using two 8-bit registers. The idea is shown in figure 21.9.

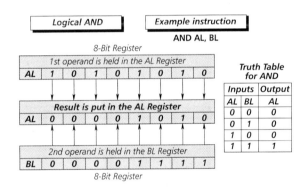

Figure 21.9

The truth table for a two-input AND function is shown at the right-hand side of this diagram. Applying these rules to each bit in the AL and BL registers, produces the result shown in the AL registers in the centre of the diagram. It can be seen from figure 21.9, the original contents of the AL register (one of the operands) is overwritten by the answer, which is placed in the same register.

The logical OR operation is also simple and is shown in figure 21.10.

> **Hint:** If it seems daunting to work out how such esoteric instructions might be used to do anything useful, refer to a book of assembly language routines. You will obviously have to get a specialised book for your particular processor, but most processors have at least one book that is suitable.

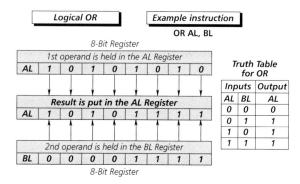

Figure 21.10

Masking

Note that the bit patterns above have *not* been chosen at random, but to illustrate an important concept in computing called **masking**. When using the logical 'AND' and 'OR' functions, we can create a **mask** which either lets a pattern of bits through, or blocks it with either 1s or 0s. Consider the *contents* of the **AL register** to be the *original pattern*, and the contents of the **BL register** to be the **mask**. The 'AND function' has let the bottom four bits 'through', and reset the top four bits, whereas the OR function has let the top four bits of the original pattern 'through' and blocked off the bottom four bits by setting them all to 1s. Masking is also used extensively in assembly language to set or reset bits without altering the patterns of other bits.

The XOR (Exclusive OR) function is shown in figure 21.11. This function is particularly useful as a check to see if all the corresponding bits in two different registers are the same or different. If the corresponding bits in AL and BL are the same, for example, then the resulting bit is reset, but if the corresponding bits in AL and BL are different then the resulting bit is set.

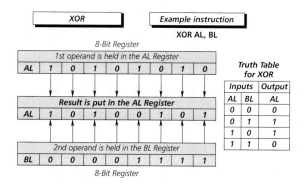

Figure 21.11

A register's contents can be negated (or inverted) by the use of the NOT function. This will change all the 0s to 1s and all the 1s to 0s. Therefore, this is one way of finding the one's complement of a number (see chapter

30). Also, if we wish to find the two's complement of a number then we can invert it and add 1 – you will see from chapter 30 that this is one method of finding the two's complement of a binary number. However, in the 80x86 range of processors, there is a NEG operation which combines these two processes into one, and thus finds the two's complement straight away.

The idea of the NOT function is extremely simple and is shown in figure 21.12.

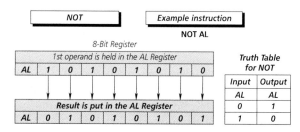

Figure 21.12

Logical shift operations

A **logical shift** instruction shifts (**moves**) each binary digit *left* or *right* and *fills up the vacating spaces with zeros*. The idea for a logical shift left is shown in figure 21.13.

A **logical shift right** is very simple too, and is shown in figure 21.14. Notice that a **carry flag** (i.e. *bit 0* of the **flag register** for the 80 × 86 processor) shown in both of these diagrams acts as a **buffer** to look at the last bit that's 'fallen off' the end.

> **Hint:** One useful way to learn assembly language programming is to work through programs that other people have written. Don't choose large ones to start with, choose the simpler well-documented routines which are only ten or twenty lines long.

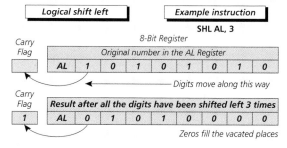

Figure 21.13

Arithmetical shift operations

There are also **arithmetic shift** instructions. These are useful for **multiplication** or **division** by *powers of two*. The arithmetic implications of these instructions, although simple in concept, need a little more thought.

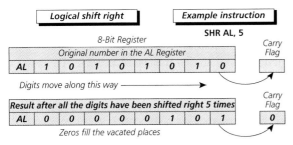

Figure 21.14

Take, for example, the number shown in the 8-bit AL register in figure 21.15.

This number is the 8-bit two's complement representation of −4 (see chapter 30). The instruction SAL AL, 2 will shift all the digits left by two places – thus having the effect of multiplication by 4 (2^2). Analyse the resulting number pattern after this operation and you will find that indeed, we have the correct 8-bit twos complement representation for −16, (the answer to −4 × 4). Therefore, an **arithmetic-shift-left** instruction is ideal for **multiplication of binary numbers** by powers of two. However, as is explained in just a moment, you must be careful to restrict the range, or the register will *not* be able to hold the appropriate information to give the correct answer.

A similar analysis with positive numbers will reveal that this method works too – again, as long as you don't go too far and exceed the range of twos-complement numbers that an 8-bit register can hold. Using an 8-bit register such as the AL register described above, would produce errors outside the range −128 to +127. It is up to the assembly-language programmer to use appropriate length registers, and to check, by an analysis of the flag register, if anything has exceeded the appropriate range.

From an analysis of the above you will see that for **arithmetic left shifts** *only*, there is *absolutely no difference whatsoever* to a **logical shift left**. Indeed, although most assemblers provide instructions like SAL shown above, there is usually no difference between the logical (SHL) and arithmetic (SAL) shift left instructions.

The **shift arithmetic right** instruction *is* different as *preservation of the sign bit* is necessary to maintain the correct answers for numbers within the appropriate range. Figure 21.16 shows

> **Hint:** Because of the specialist nature of many assembly language programs, the level of documentation you need to supply is quite large. A well commented program is all very well, but most people would need an overall plan too. Without this, few people will understand what you're trying to do.

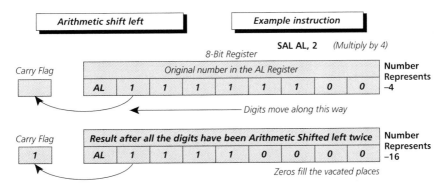

Figure 21.15

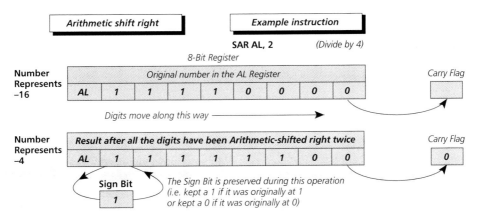

Figure 21.16

a typical example where −16 is shifted right two places, and therefore has the effect of division by 4 (2^{-2}).

You will notice that without provision for maintenance of the sign bit the two's complement representation of the number would change from being negative to being positive – thus giving the wrong answer, even though the length of the register is perfectly capable of storing this number.

Rotate instructions

Rotate instructions have several uses, the most important being that it enables the assembly-language programmer to look at numbers which are too big to be contained in a single register – as some microprocessors allow you to rotate register pairs. This scenario still applies even if the larger 32-bit registers being considered earlier in this chapter are used. An example using a 'rotate right 4-bits' instruction is shown in figure 21.17. Instead of the digits 'falling off' the end, they are directed round the path shown by the arrows and re-directed into the other end of the register.

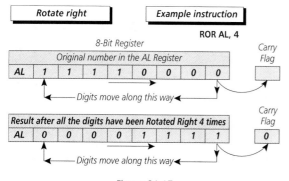

Figure 21.17

Note that the carry flag in figure 21.17 is acting as a copy of the last digit to be shifted round from the end. However, there may be some instructions available in which the carry flag acts as a 1-bit extension to the register itself. Nevertheless, the ideas associated with the rotate instruction are quite simple to understand, and we will therefore not bother with showing the rotate-left instruction format.

Bit set and reset instructions

This useful subset of instructions allows the assembly-language programmer to **set** or **reset** the contents of **registers** or **memory locations** depending on certain conditions, usually associated with the carry flag, for example. Consider the following example taken from the 80386/80486 assembly-language instruction set.

SETNO   Data   ;SET contents of the memory location labelled Data if there is NO overflow (i.e. O = 0)

When programming in assembly language you will quickly realise that the contents of the flag register will change very rapidly, probably after the execution of each instruction! Therefore, this method could provide a convenient means of storing the result at some particular instant in time, perhaps ready for later analysis. In the above case, this would mean that the memory location labelled 'Data' would have the number 01H stored in it if no overflow had occurred, or the number 00H stored in it if there was an overflow at the time the sample was taken.

You may also need to set or reset some bits inside a register at any point in time. For example, if the carry flag has been set as the result of some particular operation, then CLC is usually the instruction to clear (reset) it.

Program control instructions

For some of the time a typical assembly language program will be executed **sequentially**. This means that each instruction, one after the other, is repeatedly loaded, decoded and then executed, as was the case when discussing the simple BORIS microprocessor considered in chapter 20. Nevertheless, there are many cases where we need to control programs in much more sophisticated ways than this, and instructions are therefore needed to divert the flow of the program to different parts depending on the state of some particular condition. These essential and important assembly-language instructions are known as the **JUMP** instructions. There are many different types of JUMP instructions and a few of the more-common types are covered in this section.

Unconditional jumps

This type of instruction *forces program control* to move to some other part of the memory unconditionally. The idea is quite simple and is shown in figure 21.18. Although physically possible, it's not usually good practice to specify an absolute value for the address of a particular memory location – it is far better to use a label instead. This practice usually enables us to relocate the code more easily (i.e. run it in any part of the memory). **Non-relocatable code** is usually not a good idea because of the *lack of transferability* of the software when run on machines with different memory maps.

Conditional jumps

Many different types of jump commands are usually available, and this variety stems from the multitude of ways in which most microprocessors can **address** *different areas of memory*, and the **conditions** which apply as to whether or not the jump is made. It would take up too much space to demonstrate them all, but it's important to appreciate some typical jump conditions. You

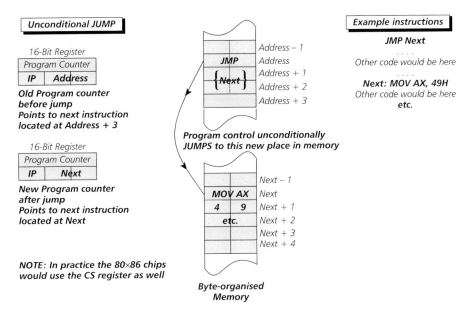

Figure 21.18

will recall that a flag register exists to flag different conditions happening inside the processors, so it's not surprising, therefore, to find that the flag register plays a pivotal role in helping to decide if jumps are to take place. Therefore, conditions like – 'jump if no overflow' or 'jump if carry set', for example, are typical of the types of conditions which may be used. Some of the jumps for the 80 × 86 range of processors are shown in the following list.

JNO	Next	;Jump if No Overflow (i.e. the O flag = 0)
JS	Next	;Jump on Sign bit = 1 (i.e. S = 1)
JCXZ	Next	;Jump if the CX flag = Zero (i.e. CX = 0)

The actual distance over which the jump may take place depends on how many bytes are used to hold the jump address. For example, if 1 byte is used, then a jump between +127 or –128 with respect to the current location could be made. However, if a 2-byte address is used, then we can go to +32,767 or –32,768. (See chapter 30 if this seems confusing.) Four bytes would be needed to cover the full 4 G Byte range possible on a microprocessor with a 32-bit address bus.

Stack operations

A **stack** is just one example of the *many* important **data structures** (see chapter 24) which are particularly useful in assembly-language programming. It's being covered here because of its importance in enabling you to understand how **control** may be *passed backwards and forwards between many different assembly-language routines*. It is the last major assembly-language concept to be considered in this chapter before going on to look at a real-life example.

The examples given in this section will not use an actual microprocessor, and will not bother with the added complications of memory being organised in byte-sized chunks. Doing this would obscure the simplicity of what is actually happening with the operation of a stack. However, should you wish to write your own working versions of any assembly-language programs making use of a stack, then you will have to look in considerably more detail to see how the system may be implemented on your particular processor. For the purposes of computing at this level, the principles are more important than the details.

Consider figure 21.19. Let's assume that the *main program* is being executed **sequentially** until the processor gets to the memory location labelled 'Address' in the main memory. This 'location' contains a **CALL** to a sub-routine called 'Start', which lives in a *different area* of the memory. The CALL instruction initiates the following sequence of operations to pass control over to the sub-routine and back again.

First the 'old' contents of the program counter (called the instruction pointer in the 80 × 86 range) is stored in a safe area of memory called the stack. The 'old' program-counter contents contain 'Address + 1' because this would have been the next memory location from which the next instruction was to be loaded if sequential operation had continued. (In practice, for byte-organised memory, the counter would have been set to a higher address to 'jump over' the next few memory locations which store the address for the call.) There is nothing special about the area of memory called the stack – it's simply a convenient place in which to store some data. The old program-counter contents must be stored because we need this address to be able to get back to the next part of the main program after the sub-routine has finished.

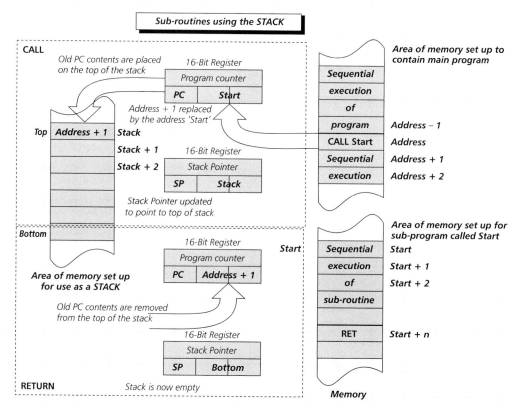

Figure 21.19

The **stack pointer** is a special register which has been set up (by the programmer) to point to the address representing the '**top of the stack**' in memory – where the old program-counter contents have been stored. Again, we will assume that the address can fit into a single memory location. In practice two or more may be needed to store this address information. The stack-pointer register itself *can't be used* to hold this address because we may have *yet another* **CALL** to a *subroutine from within the one just about to be executed.* (See in a moment.) In practice the stack area of memory could be many memory locations in size, and it is the job of the stack-pointer register to keep tabs on the memory location representing the 'top' of the stack. You can see from figure 21.19 that a label 'top' has been assigned to memory location 'stack' to help you visualise these concepts more easily. Also, as the stack obviously can't be of infinite length, another label called 'bottom' is shown which represents the address for the end of the stack.

The microprocessor carries on regardless with the fetch-decode-execute cycle (see chapter 20), but, due to the operations described earlier, now happens to be working through the **sub-program** contained in memory locations 'Start', 'Start + 1' and 'Start + 2', etc. *As far as the processor is concerned, there is no real difference between working though the main program and working through the sub-program.* However, when the **RETURN** (**RET**) instruction is encountered, this terminates the sub-program and initiates the following sequence.

The address from the 'top' of the stack (pointed to by the stack-pointer register), is removed and *placed back inside* the **program counter**. The contents of the stack-pointer register are then updated to show that there is nothing left on the stack. Hence we are now in a position identical to that which existed *before* the original **CALL** instruction was encountered. Therefore, the program can now continue as though nothing special had happened, and therefore continues with the rest of the main routine. Any other routine can be called and serviced in the same way, and in practice, many other registers might be saved on the stack too.

Interrupts

Microprocessors spend most of their time jumping in and out of routines in ways similar to those described in the last section. Indeed, much of the time hardware devices (see chapters 10, 11 and 12), will cause **interrupts** to happen. This means that a device such as the keyboard, for example, might need servicing *because* a key has just been pressed. The processor could be notified that an interrupt had just occurred. It could then place the current contents of the program counter onto the stack, load up the address of the routine to service the keyboard, carry out the servicing, then return from the service routine and carry on with what it was originally doing.

Interrupts are probably going on inside the machine many times each second, with the update of the real-time clock being a particularly good example. It's obvious that other interrupts will probably happen when a previous interrupt is in the middle of being serviced, and the stack can also be used to hold the address of the sub-routine which is being executed in identical ways to the example given in the previous section. In this way interrupts may be **nested** (*queued up*) such that higher-priority ones can be serviced immediately. Interrupts are covered in more detail in chapter 23, but figure 21.20 shows how two interrupts (represented by CALLs to Start and Next) can be serviced by making use of a stack.

As can be seen, the main routine is interrupted when a call is made to the sub-routine called Start. This is identical in principle to the way in which this subroutine was serviced in the last section. However, when dealing with the sub-routine called Start, another call is made (called a nested sub-routine) from within the subroutine already being executed. Therefore, the program-counter contents (which pointed to the next instruction to be loaded) is now placed on the new top-of-stack position, and relegates the old program counter contents (the old address to get back to the original calling routine) to second place. The stack pointer register is also updated to show the position of the new 'top' of the stack.

Control is now passed to the new routine called 'Next', and the microprocessor, as before, carries on regardless with the fetch-decode-execute cycle. The 'Next' sub-program is sequentially executed as no CALLs are made from this routine (they could have been!). Therefore, when the RET instruction is encountered, the top of the stack is popped off (*not physically removed – see in moment*), the program counter gets updated so that it can now go back and carry on with the first sub-routine called Start. The stack pointer is then altered (again by the programmer) so that the original address to get back to the main routine is ready when needed (i.e. it's ready for the time when the RET instruction is encountered at the end of 'Start'). In practice, the memory contents would not be deleted from the stack, as the stack pointers ensure that the correct addresses are removed from the stack, or overwritten by new ones which may be placed onto the stack next time it is used.

Finally, when the RET instruction in the 'Start subroutine' is encountered, the Program Counter is updated with the next address to be executed within the main routine, the stack is empty, and control then proceeds with the remainder of the main routine. The stack and other data structures are considered in more detail in chapter 24.

That's all there is to it!

If you have fully understood the previous sections then you will have a very good idea indeed of how typical microprocessors go about their business. The modern microprocessor spends all of its time jumping between different chunks of assembly-language code in exactly the ways described in this section. You will also appreciate that what's happening inside is nothing more or less than manipulation of binary digits. It's up to the programmer to decide how these digits are interpreted – it could be arithmetic on numbers, representations of colours on the screen (see chapter 11), interpreting speech (see chapter 10) or controlling a robot (see chapter 8). The power of modern microprocessors is formidable – man's ingenuity in getting binary digits to do almost anything is a remarkable human achievement.

Having understood some of the basic things that can be achieved with a typical assembly language, we now turn to the last stage in the plot – namely the mechanics of getting an assembly-language program to run on a typical computer system.

The assembler

Basically an assembler is a piece of software that converts the mnemonics into machine code ready for execution on the machine. However, a typical modern assembler does much more than this. Without an assembler program you would have to translate each assembly-language mnemonic into machine code by hand!

Did you know that . . .

Assemblers are far easier to write than compilers. There is less syntax checking and there are usually fewer instructions present than in a typical high-level language. Compilers, the other form of interpreter, are considered in chapter 32.

Suppose, for example, one line of your program was CLC on a 6502 machine. Then, after looking it up in the manufacturer's manual, you would find that the op code for this instruction is 18 hex. Therefore the binary pattern 00011000 would have to be put into the exact memory location inside the computer's main memory;

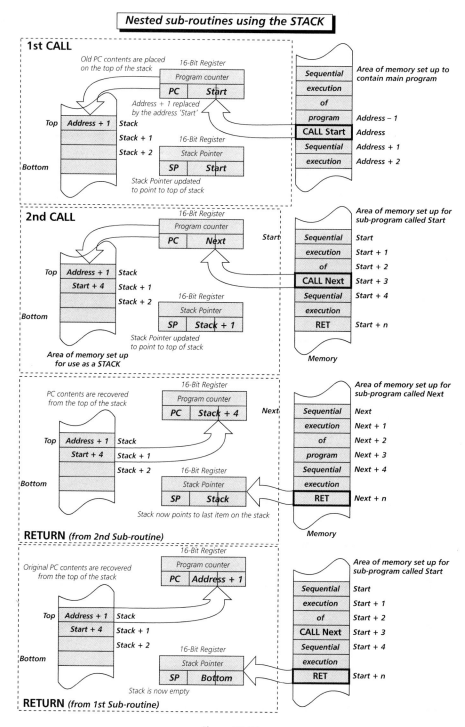

Figure 21.20

a long and tedious procedure. This process would be called hand assembly. In practice, on most computers, you would be able to enter the codes in hex, but it is still a long, tedious and error-prone task.

The assembly language mnemonics would normally have to be written on a text editor or word processor. The listing of the assembly language mnemonics is called the **source code** or the **source program**. After the assembly process has been carried out we end up with the machine-code program which is called the **object**

code or the **object program** as shown in figure 21.21. Note that the syntax of the assembly-language program is not important. What is important is to realise that each instruction produces one unique machine-code instruction that will appear in the object code. Also, it is important to realise that on a very small microcomputer several memory locations may be needed to store this instruction because of the restricted word length.

The machine on which the object code will finally run is called the **target machine**. It should be realised

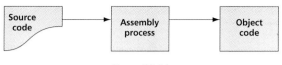

Figure 21.21

that the original source code does not necessarily have to be written on the **target machine**.

It was mentioned above that if hand assembly were undertaken then we should have to decide exactly where the instructions would be placed in memory. With an assembler, provided it has information about where in the memory to start the object code, it takes care of the positioning of all the code for you. We will now consider the main features of a typical assembler.

Main features of a typical assembler

Besides the obvious features, such as translating the source code into the object code, the main features (not necessarily in order of importance) are:

1. Enables the user to use **symbolic addressing**, i.e. the assembler will work out the address values for any labels that have been correctly used in the source program. You can give names to specific memory locations where data is to be found.
2. You can perform arithmetic (often only very simple on a micro), simply by including the appropriate signs in the source code listing.
3. You can often use different bases for your numbers e.g. base two, eight, sixteen and ten are frequently supported (as is the BCD system).
4. The assembler will alert the user to any errors during the assembly process such as incorrect instructions.
5. The user can tell the **loader program** (see later) where parts of the program or data should be in the computer's memory.
6. The assembler can produce a listing of the source code or object code, together with error messages, formatted to the user's requirements. It is essential to be able to produce a listing with comments so that you can manually work through parts of the program to sort out any bugs.
7. The assembler will work out all the necessary forward and backward references such as jumps and subroutines, a very painful process if carried out by hand!
8. Enables the user to use just one instruction to define a sequence of other instructions. It then converts these instructions into the equivalent set of machine-code instructions. These are called **macros** (see later).

Some of the above operations, such as defining directives to be used in the source program or allocating areas of memory, are not translated into machine code instructions. These extra instructions are called **assembler directives** or **pseudo-operations** because they are really instructions to the assembler and not actual code to be executed on the target machine.

Different types of assembler

Before going on to the assembly process it is important to realise that there are several different but important types of assembler available for many computers. They all translate the original source code into the final object code, but some have added facilities. Some of the more important types of assembler are:

1. **Basic assembler**. Most assemblers go through the source code producing the object code, but will ignore any forward references such as jumps (i.e. it does not know where to jump to until it has got that far in the assembly process!). This is called the first pass. On subsequent passes, the assembler will go through and resolve all the jump addresses to produce the final object code. It will also produce a data dictionary (see chapter 28).
2. **Resident assembler**. This is an assembler that runs only on the target machine, i.e. it will only translate the mnemonics into the specific machine code for the processor resident in the particular machine.
3. **Cross assembler**. Unlike the resident assembler the cross assembler is able to produce the object code that will run on a different machine.
4. **Macro assembler**. This type of assembler supports macros. Macros define a sequence of instructions with just one other instruction called a macro instruction. Every time the macro is encountered within the source code, all the necessary machine code instructions are generated. It is not like a subroutine because no branch is executed. Macros are useful because only one instruction has to be changed if a complete new routine is required when the assembler is used. However, using macros can create very long object programs if not used with care.
5. **Meta assembler**. This is an assembler that can deal with different instruction sets.

Loaders

A **loader** is a program that takes the object code (i.e. the machine code produced by the assembler) and loads it into the computer's main memory in the correct place. There are various types of loader.

1. **Bootstrap loader**. This is a loader that loads itself by using the instructions at the beginning to load the 'rest of itself'! The name bootstrap is a hangover from the days when the expression 'pull

yourself up by your own bootstraps' meant to achieve something by your own efforts, or in computing terms to achieve the loading of a large system on the basis of the effort of a smaller one. This often forms part of the system which boots up the operating system, for example.

2. **Linking loaders**. These are particularly useful as they are able to **link** together programs that have been assembled separately. For example, there may be a library of assembly language routines that can be used by other assembly language programs. An example of a typical routine may be a sort program. The assemblers that are used to produce the object code for a linking must be able to cope with what are called external references. Without this facility an error message would of course be generated.

3. **Relocating loaders**. This type of loader can load the object code anywhere in memory, as opposed to an **absolute loader**, that can't. This is obviously very convenient if many programs are being run at the same time on a system. However, the object programs that are produced must be relocatable code, i.e. programmers must ensure that no reference to an absolute memory location is used. You can't program with instructions like STA 0100H for example, i.e. store the contents of the accumulator in memory location 100 hex. These problems can easily be overcome by using labels rather than absolute addresses e.g. you would use 'STA answer' instead. Using this better method the relocating loader can move your program around anywhere in memory and it will always work.

Writing relocatable code is always the best policy. If a specific memory location is used for input/output purposes then this is also usually referred to by a name. If the manufacturers suddenly decide to update the system (they often do!) then they might decide that the absolute address of this input/output port would change. However, if you have referred to it by a standard name, then your original program should still work satisfactorily because the new operating system software should be able to cope.

An assembly-language example

Practical features of a typical assembly language

The principles covered at the beginning of this chapter are best illustrated by a practical example. First we will cover the general principles, then give a specific example making use of a typical microprocessor.

General principles

Having covered a lot of complex and detailed information, it is important to get it clear in your own mind exactly what has to happen when we go through the assembly process, i.e. what do you actually have to do to get an assembly program going? The following section outlines the typical processes that have to be carried out.

1. **The basic idea**. The problem to be solved must be broken down into a suitable form, making use of **flowcharts**, **pseudocode**, or a **clear set of written statements**.

2. **Coding the problem**. By making use of the appropriate **assembly-language mnemonics**, the code must be written either by making use of a **text editor** or a **word processor** that can produce **ASCII text**. This code must be combined with all the appropriate **directives** and **interrupts** (see in a moment) that will make it actually run on the target machine.

3. **Assembling the program**. The code produced in step 2 must be **assembled** by making use of an appropriate **assembler** for your particular machine. Such processes are considered in detail at the end of this section.

4. **Any errors?** If the assembler produces any errors, then these must be corrected by going back to step (2), changing the **source code**, and **re-assembling**. Errors detected at this stage would include invalid instructions or other **syntax errors**.

5. **Link and add macros that may be needed?** The assembler code is converted into **executable code**, i.e. code that can be run on a particular machine, by the linker, and linked with any macros that may have been called.

6. **Any execution errors?** Even though the program may assemble correctly, i.e. it is syntactically correct, it may not produce the desired results. If this is so then you will have to return to step (2) yet again, find the error, alter the source code, then re-assemble and run again.

It is most advisable to save your program on disk **before running it**. This is because certain errors can cause the machine to crash, thus destroying your program. Such errors are called **fatal errors.**

On many systems there are also **debuggers** that help you to single-step through assembly-language code as it is being run. Without these useful utilities it is often difficult, if not impossible, to see why a program does not produce the desired output. The only alternative would be to do a very tedious **dry run** by hand.

The exact details to be carried out on particular machines may vary, but they are all variations on the above theme. For example, some assemblers may not support macros, and therefore the 'adding the macros' stage might be missed out completely. The above ideas are summarised in the flowchart shown in figure 21.22.

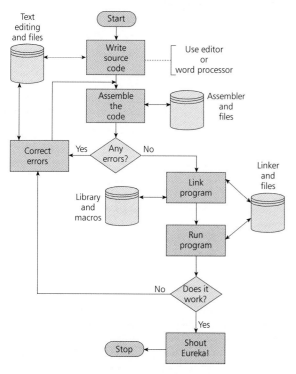

Figure 21.22

Some background information

Before using an assembly language in practice, there are a few important things to understand. This involves the mass of extra help that is usually given to program-mers when they use a particular assembler on a particular machine – help with using parts of the oper-ating system, and help with the 'nuts and bolts' of telling the computer exactly what you want it to do.

A few assembly-language instructions by themselves would not normally run properly on a computer. Extra information is required such as 'where the program will be assembled in memory'. Also, there is usually much help with carrying out common tasks, or help enabling you to get listings of your programs on the printer, etc. To undertake these routine but useful tasks requires an understanding of **directives** or **pseudo-operations**, and **interrupts**. These are briefly covered before looking in detail at the assembly-language examples.

Directives and pseudo-operations

These are operations that *do not form part of the actual program*. They **are not assembly-language instructions** in the normal sense, but **instructions to the assembler**. They will not produce machine code that forms part of your program. For example, in the **PC** system, the **END** command tells the assembler when to stop assembling. There are many other uses of **pseudo-ops** and **directives** such as telling the assembler the position in memory at which the code is to start being assembled, or convenient

ways to **define bytes** and **words**. Without help such as this, assembly-language programs would be much more tedious and difficult to write. However, remembering such details is best left to the reader when an individual assembly language (or subset of one) is studied.

Calling operating-system functions

Often there are many basic operations that need to be carried out. Examples would be putting characters on the screen, getting characters from the keyboard, opening or closing a file, printing a character, or any other of the many chores that might need to be done. It would be inefficient if you had to write all these routines from scratch, especially if they are already extensively used by the **operating system**. Therefore, most computer systems have ways of calling up the appropriate **subroutines** that reside somewhere in the operating system. Making use of interrupts usually does this, i.e. your program is **interrupted** to **call a subrou-tine** that resides somewhere else in the computer. After carrying out the required task, control is passed back to your original program. On the **PC**, **using software interrupts** carries out these calls. These calls let the user have access to routines which save the programmer the bother of having to work out all the instructions that would be necessary to carry out the operating-system-based tasks.

It should be realised **the above routines are usually called by name or number**, and not by specifying an absolute address within the machine. This is essential as it creates code that is not dependent on a particular version of the operating system. If a new version of the operating system is produced, the routine may reside at different memory locations, but the names can be used to create a vector that directs you to the new place where the subroutine is stored.

In addition to this, you can often buy **macros** on disk from a third party supplier, or write your own. These would also be able to be **called by name**, as with the above functions and SWIs (software interrupts). However, with **macros, whole chunks of code would be added to your assembled programs**, i.e. for each macro that you call, the instruction to call the macro is replaced by however many instructions are contained within the macro. Note the difference here between this and the other **procedure** or **sub-routine** calls when dealing with interrupts.

Don't forget that it's quirks like the above that ensure that low-level languages are only applicable to a partic-ular machine, unlike high-level languages which are supposed to be portable.

A specific example

In the last part of this section we will show some typical assembly-language programming. **The only way that** you can really learn about assembly-language programming is actually to do some. This example will bring out many important points, which are applicable to general assembly language programming. It should, therefore, be gone through with great care. Although the mechanics of doing things in assembly language are very different indeed from one machine to another, many of the principles are exactly the same.

> **Hint:** Don't forget to save your assembly language program before compiling and running it. Many program errors will cause the machine to crash and, under these conditions, you may not be able to retrieve your original program.

In the following example, the code used is extremely simple, making use of just a single interrupt call. We will, therefore, omit the usually essential part of developing the program from flowcharts or other methods. Here we are just giving examples of the assembly processes, and will keep the actual code used to a bare minimum.

The 8086 16-bit processor

We will now look at a CISC 8086-based processor. This is a 16-bit processor from Intel. It's interesting to note that any software developed on an 8086 system should be able to run on the much more powerful 80286, 80386, 80486 and Pentium machines, although, obviously, the more powerful 80 × 86 code will not run on the 8086 if the more advanced features have been used. We will use the 8086 for simplicity.

The internal register set of the 8086 processor is as follows:

Data registers

AH	AL	**Accumulator AX** (high and low bytes)
BH	BL	**Base BX** (high and low bytes)
CH	CL	**Counter CX** (high and low bytes)
DH	DL	**Data DX** (high and low bytes)

Pointer and index registers

SP	**Stack pointer**
BP	**Base pointer**
SI	**Source code**
DI	**Destination index**

Segment registers

CS	**Code segment**
DS	**Data segment**
SS	**Stack segment**
ES	**Extra segment**
IP	**Instruction pointer**
FlagS	**Status register**

The data registers

The **data registers** can be treated as four 16-bit registers or eight 8-bit registers: hence the layout of the above. If the 8-bit registers are used they are called AH, AL, etc. as shown above, or if the 16-bit registers are used, then they are called AX, BX, CX and DX respectively.

The segment registers

These are used primarily to keep the programs and data in separate segments of memory. This is a quirk of 8086-based processors. If you are going to learn to program on a PC machine making use of either the 8086/88 or indeed the 186, 286, 386 and 486 based 32-bit machines, then you will have to understand fully how segmentation works. These quirks ensure that low level languages for different microprocessors are totally incompatible with one another.

The instruction pointer register

The 8086 makes use of a **pipelined architecture** (see chapter 20). Separate parts of the chip fetch the instructions while another part of the chip executes a different instruction at the same time. If the results of one instruction are needed before another has been finished, then the chip will go into a wait state until the result has been worked out (a very short period of time in practice). The instruction pointer register contains the offset of the next instruction to be executed.

The pointer and index registers

These registers provide offsets that are used in conjunction with the segment registers to access parts of the memory.

The status register

This contains the flags that indicate the processor status at any particular time.

The assembly process

The features here will make use of Microsoft's MASM assembler version 5.1. You would generate your source code by making use of a suitable editor. On a PC machine you could make use of your usual word processor put into ASCII mode.

From figure 21.22 you can see that there are a number of different files involved in the assembly process. The files required, together with the appropriate MSDOS extensions might be as shown in the following sections.

A very simple program

Setting the time is a standard operation on many micros. As with most low-level languages, operations like this involve loading registers with certain numbers, and then calling the appropriate routine from the operating system.

On the PC system this would involve putting the hours, minutes, seconds and centiseconds (i.e. hundredths of a second) into the registers CH, CL, DH and DL respectively, then putting the code 2D hex into the AL register, and calling the software interrupt number hex 21. The time given by the variables would then be set.

It is necessary to **push** the AX, CX and DX registers (i.e. the 16-bit versions of the accumulator etc.) onto the stack before the interrupt is called, and then restore these registers by **popping** the contents off the stack at the end of the procedure. (See earlier for stack operations.)

We will assume that the variables **hour**, **min**, **sec** and **csec** have already been set up. (If you have MASM or an alternative version of a PC assembler, then you could find out how to add routines, which would accept appropriate input from the keyboard.) It should be obvious that the variables can take on any of the following values:

$$0 \leq \text{hour} \leq 23$$
$$0 \leq \text{min} \leq 59$$
$$0 \leq \text{sec} \leq 59$$
$$\text{and} \quad 0 \leq \text{csec} \leq 99$$

The following 8086 assembly language code forms the backbone of the 'time set' procedure. Note that ';' is used to denote a comment.

```
;
; Procedure to set up the time
;
  PUSH AX      ;Save registers on stack
  PUSH CX
  PUSH DX
;
  MOV  CH,hour ;Load values for time
  MOV  CL,min
  MOV  DH,sec
  MOV  DL,csec
;
  MOV  AH,2DH  ;Select time option
;
  INT  21H     ;Call the interrupt to set
                  the time
;
  POP  DX      ;Restore the registers
  POP  CX
  POP  AX
```

The above code would not work in isolation, there would need to be other additions such as directives etc. However, without going into unnecessary detail, we will assume that the above code is complete. The purpose of this exercise is to concentrate more on the assembly process itself.

Assembling the program

The code, together with all the directives etc. which have not been shown, would be saved on disk with an appropriate file name and an extension of ASM to denote the assembly source code. If we call the program 'Time', then the file could have been saved as:

> **Hint:** It's methods like those shown on this page that ensure that assembly language programming will be for the specialist computer scientist. You can see why programming in many high-level languages is much more user friendly.

    Time.ASM

Suppose that you want to assemble the program straight away. At the MSDOS prompt you could simply type the name of the assembler you are using. As you are using MASM, you would type:

    C>MASM

You might see a message like the following:

Microsoft ® Macro Assembler Version 5.10
Copyright © Microsoft Corp 1981, 1989. All rights reserved.
Source filename [.ASM]:_

After typing in 'Time', you would get the following response:

Source filename [.ASM]:
Object filename [Time.OBJ]:_

i.e. the computer has come up with the default suggestion of Time.OBJ for the object code. In general, the following files are required by MASM.

The minimum requirement would be:

(a) **The source code** (i.e. the original code created on your editor or word processor),

   e.g. My_Prog.ASM

(b) The **object code** (the code that will eventually run on the machine; it is produced by the assembler),

   e.g. My_Prog.OBJ

In addition you ought to have:

(c) A **listing** (i.e. a file which can help you to debug your programs by looking at some hard copy),

   e.g. My_Prog.LST

In addition you might have:

(d) A **macro file** (if you are using the macro facility),

   e.g. My_Prog.MAC

(e) An **include file** (e.g. a file containing some important data),

e.g.   My_Prog.INC

There will also be other options, which are too detailed for a first glance at MASM.

Therefore, a complete interactive dialogue for the 'Time' program might be as follows:

On screen action	Notes
Source filename [.ASM]: Time	Time is the name of the program
Object filename [Time.OBJ]:	Default object code name
Source listing [NUL.LST]: Time.LST	List is required
Cross-reference [NUL.CRF]:	Assembly process under way
50004 + 324006 bytes symbol space free	
0 Warning errors	
0 Severe errors	
No errors	

The assembly process is now complete and you have a copy of Time.OBJ (the object code) and Time.LST (the listing) on disk. However, the object code does not contain executable code, and as can be seen from figure 21.22, has to go through the linking process.

The linking process

The object code must now be translated by the linker into executable machine code. The linker would join together more than one of your programs if necessary, and resolve the external references if possible. It will also produce a listing if you have made this request. The linker is a separate program from the assembler. You usually have the choice of using the one that is supplied with your assembler, or going for a third party linker with perhaps more sophisticated facilities. For example, one type of linker from Borland enables you to handle 32-bit code for the 80386 and 80486 processors.

After the linking process has taken place, executable code will have been produced, with a file extension of EXE. This is the code that can be run directly as shown below.

Running the linker is very similar to running the assembler itself. Simply type its name from the MSDOS prompt:

On screen action	Notes
C> Link	Run the link
Microsoft ® Overlay Linker Version 3.65	
Copyright © Microsoft Corp 1983–1997.	
All rights reserved.	
Object modules [.OBJ]: Time	Specify Object code
Run file [Time.EXE]:	Default run file
List file [NUL.MAP]:	No map required
Libraries [.LIB]:	No libraries necessary

You have now created Time.EXE which can be run in the following way.

Running your program

Assuming that it works, this is the easy bit. You simply type the name of your program at the MSDOS prompt, i.e. if you are currently working on drive C, then you would proceed as follows:

```
C> Time
```

Listings of the program would produce a long list of numbers representing the memory locations, machine code instructions, the assembler mnemonics and the comments etc.

The details of the above are not important but you should now appreciate more fully how an assembler can help us to write programs in machine code using assembly-language mnemonics and a host of other extra help facilities such as directives, pseudo-ops, listings and symbol tables.

Exercise 21.1

1 What is the difference between machine code and assembly language?

2 Why do assembly-language programs written for one type of machine not run on any other? Is it sometimes possible for them to run on another machine?

3 Explain why assembly-language instructions are represented by mnemonics, and, making use of a typical example, describe why four fields are often used as the format for the representation of many assembly-language instructions.

4 What is the purpose of the following with regard to assembly-language programs?

(a) Op Code

(b) Operands

(c) Comments.

5 Explain why different modes of addressing are often encountered within a particular assembly language, making specific reference to immediate, direct, indirect and indexed addressing modes.

6 Some microprocessor manufacturers have gone for a general-purpose register set, while others have kept specific registers. Comment on the advantages and disadvantages which each approach may bring.

7 Sometimes specific registers are used, even in a more-general purpose register set. One example is the flag register. Explain what is meant by a flag register and comment on four different conditions which may be brought to the programmer's attention by the use of this register.

8 An assembly-language instruction set may be broken down into major subsets such as the arithmetic, logical and control subsets, for example. Making use of the arithmetical subset, explain how two simple one-byte-two's-complement binary numbers may be added together. Your answer should make reference to where the original numbers may come from, and where the answer may be stored. If the resultant number is too big to fit into your chosen register, how would this be handled by the microprocessor?

9 Explain how a mask may be used to prevent alteration of the top three and bottom two digits in a one-byte register. How would you then proceed to set the remaining three digits to 1?

10 Carefully explain the difference between an arithmetic and a logical shift operation. Show, by making use of the 16-bit register in the following diagram, how the contents would be altered by the following operations.

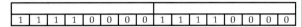

(Note you should start each operation using the bit pattern shown above.)

(a) Logical Shift Left 3 places.

(b) Arithmetic Shift Left 3 places

(c) Logical Shift Right 2 places.

(d) Arithmetic Shift Right 2 places.

11 Explain, with examples, how logical operations such as 'AND' and 'OR' may be carried out making use of registers within a processor.

12 Explain the difference between a conditional and an unconditional jump instruction by reference to a particular assembly-language instruction set with which you are familiar.

13 What is the function of the **stack-pointer register** within an assembly-language program?

14 What is an assembler, and why is it desirable to make use of one when programming in assembly language? Outline the main *advantages* from a programmer's point of view when an assembler is used.

15 Why are there different types of assembler? Make reference to the use of meta assemblers and cross assemblers in your answer.

16 A loader is often used during the assembly process – what is it and why is it useful?

17 Explain 'macro assembler', 'macro', and 'library routines' with regard to an assembly language program.

18 Give a typical scenario in which a debugger would prove particularly useful in finding run-time bugs in an assembly language program.

19 It's essential to have links between operating-system routines and assembly-language programs. Why is this the case and what advantages are to be found when making use of routines provided by the operating system?

20 If you have an assembler at school or college, make use of it to program the following tasks.

(a) Read a character in from the keyboard and print it out on the screen.

(b) Read in some characters in upper case and print them out in lower case.

End of chapter revision aid and summary

Cover up the right-hand column and see if you can answer the questions or define the terms on the left. They appear in the order in which they are covered in this chapter. Alternatively you may browse through the right-hand column to aid revision.

Into what sort of code is every operation in the computer broken down?	All activity within any computer system is ultimately broken down into operations involving binary digits called machine code.
What is machine code?	Machine code is the binary-digit language of a particular machine (computer).
Why is machine code unique?	Machine code is unique to a particular processor (microprocessor).
What is normally used instead of machine code?	Programming in machine code is a tedious, time consuming and error-prone task. Assembly language is normally used instead.
What is assembly language?	Assembly language makes use of mnemonics which represent individual machine-code instructions.
Machine code and assembly language are examples of what sort of language?	Machine code and assembly language are called low-level languages because they are close to what's happening inside the computer at a low (fundamental) level.
What is a mnemonic?	A mnemonic is simply an aid to the memory. It's easier to remember than the equivalent group of binary digits.
Will a particular assembly language work on a different type of processor?	Assembly language will only work on the processor for which it has been designed. (Assuming that another processor is not being used to emulate it!)
What characterises the particular hardware of a machine?	A particular family of microprocessors usually characterise the main hardware of particular machines. For example, Intel – IBM PC, or Motorola – Apple Mac.
What is an instruction set?	An instruction set is the set of instructions (commands available) for a particular assembly language.
What typical types of instructions would characterise an instruction set?	Instruction sets can be broken down into major subsets such as arithmetical, logical and control instructions etc.
How is the op code and assembly language instruction related?	Each assembly-language instruction is given a unique op code or operation code. An operation code is the name given to the binary code (machine code) which represents a particular assembly-language instruction.
What is a microprocessor register set?	Each microprocessor type will have a set of registers which is unique. These registers are places in which binary digits can be stored.
What is a register?	A register is a place inside a microprocessor used for the temporary storage of patterns of binary digits.
What is a general-purpose register?	Some microprocessors have general-purpose register sets while others have registers dedicated to particular tasks.
What are dedicated registers?	Dedicated registers are those such as stack pointers, accumulators, flags and index registers, for example.
Why is the size of the address bus important?	The address-bus size is important because it affects the amount of external memory which can be addressed by the processor.

Why is the size of the data bus important?	The data-bus size is important because it affects how much data can be transferred between the processor and memory at the same time. It thus affects the speed of data transfer.
How is memory usually addressed?	Memory is usually addressed in byte-sized chunks. This often makes what's going on a little easier to understand.
Into what parts is a typical assembly-language instruction split?	A typical assembly-language instruction is usually split up into four parts called fields, namely the label, op code, operands and comments fields.
Which part of the above is compulsory?	Only the Op Code field is compulsory, although the operand field is also used in most assembly-language instructions.
What is the op code field?	The op code field contains the mnemonic, which represents the operation code.
What is the operand field?	The operand field contains the source and destination information for the data.
Which part of the instruction is ignored?	The computer ignores a comment field when the program is run; it is documentation for the convenience of the programmer.
What is the label field?	The label field contains a symbolic address used for jumps, for example.
What is a symbolic address?	A symbolic address is where a label represents the address of a storage location.
What are addressing modes?	Most microprocessors have some common modes of addressing. This refers to the ways in which data can be accessed or transferred in the system.
What is immediate addressing?	Immediate addressing is where the data to be used follows immediately after the op code for the instruction.
What is direct addressing?	Direct addressing is where the contents of a memory location can be addressed directly from an instruction, usually making use of a symbolic address.
What is indirect addressing?	Indirect addressing is where the contents of another register contains the actual address to be used for accessing the data, i.e. the instruction gets the address for the data indirectly from this other register.
What is indexed addressing?	Indexed addressing is where a number contained in an index register is used in combination with some other address or addresses to determine the final address.
What common data structure can be implemented using indexed addressing?	Indexed addressing can be used to implement arrays and other data structures within memory.
What other modes of addressing exist?	Other modes of addressing exist, but are usually combinations of the types already mentioned, and are less important to remember.
What is the flag register?	The flag register holds important information regarding the status of activity within the processor. For example, has an overflow occurred?
List the basic arithmetical operations?	Arithmetical operations within an assembly language are instructions like ADD, SUB, MUL and DIV etc. which represent the basic arithmetic operations.
What number systems can be used when using the arithmetic operations?	Arithmetic operations can usually be carried out in binary, hex, decimal and BCD etc.
What is a logical operation?	Logical operations are operations such as AND, OR, XOR and NOT etc.

What is a shift operation?	A shift operation can be split up into arithmetic and logical shifts.
What is a logical shift?	A logical shift moves the digits left or right replacing the vacated spaces with zeros.
What is an arithmetical shift?	An arithmetical shift moves the digits left or right, but the sign bit must be altered if necessary to maintain the arithmetical sense of the number.
What is a rotate instruction?	Rotate operations move the digits left or right within a register, but feed one end into the other, instead of filling up with zeros or ones.
What is a bit-set instruction?	Bit set and reset instructions enable register contents or memory locations to be set or reset according to various conditions. Individual bits can be altered if masking is used, or if the register is designed specifically for this (e.g. the flags).
What is masking?	Masking is where part of the original data is protected from alteration by a particular process.
What is a program control instruction?	Program control instructions contain instructions such as conditional and unconditional jumps etc.
What is an unconditional jump?	An unconditional jump is where control is passed to some other part of the program unconditionally.
What is a conditional jump?	A conditional jump is where control is passed to some other part of the program only if a particular condition has been met.
What is a stack?	A stack is an area of memory set up to hold addresses needed by the processor to return to places from where the sequential operation of the program was interrupted. It is where control is passed to some other part of the program only if a particular condition has been met.
What is a stack pointer?	A stack pointer is a special-purpose register set up to maintain what's happening to the stack.
For what purpose are the CALL and RETURN instructions used?	CALL and RETURN instructions are used to transfer control to sub-routines contained at different memory locations. It's up to the programmer to maintain the stack.
What is a subroutine?	A sub-routine is the name given to a self-contained part of the program which executes a particular task. It helps to split up the program into smaller modules.
What is an assembler?	An assembler is a piece of software, which converts the assembly language mnemonics into the machine code which will actually run on the computer.
How is an assembly-language program built up?	The assembly-language program is usually built up by typing the assembly-language mnemonics into a text editor (a simple word processor).
What is the source code?	The assembly-language code from the text editor is called the source code.
What is the object code?	After being assembled (converted into machine code), the resulting program from the assembler is called the object code.
What is the target machine?	The machine (or microprocessor) on which the object code is intended to be run, is called the target machine.
What is symbolic addressing?	Symbolic addressing makes use of labels instead of absolute addresses.
What produces a listing of the program?	An assembler enables listings of the program to be produced easily.

What helps to trap errors?	An assembler will help with trapping errors within a program.
What works out the jump instructions?	An assembler works out all the jump references to labels.
What is a macro?	Most assemblers enable macros (one instruction replacing a sequence of others) to be used.
What is an assembler directive?	An assembler provides assembler directives (or pseudo operations) which enable the programmer to achieve a variety of tasks with ease. Examples would be selecting particular modes of operation, defining the start and stop of a macro or assigning values to particular labels etc.
What is a resident assembler?	A resident assembler is one that will only run on the target machine.
What is a cross assembler?	A cross assembler is able to assemble code to run on a different machine.
What is a macro assembler?	A macro assembler is one that supports macros, i.e. it enables a key word (the macro name) to be replaced with a whole section of code if needed.
What is a meta assembler?	A meta assembler is one that can deal with different instruction sets.
What is a loader?	A loader is a piece of software, which loads the object code into memory in the correct place.
What is a linking loader?	A linking loader is a loader that is able to link together programs that have been assembled separately. This is, of course, useful to get your own pre-written routines and other library routines joined together, for example.
Outline the main stages of the assembly-language process?	The assembly-language process involves the following stages: (1) A clear statement of the problem using appropriate techniques (see chapter 14) (2) Code the problem using a text editor. (3) Assemble the program. (4) Correct any errors if necessary. (5) Link, then add macros if necessary (6) Any execution errors will involve going back to stage (2).
What is a debugger?	A debugger is the name given to a piece of software which helps to debug (get the bugs out of) your assembly-language program.
How might a debugger be used?	A debugger often allows you to step through the program, and analyse the contents of registers etc. after the execution of each instruction. Without these utilities it would often be impossible to check what's happening when the object code is run.
How might the operating system functions be called?	Operating system functions (see chapter 22) may usually be CALLed from within assembly language programs. These often enable the assembly-language programmer to carry out mundane tasks such as 'reading a character from the keyboard', for example, without having to write the code for this particular operation.

22 A First Look at Operating Systems

Key resources

To carry out this work most successfully it's best if you have:

◆ Access to a simpler operating system like MS-DOS
◆ Access to a more complex operating system like Windows 95, RISC OS, Linux or Windows NT
◆ Access to a secure operating system like Windows NT

Concept checkpoints

◆ An appreciation of the machine architecture concepts covered in chapter 20 would be very helpful.
◆ An appreciation of the low-level languages material covered in chapter 20 would be helpful too.

Introduction

To a novice the operating system is probably the least important part of the computer – but nothing could be further from the truth. Many computers have now become so easy to use that beginners do not even realise that there is such a thing as an operating system. This is mainly due to the fact that, on many microcomputers, it is the job of modern operating-systems software to present the user with an easy-to-use front end. Most people are now very familiar indeed with GUIs such as Windows, and even small children, for example, can point with the mouse and draw a coloured picture on the screen. These simple operations belie the fact that programs of enormous complexity called operating systems are controlling such operations at the most fundamental level inside the machine.

The background to the development of operating systems is an interesting one, and goes back to the very early days of computers. The first computers were very difficult beasts to control. Each machine-code program (see chapter 20) had to be keyed in by hand, making use of a bank of binary switches called the front panel. This was a tedious and error-prone task. To gain an appreciation of this task, you must realise that there were no programs to read data from a keyboard or disk, indeed there were no computer screens or disks! The output from the computer was normally in the form of a bank of lights, or simple data typed out on a teletype (an old-style mechanical typewriter machine). Even the programs to control the teletype had to be loaded in by hand. It was no small wonder that the operators of these tedious and error-prone systems ever saw the potential of the computer under these awful circumstances.

As the electronic hardware improved, computers got faster and faster at running through their programs, but this increased speed was severely limited by the constant and often time-consuming intervention of human operators carrying out many mundane tasks such as loading new programs or stopping the computer if something went wrong. (It often did!) An *automatic* system was needed to release the operator from most of these tasks, and it was against this background that the very first operating-system software was developed. (You should now realise why they're called operating systems.) In the early days of computers, there were no minis or micros, and the original operating systems were developed for mainframe computers. Even today, the mainframe operating systems of the 70s are still influencing state-of-the-art microcomputer operating-system designs during the late 1990s and early part of the 21st century, with Unix and Linux being good examples.

The mainframe background to the development of operating systems is an important one to understand, because it's only against this background that one can appreciate the different types of operating systems such as batch processing or time-sharing. Such terms seem to have little relevance for many non-specialist users who operate in the single-user-microcomputer environment. Indeed, most micro users will probably equate operating systems with DOS – Microsoft's Disk Operating System – but this was developed much later when 8 and 16-bit microcomputers were state-of-the-art technology (the early 1980s).

Given such a complex background, we will split operating systems up into separate parts. The first, considered in this chapter, is the microcomputer operating system environment. Here we will cover the types of operating systems available. The second part, concerned mainly with minis and mainframes, covered in chapter 23, will look at the detail of different types of operating systems. The final part will be concerned with networks, which is often the bridge between the micro and mainframe world. Fortunately, many basic concepts of operating systems are common to all three scenarios. The chronological consideration of mainframe systems in the next chapter will also enable you to understand the present-day micro systems, as much of the current technology is borrowed from these earlier mainframe ideas.

Basic concepts

The variety of machines on which operating systems are designed to run is huge – anything from a single-user microcomputer through a multi-user minicomputer via a global network to a powerful supercomputer – all are controlled by different types of operating system. It is indeed fortunate that all these systems have many fundamental concepts in common, and these will now be investigated further.

Exploiting the hardware

All operating systems are designed to exploit fully the hardware on which they are to be run. It is the operating-system software which tames the raw electronic power of modern computers, and makes these computers useable by people other than specialist engineers or scientists. A useful analogy can be drawn between the operating system software designed for a computer, and the software (music) on a typical compact-disc hi-fi system. The hi-fi system by itself represents raw electronic power, but put in a CD containing your favourite software, and a complex box of electronic wizardry transforms your lounge into an orchestral hall or a rock-concert venue. You forget about the electronics and enjoy the music. So it is with a computer system – pop in the operating system, then forget about the electronics, and you are put in touch with a **virtual world** containing an environment which transforms your computer into a useful and worthwhile tool. No longer do you have to worry about how to write a character on the screen, how to output some data to the printer or how to load and save files regarding the disk drive. The operating system handles all these and many other tedious

but essential tasks, leaving you to use the computer in creative ways more suitable to human thought, productivity and leisure. However, before getting too carried away, it's wise to remember that all that has changed your hi-fi system from raw electronic hardware into an art form is some software (data which represents the music), and all that transforms your computer into a complete environment is a **computer program**. But this is where the analogy comes to an end – even though operating systems *are* simply computer programs, most will rate among the most-complex programs ever devised by man. **Multiple Virtual Storage (MVS)** for example, developed for **IBM mainframes**, is an example of a complex operating system – it gives each user a maximum **virtual memory** (see chapter 12) space of up to 32 Gbytes, and can support thousands of different users. Given that operating systems themselves are among the most-complex things that man has ever conceived, this should give you some idea of the magnitude of this enormous and fascinating human achievement.

An operating-system perspective

The **operating system** is concerned directly with interfacing to the computer's architecture (see chapter 20). You can think of an operating system in diagrammatic form as a layer, which **is on top of** or **wrapped around** the **hardware** of the computer system. However, much of the time non-specialist users of the system will not interact directly with the operating system software, but via some application package such as a spreadsheet for example. We can regard these application packages as yet another layer in our diagram placed between the end user and the operating system. This is indeed what happens, as the application package translates the user I/O (short for Input/Output) into commands which the operating system understands, then the operating system translates these commands via machine-code routines contained in the operating system into a form which the hardware of the computer understands. Figure 22.1 shows what's sometimes referred to as an onion-diagram representation, as it resembles peeling off layers of an onion to get to the middle. Although our diagram is a simple one, and different computer systems have slightly different representations, the kernel (the *innermost ring*) represents things like the **software**, which controls the device drivers. These are the drivers which drive the electronic devices such as the disk-controller chips – or **software** which contains the **network-communication protocols** *if* the operating system supports communications with a computer network (most do). For example, the popular **TCP/IP protocols** (see chapter 5) are embedded in the **Unix-operating-system kernel**. In the very centre of the ring we could have drawn an even-smaller circle representing the computer hardware.

The ring marked utilities contains many software routines such as those for saving files to disk for example, or useful utilities which help the programmer who is writing applications programs. Useful utilities (programs) might include those for re-drawing windows in a multitasking environment if the user has clicked over an icon with the mouse. There are an enormous number of sub-programs written for most operating systems. Without these programs, applications programmers would have to re-invent the wheel each time they wanted to write to a disk, read a character from the keyboard buffer, or any other of the thousands of chores that have to be carried out during the normal operation of a computer. In a nutshell, the operating system contains all these often-used routines consisting of the detailed step-by-step instructions to carry out the management of the entire memory and peripherals etc. controlled by the computer.

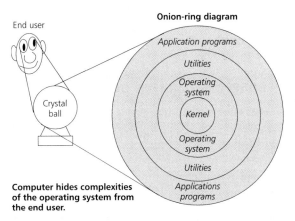

Computer hides complexities of the operating system from the end user.

Figure 22.1

Microcomputer operating system principles

We will concentrate first on the type of operating system found in a typical **microcomputer**. The mainframe operating systems will be covered in detail in chapter 23. MS-DOS is still a popular operating system, and it's relatively simple compared to windows. MS-DOS 6.0 will be used here as an example to explain main operating-system principles. Windows could have

Did you know that . . .

Over the years the PC has indeed come a long way from QDOS, the Quick and Dirty Operating System, bought up by Microsoft and made into DOS, to the Windows NT5 operating system of today. However, these new operating systems take up hundreds of Megabytes of disk space, compared to the leaner few tens of Kbytes in the early systems. Security aspects of the operating systems are now much tighter too.

been used, but MS-DOS is a simple beast in comparison, and will therefore make some of the principles easier to understand. Nevertheless, windows-based GUI systems are also covered in this part of the text where it helps to understand the concepts being covered. Earlier on the onion-diagram concept was introduced, and the onion diagram for MS-DOS 6.0 is shown in figure 22.2. As you can see from figure 22.2, MS-DOS 6.0 has been split up into 4 separate parts, and each will now be considered in more detail.

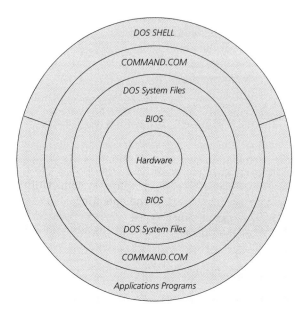

Figure 22.2

Basic Input/Output system (BIOS)

How does an **operating system** in a typical micro go about **handling** the mass of data transfers involving, for example, **mice**, **trackballs**, **disks**, **keyboards**, **monitors** (screens) and **communication devices** such as the **serial port** or **network cards**? Obviously we are communicating in complex ways with a variety of different hardware **devices** at an electronic level (i.e. the hardware as shown in the centre of the onion diagram – in this case the computer architecture based around Intel's processor). Without an operating system, it would be virtually impossible for most computer users to write programs to carry out these fundamental tasks.

Inside most operating systems, special programs have been written to help the computer user control all the various **devices**. In MS-DOS, for example, these are **the device drivers** which form part of the operating system at a fundamental level, and extend the capabilities of the BIOS (see in a

> **Hint:** If ever you need to reset your BIOS settings, you will need to remove the CMOS RAM battery and alter the position of one of the jumpers on the motherboard too. You will have to know what you're doing to perform this operation!

moment). Each device, such as the **keyboard**, has a separate **device handler**. This means, from a programmer's point of view, that all the devices look similar, and a change in device-driver name will re-direct the data to the appropriate device in hardware terms. On MS-DOS machines, the disks are slightly different in operation, and are investigated a little further in a moment. Most modern computer systems make use of **battery-backed-up RAM** (also called **CMOS RAM**) in which to store different **default BIOS** conditions for the machine at switch on. If your CMOS battery goes flat, your computer will probably respond in unpredictable ways – 'thinking it's the wrong date' would be typical, for example.

DOS system files

The DOS system files, supplied on disk, form part of the operating system, which is loaded into the computer after it has been switched on (see booting in a moment). These files are combined with the parts of the BIOS already in ROM and RAM (see chapter 12), to form a much-more comprehensive operating system. Utilities then add to the capability of the operating system still further. These and other types of files considerably extend what the operating system can do.

Booting the system

Whenever a computer system is switched on, it needs to follow a **programmed sequence of events** such as **checking that all the hardware is working and searching for any special start-up instructions**. It is the job of that part of the operating system permanently resident inside the computer (in ROM) to make sure that *other* parts of the operating system are **loaded** into

Did you know that . . .

Unless you currently have a very fast computer, it used to be quicker to boot up in the old days! There was less configuration information and the operating system loaded into RAM was significantly less massive. Today, a fully customised PC with backdrops on the desktop, many shortcuts and 'auto running of several applications and utilities' can often take between one or two minutes to boot. This is obviously frustrating if your machine has a software fault which needs constant rebooting to cure it.

memory and **started up** properly.

Getting the computer started up after switching on is called **booting the system** or, more simply, **booting**. It comes from the term 'to pull yourself up by your own boot straps', which means building up your capability from virtually nothing by using what you already know to increase your capability yet further.

This is exactly what is happening inside a computer during the switch-on sequence, because more-complex parts of the operating system are being loaded in by the other parts, thus creating a more-sophisticated system that is capable of doing very much more. At the instant you switch on your computer it can do very little – almost nothing at all. After running the boot files and loading the operating system, it has been transformed into a powerful and useful system. It has pulled itself up by its own **bootstraps**.

There are a couple of different philosophies around at the moment. The first is to supply *all* of the operating system on a **ROM** chip, as is used in the **Acorn's RISC-OS** computers and some portables – there is little alternative, for example, in the latest generation of **palmtops**. This method has the advantage that no conventional RAM is taken up with storing operating system software – some of which is quite large and could run to many Mbytes or more for the very latest windows-based systems. It is also useful in portable and palmtop machines because the computer is 'ready to go' after switching on. Nevertheless, the disadvantage is that future upgrades to the operating system require that the set of ROMs be replaced – not a job for the average computer user, and more expensive than the alternative methods. Even so, bug fixes are sometimes supplied on disk to fix bugs even when the entire operating system is stored in RAM. These modules are put into RAM and become part of the new operating system software.

The second, more-common method is to supply a very small part of the **operating system** in ROM, then supply the rest of the operating system on **disk** (which can be installed on an internal hard disk or delivered via a network if required). This is the technique used by most manufacturers, and the one that's used on mainframe computers too. The biggest advantage is that upgrades to the system are trivial – a new program is all that is required to iron out any bugs or provide a more-recent version of the system. With the trends outlined in the first part of the microcomputer section, you should be able to deduce that it's an advantage to be able to run different types of operating system. For example, 'Unix' or 'Windows NT' may be required for one job; while a real (not emulated) version of 'MS-DOS' is used for another. Supplying multiple operating systems on disk makes this sort of flexibility easier to obtain making use of the same computer hardware. Indeed, you can have multiple boot options on a PC, for example, such that it could boot up in the operating system of your choice.

Customisation of the operating system

After the operating system has been loaded, then the computer is ready and able to respond to the user's input in the normal way. However, in addition to this,

> **Hint:** Some software, without your permission, alters the settings of these crucial start-up files, often with drastic consequences for other software, which is expecting the previous information!

it is useful *to customise the computer* to your personal requirements. For example, you might want some utilities or other software to run automatically on start up, and other information, specific to any application which you may run on the system needs to be stored on disk too. This is usually carried out by what are called **boot** files. In MS-DOS there is a file called '**AUTOEXEC.BAT**', but '**CONFIG.SYS**' plays a major part here too in configuring the system to a user's specific requirements. Such files contain lists of commands to instruct the computer to go through set sequences after the operating system has been loaded and fully installed. It saves the user having to manually load software and alter settings each time the machine is switched on. If you are using a Windows GUI system, then the above can be configured still further by what used to be known as **WIN.INI** files (i.e. Windows Initialisation files). As their name implies, the WIN.INI files initialised many parameters that are specific to the Windows operating system. There were also a large number of INI files specific to many applications, but the more-recent versions of Windows now have what's called a **REGISTRY**, which is the repository of most of the knowledge regarding the initialisation of Windows and all installed applications.

Command.com

Once the operating system has been booted satisfactorily, there needs to be some way for the user to communicate with it. Part of the COMMAND.COM file is the **command interpreter** for MS-DOS, so called because it interprets commands typed in by the user. (Other parts of **COMMAND.COM** run the boot file (**AUTOEXEC.BAT**) and provide extensions to the BIOS.) A prompt (A> or C> being typical in MS-DOS) indicates that the computer is ready to accept an operating-system command from the keyboard. 'DIR', for example, would list the files in the currently selected directory, or '**DOS-SHELL**', would start the shell (see in a moment). In fact, not all commands are held in RAM after boot up, and **FORMAT** is an example of an **external command** that is classed as a **utility**. Typing a command such as 'FORMAT A:', for example, after loading the appropriate program from disk, will cause the operating system sub-program to carry out the formatting process. It would also return an error if it was not possible to format the floppy drive – you may have forgotten to put the disk in the drive! Saving and loading programs would be two other common examples of typical operating system interaction with the user via the command processor.

Simplified view of disk operations

When a file is saved to disk, for example, it is the **operating system** which has to carry out the tasks needed to accomplish this operation. The operating system will then analyse the filename you have given it. Assuming a hierarchical directory structure (see chapter 25), that the filename is valid, and that no file with the same name exists within the target directory, then the operating system will add your chosen name to the list of files within the target directory! Note that this is not enough to cause the actual data to be saved on disk, it is just a new label which is added into a table called the **File Allocation Table** or **FAT**, if we use the MS-DOS system as an example. Next the FAT has to be checked for information regarding which cluster/s is/are ready to receive

> **Hint:** Although the early versions of Windows95 still use the FAT system, later versions of Windows and WindowsNT versions 4 and 5 make use of the NTFS system. This is a more sophisticated disk structure, which allows for greater flexibility and security than is afforded by the simpler FAT system being described here.

the data, and which **tracks** and **sectors** on the **disk** (see chapter 12) make up these clusters. If these operations are successful, then the appropriate data is transferred from RAM via the BIOS. As many clusters as necessary can be allocated provided that the disk is not full. When the **file-writing** operation has been successfully completed, the FAT is updated to prevent overwriting this information when the next save operation is carried out. Reading the data back is similar in principle with the '**directory** and **filename**', and 'information contained in the FAT' being used to retrieve the data. These ideas can be seen in figure 22.3.

This is a *simplified* view of what actually happens in a typical system. It takes no account of the many things that could go wrong when carrying out operations like these in practice. For example, such errors might be a 'recently-corrupted disk surface' or an 'error in the transmitted data' (see chapter 5). In addition to this we have not covered aspects such as 'has the user attempting to gain access to the file got sufficient privilege to do so?' – a real problem in multi-user mainframe and network-operating-system environments such as Windows NT, for example.

Other types of error might be caused by mistakes in the user programs, for example, some **assembler code** (see chapter 21) attempting to address non-existent RAM, or a **Prolog program** attempting an **arithmetical operation** which results in overflow (see chapter 31). Even when running an application program, which generates user-friendly messages, it is the **operating system**'s job to pass the appropriate information over to the application program. A real operating system would have to cope with all of this and very much more. By now you should be appreciating

Plate 27

This special card fits into the motherboard of your computer, via the PCI bus. It contains fast video RAM so that graphics on the computer can be processed very quickly. The graphics card shown is the Millennium G200 SD with 8 Mbyte of graphics RAM

Plate 28 ▶

Bubble-jet printing systems from Hewlett Packard, which incorporate colour and black-and-white photocopying, colour and black-and-white printing and OCR technology. Similar printers also have the facility to fax a document directly

Plate 29

Sound systems like these are needed to complement any up-to-date multimedia system. For realism in games and hi-fi quality sound large sub-woofers (the large speakers shown) are required to get a good base response

Plate 30
Headgear and data gloves being used to interact with a computer through a virtual dummy. The computer-generated model in the background duplicates the actions of the person wearing the devices. This researcher is also wearing eye-tracking gear and has space-sensing magnets inside his clothes to interact more fully with the computer

Plate 31 ▶
A data glove being used to help control an image which is being projected into the eyes of a person wearing a virtual-reality headset. In this particular simulation, the user of the virtual-reality gear is placing tracer particles within the airflow, which is represented by the blue lines

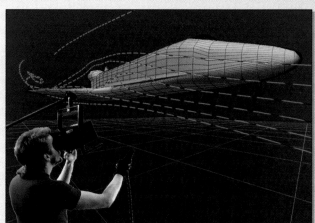

◀ **Plate 32**
The number and types of memory chips available for computers is astounding. The Kingston company, for example, produces over 1,500 memory products that are compatible with over 4,000 different types of computers from 30 different manufacturers. Shown here are SIMMs, or Single In-line Memory Modules, typical of the RAM found inside modern PCs

Plate 33 ▶
You can now record your own CDs with drives like these. The top two fit inside a standard PC and the lower one is for an external drive. Just a few years ago only large manufacturers could record CDs, but machines like these are now easily afford-able by home computer users

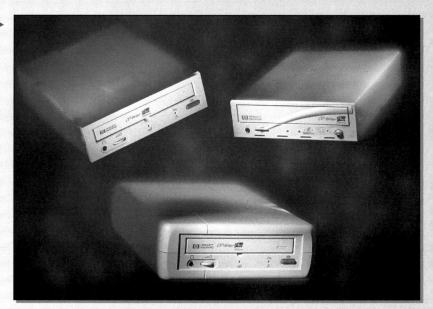

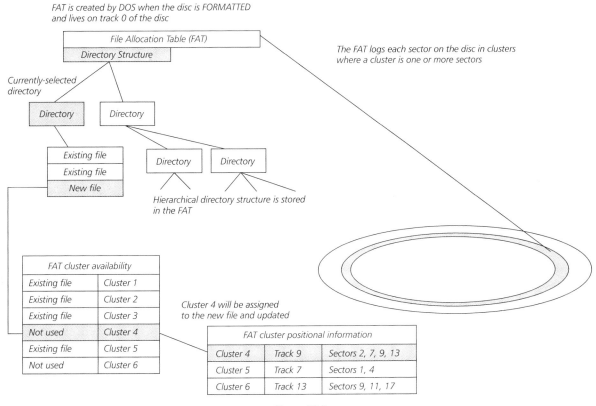

FAT is created by DOS when the disc is FORMATTED and lives on track 0 of the disc

File Allocation Table (FAT)

Directory Structure

The FAT logs each sector on the disc in clusters where a cluster is one or more sectors

Currently-selected directory

Directory

Directory

Existing file

Existing file

New file

Directory

Directory

Hierarchical directory structure is stored in the FAT

FAT cluster availability	
Existing file	Cluster 1
Existing file	Cluster 2
Existing file	Cluster 3
Not used	Cluster 4
Existing file	Cluster 5
Not used	Cluster 6

Cluster 4 will be assigned to the new file and updated

FAT cluster positional information		
Cluster 4	Track 9	Sectors 2, 7, 9, 13
Cluster 5	Track 7	Sectors 1, 4
Cluster 6	Track 13	Sectors 9, 11, 17

Figure 22.3

what a complex task it is to design modern operating systems!

In addition to the BIOS and other features mentioned in the last couple of sections, there are many **utilities** such as the 'formatting programs' already mentioned, those available for producing **statistics** such as '**disk size**' or the '**amount of RAM** available' etc. Third-party software writers also supply useful utilities, and examples of these might be programs to uninstall software which the software writers seem to splatter into every conceivable directory on your precious hard disk drive.

The DOS shell

We now consider MS-DOS again. Historically, typing in terse commands was the only way to communicate with an operating system. However, with the later versions of MS-DOS (MS-DOS 4.x +) there is an option included to load a **shell** which gives users of MS-DOS a much more user-friendly **GUI**. Just as on the Apple Mac and the later Windows PCs, DOS users could now see folders, which represent directories, and point with the mouse to carry out fundamental operations. The shell also provides a multitasking environment, which means, at last, that DOS had a way of interacting in a way that is similar to all of the other common **GUI** operating systems. Real MS-DOS can still be run alongside the Windows operating systems as described earlier in this chapter, but later versions of Windows

have integrated DOS to a greater or lesser extent. Indeed, Windows NT4 now runs many DOS programs better than the original DOS, even though the original DOS is not actually present on the machine! Indeed, as processors get faster, as memory becomes cheaper, and hard disk space becomes available at reasonable cost, it's now feasible to emulate many operating systems making use of others.

Memory maps

When considering modern microcomputers, some of the memory (RAM) is taken up with parts of the operating system. Much of the BIOS is also usually permanently resident in ROM.

Other parts of the operating system can be loaded and placed in whatever locations are decided upon by the operating-system-software writers (within available RAM limitations). Software like the disk controller or display adapter, for example, will need to go somewhere, and memory is also needed for important essentials

Hint: There can be few frequent users of PCs who have not encountered the dreaded errors like 'Page Protection Fault @ . . .'. This usually means that an errant application is trying to write to an area of the memory map that is being used by something else. If you're unlucky the machine will crash, or if you have a more sophisticated operating system like WindowsNT, then you can kill the offending application with the task manager to prevent a total crash from happening.

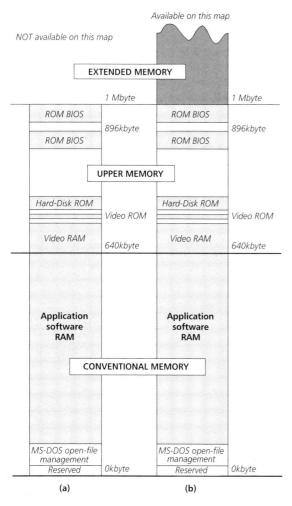

Figure 22.4

extended memory, which is real useable RAM beyond the 1 Mbyte-earlier-processor limit. This **memory map** is used by version 5.0 and 6.0 of MS-DOS and at last makes full use of the 386 and 486 processor's capabilities. The expanded memory map for this system is a simple extension as shown in figure 22.4(b) However, many software fixes had to be done to keep some older software 'happy' and 'thinking' that it was still running under the old memory maps. It is for these complex historical reasons that some programs do not function well in a modern operating system environment.

Note that different operating systems will obviously have different memory-map layouts within the same computer hardware. A **NETBIOS**, for example, would be needed if the PC were to be operated on a **LAN** (see chapter 3).

Cache memory

As is explained in chapter 12, there are two main types of semiconductor (RAM) memory. **Dynamic RAM** is fast (current access times are in the order of 40 nsec 10^{-9} sec) and is the relatively inexpensive memory used for the vast majority of RAM. There are many different-speed RAM chips, but the faster they are the more expensive they become. However, **static RAM** (or **SRAM**), which does not need to be refreshed, is faster still (current access times about 10 nsec or less) and can be used to maximum advantage if placed in-between the main memory (DRAM) and the processor as shown in figure 22.5. When used in this way, the memory in-between the processor and main memory is called **cache memory**. SRAM is not used for the entire RAM because it is more expensive than even the most expensive dynamic RAM. Although today's memory byte for byte is a lot less expensive than it used to be, the goal posts keep moving due to the increasing expectations of the users of microcomputers and the applications which they run, and the increasing power available from the microprocessor chips. A few years ago 1 Mbyte of RAM was acceptable. Today 256 Mbytes is not uncommon, tomorrow – who

such as the **stack** (see chapter 21) or **printer spooler** (see chapter 23) if one has been implemented. Anything that is added such as a **network interface card** must also have an appropriate part of the memory allocated to the **network operating system software** (see chapter 5).

To prevent the chaotic situation whereby **applications** and **utilities** could overwrite important areas of operating-system memory, it's necessary for all those concerned to have an *exact* idea of where all the operating system and applications software is to be located inside the memory of a modern computer system. This is accomplished by means of a **memory map**. A typical one for the earlier versions of MS-DOS is shown in figure 22.4(a). The first 640 Kbyte is referred to as 'Conventional memory' and the remainder up to the original 1 Mbyte-processor limit is often called 'Upper memory' as can be seen from figure 22.4(a).

Expanded memory was the first technique used to get over the 640 Kbyte MS-DOS barrier, but this was a bodge – a 64 Kbyte block called a 'page frame' could be switched in and out in 16 Kbyte sections into an area of upper memory. Later versions of MS-DOS used

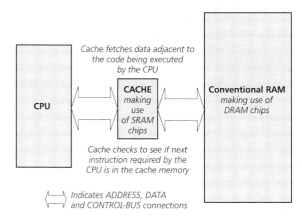

Figure 22.5

> **Hint:** Careful setting of the cache size can drastically affect the performance of your computer. If your disk keeps thrashing, then you might need to increase the cache size or, if you're unlucky, you need to get more RAM.

knows? Therefore, the cost of RAM is less of an issue.

If you analysed exactly what a typical processor spent its time doing, then you would probably find that much of the time would be taken up with execution of a linear sequence of machine-code instructions (see chapter 20). Also, for much of the time, it might be dealing with instructions that are near to the ones currently being processed. Considering the speed of today's processors, the time taken to get an instruction from memory, even though it is only a tiny fraction of a second, significantly holds up the processor's ability to get things done. Therefore, if the most-likely-used instructions are held in cache memory, then the time taken for the processor to act upon these instructions is very much reduced, due to the static RAM's faster speed. In the majority of cases the increase in speed over a machine without cache can be very significant, and most modern microcomputer operating systems and computer architectures now have cache memory as a standard feature. A typical size of external cache (see in a moment) on a microcomputer might be anything between about 256 Kbyte and 2 Mbyte.

In the last two paragraphs we have been talking of cache mounted on the motherboard (i.e. main-processor board) of the computer. However, you should also appreciate that the same techniques are used to even better effect (due to the incredibly close proximity) inside the actual microprocessors. For example, Intel's Pentium II chip has its own ½ Mbyte of cache memory inside the microprocessor itself. Because the paths between the **internal cache** and the **main processor registers** (see chapter 20) are so small (just a few mm or less), then this memory is even faster than the **external cache** referred to above.

Simple interrupts

> **Hint:** It's enlightening to compare the interrupts being considered here with the interrupts from the point of view of a microprocessor running an assembly language program. Of course, these principles are identical, because the operating system is an assembly language program being run on a microprocessor!

We are now going to consider the principles of simple interrupts on a typical **microcomputer system**.

The CPU will normally be getting on with the business of running programs until some peripheral device rudely interrupts it. It literally has to stop what it is doing and find out what device is causing the interrupt. It

will then have to jump to the routine which has been written to handle this particular interrupt and then, when the interrupting device has been satisfied, the CPU will get back to what it was originally doing.

We shall start by having a look at how the CPU of a small computer system handles interrupts in the way described above.

The interrupt may occur at any time. Therefore the processor could be in the middle of literally any operation. The processor will finish executing the current machine-code operation, then stop work on the current task. As each machine code operation takes only a few fractions of a millionth of a second, the interrupting device can usually wait this long! Inside the CPU there is yet another register called the interrupt register. It is the information held in this register, together with the information from the interrupt enable/disable register (see later) that enables the CPU to take the desired action.

The CPU must remember what it was doing, and so the **program counter** (see chapter 20) and all-important **registers** are saved in an area of memory reserved for such purposes called the stack (see chapter 21). Basically, most of the CPU registers can be pushed on to the stack. The CPU must now find out which device is causing the interrupt. There are several ways of doing this and one way is to use what is called a vectored-interrupt technique.

Consider figure 22.6. In this particular case, the interrupting device supplies a number that is then added to a fixed number as shown. This combined number then forms the address of the memory location that contains the jump address where the routine to handle the interrupt can be found. This may sound a mouthful, but it is a particularly clever way of enabling the interrupt-handling routines to be placed literally anywhere in memory. The numbers inside the memory locations which are used as **pointers** (see chapter 24) to the places where the interrupt-handling routines can be found are called **vectors**. In computing, a vector is simply a pointer, i.e. an address that will be used to point to some area of memory. This is why this method of handling

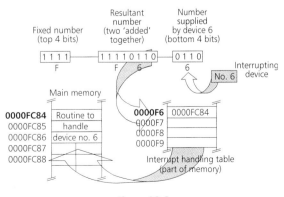

Figure 22.6

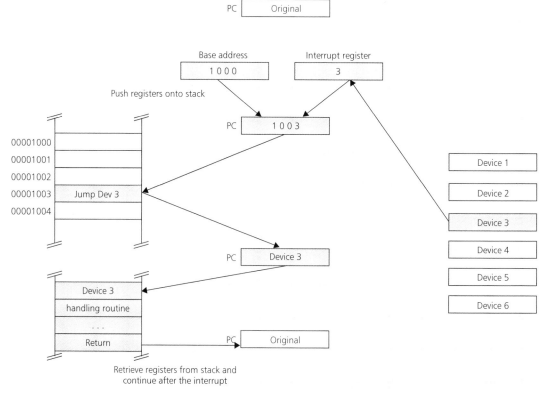

Figure 22.7

interrupts is known as vectored-interrupt handling. Consider the simple example shown in figure 22.7.

Let's suppose that we have five devices, all of which could cause an interrupt to happen. We therefore need five different interrupt vectors. Let's also assume that these vectors will be stored in memory locations 1000, 1001 and 1002 etc. inclusive as shown in figure 22.7. Finally, let us assume that each interrupting device will supply the number 1, 2, 3, 4 or 5, depending on the device causing the interrupt. Now suppose device 3 has caused the interrupt, then 3 is combined with the base address of the vectors (1000) to make 1003. The program counter is therefore set to 1003.

The computer will now fetch, decode and execute the instruction at location 1003. This is a jump instruction that points the computer to the routine which will handle interrupting device number 3. The interrupt is now being handled, and, at the end of the interrupt routine, a return-from-interrupt instruction will be encountered. This will cause the CPU to return to its original task, which it had left when the interrupt occurred. This is achieved by popping all the registers off the stack, and restoring the original contents of the program counter.

The interrupt has now been serviced and the computer has resumed its original task and is now ready for another interrupt should one occur.

One of the ideal things about the above method is that if the interrupting device, and hence the interrupt

handling routine, have to be changed, all that's necessary is to change the contents of a single memory location (the pointer) to point to the new location where the new interrupt handling routine can be found. The system is therefore very versatile and easy to update should needs change.

From reading the above it may seem that servicing an interrupt is a long process. However, this is not necessarily the case. An interrupt can usually be serviced in a few millionths of a second. Indeed, the computer can service an interrupt so quickly that the operator who is using the computer will not even notice that the program he or she is currently working on has been interrupted. Some small computers have interrupts happening hundreds of times each second. For example, it is possible to organise the keyboard so that whenever a character is typed in, the processor is interrupted to deal with it.

Handling errors

Undertaking an advanced computing course will certainly bring home the fact that computers go wrong quite frequently, especially when inexperienced users are experimenting. Therefore, much effort goes into aspects of operating-system design which try to prevent a complete crash of the system in many preventable circumstances. It would be silly, for example, if a **disk-sector error** on a floppy caused a **major crash** with loss of all data. It would be preferable if the operating system could have detected this, flagged the error to the user, then returned control to the user who could rectify the situation by changing the disk, and finally re-saving the data. There are usually an enormous number of conditions which are intercepted by the operating system and where appropriate error messages are presented to the user. However, occasionally, even the operating system gets 'confused' and a fatal crash would then take place.

Errors can sometimes be detected and corrected by the operating system. For example, by using a method such as checksums or parity (see chapters 15 and 17) an error might have been detected during the transmission of some data from memory to a disk. A re-try could be requested and the re-transmitted data might pass the check and be saved successfully. The computer user would probably be blissfully unaware that an error had even occurred. However, if after trying several times the transmitted data is still in error, then a likely hardware fault has been detected (for example, your dog might have started to chew up the external disk cables under your desk!) and an error message would then be generated by the operating system.

Operating systems are so complex that it's not possible to make sure that every single eventuality is catered for. All that can be done is to strive towards a 100% perfect system – but never actually achieve it. Nevertheless, the reliability of today's operating systems is very high, with real-time control systems being among the most reliable (see chapter 8), e.g. computer control of aircraft etc. reaching reliabilities in excess of 99.9999%.

Network operating systems

Having common operating systems on stand-alone computers is a tremendous advantage when it comes to transferring data between different machines, as the disk on one computer may be read by other computers – assuming that the same type and version of the operating system is used. However, even though the single-user-microcomputer enthusiast might be able to survive independently at home, in business and education, the sharing of information and other resources is essential. As the concept of the Earth becoming a global village comes ever closer, good communications, and especially computer communications have an increasingly important part in both business and leisure activities. Physical and radio networks (see chapter 3) are now beginning to play an increasingly important role in the distributed processing environment.

> **Hint:** You should consider the NC and network PCs as explained in chapter 3 when networks were being considered. Many billions of pounds are at stake to see who wins the network operating system war.

There is little point storing hundreds of copies of the same application software on local hard disk inside many different PCs, if the same software can be got quickly from a file server on a local network. This is, of course, assuming that you have sufficient bandwidth to do this. The ability to share expensive resources such as colour LASER printers via a printer server, a modem via an appropriate proxy server, or to share multiple stacked CD-ROM databases (see chapter 12) all put extra stress on the more-complex operating-system software. Also important is the fact that microcomputers are being used as intelligent terminals to mainframes, or using LANs, MANs and WANs to connect to mainframes which act as information providers. The network topology, hardware and communications protocols are considered in great detail in the network chapters 3 and 5. However, the need for part of the operating system to be able to deal with 'network communications' is an obvious one, and will be dealt with here for completeness of this operating-systems chapter.

DOS-based workstations

As we have used MS-DOS for the main examples in the micro-operating system section, we will again show how an MS-DOS-based machine can be used on a network from an operating system perspective.

If you are using a DOS-based machine as a workstation on a network, then it is necessary to have some additional hardware called a network interface card (NIC), and some additional network software. MS-DOS is then booted up (see earlier) at the workstation from an internal hard disk, a local floppy disk, or from the file server on the network if the network interface card has a remote-boot operating system fitted. On early versions of DOS, this network software stole 66k of the valuable 640 Kbyte of RAM that was available (see memory map in figure 22.4), but on MS-DOS versions 5.0 and later, this is no longer the case.

You can imagine the network operating system software as another layer in the onion diagram of figure 22.2, and it is also referred to as a shell, just like the bolt-on windows options. Two programs called IPX.COM and NETx.COM are the programs that have to be loaded after DOS has booted up. The boot file autoexec.bat usually runs them. These network-software programs contain the information that is needed by the workstation to communicate with the network. IPX.COM, for example, contains the data necessary to implement layers 3 and 4 of the ISO-OSI model (see chapter 5). The NIC contains the drivers necessary to interface with level 2 of the OSI model. NETx.COM is another program that interacts with DOS by running on top of DOS to create a network operating system environment for the user of the workstation (i.e. the user can then make use of the network as another disk-filing system).

It is to be appreciated that we now have several places on which to save data. We have the local hard disk, floppy disk and the network. Conventionally, drives A to E are reserved for the local hard and floppy disk, while drives F to Z are usually reserved for the network or CD-ROM drives. Once set up in this way, the network can often be transparent to the user of the system, but it should be obvious that certain **logging-on** procedures must be gone through before having access to information on a network that is perhaps common to hundreds of computers. It is usual to have to supply a **user ID** and a **password** to gain access to the system. Problems of this nature are covered in great detail in the networks chapter.

Real-time operating systems

In the operating systems considered so far, it did not matter too much if a job was delayed or if a task was carried out two seconds later rather than sooner. However, there are situations in which such a delay would be unacceptable, or even fatal. A typical but deadly example of a **real-time operating system** would be found in the embedded-microprocessor systems housed in a guided missile. Suppose, for example, that you happen to be on the deck of a warship, which unfortunately is in the path of an incoming missile. You may have just 15 seconds before impact, and you launch your anti-missile missile, which is guided by a real-time operating system. The missile just launched would have to lock onto the incoming missile and destroy it. You would not appreciate the electronics inside the missile dithering for a few seconds while the operating system decides what to do!

The above example is rather drastic but illustrates a typical example of the situation in which real-time operating systems are used. However, **real-time does not necessarily mean fast**. Although it is essential to use a real-time system where speed is of the essence, as long as the operating system can respond and process the appropriate data before some outside process could suffer, then you have what is literally a real time system. Suppose, for example, that a computer system was controlling the amount of liquid in a tank. Suppose also that the water valve must be turned off within a 1-minute period of a signal being transmitted from the sensor (see chapter 8). If the computer system responds within say, 45 seconds, and the water is safely turned off, then this is a real time system, even though it is painfully slow. However, it must be said that most real-time systems do refer to the systems in which a fast response is needed.

The majority of real-time operating systems go hand-in-hand with **process control** such as 'missile guidance' or 'controlling a chemical factory' etc. Therefore, these systems will be considered in much more detail in chapter 8 on process control.

Exercise 22.1

1 Explain how more-powerful microprocessor chips have had an enormous impact on the way that microcomputer operating systems have developed.

2 Explain how multitasking would probably be used in the context of a single-user microcomputer operating system.

3 It is now possible to run different operating systems on the same micro. Why is this an added advantage over a single operating system?

4 What is meant by an object-oriented operating system and why are they becoming important?

5 What is a BIOS in terms of a typical micro operating system?

6 Boot files are often used to start up a computer. Explain the function of the boot file and why some manufacturers do not commit their entire operating system to ROM.

7 Explain how a typical micro operating system would handle saving a file to floppy disk.

8 What is meant by a memory map in connection with a microcomputer operating system and why is it so important?

9 Explain the function of an interrupt and how an interrupt may be serviced in a typical microcomputer environment.

10 Cache memory can be used to increase the amount of work done by a computer in a given time. Explain the function of cache and how it achieves its aim.

11 The WIMP environment is much more user-friendly. Why?

12 After booting the operating system it is often useful to customise a computer to the exact requirements of a particular user. How is this done and why is it useful?

13 How can an operating system detect that an error has occurred when going about its normal tasks? Give an example of an error that could be detected by the operating system.

14 If a microcomputer is to be used as a workstation on a network, then vital software and hardware must usually be added to the system. What two things are normally needed over and above the basic operating system and hardware of the microcomputer?

15 Over the last ten years one or two operating systems have dominated the market. Why is this so and why is the situation rapidly changing in the late 1990s and 2000s?

16 What extra precautions are necessary when a network operating system has been installed in a microcomputer connected to a network?

17 Why is it possible for a novice user to not appreciate that an operating system exists inside a computer, even though the operating system is probably the most important piece of software?

18 What problems are usually encountered when attempting to transfer data between two different computers running different operating systems? How could a network help in overcoming some of these problems?

19 The early microcomputer operating systems fitted inside a few Kbytes of RAM, but some of the latest operating systems take up many Mbytes. Why is it not possible to guarantee that the complex operating system found inside a modern computer works properly? What do the companies do to help out customers when faults are found?

20 An enormous amount of progress has been made in operating systems design in the last ten years. What do you think might happen in the next ten?

End of chapter revision aid and summary

Cover up the right-hand column and see if you can answer the questions or define the terms on the left. They appear in the order in which they are covered in this chapter. Alternatively you may browse through the right-hand column to aid revision.

What is an operating system?

An operating system is a complex piece of software needed to harness the power of a computer system and make it much easier to use.

How is an onion diagram helpful when considering operating systems?

Onion diagrams conveniently display relationships between the operating system and other software (and hardware) in pictorial form.

What is distributed processing?

Distributed processing is becoming increasingly important due to the drastically increased power of microcomputers and the increasingly common and powerful networks. Sometimes different computers on the network can share the same task.

Why are microcomputer operating systems now very powerful?

Microcomputer operating systems have become increasingly sophisticated due to the enormous power increase of the microprocessors.

What is the most popular non-GUI OS.

MS-DOS is the most popular non-GUI microcomputer operating system to date. However, Unix is popular too.

What is the most popular GUI-based OS.

Many new operating systems are now in a position to become the dominant force. Windows is currently the most popular system, but this might be challenged in the future, by Linux, for example.

What advantage is there to writing an object-oriented operating system?

Object-oriented operating systems are now being written in C++ to make these incredibly complex systems more comprehensible and easy to manage.

Why is it now easier to emulate less powerful operating systems?	The new generation of microcomputers (64-bit microprocessors) are now becoming so powerful that older operating systems can be run under emulation at speeds in excess of those available on the older purpose-built hardware.
What are boot files?	Boot files are used to get the main operating system up and running, and to customise the computer for individual use.
What helps to customise a computer at start up?	Boot files such as autoexec.bat help to customise a computer to the user's requirements at start up. However, the registry is now increasingly used in Windows.
What is a registry?	In the Windows operating system a registry is a large store of information regarding hardware and software configurations for a particular machine. It customises a computer to individual requirements.
What is a memory map?	Memory maps are used to show how the operating system and other software is distributed throughout RAM and ROM.
What is cache memory?	Cache memory (fast SRAM) is used to increase the speed of instructions currently or about to be executed.
How might an operating system help with possible errors?	The operating system can be used to detect a variety of errors, some of which it is possible to correct. Even fatal errors should be handled such that the computer does not crash if possible.
What extra hardware is needed to make full use of a network operating system?	Networking capability may be added to a micro by adding a network interface card in addition to the network operating system software.
What is a shell with respect to the onion diagram?	Shells may be added in the onion diagram to show how network or windows operating systems may be added on to existing systems.
What is a real-time operating system?	A real-time operating system is one that can respond at a speed which is sufficient to process data required by an external source.

23 Larger Operating Systems

Key resources

To carry out this work most successfully it's best if you have:

◆ A visit to a large mainframe installation. This might typically be of the type to be found in a university or a large business
◆ Access to a network computer system, if possible running some NC computers in a thin client-server relationship

Concept checkpoints

◆ It's vital that you read chapter 22 before attempting to work through this chapter.
◆ Knowledge of the computer networks covered in chapter 3 is also useful when considering the thin client-server operating systems.

Mainframe computers – batch operating systems

You may recall from the introduction at the beginning of chapter 22 that the first operating systems were originally designed to alleviate the need for time-consuming human intervention. The early systems were serial in nature, in that they undertook just one task at a time. So these particular operating systems concentrated on getting jobs done one after the other as quickly as possible. These serial operating systems were known as batch operating systems, because they usually tackled a batch of jobs (programs to be run). It was the job of the computer operator to make sure that the batch of programs were put into the computer system in the right order, and other small programs, containing instructions to the operating system, were placed in between the jobs. This was the way that most mainframes operated in the early 1970s. An understanding of this is useful, not just from an historical perspective, but from the point of view of making some aspects of operating systems easier to understand today. It is easy to see where computers are going if you know where they have been in the past.

A typical sequence of jobs for a batch-processing system at a university might have included running several Fortran programs for engineering students, a few COBOL programs for business-studies students and running some machine code programs for computer-science students. You should realise that these students in the 1970s (of which the author was one!) did not sit down at terminals and type in their programs, but prepared the source code (see chapter 21) on special card-punch machines. They would then take their pile of cards to the computer centre – being careful not to drop them all on the floor! – then submit the cards to the receptionist at the computer centre main desk. If you were lucky the results of your computer program would be available the next day, and if you were unlucky the only message out of the computer might have been 'syntax error at line 10'!

The computer operator used to prepare the batch of cards in a similar way to that shown in figure 23.1, then place the entire pack into the computer system's card-reader machine. The computer's operating system would then take over, ensuring that the correct compilers were used for translating the source code into the object code for the target machine. (See chapter 21 if that was gobbledegook!)

Job-control languages

A job control language (JCL) was (and *still is* in modern computer systems) used to control the jobs being run. Job-control cards, containing the job-control-language instructions, used to be inserted

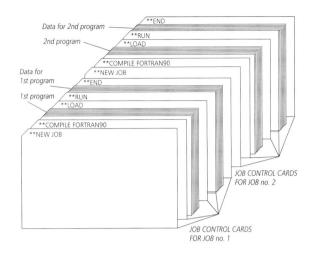

Data for 2nd program — **END
2nd program — **RUN
**LOAD
**COMPILE FORTRAN90
Data for — **NEW JOB
1st program — **END
1st program — **RUN
**LOAD
**COMPILE FORTRAN90
**NEW JOB

JOB CONTROL CARDS
FOR JOB no. 2

JOB CONTROL CARDS
FOR JOB no. 1

Figure 23.1

by the computer operator to specify things like 'the peripherals needed by the job', 'the beginning and end of the job', 'what compilers will be needed', and may also be used for 'accounting purposes'. Don't forget that mainframes were and still are expensive machines – if you use just a few seconds of CPU time then you have to pay for it! Job control languages are *still used* in the same context, but the commands are now typed into the system from a terminal, instead of being submitted on cards as in the earlier systems.

To gain a better understanding of batch operating systems you need to appreciate the advantages a batch-processing system offers when compared to no operating system at all. To do this let's assume that a Fortran program is being run. When the computer encounters the first job-control-language command, this will automatically cause the Fortran compiler to be loaded from the correct magnetic disk or tape. (Note the human operator no longer has to do this.) Next the **source code is compiled**, and if no errors are encountered, the **object code** is placed in the computer's memory at a point determined by the operating system. The object code could then be run automatically, which might, for example, cause data to be read from tape or disk, cause some output to be printed or **spooled** (see next section), and then continue to proceed in this manner until the program is finished. The operating system would probably time how long it takes the program to execute, and intervene if necessary to terminate the program. The program getting stuck in an infinite loop, for example, which has resulted from a logical error on the part of the programmer, might be cause for a program termination.

> **Hint:** To get the most out of reading this chapter you must tear yourself away from the normal PC micro-computer mentality. This chapter only makes sense when viewed in this light. A visit to a large mainframe installation operating a batch system would help considerably.

After this typical scenario the next program in the batch would be started automatically. Although the chain of events has been simplified, you can see that the mainframe computer is being utilised much more efficiently under the control of the batch-processing operating system. Without the operating system the computer operator would have had his or her work cut out just to make the above sequence of events happen manually. Even in the early days, a computer without an operating system was not a feasible proposition.

The computer operator would usually have an **operator's console,** which is the name given to a special **terminal** into which the computer operator could type instructions to terminate a job, or get a progress report on what is happening at any moment in time, for example. From this operator's terminal the computer operator could interrupt what is happening inside the computer at any moment in time, whether or not the computer was in the middle of a job.

Batch processing today

After reading the above you might think that compared to modern **multitasking windows environments** batch processing operating systems belong in the Middle Ages. However, think more carefully about problems such as processing thirty million tax demands, or working out statistics from the national census data! These and many other problems of similar and much-smaller magnitudes naturally lend themselves to batch processing, and although the input is no longer controlled in quite the same way, you should appreciate the need to process large amounts of data in a batch. This 'need' will be with us for the foreseeable future.

The strive for greater efficiency

The first operating systems were wonderful compared to none at all, but it quickly became obvious that in certain areas considerable improvements could be made. For example, if a program requested some output on a line printer (see chapter 11), then this process was very slow indeed compared to the speed at which the central processor could operate. Valuable CPU time was wasted while waiting for output on slow peripheral devices. One way round this problem was to **SPOOL (Simultaneous Peripheral Output On Line** – though nobody uses this mouthful!) the data to a tape or disk. This means outputting the data to a relatively fast peripheral, fooling the program into 'thinking' that it has printed extremely quickly, thus enabling the CPU to get on with the next task in hand. This **spooled** data was then **despooled** (i.e. sent to an actual printer) at some later stage, either under the control of the main computer or a separate computer system. In this way the average throughput of the mainframe system was significantly increased.

Accounting and accountability

Mainframes are expensive pieces of kit, and with the early operating systems any program could wreak havoc – and often did! There was nothing to stop students from printing out 5,000 Snoopy cartoons if that's what they wanted to do – if the computer operator was having his or her coffee and did not notice what was happening, then valuable resources could be deliberately or accidentally abused. To get over these problems users of the system could be **allocated levels of priority** which would prevent access to certain resources including the **allocation of time**. The computer operators, having the highest priority level, would still be able to print out as many Snoopy cartoons as they wished. Ordinary mortals, however, would be prevented from unauthorised access to designated parts of the computer, having their jobs automatically terminated by the operating system without the need for human intervention. From the computer operator's point of view this was the biggest break through in operating-system technology, as it allowed them to have their tea and coffee breaks in peace!

Did you know that . . .

It's also easily possible to implement accounting using networks and operating systems like WindowsNT. Here it is possible to log the amount of on-line time, the number of pieces of printer paper being used and a whole host of other activities.

With so many complex operations being carried out *without* the need for human intervention, it is essential to have some sort of **log** produced by the computer on the **operator's terminal**. This would be a list of **statistics** such as the 'jobs done' the 'times at which these jobs were started and finished', the 'resources' that have been used, and 'any errors' that may have occurred in a job or with the system etc. during a shift. (Mainframe computers are often used 24 hours a day, seven days a week.) Information such as this can be used to monitor the effective performance of the system, and be used for **accounting purposes** such as generating bills for the people who have made use of the system, or generating statistics about who has been using the system and when. Big Brother is definitely watching!

Multiprogramming (multitasking)

Hardware development continued at an amazing pace, and CPUs became ever more powerful and faster compared to the slower peripheral devices. We have already seen how spooling helped to solve the very-slow-printer problem, but even the much-faster tape and disk machines were starting to look pedestrian compared to the 'Warp-speed' capabilities of the CPU. An analysis of how a typical CPU spent its time would probably show that typically over 95% of time was 'wasted' in waiting while accessing peripheral units. Only the fast **RAM** was keeping up with the CPU. However, in the late 1990s this too has become a major problem (see chapter 12), and this has suggested an alternative strategy. If more than one **job** (**user program**) is resident in the machine at the same time, the CPU could then switch between **jobs** while it is waiting for a peripheral device such as a disk or tape. Why not have many users' programs all resident at the same time? The only limitation is the amount of memory needed to store all the users' programs and their data. And so the **multiprogramming operating system** was born – and this is the point where operating systems started to get more sophisticated and very complicated. Nevertheless, these ideas were so successful that multiprogramming-operating-system principles now form the basis of the most modern windows-based environments in the late 1990s, but with much more interaction between the users and the computer too.

Multitasking

To prevent multiple copies of the *same* application **programs or compilers** etc. being loaded into the machine when requested by several different users, the *same program or application* can be shared between the different **tasks** being undertaken by each user. Such a system is known as a **multitasking** operating system. Therefore, you could easily have several different programs all multitasking in which case you have a multiprogramming-multitasking operating system. However, the term **multitasking operating system** is often used to mean the same thing – when the term multitasking was coined to describe *what's happening on the latest microcomputer operating systems*, nobody bothered to notice that the same term meant something slightly different in the mainframe computer environment! Most modern multitasking operating systems are, therefore, actually multiprogramming-multitasking operating systems, and multitasking on micros means the same thing as multiprogramming. From now on we will use the term multitasking to mean the same as multiprogramming.

Batch multitasking

To keep matters simple, let's continue our chronological development of operating systems and consider the multitasking ideas applied to batch systems only. Thus batches of programs are submitted and put into the computer's 'in tray'. It is the job of the **multitasking operating system** to decide which programs to load into memory and when. The actual loading of these programs into memory causes significant **memory management** problems, and deciding which programs to load and when to run them is called **scheduling**.

Did you know that . . .

In the early days of mainframes, these large computer systems were in very secure environments and operated by scientists in white coats. Although not quite like this today, this scenario is still much nearer the truth compared to the fully distributed processing with which most people are familiar. The military and other government establishments will still have similar levels of security if the information contained on their systems is sensitive (it usually is!).

First consider the two typical scenarios shown in figure 23.2. Figure 23.2(a) shows a program that has a very high calculation content. This maths-intensive program, probably trying to solve some of the mysteries of the Universe, might monopolise the mainframe CPU for 99.9% of the ten minutes that it takes to run. The CPU is being efficiently utilised, which is one of the major objectives of this exercise, but is this efficient in terms of the throughput of jobs? Perhaps 150 other jobs could have been run in the time taken for this single program to execute!

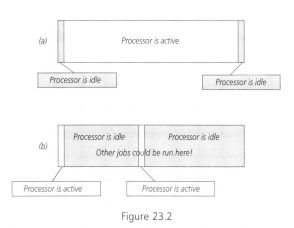

Figure 23.2

Figure 23.2(b) shows a program with intensive-peripheral activity. The CPU is not utilised very efficiently because time is wasted in waiting for other activities to take place. Other jobs could be run during the spaces indicated on this second part of the diagram. Getting the operating system to assign **priorities** to each of the jobs helps to get over these problems. However, which jobs should be run? Will they fit into available memory? When loaded will they be the 'processor intensive' or the 'peripheral intensive' jobs? If one job is not loaded what is to guarantee that it will be loaded next time round? Who decides on these levels

of priorities? You've guessed it – the operating system! Conflicting demands are therefore being made on the designers of operating systems and complex **algorithms** need to be implemented if efficient **scheduling** and **memory management** is to take place. Add to this the problems of **security** and **protection of information**. Next add **management of all the other resources** such that these conflicting demands are kept to a minimum, and at last you will *start to get a very limited idea* of the horrendous problems involved in designing 'multi-tasking operating systems' on mainframe computers.

Scheduling

A simplistic idea of **scheduling** can be gained from considering just three **jobs**, each of which have been split up into equal CPU and peripheral-time requirements as shown in figure 23.3(a). Look first at the top of this diagram which shows how the three jobs would be tackled in a simple serial fashion, with each job waiting for the previous job to completely finish. We will use 100% as the time taken for these three jobs to complete execution in this non-multiprogramming environment.

> **Hint:** Efficient scheduling is vital. The more jobs that can be processed in a given amount of time, the more money is made by the company which is operating the computer system, or the more work can be done in a given amount of time. Whichever way you view it, the result is the same.

Now consider the bottom half of this diagram. This shows the same three jobs, but this time with a multi-tasking operating system. As can be seen from the bottom of figure 23.3, Job 1 is executed immediately, while Jobs 2 and 3 are put in the queue (i.e. they are kept waiting). When 'Job 1' is waiting for a peripheral device, 'Job 2' is run by the CPU while 'Job 3' is still kept waiting. These processes continue in this way until all three jobs are completed. Although this is a contrived problem, compare the CPU and peripheral-utilisation parts of the diagram for the multitasking (bottom of figure 23.3) and the non-multitasking (top of figure 23.3) operating systems. You can see that the effective throughput of the three jobs has been made very significantly quicker when multitasking has been used, and both the peripherals and CPU have been utilised more efficiently. Note that the CPU has not done any less work, it is just that the scheduling has been improved with a corresponding increase in efficiency. If you can carry out 33% more tasks during any one day, then the computer system would be making a lot more money for its commercial operators.

Managing multitasking

We will now look at some of the methods associated with multitasking environments. To keep things simple we will not consider the use of virtual memory (see

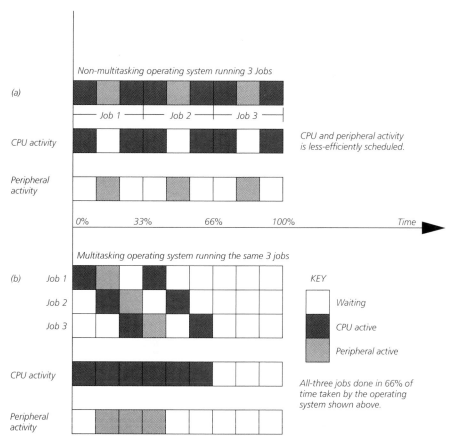

Figure 23.3

chapter 12) or multi-processors (see chapter 20) unless specified later. If several **programs** (often called **tasks** or **processes** in the context of a multitasking-operating-system environment) are resident in main memory at the same time, it is the job of another program called the **dispatcher** to set up the main processor's **program counter** (see chapter 20) so that the main processor can change between the different **tasks**. When dealing with operating systems the term 'task' is a better one to use than '**program**'. This is because not only can it refer to a user's program in the normal sense, but to the start of a new **job** (see later) in a **batch environment**, or when a new user logs on in a **multi-user interactive environment**.

Queues

A common method (see **time sharing** later) for preventing any one **task** monopolising the main processor's time, is to **interrupt** the **task** after a set period of time has been used up. At this moment the dispatcher will then suspend the operation of the task and go on to the next, putting the task just suspended into a queue. It is unlikely that this sequence of events would carry on for very long before one of the tasks themselves interrupts this smooth running. This interruption might occur by requesting a peripheral device such as a disk or printer,

or perhaps an error is generated by one of the tasks thus requiring termination of that particular task.

Figure 23.4(a) shows how such a queue is managed in diagrammatic form. Note that a **task** is either continually switched between the processor and the queue, or exits under certain conditions such as natural termination of the program or an error condition. The single FIFO data structure (see chapter 24) or queue implied in figure 23.4 is not the most efficient because this assumes that all tasks in the queue are waiting for processor time. If one of the tasks was halted because of an I/O request, then this request may not have been completed before the task gets to the beginning of the queue again. Therefore, it's efficient to implement more than one queue – one for those tasks that are waiting for attention, and another for tasks that are waiting for I/O to be completed. This idea is shown in figure 23.4(b).

> **Hint:** The important data structure called a queue is covered in detail in chapter 24. It's vital for the management of efficient multitasking.

Priorities

In practice, multiple queues would be established for most operating system designs. One advantage of a **multiple-queue** design is that this could be one method

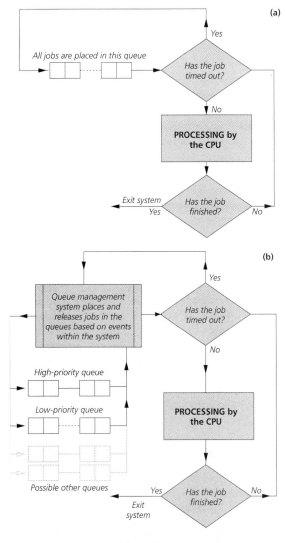

(a)

All jobs are placed in this queue

Has the job timed out?

Yes

No

PROCESSING by the CPU

Has the job finished?

Exit system
Yes

No

(b)

Queue management system places and releases jobs in the queues based on events within the system

Has the job timed out?

Yes

No

High-priority queue

Low-priority queue

Possible other queues

PROCESSING by the CPU

Has the job finished?

Yes

No

Exit system

Figure 23.4

advanced courses on operating-system design to get an overall appreciation of what is happening, and a very simple example is given in chapter 14 in the structured analysis and design section where state-transition diagrams are considered in more detail.

Concurrency problems

You saw in figure 23.3(b) how a single processor could operate in a multitasking environment. If we had *more than one* processor then each **task** (**job**) could be run in the same way, but more importantly, **tasks** could also be **overlapped**, i.e. more than one task *is* actually being carried out **simultaneously** or **concurrently**. This is an excellent idea, but creates some difficult problems to solve. You should be fully aware of the need to modularise programs (see chapter 14), as this makes for more-understandable code. However, when larger programs are spilt up into sub-programs and run as separate tasks in a **multi-processor multitasking environment**, then problems regarding synchronisation may occur, depending on the order in which the operating system decides to carry out the tasks. In chapter 20 you saw how restructuring the problems can lead to efficient utilisation of multiple processors, but with an operating system of the type now being considered it's quite different, because programmers are not writing their programs with optimisation from an operating-system viewpoint borne in mind! There are many systems in operation to get over these problems, but **optimisation of scheduling** is one of the most complex problems in operating system design. The detection and correction of operating-system errors in such an environment requires gargantuan efforts, as it is almost impossible to reproduce the set of events that may be causing a very subtle error to occur.

Deadlock

Not only must the **queues** of such **tasks** be managed, but so too must the **resources** that are allocated to these tasks. A **resource** in this context can be more easily understood if you consider it to be a **printer**, a **disk** or **tape** (i.e. **files**) etc. Life would be easy for operating system designers if there were an infinite number of these resources, as each task requesting a resource would be allocated the next one available. Due to the finite number of resources in a system, and the large number of concurrent tasks running, tasks usually have to wait until a suitable resource is free to be used.

From reading the above you might think that all that is necessary is to assign a resource to a task whenever it needs it. Unfortunately, life is not this simple. Consider, for example, the case where the **resource** happens to be a **file** which is to be **updated** (*not* simply read) by two different **tasks**. Task 2, for example, should *not be able to use the resource* (particular file) *if* task 1 already has it. If task 1 and 2 were allowed to update the file at the same

of assigning **priorities** to different tasks. **High-priority tasks** could be routed to one queue, while **low-priority tasks** could be routed to another. Multiple levels of priorities could also be implemented easily using this method. Don't forget also that without **virtual memory** (see chapter 20) all tasks must be resident in RAM simultaneously. This is wasteful if some of the tasks in RAM are not in a ready state, and this problem can be overcome by ushering some of the tasks out to a queue established on a disk. This is often known as the 'suspended queue' and consists of tasks that can be loaded back into RAM at some later stage. We can now envisage a scenario where a large number of tasks are in a great variety of different states. For example, a task could be in RAM and ready to go. Another task might be in RAM and waiting for I/O, yet another might be on disk and ready to go, and finally another task might be on disk and waiting for I/O. It is the job of the operating system to maintain all the **data structures** (see chapter 24) necessary to deal with all these different tasks and states. **State transition diagrams** are used in

Did you know that . . .

It is still possible for modern operating systems to go wrong. It is very rare indeed, but sometimes a file server or other vital part of the computer system needs to be restarted due to the operating system failing to manage resources effectively. This would obviously cause chaos in a mainframe system, but information, saved along with the current state of the system, enables the computer to restart from the point where it left off. This includes carrying on with all current tasks and users who are logged on to the system will only notice a few minutes delay before carrying on as normal with the task in hand. Using data structures called stacks, as shown in chapter 24, carries out this magical trick.

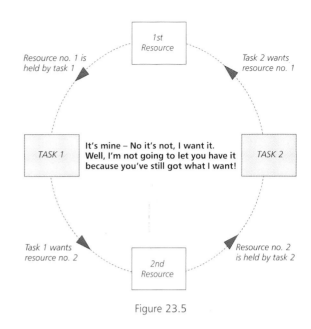

Figure 23.5

time then the resulting data would probably lose its **integrity** (a posh way of saying it could get messed up – see chapter 28). However, if task 1 were to update followed by task 2, or task 2 were to update followed by task 1, then there would be no problems as both the changes would have been recorded properly. Therefore, a system of locking has been devised whereby a resource can be locked out while it is in use by any task. This is often referred to as mutual exclusion, and for the reasons just outlined it is a desirable property in multitasking operating systems. Similar problems requiring locking would also be needed if the resources were a buffer or main memory. On more sophisticated operating systems many different types of locks are implemented to preclude certain subsets of tasks from gaining access to the resources under different sets of conditions.

There are other strategies for resource allocation such as 'a task holding on to a resource until it has been allocated another one', and other policies such as 'not being able to remove a resource from a particular task that needs it' (essential in the case of the file resource considered above). Nevertheless, all current strategies have their problems, and one is called deadlock. Deadlock is when a resource, requested by one task, is unfortunately being held by another. To compound this problem, the other task will not release the resource requested because the requesting task is holding onto the one that it wants! Each program is waiting for a response from the other!

Figure 23.5 shows this problem which is often referred to as a **circular wait** state because, without intervention by the operating system, the two tasks would go round in circles requesting resources that will never be released. Various strategies have therefore had to be implemented for preventing most cases of deadlock, for detecting if deadlock has occurred, and for overcoming deadlock if it has occurred – just another one of the million-and-one things that modern operating systems have to do!

One can imagine the scenario whereby a resource is never allocated to a particular task. The task might happen to be in a low-priority queue and the resource is being continually used by higher-priority tasks. In the extreme, the low-priority task would never come out of the computer system! Therefore, the operating system must prevent tasks being starved of resources so those tasks are carried out in a sensible amount of time.

Interrupts

One of the principle reasons why many of the techniques described above can be used is because of the ability of devices and programs to generate interrupts. For example, if the printer was busy printing out some information held in its buffer (see chapter 26) then it could carry on doing this under its own steam until it had run out of data to print. The **peripheral device**, in this case the printer, could then **generate an interrupt**, thus indicating that it needs more data, the CPU could then **service this interrupt**, then go back to what it was doing before being rudely interrupted!

Simple interrupts have already been considered in the section on microcomputer operating systems (see chapter 22), so *here we will concentrate on interrupts from a mainframe and minicomputer perspective.* You should appreciate that mainframe interrupts are much more sophisticated because the operating system can usually pre-empt what should happen to carry out many tasks efficiently, rather than 'mindlessly' carrying on with what it was doing before the interrupt occurred. It is usually implied that on mainframes all multitasking operating systems are pre-emptive multitasking operating systems. However, some very powerful micros now have this feature too.

Interrupt priorities

There are many devices that may cause an interrupt in a large computer system. For example, the operator may wish to stop the current program from being run. A printer may simply run out of paper. Perhaps the electronics that detect an imminent power failure may initiate routines to save all the current work in the few fractions of a second before the system dies. The very last example must obviously be dealt with before any of the other interrupts, even though it may not be the first interrupt that occurred. It must also be immediately dealt with even if the computer is currently in the middle of servicing another interrupt. Priorities will therefore have to be assigned to the interrupting devices so that the most important interrupts can be serviced first.

Also, interrupts may be split up into different categories. If a hardware device such as one of those described above causes the interrupt, this is called an external interrupt. There may be a fault in a program such as syntax error or arithmetic overflow. This would be a program-fault interrupt, error interrupt or program-error trap. The current program may simply run out of time because it may have got stuck in an infinite loop. This would be an example of a timer interrupt.

The external interrupts on a large computer system can be wired up so that the CPU is presented with interrupts at different levels. These are the levels of priority assigned to devices that are wired to each of these levels. Each level may be enabled or disabled (often referred to as armed and disarmed) by both hardware and software. The situation can be imagined as shown in figure 23.6.

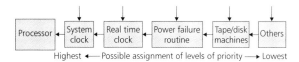

Figure 23.6

Each device on a particular level has the same priority. Therefore if two devices on level 3 cause an interrupt, the first to happen gets priority. Each level of interrupt may be totally disabled so that even if an interrupt does occur the CPU would not take any notice of it. The interrupt need not necessarily be totally disabled. For example, the interrupt may occur, but the fact that the interrupt has occurred could be registered. In this case a bit could be set to let the processor know that an interrupt has occurred, ready for when the processor can get around to dealing with it. It is useful to show the sort of thing that can

> **Hint:** After reading this section you should be able to appreciate more easily why, when printing, for example, the process might take ten times as long as normal, when everything else appears to be working properly. Most users have no idea of the many other tasks which the operating system could be handling.

happen when several devices with different priorities are causing interrupts. Let's assume, for the sake of simplicity, that there are just four interrupting devices on the system. Device number one has the highest priority, and device number four has the lowest priority. Table 23.1 shows how the CPU's time could be allocated when dealing with a typical chain of interrupting events.

It should be very clear exactly how the processor deals with the priorities that have been assigned to the various devices. To cater for differing needs each day, it is usual to be able to redefine the priorities that have been assigned to a particular task. For example, a job may not be the most efficient one to run in terms of processor time, but it may be the most important (e.g. the computer operator's pay cheque program!).

The CPU keeps track of what's happening by setting a 'bit' inside a register called the 'interrupt flag register'. If a bit is set to '1' then this could be a device for flagging the various conditions (imagine a little man jumping up and down waving a flag shouting 'device 3 needs attention'). In this way it is possible to know which devices are currently interrupting. This therefore means that the CPU can stop servicing an interrupt if a higher priority one comes along. This would be done in exactly the same way as the interruption of the original main task, by saving the contents of the registers on the stack (see chapter 24). Each time an interrupt has been serviced, the interrupt flag in the interrupt flag register can be reset so that the device may interrupt again if necessary. Finally, when all the interrupts have been cleared, the original contents of the registers pulled off the stack would be the conditions for carrying on with the main task.

It was mentioned that it is possible to disable interrupts via software control. This can be achieved by having what's called an interrupt enable/disable register. This is another register inside the CPU where bits control how interrupts in the system are handled. For example, we may have a bit inside the interrupt enable/disable register that controls device 3. It may be arranged so that if this bit is set to '1', then interrupts from device 3 (indicated by the state of the device 3 flag) will be handled normally. If this bit was set to zero, then interrupts from device 3 could be ignored.

Memory management

If many different jobs are to be resident in the computer's main memory at any one moment in time, then it's vital that the operating system prevents the programs from interfering with each other. When different programs are sharing the same memory in a computer there will always be the potential for one program to accidentally address the memory space occupied by another. If this were allowed to happen, then the programs may get corrupted with potentially disastrous results.

Table 23.1

Device 4	Device 3	Device 2	Device 1	CPU Activity	Notes (A '*' means that the device has requested an interrupt. The * is cancelled after the interrupt has been serviced. M means that the CPU is engaged in carrying out its main task.)
–	–	–	–	M M M M M M	Main task is being carried out.
–	–	–	–	M M M M M M	
*	–	–	–	4 4 4 4 4 4	Device 4 receives processor attention
*	–	–	–	4 4 4 4 4 4	
–	–	–	–	M M M M M M	Device 4 finished, main task reinstated
–	–	*	–	2 2 2 2 2 2	Device 2 receives attention
–	*	*	–	2 2 2 2 2 2	Device 3 ignored (lower priority than device 2)
–	*	*	–	2 2 2 2 2 2	
–	*	–	–	3 3 3 3 3 3	Device 3 gets attention now device 2 has finished
–	*	–	–	3 3 3 3 3 3	
–	–	–	–	M M M M M M	Main task reinstated as no more interrupts
–	–	–	–	M M M M M M	
–	–	*	–	2 2 2 2 2 2	Device 2 gets attention
–	–	*	*	1 1 1 1 1 1	Device 1 overrides device 2 service routine
*	–	*	*	1 1 1 1 1 1	Device 4 totally ignored for the moment
*	–	*	–	2 2 2 2 2 2	Device 2 reinstated
*	*	*	–	2 2 2 2 2 2	Device 3 ignored for the moment
*	*	–	–	3 3 3 3 3 3	Device 3 gets attention even though device 4 was first
*	*	–	–	3 3 3 3 3 3	
*	–	*	–	2 2 2 2 2 2	Device 2 now gets serviced
*	–	*	–	2 2 2 2 2 2	
*	–	*	–	2 2 2 2 2 2	
*	–	–	–	4 4 4 4 4 4	Device 4 at last
*	–	–	–	4 4 4 4 4 4	
–	–	–	–	M M M M M M	Main task reinstated
–	–	–	–	M M M M M M	

You will recall from the section on **scheduling** that much of the time is spent on **I/O** activities, with the processor being idle for significant periods of time. Therefore, it is the task of the memory-management system to pack as many **jobs** into the main memory as is possible. In a non-multitasking (i.e. single-user) environment you can imagine a simplistic scenario where the memory is basically split up into two sections – part for the operating system itself, and the rest for user-program space. The user's program would thus be running in an area of memory partitioned off from the operating system. This partition is fixed, as there is a need only to run a single program.

Direct memory access (DMA)

In order to manage memory more efficiently, some systems allow for the direct transfer of memory to an intelligent peripheral device, such as a disk or DVD etc., *without* going via the normal processor-system's routine. If this method is implemented it is called **DMA** or **direct memory access.**

Fixed partitioning

The simple **fixed-partition** idea could also be applied to **memory management** in the more complex **multitasking** environment. Appropriate size fixed partitions could be set up in memory, and the jobs loaded into an appropriate partition when one becomes available. These partitions could all be of the same size, or there could be a number of different-sized fixed partitions. The advantage of this system is that the algorithms for allocating user's programs to the partitions are relatively simple. An important point to realise here is that all programs 'designed to be run' in a multitasking system must be relocatable. You will recall from the machine-code section in chapter 21 that it is bad practice to write programs that write to specific memory locations. If any program is to run in any partition you should now see why this is so important.

The disadvantage of fixed-partition memory is that long queues can build up at the same time that much valuable memory remains unused, because many programs don't happen to fit into a particular partition size. Also, the programs that are occupying the partitions might be doing so very inefficiently. For example, if the smallest partition size is 500k, then a 20k program will 'occupy' all of this partition, thus preventing 480k of memory from being used effectively all the time that this program remains in memory. Also, by having a finite number of fixed partitions, you are placing an arbitrary limit on the number of tasks that the system can handle at any one time. Due to these severe limitations, fixed-partition systems are not used very often – if at all.

Variable partitioning

A better, though much-more-complex method of partitioning is to dynamically allocate the partitions as and when necessary. This is called dynamic memory partitioning. When a task is loaded it is allocated an appropriate amount of memory. You may be starting to think that we have now reached a situation where memory is being utilised very efficiently. However, when a particular task is finished and another task needs to take its place, then it is most unlikely that the two tasks are of the same size, therefore, a hole is produced in the memory which starts to become fragmented. This might not seem too bad, but as time progresses, more holes appear throughout the memory and we eventually get to a stage where the memory is being used very inefficiently indeed. Therefore, from time to time, the system has to compact all the tasks by swapping them around until we are back to the situation similar to that when the system started up.

The major disadvantage of dynamic partitioning is that this compaction process is very tedious and time consuming. You will recall that we are trying to utilise the CPU with maximum efficiency. Clearing out the memory and other housework chores such as compaction do not rate as efficient if they do not contribute to the fast throughput of the system in general.

Virtual memory

The next bright idea was to split up the memory into relatively-small sections called page frames, but in addition to this, spilt up the user programs into pages so that each page of the users' programs occupies exactly the same space as a page frame in memory. So what, you might ask! If we had split up the memory into smaller sections in the first place, and allocated as many sections as needed to each user program, then the problems with partitioning would not have occurred! This is true to a small extent, but

> **Hint:** Memory management is a complex problem in large multitasking operating systems, especially when hundreds of users could be logged on simultaneously. Virtually all computer systems, from the mainframes being described here, to the humblest of new micro systems, employ virtual memory in one form or another.

here comes the really clever part – why bother to have the user's entire program resident in the memory at the same time? If the program consists of a large chunk of code, then only a fraction of this code is ever needed to execute the current sub-set of instructions being carried out – most of the program is lying dormant in memory waiting for its big moment. It's rather like the guy in the orchestra who plays a few notes on the triangle half an hour into the main symphony. There's not much point in him being there for the first half-hour – he might as well be in the pub down the road! It would be disconcerting for the audience to watch the orchestra as the musicians kept getting up to go out to the pub, (unless they went too!), but this analogy with a virtual-memory system is a good one.

There is also an immense spin-off from this virtual-memory method in that each user program can be of enormous size – they do not have to fit into the available RAM of the computer. Therefore, a computer with an actual 1000Mbytes of RAM could, for example, be working simultaneously on 30 programs, where each program happens to be 200 Mbytes long and thus giving us a virtual RAM of 6000Mbytes.

There must, of course, be some disadvantage to the virtual memory system, and indeed there is. Some of the time the code is executed without any problems, but a branch instruction to some page of code which is not resident in RAM means that the operating system will have to load this new page. However, the operating system is not clairvoyant – how does it know which page to remove from RAM? The page just removed might be the next page that is needed. In virtual-memory systems the worst case scenario is when pages of code are continually being put into RAM and then taken out again. This unfortunate phenomenon is known as thrashing. In bad cases, the virtual-memory operating system can spend more time removing and reloading pages of code than it spends executing the programs!

As you can see from the previous sections, the problems of efficient scheduling and memory management are not trivial. Operating systems have become more complex by using combinations of these systems to optimise both resources and CPU time to get the maximum amount of work done in the minimum amount of time. With each new generation of operating system, more efficient algorithms have been developed in a heuristic way with all the benefit of hindsight from previous operating systems' development. This is just one of the main reasons why computers are becoming so fast.

Time sharing systems

In the previous sections we have considered operating systems essentially from a batch-processing point of view. Fortunately, most of the principles covered apply equally well to most of the other types of operating systems too. Still sticking with mainframes and larger computers for the time being, we will now take a look at the development of the *alternatives* to **batch processing**.

After reading the above you should appreciate that batch processing, although efficient in terms of getting vast volumes of work carried out in the minimum time, does not give the user of the system any instant feedback. The author can well remember submitting Fortran IV programs on punched cards during the morning, then eagerly collecting the output after tea in the evening, only to find that there was an error in the program. The offending card would then have to be replaced and the job re-submitted the following day. What an awful scenario for maintaining any degree of enthusiasm for the job in hand! What was needed was a system in which the user could sit down at a terminal, type in their program and get a response within a few seconds. Any error could then be corrected and the program instantly re-run. In other words, what was needed was exactly what people today take for granted with their single-user microcomputer. But don't forget – we were using a mainframe computer, *not* a micro – these had yet to be invented, and even if they had been, several hundred people would still have been itching to get their programs run on a mainframe – so this problem had to be solved anyway.

Interestingly enough, it was in this sort of environment that **BASIC** first came to the fore. This language, originally being **interpreted** instead of **compiled** (see chapter 31), was ideal for what was to be called a **conversational mode of operation**. What was needed was **an operating system** which could respond to hundreds of people sitting down at terminals running these sorts of programs. (Programs could also be compiled from these terminals but we will stick with interpreted BASIC as it makes **time sharing** much easier to understand.) It might seem an impossible feat to achieve, but

an analysis of what, typically, was happening at each terminal shows how it is feasible. Most people would be typing in their programs – a painfully slow operation compared to the speed with which a CPU can react. Even if programs were being run, more likely than not they had generated an error which meant that the student at the terminal spent the next few minutes trying to work out what was wrong. In other words, it was very unlikely that many people would be carrying out much processor-intensive activity at any one time, and even if they were, you would simply get the operating system to limit the amount of time it spent with these particular people.

The technique was to get the operating system to scan all the terminals that were on line to see if anything needed doing. If not, it simply went on to the next terminal, then the next, and the next until it came round to the original terminal again. Each time the processor allocated time to a user this was known as a **time slice**. The speed of the system compared to what was actually happening at each terminal meant that most requests were dealt with within a few seconds. A mechanical analogy of time-sharing is shown in figure 23.7.

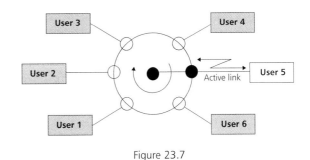

Figure 23.7

Most people are familiar with the term 'time sharing' from taking holidays abroad in villas which are rented for a few weeks of the year! However, a better analogy with the computer version would be a super-being teacher who is able to quickly run round the class sorting out the pupils' problems when they have their hands up. If the teacher acted quickly enough then each pupil would be under the mistaken illusion that they are getting the attention of the teacher all the time. So it is with the computer: most of the time all the students sitting at the terminal would be under the illusion that they are the sole user of this **multi-user operating system**. Because each person is allocated a small time slice of the computer's time, this type of system is called a **time sharing operating system**.

It's important to realise that a new set of objectives now present themselves. No longer are we trying to utilise CPU time to the maximum, but a **more-important objective** in a **time-sharing operating system** is to **maximise the speed of response** for individual users. When you realise that some mainframes were running 'batch' and 'time sharing' operating systems simultaneously, with all the compromises and conflicting conditions, you begin to realise what mind-boggling complexities these operating systems start to represent.

Protection of information

Whenever different users have access to the *same* system there is a need to protect against the misuse of information and resources. Users of the system are usually given access via a set of user IDs and passwords. There will be many different types of user, all with different levels of privilege. These could range, for example, from the computer operator who has access to almost anything, down to a first-year student user at a typical university who only has access to their own files and any software which has been placed in the public domain. It is usual for each user to have read/write access to his or her own files, but only read access to the public files. Extra security can be implemented by having hardware-only access to certain parts of the system, i.e. a certain terminal would have to be used to carry out special functions on the computer system. Most terminals within the building would not have this sort of security status.

Security has been extensively covered in the network and database chapters (see chapters 5 and 28) and will, therefore, not be repeated here. However, operating system security *is* of paramount importance – if the operating system is not secure then neither is the data held by the computer system controlled by it.

Thin client-server operating systems

After reading about operating systems in this chapter from a large-computer perspective, and after reading chapter 22 which covers operating systems from a microcomputer perspective, the last important paradigm, particularly so at the start of the 21st century, is that of **thin client-server computer operating systems**. You should be aware that **distributed processing** (i.e. conventional computers connected to a network as described in chapter 3 and chapter 5) poses very con-

siderable overheads in terms of maintenance. You should also be aware that **centralised processing** (i.e. terminals on a mainframe computer as described earlier in this chapter) does not always allow the clients to run software that would run on a conventional PC. One potential solution, becoming popular at the time of writing, is that of the thin client-server system. This system attempts to give system administrators the ease of maintenance offered by centralised systems, and the freedom of working offered to the users by distributed systems.

The problems usually associated with distributed processing stem from having local resources that can't be maintained remotely. For example, if software needs to be modified or upgraded on a hard disk, and if the 500 PCs in a particular institution need to be updated, then several scenarios exist:

1. The system administrator must go round to each of the 500 PCs and update the disk!
2. The system administrator must do a push installation from the server.
3. The system administrator can copy a disk image to each local machine.
4. The system administrator can serve the applications from a conventional file server.
5. The system administrator can update the software on the file server of a thin-client system.

The first option above is ludicrous, although, it must be said, this is the system still used in some schools and businesses today! It is one of the reasons why the thin client-server systems have been developed.

The second option is very complex, but feasible. It is, however, a nightmare if many different types of machine exist on the network, because a different push installation would be required for each type of machine! Therefore, much work still has to be done.

The third system works well, but, like the second option mentioned above, takes up a huge amount of network bandwidth, and often renders a network system unusable while it is being carried out.

The fourth option is quite efficient, but some applications are a pig to get working from a conventional file server, because they have not been designed with this mode of operation in mind.

The fifth option involves updating the file server on a thin client-server system. This is relatively easy, and is instantly available to all thin clients on the network once this has been carried out.

What is a thin client-server system?

The idea of this operating system is very similar to that of the network operating system covered earlier. The only difference is that the terminal on the network can be any suitable machine, containing any suitable hardware. All the guts of the processing are carried out on an exceptionally beefy file server, and the screen updates are sent to the client machine. Therefore, in theory, you could have Sun Workstations, PCs, Macs and Acorn systems, all running PC software over the network from a single file server. How are so many different machines able to do this? You can do this by running an operating system like 'WinFrame' from Citrix systems. In fact, at the time of writing, we are installing such a system at the author's school, which will run along side our existing Windows NT, Mac and Acorn networks.

The idea is that most of the processing is carried out at the file server, therefore, you don't need to store any software locally, or even have any hard or floppy disks locally. This scenario is nirvana for the network manager, as he or she can do all the updates from the comfort of the office, or even from the comfort of home via RAS (Remote Access Service)! The network bandwidth needed is much less than that which would be needed by a conventional PC downloading applications from a conventional file server under windows, because the big applications do not need to be downloaded at all. They are permanently resident on the file server, and much of the processing that would have taken place locally takes place there instead.

The system sounds wonderful in theory, but I have yet to be convinced that it will work as well as stand-alone PCs on a conventional network under all conditions. It will certainly be easier to maintain, but I personally feel that the network bandwidth will need to be considerable. Imagine 75 pupils all trying to load their bitmap art projects or run their avi video files from the server at the same time! I think that a 100 Mbit/sec Ethernet system would be needed rather than the 10 Mbit/sec bandwidth, which is probably adequate for word processing or vector-based applications. However, time will tell which system will be the most effective, and improvements to all types of operating system are continuing at an amazing pace. I am, for example, particularly impressed with the ability of the Citrix WinFrame system to run software like Access, Word and Excel over a 33 k modem link.

Did you know that . . .

The thin client-server model might eventually be the dominant network operating system. However, the network PC is also fighting for this share of the market. There are billions of pounds at stake for the winner of this race and if the thin client-server wins, then it could spell the end of Windows as we currently know it. However, Microsoft is also developing similar systems, so keep a careful watch if you wish to buy shares in the computer industry!

Exercise 23.1

1   Describe briefly why an **operating system** is needed for any computer.

2   List some different types of operating system used on mainframe or minicomputers.

3   With the aid of a suitable diagram, explain how the operating system links an application program to the hardware in a computer system.

4   It is often said that the operating system provides a virtual world for the computer user. Explain what is meant by a virtual world and why this description is apt.

5   Explain how a computer operator on a mainframe computer interacts with the operating system, giving some indication of a typical brief session.

6   Explain what is meant by the term 'batch processing'.

7   Multitasking and multiprogramming are often used on large computers. Explain what is meant by these terms.

8   In a multitasking operating system efficient scheduling can be used to increase productivity. Show how this may be so.

9   Interrupts form an important part of operating system design. Why are they so important and how are they used in a large operating system?

10 Compare and contrast hardware and software interrupts, giving two examples of each type.

11 Why is it necessary to assign different priorities to different interrupts?

12 Discuss how fixed and variable partitioning may be used in the memory management of a multitasking operating system.

13 Virtual memory has enormously extended the computer's ability to process a greater number of large tasks at the same time. Explain what is meant by virtual memory and how it gives a great increase in the number of tasks that can be tackled 'simultaneously'.

14 What is meant by the term thrashing in the context of an operating system?

15 Explain how time sharing can be used for giving many users access to a computer system, and how it can be used as a means of implementing a multitasking environment.

16 Explain why it is a good idea to have more than one main processor in a large computer system, and how this could help with increased reliability.

17 What functions of an operating system ensure that efficient use is made of the vast number of peripheral devices connected to the main computer.

18 The DMA controller helps to make certain aspects of the computer execute more quickly. What is meant by 'DMA' and how does it help in this way?

19 Why is a front-end processor needed on large mainframe computer systems?

20 What is the difference between distributed and centralised processing?

21 Why do you think that centralised processing was considered more important in the 1970s and early 1980s, but distributed processing was more important in the 1990s?

22 List two different methods used to help protect against unauthorised access to information on multi-user operating systems.

23 Outline the latest developments in thin client-server technology. How is this system likely to be of help to system administrators compared to the conventional distributed-processing operating systems?

End of chapter revision aid and summary

Cover up the right-hand column and see if you can answer the questions or define the terms on the left. They appear in the order in which they are covered in this chapter. Alternatively you may browse through the right-hand column to aid revision.

What is a batch operating system and why are they still used today?	Batch processing systems used on mainframes were the first operating systems and they are still popular today for running batches of jobs, such as processing utility bills.
What is a job control language?	Job control languages (JCLs) control batch-operating systems.
List a few general things undertaken by an operating system.	Operating systems help allocate resources, decide on priorities and do much housekeeping such as helping to produce logs and accounts.
What is a multiprogramming operating system?	A multiprogramming operating system can run more than one program 'simultaneously'. Literally simultaneously if there are multiple processors.
What does multitasking mean?	Multitasking is the term used to denote different tasks being run by the same program, e.g. two users are using the same database on a mainframe. However, it's also often used to mean multiprogramming, especially on microcomputers.
Is multiprogramming equally applicable to batch and interactive modes of operation?	Multiprogramming is equally applicable to batch or interactive modes such as time sharing.
How might scheduling help?	Efficient scheduling is necessary in a multiprogramming environment. It helps to make sure that everything gets a slice of the action, and this makes everything run as smoothly as possible.
What other factor helps to manage multiprogramming?	Assignment of priorities to tasks helps manage multiprogramming environments by building up efficient queues of tasks waiting to be processed.

What is deadlock or starvation?

Concurrency problems can lead to deadlock or starvation, where a resource is never allocated to a task.

What is an interrupt, and how might they be managed?

Interrupts can have different levels of priority assigned by the operating system or hardware. These help manage the computer in efficient ways giving higher priorities to certain jobs.

Why might a large amount of RAM need efficient memory management?

Large amounts of RAM need efficient memory management and this can be achieved by fixed or preferably variable partitioning.

How might memory be dynamically allocated?

The most modern systems dynamically allocate memory often by using a virtual memory environment.

What is virtual memory?

Virtual memory means that jobs can be partially stored in RAM – the rest is stored on disk. It gives the effect of having more RAM than is physically available.

What is DMA?

DMA (Direct Memory Access) enables a specialised piece of hardware to carry out data transfer between memory and peripherals.

How is buffering of help when running an operating system?

Buffering helps to match the speed of the slower peripheral devices to the fast speed of the main processors. Double buffering is normally used.

What is time sharing?

Time sharing is one method of managing a multitasking environment by allocating small time slices to each task.

What is a front-end processor?

Front-end processors are used in large computer systems to help deal with the complex communication problems with the mainframe computer.

What is a thin client-server system?

Thin client servers represent a breakthrough in the potential for managing very large network systems. It makes the management of these systems much easier. A very powerful file server actually runs the applications, and the terminal does only that processing which is necessary to update the graphics on the screen.

24 A First Look at Data Structures

In this chapter you'll learn about:

- ◆ Data structures like the linear list, stacks, queues and arrays
- ◆ Processing data by inserting and deleting items of data in these structures

Key resources

To carry out this work most successfully it's best if you have:

- ◆ Access to a high level language like BASIC, Visual BASIC, Pascal or Delphi

Concept checkpoints

- ◆ It's essential that you are a reasonably competent programmer before attempting to code the algorithms shown in this chapter. You should, therefore, have read chapters 13 and 15 before attempting to start this work.

Introduction

A study of data structures is fundamental to the study of computer science at this level. A fundamental understanding of the structure of data leads to a greater awareness of how computers can be used to process data, and this naturally leads to the development and testing of efficient algorithms to carry out these basic operations.

Typical operations carried out on data structures

There is nothing difficult about the most common data structures. Indeed, these concepts are derived from day-to-day business operations, and it is from these non-mathematical data processing businesses that much of the terminology is provided. For example, if you run a business, then it is a natural operation to add data to your files. Therefore, addition of data such as 'customer name and address' is a natural data processing operation. Similarly, a customer may have to be deleted from your accounts. Deletion of data is, therefore, another of these naturally occurring business transactions.

Each common operation is summarised in the following list. The only slightly strange term is 'traversing'. This simply means going through the set of data and, usually, undertaking some process on the way. Such a process might be generating a list of the names and addresses of all your customers who are to receive an invitation to the annual dinner party!

Common data processing operations

The following are the most common data processing operations to be carried out on basic data structures:

- Traversing the data (i.e. processing the data held in the list)
- Addition of data
- Deletion of data
- Sorting of data into some order
- Searching for a specific item of data
- Merging different sets of data.

Computer science students should easily be able to carry out any of the above operations with manual or computerised filing systems. However, what we are most interested in doing is finding *efficient* ways of carrying out the above operations when large amounts of data are involved, and *this is the fundamental importance of data structures*.

As with the operations outlined above, there are many **naturally occurring data structures**. For example, businesses have always had lists, have always stored things in **alphabetical** or **numerical order,** or have always had their own ways of doing things, given the nature of their particular business problems.

What are the most common data structures?

Data structures will allow us to carry out all the above data processing operations efficiently. To illustrate how this may be so, we will look at **lists, stacks, queues, arrays** and **trees**, etc., because these are the most common data structures. As this chapter develops, you will realise that these data structures also derive from many day-to-day business operations. For example, a queue is exactly the same as a queue in a shop, and a tree is exactly the same as the 'tree structure' or 'hierarchy' that is normally found in a business or a family tree. Therefore, typical things to be tackled might be 'how to **delete** data from a **linked list**', or 'how to **add** data to a **hierarchical** data structure', for example.

The **efficiency** spoken of above is usually measured in terms of **how much time a particular operation takes**. For example, what is the average time to find a random item of data from a data structure containing 50,000 items? The other measure of efficiency is **how much memory is taken up** on the computer. However, this is a lot less important than it used to be, as many megabytes of RAM are now common. Even so, if the entire data structure can be fitted into RAM, then the results will be available a lot faster than if we have to write to disk.

Did you know that . . .

About 30 years ago, saving memory was vitally important. Programmers would do virtually anything to save one or two bytes and it is against this background that the millennium bug was born. Two bytes of data were saved for each entry by not having the 19 figures in a date like 1951.

Searching, sorting and merging are covered in other chapters. Here, we will look in detail at the first three techniques mentioned in the above list. In most cases, simple examples will be given, **algorithms** will then be developed, and **pseudocode** examples given at the end of each section. In the more complex cases, **dry runs** are also included. After reading through this and the other relevant chapters, you should have enough experience to develop and code your own algorithms, write some appropriate pseudocode, then code these ideas using a high level language of your choice.

In fact, the writing of pseudocode is now becoming very popular in computer science examinations at this level. It is worth spending much time on this work as it forms a major part of many syllabuses. **When working**

through any textbook you will find that different authors will do things in slightly different ways. However, there is no substitute for applying a mass of common sense to the problems, as the underlying principles are often not difficult.

What students do find most difficult is to be consistent about terminology, and meticulous in their testing of algorithms. It does not matter too much about what you call the pointers or lists, etc. What is important is that you explain what you are doing, and then *write enough comments* in the pseudocode to enable your teachers and examiners to work out exactly what you are actually doing.

You must make sure that the **algorithms work for all possible cases**. If there is some case for which your algorithm will not work, then say so. It is often the case in an examination that you are asked to state any assumptions that you have made. It is also a very good idea to do this even if you have not been asked. The exact ways in which these data structures are processed will depend to a very large extent on the software that you have, but the principles are the same.

Linear list

The following description may seem a little long-winded considering we are only going to talk about six numbers! However, some important concepts will be introduced which will be assumed without explanation for the more complex data structures that follow.

One of the simplest forms of data structure is a linear list, and in fact a linear list can be thought of as a **one-dimensional array**. It is easier to consider these data structures by means of simple examples, rather than introduce them as complex mathematical relationships. As an example of a linear list, consider the following sales figures for the month of March for five different sales personnel selling Bradbury's chocolates:

> **Hint:** Students often fail to appreciate some of the simpler structures which are present in lists of information. Failure to be able to spot structures and patterns within the data will make this work more difficult. Get all the practice you can by actually coding these methods in a high-level language of your choice.

Bradbury's Chocolates	March Sales Figures
Salesperson	Sales (thousand boxes)
Smith	2.3
Jones	1.9
Anson	6.4
Talbot	5.0
Bartlett	3.9
Carter	0.0

This list of numbers forms what is called a linear list, i.e. '2.3, 1.9, 6.4, 5.0, 3.9 and 0.0'. If you were presented with the raw data '2.3, 1.9, 6.4, 5.0, 3.9 and 0.0', then it would be meaningless in itself, until the structure given by the above table was applied to it. When we do this the **data** *becomes* **information** – i.e. '3.9' means that 'salesperson Bartlett has sold 3900 boxes of Bradbury's chocolates in the month of March'.

The above linear list is not in any particular order. It would be possible to rearrange the data so that other information could be more easily obtained from it. For example, we may want to know who sold the most chocolates and who did next best etc. In this case the rearrangement shown in table 24.1(a) would be most appropriate. Other information might be found more easily if the names of the people were in alphabetical order. In this case the arrangement shown in table 24.1(b) would be convenient.

All these arrangements of the data still form a linear list, but some are more useful than others. In this chapter we will seek ways of extracting information such as that shown in table 24.1, without having to physically move the data around in the ways that we have shown. To be able to do this we must refer to the data within the list in a very general way, and one that is suitable for representation on a computer.

The linear lists we have just considered contain only six sets of information. In general, a linear list may have N sets of information, where N >= 0. Let's give a general name to each element, where 'S' might be a good choice representing 'Sales'. Each item in a linear list is referred to as an **element**. We can use a **subscript** to uniquely identify each element (sales figure) as follows:

> **Hint:** You will almost certainly find that you need to dimension any subscripted variables that you use in a particular high-level language. This is usually done at the variable-declaration stage at the beginning of the program or procedure.

If we assume the original list 2.3, 1.9, 6.4, 5.0, 3.9, 0.0 then:

$S(1) = 2.3$, $S(2) = 1.9$ and so on until $S(6) = 0.0$

Data can be stored inside computers as a linear list. In fact the use of the subscript to uniquely identify each element within the list corresponds very closely to the address used for the storage locations inside a typical computer. So, it is convenient if we think about the values of each element as being put inside a box whose address is given by the subscripted element as shown in the following table.

Linear list S	
S(1)	2.3
S(2)	1.9
S(3)	6.4
S(4)	5.0
S(5)	3.9
S(6)	0.0

A 'general element' within the list can be referred to as the 'ith element'.

Hence, if i = 3, then we are referring to the 3rd element which is $S_{(i)} = S_{(3)} = 6.4$

A set of related variables such as those in the above linear list is also known as a **vector S of size N**. The name derives from the fact that in mathematical terms, a **vector** is the name for a **one-dimensional array**, i.e. a list.

As can be seen from table 24.1(b), a linear list may often be in some convenient order such as alphabetical, for example. However, if we wish to **add** an item of data in the middle of the **list**, then all the data *after* the item to be inserted would have to be moved to make way for the new item of data. Similarly, if we were to **delete** an item of data from a **linear list**, then there would be a **free space**, and all the items of data after the item that has just been removed would have to be moved up.

It would be possible to develop algorithms to do this, but they would not be used in practice, and would be very inefficient if large amounts of data were involved. It is far better to concentrate your efforts on understanding the **pointer systems** to be introduced in the next few sections. These show how new, *more sophisticated* **data structures**, *enable us to insert and delete items of data without having to move any of the existing data.*

Table 24.1

Salesperson	Sales (thousand boxes)	Salesperson	Sales (thousand boxes)
Anson	6.4	Anson	6.4
Talbot	5.0	Bartlett	3.0
Bartlett	3.9	Carter	0.0
Smith	2.3	Jones	1.9
Jones	1.9	Smith	2.3
Carter	0.0	Talbot	5.0
(a)		(b)	

Stacks

A **stack** is one of the methods used to insert and delete items from a linear list, but other, more sophisticated methods, will be considered later in this chapter. The concept of a stack is of fundamental importance in computing as it is used in so many different applications, and the principle of a stack is illustrated in the following example.

Consider the numbers in the list 23, 54, 10 and 90. When talking of a stack we will refer to the '**top** of the stack' or the '**bottom** of the stack', and so the numbers will be set out vertically, to reinforce this point visually. The list now becomes like that shown below.

> **Hint:** If you find encoding these data structures quite easy, why not add some animation routines which show the numbers moving around on the screen as the algorithms are progressing. This would also make a great teaching aid.

    23
    54
    10
    90

If we now add a number (such as 77) to the stack, it is **pushed** onto the top of the stack. The stack now becomes as shown below.

    77
    23
    54
    10
    90

The phrase '**pushed on to the top of the stack**' is the one used with stacks to indicate that an item of data has been added to the stack. If an item is to be removed from the stack then it is said to be '**popped off the stack**'. Using this system, the 'last number in' is always the 'first number out'. The system of storing this list of numbers is called a **LIFO stack (Last In First Out)**. A LIFO stack is often compared with a pile of plates in a canteen. After washing up the plates, the last plate will be placed on to the top of the stack. The next plate to be used will be taken from the top of the stack, i.e. a LIFO stack.

Any reader familiar with machine code programming will realise that the terms PUSH and POP are often included in the assembly language mnemonics exactly for this purpose.

Although the dinner-plate theory is conceptually correct, in practice a stack would be built up in the computer's memory using a **pointer system**. A pointer is simply a number used to point to an item of interest, so it may be used to point to the *memory location* inside the computer that indicates the top of the stack. Used in this way, it is called a **stack pointer**. Let's assume that we have six memory locations as shown in figure 24.1.

These six memory locations are shown as boxes, and represent our LIFO stack. Only three items of data 13, 24 and 53 are currently on the stack. These numbers were placed on to the stack in the order shown, and hence 53 will appear at the 'top' of the stack. The stack pointer will therefore be pointing at the memory location containing the number 53 as shown in figure 24.1(a). Let's now suppose that a new number, 11, is pushed on to the stack. The situation now becomes as shown in figure 24.1(b). If the next operation is a pop then the number 11 will be popped off the top of the stack, giving the situation shown in figure 24.1(c). Finally, if another pop is carried out, we get the situation shown in figure 24.1(d).

If the stack becomes 'empty' or 'full', then an error message would have to be generated. Such techniques might set the stack pointer to '–1' so that the next pop operation could report an error.

Processing data in a stack

To implement a stack system in memory is relatively simple, and the algorithms in this section perform the operations **PUSH** and **POP** on an area of memory called **STACK**.

In the **pseudocode algorithms**, the following terminology will apply:

> **Hint:** When coding your own algorithms, you should always include information similar to that shown at the beginning of the next page. It makes the resultant code far easier to understand.

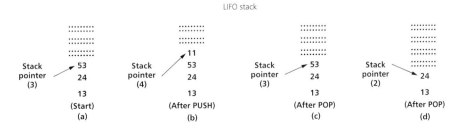

LIFO stack

Stack pointer (3)	53	Stack pointer (4)	11	Stack pointer (3)	53	Stack pointer (2)	
	24		53		24		24
	13		24		13		13
	(Start)		13		(After POP)		
	(a)		(After PUSH)		(c)		(After POP)
			(b)				(d)

Figure 24.1

Stack_pointer	variable used to indicate the current top of the stack.
Maximum	used to determine when the stack is full.
Minimum	used to determine if the stack is empty.
Data	item of data to be **pushed** or **popped**.
STACK	general name for the stack contained in memory.
STACK(Stack_pointer)	subscripted variable representing the data at the current stack pointer, i.e. it is an **identifier** for data on the stack.

The above are parameters that are passed over to 'generalised stack maintenance procedures' **called PUSH** and **POP**.

Pseudocode to PUSH a new item of data on to the top of the STACK

The code is relatively obvious; the only thing to check here is that there *is actually room* to put another item of data on the top of the stack. If this is not possible, then an **error message** must be generated, as an **overflow** has occurred.

The procedure assumes that an array **STACK(N)** has already been set up, and the procedure is to be called by using:

```
PUSH(Stack_pointer, Maximum, Data)
```

The actual **pseudocode for the PUSH procedure** is as follows:

```
PROCEDURE PUSH(Stack_pointer, Maximum,
                              Data)
  (*Check if the stack is already full*)
  IF Stack_pointer = Maximum THEN
     PRINT No room on the stack
     EXIT PROCEDURE
  ELSE
  (*Push data item on to stack*)
     SET Stack_pointer = Stack_pointer +
                                       1
     SET STACK(Stack_pointer) = Data
  ENDIF
END PROCEDURE
```

Pseudocode to POP an item off the STACK

Here it should be obvious that the stack cannot **overflow** from this operation. However, there might be no items of data on the stack, in which case we cannot remove any more data.

The pseudocode procedure is to be called by using:

```
POP(Stack_pointer, Minimum, Data)
```

The actual **pseudocode POP procedure** is as follows:

```
PROCEDURE POP(Stack_pointer, Minimum,
                              Data)
  (*Check if the stack is already
                          empty*)
  IF Stack Pointer = Minimum THEN
     PRINT The stack is already empty
     EXIT PROCEDURE
  ELSE
     (*POP data off of stack and adjust
                          pointer*)
     SET Data = STACK(Stack_pointer)
     SET Stack_pointer = Stack_pointer -
                                       1
  ENDIF
END PROCEDURE
```

If the stack is not empty, then the procedure is exited with **data** containing *the information that was on the top of the stack*.

Queues

A **queue** is very similar in principle to the operation of a stack. Indeed, a queue is often called a FIFO stack (First In First Out). The principle of operation of a queue is exactly the same as the principle of a 'normal queue' waiting to be served in a shop, i.e. the first in the queue would be expected to get served first, and therefore be the first out. Hence the name **FIFO stack**. To implement the queue in memory the techniques demonstrated in figure 24.2 are used.

> **Hint:** If you wish to build up an animated teaching aid as suggested earlier, then combining the LIFO and FIFO stacks into one program with an option to choose the method is a good idea. It saves the teacher having to load up a separate program to demonstrate each of these techniques.

The start position, shown in figure 24.2(a), shows three numbers in the queue. Number 13 is at the head of the queue, indicated by the **start pointer**, and 53 is at the end of the queue, as indicated by the **stop pointer**. 13 was placed first in the queue, and has therefore been waiting longest. However, the number 13 has not physically moved. It has remained in its position at the top of the queue.

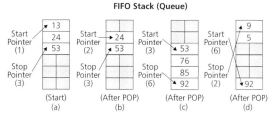

Figure 24.2

Figure 24.2(b) shows what happens when 13 is popped off the queue (i.e. the number 13 has been **served**). Notice again that the data does not move, it is just the **pointers** that have been altered.

If three more numbers 76, 85 and 92 are pushed on to the queue, and then another number is popped off, we end up with the situation shown in figure 24.2(c). Any data added to the queue must now be put into position number 1, and the pointers altered accordingly.

Figure 24.2(d) shows the situation after three more numbers have been popped off, and two more numbers, '9' and '5' have been added. A **circular list** arrangement has therefore been established using these pointers, i.e. when you have run out of space at the bottom, you simply start again at the top.

Queues are particularly easy to implement in practice (it is a simple matter of updating the two pointers). They are useful, together with random numbers and statistics, for producing simulations of real life queuing systems such as simulating how many petrol pumps are necessary in a garage forecourt, given that customers arrive at a particular rate and should not be kept waiting too long (see chapter 18).

Processing data in a queue

In this section we show a couple of **pseudocode algorithms** to INSERT an item of **Data** into a QUEUE, and to DELETE an item of **Data** from a QUEUE.

In the **pseudocode algorithms** the following terminology will apply:

Start_pointer	variable used to indicate the start of the queue.
Stop_pointer	variable used to indicate the end of the queue.
Size	variable that represents the size of the queue (i.e. how many data elements are contained in the queue).
Data	item of data to be pushed or popped.
QUEUE	general name for the queue contained in memory.
QUEUE(Pointer)	subscripted variable representing the data at the current pointer position i.e. an **identifier** for the data in the queue.

The above are parameters that are passed over to generalised stack maintenance procedures called INSERT and DELETE.

Procedure to INSERT some data into a queue

As with the stack, we must ensure that **overflow** does *not* occur. Therefore, we will have to test for this condition on entry to the INSERT procedure. The checking to see if the queue is full is slightly more complicated:

The first case shown in figure 24.2 is easy, we can simply state:

IF the **Start_pointer = 1** AND the **Stop_pointer = Size, then the queue is full**.

However, this will not work for the other cases. Observation of the conditions in Figure 24.2 (b), (c) and (d) will show that the condition:

IF the **Start_pointer = Stop_pointer + 1 THEN** the **queue** is also **full**.

These two conditions are, therefore, used to check if the queue is full at the start of the INSERT procedure.

When the queue is empty, setting the start pointer to 0 will indicate this. (Note that location zero does not exist in the queue.)

In the following we assume that a queue, **QUEUE(N)** has already been set up. The procedure will be called by using:

```
INSERT(Size, Start_pointer,
    Stop_pointer, Data)
```

The actual pseudocode for insertion of data is shown in figure 24.3.

Procedure to DELETE some data from a queue

As with the stack system, we must ensure that underflow does not occur, i.e. we cannot remove an item of data from an empty queue! Also, if the queue becomes empty after an item of data has been removed, we must ensure that the start pointer is set to zero, as this would be needed by the INSERT procedure shown above to initialise the queue.

Testing if the queue is empty is easy, as is the extraction of the data. However, we must ensure that when only one item is originally in the queue, we set the start pointer to zero as described above.

The procedure will be called by using:

```
DELETE(Size, Start_pointer,
    Stop_pointer, Data)
```

The actual pseudocode for deleting from the queue is shown in figure 24.4.

```
PROCEDURE INSERT(Size, Start_pointer, Stop_pointer, Data)
(*is queue full?*)
IF Start_pointer = 1 AND Stop_pointer = Size OR Start_pointer = Stop_pointer + 1 THEN
                   PRINT Queue is already full
                       EXIT PROCEDURE
                   ENDIF
                   (*Check to see if queue is empty*)
                   IF Start_pointer = 0 THEN
                       (*initialise queue*)
                       SET Start_pointer = 1 and SET Stop_pointer = 1
                       (*Queue not empty, update pointers*)
                   ELSE
                       IF Stop_pointer = Size THEN
                               SET Stop_pointer = 1
                               (*Put Stop_pointer back to beginning*)
                       ELSE
                               SET Stop_pointer = Stop_pointer + 1
                               (*Update Stop_pointer*)
                       ENDIF
                   ENDIF
                   QUEUE(Stop_pointer) = Data
                   (*Store Data in queue*)
END PROCEDURE
```

Figure 24.3

```
PROCEDURE DELETE(Size, Start_pointer, Stop_pointer, Data)
    (*The queue is empty*)
    IF Start_pointer = 0 THEN
       PRINT The queue is empty
       EXIT PROCEDURE
    ELSE
       (*Queue not empty*)
       Data = QUEUE(Start_pointer)
       (*Get data from the front of the queue*)
       IF Start_pointer = Stop_pointer THEN
               Start_pointer = 0
               (*Only one item was in the queue*)
               Stop_pointer = 0
               EXIT PROCEDURE
       ENDIF
       (*More than one data item was in queue*)
       IF Start Pointer = Size THEN
               Start_pointer = 1
               (*Put Start_pointer back to beginning*)
       ELSE
               Start_pointer = Start_pointer + 1
       ENDIF
    ENDIF
END PROCEDURE
```

Figure 24.4

Arrays

An array is simply an ordering of data elements so that information may be extracted from them. In the case of the linear list shown earlier, we saw an **example** of a **one-dimensional array**. More complex data structures can be expressed by making use of two- (or more) dimensional arrays.

Hint: An array is one of the most important data structures. Make sure that you understand it completely and are able to program arrays using a high-level language of your choice. Most computers support many more dimensions and it's fun to try out several more than the two being described here.

An example will help clarify the situation. We will again use Bradbury's chocolates, but this time we will represent the sales figures for the first six months of the year. The following table should be self-explanatory:

Bradbury's chocolates: First half-year sales figures

Salesperson	Sales (thousand boxes)					
	Jan	Feb	Mar	Apr	May	Jun
Anson	4.7	3.8	6.4	4.6	0.0	4.3
Bartlett	5.1	0.0	3.9	3.7	4.1	3.9
Carter	3.9	4.8	0.0	4.0	5.3	4.1
Jones	0.0	2.8	1.9	3.1	2.6	0.0
Smith	0.9	1.7	2.3	1.5	1.2	2.7
Talbot	4.2	3.6	5.0	0.0	3.4	3.8

The size of an array depends on the number of **rows** and **columns**. In the above case, we have a 6×6 **array**. (Just take note of the figures only.) If we use 'S' to represent the sales elements, and if a **double subscript notation** is used to uniquely identify each individual element within the array, then we may categorise the elements like the examples that follow:

$S_{(1,2)} = 3.8$ i.e. Anson's February sales figures
$S_{(3,4)} = 4.0$ i.e. Carter's April sales figures

using $S_{(row,column)}$ to refer to each element within the array. This is the convention that is always used.

As mentioned above, the process can be extended into further dimensions. Although more difficult to draw, one could easily imagine a set of sales figures for the whole year set out as above in a **two-dimensional array**. The next year's sales figures could then be set out as yet another two-dimensional array. Finally we can imagine it to be behind the previous year's (i.e. in the third dimension). The system could then work as follows:

$S_{(1,2,1)} = 3.8$ Anson's February sales in the 1st year;
        i.e. $S_{(Anson, February, 1st year)}$
$S_{(3,6,4)} = 8.7$ Carter's June sales in the 4th year.

Three or more dimensions may be difficult to imagine or draw, but it is very easy to use them, we simply write down what each dimension means as in the above example. Most high level languages support many more than two or even three-dimensional arrays. However, it should be remembered that a massive amount of memory can be consumed for large multi-dimensional arrays e.g. a five-dimensional array containing 10 elements in each dimension would need:

$10 \times 10 \times 10 \times 10 \times 10 = 100\ 000$ locations (assuming that each number could be stored in just one memory location).

Even arrays must still be represented inside the computer as a **linear list** (i.e. a one-dimensional array). Don't forget that the nature of primary storage *is* simply a linear list. To represent an array in the computer's memory requires **mapping** each element of the array on to the corresponding **locations** that will store the array. The idea is as follows:

Consider the simple 3×4 array with an identifier T.

$$T = \begin{matrix} 10 & 21 & 37 & 31 \\ 35 & 22 & 14 & 66 \\ 13 & 82 & 26 & 94 \end{matrix}$$

Using **row-by-row mapping** we get:

	(1,1)	(1,2)	(1,3)	(1,4)	(2,1)	(2,2)	(2,3)	(2,4)	(3,1)	(3,2)	(3,3)	(3,4)
T	10	21	37	31	35	22	14	66	13	82	26	94

Or using **column-by-column mapping** we get:

	(1,1)	(1,2)	(1,3)	(1,4)	(2,1)	(2,2)	(2,3)	(2,4)	(3,1)	(3,2)	(3,3)	(3,4)
T	10	35	13	21	22	82	37	14	26	31	66	94

It is the above sort of processes that have to be tackled by the computer when you use a **dimension statement** in a high level language such as BASIC. The statement: DIM T(3,4) would be the information that the computer uses to reserve an area of memory using methods similar to those shown above. If you refer to an element in the array such as T(2,1), then the computer knows exactly where that element can be found.

The above methods are often useful when programming in a low-level language (see chapter 21) as no help with array structures is available. We therefore have to devise our own system for accessing the stored information, and this can easily be done in the following ways.

The only things that we know about the elements in the array are the row and column numbers. Similarly the only things we know about the memory locations are the 'first location' and the 'number of locations needed', i.e. the number of elements within the array.

We next have to choose to map either row-by-row or column-by-column as demonstrated above.

The absolute addresses of the memory locations are usually irrelevant so we will use the label MEMstart to indicate the start of the array in MEMory. The address of an element such as T(R,C) will be denoted by ADD T(R,C), i.e. the ADDress of 'the element of T' in the 'Rth Row' and 'Cth Column'.

Let us assume row-by-row mapping. Taking some typical examples of where the data would be stored, we can build up the following picture of the data structure in memory:

Memory location		Array element	Data
Base address + Offset		T(RC)	
MEMstart	+0	T(1,1)	10
MEMstart	+1	T(1,2)	21
MEMstart	+2	T(1,3)	37
MEMstart	+3	T(1,4)	31
MEMstart	+4	T(2,1)	35
MEMstart	+5	T(2,2)	22
MEMstart	+6	T(2,3)	14
MEMstart	+7	T(2,4)	66
MEMstart	+8	T(3,1)	13
MEMstart	+9	T(3,2)	82
MEMstart	+10	T(3,3)	26
MEMstart	+11	T(3,4)	94

From the above patterns we can establish a general expression to indicate where in memory a general element T(R,C) would be stored, i.e. to find ADD T(R,C).

We must use the R and C numbers in the **array element** column to generate the offset from the base address called MEMstart. Concentrate on the C numbers in the array-element column of the above table. You will notice that the numbers form a cycle (1,2,3,4), (1,2,3,4) etc. Also you will notice that these C numbers conveniently go up in steps of 1, although to generate a suitable offset we really need to use (C − 1). Hence (C − 1) will form part of our final expression:

OFFSET = ????? + (C − 1)

The unknown part of the offset expression must be some function of R. Now R must not contribute anything

> **Hint:** The methods being described here are very useful for assembly language programming too. Arrays and other data structures play a vital part in low level language programming.

to the first four addresses as 0,1,2 and 3 from the (C − 1) part do this already. Hence when R = 1, we need '0' generated for this unknown part. When R = 2 we need 4 generated, or when R = 3 we need 8 generated. The function 4(R − 1) will generate these numbers, i.e. when R = 1 we get 0, or when R = 2 we get 4 etc.

Combining these two expressions we get:

Offset = 4(R − 1) + (C − 1)

A few tests will confirm this expression:

T(1,1) Here R = 1 and C = 1
Therefore offset = 4(1−1) + (1−1) = 0+0 = 0
T(2,3) Here R = 2 and C = 3
Therefore offset = 4(2−1) + (3−1) = 4+2 = 6

T(3,4) Here R = 3 and C = 4
Therefore offset = 4(3−1) + (4−1) = 8+3 = 11

We can also confirm that these answers agree with those given in the original table.

Hence the memory address at which an element T(R,C) would be stored is:

ADD T(R,C) = MEMstart + 4(R − 1) + (C − 1)

If we were to study several different sizes of arrays having M rows and N columns then you would find the following general form of the above for row-by-row mapping:

ADD T(R,C) = MEMstart + N(R−1) + (C−1) (where N = number of columns)

or for column-by-column mapping:

ADD T(R,C) = MEMstart + M(R−1) + (C−1) (where M = number of rows)

Processing data in arrays

Arrays are also useful in **high level languages**. As with all **data structures**, the usefulness is reflected by the needs of the business or application that is to make use of the data. As an example, consider a firm of four computer consultants. They all have their own customers, but make use of the same computer system for processing their transactions. Let the names of the consultants be Bradley, Faithful, Prakash and Whyte.

You could have **four different arrays** called **Bradley, Faithful, Prakash and Whyte**. Suppose we treat these as one-dimensional arrays, each having ten elements (not much room for expansion but it makes the diagrams simpler!). Then these could be represented as follows:

Data structure 1			
Bradley	**Faithful**	**Prakash**	**Whyte**
1 Cole	1 Brasier	1 Luscombe	1 Dixon
2 Collis	2 Greenwood	2 May	2 Patrick
3 Gray	3 Jordan	3 Moon	3 Phelps
4 Pegden	4 Sidders	4 Godden	4 Saggers
5 Tonkin	5 Widgery	5	5
6 Williamson	6	6	6
7	7	7	7
8	8	8	8
9	9	9	9
10	10	10	10

Therefore, **Faithful(2)** would refer to the customer Greenwood, who has 'Faithful' as their computer consultant.

The above data structure is only one of many possible arrangements when making use of arrays. For example,

CUSTOMER and CONSULTANT might be a better alternative as follows:

Data Structure 2

	Customer	Consultant
1	Brasier	Faithful
2	Cole	Bradley
3	Collis	Bradley
4	Dixon	Whyte
5	Godden	Prakash
6	Gray	Bradley
7	Greenwood	Faithful
8	Jordan	Faithful
9	Luscombe	Prakash
10	May	Prakash
11	Moon	Prakash
12	Patrick	Whyte
13	Pegden	Bradley
14	Phelps	Whyte
15	Saggers	Whyte
16	Sidders	Faithful
17	Tonkin	Bradley
18	Widgery	Faithful
19	Williamson	Bradley

In the above structure, CUSTOMER(7) would refer to Greenwood, which in turn would refer to CONSULTANT(7), which gives Faithful, Greenwood's consultant. Finally, a pointer system that points to the location in a customer array can be set up. Each of the three consultant's pointers points to the start address of the 'position in the array where the information is stored'. Extra information regarding the number of clients that each consultant has, is stored along with the pointer information. One representation is as follows:

Data structure 3

Consultant	Number of customers	Pointer	Customers
1 Bradley	6	1	1 Cole
2 Faithful	5	100	2 Collis
3 Prakash	4	200	3 Gray
4 Whyte	4	300	4 Pegden
			5 Tonkin
			6 Williamson
			7
			....
			100 Brasier
			101 Greenwood

Data Structure 3 continued

Consultant	Number of customers	Pointer	Customers
			102 Jordan
			103 Sidders
			104 Widgery
			105
			.....
			200 Luscombe
			201 May
			202 Moon
			203 Godden
			204
			205
			.....
			300 Dixon
			301 Patrick
			302 Phelps
			303 Saggers
			304
			305
			....

The above structures all have their advantages and disadvantages. The usefulness of each depends on how information contained within the data structure needs to be accessed. For example, what would be the case if the customers wanted to swap consultants? In data structure 1 it would be a simple case of altering one item of information. If each consultant wanted to process all their clients separately, then data structures 1 or 3 would be best. If the office has to process all the consultant's accounts each month, then data structure 2 would be a good idea. But what if the accounting systems were different for each consultant etc.?

Arguments such as the above have to be weighed up when implementing data structures on a computer. As stated at the beginning of this chapter, it is the particular business applications that dictate the most efficient ways in which to store the data.

Pseudocode to process data held in an array

As an example, take another look at the data structure 3 for the computer consultancy service. Suppose, for example, we wish to process the monthly bills for Whyte. This can be done quite simply using the following pseudocode.

The terminology in the pseudocode algorithm is as follows:

Start_pointer = pointer set to the start of the consultants list in the array CUSTOMERS.

C = **Consultant number**, e.g. Prakash = 3, Bradley = 1, etc.

N = **Number of Customers** derived from associating the position of the consultant with the number of their customers.

```
(*Set start pointer to beginning of
list*)
Start_pointer = Pointer(C)
(*Deduce the end of the list*)
Stop_pointer = Start_pointer + N
(* Process customer information*)
```

```
FOR count =   Start_pointer TO
Stop_pointer
    PROCESS CUSTOMER(count)
NEXT count
```

Addition and deletion of data is considered in great detail **when dealing with linked lists and trees** in the next chapter. As with the **linear list** (which is really a one-dimensional array), addition and deletion of data involves moving many data items and becomes inefficient for huge amounts of data.

Exercise 24.1

1   Explain what is meant by the following terms:

(a) Linear list

(b) Circular list

(c) Stack (LIFO and FIFO)

(d) Queue

(e) Array.

2   Using a pseudocode language of your own choice, and the following simple numerical data structure:

6, 18, 31, 46, 52

devise suitable algorithms, to implement the following:

(a) A linear list

(b) A circular list

(c) A LIFO stack

(d) A FIFO stack

(e) A queue.

3   Using a high-level language of your own choice, turn the pseudocode algorithms developed in question 2 into fully working programs. You need only a simple printed output to show how each of the algorithms cope with the addition and deletion of data. Your structure must not only be able to cope with both the addition and deletion of data, but also with empty and full sets. Allow for a maximum of 10 items of data.

4   If you are good at programming, attempt to make animated versions of the algorithms in question (3) into fully blown teaching aids! You can, for example, make good use of graphics, and of a Windows interface like Micosoft's Visual Basic. You can show how the numbers get put into and taken out of the right places.

N.B. You should be aware that this exercise could represent many hours of work.

End of chapter revision aid and summary

Cover up the right-hand column and see if you can answer the questions or define the terms on the left. They appear in the order in which they are covered in this chapter. Alternatively you may browse through the right-hand column to aid revision.

What is a data structure?	A data structure is a *logical way* of organising data.
Describe the most common operations carried out on a data structure.	*The most common* data-processing operations are traversing data, addition and deletion of data, sorting, searching and merging.
What is a linear list?	A linear list is a one-dimensional array data structure.
What is a vector?	A linear list is also known as a vector.
What does a stack mean?	A stack is an area of memory set up as a temporary storage for data. A stack has a logical top and bottom, which represent the places at which the *beginning and end* of the data can be found.
How might a stack be implemented?	Stacks are implemented by pointers which point to specific areas of memory.
What is a pointer?	A pointer is simply a *data element that indicates the position of some other data element* (e.g. the data element that points to the top of the stack).
What does the term 'push' mean?	Push is the term used to indicate that data has been *placed* on *the stack*.
What does the term 'pop' mean?	Pop is the term used to indicate that data has been *removed from the stack*.
What is a LIFO stack?	A LIFO stack is a Last-In-First-Out stack.
What is a FIFO stack?	A FIFO stack is a First-In-First-Out stack.
What is an array?	An array is the name normally given to a two-or-more dimensional set of data.
How might an array be mapped on to typical memory locations?	The data inside two-dimensional arrays can be mapped onto memory locations by using row-by-row or column-by-column mapping.

25 Further Data Structures

Key resources

To carry out this work most successfully it's best if you have:

◆ Access to a high-level language like BASIC, Visual BASIC, Pascal or Delphi

Concept checkpoints

◆ It's essential that you are a competent programmer before attempting to code some of the algorithms in this chapter. You need to have read chapters 13, 15, 18 and 24 before proceeding with this work.

Introduction

Simple data structures have already been considered in chapter 24. Here we will look at more sophisticated data structures using complex pointer systems.

Linked lists

In a linked list the structure of the data does not necessarily reflect the way in which the data is stored in the computer's memory locations. A linked list uses the important concept of pointers, where a **pointer** is simply a number stored in memory that points to the location where another item of data is to be found.

Consider the example about the Bradbury's chocolates sales people, already used for the simple data structures covered in chapter 24. The original list was not in any particular order. We could rearrange the list so that the sales performance could be analysed, and then rearrange it again so it is in alphabetical order of names. However, with the simpler data structures already covered, this was achieved by completely rearranging the relative positions of the data as shown in Table 24.1.

Consider now a new method, where we will make use of some pointers. Using this new method, the data need not be moved at all to extract exactly the same information. The idea is as follows.

Bradbury's chocolates: March sales figures				
Salesperson	Memory location	Sales data	Alphabetical pointers	Best salesperson pointers
Smith	1	2.3	3	3
Jones	2	1.9	5	4
Anson	3	6.4	6	5
Talbot	4	5.0	2	1
Bartlett	5	3.9	1	2
Carter	6	0.0	4	6

The absolute values of the memory locations where the sales data is stored are unimportant. They have, therefore, just been called 1,2,3,4 etc. for convenience. The alphabetical pointers point to the memory location that holds the next item of data in the alphabetical list. If we read off the alphabetical pointers from top to bottom we get 3 (the location where Anson's figures are stored), 5 (the location where Bartlett's figures are stored) etc. We get a list of the sales data in alphabetical order without having to physically rearrange the data in such a way. The situation is shown in figure 25.1(a).

Alphabetical linked list

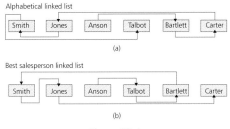

(a)

Best salesperson linked list

(b)

Figure 25.1

Figure 25.1(b) shows the same idea for the best sales-person pointers.

The lists are simply called **linked lists** because they are linked together by pointers.

An important point to realise from the diagrams above is that each of the boxes represents a **record**. A record is simply a set of related data. If the record contains more than one item of data (as is the case with 'Anson' and '6.4', Anson's sales figures) then the record is split up into **fields**. The example just considered could have two fields; one containing the 'surname Anson' and one containing the 'data 6.4'. However, we could include the year's sales figures, in which case there would be 13 fields to the record; one containing the 'surname Anson' and 12 others containing the 'monthly sales figures' for January through to December.

> **Hints:** To round off your knowledge of important data structures, after having read chapters 24 and 25, you should look at the file handling chapters too.

The way that the records are split up into fields is entirely the responsibility of the programmer, and will be considered in some detail in the chapter on **file handling**.

It would be sensible to choose an item of data within the record to be the one that describes that record most conveniently. In the case of our example, the name Anson would seem a sensible choice. Hence the field Anson, or more generally the 'surname field' will become what is known as the **key field**. In practice the surname might not be unique, and an ID number would be more sensible. However, in these examples, there are no duplicate surnames, and so this should be satisfactory in this case. Also the sales data associated with this key field will not be shown from now on.

For the purposes of this chapter we will now consider the record to be one big chunk of data, together with some pointers to form specific linked lists.

*It is usual when considering data structures to represent the records in similar ways to that shown in the following example. The details of the records are unimportant, as we are mainly concerned only with the pointer structure. Used in this context, the record is often called a **node** or a **cell**. An example is shown in the following table.*

Node or cell representing Jones's data and pointers	Key field	Alphabetical pointer	Best sales pointer
	Jones	1	6

Note that the above pointers are **actually stored with the node data,** and must, therefore, reflect where you go after visiting the node called 'Jones'.

For example, **Jones's alphabetical pointer is now 1**, because the **next person** after Jones in the alphabet is **Smith**, who is **stored at 'memory location 1'**. (See the table on the previous page.) Similarly, **Jones's best sales pointer is 6**, because, **after Jones**, the **next best sales person is Carter**, who lives at **'memory location number 6'**. This new, and more convenient way of using the pointers will be used in the next table, where each row of the table reflects the node structure within the list. You may have as many pointers as necessary.

To make use of such a list the computer must know where the list starts. A separate pointer, known as the **start pointer, start cell** or **header** (head of the list) is used. This is simply another memory location or, for the purposes of this chapter, another box. Similarly, as the end of the list must also be known, it is usual to have a **finish pointer**. Again this will simply be a number in a box. Often, in practice, the last pointer in the list would be set to 'zero' or some other suitable symbol to indicate that no data follows.

The complete list for the March sales, together with all the headers and end pointers is shown in figure 25.2.

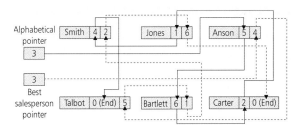

Figure 25.2

You can obviously see that the above diagram gets a little unwieldy, due to the many arrows and pointers, and so a tabular arrangement of the above is often used. This new tabular layout is as follows, and the 'Jones node' is highlighted to show the relationships just established in the last section. (Table continues.)

	Physical position	Key field	Alpha pointer	Best sales pointer
Alpha header **3**	1	Smith	4	2
	2	Jones	1	6
	3	Anson	5	4

	Physical position	Key field	Alpha pointer	Best sales pointer
Best sales header				
3	4	Talbot	0 (End)	5
	5	Bartlett	6	1
	6	Carter	2	0 (End)

Important note: Don't forget that the new method of storing the pointers implies that the '**alphabetical' and**

'**best-sales pointers' in the above table are not to be read from top to bottom** as was the case with the table at the beginning of this chapter. They must be followed by threading your way from the 'start pointers' (headers) and working through the list. In this way, you should see how this new representation generates all the same numbers that were used in the original list on page 509. The table above is simply a more convenient tabular arrangement of the information given in figure 25.2. It also gives the information in a more convenient form for programming, as it shows the 'pointer information' which would be held in each record (i.e. in each row of the table above).

Altering records in linked lists

In the above examples we have not considered the possibility that new data will have to be added, or old data deleted from the list. One of the biggest advantages of linked lists is in the ability to make 'additions' or 'deletions' *without having to move any other items of data*. The only parts of the list that change are the pointers.

No attention has yet been paid to the fact that it is highly likely that there will be more memory left. The end pointers (0 in our examples) refer to the end of data; they do not necessarily refer to the end of memory. In fact it is usual to have a pointer that points to the 'next free storage location', and this pointer will therefore be known as the **free storage pointer**. The idea is shown in figure 25.3.

Deleting data from a linked list

Suppose that we wish to delete the salesperson called Smith. We can do this by altering the pointers shown in the diagram of figure 25.3. Again only the alphabetical pointers will be shown. Figure 25.4(a) shows before deletion and figure 25.4(b) shows after deletion. Note the way in which the pointers have been changed.

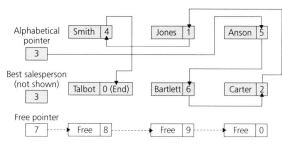

Figure 25.3

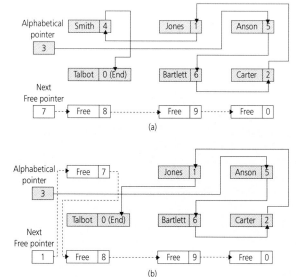

Figure 25.4

1. Jones pointer is altered to point to Talbot. This leaves the 'Smith node' free to be added to the list of 'free nodes', i.e. Smith now becomes the new free node.
2. The pointer of this new free node is now altered to point to where the free storage pointer is pointing.
3. The free storage pointer is now altered to point to the new free node; i.e. the node that used to be called Smith is now first in the free node list.

It can be seen that slight modifications to the above algorithm would be necessary if the data to be deleted was the first or last in the list. In such cases it is a simple matter to check for this and alter the header or the last free pointers accordingly.

Similarly, one could easily develop algorithms to insert a node into any part of the list. Again you

would have to consider the case of the new node to be inserted somewhere in the middle of the list as slightly different from the data to be inserted at the beginning or the end of the list.

Adding data to a linked list

As an example, we will start again with the original list, then insert another salesperson called 'Cummings'. The before and after pointer situations are shown in figure 25.5.

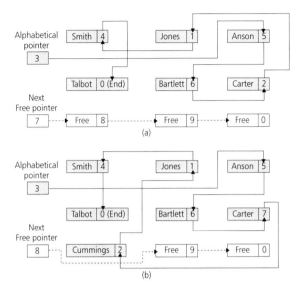

Figure 25.5

The procedure goes along the following lines:

1. Determine where in the list the node is to be inserted. *(This is obviously in between Carter and Jones.)*
2. Store data at the position indicated by free storage pointer.
3. Alter free storage pointer to point to next free location.
4. Alter Carter's pointer to point to Cummings.
5. Alter Cummings' pointer to point to Jones.

Again, slight modifications will be necessary if the data is at the beginning or end of the list, or if no storage space is available, in which case the free storage pointer would have been set to zero by the previous operations. One could build up a complete set of algorithms (see next section) to deal with each possible set of circumstances and then incorporate them all into a flowchart to maintain this data structure. It is not necessary to understand the principles on which these data structures are based unless you wish to incorporate them into a program. In such cases you will be forced to write the algorithms and flowcharts anyway!

In practice, to insert items of data in the way described above would require such techniques as following the pointers and checking to find the exact place for insertion. Once found (probably using string comparisons on the key fields), you make a note of the pointers for the data, just before the place you are inserting, so that stages (4) and (5) above then become a relatively simple matter.

Processing data in a linked list

Linked list systems can be processed by making use of the algorithms shown in the next section.

The following terminology will apply:

Pointer	=	Variable used as a pointer to each node.
start	=	Address of start pointer.
finish	=	Address of finish pointer.
LIST	=	General name for the list contained in memory.
LIST(Pointer)	=	Subscripted variable representing data at *current node* pointed to by *pointer*, i.e. the **identifier** for a specific item of data.
LINK(Pointer)	=	Subscripted variable used as an **identifier** for the current pointer data, i.e. the number which is used as the link pointer (see traversing a linked list for explanation).

Traversing a linked list

The following pseudocode shows how a typical linked list may be traversed. As traversing the list is usually done for some specific reason, we will print out the data contained at each node.

The following procedure assumes that a list called **LIST(N)** has already been set up. In addition to this, one easy way to set up the **link pointer system** is to establish *another list identical in structure to the first*. However, this one contains the **link pointers**, and will therefore be called **LINK(N)**. It is easy to visualise as shown in figure 25.6.

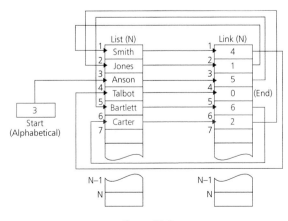

Figure 25.6

Procedure to print out all the data in a linked list

By referring to the diagram of figure 25.6, you should easily be able to see that the following pseudocode is all that is necessary to print out the entire list.

```
PROCEDURE PRINT(start, finish)
  Set Pointer = start
          (*Point to beginning of list*)
  REPEAT
     PRINT LIST(Pointer)
         (*Node information printed out*)
     SET Pointer = LINK(Pointer)
             (*Set Pointer to new link*)
  UNTIL Pointer = finish
               (*Last node printed out*)
END PROCEDURE
```

Notice that we passed the parameters about the start and finish pointers to the procedure. The same procedure could then be used for different pointers such as 'best sales' and 'alphabetical', etc.

If the data consisted of just the names of the salespersons, and if the start pointer was put equal to the 'best sales' pointer, then a list would be obtained of the 'best sales' people in descending order. Of course the figures and anything else could also be printed out if this formed part of the data for each record.

Procedure to search for an item of data in a linked list

To **search** a linked list is just as easy. For example, we might want to print out all the information connected with *Talbot*. If, in this case, Data = Talbot, the pseudocode for *finding and printing out Talbot's information* could be as follows:

Note in the following case, **Data = Talbot**
When **Pointer = 0**, we are at the **end of the list**

```
PROCEDURE SEARCH(Start, Data)
  SET Pointer = Start
          (*Point to beginning of list*)
  REPEAT
     IF Data = LIST(Pointer) THEN
                       (*Match found*)
       Print out the data at node
       EXIT PROCEDURE
     ELSE
       SET Pointer = LINK(Pointer)
             (*Set pointer to new link*)
     ENDIF
  UNTIL Pointer = 0
                        (*Last node*)
  PRINT Information can't be found
                        (*No match*)
END PROCEDURE
```

As you can see from the above, it is relatively easy to write procedures to interrogate linked list data structures. Many other examples could be developed and the reader should feel confident in being able to do so. It is slightly more complicated to add or delete data from a linked list, as the free pointers also have to be taken into account. The following is an example of one method of deleting data from a linked list.

> **Hint:** Don't be content with just reading through this work. You need to write some code in a high-level language of your choice. If you do this and get these algorithms working, then you will understand the work much better.

Procedure to delete data from a linked list

The pseudocode for deleting Smith from a linked list is as follows:

Note: In addition to previous definitions, in the following case:

Data	= Smith
Previous_Pointer	= Link pointer from *previous node* (see explanation in a moment).
LINK(Pointer)	= subscripted variable used as an **identifier** for the Link pointer in the same way as before (see last algorithm).
Free_Pointer	= Pointer to the *next free node*.

The following should be read in conjunction with figure 25.4, as this gives a visual indication of what is actually happening. Don't forget that as we go through the list, we must keep a note of the previous node's pointer because, if we find the node we wish to delete, then the previous node's pointer becomes important in the deletion process.

We must **first traverse the list, checking the data at each node to see if it is the one to be deleted. To delete a node from a linked list requires altering the pointers from the previous node to point to the node after the node to be deleted.** We must also allocate the **freed node** to the **next free pointer list.** As shown in the diagram, we will assume that the freed node will go at the beginning of the free node list. The swap routine in the algorithm will swap any pointers that are necessary.

The situation is slightly more complex if the node to be deleted happens to be the first node in the list, or the last node in the list. This is allowed for in the pseudocode algorithm that follows.

In the following algorithm, if Data = Smith, then it should carry out the processes shown in figure 25.4.

Again it is assumed that **LIST(N)** and **LINK(N)** have already been set up, and are being used in exactly the same way as shown in figure 25.6. The only difference here is that we now have a free pointer system as well, and are thus keeping a note of the previous node's pointer.

The actual pseudocode algorithm for the 'delete procedure' is shown in figure 25.7.

```
PROCEDURE DELETE(Start, Free_Pointer, Data)
   Pointer = Start                                    (*Point to beginning of list*)
   Previous_Pointer = Start                           (*No previous pointer yet*)
                    (*Main procedure for node deletion and adding to next free list*)
   REPEAT
     IF Data = LIST(Pointer) THEN                     (*Node for deletion is found*)
       IF Previous_Pointer = Start  AND Pointer = Start THEN
                                                       (*1st node to be deleted*)
         temp = Free_Pointer
         Free_Pointer = Previous_Pointer
         Start = LINK(Pointer)
         LINK(Pointer) = temp
                             (*1st node deleted and assigned to free list*)
       EXIT PROCEDURE
       ENDIF
       IF LINK(Pointer) = 0 THEN                       (*Last node to be deleted*)
         temp = Free_Pointer
         LINK(Previous_Pointer) = 0
         Previous_Pointer = 0
         Free_Pointer = Pointer
         LINK(Pointer)  = temp                         (*New end of list set up,
         EXIT PROCEDURE                      deleted node assigned to free list*)
       ENDIF                                           (*Middle node to be deleted*)
         temp = Free_Pointer
         LINK(Previous_Pointer) = LINK(Pointer)
         Free_Pointer = Pointer
         LINK(Pointer) = temp
                             (*Middle node out of list and assigned to free list*)
       EXIT PROCEDURE
     ELSE                                              (*Update pointers for next node*)
         Previous_Pointer = Pointer
         Pointer = LINK(Pointer)
     ENDIF
   UNTIL Pointer = 0                                   (*Node not in list*)
  PRINT Node requested has not been found
  EXIT PROCEDURE
```

Figure 25.7

In practice the algorithm in figure 25.7 would need to check if the initial list was empty, and, if merged with an algorithm to add data to a linked list, would have to have slight modifications. Again the reader should be able to add to and modify the above procedure to carry out a variety of tasks.

Circular or ring lists

In the last example we saw the use of **end pointers** to indicate the end of a list. Such an example occurred when following alphabetical pointers through the records. Instead of terminating the list with either a zero or some other suitable character we can arrange a pointer to point back to the beginning of the list. A **circular list** using such a pointer system for the March sales of Bradbury's chocolates would be as follows:

	Physical Location	Key Field	Alpha Pointer	Best Sales Pointer
Alpha Header 3	1	Smith	4	2
	2	Jones	1	6
	3	Anson	5	4
Best Sales Header 3	4	Talbot	3 (New pointer)	5
	5	Bartlett	6	1
	6	Carter	2	3 (New pointer)

Note that the end-of-data pointers (they used to be zero), are now pointing to 3, as Anson heads *both* the alphabetical and best sales lists. The table should be compared with the table for the simple linked list shown earlier. The advantage of using a circular list over the simple linked list is that we are able to investigate the nodes as many times as we please by literally going round in circles! Note that we still need the alphabetical and best sales pointers or we would have no indication of where each list starts. Similarly, we would still need the free storage pointer to indicate where extra data is to be stored.

Two-way linked lists

It is often desirable to be able to go both in the forward and backward directions by making use of pointers. As an example, consider our alphabetical salesperson list used many times in the last few sections. As well as having a list of alphabetical pointers, a **two-way linked list** would also have reverse-order alphabetical pointers. This enables us to go both backwards and forwards in the list with ease. A two-way circular linked list system using both forward and backward pointers on the alphabetical and best sales lists for March would be as shown in table 25.1.

Using a two-way linked list (circular or simple) enables us to quickly go both ways in the list to search for data, and to make lists in either forward or reverse order. However, the process is relatively slow compared to other more sophisticated methods if large amounts of data are stored, and if random data must he sought quickly. The linked list system is ideal for listing large amounts of related data such as alphabetical order or sales figures. Other pointer systems could be set up to indicate length of service to the company, age etc.

> **Hint:** Entire databases can be built up using a combination of the structures shown in chapters 24 and 25 and with the structures contained in the file handling chapters too. Don't forget that commercial database systems make all these operations transparent to the end user.

Tree structures (hierarchical data structures)

Often data does not conveniently fit into a list structure, and other structures such as the **hierarchical data structure** shown in figure 25.8 are used. Such a data structure would be useful for storing items of data in the automobile industry, for example. In such a system, an alphabetical listing of all the component parts of the car would be less efficient compared to representing the system as a hierarchical data structure as shown in the diagram.

> **Hint:** The more experience you can gain with different data structures, the happier you will be when applying them to your project work. Don't forget that spotting such patterns in the data is the key to all this work.

Table 25.1

	Physical Location	Key Field	Alpha Pointer	Reverse Alpha Pointer	Best Sales Pointer	Reverse Best Sales Pointer
Alpha Header 3	1	Smith	4	2	2	5
	2	Jones	1	6	6	1
	3	Anson	5	4	4	6
Best Sales Header 3	4	Talbot	3	1	5	3
	5	Bartlett	6	3	1	4
	6	Carter	2	5	3	2

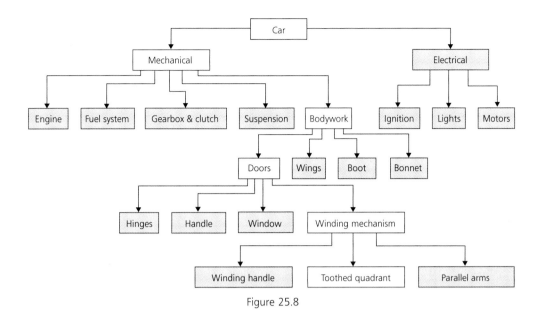

Figure 25.8

The complete data structure is not shown, as it would be impossible to fit such a vast quantity of information on to a single page. However, a typical path is shown to obtain information about a toothed-quadrant gear, which is used to wind the car window up and down.

First the appropriate car file is located; the manufacturer, model and year would determine this. Next the mechanical section is chosen because the winding mechanism for the window is mechanical. Going down the hierarchy we chose bodywork, doors, winding mechanism and finally toothed quadrant.

Many data structures in real life, from family trees to a fully structured program (i.e. split up into simpler modules and these modules are then split up into submodules etc.) can be represented as hierarchical data structures.

A hierarchical data structure is called a **tree** (compare it with a family tree). Each part of the tree that contains data is called a **node** (in the same way that we used the term for lists). Much terminology from trees is used to describe various parts of the structure. For example, the most important node (i.e. the node at the beginning of the tree structure) is called the **root node**. Therefore, 'Car' would be the root node for the tree structure shown in figure 25.8. The lines that connect the nodes are called **branches**. Consider the root node of the structure in figure 25.8. You will see that there are two branches, one leading to the mechanical node and the other to the electrical node. Car is called the **parent node** and mechanical and electrical are called **children nodes**. Now mechanical and electrical are the children of 'car', but mechanical is the parent of 'engine', 'fuel system', 'gearbox and clutch', 'suspension' and 'bodywork' etc.

Each part of the tree that consists of parent and child nodes (such as mechanical) is called a **subtree**. Similarly bodywork would be another example of a **subtree**.

At the bottom of a tree we end up with a child node that has no children. This is termed a **leaf node** (imagine them to be the leaves on the top of the tree when the tree structure is turned upside down such that the root is at the top). Leaf nodes are also known as **terminal nodes**.

As can be seen from the tree structure of figure 25.8 some parents have a number of children. Therefore, the relationship between these children would be that of brother or sister. **Brother** and **sister nodes** are said to be on the same **level** of the subtree.

Tree structures are often used for storing vast amounts of data, such as is found in **databases**.

To represent a tree structure on the computer, extensive use is made of **pointers**. It is usual to start at the root node then follow the pointers through to find the particular item of interest.

Each node has pointers indicating any other nodes on the same level and to point to any subtree that may exist for that node. The general form of a node will therefore be as follows:

Subtree pointer	Data associated with this node	Pointer to same level nodes

For simplicity let us consider the 'Bodywork subtree' shown in figure 25.8. This is reproduced with pointers in figure 25.9.

Although such data structures are convenient for quickly locating data related in this way, it is more complex to add and delete nodes compared with linear lists. It is usual to implement some form of stack (see chapter 24) so that the route through the tree can be traced back to previously visited nodes.

The zeros used in the tree in figure 25.9 indicate the end of list in exactly the same way as those used for linked lists.

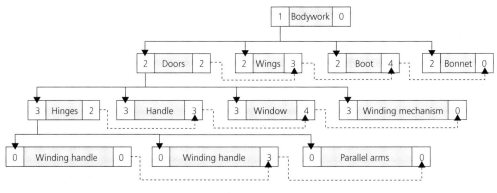

Figure 25.9

Binary trees

These are special types of tree where the parent is only allowed to have a maximum of two children. **Binary tree structures** are implemented using pointer systems in similar ways to the node pointers used with linked lists. The node structure for a typical node in a binary tree diagram would be as follows:

Left pointer	Data to be contained in the node	Right pointer

The main point to note is that each node in the structure contains left and right pointers and either of these pointers may be set to indicate the end of the structure. As an example, consider the following list of names:

Poon, Derry, Smith, Ashton, Wray, Taylor, McCulloch

We may wish to store the data using '<' or '>', together with the first letter of the name, i.e. 'Poon' > 'Derry' because 'Poon' comes after 'Derry' in the alphabet.

Let's suppose that Poon is the root node. This would be as follows:

Poon

Now 'Derry' is the next item from the list to be added. As Derry < Poon, Poon's left pointer is used to point to Derry. The structure now becomes:

Smith is next in the list, as Smith > Poon, therefore, Poon's right-hand pointer points to Smith as follows:

Derry — Poon — **Smith**

Ashton is next. As Ashton < Poon, we follow Poon's left-hand pointer and arrive at Derry. As **Ashton** < Derry we

make Derry's left-hand pointer point to the new node Ashton. The tree is now as follows:

Poon — Derry — Smith, **Ashton**

In a similar way all the other nodes are added to build up the complete binary tree. The results are as follows:

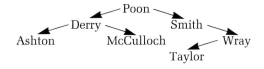

Traversing tree structures

Some interesting and efficient ways of extracting data from tree structures depend on the way in which the tree is **traversed**, i.e. the 'routes which are taken through the tree to visit the various nodes in a definite order'. There are several standard techniques for traversing trees, all of which are useful for specific purposes. For example, the **postorder traversal** method is commonly used for converting from **infix** to **reverse Polish notation** (see chapter 32). The tree shown in figure 25.10 will be used in each case to indicate the traversal method being used.

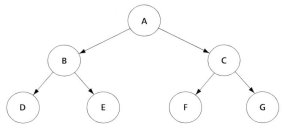

Figure 25.10

> **Hint:** You will need to have understood recursion when this was covered in chapter 18. Make sure you are competent with these procedures before attempting the algorithms that follow.

For each method the nodes will be listed in the order in which the tree has been traversed. A simple three-stage algorithm is also given in each case. In each case the definitions are **recursive** (see chapter 18). As far as we are concerned, this means that they can call themselves. For example, if the left-hand subtree is to be traversed, then the three-stage algorithm will call itself to perform the traversal of this subtree. It may seem complex, but the process is really very simple.

Preorder traversal

1. Start at the root node.
2. Traverse the left-hand subtree.
3. Traverse the right-hand subtree.

As this is the first example it will be explained in detail. Performing stage (1) of the algorithm, the list becomes:

A   i.e. write down the root node

Part (2) involves traversing the left-hand subtree. Now we effectively call the routine again because we want to perform a **preorder traversal** of this left-hand subtree.

Part (1) of this second level then starts at the new root node. As the root node of the left-hand subtree is 'B', then this is listed. The list now becomes:

A B

Part (2) involves traversing the left-hand subtree, but this time it is simply a terminal node 'D'. We therefore add D to the list, and it becomes:

A B D

Part (3) involves traversing the right-hand subtree. This is again a terminal node E. The list now becomes:

A B D E

We have now performed part (2) of the original set of instructions. We therefore proceed to part (3), which states 'traverse the right-hand subtree', i.e. the subtree with the root node C, and the definition now recursively calls itself again as above. The complete list for a preorder traversal will therefore be:

A B D E C F G

Inorder traversal

1. Traverse the left-hand subtree
2. Visit the root node
3. Traverse the right-hand subtree

Applying the recursive definition to the tree in figure 25.9 we get the following list for inorder traversal:

D B E A F C G

Postorder traversal

1. Traverse the left-hand subtree.
2. Traverse the right-hand subtree.
3. Return to the root node.

Applying the recursive definition for postorder traversal we get the following list:

D E B F G C A

The names **preorder, inorder** and **postorder** are obtained from the position in which the root node is visited with respect to the other operations. In the preorder traversal it is visited during the first stage (1). In the inorder traversal the root node is visited in the middle, stage (2). Finally, in the postorder traversal, the root node, stage (3) is visited at the end.

Examples

(1) As an example of the application of traversal methods, consider the binary tree shown at the beginning of the binary tree section consisting of seven different names, i.e.

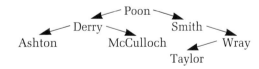

The tree was originally constructed using the standard '<' and '>' tests on letters of the alphabet. If we perform an **inorder traversal** on the above tree we get:
Ashton, Derry, McCulloch, Poon, Smith, Taylor and Wray

We have now produced an alphabetical list of the data contained in each node. Magic!

(2) As another example of how these traversal methods can be used, consider the INFIX (see chapter 32) algebraic expression: $X = 3 * Y + (Z \uparrow 2 - Z)$. This may be expressed as a binary tree as shown in figure 25.11. (You may wish to come back to this example when you understand its significance more readily.)

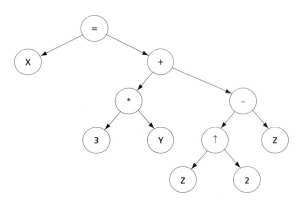

Figure 25.11

Processing data in trees

We will now develop a method for traversing a tree structure using **preorder traversal**. Make sure that you have understood what is meant by preorder traversal, and make sure that you are familiar with the **stack data structure** covered in chapter 24.

Pseudocode to traverse a tree using preorder traversal

First, a brief reminder of **preorder traversal**:

1. Start at the **ROOT** node.
2. Traverse the *left-hand* subtree using **preorder** traversal.
3. Traverse the *right-hand* subtree using **preorder** traversal.

To convert this to **reverse Polish** we traverse the right-hand subtree using postorder traversal, listing the nodes when this part of the traversal is complete. The **reverse Polish expression** can be found in seconds when you have had some practice. However we will build it up slowly to illustrate the traversal method.

Hint: If you have covered the work on reverse Polish notation, why not write some code to carry out conversion between infix and reverse Polish notation. This should provide you with a challenge for a few hours.

We traverse the **right-hand subtree**. The root node of this subtree is the + node. Now this can't be written down in one lump and so we apply the algorithm again (the recursive definition).

Traverse the left-hand subtree. The root node of this subtree is now the * node. Hence applying the algorithm again, we traverse the left-hand subtree. We have finally arrived at a terminal node, which is 3. Hence the expression becomes:

3

Traverse the right-hand subtree (which is simply the Y). Hence the expression becomes:

3 Y

We now return to the root node of the subtree, which is *. Hence the expression becomes:

3 Y *

Next we return to the root node which is + and traverse the right-hand subtree. In this way the rest of the expression can be built up as follows:

3 Y * Z 2 ↑ Z – +

This is the reverse-Polish expression for X.

As we are traversing the left-hand subtree we shall have to come back to the root of the subtree eventually so that the right-hand subtree may be traversed. The **STACK** will be used as a **temporary store** in which to place the addresses of the nodes, which must be visited on our return journey. We must, therefore, *initially* set **the STACK to zero**. In the following algorithms we have made use of a stack, but will not check to see if the stack will overflow. These techniques have already been covered earlier in chapter 24, and will only make what we are trying to do appear more complex. You can easily add these checks at a later stage when the tree-traversal algorithms are working for simple sets of data.

Having undertaken a preorder traversal of the tree shown in figure 25.10, you will recall that as each node is visited it must be processed. As an example, in the algorithm that we are developing, the *process* that will be carried out is '*print the data contained at each node*'. We should, therefore, end up with the same sequence of letters: **ABDECFG** after working through the final pseudocode algorithm.

When proceeding down the left-hand path of the tree, as well as processing each node visited as described above, we must push any right-hand child nodes that we find onto the top of the stack. This process must continue until we get to a **leaf node**, whereupon this leaf node is processed. To progress down the subtree we must follow the **Left_Pointers**. We will know we have hit a **leaf node** because, at this stage, **Left_Pointer = 0**.

After reaching a leaf node we must backtrack by **popping** the address off the stack. However, each time we remove an address from the stack we must check to see if it is zero. If it is, we have finished, if not, we assign our pointer to this new address from the stack and must then go through the same process again with the new pointer from the stack as our new starting point.

In the **pseudocode algorithms**, the following terminology will apply:

Pointer	= Variable used as a pointer to each node in the tree.
STACK	= A stack implemented as described earlier in this chapter.
STACK(Stack_Pointer)	= Subscripted variable used as an identifier for the data on the stack pointed to by the current stack pointer.
PUSH and **POP**	Used as described in the section on stacks.
ROOT	= Root node of the tree.
TREE(Pointer)	= Subscripted variable used as an identifier for the data at the node pointed to by the current pointer.
Left_Pointer	= Pointer to left child of TREE(Pointer).
Right_Pointer	= Pointer to right child of TREE(Pointer).

It is assumed that **STACK(N)** and **TREE(N)** have already been set up.

We must start at the root of the tree, and therefore the **Pointer** must be **SET** initially to the **ROOT**.

If we arrange the following algorithm carefully, then the STACK should be empty only at the start and when the *complete tree* has been traversed.

The final pseudocode algorithm can be developed as shown in figure 25.12.

To help you understand the above algorithm, consider the following **dry run** with the data from figure 25.9.

Note that *each node is called by its contents*, A, B, C, D, etc. Note also that **Ra** denotes the **Right_Pointer of Node** A and **Le** denotes the **Left_Pointer associated with Node E**, etc. 'A' and 'B' are simply the pointers to these nodes, i.e. if we are dealing with the root node, then the pointer must be at A.

The **dry run** for **preorder traversal** using the **pseudocode algorithm** with the **data** from **Figure 25.10** is shown in Table 25.2.

```
PREORDER(ROOT)              (*initialisation of pointers and stack*)
SET Pointer = ROOT
Stack_Pointer = 0
REPEAT
                        (*Get data and pointer info from node*)
   PRINT TREE(POINTER)
IF Right_Pointer <> 0 THEN      (*First time node has been visited*)
                    (*Deal with right child node*)
      Stack_Pointer = Stack_Pointer + 1
      STACK(Stack_Pointer) = Right_Pointer      (*PUSH onto STACK*)
ENDIF
IF Left_Pointer <> 0 THEN (*Set pointer to traverse left subtree*)
      SET Pointer = Left_Pointer
ELSE              (*Arrived at a leaf node*)
      SET Pointer = STACK(Stack_Pointer)       (*POP off STACK*)
      Stack_Pointer = Stack_Pointer - 1
ENDIF
UNTIL Pointer = 0        (*Top of stack is empty, tree has been traversed*)
END PROCEDURE
```

Figure 25.12

Table 25.2 (continues)

Pointers			Stack Pointer	Contents of Stack	Processing Results	Comments
L	Ptr	R				
La	A	Ra	0	–	–	Initialisation
La	A	Ra	0	–	A	Processing carried out on root node
La	A	Ra	1	Ra	–	Save right child on stack
Lb	B	Rb	1	Ra	–	Update pointers
Lb	B	Rb	1	Ra	B	Processing carried out on node B
Lb	B	Rb	2	Rb Ra	–	Save right child on stack

Table 25.2 (continued)

Pointers			Stack Pointer	Contents of Stack	Processing Results	Comments
L	Ptr	R				
Ld	D	Rd	2	Rb Ra	–	Update pointers
0	D	0	2	Rb Ra	D	Processing carried out on Node D
			–	–	–	Note Ld and Rd = 0
0	Rb	0	1	Ra	–	POP off stack
0	E	0	1	Ra	–	NB pointer been set to E (i.e. RH-pointer of B)
0	E	0	1	Ra	E	Processing carried out on Node E
			–	–	–	NB Le and Re = 0
0	Ra	0	0	–	–	POP off stack
0	C	0	0	–	–	NB pointer been set to C (i.e. RH-pointer of A)
Lc	C	Rc	0	–	C	Processing carried out on node C
Lc	C	Rc	1	Rc	–	Save right child on stack
Lf	F	Rf	1	Rc	–	Update pointers
0	F	0	1	Rc	F	Processing carried out on node F
			–	–	–	Note Lf and Rf = 0
0	Rc	0	0	–	–	POP off stack
0	G	0	0	–	G	Processing carried out on node G
0	0	0	0	–	–	Main pointer = 0
–	–	–	–	–	–	Algorithm is therefore terminated

Pseudocode to traverse a tree using inorder traversal

First, a brief reminder of **inorder traversal**

1. Traverse the *left-hand* subtree using **inorder** traversal.
2. Visit the **ROOT** node.
3. Traverse the *right-hand* subtree using **inorder** traversal.

The ideas are obviously very similar to those encountered when carrying out the **preorder traversal** earlier. However, inorder traversal is a little trickier. Even so, after following through the dry run given after the algorithm, you should be able to understand the ideas.

As before, the 'Pointer' will be used to direct the processing of data. This time however, we will carry on down the 'left-hand side of the tree' pushing each node on to the stack. We will then continue in this way until we reach a leaf node, in which case this is the 'root' of the left-hand subtree, and the data at this node will therefore be processed.

We then backtrack to the root node of the left-hand subtree, popping each item off the stack until the stack is empty. However, when popping an item off the stack, if a right child is found, this must then be processed by calling the original algorithm again, but this time with the pointer set to the new Right-Pointer instead of the root.

It should be noted that recursion is used in the following algorithm, i.e. the procedure calls itself (see chapter 18).

In this **pseudocode algorithm**, as before, the following terminology will apply:

Pointer	= Variable used as a pointer to each node in the tree.
STACK	= A stack implemented as described earlier in this chapter.
STACK(Stack_Pointer)	= Subscripted variable used as an identifier for the data on the stack pointed to by the current stack pointer.
PUSH and **POP**	= Used as described in chapter 24 on stacks.
ROOT	= Root node of the tree.
TREE(Pointer)	= Subscripted variable used as an identifier for the data at the node pointed to by the current pointer.
Left_Pointer	= Pointer to left child of TREE(Pointer)
Right_Pointer	= Pointer to right child of TREE(Pointer)
PROCESS	= Part of the algorithm which may call itself. It has therefore been written as a separate procedure.

The pseudocode algorithm is shown in figure 25.13.

```
PROCEDURE INORDER(ROOT)      (*initialisation of pointers and stack*)
   SET Pointer = ROOT
   Stack_Pointer = 0
   PROCESS                        (*Call the process procedure shown below*)
END PROCEDURE
PROCEDURE PROCESS
   REPEAT
        Stack_Pointer = Stack_Pointer + 1 (*Push data on to stack*)
        Stack(Stack_Pointer) = Pointer    (*Update pointer to get to next node*)
        Pointer = Left_Pointer
   UNTIL Left_Pointer = 0(*Arrived at leaf node as left pointer = 0*)
   PRINT TREE(Pointer)    (*POPS node data off the stack*)
   Pointer = STACK(Stack_Pointer)
   Stack_Pointer = Stack_Pointer - 1
   REPEAT                         (*Process the data in the node*)
        PRINT TREE(Pointer)
        IF Right_Pointer <> 0 THEN        (*Traverse right-hand subtree?*)
            Pointer = Right_Pointer
            PROCESS       (*Recursive call to this procedure*)
        ELSE                      (*POPS node off the stack*)
            Pointer = Stack(Stack_Pointer)
            Stack_Pointer = Stack_Pointer - 1
        ENDIF
   UNTIL Left_Pointer = 0
END PROCEDURE
```

Figure 25.13

Table 25.3 (continues)						
Pointers			Stack Pointer	Contents of	Processing	Comments
L	Ptr	R		Stack	Results	
La	A	Ra	0	–	–	Initialisation
La	A	Ra	1	A	–	Push data onto stack
Lb	B	Rb	1	A	–	Update pointers Lb <>0
Lb	B	Rb	2	BA	–	Push data onto stack
Ld	D	Rd	2	BA	–	Update pointers Ld = 0
Ld	D	Rd	2	BA	D	Process data
Lb	B	Rb	1	A	–	Pop data and update pointers
Lb	B	Rb	1	A	B	Process data Lb <> 0 Rb <> 0
Le	E	Re	1	A	–	Update pointers
*** Procedure calls itself to traverse the right-hand subtree ***						
Le	E	Re	2	EA	–	Push onto stack
–	0	–	2	EA	–	Update pointers
						No processing as node data does not exist
Le	E	Re	1	A	–	Pop off stack
Le	E	Re	1	A	E	Process data Re = 0
La	A	Ra	0	–	–	Pop off stack
La	A	Ra	0	–	A	Process data La <> 0
Lc	C	Rc	0	–	–	Update pointers
*** Procedure calls itself to traverse the right-hand subtree ***						

Table 25.3 (continued)

Pointers			Stack Pointer	Contents of Stack	Processing Results	Comments
Lc	C	Rc	1	C	–	Push onto stack
Lf	F	Rf	1	–	–	Update pointers Lf = 0
Lf	F	Rf	1	C	F	Process data
Lc	C	Rc	0	–	–	Pop off stack
Lc	C	Rc	0	–	C	Process data Rc <> 0
Lg	G	Rg	0	–	–	Update pointers
*** Procedure calls itself to traverse the right-hand subtree ***						
Lg	G	Rg	1	G	–	Push data onto stack
–	0	–	1	G	–	Update pointers
No processing as node does not exist						
Lg	G	Rg	0	–	G	Process data Rg = 0
Lg	G	Rg	0	–	–	Pop off stack
			END CALL			
			END CALL			
			END CALL			
		End of original procedure			

Pseudocode to traverse a tree

Having gone through the last two traversal methods in great detail, it is left to the reader to develop the final method. The method is a little more complicated than the previous two algorithms. (Teachers take note: it makes a great assignment!)

Networks

Networks are data structures that allow more complex interconnections than are possible using linked lists or trees. An example of a network is shown in figure 25.14.

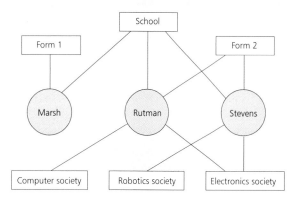

Figure 25.14

For simplicity the network shows just three pupils of a school, together with two forms and three school societies. From the network the relations between the

various nodes can be seen. For example, Marsh is a member of Form 1, but belongs to no society. Rutman is a member of Form 2 and belongs to the computer society and the electronics society.

Network data structures have been used extensively in the implementation of **database systems** because of the vastly increased flexibility over the more limited hierarchical data structures. They are difficult to maintain (i.e. difficult to modify because of the spider's web of pointers) and techniques known as **relational structures** (see chapter 29) are rapidly becoming more popular. However, these will be covered in more detail in the chapter on databases.

Hash tables

We have seen how data may be stored in lists and trees, and how data may be represented in memory as a linear list. The previous methods are good for finding data that has structure such as a hierarchy, but not so useful for storing and accessing data in more **random** ways. Suppose, for example, that we have a table consisting of 1,000 elements (initially empty) as shown in figure 25.15(a).

Suppose now that we run a club with no more than 1,000 members each with a five-digit secret membership code. The problem is, how do we map the membership code (the key field) to these 1,000 storage locations in the table? One method that gives very quick access to the stored data is called **hashing**.

> **Hint:** Many students understand and remember hashing for the examinations, but fail to apply similar methods in their projects when it would be useful to do so.

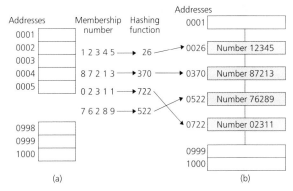

Figure 25.15

We must first think up a **hash (or hashing) function**. This is simply a set of rules that, when applied to the five-digit key field, generates the appropriate address in the table.

Consider the hash function to be a pointer that is used to point to the location where the appropriate data may be found. A generalised hash function is used in the following way:

Address = hash function (key field)

As an example, let us consider the following hash function:

Hash function = key field is **squared**, then take **right-hand three digits** and finally **ADD 1**

Consider the member who has a secret membership code number of 12345.

Applying the above hashing function we get:

Original number	Number squared	Right-hand three digits	Right-hand three digits ADD 1
12345	152399025	025	26

Therefore, the address of membership number '12345' is '26'.

The above is shown in figure 25.12(b) together with the three other membership numbers worked out below.

Original number	Number squared	Right-hand three digits	Right-hand three digits ADD 1
87213	7606107369	369	370
02311	5340721	721	722
76289	5820011521	521	522

One disadvantage of hashing functions is their ability to generate the same address within the table for different key fields. This is termed a **collision**. From the above it should be reasonably obvious that collisions will occur if the last digits in the membership number are the same. As an example, consider the following three membership numbers.

Original number	Number squared	Right-hand three digits	Right-hand three digits ADD 1
83123	6909433129	129	130
95123	9048385129	129	130
07123	50737129	129	130

We can see that all three unique membership numbers have generated the same address at which to store the data. One method to get over this is to make use of an **overflow table**. The idea is shown in the following table.

Membership number	Hashing function	Addresses	Contents of the 1,000 addresses	Overflow table space
12345	26	1	–	95123*
87213	370	...	–	07132
83123	**130**	...	–	–
95123	**130**	26	12345	–
07123	**130**	...	–	–
02311	722	...	–	–
76289	522	**130**	83123 *	–
–	–	...	–	–
–	–	370	87213	–
–	–	...	–	–
–	–	522	–	–
–	–	...	–	–
–	–	722	–	–
–	–	...	–	–
–	–	...	–	–
–	–	999	–	–
–	–	1000	–	–

We can see that membership number 83123 came first. It therefore occupies the free location 130. Now the next number to generate the same address is 95123. This is then stored in the overflow table, which is linked to the original address 130 by a pointer system. The * at the end of the data indicates that an overflow table exists, or, if it is already in the overflow table, then it indicates a pointer that points to the next entry in the overflow table.

Devising the hashing functions

In the above section we said 'think up a hashing function'! In fact there are thousands of different possible functions, some of which are more suitable for particular applications than others. It is usual to try to obtain an even distribution of data throughout the table. This is because a bias towards one end or the other would produce more collisions than necessary. Several standard methods for choosing hashing functions have been developed and some are shown in the following sections.

Methods using modulo arithmetic

A common method used to generate addresses uses the **modulo** function (see chapter 18). This is convenient as it enables us to generate the exact number of addresses easily and quickly. For example, if we had just fifty locations in memory, then 'MOD 50' would produce the numbers '0 to 49' from any **numeric field**. Similarly, if we had 1000 memory locations, we would then use 'MOD 1000' to produce the numbers '0 to 999' for any numeric field. Hence a general hashing function using modulo arithmetic might be of the form:

Address = (Key field)MOD N + 1

We have stressed that this is for numeric fields. However, it can be applied to non-numeric fields if an appropriate coding method is used. As an example, let us assume that we use an alphabetic key field consisting of five letters. We could use the ASCII code (see chapter 12) for each number and build up the numbers that can be used in the hashing function.

Non-numeric field	= F	R	E	D
ASCII codes	= 70	82	69	68
	(ASCII code for F in decimal is 70 etc.)			
Numeric equivalent	= 70826968			
Addresses (MOD 1000)	= 968			

Hence, FRED would be stored in location 969.

Radix conversion

You might realise that a **radix** is simply the name given to a number base (see chapter 30). Any base greater than ten can be used and hence we will use base thirteen in our example.

Example

Let the original key be 2 3 1 6.

We assume that the above number is in base thirteen and proceed to convert it into base ten. If a base < ten is used you may get high digits that would be impossible in that base!

1×13^3	$+1\times13^2$	$+1\times13^1$	$+1\times13^0$	Columns headings in base 13
2	3	1	6	Original number (Multiply)
4394	+ 507	+ 13	+ 6	**4920** **Result**

If the range of addresses is too large (as will probably be the case above), then it is usual to **truncate** the number to the required number of digits. Thus, if three digits were required in the above example, then 2316 would generate the address 920.

Mid-square method

Another popular technique is to **square** the **key field** and take N digits out of the middle of the result, and an example now follows.

Suppose that we are dealing with a four-digit key field. The maximum number of digits that this can generate when squared is eight, i.e. 9999 × 9999 = 99980001. Therefore a number which, when squared, does not generate eight digits, is packed with leading zeros.

Let us choose to take the middle four digits out of the squared number.

The key field 1210 would generate the following address:

1210 × 1210 = 01464100

Therefore the middle four digits = 4641, which is the required address.

Exercise 25.1

1 What is a tree structure and why is it of fundamental importance in computing? Briefly explain and give examples of the following terms when applied to a tree structure:

(a) Subtree

(b) Node

(c) Terminal nodes, child node, parent node, sister node and root node.

(d) Give two examples of data that would naturally lead to a hierarchical structure.

2 A binary tree is a special type of tree structure. Outline the conditions that must be obeyed for a tree to be a binary tree and give an application of a typical binary tree structure.

3 There are various ways of traversing tree structures. These include:

(a) Preorder traversal

(b) Inorder traversal

(c) Postorder traversal.

Using the following tree structure write down the order in which the node data would be listed using the three traversal methods described above.

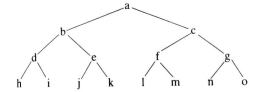

4 What are the main differences between a **network** data structure and a **tree** data structure? Which would be the most appropriate structure for a database and why?

5 (a) What is meant by the term '**hash table**'? Give an example by making use of a suitable hashing function of your own choosing.

(b) What is meant by the term '**overflow table**' when using hashing functions. What happens when the overflow table overflows?

6 Describe a suitable data structure that could be used to implement a directory on a disk. You must make sure that your directory can cope with file extensions, i.e. files of the type PASCAL.SORT1 would represent a program SORT1 that is an extension of the Pascal directory.

The following ideas can be used for more practice in writing algorithms for data structures. They are of a similar degree of difficulty to the examples given in this chapter. With suitable extensions they could form the basis of an A-level project. You will also have to develop the code to set up the appropriate data structure in the first place.

7 Using a suitable high level language, develop algorithms and produce code to solve the following problems.

(a) Create a binary tree using the names of people in your class. Choose a suitable root node (i.e. someone whose name is roughly in the middle of the alphabet) and create the tree as shown on page 518.

(b) Perform an in-order traversal and check that the names come out in alphabetical order.

8 (a) Devise the code necessary to input an INFIX string and build up a suitable tree structure as shown on page 518.

(b) Perform a post-order traversal and check that the expression comes out in the correct 'reverse Polish' form.

End of chapter revision aid and summary

Cover up the right-hand column and see if you can answer the questions or define the terms on the left which are covered in this chapter. Alternatively you may browse through the right-hand column to aid revision.

Describe the function of a linked list.	Linked lists make use of *one or more* pointers assigned to different functions such as alphabetical or increasing-numeric etc.
What is a circular list?	Circular or ring lists may be set up by appropriate pointer systems, connecting the end and beginning of the list.
What is a two-way linked list?	Two-way linked lists allow data to be traversed in both directions.
What is a tree structure?	A tree structure is a hierarchical data structure.
What is a root node?	The root node is at the 'base' (top!) of the tree. A node refers to a specific data item or items (which may include pointers too).
What is a parent node?	A parent node has other *subordinate nodes* called children nodes.
What is a leaf node?	A leaf node is a child node with no further children.
What are brother and sister nodes?	Brother or sister nodes are *nodes, which have the same parent.*
What is a sub tree?	A sub-tree consists of parent and child nodes, which form just a part of the main tree structure.
What is a terminal or leaf node?	A terminal node is the same as a leaf node and indicates that no children are present.
What is a branch?	A branch is the name of the route taken from a parent to a child node.
Describe a binary tree.	Binary trees are trees in which a *maximum of two children per parent* is permitted.
List three ways in which tree structures can be traversed.	There are *several methods* of traversing tree structures, namely pre-order, in-order and post-order traversal.
Describe preorder traversal.	Preorder traversal visits the root, left-hand sub-tree, then right-hand sub-tree.
Describe inorder traversal.	Inorder traversal visits the left-hand sub-tree, root, and then right-hand sub-tree.
Describe postorder traversal.	Postorder traversal visits the left-hand sub-tree, right-hand sub-tree then the root.
How might sorting be carried out with a binary tree?	'Sorting' into order can be accomplished by using in-order traversal of an *appropriately set up* binary tree.
How might infix be converted to postfix?	Infix may be *converted to* reverse Polish (postfix) by using post-order traversal or an appropriately set up tree.
What is a network data structure?	Networks are *partially or fully interconnected* data structures.
What is a relational data structure?	Relational data structures are considered in the database chapter. They are defined by special tables.
What is hashing?	Hashing is a technique for random access of stored data. Applying a hash function to a key element within the data – bank account number, for example generates an address.
What is modulo arithmetic?	Modulo arithmetic methods are popular for devising suitable hashing functions. It is the clock arithmetic as described in chapter 18.
What are the radix conversion and mid-square methods examples of?	Radix conversion and the mid-square methods are also other popular hashing techniques.

26 File Handling and Organisation

In this chapter you'll learn about:

- Serial and sequential file handling methods
- Direct and indexed sequential files
- Creating, reading, writing and deleting records from a variety of file structures
- Creating code to carry out the above operations

Key resources

To carry out this work most successfully it's best if you have:

- Access to a high-level language that supports serial and random access file handling like the later versions of BASIC and Pascal, Visual BASIC or Delphi
- Access to the COBOL language would be a particular advantage if you are lucky enough to have a suitable compiler

Concept checkpoints

- It's essential that you understand the concept of pointers, as covered in chapters 24 and 25, when data structures are being considered.
- It is also essential you that you are familiar with structure diagrams like those developed by Nassi and Schneidermann as covered in chapter 14.
- An appreciation of the work covered in chapter 19 would also be useful.

Introduction

A file is such an important data structure that two chapters are devoted entirely to it. Few activities take place in computing without reference to a file – be it a database file, a word-processor file or indeed any other application-based or program-based files. **One often hears a huge variety of terms like 'file allocation table' (see chapter 22), a 'COBOL file', 'file-management utilities', 'file names', 'file servers', 'file types' and 'file maintenance', for example. The thing which all of these terms have in common is that they are all usually referring to data structures for external storage systems such as disks, tapes, CD-ROMs, DVDs etc.** Although it is easily possible to create and process files entirely within memory, one advantage of file data structures is that they are designed to cope with vast amounts of data in a single structure. Typically this structure is many Mbytes, but often several Gbytes or even larger. For much of the time, complete files cannot be fitted into the available amount of RAM on the majority of computer systems.

It's most important that you have read and understood chapters 24 and 25 on data structures, and also have an appreciation of some of the work covered in chapter 19 when sorting and searching techniques are discussed in detail. Many of the principles and concepts built up in this chapter rely on work that has been covered in these and previous chapters.

What is a file?

A **file** is *logically organised* (see in a moment) *as* **a collection of records**, and *usually* contains **related information**. A file is, therefore, **a collection of related information** stored on some suitable storage medium. Such concepts are not difficult to understand. Most people would use similar terms in the everyday sense of the words. The ideas of 'customer files', 'criminal-record files' or 'stock files', for example, would be understood by the majority of people. These terms have literally been borrowed from office terminology where files (folders containing information) are stored in filing cabinets in ways similar to that shown in figure 26.1. These days, however, more and more data in the form of files are being stored on computer disks and tape. Throughout this chapter we will be looking in detail at the anatomy of these files, and the ways in which the data stored within these files can be processed efficiently.

A file's **logical organisation** relates to the ways in which it is **logically** broken up into smaller self-contained units called **records**. For example, if we are dealing with a customer file, then each customer would probably have his or her own record, shown as a 'record card' in the case of figure 26.1. On the other hand, the **physical organisation** of a file refers to the ways in which *the file is physically stored on a disk or tape*. It deals specifically with the ways in which the information is **mapped** onto the **physical blocks**, and

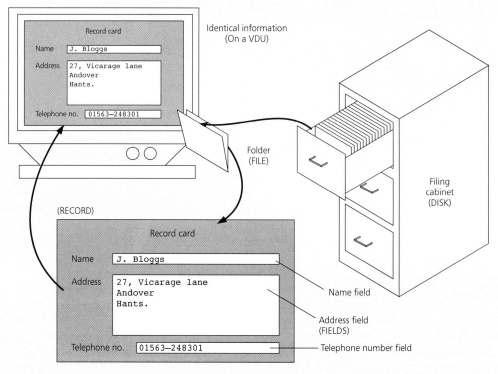

Figure 26.1

eventually onto the **tracks** and **sectors** (see chapter 12) on a disk, for example. However, this physical organisation can be forgotten about for the time being, it is covered in chapter 12.

Did you know that . . .

In the early days of file handling, virtually all files were processed on large tape machines. These sequential access methods have found their way into the most modern of file handling procedures because the methods, developed back in the 1950s and 1960s, are still just as applicable today. It's nice to know that something you learn in computing is not going to be out-of-date soon!

Each **record** usually contains information, which *has been further split up into smaller logical units* called

fields. Figure 26.1 shows a record card with three separate fields, namely 'customer name', 'address' and 'telephone number'. Many students have little experience of using magnetic tape, but it's easy to visualise what's happening here too by considering figure 26.2. In this diagram we can see that the customer file has been split up into 'customer identity number', 'name', 'address' and 'amount outstanding' fields. The only problem with tape, as we shall see later, is that all the records have to be cycled through until you get to the one that you need. This could often take a long time (in computer terms of course), but don't dismiss tape as a viable and efficient file-storage and data-processing medium on large systems, it is often very efficient, fast and cost effective if used in the correct way.

Of course, a **field** is *not* the smallest item of data within a **file**; the contents of most fields are further subdivided into **characters**.

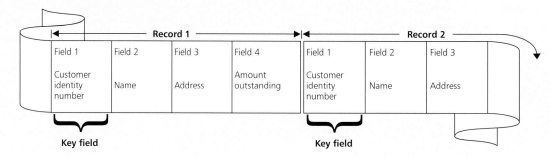

Figure 26.2

Logical file organisation

There are *several different types* of **file organisation**, each being efficient in its own way for certain types of operation, and each more or less efficient – or indeed impossible to use – with different types of secondary storage media. The **four main types of file organisation** are shown in the following list (although alternative names are sometimes used) and each type is explained in the next few sections.

(1) **Serial access**
(2) **Sequential access**
(3) **Direct access**
(4) **Indexed sequential**

You may come across other file organisations such as 'indexed' or 'binary search' for example, and these variations on the above themes are covered later in this chapter.

Serial access files

When this type of file organisation is used **each record is stored one after the other with no regard to any logical order**. *In other words – each record is stored one after the other in a higgledy-piggledy way.* Files organised like this are often the inevitable consequence of day-to-day operations such as reading raw statistical data or collecting data from questionnaires and the like. Serially organised files therefore usually consist of unprocessed records waiting for some operation such as 'sorting', for example, to be carried out. However, if the same processing has to be carried out on all records then serial-access files are just as efficient as any other method.

To *access data within a serial file* the concept of a **pointer** must be well understood. Pointers have already been covered in some detail in chapters 24 and 25 when other **data structures** are considered, and therefore it's not too surprising that pointers are used within files too. A file is just another example of a data structure – albeit usually implemented on an external device. Figure 26.3 shows a serial-access file in which the pointer has been placed at the beginning of the next record, marking the next position within the file ready for processing.

Most high-level languages have mechanisms for **pointer** and **file manipulation**, but *few have the sophisticated file-handling facilities of* **COBOL** (see chapter 15). Some versions of **Pascal**, for example, are limited to **serial or sequential access files only**, and the facilities in

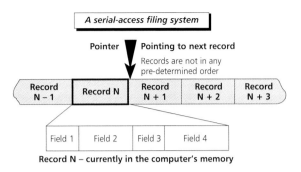

Record N – currently in the computer's memory

Figure 26.3

some versions of BASIC are literally – just as basic! It is, however, *essential* **that you have some high-level programming experience of file-handling** – programming by making use of a 4GL database language only would give you insufficient insight into what's going on at a fundamental level. If you have access to Microsoft's **Visual BASIC**, for example, then this *will* enable you to program using **random-access file** techniques. However, these more advanced techniques are the subject of the work covered in chapter 27, where you will find examples that can be developed into complete working systems in appropriate high-level languages of your choice. This chapter deals only with processing serial and sequential access files, and algorithms for these simpler file structures are covered in this chapter too.

Sequential access files

This file-access method operates on *a file, which has already been put into some pre-determined* **sequence**. For example, it might be 'ascending order of bank-account number', 'alphabetical order by name', or 'ISBN number' for books. It is usual for the field associated with the sort order to be termed the **key field**, and these ideas are shown in figure 26.4.

This file must have been sorted into order using techniques similar to those covered in chapter 19. However, *if the file to be sorted is too big to fit into available RAM,* then **other techniques**, *covered later in this chapter* can easily be used instead.

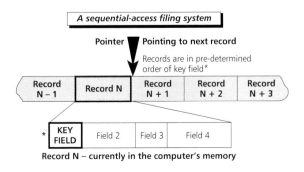

Record N – currently in the computer's memory

Figure 26.4

Sequential files are extremely efficient for **batch processing** (see chapter 23) operations such as working out quarterly service bills for water, electricity and gas, for example. If the information in a sequential file needs to be **updated** (see later in this chapter), then it is very *efficient* to make use of a **sequential file** *if* the **amendments file** or **transaction file** *is also in the same order*. It should be noted that *if* a **magnetic tape is being used, then 'serial' or 'sequential file organisation' is the** *only option* available. Even so, it is possible to implement such file systems in more efficient ways if they are used on a direct-access storage medium such as disk.

Direct access files

A **direct-access file** (also called a **random-access file**) means that *it's possible to* **directly access a record** *without* having gone through any previous records. Conceptually, *instead of visualising the system as a long list of records* – as in the previous two sections, a direct-access file can be thought of as an **array**-type data structure (see chapter 24). The idea is shown in figure 26.5. As can be seen from the diagram, this method relies on the fact that each record is referenced by a unique address on the particular storage medium. Therefore, only direct access media such as disks are suitable for this method of access. You should take particular note that it's possible to put the pointer at any address without the need to sequence through any of the previous addresses.

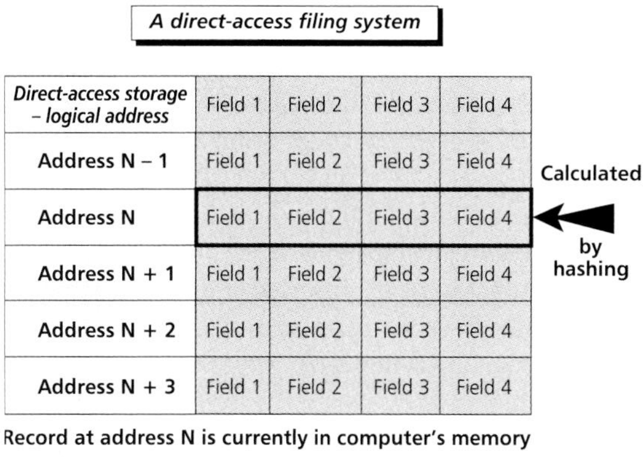

A direct-access filing system

Direct-access storage – logical address	Field 1	Field 2	Field 3	Field 4
Address N – 1	Field 1	Field 2	Field 3	Field 4
Address N	Field 1	Field 2	Field 3	Field 4
Address N + 1	Field 1	Field 2	Field 3	Field 4
Address N + 2	Field 1	Field 2	Field 3	Field 4
Address N + 3	Field 1	Field 2	Field 3	Field 4

Calculated by hashing

Record at address N is currently in computer's memory

Figure 26.5

The *addresses for the location of each record do not have to be contiguous*, and can be calculated by a variety of methods including **hashing** (see chapter 25), or methods making use of **hierarchical** or other data structures such as the **binary search** shown in chapter 19. Hashing is the most direct and therefore the quickest of the record-location methods. Eventually, the calculated address would have to be mapped onto the physical device such as the disk or CD-ROM, and this is covered in more detail when physical records are covered in chapter 27.

Indexed sequential files

This system *organises the file into some* **sequential order**, usually based on the **key field**, very similar in principle to the sequential files explained earlier in this chapter. However, it is *also possible* to *randomly* (i.e. *without* having to sequence through all the records which appear before the one you want) *access the* **records** by using a separate index file as shown in figure 26.6. The example shown here has a file, in which the **key field** is breakfast cereals, together with the names of the people who eat these particular cereals for breakfast.

For example, if the people who like Coco Pops need to be processed (or a person who likes Coco Pops needs to be found), the index file is searched for the Coco-Pops entry. Next a **pointer** *from* the **index file** is followed to find the *first* Coco-Pops record (Digby in this case) and finally **other pointers** are followed until the *end* of the **Coco-Pops list** of records is encountered. This condition is given by the 'Issac record' in this sequential file, because the next entry points to Shreddies, which is alphabetically beyond Coco Pops.

It is possible to set up more than one index in an indexed-sequential file if this is thought desirable, but the **primary index** is the one in which the **sequential order of the file** was *first established*.

One major disadvantage with **sequential files** on **serial-access media** such as tape is that *a complete rewrite of the entire file* has to be done if a new record needs to be added. However, with an **indexed-sequential file on disk**, this is *not* the case. Any new addition can be put into an **overflow table** as shown in figure 26.6, and the pointers pointing to the overflow table can be set up in ways similar to those when dealing with **linked lists** in chapter 25. As shown in figure 26.6, each record has an extra field (normally invisible to an application) which points to an overflow table if it needs to be used after the initial file has been created.

After many updates, the pointer arrangements are bound to become very messy. The **overflow table** will fill up, and it's usual to run a program which would merge (see later) the overflow table with the **main sequential file** to produce a **new indexed-sequential file** *ready to start afresh* with a **new overflow table**. The techniques for this merging process are covered later in this chapter.

Why an index is useful

At this stage some students might feel that *searching an index file* for an entry is *not* very much different to *searching the actual file* for an entry. However, in practice, nothing could be further from the truth. It's interesting to calculate how many comparisons would be needed, on average, to find a record of interest if an **index** is used, compared to the number of comparisons

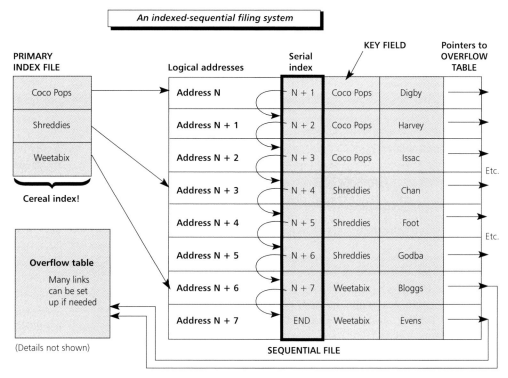

Figure 26.6

that would have to be made on the same size file if *no index* (i.e. a **sequential file**) is used. Obviously these are only average figures, but it does give a good indication of the enormous difference. The general idea is shown in Figure 26.7, and is explained as follows.

Figure 26.7 shows a typical large file with 1,000,000 records. Without any index at all, to find any record of interest would, therefore, on average, take about 500,000 comparisons. You can see that this method would be slow, even on disk! However, suppose that we now have just a single index in which there are 1,000 entries, roughly equally spaced over the entire range of the file. To search for an entry in the index would take on average 500 comparisons. Now assuming that the main file is split up into 1,000 equal parts, one part for each index entry, then each part can be assumed to have, on average, a sub list of 1,000 records. Now again on average, a further 500 comparisons would be needed to find the item of interest in this sub list of the sequential file. This makes 1,000 comparisons **needed altogether**, *compared to the original* **500,000 comparisons needed without an index**. Therefore, on average, a single index in this particular example has increased the search speed by a factor of 500! You can now see why the addition of an index is extremely useful.

It should be obvious that *this file-handling system can only be implemented on* **direct-access storage media**, because some parts of the system rely on the fact that you can go straight to a logical address without having to stop and investigate any previous addresses on the way.

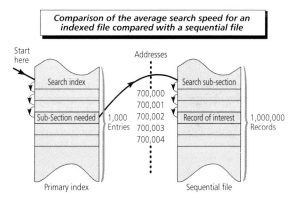

Figure 26.7

Operations with files

Files must obviously be **created** in the first place, usually need **updating** at regular intervals, might have to be **merged** with other files, or individual records might have to be **amended**. New records might have to be **added** and old records **deleted**, or the contents of a file might have to be **sorted** into a different order. Files have to be **searched** for specific criteria and often have to be **backed up** for security purposes. Typical operations like these will now be looked at in a little more detail, together with a brief description of some algorithms required to tackle some of these jobs.

The *ways in which files can be processed* **depends to a large extent on the file organisation** *and* **on the** storage media on which the file is to be held. If we are updating a file on tape, then one or more tape files usually act as the input/s. Another (different) tape file must act as the output. Similar methods can also be used on disk, but direct access methods such as indexed-sequential would need to be updated in different ways again, as the index-pointer mechanisms will need to be maintained in ways similar to those shown in chapter 25. We will now look at processing data in serial and sequential files.

Processing data with serial and sequential access files

These methods are *predominantly* used for **tape-based systems**, but can also be used efficiently on disk systems for some types of operation. Don't forget also that some high-level languages such as the early versions of **Pascal and BASIC**, treat *all files* **as if they are on tape-based systems** – even when they are actually on disk!

File creation

Any **data structure** needs to be **created** in the first place, and a **file** is obviously no exception. Let's suppose, for the sake of argument, that we wish to **create a file called 'Students'** *consisting* of student names and initials, *together with the grades* for each of five compulsory subjects – being 'Maths', 'Programming', 'Analysis', 'Electronics' and 'Systems'. The mark for each subject is an **integer** value from *0 to 100 inclusive*. The

> **Hint:** It does not matter if you don't have access to a COBOL compiler. You can use whatever suitable high-level language is at your disposal. COBOL has been used here to demonstrate the principles, but learning some new syntax for your particular language should not cause too many problems for computer science students.

'**name field**' is to be **20 characters long**, containing the surname, followed by the '**initials field**' consisting of **5 characters**, being **initials** separated by **full stops**. A typical record would therefore be as shown in figure 26.8.

We have already seen how to create file record definitions in **COBOL** (see chapter 15), and a typical one for the students' file could therefore be as follows.

```
01      STUDENT.
        02      NAME.
                03   SURNAME   PIC X(20).
                03   INITIALS  PIC A(5).
        02      MARKS.
                03   MATHS     PIC 999.
                03   PROG      PIC 999.
                03   ANALY     PIC 999.
                03   ELECT     PIC 999.
                03   SYST      PIC 999.
```

COBOL would also have to know that this is a **serial-access file**, because COBOL can cope with direct-access files too. This definition is easily achieved by using the **environment division** (see chapter 15). Note that COBOL does *not* differentiate between serial and sequential files when it comes to the file definitions. A typical environment-division definition is, therefore, as follows.

```
ENVIRONMENT DIVISION.
INPUT-OUTPUT SECTION.
SELECT STUDENTS ASSIGN TO
  "C:STUDENTS.DAT"
* Assigns file called students to drive
  C with a suitable secondary filename
  for Data files.
ORGANISATION IS SEQUENTIAL
ACCESS MODE IS SEQUENTIAL.
```

Writing data to a file

To *create a file* we must first **write** some information to it. In most high-level languages, including COBOL, BASIC and Pascal, for example, a command called 'OPEN' (or a variation on this theme) is used to **open**

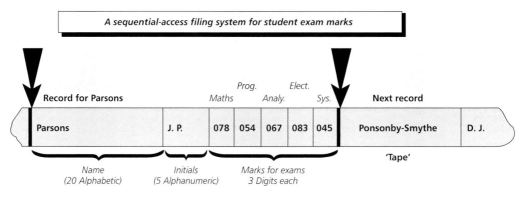

Figure 26.8

up a file for reading or writing. Similarly, when *all file activity has finished*, it is usual to **CLOSE** all the files. Opening a file prepares a file for processing – it usually involves operations like automatically positioning the pointer at the beginning of a file, which is usually transparent to the programmer. Similarly, **closing** a file ends all the connections between the file and a particular program. Closing a file for the first time will write an **end-of-file marker (EOF)**, which is a special character/s that indicates to the system that there is *no more data* in the file after the record that has just been read. The EOF marker is useful when reading data from files; you don't need to know exactly how many records are present within a particular file, all that is necessary is to loop until the EOF is reached.

Let's suppose that we are now going to **create the file**, and *at the same time* **enter data regarding the students' names and examination marks** – this is not necessarily the most efficient way to proceed, but it keeps things extremely simple *and illustrates all the appropriate principles*. Let's also assume that a dummy-data entry for surname of "ZZZ" will be used to terminate the proceedings. A structure diagram for the procedure division is shown in figure 26.9.

A complete COBOL program, based on the environ-

> **Hint:** Don't forget to close a file after you have finished with it. Leave it open, and you will have problems the next time you try to access the data contained in the file.

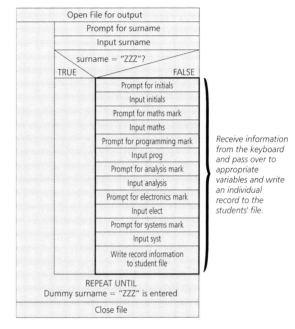

A structure diagram for writing the students' records in the student-examination-mark file

Figure 26.9

ment and data divisions in the previous sections, together with the procedure division outlined in the above Nassi-Schneidermann diagram is shown in figure 26.10.

```
IDENTIFICATION DIVISION.
  PROGRAM-ID.      WRITE-STUDENTS.
  AUTHOR.   KING KONG.
  *
  ENVIRONMENT DIVISION.
  INPUT-OUTPUT SECTION.
  FILE-CONTROL.
      SELECT STUDENTS ASSIGN TO "C:STUDENTS.DAT"
      ORGANISATION IS SEQUENTIAL
      ACCESS MODE IS SEQUENTIAL.
  *
  DATA DIVISION.
  FILE SECTION.
  FD STUDENTS.
  01     STUDENT.
         02     NAME.
     03  SURNAME    PIC X(20).
     03  INITIALS   PIC A(5).
         02     MARKS.
     03  MATHS      PIC 999.
     03  PROG       PIC 999.
     03  ANALY      PIC 999.
     03  ELECT      PIC 999.
     03  SYST       PIC 999.
  *
```

Figure 26.10 (continues)

```
PROCEDURE DIVISION.
FILE-WRITE.
      OPEN OUTPUT STUDENTS.
      PERFORM UNTIL SURNAME = "ZZZ"
  DISPLAY "Please enter the student's surname"
  ACCEPT SURNAME
  IF SURNAME NOT = "ZZZ"
      DISPLAY "Initials"
      ACCEPT INITIALS
      DISPLAY "Maths mark?"
      ACCEPT MATHS
      DISPLAY "Programming mark?"
      ACCEPT PROG
      DISPLAY "Analysis mark?"
      ACCEPT ANALY
      DISPLAY "Electronics mark?"
      ACCEPT ELECT
      DISPLAY "Systems mark?"
      ACCEPT SYST
      DISPLAY "Done"
      WRITE STUDENT
      DISPLAY SURNAME "'s record has been written to file"
  END-PERFORM.
CLOSE STUDENTS.
DISPLAY "File has now been created and closed"
STOP RUN.
```

Figure 26.10 (continued)

The above program should be relatively easy for students to interpret, even if you have never done any COBOL. After it has been run, a file called 'Students. DAT' exists on drive C (one of the hard disks), and contains a serial-access file of the students and grade *information in the order in which they were entered from the keyboard.* You should take special note that, *for the sake of* **simplicity, no validation routines were used** when the marks were entered. Similarly, **there was no error checking of any sort** to handle the situation if something should go wrong with data entry or with writing the data to the file – this is extremely bad practice and should not be emulated in your projects! Note also that if a *proper* **sequential access file** is required then the **serial file** will have to be sorted making use of methods such as those shown in chapter 19 or later on in this chapter.

Once a file has been created you will probably want to interrogate it – there's not much point in creating it otherwise! Again, the concepts are common to most high-level languages, and assuming that the file has been opened for reading, a command called **READ** (or a variation on this theme) can be used to extract data from the file.

Reading data from a file

Files are usually read by programs *other than those* that created them. You must also appreciate that *there's no* *magical structure that has been stored along with the data on a tape or disk.* Therefore, **the program that reads the file needs to know which data structure was used when the file was created.**

A structure diagram for reading data from the student file, then calculating and outputting the average mark

| Open file for input |
| Set end-of-file NOT true |

EOF TRUE?

YES   NO

Read student-record details
Output titles for student's name
Output name from file
Output titles for exam marks
Output marks from file
Calculate average mark
Output titles for average
Output average mark

Receive information from each record in the student file. Output name and marks, calc. and output average mark.

REPEAT UNTIL
end-of-file is encountered

Close-file

Figure 26.11

Whichever high-level language is being employed, the original structure used must be explicitly stated again. With this information the program which reads the data then knows what patterns of data to expect on the disk or the tape, and the data will be interpreted correctly. Suppose, for the sake of argument, we now wish to read information about all the students from the students' file created earlier in this section, print out the students' names and examination marks, calculate the averages, and then output these too. A simple structure diagram for the procedure division of this program could be as shown in figure 26.11.

A complete COBOL program based on the above analysis is shown in figure 26.12.

```
IDENTIFICATION DIVISION.
PROGRAM-ID.          READ-STUDENTS.
AUTHOR.     GODZILLA.
*
ENVIRONMENT DIVISION.
INPUT-OUTPUT SECTION.
FILE_CONTROL.
   SELECT STUDENTS ASSIGN TO "C:STUDENTS.DAT"
   ORGANISATION IS SEQUENTIAL
   ACCESS MODE IS SEQUENTIAL.
*
DATA DIVISION.
FILE SECTION.
FD STUDENTS.
01     STUDENT.
       02     NAME.
   03  SURNAME     PIC X(20).
   03  INITIALS    PIC A(5).
       02     MARKS.
   03  MATHS       PIC 999.
   03  PROG PIC 999.
   03  ANALY       PIC 999.
   03  ELECT       PIC 999.
   03  SYST PIC 999.
*
WORKING-STORAGE SECTION.
01  EOF-FLAG   PIC X.
    02  EOF        VALUE IS "F".
    02  NOT-EOF    VALUE IS "T".
01  AVERAGE        PIC 999V99.
*
PROCEDURE DIVISION.
FILE-READ.
OPEN INPUT STUDENTS.
SET NOT-EOF TO TRUE.
PERFORM UNTIL EOF
    READ STUDENTS
      AT END
         SET EOF TO TRUE
      NOT AT END
            DISPLAY "Student name"
            DISPLAY NAME
            DISPLAY "Examination marks"
            DISPLAY MARKS
            COMPUTE AVERAGE = (MATHS + PROG + ANALY + ELECT + SYST)/5
            DISPLAY "Average mark is" AVERAGE
            DISPLAY
END-PERFORM.
CLOSE STUDENTS.
STOP RUN.
```

Figure 26.12

Notice the use of the **EOF (End of File) variable** mentioned earlier in this section. *See how it has been used to terminate the loop when the end of file has been detected.* The extended read statement READ...AT END.... NOT AT END acts as an 'IF-THEN with EOF check' type statement when reading files in COBOL. Notice also that displaying (outputting) 'NAME' will display the sub-fields 'NAME' and 'INITIALS', and displaying 'MARKS' will display all of the sub-fields in this group, namely, 'Maths', 'Prog', 'Analy', 'Elect', and 'Syst' – another nice feature in COBOL.

A more sophisticated example of DP

Having created a serial-access file and read back the data, we will now concentrate on slightly more realistic and sophisticated data processing. Complete COBOL programs take up a lot of space, therefore, *only* the **procedure divisions** will be given *if* **COBOL** is to be used in an example, and often just a COBOL-like-pseudocode algorithm will be given. It is left to the reader to develop these into fully-working COBOL or other high-level language programs of their choice.

Searching

Searching a file is of obvious fundamental importance and carrying out these processes in practice is relatively trivial. All that is necessary is to sequence through the file, record-by-record, until the required match is found, *or* until the **end-of-file** (see last section) has been reached – in which case, tough luck, there is no match! The search criteria may be simple, such as a 'customer name', for example, or it may be more complex involving a combination of Boolean operators (matching criteria strung together with 'ANDs', 'ORs', 'NOTs' or other Boolean operators).

> **Hint:** There are many pages dedicated to different search routines and these can be found starting in chapter 19.

Using the student-examination file created in the last section, we might, for the sake of argument, want to identify all those students who have marks below 40% in any examination. We can then inform them that they must retake this/these particular exam/s again before the start of the next term if they wish to carry on! Also, on a more-positive note, we want to identify all those students who have passed, congratulate them and notify them accordingly. To keep you on your toes regarding different forms of structured analysis and design, a JSP diagram (see chapter 14) is used to express the guts of this particular algorithm. This is shown in figure 26.13.

A typical algorithm using COBOL-like pseudocode for the procedure division follows shortly. Note that some procedures, such as the ones shown inside the dotted lines have been modularised (coded once only and called up when needed). In COBOL, the word

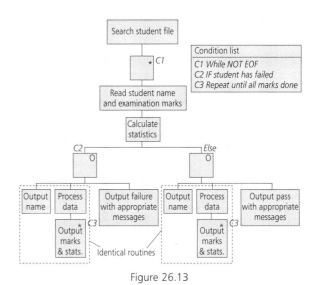

Figure 26.13

'PREFORM' followed by the name of the procedure to be performed acts as a procedure call. These procedures have not been covered in detail, as they contain relatively trivial code and should easily be able to be worked out by most readers. It should also be obvious that these procedure definitions would also be needed for the following programs to work in practice.

```
OPEN INPUT STUDENTS.
SET NOT-EOF TO TRUE.
PERFORM UNTIL EOF
    READ STUDENTS
      AT END
          SET EOF TO TRUE
      NOT AT END
          PERFORM STATS-CALCULATIONS
      IF FAIL is TRUE
          PERFORM WRITE-HEADINGS-AND-NAME
          PERFORM PROCESS-DATA
          PERFORM OUTPUT-MARKS-AND-STATISTICS
          PERFORM FAIL-PROCEDURE
          ELSE
          PERFORM WRITE-HEADINGS-AND-NAME
          PERFORM PROCESS-DATA
          PERFORM OUTPUT-MARKS-AND-STATISTICS
          PERFORM PASS-PROCEDURE
END-PERFORM.
CLOSE STUDENTS.
```

Obviously the middle parts contain many lines of code, but these are of little consequence to a chapter on file handling. Most readers should be able to develop the above pseudocode into code in a high-level language of their choice.

Updating records

Updating a file involves things like **addition** of a new record, **insertion** of a new record, **changing information** *within* an existing record, or the **deletion** of a particular record. With **serial or sequential-access files** some of *these operations are not as trivial as might appear at first sight.*

Don't forget that we are currently dealing with files as though they are stored on tape. Therefore, we can't just pop a record in at some point within a sequential file *without* **physically moving** all of the other records out of the way to make space for the new one. The idea is shown in figure 26.14.

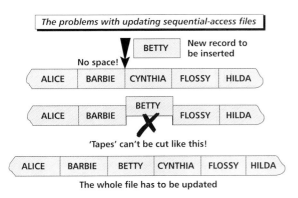

Figure 26.14

Inserting records

If you *imagine* that the **files are physically on tape**, as shown in figure 26.14, then you will easily appreciate the principles involved. Don't forget the fact that some files in large computer systems will be on tape, and some versions of languages like BASIC and Pascal arrange their file handling like this, even though they are on disk.

Whenever you make use of a cassette tape recorder at home, for example, *if you are going to record anything from an existing tape* then **one tape must act as the master and another tape must act as the copy**. You can't have the same tape simultaneously recording something from itself to itself! With this borne in mind, it should be

relatively obvious that the same principles must apply to altering records on a serial-access medium, or a serial or sequentially organised file structure on a direct-access medium.

Whenever a record needs updating – even if it's only a single record – then the entire file will

> **Hint:** You should compare and contrast the methods being covered here with the methods to insert and delete records in the data structures held in RAM. These methods have been covered in chapters 24 and 25.

need to be rewritten! However, don't forget that these ideas should not be alien – if you add just a 'single full stop' to the middle of a large word-processor document, for example, then the whole document will have to be saved again – things are not so daft as they might originally sound.

On systems where *many transactions* may have taken place (such as 35,000 customers paying their electricity bill), it's usual to build up these transactions on a *separate* **transaction file**, which is then **sorted** into a *suitable sequential order* – perhaps by customer number. At the end of the day, for example, this **transaction file** is then *used to update* the **master file** (also sequentially organised in the same way) so that a **new master file** is produced which contains the latest information. These ideas are shown in the systems flowchart of figure 26.15.

The updating process shown in figure 26.15 would consist of reading the sequentially organised files by getting the first record from the master file, and then comparing it with the first record in the transaction file. If a match is found, we then update and copy the results to the new master file, or, if no match has been found, copy the record from the master file without alteration to the new master file. We then get the next record from the master file, and carry on with the method until all records in both files have been processed. There is, however, an added complication. If, for example, a brand-new record exists within the transaction file that was not present within the master file, then this situation

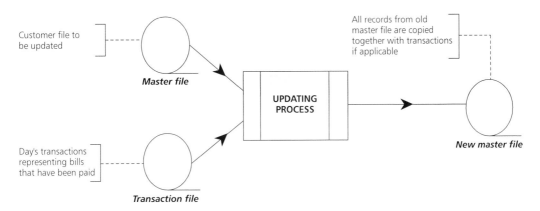

Figure 26.15

has also to be dealt with by the following code. Also, if the transaction file runs out of records, we still have to transfer the remaining master-file records to the new master-file. Alternatively, if the master file runs out of records, and there are still some records left in the transaction file (obviously new customers), then the remainder of this file will need transferring too. Unfortunately, it all makes for a more-complex-looking algorithm.

The above paragraph is a bit of a mouthful, therefore an **algorithm** to carry out these transactions using **COBOL-like pseudocode** has been developed as shown in figure 26.16.

```
OPEN MASTER-FILE for INPUT
OPEN NEW-TRANSACTION-FILE for INPUT
OPEN NEW-MASTER-FILE for OUTPUT
READ MASTER-FILE-RECORD INTO MASTER-RECORD
READ TRANSACTION-FILE-RECORD INTO TRANSACTION-RECORD
* Need to get first records from each file
* Working records are called MASTER-RECORD and TRANSACTION-RECORD
WHILE NOT END-OF-MASTER-FILE AND NOT END-OF-TRANSACTION-FILE
    IF KEYFIELD-MASTER-RECORD < KEYFIELD-TRANSACTION-RECORD
        *No update necessary for this record
        WRITE MASTER-RECORD TO NEW-MASTER-FILE
        READ MASTER-RECORD INTO MASTER-RECORD
    ELSE
      IF KEYFIELD-MASTER-RECORD = KEYFIELD-TRANSACTION-RECORD
        *Update the record before writing
        PERFORM UPDATE procedure
        WRITE MASTER-RECORD TO NEW-MASTER-FILE
        READ MASTER-FILE-RECORD INTO MASTER-RECORD
        READ TRANSACTION-FILE-RECORD INTO TRANSACTION-RECORD
      ELSE
        KEYFIELD-MASTER-RECORD > KEYFIELD-TRANSACTION-RECORD
        *New record to be added
        PERFORM NEW-RECORD procedure
        WRITE NEW-RECORD TO NEW-MASTER-FILE
        READ TRANSACTION-FILE-RECORD INTO TRANSACTION-RECORD
      END IF
    END IF
ENDWHILE
WHILE NOT END-OF-MASTER-FILE
  * Transfer any remaining master-file records to new master file
  WRITE MASTER-RECORD TO NEW-MASTER-FILE
ENDWHILE
WHILE NOT END-OF-TRANSACTION-FILE
  * Transfer any remaining transaction records to new master file
  * New record/s to be added and transferred to new master file
  PERFORM NEW-RECORD procedure
  WRITE NEW-RECORD TO NEW-MASTER-FILE
  READ TRANSACTION-FILE-RECORD INTO TRANSACTION-RECORD
ENDWHILE
CLOSE MASTER-FILE TRANSACTION-FILE NEW-MASTER-FILE
```

Figure 26.16

That was a bit of a mouthful too! As you can see, updating a serial file is no trivial matter! If you are brave enough, you may wish to code the above pseudocode algorithm into a high-level language of your choice. Don't forget that all of these techniques can be done on disk too – it's no use saying you can't do it because you don't have a tape system!

Deleting records

We could easily have included records for deletion into the above algorithm. Instead of assuming automatically that all new records would be added, we could simply not copy the record across if instructed to delete it. That was easy!

Merging files

This is typical of many transactions that take place in the data-processing industry. For example, it may be that two master files need to be merged into one larger file. In fact, *this is the way that sorting can be accomplished* if the file is **too big** to fit into available RAM. The file can be split up into two parts, or indeed any number of smaller files such that these smaller files *will* fit into RAM. Each of the files is then sorted and written as a new sequential file.

The next stage of the process is to **merge** two of the files *using techniques almost identical to those shown in the updating process earlier* – in fact, the process is slightly simpler as no processing has to take place. The two files are simply interrogated sequentially and output to produce a single new master file. This new master file is then combined with another of the tapes in an identical way, to produce an even-newer master file consisting of three or more of the original tapes, if necessary. The process then continues until all original sorted tapes have been merged onto a single master file. The only limitation is the amount of data which can be fitted onto a single tape – and that's quite a lot of data (see chapter 12). If it does not fit onto a single tape, then many tapes can be sequenced together also. However, this would require manual intervention if only one tape drive was available.

Generations of files

One *advantage* of serial and sequential file processing is that *after any updates* you *still have* the **original files intact**. This may not sound too revolutionary, but consider the situation for a moment and you will realise that it's possible to backtrack in some cases of error! It is often useful to be able to do this whereby the original files are kept as well as the new files. This leads to the idea of generations of files, and the concept is shown in figure 26.17.

The **original master file** is renamed to the **father file** when a **new master file** (called the **son**) has been produced from it. Similarly, when the **son** is used to produce *yet another* **new master file**, the **son** *becomes the* **father** and the *original father* therefore becomes the **grandfather file**. We could go on with great-grandfather files but we have to stop somewhere otherwise the world would be full of tapes. Three generations is usually the norm, with the grandfather file being 'killed off' when the great grandson is born. Euthanasia *is allowed* when serial or sequential files are being used!

> **Hint:** As very large hard disks become cheaper and Terabyte disk farms become the norm in mainframe installations, it's usual to mirror large files on another disk rather than keep several generations as described here. However, these methods will still be used in the foreseeable future.

When to use serial and sequential files

After reading the above your immediate answer might be to say **never!** Nevertheless, such file organisation is *ideal* for **large-volume batch production** of data. Such methods are still extensively used on mainframes today *because* they are extremely cost effective and efficient for many data-processing tasks.

Don't forget that serial access files have a role to play too. Not only in acting as an input queue to some particular processing task, but they can be used in their own right when carrying out the **same process** to *all records within a file*. In this case the records do not have to be in any particular predetermined order.

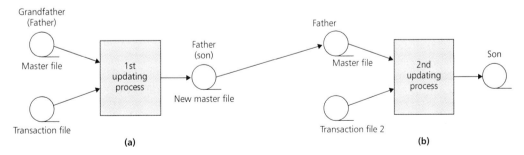

Figure 26.17

Exercise 26.1

1 Define the following terms associated with computer files:

(a) Character

(b) Field

(c) Record

(d) File.

2 Compare and contrast the following file-organisation methods:

(a) Serial access

(b) Sequential access

(c) Direct access or random access

(d) Indexed sequential access.

3 Carefully explain the following terminology associated with files:

(a) File creation

(b) Updating

(c) Merging

(d) EOF.

4 The idea of a pointer is of paramount importance. What is a pointer and how is it used in association with file data structures?

5 What is a key field?

6 What do the following mean:

(a) An index

(b) An overflow table

(c) A linked list?

7 Carefully describe a sequential file updating process making sure to refer to the master file, new master file and transaction file in your explanation.

8 Explain what is meant by a hashing algorithm in association with reading data from a file.

End of chapter revision aid and summary

Cover up the right-hand column and see if you can answer the questions or define the terms on the left. They appear in the order in which they are covered in this chapter. Alternatively you may browse through the right-hand column to aid revision.

What is a file?

A file is a collection of related information, which is processed as a single unit that is further divided into records and fields.

How does a file differ from the other types of data structure?

Files are data structures which are usually used to process information on a secondary-storage medium.

From what two viewpoints is a file considered in terms of its organisation?

A file can be considered to be organised either logically or physically in the form of records or blocks as described in chapter 27.

What is a record?

A record is a subset of a file which can be treated as a single-unit of related information. For example, each customer would probably have a single record.

What is a field?

A field is a subset of a record containing a single unit of information such as 'customer name', 'amount outstanding' or 'age'.

Name four basic types of file organisation.

Logical file organisation can be split up into four main different methods, namely serial, sequential, direct and indexed-sequential.

What is a serial file?

Serial files are organised such that there is no pre-determined order to the records.

How might a serial file be produced?

Often a serial file is the inevitable consequence of data collection before processing takes place.

What is a sequential file?	Sequential files are organised so that the *records are arranged in order of a key field*.
What is a key field?	A key field is the *field chosen to identify a* record.
What two types of file organisation are supported on serial media such as tape?	Serial and sequential file organisations are the only two structures that can be used with magnetic-tape systems, but they can be used efficiently on disk-systems too.
What is a direct access file?	A direct or random-access file is one in which it is possible to get to the record of interest without having to go serially or sequentially through any others.
What is an indexed sequential file?	An indexed-sequential file is one in which a sequentially-organised file on a direct-access medium can be accessed by means of one or more indexes.
Name some typical operations, which are carried out when using files.	Typical operations with files involve the creation, updating by altering, adding or deleting data, merging with other files, searching, sorting and backing up.
How is a file created?	Creation of a file involves using a high-level language or application to create an appropriate data structure such as sequential or random access for example.
What does updating mean?	Updating involves changing information in a file by altering one or more records.
What disadvantages are there when attempting to update a sequential file?	The addition or deletion of records when using serial or sequential files involves a complete re-write of the original file.
What are the names of the three files used when updating sequential files?	Insertion and deletion of data on serial or sequential files involves the use of three files – a master file, a transaction file and a new master file.
What is a master file?	The master file is the original (unmodified) copy of the data.
What is a transaction file?	The transaction file contains details of the amendments.
What is a new master file?	The new master file contains copies of the original master-file records together with the amendments necessary from the transaction file.
What are the names given to the generations of files?	Several generations of files are usually kept for data integrity purposes. These three generations are referred to as grandfather, father and son files.
What is a son file?	A son file is the newest generation master file.
What is a father file?	A father file is the old master file used to produce the son file.
What is a grandfather file?	A grandfather file is the oldest generation of master file, from which the father file was produced. The grandfather file is ditched after a great-grandson has been produced.
What does merging mean?	Merging files is the process of joining two sequentially-organised files record-by-record transferring them in the correct order to the new master file.
How can files too large to be fitted into available RAM be sorted?	Sorting of very large files can be carried out by sorting separate subsets of the large file, then joining them together by making use of a merging procedure.

27 Further File Handling

Key resources

To carry out this work most successfully it's best if you have:

◆ Access to a high-level language that supports direct access files, such as the later versions of BASIC and Pascal, Visual BASIC or Delphi

Concept checkpoints

◆ It's essential to have read chapter 26, which covers the basic file-handling operations.

◆ It's also useful to have knowledge of the linked-list structure covered in chapter 25.

Direct-access or random-access files

Direct-access or random-access files are supported only by direct access media such as magnetic disks or magneto-optical disks (see chapter 12). However, it should be remembered that all sequential and serial accessing of files, as carried out in the last chapter, could be carried out on disk-based files too.

You may (or may not if you found the work difficult!) be pleased to know that the principles of direct-access files are very similar to those covered in chapter 25 when linked lists were being studied. Updating, inserting and deleting data in a linked list is similar to updating, inserting and deleting records in direct-access files.

Instead of the logical positions in a linked list being mapped onto physical memory locations, the logical addresses within a direct-access file are mapped onto physical locations on the storage devices. The ability to do this with an external storage device opens up more possibilities for more flexible arrangements regarding file handling. For example, we can make use of hashing (see chapter 25) for very fast recovery of arbitrary data from a direct-access file – no longer do we have to serially search the file until we get to the record of interest.

We need to devise a suitable **hashing** or **hierarchical algorithm** (e.g. a **search** as shown in chapter 25) to calculate the address at which the record is going to be placed in our direct-access file. (It's then up to the system software to translate this logical address into a physical address on the disk, as can be seen later). The **logical-record-address numbers** that we have calculated from the algorithm would usually refer to a **relative address**, this being a number, which represents how far the record is 'in' from the beginning of the file. The idea is shown in figure 27.1

The **COBOL language**, for example, allows access by what's called a **relative key**, and, if this technique is to be used, the file-control section of the environment division might have something similar to the following.

```
ENVIRONMENT DIVISION.
INPUT-OUTPUT SECTION.
FILE-CONTROL.
    SELECT STUDENTS ASSIGN TO "C:STUDENTS.DAT"
    ORGANISATION IS RELATIVE
    ACCESS MODE IS RANDOM
    RELATIVE KEY IS RECORD-NUMBER
```

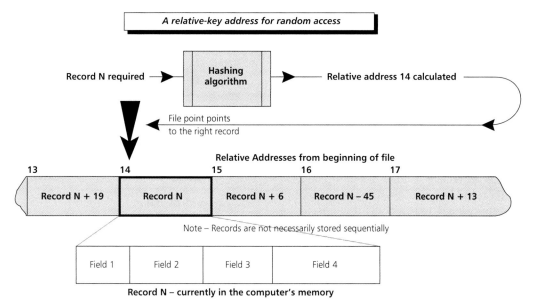

Figure 27.1

Updating records in direct access files

The **updating** processes here are *not* too difficult to understand. A record is read from the disk, processed in some particular way, then rewritten to the *same* logical storage address. These concepts are, in fact, easier to understand (though not necessarily easier to implement in practice) than the serial and sequential file systems considered in chapter 26. You will probably recall that in chapter 26 we have either **opened a file for input**, *or* **opened a file for output**. You will also recall that it was *not possible* on a **serial** or **sequential system** to have the *same file doing both*. (Remember the cassette-tape example!) **When updating a direct-access file**, *the file must be* **opened for both input** *and* **output**. Again, when using COBOL language, the same file may be opened for input and output simultaneously.

Inserting a record

Insertion could be a simple case of *calculation of an address* from the *key field* by **hashing**. However, as was seen in chapter 25 when hashing functions are considered, *if a clash occurs* then some sort of **overflow structure** will need to be maintained to insert the record in an alternative place. There are a variety of methods for being able to do this, with a flag indicating whether a space is occupied or free being one option. For example, in COBOL, a particular file-status code indicating an error is returned if an illegal attempt (i.e. an insert not an update) is made to write a record over the top of one which already exists. It is up to the programmer to trap this error, then make alternative arrangements for putting the record somewhere else.

Deleting a record

Notice that **record 'deletion' was not an option** in **serial-access file systems**! If we wanted to delete a record it simply meant that we did *not* copy the record to the new master file! Nevertheless, some implementations of sequential files based on disks do allow for additions and deletions to be made. This is done by means of an overflow table similar to the type used when the indexed-sequential files were being considered. Merging of the overflow table and main file would then have to be done at some later stage. However, back to the direct-access files – deletion can easily be accomplished when using this file type. Record deletion is simply a case of having some indication that the space occupied by the deleted record can now be returned to the pool of available space – the methods are very similar indeed to those shown when linked lists were covered in chapter 25. It is not usual or necessary to delete the physical record – we could not care less whether a sector on a disk, for example, contains irrelevant data or just groups of zeros which may indicate that it is empty. The record is only **logically deleted** – this means that the old data remains there until it's overwritten by something new. Some systems would be organised such that deleted data would simply remain unused, until some clean-up utility reclaiming this space was run at a later stage.

When to use direct access files

Direct-access files are really the *only sensible options* for **interactive systems** that deal with **on-line queries** where a response time would be expected within seconds. These file systems are the only ones with the appropriate speed necessary, especially if the database (file) is very large. Also, with direct-access files, **on-line transactions from menu-driven systems** within a GUI environment are an attractive option for more user-friendly systems. If *very quick response* is needed then *only* a **direct-access file** will do.

Processing data in indexed-sequential files

These ideas are extremely simple when applied to direct-access file handling, and are identical in principle to looking up an index in this book. If you have the name of the topic in which you are interested – say 'nano technology', for example – you look it up in the index, find the page number, then go straight to the right place in a sequentially-organised file, i.e. the sequential pages of this book. Just like this book, these indexed sequential files have all the advantages of sequential batch-processing organisation, together with a fast-access mechanism by making use of an index. The initials **ISAM** are often used in this context, and stand for **Indexed Sequential Access Method**.

It's of paramount importance to realise at the outset that the *sequential nature* of **indexed-sequential files** *is not subject to the restrictions of ordinary sequential files* such as those found on tape, for example. With an **ordinary sequential file** the file is **literally stored sequentially** on the storage medium. This means that you can't insert or delete records *without having to reorganise the entire file* in the ways described in chapter 26. However, with an **indexed-sequential file**, as was shown in figure 26.6, the **overflow table and pointer system** make it possible to update the records without a rewrite.

It's also important to realise that sequential processing *is* extremely fast for **batch-processing-type activities**. For example, suppose you are processing the monthly-payroll program in alphabetical order of employee. There's not much point in using a direct-access file, and hence calculating each logical address by hashing – by dealing with the problem **sequentially**, the next record required would be the one currently after the record being processed in the sequential list. However, if a particular employee has a query on his or her salary, for example, then you do need to go directly to the required record, and in this case you could follow a suitable index system. Therefore, assuming that appropriate and efficient indexes are created, **this system capitalises on the benefits of both sequential and random access**. In practice, for the reasons just stated, indexed-sequential files are *the* most popular in the data-processing industry. It is normal to have a **separate file for the data** and a **separate file for the index**.

COBOL, for example, maintains all of these systems in ways that are reasonably transparent to the programmer.

The following slice of an environment division from a typical COBOL program deals with a file that can be accessed both sequentially and randomly.

```
ENVIRONMENT DIVISION.
INPUT-OUTPUT SECTION.
FILE-CONTROL.
    SELECT STUDENTS ASSIGN TO
    "C:STUDENTS.DAT"
    ORGANISATION IS INDEXED
    ACCESS MODE IS DYNAMIC
    RELATIVE KEY IS RECORD-NUMBER
```

The keyword **dynamic** in the above COBOL code indicates that **the indexed file can be accessed both sequentially** *and* **randomly**. The **organisation** must be specified as **indexed** (meaning indexed-sequential in COBOL) or the file will be assumed to be sequential. Note also how statements such as those given in the above code add to the self-documenting aspects of COBOL. We have stated on many occasions that **COBOL** is *the* data-processing language – after covering the examples in chapter 26, and looking at the above, you can start to see why.

> **Hint:** Even though you would not be expected to make use of COBOL, it's quite likely that some projects could require random updates of files in a high-level language like Visual BASIC.

Another advantage of indexed-sequential mode is that the software, which controls the system, ensures that only those records that are occupied take up space on the disk. This should be contrasted with direct-access files where much space is taken up with empty records and overflow areas waiting to accept data in places which have been calculated by the hashing algorithm.

Creating an indexed sequential file

One method of creation involves creating a **sequential file** in ways identical to those shown earlier in chapter 26, then *reading the records* from this **sequential file** and *writing them*, together with an **index**, as an **indexed-sequential file**. We have already seen how to produce a sequential file in some detail, and COBOL provides several other facilities to enable index files to be built up using the principles just described. However, the detailed analysis and creation of such an index making use of a language such as COBOL is beyond the scope of your work at this level.

Updating, inserting and deleting

Once the index has been built up in the ways described in the last section, other routines to update delete and insert records, for example, can be devised. Don't forget, however, that there are *two types* of access mechanisms – **sequential** and **random**. Therefore, *different* algorithms would have to be developed for updating by these different mechanisms. Again, COBOL would help considerably by automatically coping with some of the hassle for us. For example, if an indexed-sequential file is to be accessed sequentially, as long as the environment division specified that the **file type is indexed**, *and* that **access is sequential**, then the algorithms already established for accessing data in a sequential file would work – this saves one hell of a lot of work.

To access records randomly from an indexed-sequential file using COBOL involves a special form of read statement together with assigning a key field within the program. The computer searches the index for a key, which is the same as the key-field in the program, and, when found, the record can then be read directly (randomly) from the data file that is associated with the index. The modified form of read statement also includes what to do if the desired key is invalid.

It is not appropriate at this level to consider detailed algorithms for random updates of indexed-sequential files making use of the more advanced COBOL features. Nevertheless, you should now have a very good idea of all the principles that are involved, and realise that languages like COBOL, for example, provide the necessary infrastructure to create, interrogate, delete and insert records both sequentially and randomly on multiple indexes when using indexed-sequential files.

General terminology associated with files

Fixed and variable length records

Hitherto we have implied that each record within a file is of **fixed length**. This makes life much easier, because the computer can more easily process the data in record-size chunks that are *all the same*. It is possible to set up a system whereby the records are all of a **variable length**, and although this does save some storage on the secondary storage media being used, the added complexity of the system is often not worth the bother. A more-complex pointer system would be needed, and data regarding the length of a record may have to be stored along with the actual data within each record. On some systems, such as the **relational database systems** covered in chapter 28, it is a requirement of **normalisation** (see chapter 28) that all records be of fixed length. However, in examinations, it's popular to comment on the relative merits of both fixed and variable-length systems.

If you are using a **fixed-length system** then each record may be accessed more efficiently and quickly by making use of the pointer systems covered so often in other parts of this book. Pointers can be set at regular intervals, and updating the records is therefore much easier. However, it is not so efficient in terms of storage

of information, as unnecessary space may be wasted. With a **variable-length record**, no space is wasted, because each record is just the required number of digits to store the data. However, it would normally take longer to access the data in a variable-length record, because extra information is needed on its size, and therefore the positions of the pointers needed. Sometimes, the length of each record might be stored along with the record itself. Therefore, when this information at the beginning of the record is read, the number of bytes belonging to this record is determined.

Estimation of file size

You may be asked to calculate the length of files for your projects, or in an examination question. If it is a fixed-length record system, then you multiply the number of bytes in each record by the estimated maximum number of records that will be required. You will then need to add a few more bytes for information such as the file headers, end of file markers and other similar house keeping functions. You will also need to remember what sort of character representation is needed for each type of data such as 'Boolean', 'integer numeric' or 'character' to name but a few. Let's consider an estimation of the **file size** for the following data regarding a database having a maximum of 100,000 records. The data stored on each for each record is as follows:

- Surname
- First name
- Date of birth
- Age
- Address
- Notes

Let's assume that we will be using fixed-length records. You will need to estimate the number of bytes needed for each of the above. For the sake of argument, let's assume 25 characters for each of the surname and the first name. Let's also assume 20 characters for each line of a 5-line address (giving 100 characters for the address). Let's assume that there will be 500 characters needed for the notes. Now age can be coded as an integer, probably needing only 1 byte. (This gives a maximum of 255). Date could be encoded as 4 bytes (to be millennium compliant). Therefore, we will need $25+25+4+1+100+500 = 655$ bytes for each record.

Now 100,000 records, each needing a space of 655 bytes will be 65,500,000 bytes. Not forgetting that a real Mbyte is 1024x10244, you can specify a probable maximum file size of 65 Mbytes, which would include enough for overheads too.

Other file terminology

Other terminology associated with files from a more-general point of view is covered in this section. For example, there are several different types of file whose names have been coined from the context in which they are used, rather than from any fundamental file-organisation principles like the sequential or direct-access methods considered earlier. We now investigate some additional commonly used terms.

Data files

All files are **data files** – because all files eventually contain just a sequence of digits stored as data! However, this is *not too helpful*, and so extra terminology is used to distinguish between files used for different purposes. Most of the files referred to since the beginning of this chapter are examples of data files. Data files can more usefully be described as files of related data in which the data has been organised in some particular way – usually in the form of records and fields, and arranged by a *file-access method* such as sequential or random, for example. In any examination assume that this is the definition which is required, but data files also have more specific meanings when used in more specific contexts.

Backup files

When using serial or sequential-access files, together with the grandfather-father-son principle, it is possible to recover from many different error situations. However, when using direct-access, file records can inadvertently be overwritten, with no means of recovery. Therefore, copies of the files should be made at frequent intervals and these copies are called **backup files** for obvious reasons.

Scratch files

This is a **file that contains temporary data**. For example, suppose that a sequential file has been created with the sole purpose of being used as a source file to generate an indexed-sequential file (see earlier). When the indexed-sequential file has been created then there is no need for the original sequential file. The original file was simply a **temporary file** or a **scratch file**.

Indexed files

This name is often used to denote a file that has **multiple indexes**. Such systems are more common in **database applications** and in the context of system software such as operating systems, for example.

Hashed files

This is just an alternative name for a file, which is accessed by means of a suitable hashing function. It is no different to the direct or random-access files considered in this chapter.

Binary search

This is an alternative file-access mechanism and is based on searching for the address of a record in ways identical to searching a binary tree that are covered in chapter 25.

Hierarchically-organised files

Most modern operating systems enable the user to structure files so that their organisation is **hierarchical**. This is exactly the same idea as the hierarchical (tree) data structures covered in chapter 25. In the early days of disk-operating systems the user was restricted to a single directory in which all files were listed. Manually finding files on such systems was a slow and painful process, and the concept of hierarchical directories was borne.

> **Hint:** You should always organise your directory structure in a logical, hierarchical way. It's amazing how many students still organise their work badly and therefore can't find items of data which they need quickly. It saves a lot of time in the end.

Figure 27.2 shows a typical directory structure with which most windows-based operating system users will be familiar. It shows just a tiny fraction of the directory structure of one of the author's hard disks. As an example, the route to the file containing the very drawing at which you are looking (figure 27.2) has been shown. Follow through the route, which starts at the root (base directory) of the structure. (Don't forget that it's called the root because the structure is an upside-down tree in which the top part forms the root.) The path name for the drawing file called 'root' is

```
C:\Publishing\StanleyThornes\ALevel\
4thEd\Files2\Root
```

Notice that in some systems the directories might have to be labelled slightly differently. Stanley Thornes, for example, is too many characters for a directory name in some MS-DOS based systems and so, in practice, it might be called Stanley. The path name illustrated would not work on MS-DOS systems because of this. Different operating systems have slightly different notation, but the ideas are the same, and the latest versions of Windows do not suffer this limitation.

Without a hierarchical structure of the sort described above, thousands of files would have to live in the same directory – together with all the limitations that this would impose regarding file names. It's not possible, for example, to have two file names which are identical within the same directory. I have an admin directory for school, an admin directory for each of the publisher directories, an admin directory for business and several admin directories for other purposes. If they

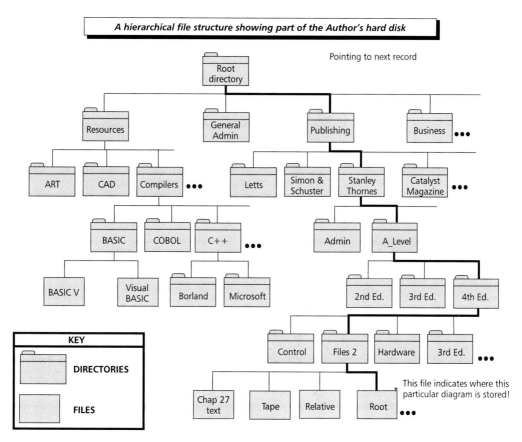

Figure 27.2

were all in the same directory then the only way of getting over the problem on some systems would be to make use of extensions to the file names such as Admin.sch for school and Admin.sta for Stanley Thornes publishers, for example. This is an extremely messy method of file organisation and the hierarchical-file structures offered by today's modern windows-based operating systems make life very much easier.

You should note that it is only possible to have an actual **file** (i.e. an **object** containing things like a **word-processor document**, or an **application** for example) as a **leaf node** in the system. All **parent nodes** are **directories**, not files. In most windows-based systems it is usual to have different file types for each application, and thus each file type can have unique icons assigned to them. In this way it's easy to identify a file by simply looking at the picture.

The link to the physical organisation of files

Hitherto in this chapter we have *concentrated entirely* on the **logical organisation** of files from a *programmer's point of view*. Nevertheless, it will be obvious to most readers that all the data being processed, irrespective of the file-organisation methods being used, will have to be stored on some suitable media such as magnetic disk or magnetic tape, for example. No well-rounded overview of file handling on modern computer systems would thus be complete without this final link in the chain being investigated. During the next section we will, therefore, take a brief look at how data eventually gets put onto or read from the storage media – be it tape, magnetic or optical disk, or CD-ROM. In fact, you will probably be quite surprised that, *given the variety of secondary-storage hardware that it's possible to interface to a computer* system, **the way in which the system software treats them all is remarkably similar**. It should be noted that the next section should also be read in conjunction with the storage-devices covered in chapter 12, where the physical attributes of the disks and tape being used in the next section are explained in more detail. All the principles about to be discussed can be applied to all storage media such as disks and tape, but a specific example will make things far easier to understand. At the end of this example we will then show *why* all these ideas can be applied to any system.

As serial and sequential files were handled first, we will first take a look at an *example* of a **tape-based system**. However, don't forget that these are general principles being established here so don't think that this section is irrelevant!

Blocks of data

As you will have gathered from reading chapter 12, tape systems on a large computer bear little resemblance to the audio-tape machines used at home. Unfortunately, however, like the audio and videotape systems that are used at home, computer-based tape formats also come in a variety of incompatible formats. Nevertheless, many of the *principles* of storing data on tape are *similar*, irrespective of the format being used. We will now concentrate on *typical* relationships between the **logical-files** considered earlier in this chapter and the **physical blocks of data** on the tape.

A mainframe tape example

Figure 27.3 shows a typical ½-inch-wide 9-track tape format, as is found on some mainframe computers. This particular format would probably make use of the EBCDIC code (see chapter 12), but different 7-bit codes are also sometimes used. As can be seen from the top of the diagram, just part of the tape is being used to store a logical file. It might be one of the serial or sequential files created by a COBOL program considered earlier in chapter 26. This large file has been considerably expanded so that only a small section of it can be seen on the second level of the diagram. Now the file is so big that it obviously can't be dealt with all at the same time, therefore, the tape has split up the file into **physical records** (nothing to do with the logical records in the file), which are called **blocks**. However, on some systems, as in the system shown in figure 27.3, a physical record can be made up of several physical blocks – it simply depends on the type of system being used.

It's most important to realise that a **physical record** (or block or *group* of blocks depending on the system being used) *is the size of the chunk which is used by the hardware to transfer data in and out* of the system. *This is what a physical record means.* It is literally the chunk of data that gets taken in or spewed out to the tape machine in this particular case.

If, as is likely *because of the relative sizes*, several **logical records** fit into a **physical block**, then the number of logical records that can be fitted into the block is called the **blocking factor**. Therefore, in figure 27.3, a blocking factor of 4 has been used because 4 logical records, as shown on level 3 of the diagram, have been fitted into a single physical block. If one logical record fits into a single physical block then blocking would

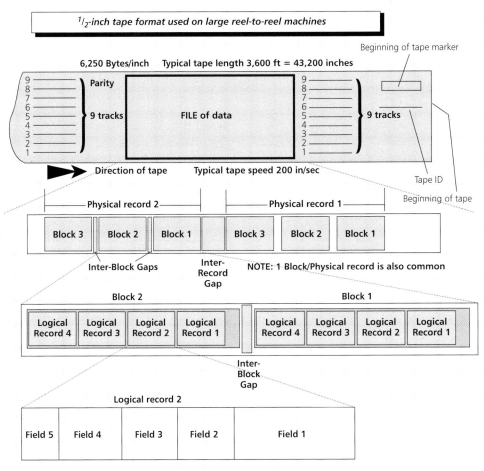

Figure 27.3

not need to be used, and the blocking factor would be equal to 1.

It should be clear that some gaps (i.e. bits of the tape not containing logical data) will inevitably appear on the tape. This means that not every inch of the tape can be used to store useful information, and so the amount of data on the tape is less than would appear from a calculation of bit density times length. Nevertheless, blocking helps to save waste space on the tape. Much space would be wasted if a single logical record of length considerably less than a single physical record was stored in the space occupied on the tape by a single physical record.

Buffering

Buffering is used to *convert* the **physical blocks** or **physical records** *into* the **logical records** used by the **application software**. It is usually the function of the **operating system software** to *carry out these operations* automatically. The idea is shown in figure 27.4. Physical blocks on the storage device (tape in this case) are transferred into an area of main memory called a buffer.

The operating system software (i.e. appropriate add-on device drivers for the hardware being used), then converts the data into the logical records needed by the application. This is usually transparent to the application. The application simply saves or loads the records in this format, and the buffer, operating-system software and hardware interface takes care of how the logical records are mapped onto the hardware device being used.

These ideas are important, because they can be applied to any secondary storage device. It's up to those parts of the operating system which control the interface hardware to make sure that the data gets put onto the storage device in an appropriate format. In this way **any device, even those yet to be invented, can be mapped onto any application software** – magic!

Only a single buffer has been shown above, but it's usual for the operating systems to employ **double buffering** if a faster speed of response is required. This simply means that one physical block can be interrogated whilst another is being loaded or saved by using a second buffer area in main memory.

Disk based systems

We could have started off this section with a different scenario regarding a typical disk, being made up of tracks and sectors as described in chapter 12. However, we would then have suggested that a **block** of data from the disk, mapped onto **sector** and **track addresses** (or cylinders in the case of larger disks), can be read into an area of memory called a buffer. We would then have gone on to suggest that it's the job of the disk interface part of the operating system to map these physical blocks held in memory into the logical records also held in memory, so that a logical record can be used by an application or appropriate high-level language. We would have ended up with a diagram identical in principle to that of figure 27.4.

Other systems

As you can see from the above, **blocks of data are buffered into the system and interpreted by the operating-system's software**. Therefore, apart from the obvious restrictions of the physical media such as not being able to operate an indexed-sequential file on a tape, for example, the whole process is transparent to the application or language being used. The idea of blocks of data and buffering apply from the fastest of mainframe tape drives to the humblest cassette-based tape streamers. As can be seen from chapter 12, the physical formats and physical methods of storage and retrieval are very different for each type of secondary-storage device, but the principles of **block-data transfer**

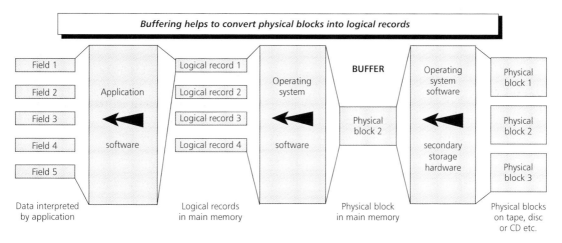

Figure 27.4

and **buffering** allow us to work with them all. Mapping physical records or blocks to logical records is done in this way for all secondary storage media, and file handling is thus made much simpler from a user's point of view.

File maintenance

Students at this stage of their course should need no reminding of the need for backup and other general file maintenance. It's inevitable that systems will crash – eventually. As more and more companies rely on computerised information processing the need to maintain a backup policy is essential. On larger systems complete disks will be backed up as a matter of course, and archives of tapes kept in separate buildings. But on microcomputers too its essential that important parts of your hard disk are backed up, or the complete hard disk is tape streamed (see chapter 12). Other systems such as RAID (shown in chapter 12) can be of tremendous advantage in keeping your computer data on files intact.

The drive-you-mad car company

In examinations (fortunately for many students!) there is usually little time to develop any but the most simple of algorithms relating to file processing. However, extended exercises, required by some of the boards in addition to project work, can provide an environment where your programming skills are tested to the limit. You are usually given a few months to come up with solutions to these exercises, but under examination conditions you are expected to come up with some reasonably sensible data structures in the limited amount of time available.

The drive-you-mad car company example can be considered with these scenarios in mind, and covers work, which might typically be expected under examination or extended exercise conditions. The actual example is obviously longer than would be expected from an examination question, but this is so that a number of appropriate questions can be covered.

Example

The drive-you-mad car company is a car hire firm, which operates a fleet of three main types of car. There is an executive model (rather expensive but would easily impress the girlfriend/boyfriend), a medium priced family saloon and a budget priced small economy car.

At present the firm runs a manually operated system with three card-index files and some books. These files are simply referred to as A, H and S. A contains the cars AVAILABLE for hire, H the cars already on HIRE and S contains cars that are out of action because they

are being SERVICED. Within each card index there are three different colours used to sort out the executive (exec), family (fmly) and budget (budg) cars. These are green, pink and blue respectively. It is company policy to make sure that the last car returned should be the last to be used again. In other words, the car, which has been standing in the garage longest, should be the next car to be hired, or some car might never be used!

At the beginning of each day the manager goes through the cards to establish which cars are needed for that day's hire. The cards are arranged in chronological order so that the cars to be used that day are at or near the front of the queue. A list of possible future bookings is also included with the card so that double booking is not possible. If a customer books in advance, then the 'name and address of the customer', together with the 'type of car booked' and the 'dates' are recorded in the hire book. If a customer books a car and wishes to drive it away immediately, then the name and address is again entered on the appropriate page in the hire book.

The car hire firm has several branches and is considering expansion. However, it is not envisaged that there will ever be more than a total of 1000 cars. It should be possible to book in advance any type and quantity of cars on a daily basis for any number of days.

The current manual system

First consider the existing manual system. Typical information on each card consists of the following:

Example		Future bookings	
		Date	Number of days
Type of car	*Executive*		
Registration number	*S 463 YKL*	*19/12/98*	*3*
Mileage	*38 971*	*30/12/98*	*6*
Mileage at last service	*35 120*	*13/01/99*	*1*
		19/02/99	*1*
		21/03/99	*4*
		Etc.	

The mileage is updated every time the car is returned from a hire commitment, and the cars are serviced every 5000 miles if possible. The cards are often in a tatty condition because the figures written on them are rubbed out and changed! When a card becomes too tatty it is replaced. You are to design a satisfactory system that could be implemented on a digital computer. You must explain in detail the files you propose to use, and the detailed structures of *two* of these files. Also, give an example of how a typical transaction using these files might take place.

What other functions (not mentioned in the question) could be performed by the introduction of the system that you have proposed?

Solution

You may think that the following solution is very long winded for a typical long exam question, and you are probably right! However, 75 per cent of the following text explains the approaches that can be used, and provides an excellent base from which to understand similar problems.

First notice that you are not asked to design the entire system in detail. That amount of work would rate as a complete project and not an examination question! Note also that you are asked only to give details of two particular files, and one particular transaction example.

When starting complex problems such as the above it is always a good idea to get an overview of the existing system, with special reference to the way in which data can be moved around from one 'file' to another. The table below shows how the three manual files A, H and S might be altered for some typical transactions, and figure 27.5 shows how the old manual files were operated.

Typical transaction	Consequence
The purchase of a new car.	Add new record to file A.
A car is hired.	Car is removed from file A, and placed into file H.
A car is returned.	Car is removed from file H and placed into file A.
A car is scrapped.	Car is removed from file A, H or S, according to why it is being scrapped (e.g. age or accident etc.).
A car is removed for a service.	Car is taken from A and placed in S.
A car has been serviced.	Car is taken from file S and placed in file A.

A: Cars Available   H: Cars on hire
S: Cars in for a service

In essence the manual system consists of nine files: one 'executive', one 'family' and one 'budget' file for *each* of the 'available', 'hired' and 'service' categories. When using a computer, it would not be necessary to physically move the data (entire card) from one file to the other. It would be more efficient to set up flags to indicate 'if the car was available for hire', was 'actually hired', or was 'in for a service'. It would make the situation easier to manage, plus increase the access speed, if there were *three separate files* for each of the categories; 'executive', 'family' and 'budget'. In this way, it is only necessary to consider the data structure for one of them. The other two are set up in an identical manner! Always look for dodges like this in an examination question, it can save you a great deal of time and effort.

First consider the information to be contained in a typical **field**. As there will be three separate files, one for each type of car ('exec', 'fmly', 'budg'), it is not necessary to identify the type of car as this will be implicit from the file in which it is located. The **key field** could therefore be the 'car registration number', but mileage and 'last-service mileage' will also be needed. The most complex task is to arrange the future booking for each car. This will have to be thought out in some detail, and is looked at in the next section.

Future booking

The computer will have to keep a table of 'which cars are booked on each day' and 'future bookings'. It is *not* necessary to book a specific car, only a specific type of car. Therefore, the system can be simplified considerably. All that's necessary is to make sure that there is not more than the available number of each type of car booked on any particular day.

It should be possible to hold the number of cars of each type in a simple **array** (see chapter 24). If a new car is requested on a particular day, then this array must be consulted before the booking can be confirmed.

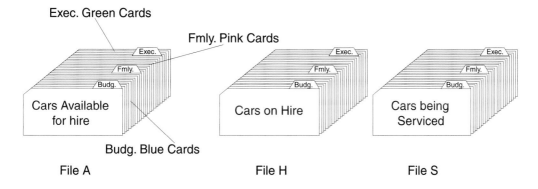

Figure 27.5

As bookings can be carried out in advance, there will have to be a number of these totals, one for each day. The system could work as follows:

Table shows current day number where '1' would be 'Today'

	1	2	3	4	5	6	7	8	9	10	11	12	13	14	15
Exec	12	8	7	1	2	2	1	1	1	1	1	1	0	0	0
Fmly	45	13	4	0	5	4	2	0	0	0	0	0	0	0	0
Budg	76	52	25	13	8	1	0	0	0	0	0	3	0	0	0

Max Executive = 100:   Max Family = 230
Max Budget = 350:

The current day could be numbered as day 1 (i.e. from 0700 to 0659.59). At the beginning of each day, all the totals for that day would have to be updated. The future days will then be numbered as 2, 3, 4, 5, 6 etc., so a car booked from 'day 1' for 'five days', for example, will increment the 'day 1, 2, 3, 4 and 5' totals by 1.

The above table shows that for the current day, there are already 12 'exec' cars, 45 'fmly' cars and 76 'budg' cars on hire. Or, in three days time (day 4) there are already 13 'budg' cars booked.

At the beginning of each day, the computer must update the above array so that over booking does not occur. 'Day 2 will then become day 1', and 'day 3 will become day 2' etc. All the figures in the above array will shift left with the passage of time. Underneath are the variables 'Max executive' etc. that show the total number of cars that the company owns. As far as the record is concerned, all that is necessary is to have a flag that is set if the car is available for hire; another flag could determine if it is in the service department. These flags will be altered when a car is hired or returned.

The company will have to establish how far in advance it would be sensible to accept bookings, so that the **dimension** of the array (see chapter 24) can be deduced. It would seem unnecessary to have a large array, as most of it would be empty. However, it must also be possible, perhaps by some alternative method, to make sure that a booking could be established months in advance if necessary. A separate file could be used for this purpose if this was felt to be necessary.

The company's policy of making sure that the last car returned should be the last one to be used again can easily be established by the use of a **circular list** (see chapter 25). In other words, when the last car in the list has been hired, you are automatically referred to the first car in the list. We therefore need to set up a system of pointers in each file, and this will have to be accommodated within the record structure.

A typical record structure for each car could therefore be as follows:

Reg. No.	Available flag	Service flag	Mileage	Last service mileage	Next-free pointer
S 463 YKL	1	0	38971	35120	003

Note: For the flags (1 = YES and 0 = NO)

If the above record is in the 'exec file' then it would indicate that the executive car S 463 YKL was ready for hire, had done 38,971 miles, and was not due for a service. The next free pointer indicates that the next 'exec' car that is to be hired can be located at record number 003 within the 'exec file'.

The file structure

Having considered the information that is to be contained in each record, we can now consider the file structure. As there is a maximum of only a few hundred cars in each file, then complex accessing methods, to gain super fast access to each record, are not necessary. A sequential access method using the pointer system hinted at above would produce a response within a few fractions of a second, which is easily fast enough for this application.

Circular list

To maintain the **circular list** principle, there must be a **header pointer** (pointer to the beginning of the list), and a **tail pointer** (pointer to the end of the list). If a new car is added, then this can be inserted after the tail (in the position indicated by the **free-space pointer**) so the new car now becomes the new tail, and the free-space pointer is altered accordingly. If the head and the tail become coincident, we have run out of cars! Also, when the car at the tail end of the list has been hired, the car at the head of the list will be the next one to be chosen (hence the circular list).

Using the pointer systems

We have seen that to maintain our circular list we need a header, tail and free space pointer. We will also need some indication that we have reached the end of a list. For example, in situations where no more free space is available (unlikely as the limit of the file should exceed the limit of the number of cars it's possible to have), or there are no more cars available for hire, any car that is scrapped can then have its record removed, and the space returned to the free-space stack. As an example, consider the exec file (the other two are identical in principle) the beginning of which, at a certain day, might be as shown in table 27.1.

Table 27.1

Comments	Record number	Reg. No.	Available flag	Service flag	Mileage	Last service mileage	Next pointer
Available pointer (header) points to here ⇒	0001	S 463 YKL	1	0	38971	35120	0025
Hire pointer (header) points to here ⇒	0002	R 768 TDF	0	0	12987	10090	0003
	0003	R 342 TYT	0	0	46981	45003	0123
Service pointer (header) points to here ⇒	0004	S 234 VTY	0	1	10234	5178	0067
	...						
Next car available after S 463 YKL	0025	*Car available for hire in list after S 463 YKL has been hired lives here*					
	...						
Next car to be serviced after S 234 VTY	0067	*Car in the garage being serviced after S 234 VTY lives here etc.*					
	...						
	...						
Next car in the on-hire list after R 342 TYT	0123	*Car in the garage on hire list after R 342 TYT lives here etc.*					
	...						
	0226						
	...						
	1000						

Available Header = 0001   Hire Header = 0002   Service Header = 0003

From the above table you can see that in the 'exec file', S 463 YKL is the first car available should an 'exec' car be required for hire. If it were needed immediately, then this would be removed from the available list and placed on the hired list. This can be achieved simply by updating the available header. Similarly, the car at the end of the on hire list (given by the on hire footer pointer not shown here) can be altered accordingly. Note that the data has not been physically moved (as was the case in the manual system), in the new case only the pointers have been altered. The above situation with regard to the pointers is shown in figure 27.6. Figure 27.6(a) shows the pointers before hire of the car in record 1, and figure 27.6(b) shows the situation after hire. If the car was to be booked in advance, then the appropriate checks must be made and, if a car is available, a booking confirmed by incrementing the appropriate element in the array. Also, the 'names and addresses' of customers must be entered into the customer record so that bookings can be confirmed on arrival when customers come to pick up the cars.

Customer name and address file

Let us now consider the customer name and address file (i.e. the information usually contained in the book under the manual system). This will simply be a record of the names and addresses of the customers, together with the dates of hire and the type of car hired. It may be a good idea to store this in chronological order, i.e. in date order. This would mean that if a car were hired

on 16/12/1999, for example, then this would be the way in which a customer can be traced. This file would get very large if no data were ever deleted from it. We must, therefore, establish a company policy on how long it wishes to keep old records. They must be kept for some time in case of enquiries over payments or police enquiries etc. Perhaps it would be an idea to keep them on disk for a few weeks, then back them up to tape and keep them for a few months or a few years if necessary.

We now assume that all customers' names and addresses are to be stored on disk. Also, a flag can be set to indicate whether or not the car has been taken, and if it has been taken, whether or not it has been returned. If both of these flags are set then, on the appropriate scan of the disk, the record may be removed and archived to tape in the way described in the previous paragraph.

Structure of the name and address file

As we have already mentioned, it might sometimes be necessary to interrogate the files in other ways on special occasions, such as a police enquiry. However, the main point of this file is to give a rapid response to the car-hire salesperson in the showroom when a customer comes to book a car, or to pick up a car that has previously been booked. Therefore, a file with fast access by date, and reasonably rapid access by customer name within that date, would be ideal. It would be a good idea to have a separate file for each date. In this

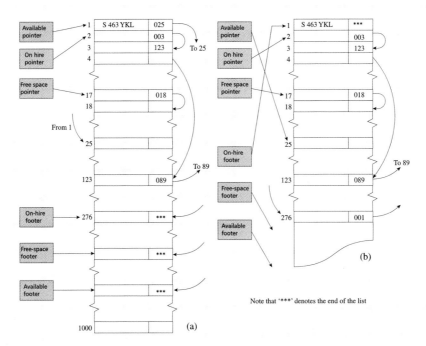

Note that '***' denotes the end of the list

Figure 27.6

way, access by date would be almost instant. It may be necessary to have two or three months ahead on disk and the old files (again in chronological order) archived to tape. If a car is to be booked for more than two or three months (very unlikely at the prices that will have to be charged to recoup the cost of the new computer system!) then this will have to be considered as a special case.

Let us consider a typical date: 22/11/1999, for example. As this file will be called 22/11/1999 then the date need not be stored in any of the records. A typical record structure for this file would therefore be as follows:

Surname	Initials	Address
Bradley	*R.J.*	*My address*

Type of car	Reg. No.	Hire from	Hire to	Car taken	Car returned	Damage
Exec	*S463YKL*	*22/11/ 1999*	*16/12/ 1999*	*1*	*0*	*0*

1 = Yes, 0 = No

As you can see from the above table, the record structure is simple. Let us now consider the file structure in more detail.

It is unlikely, but a maximum of 1000 enquiries may have to be dealt with in any one day. This would assume that all cars were booked out on a particular day, and no cars were being serviced. It will be usual for there to be a morning rush, and therefore many enquiries based on surname and initials will have to be dealt with quickly. Now access to the date is very quick, as a separate file is used for each day. It there-

fore only remains to sort out the structure of each date file.

With up to 1000 names possible, it might take too long for a serial-file arrangement, i.e. one record after the other with no regard to order. Also, if several enquiries were to be made at the same time from different terminals, then the search time might be particularly slow. One possible method would be to implement a pointer structure that is based on a binary tree. The idea can be seen in chapter 15. Using this system, we could set up a hierarchical data structure for the initial letters of the surnames as shown in figure 27.7.

When a particular initial letter is encountered, then a simple serial access list for each group of surnames beginning with the same letter should be adequate.

To summarise the above, to locate, insert or delete a record on the computer:

- Load appropriate date file.
- Search binary tree for the initial letter of surname.
- Serially search the sublist for surname and initials that match.

How do these files interact?

To explain how the system will operate, consider the following scenario:

1. At the beginning of each day (just before the showroom opens) the computer does various housekeeping facilities, such as archiving unwanted date files and setting up the variables for the date and pointers. This will be known as initialising the system.

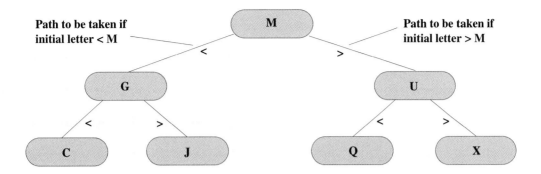

Path to be taken if initial letter < M

Path to be taken if initial letter > M

Figure 27.7

2. During the morning the cars that have been left overnight are checked in by the staff, visually checked for damage, and have the new mileage recorded on a special data capture form designed for data entry into the system. If you had enough money to spare then this could be done with a bar-code system and radioed back to the office!

3. When the data is entered into the computer system, the computer will automatically adjust the appropriate flags (e.g. no damage) and check if any cars need a service, as follows:

Mileage >= Last service + 5000

If a car is in need of a service, when the car is taken off the 'on hire list' and is put on the 'service list', a suitable printout is provided so that the service manager can arrange the appropriate schedules.

4. When customers come to pick up a car the showroom salesperson will ask them if they have booked. If they have, he or she will initiate a search for the surname and initials on the current date file. If the customer has not yet booked, then the salesperson will check if a car is available (by getting the computer to check the current totals in the array). If a car is available, the computer will insert the appropriate record in the current date file by searching through the binary tree structure until the appropriate place for the insertion of the record is found.

5. If a customer requires a future booking, then the appropriate date file is loaded, and modifications made to the records in an identical way to that described for a current date booking. If the booking is too far in advance, then special arrangements will need to be made.

6. When a car has been returned from the service department, the appropriate data is fed into the computer, and the flag changed so that the car may be added to the footer of the available for hire list. Of course, all the appropriate pointers must

be altered in a similar way to that described at the beginning of this example.

7. If a car is scrapped, then the appropriate record is deleted and returned as free space to the system.

With many of the above operations it's likely that an appropriate printout will be necessary, such as customer receipts, cars to be serviced and the number of cars needed for a specific day, for example.

We have now described a brief outline of the possible ways in which some files may be set up to computerise the drive-you-mad car company. The example also asked you to describe a typical transaction that might take place using these files. We will now develop a possible flowchart to show how a car may be booked and taken away immediately.

The part of the algorithm to perform this operation is shown in figure 27.8. Figure 27.8 assumes that the system has already been initialised. It would be likely that this routine would be called from a main menu.

One major point that has *not* been covered above is that it has been assumed that several terminals would be able to access the files at the same time. This is possible on most systems, but care should be taken when any data is being recorded on a file – i.e. if any pointers are being altered, then no other user should access the system during this critical time (usually only a few fractions of a second). However, once the new pointers have been established, the next user may use the next record in the list.

The final part of the question asks what extensions to the system do you see as possibilities. Some of the most obvious attributes not mentioned in the example concern the accounting procedures. No mention was made about how customers would be billed for the hire and how receipts are produced. It would easily be possible to include some sort of accounting procedure, possibly by an extension of the customer name and address record, as this has all the information necessary (i.e. type of car and number of days, customer name and address) to produce the required bill. Things

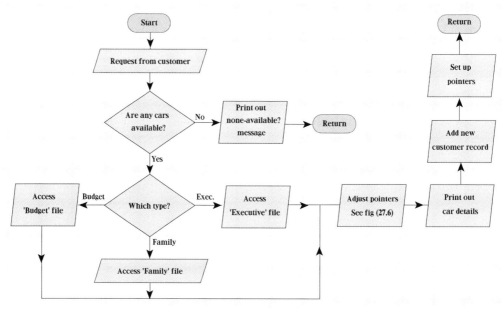

Figure 27.8

like this could typically be included on an extended exercise basis.

Other obvious things that could easily be produced are a variety of statistics relating to running of the business. These might be graphs of the 'number of cars hired', 'type of cars' and 'branches hiring the most'. Similarly, an 'analysis of profit' could easily be worked out. Such systems would obviously not be carried out at the same time as the on-line enquiries, but would be carried out overnight in a batch-type mode of operation.

Exercise 27.1

1 Explain the following terms:
   (a) Backup files
   (b) Hashed file
   (c) Hierarchically-organised file
   (d) Scratch file.

2 Describe the difference between **logical** and **physical records**, making sure to make use of the term **blocking factor** in your explanation.

3 What is meant by the term **file maintenance**?

4 Why are **buffers** often used when accessing files?

5 Using a suitable **high-level language**, write a program which reads positive and negative integers from a serial-access file, then copies the positive numbers into one output file and the negative numbers into another output file, both of which are serial access. You may assume that the files can be held in memory.

6 *Two files* contain data in *sorted order*. Each file is able to be loaded into the computer separately.

However, the combined sorted file is too big to fit in memory. Describe a method that could be used to produce a large file containing all data sorted into order.

7 A hamburger joint produces a sequential-access file for each transaction made at the till. The item code followed by the quantity is entered, one after the other, for each item sold, e.g. the entry 2,3 might mean that 3 cheeseburgers have been sold because 2 might be the code for a cheeseburger. Write a program which interrogates the file and prints out, in order of code, how many of each item has been sold. State any assumptions you make.

8 In a high-security system **data integrity** is of paramount importance. Data is already validated on entry, but two operators create the same information in two separate files. Assuming that the files are organised sequentially as pure text files, devise and test an algorithm, which **verifies** the files by seeing if there are any differences between the two files. If the verification fails the system should output a suitable error message.

End of chapter revision aid and summary

Cover up the right-hand column and see if you can answer the questions or define the terms on the left. They appear in the order in which they are covered in this chapter. Alternatively you may browse through the right-hand column to aid revision.

What is a direct or random-access file?	A direct or random-access file accesses records by means of a hashing function or hierarchical data method such as a binary search. It is a file in which data can be accessed without having to go through all the previous data.
What is a hashing function?	Hashing functions generate a range of addresses, which provide relative keys for accessing the data by reference to an address.
What type of media can support random access files?	Direct or random-access files can only be supported on secondary storage media with *direct-access capability* such as disks.
What is a relative key?	A relative key is a system whereby logical records can be directly accessed by reference to the first record in the file, which is usually labelled record zero or one.
What is an indexed-sequential file?	An indexed-sequential file is accessed by means of one or more indexes held as separate data structures.
How is an index built up for an indexed-sequential file?	The index in an indexed-sequential file needs to be built up by the programmer or application such as a database.
How do high-level languages differ in their ability to support files?	Many high level languages, such as early versions of Pascal and BASIC, have limited file handling capabilities, but the COBOL language is rich in a huge variety of file-handling techniques.
How do the algorithms for file handling relate to other data structures?	The algorithms designed for file handling rely heavily on algorithms developed to maintain linked-list data structures, and the algorithms for sorting and searching.
What is a data file?	A data file is the name given to a file organised in ways considered in this chapter. The name is used to distinguish these files from other common file types.
What is a backup file?	A backup file is a direct copy of an existing file made for data integrity purposes.
What is a scratch file?	A scratch file is a file containing temporary data that is deleted after it has served its purpose.
What is an indexed file?	An indexed file is the name sometimes used for an index-sequential file with multiple indexes.
What is a hashed file?	A hashed file is the name sometimes used to denote a direct-access file, which is accessed by a hashing function.
What is a hierarchically-organised file?	A hierarchically-organised file is the name given to the file structure often associated with hierarchical directories in modern WIMP systems.
What is a logical record?	A logical record is a record viewed from a programmer's point of view. It is the record created by the high-level programming language or application.
What is a physical record?	A physical record or block (sometimes a group of blocks) is the unit used by the secondary storage medium being used – it usually contains several logical records.
How are physical and logical records related?	A logical record is mapped onto the physical record by the operating system software and interface hardware for the secondary storage medium being used.

What is a block?

A block, often the same as a physical record, is a unit used by the operating-system-hardware interface to transfer a chunk of data to or from the secondary storage device being used.

Describe blocking.

Blocking is the term used when more than one logical record fits into a block or physical record.

What is a blocking factor?

The blocking factor is the number of logical records which fits into a physical record or block.

How do buffers help in relation to files?

Buffers are used to help map the physical records and blocks used by the hardware to the logical records used by the high-level language and applications software.

How do blocks and buffers help with different secondary storage media?

Blocks and buffers enable any secondary storage device, such as tapes, disk and CD-ROM, to be treated in very similar ways.

28 A First Look at Databases

Key resources

To carry out this work most successfully it's best if you have:

◆ Access to a modern database creation package such as Microsoft's Access or Lotus Approach, for example. For the purpose of this chapter only, the database being used does not need a relational capability (see chapter 29)

Concept checkpoints

◆ A familiarity with the organisation of manual systems in a filing cabinet would be useful.

◆ An appreciation of the material covered in chapters 22 and 23 on operating systems, and chapters 26 and 27 on file handling would be useful.

Introduction

Databases have improved considerably over the years. As micros have become more powerful, and networks more prolific, we are able to apply very sophisticated database concepts that used to be possible only in the mainframe-computer-system environment. **Software packages like Microsoft's Access have meant that ordinary users can now produce elaborate databases with GUI-based front ends that hitherto would have taken a team of skilled systems programmers months to complete.**

Databases are so important that a significant proportion of this book is devoted to their use, and, even though a database is only an application in the normal sense of the word, its use permeates all corners of an organisation. If not properly set up and maintained, then the company which tries to makes use of it could literally be thrown into desperate trouble. If, however, the database is well thought out, well set up and efficiently maintained, it could easily give the managers of the company the information they need to make informed decisions at the appropriate times. **Databases range from packages found on micros, to enormous large-volume transaction systems connected to mainframe computers via high-speed links. It is no longer unusual for large multinational companies to have databases containing literally Tbytes of important information. When mainframes holding vast databases link together with sophisticated communication systems, you start to realise the potential for this vast and very sophisticated global-information system of which the Internet is starting to give us a flavour.**

Background information

Before the advent of the ideas behind a modern database, it was common for different divisions within a business to run most of their affairs independently. If we were to go back and consider a typical company at that time, then different departments such as 'sales', 'marketing', 'accounts' and 'production', would probably have managed their own separate manual or computerised systems. It's likely that there would have been much **duplication of data**, and little opportunity for automatically passing information between their totally **incompatible systems**! To transfer data they would probably have to have **physically re-typed the data** into one of the different computer systems, or written out separate forms for each department if the system operated manually.

If management wanted an overall view of the company, they would have to have **collated lots of information** from many disparate departments before the appropriate statistics could be obtained. This process was often **too laborious** to be considered, and thus vital information in the decision-making process could be lost. Even commonplace information such as 'how many customers live in the South East of England?' for example, would probably have been beyond the capability of most of the older computerised and manual systems – unless this particular question had been anticipated and pre-programmed when the original system was conceived. It is against this sort of unsatisfactory background that the modern database ideas were born.

The modern database

Put simply, a **database** is a **collection of interrelated data** – rarely (perhaps on a simple micro system) containing just a single file, but more often containing a collection of several or even **many files**. If a database can work only on one file at a time, then it is called a **flat-file** database. In addition to these basic files which can be **modelled** in a variety of ways, there would be some **program** or a **set of programs** to carry out operations such as **data entry**, and generate **queries** which can extract a variety of information specified by the users of the system. At the most basic level, an 'address book', or even a 'list containing telephone numbers' could be regarded as examples of *very simple* databases. However, in this particular chapter, we will take a general look at **DataBase Management Systems** (**DBMS**). For those undertaking further database work, chapter 29 will cover the theory in more detail, looking at the **hierarchical** and **network** database models. Chapter 29 also takes a **special look** at **relational databases** and the **RDBMS**, which are now available on modern computer systems. Relational databases have become *the* most versatile and popular databases due to the versatility of this system, and the increased power of the current computer systems needed to implement it.

When databases are undertaken within the **DBMS environment**, computerisation *should* ensure that the database is much more convenient to operate. The DBMS should also ensure that it's more efficient to enter and extract the data than was the case with the older manual or computerised systems based on files, which had no 'interaction capability'. Indeed, a properly constructed and well-maintained database should be such that the **overall usefulness** of the system is far greater than the sum of its parts. Databases usually change over a significant period of time, and as the needs of an organisation develop, so too must the flexibility of the computerised database structures used to model a company.

We will now look at some of the facilities offered by modern database systems, and look at the **setting up** and **maintenance** of these systems. Examples will also be given so that you will gain an idea of the typical processes involved. The **advantages** and the **disadvantages** of making use of such systems should always be borne in mind too, and although there are many advantages, you must make sure that you are always aware of the potential database pitfalls – never forget the true saying:

> *To err is human, but to really foul things up you need a computer!*

This is particularly true when it comes to constructing huge databases on which a company may well rely for its day-to-day operation – the **database administrators** (people who set up and run the database) in industry today certainly have an awesome responsibility.

Why use a database?

It is very much easier to make use of a 'proprietary database system' than to attempt to program a similar 'set up' from scratch making use of an appropriate high level language like **Visual BASIC** or **Delphi**. The database system takes care of all the complex file handling and pointer manipulation that is necessary to build up a speedy and efficient system, and handles all the user interfaces such as the menus etc. with ease. In conjunction with other specially written languages such as **DMLs** or **SQLs**, the database system copes easily with the numerous and involved **queries** that are often requested by the users of such systems.

A modern database also allows **applications** and **high-level languages** to link to the data in such a way that the **structure of the database** is transparent to the application. This has led to powerful **integrated systems** being set up and used in many businesses. An 'integrated system' means that it's easy to pass information from one system to another without having to manually transfer the data. Indeed, if well set up, then this transfer process should also be automatic and transparent to the users of the system. In this way lengthy delays within an organisation are avoided. Many databases also allow external programs and routines to be called from within the database. In this way it is possible to 'bolt on' the most sophisticated user-generated routines that can customise the database to the exact requirements.

If the company mentioned in the background-information section earlier had an **integrated database system**, this would mean that information could be shared between different departments very easily. Moreover, with an appropriately set up system, each department would have a view not too dissimilar from that which they had when they operated independently! When viewed from a departmental perspective, each

Did you know that . . .

Databases have indeed come a very long way over the last couple of decades. From specialist, difficult to use packages, which were limited in operation, to easy to use relational databases, which can be set up by using a variety of Wizards which help the novice to set up the most sophisticated systems. However, you will still need to be an expert to set up a complex database system for a large company.

department has a unique view, which relates only to the way the database is set up for them. Therefore, the marketing perspective of the database is very different from the sales perspective of the same database, even though they share some common information. These ideas are simple, and are represented in the Venn diagram shown in figure 28.1. You can see that all the data, which belongs to a specific set, are labelled in their own 'data worlds'. However, each data set will overlap with other data sets from different 'data worlds' – it is in this way that much data duplication is avoided.

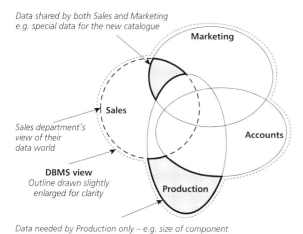

Figure 28.1

You should note also at this stage that much data couldn't be viewed from unauthorised places. For example, it would not be desirable for 'marketing', 'sales' or 'production' to have access to information regarding 'employees salaries', for example. This information would therefore live in that part of the database to which only the 'accounts department' would have access.

The database management system

The **DBMS** is basically lots of complex software, which **controls all aspects** of database management. For example, a **database** will need to be **defined**, it needs to be **created**, efficiently **maintained** and **managed**, and it needs to be **accessed**, **interrogated** and **backed up**. **Queries** need to be made in which information can be extracted for **reports** – and this is just a flavour of some of the functions carried out by a modern **DBMS**. It also provides the **interface** between the data and the users – for example, it would probably allow you to create powerful **GUI-based** systems that enable non-specialist

users to easily enter data into the system or to carry out standard queries. It allows you to interface a variety of high-level languages via suitable language extensions and provides **multiple levels of security** etc. Together with an **SQL**, or **Data Query Language (DQL)**, it provides management with a powerful analytical tool that can handle most aspects of their data-processing business, because the **database** literally *is* their business. The general idea of a typical database management system is shown graphically in figure 28.2.

How is the system organised?

As can be seen from figure 28.2, the **DBMS** provides the necessary **links** between the **data** stored on magnetic disk or other suitable secondary storage medium, and the external **software interfaces** such as **applications programs** etc. As you can see from the diagram, the **database management system** also provides an appropriate **interface** between other **applications** that might want to make use of the data in the database system.

For example, a high level language may wish to use the facilities of the **DBMS** so that it can store and retrieve data for its own particular application. Modern versions of **COBOL**, for example, have been extended to include special commands, which deal specifically with databases.

The DBA

A person called the **DataBase Administrator** or **DBA** (shown by the very special user D in figure 28.2) will be in charge of the database design and maintenance. He or she is the 'big-boss person' and will set up a **database schema**, which is the **grand design** of the **overall database**. This design or schema would make use of the **data models** covered in chapter 29.

This DBA is in a very powerful position and has great responsibility. He or she will need extensive knowledge about the nature of the business, and also about the particular company concerned. It's

the DBA's responsibility to maintain the database, and this involves operations like altering the structure of the database as the business expands into new areas. You should note that it does not involve the entry of data itself, except, perhaps, for test purposes. The inexperienced users shown in figure 28.2 would carry out ordinary data entry. As the DBA is able to do *anything* to the database, they are given the **highest level of security**

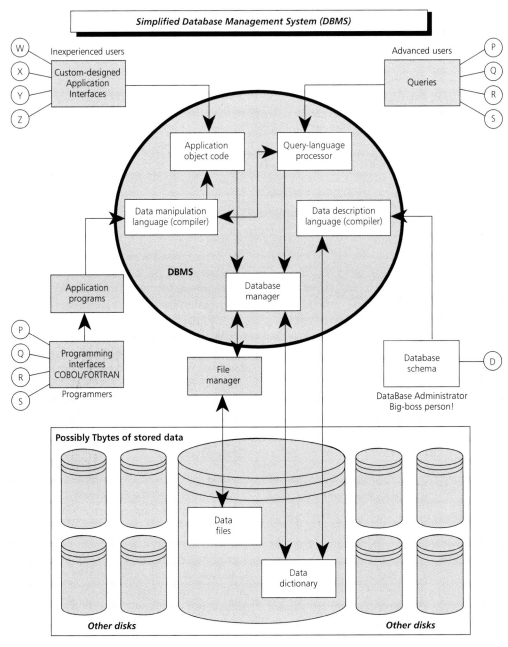

Figure 28.2

possible. The **database management system (DBMS)** would allow the **database administrator** to set a password as soon as the creation of the database is underway – if this is *not* done then anybody might be able to gain unauthorised access to the data or the structure of the database.

The schema

The definition of the entire database or **schema** can be thought of as being viewed from several different **levels** called **subschema**. The *first level* is the **conceptual level**, which describes the data as seen by the **application** that is making use of the DBMS (i.e. this could be thought

of as the different 'database views' which people using the database might have). The **second level** is called the **logical level**. This describes how the relationships will be represented in the **logical structure** of the database. Finally, the **third level**, called the **physical level**, describes how the data will be stored on the **physical media** such as **primary** or **secondary storage** devices. The schema is, therefore, a detailed description of the database, which is used by the **DBMS**.

Data definition language

Many of the above **subschema** would also be split up into further **subschema** with defined roles such as 'which users will have access to which data' etc. The principles make use of the ideas shown in figure 28.1 at the beginning of this chapter. The database schema would be modelled by the DBA with the help of a special language called the data definition language or, alternatively, the data description language (DDL). The data definition language helps to define the structure of the files. One example of just part of a data definition language would be the **SQL** which is used to define queries. In addition to the above, the data definition language would help to describe attributes such as 'record layouts', 'fields' and 'key fields', and other things such as 'location of the files'. Therefore, the **data definition language** helps the **DBA** to define the **logical structure** of and **files** within the database, which is then used to construct tables that are held in the **data dictionary**.

The data dictionary

The **data dictionary** can be regarded as a **description of the database itself** (not the actual data – that is held in the **data files**). This would help to **map** the **logical database** onto the **physical-level** storage devices, help sort out who has access to what data for security purposes, and help with any validation such as checking to see if the data actually exists. It would also help to make sure that adequate schemes are in operation for recovery in the event of errors such as disk crashes or fire. The data dictionary can be thought of as containing data that describes the databases, and therefore enables the DBA to maintain overall control of the system.

The file manager

As you will appreciate from reading chapters 22 and 23 on operating systems, the file manager would be that part of the **operating system** which allows physical access to the data stored on the disks in this particular database example. Therefore, this manages access to the data at the physical-level subschema. The file manager interfaces the data stored on disk with the software requesting particular data. Therefore, the logical structures used at the higher levels of file management would be identical to those covered in chapters 26 and 27 when files and file-handling techniques were looked at in some detail. You should note also that there are no special methods of storing files other than those covered in chapters 26 and 27. It's the job of the DBMS to convert the data presented to the users. This is done via the schema, and the logical-file structures such as indexed sequential, for example. The data is broken down further by the buffering systems mentioned in chapter 27, and eventually converted to the physical ways in which the bytes of data are actually stored on the secondary storage media. This is covered in chapter 12.

Data manipulation language (DML)

The **data manipulation language** (DML) provides a comprehensive set of features to allow modification to the data contained within the database. Some of the facilities provided by the DML are intended only for the DBA, but other facilities such as parts of the **query language** (see in a moment) allow all users to carry out common operations such as retrieving and modification (if they have appropriate security clearance) of data. You should realise that large database systems will probably have multiple users, and these conditions usually bring extra problems. For example, different users can't carry out updates on the same record at the same time. Therefore, a process called **record locking** is used whereby a record in the process of being updated is not available to other users during this editing period.

There are two current types of DML supported by most DBMS, and these are related to the procedural (**imperative**) and non-procedural (**declarative**) language types as typified in the high-level languages principles chapter 13. You may recall that **4GLs** (see chapter 13) typified the non-procedural DML types, and it's these which allow users to access data in very easy ways. However, as described in the high-level language chapter, no language is an island unto itself, and most DMLs have aspects of each. Advanced users would build up their own algorithms enabling them to use the database in innovative ways, but the inexperienced users would make do with the simpler aspects of the DML to retrieve data in standard ways. You should not forget that the programmers or the DBA could write their own code which might calculate statistics, for example, which could then be called up as a **macro** (see chapter 21) by inexperienced users of the system. Typically, on a micro running Microsoft Access, for example, you could write routines using VBA (Visual BASIC for Applications), a subset of Visual BASIC which allows very sophisticated processing to be carried out on data contained within the Access database.

The query language

Part of the facilities provided by the DML enable the end users to execute queries, and this is specifically referred to as a **query language**. In some systems the DML and the query language are one and the same thing. It is the job of the **query processor** in the **DBMS** to take the queries written by the users and to change them into a form that can be used inside the DBMS to activate the interface with the other systems described above. The query processor must also communicate with the DML so that appropriate queries produced from the high-level languages or other applications may be converted into the application code necessary to communicate with the database manager at the appropriate level – follow the arrows in figure 28.2. Specific examples of queries are covered in the practical section when different systems are looked at during the next few sections.

Commercial database applications

This section relates to the material covered in the business-applications section of chapter 6. However, as you can see from reading the first few parts of this chapter, an understanding of database systems requires a little more technical knowledge! This is why it is being covered now. The following examples make use of the Microsoft Access database, a common database system used in many businesses and educational establishments. Here we will concentrate on the easy-to-understand front end to the system. However, bear in mind the work that had to be undertaken by Microsoft! The sorts of things described at the beginning of this chapter are actually required to get the database system working – it's as well that this is transparent to non-technical users.

Creating the database

Much design work needs to be done before starting a database, but the objective here is to show the mechanisms which enable you to create your own powerful database systems. Figure 28.3 shows part of a very simple database regarding pupils at a school. You can see that a 'Student ID number' has been entered as the **key field**, (the same idea when file handling was covered in chapter 26). Next 'Surname' and 'House' have been entered as **strings**. Finally, the 'Form' is being created by a **Wizard**, which is prompting you to enter a list of possible form entries such as 3a and 3b etc.

The thing to appreciate here is how this particular application package makes it relatively easy, even

for novice users, to create complex data structures with little knowledge of computer science. From reading the beginning of this chapter you should appreciate what this simple GUI-based front end is creating, and from reading the file-handling chapters

> **Hint:** Although Microsoft Access has been used in these particular examples, any competent database system would be adequate for the purposes of this chapter, where no relational elements are needed.

you should know what sort of data structures are being created on disk.

After going through the motions, accepting little or no responsibility for layout (i.e. leaving it up to the database design Wizards), you could end up with a simple GUI-based front end as shown in figure 28.4. Here you can see that we have a workable design which has created a record-card type filing system which displays the fields (the boxes into which the data is to be typed). The field descriptions, giving the user who will enter the data an idea of what to enter have also been set up. The ability to use some pull-down lists to save typing in data which belongs to a finite and predictable set such as 'forms' (e.g. you might have a set of forms 3a, 3b, 3c etc.) is also useful. We have not made use of any of the fancy facilities that are available such as inserting a photograph of each student or inserting music or video clips, for example. This is indeed a measure of a modern database application package like Access. It really does make the creation of very complex databases relatively simple for the non-specialist.

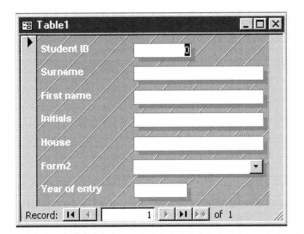

Figure 28.4

Entering the data

To program something of the above complexity from scratch, even using a GUI-based language such as Visual BASIC, Delphi or Visual C++, would take an experienced programmer many hours to accomplish, and would easily constitute an advanced-level project

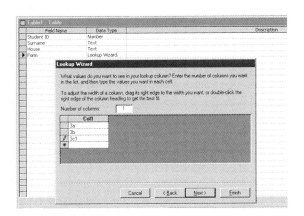

Figure 28.3

if done properly. *An inexperienced person can carry out the same work using 'Wizards' and a 'database application program' in minutes!* However, don't get too carried away – you will need to be very skilled, have a lot of experience, and need to spend a lot of time if you are going to create a big database application using such a package. It's just that the beginner *can* create *very simple* databases very easily, and this is just one of the advantages of these systems. Inexperienced users can get a system up and running quite quickly. Entering the data then becomes quite a trivial (if tedious) operation. This is aided by the data-entry screen, and the addition of video-recorder type controls for going backwards and forwards through the records.

Validation

Validation (checking to see if the data entered is valid in the context in which it is being used) is also easy to set up in such systems. For example, in this simple database, the Student ID has been forced to accept only positive numbers in the range of 0 to 9999 inclusive as shown in figure 28.5 where a negative entry has been attempted. The computer has detected that the number entered is not in the range defined by the person who has set up the database.

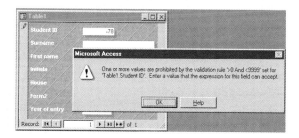

Figure 28.5

You should realise, of course, that a number 0 would probably not be a very sensible student number. Therefore, the range should perhaps be restricted to numbers between 1000 and 9999, for example, thus giving each student a unique 4-digit number. Problems like this are the sort of thing which should be covered at the database design stage, and is the reason why much thought has to go into the design of the database *before* any work is carried out at the computer. Nevertheless, trivial alterations to validation ranges such as this are easy to do post implementation. Other problems, like adding or deleting records, might be less trivial to implement after you have set up the entire system.

> **Hint:** Failure to validate data at every conceivable opportunity during the data entry phase would loose you a lot of marks in your project. The validation rules should be finalised during the design stage.

Alternative input of data

Most modern databases allow the designer of the database to specify alternative ways of entering data. For example, at the author's school we have devised a program which acts as a questionnaire to determine the IT experience of new pupils. Many of the responses to the questions are limited to multiple-choice types, and therefore each question would have a limited number of answers. Most of the questions, of the type shown in figure 28.6, have been designed such that the student can 'point with a mouse and click a button' for easy entry of the data. This is far better than typing in the words which, due to errors, would be far more difficult to analyse when it comes to reporting the results of the survey. Notice that question (1) allows for a single response only, but question (2), (3) and (4) allow for multiple responses if necessary.

Notice also the 'pull down menu' boxes for the responses to the 'house', 'form', and 'year of entry' options. The person entering the data would only be able to type a valid option, or 'click over the arrow' and be presented with a valid list from which to choose. If the student actually clicked over 3C4, then it would replace any entry, which could have already been typed into the box by mistake.

Extracting information

A database can take the information from the data files and, using a set of **relational operators** (see in a moment) like **arithmetical operators**, **comparison operators** and **logical operators**, can create new **files** or **reports** containing information based on any **matching criteria**. This means that a database gives you a totally *ad hoc* ability to extract virtually any information (assuming it's there), given that you can define what you want in terms of '=' 'AND', 'OR', '<' and '>' etc. A subset of relational operators is shown in the table overleaf.

The results of these operations would usually return a **true** or **false** value, or be used as a **flag** in which to choose a record or otherwise. As you can see from the examples, it is also usual to have the **set operators** such as **union (OR)**, **intersection (AND)** and **difference** etc. (**Difference** means the values in one set which do **not** belong in the other set.) A typical **query** would allow the user to **list** and **print out** selected information from the database making use of expressions built up by these **operators**. It's also usually possible to perform **count** and **sum** operations etc. on

> **Hint:** Some companies would buy an entire network and computer system simply on its ability to support a database like Microsoft's Access, for example. Many companies use this, together with a suitable file server, as a basis for local and wide-area network information distribution and processing.

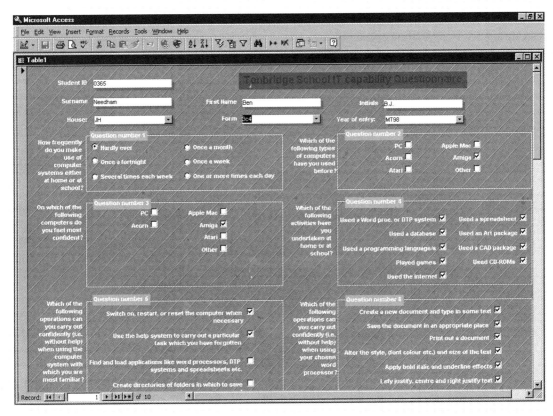

Figure 28.6

Example relational operators	Symbol	Examples
'Equals'	=	Teacher = "Bloggs"
'Less than'	<	Name < "Cooper"
'Greater than'	>	Quantity > 3
'Less than or equal to'	<=	Salary <= 50000
'Greater than or equal to'	>=	Tax >= 40
'Not equal to'	<>	Form <> "3a"
'And'	'And'	(Form = "3a") And (Name = "Tom")
'Or'	'Or'	(Form = "3a") Or (Form = "3b")
'Not'	'Not'	Countries = Not "UK"
'Is like'	'Like'	Like "Brad*"
'Lies between'	'Between'	Date Between #01/01/1999# And #01/01/2000#

the data as it is being extracted, and all of the expressions which are formed can be combined with programming constructs (see chapter 13) such as '**If**', '**While**' and '**Do**' etc.

These principles are usually very easy to apply in practice. For example, if you were dealing with a typical school database, and if you wish to apply a query such as 'Find all the people in "Weldon House" (Codename WH) whose first name happens to be Nick', then a simple interface to achieve this is shown in figure 28.7. This is the equivalent to typing in a command like: (House = "WH") AND (First Name = "Nick"). Note the facility to add more conditions, making use of 'Or' in the final line of the query window in this particular example. This simple way of operating for novice users is often called **query by example** or **QBE**.

A **query** is the name given to one or more commands written in a **data query language**. It effectively tells the database how the data is to be manipulated, and any other actions that should be taken. The **data query language** (DQL) would actually make use of the **data manipulation language** (DML) and the **data description tion language** (DDL) to access the physical data within the database.

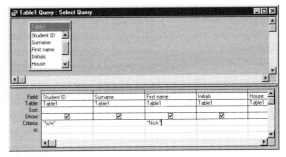

Figure 28.7

Use of 4GLs

Figure 28.7 provides a much-easier human computer interface (HCI) than the conventional SQL language. The **structured query language** (e.g. a **4GL**) to achieve the same result in Microsoft Access would be:

```
SELECT DISTINCTROW
Table1.House, Table1.Surname,
Table1.[First Name], Table1_1.Initials,
Table1.[Student ID]
FROM Table1, Table1 AS Table1_1
GROUP BY Table1.House, Table1.Surname,
Table1.[First Name], Table1_1.Initials,
Table1.[Student ID]
HAVING(((Table1.House)="WH")AND((Table1
.[First Name])="Nick"));
```

assuming, of course, that you wish to accept the other default operations. This is a classic example of the difference between a typical custom-designed application interface for inexperienced users, and the SQL language used as a programming language in it's own right. Notice that the above query is declarative in nature, although advanced users may use the imperative nature of the SQL to provide their own more-advanced facilities.

A feature for more advanced users, which might be available in a typical 4GL, could be 'delete all the records of customers who have not had any transactions with the company for the last ten years'. The procedure, as defined by the data query language, might be something along the following lines.

```
for  CUSTOMERS;
  if highest of INVOICES DATE
   < 01/01/1989 then
        delete records
  else
        delete records in INVOICES
with (DATE<01/01/1988)
  end
end
```

The above procedure will search the customers' INVOICES held in the database and determine if the **highest value** for the **date field** selected from the records within a related file has a value that is **less than** the **target date**, if so, then the record will be deleted. However, there may be transactions older than this date with customers that also have more recent transactions. The second part of the above procedure will delete just the old parts of the customers' records without deleting any later information.

Just as a matter of interest, it is this sort of thing that could cause problems regarding millennium compliance. If the dates were written using just two numbers for the year as DATE <01/01/84, for example,

does 84 mean 1984 or 2084? When we get to the year 2000, if such a routine is run, then all records < 2084 could be deleted by mistake!! You can now see why it's called the **millennium bug**!

As you can see, learning a query language could take a long time, therefore, the rest of this section will concentrate on the sort of things that can be done without going into actual details.

Some other functions

Many of the **mathematical functions** found on a scientific calculator are automatically available from many databases, i.e. **sin**, **cos**, **tan**, **square roots**, **logs** and many others can be used in conjunction with numerical data. In addition to the mathematical functions, there may be specialist **financial functions**. For example, '**future values**' and **interest** etc. may also be available. There is also usually a wealth of **statistical functions** such as **mean** and **variance**. The user is, of course, often able to set up any function that they desire by defining it themselves.

Time and date calculations

As shown above, calculations can be made on information contained in the form of date. It is also usual to provide the ability to give similar functions with time. Both American and British systems for date can be catered for, and most modern systems should now be millennium compliant, although many of the old databases are not. It has been estimated that it might cost up to $4,000,0000,000 dollars to correct the entire problem world-wide, unless someone comes up with an ingenious solution in the meantime. (Lots of opportunity for you here if you are reading the book before the year 2000!)

Wild cards

The ability to search a database is of paramount importance, and much effort would be put into constructing the procedures to search the database. To help out there would probably be a system, which makes use of what are known as **wildcards**. There could be several different types of wildcards in a typical system, but often an '*****' (**asterisk**) would mean 'any number of characters' and a '?' would mean a single character, just like in the MS-DOS system. Therefore, if you wanted to search for all names beginning with 'BRAD' you might use the following procedure.

```
for CUSTOMERS with LAST NAME = 'BRAD*'
list records
end
```

The above would make sure that names like – **Bradbrooke, Bradbury, Bradley, Bradford, Bradshaw** and **Brady** would all be included in the output from the above search.

Reports

A **report** can be generated as the result of a **query**. It is usually possible to format the output to the user's requirements. This output can usually be directed to the screen, the printer or a file. As with the searches, it would be usual for non-technical users to have a set of pre-defined reports, which they use for the day-to-day operation of the database. However, the **database administrator** or other **power users** (users with sufficient knowledge and privilege) can also define their own unique reports. Many **utilities** such as **pre-defined templates** make report generation relatively simple. Also, as with the import facilities described earlier, there are usually many formats in which data can be exported to other normally incompatible systems by making use of the report generators. Data could be exported into word processors, spreadsheets, transmitted over networks or transported

> **Hint:** Students usually do reporting very badly. Some fail to understand that queries and reports are usually the whole point of setting up the database in the first place. Also, make sure that the outputs from your reports are attractive. They should almost look as if they have been designed on a DTP system!

to other systems such as mini and mainframe computer systems.

Taking a typical example from Microsoft Access, and after defining a suitable query such that only appropriate data may be found, the next job would be to define how the report is to be formatted or laid out. A typical simple layout for some test data is shown in figure 28.8. Here you can see the default options chosen by the system. To complete the task, you could change the heading from 'table 2' to something more suitable, delete any unnecessary information in the page header and page footer areas, and delete any details not needed in the main body of the text.

After carrying out the operations suggested in the last section, and then executing the query, we could get results similar to those shown in figure 28.9. You could then save this report in its edited form, so that it may be recalled by name and executed much more quickly at a later stage. There are also many more options that we have not shown – experiment for yourself if you have this system at your school or college. It's very easy to use.

> **Hint:** If you get an opportunity, have a look at some of the specialist computerised databases that have been designed for companies like estate agents. Here database searches are combined with maps of the local area, to quote just one very small part of a very large system.

Other typical systems

Typical systems around at the time of writing include the **DB2 (Database 2) DBMS** system developed by IBM for use on its large mainframe computers. This database is fully relational and uses most of Codd's (see chapter 29) relational data models. It allows many users to have access to many databases by using standard

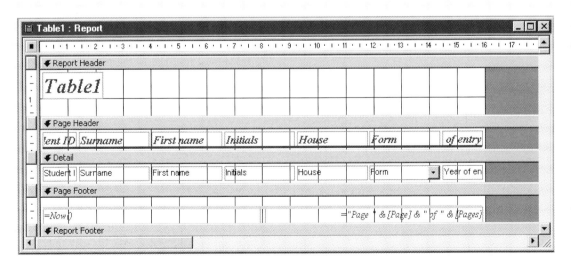

Figure 28.8

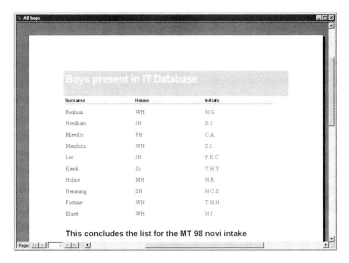

Figure 28.9

SQL procedures. It's also possible to embed **SQL commands** in languages such as **COBOL II**, **FORTRAN 90** and yes, even **BASIC**! In addition to this, APL and the system/370 assembly language also support SQL. These systems are also supported on most IBM **operating systems.** From the powerful **MVS/370** mainframe, (**multiple virtual storage**, see chapter 23 for virtual storage systems), via **DOS** and the latest **OS/2**, Linux and **Windows** operating system for the Pentium-based 586 microprocessors.

You should now appreciate the task in front of the database administrator! You should also now fully appreciate why extensive systems analysis would be necessary over a period of many months if you were to store the information regarding a medium or large company. It should be obvious that no single person would be able to cope with such extensive computerisation by him or herself, and therefore a team of computer specialists would work on the problems over an extensive period of time.

You will remember that, at the beginning of this chapter, we said that databases could permeate an entire company. You should now see why.

Security of the database system

There are two different aspects of security to consider: the **physical security** of the data, i.e. the disks on which it is stored etc. and the **prevention of unauthorised access**.

Physical security of data

This means recovering from errors if a disk gets corrupted, or making sure that most of the database can be restored in the event of a fire etc. If one of the disks containing the database becomes corrupted then there should be facilities to recover the database so that a minimum of information is lost. This will in turn depend on the volatility of the data contained in it. Typical backups might be made daily, weekly, monthly or at intervals which particularly suit the organisation and database.

The backed-up data must be stored such that it can't become corrupted through heat or external magnetic fields etc. It should preferably be stored in a fireproof container in a different building. However, there are other alternatives – having a complete backup computer system in another building, or some other techniques involve making use of **RAID** or **tape streamers** (see chapter 12). However, the storage and fire security precautions are similar for all such systems.

The obvious must also not be overlooked. Don't forget that the disks or tapes etc. could literally be stolen from the room in which they are stored. Therefore, the room must be locked, and the personnel who are allowed access to the main computer room, or access to the main administrative terminals linking to the database must have a high level of security. The administrative terminals are those from which only certain operations, usually carried out by the DBA are allowed. You can compare this with *direct access* to a file server on a network, for example.

Preventing unauthorised access

This is the security which is used to **prevent illegal access** to the data by unauthorised users or hackers. This is normally under the control of the **database management system** and the system is set up by the **DBA**.

Some systems allow you to set several different levels of security and typical ones are shown in the following table.

Security type	Level	Typical situations
Highest	1	DBA only – access to all functions and data.
High	2	Access to all options except database administration.
Medium high	3	View, enter and delete all records, can define and run reports. Able to import and export data to other systems. Define, run and save reports.
Medium	4	View, enter and delete some records, can define and run some reports but not save them.
Medium low	5	Various levels of view security and write security depending on the job description of the user.
Low	6	As for 5, but with even lower priority.
Very low	7	View very low security records only, can't change any data, but may be able to run a few reports.

Although the security levels in the above table sound like the temperature settings on an oven, their use is quite simple. You are only able to do things to the data that has been allowed by your level of security. If for example, the **view security** of a **particular field** had a security rating of **medium**, then anyone with **medium**, **medium high**, **high** and **highest** security levels would be able to observe the data. The **medium low**, **low** and **very low** security people would not be able to see it. These levels of security are usually defined as the database is being created by the DBA.

Sensitive data may also be encrypted as described in chapter 9. If the key accompanying the data is long, then it's virtually impossible to crack the codes and read the data.

Every action such as **reading**, **updating** and **deletion** etc. can have *different* security levels assigned to them on data in a particular field. Therefore, you can usually specify which fields are visible or invisible to a particular user, and what type of access the user may have on each field. This information can then be used by the system in the form of a look-up table when the different users make requests. Databases have to have sophisticated levels of security as many different people can have access to the same database. You would not, for example, want the catering manager to have access to everybody's salary information. However, they may well have a high security level on a field, which relates to the restaurant bill for the month. The amount of money in this field might well be related to the salary field by showing up as a debit from the salary cheque. Don't forget that this is what good database design is all about, the ability to share the data, but each department has it's own view of the data and its own security permissions.

Disadvantages of using a database

We have already covered many of the possible disadvantages of using databases throughout this chapter. Even so, you must not loose sight of the biggest potential danger of all – **catastrophic failure**. This is the sort of failure that happens when a disk sector gets physically damaged and important data (possibly containing some of the important pointers etc.) is lost. Major contingency plans for recreating as much of the database as possible must be put into action. There must be an appropriate **emergency plan** that is worked out during the systems analysis phase. This must include how the business or organisation is to operate while the system is down. (i.e. while the hardware is being mended and the database is being restored). Suitable backup procedures such as those described in this chapter must obviously be carried out. Fatal errors *will always occur* and must be allowed for by good planning.

Database recovery

At some stage it's likely that a system will fail for a variety of reasons. This failure could occur in the middle of entering data into a database, and either the current transactions or larger parts of the database might become corrupted. It is usual for the **DBMS**, and indeed the **operating system** itself to keep files of information that can be used to re-establish the stable conditions that occurred just before the disaster happened. In this way it's possible for the loss of data to be absolutely minimal. In an ideal world, this would mean loss of only the last few transactions, which can easily be re-established manually when the system is up and running again.

One method, called a **checkpoint**, is to keep a copy of the computer's memory, which is periodically saved to disk. In addition to this, the contents of the processor's (or processors') registers (see chapter 20) can be saved on disk too. *If the system should fail, then this checkpoint method can be used to re-establish the exact conditions of the computer at the time of the last checkpoint.* The system could then be fixed, (which in the simplest case might involve only a re-start of the computer system), and the memory and hardware registers can be put back to what they were at the time of the last checkpoint. Processing can then continue, with the loss of only that data which has been entered between the last checkpoint and the system failure. On some systems a **transaction log** (see in a moment) could be used to help automatically recreate these transactions if necessary.

Sometimes the DBMS itself might be the cause of the fault, in which case the **transaction log** might be all that's needed to aid recovery. The transaction log is simply a record of the transactions, which have occurred, since the log was created. In the event of a disaster, all transactions in this log may be used to recreate the system almost up to the state at which the disaster occurred. The open transactions may be lost, because these would probably not have been written to the log due to the system crash. Obviously these systems are not intended to replace the backups that are made of the database at frequent intervals. Indeed, in the event of a total disk crash, the backup system may be all that's recoverable. The term **rollback** is used to denote the operation of returning to a stable condition after a disaster.

Data Protection Act 1998

Having read through this chapter, and in conjunction with chapters 3 and 5 on data communication systems, you should now be in a position to fully appreciate the consequences of storing information in computer systems. The potential for the misuse of such data is enormous. Computer crime (see chapter 9) can have some very tempting rewards for unscrupulous people, or, quite simply, genuine mistakes can be made. These are usually in the form of human error, or, when it's not possible to completely validate and verify the data entered into the system. It is, therefore, fitting to end one of the major database chapters with a brief look at an act of parliament that legislates for the conduct of people and organisations that hold personal data about individuals. This is called the **Data Protection Act** and was in **full force from late 1987**. However, it was revamped in 1998 and Schedule 1 and 2 of the Act are as follows.

SCHEDULE 1

THE DATA PROTECTION PRINCIPLES
PART I
THE PRINCIPLES

1. *Personal data should be processed fairly and lawfully and, in particular, shall not be processed unless–*
   (a) at least one of the conditions in Schedule 2 is met, and
   (b) in the case of sensitive personal data, at least one of the conditions in Schedule 3 is also met.
2. *Personal data shall be obtained only for one or more specified and lawful purposes, and shall not be further processed in any manner incompatible with that purpose or those purposes.*
3. *Personal data shall be adequate, relevant and not excessive in relation to the purpose or purposes for which they are processed.*
4. *Personal data shall be accurate and, where necessary, kept up to date.*
5. *Personal data processed for any purpose or purposes shall not be kept for longer than is necessary for that purpose or those purposes.*
6. *Personal data shall be processed in accordance with the rights of data subjects under this Act.*
7. *Appropriate technical and organisational measures shall be taken against unauthorised or unlawful processing of personal data and against accidental loss or destruction of, or damage to, personal data.*
8. *Personal data shall not be transferred to a country or territory outside the European Economic Area unless that country or territory ensures an adequate level of protection for the rights and freedoms of data subjects in relation to the processing of personal data.*

At the time of writing, point 8 is particularly contentious, as the USA does not have all appropriate EEC provisions in place! This makes commerce with the USA particularly interesting.

SCHEDULE 2
CONDITIONS RELEVANT FOR PURPOSES OF THE FIRST PRINCIPLE: PROCESSING OF ANY PERSONAL DATA

1. *The data subject has given his consent to the processing.*
2. *The processing is necessary–*
   (a) for the performance of a contract to which the data subject is a party, or
   (b) for the taking of steps at the request of the data subject with a view to entering into a contract.
3. *The processing is necessary for compliance with any legal obligation to which the data controller is subject, other than an obligation imposed by contract.*
4. *The processing is necessary in order to protect the vital interests of the data subject.*
5. *The processing is necessary–*
   (a) for the administration of justice,
   (b) for the exercise of any functions conferred on any person by or under any enactment,
   (c) for the exercise of any functions of the Crown, a Minister of the Crown or a government department, or
   (d) for the exercise of any other functions of a public nature exercised in the public interest by any person.
6. *(1) The processing is necessary for the purposes of legitimate interests pursued by the data controller or by the third party or third parties to whom the data are disclosed, except where the processing is unwarranted in any particular case by reason of prejudice to the rights and freedoms or legitimate interests of the data subject.*
   (2) The Secretary of State may by order specify particular circumstances in which this condition is, or is not, to be taken to be satisfied.

Schedule 3 and much other information on the Act can be found at http://www.hmso.gov.uk/acts/acts1998/80029--o.htm

The Computer Misuse Act

Another legal milestone was introduced when the **Computer Misuse Act** came into being in 1990. For the first time **hacking** and other such criminal activity became illegal. Before the advent of this particular act the only criminal offence being committed by someone who broke into a computer system was theft of electricity!

With the proliferation and use of the Internet, the opportunities for computer criminals multiply every day. The law is finding it increasingly difficult to keep pace with technological change, and we can expect more computer legislation in the future.

Exercise 28.1

1 What makes a **database** very much better than an unrelated collection of files holding information on a computer system?

2 What is a **flat-file** database?

3 Define the following terms in relation to a database:

(a) **DDL**

(b) **DML**

(c) **DBMS**

(d) **Data dictionary**

For each of the above, briefly describe the function it carries out within the database system.

4 Outline the role of a **DBA**.

5 Briefly outline the main stages which have to be undertaken when creating a simple database using a proprietary package.

6 What is the difference between a **QBE** and an **SQL** method of generating a query?

7 Suggest some validation checks which might be useful for the following data:

(a) The age of a pupil in school.

(b) A quarterly electricity bill for domestic users.

8 How is it possible to prevent unauthorised access to certain parts of the database without blocking key personnel?

9 Outline two rights which you have under the Data Protection Act of 1998.

End of chapter revision aid and summary

Cover up the right-hand column and see if you can answer the questions or define the terms on the left. They appear in the order in which they are covered in this chapter. Alternatively you may browse through the right-hand column to aid revision.

Define what is meant by a database.	A database is a collection of related information, organised such that efficient data processing may be carried out on the data contained in it. It's possible to arrange a centralised database so that each department in an office or factory etc. has its own specific view of the data contained in a large database. Large databases form the hub of many companies, with the information contained within the database vital for many different aspects of the business.
What is meant by a DBMS?	A DBMS is a DataBase Management System. A DBMS is a very powerful piece of software, which helps to design, build and maintain a database.
What is a flat-file database?	A flat-file database is one that can operate on one file only. Compare with a database that can operate on many files, e.g. a fully relational database (see chapter 29).
Describe what is meant by a schema.	A schema is the name given to the logical definition of a database.
What is a subschema?	A subschema defines a specific sub-section of database that a particular program, for example, might use.

What is a DDL?

A DDL or data description language is used for describing data and the relationships between data in a database, e.g. field descriptions or file locations etc.

What is a DML?

A DML or data manipulation language is used for manipulating data within a database, e.g. updating, deleting, or creating etc.

What is a data dictionary?

The data dictionary contains data about the 'data in the database'.

What does the file manager do?

The file manager is part of the OS, which helps to map the logical file structures onto the physical storage devices.

Who is the DBA?

The DBA is the DataBase Administrator. This is the person who is responsible for the design, implementation and maintenance of the database. (Note: not usually the same as the people who enter the actual data!)

What is an SQL?

An SQL is a structured query language – this enables queries to be carried out efficiently by writing simple or complex programs.

What is meant by QBE?

QBE, or query by example is an alternative to SQL.

How is a database usually constructed?

Databases are created by using specialist applications packages, and information can be extracted from a database by means of a query.

What is a relational operator?

A relational operator is used to help specify queries in a database. The relational operators are : $<$, $\leq$, $<>$, and $\geq$ etc.

What is a set operator?

The set operators OR, AND and NOT also help to define database queries.

What is a transaction log?

A transaction log is a file of recent transactions that is kept by the system as an aid in the event of a disaster. It can also be used to build up an audit trail.

What is a checkpoint?

A checkpoint is a file, kept by a system such as a DBMS or the operating system, which holds information about the state of a computer such as the memory and registers, for example. It is used in the event of a system crash to aid recovery.

What is rollback?

This is the term used to describe the process of disaster recovery. It is when you rollback to a previously stable version of the system after repairing the system.

What is the Data Protection Act of 1998?

The Data Protection Act 1998 is an Act of Parliament that protects people from harm due to misuse of data held about them in a computer system. For the first time, similar systems are in operation throughout the whole of the EU.

29 Further Databases

In this chapter you'll learn about:

- Modelling data
- Hierarchical and network databases
- Relational databases
- First, second and third normal forms

Key resources

To carry out this work most successfully it's best if you have:

- Access to a relational database like Microsoft's Access, for example

Concept checkpoints

- It's essential that you read chapter 28 where the basic ideas of databases are covered.
- An appreciation of the material covered in chapters 22 and 23 on operating systems, and chapters 26 and 27 on file handling would be useful. A knowledge of chapters 24 and 25 is needed here too.

Introduction

This second database chapter will look at the fundamental principles on which database design is built. We will look at typical database models, but concentrate most on the RDBMS (Relational DataBase Management System) model. We will also show how normalisation can make a big difference to the efficiency with which the data in a relational database can be stored and handled. Before starting this chapter you should realise that some of the technical details appropriate to many parts are covered in other chapters such as file handling and data structures. It is not recommended that you read this chapter before becoming familiar with these other basic concepts. We will start by having a look at the logical data structures on which a database depends, and at the theoretical models, which describe how the data within the database are related at a fundamental level. These models show how data is linked or related to other data inside the database. Most of the structures can be expressed in the form of diagrams, although the relational databases make use of tables, and some databases may use a combination of several of these techniques. First let's look at modelling the basic data.

Modelling data

An often-used term in database design is the relationship. The idea behind a relationship is exactly the same as the **mathematical relationships** you may have covered in your elementary mathematics courses – but if you've forgotten, or did not cover them in the first place, the ideas are very simple and are summarised in, figure 29.1. In database theory, this relationship is often described as a **link**, a **dependency** or some sort of **association** between two **entities** – all these terms are defined very shortly.

When considering the different database models, the ideas connected with **relationships** will crop up quite often, as the association between different data items is fundamentally important. An understanding of the above **relationships** will help considerably, especially when trying to explain why things can or can't be accomplished easily when a particular database model is being used. This will help you choose which particular model might be most appropriate in different situations.

When undertaking **database design**, any 'concrete or abstract occurrence' represented within the database is usually called an **entity**. In the database at your school or college, for example, **you** would be regarded as an **entity** because you are important from the school's point of view – you are effectively a 'customer' and the 'product' you're receiving is hopefully a good education. With most of the work undertaken at this level, an **entity** can be regarded as being the same as a **record**. Therefore, your record within the school or college database uniquely defines you in terms of the information which the school or college is holding. We can then go on to give any entity **named attributes** – and simplifying matters again, these attributes which together constitute the **entity** can be regarded as being the same as the **fields** within a **record**.

Sometimes it's not possible to have one entity without the existence of another. For example, in a **tree data structure** it's **not possible** to have a **child** without a **parent**. In a database, for example, it would probably not be sensible to have an 'order' in existence without a 'customer', and this sort of constraint can be built in at the database-design stage. This particular data relationship is called **dependency**, and defines a relationship in which the existence of one entity is entirely dependent on the existence of another. Specifically this sort of dependency is an important consequence of data being modelled with the **one-to-one** and **one-to-many relationships**, which can be confirmed by looking at the top half of figure 29.1. Take away any entity on the left of these diagrams, and the ones mapped from it on the right hand side cease to exist. The main things of importance when dealing with relationships are the **direction** of the **relationship**, as shown in figure 29.1, and the **associations** (i.e. the **types of connections** between the entities such as **one-to-one** or **many-to-one** etc.) of the relationship which are also shown in 29.1.

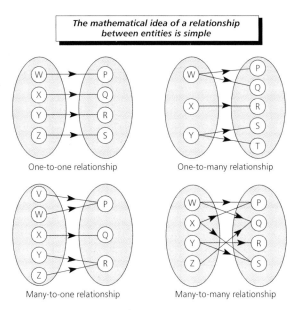

The mathematical idea of a relationship between entities is simple

One-to-one relationship

One-to-many relationship

Many-to-one relationship

Many-to-many relationship

Figure 29.1

We can show all the **relationships** mentioned in the last section, and the **entities** and **attributes** just introduced on special diagrams. There are several different types of these diagrams in existence, but some simple ones are shown in figure 29.2. Here you can see the **relationships** and **dependencies** between the **database entities** 'Component', 'Order' and 'Customer' for

a typical component supplier. Figure 29.2(a) shows a diagram in which the **entity dependencies** are outlined, and figure 29.2(b) shows two simplified **entity relationship** or **ER** diagrams.

If the entities in figure 29.2(b) were expanded to show the format of the information contained within, then the attributes could also be shown.

In figure 29.2(a) the **relationship** between the component and order is **many-to-many** because a single order can include a large number of components, or a single component may be included on a large number of orders. The path between order and customer, however, is a **many-to-one relationship**, because one customer may have many orders, but a single order obviously can't have many customers. Diagrams such as these often help to clarify the relationships between entities. In figure 29.2(b), the relationship 'consists of' is a many-to-one type as an order may consist of many components, but a component can't consist of many orders. Most of the diagrammatic representations are common sense, but you do have to think *very carefully* about the **entities**, **relationships** and **attributes** to draw them properly. Indeed, *this is the whole point of using them* – not to explain the obvious, but to map out how data is related in some detail, especially in terms of the direction of the mapping.

The basic database models

A **database model** is simply a model of the various ways in which the data within a database may be **structured**, i.e. the **logical structure** and *not* the way that it is stored on any particular storage medium. (Don't forget that the way that the data is actually stored is referred to as the **physical structure**, and this is covered in chapter 12.) You have already covered many **data structures** in chapters 24 and 25, and understanding the work in chapter 25 means that you are already well on the way to an understanding of all the database models.

In chapter 24 we looked in detail at **linear lists, linked lists, stacks** and **arrays** etc. and you should, therefore, know that **logical data structures** such as these enable **pointers** (or **links**) to be maintained such that the information stored can be navigated quickly, and the data processed efficiently. You should also note that the term **data model** need not apply just to databases, but to any **formally defined structure** which represents data, usually at the logical level.

> **Hint:** In chapter 28 we made a point of stressing how simple it is for the novice to design a sophisticated database application. In this chapter, you will learn some of the more advanced theory, which supports the view that you need to be an expert to undertake good database design.

Although there are others, the three main types of **database models** to be covered at this level are as follows:

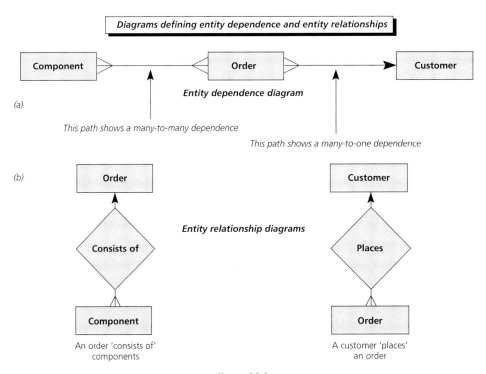

Diagrams defining entity dependence and entity relationships

(a)

Component ▷———◁ Order ▷————▶ Customer

Entity dependence diagram

This path shows a many-to-many dependence

This path shows a many-to-one dependence

(b)

Order

Entity relationship diagrams

Consists of

Component

An order 'consists of' components

Customer

Places

Order

A customer 'places' an order

Figure 29.2

- **Hierarchical database model**
- **Network database model**
- **Relational database model**

Traditionally, the **hierarchical** and **network data models** allowed for very fast, but more limited access to data contained within the database. They were ideal for specific queries of the sort that were carried out most often. These impressive speeds were, therefore, ideal for on-line transactions where certain information is needed quickly from a vast amount of data. On the other hand, the **relational database** was good at dealing with the *ad hoc* query, but was quite slow in comparison with the other two models.

On microcomputers, the most extensively used of the above three models is the **relational database**; however, the much faster **hierarchical** and **network databases** found on many mini and mainframe computers also allow some powerful **relational capabilities**. As is usual in computer science, much development goes on, and the rules get changed to a certain extent. More recently, the versatility and power of a relational database has been brought to mainframes with a vengeance. The latest relational databases for some of the largest mainframes are approaching the speed of the fastest hierarchical and network database models. As the techniques get refined over the next few years, these relational-database speeds are likely to be in excess of those for the other techniques. It seems, therefore, that in the foreseeable future, **very high speed, powerful relational databases** will rule, from the humble micro, up to and including the largest mainframes and super-

computers. Powerful companies such as IBM and Microsoft have also put their full weight behind such projects to ensure that this will be so! We will now look at each model in detail.

An example structure

A very simple generalised data structure will help to give an instant impression of the data structure used for each model. However, to make life easier, after introducing the concepts, we will use just **one small data set** to illustrate how the **three different database models** can be visualised and therefore compared. The data for this simple model will consist of the surnames, first names and towns of people who have accounts in a small building society. An alphabetical list of just a few of the account holders is shown in Table 29.1. As you can see, some customers have more than one account, and Kevin Mills from Croydon has actually got three! In fact, one of Mills' accounts is a joint-business account,

> **Hint:** Together with the work covered in the data structures and file handling chapters, this work on database structures completes your knowledge of data structures at this level. You should now be able to model most of the data that you will normally encounter.

which he shares with Sindy Norton, who is a co-director in the Mills & Norton Company. Look out for how these aspects of the data set are handled when using the different database models.

Table 29.1 Data to be used for a comparison of database-modelling methods

Surname	First name	Town	Account Number	Balance (£)	Interest (£)
Desmond	Carol	Tonbridge	0135	1,500.67	120.53
Lewis	Sheila	Brighton	0267	1.75	0.14
Lewis	Sheila	Brighton	0078	160.34	12.82
Mills	Kevin	Croydon	1016	12,786.00	1,022.88
Mills	Kevin	Croydon	1143	9,430.45	754.44
Mills	Kevin	Croydon	1209	172	13.76
Norton	Sindy	Bromley	1016	12,786.00	1,022.88
Manning	Brian	Chatham	1782	16,897.21	1,351.77

The data contained in table 29.1 can be handled in a variety of ways, but let's suppose, for the sake of argument, that we wish to split up the information in the above table into **two different entities**. These two entities are a **personal-information entity** with attributes 'Surname', 'First name' and 'Town', and an **account-information entity** being made up of the attributes 'Account number', 'Balance' and 'Interest'. A simple dependence diagram for this structure is shown in figure 29.3. In the next few sections we will concentrate on the three main models outlined earlier. Don't forget that one of the requirements is to compare and contrast these models as you are progressing through the work.

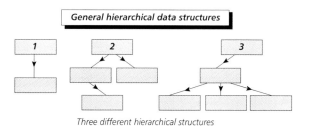

General hierarchical data structures

Three different hierarchical structures

Figure 29.4

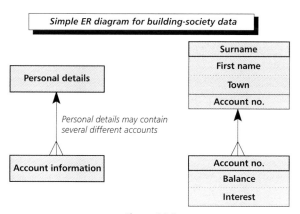

Simple ER diagram for building-society data

Personal details

Personal details may contain several different accounts

Account information

| Surname |
| First name |
| Town |
| Account no. |

| Account no. |
| Balance |
| Interest |

Figure 29.3

You should be very familiar with these types of data structures – they're identical to that of the **tree structures** covered in chapter 25, and the hierarchical structure making use of the building-society table is shown in figure 29.5. All these structures mirror the **parent-child** or **superior-subordinate** relationships that are typical of those found in a family tree. The **nodes** in the building-society structure correspond to particular instances of **entities** in the hierarchical database, and the sub-sections of a node, such as 'surname', 'first name' and 'town' etc. correspond to examples of particular **attributes** – in this case attributes for the personal-details entities.

> **Hint:** Most databases you will encounter on the micros that you have at school will be of the relational variety. Even if they don't have full relational update facilities, it's almost certain that they will store the data in the form of tables which you will see later on in this chapter.

The hierarchical database model is ideal for modelling the **one-to-many relationships** between **entities** found naturally in many organisations, and it's obviously ideal for **one-to-one relationships too** – which are just a special case of the one-to-many relationships. Another example already established is considered when storing all the parts that go into the making of a car. The root node could be the car itself, which could then be split up into further sub-systems consisting of engine, gearbox and body etc. The body could then be

The hierarchical database model

The logical structure of a **hierarchical database** is, not surprisingly, based on a **hierarchical data structure** (see chapter 25), and typical general examples can be seen in figure 29.4.

further split up into doors, bonnet and boot etc. This diagram is shown in figure 25.8 where **hierarchical data structures** were considered in detail. You may be surprised at how many real-life data structures can be modelled hierarchically, and the speed with which data can be found is remarkably fast. You should notice also that, for a hierarchical data structure, *each entity can only have one owner*, therefore, other types of relationship can't be modelled using a hierarchical database. Note too that the **hierarchical data structure** is just a **particular case** of the more **general network data structure** to be considered in the next section.

A **hierarchical database model** would be a database that has been set up based on a **hierarchical data structure**. **Links** or **pointers** would be established in the ways already covered in chapter 25, which enable *very fast* searches and processing of data items based on these naturally occurring structures. A typical example of a hierarchical database system is **IMS/VS** – the Information **M**anagement **S**ystem / **V**irtual **S**torage database found on many IBM mainframes. However, better facilities are offered with the later version **IMS/R**, the **relational** version of IMS.

Advantages and disadvantages

When choosing a particular database model, the designer must always be aware of the limitations imposed on the users by the structure which he or she has chosen. For example, if a database is implemented making use of a hierarchical database model, and if a parent within the structure is deleted, all the children are deleted too. This may be an advantage, in which case this particular operation is efficient and very quick, or it may be a disadvantage, in which case some other database model should have been chosen to represent the data more realistically. In a similar way, we can't add a record to a hierarchical database that has no parent. This may not be an inconvenience, or it may be a disaster. More specifically, when representing the building-society data, the shared account between Mills and Norton is represented as two separate nodes – this will cause potential problems when updating balance etc. It's up to the database designer to make sure that he or she knows what the future requirements will be, and this is usually determined by extensive **systems analysis**. Later we will see how different database models might be able to cope with these problems.

The network database model

You should note that, in this chapter, this refers to the '**logical structure of the database**' and *not* to the use of a database over a computer network. (The use of networks is covered elsewhere, and the use of **any type** of database over a network presents additional problems due to **multi-user access**.) So, not forgetting that a network database model has nothing to do with

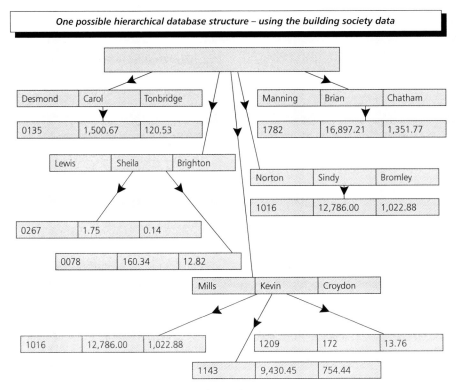

Figure 29.5

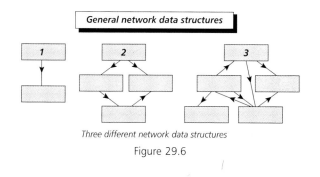

General network data structures

Three different network data structures

Figure 29.6

physical networks, figure 29.6 shows some generalised network structures.

Any **record** or **node** in a **network structure** can be accessed from starting at the **root node**. However, there is usually a much more complex **pointer** (**link**) system to maintain than was the case when using the simpler hierarchical data structure. Note that unlike a hierarchical data structure, when using a **network data structure**, a record *can have* **multiple owners**, except, of course, for the root record.

This is a little like the *impossible situation* where a child node can have many parent nodes, but it's much more sensible to think of it as a supplier-customer relation. For example, one supplier may have three or four customers, but it's also possible for a customer (one of the child nodes of the original supplier), to be a supplier to other customers *including* the one which originally supplied them. This scenario would be impossible to express as efficiently with a hierarchical data structure. Note also that there may well be alternative routes to get to some data items.

Making use of a network data structure to model the building-society data shown earlier, this particular network data structure is shown in figure 29.7.

Hierarchical database models are ideal for **one-to-many** and **many-to-many relationships** between the different **entities** held in the database. In both **network** and **hierarchical databases**, records in one file may **point** to the locations of records in other files.

A set of standards was set up for **network databases** by CODASYL. This is an acronym for the **COnference on DAta Systems Languages** – an American organisation made up from interested parties, which originally developed **COBOL**. CODASYL defined extensions to **COBOL's DATA division** (see chapter 15), so that it's possible to set up records which are related by **links**. This means that you can **sequentially access non-sequential** information very quickly by following the pointers. The DBTG (DataBase Task Group) of CODASYL has also brought out new proposals in the last couple of years.

Examples of network databases are **DBOMP**, the **DataBase Organisation and Maintenance Processor** and **IDMS**, the **Integrated Data Management System**. Both of these systems operate on **mainframe** computer systems.

Advantages and disadvantages

As with the hierarchical database model, all the relationships between the entities must be defined at the time the database is designed. Also, there are one or two extra complications, involving the maintenance of the database. For example, with a hierarchical database, if a record is deleted which involved pointers to others records, then these records too would also be deleted. However, with a network database model, pointers can go to other records, which may not need to be deleted. Therefore, the maintenance arrangements are complicated by the more-complex data structures involved.

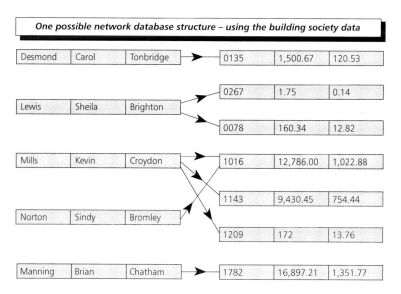

One possible network database structure – using the building society data

| Desmond | Carol | Tonbridge | 0135 | 1,500.67 | 120.53 |

| Lewis | Sheila | Brighton | 0267 | 1.75 | 0.14 |
| | | | 0078 | 160.34 | 12.82 |

Mills	Kevin	Croydon	1016	12,786.00	1,022.88
			1143	9,430.45	754.44
Norton	Sindy	Bromley	1209	172	13.76

| Manning | Brian | Chatham | 1782 | 16,897.21 | 1,351.77 |

Figure 29.7

The relational database model

Due to the primary importance and popularity of the relational database, we will be looking in much more detail at this particular system. Even though the network and hierarchical database models are still used, at some time in the future it's most likely that all database models will be relational – at least until somebody comes up with a better idea.

The relational database is unusual in so far as it's not a structure based on the idea of a structure diagram together with a suitable pointer system, and therefore we can't possibly show some generalised relational-database structures as we did with the other two models. However, it's interesting to note that whatever database structure is used, it will eventually have to be mapped onto a conventional file structure (see chapters 26 and 27) so that it can be stored on a suitable secondary storage medium. We will now go straight into a specific relational database example using the building society data shown earlier. One possible layout of this data is shown in table 29.2.

As you can see, in this case we have a collection of two tables, which match the ways in which the data was originally split up in figure 29.3. The organisation of the database in this sort of way is known as a schema, and the above schema, although chosen by a common-sense method, is not a particularly good one! The reasons for this will soon become obvious – but first let's introduce some new terminology.

Each table is made up of rows and columns that represent a special idea called a relation. Using terms that have been previously defined in this chapter, a relation is, therefore, a set of entities that have the same attributes. Each entity in the 'Personal table', for example, has the same attributes 'Surname', 'First name', 'Town' and 'Acc. no.' as described by the column headings in the table. It's usual to make the connection between these tables and the records, fields and files with which we are all more familiar (see chapters 26 and 27). Each entity in a table usually corresponds to a record in a file, and each attribute, being a subsection of a record, must therefore correspond to a field. Finally, the relation or table itself usually corresponds to a file. In a relational database, relations are now defined in terms of these special two-dimensional tables, or, putting it simply, a table is literally a relation. You should note at this stage that the term 'relation' as defined here should not be confused with the term 'relationship', as used in many other contexts throughout this chapter.

Each column must have a unique name like 'Surname', and 'Town', for example, just like fields in a record must also have a unique name. Nevertheless, column names can be used again in other tables, and this will prove essential when we need to establish links between the different tables a little later. It's important to realise that the order in which the entities are entered into the tables is of no consequence whatsoever. Whenever we need to establish a new set of data from a relational database, a brand-new table is produced by the relational-database system, which matches the new requirements. In other words a new file of information is produced each time.

Don't forget that we used some ordinary common sense to arrange the two tables. However, in the relation which we have called 'Personal', we have implied that 'Surname' is important, because that's the principle way by which each entity within 'Personal' is intended to be identified. 'Surname' is therefore called the primary key for 'Personal', and, by a similar argument, 'Account number' would be the primary key for 'Account'. Nevertheless, there is a major problem here – a primary key is intended to be a unique identification for a particular record, entity or row. It should, therefore, act as a unique identifier for each row of information within a table. In practice, surname would

Table 29.2 One possible relational database structure – using the building society data

Surname	First name	Town	Account Number	Account Number	Balance (£)	Interest (£)
Desmond	Carol	Tonbridge	0135	0135	1,500.67	120.53
Lewis	Sheila	Brighton	0267	0267	1.75	0.14
Lewis	Sheila	Brighton	0078	0078	160.34	12.82
Mills	Kevin	Croydon	1016	1016	12,786.00	1,022.88
Mills	Kevin	Croydon	1143	1143	9,430.45	754.44
Mills	Kevin	Croydon	1209	1209	172	13.76
Norton	Sindy	Bromley	1016	1016	12,786.00	1,022.88
Manning	Brian	Chatham	1782	1782	16,897.21	1,351.77

'Personal' relational table   'Account' relational table

not be sufficient because it's probably not going to be unique. It would usually be far better to use account number – but, as the more astute readers will have seen, for joint accounts this is not unique either! Oh dear! Problems like this are sometimes a little awkward to sort out, and a more-efficient arrangement of the tables will be needed to solve them. This process of efficient arrangement of the tables is called **normalisation**, and is explained in detail later. For the moment we will ignore these potential pitfalls, and carry on working with unnormalised data for the purposes of introducing the rest of the terminology.

A **shorthand notation** has been developed for representing these tables by making use of the attribute names in a simple list. Using this shorthand notation, the **primary key** is indicated by underlining the appropriate attribute. The shorthand notation for the relation called 'Personal', for example, would therefore be as follows:

Personal (<u>Surname</u>, First name, Town, Account number)

As you can see from the above, each attribute (column heading) is contained in a named list, separated by commas, with the primary key underlined and the name of the relation (table) to the left of the brackets. The **primary key** does not have to be the first column in the table as the order does not matter. Using the same techniques, the shorthand notation for the relation called 'Account' would be represented as follows:

Account (<u>Account number</u>, Balance, Interest)

These and many other **ideas** for the **relational database** were first proposed by Edgar Codd back in the 1970s. His ideas put database systems on a sound theoretical basis, which has also had spin offs in other computer-science fields such as **artificial intelligence** (**AI**) and **natural language analysis**. Codd was a mathematician who worked for IBM, and it's therefore not surprising that some modern-mathematical ideas have come over in his **relational database models**. For example, Codd called a **row** from a **table** a **tuple**! – and this is the term which is often used today – in fact it's the preferred term in more advanced computer-science courses. It's used in preference to the word 'row', which may or may not be anything to do with a relation. If you are wondering why the strange name 'tuple' is used, then reading the next section on 'tuples' will help to explain. If you're not curious you may skip over the next section!

Tuples

In this chapter we have defined a **relation** as being represented by a **2D-table** – this is, in fact, **exactly the same** as the definition of a **relation** using more formal mathematical theory – minus the very complex set-theory terminology that would be used to back up these ideas. Consider the following.

You should all be familiar with the idea of a set – for example, the 'set of hex digits' consists of 0 to F inclusive, and the 'set of months' would consist of January to December inclusive. Therefore, making use of some typical abbreviations, we can write out these sets as follows:

```
Hex digits =
       {0,1,2,3,4,5,6,7,8,9,A,B,C,D,E,F}

Months = {Jan, Feb, Mar, Apr, May, Jun,
       Jul, Aug, Sep, Oct, Nov, Dec}
```

Relating this to our database theory, the **entity** months, for example, can have any of the **attribute values** listed in the above set. No problems so far! The more rigorous mathematical definition of a relation also takes into account the **range of possible values** that each **attribute** may have, and this is obviously useful for database systems too. In mathematics 'sets of permitted values', like those shown in the above examples, are called **domains**. We can easily denote a domain by a single letter, therefore, D_M might represent the domain of months, or D_H might be used to represent the domain of hex digits.

You have all done enough computer science to realise that **domains** and **sets** are **very important concepts** and exhibit strong connections with database ideas. For example, using the building-society data from the tables in figure 29.9, we could denote the domain of 'all possible Surnames' as D_S, the domain of 'all possible First names' as D_F, 'all possible Towns' as D_T and 'all possible Account numbers' as D_A. Mathematically, we can express the relation 'Personal' as being a **subset** of

$$D_S \ x \ D_F \ x \ D_T \ x \ D_A$$

which defines **all possible values** for each of the rows that we can have in the relation we call 'personal'. The 'x' sign in the above domain does **not** mean multiplication, but is called a Cartesian product, and is from a branch of mathematics called relational algebra. A **Cartesian product** means the set of all ordered pairs, and the following example will make this concept quite clear.

> **Hint:** When studying computing beyond this level, there is much to learn in terms of new mathematics such as that being considered here. You should make sure that you like such topics and are completely at ease with other topics like the lexical analysis covered in chapter 32 before you commit yourself to studying the subject at this level.

If A = {Tom, Dick, Harry} and B = {1,2} then the Cartesian product, A x B would be the set of all possible values of ordered pairs that each two-attribute row may take on.

```
A x B = {(Tom,1), (Tom,2), (Dick,1),
    (Dick,2), (Harry,1), (Harry,2)}
```

We obviously could not have all possible combinations occurring in practice, or else unrelated people would be allowed, for example, to have the same bank account number! This is why the phrase 'subset of' was used when we mathematically defined 'personal' a moment ago.

If we take a particular 'row' at random from the relation called personal, such as

```
(Norton, Sindy, Bromley, 1016)
```

for example. Then we can represent this, or any other 'row' more generally as

$$(X_S, X_F, X_T, X_A).$$

Codd called this a 4-tuple, because an 'n-tuple' is the correct mathematical term for a row, consisting of n attributes, extracted from a relation defined in terms of the Cartesian products of the individual domains as described above. However, the term 'tuple' is now generally used in preference to the term 'n-tuple'. Furthermore, X_S means that this particular attribute belongs to domain D_S, and X_F belongs to the domain D_F etc.

Now you are probably thinking that all this mathematical theory is an awfully long-winded way of expressing the obvious. Nevertheless, you are possibly not aware of the fact that there are branches of mathematics called 'tuple relational calculus', and 'relational algebra', which take relational-database theory far beyond that which we have outlined here. In fact, these important mathematical theories form most of the groundwork on which many relational database ideas depend, including the powerful relational queries, normalisation (see next section) and most other things which we will take for granted throughout the remainder of this chapter.

Relational databases are very powerful because they are formed on the basis of a very sound mathematical reasoning. Codd's mathematical theories of relational-database systems have built up some extremely potent ideas, which, in recent years, have ensured that virtually the entire database market has moved towards his ideas of relational database models. The hierarchical and network databases considered earlier have no mathematical footing – they have been built up from *ad hoc* and heuristic techniques. Another area of computing in desperate need of the full mathematical treatment is 'determination of absolute correctness of algorithms' – but this has yet to be developed, but see the next best thing when white-box testing is explained at the end of chapter 17. Relational calculus and relational algebra are the theories, which gave the relational database its name – and you now know why the term tuple is used!

Normalisation

In 1970, Edgar Codd defined certain **constraints** (i.e. defined certain limits and conventions) that **relations**

Did you know that . . .

Access provides many aspects of normalisation. For example, if you have unnormalised data in your tables, running the normalisation wizard will split up the tables so that the data is stored more efficiently. This is a real bonus for the relatively inexperienced user.

---

in a **relational database** should obey. If a database conforms to these constraints then it is said to be **normalised**, or is in **normal form**. **Normalisation** is a way of ensuring that the data is processed more efficiently in a relational database, and any *ad hoc* query can be processed.

Normalisation simplifies the relational tables by reducing the relations to their simplest forms, and therefore making these relational tables easier to handle. Only one table in the database should represent each entity, but the problems are usually associated with deciding which entities to use, and what attributes each entity should have. After normalisation, maintenance of the database should be less hassle, and queries (see later) should be able to be carried out more quickly. It should also eliminate the need to restructure the entire database when new and unexpected demands are made of the system, and should preserve relations when any changes are made. For example, in this chapter we have already seen how it might **not be possible** to represent a relationship between different data items easily – if at all, and we have also seen how **deleting** some items of data may cause others to be **unintentionally** deleted too.

There are **five normal forms** (plus lots of others too!), although **not all of them are commonly used**, and only the first **three** are of any importance to many systems analysts. However, for the purposes of work at this level, you need only to be able to appreciate that there are **three major stages of normalisation**, and be able to carry out these important processes on simple tables **in the right order**.

An example

A new data set, more suited to those of you who like eating, will be used to show the processes of normalisation, and this is outlined in figure 29.10. This data refers to the orders for delivery of cakes and pies etc. for a local baker. The local baker has been carrying out these processes for years, but now wishes to computerise the system. Figure 29.10 is typical of the sort of information, which may be given to the delivery person and held in the baker's computer system. However, in its current form, it's not arranged in ways which allow for efficient processing by using a relational database. It has not yet been normalised to conform to Codd's set of rules.

Table 29.3 Data to be used for carrying out the normalisation processes

Order no.	Acc. no.	Customer	Address	Date	Item	Quantity	Item price	Total cost
7823	178	Dick's Cafe	27 Nights Close, Tonbridge	16/7	Bakewell Tart	20	0.15	12.35
					Danish Pastry	13	0.20	
					Apple Pie	45	0.15	
4633	562	Harpers	12 The Drive, Tunbridge Wells	16/7	Danish Pastry	120	0.20	24.00
2276	167	Pie Crust	3a High Street, Maidstone	17/7	Apple Pie	130	0.15	56.50
					Cherry Pie	100	0.18	
					Steak Pie	30	0.50	
					Danish Pastry	20	0.20	
1788	032	Sloggers	17 Maple Avenue, Maidstone	18/7	Apple Pie	15	0.15	12.25
					Danish Pastry	50	0.20	
7120	289	Dibble & Son	The Pound, Tonbridge	18/7	Apple Pie	20	0.15	7.50
					Chocolate Log	3	1.50	

Don't misunderstand what's happening here – we're not trying to tell the delivery person that they must have the data in a different form to that which they find useful. In fact we can easily print out the data in **any** form, including the form shown in table 29.3 if this is desired. We are simply restructuring the data for efficient computer analysis in terms of storage, updating and processing the information.

First normal form

The first stage of **normalisation** is to make sure that any **attributes** (fields) with **multiple** (or repeating) **values** are removed so that the **records (entities or rows)** are **all the same length**.

Fixed-length records (see chapter 27) are far easier to deal with than variable-length ones – the results of queries, for example, will be obtained much more quickly if the computer system does not have to look and see where a particular record ends. To remove a repeating group is quite simple – we first identify it (or them), then eliminate the repetition by putting this group (or groups) in an **alternative relation** (table).

As an example, carefully consider the baker's data in table 29.3. Looking at the first entity for order number 7823, we can see that the 'Item', 'Quantity' and 'Item-price' attributes **all** contain multiple-value entries. So what! – the three different types of cakes ordered by Dick don't seem to be causing too much harm – but what if

> **Hint:** Putting data into normal form is simply another way of structuring the data so that it is stored more efficiently, maintained more easily and avoids unnecessary redundancy.

Dick's cafe wanted 103 different items? Would the 'item attribute' (don't forget that it's only a single field in a record!) be able to cope? I doubt it. We need to alter this **relation** so that all **records (entities)** are **of the same length**, and the only possible way to do this is to remove the offending data from the original table and put it somewhere else. Harper's looks OK at the moment, as

there's only a single item, but it's still a problem because tomorrow it might contain repeating values like all the others.

Where do we put all the data that has been removed? We invent a further relation, which relates the 'order number' to the cakes that have been purchased. This new relation will be made up from the offending parts of the original table. The results of these operations can now be expressed as two separate tables, and these two **relations**, which are given the names '**orders**' and '**items purchased**', are shown in table 29.4 – they are now said to be in **first normal form**. Alternatives are available in which repeating groups can be catered for, and some advanced relational databases allow attributes to specify relations themselves! This means that a single attribute can refer to a whole table, and this is ideal for the emerging **object-oriented relational databases**. It's important to note that there must be some sort of link between these two tables, and this is shown by the 'Order number' attributes being repeated in each table. If this linking is not done then the **tables** would **not** be **related** to each other.

The **shorthand notation** for these two tables in **first normal form** is as follows.

> **Orders (Order no., Acc no., Customer, Address, Date, Total cost)**
>
> **Items purchased (Order no., Item, Quantity, Item price)**

Second normal form

As this process is carried out **after** the first normal form, this obviously assumes that you have got your data into the first normal form before you start! So, in addition to this requirement, the second normal form states that all the **attributes** in an **entity** must be **functionally dependent** (have a **unique association**) with the primary key for the purposes of identification.

This posh term **functional dependency** means that there must be **only** a **one-to-one dependency** (see

Table 29.4 First normal form for the bakery data

Relational table for orders

Order no.	Acc. no.	Customer	Address	Date	Total Cost
7823	178	Dick's Cafe	27 Nights Close, Tonbridge	16/7	12.35
4633	562	Harpers	12 The Drive, Tunbridge Wells	16/7	24.00
2276	167	Pie Crust	3a High Street, Maidstone	17/7	56.50
1788	032	Sloggers	17 Maple Avenue, Maidstone	18/7	12.25
7120	289	Dibble & Son	The Pound, Tonbridge	18/7	7.50

Note: These two colums show relational information

Relational table for items purchased

Order no.	Item	Quantity	Item price
7823	Bakewell Tart	20	0.15
7823	Danish Pastry	13	0.20
7823	Apple Pie	45	0.15
4633	Danish Pastry	120	0.20
2276	Apple Pie	130	0.15
2276	Cherry Pie	100	0.18
2276	Steak Pie	30	0.50
2276	Danish Pastry	20	0.20
1788	Apple Pie	15	0.15
1788	Danish Pastry	50	0.20
7120	Apple Pie	20	0.15
7120	Chocolate Log	3	1.50

earlier) for **each attribute** mapped **from** the **primary key to the attribute**. In other words, **just making use of the primary key must uniquely identify each attribute** – if this is not the case, then it's not in second normal form. Therefore, to test for **functional dependency**, we have to test each particular attribute in turn, and check that only a one-to-one dependency exists with respect to the **primary key**. If, for example, we have a **primary key** of '**order number**', then we know that **each order number is uniquely associated with just one 'total cost'**. You can't have several different total costs in an order! **Don't think about this the wrong way round** and try and associate a **total cost** with an **order number**. Many different orders may have the same total cost. Get this vital one-to-one dependency the wrong way round and you will become very confused indeed – you will begin to think that the desired functional dependency does not exist!

This whole idea sounds awfully complex, but let's look at another example. Consider the first-normal-form data for the bakery at the top of table 29.4, and examine the **relationship** between the **primary key** we called '**order number**' and '**Dick's cafe**' as a specific example of the attribute '**Customer**'. We now proceed along the following lines. An entity-dependence diagram between 'order number' and 'customer' is shown in figure 29.8(a) – because 'Dick's cafe' is able to place many orders, the customer name does obviously **not** have a unique association with order number. Therefore, the one-to-one dependency (the condition for being **functionally dependent**) has **not been satisfied** for this particular attribute at least, and the data in the relational

table for 'Orders' is, therefore, **not yet** in **second normal form**.

Changes must therefore be made, and we can, in this particular case, change the **primary key** from '**Order number**' to '**Account number**'. Now the **customer is uniquely associated** with an **account number**, and figure 29.8(b) demonstrates this functional dependency. Therefore, *if* we invent a new relation called 'Customers', the required functional dependency can be achieved by extracting the 'Account number', 'Customer name' and 'Address' from the original relational table

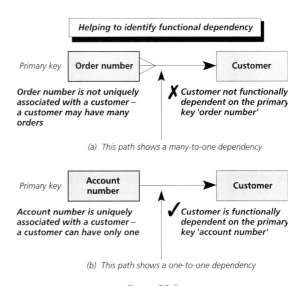

Helping to identify functional dependency

Primary key | **Order number** ⟶ **Customer**

Order number is not uniquely associated with a customer – a customer may have many orders

✗ Customer not functionally dependent on the primary key 'order number'

(a) This path shows a many-to-one dependency

Primary key | **Account number** ⟶ **Customer**

Account number is uniquely associated with a customer – a customer can have only one

✓ Customer is functionally dependent on the primary key 'account number'

(b) This path shows a one-to-one dependency

Figure 29.8

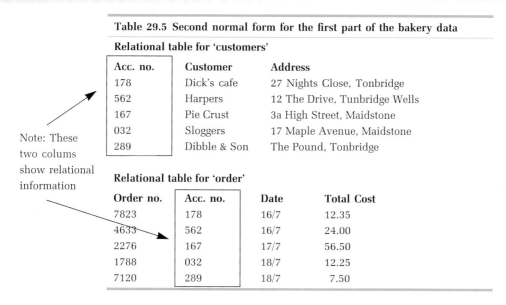

Table 29.5 Second normal form for the first part of the bakery data

Relational table for 'customers'

Acc. no.	Customer	Address
178	Dick's cafe	27 Nights Close, Tonbridge
562	Harpers	12 The Drive, Tunbridge Wells
167	Pie Crust	3a High Street, Maidstone
032	Sloggers	17 Maple Avenue, Maidstone
289	Dibble & Son	The Pound, Tonbridge

Note: These two colums show relational information

Relational table for 'order'

Order no.	Acc. no.	Date	Total Cost
7823	178	16/7	12.35
4633	562	16/7	24.00
2276	167	17/7	56.50
1788	032	18/7	12.25
7120	289	18/7	7.50

(top of table 29.4). The table for this new relation to be called 'Customers' is shown in table 29.5.

As you can see from this new table at the top of table 29.5, the account number uniquely determines the customer, and the account number uniquely determines the address, therefore, in this particular table; **all these attributes** are **functionally dependent** on the new **primary key**. Therefore this **relation** is now said to be in **second normal form**.

The data, which has been removed, is shown in the relation (table) called 'Order' at the bottom of table 29.5. However, we need a link from 'Customers', and 'Account no.' serves this purpose admirably. Looking in detail at this new table, we see that the primary key called 'Order' uniquely determines 'Account no.', 'Date' and 'Total cost'. Therefore, **this table too is now in second normal form**. The shorthand form for these two new tables is as follows:

Customers (<u>Acc. no.</u>, Customer, Address)

Orders (<u>Order no.</u>, Acc. no., Date, Total cost)

You should note that sometimes it's necessary to include more than one attribute in the primary key in order to achieve functional dependency. *If* the **primary key** *does* contain **more than one attribute**, then **functional dependence** is **relative to all attributes** contained within the **composite primary key**, and this particular situation happens in the next part of this example.

Finally, we have to operate on the other first-normal-form relation for the bakery shown at the bottom of table 29.4. Now this table illustrates a common problem, which we have not yet encountered – it's **much more difficult** to choose a suitable **primary key**. For example, if we choose 'Order no.', then there is no unique association with either 'Item', 'Quantity' or 'Price'. If we choose 'Item' to be the primary key, there is no unique association with 'Order number' and 'Quantity' – and 'Quantity' and 'Price' are even less-

likely candidates for the primary key! The way out of this dilemma is to choose a **primary key** that has **more than one attribute**.

If, for example, we create a **composite primary key** consisting of the attributes '**Order no.**' and '**Item**', then this new primary key can be used to establish functional dependency very easily. For example, consider a 'Bakewell tart' belonging to 'Order number 7823'. In this case the '**Quantity**' (of '7823-Bakewell tarts') is now functionally dependent on the composite primary key, because order number 7823's Bakewell tarts are uniquely associated with the quantity 20.

The **item price** is obviously functionally dependent on **item**, but **not** on the 'order no. and item' composite primary key, because many different composite primary keys will be associated with the item price. Therefore, to rectify this final problem, a small table consisting of item as the primary key will be needed. Note that the attribute item provides the necessary link between these two tables, and order number acts as the link to the previous tables. We will not bother to show these two new second-normal-form tables in full, as they are defined completely by the standard shorthand notation as follows.

Part order (<u>Order no.</u>, <u>Item</u>, Quantity)

Item (<u>Item</u>, Item price)

We have, therefore, established **four relations** for the bakery data, **all** of which are now in **second normal form**.

Third normal form

Don't forget that we must make the assumption that all tables are already in second normal form, so, given this obvious requirement – Codd's third normal form states that there should be no **functional dependencies** (**unique associations**) existing between **attributes** (or groups of attributes) that could **not** possibly be used as an alternative to the **primary key**.

One of the things which Codd's third normal form helps to eliminate is unintentional deletion of data, and a simple example will help to explain. Consider figure 29.9(a). We already know that each **attribute** in this **entity** must be **functionally dependent** on the **primary key**, for if this were **not the case**, then the relation would **not** be in **second normal form**. However, **all these attributes** could be used as **alternative primary keys** – simply because of the **very strong relationship** between them. Forget for the moment that 'surname', for example, might be duplicated, and therefore be a possible bad choice primary key, it's the idea of the very strong relationship that counts. For example, the surname could determine the account number, or the address could also determine the account number. Here there should be no particular deletion problem as deletion of any one of these attributes would surely require the deletion of the rest. However, for attributes that could **not** be used as **alternative primary keys**, we do have a considerable problem, which must be eliminated, and this is demonstrated in the following section.

Next consider figure 29.9(b), again we already know that each **attribute** in this **entity** must be **functionally dependent** on the **primary key**, for if this were **not the case**, then the relation would **not** be in **second normal form**. But, in addition to this **functional dependency**, let's suppose that there happens to be another functional dependency between some other **non-identifying**

attributes (i.e. between **attributes** that could **not possibly** function as **alternatives** to the **primary key**) This particular functional dependency is shown by the arrow next to the cross. Because the attribute 'Supplier' is functionally dependent on 'Component' – elimination of the 'Product' will cause the supplier to be eliminated too! This might prove to be disastrous **if** this particular supplier happens to supply the same component for other products! If this type of relationship exists then it's called a **transitive dependency**.

If this sort of thing happens in a relational database then the relation can be split up yet again into different relations, and one possible change is shown in figure 29.10. Here we can see that elimination of the original product will **not** cause the supplier to be eliminated, and this would ensure that the data is now in third normal form.

Returning to the first two tables of the bakery problem, we can see that all attributes in the table at the top of table 29.5 could be used as alternative primary keys, and therefore this relation is already in third normal form. The table at the bottom of table 29.5 contains no non-identifying attributes. Therefore, we must check to see that there are no functional dependencies (unique associations) existing between them. A careful examination of the 'Account no.' 'Date' and 'Total cost' will reveal that none of these are functionally dependent on each other, and therefore no alterations are necessary. Therefore, **this particular table is already in third normal form**. The remaining two tables, shown in shorthand form a little earlier, are also no problem. Therefore, **all tables** are actually in **third normal form**. More practice with third normal form is given in the following exercise.

That's all there is to normalisation!

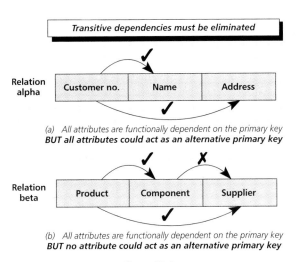

(a) *All attributes are functionally dependent on the primary key*
BUT all attributes could act as an alternative primary key

(b) *All attributes are functionally dependent on the primary key*
BUT no attribute could act as an alternative primary key

Figure 29.9

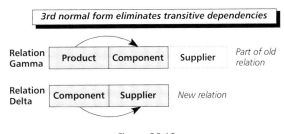

Figure 29.10

Exercise 29.1

1   Write down the **type** of **relationship** that exists between the following entities.

   (a) Car   Driver

   (b) Car   Registration number

   (c) Bank account   Customer

   (d) Mother   Children

   (e) Brother   Sister

2   Using a **hierarchical database structure**, show how it might be possible to model the books in a library. Would this be an efficient structure? Why would a network structure probably improve the situation?

3   Show how a typical **network database structure** might be used to model the pupils in a school or college.

4   Why is a **relational** database very different indeed from the **hierarchical** and **network** databases?

5   Define the following terms in relation to a relational database.

   (a) Attribute

   (b) Entity

   (c) Relation

   (d) Primary key

   (e) Tuple

   (f) Normalisation

6   What do the terms 'functional dependency' and 'transitive dependency' mean? Give an example of each.

7   What is meant by a **variable-length record**, and why is it best **not** to make use of variable record lengths in a **relational database**?

8   Consider the following data, which shows a **single student record**.

Pemburyshire College of Advanced Technology

Student name   Nick Codswallop   **Student ID**   317256

Address   123 Oak Road, Seven Oak Green, Wellington MN12 6TH

Home phone number   081-278-162251

Company   Southern Sewage

Company phone number   0903-356-198726

Subject code	Subject name	Grade	Teacher	Department
DENCS1a	Computer science	A	RJB	Computing
DENEL1c	Electronic systems	B	DLF	Electronics
DENPH1b	Physics	B	RIL	Physics
DENMA1d	Mathematics	A	NJL	Mathematics
DENHM1c	Higher mathematics	B	TAG	Mathematics
DENTE1a	Technology	A	AJH	Technology
DENGE1e	General studies	E	DEB	English

Derive a set of **tables** to show the above data in first, second and third normal form. There is a potential problem with the data as shown above. What is this problem, and what data could be added to overcome it?

9   Describe the difference between a declarative SQL used to define a query and a typical user-friendly HCI to achieve the same result with inexperienced users.

10 Outline the essential security measures to be undertaken when setting up a database in a large company.

11 Use a database system, which you have at school or college to set up a database listing the names and subjects taken by the pupils in your class. Use an SQL to make a report containing each student under all the different subject headings which are taken by the students, e.g. a heading of 'Maths' followed by all that take maths, followed by a heading of 'Computer science' followed by all those who take computer science etc.

End of chapter revision aid and summary

Cover up the right-hand column and see if you can answer the questions or define the terms on the left. They appear in the order in which they are covered in this chapter. Alternatively you may browse through the right-hand column to aid revision.

Describe what is meant by a database.	A database is a collection of related information, organised such that efficient data processing may be carried out on the data contained in it.
How might different departments make use of the same database?	It's possible to arrange a centralised database so that each department in an office or factory etc. has its own specific view of the data contained in a large database.
Why are databases important to a company?	Large databases often form the hub of many companies, with the information contained within the database vital for many different aspects of the business.
What is a mathematical relationship?	A relationship is a link, some sort of association or some dependency between two or more attributes.
Name different types of mathematical relationships.	Relationships can be of the type one-to-one, one-to-many, many-to-one or many-to-many.
What is an entity?	An entity is any concrete or abstract occurrence defined in a database and can be regarded as a record, e.g. customer record or criminal record!
What is an attribute?	An attribute is part of a record, and can be regarded as being the same as a field within a record.
What is meant by the term dependency?	A dependency can be regarded as a particular relationship in which the existence of one thing depends upon the existence of another.
What is an association?	An association is the type of connection between entities and usually defines one of the standard relationships.
What is shown on an entity dependence diagram?	An entity dependence diagram shows the relationships between entities in terms of how the existence of one depends on the existence of others.
Into what shape boxes are entity relationships placed on a diagram?	An entity relationship diagram shows the relationships between entities; the relationships are usually placed in diamond-shaped boxes.
Name three different types of database structures.	There are several different types of database including hierarchical, network and relational databases.
What is a hierarchical database?	A hierarchical database is modelled on a tree structure in which each parent can have many children. It is therefore ideal for one-to-many relationships.
What is a network database?	A network database is modelled on a partially or fully interconnected structure in which pointers may operate in a variety of modes. Unlike the hierarchical database, each record can have multiple owners.
What is a relational database?	A relational database is a database built up around relations.
How are relations represented in a relational database?	A relation is basically a two-dimensional table where rows (tuples) represent logical records, and column entries represent the attributes of a particular entity.
What is a table in a relational database?	A table in a relational database corresponds to a file.
What is a tuple?	A record in a relational database is referred to as a tuple, and corresponds to a row from a relational table.

Why is the term tuple used?	A tuple is used instead of 'row' because it's the correct term from the tuple relational calculus and relational algebra – the theories on which relational databases depend.
What is a domain?	The set of all possible values that an attribute may take on is called a domain.
What is the shorthand notation to indicate the primary key in a relation or table?	Relations or tables may be written in shorthand notation with the primary key underlined. It consists of the name of the relation followed by attributes, separated by commas, in a list contained in brackets.
What is meant by the primary key?	The primary key is the key by which the relational table is best identified. It's often the first column in the relation, but this need not be so.
What condition must the primary key satisfy?	The primary key should uniquely identify each record if problems of duplicates are to be avoided.
Might a primary key have more than one attribute?	A primary key may consist of more than one attribute if this helps to establish functional dependency. It's often necessary to do this.
How is a database normalised?	Relational databases may be normalised by application of Codd's rules.
What is meant by normalisation?	Normalisation is a set of rules developed by Codd which result in more efficient data organisation, more efficient storage and the simplification of the database.
Describe the process of putting a database in first normal form.	The first normal form states that any attributes with multiple or repeating values are removed so that all entities (records) are the same length.
Describe the process of putting a database in second normal form.	The second normal form states that all attributes in an entity must be functionally dependent on the primary key.
What is meant by being functionally dependent on the primary key?	Functionally dependent (on primary key) means that there should be a unique association between the primary key and the attribute. Thus the primary key should be able to uniquely identify an attribute if functional dependency exists.
Describe the process of putting a database in third normal form.	The third normal form states that there should be no functional dependency existing between attributes or groups of attributes that could not be used as an alternative primary key, i.e. there should be no transitive dependencies.
What is meant by a transitive dependency?	A transitive dependency means that if A is dependent on B, and B is dependent on C, then A is dependent on C also. This often has to be avoided if unnecessary data deletion is to be avoided.

30 The Binary Number System

In this chapter you'll learn about:

- Using the binary, octal and hexadecimal number systems
- Carrying out arithmetic using any of the above number bases
- How fractional and negative numbers can be represented in binary and hexadecimal
- Fixed point binary notation
- BCD notation

Key resources

To carry out this work most successfully it's best if you have:

- Access to a calculator that handles binary, octal and hexadecimal operations

Concept checkpoints

- This work does not depend on any work that has been previously covered.

Introduction

So much in computing (and indeed in society today) depends on a comprehensive mastery of the way in which data can be manipulated and stored. From the understanding of some of the algorithms used to solve problems in the most sophisticated high level languages, to an understanding of the most intricate detail in an individual chip inside the computer, all this knowledge depends on a thorough understanding of the way in which binary code in its most simple and advanced forms can be used to represent data.

This chapter will take you from the birth of the binary system through to many of the ingenious ways of representing and manipulating numeric data types. Other non-arithmetic data types are considered at frequent intervals throughout the rest of this book.

The binary system

The **binary system** (also called **base two**) has just two states: usually called '**off**' and '**on**' or '**0**' and '**1**'. The reason why this system is so important is that it is the simplest system to implement in practice using the electronic technology available today. It is relatively easy to detect very quickly if a circuit is switched on or off. It would be a much more difficult task to detect levels in-between these two extremes. Hence binary is ideal for use in modern electronic digital computers. In fact, if you worked out the optimum base for a computer mathematically, in terms of the cost of storing numbers that could be represented with complete disregard for what could be built in practice, you would find that a base of two or three (or 2.718 281 828 4 to be exact!) is optimum. Mathematicians may recognise this number as being e (the base for natural logarithms). Also, a 2-bit code is the minimum necessary to be able to transmit any information. The case for binary is, therefore, proved.

To understand the binary system it is useful to think more carefully about a system with which most people will be more familiar, i.e. the **decimal system** or **base ten**. The decimal system of numbers is also known as **denary**.

When you learnt to count in base ten you would have been told that the symbols to be used are the set of numbers {0, 1, 2, 3, 4, 5, 6, 7, 8 and 9} i.e. you have ten different symbols when using base ten. You would also have been told that the column headings above each number, starting at the right, represent units, tens, hundreds and thousands etc. Therefore the number:

Th	H	T	U
1	0	7	3

would represent one thousand, no hundreds, seven tens and three units, making a number that is called 'one thousand and seventy three'. In base ten, each column heading to the left is obtained by multiplying the previous column heading by ten i.e. the number representing the base in which we are currently working.

Now consider the **binary system**. Here just two symbols are used: '0' and '1'. Therefore, any number must be represented using 0s and 1s only. This time the column headings will be (from right to left) 1s, 2s, 4s, 8s, 16s, 32s, etc. To obtain the next column heading, the number is 'multiplied by two', which is simply the base in which we are currently working. Any column headings in **any number base** can be obtained by starting with the unit's column, and multiplying by the base in which you are working. Therefore, in base sixteen (a number base with which you will soon become familiar), the column headings would be 1s, 16s, 256s, 4096s, etc. Getting back to the binary system, the following number

16s	8s	4s	2s	1s
1	0	1	1	1

would represent '**1 lot of 16**', '**0 lots of 8**', '**1 lot of 4**', '**1 lot of 2**' and finally '**one unit**'. There is no point inventing a name for such a number, unless it is going to be the major system used by everybody. Therefore, we manipulate numbers in binary when doing computing, but might convert them into decimal numbers if we wish to have a 'human' idea of the magnitude (size) of the number.

When dealing with number bases it is important not to confuse the base of the number in which we are working. For example is '101'equivalent to 'five', 'one hundred and one', or 'two hundred and fifty seven'? The first answer assumes binary, the second answer assumes decimal and

Did you know that . . .

If humans had evolved into creatures with just one finger on each hand, we would probably count in binary, just like computers!

the third answer assumes base sixteen! To get over this problem, a useful subscript notation has been developed. If there is any chance of ambiguity then the number base is written at the end of the number as a subscript:

Therefore, 101_2 means base two, and 1011_{16} means base sixteen.

If no subscript is used, then it is usual to assume that base ten is being implied. However, in sections where there is no ambiguity as to the base in which we are working, the subscript is often omitted, even if we are working in binary or hex.

Counting in binary

It's most important to be able to count in binary, and the system is simple, as the following example shows. To start with we simply count up in decimal, and write down the binary representation of the decimal number as described above:

Decimal		Binary	Comments
1 decimal	is	1 binary	One lot of 1
2 decimal	is	1 0 binary	One lot of 2 and no lots of 1
3 decimal	is	1 1 binary	One lot of 2 and one lot of 1
4 decimal	is	1 0 0 binary	One lot of 4, no lots of 2 and no lots of 1

This sequence is extended in table 30.1.

Table 30.1

Decimal number		5-bit binary number					Decimal number		5-bit binary number				
Tens	Units	16s	8s	4s	2s	1s	Tens	Units	16s	8s	4s	2s	1s
0	0	0	0	0	0	0	1	6	1	0	0	0	0
0	1	0	0	0	0	1	1	7	1	0	0	0	1
0	2	0	0	0	1	0	1	8	1	0	0	1	0
0	3	0	0	0	1	1	1	9	1	0	0	1	1
0	4	0	0	1	0	0	2	0	1	0	1	0	0
0	5	0	0	1	0	1	2	1	1	0	1	0	1
0	6	0	0	1	1	0	2	2	1	0	1	1	0
0	7	0	0	1	1	1	2	3	1	0	1	1	1
0	8	0	1	0	0	0	2	4	1	1	0	0	0
0	9	0	1	0	0	1	2	5	1	1	0	0	1
1	0	0	1	0	1	0	2	6	1	1	0	1	0
1	1	0	1	0	1	1	2	7	1	1	0	1	1
1	2	0	1	1	0	0	2	8	1	1	1	0	0
1	3	0	1	1	0	1	2	9	1	1	1	0	1
1	4	0	1	1	1	0	3	0	1	1	1	1	0
1	5	0	1	1	1	1	3	1	1	1	1	1	1

It is tedious to build up a table, but the decimal values and the patterns established above should be understood and remembered. To count in binary we simply start with 00000, to the required number of digits. The unit's column changes like '0, 1, 0, 1, 0, 1' etc. The two's column has 'two 0s' followed by 'two 1s' followed by 'two 0s' etc. The four's column has 'four 0s' followed by 'four 1s' followed by 'four 0s' etc. The eight's column has 'eight 1s' followed by 'eight 0s' etc. This system of patterns is particularly useful, it is very easy to make a mistake when filling in tables of this nature, and recognition of this pattern will help to reduce them.

It would be unrealistic to start from 0 if the binary number we wish to obtain is large. In this case, the column headings can be used, together with a little common sense as follows:

Suppose we wish to express the decimal number 183 as a binary number.

1. Write down the binary column headings until the value of the column heading exceeds the magnitude of the number you are converting. (In this case 256 is bigger than 183.)

256	128	64	32	16	8	4	2	1

2. Next write down a 1 underneath the maximum number that can be subtracted from your original number. In this case it is 128.

256	128	64	32	16	8	4	2	1
	1							

There is one lot of 128 in 183 with 55 left over.
3. Move along to the next binary column heading that can be taken away from the remainder of (2) above. Now '64' is too big, therefore 32 must be taken away from 55. A '0' is written underneath the '64 column' (because we have no lots of 64) and a '1' is written underneath the '32 column', as there is one lot of 32 in 55.

256	128	64	32	16	8	4	2	1
	1	0	1					

There is one lot of 32 in 55 with 23 left over.
4. The process is continued until the remainder is zero. This will always be the case with **integer** (i.e. whole) numbers. Continuing the above, the final result obtained would be:

256	128	64	32	16	8	4	2	1
	1	0	1	1	0	1	1	1

Therefore $183 = 10110111_2$

The above is obviously just one method of converting between base ten and binary. A useful check to see if the answer is correct, and a method of converting between binary and base ten, is to add together all the column headings with a 1 underneath them, and see if the sum of these numbers is the same as the original number.

i.e. $128 + 32 + 16 + 4 + 2 + 1 = 183$
(thus confirming that the answer is correct). This is always a good idea in an important examination.

Conversion between decimal and binary using repeated division

Another popular method for conversion between base ten and binary is repeated division by two. In fact the idea will work for any base. For example, if you were using base eight, repeated division by eight would be used instead. The method is particularly suitable for computerisation in conjunction with MOD and DIV commands in most versions of high level languages such as BASIC. (MOD gives the remainder after division and DIV gives the whole-number part of the result of a division.) As an example, consider converting 183 to binary again. A suggested layout is as follows:

Division sums		Remainders		Operation being carried out	Result of operation
2	183	–		–	2 goes into 183... 91 times with 1 left over
2	91	Remainder 1	1	2 goes into 91....	45 times with 1 left over
2	45	Remainder 1	1	2 goes into 45....	22 times with 1 left over
2	22	Remainder 1	1	2 goes into 22....	11 times with 0 left over
2	11	Remainder 0	0	2 goes into 11....	5 times with 1 left over
2	5	Remainder 1	1	2 goes into 5....	2 times with 1 left over
2	2	Remainder 1	1	2 goes into 2....	1 time with 0 left over
2	1	Remainder 0	0	2 goes into 1...	0 times with 1 left over
	0	Remainder 1	1	End of sum.	

Consider the top part of the above ladder of division sums (the first two columns). Two goes into '183' '91 times' with 'one unit left' over. The remainder at the top of the ladder in the third column represents this unit. Therefore, in the final binary number, this digit represents 2^0 or 1 (i.e. a '1' in the unit's column of the answer). Next we divide by two again. This means 'four goes into the original number 45 times' with 'one lot of 2 left over' (plus the original unit found above of course). Hence the second remainder means that there is a 1 in the 2's column of the answer.

Continuing the above argument, we can see that the answer is the vertical column of remainders with the least significant bit at the top. The final answer must therefore be this vertical column of remainders read from bottom to top.

	1×128	0×64	1×32	1×16	0×8	1×4	1×2	1×1
Binary no.	1	0	1	1	0	1	1	1

Example

Convert 25 into binary using the method of repeated division by 2.

```
2   25
2   12   r 1
2   6    r 0
2   3    r 0
2   1    r 1
2   0    r 1        Therefore 25 = 11001
```

Simple binary arithmetic

On many occasions it is useful to be able to add, subtract, multiply and divide in binary. The following is therefore included for completeness, and to allow people who are rusty to brush up on this topic before proceeding further. However, these topics are obviously included in the computer science syllabus for people who have not covered them before. Plenty of examples are included in the end of chapter exercises, but don't forget you can use a calculator (put into binary mode) for most of these examples too!

Addition of binary numbers

The main points to remember are that the answer can only contain 0s and 1s, and you carry 'groups of two'. Consider the following sum:

	1	1	1	0	1	0	
	0	1	1	0	1	1	+
	1	0	1	0	1	0	1
	1	1	1		1		

All possibilities with two digits are covered in the above sum. The main point to realise is that if the digits you are adding equal 2 then you carry 1 (i.e. one lot of 2 into the next column).

Example

Add together the binary numbers 10101, 101, 110011, and 101101. The layout used in the above example is recommended.

0	1	0	1	0	1	
0	0	0	1	0	1	
1	1	0	0	1	1	
1	0	1	1	0	1	+
1	1	1	1	0	1	0
1	1	1	2	1	2	

A point of confusion, which often arises, occurs in the unit's column. When the digits are added we end up with 4. This is simply 'two lots of 2', and therefore a '2' is carried into the next column. It is permissible to write down 2, even though this number does not exist in binary. This is not a fiddle – it's exactly what would happen in a decimal sum if the units column was so large that you were to end up with 273, say. You would write down 3, and carry 27 (i.e. 27 lots of ten into the 10s column).

Subtraction of binary numbers

At least with subtraction we can only have two rows! As long as we remember that when we 'borrow 1' from the previous column it is really twice as big, there should be no problems. Consider the following example:

			0	2			
1	1	1	0	1	1	
0	1	0	1	0	1	–
1	0	0	1	1	0	

Example

Evaluate 10011 − 1111

0	2	1	2		
1	0	0	1	1	
0	1	1	1	1	–
0	0	1	0	0	

Therefore, 10011 − 1111 = 100

No difficulties occur until the third column is encountered. Here we need to borrow a '1' from the previous column. As there is no digit to subtract from in the third column, the third column has to borrow a '1' from the fourth column. Now the fourth column has no digit either, therefore, we move along until we find a digit from which to borrow. One is found in the fifth column. Therefore, the fourth column borrows 'one lot of 2' from the fifth column. Making the '0' at the

> **Hint:** You won't find specific questions on this section in computing examinations, but it helps to make some of the work much easier.

top of the fourth column into a 2 shows this. The third column can now borrow 'one lot of 2' from the fourth column. This is shown by making the zero at the top of the third column into a 2, and reducing the 2 at the top of the fourth column into a 1. The sum can then proceed in the normal way.

Multiplication of binary numbers

This is really very easy when compared with subtraction. If you can manage the once-times table then this is all that's needed, i.e. we have only to work out 1×0 or 1×1. The multiplication sum is set out in the standard way with 0s being inserted every time you move to the next digit of the multiplying number. However, remember that the adding up of the subtotals has to be done in binary, as shown in the binary-addition section.

Example

Evaluate 1010111×1011

```
        1 0 1 0 1 1 1
          1 0 1 1   x
    _____
        1 0 1 0 1 1 1
      1 0 1 0 1 1 1 0
  1 0 1 0 1 1 1 0 0 0   +
  _____
  1 1 1 0 1 1 1 1 0 1
    1 1 1 1 1 1 1
```

It can be seen that the process is quite simple. It may also have been noticed that the original number was simply shifted over to the left – once for the second digit, and three times for the fourth. In binary a shift left is the same as a multiplication by two. This is because the digits are written under the new column headings, one place to the left, which are twice as big. This shifting is a process which will be of fundamental importance if you study machine code and assembly language as shown in chapters 20 and 21.

Division of binary numbers

Although a little more complex than multiplication, it is still relatively simple. This simplicity stems from the fact that the answer can only contain the digits 0 and 1. The layout is as follows:

Example

Evaluate 11100001 / 101

```
              1 0 1 1 0 1
      _____
1 0 1 | 1 1 1 0 0 0 0 1
        1 0 1
        _____
          1 0 0 0
          1 0 1
          _____
            1 1 0
            1 0 1
            _____
              1 0 1
              1 0 1
              _____
                  0
```

The layout is that of a classic division sum. The details of the subtraction processes have not been shown for reasons of clarity. If the above sum had yielded a fractional answer, then binary fractions (see later) should be used.

Other number bases

Octal

If the principles of the last few sections have been well understood, it's relatively easy to extend the concepts of the four basic rules to any other number base. However, in computing, only two other number bases are of any importance. These are **octal** (base eight) used occasionally, and **hexadecimal** (base sixteen) used *very frequently*. In octal we have eight different characters:

$$\{0, 1, 2, 3, 4, 5, 6, 7\}$$

We use the column headings 1s, 8s, 64s, 512s etc. Some octal examples now follow:

> **Hint:** Don't forget that most calculators can be set up to work in the most common number bases. Even the scientific calculator that comes free with Windows, for example, can do sums in binary, octal and hexadecimal, as well as the traditional decimal used by the majority who don't study computing.

```
a. 2 3 4            b.   2 14
      1 7  +            2 3̶ 6̶
    _____            1 2 7  –
    2 5 3            _____
                       1 0 7
```

```
c.    1 3 6         d. 2 4 6 | 2 6 0 0 3 2       1 0 3 7
        3 4  x                 2 4 6.....
      _____                _____
      5 7 0                      1 2 0 3
    4 3 2 0                        7 6 2
    _____                    _____
    5 1 1 0                        2 2 1 2
    1 1                            2 2 1 2
                                   _____
                                       0 r 0
```

(Not easy to think about! Don't forget that the subtraction is done in base 8.)

Hexadecimal

Hexadecimal comes into its own when it's necessary to deal with large groups of binary digits. It is, therefore, most important that **hexadecimal** (or more simply hex) is well understood. All the previous principles of number bases still apply, and the only novelty with hex is that we have to use sixteen different symbols. Binary needs two, decimal needs ten, and therefore hex must have sixteen. The sixteen different symbols used are:

{0, 1, 2, 3, 4, 5, 6, 7, 8, 9, A, B, C, D, E, F}

Here 'A' represents ten, 'B' represents eleven and so on until 'F' which represents fifteen.

Some hex examples now follow:

```
                              D  29
  a. 1 2 7          b. B  E̶  D̶
     5 0 A +           7  0  F  –
     6 3 1            4  D  E

                                     B E 3
  c.    A 0 B        d. A 7 | 7 C 1 1 5
        3 9 x               7 2 D
     5 A 6 3               9 4 1
   1 E 2 1 0               9 2 2
   2 3 C 7 3               1 F 5
                           1 F 5
                               0
```

It must be stressed that not many people would attempt the octal or hex division sums outlined above! It would be far less damaging to the brain to convert to base ten, perform the division and then convert the answer back to the appropriate base. However, division in binary is important because it gives an insight into how the computer might tackle such problems.

Conversion between octal, hex and binary – quick method

Any number base can be converted to any other by first changing it into base ten. To convert binary into hex, first convert binary into base ten and then convert the base ten number into hex using the methods described earlier in this section. However, there is a much quicker method, and this should be used in preference to the long way round. The methods are simple because of the strong relationship between binary, octal and hex.

Each group of four binary digits represents numbers from 0 to 15 inclusive. Each hex digit also represents numbers from 0 to 15 inclusive, and so there is a one-to-one relationship between a hex digit and a group of four binary digits. The principles can be stated as follows.

To change a binary number directly into hex, split up the binary number into groups of four digits starting at the right hand side of the number. Next write down the hex equivalent for each group of four binary digits.

Example

Change $39A4_{16}$ into binary.

3	9	A	4	Numbers converted into groups of 4 binary digits
0011	1001	1010	0100	Binary digits representing hex digit

Therefore, $39A416$ is 0011100110100100_2

The principles are very similar for octal, but here three binary digits are used instead of four.

Example

Change 10110011000_2 into octal.

010	110	011	000	(Split up octal numbers into 3s from the right)
2	6	3	0	Octal digit representing the binary digits

Therefore, 10110011000_2 is 2630_8

Binary coded decimal

There are several other types of binary representation which can occur inside computers. One of the most important is called **binary coded decimal**. This is because each decimal digit has its own special binary code. There are several different types of binary coded decimal (**BCD**), but we will consider the most common which is called the **8421 weighted code**.

Let us use the example of representing 3591 in BCD. Each decimal digit is written as it appears in the decimal number, i.e.

3   5   9   1

Each digit is then coded into binary as follows:

3	5	9	1
0011	0101	1001	0001

It is called the '8421 weighted binary coded decimal' because each digit is encoded using four binary column headings with weightings 8421 (i.e. like a normal binary number). However, you can see that the system is not a number base in the sense that 'binary', 'hex' and 'octal' are.

As the maximum decimal digit that can occur is 9, the maximum code that can be represented using each of the 4 bits is 1001. This means that 1010, 1011, 1100, 1101,

1110 and 1111 are effectively redundant. Therefore, this type of code is inefficient in terms of the numbers that it can store for a given number of digits used.

If you are wondering why such a code is used, then you will see that it comes into its own when binary numbers have to be electronically decoded to operate displays such as those found in pocket calculators. As an example, consider the pure binary and BCD representation of the number 3591 shown above.

i.e. binary for 3591 is 111000000111_2 but BCD for 3591 is **0011010110010001BCD**

Each number must be decoded so those decimal digits representing 3, 5, 9 and 1 are presented with the correct codes. In the case of the pure binary number, considerable manipulation will have to be done (i.e. a binary to decimal conversion). However, in the case of the BCD number, all that is necessary is to split the number up into groups of 4 bits, starting from the right, and then feed the codes directly to the digits as shown:

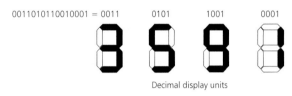

0011010110010001 = 0011   0101   1001   0001

Decimal display units

Figure 30.1

Binary fractions

The processes introduced in the last few sections can be extended to include fractions with few problems. If you consider the column headings for binary numbers, then you will realise that, from left to right, the column headings get smaller by a **binary** factor of two, i.e. 8s, 4s, 2s, and 1s. If we continue this process of dividing by two, then we get the **fractional headings** 1/2, 1/4, 1/8, 1/16 etc. The **binary**

point separates the fractional and whole number part as follows:

Integer part							Fractional part				
32	16	8	4	2	1	.	1/2	1/4	1/8	1/16	1/32
1	0	1	0	1	0	.	0	1	0	1	1

Therefore, the number shown above must be treated in two parts.

1. The **whole number** or **integer** part can be treated using the methods of the previous sections, i.e. to find the decimal value we add: $32 + 8 + 2 = 42$.
2. The **fractional part** can be found using similar methods, i.e. $1/4 + 1/16 + 1/32$.

It is usual to express these fractions as decimals.

Therefore we get $0.25 + 0.0625 + 0.03125 = 0.34375$.

The values are now added together to get 42.34375.

Therefore $101010.01011_2 = 42.34375$

It is useful to have a table of some of the more common binary fractions and this is included for your convenience in table 30.2.

Representation of negative numbers

Negative numbers are essential and any computer not capable of dealing with them would not be particularly useful. There are several methods which can be used to represent negative numbers in binary. One of the most common methods used can be explained with reference to a car 'milometer'. Let us assume that we have a three-digit decimal car milometer as shown in figure 30.2(a).

If we start the monster truck on the starting grid shown, with the milometer set to 000, then after 23 miles the car milometer would register 023. This system could record positive numbers up to and including 999 miles.

Table 30.2

Binary fraction	Fraction	Decimal fraction	Binary fraction	Fraction	Decimal fraction
0.1	1/2	0.5	0.000001	1/64	0.015 625
0.01	1/4	0.25	0.0000001	1/128	0.007 812 5
0.001	1/8	0.125	0.00000001	1/256	0.003 906 25
0.0001	1/16	0.062 5	0.000000001	1/512	0.001 953 125
0.00001	1/32	0.031 25	0.0000000001	1/1024	0.000 976 562 5

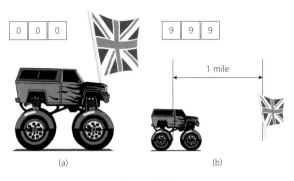

Figure 30.2

However, the system would break down if we did 1000 miles because the milometer would read 000 again.

Let us now use the same milometer, but this time invent a way to record negative distance as well. If the car starts off at the grid as shown in figure 30.2(a), then if we set the same milometer to 000 again, but drive backwards, then after 1 mile the reading would be 999. We can use 999 to represent –1 (i.e. 1 mile in the reverse direction). Of course we could not let 999 represent 999 miles in the forward direction as well, and so our range of numbers in the forward direction would be more limited. The principle of using the milometer in this way is shown in figure 30.2(b).

Let us now consider a 'binary milometer'. However, we will call it a **register** as this is the name given to the place where such numbers would be stored inside the computer. For simplicity our register will have just **4 bits** (**binary digits**). If we now analyse the possibilities using just 4 bits we get the results in the following table:

Register number					Decimal equivalent
	1	0	0	0	–8
	1	0	0	1	–7
	1	0	1	0	–6
Negative numbers	**1**	0	1	1	–5
(Backwards)	**1**	1	0	0	–4
	1	1	0	1	–3
	1	1	1	0	–2
	1	1	1	1	–1
Start here....	**0**	0	0	0	0
	0	0	0	1	1
	0	0	1	0	2
(Forwards)	**0**	0	1	1	3
Positive numbers	**0**	1	0	0	4
	0	1	0	1	5
	0	1	1	0	6
	0	1	1	1	7

If a 4-bit binary number were used in the conventional way, 0000 to 1111 would give us sixteen different combinations of numbers from 0 to +15. Using the above method we still have sixteen unique numbers (–8 to +7) but the range in the positive direction is reduced.

At first sight it may seem difficult to distinguish between positive and negative numbers until you realise that **all negative numbers start off with 1** and **all positive numbers start off with 0**. This method of representing numbers is called **two's complementation** for reasons soon to become obvious.

Before dealing with complementation more formally, a quick method of obtaining the answers will now be introduced. It is a method, which can be used in preference to the other methods if you are not asked specifically to prove what you are doing.

Two's complement, a quick method

It would be inconvenient to have to draw out a table similar to the above to find the binary representation of a particular negative number. Suppose, for example, we wish to find the two's complement 4-bit representation for –6. From the above table we can see that the answer is: 1010. However, consider the following method.

1. Write down the positive binary number using 4 bits, i.e. for '–6', we would write the binary number for '+6'.

Therefore 6 becomes 0110 using 4 bits.

2. Starting at the right hand side, rewrite this number up to and including the first 1. For 0110 this would mean writing down 1 and 0.

Therefore the right hand two digits only are written down: 10.

3. For the remainder of the number (i.e. all the digits to the left), change the 0s for 1s and 1s for 0s. Therefore the number becomes:

1010 which is the required answer. It's as simple as that.

Example

Write down the two's complement 8-bit representation for –39.

39 in binary is...	**0 0 1 0 0 1 1 1**	Using 8 bits
	1	Write down above number from right, up to and including the first digit that's a 1.
	1 1 0 1 1 0 0 1	Change all other 0s for 1s and 1s for 0s

Hence –39 = 1 1 0 1 1 0 0 1

Besides being able to represent negative numbers in binary, it is possible to subtract numbers by adding the complement, i.e. 59 + (–32) is the same as 59 – 32. Therefore, all the electronic circuits designed for adding inside a computer chip can be used for subtraction as well. It is for this reason that complementation is of such fundamental importance in computing.

Complementation, a more formal approach

Complementation (for the purpose of this chapter) is a way of representing numbers (particularly in binary) that enables us to subtract these binary numbers by using the process of addition, i.e. we find the complement of the number that we wish to subtract, then add it to the original number instead.

There are two important methods of complementation.

The radix-minus-one complement

A radix is just the posh name for **base**. Hence, if we are working in binary, then the **radix-minus-one's complement** becomes $2 - 1 = 1$, i.e. the **one's complement**. To obtain the one's complement of a binary number each digit is subtracted from 1 or inverted.

i.e. the one's complement of 101001 is 010110 (111111–101001)

The radix complement

In binary, this would become the **two's complement**, i.e. the method used in the table for the binary mileometer shown earlier. To obtain the two's complement we simply add 1 to the ones complement.

i.e. the two's complement of 101001 is 010110 + 1 = 010111

However, don't forget the quick method mentioned earlier.

Examples

(1) Find the radix-minus-one's complement of 1011100110000

Answer: 0100011001111   Subtract each digit from 1 or invert each digit.

(2) Find the radix complement of 100110011

Answer: 011001101   Quick method

(3) Use the one's complement method to work out the following subtraction by addition:

101110001 – 101100 (Note the 'fiddle' needed when using this method.)

The one's complement of 101100 is 010011
The one's complement of 000101100 is 111010011

Therefore work out:

```
1 0 1 1 1 0 0 0 1
1 1 1 0 1 0 0 1 1 +
─────────────────
1 0 1 0 0 0 1 0 0
```

This carry must be (1) taken to the other end and added on!

```
1 1 1 1     1 1
1 0 1 0 0 0 1 0 0
              1 +
─────────────────
1 0 1 0 0 0 1 0 1
```

(Adding on the carry at the other end)

You will often find that 'fiddle factors' such as the above have to be applied to get the right answer. However, for a given number of bits it can easily be shown that by adding round the carry the right answer is obtained in every case.

(4) Use the two's complement method to work out 101110001 – 101100.

The two's complement of 101100 in 9 bits is 111010100 (using quick method).

> **Hint:** Remember that all data inside a machine are represented as binary digits. We can't use a minus sign, therefore ingenious coding methods have been used to overcome this problem. All numbers, positive or negative, must be represented by a string of 1s and 0s.

Therefore work out:

```
1 0 1 1 1 0 0 0 1
1 1 1 0 1 0 1 0 0 +
─────────────────
1 0 1 0 0 0 1 0 1
```

Carry is ignored (1)   1 1 1 1

This time the carry is not taken to the other end, as was the case with the one's complement method. If you think that the two's complement is easier because there is no digit to add on, don't forget that to find the two's complement the one's complement must first be found, and then a digit must be added on the two's complement! This is the way a machine would do it. However the two's complement method has other advantages over the one's complement too, and one of these advantages is covered in the next example.

Consider the representation of zero in both systems:

Using 4 bits the two's complement of 0000 (zero) is 0000
(i.e. 1111 + 1 but the carry is lost), but the one's complement of 0000 (zero) is 1111.

Now consider the representation of –1 in both systems:

Using 4 bits the two's complement of 0001 (+1) is 1111. But the one's complement of 0001(+1) is 1110.

Working out a few values each side of zero the following table can be built up:

Number	One's complement	Number	Two's complement
+ 3	0011	+ 3	0011
+ 2	0010	+ 2	0010
+ 1	0001	+ 1	0001
Zero	0000	Zero	0000
Zero again!	1111	−1	1111
−1	1110	−2	1110
−2	1101	−3	1101

We can see from the above table that we have a redundant zero when using the one's complement method. This is one more of the reasons why the two's complement is used in preference to the one's complement method.

Explicit sign method

There is one final method that is often used called the **explicit sign method**. It is also called the **sign and magnitude** method. When using one's and two's complement methods the sign of the number was taken care of implicitly when applying the rules for each method. The explicit sign method is very easy to understand – it is simply an ordinary binary number with one extra digit placed in front to represent the **sign**. Again a '1' is used for negative numbers and a '0' is used for positive.

Example

Express + 13 and −13 using the explicit sign method and 8 bits.

Now 13 in binary is 1101 = 0001101 (using 7 bits for the actual number)

Therefore +13 = 00001101, and −13 = 10001101

Negative binary fractions

These are really a combination of previous methods, and should be easy to understand.

Example

Find a two's complement representation of $(-13\frac{5}{16})$ using 5 bits for the integer part and 4 bits for the fractional part.

First the whole number part: +13 = 1101 = 01101 (5-bit integer part)

Next the fractional part:

$\frac{5}{16} = \frac{1}{4} + \frac{1}{16}$ 　 = 0.01 + 0.0001

　 = .0101 (4 bits for fractional part)

Therefore: $+13\frac{5}{16}$ = 01101.0101

Therefore: $-13\frac{5}{16}$ = 10010.1011 (two's complement representation)

Fixed point binary numbers

In the last few sections we have not been too bothered about the number of digits required for the number represented, or the position of the binary point within the number. In practice the register holding the number is of fixed length, and therefore many compromises may have to be made. The situation can be compared to an electronic calculator. If only ten digits are available on the display, then we can't possibly display an eleven-digit number. The size of register will therefore affect the range of numbers that can be displayed. There are methods available to increase this range, but at the expense of one or two other desirable attributes (see chapter 31).

There are two major types of fixed point representation – **integer** and **fractional**. We will now consider these two systems in more detail.

Integer fixed point representation

We will assume an 8-bit register (a sensible choice as many computers work in 8 bits or multiples thereof) and two's complementation will be used throughout. The register is therefore as follows:

It is important to be able to evaluate the limitations of such a system, e.g. what is the largest number that can be held in the register? What is the smallest? This can easily be worked out by filling the register up with the appropriate bits and having a look to see what happens.

> **Hint:** Real machines have only a finite number of digits with which to represent an actual number. Therefore, there will be limitations to which numbers can actually be represented in terms of maximum and minimum values, etc. This important concept enables you to understand how errors can be introduced.

First the maximum positive number:

01111111   i.e. +127

(Don't forget that the sign bit at the beginning must be 0 to be positive in two's complement.)

Next the minimum positive number:

00000001   i.e. +1

(Zero is neither positive nor negative!)

The smallest magnitude negative number:

11111111   i.e. −1

(Don't forget the car milometer if the above is confusing. See earlier.)

Finally, the largest magnitude negative number:

10000000   i.e. −128

If the above was difficult to understand, you need more practice using two's complement notation.

If we look at the above results then we can see that the **range** of numbers (i.e. from largest to smallest) is +127 to −128 inclusive.

It would be more useful to express the relationship in terms of powers of two, because this can then be extended to evaluate the numbers for any register with N bits:

For our 8-bit register
$$-2^7 \leq \text{range} \leq 2^7 - 1$$

Therefore for an N-bit register
$$-2^{N-1} \leq \text{range} \leq 2^{N-1} - 1$$

Exercise 30.1

1   (a) Convert the following **binary** numbers into **denary**:

   (i)   1010   (ii) 101000

   (iii) 11111111   (iv) 010100111011

   (b) Convert the following **denary** numbers into **binary**:

   (i)   27   (ii) 128

   (iii) 789   (iv) 176 891

2   Convert the following **base ten** numbers into **binary** making use of the **repeated division method**.

   (a) 13   (b) 127

   (c) 357

3   Work out the following **binary** arithmetic:

   (a) 1000 + 101

   (b) 1011 + 1110

   (c) 10011 + 10011 + 101011

   (d) 1001011 + 100110 + 110111 + 011 + 1101

   (e) 1111 − 101

   (f) 1010 + 101

   (g) 10000000 − 1001100

4   Work out the following **binary** arithmetic:

   (a) 101 × 11   (b) 10110 × 1011

   (c) 101 × 10 × 101   (d) 11010 × 1011

   (e) 10010 / 10   (f) 1001011 / 101

   (g) 1001011101 /1110

5   Work out the following **hexadecimal** arithmetic:

   (a) 192 + 76   (b) A73 + B412 + 52D

   (c) 170 − 36   (d) BED − ABC

   (e) 127 × 79   (f) CAD × BOD

   (g) 19E / 12

6   Work out the following **octal** (base eight) arithmetic:

   (a) 17 + 234   (b) 2732 − 156

   (c) 123 × 456   (d) 77 / 25

7   Convert the following **binary** numbers into **hexadecimal**:

   (a) 10101011

   (b) 11110000

   (c) 11110000

   (d) 1001100101010100

   (e) 10110

   (f) 1010101

8   Convert the following **hexadecimal** numbers into **binary**:

   (a) 160   (b) 279

   (c) FF60   (d) FBFF

9   Convert the following **octal** numbers into **binary**:

   (a) 160   (b) 275

   (c) 1234   (d) 7531

10 Convert the following **hexadecimal** numbers into **octal**:

   (a) 281   (b) F7BB

   (b) ABCD   (d) 1000

11 Convert the following **octal** numbers into **hexadecimal**:

   (a) 731   (b) 100

   (c) 6661   (d) 7070

12 Represent the following numbers in the BCD 8421 weighted code:

   (a) 101010 (binary)   (b) 746 (octal)

   (c) A4F (hex)

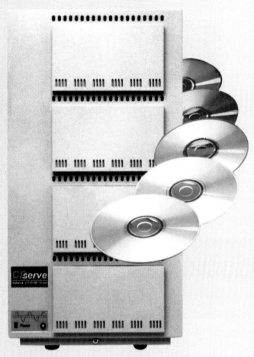

◀ **Plate 34**
Up to 255 users, via a network, can access the Avantis CD-ROM server shown here. A maximum of 300 different CDs can be used at the same time, but fast network connections are required to prevent the entire system from grinding to a halt!

▼ **Plate 35**
Linear tape fulfils an important role in the mainframe environment. This digital-linear-tape library system can handle up to 80 DLT drives and 1630 cartridges for a native data transfer rate of 1.44 Terabytes/hour, with a storage capacity of 57 Terabytes

▼ **Plate 36**
The Fujitsu F6457 magnetic tape library system, for use on the Fujitsu mainframe and super computers, can store up to 48,508 tape cartridges, giving many Tbytes of information, and has a data transfer rate of 3 Mbyte/sec. The recording density is 75,742 Bytes/inch

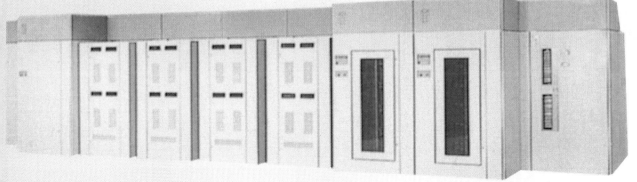

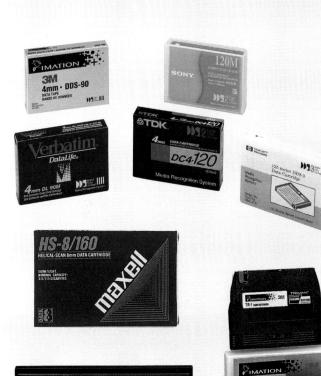

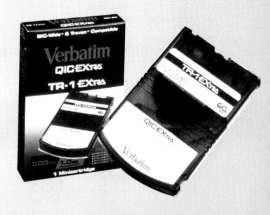

Fractional fixed-point representation

Again, two's complementation will be used, but this time the binary point will be in the position shown (in fact the binary point may be in any desired position within the register):

First the maximum positive number: 0.1111111

The best way to describe the above is
$$1 - 1/2^7 \text{ i.e. } 1 - 1/128 = 0.992\ 187\ 5$$

Next the smallest positive number: 0.0000001

This time the number is simply
$$1/2^7 \text{ i.e. } 1/128 = 0.007\ 812\ 5$$

Next the smallest magnitude negative number:
$$1.1111111$$

The two's complement of the above is 0.0000001 therefore the number is
$$-1/2^7 \text{ i.e. } -1/128 = -0.007\ 812\ 5$$

Finally, the largest magnitude negative number:
$$1.0000000$$

Therefore, the number is –1 (the two's complement of the above number is the same).

As we are dealing with fractional numbers, there will be many numbers (most, actually) that we can't represent exactly. For example, the largest magnitude negative fraction that can be represented is 1.0000001.

The two's complement of the above is
$$0.1111111 = -(1 - 1/27) = -(1 - 1/128)$$
$$= -0.992\ 187\ 5$$

Therefore numbers between this and –1 cannot be represented. The consequences of this are dealt with more fully when **accuracy** and **errors** are dealt with in chapter 31.

Exercise 30.2

1 **Change the following** decimal fractions **into** binary fractions:

(a) 0.25   (b) 0.031 25

(c) 1.5   (d) 15.375

(e) 13.5625   (f) 67.0468 75

2 Represent the following **decimal** numbers using 8-bit **two's complement** representation:

(a) –4   (b) –13

(c) –69   (d) –123

3 (a) Represent the following **binary** numbers using **one's complement** 10-bit representation:

(i)   1001   (ii) 110111

(ii) 0110001001

(b) Represent the following **binary** numbers using 10-bit **radix complement** notation:

(i)   1001

(ii) 110111

(iii) 0110001001

4 Represent the following **decimal** numbers using a 12-bit explicit sign representation:

(a) +128

(b) –50

(c) –196

5 Find the **two's complement** representation of the following **real numbers**: (use 8 bits for the **integer part** and 4 bits for the **fractional part**)

(a) –63.25   (b) –17.625

(c) –113.1875

End of chapter revision aid and summary

Cover up the right-hand column and see if you can answer the questions or define the terms on the left. They appear in the order in which they are covered in this chapter. Alternatively you may browse through the right-hand column to aid revision.

Describe the binary system.	The binary system has just two stable states – 'on' and 'off' or '1' and '0'.
Why is the binary system used in computers?	The binary system is used in computers because it's easy to represent these two states using electricity.
What is denary?	The decimal or denary system is also called base ten. It is the 'normal' system of counting.
Which symbols does binary use?	The binary system uses just *two symbols* {0,1}.
Which symbols does the decimal system use?	The decimal system uses *ten symbols* {0,1,2,3,4,5,6,7,8,9}.
Name a mechanical method whereby decimal can be converted into binary.	Conversion *between decimal and binary* may be accomplished by using repeated division.
Can normal methods be used for arithmetical operations in binary?	Binary numbers may be added, subtracted, multiplied and divided using methods *identical in principle* with normal decimal arithmetic.
What is hexadecimal?	Hexadecimal (or hex) is another name for base sixteen.
Which symbols are used in base sixteen?	Base sixteen uses *sixteen symbols* {0,1,2,3,4,5,6,7,8,9,A,B,C,D,E,F}.
What is octal?	Octal is another name for base eight and uses the symbols {0,1,2,3,4,5,6,7}.
Is there an easy way to convert between binary, octal and hexadecimal?	Conversion between binary, octal and hex is trivial because of the relationships between these bases.
What is BCD?	Binary coded decimal or BCD is a method of coding each decimal digit separately using an 8–4–2–1 weighted binary code.
How are fractions represented in binary?	Binary factions are a simple extension to ordinary binary numbers. A binary point is used *instead* of a decimal point.
How are negative numbers represented in the binary system?	Negative numbers may be represented in binary using a variety of techniques including explicit sign, one's complement and two's complement.
What is two's complement?	Two's complement is the *most versatile method* although many other forms which are extensions of this principle exist on real computers.
What are fixed-point binary numbers?	Fixed-point binary numbers are used to represent integer and fractional numbers, with limited range but greater precision.

31 Further Binary Systems

Key resources

To carry out this work most successfully it's best if you have:

◆ Access to a calculator which can operate in binary and hex modes

Concept checkpoints

◆ It's essential that you have read, and completely understood, chapter 30 on binary arithmetic.

Introduction

This second chapter on binary number systems will introduce the concepts of floating point binary numbers. These numbers are used to extend the range of numerical data on modern computer systems, without which most of the engineering, scientific and mathematical calculation could not be undertaken.

Floating point representation of binary numbers

This is a more versatile system than fixed point representation considered in chapter 30. To understand it we need to recall that numbers can be split up into two parts called a **mantissa** and an **exponent**. As an example consider the following number written using the mathematical technique called standard form (the same as scientific notation on most calculators).

$$1.637 \times 10^{50}$$

Here 1.637 is called the **mantissa**, and 50 is called the **exponent**. You will recall from your mathematics that such a number means that the decimal point in the mantissa has to be moved 50 places to the right (for a positive exponent). Therefore, the equivalent number to the above would be:

163700000000000000000000000000000000000000000000000000

You will agree that the range is considerably extended! However, the precision has been sacrificed. It is usual to make a compromise between the bits used for the mantissa (more precision) and the bits used for the exponent (more range). It is fortunate that it's unusual to require a vast range *and* to be highly precise. (If you require such precision and range, as would be the case with calculation of large primary numbers, for example, then special machine-code routines would have to be written.)

The term **floating point** is derived from the fact that to build up the final number (as above) the point floats along (it is moved by you!) until it rests in the final place.

Let us consider an example, which uses a 16-bit register. We will assign 10 bits for the mantissa and 6 bits for the exponent. This is shown as follows:

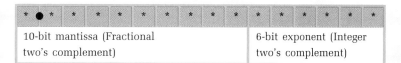

| 10-bit mantissa (Fractional two's complement) | 6-bit exponent (Integer two's complement) |

As can be seen, the mantissa will have a 10-bit fractional representation in two's complement, and the exponent will use an integer two's complement representation. Therefore, the methods used will be a combination of the two previous sections on binary fixed point notation, both fractional and integer, as described in chapter 30.

Consider the following number contained in our 16-bit floating-point register

0.1 0 1 1 0 0 1 0 0 | 0 0 0 1 0 0

The number must be decoded in two parts.

1. The mantissa, 0.101100100, is simply rewritten in the same form.
2. The exponent, 000100, is binary for 4. This means that the binary point in the mantissa has to be moved four places to the right, using the convention that + means move right.

Combining the above two stages.

The final answer is therefore: 01011.00100 i.e. 11 1/8

Therefore: 0.101100100 | 000100 represents 11.125

Example

> **Hint:** Think about the scientific notation and standard form used on calculators and in elementary mathematics. These ideas are very similar.

Using the same floating point representation as above, determine the decimal number for the following floating point representation, assuming the same layout as before.

1.100110000 | 111100

1. This time the mantissa is a negative number (two's complement and the sign bit is 1). Therefore we will have a negative answer.

   The two's complement of 1100110000 is 0011010000

   Therefore, the mantissa becomes −0.011010000

2. The exponent is also negative. Now the two's complement of 111100 is −000100 = −4. Therefore, we move the binary point four places to the left.

Altering the original mantissa we get −0.00000110100.

Now 0.00000110100 = 1/64 + 1/128 + 1/512

= 0.015 625 + 0.007 812 5 + 0.001 953 125

= 0.025 390 625

Therefore: 1.100110000 | 111100 = −0.025 390 625

Let us now consider a consequence of using this system.

Consider the following three numbers represented using our 16-bit register:

(a) 0.100000000 | 000010

(b) 0.010000000 | 000011

(c) 0.001000000 | 000100

Number (a) above is $0.100000000 \times 2^2 = 010.0000000 = 2$
Number (b) above is $0.010000000 \times 2^3 = 010.0000000 = 2$
Number (c) above is $0.001000000 \times 2^4 = 010.0000000 = 2$

i.e. they are all different representations of 2.

This is obviously not a satisfactory state of affairs. Also, if there are leading zeros before the most significant figures in the (b) and (c) representations above, then it is possible that some less significant digits will be lost, thus causing an unnecessary error. For example, if 0.100000101 had been used then this can be represented using (a), but not using (b) and (c) because the last digit would be lost. This would cause a slight difference in the value of the final number, and would not be sensible if it was not necessary to lose this digit.

To overcome the problems of many different representations of the same number, and to keep results as accurate as possible, a technique called **normalisation** is used.

Normalisation (standardisation)

The precision of the floating point representations just described depends on the number of digits that can be held in the mantissa. It is a waste if the number is stored in such a way that any precision is lost, given the fixed number of digits that are available.

> **Hint:** Normalisation has been used when considering databases and appears in other parts of computer science too. Normalisation is just another way of storing numbers. It is much more efficient than storing numbers which have not been normalised.

For positive numbers, there must be no leading zeros to the left of the most significant bit. This obviously must exclude the sign digit or it would be a negative number!

Thus (using 10 bits) the number:

0000011111 would be represented in the mantissa as 0.111110000

The exponent would obviously have to be altered to compensate for this change.

For negative numbers, there must be no leading 1s to the left of the most significant bit. (If you think about two's complement negative numbers then the '0' becomes the significant bit.) This must obviously exclude the sign bit or it would be a positive number.

Thus (using 10 bits) the number:

1111100100 would be represented in the mantissa as: 1.001000000

Again the exponent would have to be altered to compensate for this change.
Normalisation therefore ensures that the maximum possible accuracy with a given number of bits is maintained, and also ensures that only a single representation of the number is possible, i.e. it is a standard form which optimises the way in which the number is stored. It can also be used to detect if error conditions such as 'underflow' or 'overflow' occur (see the errors section later in this chapter).

Examples

Using a 16-bit register (10-bit two's complement fractional mantissa, and 6-bit two's complement integer exponent) as before, express the following numbers in normalised form:

   (1) 123   (2) 0.1875   (3) −15/32

Example 1

123 in binary is 0001111011 (10 bits).

Therefore, the normalised mantissa will be 0.111101100

The binary point will have to be moved seven places to the right to make the normalised mantissa back into the original number. Therefore, the exponent will be 7, which in binary is 000111

Hence the normlised form for 123 is 0.111101100 | 000111

Example 2

0.1875 = 1875/10000 = 75/400 = 3/16 = 2/16 + 1/16 = 1/8 + 1/16

Therefore, 0.1875 = 0.001100000 (10 bits).

Therefore, the normalised mantissa will be 0.110000000

The binary point will have to be moved two places to the left to make the normalised mantissa back into the original number.
Therefore, the exponent will be −2. Now the exponent must be represented in two's complement integer notation using 6 bits.
Now 2 in binary (6 bits) is 000010.
Therefore, −2 = 111110
Therefore, the exponent will be: 111110

Hence the normalised form for 0.1875 = 0.110000000 | 111110

Example 3

−15/32 is a negative number, we therefore need the two's complement of +15/32 to represent it.
  Now +15/32 = 1/4 + 1/8 + 1/16 + 1/32 = 0.011110000 (10 bits).

The two's complement of 0.011110000 is 1.100010000.

Therefore, the normalised mantissa will be 1.000100000.

The binary point will have to be moved one place to the left to make the normalised mantissa back into the original number. Also, don't forget that if the number is negative, when the point is continuously moved to the left, leading 1s and not 0s would have to be introduced.
Therefore, the exponent will be −1. The two's complement of +1 (000001) using six digits is 111111.
Therefore, the exponent will be: 111111

Hence the normalised form for −15/32 = 1.000100000 | 111111

One thing to notice about all the normalised numbers is the first two digits (the sign digit and the next one) will always be different. This can be used as a check to see if the number is, in fact, in normalised form.

Range of normalised floating point numbers

As with fixed point, it is essential to be able to determine the largest and smallest numbers that a given register combination can hold. The rules in the previous section on normalisation should be well understood.
To keep the ranges of the numbers to a reasonable level, let's consider a 10-bit register which uses 6 bits for the two's complement fractional mantissa, and 4 bits for the two's complement integer exponent see figure 31.1.

Figure 31.1

Example 1

First the maximum positive number. This will need the largest positive mantissa and largest positive exponent.

  0.11111 | 0111

The exponent requires the binary point to be moved seven places to the right.

Therefore, the mantissa now becomes:

01111100. = 124

Therefore, the largest positive number is +124.

Example 2

Next the minimum positive number. This will be when the smallest positive mantissa and largest negative exponent occurs.

0.10000 | 1000

Note that (0.00001) would not be a normalised number. The two's complement of the exponent is 1000, and thus the exponent requires that the binary point be moved eight places to the left. Therefore, the mantissa now becomes:

0.000000001 = 1/512 = 0.001 953 125

Therefore, the smallest positive number is +0.001 953 125.

Example 3

The smallest magnitude negative number can be found by having the smallest magnitude negative mantissa and the largest negative exponent.

1.01111 | 1000

Note that 1.01111 is the smallest possible negative mantissa in standard form. 1.11111 is not a normalised number. The exponent requires that the binary point be moved eight places to the left. Therefore the mantissa becomes:

1.1111111101111

Note 'leading 1s' are required for negative numbers. The two's complement of this number is

0.0000000010001

This number is binary for +1/512 + 1/8192 = 17/8192 = 0.002 075 195 313 (to twelve decimal places).

Therefore, the smallest magnitude negative number is −0.002 075 195 313

Example 4

Finally, the largest magnitude negative number occurs with the largest magnitude negative mantissa

> **Hint:** It's interesting to compare the range of real numbers in your favourite high-level language. For example, in Microsoft's Visual BASIC, single-precision positive numbers go from 1.401298×10^{-45} to $3.402823 \times 10^{+38}$

and the largest positive exponent.

1.00000 | 0111

The two's complement for the negative mantissa is 1.00000.

The exponent requires that the binary point be moved seven places to

the right, therefore the mantissa becomes:

10000000. = 128

Therefore, the largest magnitude negative number is −128.

The range for the 10-bit register using a 6-bit two's complement fractional mantissa and 4-bit two's complement integer exponent is therefore:

−128 ≤ negative range ≤ −0.002 075 195 313
+0.001 953 125 ≤ positive range ≤ +124

Working through the above theory you may have lost sight of the fact that zero (000000) is not a normalised number! It does therefore not exist in normalised float-ing-point numbers! To get over this slight problem, the computer will normally use the smallest positive number. In the above case this is only 0.001 953 125, a pitiful representation of zero! However, it is usual to have many more digits to represent floating point numbers, even on the humblest of microcomputers. The smallest positive numbers are, therefore, very small indeed. In practice less then 10^{-60} is typical. However, if you use integer numbers, then zero would be permissible.

Further arithmetic with floating point numbers

It will be convenient if we now keep the same floating point representation for all the different examples. This will make it easier to understand the principles involved. *Therefore, we will now use a 12-bit register having an 8-bit fractional two's complement represen-tation for the mantissa, and a 4-bit two's complement integer representation for the exponent.*

Addition and subtraction of floating point numbers

First consider the decimal sum: 123.45 + 1.6589. Before you can add the digits together you must line up the decimal points as follows.

123.45
 1.6589 +

The same principles will apply to binary numbers. We must make sure that the binary points are 'underneath' each other before adding the digits.

Example 1

Add together the following normalised floating point numbers, and put the answer in normalised form.

0.1001000 | 0010 + 0.1111000 | 0100

For the first number, the exponent requires that the binary point is moved two places to the right. Therefore, this number now becomes: 010.01000

In the second number, the exponent requires that the binary point be moved four places to the right. Therefore, this number now becomes: 01111.000

Adding these two together:

```
    0 1 0 . 0 1 0 0 0
  0 1 1 1 1 . 0 0 0 0 0 +
  _____
  1 0 0 0 1 . 0 1 0 0 0
      1 1 1
```

The result is now 10001.01. (Do a quick decimal check 2.25 + 15 = 17.25)

To normalise the result we would need to move the binary point five places to the left. The number would now become 0.1000101. When written in this form we need an exponent of +5 to make the normalised answer correct. Therefore, the exponent will be +5 or 0101.

The normalised answer is, therefore,
0.1000101 | 0101

Note, if more digits than are available were needed, then the least significant digits would have to be chopped off or rounded (see the section on errors later in this chapter).

Example 2

Subtract these numbers and give the answer in normalised form:

0.1100000 | 0001 – 1.0100000 | 0000

Note that the second number is negative (sign bit is 1) therefore, the answer should be positive. For the first number, the exponent requires that the binary point be shifted one place right. Therefore, this number becomes 01.100000

Now the exponent of the second number requires that the binary point is not moved. Therefore, this number becomes 1.0100000. We can perform the subtraction by adding the complement of this second number. The two's complement of the second number is: 0.1100000

We now line up the point and 'subtract' the numbers:

```
  1 . 1 0 0 0 0 0
  0 · 1 1 0 0 0 0 +
  _____
1 0 . 0 1 0 0 0 0
              1
```

(Do a decimal check on the correct answer +1.5 – (–0.75) = 2.25 as shown in above sum.)

To normalise the answer we write 0.1001000 and the exponent needs to be +2.

Therefore, the normalised form of the answer is
0.1001000 | 0010

Multiplication and division of floating point numbers

This is one of those rare occasions when something is extremely simple for once! The only thing to remember here is that **double-length registers** may be needed to hold the result of a product.

Again consider a decimal analogy:
Suppose we wish to work out $(4 \times 10^2) \times (2 \times 10^3)$

From our mathematics we remember that we can write $4 \times 2 \times 10^2 \times 10^3$

We can multiply the powers of ten by adding the indices. Therefore, the sum becomes:

$(4 \times 2) \times 10^5$

Therefore, we **multiply** the original numbers and **add** the indices. The same can be done with binary floating-point numbers as follows:

Multiply the mantissa of each number and add the exponents. Put the two decimal numbers into normalised form. Multiply them together and put the answer in standard form.

Example

Work out 12×9

The binary for 12 is 1100. Therefore, in normalised form we get   0.1100000 | 0100
The binary for 9 is 1001. Therefore, in normalised form we get   0.1001000 | 0100

Multiply the mantissa:

```
  0 . 1 0 0 1
    0 . 1 1 ×
  _____
    1 0 0 1
  1 0 0 1 0 +
  _____
0 . 0 1 1 0 1 1
```

Remember from your early school days the rule for 'counting up the number of figures after the point in the question', and then 'making sure that there are the same number of figures after the point in the answer'. It works in binary too.

Therefore, 0.11 × 0.1001 = 0.011011

The normalised form of the above is: 0.1101100 | 1111 (exponent of –1)

Next add the original exponents (the easy part!):
0100 + 0100 = 1000

> **Hint:** Don't forget you can use a calculator to work out the fractional sum by multiplying 1011 x 11, then putting the binary point in the right place. In the sum shown here, you count back six places from the right of the number (putting in extra 0s if required), because there are 6 figures after the binary points in the question. This should be remembered from your elementary mathematics days!

Now incorporate this with the normalised mantissa. Note that the sum of the previous exponents will have to be added to the −1 produced from the normalised mantissa. Therefore, the new exponent will be:

```
1 0 0 0
1 1 1 1  +
―――――
0 1 1 1
```
     i.e. 1000 + 1111 = 0111 using a 4-bit exponent.

Carry is
lost   (1)

Therefore, the new mantissa becomes 0111

Hence the final answer is 0.1101100 | 0111

In pure binary this is 01101100 = 108

Note that the system can only handle numbers up to +128. If we had tried to work out 12 × 11 then we would have obtained the wrong answer. This would have been a case of **arithmetic overflow** (see later in this chapter).

Division of floating point numbers is performed in a similar way. The only difference is that the mantissa of the first number is divided by the mantissa of the second, and the exponents are subtracted.

Multi precision

If greater precision is required, then **words** (the collections of binary digits which we have been using) can be joined together to form longer words. For example, two 8-bit words can be joined to form a 16-bit word, thus giving a large increase in the number of significant figures. Such a technique is known as **double precision.** Three words joined together would give us **triple precision.** The collective term is simply known as **multi-precision**. In Microsoft's Visual BASIC, for example, negative-double-precision-floating-point numbers have the following range.

  $-1.79769313486232 \times 10^{+308}$ to
                      $-4.94065645841247 \times 10^{-324}$

Computer-based arithmetic procedures

After wading through many of the previous sections you will be aware of the fact that computer arithmetic in its many forms is a combination of shifts (left and right), adding, adding complements and fiddle factors. It is beyond the scope of this book to go into too much detail on complex computer arithmetic, but some elementary computer-based methods are included in some syllabuses.

The restoring method (binary division)

Let us assume that we are going to work out 39/3 = 13 in binary. To save us using long groups of names like 'the number which we are dividing by' we will use the correct terminology. In any division sum it is:

$$\frac{\text{Dividend}}{\text{Divisor}} = \text{Quotient, and Remainder (if necessary)}$$

Therefore, in the above sum, 39 is called the **dividend,** 3 the **divisor** and 13 is the **quotient**. There is no **remainder**. We would normally set out the sum as follows:

```
        0 0 1 1 0 1
   1 1 | 1 0 0 1 1 1
         1 1 . . .
        ―――――
         1 1 . . .
         1 1 . . .
        ―――――
           0 1 1
           1 1
        ―――――
           0 r 0
```

The bits in the quotient will be called **quotient bits.**

Note the number 01 is used as though we are going to start the sum again using 01, and eventually 011. As the 'new dividend' these numbers are called **partial remainders.**

A very considerable amount of insight has gone into the above sum. For example, in the very first part we would mentally ask ourselves if 11 goes into 1. The answer is obviously no because 11 is bigger. However, a computer could not mentally do this and would, therefore, have to do some test on the numbers. One way would be to try the subtraction to see if it worked. If it did not, you could **restore** the dividend and move along to the next group of digits to try again. This forms the basis for what is called the **restoring method**. The method is demonstrated using the 39/3 example again. Let's use an 8-bit integer two's complement representation.

When the divisor (11) is subtracted we will add the two's complement. Now the two's complement of 11 is 101 (must have a 1 in front or it would not be a negative number). Therefore, this number will be added to the appropriate part of the dividend:

We cannot shift the divisor right any more unless we introduce more digits and a binary point. The above shows that 3 goes into 39 exactly 13 times, i.e. no remainder. If there were a remainder it would be contained in this last number. The answer is obtained by building up the quotient bits shown in table 31.1.

Quotient bit number   1 2 3 4 5 6
                              0 0 1 1 0 1   i.e. the answer is 13

We will now summarise the above procedure so that an algorithm can be formulated. The following must be read in conjunction with the working out of the binary sum in table 31.1:

Table 31.1

Instructions	Carry bit	Sign bit	Rest of number							Comments
Start with the dividend		0	0	1	0	0	1	1	1	i.e. +39
Place divisor under appropriate digits		1	0	1						Two's complement of +3
Subtract by adding two's complement		1	1	0	0	0	1	1	1	Sign bit is negative so did not work.
Restore the original number		0	1	1						Set quotient bit (1) = **0**
Carry is lost	1	0	0	1	0	0	1	1	1	Original number is restored
Shift divisor right one place		1	1	0	1					Leading 1s inserted for negative number
Subtract by adding twos complement		1	1	1	1	0	1	1	1	Sign bit is negative so did not work.
Restore the original number		0	0	1	1					Set quotient bit (2) = **0**
Carry is lost	1	0	0	1	0	0	1	1	1	Original number is restored
Shift divisor right one place		1	1	1	0	1				Leading 1s inserted for negative number
Subtract by adding two's complement	1	0	0	0	0	1	1	1	1	Sign bit is positive so it worked!
New partial remainder is now		0	0	0	0	1	1	1	1	Set quotient bit (3) = **1**
Shift divisor right one place		1	1	1	1	0	1			Leading 1s inserted for negative number
Subtract by adding two's complement	1	0	0	0	0	0	0	1	1	Sign bit is positive so it worked!
New partial remainder is now		0	0	0	0	0	0	1	1	Set quotient bit (4) = **1**
Shift divisor right one place		1	1	1	1	1	0	1		Leading 1s inserted for negative number
Subtract by adding two's complement		1	1	1	1	1	1	0	1	Sign bit is negative so did not work
Restore the original number		0	0	0	0	1	1			Set quotient bit (5) = **0**
Carry is lost	1	0	0	0	0	0	1	1		Last working number is restored
Shift divisor right one place		1	1	1	1	1	0	1		Leading 1s inserted for negative number
Subtract by adding two's complement	1	0	0	0	0	0	0	0	0	Sign bit is positive so it worked!
No digits are left!		0	0	0	0	0	0	0	0	Set quotient bit (6) = **1**

(a) Start at the most significant end of the dividend i.e. shift the divisor left until the most significant bit of the divisor lines up with the most significant bit of the dividend.

(b) Next subtract (by adding the two's complement) the divisor from the three most significant bits of the dividend (or four for a four figure, five for a five figure divisor etc.).

(c) If the result of the subtraction in (b) is positive, put a 1 in the most significant bit of the quotient. If the result of the subtraction in (b) is negative, put a 0 in the most significant bit of the quotient

(d) If a 0 was put in (b) we restore the quotient by adding back the divisor or shifted divisor. If a 1 was put in (b) then we leave the partial remainder alone.

(e) Next shift the divisor one place to the right and repeat the above process making sure that the 0 or

1 in (c) above is put in the next most significant bit of the quotient.

(f) The only problem is how to know how many shifts right of the quotient we must make. To solve this problem, we shift the divisor left at the start of the procedure until a 1 appears in the most significant bit of the register. If we record the number of shifts that were necessary, then this will be the number of shifts right that are necessary.

Consider the following example, which reflects what's happened during the above process:

We started with a divisor of 3, i.e. in 8 bits: 00000011
Shift left until a 1 appears in the most significant bit, i.e. 01100000 (note the number must still be positive).
Five shifts left were necessary. Therefore, five shifts right were needed in the above problem.

Exercise 31.1

1. (a) Explain the difference between **fixed and floating point** numbers. What are the **advantages** and **disadvantages** of each system?

   (b) Clearly explain the functions that the **mantissa** and **exponent** have in **floating point** number representation.

   (c) Why is **normalisation** necessary when representing numbers in floating point form?

2. Using an **integer fixed point binary two's complement** representation with a 12-bit register, work out the following:

(a) What is the **maximum positive number** that can be stored?

(b) What is the **minimum positive** number?

(c) What is the **smallest magnitude negative number**?

(d) What is the **largest magnitude negative number**?

3 Using a **fractional fixed point binary two's complement representation** and a 10-bit register, and assuming that the **binary point** is in the position shown:

* • * * * * * * * *

If **normalization is ignored**, work out the following:

(a) What is the **maximum positive** number that can be stored?

(b) What is the **minimum positive** number?

(c) What is the **smallest magnitude negative number**?

(d) What is the **largest magnitude negative number**?

4 A 12-bit register is split up such that 8 bits are used in **fractional two's complement** representation to represent the **mantissa** and the remaining 4 bits are used as an **integer two's complement** representation for the exponent as follows:

* • * * * * * * * / * * * *

Mantissa   **Exponent**

Using the above register represent the following numbers in **normalised** or **standard form**:

(a) +1   (b) +9

(c) −3   (d) −30

(e) 0.125   (f) −0.015 625

5 Using a **fractional floating point two's complement binary representation** with a 16-bit register, split up into a 10-bit **mantissa** (two's complement fractional) and a 6-bit **exponent** (two's complement integer). Assuming that your answers must be **normalised** work out the following:

(a) What is the **maximum positive** number that can be stored?

(b) What is the **minimum positive** number?

(c) What is the **smallest magnitude negative number**?

(d) What is the **largest magnitude negative number**?

6 Explain the differences in the techniques of carrying out **addition** and **subtraction** when compared to carrying out **multiplication** and **division** using **fractional floating point binary two's complement representation** of numbers. Make specific references to how the **mantissa** and **exponents** play their particular parts.

7 Use the **restoring method** for carrying out the following **binary** divisions:

(a) 48/8   (b) 51/6

Errors in computer arithmetic

In previous sections the numbers have been carefully chosen so that 'right answers' were obtained when the various methods of arithmetic were being tried out. It must be realised that the number of bits available to perform the arithmetic is limited, and therefore errors will occur because the numbers will probably have to be simplified in some way. The representation of the numbers, i.e. 'fixed' or 'floating point', has a major effect on the accuracy that can be achieved with a given number of digits. Errors that are introduced because of the way that the numbers are represented inside the computer are called **computational errors**. If we are able to understand why these errors occur, then it is often possible to design algorithms to minimise these errors. Other types of errors, e.g. data being entered into the computer the wrong way round, etc., will be treated in other parts of this book.

Let's think of the real numbers in terms of the following graphs. Here we simply have real numbers represented graphically from 0 to 10.

0   1   2   3   4   5   6   7   8   9   10

If we were to zoom in on part of the above range, say from 1 to 2, then we could expand the range between 1 and 2 as shown in the following diagram.

1.0   1.1   1.2   1.3   1.4   1.5   1.6   1.7   1.8   1.9   2.0

Did you know that . . .

There is a variation on the old saying, 'To err is human, to forgive is divine'. It's . . .

'To err is human – to really foul things up you need a computer!'

We could continue this process further and look at the range between 1.3 and 1.4:

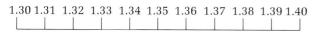

1.30 1.31 1.32 1.33 1.34 1.35 1.36 1.37 1.38 1.39 1.40

The process can be extended indefinitely. Thus, we can see that we have an infinite supply of real numbers. Therefore, no computer could possibly represent all of the real numbers, even in the small range 1.3 to 1.4! As an example, consider a 3-bit-fixed-point register. In two's complement we could only represent the following:

Register representation			Actual number
0	1	1	+3
0	1	0	+2
0	0	1	+1
0	0	0	0
1	1	1	−1
1	1	0	−2
1	0	1	−3
1	0	0	−4

If we wished to express 2.75 in the above system then it could not be done exactly. Now 2.75 can be represented exactly in binary as: 010.11. If we chop off the last two digits then we would get 010 (i.e. 2), or if we used a method of rounding up, then we would get 011 (i.e. 3). Therefore, in the above system 2.75 would have to be represented as 2 or 3.

In a real computer the range of numbers would be vast compared with the above representation, and precision would be considerably improved due to the very large increase in digits available. However, the same principles of finding and working out the errors will still apply.

Some terminology used with errors

It is important to define a few terms and concepts used in error analysis before proceeding any further.

Precision

This is the term associated with the word length (i.e. the number of bits) that is available to represent a given number. As an example, consider an 8-bit register. Any number that is contained inside this register can only be precise to one part in 256. The term precision should not be confused with the term accuracy, which indicates the 'degree of correctness'.

Accuracy

This is a measure of the closeness of an approximation to the exact or true value. This term should not be confused with precision, which is related to the degree of detail (i.e. the number of digits) that is being used in a number.

A simple example is all that's necessary to clarify the difference between accuracy and precision. Suppose we have to represent the number 7 in pure binary using four digits. Seven can be represented exactly (i.e. without error) as 0111. Next suppose that the fraction 0.10101010101 is to be represented using 8 bits. The number would become 0.1010101. There has been an error introduced when representing the original number.

The second representation above, containing the error, is more precise (i.e. 8 bits instead of 4) but it is less accurate.

Range

The range is the set of all numbers that can be represented by a particular system. For example, using a 4-bit two's complement integer representation, the range of numbers would go from −8 to +7 (see chapter 30). The range can also be expressed as the difference between the largest and smallest values. Therefore −8 to +7 could also be expressed as a range of 15 [(+7) − (−8)].

Resolution

This is simply the magnitude of the difference between the last two (least significant) adjacent digits or numbers, e.g. for a three-digit decimal representation, the range may go from 000 to 999. Over this entire range the resolution would be 1, because the difference between the last two adjacent integer values is 1. Obviously for other representations, like floating point, the resolution is not constant over the entire range and varies according to the value of the exponent being used.

Truncation

Also known as **rounding** down. This is one of the methods for dealing with situations where the precision is not adequate to represent all digits in the number to be stored. As an example, suppose we wish to store the decimal number representing π (i.e. 3.141 592 653...), but only five digits are available. If the number is truncated then this means that all the digits after the fifth are to be dropped, i.e. the number 3.141 592 653 ... would be represented in five digits as 3.1415.

Truncation error

This is the error that results from the use of the truncation process. For example, if the number 273.1473 is represented as 273.14, then the truncation error would be 0.0073.

Rounding

This is a method which tries to select a value nearest to the original value of the number. It is the method with which most people will be familiar from mathematics. In the decimal system the following rules would apply.

If the number after the last digit to be represented is 5 or more, then increase the previous digit by 1. If the number after the last digit to be represented is less than 5, then truncate (see above).

e.g. 21.7348 would be 21.735 to five significant figures or 21.73 to four significant figures.

In binary, if the digit after the last digit to be represented is a 1, then increase the previous digit by 1, otherwise leave the previous digit alone.

Overflow

This occurs when a computation has produced an answer that is too big to be represented in the system. For example, if we had a 4-bit integer two's complement representation then the range is –8 to +7. However, if we worked out 3×5 then this would produce an answer of 15, i.e. a number which is too big to be represented in our 4-bit system. This happens so often with multiplication that double length registers are needed to hold the answer. If the system did not detect that an overflow had occurred, then large errors could easily be made, e.g. in the above example $3 \times 5 = 1111$, the number would be taken as –1 instead of +15!

Underflow

If an answer that is smaller than the smallest number that can be represented by the system is produced, then underflow has taken place. It's possible to generate an error message but often the system uses the number zero instead.

Errors introduced from decimal to binary conversion

Most decimal numbers are converted into binary and therefore, for the majority of numbers, an error will be introduced at this stage before the numbers are even used in any calculations.

Consider the following. If the decimal fraction 0.75 is converted into binary, then no error occurs because 0.75 can easily be represented as 0.11. However, most numbers are not multiples of binary fractions and will not be able to be expressed exactly, irrespective of the number of binary digits available. For example, the number 0.1414, using 8 bits, would be represented as shown in table 31.2.

Subtracting the two digits representing the number from the actual number we get a difference as follows.

$$
\begin{array}{r}
0.1414 \\
0.1250 \; - \\
\hline
0.0164 \\
0.015625 \; - \\
\hline
0.000775 \\
\hline
\end{array}
$$

Hence 0.1414 = 0.00100100 (8 bits).

But 0.00100100 is actually 0.015 625 + 0.125 = 0.140 625.

Therefore 0.1414 has been represented as 0.140 625 in 8 bits. Errors like this happen when most decimal fractions are input to a computer. However, it is usual to have a large number of binary digits, and this means that the decimal number is represented to a sensible number of decimal places.

Error classification

There are two important ways in which computational errors can be described. It is really common sense, but can be expressed as follows:

1. Actual error = exact value – computed value

Here the **exact value** would be the value obtained in theory without any error. The **computed value** is the value obtained from the computer after it has been processed, e.g. we might have a decimal to binary conversion error, followed by a truncation error, followed by a binary to decimal conversion error.

2. Relative error = actual error / exact value

Therefore

relative error = (exact value – computed value) / exact value
(Combining (1) and (2) above)

Table 31.2

0.5	0.25	0.125	0.062 5	0.031 25	0.015 625	0.007 812 5	0.003 906 25
0	0	1	0	0	1	0	0

The actual error could be very misleading, e.g. an error of 0.000001 sounds better than an error of 10. However, it depends on the size of the original number. Hence the need for relative error. In practice it is likely that we may not know the exact value, and hence we have to use the approximation:

relative error = estimated error / approximate value

This would be used in examples such as 'If 180 has been given correct to three significant figures, what is the maximum relative error?' (see later).

3. Absolute error = |actual error|

(Note | | means modulus)

4. Absolute relative error = |relative error|

(This is similar to percentage error.) The last two formulae are simply the previous two without any regard to the signs of the error; it is usual in many cases to concentrate on the magnitude of the error.

5. Percentage error = relative error × 100 per cent

Example 1

Find the actual and relative error when 1/3 is approximated to 0.333.

Now the exact value $= 1/3$
and computed value $= 0.333$
Hence actual error $= 1/3 - 0.333$
$= 1/3 - 333/1000$
$= (1000 - 999)/3000 = 1/3000$
Therefore actual error $= 1/3000$
Relative error $=$ actual error/exact value
$= 1/3000 / 1/3 = 1/3000 \times 3/1$
$= 3/3000 = 1/1000$

Hence relative error $= 0.001$

Example 2

The sum '4.39 + 0.798' is to be worked out using only three significant figures. Find the actual and relative errors if truncation is used.

4.39
0.798 +
─────
5.188   (This value is truncated to 5.18)
─────

The exact value is 5.188 and the computed value is 5.18.

Therefore actual error $= 5.188 - 5.18 = 0.008$
Hence relative error $= 0.008/5.188 = 0.001\,542$

Finding maximum errors

It can be seen from the above that it is simple to calculate each error for a given number if necessary. However, every different number would produce different values for error. It would be more useful to calculate the **maximum error** that is likely to occur in a given situation. The same terminology is used, but this time we calculate **maximum actual or relative error**.

It is important to realise that the maximum actual error that can occur is very simple to work out. For decimal numbers it is simply 'put a 5 in the digit after the required number of places'. As a demonstration, we will choose a situation where **rounding** occurs with decimal numbers.

Did you know that . . .

The arithmetic bug in the original Pentium was due to some errors in a look up table – a method being used by Intel to speed up the Pentium chip compared with the other chip competitors at the time. Intel offered free Pentium upgrades to all those users who requested it!

Let the exact decimal number vary over the range 0.120 to 0.130, as shown in table 31.3. Also, let there be only two figures after the decimal point available to represent the number.

From the table we can see that the maximum absolute error that can occur is 0.005 so 5 is put in the column after the last digit that can be represented, in this case, the third column. The following patterns for decimal numbers can therefore be established:

Typical decimal number	Maximum absolute error
0.3	0.05
0.72	0.005
0.769	0.0005
0.2856	0.00005

As an example, consider working out the maximum relative errors for the decimal numbers 0.017 and 0.916 when computed to two decimal places:

(a) Actual value $= 0.017$
Computed value $= 0.02$
Max absolute error $= 0.005$
Max relative error $= 0.005 / 0.017$
$= 0.2941$

Table 31.3

Exact value	0.120	0.121	0.122	0.123	0.124	0.125	0.126	0.127	0.128	0.129	0.130
Computed value	0.12	0.12	0.12	0.12	0.12	0.13	0.13	0.13	0.13	0.13	0.13
Absolute error	0.000	0.001	0.002	0.003	0.004	0.005	0.004	0.003	0.002	0.001	0.000

(b) Actual value = 0.916
Computed value = 0.92
Max absolute error = 0.005
Max relative error = 0.005 / 0.916
= 0.005459

The maximum relative error for any given number will, therefore, increase, as the actual number becomes smaller. In the worst case of all the maximum relative error could be 1. The relative error will always be less than or equal to the maximum relative error.

(1) 0.072 71 is rounded to four decimal places.
Maximum absolute error 0.000 05.
Maximum relative error 0.000 05/0.072 71
= 0.000 687 7

(2) 12.727 is stored to four significant figures.
Maximum absolute error 0.005.
Maximum relative error 0.005/12.727
= 0.000 392 9

Examples

Find the maximum 'absolute' and 'relative errors' of the following:

Exercise 31.2

1 (a) What is meant by **errors** when applied to computer arithmetic?

(b) Explain the difference between **accuracy** and **precision**.

(c) What do the terms **overflow** and **underflow** mean?

(d) Find the **relative error** when 5/7 is represented correct to three decimal places

(e) Find the **actual** and **relative errors** when 2.31×5.82 is truncated to four significant figures.

(f) Find the **maximum absolute error** when 0.2753 is computed to three decimal places.

2 Find the **worst possible relative error** when 29.1 is subtracted from 108.3.

3 When the numbers 31.8 and 2.16 are added together the arithmetic is to be restricted to only three decimal digits. Work out the possible range of values of the answer and give the answer correct to two significant figures.

4 In the following, **a** can be found by using the formula:

$a = (h^2 - b^2)$

Now $h^2 - b^2$ can be worked out in the following two different ways:

(1) $(h \times h) - (b \times b)$ or   (2) $(h + b)(h - b)$

Using the figures h = 3.2 and b = 2.8, work out the relative percentage error when each method is used if the machine on which the algorithms are executed is accurate only to two significant figures.

End of chapter revision aid and summary

Cover up the right-hand column and see if you can answer the questions or define the terms on the left. They appear in the order in which they are covered in this chapter. Alternatively you may browse through the right-hand column to aid revision.

What is a floating point binary number?	Floating point binary numbers are numbers with mantissa and exponent parts used to represent a wider range of numbers with less precision.
What is a mantissa?	A mantissa is that part of a number which represents the digits in a number.
What is an exponent?	The exponent is that part of a number which represents the power (i.e. the number of places that the binary point has to be moved from it's current position to determine the value of the final number).
How might normalisation help?	Normalisation is a method of preventing loss of accuracy and multiple representations of the same number.
What is meant by the term precision?	Precision is a term associated with the word length.
Define the term accuracy.	Accuracy is a measure of how close to a real value we can get.
What is meant by the term range?	Range is the difference between the largest and smallest values.
What is meant by the term resolution?	Resolution is the magnitude of the difference between the last two adjacent digits.
What are truncation errors?	Truncation errors are errors due to truncation (i.e. chopping off digits).
What is meant by rounding?	Rounding is where the digit after the last one of interest is examined and some rule is applied which may alter the previous digit.
Define overflow.	Overflow occurs when a number is too big to be represented by the system.
Define underflow.	Underflow is when a number is too small to be represented by the system.
What is the actual error?	Actual error = exact value − computed value
What is the relative error?	Relative error = actual error/exact value
What is the absolute error?	Absolute error = $\vert$ actual error $\vert$
What is the absolute relative error?	Absolute relative error = $\vert$ relative error $\vert$
What is the percentage error?	Percentage error = relative error × 100%

32 Language Translation

Key resources

To carry out this work most successfully it's best if you have:

◆ A reverse Polish notation calculator. The Hewlett Packard company used to produce the most, but you can also find these types of calculator simulated on a computer

◆ If you don't have a reverse Polish notation calculator, you might be able to program your own after reading this chapter!

Concept checkpoints

◆ It's imperative that you understand the concept of a stack before covering Polish notation. This is covered in chapter 24.

◆ You will need some knowledge of the data structures from chapter 25.

Introduction

This chapter looks at some of the ways in which languages are transformed into a form that can be run on a computer system, and some of the methods that are used to check to see if the rules of a language have been obeyed and applied correctly.

Anyone who uses a computer system must be using some form of language to control it. Therefore, a study of language itself is fundamental to the study of computer science. However, this topic is not an easy one, and is therefore not covered in great depth at this level.

It is the job of the computer language to interface with the computer user in such a way that the hardware of the computer system is completely disguised. In this way, the user does not see the hardware of the machine, but a computer running 'COBOL', 'Java' or 'Pascal', for example.

We mentioned at the beginning of chapter 13 that computer languages are not like natural languages such as English, but are a class of **formal** languages. Even so, many of the techniques of language analysis that are used for natural languages can be used to help define the formulation and manipulation of computer languages.

First, it is obvious that statements that constitute parts of high-level languages bear little relationship to the actual control of the computer at machine code level. For example,

PRINT TAB(3,7) "Good Morning."

masks the complexity of the actual processes that go on inside the machine to cause the string 'Good Morning' to appear on the output device at the desired tab position. Therefore, some method of **translation** is needed, that must act upon code such as that shown above, to produce the desired machine code that will perform this operation and therefore get the job done. The general name for software that translates 'source code' into the 'code that can be run directly on a machine' is a **translator**. The situation can be summarised in figure 32.1.

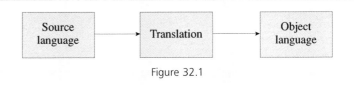

Figure 32.1

The code that is input to a translator is called the **source language (or source code)** and the code that is output from the translator is called the **object (or target) language**.

The three common forms of translators are **compilers**, **interpreters** and **assemblers**, but assemblers have already been covered in detail in chapter 21. It is the job of these translators to turn the source code into object code by following strict sets of rules specified by the designers of language being translated.

An **interpreter** is a translator that goes through the processes of translation every time the program is run. Indeed, **interpreters** such as those found running some versions of BASIC, translate one line of the program at a time. If these lines of code happen to be inside a particular loop structure, if the loop is to be executed 1000 times, then the lines must be interpreted 1000 times! This means that *all* the stages of translation, including checking, will have to be gone through many times, and this is the main reason why most interpreters are very slow compared to compilers.

A **compiler** is a translator that goes through the translation process only once. The object language is then saved, and next time the program is run it does not have to be **recompiled**. Although compilers are very much faster than interpreters are, if the source language has to be modified, then the whole program must be recompiled. This means that compilers are not as convenient as interpreters are for program development and debugging. Nevertheless, this is the way that most professional programming environments such as C++, for example, are organised.

Did you know that . . .

In the early days of computing all high-level languages were compiled. It was the advent of BASIC working in a time-sharing environment that brought about alternative methods of translation like interpretation.

The processes of **compilation** and **execution** can be seen in figure 32.2(a) and figure 32.2(b) respectively. Figure 32.2(a) shows the source program, i.e. BASIC, Pascal, or Java, etc. being **compiled**, and the details of this compilation process will be covered shortly. A different compiler would be needed for each high-level language that is to be run on the machine, and a large machine may have many different high-level language compilers. Besides producing the **object program**, a listing of the **source program** is often required at compilation stage, and there are many other aids to help develop the programs too.

Figure 32.2(b) shows the object program being executed by the CPU, i.e. this is a **machine code program** (see chapter 20) that is resident in the computer. If the object program needs any additional data, such as files, for example, they would have to be stored in appropriate places so that the resident machine code could work with this data in convenient ways.

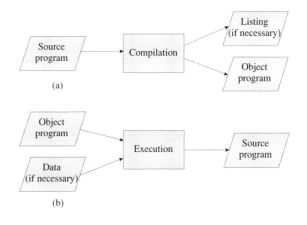

(a)

(b)

Figure 32.2

Compilation

It should be obvious from reading the above that the compiler itself must be a very complex piece of software. Indeed, most compilers on large computer systems take many years to write.

The **compilation process** can be split up into several stages. These are as follows.

1. **Lexical analysis**
2. **Syntax analysis**
3. **Code generation**
4. **Code optimisation**

Lexical analysis

Lexical analysis is the first stage of compilation. A **lexical analyser** is a part of the compiler program that breaks up the input presented to the compiler into chunks that are in a form suitable to be analysed by the next stage of the compilation process.

For example, if different peripheral devices have been used to input a program into the computer system, it is the job of the lexical analyser to standardise these different source codes into a form that would be identical for the next stage of the compilation process. For example, if two identical programs were to be run on a computer, but one program was stored on disk and the other on magnetic tape, then the codes that represent these programs may be slightly different. The lexical analyser ensures that these codes are changed into a form that is the same for each peripheral device that may be used to input source programs into the system.

When the strings of characters representing the source program are broken up into small chunks, these chunks are often known as **tokens**. The source code has therefore been **tokenised**. It is usual to remove all redundant parts of the source code (such as spaces and comments) during this tokenisation phase. It is also likely in many systems that **key words such** as 'ENDWHILE' or 'PROCEDURE' etc. will be replaced by more efficient, shorter tokens.

It is the job of the lexical analyser to check that all the key words used are valid, and to group certain symbols with their neighbours, so they can form larger units to be presented to the next stage of the compilation process. This is because the characters of the source program are usually analysed just one at a time. Characters such as '+' or 'x' are known as **terminal symbols** in their own right, but other characters such as 'P', 'R', 'I', 'N' and 'T' may have to be grouped together to form the token for the **reserved word** 'PRINT'.

As errors can be detected during this first phase of compilation, facilities to generate an **error report** must also be provided.

Syntax analysis

Syntax analysis is the second stage of compilation and determines whether the 'string of input tokens' form valid sentences etc. (i.e. it checks the grammar to see if all the rules of syntax are being obeyed). At this stage, the structure of the source program is analysed to see if it conforms to the context-free grammar for the particular language that is being compiled. It basically breaks up the statements into smaller identifiable chunks that can be acted upon by the computer when it executes the final program. It would also include finding out things like 'whether the correct number of brackets has been used in expressions', and determining the priorities of the arithmetical operators used within an arithmetic expression, for example. This process is also called **parsing**, and is carried out by that part of the compiler called the **parser**.

Did you know that . . .
One of the first compilers was invented in 1952 at the University of Manchester.

The syntax of any high level language is expressed as a set of rules. For example, in Pascal, the **syntax diagram** is often used. This is simply a convenient way of expressing the syntax of a language (syntax definition). In Pascal, the syntax diagram for an **identifier** is shown in figure 32.3.

From figure 32.3 it is easily seen that 'A', 'H7', 'ASS31' and 'ABC12U' are all valid identifiers, but '1B', '17' and '17BY14' are not, because they all start with a number. Other forms of syntax definition, using the Backus Naur Form (BNF), will be developed later in this chapter. As errors in syntax can be generated during this syntax analysis phase, the ability to print error reports is also necessary. It is also at this stage that a **dictionary** is generated. This is simply a list kept by the compiler of

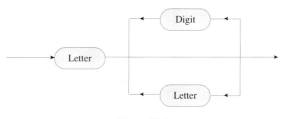

Figure 32.3

the variables used by the program, the variable types such as 'numerical', 'integer', 'real', 'complex' or 'logical', for example, and the place in memory at which these variables can be found. All the information stored in the dictionary will be needed later when the object program is run. The actual details of this syntax analysis phase of compilation will be covered shortly.

Code generation

Code generation is the phase of the compilation process where the code specific to the target machine is generated. As the code is **machine code,** then it is usual for several machine-code instructions to be generated for each high-level language instruction.

As an example, consider the following simple line in a BASIC program:

LET length = 2*(side1 − side2) + 4*(side3 − side4)

Now the keyword LET is optional, and would, therefore, have been removed during the **lexical analysis** stage. The resulting statement might now be as follows:

length = 2*(side1 − side2) + 4*(side3 − side4)

The 'side1', 'side2', 'side3', 'side4' and 'length' variables will have been created in the **dictionary** mentioned earlier during the syntax analysis stage. The dictionary will contain the variable name, the variable type and where in memory this variable can be found so that the machine code program can load it. Therefore, for the above line, the dictionary used by the compiler may have entries similar to those shown in the following table.

Variable name	Variable type	Memory location
length	Numeric	F B F F
side1	Numeric	F C 0 6
side2	Numeric	F C 0 D
side3	Numeric	F C 1 4
side4	Numeric	F C 1 6

As well as building up dictionary tables like the above, routines from the system library may often have to be called up. Functions such as 'square roots' or 'sine' might be needed so often that the machine code to deal with them is stored in the system library.

If we now imagine some fictitious assembly language (see chapter 21) with mnemonics ADD, SUBTRACT and MULTIPLY etc., then the following assembly-language code might be generated for the single line of BASIC.

LOAD	sidel
SUBTRACT	side2
MULTIPLY	2
STORE	temp
LOAD	side3
SUBTRACT	side4
MULTIPLY	4
ADD	temp
STORE	length

In the above assembly language program, '**temp**' is simply a location used by the computer to store a '**temporary** answer' during a calculation. In fact, actual machine code would be produced by the compiler, but a list of hex or binary numbers is not so enlightening as the above for showing the principles of how the object language might be generated.

Code optimisation

Often the code produced by such methods is not the best that can be obtained. This is a consequence of trying to construct machine code from a high-level language. It's often possible to generate more efficient machine code by carrying out a process called **optimisation**. However, it is still very unlikely that even the best optimisers can produce code that would be as good as hand-optimised code. Usually, it is not worth going to these extraordinary lengths to improve the final product, but if speed or efficiency is of paramount importance as might be the case with a real-time system (see chapter 8), then there may be no choice.

Methods of syntax definition

One advantage of being the **user** of a language is that even if you don't understand all of the language, you can try 'bits' out to see if they work, and let the interpreter or compiler throw error messages at you if necessary. There is, however, no such luck if you have to write the language or the compiler in the first place! Therefore, formal methods have to be developed to completely describe the syntax of a language before it is written and implemented. One of the most common methods for defining syntax was developed by John Backus, and was originally called the **Backus normal form**. It was later pointed out that it was not normal from a mathematical point of view, and so became known as the **Backus Naur form**. This gave recognition to the work of Peter Naur, who did much work using this syntax definition method to define the original ALGOL language. The letters **BNF** are an abbreviation for **Backus Naur Form** and will be used whenever necessary. Any language (such as BNF) which is used to describe the syntax of a computer language is known as a **meta language**.

BNF notation

The BNF notation is quite simple, and involves a list of statements, which define symbols that represent the language.

As a start we need to define the symbol ':: =' to mean 'is defined by'

Hence LHS ::= RHS

would read the 'left-hand side is defined by the right-hand side'. The symbol ':: =' is an example of what's called a **meta symbol**, i.e. a symbol which is used in a meta language.

The second important meta symbol is '|', which means 'OR'.

For example, LHS::= A|B would read as the 'left-hand side is defined by A OR B'.

The third part of the basic notation involves the use of corner braces '<' and '>'. These braces are used to define what are called **meta variables** or **syntactic variables** (or even metasyntactic variables!).

This sounds horribly complex, but consider the following simple example:

<hexdigit> ::= 0 | 1 | 2 | 3 | 4 | 5 | 6 | 7 | 8 | 9 | A | B | C | D | E | F

Therefore a 'hexadecimal digit' is defined by a '0' or '1' or '2' or '3'...etc.

<hex digit> is known as a **meta variable**.

The symbols such as 0,1,2,3, etc. in the above example are known as **terminal symbols**.

Once a meta variable has been defined, it can then be used to form the next part of a more complex definition of the syntax of the language. For example, to define an integer we may use the following.

<digit>   ::= 0 | 1 | 2 | 3 | 4 | 5 | 6 | 7 | 8 | 9
<integer> ::= <digit> | <digit><integer>

Therefore, an 'integer' is defined by a 'digit', or a 'digit and an integer'.

Groups of definitions such as these are known as **productions**. From these productions we can see that an integer can consist of as many digits as necessary. There are more meta symbols, but the above three are sufficient to define many of the simple syntax structures of a language. EBNF is covered later in the chapter.

Methods of syntax analysis

Having defined how to use BNF, we can now see how the **parsing** (**syntax analysis**) stages can be carried out.

The parsing process breaks down the original sentence written in the language to see if it is legal or illegal. A sentence is simply a part of a language such as a single line in a BASIC program. To give an example of the parsing process, consider a simple example using car registration numbers.

Consider the following productions:

Rule 1 **<car registration>** ::=
<letter><digit><digit><digit><letter><letter>
<letter> | **<letter><letter><letter><digit><digit>**
<digit> **<letter>**

Rule 2 **<letter>** ::=
A | B | C | D | E | F | G | H | I | J | K | L |
M | N | P | R | S | T | V | W | X | Y

Rule 3 **<digit>** ::= 0 | 1 | 2 | 3 | 4 | 5 | 6 | 7 | 8 | 9

We will now parse the 'car registration number' T463YKL to see if it is legal.

```
   T      4      6      3      Y      K      L
<letter><digit><digit><digit><letter><letter><letter>
                <car registration>
```

Productions used
Rules 2,3,3,3,2,2, and 2
Rule 1

As each of the above forms one of the valid definitions of <car registration> (from Rule 1) we can see that the syntax analysis has been successful.

Another method is by means of a parse tree and this is shown in figure 32.4. This shows that it's possible to start off with the production <car registration>, and end up with the legal terminal symbols 'T463YKL'. If the registration number had been 'T463UKL' then the parse would have failed because we would have ended up with an illegal letter 'U'.

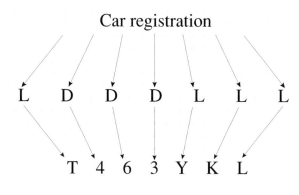

Figure 32.4

Example using BASIC

We will now look at a computer-based example using a simplified conditional branch from the BASIC language. Consider the following example of a conditional branch statement.

'IF test < 20 THEN 400'.

If we now formally express this type of simplified statement using BNF notation, we get something along the lines shown in table 32.1.

One can see how the definition of even this simplified form of conditional branch can become complex very rapidly. For example, we have only very simple variables such as 'A' or 'B7' etc. and have not even considered the use of strings. Good compiler designers certainly deserve one's admiration for the sheer enormity and complexity of their task.

We can now apply the above productions (rules) to see if the following BASIC statements are valid, and this has been done in table 32.2(a).

(a) 250 IF X < 20 THEN 400

(b) 270 IF 30 > X THEN 400

Table 32.1

Rule 1	<conditional branch statement>	::=	<line number> IF <condition> THEN <line number>
Rule 2	<condition>	::=	<variable><relation><constant>
Rule 3	<line number>	::=	<integer>
Rule 4	<integer>	::=	<digit> | <digit><integer>
Rule 5	<digit>	::=	0 | 1 | 2 | 3 | 4 | 5 | 6 | 7 | 8 | 9
Rule 6	<variable>	::=	<letter> | <letter> <integer>
Rule 7	<letter>	::=	A | B | C | D | E | F | G | H | I | J | K | L | M | N | O | P | Q | R | S | T | U | V | W | X | Y | Z
Rule 8	<relation>	::=	< | > | = | <= | >= | <> |
Rule 9	<constant>	::=	<signed integer> | <integer>
Rule 10	<signed integer>	::=	+ <integer> | – <integer>

Table 32.2

(a) 250 IF X < 20 THEN 400							Productions applied
250	IF	X	<	20	THEN	400	
<line number>	IF	<letter>	<relation>	<integer>	THEN	<line number>	3,7,8,4 and 3
<line number>	IF	<variable>	<relation>	<constant>	THEN	<line number>6,9	
<line number>	IF	<condition>			THEN	<line number>	2
		<conditional branch statement>					1

(b) 270 IF 30 > X THEN 400							Productions applied
270	IF	30	>	X	THEN	400	
<line number>	IF	<integer>	<relation>	<letter>	THEN	<line number>	3,4,8,7,3

Therefore, we have a valid conditional branch statement, i.e. one that has passed the syntax analysis stage.

You might think that it's a wild guess to go straight to <line number> at the beginning, and not to go via <digit>, <integer> and <line number>. It was done this way because the compiler would have found the key words 'IF' and 'THEN', and tried to see if the statement is a conditional branch. Let's now see what happens with the second example, shown in part (b) of table 32.2.

The parse has already failed as <condition> can never be obtained using any of the rules. This is because a <condition> cannot start off with an <integer>, i.e. there are no rules above that can turn an <integer> into a <variable>. Therefore, this second statement has failed the syntax analysis stage, and is an invalid statement.

The parse tree for statement (a) can be seen in figure 32.5(a) and the parse tree for statement (b) can be seen in figure 32.5(b).

Methods of parsing

It can be seen from the above that under certain conditions it may easily be possible to end up with an ambiguous parse. You may recall from other parts of this book that one of the essential requirements of a computer language is that it is unambiguous. Therefore, methods that can't possibly produce ambiguous languages must be used, and this is one of the challenges of good language design. One simple method is to start at the left-hand side of the statement to be parsed, and replace each element with the appropriate meta variable. We then proceed in the same way, always working from the left, and always replacing multiple meta variables with a more comprehensive meta variable where possible. This simple technique of working methodically from left to right is called **canonical parsing**. If you're wondering, the word 'canonical' simply means **standard form**, and is sometimes used when talking about the standard (canonical form) of a statement in a programming language. The word is also used when making sure that data in a database does not contain any redundant data, by defining a suitable schema.

Consider the following simple examples to show how canonical parsing works.

Parse example (1)

A decimal number may be defined using BNF notation as shown in table 32.3.

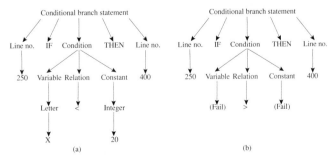

Figure 32.5

Table 32.3

					Production number
\<decimal number\>	::=	\<point\>\<number\> | \<number\>\<point\>\<number\>			1
\<number\>	::=	\<digit\> | \<number\> \<digit\>			2
\<digit\>	::=	0 | 1 | 2 | 3 | 4 | 5 | 6 | 7 | 8 | 9			3
\<point\>	::=	.			4

Table 32.4

3.142						Production used
3	.	1	4	2		
\<digit\>	.	1	4	2		3
\<number\>	.	1	4	2		2
\<number\>	\<point\>	1	4	2		4
\<number\>	\<point\>	\<digit\>	4	2		3
\<number\>	\<point\>	\<number\>	\<digit\>	2		2
\<number\>	\<point\>		\<number\>	2		2
\<number\>	\<point\>		\<number\>	\<digit\>		3
\<number\>	\<point\>		\<number\>			2
	\<decimal number\>					1

Using a **canonical parse**, we can see if '3.142' is a valid decimal number – see table 32.4.

The sequence of productions applied is shown in the last column. It is not possible to generate any other sequence if canonical parsing is used.

Parse example (2)

Sometimes the language definition may not be satisfactory, as in the next set of productions:

Language definition number 1
\<expression\> ::= \<variable\> \| \<expression\>
                \<operator\> \<expression\>
\<operator\> ::= + \| * \| ↑
\<variable\> ::= W \| X \| Y \| Z

Consider the 'expression' W * X + Y ↑ Z
Applying a canonical parse we get:

W	*	X	+ Y ↑ Z
\<variable\>	*	X	+ Y ↑ Z
\<expression\> \<operator\>		X	+ Y ↑ Z
\<expression\> \<operator\>		\<variable\>	+ Y ↑ Z
\<expression\> \<operator\>		\<expression\>	+ Y ↑ Z

We can see without proceeding further, that 'W * X + Y ↑ Z' would be evaluated from left to right, thus not obeying the normal rules of precedence, i.e. a successful canonical parse would have taken place with the '+' taking priority over '↑'. Thus, the original definition of the language will need to be changed, and this is done in the following way.

A new set of productions could be:

\<expression\> ::= \<term\> \| \<expression\> + \<term\>
   \<term\> ::= \<factor\> \| \<term\> * \<factor\>
  \<factor\> ::= \<primary\> \| \<factor\> ↑ \<primary\>
\<primary\> ::= \<variable\>
\<variable\> ::= W \| X \| Y \| Z

Let us now perform a canonical parse on W * X + Y ↑ Z again.

Step							
1	W	*	X	+	Y	↑	Z
2	\<variable\>	*	X	+	Y	↑	Z
3	\<primary\>	*	X	+	Y	↑	Z
4	\<factor\>	*	X	+	Y	↑	Z
5	\<term\>	*	X	+	Y	↑	Z
6	\<expression\>	*	\<variable\>	+	Y	↑	Z
7	\<expression\>	*	\<primary\>	+	Y	↑	Z
8	\<expression\>	*	\<factor\>	+	Y	↑	Z
9	\<expression\>	*	\<term\>	+	Y	↑	Z
10	\<expression\>	*	\<expression\>	+	Y	↑	Z

We can see that \<expression\> * \<expression\> is not defined, and therefore the parse has failed at this point. We now backtrack to step 5.

5	\<term\>	*	X	+	Y	↑	Z
6	\<term\>	*	\<variable\>	+	Y	↑	Z
7	\<term\>	*	\<primary\>	+	Y	↑	Z
8	\<term\>	*	\<factor\>	+	Y	↑	Z
9		\<term\>		+	Y	↑	Z
10		\<expression\>		+	Y	↑	Z

11	<expression>	+ <variable> ↑ Z
12	<expression>	+ <primary> ↑ Z
13	<expression>	+ <factor> ↑ Z
14	<expression>	+ <term> ↑ Z
15	<expression>	↑ Z

Here we can see that '<expression> ↑ anything' is not defined. We now backtrack to step 13.

13	<expression> + <factor> ↑ Z
14	<expression> + <factor> ↑ <variable>
15	<expression> + <factor> ↑ <primary>
16	<expression> + <factor>
17	<expression> + <term>
18	<expression>

We have finished at last! You can see how the definition of the language forced '↑' to be evaluated before being added to the rest. Similarly '*' took precedence over '+'. This is an example of how the new language definition coped with the problem outlined earlier.

Parse trees

A **parse tree** or syntax tree is another method of determining whether an expression is ambiguous or not. If two trees can be drawn for the same expression then the expression is ambiguous. Consider the examples described above again.

Example (first language definition)

W * X + Y ↑ Z

The parse tree is as shown in table 32.5.

As it is possible to draw two completely different syntax or parse trees, and still end up with a valid expression, then the language definition is ambiguous, as was found out by canonical parsing in the last section.

Example (second language definition)

However, using the second language definition: W * X + Y ↑ Z shown in table 32.6:

This time we have a unique parse tree. Try to devise another, but make sure that you stick exactly to the improved language definition!

EBNF

The BNF system suffers from quite a few limitations, although they were purposely kept from the reader in the last few sections. For example, what happens if the language you are trying to define contains some of the meta symbols like '<','>' or '|', for example? Also, among many other things, there is no place for comments, which are often added informally by experienced users at the side of existing BNF definitions. Over the past few years, programmers have therefore added more symbols to the BNF notation, and changed other parts of BNF to make it more versatile. These

---

Table 32.5

			<expression>		
	<expression>		<operator>	<expression>	
<expression>	<operator>	<expression>	+	<expression> <operator> <expression>
<variable>	*	<variable>		<variable> ↑ <variable>
W		X		Y Z

However, it is easily possible to end up with a completely different parse tree:

	<expression>			
<expression>	<operator>		<expression>	
<variable>	*	<expression>	<operator>	<expression>
W		<variable>	+	<expression> <operator> <expression>
				variable> ↑ <variable>
		X		Y Z

Table 32.6

		<expression>		
	<expression>	+		<term>
<term>	*	<factor>		<factor>
<factor>		<primary>	<factor>	↑ <primary>
<primary>		<variable>	<primary>	<variable>
<variable>		X	<variable>	Z
W		Y		

extensions have become known as **Extended Backus Naur Form**. (Or sometimes **Extended Backus Normal Form**.)

It is beyond the scope of this book to go into all the possible details regarding **Extended Backus Naur Form**, but simple uses of it are now present in some 'A' level syllabuses. A complete definition of EBNF is more appropriate to a computer science degree course, and if you are interested in the complete works, then have a look at the ISO (International Standards Organisation) 14977 definition developed in 1996. EBNF has been around for many years, and is a more comprehensive metalanguage than the original BNF. However, for the purposes of 'A' level, the following few simple definitions regarding the syntax, together with some simple examples showing the main differences between the two systems should be sufficient if you are expected to undertake EBNF in your syllabus. You should also note that there will always be minor variations in the way that these metalanguages are used by different organisations which describe the syntax of a variety of computer languages.

- EBNF enables you to show items that appear zero or more times by using {}.
- Literals (see chapter 13) are enclosed within quotes, and syntatic variables are plain text. (*Compare this to BNF where literals are plain text and syntatic variables are enclosed in angle braces.*)
- The '=' (instead of '::=' as in BNF) is used to represent 'is defined by'. (*Some definitions of EBNF actually use ':==' instead. However, it is particularly obvious if this is happening!*)
- [] are used to denote optional elements.
- EBNF also allows for comments to be added. (* *This would be a comment**)
- You can group choices more easily than in BNF by making ordinary use of brackets in the ordinary sense (i.e. similar to the use of brackets in mathematics).
- The users of the system may extend EBNF even further! (*This is because EBNF can be used to define its own syntax.*)

The above all adds up to a comprehensive metalanguage which enables language designers to express syntax more easily. Indeed, EBNF can define things that are impossible to define using BNF alone. Some *very simple* EBNF examples are now compared with BNF examples where appropriate, and this should give readers a taste of how EBNF is used. We will look at examples very similar to those covered in the BNF section earlier in this chapter, and you should not attempt to read this without an understanding of the BNF system and its uses.

(a) A vowel
In **EBNF**
vowel = "A"|"E"|"I"|"O"|"U"

(Notice how the syntatic variable is in plain text, and the literals are within quotes.)

(*In BNF*
<vowel> ::= A | E | I | O | U)

(Compare this to the *same* BNF definition where the syntatic variable is in corner braces and the literals are plain text.)

(b) An integer
In **EBNF**
digit = "0"|"1"|"2"|"3"|"4"|"5"|"6"|"7"|"8"|"9"
integer = digit {digit}

(Notice how the {} are used for repetition. The part within the {} can be repeated zero or more times – therefore, an integer may be any number of digits.)

(*In BNF*
digit ::= 0 | 1 | 2 | 3 | 4 | 5 | 6 | 7 | 8 | 9
<integer> ::= <digit> | <digit> <integer>)

(*Note how BNF has to use a recursive definition to enable it to cope with repetition.*)

(c) Repetition of a sequence of the letter z.
In **EBNF**
Sequence = {'z'}

(As {} is used to denote zero or more occurrences of what's inside them, the sequence defined here can mean 'z' or 'zz' or 'zzz' etc.)

(*In BNF*
<Sequence>::=z | zz | zzz | ....)

(This is where we would have to cheat by putting a comment at the side saying that this can go on forever – Note that the . . . dot's are not really part of the BNF definitions.)

(d) The inclusion of optional elements
In **EBNF**
Sequence = 'x' 'y' [z]

(The sequence here could be 'xy' or 'xyz')

(*In BNF*
<Sequence>::=xy | xyz)

(e) Letters of the alphabet
In **EBNF**
Letter = ("A" . . . "Z" | "a" . . . "z")

(The "..." here are used to denote implied obvious sequences together with the brackets which are used for grouping)

(*In BNF*
<Letter> ::=
$A|B|C|D|E|F|G|H|I|J|K|L|M|N|O|P|Q|R|S|T|U|V|$
$W|X|Y|Z|a|b|c|d|e|f|g|h|i|j|k|l|m|n|o|p|q|r|s|t|u$
$|v|w|x|y|z$)

(f) Unsigned decimal number (*No scientific notation to be catered for here*)

In **EBNF**

unsigned decimal number = digit {digit} "."
digit{digit}
digit = ("0".…."9")
(*In BNF*
<unsigned decimal number> ::= <digits> . <digits>
<digits>::= <digit>|<digit><digits>
<digit>::= $0|1|2|3|4|5|6|7|8|9$)

Notice that the elegance of the EBNF format is starting to come out over the BNF format for the same definitions. Modern compiler designers now prefer EBNF to BNF when it comes to defining the syntax of a language. Finally a definition of 'number' using EBNF from a computer language called 'Parallaxis III' is given in the following example. EBNF is actually easier than BNF once you get used to it.

Number = Integer | Real
Integer = Digit{Digit} ["D"] | OctalDigit {OctalDigit}
("B"|"C") | Digit {HexDigit} "H"
Real = digit {Digit} "." {Digit}[ScaleFactor]
ScaleFactor = "E" ["+"|"–"] Digit {Digit}
HexDigit = Digit "A"|"B"|"C"|"D"|"E"|"F"
Digit = OctalDigit "8"|"9"
OctalDigit = "1"|"2"|"3"|"4"|"5"|"6"|"7"

Exercise 32.1

1 (a) Why is a **translation** process necessary when computer languages are used?

(b) Name *three* common types of translator.

(c) Explain the *major* differences between the three types of translators outlined in (b).

2 The **compilation** process can be broken up into *three* main stages:

(a) **lexical analysis**

(b) **syntax analysis**

(c) **code generation**.

Outline why these three stages are necessary and give an example for each of the above stages using a language of your choice.

3 When using a **compiler** the following terminology is often encountered:

object program, source program, tokens, parsing, dictionary, terminal symbols, optimisation.

Write at least one sentence on each of the above parts to show that you fully understand the meaning of each term.

4 **Backus Naur form** is one method of defining syntax. Using a high level language of your choice show (by being as detailed as you can), how BNF notation can be used to define the following:

(a) **Identifier**

(b) **String**

(c) **Unsigned real number**

5 Define the syntax of parts (a), (b) and (c) in question **4** making use of **syntax diagrams**.

6 Consider some typical telephone directory entries:

Hopkins A.B.C., 32 Relbridge Close   Pembury 123456

Williams Rev, F.V., 1 Davidson Road   Brighton 78152

It can be seen that each entry is split up into two fields as follows

Surname | [title] | initials, | [number] | street | town | telephone number

The attributes in brackets '[ ]' are optional, i.e., we could easily have

Blogg B.C., Oak Farm Ashford 253

Devise a set of productions using Backus Naur form which, when applied to typical telephone entries, will determine the legality or otherwise of the entry.

By making use of a canonical parsing method apply the productions you have devised to show that:

Brown Y, 271 Kingsway   Exeter 736442 is legal and

Zoe P.J., 274 Bognor 817325 is not.

7 Outline the differences between BNF and EBNF.

Parsing arithmetical statements

It makes the design of compilers easier if the arithmetic expressions are presented to the compiler in what is called **reverse Polish notation.** This form of notation will now be investigated.

Polish and reverse Polish notation

Jan Lukasiewicz (you can easily see the reason why it is called Polish notation!) developed Polish notation! Polish notation is also known as **prefix notation,** because each operator *precedes* its operands. You are warned that to appreciate this notation fully, the concept of a **stack** (see chapter 24) should be well understood.

For example, instead of writing 'X + Y', '+X Y' is written.

'+X Y' is interpreted as follows:

You have two numbers, 'X' and 'Y'. The operator, which precedes the numbers tell you what to do with them. Therefore, in the above case, the numbers must be added together.

Hence +3 5 = 8

Polish notation has the advantage that there can be no ambiguity in the way that an arithmetic expression is worked out. It also needs no parentheses to separate the different parts.

Reverse Polish notation

Another form of notation, called **reverse Polish** (or **postfix) notation** is very similar in principle to Polish Notation, and also forms a parentheses-free system. However, this time, reverse Polish notation is particularly suited to computerised methods because of the ability to deal with such expressions easily by using a **stack** (see chapter 24).

An example will make things clear. We may write down a 'normal' arithmetic expression, for example, as follows:

$(3 + 5) \times (9 - 7)$

This is called **infix notation,** because all the operators are *inside* the expression. To work this out, we apply the rules of precedence, i.e. brackets, exponentiation, multiplication and division. Therefore, we would end up with an answer of 16 for the above example.

Hint: The very first calculators that appeared on the market all used reverse Polish notation. If you look at one of these old machines you will see that it has not got an 'equals sign' nor has it got any brackets. However, if you were good at using these types of machine, you could often get complex arithmetic done much more quickly compared with a conventional calculator.

$$(3 + 5) \times (9 - 7)$$
$$= 8 \times 2 = 16$$

If we were to work out this problem using a low-level computer language, then we would have to do something along the following lines:

LOAD	3
ADD	5
STORE	temp
LOAD	9
SUBTRACT	7
MULTIPLY	temp
STORE	result

However, let us consider the logical order in which a sum such as this should be worked out:

$$(3 + 5) \times (9 - 7)$$

- Get the number 3 (1st part) and then get the number 5 (2nd part).
- Add them together (3rd part).
- Get the number 9 (4th part) and then get the number 7 (5th part).
- Subtract the above (9 − 7) (6th part).
- Finally, multiply the number from the 3rd part by the number from the 6th part (7th part).

Now consider the same problem again, but this time using reverse Polish. Using reverse Polish or postfix notation we would write:

$$3 \quad 5 \quad + \quad 9 \quad 7 \quad - \quad \times$$

This leads to the following two simple rules for evaluating such expressions.

(1) The next symbol encountered must be loaded on to the stack if it is an operand, i.e. 'a number or variable, which is to be operated upon'.
(2) If the next symbol to be encountered is an operator, i.e. '+' or '−', etc. then carry out the required operation on the top two items in the stack. The result of this operation must be left on the top of the stack.

Carrying out the above algorithm for the numbers shown above we get the results shown in table 32.6.

We now read the answer from the top of the stack, i.e. 16.

The above is not really just a weird and wonderful set of rules; it's simply the way that the expression would be worked out logically. It corresponds exactly with the logical order of working out the sum. In fact, reverse Polish notation is more natural than the usual infix notation with which we have all become so familiar. A few calculators use reverse Polish notation as their normal mode of operation, as it does away with the clumsy brackets so often needed in lengthy calculations.

Table 32.6

		Stack contents	
Part (1) 3 is an operand	(Put on stack)	[3]	top
Part (2) 5 is an operand	(Put on stack)	[5] [3]	top
Part (3) + is an operator	(Perform operation on top two numbers in stack and leave the result on the top of the stack)	[8]	top
Part (4) 9 is an operand	(Put on stack)	[9] [8]	top
Part (5) 7 is an operand	(Put on stack)	[7] [9] [8]	top
Part (6) – is an operator	(Perform operation on top two numbers in stack and leave the result on the top of the stack)	[2] [8]	top
Part (7) x is an operator	(Perform operation on top two numbers in stack and leave the result on the top of the stack)	[16]	top

Conversion between infix and reverse Polish notation

One novel way of converting from **infix** to **reverse Polish** makes use of **trees** (see chapter 25). First the **reverse Polish notation** expression is written down as a binary tree. Next, you undertake a **postorder traversal** of the tree (see chapter 25). Finally, the nodes visited are written down, and the result is the original expression converted into reverse Polish notation.

Example (1)

As an example, consider the following infix algebraic expression:

X = A * B + C/D

The binary tree for this expression is shown in figure 32.6. You should note that to form the binary tree, we put the '=' sign as the root node. The left-hand side of

the expression (simply X in this case) forms the 'left-hand subtree' and the right-hand side of the expression forms the 'right-hand subtree'. The lowest precedence operators (i.e. + or – etc.) form the next level of the tree. The tree is continually formed in this way until the terminal symbols form the leaf nodes of the tree. If we now visit each node of the right-hand subtree using the postorder-traversal method (see chapter 25) then we get the following list:

A B * C D / +

It is easy to remember that **postorder traversal** is required, as **reverse Polish** is the same as **postfix notation**.

Notice that, in these examples, with the equals sign at the root node, the **right-hand subtree becomes the required reverse Polish notation expression**, and the X, being the left-hand subtree, is equivalent to it.

Example (2)

As another example, let's see how to convert the following into reverse Polish notation:

X = 3 * (A + B + C) – (F – G)/5 + 2 * (D – E)

The binary tree for the above expression is shown in figure 32.7. Figure 32.7 may seem a complex tree, but it's really very easy once you get used to the principles involved. For example, concentrate on the right-hand subtree of the tree. This shows how the author formed it.

First the '=' sign was put at the root, and the left-hand side easily dealt with. After this the first '–' sign in the expression is chosen. This acts as a root for the next subtree. Therefore, the left-hand side of this subtree becomes the part of the equation on the left of this minus sign, and the right-hand side of this subtree becomes the part of the equation to the right of the minus sign.

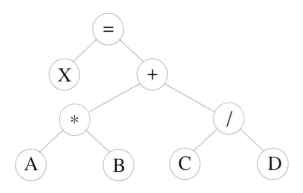

Figure 32.6

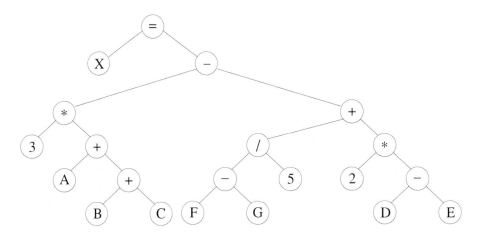

Figure 32.7

Note: We did not *have* to choose the minus sign. The '+' sign between the 5 and 2 would have done just as well, as this is a low precedence operator too. The other signs are within brackets, which mean that they must have the highest precedence, because the brackets must be worked out first (the whole point of using brackets!).

Next consider the part of the equation to the left of the minus sign, this forms a subtree, the root of which is the '*' sign i.e. the lowest precedence operator. 3 is to the left of this '*' sign and therefore forms the left-hand subtree. '(A + B + C)' is to the right of this '*' sign, and therefore forms the right-hand subtree. We continue in this way until all the terminal symbols have been arrived at. As long as you keep track of what you are doing, it's really quite straightforward.

To convert the expression we now do a postorder traversal of the right-hand subtree. This then gives us the reverse Polish notation expression which is as follows:

3 A B C + + * F G – 5/2 D E – * + –

If you think that the above looks messy, don't forget that it was the logical way that the sum would have been worked out. Also, don't forget that reverse Polish notation is used because it is ideal for solution by a low-level language making use of a stack. Therefore, it is a simple matter for the computer to evaluate it. Finally, and most importantly, once the expression has been converted to reverse Polish notation, the computer has only to scan the expression once to evaluate it. Compare this with how many times it is necessary to scan the original expression containing the brackets when using infix notation. Before proceeding further, let's remind ourselves of the normal mathematical rules of **precedence**. They are outlined in the following table.

Operators		Normal precedence
'Unary operators' and '()'	Unary +, Unary – & brackets	Highest
'↑'	Exponentiation	Very high
'*' and '/'	Multiplication and division	High
'+' and '-'	Addition and subtraction	Low
'='	Equals	Lowest

Note: the terms '**Unary +**' and '**Unary –**' mean '+' and '–' signs associated with a single operand like '–3' or '+6', for example. If we had an operator like '+' associated with two different operands ('2+3', for example), then it would be a 'binary +' or a 'binary –'. Note also that '>', '<', '<=', '>=' and '<>' have the same precedence as '='. Also, the logical operations 'NOT', 'AND' and 'OR' have decreasing orders of precedence, even lower than the '=' sign shown in the above table. However, to keep matters simple, only the signs used in the above table will be used in the examples that follow.

In many high-level languages, where a unary minus occurs (–7 or –3 etc.), we usually have to enclose this in brackets. In high-level languages we must not use expressions like 'X = A * –B'. We must rewrite it as 'X = A * (–B)'. The brackets then make sure that B is multiplied by –1 first. However, this is only another way of assigning 'unary –' and 'unary +' the highest precedence, as is confirmed by looking at the above table. To keep matters simple, we will not make use of the unary + or – or the logical operators in the examples that follow.

It is usual to assign numbers to the precedence of an operator from 0 (representing lowest precedence) to a number representing the highest precedence. Therefore, we could assign the numbers shown in the following table, which will lead to successful evaluation of expressions.

Operator	Precedence
() and ↑	3
* and /	2
+ and −	1
=	0

Developing the algorithm to convert from infix to reverse Polish notation

The basic process that must go on when converting from infix to postfix is quite simple, the operator must be taken from the place inside the two operands, and be placed post (i.e. after) the two operands. For example:

X + Y must become XY+

This is all very easy with a simple equation, but obviously gets much more complex depending on the complexity of the original infix expression. The following example will take a lot of concentration, but if worked through very carefully, considering each point in detail, the final algorithm should make sense.

Worked example

Consider the more complex infix string:

V + W ↑ X * Y / Z

First we read the variable V (i.e. an operand). We output this to the postfix string.

Situation so far:	Infix string	Postfix string	Stack
	V+W↑X*Y/Z	V	(empty)

Next we read the operator (i.e. '+' in this case). Now 'V' must be the preceding operand, but we must now find out what other operand is to be used with 'V'. Therefore, we must save this '+' until we have found out the next operand, so that we can place it in the postfix string. The + is therefore saved on the stack.

Situation so far:	Infix string	Postfix string	Stack
	+ W ↑ X * Y/Z	V	+ (top)

Next the variable 'W' is read. We output this to the postfix string:

Situation so far:	Infix string	Postfix string	Stack
	W ↑ X * Y/Z	VW	+ (top)

The operator '↑' is read. However, '↑' has a higher priority than '+' (the last operator on the stack). Therefore, the 'W' belongs to the exponentiation and not the plus. The '↑' is therefore saved on the stack so that we can find out the other operand to go with it.

Situation so far:	Infix string	Postfix string	Stack
	↑ X * Y/Z	VW	↑(top)
			+

Next the variable 'X' is read. This is output to the postfix string:

Situation so far:	Infix string	Postfix string	Stack
	X * Y/Z	VWX	↑(top)
			+

Next the '*' is read. However, this has a lower priority than the operator currently at the top of the stack. Therefore, the 'X variable' must be the one that belongs to the 'exponentiation'. Therefore, the exponentiation is output to the postfix string.

Situation so far:	Infix string	Postfix string	Stack
	* Y/Z	VWX↑	+ (top)

The next character in the infix string is '*' (as shown above). Before the exponentiation messed up our train of thought, we were trying to find the second operand for the addition. We must therefore return our thoughts to looking for this second operand. It is obvious from looking at the infix expression, that it is the whole of the right-hand of the expression! i.e. 'W ↑ X * Y/Z'. Let's carry on and see if this works out in this way.

We have just read the multiplication operator. This is compared with the addition operator on the stack. Since this multiplication has a higher priority than the addition operator, the W ↑ X part must be the first operand for the multiplication. Therefore, we must now look for the second operand for this multiplication. The '*' sign is therefore placed on to the stack while the search takes place:

Situation so far:	Infix string	Postfix string	Stack
	*Y/Z	VWX↑	*(top)
			+

The next character to be read in is the variable, 'Y'. This is output to the postfix string:

Situation so far: **Infix string**   **Postfix string**   **Stack**

                    Y/Z   VWX↑Y   *(top)
                                                    +

Next the operator '/' is read. Now this has the same priority as the '*' operator at the top of the stack, therefore the '*' sign can now be output to the postfix string:

Situation so far: **Infix string**   **Postfix string**   **Stack**

                    /Z   VWX↑Y*   + (top)

As the '/' operator has a higher priority than '+' at the top of the stack, the operator is saved on the stack.

Situation so far: **Infix string**   **Postfix string**   **Stack**

                    /Z   VWX ↑ Y   /(top)
                                                      +

Finally 'Z' is read and output to the reverse Polish string:

Situation so far: **Infix string**   **Postfix string**   **Stack**

                    Z   VWX ↑ Y * Z   /(top)
                                                  +

As there are no more characters to be read, the contents of the stack are output to the string. First the '/' operator:

Situation so far: **Infix string**   **Postfix string**   **Stack**

                                VWX↑Y* Z/   +(top)

And finally the '+' operator:

Situation so far: **Infix string**   **Postfix string**   **Stack**

                                VWX↑Y* Z/+   (empty)

The reverse Polish notation for the original expression can now be seen above.

The algorithm is summed up in the flowchart shown in figure 32.8. From figure 32.8 we can see that the algorithm shown in the flowchart also copes with brackets within the expression.

Try using the flowchart with '(A + B)/(C + D)'.

Note: as before, spaces have been shown within the expression simply to clarify the expression. These spaces do not count as a space until the end of the equation is encountered.

Using the flowchart you should obtain the following postfix (reverse Polish) string:

Symbol being considered	Postfix string	Stack	Comments
(		(	
A	A	(	
+	A	+(	Note: '+' has higher priority than left brackets already on the stack This is because the expression within the brackets must be evaluated first.
B	AB	+(	
)	AB+		Note: top of stack removed
/	AB+	/	
)	AB+	(/	
C	AB+C	(/	
+	AB+	+ (/	
D	AB+CD	+ (/	
)	AB+CD+	(/	
	AB+CD+	/	
	AB+CD+/		Note stack empty

Therefore, the postfix string is AB+CD+/

You should confirm that this is the answer that would have been obtained if a binary tree structure had been used to obtain the postfix string.

One of the things that may cause confusion with the above happens when the '+' operators are encountered. When working through the flowchart one is presented with the question, 'Is operation of higher precedence than that on stack?' One's immediate reaction is that the answer is yes. However, if you think about it, if the top of stack contains a '(' then any operator coming after it must have a higher precedence, so that the expression within the brackets can be evaluated. Of course if another '(' is encountered, this would then be entered on to the stack in the standard way.

After ploughing through the above you should have a good idea of some of the basic principles that are involved when translators have to convert the source language into the object language for both arithmetical and non-arithmetical processes.

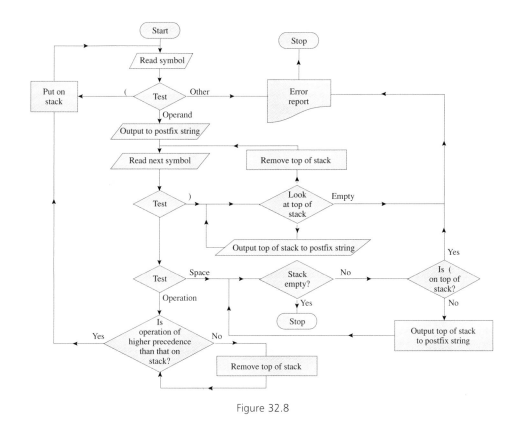

Figure 32.8

Exercise 32.2

1 Convert the following expression into **reverse Polish** (postfix) expressions:

(a) P*Q + (R – S)*T

(b) (M + N) *(0 – P)

(c) W+X*Y/Z

(d) (x + y/z) / (u – v)

(b) X Y Z / S × T + –

(c) x y + r s – × t / * *

(d) A B + 3 F G – H / * K F G – * – –

2 Convert the following **reverse Polish** expressions into **infix** (normal) form:

(a) AB+CX

3 By making use of an appropriate stack, show how the following **postfix** arithmetic would be evaluated:

(a) 9 3 – 2 /

(b) 12 9 – 16 20 – *

(c) 11 3 2 ↑ + 7 6 3 / – /

End of chapter revision aid and summary

Cover up the right-hand column and see if you can answer the questions or define the terms on the left. They appear in the order in which they are covered in this chapter. Alternatively you may browse through the right-hand column to aid revision.

What are natural languages?   Natural languages are languages such as English or French etc.

What are formal languages?   Computer languages belong to a class known as formal languages.

Are natural languages context sensitive?   Natural languages are context sensitive and this is why a great deal of expression can be built into them. However, they are sometimes ambiguous.

Are formal languages context sensitive?	Formal languages are not context sensitive and are unambiguous. They currently can't be used for such a rich diversity of expression.
What is a source language?	A source language is the high-level code written by the computer programmer.
What is an object language?	An object language is the code in a form that the machine can understand.
What is a translator?	A translator is needed to convert a source language into an object language.
Name the three most common types of translators.	Assemblers, interpreters and compilers are the three main types of translator.
What does an assembler do?	Assemblers convert assembly-language mnemonics into machine code.
What does an interpreter do?	Interpreters convert each line of the source code into the object code as the program is being run. This gives a better interactive environment but is slower.
What is a compiler?	A compiler converts the entire source code into machine code so that it can be run on the machine without further translation. However, error correction is tedious.
Name the three main stages in which compilation is split.	The compilation process can be split up into three sections – lexical analysis, syntax analysis and code generation.
What is the lexical analysis phase?	The lexical analysis phase breaks up the source code into logical chunks ready for the next stage of analysis. The resulting chunks are often called tokens.
What is a token?	A token represents the *smallest independent part of a program* which has some meaning such as a key word or variable etc.
Describe what happens during syntax analysis.	The syntax analysis phase determines if the string of input tokens passed via the lexical analysis phase *forms a valid sentence.*
When is the dictionary generated?	A dictionary is generated during the *syntax analysis phase.*
What is a dictionary?	A dictionary is simply a list of variables etc. used by the compiler.
What happens during the code generation phase?	The code generation phase generates the machine code from the information passed over from the lexical and syntax analysis phase – the dictionary is also consulted.
How is further optimisation achieved?	Further optimisation can often be achieved by the use of special software.
What is BNF?	Backus Naur Form (BNF) is one method used to *describe formally the syntax* of a language.
What is a meta language?	A meta language is the name of a *language used* to describe the syntax of another *language.*
What is a meta symbol?	A meta symbol is the name given to the symbols in a meta language.
Write down the standard BNF symbols.	BNF meta symbols are '::=', ' | ', '<' and '>'.
What are the extended BNF metasymbols?	Extended BNF uses '{ }' to denote repetition, '[ ]' to denote optional elements and '( )' to enable grouping. Comments may also be added using '(*' and '*)'.
Distinguish between literals and meta-variables when using BNF and EBNF	In BNF, literals are plain and meta-variables are in angle braces. In EBNF meta variables are plain and literals are put in quotes.

Images generated mathematically using
fractal geometry

◀ **Plate 39**
A deep zoom of the **Mandlebrot** set

Similar images can be found by visiting the
Geocities World Wide Web site at
http://www.geocities.com/CapeCanaveral/2854/
gallery.html

Plate 40 ▶
This famous **fern** shows how nature can
be modelled using mathematics. It's also
possible to build up larger plants, trees,
or forests of trees, which can be used in
construction of fractal landscapes

◀ **Plate 41**
A **Julia Set** is a mathematically generated
image very similar to the Mandelbrot set. This
time the constant is fixed and the complex
part of the equation varies

Plate 42 ▶
This part of the fractal shows a
close-up of an interesting area of
the Mandlebrot set

If you wish to generate your own
images like those shown on this
page, then you need to study the
work covered on **Iteration**
in chapter 18

▲ **Plate 43**
Saturn Rise
by Ken Musgrave

A stunning sequence of fractal-generated images produced by Ken Musgrave. These are the products of a brilliant mathematical imagination and much computer-processing power. The images you see here and other similar images can be found on the World Wide Web by visiting the Fantastic Fractals site at

http://library.advanced.org12740/ms cie4/index.html.

▲ **Plate 44**
Night III
by Ken Musgrave

The mountains and seas are generated as wire-frame images. They can then be ray-traced, but to get fractal-based images looking this good, intervention by a skilled artist is required to add the finishing touches. Other objects occurring in nature can be modelled using fractals, for example flowers, trees, and the human nervous system.

◀ **Plate 45**
Lethe III
by Ken Musgrave

What is parsing?	Syntax analysis is known as parsing. Parsing breaks down a sentence to see if it is legal.
What are productions?	Productions are the names given to the rule definitions which define syntax using the BNF and EBNF systems.
How is the parsing process carried out?	Parsing can be carried out by hand using common sense or parse trees.
What is canonical parsing?	Canonical parsing is a *general rule enabling a machine to carry out parsing* in a methodical way.
What is reverse Polish notation?	Reverse Polish notation is a notation in which the operator is placed after the operands as in postfix notation.
What data structure is used to implement reverse Polish notation?	Reverse Polish notation is a *parenthesis-free notation* and can be easily manipulated by a data structure called a stack.
How might parsing an arithmetical statement be undertaken?	Parsing arithmetical statements is often carried out by using reverse Polish notation.
What is Polish notation?	Polish notation is a prefix notation, e.g. + X Y.
What is infix notation?	Infix notation is a 'normal' notation, e.g. X + Y.
What is postfix notation?	Reverse Polish notation is a postfix notation, e.g. X Y +.
How might we convert infix to reverse Polish making use of a binary tree?	Postorder traversal of a binary tree *converts infix to reverse Polish.*

33 Computer Science Projects

Introduction

Specialist project work forms a major part of most computing courses. At this level it is usual to allocate about one third of the total marks for this important component. Treat computing projects with some care, and don't view them in the same light as writing large essays or researching some extended topic. Thinking in this way leads to the mistaken impression that the project can be researched and completed within a few weeks – this is usually not so. To do well on the project work you will need to have planned it over a significant period of time. I would suggest that you start to think about what you want to do about a year before the final deadline. This will give you time to change your mind before it's too late!

The nature of computing projects

Some students are used to cramming – they believe that *extremely hard work* over a *limited period of time* will produce good results. They may be used to this mode of operation because they usually write their essays or do other short-term research or examination revision in this way. An intense couple of weeks spent researching and writing an essay, for example, does work with some people. However, with computer science projects, even the brightest and best-intentioned students often damage their chances considerably by applying the same overall philosophy to their computer science project work. They are assuming that they can learn complex packages or languages in a couple of weeks. They are assuming that the algorithms they choose to solve their problems will work first time! They are assuming that the computers on which they are working will be faultless in operation when they need them and work exactly as expected – they rarely do! They are also assuming that nobody else will be using the facilities when they decide that it's time for them to spend a long session at the computer! *They are usually mistaken on all counts*, so make sure that you are not one of these students.

Although it's human nature not to start things until the very last minute, you *must* be well disciplined and start to work hard on your project early on, with serious work being undertaken at least two terms before it's due to be handed in. If for any reason you complete it early, so what? You will have some extra time on your hands, which will usually prove to be invaluable in a period when mock examinations and shorter but more intense projects in other subjects might be taking place. With modular 'A' levels, GNVQs and other courses, you must manage your time effectively and plan your workload many months in advance.

It's also advisable that you should not go to the other extreme of working ridiculously hard on your project over such a long period of time that your other work starts to suffer. Many students do get carried away with their projects because interesting projects can and

In this chapter you'll learn about:

- The nature of computer science projects
- How to choose a project
- How to conduct the project over an extended period of time
- How to maximise your chances of getting good marks
- How to write up the report
- The importance of the project marking scheme

Key resources

To carry out this work most successfully it's best if you have:

- Access to the project-marking scheme for your board
- Some exemplar work from previous years if this is available
- Specimen projects from your examination board
- Access to your project supervisor!

Concept checkpoints

- Project work involves many concepts from other parts of this book. It is usually undertaken at the beginning of the second year of a two-year course.
- Some techniques needed for your project may not be covered in the theory lessons before you have to start on the project. You will often have to learn these new skills independently if you are to make progress on the project work.

indeed do become addictive, especially if they are going very well. If you start to feel that you are falling into this all-too-familiar trap, then you have probably chosen a project which is too complex, or one that is too long. Both are inappropriate if it means that you have to spend a disproportionate amount of time on your computing project.

There may be other reasons for wanting to spend several hundred hours on a project, but don't blame it on your computer science course if you have chosen to do this! It is not usually a requirement of the course, or indeed of any course. Some students may feel that the time spent is justified because they may be entering their project into a national competition, may be writing a project which they intend to develop into a saleable item, or may be thinking of starting up their own software house. All these things have been done under the umbrella of a computing project at this level! Web site design seems to be quite popular since the Internet and Intranets have caught on in a big way, and designing impressive web sites is quite easy and lucrative for students who have good ability in computing.

From the examination point of view you should realise that most of the effort should be put into a thorough understanding of the theory papers, as this is the most effective way of spending your time if you are aiming to maximise your marks. For example, a very good project might score about 80%, whereas a superb project might score about 90% or more! Now we are arguing about 10% of the marks in a component of the examination, which represents about 30% of the total. Therefore, this huge difference in effort put into your project is only getting you about 10% of 30% which is 3 marks in the final examination! This type of mark could easily be achieved by learning an extra couple of facts and writing about them in the exam! This process, which might take only a few minutes, will give you the same results, and this is a sobering thought! However, don't go to the other extreme, and hand in a project into which little or no effort has been put. You might think that you can score very highly from the theory papers, but you are gambling on doing exceptionally well. This attitude to life will probably mean that you will have problems later on when it comes to undertaking work which, in your opinion, might not be so important. The best idea is to strike a balance between doing little and working too hard. Always err on the side of hard work – if you have a bad day when doing the examination, or if the paper turns out to be harder than you thought, then you will be glad of all the extra project marks that you can muster. I have known few students who have regretted the effort put into the project work.

Where to begin?

This is often the hardest part of your project – deciding what to do! I advise my students to think up about half a dozen totally different possible projects, and then start to think about each one in more depth. Starting to analyse the problem as described in the project-analysis section later in this chapter helps you to do this. Sometimes you will find that good ideas fizzle out because you can't think about them in the detail required, they become boring or tedious, too complex or too simple, or you can't find enough information. Also, the computers you have at school or college might not support the sort of project you envisage. The idea might have been done so often before that your teacher will probably be sick in a bucket if another of his or her students decides to hand in yet another dating-agency database, for example. Other ideas, which might seem slightly silly at the start, often bear fruit in unexpected ways, especially if you talk to other people who might be experts in your chosen project area. It's essential that you have an extended talk with your teacher or lecturer regarding your final choice, and it's most important that whatever is chosen fits exactly into the mark scheme (see next section) that you will be using. It is always a good idea to do projects for other people, and many examination syllabuses now insist on this condition. Never start on a project for yourself, because you lose the impetus of information gathered from interviews, feedback from different users, and the constructive criticism which can only be sensibly obtained from a third party.

> **Hint:** Talk to your parents, teachers or lecturers, they will often have good ideas for computer-based projects. With new software tools available like Delphi, Visual BASIC, Visual Java, Visual C++ and web-site tools, you are now able to develop very professional looking projects.

Sometimes you will find it profitable to combine your computer-science project with other courses, so that the project you are doing for computing can be used to provide data for other subjects. This is sometimes a good idea as much of the research done might go towards two different courses! However, there are great dangers if you are not very careful indeed. It's most unlikely that any single project would satisfy two different pieces of coursework, although 'hardware for a technology course', together with 'software for computer science' is one noteable exception. Different aspects of your project will usually be irrelevant as far as each subject is concerned, and you need to be skilful if you are to satisfy all criteria for both examinations. Obviously we are not envisaging the same report being submitted for both projects. For example, a detailed analysis of how the computer is used to solve a problem would be irrelevant in a geography report. Similarly, a

> **Hint:** The technique of brainstorming will often help you to choose a project. You write down literally anything which comes into your head for a period of about 5 minutes. You then look through the list of things to see if any are sensible.

detailed analysis of the geographical interpretation of data would be irrelevant on the computer-science side. Don't forget also that projects usually have to be chosen at different times for different subjects, and you need to plan well ahead if you are thinking of going down this particular route.

It's obviously an advantage if you are trying to solve a real-life problem. Indeed, I think it's almost essential that you do so. Solving real problems makes the specification sections of the project easier to write, gives you something definable to achieve, and usually produces something that might be useful in the end. However, you must not commit yourself to producing a fully working system for anyone. The people for whom you are working often get excited because they are having a pet project undertaken by a capable computer science student. They look forward to having some utility, application or program, which will enable them to solve their particular problem. Unfortunately, the truth is more likely to be that the project may never be working completely! You must remember that you can't put in the time and effort needed to fully support some future system. You should be concerned with the all-important 'getting your project to a standard good enough for your examination'. You are not in the business of sorting out many of the problems that may arise due to the implementation of your newly written system. You must explain to the people concerned that if the project works perfectly then this is a bonus, you will probably be leaving school or college soon after the project is finished, and there may be no support at all for continued use of the project after you have gone! When people view projects in this light, it removes the pressures that so often lead to the scenarios outlined earlier.

It's absolutely essential that you choose a project in which you are interested, and there are bound to be many projects that fall into this category. If you can think of none, then I suggest that you might be doing the wrong course! There will be times when you feel like throwing your project out of the window in frustration, and if there is no real interest in what you are trying to achieve then you will become disillusioned, not only with your project, but with computer science as a subject. Choosing an interesting and appropriate project is essential. It will affect your attitude to your work over an extended period of time. There is no recipe for choosing the right project for you particularly, but some of the projects, which have been done at my schools in the past, include the following:

- Designing a school or college web site.
- Producing a database for a local small business.
- Designing a virtual tour of your school or college using touch-sensitive screen input.
- Design of an electronic notice-board system for use around the school or college.
- Designing a special calculator and other utilities for visually handicapped people.

- Creating a learning package showing animated sort and search routines.
- Designing a pseudo low-level language assembler.
- Creation of a stock control system for a school shop.
- Creation of an ordering, invoicing and charging system for school or college departments.

Another golden rule is that you should not usually try to do something that can be done more easily in other ways, unless there is a compelling reason, such as not being able to afford a particular package. A typical illustration of this scenario would be the student who wrote a picture-drawing package in BASIC. Using this package you are able to draw squares, lines, circles, ellipses, etc. and build up pictures making use of these basic shapes! But why bother? Even the simplest of CAD packages in the public domain undertake these tasks very well. The whole object of the exercise seems so pointless. It is for reasons like this that it's suggested you solve a real-life problem – you are less likely to fall into this particular trap!

> **Hint:** Look around the school or college where you are studying. Ask the staff if there are any administrative tasks that could be done more efficiently using a computer. This is often a good source of fruitful ideas.

The marking scheme

It's most important that you adhere strictly to the scheme which is going to be used for marking your particular project. As an example, consider the proposed 'Year 2000 marking scheme' for AEB. It consists of the following headings.

Analysis	Design	Technical solution
System testing	System maintenance	User manual
Appraisal	Quality of language	

Each section, is allocated a different mark, and is further split up into useful subsections. For example, the **Design section** should include the following.

- A realistic appraisal of the feasibility of potential solutions and justification of the one chosen.
- Definition of the data requirements.
- Design of the user interface including input/output, forms and reports.
- The method of data capture and entry including validation.
- The record structure, file organisation and processing.
- The database design.
- Information about the security and integrity of data.
- The system security (access control).
- The system design.

- Program/module specification (not detailed algorithm design).

Some boards split up the projects into sections for AS and A, and some boards will have exercises to make sure that you demonstrate your programming expertise on a set range of mini projects. In this latter case, the main project is usually allocated proportionally fewer marks. Coming back to the main headings described above, marks range from describing how 'demanding problems have been clearly identified and desired outcomes have been achieved' to 'there is no work of the appropriate standard'! **Students should know how the scheme will be applied, and be particularly vigilant regarding all the known requirements.** For example, expressing an opinion that 'your project is working very well indeed' is unlikely to get you any realistic marks in the testing section – even if your project supervisor has seen your 'perfect project'! You must realise that *the moderator usually sees only the written project report*, and it is this alone which determines your marks. If you have not written down that you have tested the system, have not backed up your claim to test the system with suitable data and results, then you will probably get no marks at all, *even if your system is actually working perfectly*. This is a sobering thought, and outlines the importance of adhering exactly to your particular marking scheme. It's essential that you have the actual marking scheme well in advance of starting the project; in this way you can write up the project in exactly the right way as you are proceeding through the analysis and design sections months before the project is due to be finished.

The written report

This is the single most important piece of evidence to support your project. It is usually this piece of written work alone which will be the biggest determining factor regarding your final grade for the project. The application used or the program that you have written, is almost of secondary importance compared to the written report. Obviously your program or application will need to be undertaken in depth or you will have nothing to write about! However, it's the analysis, design, testing, documentation and the like which accompanies your written report which will be important, not only in its ability to impress the moderator, but in conveying what you have done, how you have done it and the results you have achieved. **The importance of this written report can't be overestimated.** A satisfactory project with a well-written and presented report will earn the student more marks than a superb project with a badly written or mediocre report. Don't forget it is the written project report which explains most of the work you have carried out – not the lines of code which constitute your actual project. You must, therefore, not spend so long trying to get your actual project working that you leave insufficient time to write the report. It's far better to stop your project altogether and concentrate on the report some considerable time before your project is due to be handed in. It's far better still to actually write up the report as you are going along – in this way you are less likely to forget why you have decided that things should be done in particular ways.

Project analysis

This very important stage is the detailed thought which needs to be put into your project, *some of which should be undertaken before making the final commitment* to any particular project. It is only by carrying out such analysis that you are able to determine the feasibility of your project, and hence how complex it's likely to be. It will also determine whether it will involve the sorts of things that you are able to do, and whether it's got enough scope to keep you interested for six months or more. Try also to make the project more open ended; in this way you are likely to be able to choose subsections which, if there is time, can be added on later. It will also give you scope to write about possible extensions when you come to do the 'possible improvements' at the end of your write up. All these are important considerations, and **time spent undertaking this analysis will be time well spent, even if you come to the conclusion that you will need to change your choice of project rather rapidly!**

When you have decided on a particular project, much more analysis needs to be done before you sit at the computer and start to do any practical work. The best way to get marks on your project is to analyse it in detail, then do some more analysis until you think you have covered every aspect – finally, do some more analysis! However, don't let this sort of analysis stifle any prototyping that might be necessary. Don't forget that some of the people for whom you are designing the project might not know exactly what they want, and designing a few 'mock ups' of possibilities is often a great help.

Your analysis should include the HCI (see chapter 8), and perhaps a detailed investigation into the existing practices that might currently be carried out in some manual version of your project, if this is appropriate. If you can compare your proposed system with an inferior manual system, then you can pick up a good many marks later on. However, if you can't make your system better than an existing manual one, then there's not much point in trying to proceed any further with your project – choose another! A classic case here, for example, would be setting up a database that gives no advantage over the same information presented in a book. Indeed, I have known situations where the information presented in a book is preferable, because a computer is not always available when the people who were to operate the system needed to use it!

Don't forget to have a detailed look at the 'Corpus-Crumbly' systems analysis of a library in chapter 16. This and other systems-analysis examples are worth reading before doing your own systems analysis on your project – they provide you with typical ways of tackling many different problems of the sort that you are likely to encounter.

The method of solution

The analysis part of your project can and indeed should be written up as you go along. Why bother to wait until you have got the thing working – much of the analysis will not change that much – and if it does, then this will give you ample opportunity later on to discuss in detail why you have made these changes. This all adds to the interest of the project and will enable you to score very highly when an overall assessment of what you have accomplished is done.

> **Hint:** Make sure that you apply many of the methods which you have learned from this book. If you wish to start work on your project early, then make sure you have read chapters 14, 16, and 17.

You must not forget the extensive range of analytical techniques covered in chapter 14. Use a large variety of appropriate techniques, and *make sure that your analysis is well structured and above all modular.* There will be times throughout your project when you come to a dead end, lose inspiration, or find that you lack information to carry on with some particularly detailed section. If you have modularised your project, you can concentrate on another part, and be sure in the knowledge that it will interface with all the others. You can then go back to the part that was causing you problems at a later stage.

There are many techniques covered throughout this book, and you would be well advised to apply them to appropriate parts of your project where necessary. It does not matter if you have not covered a particular topic if it is needed for your project. Read about it, learn it and use it. Indeed, there will probably be some techniques which you will never cover in class – don't worry, this is the whole point of undertaking projects – to enable you to do some further research, and to apply appropriate techniques. By doing this you will score highly for your methods of solution. However, don't forget to acknowledge the source of all routines or algorithms used in your project; it's unlikely that you will have thought up some wonderful new ways of solving a particular problem. Your project supervisor will probably have seen these methods before, and he or she will not be fooled into thinking that it's your original work!

Testing the system

This is often the weakest section in the report. Even able candidates with wonderful projects throw away marks at this important stage. With no sensible test strategy you have probably limited yourself to about 80% of the marks, assuming that you have produced a project which is perfect in all other respects. This is a stupid waste of time and energy. You must think up a suitable strategy for testing individual modules at an early stage. It's far easier to think up suitable tests before you have written the modules. Many students get their modules working before deciding on a suitable test strategy. They then wonder why any testing is needed at all! They will say that the module obviously works, and promptly throw away marks that would have been awarded by the mark scheme for the development of a suitable test strategy!

Don't forget that you should devise suitable test data, and look out for unusual as well as usual situations regarding data entry. Don't forget the **validation**, **verification CRCs**, **hashing** and other paraphernalia which usually go into making sure that data entry, recovery or transmission is carried out correctly. Many students fail to apply what they have learnt in the theory lessons – a sure way to loose valuable marks. The section at the end of chapter 17 is ideal for this purpose.

Documentation

This is essential and should be split up into two parts for most systems. First there is the user documentation, and this refers specifically to the instructions needed to operate the system. It should be non-technical and as easy to follow as possible. Secondly, there is the technical documentation, of which much of your project report will form a major part. It is intended to enable a competent person to be able to correct any errors in, or modify any part of your project in your absence! This is difficult for students at school or college to cover due to lack of time. However, with well-structured analysis and design sections, and with a well-documented program listing, there should be few problems in practice.

Does it work?

In many cases the answer will be almost! However, you will probably not fail because of this, assuming that you have taken the advice outlined in this brief chapter. Don't forget that you have a deadline to meet. It can't be extended, or you will not get the project report completed in time for marking! This is an unrealistic scenario – in real life an extension of a month or two on a project might be all that is needed to get the system fully working. Your teachers and the board realise these problems and the mark schemes are arranged accordingly so that students who have worked hard and undertaken all the correct procedures will get high marks in the project work, even if the overall project is not working completely. However, don't use this as an excuse for starting the project late. There is a big difference between laziness and lack of completion due to other problems. Your lecturer will take this into account based on his or her knowledge of how you have conducted yourself throughout the duration of the project.

Presentation

Finally, a word is in order about the presentation of the written report. Do use a DTP system or powerful word processor to produce your final report. Tatty hand-written documentation is really no longer acceptable from advanced computer science students. All students should be capable of a professional standard of documentation without too much effort. Don't forget also that marks are usually deducted for bad spelling, punctuation and grammar. Use the spelling and grammar-checking facilities on packages like Word, for example.

Indeed, if you follow the advice given earlier in this chapter, then you will already have a lot of text on the computer, because this has been produced as you are going along. The final report should, therefore, consist of a collating exercise, with added notes and diagrams. Indeed, do the diagrams on the computer as you are going along too. CAD packages should also be familiar to students at this level. Hand-written documentation is usually an indication that the project was completed in a rush, probably at home, in the Easter holidays before the report was to be handed in!

> **Hint:** A well-presented report goes a long way to giving the impression that you know what you are doing. Use this fact to your maximum advantage and make sure that it's easy for the moderator to find important information.

Don't forget also that the moderator is a busy person – it is essential that he or she is able to find things quickly. If you hand in a well-written and presented report, complete with an appropriate index which shows all relevant sections which relate exactly to the marking scheme (i.e. analysis, testing, user documentation, conclusions etc.) then you are more likely to be viewed sympathetically when it comes to the allocation of marks. Moderators are not going to spend a disproportionate amount of time trying to find some esoteric information buried deep in a poorly produced document. If they can't find information after a reasonable amount of time, they will realistically assume that it's not there – a stupid waste of your time as you will, in effect, be throwing marks down the drain. As with most things to do with projects, **forward planning and steady work over a long period of time is the key to success in this vitally important area.**

End of chapter revision aid and summary

Cover up the right-hand column and see if you can answer the questions or define the terms on the left. They appear in the order in which they are covered in this chapter. Alternatively you may browse through the right-hand column to aid revision.

Why are computer-science projects important?	Projects form a major part of most computing courses – they should be taken seriously because they account for about 30% of the final marks.
What makes computing projects fundamentally different?	Computing projects are of a different nature to the majority of other projects – a single project is usually carried out over an extended period of time.
Why must you start early?	Don't wait until the last moment before starting your project – cramming and hard work over the space of a week or two will not be sufficient.
Computing projects can become addictive. Why is it usually not a good idea to spend too long on them?	Don't spend a disproportionate amount of time on your project – no course demands that you spend hundreds of hours making sure that your project is perfect.
How do you choose a suitable project?	Although you need to do a good project, the difference between an excellent and a very good project is often not worth the extra effort – you would be far better to concentrate a similar effort on the theory papers. Choosing a project may not be easy for many students. Start off by thinking up half a dozen projects, then start to analyse each one in depth and decide on the best.
Can projects be combined with other subjects?	Computing projects may be combined with other subjects, but you can't use the same report for each, and some parts will be irrelevant to the other.
Why solve a real-life problem?	Solve a real-life problem if possible – it's easier to be objective about what you are trying to achieve, and easier to measure the results of your progress.
Does it have to work properly?	Don't promise anyone that you will produce a fully working project, which will solve his or her problem. The chances are high that it won't – simply through lack of time.
Can it be done more easily without a computer?	Try not to emulate things that can be done in much easier ways – unless there is some compelling reason to do so.
Know your marking scheme well.	Get a copy of the marking scheme and get to know it well. Make sure that all required sections are covered in the detail required by the examining board.
Is the written report as important as the work on the computer?	The written report is the most important single piece of evidence, which represents your project. Often it's the only part that the moderator will see.
Use all the necessary analytical techniques in this book.	Analyse your project making use of all the analytical techniques that have been used in the book – plus others if you find them to be useful.
Can you do too much analysis?	It's virtually impossible to carry out too much analysis in the initial stages of project design. All the hard work done then will pay huge dividends later.
Modularise your project.	When explaining your chosen methods of solution make sure that the methods are structured and modularised. Don't forget to include test procedures before designing the modules – they're much easier to think about then.

Look at other projects.

The Corpus Crumbly case study in chapter 16 is essential reading before starting the analysis of your project.

Make sure you test the system very thoroughly indeed.

Testing the system is of paramount importance. Most students loose marks on this aspect of their project – use abnormal as well as sensible data, and validate, verify and use CRCs etc. where it is a good idea to do so.

Include all the necessary documentation.

Appropriate documentation should accompany the project. User documentation should be non-technical and simple.

What additions might be needed in the technical documentation?

Technical documentation might be needed in addition to parts of the report – for example, an explanation of some particular method not usually associated with computing.

Should your code be self-documenting?

Much of your report, including any programs, should be self-documenting if written in appropriate ways, and should form part of the technical documentation.

It's best to be reasonably honest about what has occurred.

When doing an appraisal of your system you must be honest (most of the time!). The examiners will realise that you are learning the subject, that with hindsight you would probably have done it differently, and above all don't expect the project to work perfectly. If it does then that's an added bonus.

Don't forget that marks may be lost for spelling and grammatical errors.

Hand in a neat and well-documented report – it should include an index which relates to all sections required in the marking scheme. Use the spell checking and grammar analysis that your word processor provides.

34 A Selection of Exam Questions

Questions from all examination boards

NOTE: *These contain a mixture of modular and full 'A' level or equivalent standard questions. Some examination boards have now merged under a different name.*

1 When completed later this year, Silverpools is going to be the largest out-of-town shopping centre in the country. It will consist of a number of interlinked buildings, each one capable of being divided flexibly into shops, entertainment areas and restaurant areas. In addition, Silverpools will have a security and management centre to which each building will be connected.

   The firm that is developing Silverpools has developed a standard 'building block' on two floors. Each 'building block' has service passages, lifts, moving ramps, and standard infrastructure such as electricity and water, and cabling for a local area network. A security and control office is also included.

   (a) Explain how you would use a Computer Aided Design (CAD) package to produce a 3-dimensional model of one of these standard 'building blocks'. [8]

   (b) What input and output facilities would you need to enable the developers of Silverpools to see their ideas [5]

(University of Oxford Delegacy of Local Examinations – Modular Computing – Graphical and Real Time Applications, 1998)

2 In a certain graphics mode, a microcomputer uses four binary digits (bits) to contain colour information about one point or *pixel* on the screen display. For instance, 0000 represents black and 0011 represents green.

   Each memory location in the computer contains 32 bits, and the screen size is 1024 by 1024 pixels.

   (a) (i) State the number of different colours (including black) which this system can support. [1]

   (ii) If each memory location stores data about as many pixels as possible, how many will be needed for the entire screen. (Note: you can either give an exact answer or a number of kilo-bytes.) [2]

   (b) The computer also has an enhanced colour graphics mode where each memory location contains colour information about only **two** pixels. How many colours can be supported in the enhanced colour mode? [2]

(Welsh Joint Education Committee – Modular Computing, Algorithms and Structures, May 1997)

3 (a) Define the term algorithm. [2]

   (b) Outline two methods, which can be used to define and describe an algorithm. [2]

   (c) Consider the following simple sort algorithm, intended to sort the integer array x[1..n] into ascending order.

```
repeat
    done = 1
    for i = 1 to n-1
        while x[i]≥x[i+1]
            temp = x[i+1]
            x[i+1]=x[i]
            x[i] = temp
            done = 0
        endwhile
    endfor
until done = 1
```

   Assume that a set of n integers is input to the algorithm. The algorithm will fail under certain circumstances. State what these circumstances are and the manner in which the algorithm will fail. Indicate an alteration to the algorithm which will solve this problem. [3]

(Welsh Joint Education Committee – Modular Computing, Algorithms and Structures, January 1997)

4 In a chemical processing plant the temperature of a tank is being monitored by computer.

   Identify, and explain the purpose of, two pieces of hardware which are essential to this monitoring process. [4]

(NICCEA Computing, Paper 1, May 1997)

5 Explain, with the aid of an example, what is meant by a real-time operating system. [4]

6 In terms of the fetch-execute cycle, describe how conditional jumps are executed. [4]

7 Explain the advantage of using an interpreter rather than a compiler in the development of a program   [4]

8 Distinguish briefly between the lexical analysis and the syntactical analysis stages of the compilation of a program.   [4]

(All four questions above are from an NICCEA Modula Computing, Paper 1, May 1997)

9 A small business has a basic word-processing package for its microcomputer. The package only provides facilities to type, edit, print, load, save and format. The business wishes to buy a new word-processing package and you have been asked to advise them on a suitable choice.

(i) Describe three additional features of the new package which could be useful to the business.

(ii) For each feature, suggest how the business could benefit from its use.   [9]

(NEAB A and AS Modular syllabus, May 1997)

10 An eight-bit register contains two four-bit codes (bits 0 to 3 and bits 4 to 7).

7 6 5 4 3 2 1 0

Describe how, using shifting, and masking, copies of each of these four-bit codes can be obtained from the register.   [4]

11 Using the four digits 4764, explain how a check digit can be generated. Using the resultant five-digit number, explain how a validation program would check the validity of that number.   [5]

12 For each of the following search methods, describe how it determines that a record being searched for is not in the file or list being searched.

(i)   Linear search – records not in order

(ii) Linear search – records in order

(iii) Binary search (binary chop)   [6]

(All three questions above from an NEAB AS and A Paper 1, May 1997)

13 Most database management packages allow conditions to be associated with the fields of a record. These conditions are specified during the design stage.

An application using such a package has records containing the following fields:

part_number, description, number_in_stock, unit_cost, value_of_stock.

Explaining your decision, choose from these fields:

(a) one which must be unique;

(b) one which must be calculated;

(c) one which is always required (mandatory).   [3]

14 A firm uses an existing database to send a word-processed, personalised letter to all its customers telling them of a new product.

(a) What is the term used for this process?   [1]

(b) Draw a data-flow diagram for this process.   [3]

15 Give one appropriate use with clear justification for:

(a) Floppy discs

(b) Hard discs

(c) CD_Roms.   [6]

(All three questions above are from an AEB A level Paper 1, May 1997)

16 A program is to be written to help three-year old children recognise the numbers from 1 to 10.

A procedure exists called STAR, X,Y where X and Y are both whole numbers, which will print X stars (from 1 to 10) on the screen in colour Y. The colour Y can be:

0	Black
1	White
2	Red
3	Green

Black is the colour of the background screen. This means that STAR, X, 0 will rub out X stars that were on the screen.

(a) Using pseudocode or otherwise, construct an algorithm which will:

• Choose the number of stars and the colour at random

• Display the number of stars and the colour at random

• Display the number of stars

• Allow the child to input their answer

• Provide a suitable message dependent upon their answer, and then

• Clear the screen before the next question.

The algorithm should ask ten questions and then give a score of the number of correct answers.

You may assume that a suitable random number generator exists, but you should specify its output.   [15]

(b) How can your algorithm be changed to allow beginners to have more chance of a lower number of stars? [4]

(c) If the program were to be used with a number of children during a play session and an adult wanted to know how each of the children had scored, then the scores and names would need to be stored. Suggest a suitable structure for storing this data. [6]

(UCLES Computing, Paper 2, May 1997)

17 (a) What is meant by the following terms?

(i) Entity

(ii) Attribute [2]

(b) The following tables represent a relational database.

Stock

Product code	Number in stock	Supplier code	Supplier name	Supplier location	price
123	12	5689	Johnston's	Crewe	12.95
456	67	3257	CYC Ltd	London	6.00
678	46	9654	Hands & Co	Newcastle	4.60
396	35	3257	CYC Ltd	London	0.35
765	68	5689	Johnston's	Crewe	0.68
245	0	3257	CYC Ltd	London	1.50

Sales

Product code	Number sold
123	3
456	1
678	4
456	7
396	5
456	1
678	1
456	2

(i) What type of relationship exists between the stock table and the sales table? [2]

(ii) The above database has been partially normalised. Redraw that database so that data duplication is reduced further. Show clearly any additional tables, relationships and primary keys in your solution. [9]

(NEAB A level, Paper 2 May 1997)

18 A Company is storing details of its customers on a database. Describe three obligations the company has under the Data Protection Act. [6]

19 Explain what is meant by

(i) a declarative computer language,

(ii) an imperative/procedural computer language,

(iii) a functional computer language. [6]

20 (a) Describe the essential features of the following data structures:

(i) a queue,

(ii) a stack. [4]

(b) Using a diagram, explain how a queue is implemented in an array. [3]

(c) Using pseudo-code, give the steps needed to add data to a queue, which is held in an array. The queue cannot contain more than 10 items of data at any one time. [4]

(All three of the above questions are taken from an NEAB A level, Paper 1, May 1997)

21 (a) Explain the difference between an iterative and a recursive solution to a problem. [2]

(b) Given two positive integers M and N, the function GCD(M,N) is defined by

(i) If M<N swap M and N.

(ii) Divide M by N and let R be the remainder. If R = 0, N is the answer.

(iii) Set M=N, N=R and go back to step (i).

Produce a recursive solution for GCD(M,N) using pseudocode. You may assume the availability of an operator REM where a REM b returns the remainder when a is divided by b. [6]

(UCLES Computing, Paper 2, November 1997)

22 A software house has written a system and provided documentation for a user organisation. Identify and describe four components of this documentation. [8]

23 Briefly describe two techniques which are employed to help compensate for the speed differences between the CPU and the various input and output devices which communicate with them. [4]

24 When deciding which file structure to use for a particular application, one must choose between fixed length and variable length records.

(a) State two advantages of using fixed length records. [4]

(b) Describe one example when it would be more appropriate to use variable length records. [2]

(All three of the above questions are taken from London Examinations Computing, Paper 1, May 1997)

25 (a) What is an interrupt? [2]

(b) Give two reasons why an interrupt might occur. [2]

26 The binary pattern 1010 1011 0111 can be interpreted in a number of different ways.

(a) State its hexadecimal representation.   [1]

(b) State its value in denary if it represents a two's complement-floating-point number with an eight bit mantissa followed by a four bit exponent.   [3]

27 Data can be grouped into packets for transmission over a network. State three items, in addition to the data, that each packet should contain.   [3]

28 (a) Distinguish between *security* and *integrity* of data.   [2]

(b) Name two methods by which the integrity of data may be maintained.   [2]

(The above four questions are taken from AEB Paper 2, May 1997)

29 Consider this press cutting:

'By the year 2005, most children will get all their education via the Internet'.

(a) Giving two reasons to support your views, describe the extent to which you agree with this statement.   [2]

(c) Assume that this prediction does eventually come true. Comment on the potential effects of this change on the students.   [2]

30 A 'hacker' is a person who gains or attempts to gain unauthorised access to a computer system.

(a) Passwords are often used as a security measure to try to prevent unauthorised access. Describe three ways in which a password system can be made as secure as possible.   [3]

(b) Describe in detail two ways in which a hacker could benefit financially from unauthorised access to a computer system.   [4]

31 (a) A word-processing package contains the following facilities amongst others.

(i) Spelling checker.   [2]

(ii) Index production.   [2]

(b) A spreadsheet package contains the following facilities amongst others.

(i) Sorting   [2]

(ii) Macros   [2]

Describe these facilities.

(All three questions above are taken from an NEAB AS and A paper, Specimen question paper for computing 1999/2000)

32 When a subprogram is called some of its parameters may be passed by value and others passed by reference.

(a) What is a parameter?

(b) Distinguish between passing by value and passing by reference, and explain when each may be used.

33 (a) Explain what is meant by Computer Aided Software Engineering (CASE).

(b) Describe four distinct facilities you would expect to find in a CASE system.

34 A company has a policy of only transmitting encrypted data when public telephone lines are involved in the data transfer. When transmitting low security data each block of ten characters is reversed before the transmission. Thus the twenty characters

THE RED CAT RAN AWAY

Would be transmitted as

AC▽DER▽EHTYAWA▽NAR▽T

(N.B the ▽ represents a space. A space counts as a character.)

Develop an algorithm, which takes a file of text and encrypts it prior to transmission. The following commands are available.

READ(char) – transfers a character from file to the variable char. An attempt to READ a character beyond the end of the file will set an EOF flag.

WRITE(char) – transfers contents of the variable char to file.

OPENIN(filename) – opens a file in Read Only mode.

OPENOUT(filename) – Opens a file in Write Only mode.

CLOSE(filename) – closes a file.

(All three questions above are taken from an NEAB AS and A paper, Specimen Question Paper for Software and System Development Module 1999/2000)

35 Describe two ways of achieving parallel processing.   [4]

36 Either of the following two computer systems could be used in a large government department to perform administrative tasks.

System A – a centralised multi-access, mainframe computer system with terminals, a centralised printer and a large disk storage.

System B – a ring network of microcomputers with a file server and a number of shared printers.

(a) Describe in detail how the multi-access capability of System A could be implemented using time slicing.   [3]

(b) System A also has a multi-programming capability. Describe in detail the operating system components which would be needed to implement this. [6]

(c) Describe the differences in the methods used by the respective operating systems to control access to the shared facilities in systems A and B. [6]

37 Discuss, in the form of an essay, the development of programming languages from the early machine codes of the 1940s to the fourth generation languages of today. [15]

(All three questions above are taken from the London Advanced Level Computing, Paper 2, May 1997)

38 The automatic cash dispensing machines used outside some banks contain two separate printing devices. One is used to print receipts for customers, on request. Suggest how the second is used, and why it is necessary. [2]

39 A vowel string in a high level programming language has its syntax described in Backus Naur Form as follows:

<vowel string>::= <vowel>|a<vowel>a| e<vowel>e|i<vowel>i|o<vowel>o|u<vowel>u

   <vowel>::= a | e | i | o | u

(a) State, with reasons, whether each of the following character strings is a valid vowel string.

sting

aea

eae

AEA

sds [3]

(b) ROTATOR is a palindromic word because its letters, when taken in reverse order, give the same word.

Make simple changes to the rules given above, so that a string of vowels of any length is a valid vowel-string if and only if it is palindromic. [4]

40 Some of the steps in computerising an existing manual system are:

● Systems analysis

● System design

● Programming

● Testing

● Changeover to the new system

● Operation and maintenance

(a) Describe three aspects of the existing manual system, which would have to be investigated so that the analysis could be carried out. [3]

(b) Briefly describe four tasks which will be performed during the design process. [4]

(c) Explain how it is possible for all the individual component modules to pass their tests and yet for the system still to fail. [3]

(d) The changeover to the new system from the manual system can be achieved in three ways:

(i) immediate change;

(ii) running the manual and computerised systems in parallel ;

(iii) gradually introducing the new system one sub-system at a time.

In each case, state an application for which the technique is most appropriate. [3]

(e) Briefly describe the responsibilities of the systems analyst once the system is operational. [2]

(All three questions above are taken from London Specimen Paper for Advanced Level Computing, 1998)

41 At the end of each year a hospital archives all its patients records to magnetic tape, only the records relevant to the current year being maintained on-line on disc storage. It is now proposed to replace the magnetic tape records by COM.

Explain what is meant by COM and evaluate the hospital's decision. [6]

42 (a) A register contains the ASCII characters 'A' and 'B' as follows:

0100000101000010

Explain how shift operations can be used to:

(i) reverse the order of the characters in the register and [2]

(ii) replace the first character in the register with eight zeros leaving the second character unchanged. [2]

(iii) Show how masking can be used to achieve this second result. [4]

(iv) If the binary pattern is interpreted as a twos complement integer, show how shifting can be used to perform simple multiplication and division. [4]

(b) Indirect and indexed (or modified) are two modes of addressing found in assembly languages. Describe, with the aid of examples, how each of these addressing modes differs from direct addressing and state one reason why each is required. [8]

(The above two questions are taken from NICCEA Computing, Paper 1 (Computer System), Specimen Paper for 1998)

43 A binary tree is illustrated below:

Towns

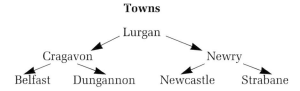

Indicate the output when the contents of each node are printed out using pre-order traversal:

Write out the contents of the node

Process the left subtree

Process the right subtree [6]

(a) What is meant by top-down design? [2]

(b) Give two clear advantages of using top-down design in the production of good quality software. [4]

44 Once a program has been coded it must be debugged and tested before being implemented.

(a) Distinguish between debugging and testing a program. [4]

(b) Name a software utility, which can assist software debugging. Describe two features of such a utility. [5]

45 The following is a design for a simple version of the exchange sort or bubble sort algorithm which sorts an array of N integers into ascending order. The variables i and $Pass$ are of type INTEGER.

1   loop for Pass from 1 to N −1

2   loop for i from 1 to N−1

3   if the ith element of the array is greater than the (i+1)th element

4   then

5   exchange the ith and the (i+1)th elements

6   ifend

7   loopend

8   loopend

(a) The following array of seven integers is sorted using this algorithm.

    23 35 26 20 46 33 54

Draw a sequence of similar diagrams showing the status of the array at the completion of each pass (that is, each time the inner loop is completed). [8]

(b) Provide a sequence of instructions, which will achieve the exchange specified in step 5. Indicate the name and type of any additional variable(s) required. [4]

(c) Suggest two ways in which the given algorithm may be made more efficient. It is not necessary for you to incorporate these changes into the algorithm. [6]

(The above three questions are taken from NICCEA Computing Paper 1 (Software techniques and tools) specimen paper for 1998)

46 A garden centre has invited a computer consultant to advise on the computerisation of its business. The business grows over 300 varieties of plants for sale to the general public. With the consultant's help the centre has been able to identify two key areas that would benefit from computerisation. These are as follows.

– Environmental control of climate inside greenhouses, e.g. temperature, humidity, light levels, soil moisture content and automatic watering of plants in the open.

– Sales processing.

(a) Describe three methods that the consultant might have employed when analysing the requirements of the garden centre business. [3]

(b) For the environmental control many sensors will be needed. The consultant advised connection via a multiplexor to a microcomputer operating in real time and containing in its interface a single analogue to digital converter (ADC).

(i)   Why is an analogue to digital converter needed? [2]

(ii) What is meant by the phrase real-time operating system? [2]

(iii) State two reasons why a multiplexor is needed. [2]

For sales processing, the consultant proposed that the following data about stocked plants be recorded in a computer based on-line file, PLANT.DAT, with the following record structure:

    Catalogue number

    Plant name

    Quantity in stock

    Current price

Catalogue number is a unique five-digit number.

In addition, the computer is to print catalogue numbers in bar-code form onto labels, which are attached to each plant for sale. Initially, sales are to take place from a single terminal using a bar-code reader connected to the computer system. The field <quantity in stock> of PLANT.DAT must be adjusted accordingly at the time of each sale.

(c) (i) Explain one advantage and one disadvantage to the garden centre deriving from the use of a bar-code reader. [2]

(ii) Describe the file organisation for the file, PLANT.DAT, which would enable sales of plants to be processed quickly. Justify your answer. [4]

(iii) Describe the basic computer processing that must be done for each item when a sale is made. What use might be made of the plant name?   [5]

47 A multi-user, multi-tasking, virtual memory operating system is installed in a minicomputer system. The operating system supports multi-programming. The minicomputer is used both for batch and interactive work.

(a) Explain the differences between:

(i) multi-programming, multi-access and multi-tasking;

(ii) interactive and batch programs.   [5]

(b) (i) Describe the two main functions of a scheduler in such an operating system.   [2]

(ii) Describe two different events that lead to the scheduler being invoked.   [2]

(iii) Describe two of the objectives of the scheduler when assigning job priorities in this system.   [2]

(iv) Describe a suitable scheduling algorithm and explain how it satisfies at least one of these objectives.   [4]

(c) Explain the term virtual memory.   [5]

(The above two questions are taken from AEB Computing, AS and A Specimen Papers for 1999)

48 Ayemouth College uses a number of stand-alone microcomputers with hard drives and floppy drives to which both staff and students following specialist IT courses have access. There is also a computer network, available to all students, which is used to support other subjects. Software available on this network includes word processor and subject-specific applications.

Three major problems have become apparent to the systems manager:

(i) The import of viruses to both systems.

(ii) The security and protection of the files stored on the systems by both staff and students.

(iii) The transfer of files from one system to the other.

Suggest how the system manager could address these problems.   [9]

49 A supermarket sells a large number of items. Details of these items are stored on a fully indexed file. This file is accessed using multi-level indexes containing the bar codes.

When a item is purchased at the checkout, the barcode is read by a barcode reader. This barcode identifies the item. The computer needs to find the record corresponding to the barcode as quickly as possible.

(a) Assuming that these barcodes are 6 digit numbers between 100 000 and 999 999, describe, using a diagram, the index structure used.   [5]

(b) Using pseudo code or otherwise, describe an appropriate method of searching the index for a specific barcode. Ensure that your algorithm can handle error conditions, and that it produces a suitable response.   [10]

(The above two questions are taken from UCLES Computing, Paper 2 for 1997)

NOTE: Important terms in each definition that appear in **bold type** *are also defined in the glossary*.

Absolute address – A number used to fix an **address** in **memory** without the need to be modified.

Access – Microsoft's main **database** system.

Access privileges – The permissions granted to a user of a system when they log onto the system. The administrator usually has the highest privilege level.

Access time – Time taken to locate a particular item of data.

Access time (disk) – Seek time + Search time + read/write time.

Accumulator – A **register** inside the **CPU** in which temporary **data** is stored.

Accuracy – The difference between the **actual** and **computed value**.

Acorn – British-based computer company (now owned by Olivetti) – manufacturer of the Archimedes and **RISC PC**. First company to bring **RISC**-based computing to the general public in the UK.

Acoustic coupler – A device used for sending information down a telephone line making use of a standard handset.

Acronym – A term used to describe deriving a word from the letters at the start of other words, e.g. **BASIC** is an acronym for Beginners' All-purpose Symbolic Instruction Code.

ActiveX – A software component, developed by Microsoft, to develop interactive components for use on the **Internet**. Like **Java**, it does not matter which computer runs the component as long as it is capable of running a suitable web browser like **Internet Explorer**.

Activity (file) – The percentage of the **file** processed in any one **run**.

Actual value – the exact (theoretical) value of a number. It normally acts as a reference to enable the calculation of **errors**.

Ada – relatively recent **high-level language** developed with the US military and ideal for **real-time** and/or **embedded applications**.

Address – A number used to locate a position in **memory** or some other device.

Address bus – The lines (wires or copper tracks on a **PCB**) along which the **address** signals travel.

Address modification – Used in **machine code** and **assembly language** programming where an address is transformed into another, e.g. **relative addressing**.

Addressing modes – The different ways in which a **microprocessor** is allowed to calculate an **address**.

AI – **Artificial Intelligence**. That which all good computers have!!

ALGOL – ALGOrithmic Language – an early **high-level language** from which other languages, such as **FORTRAN** and **Pascal**, are derived.

Algorithm – A set of instructions or procedures for solving a problem. This could be in the form of a picture, pseudocode or other form of prose.

Alias – used with e-mail to describe an alternative name which gets converted into a real e-mail address. For example, 'Mickey' could be an alias for 'mickey-mouse@disney.com'. You can also make use of an alias in many other computing contexts.

Aliasing – A term used to describe the jagged edges which are typical of **bit-mapped graphics** on a computer.

ALOHA – This is Hawaiian for hello, and is the **radio-based computer network** that links the Hawaiian islands. **Radio networks** are becoming increasingly popular for permanent connection to **networks**.

Alpha chip – A very fast processor created by the Digital Equipment Company (now taken over by Compaq).

Alpha testing – Testing a new product in a laboratory setting before being released for **beta testing**.

ALT – A special key on the keyboard, which is used in combination with other keys for special effects, e.g. **CTRL/ALT/Delete** might enable you to log on.

AltaVista – One of the search engines used on the **World Wide Web**.

ALU – **Arithmetic Logic Unit**. Part of the **CPU** that performs **arithmetical** and **logical operations**.

Analogue – Something pretending to be something else.

Analogue MODEM – Used to denote the conventional **modems** which change digital computer signals into the analogue sounds to send over a conventional phone line.

Analogue signal – A continuously variable signal – contrast with a **digital signal** (varies in discrete steps).

AND gate – A **logic gate** whose output is '1' only if all inputs are '1'.

Animated GIF – A sequence of **GIF** images, which, when displayed in a suitable **web browser**, will give the appearance of motion.

Animation – Creating the illusion of a moving sequence by using a series of still images as is done in the movies. There are many animation software packages.

ANSI – The American National Standards Institute.

Anti-aliasing – Inserting light-grey squares into the jagged edges of a graphic to give the appearance of a smoother transition. Used extensively to display high-quality text on the screen.

API – Application Programming Interface. This is a way of calling up **operating system** routines from within a program like **Visual Basic** or from other **applications**. It enables programmers to make use of routines written for the **Windows** operating system, for example.

APL – A Programming Language – a high-level language used in engineering and science.

Apple – American-based computer company – the first to establish **windows** in the commercial world.

Application – See **Applications package**.

Application layer – The top level in the **ISO OSI model** for network protocols.

Applications package – **Software applications** such as **DTP**, **CAD** and **spreadsheets** etc.

Applications programmer – The person who writes the code to produce applications such as word processors or spreadsheets etc.

Archive – A copy of a file for long-term storage (ie little used).

Arithmetical operations – Add, subtract, multiply, divide etc.

Arithmetical shift – **Bits** move left or right but the sign bit is preserved.

ARM – Acorn's Risc Machine – now called Advanced Risc Machines, and owned by Intel.

ARPANET – Advanced Research Projects Agency NETwork. A very large **mesh network** – now part of the **global network**. It was from **ARPANET** that ideas for the **Internet** were initially developed.

Array – A series of **data** items arranged in a useful way and is usually referenced by an index.

Array element – One of the data items within an **array**.

Array processor – **Parallel processors** under the control of the same **CPU**. Now being superseded by **massively parallel processing**.

Art package – See **Paint package**.

Artificial intelligence – Use of computers involving 'human like' abilities such as visual perception, speech recognition and natural language analysis etc. Philosophers will argue for many years as to what constitutes intelligence – it's not yet certain as to whether machines will ever be able to be intelligent.

Ascenders – Parts of the lower-case text which rise above the 'normal area'.

ASCII – American Standard Code for Information Interchange. An agreed set of codes for each **character**.

ASDL – **Asymmetric Digital Subscriber Line** – A digital link, using a conventional phone line but with special equipment at the client and telephone exchange ends. Speeds of up to 9 Mbit/sec are possible.

Aspect ratio – The ratio of the width to the height e.g. 4 : 3 for normal TV or 16 : 9 for widescreen TV.

Assemble editing (video) – Assembling a sequence of automatically-controlled recordings.

Assembler – Program that converts **assembly language mnemonics** into **machine code**.

Assembler directives – Pseudo operations which enable the **assembly-language** programmer to carry out operations such as calling **macros** which might form part of the operating system, for example.

Assembly language – programming making use of **mnemonics** instead of **machine code**.

Assignment operator – Usually ':=' or '=' depending on language.

Association – the type of connection between **entities** to define one of the standard **relationships**.

Associative store – Associating stored information with regard to its contents rather than with an absolute **address**.

Asynchronous transmission – The transmission of data where the receiving and transmitting ends are not synchronised – **start** and **stop bits** are usually added.

ATM (1) – Automatic Teller Machine – Hole in the wall from which you can get money with an appropriate card – used in banks and building societies etc.

ATM (2) – Asynchronous Transmission Mode – A network **protocol** which deals with computer data, video and voice.

A to D converter – **Analogue** to **Digital** converter. Converts analogue to digital signals.

ATOM – A smaller unit of a LIST in the language **LISP**.

Attachment – a **file** which is attached to an e-mail document. Used to send pictures and computer programs, for example. The attachment must usually be **encoded** using a system like **UUencoding**, for example.

atto (a) – Multiplier representing 1×10^{-18}

Attribute – Part of a **tuple**, **row**, or **record** in a **relational table** (**relation**).

Audit trail – This is a record of things that have happened in a computer system like a **DBMS**, for example. Typical things that might be set up include who has entered or deleted data, when these transactions took place, and from what terminal the transaction was carried out.

Authoring language – Language used to program an **authoring system**.

Authoring system – A system to enable non-specialists to build up control systems for **interactive video** systems or **hypertext** systems and other **multimedia** presentations.

Auto boot – Running a special **program** which sets up your machine on start up.

Autoexec.bat – A **file** which contains a **batch** of commands each of which is executed on start up.

Autostereogram – Seeing a 3D image in a 2D picture by clever arrangement of patterns and shapes.

Auxiliary store – See **secondary store**.

AZERTY keyboard – The standard French keyboard. Compare this to the QWERTY British/American layout.

Back drop – Picture or other suitable material as a backing for charts or other presentation material.

Background printing – A computer printing a document whilst (usually) doing something else.

Backing store – See **secondary store**.

Backup copy – Copy which is identical to the original but stored in a different place for safe keeping.

Backup file – An identical copy of another **file** used for security purposes.

Backup store – Store used to back up information, e.g. a cassette tape, **DLT** or **QIC** etc.

Backward pointer – A **pointer** indicating the way back to the previous **node** in a data structure.

Band printer – A **line printer** making use of a rotating metal band containing an embossed **character set**.

Bandwidth – Physical limitations imposed on a communication system – usually expressed in **bits**/sec.

Bar code – A code using lines of varying thickness to represent a unique produce code.

Bar code reader – A device for reading **bar codes**.

Barrel printer – See **drum printer**.

Baseband – A method of sending a signal at its original frequency.

Baseline – A line on which text rests. Used in **DTP** and **word-processor** systems.

BASIC – Beginner's All-purpose Symbolic Instruction Code. A popular high-level language.

Batch entry – A method where the data to be entered into the **computer** system is entered **off line**.

Batch operating system – An **operating system** that supports **batch processing**.

Batch processing – A **system** where the **jobs** are usually submitted and **run** in **batches** – i.e. several at the same time.

Baud rate – The number of signal transitions per second.

Baudot – A scientist who carried out much work on signal transmission – Baud rate is named after him.

BBS – Bulletin Board System – A message system, usually on the Internet or on an Intranet.

BCC – Blind Carbon Copy – Used on **e-mail** systems to send a copy to another person without the original recipient knowing about it!

BCD – Binary Coded Decimal.

Benchmarks – A performance test for hardware or software in a **computer system**, e.g. speed etc.

Beta testing – Testing a new product on users before it's released officially.

Bezier curves – A type of mathematically-defined curve that obeys certain conditions at its end points. Useful in **Art** and **CAD packages**.

Bin – Short for **binaries** or **binary files**. A typical use might be a **cgi-bin**, a binary executable file on an **HTTP** server.

Binary – A two-state system – usually expressed using the digits '0' and '1' but any two states could be used.

Binary adder – A **logic circuit** that adds **binary digits** together.

Binary code – Groups of **binary digits** to perform some specific function – e.g. **ASCII** or **EBCDIC**.

Binary Coded Decimal – **Binary** code in which each digit is coded separately using four **binary digits**.

Binary counter – A **logic circuit** used to count up or down in binary on the application of a **clock pulse**.

Binary digit – A '1' or a '0' – also called a **bit**.

Binary file – A file containing executable binary code.

Binary number – A number made up out of binary digits.

Binary pulse train – A voltage which alternates with time between the '0' and '1' levels being used.

Binary search – A **search** technique which repeatedly splits up a list into left and right-hand sublists, and concentrates only on the half of the list which contains the data.

Binary tree – A **tree structure** where each **node** is allowed a maximum of two **children nodes**.

BinHex – A system (used on Macs) for transmission of information over systems which make use of the 7-bit ASCII set (i.e. **e-mail** and **Newsgroups**).

Biocomputers – **Computers** made out of organic molecular electronics. Genetically engineered protein is one example.

BIOS – **Basic Input Output System** – part of the **operating system**, usually housed in **ROM**.

Biosensors – Systems developed to enable **computers** to **taste** and **smell** etc.

Bistable – A circuit with two stable states. Term also used to denote a **flip flop**.

Bit – **Binary** Digit.

Bit map – **Computer memory** that represents a **graphic** image or text in a **font** etc.

Bit-mapped font – **Fonts** made up from a map of **pixels** in a similar way to **bit mapping** on screen.

Black-box testing – The software under test is split up into identifiable **modules**, each having one or more inputs and one output. A box is drawn, with inputs (**variables**) on the left, and the output (**variable**) on the right. A table is then drawn, into which salient values of the **variables** under test (like maximum and minimum etc.) are input. Some comments are then put into the table to explain the special conditions under which the tests on each variable are being carried out. This documentation provides evidence that methodical testing has been undertaken.

BLAISE – The British Library Automatic Information SErvice.

Block (1) – A data storage area on a **secondary storage** device. See **physical record**.

Block (2) – Part of a **program**.

Block structured language – A language which allows structured **programming** in **blocks**, i.e. **variables** can be declared to be valid within one block etc.

Blocking – A method which is used to increase the speed and efficiency with which **data** may be read from and written to various devices such as **disk** or **tape**.

Blocking factor – The number of **logical records** per **block**.

BNF – **Backus-Naur Form**. A **metalanguage** used to define some computer languages.

Boolean algebra – An algebra developed by George Boole for dealing with **logical expressions**.

Boolean variable – Can be only true or false (i.e. one of two values).

Boot up – Getting the computer system started – can also be used to load utilities and other software.

Booting – Synonymous with **bootstrapping**.

Bootstrap – A term used where a simple **program** starts off other bigger programs. It is usually used to **boot** up the **operating system** and some other software to customise the system or load applications.

Bootstrapping – The process of loading the **operating system** into the **computer**.

BORIS – The Beginner's Optimised Reduced Instruction Set **microprocessor**! – See chapter 20.

Bot – This is a piece of software which can be set up to search the web for specific information. The little **robot** is run in a **batch** mode, often during the middle of the night, and then you can see the results of the search at some convenient later time.

Bottom of stack – The position of the last number on the **stack** – usually accessed by the **stack pointer**.

Bottom-up approach – Method of solving a problem by concentrating on the detail first – used for **testing** and **prototyping**.

bpi – Bits per inch – measure of storage density on **magnetic tape**.

Bps – **Bytes** per second.

bps – **Bits** per second.

Branches – The lines that connect the **nodes** on a **tree structure**.

Breakpoint – A point within a program which terminates execution so that the programmer may examine the state of any **variables** etc. – used to help **debug** programs.

Broadband – A method of communication which uses different frequencies to send signals simultaneously by methods such as **FDM** – contrast with **baseband**.

Broadband network – A network which makes use of a **broadband** system for transmission of the packets of information.

Brother node – A **node** in a **tree structure** having the same **parent** – also called a **sister node**.

Bubble-jet printer – See **Ink-jet printer**.

Bubble memory – A type of **memory chip** not based on **semiconductor** technology but using magnetic bubbles in a garnet crystal. Not quite **random-access memory**, although still very fast.

Bubble sort – A **sort algorithm** where the sorted items float to the top of the list.

Bubble store – An alternative memory technology using magnetic bubbles in a garnet crystal.

Bucket – A number of **sectors** or **blocks** on a **disk**.

Buffer (1) – An area of **memory** used to temporarily store data. Usually used to match devices that work at different speeds, such as **CPU** and **disk**.

Buffer (2) – Some extra **memory** inside a **peripheral device** such as a **printer** – see (1) for reason for use.

Buffer (3) – A **logic circuit** that can be used to isolate signals from the **bus system**.

Buffer (4) (file) – The area of **memory** where a **physical record** from a **file** is stored. Each **physical record** may have several **logical records**.

Bug – An **error** in the **program** or an 'undocumented feature' if it does anything remotely useful!

Buggy – A small robot which is usually controlled by a micro – runs around on wheels.

Bulletin board – A **computer** set up to receive and distribute messages over a **network** or phone system.

Bus – A parallel group of wires, usually 16, 32, 64 or 128 bits wide.

Business data processing – Use of computers for accounting and stock control etc.

Business graphics package – Changes numerical data into graphs and charts etc.

Bus network – A **network topology** described by a main spur with computers connected at various points.

Byte – Eight **binary digits**.

C – A popular **high-level language** suitable for complex **systems programming** because it has much low-level language support.

C++ – A popular **object-oriented high-level language** which is a superset of **C**.

Cache – A very fast expensive **semiconductor memory** (faster than **main memory** if **SRAM** is used).

Cache (Disk) – An area of **main memory** set up to hold **data**, which would normally be accessed on **disk**.

Cache (Internal) – An area of **memory** inside a **microprocessor**. Used to save time in accessing **RAM**.

Cache (Main) – An area of **memory** making use of **SRAM**.

Cache memory – A very high-speed **memory** used to store the most-often accessed instructions.

CAD – Computer Aided Design – **Object oriented graphics package** that is ideal for design engineers and architects etc. The data is often exported to support **CAM** and **CIM**.

CAD/CAM – The integration of the **CAD** and **CAM** processes.

CAFS – Content Addressable File Store. (See **Associative Store**.)

CAI – Computer Aided Instruction – same as **CAL**.

CAL – Computer Aided Learning (or Computer Assisted Learning).

CALL – Statement used to **call** a **subroutine** or **procedure** etc.

CAM – Computer Aided Manufacture – The use of computers in all stages of manufacturing (e.g. numerically controlled machine tools etc.).

Cambridge Ring – One type of ring network.

Canonical parsing – A mechanistic way of getting a **machine** to carry out **parsing**.

Caret – The flashing **cursor** indicating where typed input is to be placed.

CareWare – Software which is distributed free on the proviso that the user donates some money to a good cause specified by the author.

Carrier – The radio wave which carries the **computer data** over a satellite or other radio link.

Carry flag – A **flag** inside the **flag register** used to show that a carry has been generated.

Cartesian product – If we have two sets called X and Y, then the Cartesian product is the set of all ordered pairs – a nice way to think of this is that if each set is the set of real numbers, then the Cartesian product of these two sets is the set of all Cartesian co-ordinates on a piece of graph paper of infinite size.

CAS – Content Addressable Store. (See **Associative store**.)

CASE – Computer Aided Software Engineering – **Software** to help with **systems analysis** design, and testing.

Case statement – An alternative to nested **if-then statements**.

Case study – A (usually) detailed **systems analysis** or study made on a specific system.

CC – Carbon Copy – Used on **e-mail** systems.

CCD – Charge Coupled Device.

CD – Compact Disc.

CD-DA – Compact Disc-Digital Audio – The original CD.

CDI – Compact Disc Interactive – One standard for **interactive video systems**.

CD-E – Compact Disc-Erasable – This type of CD may be re-recorded. However, it can't be read back by a conventional CD drive, only by a drive which is of the same type as that which recorded the signals.

CD-R – Compact Disc-Recordable – Enables the user to record information on a special CD, which can then be played back on a normal CD player.

CD-ROM – Compact Disc-Read Only Memory – An **optical disk** which can store video, audio and computer data.

CD-ROM master – Master **CD-ROM** disc from which copies can be made.

CD-ROM-XA – The Extended Architecture version for the PC.

CELL (1) – The name sometimes given to the **record** in a **file** – used when dealing with **pointer systems**.

CELL (2) – The intersection of a row and column in a **spreadsheet**.

CensorWare – Software which imposes restrictions on the users of the system. Used on Internet sites and Newsgroups, for example.

Centralised network – All communications go via a central **node**.

Centralised processing – Using a centralised computer facility as opposed to **distributed processing**.

Centronics parallel port – a common **interface** standard for connection of a **printer**.

CGA – Colour Graphics Adaptor – IBM PC adaptor standard.

CGI script – Common Gateway Interface script – A way of handling interactive input from the users of an HTML page. The information gathered might be put into a **database**, for example.

Channels – A set of convenient links, which can be viewed in a **web browser**, like **Internet Explorer**, for example. It enables you to surf the **web** making use of a TV-channel type service.

Character (1) – A letter, number or symbol which goes to make up a **character set**.

Character (2) – The smallest unit of **data** that can exist in a **file**.

Character code – A **binary code** such as **ASCII** or **EBCDIC**.

Character font – The style for a particular **character set** e.g. Gothic or Times Roman.

Character graphics – system such as that used to create **teletext**-type images and text.

Character set – A set of characters e.g. alphabet (upper and lower case) plus numbers.

Character variable – See **string variable**.

Charge coupled device – An **MOS** device similar in principle to **bubble memory**.

Charting package – Application to produce **charts** and graphs from numerical data.

Check digit – See **check sum**.

Checkpoint – This is a **file** that determines the state of a system at any particular moment in time – it can be used to re-establish the state of the system in the event of the system becoming corrupt. The computer's memory and the registers from the processor(s) are often kept in the checkpoint file.

Check sum – Extra data, derived by applying some suitable **algorithm**, is sent along with the message as a check on the **integrity** of the received message.

Chief systems analyst – The person in charge of the **systems analysis** team.

Child node – A **node** in a **tree structure** that has a **parent node**.

Chip – An alternative term for an **integrated circuit**.

CIM – Computer Integrated Manufacture – All the data from the design via the construction of artifacts to stock control etc. is processed and carried out by a centralised **database**.

Ciphertext – The **encrypted** text which can't be **deciphered** without a **key**.

Circuit switching – A method of sending messages where a dedicated physical path exists between the sending and receiving **computer**.

Circular list – a list whose **pointers** are arranged such that the **header** is joined onto the **footer**.

Circular wait state (OS) – A **deadlock** condition where two tasks are competing for the same resources. See **Pre-emptive multitasking**.

CISC – Complex Instruction Set Computer – Contrast with **RISC**.

Clashes – See **collision**.

Classes (C++) – A group of **objects** which share a common definition.

Cleartext – Also called **plaintext** – the input to a **cryptographic system**.

Clerical errors – Common errors when people enter data into a computer system, for example 'Clark' typed instead of 'Clarke'.

CLI – Command Line Interpreter.

Client (1) – A customer – used in the context of a client for a **system's analyst**, for example.

Client (2) – A **user** on a **network** which is connected to a **file server**.

Client-Server Architecture – The name given to an environment in which networked **fat** or **thin clients** interact with the **file server**.

Clip Art – The collection of art work that is used for **word processors** and **DTP documents**.

Clock – A crystal-controlled oscillator to produce the **clock pulses** inside a computer.

Clock pulse – A **binary pulse train** used to activate some condition at a precise moment in time. It is used to control the timing of the **CPU** and other systems.

Clock rate – The speed of the clock in **Hz**.

Clones – A computer manufactured by a third party which performs in ways identical (or better) than those computers manufactured by the original maker of the system.

Closed loop mode – A type of **feedback** in which the output is monitored to modify the input.

CMOS – Complementary Metal Oxide Silicon – A fabrication technique used for silicon chips.

CMOS RAM – **Memory chips** used on **mother board** to hold **configuration** data. Usually they hold the data in the memory by the use of a lithium battery which lasts for yonks.

CMYK – **Cyan Magenta Yellow** and **Key** – Colour model used in the printing industry.

CNC – Computer Numerical Control – Drilling machines etc. controlled by a computer. These ideas are central to an automated factory which makes extensive use of **CAD/CAM** and **CIM**.

COBOL – COmmon Business Oriented Language.

COBOL 97 – Latest version of the COBOL language.

CODASYL – COnference on DAta SYstems Languages – The organisation which originally developed COBOL.

Codd – Edgar Codd defined conventions which, if obeyed, result in an efficient **relational database** structure. There are five basic **normal forms**, although all of them are not normally used.

Code – Another name for the program instructions.

Coding – Solving a problem using a computer language.

Collision – A **hashing function** generating the same **address** for different **data**.

Colour correction – Compensation for incorrect colour rendition in a video or computer-based image.

Column by column mapping – A method of representing a two-dimensional **array** in **store**.

Combinational logic – A **logic circuit** in which the output depends only on the current combination of inputs – compare with the **sequential logic circuit**.

COM – Computer Output on **Microfilm**.

COM reader – A machine which can read computer output on **microform**.

COM recorder – A machine which transfers data from the **computer system** (disk etc.) onto **microform**.

Command.COM – The command interpreter for MS-DOS – it controls the 'system prompts' and interprets commands from the **keyboard**.

Command line interpreter – Part of the operating system which interprets commands typed in at the keyboard.

Comments – Text added for **documentation** purposes – ignored by the **interpreter, compiler** or **assembler**.

Commissioning – Installing and setting up a new **computer system**.

Communications controller (OS) – The system used to control communication between a **mainframe** or **mini** and the **terminals** trying to access the system. On a **mainframe** it's called a **front-end-processor**.

Communications package – **Software** to drive a **MODEM** for communication with **databases** and **bulletin boards** etc. usually on the Internet or an Intranet.

Compaction (Disk) – The gathering together of unused **sectors** into a contiguous space on the **disk**.

Compaction (OS) – Gathering together bits of unused **memory** in a **dynamic-memory partitioning system**.

Compilation – The process of changing the **source code** into the **object code**.

Compilation error – An error which has been detected during the **compilation** of a program.

Compiler – A **program** which **translates** a **high level language** into **machine code**.

Complementation – One way of representing negative (and positive) numbers using the **binary** system.

Complex Instruction Set Computer – A **computer** based around a **CISC microprocessor** which has a complex (very large) **instruction set** for its **assembly language**. Contrast with **RISC**.

Complex number – A number having a real ('ordinary') and an imaginary part. The imaginary part is plotted at 90 degrees to the ordinary part. A typical number would be written as x + iy.

Compressed file – A file which has been compressed (made smaller) by a utility such as **WinZip**.

Compression techniques – Techniques used to fit a quart into a pint pot! – often used to increase the data capacity of **disks** and get over the problems of limited **bandwidth** on **network systems**. Various standards exist such as **GIF**, **JPEG** and **MPEG** etc.

CompuServe – One of the companies providing facilities to access the **Internet**.

Computed value – The value of a number after a computer has processed it. It may be different from the actual value because of the introduction of errors from the **computer** system.

Computer – A processor of **information**. Processed information forms the basis of knowledge itself.

Computer Aided Design – Use of **computers** to aid design and other related processes.

Computer Aided Learning – Special **interactive** teaching packages.

Computer Aided Manufacture – Use of **computers** to design and build artifacts.

Computer Aided Software Engineering – **Software** to help with **systems analysis**, design, and testing.

Computer crime – The process of using a computer to carry out criminal activities.

Computer Misuse Act – Legislation introduced in 1990 to curb misuse of computers – e.g. injecting **viruses** and other forms of **hacking** etc.

Computer operator – A person who controls the day-to-day operation of the **computer** such as loading programs or putting paper in the printers – it's a term usually associated with minis and mainframes.

Computer program – A set of instructions which tells the computer what to do.

Computer Services Department – The **data processing** personnel for a company.

Concatenate – To join together two or more **strings**.

Concept keyboard – A **keyboard** which can have specialised overlays to perform functions with specialist **software**, e.g. pictures can be used on the keyboard etc.

Concurrency (OS) – Carrying out different operations at the same time or within a specified period (usually quite short).

Concurrent – tasks being carried out at the same time.

Concurrent Pascal – Version of **Pascal** which supports **parallel processing**.

Conditional jump – **Jump** to another part of a **program** on a condition such as an **overflow** being set.

Config.sys – An **MS-DOS** file which contains important operating system information to help set up the system to specific requirements.

Configuration – The way in which a **system** has been set up – e.g. 8 Gbyte disk – **SVGA** mode etc.

Constant – A value that does not vary.

Construct – A **syntactic** structure used in a language – e.g. a **conditional** or **loop construct**.

Content Addressable Store – See **Associative memory**.

Continuous variable – A **variable** that can have any value between various limits.

Control bus – The lines along which the control signals travel.

Control character – A character which is not printed but causes some other action to take place.

Control software – **Software** used to manage a **control system**.

Control structure – Structures such as **if-then**, **case** and **do-while** etc.

Control system – The integration of a **computer** and other **peripherals** to control machinery and plant.

Control unit – Part of the **CPU** – it controls the timing and routing of signals inside the **CPU**.

Conversational mode – An **interactive system** in which the **computer** and **user** are 'talking', e.g. an **interpreted BASIC** environment.

Cookies – Information stored locally on your hard disk and used by ISPs or Internet sites you have visited to create customised pages or help find out information about you!

CORAL – COmmon Real-time AppLication-language used for **real-time control systems**.

CORE store – A form of **primary storage** in which tiny doughnut-shape ferrite rings are used as the means of storage – now mostly out of date – also (rarely) the name given to **primary store**.

CPA – Critical Path Analysis.

CPU – Central Processing Unit.

cps – **Characters** per second.

Crash (1) – The system has unfortunately gone gaga and you will have to reset the machine!

Crash (2) – The disk heads have gouged a path through your valuable data stored on the surface of the disk – You will have to make use of the backup copy which you recently made!

CRAY – A computer manufacturer specialising in making ultra-fast supercomputers, e.g. the Cray T3E1200 (2.5 Tflops).

CRC – Cyclic redundancy check.

Critical path analysis – A time and resource management technique for large projects.

Cross assembler – One which produces assembly-language code that is to be run on another **machine**.

Cross compiler – One which produces high-level-language code that is to be run on another **machine**.

CRT – Cathode Ray Tube – The main screen in a computer monitor.

Cryptographic system – A system which uses **cryptography**.

Cryptography – The art of data **encryption** and **decryption** – keeping transmitted messages secret.

CSO – Colour Separation Overlay (Video) – Used for trick shots with false backgrounds, e.g. making superman appear to fly over a New York background.

CSV – Comma Separated Variable – A format for passing data between applications packages.

CTRL – The control key on the keyboard. Used in conjunction with other keys to produce special effects.

Cursor – The movable symbol on the **VDU** that indicates your current position on the screen.

Cursor keys – Special keys which control the direction of the **cursor**.

Cyan – The 'turquoise blue' colour obtained when Green and Blue light are mixed.

Cybercafe – A place which gives access to the Internet over a cup of coffee.

Cybernetics – The science of **robotics** and **AI**, particularly to do with mimicking human characteristics.

Cyberspace – Name for the space created by a **VR system** – the environment in which one is virtually present. Also used as a general name describing the electronic world of information.

Cyclic redundancy check – A mathematical **error** checking technique for transmitted data.

Cylinder – Concentric **disk tracks** (one on top of the other) form a **cylinder** on a **disk pack**.

Cylinder number – Each **cylinder** within a **disk pack** has a unique number.

Daisy wheel – The daisy shaped wheel around which the characters are embossed, as in a **daisy wheel printer**.

Daisy wheel printer – A high-quality printer using a daisy-wheel mechanism as found in typewriters.

DAT – Digital Audio Tape – One method of tape backup used on micros.

Data – The raw material on which the **computer** operates.

Database – A (usually complex) system containing many different but interconnected **files** from which complex information can be extracted, usually by means of a **query language** (**SQL**) or **DML**.

Database Administrator (DBA) – One who looks after and maintains a **database**.

Database Management System – A complex piece of software which enables the DBA to maintain and manage the **database**.

Data bus – The lines along which the data signals travel.

Data capture – The general term for gathering data together to be fed into the computer system.

Data compression – See **Compression**.

Data controller – Person in charge of the **data-control staff**.

Data control staff – The people who make sure that all the jobs to be entered by the **data entry staff** (clerks etc.) are in the correct place with nothing missing etc.

Data Description Language – A language used to describe the data in a **database**. It describes the data at various levels of abstraction.

Data dictionary – Holds the definitions of the descriptions of the data within a **database**.

Data encapsulation (C++) – **Objects** contain both **data** and **functions**.

Data encryption – See **Encryption**.

Data entry staff – People in a **data processing** department who look after and enter the data into a computer system.

Data export – See **export**.

Data file – A **file** consisting of **data** that is usually used by a **program file**.

Data flow architecture – One of the techniques of **parallel processing**.

Data flow diagrams – Special diagram to show interaction between **data** and processes.

Data flow graph – A technique of splitting up a problem ready for solution by **parallel processing**.

Data glove – A **virtual-reality** input device worn on the hand and used to control **virtual worlds**.

Data hiding (C++) – Only **member functions** have access to private data within their own **class**.

Data integrity – Making sure that the **data** is correct.

Data import – See **import**.

Data link layer – See **link layer**.

Data logger – A device (and software) for interfacing a **computer** to specialist input devices such as **pH sensors**, for example.

Data logging – The automatic capture of data by using a **data logger**.

Data preparation – Entering the **raw data** into the system (usually into machine readable form).

Data preparation supervisor – The person in control of the **data entry staff**.

Data processing (DP) – The arrangement of **raw data** into a form that is useful for other purposes.

Data processing manager – The person in charge of the **DP department**.

Data Protection Act 1998 – The government act that lays down guidelines for personal **information** stored in **computer systems** – it gives people the right to see stored data which affects them, and now includes extensions specific to the Internet.

Data types – different types of **data** in a **high-level language** e.g. **array**, **Boolean**, **character** etc.

Data security – Making sure that data is not misused or observed by the wrong people.

Data structures – The organising of **data** in special ways so that efficient processing may take place.

Datazooming – Press and hold the shift key while rotating the wheel on an **Intellimouse**, and you can jump backwards and forwards between pages displayed on a **web browser**, for example.

Daughter board – An accessory board such as a sound or video card which plugs into the **mother board**.

DB2 – IBM's powerful **relational database** system for **mainframes**.

DBA – The Database Administrator.

DBMS – DataBase Management System.

DBOMP – **DataBase** Organisation and Maintenance Processor – A **network database** for a **mainframe**.

DDE – Direct Data Entry – For example the use of a **key-to-store** system.

DDL – Data Description Language.

Deadlock (OS) – A resource being requested by one **task** is held by another.

Debuggers – Special **software** that helps you to **debug programs**. They often allow you to single step through a **machine code program** and see the effects on each **register** etc.

Debugging – Removing **errors** from **systems** or **programs**. Also applies to **hardware**.

Debugging time – Empirical rule stating that **debugging time** = programmer time x (number of lines of code)^2

DEC – The Digital Equipment Corporation – A major computer manufacturer.

Decimal system – Base ten using the digits 0,1,2,3,4,5,6,7,8,9.

Deciphered – The **encrypted** text is decoded.

Decision tables – A tabular arrangement of conditions and actions.

Decision trees – A sideways **tree structure** showing conditions and actions – an alternative to using **decision tables**.

Declaration – Declaring **variable** types at the beginning of a **program**.

Declarative language – A type of language where you do not have to explicitly state how the output is to be derived from the inputs. Used in **fifth generation languages** like **Prolog**, for example. **HTML** is an example of a declarative markup language.

Decode (1) – Extracting the original data from an **encoded** message.

Decode (2) – Term used to indicate when a **machine-code instruction** is being analysed to determine its function.

Decoder – A **logic circuit** that changes a code from its **encoded** form back to its original form.

Decryption – Changing a gobbledygook message back into ordinary text making use of a suitable **algorithm** and a **key**.

Default values – Sensible values chosen by the computer in the absence of other information from the **user**.

Delphi – Borland's visual programming environment which can produce **GUI**-based front end programs which are programmed in **Pascal**.

Demodulation – Changing a signal back into its original form.

De Morgan's law – A useful law in **Boolean algebra** for helping to simplify **logical functions**.

Denary – The name for the decimal system.

Dependency – A **relationship** in which the existence of one thing depends on the existence of another.

Derived class (C++) – A **class** that exhibits all the characteristics of the **base class** and some others in addition.

Descenders – Part of the text which goes below the **baseline.**

Design Structure diagram – A BS6244 alternative to basic **flowcharts**.

Desk Top Computer – A **microcomputer** such as the **PC**.

Desk Top Publishing – **Software** that gives a **computer** the power to manipulate virtually any characteristic of **graphics** and text on the screen.

Despooling – The process that extracts all the **spooled data** from **disk** or **tape** and carries out the appropriate processing such as printing, for example.

Device address – The **address** which, when put on the **bus**, causes the device to become active.

Device handler (OS) – A **program** which handles communications between the **operating system** and different devices such as the **keyboard**.

Dhrystones – A **benchmark** test for general instructions.

DHTML – Dynamic HyperText Markup Language. **HTML** with dynamic extensions.

Diagnostics – General name for **debugging tools** and the like for helping to find **bugs** in the **system**.

Dictionary (1) – A list of **variables** and other useful information **compiled** during the **syntax analysis** phase.

Dictionary (2) – A word list used to check the spelling in a **WP** or **DTP** system.

Dictionary (3) – Data about the data stored in a **database** – called the **data dictionary**.

Differentiation (maths) – The process of finding the derivative which is essentially the gradient of a graph at some particular point.

Digital – Varies in discrete steps.

Digital camera – A camera which does not make use of film, but records the light intensity on special chips housed in the camera. The images are then downloaded into the computer for processing.

Digital computer – A **computer** that operates on **digital** signals, i.e. almost all computers.

Digital MODEM – The newer breed of **modem** which transmits a digital signal over a link such as a specially-equipped phone line, power cable, cable company link or satellite link.

Digital plotter – A **plotter** which works on an absolute (x,y) co-ordinate system – e.g. move to 234,5678.

Digital signature – This is a method by which you can 'guarantee' that the people who send you information are actually who they say they are. It is therefore an electronic version of the 'trusted' signatures used when you send a letter by **snail mail**.

Digital TV – The latest type of television on which you can view an enormous number of channels and, with an extra box, can surf the **Internet**.

Digital Versatile Disk – Also called Digital Video Disk – A high-density double-sided CD-ROM format.

Digitisation – See **quantisation**.

Direct access – Any item of **data** can be found without having to go **sequentially** through the entire list.

Direct access files – See **Random access file**s.

Direct access secondary storage – **Storage** where the **data** can be accessed directly, e.g. **disks**.

Direct addressing – A mode of **addressing** in which a **memory location** is used to directly specify an **address**.

Directed graph – A **graph**, similar to a **state-transition diagram**, consisting of **nodes**, arcs and arrows can be drawn from a consideration of the **structure** of the **module** under test. The nodes represent entry and exit points to and from sub-structures within the software. The directed arc (the arc with an arrow on it) from one node to the next represents the code between the **nodes**. **Loops** represent '**while conditions**' and 'multiple arcs' can be used to represent '**if-then** conditions', for example. See white-box testing.

Direct entry – A method where **data** is entered into the **computer system on line**.

Directive – A special instruction to an **assembler**. See **assembler directives**.

Directory – Information about the **files** stored on **magnetic disk**.

Directory file structure – See **hierarchical file**.

Disassembler – Software which attempts to extract the **object code** from the **source code** – it's often impossible to get a correctly disassembled output. Many **debuggers** have this facility.

Discrete variable – A **variable** that can only have a discrete set of values.

Disk – A **direct-access storage** device.

Disk cache – **Semiconductor RAM** used to speed up **disk** access.

Disk cartridge (1) – Mainframe – A single (removable) 14in-disk housed in a plastic container.

Disk cartridge (2) – Micro – A removable hard disk drive such as the **SCSI** cartridge system.

Disk drive – The **peripheral storage device** which houses the **magnetic** or **optical disk**.

Disk pack – A large **hard-disk system** using a stack of 14in disks on a common spindle and accessed by a least one **read/write head** per disk surface. **Data** is stored in **cylinders**.

Distributed network – A **network** with many independent interconnections.

Distributed processing – Different **computers** *handling their own work*, but also helping to manage common resources on the network, or even sharing work on the same problem.

Divergence (iteration) – The actual solution gets further away from the theoretical solution.

DLT – Digital Linear Tape – One format of tape backup, now popular as DLT libraries on large **mainframes.**

DMA – Direct Memory Access – Access to memory not under the direct control of the main processor.

DMA controller (OS) – A special **microprocessor** used to handle Direct Memory Access.

DML – Data Manipulation Language – Language used to access data in a database.

Documentation – **Information** written about **programs** or **applications** etc. Ranges from simple manuals through to a complex technical description.

Domain name (1) – The name given to an organisation which is connected to the Net. For example, microsoft.com would be Microsoft's domain name. It can refer to a single computer or a group of computers which constitutes the Internet site.

Domain name (2) – Used on some **LANs** to define security and other policies for users of the network. It also refers to logical groups of computer on a LAN, which is of some administrative convenience, e.g. sales and marketing etc.

DOS – Disk Operating System.

Dot matrix printer – A **printer** which fires tiny pins through a ribbon thus forming the characters by dots.

Double buffering – A technique of using two **buffers** to speed up input/output.

Double precision – Using a double **word length** to increase the **precision** of calculations.

DP – Data Processing.

dpi – dots per inch – A measure of print quality.

DQL – Data Query Language.

Draft copy – copy used to check work before the final copy is made. Often a lower-quality output would be used, e.g. a 300 dpi laser printout to check a book which will be typeset at 1200 dpi.

DRAM – Dynamic Random Access Memory – The most common type of **RAM**. Various types such as EDO and SDRAM etc. are available.

DRUM plotter – A device in which a pen moves across a rotating drum to produce **graphics** output.

DRUM printer – A type of **line printer** that utilises a revolving drum.

Dry run – The process of working through a program *by hand* to see what the answers should be.

D to A converter – A **digital** to **analogue** converter – converts **digital** to **analogue** signals.

DTP – Desk Top Publishing.

Dumb terminal – A **keyboard** and **VDU** with little or no processing power. The processing has to be carried out by the computer to which the terminal is connected.

Dump – The copying of a **file** to **disk** or the **printer** etc.

Duplex – A two way (only one way at a time) communication system.

DVD – See **Digital versatile (or video) disk**.

Dynamic memory partitioning (OS) – Allocation of memory partition in an *ad hoc* way according to need.

Dynamic RAM – Memory that has to be **refreshed** to maintain its contents.

EAN – European Article Number – One type of code used with the **bar-code** system.

EAROM – Electrically Alterable Read Only Memory.

EBCDIC – Extended **Binary Coded Decimal** Interchange Code – Often used with IBM tape systems on mainframes.

EBNF – Extended Backus Naur Form – More versatile alternative to **BNF** as it has a few more symbols and can be used to define its own syntax.

ECONET – One of Acorn computer's **LANs**.

Editor – Name for the **software** which can display and edit text.

Editing – Changing attributes of text in a WP or DTP document, for example.

EDORAM – **Extended Data Out Random Access Memory** – A faster form of RAM.

EDP – Electronic Data Processing.

EEROM – Electrically Erasable Read Only Memory.

EFT – Electronic Funds Transfer – Use of IT to transfer money from one account to another.

EFTPOS – Electronic Funds Transfer at the Point Of Sale.

EGA – Enhanced Graphics Adaptor – IBM PC video standard now largely replaced by better ones.

EIDE – Enhanced Integrated Drive Electronics. Upgraded version of the **IDE interface**.

EISA – Enhanced Industry Standard Architecture – An enhanced version of **ISA** bus system.

Electrically Alterable Read Only Memory – A **ROM** in which locations can be electrically altered without having to reprogram the whole **chip**.

Electrically Erasable Read Only Memory – A **ROM** which can be erased electrically instead of making use of UV light.

Electronic data processing – See **Data processing**.

Electronic encyclopaedia – An encyclopaedia stored on **CD-ROM** or some other suitable media.

Electronic mail – The ability to send and receive documents via suitable networks. (Including the telephone-**network** system and hence the **Internet**.)

Element – An item in an **array**.

E-Mail – Electronic mail.

E-Mail address – The unique address given to the mail box for each user who has an e-mail account. It typically uses the '@' sign as in the following example – mickey-mouse@disney.com.

Embedded microprocessor – A **microprocessor** system which is dedicated to one particular task such as controlling a washing machine.

Embedded system – A **system** which contains an **embedded microprocessor**.

Emulation – One **computer** system pretending to be another.

Emulator – **Hardware** or **software** or a combination of both carrying out the **emulation** process.

Encode – Putting **data** into some sort of code.

Encoder – A **logic circuit** which changes the **data** into a code suitable for **machine** entry.

Encryption – Changing 'ordinary – message text' into gobbledygook using a **key** and a suitable **algorithm**.

Encryption key – What's needed to decipher an **encrypted** message.

Endless loop – See **Loop endless**.

Engine – Simply another term for a processor. (**Hardware** and **software**.)

Entity – A concrete or abstract representation of data held in a **database** which corresponds to a **record**.

Entity dependence diagram – Pictorial way of showing how one **entity** depends on others, and the **association** between each **entity**.

Entity relationship diagram – Pictorial way of showing relationships between entities. **Relationships** are usually shown in diamond-shaped boxes, and **entities** in square boxes.

Enumerated data type – a data type in which a list of data (e.g. mon,tue,wed) indicates the data set.

EOF – End Of File.

EPROM – Erasable Programmable Read Only Memory.

EPS – Encapsulated PostScript – A PostScript file format that can be used to transfer editable files from one hardware or software platform to another. Sometimes it's the only way to transfer a complex graphic.

Equivalence gate – See **XNOR gate**.

Erasable Programmable Read Only Memory – A **PROM** that can be erased using ultra-violet light.

Ergonomic keyboard – **Keyboard** specifically designed to overcome problems such as **RSI**.

Ergonomics – The relationship between humans and their interaction with systems such as computer systems, for example.

Error (1) – A mistake.

Error (2) – (**absolute relative**) = | relative error |

Error (3) – (**absolute**) = | actual error |

Error (4) – (**actual**) = Exact value – computed value.

Error (5) – (**percentage**) = Relative error x 100%

Error (6) – (**relative**) = Actual error/exact value.

Ethernet – An industry standard **LAN** popular for connecting **PCs** and most other machines.

European article number – A **bar code** method for coding goods as found in the UK.

Even parity – An even number of '1s' in each transmitted code acts as a check on **data integrity**.

Exa (E) – Multiplier representing 1×10^{18}. (Computing alternative 1024^6.)

Exclusive OR gate – An **OR gate** that does not give an output (of 1) when all inputs are at '1'.

Execute – To carry out the instructions in a **program**.

Execution error – An **error** which occurs when the **program** is **running**.

Executive – See **operating system supervisor**.

Excel – Microsoft's main **spreadsheet** program.

Exhaustive testing – Testing every possible thing that can happen to a computer system under test. For very large systems, this would take an infinite amount of time, and is therefore impossible.

Expansion slots – Places inside a **PC** which help to enable **peripherals** to be connected to the **system**.

Expert system – A specialist problem-solving **system** programmed with knowledge from human experts.

Explicit sign method – A way of assigning a **sign bit** at the beginning of a **binary number**. Contrast with the **two's complement** method.

Exponent – Indicates the power of a number, e.g. in 10^3, 3 is the exponent.

Export – Getting data from your computer system to another computer system.

Expression – Part of a language **construct** used to calculate a single value from one or more **operands**.

Extended ASCII – Making use of the **parity bit** to extend the **ASCII code** – 128 extra codes are generated.

External database – A **database** accessed via a **LAN** or **WAN**, often making use of the phone system and a **MODEM**.

External devices – A device which is connected to the system such as **printers** and **keyboards**.

External interrupt – An **interrupt** caused by an **external device**.

External sort – A **sort algorithm** used when the **files** to be **sorted** are too large to fit in **main memory**.

E13B – The system of numbers used at the bottom of bank cheques for **MICR**.

Factorial – A mathematical sequence of numbers such that N! = N(N–1)(N–2)(N–3)...3.2.1 and 0! = 1.

Fast ethernet – 100Mbit/sec **ethernet**.

Fast SCSI – A SCSI II interface giving about 10Mbytes/sec.

Fast wide SCSI – A SCSI II interface giving about 20Mbytes/sec.

Fatal error – An **error** which would terminate the **execution** of a **program**.

FAT (OS) – File Allocation Table – A file used by **DOS** to allocate space on a **disk** and to help locate and manage the **files**.

Fat client – A PC with a hard disk and the ability to do all the processing, which is connected to a network. Applications may be loaded from the local disk or the network **file server**.

Father file – The name given to the current **master file** when being used in conjunction with the **transaction file** to produce the new **master file**.

Favourites – Pages that a user would frequently visit on the web can be added to your favourites. This saves you having to type in the **URL** each time you visit the site.

Fax – Short for facsimile. Sending pictures down the telephone line. (However, it's obvious that text can also be sent.)

FDDI – Fibre Distributed Data Interface – High-speed **fibre-optic networks**.

FDDI II – The later '1 Gbit/sec version' of **FDDI** technology.

FDM – Frequency Division **Multiplexing**.

Feasibility study – Part of the **system life cycle** which examines possible solutions to **systems** problems.

Feedback – Part of the output signal is fed back to modify the input signal.

Femto (f) – Multiplier representing 1×10^{-15}

Fetch – Term used to indicate that a **machine code instruction** is being fetched from memory.

Fetch-decode-execute cycle – The repetitive tasks always being undertaken by a **microprocessor** when it's switched on. Often shortened to just the fetch-execute cycle.

Fibre optic – A cable made out of plastic or glass fibre, useful for **computer** communication systems.

Field – A group of characters that represent a single item of **data** in a **file**.

Field width – The number of **characters** stored in a particular **field**.

FIFO – First In First Out.

FIFO stack – A **stack** designed to operate on the **FIFO principle** – also known as a **queue**.

Fifth-generation language – **Declarative languages** such as **Prolog** and **LISP**.

File – A collection of **records** that are related in some way and are contained in a single unit.

File creation – Setting up a new **file** so that it is ready to accept **data**.

File maintenance – Keeping the contents of **files** in an efficient state and making **backups** etc.

File manager – Part of the **OS** which maps the logical onto the **physical-level subschema**.

File security (1) – The arrangements made to prevent unauthorised access to **files**.

File security (2) – The physical safety of **files** such as placing them in fire-proof safes.

File server – **Computer** on a **network** from which the **files** are served.

Filter – Software, which allows you to filter out undesirable content on the **Internet**. It's useful for schools and parents to prevent children from seeing unsuitable material when surfing the **net**.

Finger-print entry – A smaller version of the **palm print** system. Used for gaining entry into secure sites. Only a single finger need be inserted into the machine.

Finish pointer – A **pointer** that points to the end of a **list**.

Firewall – A system that helps to prevent the threat of hacking into a company's network by unauthorised external (or internal!) personnel.

Firmware – The **software** stored in **ROM**.

First-Generation Language – **Assembly languages** and **machine code**.

First Normal Form – **Attributes** with multiple or repeating values must be removed so that all **tuples** (**records**) in a **relation (table)** are of the same length.

Fixed-length field – A **field** in a **file** where the number of **characters** can't be varied.

Fixed-length record file – All **records** in the **file** are of fixed length – not necessarily the same length.

Fixed partition – A section of **memory** of fixed size, usually used in **multi-user systems**.

Fixed point number – The decimal point can't be altered by an **exponent**.

Fixed spacing – Text as would be produced on a mechanical typewriter.

Flag – A **bit** inside a **register** which is set if a particular event has happened, e.g. the **overflow flag**.

Flag register – A **register** whose contents are made up of many **bits** – all acting as **flags**.

Flaming – The act of sending abusive **e-mail**.

Flash ROM – A **ROM** which can be programmed *in situ* by smaller voltages. Used extensively in peripheral devices such as **MODEMs** etc. to upgrade the chip without changing it. Can also be used for the **BIOS**.

Flat-bed plotter – A device which controls a pen moving over a flat piece of paper (x,y co-ordinates).

Flight simulator (1) – A software package on a microcomputer, like Flight Simulator 98 from Microsoft, for example. A good deal of learning can be carried out using these **packages**, as they are very realistic.

Flight simulator (2) – A large and expensive computer-controlled system set up to enable pilots of real aircraft to be trained under conditions that would not normally occur in practice. These flight simulators cost millions of pounds.

Flight yoke – An external control panel which simulates the controls at the cockpit of an aircraft. It can be interfaced to your computer to make using a flight simulator more realistic.

Flip flop – A **sequential logic circuit** which is used as a **storage** element and is found in **counters** and **shift registers**.

Floating point accelerator – See **maths co-processor**.

Floating point number – A number with a **mantissa** and an **exponent**. Contrast with **fixed point**.

Floppy disk – A small flexible version of a **disk**, mainly used on **microcomputers** – there are several formats, and the size of floppy in use today is mainly 3.5in.

Flops – **FLOating Point** operations per Second – A measure of a computer's processing speed.

Floptical disk – The name sometimes given to the latest high capacity 'floppy disks', which use optical technology.

Flowchart – Pictorial representation of an **algorithm** – different types exist, e.g. **program flowcharts**, **systems flowcharts** and **design structure diagrams** etc.

FMV – Full Motion Video – Used to describe VHS-quality movies encoded using **MPEG** 1 or 2 onto a **CD-ROM** or **DVD**.

Font – The name given to a **typeface** e.g. Times New Roman.

Font card – The smaller version of the **font** cartridge found in **printers**.

Font cartridge – A plug-in module used for extra **fonts** on some **LASER** or **dot-matrix printers**.

Footer (1) – A **pointer** that points to the end of a **list**.

Footer (2) – The line of text at the bottom of a document (below the main body of text).

For loops – **Loop structure** based on a counter which controls how many times the loop is executed.

Force feedback joystick – A joystick which can be controlled from the computer to produce effects like 'vibrations' if, for example, an aircraft in the flight simulator which you are using is about to stall.

Form – **HTML** method of getting information back from the users who are browsing through **Web** pages.

Formal language – Unambiguous **context-free language** used on current generations of **computers**.

Format – The layout of a document or file etc.

Formatting (1) – Preparing a **disk** ready for storing data.

Formatting (2) – Laying out text in a word processor using a variety of techniques such as **justification** etc.

FORTH – **High-level language** suitable for **control**.

FORTRAN – FORmula TRANslator – A **high-level language** suitable for maths, science and engineering applications.

FORTRAN 90 – A modern version of **FORTRAN** that supports **concurrent** programming.

Forward pointer – A **pointer** indicating the way forward to the next **node** in a data structure.

Fourth-generation language – Languages used in **spreadsheets** (macros) and **databases** (SQLs) etc.

FPU – Floating Point Unit – Same as a maths co-processor, i.e. hardware used to speed up numeric calculations. Now usually housed in the main micro-processor.

Fractal – A simple unit that is used to build up other, more-complex units. Each unit is similar to its components.

Frame – A guide for the text in a **DTP system**.

Free-storage pointer – A **pointer** used to indicate the next free location.

FreeWare – Software which is distributed free of charge.

Frequency – Cycles per second – measured in **Hz**.

Front-end processor – Another **computer** used to control the input/output operations of a larger system.

FrontPage – Microsoft's all-singing all-dancing **HTML** web editor, explorer and site-creation package. You can use it just like a **word processor** to create the pages, or make use of an extensive collection of **wizards** to build up impressive **web sites** in a minimum amount of time.

FTP – **File Transfer Protocol** – A common system used for transferring files over the **Internet**.

Full adder – A **logic circuit** that adds two **binary digits** that can cope with a carry from the previous bit.

Full duplex – A simultaneous two-way communication system.

Fully dependent – See **Functional dependency**.

Function – Something which is used to call up a **subroutine** during **compilation**, for example 'sin' (sine), 'sqr' (square root), or 'eof' (end of file).

Functional dependency – a unique association **one-to-one relationship** only.

Functional language – A **paradigm** based on **parameters** being passed to **functions**.

Fuzzy logic – A type of logic which, instead of **Boolean** true/false scenarios, is able to cope with less cut-and-dried concepts such as 'tall' or 'short', for example.

Gantt charts – Calendar-type charts which show the proposed or actual progress of a project using horizontal bars.

Gate – **AND**, **OR** and **NOT gates** etc. built up from electronic circuits. They control the actions of digital signals presented at the inputs to these gates. The output depends on the combination of inputs.

Gateway – A **computer** that is used to connect different **networks** together so that larger networks may be formed. For example, the **Internet** is formed by the interconnection of many other networks.

Gbit Ethernet – 1000 Mbit/sec **Ethernet**.

Gbyte – See **Gigabyte**.

G code – The code consisting of numbers and letters used to control a **CNC** machine.

General-purpose register – A **register** that is not assigned to any particular task, although it may be used for special purposes when some instructions are being carried out.

GIF – Graphics Interchange Format – A **compression** standard for **graphics files** developed for use when downloading files from **bulletin boards** or **HTML pages** on **networks** like the **Internet** or an **Intranet**.

GIF animation – A series of **GIF** images played in sequence to give the illusion of animation. Used extensively for constructing animations on **HTML** pages.

Giga (G) – Multiplier representing 1×10^9. (Often-used alternative in computing $1024 \times 1024 \times 1024$.)

Gigabyte – $1024 \times 1024 \times 1024$ bytes of data.

GigaFlops – 10^9 **Flops**.

Global communications network – A world-wide connection of **computers** such that **computer data** can be transmitted from any **machine** to any other **machine**.

Global variable – A variable which is available to all of the program – contrast with **local variable**.

GOPHER – An **Internet** tool designed to help navigate and browse through the **network**.

GOTO – An unconditional **jump**.

Grammar checker – Accessory for **WP**, **DTP**, spreadsheet and other systems. It is context sensitive.

Grandfather-father-son – A method of **backing up** in which three generations of **files** are kept.

Grandfather file – A **master file** two generations old.

Graphics – Pictures that can be manipulated on the **computer**.

Graphics Interchange Format – See **GIF**.

Graphics tablet – A device to transfer a picture into the computer by moving a pen across the tablet.

Gray code – A code where only one digit changes between transitions when the code is used for counting.

Grey-scale image – A 'black and white' image made up from many shades of grey.

GUI – Graphical User Interface – **WIMP**-based computer interface, e.g. **windows**, for example.

Hacker – A person who illegally breaks into or tampers with computer systems.

Hacking – The unauthorised use of computer equipment.

Half adder – A **logic circuit** which adds two **binary digits** but can't cope with a carry from the previous column.

Half duplex – Two way communication, but only one way at any one time.

Handshaking – A **protocol** used when communication with **peripheral** equipment is taking place.

Hard copy – A printout, usually on a piece of paper.

Hard disk – See **Magnetic disk drive**.

Hardware development – The process of developing new **hardware**.

Hardware test programs – **Programs** that are run to diagnose a fault in the **computer hardware**.

Hard wired – A **system** which is programmed by the hardware (e.g. wire links etc.) and can't be altered.

Hash table – A table which contains data stored by means of a **hashing function**.

Hash total – See **check sum**.

Hashing – See **hashing functions**.

Hashing functions – A set of rules that generates a storage **address** – usually applied to a numeric **key field** or by using some numeric relationship such as **ASCII** or **EBCDIC** etc. on a **string field**.

HCI – Human Computer Interface – The art of human interaction with a **computer**.

Header (1) – The line at the top of a page in a **DTP** or **WP system** (above the main body of text).

Header (2) – A **pointer** that points to the beginning of a **list**.

Header (3) – **Digital data** that contains **information** such as the destination etc. for a message transmitted over a **network**.

Header label record – The **record** of the beginning of the **tape** which identifies the **tape**.

Heat-sensitive printers – **Printers** which use special heat-sensitive paper brought into contact with hot pins.

Help system – A self-help system which is built into many modern **applications**. One may ask questions or search an index.

Hertz – Cycles per second.

Heuristic programming – A programming method based on rules of thumb and learning from previous experience.

Hex – short for **hexadecimal**.

Hexadecimal – Base sixteen, uses the characters 0, 1, 2, 3, 4, 5, 6, 7, 8, 9, A, B, C, D, E and F.

Hierarchical database – A **database** built up on a **hierarchical data structure**.

Hierarchical data model – The **tree**-type **data structure** model.

Hierarchical data structure – The structure that is derived from the principles involved in a family tree.

Hierarchically-organised file – A file based on **hierarchical data structures**.

High-level languages – English-like language such as **COBOL, Pascal** or **BASIC**, for example.

High-resolution graphics – Computer pictures with a lot of detail.

HIPO chart – Hierarchical Input Processing Output – a form of **structure diagram**.

History – Information, held by your computer, which enables you to load recently-visited web pages by holding them in **cache** on **disk**.

Hollerith code – The code used on 80-column punched cards.

Home page – The name given to a **web site**, set up by the **user** (or the manufacturer of the web browser) which is used as the **default** page when you first load your **web browser**.

HRG – High Resolution Graphics.

HSV – Hue Saturation Value – A colour model used by artists making use of hues, tints and tones, used on some **DTP systems**.

HTML – **HyperText Mark-up Language** – A page description language used to create **Web pages** which can be viewed by **Web browsers**.

HTML editor – A software package specifically designed to help construct HTML pages. Many of the later versions are full **WYSIWYG** with many other useful utilities. See **FrontPage.**

HTML link – See **Hypertext link**.

HTTP – **HyperText Transfer Protocol** – *The* **protocol** commonly used by many **Web browsers**.

Hub – Hardware placed on a network to allow computers to be connected to the network. Typically used for connecting PCs to **Ethernet**. One hub may connect a dozen machines to a spur to form a **tree network**.

Human Computer Interface – See **HCI**.

Human readable – **Data** that is in a form that can be read by humans.

Hypermedia – A **system** making use of **computer data**, video and audio etc.

Hypertext – A sub-set of **hypermedia** where textual information can be set up by associating parts of the data with other ideas – useful for research that needs carrying out on the text.

Hypertext link – The graphic or text-based reference which, when clicked with the mouse can generate a new address to transport you somewhere different on an **Internet** or **Intranet** system.

Hz – Abbreviation for **Hertz**, or cycles per second.

I/O – Input/Output

IAP – Information Access Provider – An alternative name for an **ISP** or **Information Service Provider**.

IAS – Immediate Access Store – The **primary** or **main storage** inside a **computer**, i.e. **RAM.**

IBG – Inter-Block Gap – Gaps inbetween the **blocks** of data on a **tape system**.

IBM – Big Blue or International Business Machines – This used to be the largest computer company in the world.

IC – Integrated Circuit – The alternative name for a **silicon chip** – also called a **chip**.

ICL – International Computers Ltd. – A British based manufacturer of computer equipment.

Icons – The pictures used in the **WIMP environment** to help with selection of various actions.

IDE – Integrated Drive Electronics – A **disk-interface** standard.

Identifier – One or more **characters** which are used to identify an element in a **high-level language**.

IDMS – Integrated Data Management System – A **network database** for a **mainframe**.

iMac – **Apple's** revolutionary design of computer which is **Internet** ready. However, it does not come with a floppy disk as standard.

Immediate access store – Same as **primary store** or **main store**.

Immediate addressing – A mode of **addressing** in which an **address** is specified by an immediate **operand** (a number immediately after the **Op code**).

Immediate mode – Execution of a command from outside a program, e.g. typing in a command from the keyboard which can then be directly **interpreted** by the **operating system**.

IMP – Interface Message Processor.

Impact printer – Any **printer** relying on a hammer or pin etc. impacting on a ribbon to produce a **character**.

Imperative languages – Ones in which sequences of instructions called **imperatives** are given to the computer. Typifies telling the computer *how* to do something. Also called **procedural languages**.

Import – Getting data from another computer system into your computer system.

IMS – IBM's Information Management System database on a **mainframe computer**.

IMS/R – Relational version of IMS.

Incremental plotter – A **plotter** which works on co-ordinates which are relative to the last position used.

Index (1) – A number, usually held in an **index register**, that represents an offset.

Index (2) – A reference used to help locate **records** and **files** on a **disk** or **CD-ROM** etc.

Indexed addressing – An **addressing mode** in which several **registers**, including an **index register** are combined to produce the actual **address** – it's useful for setting up **stacks** and **queues** etc. The **absolute address** is a base address plus an **index**.

Indexed sequential file – A **sequential file** in which the **records** are pointed to by **pointers** held in an **index**.

Indirect addressing – An **addressing mode** in which an **address** is calculated indirectly, usually by specifying a **memory location** and a **register**.

Infix notation – Normal algebraic notation where the operator appears inbetween the operands, e.g. P + Q.

Information – Information is **Data + Structure**.

Glossary of Terms Used in this Book **669**

Information superhighway – A **global network** which will eventually transmit computer data, audio and video etc. Also, a common name used for the **Internet**.

Information technology – Applying computer technology to the solution of a wide variety of problems.

Infrared interface – An interface, usually used on a printer, a portable computer, **PDAs** and **palmtops** etc., which enables you to connect to a peripheral device without the need for a cable.

Infrared mouse – A mouse with no connecting lead.

Inheritance (C++) – Passing on characteristics from a parent class to a child class.

Initialise – Making sure that all **variables** and **constants** etc. are set up correctly before the rest of the program is run.

Ink-jet printer – Printer technology which squirts ink from a nozzle to form the text or **graphics**.

Inorder traversal – A method for traversing (moving around) a **tree structure**, visiting the left-hand, **root** and right-hand subtrees in this order.

Input – **Data** to be entered into the **computer system**.

Input Peripherals – Devices such as **keyboards**, **mice**, **scanners** or other data-input technology.

Insert edit (video) – Inserting a new video image into the middle of an existing recording.

Insertion sort – A simple and straightforward **sort algorithm** – items of data inserted in the correct place.

Instruction pointer – See **Program counter**.

Instruction register – A **register** which contains the current instruction being **executed** by the **program**.

Instruction set – A set of **assembly language mnemonics** which represent the machine code of a particular **computer**, e.g. instructions for Motorola's 68000 or Intel's Pentium range of microprocessors.

Integer – A whole number.

Integrated Circuit – Same as **IC** or **silicon chip**.

Integrated software package – **Software** which usually has a **word processor**, **database** and **spreadsheet** integrated into the same system.

Integrated system – A **system** in which it is easy to pass **data** between one part and another.

Integration (maths) – The process of finding the area 'under' a graph between two given points.

Integrity – making sure that transmitted **data** or **data** entered into a system is correct.

Intel – A large-scale manufacturer of **chips** and **microprocessors**. Inventors of the famous 80×86 range of processors and the **Pentium** etc.

Intelligent bridge – A bridge on a network which can route network traffic and prevent some stations on one network from interacting with some stations on another. Useful for security and traffic management.

Intelligent terminal – A **terminal** that is capable of doing much local processing.

Intellimouse – One type of mouse which gives you extra functionality. An extra 'wheel' on the mouse enables you to scroll up and down a long page, for example.

Interactive – The user can **interact** with the system – contrast with **batch**, for example.

Interactive video – Video based on a **CD-ROM** or **DVD** system in which the **user** can **interact**.

Inter-block gaps – The gaps between **blocks** on a **tape system**.

Interface (1) – Special electronic circuits to help connect different **peripherals** and other devices like **transducers** to the **computer system**.

Interface (2) – The interaction between people and **computers**, e.g. the **HCI** that an **operating system** might present to the user.

Interface message processor – Another name for a **node computer** on a **network**.

Internal sort – A **sort** that can be accomplished by using the **main memory** in a **computer system**.

Internet – A **global network** of other **networks** which forms one basis of the **information superhighway**. It is a **packet-switched network** consisting of many small **networks** interconnected via **gateways**.

Internet backbone – The physical parts of the network which form the fastest and highest-**bandwidth** links for the **Internet**. The cable, fibre or satellite links used by the **ISPs** and for international communications.

Internet Explorer – Microsoft's **Internet browser**.

Internet Service Provider – See **ISP**.

Interpreter – A **program** which **translates** a **high-level language** into **machine code** in an **interactive** environment. It is slow as each line is **translated** each time it is encountered.

Inter-record gaps – The gaps between **records** on a tape **system**.

Interrupt – The **CPU** is interrupted from what it is doing so that something else may receive attention.

Interrupt disabled – The **CPU** pays no attention to **interrupts** when they occur.

Interrupt enabled – The **CPU** pays attention to the **interrupts** when they occur.

Interrupt flag register – A **register** in which the **bit** patterns are used as **flags** to represent the state of many operations, e.g. **overflow** or **underflow**, **carry** generated etc.

Interrupt handling routine – The **software** which has been written to take control once an **interrupt** has been initiated.

Interrupting device – The device which has caused the **interrupt**, e.g. the **disk** or the **printer** etc.

Interrupt priorities – The priority assigned to different **interrupts** in the **system**. There may be devices which have a high priority and others which have a low priority.

Interrupt request – A device has requested an **interrupt**.

Interrupt servicing – The process of handling an **interrupt**.

Interrupt vector – A **pointer** used to point to the place where the **interrupt** handler resides in **memory**.

Intranet – A **web site** set up for *internal use*, usually within a company or an educational establishment etc. This is a closed site which may be accessed from the outside if the hardware, software and passwords are known. It is an efficient way of disseminating company information to employees and visitors.

Inverter – See **NOT gate**.

IP (1) – **Internet Protocol** – the protocol used for connection via the Net or a LAN. It forms part of the popular **TCP/IP protocol** which helps to route the information across the networks.

IP (2) – **Information Provider** – an alternative name for an **ISP** or an **IAP**.

IP address – This is a unique 32-bit number which identifies your computer when connected to the Net.

IRG – **Inter-Record Gap**.

ISA – Industry Standard Architecture – A 16-bit bus system for the IBM PC and its clones.

ISDN – **Integrated Services Digital Network** – A fast transmission system which can handle audio, video, computer and other forms of data.

ISO – The International Standards Organisation.

ISO OSI model – The ISO model for Open-Systems Interconnection. A seven-layer model for the standardisation of **network** interconnection.

ISP – **Internet Service Provider** – Organisations such as **AOL**, **Compuserve** or **MSN**, for example, which provide user-friendly access to the **Internet**, usually via local **POPs**.

IT – **Information Technology**.

Iteration (1) – **Looping**.

Iteration (2) – A mathematical method of solving problems by **numerical analysis**.

Jackson Structured Programming – A method developed by Jackson to show sequence, **iteration** and selection on a **structure diagram**.

JANET – The Joint Academic NETwork – A large **PSN** in the UK used by universities and industrial research establishments to communicate via computer and send **e-mail** – now part of the **Internet**.

Java – Programming language developed by Sun Microsystems. It is ideal for creating programs which work over the **Internet**, but Java is a fully blown **object-oriented language** in its own right.

Java Applet – A Java class that is loaded and interpreted by a suitably equipped Web browser. It is used to create fancy effects on **HTML Web pages**.

Java Byte Code – The intermediate stage of the Java code before being translated into the final language to run on the **target machine**.

JavaScript – an **interpreted language**, which can be **embedded** inside **HTML pages**. With a suitably equipped **Web browser**, very fancy effects, not possible by using HTML alone are now easily possible with JavaScript.

JCL – Job Control Language – The language in which a **job-control program** is written.

J-K flip flop – A versatile **flip flop** used in electronic **counters** and **shift-register** circuits.

Job – The name given to a **program** (or set of work which can be regarded as a single unit) which is to be **run** on a **computer system**.

Job-control language – The language in which the **job-control program** or **job-control commands** are written.

Job-control program – A sequence of **job-control commands** used by the machine operator to **run** a **batch** or **jobs** and do other **tasks**, usually on a **mainframe computer**.

Joint Photographic Experts Group – See **JPEG**.

Joystick – A device to control the **cursor** or other functions by waving a stick in two (or three) dimensions. Useful for computer games, flight-simulators and **VR** etc.

JPEG – The **Joint Photographic Experts Group** – One method for storing and compression of coloured graphics images.

JSP – **Jackson Structured Programming**.

Jump – Transfer of control from one part of a program to another.

Justification – Term used to denote alignment in **WP** and **DTP** systems, e.g. left or right justified text.

Just-in-time – Production techniques where components arrive just in time to be used in the factory.

J++ – One version of the Java language.

K – Short for **kilo**. Multiplier representing 1 x 10^3. (Often used computer alternative is 1024.)

Karnaugh maps – A pictorial way of simplifying certain types of **Boolean functions**.

Kbyte – 1024 bytes of data.

Kernel (OS) – An alternative name for the nucleus of an **operating system**. It's the part of the operating system which performs the most basic of operations.

Kerning – A term for altering the gap between text by small amounts. Useful for large point sizes.

Key (1) – The pattern needed to unlock **ciphertext**.

Key (2) – The information for totally-black text in the **CMYK colour model** used by printers.

Keyboard – Device for entering text manually into the **computer system**. English keyboards are of the **QWERTY** type. A variety of different keyboards now exist for overcoming **RSI** problems.

Key field – The most-important **field** which uniquely identifies a **record**.

Key-to-disk – A machine to get data from the **keyboard** to a disk without using the main machine.

Key-to-store – General name for a machine to get data from the keyboard to a storage device such as **disk**, **tape** or **CD-ROM** etc. without using the main machine – ideal for **batch processing**.

Key-to-tape – A machine to get data from the keyboard to a tape without using the main machine.

Kilo (k) – Multiplier representing 1 × 10^3. (Often-used alternative in computing 1024.)

Kilobyte – 1024 bytes.

Knowledge-based system – See **Expert system**.

Label – A means of identification used in a program, e.g. JUMP to the label 'Next'.

Landscape – A sideways document in which the longest side is at the top.

Laptop – A portable computer.

LASER – Light Amplification by the Stimulated Emission of Radiation.

Laser disk – Name for the 12 in version of the **CD-ROM** – Largely superseded by the 12 cm **CD-ROM** and **DVD**.

Laser disk player – Name for the machine which handles the 12 in optical laser disks.

Laser engine – The name given to the part inside a laser printer which gives it its characteristics.

Laser printer – Page printer based on laser technology.

Laser scanning mechanism – System to read bar codes at **EFTPOS** terminals.

Latency – See **search time**.

LCD – **Liquid Crystal Display** – Screen used mainly on portable equipment.

Leading (DTP) – Space between the lines on a document.

Leaf node – **Terminal node** on a **tree structure**.

Leased line – A permanently-open connection to the **Internet**. You may use the system for 24 hours a day without incurring phone bills. However, the leased line is quite expensive to rent.

Least significant bit – The **binary digit** at the end of a **binary** number having the least place value.

LED – Light Emitting Diode – A semiconductor which emits light – used for displays, especially 7-segment LED displays as used in control panels to display numbers.

LEP – Light Emitting Plastic – A relatively new medium for the production of computer screens. It is cheap to produce and can be moulded into a variety of shapes.

Lexical analysis – The first stage during **compilation**.

Library – A collection of routines which are accessible to a programmer.

Library routine – A routine which is stored within a library. It is usual for often-used routines to be linked to programs when the program is run.

Light pen – A pen-shaped device which enables you to 'write' directly on the **monitor** screen.

Linear congruential method – A method of generating **pseudo-random numbers** with very long cycle lengths.

Linear list – A two-dimensional **array**.

Linear search – The most simple **search algorithm**.

Linear structure – one set of instructions carried out one after the other in a linear sequence.

Line editor – A simple **text editor** which can handle only one line of text at a time.

Line printer – A printer which prints 'one line' at a time, e.g. chain or drum printer.

Link layer – The second layer in the **ISO OSI network model**.

Linked list – A **list** whose structure is defined by **pointers** and not physical locations.

Linking loader – A **loader** that is able to link together programs that have been assembled separately.

Linotronic printing – Professional printing system (often 1200 dpi resolution) used for books etc.

LIPS – Logical Inferences Per Second – A **fifth-generation** measure of computer performance.

Liquid crystal – A crystal in a liquid or solid state which can be altered by an electrostatic field.

LISP – A **high-level computer programming language**.

List – A set of **data** arranged into some order.

Literal – A **symbol** (**lexical** unit) in a **programming language** which is itself used as **data**.

Liveware – Silly term for *people* who use the system – compare with **software**, **hardware** and **firmware**.

Loader – A **program** that loads part of the **operating system** or other previously-assembled program into **memory**.

Local Area Network – A **network** in the same building or the same locality (up to about 1km).

Local variable – A **variable** which is recognised only within a **procedure** or a **block**.

Logical error – An error in the logic of a program – compare with **syntax** and **execution errors** etc.

Logical operations – **AND**, **OR**, **NOT**, **NAND**, **NOR**, **XOR** and **XNOR**, **shift left** and **shift right** etc.

Logical record – A **record** viewed from a **software** point of view.

Logical shift – **Bits** in a **register** are moved right or left with zeros filling the vacated spaces.

Logic bomb – A type of catastrophic computer **virus**.

Logic circuit – A circuit made up from **logic gates**.

Logic gate – An electronic circuit designed to perform a specific function such as **AND**, **OR** and **NOT** etc.

Logo – A **high-level language** used extensively by children to create patterns and thus learn to program the computer. However, it's also a powerful **high-level language** in its own right – most famous for it's **turtle graphics**.

Log off – The process of signing off from a computer system so that the logical connection is severed.

Log on – The process of identifying yourself to a **computer system**.

Long haul network – An alternative term for a **WAN**.

Look up table – A table in which a value is given depending on the value of some other variable, e.g. conversion of a bank account number into a customer name could be done with a look-up table.

Loop – Part of a **program** which may be executed many times.

Loop, endless – See **Endless loop**.

Loop network – A physical **ring network**.

Lower case – Small letters (not capitals).

Low level language – **Machine code** or **assembly language**.

LSB – Least Significant **Bit**.

LSI – Large Scale Integration – Between 500 and 20,000 transistors per chip.

Machine – Alternative name for the **computer**.

Machine architecture – The way in which the internal guts of a particular **machine** are organised.

Machine code – The **binary** or **hex digit**s used to **program** the machine at a fundamental level.

Machine language – Same as **machine code**.

Macro – A single instruction which is replaced by a group of other instructions. It is now used in many contexts from assembly language to carrying out sequences of operations in a **word processor**, for example.

Macro assembler – An assembler that supports **macros**.

Macro instruction – See **Macro**.

Magenta – The 'crimson' colour obtained by mixing red and blue light.

Magnetic bubble memory – See **bubble memory**.

Magnetic disk drive – **Data** is recorded on concentric tracks on both sides of a rotating magnetic surface. See **floppy disk** and **Winchester disk**.

Magnetic media – Media such as **magnetic disks** and **magnetic tapes** etc.

Magnetic tape – A **serial-access** medium on which a large amount of **data** can be stored cheaply. Many different **tape** formats exist, and tapes are used for **serial files** and **backup** purposes.

Magneto-optical drive – Technique to increase **data** storage making use of **LASER**s in conjunction with magnetic media.

Mail box – A place on a **disk** (usually on a **file server** or other **computer**) where **e-mail** can be stored.

Mailing list – A list used by an **e-mail system** to send the same message(s) to many different people whose names are on the mailing list.

Mail merge – Combining standard letters with **database** information to produce 'personalised' letters.

Mail server – A **file server**, typically used on a **LAN**, which receives all the mail before distributing it to each person when they log on to the local mail system.

Mainframes – The largest of **computer** installations.

Main memory – See **Primary store**.

Main store – The computer's **RAM**. – See **Primary store**.

Maintenance – Keeping a system up to scratch after it has been installed (software and hardware).

Maltron keyboard – An **ergonomic keyboard** of very unusual design. Compare with the **QWERTY** and **AZERTY** keyboards.

MAN – Metropolitan Area **Network** – Longer than a **LAN** but shorter than a **LHN** or **WAN**.

Mandelbrot – IBM mathematician who discovered the Mandelbrot set.

Mandelbrot set – An analysis of the boundary of a mathematical function using complex numbers. Worlds of infinite beauty and complexity may be explored using colours and a computer.

Mantissa – The numbers representing the fractional part of a **floating point number**.

MAR – **Memory Address Register**.

Mark-sense reader – A machine capable of reading a source document on which marks are made with an HB pencil. Used for marking multi-choice examination material.

Masking – The ability to prevent alteration of certain **bits** inside a **register** when the rest of the **register** is being updated.

Massively parallel processing – A technique whereby many different microprocessors are connected together to form a single **CPU** as would typically be found in a **supercomputer**, for example.

Master control program – See **Operating system supervisor**.

Master disk – **Disk** containing the original copy of **software**.

Master file (1) – A **file** of information which is used in conjunction with a **transaction file** to produce a **new master file**.

Master file (2) – A **file** used for reference only or the **original file** from which copies are made.

Master tape – **Tape** containing original material.

Mathematical model – A model, usually on a computer, which is based on equations that can be run either by a **spreadsheet** or other program etc.

Mathematical typesetting package – A text processing system designed for maths and chemical formulae.

Maths co-processor – A bolt-on number crunching chip to carry out high-speed maths. Some powerful processors already have these facilities built in.

Matrix – A rectangular **array** of elements.

Mbyte – See **Megabyte**.

M/c – An abbreviation for **machine**, i.e. the **computer.**

MDA – Monochrome Display Adaptor – an IBM PC adaptor for single-colour text.

MDR – **Memory Data Register**.

Media – The name for the disks and tapes or paper etc. on which data can be stored.

Mega (M) – Multiplier representing 1×10^6. (Often-used alternative in computing 1024×1024.)

Megabit modem – The name used for the **digital modem** which is used with the **ADSL** or mains electricity distribution systems, for example.

Megabyte – 1,048,576 bytes (1024×1024).

Member functions (C++) – Functions which are members of a particular **class**.

Memory – See **Primary storage**.

Memory address register – A **register** holding the **address** of the most current **instruction** or **data** taken from or put out to **memory**.

Memory data register – A **register** holding the most-recent **data** taken from or put out to memory.

Memory location – One of the 'pigeon holes' into which data can be stored.

Memory management – The name given to the techniques used to manage the **memory** when more than one **task** is being undertaken.

Memory map – A diagram showing how the computer's memory is split up to hold different programs or parts of the **operating system** etc. It's a map of the memory utilisation.

Merging – The joining of two **data** sets.

Mesh network – See **distributed network**.

Message switching – A permanent path is set up between two node computers which can be used for short-duration messages – these paths are then instantly available for other traffic – compare with the **circuit-switching** systems used for the public telephone networks.

Meta assembler – An assembler which **assembles** code for many different **instruction sets**.

Metalanguage – A language used to describe another language, e.g. **BNF**, or **EBNF**.

Metal Oxide Silicon – One of the fabrication techniques used in the manufacture of **silicon chips**.

Meta symbols – The symbols used in a **metalanguage** like **BNF** or **EBNF**.

Michaelangelo – A virus which is activated on March 6th, but also used as a generic name for other viruses of this type.

MICR – Magnetic Ink Character Recognition – For example the **E13B** character set at the bottom of bank cheques.

Micro – Same as **Microcomputer**.

micro (μ) – Multiplier representing 1×10^{-6}.

Micro-code – A further level below conventional machine code used to customise your own instructions.

Microchip – Same as chip.

Microcomputer – A **computer**, built up around one or more **microprocessors** as the main **CPU**.

Microfiche – A rectangular photographic card on which frames of information are stored.

Microfilm – A photographic technique for reducing documents in size and storing them on film.

Microform – A collective term for **microfilm** and **microfiche**.

Micro-instruction – See **Micro code**.

Microprocessor – Most of what's required to implement a computer system on a **single chip**.

Microprogramming – Programming making use of **micro-code** – several of these **micro-code** instructions would make up a **machine-code** instruction.

MicroProlog – A version of the **high-level language Prolog** for **micros**.

Microsoft – The largest software company in the world. Authors of **MS-DOS**, **Windows**, **Excel** and other best-selling blockbusters.

MICR reader – A device used to read **MICR** documents. Bank cheques are the best example.

MIDI – Musical Instrument Digital Interface – a standard for connection of musical instruments to a computer system.

Mid-product method – A method for generating **pseudo-random numbers**.

Mid-square method – A type of **hashing function**.

Millennium bug – An unfortunate consequence of storing the date as two digits instead of four. Thus computers can't tell the difference between 1900 and 2000 because both are stored as 00!

milli (m) – Multiplier representing 1×10^{-3}.

MIME encoding – Multipurpose Internet Mail Extensions – A system for sending information across systems which make use of only the 7-bit **ASCII** set (i.e. **e-mail** and **Newsgroups**).

Mind mining – The process of putting human knowledge into an **expert system**.

Mini – Same as **minicomputer**.

Minicomputer – A computer half way between a **micro** and **mainframe** in terms of performance and facilities. The term is getting more difficult to apply as micros become more powerful.

MIPS – Millions of Instructions Per Second – A **computer benchmark** measurement.

Mirror-reflecting gray code – A type of **gray code** used to generate the numbers for **Karnaugh maps**.

MMX – MultiMedia eXtensions – An enhancement to the Pentium chip which makes it faster for multimedia and communications applications.

Mnemonic – An aid to the memory. Usually used for **assembly language instructions**.

MODEM – **MOdulation-DEModulation** – A device used for sending and receiving data using the phone line. It converts data into audible tones so that the ordinary telephone lines can be used.

MO drives – See **Magneto-Optical drives**.

MODULA II – A high-level language which is derived from **Pascal** – ideal for concurrent processing.

Modular programming – Breaking up larger programs into smaller modules.

Modulation – Changing a signal into a form suitable for transmission.

Modulo arithmetic – Clock arithmetic where the numbers go round in cycles, e.g. MOD 4 would be 0,1,2,3,0,1,2,3,0,1 etc.

Monitor (1) – **Computer VDU**.

Monitor (2) – The **operating system supervisor** of a **microcomputer**.

Monte-Carlo method – Method used for finding an area under a graph making use of **pseudo-random numbers**.

Morphing – Changing one **computer graphic** into another in a defined way.

MOS – Metal Oxide Silicon – A fabrication technique used for **silicon chips**.

Most significant bit – The **binary digit** at the end of a **binary** number which has the largest place value.

Most significant digit – Same as most significant **bit**.

Mother board – The main **PCB** inside a **microcomputer**.

Motorola – A large scale **chip** manufacturer. Famous for the 68000 range of Apple Mac processors.

Mouse – Pointing and switching device for computer input – ideal for a **windows** environment.

Moving Picture Experts Group – See **MPEG**.

MPEG – The **Moving Pictures Experts Group**. A standard for the **compression** and storage of video and computer-animation material. There are several different MPEG standards.

MSB – **Most Significant Bit**.

MS-DOS – MicroSoft's non-GUI based **Disk Operating System**.

MS-DOS Shell – **MSDOS** system to provide simple **GUI** and **multitasking** from **DOS**.

MSI – Medium Scale Integration – Between 10 and 500 transistors per chip.

Multi-access – More than one **user** having access to a **system** at the same time.

Multimedia – The buzz word indicating the amalgamation of text, computer data, audio, video and any thing else that you can think of into a single system.

Multi-mode operating system – An **operating system** which supports more than one mode of operation – e.g. **batch** and **multi-access**.

Multiple buffering (OS) – Use of two or more **buffers** to speed up communication between the **processor** and **peripheral** devices.

Multiple bus systems – A system in which two or more **bus systems** operate in parallel to speed up data transmission.

Multiplexer – A device that carries out **multiplexing**.

Multiplexing – A process of sending many signals down the same line at the same time or apparently at the same time.

Multiprocessing – More than one **CPU** is used inside the **computer** at the same time.

Multiprogramming – More than one **program** can be operated on at the same time or apparently the same time. (Depends on whether the system has more than one **CPU**.)

Multiprogramming operating system – An **operating system** that supports **multiprogramming**.

Multiscan monitors – See **Multisync monitors**.

Multisync monitors – A **VDU** with a variable (and usually higher) range of scanning frequencies controlling the **Raster** scan display.

Multitasking (1) – **Micro** – doing more than one thing at the same time or apparently at the same time.

Multitasking (2) – **Mainframe** and **mini** – many user's data being serviced by the *same* program.

MVS – Multiple Virtual Storage – An **operating system** developed for **IBM mainframes**.

NAND gate – A **logic gate** which is **NOT(AND)**.

nano (n) – Multiplier representing 1×10^{-9}.

Nano-technology – Technology carried out at nanometre scale – small **robots** can be constructed so that they may be injected into the human body, for example.

Nassi-Schneidermann diagram – One type of **structure diagram**.

Natural language – A context-sensitive language such as English or French.

Navigator – A web-browser program which helps to surf the **Internet** and developed by Netscape.

NC-Networked Computer – A cost-effective computer designed to be operated over a network. Only those parts of the software needed by the user are downloaded on demand. It is used in conjunction with languages such as **Java**.

Near Letter Quality – A technique used to improve the output from **dot-matrix printers**.

Near Photographic Quality – The highest quality associated with the best colour **laser printers**.

NERIS – National Educational Resources Information System – **External database** of educational resources.

Nested if-then – **If-then statements** within other **if-then statements**.

Nested loop – Loops within other loops – don't forget that certain rules must be obeyed.

Net – Often used as a shortened name to describe the **Internet**.

Netiquette – The rules one should abide by when trying to be polite on the **Net**. For example, don't use capitalisation – IT'S REGARDED AS SHOUTING!

Network (1) – Many **computers** linked together and sharing the same resources such as **file servers, teletext servers** and **printer servers** etc. It can also refer to a network of networks such as the **Web**.

Network (2) – A **data structure** that enables any relation between **nodes** to be implemented.

Network architecture – See **network topology**.

Network database – A **database** built up using a **network data model**.

Network data model – A **data structure** in which any **node** can be connected to any other.

Networked computer – See **NC**.

Network hub – See **hub**.

Network layer – The 3rd level of the **ISO OSI network model**.

Network Manager – The person who is responsible for the efficient operation of both the **hardware** and **software** on the network.

Network operating system – An **operating system** that supports the use of a **network**.

Network topology – The various physical layouts of the **networks** from a **typological** point of view.

Neural network – Circuits or **software** set up in ways similar to a simplified operation of the human brain.

Newsgroups – Tens of thousands of different groups exist to exchange material on just about any topic under the sun. A few of these newsgroups are notorious for their subject content, and some of them contain illegal material.

Newton – Apple's **PDA** computer with **pen-based input**.

Nibble – Half a **byte**, i.e. four **bits**.

NIC – **Network Interface Card** (IBM PC).

NLQ – **Near Letter Quality**.

Node (1) – The name given to the **record** in a **data structure**.

Node (2) – A point at which different **networks** are interconnected.

Node computer – A **computer** placed at the **node** of a **network** to handle communications.

Non-equivalence gate – See **Exclusive OR gate**.

Non-impact printers – **Printers** such as **lasers** or **bubble** jets which don't have hammers or pins.

Non-interactive processing – Processing that does not require **user** intervention.

NOR gate – A **logic gate** which is **NOT(OR)**.

Normal form (1) – A set of rules regarding Codd's **relational database** system. See **first**, **second** and **third normal** forms of a **relational database**.

Normal form (2) – A **floating point number** after it has been **normalised**.

Normalisation (1) – Putting a **floating point number** into **normalised form**.

Normalisation (2) – Setting up a **database** to Codd's **normal forms**.

Normalised – Changing something into a form which is more efficient.

NOS – Network Operating System.

NOT gate – A **logic gate** which has an output which is the inverse of the input.

NPQ – **Near Photographic Quality**.

NTFS – **NT (New Technology) Filing System** – The filing system used by the **Windows NT** operating system.

Numerical Analysis – Building up complex **numerically-based models** so that a variety of mathematical tasks may be accomplished, e.g. **numerical integration** or **differentiation**, finding roots etc.

Numerical integration – The process of finding areas under a graph.

Numeric control – The computer control of drills, lathes and milling machines etc. (see **CNC**).

Numeric data – **Data** consisting of numbers only.

Numeric keypad – Part of the keyboard used specifically for entering numbers.

Nyquist's criterion – Sample at twice the highest rate of the frequency of interest when **digitising analogue** signals.

Object – Used in **Object Oriented Programming** to encapsulate the **variables** and data into one **entity**.

Object code – The **machine code** ready to be **executed** on a computer.

Object linking and embedding – A **system** which can transfer data backwards and forwards between **packages** at the flick of a mouse button. Useful for getting a diagram from a **DTP package** into a **CAD package**, then editing it and putting it straight back into the **DTP package**, for example.

Object oriented (1) – The use of **objects** to perform **tasks**.

Object oriented (2) – **CAD package** technique representing **objects** by mathematical equations.

Object-oriented programming – A complete programming methodology in which **objects** form the basis of many operations.

Object program – The output from an **assembler** or **compiler**.

Objects (C++) – A **data object** – a strictly-controlled **data structure** (see **object**) which makes programs easier to develop on complex systems.

OCR – Optical Character Recognition.

Octal – Base eight – uses the digits 0,1,2,3,4,5,6,7.

Odd parity – An odd number of 1s in the transmitted code as a check on data **integrity**.

OEM – The Original Equipment Manufacturer – company that makes the equipment that could be used by other companies in their products.

Off line – Not under the control of the **computer**.

OHP projection – Device placed on top of the Over-Head Projector to project a computer image on a standard OHP screen.

OLE – **Object Linking and Embedding**.

OMR – Optical Mark Reader – Same as **mark-sense reader**.

Ones complement – One less than the **twos complement**.

Onion diagram – Means of viewing the layers of **operating system software** and other applications.

On line – Under the control of the **computer**.

On-line banking – Using a PC from home or the office to view bank statements, pay bills, transfer money or just to see how broke you really are!

OOP – **Object Oriented Programming**.

Op code – Short for **Operation Code**.

Open-loop mode – No **feedback**.

Open system – A network system designed to cope with all types of manufacturers' hardware and software connected together.

Operand – Something on which an operation is performed, e.g. in SQR(4) = 2, '4' is the **operand**.

Operating system – The extremely complex **software** which controls a **computer**, and provides the interface between the **user**, **programs**, **applications** and the **hardware**.

Operating system supervisor – The **software** that controls the organisation of the **operating system**.

Operational research – The use of mathematical and scientific methods to help manage decision making.

Operation code – The **binary** code which represents a **machine-code** operation.

Operations manager – The person in charge of a **data processing department**.

Operator – The person who is operating the computer – same as **User**.

Optical Character Recognition (1) – A device to read carefully prepared hand written documents or typed text into the computer and change it into **ASCII** or other text.

Optical Character Recognition (2) – A device to read special characters on a source document. Sometimes used on **turnaround documents**.

Optical disk – A **disk** in which **data** is read by a **laser** – **CD-ROM** and **DVD** are the best examples.

Optical methods – Methods making use of light to perform their primary function.

Optical wand – See **bar-code** reader.

Optimisation – Producing the most efficient output from a **compiler** or **assembler**. It rarely equals hand-optimised code.

Order – The size of a **matrix** in rows and columns, e.g. (4,3).

OR gate – A **logic gate** whose output is '1' if any of the inputs are '1'.

OS – **Operating System**.

OSI – **Open Systems** Interconnection – An **architecture** for the interconnection of **computer networks**.

OS/2 – An **operating system** developed by **IBM** for their personal computers.

Outline font – Maths definitions used to create infinitely-scalable **fonts** (also called true-type fonts).

Output – The **data** from a **computer system**.

Output peripherals – Devices such as **printers** and **plotters** which output **data**.

Overflow – A number too large to be represented by the **computer system** has occurred.

Overflow flag – A **flag** inside the flag register indicating that an **overflow** has been detected.

Overflow table – A method of dealing with **collisions** when using a **hashing function**.

Package – See **software package**.

Packet – A defined chunk of data used on a **message-switching network**.

Packet switching network – A **message**-switching **network** in which messages are split up into convenient packet-sized chunks ready from transmission. Contrast with **circuit-switching networks**.

Paddle – A one-dimensional **joystick**.

Page – A **block** of **memory**.

Page-description language (1) – A language which describes every attribute on the printed page. Used for some types of **laser** and other **printers**. **PostScript** is a common example.

Page-description language (2) – A language like **HTML** used to describe every attribute on a **Web page**.

Page printer – A **printer** where a page is apparently printed all at the same time, e.g. a **laser printer**.

Paint package – A **pixel based art package**. Some **object-oriented packages** can now produce similar effects.

Palette – The range of colours normally available on the computer at any one time.

Palm print scanner – A machine onto which the palm of your hand is placed. A scan is then made, and salient features of your prints are compared to stored images. It is used mainly as a measure for entry into high-security installations.

Palmtop – A small hand-held computer.

Paradigm – Organising principles used in the design of **high-level languages** or other systems.

Parallel adder – A **logic circuit** which adds together two **binary** numbers in parallel.

Parallel data – **Data** in which several **bits** are sent simultaneously along different communication channels.

Parallelism – The art of doing more than one thing at the same time.

Parallel processing – **Architecture** enabling more than one thing to be done at exactly the same time. Need more than one **processor** to accomplish this.

Parallel transmission – Several signals are sent simultaneously.

Parameter – A **variable** that has temporarily assumed a constant value for the purposes of being passed on to a **subroutine** or **procedure** etc.

Parametric CAD – **CAD package** which allows diagrams to be expressed in terms of **parameters**, which express relationships between parts of the diagram. Animation is possible using **parametric CAD**.

Parent node – A **node** in a **tree structure** which has **children**.

Parity – A method used to ensure the **integrity** of received **data**. **Errors** can be detected and a retransmission requested – 2D parity can theoretically correct data which has been incorrectly received.

Parity check – Making use of **parity** to check **data integrity**.

Parity bits – Same as **parity digits**.

Parity digit – The extra **parity bit** added for the purpose of **parity** checking.

Parity track – A **track** on **magnetic tape** used to hold the **parity bits**.

Parsing – Seeing if the rules of **syntax** have been obeyed.

Partition – Part of **memory** set aside to hold set **data** or **programs** etc.

Partition sort – See **quick sort**.

Pascal – **High level language** named in honour of the mathematician Blaise Pascal.

Passing by reference – Value of the **variable** gets changed as the actual variable is *referenced* and is therefore irrevocably altered by the **procedure**.

Passing by value – *Value* of the **variable** used to pass the **parameter** to the **procedure** is *not altered* because a copy (i.e. a different variable) has been used to receive the information.

Password – A code which is checked for **integrity** on entry to a secure system.

Patch – A bug fix to get round an error in a program until the next version is produced. Also used as a term which applies to slight modification of the original code for some specific user requirement.

Pbyte – See **Petabyte**.

PC (1) – Personal computer – used to be **IBM PC** or compatible, but now a generally used term for a micro.

PC (2) – **Program Counter**

PCB – **Printed Circuit Board** – A fabricated board to hold and connect the **chips** and other electronics.

PCI – **Peripheral Component Interconnect** – a 64-bit bus system for the IBM PC and its clones.

PCM – **Pulse Code Modulation.**

PCMCIA – The Personal Computer Memory Card International Association – The standard for the credit-card-size interface for **modems**, **faxes**, **disk drives**, **network** and adaptors etc. which plug into **portable computers** – it's so small that the normal connection leads wont fit into it!

PD – Public Domain – it's free!

PDA – Personal Digital Assistant – Integration of an organiser with a simple palm-top computer.

PDL – Page Description Language – e.g. **PostScript**.

PDS – Public Domain Software – Software you don't have to pay for.

Pen Input – Use of a pen as the main input medium instead of a **keyboard** – ideal for **PDAs**.

Pentium – Intel's '80586' processor, called the **Pentium** to overcome copyright problems.

Pentium Pro – Intel's successor to the **Pentium**.

Pentium II and III – The successor to the **Pentium Pro**.

Peripherals – Devices connected to the main **computer** such as **disks**, **keyboards**, **printers** etc.

PERT chart – A chart showing events and activities, times and resources enabling **critical paths** to be evaluated.

Peta (P) – Multiplier representing 1×10^{15}. (Computing alternative 1024^5.)

Petabyte – $1024 \times 1024 \times 1024 \times 1024 \times 1024$ bytes of data.

PGP – **Pretty Good Privacy** – One of the best **public-key encryption algorithms**.

pH – Numerical scale depicting acidity or alkalinity, 7 is neutral.

Phoneme – A basic unit into which speech can be split up.

Photo CD – Developed by Kodak – A system used to store still images on CD.

Physical layer – The most basic layer of the **ISO OSI network model**.

Physical record – A **record** whose size is convenient from a **hardware** point of view. Several **logical records** will probably fit into a **physical record**. Also called a **block**.

pica – Measure used by typesetters. 1 pica is 12 **points** and 72 points is 1 inch.

pico (p) – Multiplier representing 1×10^{-12}.

PILOT – Programmed Inquiry Learning Or Teaching. A specialist computer language for **CAL** applications.

PIN – Personal Identification Number.

Pipeline architecture – A technique of **parallel processing** where different instructions are **fetched**, **decoded**, and **executed** at the same time.

Pipelining – See **pipeline architecture**.

Piracy – Illegal theft of **computer software**.

Pixel – A picture element – often the smallest element which goes into making up a picture.

Plaintext (1) – See **Cleartext**.

Plaintext (2) – Basic **ASCII** text.

Plated-wire store – 'Bullet proof' storage used in harsh military environments and black boxes on aircraft.

Platform – Term used to describe a **hardware** or **software** environment, e.g. an **Intel** platform or a **Unix** platform.

Plotter – A device that produces high-quality **hard copy** for **CAD packages**. Large sizes and hence cost effectiveness are the only advantage these devices have over the current colour **laser printers**.

PNG – **Portable Network Graphics** – An alternative to the **GIF format**. It has a better compression ratio and no royalties need to be paid as would be the case if you are developing a package to produce **GIFs**.

Pointer (1) – The contents of a **register** or **memory location** which is used to point to some other location.

Pointer (2) – The **icon** on the screen that's moved around by the **mouse**.

Point Of Presence – See **POP**.

Point Of Sale Terminal – A **computer terminal** specifically designed for use in a shop. It will probably have integral **bar code readers**, links to a **computer** and links to the phone system etc.

Point size – A measurement used for the size of text in a **DTP system**. There are 72pts in 1 inch.

Polish notation – Prefix notation – **arithmetical operators** appear before the **operands** e.g. + P Q means P+Q in 'normal' terminology.

Polling – Taking a poll to see if any **peripherals** need attention.

Pop (1) – Terminology for removing a **data** item from a stack.

POP (2) – **Point of Presence** – A link provided locally so that people may access the **Internet** for the cost of a local phone call.

POP (3) – The Post Office Protocol – One of the protocols for connecting to the **Internet**.

Port – A connection on the periphery of a **computer** in which signals can be fed into and/or extracted from the system.

Portable (1) – A portable computer.

Portable (2) – Being applicable to more than one **computer system**, e.g. a **high-level language**.

Portable Network Graphics – See **PNG**.

Portrait – A document view with the shortest side at the top.

POS – **Point Of Sale**.

Postfix notation – see **Reverse Polish notation**.

Post-order traversal – A method for traversing (moving around) a **tree structure** visiting the left and right **sub trees** and then the **root**.

PostScript – A popular **page-description language**.

Pot – Same as potentiometer.

Potentiometer – An electronic component used to vary an analogue voltage.

Power Open System (OS) – An operating system developed for the Power PC-based machines.

PowerPC – A collaboration between **Apple**, **IBM** and **Motorola** to produce a range of **RISC**-based **machines** based around the PowerPC chip.

PowerPoint – Microsoft's main **presentation package** software.

Power user – Someone who is a very advanced and technically-competent user of the **system**.

PPM – **Pulse Position Modulation**.

PPP – **Point to Point Protocol** – One of the common **communications protocols** used by **ISPs** to connect your **MODEM** to the **Internet**. See also **SLIP**.

Pragmatics – Other aspects (besides **syntax** and **semantics**) of a language implementation such as efficiency, practicality and ease of use etc.

Precedence – The order of priority in evaluation of an **arithmetical** or **logical expression**.

Precision – A term usually associated with **word length** – something can be expressed with great **precision** but need not necessarily be **accurate**.

Predicate – A logical relationship.

Pre-emptive multitasking – A technique used by the operating system to make sure that no single resource monopolises all the resources.

Prefix notation – See **Polish notation**.

Pre-order traversal – A method of traversing (moving around) a **tree structure** visiting the **root** first, followed by the left and right-hand **sub trees**.

Presentation layer – The sixth layer of the **ISO OSI network model**.

Presentation package – **Applications package** to produce presentations using a mixture of text, graphics charting, back drops, audio and video data.

Pretty Good Privacy – See **PGP**.

Primary key – the key by which a **table** in a **relational database** is best described – The primary key may contain several **attributes** if **normalisation** is to be achieved in practice.

Primary storage – The main **semiconductor storage** inside a **computer system**. This is usually very fast **RAM** but **cache** is often quicker still, being made up of **SRAM**.

Printer – A device for obtaining **hard copy**.

Printer spooler – A device for accepting print output in a queue, and then sending the output to the **printer** in an orderly way.

Print head – That part of the **printer** which is the actual printing mechanism.

Print server – A computer set up to act as a **printer spooler**.

Priorities (1) – The **computer operator** can assign a **priority** to a **job** so that it can override **operating-system** scheduling procedures. The operator's pay check program has the highest priority in this mode!

Priorities (2) – The **operating system** can assign **priorities** to tasks to maximise the efficiency of the system in terms of resources being efficiently used etc.

Priorities (3) – **Interrupting devices** may have **priorities** assigned according to the urgency with which the interrupts must be serviced.

Private (C++) – **Data** which is only associated with a particular **class**.

Private key – The private key which a user keeps secret. He or she uses this key to **encrypt** messages, which may be decrypted by anyone having the appropriate **public key**.

Probability – A number between 0 (which represents impossible) and 1 (which represents certainty).

Procedural languages – Languages like **BASIC** or **Pascal** which make use of **procedures** or groups of statements.

Procedure – A separate section of the **program** designed for some specific purpose. Unlike a **function** it can receive and return multiple values.

Process control – Using **computers** to monitor industrial tasks such as a chemical works.

Productions – Rule definitions used to define syntax using **BNF** or **EBNF**.

Program – A set of **instructions**.

Program counter – A **register** to keep track of the current position in a program. Same as **sequence control register**.

Program documentation – **Documentation** which accompanies the program to explain how it works at a technical level.

Program execution – running the **program** so that it may carry out it's instructions.

Program file – A **file** which is literally a **program**. As opposed to a **data file**, for example.

Program flowchart – A **detailed flowchart** which outlines how a **program** works and can hence be used to help develop the **program**.

Programmable Read Only Memory – A **chip** that can be permanently programmed to the **users** requirements.

Programmer – The person who codes the **programs**, usually from the information provided by the **systems analyst**.

Programmer time – 'Average' time taken for a programmer to do a 'job' – Good programmers have smaller values for programmer time.

Projection TVs – Large screen projection of computer and other images.

Prolog – PROgramming in LOGic – A **fifth-generation language**.

PROM – **Programmable Read Only Memory**.

Prompt – A **character** used to prompt the **user** of an **interactive system** to input **data**.

Proportional spacing – Variable gaps between the characters in text – generally looks better than fixed spacing, but fixed spacing is good for program listings.

Protection – The prevention of unauthorised access to the **computer system**.

Protection ring – A **ring** which must be placed on a reel of **tape** if data is to be written to it.

Protocol – A set of rules by which communication is possible between two points if both ends are obeying the rules. **PPP** and **SLIP** are two examples of different sets of rules or protocols.

Prototyping – Making a mock-up of parts of the system for early evaluation and possible modification.

Proxy server – A computer set up so that users of a **LAN** may have simultaneous use of the **Internet**. From the **ISP's** point of view, only a single account is needed. From the **LAN** point of view many different people can surf the net at the same time.

Pseudocode – A **high-level-language-like** code used to help develop **algorithms**.

Pseudo operations – See **directive**.

Pseudo random numbers – A number pattern that repeats itself every so often. The secret is to make the pattern so long that nobody notices – it therefore looks like a real random number.

PSN – **Packet Switched Network**.

PSS – Packet Switched System – same as a **PSN**.

Public (C++) – **Data** which is available to all **classes**.

Public domain – Software which is free!

Public key – This is the key that any member of the public may use to send encrypted messages to the person to whom the key belongs. The **private key** is needed to decrypt the message.

Public key encryption – A system which uses a **public key** to encrypt the data and a **private key** to decrypt the data. It is also used as a system which can verify **digital signatures** which have been created with the private key, and thus authenticate the message originator.

Puck – Input device for use on a **graphics tablet**.

Push – Term used to denote an item of data being put onto the **stack**.

PWM – **Pulse Width Modulation**.

QBE – Query By Example – An alternative to **SQL** for **database queries** whereby a user sets up queries by specifying fields to use etc. usually by means of pictures representing various attributes.

QIC – Quarter Inch Cartridge – System of tape **backup** used on **micros**.

Quantisation – The process of converting to discrete levels when converting an **analogue** signal to a **digital** one.

Query – Requesting information from a **database** – usually in the form of an **SQL** or **Query By Example**.

Queue (1) – A **FIFO stack**.

Queue (2) (OS) – The **batch** of **jobs** waiting to be processed in a **batch** environment.

Queueing theory – A **simulation** technique for analysing **data** associated with **queues**.

Quick sort – A special sort **algorithm** which is quick for long lists of data.

Quinkey – A special **keyboard** design for one-handed data entry.

QWERTY – The English and American keyboard layouts – look at letters along the top row. Not all keyboards are alike – France uses the **AZERTY** keyboard and the Chinese keyboard can only be imagined!

Radio networks – A **computer network** making use of radio waves as the **carrier** of the information.

Radix – Another name for a **number base**.

Radix conversion – One type of **hashing function**.

RAID – Redundant Array of Inexpensive Drives – Used to increase reliability of **file servers** – A mirror image of the data is stored on one or more backup disks.

RAM – **Random Access Memory**.

Random access – The time taken to access any location is not dependent on position.

Random access files – Any **record** may be read without having to read all the previous **records**.

Randomisation algorithm – An **algorithm** used to determine the **physical address** at which **data** can be stored.

Random numbers – A number sequence in which the next number chosen does not depend on the previous number, and all numbers are equally likely to occur.

Range – The difference between the largest and smallest values.

Raster scanning – Mechanism used in most conventional **computer monitors** to drive the electron beam in the **CRT** to make up the picture.

Raw data – **Data** that has been collected but not processed in any way.

Ray tracing – A technique of generating realistic-looking images by following paths of light reflected from the objects in the picture.

RDBMS – **Relational Database** Management System.

Read – Term used to get access to data stored in memory or some other suitable storage device. The act of reading does not destroy the data but makes a copy of it.

Read head – The part of a **tape** or **disk** which reads data from the magnetic surface.

Reading – The process of accessing **information** from **memory** or a **file** etc.

Read Only Memory – **Data** is permanently stored inside the **chip** or other medium. It can't be removed.

Read/Write – The control signal used with a memory chip to determine whether a Read or Write operation is to take place.

Read/Write head – The same head is used for the read and write operations.

Read/Write time – The time taken for a read or write operation to take place.

Real number – A number with a fractional part.

Real time – A **system** which can respond in an appropriate amount of time – usually very quickly, but not necessarily so. Modern definitions are now including reliability together with response speed.

Real-time clock – An electronic circuit which keeps the time of day. This information may be used by software to display clocks or activate **control systems** etc.

Real-time operating system – An **operating system** that supports this mode of operation.

Record – A self-contained part of a **file**, usually made up of several **fields**.

Record locking – A system, common in **distributed processing** where only one user is allowed to access a **record** at any particular time. This is essential if a write operation is taking place.

Recursion – A programming technique where a routine is written such that it may call itself.

Recursive algorithm – One that can call itself.

Reduced instruction set – The **assembly language** consists of fewer simple instructions taking only a few **clock cycles**. The very-complex complex instructions common on **CISC** processors are not present.

Refresh – The process of topping up **DRAM** with charge – contents would leak away if this were not done.

Register – A special electronic circuit (highest access speed) where data can be stored for a specific purpose. **Registers** are usually inside the main **CPU**.

Register addressing – An **addressing mode** making use of **registers** to specify the **address**.

Relation – A *two-dimensional* **table** in a **relational** database. Tuples or **rows** correspond to **entities** or **records**, and each *subsection* of a **tuple** corresponds to a **field**. The **table** corresponds to a **file**.

Relational algebra – An algebra which deals with **relations** using operations with sets.

Relational calculus – A branch of mathematics which deals with the generation of new relations from existing ones. It is the link to the idea of a tuple in Codd's **relational database** theories.

Relational database – A **database** built up on a set of **relational tables**.

Relational data model – A **data structure** making use of a set of **tables**.

Relational operator – '=', '<', '>', '**AND**', '**OR**' etc.

Relational table – A 2-dimensional **table** in a **relational database**.

Relationship – A link, or some sort of **dependency** or **association** between two or more **attributes**. One-to-one, one-to-many, many-to-one and many-to-many relationships are common.

Relative address – An **address** calculated by adding a number to a base **address**.

Relative key – A system whereby **logical records** in a **file** can be accessed by reference to the first **record** in the file.

Relocatable code – **Programs** that can run in different parts of the **memory**.

Remote access – Getting access to a computer system from a place removed from the main installation.

Rendering – A term used when creating a realistic looking image. You can, for example, render textures such as shiny metal or wood, or render skin tones or 'surface of water' etc. When applied to models inside a **CAD** system, the mathematical objects can look as though they are actually real.

Repeater – Hardware on a network or communication system which receives, boosts and retransmits a signal to the next part of the system.

Repeat until – Statements in loop are **executed** and **Boolean** condition checked at the end to see if termination is required.

Report – The output to the screen or a file from a **database query**.

Report generator – A program that allows non-specialist users to generate reports from a database.

Research and development staff – The staff who do research into the **computer systems** of tomorrow.

Reserved word – A **key word** used in a **high level language** to perform a specific function.

Reset – Make a **bit** = 0.

Resistor – An electronic component used to alter the current or voltage.

Resolution (1) – A measure of how closely one can get to some ideal, e.g. **high-resolution graphics** are more realistic than low-resolution graphics.

Resolution (2) – The number of discrete levels when **digitising** an **analogue** signal.

Resolution (3) – The magnitude of the difference between the last two **bits** representing a number.

Retina scanner – The user of the machine looks into a 'binocular type tube'. The retina of the eye is scanned, and features of it are compared to stored images. It is used mainly as a measure for entry into high-security installations.

Return – Instruction to return from a **subroutine**.

Reverse Polish notation – Same as **postfix notation** – operator appears after the operands e.g. P Q + means P + Q.

RGB – Red, Green and Blue – One of the additive colour models used in a computer system.

Ring – A loop of cable which is used in some types of physical **ring networks**.

Ring list – See **circular list**.

Ring network – A **network** based on a circular loop of cable – a **token-ring network** is not necessarily wired as a physical ring network.

RISC – Reduced Instruction Set Computer – Complex instructions not present in the instruction set.

RISC computer – A **computer** based around a **RISC microprocessor**.

RISC microprocessor – One which has a **reduced instruction set** as it's **assembly language**.

Robot (1) – Devices used to carry out specialist functions, usually in an industrial environment.

Robot (2) – Device intended to mimic human-like qualities – still some way into the future.

Robotics – Intelligent **computer control** of mechanical machines.

Rogue value – A value which can't possibly be interpreted as being part of a data set – used to terminate the execution of some particular part of the program.

Rollback – This is the term used to describe going back to a previously stable state after a system crash. It can range from using backup copies in the event of a total hard disk failure, to using **checkpoints** and **transaction logs** in the event of less catastrophic failures.

ROM – Read Only Memory.

ROM cartridge – A cartridge containing a **ROM** which can plug into a **micro** or games machine.

Root (maths) – The solution to an equation expressed as f(x) = 0.

Root directory – The base **directory** in a hierarchical **data structure**.

Root node – The first **node** in a **hierarchical data structure**.

Rounding error – The **error** due to **rounding up** or **rounding down**.

Router – A hardware device used to connect many computers on a **LAN** to the **Internet**. It can also be used to enable many different computers to route messages by the most efficient routes.

Row – Same as a **tuple** from a **relational table** – corresponds to a record in a **relational database**.

Row-by-row mapping – A method of representing a two-dimensional **array** in **main store**.

RSI – Repetitive Strain Injury – Problems due to excessive periods at badly-designed **HCIs**.

RS 232 and RS 423 – **Serial port interfacing** standards.

RTF – Rich Text Format – One way of getting text together with styles and tab settings etc. from one word processor to a different type of word processor.

Run – The term used to denote that a **program** or other **job** is being carried out.

Sampling frequency – The rate at which **analogue data** is sampled for conversion in an **A to D converter**.

Scanner – A hand-held or desk-top device used to **scan** images and text into a **computer**.

Scheduler – **Operating system software** which determines the **schedules** for a **job**.

Scheduling – The techniques used by the **operating system** to allocate **CPU** time in a **multi-tasking** or **multi programming multi-access** environment, e.g. **time sharing**, for example.

Schema – The logical definition of a **database**.

Scratch file – **File** used for temporary storage of **data**

SCSI – Small Computer Systems Interface – An **interface** standard for **microcomputers**.

SCSI 2 (or SCSI II) – A faster and higher-spec. version of SCSI.

SDRAM – Synchronous Dynamic Random Access Memory – A faster form of **DRAM** which can run at higher **clock speeds**, and thus make the memory go at a faster rate.

Search engine – A program which **searches** a document or one of the programs on the **WWW** which searches for items of interest.

Searching – Finding a specific item of data from a **list**.

Search length – The average number of **data** comparisons that must be made to **search** for an item of **data**.

Search time (disk) – The time taken for the head to move and the disk to rotate until the head is over the required data.

Search time (searching) – The average time taken to find an item of **data** in a **list**.

Secondary store – Storage for **data** that is not needed so quickly, e.g **disk**, **tape**, **CD-ROM** and **DVD**.

Second-Generation Language – Unstructured **high-level languages** such as early versions of **BASIC** or **FORTRAN**.

Second normal form – All **attributes** in an **entity** must be **functionally dependent** on the **primary key**.

Sector – **Disk track** is split into sub-sections called **sectors**.

Sector number – Each **sector** has a unique number associated with it.

Secure data transaction – An electronic data transaction in which **encrypted** data is sent. It is used for on-line banking and for on-line transactions when using the **web**.

Seeds – The numbers used to start off a **pseudo-random-number** sequence.

Seek time (disk) – Time taken for the **head** to move to the right track.

Semantics – The meaning applied to a language.

Semiconductor – A material having an electrical conductivity half way between that of an insulator and a conductor. Specially treated semiconductors are used to manufacture **silicon chips**.

Semiconductor store – Same as **RAM** or **main store** or **primary store**.

Senior programmer – The person in charge of a programming team.

Sensors – See **Transducers** (input).

Sequence control register – Same as the **program counter**.

Sequential access – The complete list of **data** must be searched until the required item is found.

Sequential access file – **File** in which **records** are stored, one after the other in some pre-determined order.

Sequential logic circuit – A **logic circuit** whose outputs depend on previous inputs.

Sequential search – See **linear search**.

Serial access file – A **file** in which **records** are stored one after the other with no regard to order.

Serial adder – A **logic circuit** which adds together **binary digits serially**.

Serial data – **Data** which is treated one **bit** at a time.

Serial data transmission – The transmission of **data** along the same line, often using a single channel only.

Serial file – A **file** which is not in any special order.

Serial operating systems – see **Batch operating systems**.

Serial printer – A **printer** which prints one **character** at a time.

Serial transmission – One **bit** of **data** is sent at a time.

Session layer – The fifth layer of the **ISO OSI network model**.

Set – Make a **bit** = 1.

Shareware – Software in which the user of the program is supposed to pay a small fee to the author of the software after trying it out, if they intend to carry on using it.

Shell – A layer of an **onion diagram**.

Shell sort – A sort **algorithm** developed by Donald Shell.

Shift leader – A person who leads a team operating a **mainframe computer** on a shift.

SID – Standard Idiot Test – Getting an 'idiot' to test your **programs** – normal people are usually just as effective!

Sign and magnitude – Method of representing positive and negative **binary numbers**.

Signature – Data used for the purposes of identification, specifically with **e-mail** communications and **on-line** transactions.

Sign bit – A binary digit at the beginning of a binary number, not having any bearing on the magnitude of the number but used exclusively for the allocation of +ve or –ve. Usually a '0 is positive' and a '1 is negative'.

Silicon – A **semiconductor** material.

Silicon chip – An electronic component containing **transistors** and other components made from silicon and other materials, and housed inside a small package called an **integrated circuit**.

Simplex – Communication in one direction only.

Simulation – A computer system that is pretending to be something else. Following a **mathematical model** usually carries out the simulation. A good example would be a **flight simulator**, but economic and other simulations are common.

Sister node – See **brother node**.

SLIP – **Serial Line Internet Protocol** – One type of protocol commonly used by the **ISPs** to connect your **MODEM** to the **Internet**. See also **PPP**.

SLSI – Super Large Scale Integration – More than 100,000 transistors per chip.

Smalltalk – An **object oriented programming language** – still going strong – a popular alternative to **C++** for some people.

Smart card – A credit card device which contains a simple **microchip**.

Smart key – A device which looks like a key, but carries a **microchip** such that it can carry out the same functions as a **smart card**. Often used in high-security buildings.

Smart terminal – One which has some local processing ability.

Smell input – Gas detectors used as input devices interfaced to an appropriate **computer system**.

Snail mail – Derogatory term used to describe the conventional mail system when compared to the speed of **e-mail**.

Soft copy – The output on a **VDU** screen.

Soft keys – The **function keys** or user-defined keys on a **keyboard**.

Software – The **programs**.

Software development – The process of developing new and better **software**.

Software engineering – Methodology which embraces **documentation**, **maintenance**, **testing**, **debugging**, and development of a **system** making use of a variety of **software engineering** tools (**CASE**).

Software houses – The companies that develop **software**.

Software packages – **Applications packages**.

Son file – The latest generation of **master file**.

Sorting – Putting **raw data** into some pre-determined order, e.g. alphabetical.

Soundex – A 'sounds like' search on a **database**.

Source document – A document on which the source data to be entered into the **computer** may be found.

Source program – **Program** before being **assembled** or **compiled**.

Speech input – **Data** entered by means of the human voice.

Spell checker – Usual accessory on most **WP** and **DTP systems**. Unfortunately not context sensitive. (See **grammar checker**.)

Spooling (1) – Sending several **files** to the **printer** so that the main **processor** is relieved of the task.

Spooling (2) – A process which gathers together **jobs** to be **run** and puts them on a fast access medium ready for **batch processing**.

Spreadsheet – An **applications package** to model financial, mathematical and other scenarios.

Sprite – A picture made up of **pixels**.

SQL – **Structured Query Language**.

SRAM – **Static Random Access Memory** – The fastest type of **RAM** which does not need to be **refreshed**.

S-R flip flop – A **logic circuit** with set and reset inputs.

SSI – Small Scale Integration – Less than 10 transistors per chip.

Stack – An area of **memory** used to contain temporary data.

Stack pointer – A number (usually inside a **register**) used to maintain the **stack**.

Start bit – Extra bit sent as an aid for synchronisation purposes in a **serial** transmission link.

Star topology – A fast and secure method of connecting computers on a **network**.

Start pointer – A **pointer** used to indicate the beginning of a **list**.

Statement – A **high-level language** program instruction.

State transition diagram – A diagram to show physical or logical states in a system, and the possible transitions between them.

Static RAM – See **SRAM.**

Status register – See **Flag register**.

Stepper motor – A motor that moves a set angle in response to a pulse from a **digital** system.

Stock control – An **application package** for controlling this aspect of the business.

Stop bit – A bit used to indicate the end of a group of bits in a **serial** link.

Storage – Same as **memory**.

Storage partitioning – A form of **memory management**.

Store – See **primary store.**

Story – A text file in a **DTP system**.

Strain gauge – A **sensor** that can be used as an input **transducer** to detect pressure applied.

Streaming – The processing of data in a continuous stream. This is becoming increasingly popular on the Internet for processing sound and real-time video images.

String – A set of alphanumeric **characters** and other punctuation etc.

String variable – A **variable** that can consist of a string of **characters**.

Strong encryption – Encrypting using very long **keys** makes it virtually impossible to guess the codes, even with the most powerful **supercomputers** spending hundreds or thousands of years on trying to solve the problem by guessing.

Structure diagram – A better alternative to **flowcharts** to pictorially establish a structure for many types of **algorithm**.

Structured programming – A methodology used to ensure good programming style, which in turn maintains understandability and maintainability etc.

Structured Query Language – A language by which information in a **database** may be accessed.

Style (1) – *Italic*, **bold** or underlined etc.

Style (2) – Name given to a set of attributes applied to text within a **word processor**.

Stylus (pen input) – A device used to write on the screen. Often no more than a pointer.

Subroutine – A self-contained part of a **program** usually designed to accomplish a specific task.

Subschema – The conceptual, logical and physical levels into which a **database** may be split up.

Subscripted variable – **Variable** used to describe a **vector** or an **array** – e.g. Position(3,2,4).

Subtree – **Tree structure** that consists of **parent** and **children nodes** extracted from a larger tree structure.

Supercomputer – The fastest and most powerful computers available. Used to carry out maths-intensive applications such as forecasting the weather or creating realistic **ray-traced** images.

SuperJANET – A higher **bandwidth** and more versatile version of **JANET**.

SVGA – An enhanced version of the **Versatile Graphics Array (VGA)**. 256 to full 24-bit colour depending on hardware available.

Switching algebra – An algebra which helps to realise **logical functions** making use of switches.

Symbolic address – The use of **symbols** (characters) to represent an **address**, e.g. a label.

Symbol table – A table used by **compilers** and **assemblers** which stores the relationships between the **symbolic addressing** used by the programmer and the **machine addresses** on the actual **machine**.

Synchronous burst RAM – A technology which attempts to speed up memory access by a small amount.

Synchronous transmission – The transmission of data where the sending and receiving ends are in synchronisation.

Synonyms – See **collision**.

Syntax – The rules which govern the structure of a language.

Syntax analysis – The stage during **compilation** when the rules of the language are being checked for a particular program.

Syntax diagram – Pictorial alternative to **BNF** and **EBNF** for describing the **syntax** of a language.

Syntax error – A breach of one of the rules of **syntax**.

System – The **computer system** as a whole or some other more comprehensive definition including much hardware and software. (See **Control system**.)

System life cycle – The classic stages of **systems analysis**.

Systems analysis and design – The **analysis**, **design**, **testing**, correcting and **maintenance** of a system.

Systems analyst – The person who carries out the **systems analysis** phase.

Systems flowchart – A **flowchart** with extra systems-type **symbols**.

System software – **Software** such as the **operating systems** and **utilities**.

Systems programmer – The person who writes code for **operating systems** and the like.

TA – **Terminal Adapter** – A piece of hardware for connecting your computer to the **Internet** making use of an **ISDN link** instead of the slower **MODEM** connection.

Table (1) – **Rows** (**tuples**) and columns containing **attributes** which represent a **relation** in a **relational database**.

Table (2) – A special feature for helping to provide a tabular arrangement in an **HTML** document.

Tape cartridge – A small **cassette**-type **tape** system used for **backup** on **micros**.

Tape library (1) – The name given for the store of **tapes**, usually associated with a **mainframe**.

Tape library (2) – The name given to the large **DLT** libraries available on some **mainframes**. The high-availability types give 'on-line' access to vast quantities of data stored on DLT tapes which are in the drives held in the library.

Tape streamer – **Tape system** used for **backing** up **hard disks**, usually on a **micro**.

Target machine – The **machine** on which the code is intended to **run**.

Tbyte – See **Terabyte**.

TCP/IP – Transmission Control **Protocol** / **Internet Protocol** – A popular interconnection between **LANs** and **WANs**.

TDM – Time Division **Multiplexing**.

Technical documentation – Detailed documentation to enable other programmers to modify the system.

Technical support – That which most software companies will give you for a limited period of time after you have purchased their **software package**. It often takes ages waiting in a telephone queue to get through, and the phone calls are sometimes charged at premium rates. Some companies charge a great deal of money for continued technical support.

Teleconferencing – See **video conferencing**.

Teleprinter – A special **machine** with an integral **keyboard** and **printer** for sending and receiving messages.

Teletext – **Data** transmitted along with conventional TV signals – **decoded** and displayed on TV screen, local microcomputer, or via a **teletext server** on a **computer network**.

Telex – A system of communication making use of **teleprinters**.

Tera (T) – Multiplier representing 1×10^{12}. (Often-used alternative in computing 1024^4.)

Terabyte – $1024 \times 1024 \times 1024 \times 1024$ bytes of information.

Teraflops – 10^{12} FLOPS – A **fifth-generation** performance measurement.

Terminal – Special **hardware** or more commonly a **microcomputer** running **terminal-emulation software** which enables it to communicate with a **mainframe** or **external database**.

Terminal-emulation software – **Software** that enables a standard **micro** to act as a **terminal** for external communications.

Terminal node – A **node** in a **tree structure** which has no **children**.

Test data – **Data** used to test input to a **system** – care and thought need to be put into the choice of **data**. (See **black-box testing**.)

Testing – Going through the processes of making sure that a **program** or **system** works perfectly. For large and complex systems it's impossible to do exhaustive testing, but see the **white-box** and **black-box testing** methodologies.

TEX – Donald Knuth's mathematical **typesetting** package.

Text editor – A simple **word processor** used to construct **source code** for **high** or **low level languages**, or to create documents for **e-mail** etc.

Thesaurus – Usual accessory to **WP** and **DTP** system containing synonyms.

Thin client – A machine connected to a network which is unlikely to have a local hard disk. Most of the processing is carried out on a very powerful network **file server**. As virtually all of the processing is carried out on the file server, only information needed for screen updates is sent to the thin client machine.

Third-Generation Language – Structured languages such as later versions of **BASIC** and **Pascal** etc.

Third Normal Form – There should be no **functional dependencies** existing between **attributes** that could not be used as an *alternative* to the **primary key** – these are called **transitive dependencies**.

Third party – A supplier, other that the original manufacturer of the system who supplies **software** or **hardware** for the system.

Thrashing – An unfortunate consequence of using a **virtual-memory system** whereby code is continually being brought in and sent back to the **disk**.

Throughput – The amount of work being done by a **system**.

TIFF – The Tagged Image File Format – A popular **graphics** interchange format originally designed to handle **scanned** images.

Time division multiplexing – A technique which sends more than one signal down a communication line by allocating time slots to each signal.

Timer interrupt – A **job** has **run** out of time on the **CPU** – usually by getting stuck in a **infinite loop**.

Time sharing system – Each **job** or **user** is allocated a fixed amount of time, usually on a rotating basis.

Time slice – An amount of time allocated to a **user** in a **time-sharing system**.

Token (1) – An electronic **token** (special message) used in a **token-ring network**.

Token (2) – The smallest independent part of a **program** which has some meaning.

Tokenising – Replacing **high-level language** code by more efficient **tokens**.

Token ring network – A **computer network** in which an electronic **token** has to be grabbed before communication is possible.

Toolbox – That part of the screen of an application which displays the tools which are available within a particular application, e.g. a **CAD toolbox** would have special shape-drawing tools etc.

Top-down approach – Method of designing a solution to a problem by splitting it up into sub-problems.

Top-down design – Same as **top down approach**.

Top of stack – The first number on the **stack**.

Topology – Properties in terms of the shape and interconnections etc. The London underground map is a topological representation of the underground system, for example.

Touch screen – A **VDU** in which criss-crossing infra red beams may be broken by pointing a finger at the screen. Often used for easy selection of on-screen menus.

Tournament sort – A sort **algorithm** making use of a **binary tree**.

Trace – A system to help find out in what order a **computer** is **executing** a **program**.

Track (1) – Concentric **tracks** on a **floppy** or **hard disk**.

Track (2) – Continuous spiral on a **CD-ROM disk**.

Track (3) – Linear track on a **tape**.

Trackball – A device in which a ball is rotated to move the **cursor** on the screen. An upside-down mouse!

Track number – The number assigned to a **track** on a **disk**.

Transaction file – A **file** of **transactions** used to update the **old master file** to produce the **new master file**.

Transaction log – A file which records transactions, either with a view to producing an audit trail or to aid recovery in the event of a disaster.

Transactions – Generally used to denote new business information ready to be input to the **system**, e.g. things sold in a shop or factory, or stock brought into the warehouse on a certain day etc.

Transducer – A device that converts energy from one form into another.

Transducer driver – Circuit which boosts an electrical signal to drive outputs like motors, solenoids and heating elements etc.

Transducer (input) – A device that converts a physical quantity into an electrical signal e.g. a pH sensor.

Transducer (output) – A device that converts an electrical signal into a physical quantity e.g. a motor.

Transistor – A tiny electronic component used as a fast switch inside a computer.

Transitive dependencies – If A is dependent on B and B is also dependent on C, then A is dependent on C, and a transitive dependency is said to exist. It can often lead to unintentional deletion of data in a **database**.

Translator – **Software** which converts one language into another, e.g. a **compiler**, **interpreter** or **assembler**.

Transport layer – The fourth layer in the **ISO OSI network model**.

Transputer – A special **microprocessor** or an arrangement of **microprocessors** for **parallel processing**.

Traversal – Moving around a **data structure**.

Tree – A **hierarchical data structure**.

Tree network – The **topology** of a network when **hubs** are used to join several computers to an **Ethernet network**, for example.

Tree sort – See **tournament sort**.

Tree structure – A **data structure** making use of a **tree**.

Tri-state buffer – An electronic circuit which is used for routing. It has three states: '0', '1' and 'off'. Here 'off' represents a high-impedance state.

Trojan horse – One type of computer **virus**.

True-type fonts – See **outline fonts**.

Truncation error – An **error** due to 'chopping off' some of the 'less-significant digits'.

Truth table – A list of the relationships between the outputs and inputs of a **logic circuit**.

TTL – Transistor-Transistor Logic – One type of fabrication technique used in logic **chips**.

Tuple – The correct term for a **row** or **record** from a **relational table**. Called a **tuple** because it's the *correct term* from relational calculus and relational algebra from which **relational databases** are derived.

Turing – A mathematician who did much pioneering work in computing.

Turing test – A test to see if a computer has intelligence.

Turnaround document – A document, output from a **computer system**, which is intended to be fed back into the system at a later stage.

Turtle – A little **robot** which acts as a plotter when doing turtle **graphics** in **Logo.**

Turtle graphics – Drawing pictures using the **high-level language Logo**.

TWAIN – Tool Without An Interesting Name! – A scanner interface standard.

Twos complement – A method of representing positive and negative numbers in **binary**.

Two-way linked list – A **list** which has both **forward** and **backward pointers**.

Typeface – The characteristics of machine-generated text, e.g. Times, Helvetica etc.

Ultrix – DEC's version of **Unix**.

Unconditional jump – A forced **jump** to another place in the **program** with no pre-conditions.

Underflow – A number too small to be represented by the **system** has been encountered.

Universal Product Code – The American equivalent of the **EAN bar-code system**.

Universal Serial Bus – A relatively new **serial bus system** for the connection of external devices to microcomputers. Many more devices can be connected using this system compared to the conventional **ports**. For example, 127 external devices can be connected to a single USB **port**.

Unix – A popular and long-lasting operating system used in the professional world for **micros**, **minis** and **mainframes**. Linux is a derivative from this.

UPC – **Universal Product Code** – The American equivalent of the **EAN bar-code** system.

Updating – Replacing, adding or deleting information (especially in a **file**) for more recent information.

Upgrade – Changing parts (or all!) of the **hard-ware** or **software** for later and hopefully better versions.

Upper case – Capital letters only.

UPS – **Uninterruptible Power Supply** – Used to prevent **volatile RAM** losing its contents in the event of a power failure. Some systems will not allow you to keep on computing – it only lasts a few seconds. Other systems will keep you going for twenty minutes or longer.

URL – **Uniform Resource Locator** – The path which contains the address at which a particular resource is located on the **Internet**. For example, HTTP://www.ft.com would be the URL used by the **Web browsers** to locate the Financial Times.

USB – **Universal Serial Bus**.

Usenet – A large group of **Internet** users who communicate using the **UUCP protocols**. Virtually any topic of interest is covered.

User – You!

User-defined keys – Special **keys** on the **keyboard** which can have effects programmed by the **user**.

User documentation – The manuals (usually non technical) for the **users** of the system.

User friendly – A computer system that is supposed to be easy to use, e.g. a windows-based system.

User interface – That part of the **system** which interacts with the **user**. See **GUI**, **WIMP** and **HCI**.

Utilities – **Software** such as disk **formatters**, **viral killers** and parts of the **operating system**.

UUCP – **Unix to Unix Copy Protocol** – The system used by the **UseNet Newsgroups**.

UUencode – A **Unix**-based coding system which allows transmission of any information over systems which make use of the 7-bit **ASCII** set (i.e. most **e-mail** or **Newsgroup** transmission systems). See also **MIME** and **BinHex**.

Validation – **Data** is checked to see if it is sensible in the context in which it is being used, e.g. a date is not entered as 31/2/1999.

Variable – A **data** item that can take on a range of different values.

Variable-length field – A **field** in which the width depends on the number of **characters** entered.

Variable-length file – The **file** length depends on the number of characters entered into it. Compare to a **fixed-length file** in which dummy **data** is used to create the maximum-length file from the start.

Variable partition – A proportion of the **memory** which is varied in size by the **operating system**.

Variable type – The type of variable such as **integer**, **floating point**, **enumerated** or **string** etc.

VAX – Virtual Address eXtension – **DEC's** range of **minis**.

VBA – **Visual Basic for Applications** – This is a version of Visual Basic based on **Macros**. It is the programming language which accompanies applications like Word, Excel, and Access, for example.

VBScript – Microsoft's **Visual Basic Scripting language**, used for writing customised routines as an add on to many Microsoft applications. It also does similar things to **JavaScript** if you have a suitably equipped Web browser.

VCR – Video Cassette Recorder.

VDSL – **Very high data rate Digital Subscriber Line** – Maximum of 52 Mbit/sec is possible using this technology over phone lines with special equipment in the exchange and the client end.

VDU – Visual Display Unit – Same as a **monitor**.

Vector (1) – A one-dimensional **array**.

Vector (2) – A pointer used to hold the address of a routine which is resident somewhere else.

Vectoring – System used to transfer control from one part of the program to another by an **address pointer** which is called a vector. The **vector** can be altered so that the routines may be held in different parts of the memory for different operating system versions, for example.

Vector processor – Special **hardware** for calculations on **vectors**.

Verification – A check to see if data has been entered correctly, e.g. the name 'Clark' might be entered as 'Clarke'.

VESA – Video Electronics Standards Association – A group of PC manufacturers who have set a standard for video adaptors.

VGA – Versatile Graphics Array – One type of graphics standard (several actually!) on an **IBM compatible PC**. 256 colours in low resolution or 16 colours in high resolution – **SVGA** is better.

VHS – Vertical Helical Scan – *The* most popular format for video tapes.

Video adaptor – A circuit generating all the signals required to generate text and/or pictures on the computer's **raster display**.

Video conferencing – Eyeball-to-eyeball communications via a **computer network**. Now available over an **ISDN link** on the **Internet**.

Video digitiser – Video camera linked to a computer to **digitise** an image. You will need a special card and software to operate the system.

Video phone – Sound and **real-time** vision via the telephone or other network.

Video RAM – Fast RAM which is often used in a graphics card on a PC.

Videotex – Interactive system in which text and low-res **graphics** etc. can be exchanged via a **network**.

Viewdata – Same as **Videotex**.

Virtual machine (1) – A **machine** that utilises **virtual-memory techniques**.

Virtual machine (2) – The **user's** perception of a **machine** that is remote from the actual **hardware**.

Virtual memory – Use of **disk** to give the illusion that you have lots more **RAM**.

Virtual peripheral – A **peripheral** that is shared by many **users**, e.g. a **printer server**.

Virtual reality – A computer-simulated world interacting with the **user** via **data gloves** and special **helmets** etc.

Virtual world – The illusion created by **VR**.

Virus – **Software** which is illegally injected into a system which often has annoying or even catastrophic results. It is designed to propagate itself and infect other computer systems too.

Visual Basic – Microsoft's **GUI**-based developer environment making use of **BASIC** together with all the tools and programs to create fully WIMP-based programs which can be compiled into useful application code.

Visual C++ – Microsoft's **GUI**-based developer environment making use of C++ together with all the tools and programs to create fully WIMP-based programs which can be compiled into useful application code.

Visual display unit – The name for a computer screen, monitor or VDU.

Visual Java ++ – A visual programming environment for Microsoft's Java.

VLSI – Very Large Scale Integration – Between 20,000 and 100,000 transistors per chip.

VMS – Virtual Memory System.

Voice input – Human voice used to control a **machine**.

Voice output – Synthesised human speech.

Voice print – The use of the human voice as a security measure, usually for gaining access to a secure system.

Voice systems – System used on the **Internet** for the **real-time** transmission of voice data.

Volatile store – **Memory** that looses its contents if the power is removed from the system.

Volatility (file) – The frequency with which updates are performed.

von Neumann – A mathematician who did much pioneering work on computers.

von-Neumann bottleneck – The queueing up of all the instructions waiting to be processed.

von-Neumann concept – The cycle of **fetching**, **decoding** and **executing** instructions one at a time.

VR – Virtual Reality.

VRAM – Video RAM – RAM used for the display of video information – usually incorporated on a graphics display adaptor card.

VRML – Virtual Reality Modelling Language – You may explore 3D worlds on a suitably equipped **Web browser** if the source code is written in this language.

VTR – Video Tape Recorder.

WAN – **Wide Area Network**.

Wand – Also called optical wand-device to read **bar codes**.

Weak encryption – Making use of encryption methods which are difficult for ordinary people to crack. However, if you have a large and powerful supercomputer, then these codes may be easily broken in a sensible amount of time. Some governments advocate this method so law-enforcement agencies may crack the codes.

Web – The **World Wide Web** or **Internet**.

Web browser – The software used for surfing the **Net**. Common examples are Netscape Navigator and Internet Explorer.

Web crawler – One of the **Internet's search engines**.

Web page – A page constructed, usually by using the **HTML language**, which enables graphics, text and other fancy effects to be displayed by using a **Web browser**.

Web site – The collection of **HTML** pages, which make up a site for a particular company or individual etc. Each site needs a unique **domain name** on the **Internet**.

What-if analysis – Modelling scenarios on a **spreadsheet** to see what the effects of changes might be.

Whetstones – A **benchmark** test for **floating-point operations**.

While loop – Checks **Boolean** condition before executing loop statements.

Whiteboard – System used to transmit doodles over the **Internet** while you are using a **voice** or **video system**.

White-box testing – White box testing is applied to the software **module** under test by identifying the paths through the project. This is done by creating a **directed graph** from the sub-modules of the module under test. (Using the 'loops' and 'self-contained chunks of linear code' etc. as a guide.) Once the directed graph for the module has been created, the paths through the code can be established by counting up the number of regions in the graph, and applying some common sense. Once all of the unique paths through the code have been documented, **black-box testing** methods are applied to each of these paths.

Wide Area Network – A long-range network making use of public lines such as the telephone system.

Wildcard – A character which can be used to replace a group of other characters – usually used in a search.

WIMP – **Windows Icons Mouse Pointer** – The familiar **desktop** operating environment.

Winchester disk – A **hard disk** making use of **Winchester** technology. Now just called a hard disk.

Window – A part of the screen through which you can see either a separate application or some other scene such as a **directory**, for example.

Windows CE – A cut down version of windows for use on **palm tops** and **PDAs**.

Windows NT – Windows New Technology – Another windows operating system for the **IBM PC**. However, it's much more robust and secure than Windows 95 or 98 and is to be renamed Windows 2000.

Windows RAM – An efficient way of utilising RAM in a Windows environment.

Windows 3.1 or 4 – A **windows**-based **operating system** for the **IBM PC**. Now superseded by Windows 95, Windows 98 and Windows 2000.

WinZip – One of the standard file-compression utilities.

Wire-frame modelling – Building up 3D images just using the outline edges.

Wizard – A method of helping you to achieve a set task with which you might not be familiar. A typical wizard will choose **default** or sensible values to get you going unless otherwise stated.

Word (1) – The number of bits that can be handled by the **CPU** at any one time. Usually 8, 16, 32, 64 or 128.

Word (2) – Microsoft's main **word processing** system.

Word length – The number of **bits** capable of being handled by a computer at any one time, e.g. how many bits can be transferred from **memory** to the **CPU**.

Word processor – An **applications package** used for the creation of mainly text-based documents.

Working tape – Tape used to store current data.

Workstation (1) – Name used for high-performance **microcomputer**.

Workstation (2) – Name used for a terminal on a network.

World Wide Web – The name given to the 'network of networks' called the **Internet**.

WORM – Write Once Read Many times – One type of **optical disk**.

Worm – A type of **computer virus**.

WP – **Word Processor**.

WRAM – **Windows RAM** – RAM organised efficiently for use in a Windows environment.

Write – Term used to make a record of **data** in **memory** or on some suitable storage **medium**. The act of writing data will usually destroy (overwrite) any data that used to be stored in the same place.

Write head – The part of the **disk** or **tape** which writes the **data** to the magnetic media.

WWW – The entirety of all **pages** (**hyperlinked documents**) that together make up the resources available on the **Internet**.

WYSIWYG – What You See Is What You Get – Screen contents reflects what would be printed out.

Xerographic printer – **Printer** making use of the Xerox photocopying techniques.

XNOR gate – A **logic gate** which is a **NOT(XOR)** gate.

XOR gate – A **logic gate** which is similar to an **OR gate** but excludes the situation where all inputs are 1, which in this case gives a 0 out.

Ybyte – See **Yottabyte**.

Yotta – Multiplier for 1×10^{24}.

Yottabyte – $1024 \times 1024 \times 1024 \times 1024 \times 1024 \times 1024 \times 1024$ bytes of data.

Zbyte – See **Zettabyte**.

Zetta – Multiplier for 1×10^{21}.

Zettabyte – $1024 \times 1024 \times 1024 \times 1024 \times 1024 \times 1024$ bytes of data.

Zip drive – A 100 Mbyte removable drive developed by Iomega.

4GL – Fourth-generation language.

68000 – The range of **microprocessor chips** from **Motorola**.

80 × 86 – The range of **CISC microprocessor chips** from **Intel**.

To cut down on the enormous amount of space that would be required, the answers given here are printed in a smaller font and kept <u>very brief</u> indeed – <u>students should expand considerably on the given information when answering questions or doing their own work</u>. One or more page number references are also provided where the relevant extra information can be found in the chapter being studied, and other relevant and related chapter and page references are also given. Additional reference material is sometimes quoted along with the answers to enable students to investigate the subject further if necessary. Some questions are of the open-ended research type and therefore have no answer in the following sections.

Answers to exercise 2.1

1. (a) **Input**, **Processing** and **Output**. The computer system and sub-sections of it can be categorised for analysis in separately identifiable chunks. Division between **hardware** and **software** is also important.

   (b) A **compiler** – it is **software** – *the rest* are examples of **hardware**.

2. **Information** is obtained from **raw data** after some suitable **structure** has been applied to it.

3. Examples only are given – your answers will depend on your own systems.

   (a) MJN Pentium 750, Acorn RISC PC, Sun SparcStation, GateWay Pentium II 500MHz etc.

   (b) VisualBASIC, BASIC VIII, Pascal, Delphi 4, Borland C++, COBOL 97, FORTH, Logo, Java ++, Prolog etc.

   (c) Adobe Acrobat, AutoCAD 14, AutoRoute Express, Corel-Draw 8, FrontPage 98, Lotus Freelance Graphics, Math-CAD 7, Office 2000 Professional, Quark Express 4.0. etc.

   (d) Varies between 64 MB and 256 Mbyte depending on micros.

   (e) Windows 3.1, Windows 2000, Windows NT4 and Linux, System 7, RISC-OS 4.0, Unix, Ultrix, Novell, OS/2 etc.

   (f) Ethernet – 10 Mbits/sec, Econet – 200 k/sec, FDDI – 1000 Mbits/sec, Fast Ethernet – 100 Mbits/sec and Gbit Ethernet etc.

4. 1st – Valves, 2nd – Transistors, 3rd – SSI, 4th VLSI, 5th – Knowledge-based machines with AI.

5. (a) Micro-desktop, few peripherals, single user, cheap, easy to use etc. price to about £5,000, much more for high-end servers.

   (b) Size between micro and mainframe, multi-user, expandable, £20,000+, floor or large desktop etc.

   (c) Mainframe – Large floor-standing, lots of peripherals, many users, £100,000+ etc.

   (d) Laptop – small, portable, all peripherals in the same box if possible. Communication with peripherals like printer via an infra-red link etc.

6. A processor/s in which more than one thing can be achieved at literally the same time.

7. Any information can be coded into binary e.g. '10011000' might mean the colour red or '10111001' might mean 'switch on the coffee pot'. By following coded instructions in binary, and with the appropriate peripherals attached, it is possible for a computer to do many different tasks.

8. Candidates for possible consideration would be VR (see page 172), AI (see page 172) or nanotechnology (see page 133), for example.

Answers to exercise 3.1

1. The advent of cheap network hardware and software, the proliferation of distributed processing, higher bandwidth links, better communication systems, cheaper telephone calls and the Internet to name but a few.

2. **LAN** – Local Area Network – up to about 1km/network although multiple networks may be connected by bridges – under control of individual institutions.

   WAN – Wide Area Network – making use of public service networks from BT or Mercury etc. National and international in scope.

3. Several file servers and print spoolers, access to a wide range of software served by fat or thin clients, access to Intranets and the Internet via a proxy server. Access to specialist peripherals such as video digitisers and scanners that can transfer pictures via the network.

4. It's hard to keep many disk-based fat client workstations going due to admin overheads. New strategies include maintaining the system from a central resource by having diskless workstations.

5. NC is a Network Computer, usually a diskless workstation working in a thin-client architecture. A Network PC is a normal disk-based fat client operating more conventionally on a network. There are low maintenance options being developed for this configuration too.

6. Bandwidth is the rate at which information can be transmitted across the network system. If the bandwidth is insufficient the system is slow or may not work at all.

7. You would need to present a user ID and a password, which would then log you onto an appropriate file server with an appropriate security clearance. The password would not be shown on screen at log on.

8. In a high-security network, or when speed is of great importance.

9. Bus, Star, Tree, Ring, and Mesh.

10. (a) At lesson-change time many students are logging off while others are trying to log on for the next lesson.

    (b) Some students might deliberately try to damage the system.

11. Creation and deletion of user accounts. Backing up of system and user files. Maintenance of any hard disks connected to the network. Setting up of the security policies. Installing new applications and licensing etc.

12. Because it's become cost effective and is relatively fast.

13. The hardware needed to physically connect the PC to the network.

14. By having routers and/or bridges, which can boost the signals to cover greater distances.

15. Setting up an Intranet, video conferencing and e-mail. Each system relies on communication between different machines, and a network is ideal for this.

16. Normal PC users can connect to an ISP via a MODEM and phone line. Also, via a proxy server it's possible to connect from a LAN to the outside communication system using a phone or ISDN line, for example. This then allows access to an ISP which usually has a computer connected to the Internet backbone. Once on this vast network you have access to millions of sites.

17. The site is very busy.

18. Answer depends to a large extent on what you have at school or college.

Answers to exercise 4.1

1. A computer or WebTV, an account with an ISP, like AOL or CompuServe. A modem, a telephone line, ISDN line or an Ethernet card connected to the new megabit modems for links via ADSL, satellite or mains electricity, for example. In addition you will need software drivers for the modem, and software to the net like Internet Explorer or Netscape Navigator, for example.

2. LAN based connection to the net will need a proxy server to manage the multiple-user to single communication line aspects of the system. In addition to this, there will need to be a mail server, which handles the collection, distribution and sending of e-mail. Apart from firewall security, all the software needed is similar to a single user.

3. Typically you can send and receive mail, send to single or multiple users, which may be set up either by an address book or locally. You can send attachments, and have all the usual spelling checking and similar WP facilities.

4. Advantages – Fast, cheap and secure if encryption is used.

   Disadvantages – Need a computer, can be intercepted, and can be more difficult to verify unless a digital signature is used.

5. On-line charges such as hourly or monthly rate etc. Whether they have a POP in your area, the number of unique e-mail addresses provided, access or otherwise to material which might not be desirable.

6. e-mail, large numbers of forums, news services, on-line support, telephone support, access to newsgroups, connection to the www.

7. Search engines are databases, which contain information about a huge number of sites; they can be used to provide you with a suitable list of hypertext links on response to a key-word search. Boolean function and advanced search facilities make finding information much easier.

8. A URL is a Uniform Resource Locator. It is the address at which a resource is located. For example, the author's school is at

   http://www.tonbridge-school.co.uk

9. There are many search engines. Software like WebSeeker, for example, can search many search engines simultaneously, correlating all the results and eliminating duplicate entries.

10. You download the required information to disk, then surf your disk without paying any phone bills.

11. Voice-to-voice and video links are possible using appropriate software and hardware. Obviously a microphone and video camera are needed for video, a special interface, and the software to manage the pictures and sound over the Internet link. International calls can be made for local rates, but you would have to agree beforehand on the time of communication. Video is slow unless you have a fast link.

12. An increase in bandwidth, improved compression algorithms and the increasing use of streaming.

13. More than two people can talk to each other at the 'same time'. Facilities like white boards and clipboards to view each other's screens or to scribble notes with a graphics tablet or a mouse.

14. UseNet newsgroups can be set up by anybody. They discuss virtually any topic under the sun. They are controversial because people use them for illegal activities such as distributing child pornography or instructions on how to make a bomb, for example.

15. Unless strong encryption is used (it's illegal in some countries) then anyone with the appropriate equipment can intercept and read e-mail, credit card numbers or bank account details. Information can also be easily logged about where individuals have been on the net.

16. HTML allows users to link to other web pages at the click of a button. The latest versions of HTML and DHTML are overflowing with features like sound, animation, video clips and the ability to send information back to the host site. Also, languages like VBScript, JavaScript and Java enable an HTML page to do virtually anything that's possible on the computer.

17. GIF – good for 256 colour images – fast to download. JPEG – good for photographs, more than 256 colours, compression varies between about 20:1 and 100:1. An animated GIF is a sequence of GIF images encoded into a single GIF file. When viewed with a browser it gives the appearance of motion.

18. VRML is the Internet's Virtual Reality Modelling Language. A suitably equipped browser will enable the user to interact with 3D worlds. VRML is effective in training, games, estate agents, CAL and scientific investigation.

19. Small but powerful programs may be run giving interactivity and facilities beyond those offered by standard HTML and DHTML.

20. Java can give you complete functionality over the Web; this can be taken so far that a Java enabled browser might be all you need to do computing in the future! Applications or parts of applications could be downloaded from the Web in ways similar to the thin-client systems.

21. They make very fancy effects like rotation of 3D objects or an interactive calculator possible. Only the imagination and ability of the people who are programming the system limit you.

22. Complete interactive environments with whole body suites, VR helmets and data gloves giving Web pages extra interactivity. The Web may deliver standard lessons for education, and teachers will be able to get the work marked automatically! Reports could be generated too.

Answers to exercise 5.1

1. Half and full duplex.

2. The number of bits/sec. The transmission Baud rate will include overheads for things like check digits or parity, for example. Therefore, the actual information transmitted is less than that which might be expected.

3. The analogue telephone line was originally designed for speech, which is an analogue signal. Computers work with digital data, the modems change the signals into the appropriate forms.

4. Modulation means changing some aspect of a signal so that information is imparted. Frequency modulation means that one frequency could represent a '1' and another frequency could represent a '0'.

5. (a) Time division multiplexing is one way of sending multiple signals over the same line using small periods of time called a time slot.

   (b) ADSL is Asymmetric Digital Subscriber Link. A technology that allows you to receive at a much faster rate than you can transmit.

   (c) Data encryption allows you to send messages, which, even if intercepted, would be difficult or impossible to crack.

6. Circuit switching is the conventional phone line, where you have a dedicated line for the duration of the call. Message switching is where a message can be sent via any available route. Messages are split up into packets so that no one computer can hog the network.

7. A buffer is an area of memory. It can be used to receive and store a large amount of information, which can then be retransmitted at a different Baud rate.

8. To allow the equipment of many different manufacturers to talk to each other. You also need software standards too.

9. 7 layer model

   Layer 1 – Physical – Physical connections

   Layer 2 – Data Link – Integrity of transmission (error detection)

   Layer 3 – Network – Establish routes and packet sizes

   Layer 4 – Transport – Delivery of packets, major error recovery

   Layer 5 – Session – Manages dialogues between send and receive stations

   Layer 6 – Presentation – Data encoding and some syntax

   Layer 7 – Application – Language and higher-level syntax

10. TCP/IP is the protocol used with the Internet. ATM is a communications protocol designed for computer data, voice and video. It is used mainly by the phone companies, but can also be used on LANs.

11. Parity checks used mainly for checking individual bytes of information, no good for long messages. CRC checks very reliable for long message, but a re-transmission is needed if an error is detected.

12. Software security would involve the use of passwords, encryption and various levels of access depending on the password. Hardware security would involve palm print or retina scans. The physical position of the equipment, burglar alarms and door locks etc. should be considered too.

13. Radio link via satellite to portables in the jungle would be the best option. Encryption is essential, and passwords would be needed in case the equipment got into the wrong hands.

Answers to exercise 6.1

1. Computers are used for business because they help to save money. This can be done by increasing the efficiency with which information can be processed and handled, by reducing the number of staff needed, and by enabling communication between different sites.

2. People may not be fully IT literate when new systems are introduced. Failure by management to understand these difficulties could lead to disillusion with the new systems. Sometimes the new systems are difficult to get working, and the London Ambulance Service has experienced this as has the Southampton Air Traffic control system, for example.

3. Edit, justify, apply styles, effects, colour, check spelling and grammar, mail merge, e-mail, apply bullets, format the document, use templates and master pages, insert pictures, make multiple copies, send over the net, insert tables and objects like spreadsheets and databases etc.

4. WP suitable for all the tasks outlined in question (3). A DTP system is more suited to page layout for complex magazines and the like.

5. Can be instantly edited, can be merged with other text, can be sent over the net, can be proof read by the computer etc.

6. It's usually easier to transfer information if the WP forms part of an office suite like Microsoft's Office 2000 or Lotus SmartSuite 99, for example.

7. Mail merge – putting names and addresses and standard paragraphs into many different letters automatically.

   Macros – Automating a set sequence of operations which may be recorded by the user and called up with the press of a button.

Templates allow a house style to be loaded so that any new document being produced adheres to the styles without having to set them up each time a new document is needed. Simply load the template.

8. It enables mathematical models to be built up on anything from working out pocket money to simulating a queue in a large supermarket. These sheets are useful because, once set up, they allow the users to experiment using 'what if' scenarios. The spreadsheet has revolutionised financial planning because it would take too long to carry out these processes by hand.

9. Applying maths to numbers in cells, sorting lists into order, plotting charts, carrying out macros, database functions, programming the sheet using a script language, displaying pictures, formatting numbers and text in ways similar to that of a WP. Filtering data, applying validation rules, processing demographic data, formatting numeric data, creating colourful display to help clarify the data, applying logical and lookup functions, date and time calculations, correct spelling, create links to other sheets etc.

10. Cells may be selected in the sheet and then pasted into a WP in a variety of forms including screen captures, real data, CSV, and other formats exist for both databases and WPs.

11. A variety of scenarios may be modelled and, based on the responses of the users (soldiers), different paths and hence different outcomes may be pursued. You can imagine battle simulations being carried out, for example.

12. Graphics are used for an enormous number of different purposes from colour laser printing, via quick downloads on the web to high-quality video images. These techniques have conflicting requirements. Also, each manufacturer might invent a new system suitable for their particular package. It's essential to be able to exchange data, therefore, packages support many different formats allowing conversion between them.

13. Queries, Orders, Reports, Stock control, Goods inwards, Supplier.

14. Supplier – names and addresses, reliability etc.

    Goods inwards – Quality control, damaged goods to return etc.

    Reports – Reports to managers on state of stock or delays etc.

15. A *small selection* is as follows:

    Type of goods – food, clothes etc.

    Sub categories of each such as vegetables, dairy etc.

    Exact name of goods, Bar code, Supplier, Stock level, Price (supply price and selling price), Goods out of stock, Quantity in stock, Minimum order stock, frequency of sales, sell-by dates, special offers etc.

16. Export of data for reports, production of invoices, production of sales statistics, consequent analysis of these statistics etc.

17. Likely volume of transactions, network connection to other branches, connection to stock-control systems, security systems, tills and cash transfers, payment by credit card or debit card, able to work in multiple currencies such as the Euro, for example.

18. Essential for monitoring what's going on, and for passing statistics to other branches or head office. Can also help with security issues like vandalism and burglary, for example.

19. Cash for customers at point of sale, special offers and information for card-holding customers, customers able to check bank balance etc.

20. Physical security of cash is paramount. Electronic security via magnetic stripe and pin.

21. Self-help via application packages is ideal if the user has forgotten the odd trick or needs to learn one or two new ideas. Training via video, CD-ROM and the net is possible for longer periods. Word of mouth from an expert is useful, and proper staff training periods can help to start the ball rolling.

Answers to exercise 7.1

1. A pixel-based art package is made up of lots of tiny squares called pixels. An object-oriented CAD package is based on mathematically defined objects such as lines and circles etc.

2. Copy, Cut, Paste, Shapes, Libraries, Line styles, Hatching, etc.

3. Flood fill, paint brush styles, special effects like blur or drop shadows, deformation like perspective, cylinder or sphere etc.

4. When mapping out initial ideas.

5. The integration of CAD and CAM means that information from the drawings can be used to generate manufacturing data for CNC machines, or be used to generate information for stock and invoice purposes etc. Many so-called less developed countries may not make use of CAD/CAM because the infrastructure needed has not been set up and labour is cheap.

6. CNC is Computer Numeric Control. Special machines can accept codes, generated from computers, which control the action of lathes and milling machines used in the manufacture of components.

7. A robot without feedback must assume that the pieces are always put down in precise positions. It will not be able to detect if a chess piece is missing, for example. A robot with feedback could tell if a piece was not in the right place, or be able to tell if a piece has not been captured correctly by the grab, for example. Sensors such as strain gauges could detect the pressure applied when a piece is picked up, and optical sensors could detect the presence or absence of a piece on the board.

8. Ray tracing calculates the colour and other attributes such as intensity of light etc. falling on objects in the computer-generated picture. Textures can be simulated such as metallic or wood, and reflections in these materials simulated using this technique. Rendering is the general name given to a 3D graphics simulation, which incorporates the effects of light etc. such as that obtained from ray tracing.

9. (a) Detection of sound is easy, the interpretation of the sound is difficult, but understanding continuous speech is now quite advanced.

   (b) Video images can be captured easily, but interpretation of the image is still in its infancy. Fuzzy logic is helping with these problems.

   (c) Chemical analysis of smells is still in its infancy, but detection of certain chemicals to set alarms in computer control is quite advanced.

   (d) Touch is quite advanced in that sensors can detect very small pressures applied to strain gauges, for example.

   (e) Tasting is still not advanced, and is based on chemical analysis of bitter and sweet etc. However, computers are used to detect if certain wines and champagnes are genuine.

10. This is due to the intense number of mathematical calculations that have to be completed to get a weather forecast in a sensible amount of time.

11. Depends on the game. (Have fun!)

Answers to exercise 8.1

1. Transducers are devices to convert one form of energy into another – specifically, for computer systems either physical quantities into electrical signals, or electrical signals into physical quantities.

2. A device, which is used to convert signals from any form into a form that the computer can understand, or to convert computer signals into any other suitable form, e.g. disk-drive interface, printer interface, sound or video card, network interface etc.

3. To connect a range of peripheral devices.

4. INPUT – pH sensor, light sensor, microphone, gas detector, temperature sensor. OUTPUT – loudspeaker, motor, light bulb, solenoid, buzzer. Solenoid is digital – rest are analogue, but may be operated digitally in special circumstances, e.g. motor or bulb can be on or off, but they are still analogue devices in nature as they can be gradually increased in speed or brightness.

5. Serial – data is sent one bit after another down the same transmission medium – ideal for long distances.

   Parallel – two or more bits sent simultaneously down different wires or other media – ideal for communication inside the computer, i.e. short distances.

6. Start and stop bits, and transmitting at a given baud rate, see page 143.

7. Digital – varies in discrete steps – logic-gate output. Analogue – continuously variable – sound.

8. 12 bit – hence 4096 discrete levels for quantisation of analogue signal. Resolution determines how near we can simulate the intended analogue signal. See page 144.

9. Feedback – paying attention to what is actually happening by monitoring suitable signals derived from input transducers – without this ability, safety may be compromised as wrong assumptions about what is happening could be made, e.g. the computer might have switched off a motor but it's still going!

10. A computer-control system has a fully blown micro, mini or mainframe controlling the process, whereas an embedded system has only a microprocessor with memory etc. dedicated to a particular task. Examples of embedded systems are video recorders and cameras; examples of micro-controlled systems could be PCB drilling machine or CNC milling machine. PC control more versatile – embedded is cheaper.

11. Stepper motors can move in discrete steps under the control of a digital signal. Ideal for computer control. Ordinary D.C. motors require analogue voltage for speed control.

12. Tri-state means on, off or high impedance. Used to route signals along the bus system – Tri State can prevent data for disk drive from reaching the printer, can also determine the direction of data. See page 151.

13. Real time-system must respond quickly enough to react to some external event. Engine management system in a car is a good example. Software routines take a finite time for execution and may be too slow.

14. A critical temperature is reached inside a nuclear reactor. The shutdown procedure must be activated immediately. Data integrity (correctness) and reliability are just as important as raw speed.

15. HCI – Human Computer Interface. People often form an integral link in a control system, and speed of reaction and interpretation of data by the human operators is important. The design of the interface should ensure that smooth and stress-free operation is possible.

16. Perfect coffee maker is shown in the diagram on the next page – assume that milk is put into the cup before the coffee is added – sugar is added last.

Answers to exercise 9.1

1. Depends on your database.

2. Points for – Freedom of information, access to a vast range of material, share interests with other people, information instantly available, very easy to search for any information, international boundaries are broken down. Ideal for disabled people who are housebound, people who work from home, or people who find it difficult to interact with others.

   Points against – Criminals can exchange information very easily, children may have easy access to information which they should not see, illegal material may be imported due to the international nature of the Internet.

3. (a) ISPs can prevent people from having access to some of the material by filtering it from their systems.

Automatic coffee-making machine

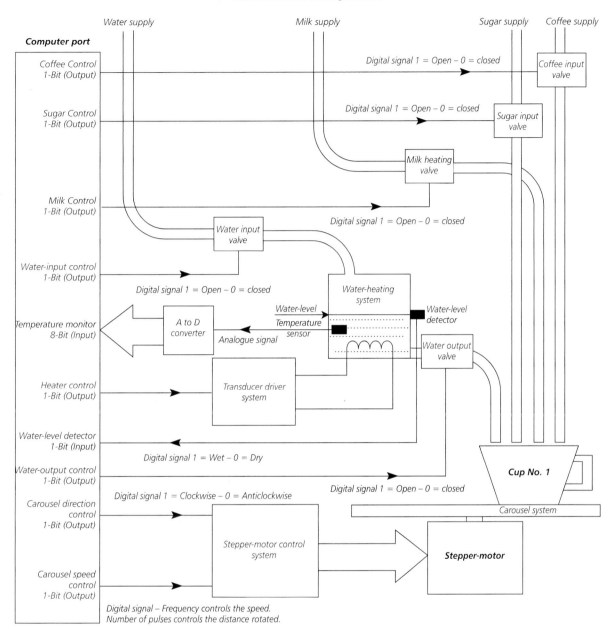

(b) Probably not!

(c) Many serve a useful purpose and should not be banned. Only those who are operating illegally should be banned.

(d) Definitely not. People would find other ways to trade the material.

4. (a) This scenario will be with us within a few years. VR helmets, data gloves and whole-body suites are already with us. When the price comes down this will be an increasing problem.

(b) VR can be of great use in education and training, helping people to be virtually present in a variety of environments hitherto much too expensive to visit, e.g. the surface of Mars. However, all these advantages can be used for illegal activities too.

(c) VR could, for example, be used to enable scientists to explore complex molecular structures by being telepresent inside the actual molecules. This could enable them to understand the interaction between the structures more easily, for example.

(d) Act out historical battles, be telepresent in dangerous environments, experience travel without actually going there etc.

(e) It's possible to interface a range of exercise machines to the computer, which, in addition to the virtual worlds being created, could give the user exercise too. For example, a user could be running along the beach in the south of France, could be engaged in a famous football match, or be rowing down the river in Cambridge. In the last example, the rowing machine could have sensors, which could control the speed of the simulation depending on the speed at which the user is rowing.

5. (a) More powerful and faster computers, clever software simulation, and massive expert-system databases, together with hardware developments like neural networks and fuzzy logic, for example, favour the AI argument. Limits of the algorithmic approach to problem solving (irrespective of future technology or speed) favour the people who believe that computers will never be able to think.

(b) If computers were more intelligent than humans are, then it might be possible for computers to solve problems that are currently beyond the capacity of humans to solve. This could have tremendous advantages in medical research, for example.

(c) If computers did ever evolve into an independent-thinking entity, then it might not be for the benefit of humanity. If this happened, it might be difficult for humans to control these machines. It depends on how much autonomy the machines were allowed to have.

6. Physical damage – backups kept on different disks, in different locations and in fireproof safes. Theft might be physical, in which case burglar alarms, locks and key-entry devices would be needed. However, it also might be logical, in which case passwords, encryption and database protection are needed. To prevent misuse of data you need to have both the physical and logical protection described above, plus protection against computer viruses too.

7. A worm virus gradually gobbles up computer memory. Therefore, at some later date after infection, applications that used to work well may no longer run due to lack of memory, even though the actual memory has not changed. You need to ensure that the latest virus protection software is installed, but this is no guarantee that you will be free from infection, as new viruses are being developed each day.

8. Change the date!

9. Weak encryption enables ordinary users to transmit information with a good degree of security. However, anyone with sufficient computing power, like the CIA, for example, would be able to crack the codes. Strong encryption is almost impossible to crack, and is widely available on the Internet; this means that governments can't crack these codes, and this in turn means that people carrying out illegal operations on the net are protected.

10. Only you have your private key, which is capable of decrypting a message. It does not matter that everybody else has your public key, because this can only be used to encrypt messages.

Answers to exercise 10.1

1. (a) Standard method is to use a mark-sense reader and appropriate source documents. (See page 198.)

(b) CAD – Any GUI-friendly device such as a mouse, trackball or light pen. However, a puck in combination with a graphics tablet is probably the most versatile, especially when part of the tablet is set up as a concept keyboard. (See pages 185, 187, 189 and 190.)

(c) The data glove is probably the most common but part or whole body suits are being developed which can monitor movements of any part of the body, and place the body with respect to some co-ordinate system operating within the computer. (See pages 207 and 208.)

(d) Bar codes, LASER scanners, magnetic stripe cards and smart cards all have a part to play in using computer-input peripherals for control of Electronic Funds Transfer at the Point Of Sale. Some new radio-tag systems can now tot up the contents of the trolley without removing the goods!

(e) A flatbed scanner can scan text and pictures into the computer as a bit-mapped image. Special software can then analyse the textual parts of the scanned image and turn it into ASCII text, bit-mapped or true-type fonts ready for production of CDs.

(f) Flatbed scanners or high-quality video digitisers are both capable of producing the required image quality, with expensive flatbed scanners being the highest quality possible. A digital camera is also useful.

(g) Any MIDI-based keyboard together with an appropriate MIDI interface and suitable software would be able to capture data played by the musician in real time and output the music in an appropriate form. For example,

the Sibelius software for the Arc, Mac and IBM range of PCs.

2. Due to the increased awareness regarding RSI, ergonomic keyboards are becoming more popular.

3. Turnaround documents such as those used for electricity-meter reading, for example, can be used to input the readings either as a mark in a box or neatly written characters which can be recognised by the computer.

4. A concept keyboard could be configured to respond to picture overlays placed on top of the tablet – when a child pushes one of the pictures the computer can be made to respond in an appropriate way.

5. Electronic Funds Transfer at the Point Of Sale – 'cash' transactions are carried out electronically. Advantages are shops do not keep so much money that can be stolen, fraud is less likely, it's often quicker and more convenient for the customer etc.

6. (a) Different types of keyboards to be considered in your explanation are ergonomic, Maltron and other different layouts, different language keyboards and concept keyboards.

(b) Mouse and trackball input devices have made GUIs much easier. Alternative 'use of the cursor keys' is less satisfactory. Ease of use for graphics-based input, art packages, menu selection, more intuitive interface, less command-driven input and hence computers easier to use etc.

(c) Pressure-sensitive graphics-tablet based input is an alternative for getting hand-sketched material into the computer system. Artists find the medium reasonably intuitive, good accuracy to less than 0.1 mm is possible, handwriting input handled, strokes of stylus (pen) combined with extra buttons make for a large set of alternatives such as deletion, colour, change of thickness etc.

(d) Video card together with a single video recorder or DVD and powerful computer can now replace an entire edit suite. Video processing possibilities only limited by software and can thus be upgraded without change of hardware. Non-linear editing possible, no degradation on multiple edits etc.

(e) Need multiple sensors capable of detection of chemicals in the wine, which give it its characteristic taste. (See chapter 8 for interfacing these devices.) Algorithms to relate good and bad wines to chemical content necessary to analyse results.

7. For – most people can speak faster than they can type, easier form of input, more natural form of input, ideal input medium for some disabled people, ideal input if hands are occupied with other tasks at the time (e.g. both hands might be fully occupied with a computer-control system).

Against – noisy in an office environment (imagine 20 people shouting at their computers!) many different words sound the same, people might have a cold, thousands of people are already trained to type, some operations would be incredibly tedious with voice-only input. Imagine telling a word processor to put text into underlined-and-centred-bold-italic Times in 22.5pt! Pointing and clicking may be far easier.

8. PDAs, such as Apple's Newton, for example, make use of pen-based input and are thus ideal pocket-sized communication and data processing centres. Note pads, diaries, simple databases, simple spreadsheets and word processors all fit neatly into this category, along with specialised software for business personnel. Fax, video communication links and computer communications connect this device to the information super highways of the future. PDAs of tomorrow will be doing what micros are doing today.

9. Smart cards and smart keys (see page 165) are least susceptible to tampering and are thus more secure. They are also more versatile and robust. Smart keys can hold sophisticated programs giving access to a wide range of different areas. PIN numbers, finger print, voice print or retina scans could add to security.

10. Office PCs tend to be low-volume data, often entered by hand directly into an application. Mainframes tend to be large-volume data entry, often carried out in batch processing mode. (See page 484.) Office PCs tend to be stand-alone or networked, mainframe input tends to be via terminals, micros acting as terminals or via a network.

11. A bit-mapped image stores the image as many tiny pixels associated with a co-ordinate position on the page. Each pixel has an associated colour. When viewed at normal size an illusion of a picture is created. To get text into a form understood by a computer, complex algorithms have to be applied to the probable text outlines and correlation with previous images representing the patterns of the text is undertaken. If the correlation is high the text is assumed to be of a particular character and font.

12. Sensors are available and others can be developed which convert limited movement into an electrical signal, which can be interpreted by a computer system. Such input techniques are discussed in chapter 8. Appropriate software displaying menus can activate choices based on what's happening to a pointer on the screen, what noises are being made, or what buttons may have been pressed on a special input unit.

Answers to exercise 11.1

1. Computer monitors – high quality, high-resolution, non-interlaced. Domestic TVs – 'low' quality, less resolution, usually interlaced raster scan. Monitors are also low radiation, multisync touch screen etc.

2. A system that uses 1 byte per RGB colour thus having 3 bytes or 24 bits giving 16,777,216 colours.

3. Each memory location in Video RAM contains bits, which are used to describe the grey scale or colour of a pixel on the screen. Each memory location is mapped to a physical position on the screen. (See page 217.)

4. CRT – very high quality, bright, high resolution uses much energy. LCD, usually small, not so bright, less resolution, uses far less energy. CRT mainly for desktops – LCD mainly for portables but expensive LCDs now available for desktops.

5. Touch-screen useful for pointing finger at screen when making a choice from a menu. More user friendly and ideal for shopping malls and the like – a mouse would probably get stolen!

6. Typewriter – slow, manual operation only – dot matrix printers together with WP replaced typewriters, able to do graphics. LASER printers able to do high quality work, colour now possible etc.

7. A bit-mapped font uses a map of pixels to generate the shape, outline fonts use maths definitions.

8. They are extremely fast for high-volume output.

9. See colour model on page 227. Cyan, Magenta, Yellow and Black Toners are combined to produce a range of colours which can be used to produce 24-bit or 32-bit (+ 8 for the black) images.

10. A5 paper size is 8.27in by 5.23in. At 300dpi this gives 300x300x8.27x5.23 = 3892689 dots. Monochrome image would take 3892689/8 = 486586 bytes. Coloured image = 3 x 486586 = 1459758 bytes. The black image (assuming the CMYK model is used) will need another 486586. Therefore just over 2 Mbytes would be needed. However, in practice, because colour on paper is simulated by spacing dots further apart, considerably less than this 2 Mbytes would actually be needed.

11. Skilled typesetters have been replaced by DTP operators. More scope for small publishing companies. Very much more scope for individuals with computers to publish documentation.

12. For up to A3 size probably. Larger than this probably not, due to the enormous expense of the LASER printer. Architects often use A2 and A1 sizes or larger, plotters go considerably larger than this, and can be the size of a small room.

13. Still popular in libraries and garages etc. It saves a vast amount of space on information storage and is also very cheap.

14. (a) Plotter (b) Linotronic (c) LASER or bubble jet (d) LASER or bubble jet (e) Thermal or dot matrix.

15. Can save memory by specifying white space in alternative ways. Can make use of lower-bandwidth networks, save money on phone or satellite bills if information can be sent in less time.

16. (a) Voice output. (b) Braille output – can be used with suitable interface.

Answers to exercise 12.1

1. Cheap, fast and plenty of it!

2. A pigeonhole concept is used as a description of primary storage where each unique physical memory location has an associated address. The word length determines the number of bytes held in each location, and the data bus is usually of sufficient width to make sure that the contents of a single memory location may be transferred in one go. The width of the address bus determines the memory capacity. (See page 242.)

3. The program currently under execution is held in primary storage. The fetch times for each instruction have a significant effect on the execution speed of a program. Cache memory can be used if necessary.

4. RAM – Random Access Memory, used for primary storage. (See page 242.) ROM – Read Only Memory used for parts of Operating Systems and other programs which don't change. (See page 244.) Embedded systems (see page 149) would probably be ROM only. Few if any systems these days are RAM only, as manual code would have to be typed in to boot the system. (See page 473.)

5. Volatile means that the contents of the memory will be lost if the power is removed. Use an Uninterruptible Power Supply (UPS) if important data might be lost. (See page 243.)

6. SRAM – Static Random Access Memory. Common use is for cache memory as it's faster than DRAM.

7. A memory map maps out important parts of RAM and ROM used for specific purposes. Without it important areas of memory could be inadvertently overwritten for other purposes.

8. EPROM – Erasable Programmable Read Only Memory. Used for experimental software development, ideal for small batch production and testing of operating-system ROMs before being committed to blowing a real ROM. Ideal for development of embedded systems (see page 149.)

9. ASCII – The American Standard Code for Information Interchange. A code developed to allow different computers to share information by recognition of a common code. Compare with EBCDIC, and extended ASCII. (See pages 247 and 261.)

10. Backing store such as tapes, magnetic disks and optical disks etc.

11. Direct and sequential access modes of operation.

12. Your answer should address the problems of physical disk sizes, different disk formats, different operating systems and different data storage mechanisms used by different applications.

13. Floppies have less expensive and simpler mechanisms and are open to the atmosphere, therefore the track density is far less than for a hard disk, for example, which is housed in a hermetically sealed unit free from dust, smoke and other debris.

14. Number of surfaces, track density, sectors/track and bytes/sector. Bus parameters (e.g. width and speed) and interface electronics limit the computer's ability to extract data from the disk at the maximum rate. Also the disk's physical parameters such as seek time and read/write access time plus the speed of rotation etc.

15. CD-ROM disks are very cheap, made even cheaper by the popularity of compact-disc audio systems. A large amount of data can be stored on each disc, therefore ideal for the distribution of software.

16. Speed of access is the biggest problem, and writable CD-ROM systems are currently expensive (but getting cheaper). Data storage capacity is also going to be a problem at some time in the future. Multiple spin speed drives (e.g. 48×) have overcome data-transfer speed problem, and blue laser or multiple layers will quadruple the storage capacity. Compression is currently used to pack in more data.

17. As usual in the computer world different manufacturers develop different systems independently. The problems with CD-ROM drives are quite bad because they are also used for home entertainment and other systems – and all these need to be compatible in multimedia systems.

18. Disks may be quite fast, but compared to CPU speeds they are painfully slow. Therefore, an area of memory acting as a buffer significantly decreases data access times if the appropriate parts of the disk are stored in the cache memory.

19. Tapes are still the cheapest storage medium in terms of cost/byte. Vast quantities of data are currently stored on tape, and the medium is ideal for batch processing. However, DLT libraries give a good high-availability factor, and will ensure that tapes go on for many years to come.

20. The physical records stored on the secondary storage media are such that the most efficient transfer size to the physical media is set up. The logical record used within an application or a program etc. will not usually relate to the size of the physical records. Therefore a buffering system is used to translate the physical access requirements to the logical (application or program's) requirements (see page 550).

21. Tapes on micro are generally used for backup purposes. Tapes on mainframes are usually used for batch-processing and sequential file handling (see chapter 26) operations.

Answers to exercise 13.1

1. Makes the machine easier to use. Complex problem-oriented solutions as opposed to machine-oriented solutions are possible. Software development is significantly easier and faster.

2. No single language can cope with the vast range of requirements from embedded system control (see page 149) via advanced mathematics to business administration etc. – the language would be too cumbersome.

   (a) Typifies telling the computer how to do something by using instructions called imperatives.

   (b) Typifies telling the computer what to do (not exactly how to do it).

   (c) Typifies languages expressed in terms of functions or procedure calls.

   (d) Makes use of objects which are classes describing both data and operations.

   N.B. Most languages contain one or more of the above paradigms.

3. It's a whole design philosophy approach to programming and systems analysis (see chapters 16 and 17).

4. (a) 3rd (b) 1st (c) 2nd or 3rd depending on version (d) 5th (e) 2nd (f) 4th.

5. BBC BASIC used for all examples.

   (a) A variable is an identifier, which can take on a range of different values – but only one at a time!

   Variable name examples – x, fred, Name$, x_value, radius_of_circle.

   (b) An identifier is a set of one or more characters used to identify a data element such as a variable, an array or a function etc.

Identifier examples – stock(n), 45.3, balance_of_account, 3.141592654, y12.

(c) Reserved words are key words, which can't be used for identifiers – however, BBC BASIC allows this if lowercase letters are used.

Reserved word examples are – COUNT, VOICES, PLOT, FILL, SOUND.

(d) Built-in maths functions are identifiers that call up prewritten functions.

Maths-function examples are COS, SQR, LOG, EXP, TAN etc.

6. (a) A diagram which defines the syntax of a language pictorially – as opposed to using techniques such as BNF or extended BNF etc. (see chapter 32).

   (b) It is easier to follow by people who are not experts in compiler design. See Pascal syntax diagram on page 276.

   (c) BNF – Backus Naur Form. (See page 621.)

7. Different data types give rise to different characteristic sets of possible values. Explicit data types might be INTEGER or STRING – only rules applying to that data type may be applied – it thus gives a more rigorously enforced structure to the program.

8. BBC BASIC is used for the following definitions.

   (a) for loop

   FOR <variable> = <expression> TO <expression> [STEP expression]

   Valid statements

   NEXT <variable>

   (b) while loop

   WHILE <expression> (Never executed if expression is false)

   Valid statements

   ENDWHILE

   (c) repeat – until loop

   REPEAT   (Always executed at least once, even if expression is TRUE)

   Valid statements

   UNTIL <expression>

9. BBC BASIC used for the following examples.

   (a) Data types are NUMERIC – Integer, Floating point. BOOLEAN, STRING, ARRAYS (Subscripted variables), FILE (Simple pointer)

   (b) Ranges of numeric data types are

   INTEGER –2147483648   to +2147483647

   Floating point –1.7 x 10^{38} to +1.7 x 10^{38}

10. (a) Boolean – used for TRUE/FALSE values only.

    (b) Integer – Numeric values, whole numbers only, limited range but good accuracy.

    (c) Real – Numeric values, large range, limited accuracy if floating point is used.

    (d) String – Alphanumeric character storage, limited length, can't do arithmetic on numbers but can concatenate strings, search for characters, used to help sort data into alphabetical order etc.

Answers to exercise 13.2

1. A list of values that the variable can assume, e.g. Tom, Dick or Harry.

2. BBC BASIC VII – DIM structure(5,3) would define a two-dimensional array named structure. To access the element in the 2nd row and the 2nd column use the variable structure(2,2).

3. The pointer data type holds a number, which can be used to point to a memory location, an element within an array, an element within a record or a file, or a position within a

string etc. By changing the pointer number we can access different data items set up using the rules of a number of different structures.

4. A condition, such as the value of a variable, for example, is tested, and if the condition is TRUE (Boolean function) then a JUMP to a different part of a program is carried out. For example, using BBC BASIC – IF test >= maximum THEN PROCreset – calls the reset procedure if test >= maximum.

5. WHILE is never executed if the condition is FALSE, whereas REPEAT – UNTIL will always be executed at least once, irrespective of whether the condition is TRUE or FALSE.

6. Loops can only be nested within themselves, they can't overlap (see diagram on page 288).

7. Excessive use of the GOTO can lead to unwieldy and unreadable programs. It's often extremely difficult to follow the logic of a program, which is liberally sprinkled with GOTOs. Use only on error conditions.

8. Case statements are more readable, and are easier to use when constants are used for the test condition, nested IF – THEN statements are more versatile, unless the language supports ranges within case statements.

9. A function is used as a subroutine that returns the value of a single variable, a procedure is a subprogram which can have many parameters passed over to it and returned from it.

10. BBC BASIC

```
INPUT"Radius of circle ";rad
Area = FNArea_of_circle(rad)
PRINT "Area of circle of radius";" ";rad;" is";Area
END
DEF FNArea_of_circle(radius)
= PI * radius^2
```

11. BBC BASIC

```
DIM x(5)                DEF PROCaverage
PRINT"Input five numbers"   LOCAL Total, count
FOR count = 1 TO 5      Total = 0
 INPUT x(count)         FOR count = 1 TO 5
 NEXT count             Total = Total
                          + x(count)
 PROCaverage            NEXT count
 PRINT"The average is   average = Total/5
  ";average             ENDPROC
END
```

12. The scope of a local variable is defined and recognised only locally by a unit of the program such as a procedure, a global variable is recognised and can be altered by any part of the program.

13. Passing by value means that the variable being used to transfer the value to the procedure does not get altered itself, only its **value** is **passed**. Passing by **reference** means that the variable being used to pass the parameter does get **referenced** and therefore *irrevocably altered* by the procedure.

14. It makes the program much easier to understand by both the programmer and any people who have to modify the program at a later stage. It adds to the self-documenting nature of structured programming.

15. GUI based front ends like Microsoft Visual Basic or Borland's Delphi, for example, enable users to interact with multi-tasking operating systems by making the front end easier to use. The user does not have to get involved with the tedious details of windows design, but can manipulate the systems with a mouse, and get the system to generate the data. This gives a very easy interface to the user's code, which is controlling the system.

Answers to exercise 14.1

1. (a)

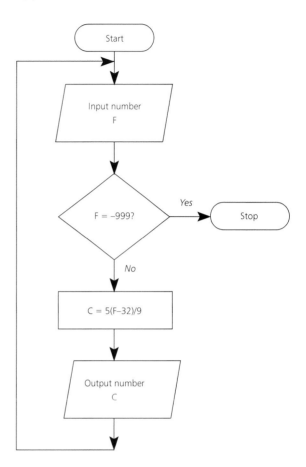

(b) Figure overleaf
(c) Figure overleaf
(d) Figure overleaf
(e) Figure overleaf

2. (a) Figure overleaf
(b) Figure overleaf
(c) Figure overleaf
(d) Figure overleaf
(e) Figure overleaf

3. Pseudocode algorithms can easily be derived from the final code in question 4.

4. NB All code in BBC BASIC VII

(a)
```
REPEAT
   INPUT f
   c = 5*(f − 32)/9
   IF f<> − 999 THEN PRINT c
UNTIL f = −999
```

(b)
```
count = 0
INPUT number
smallest = number
largest = number
REPEAT
   count = count + 1
   INPUT number
   IF number>largest THEN largest = number
   IF number<smallest THEN smallest = number
UNTIL count = 10
PRINT largest,smallest
```

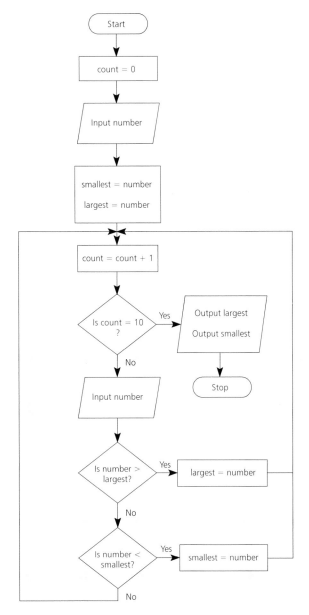

Figure for question 1(b)

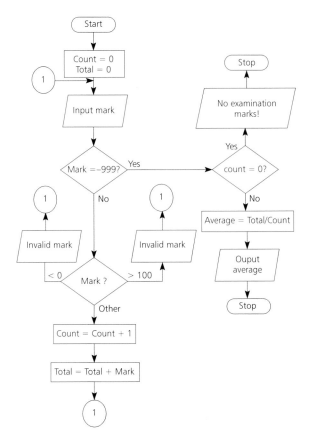

Figure for question 1(c)

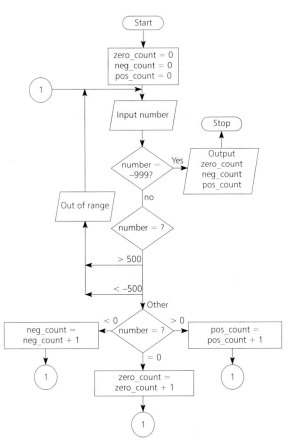

Figure for question 1(d)

4. (c)
```
ON ERROR PRINT ERL,REPORT$:END
count = 0: Total = 0: mark = 0
REPEAT
  flag = 0
  INPUT mark
  IF mark <> -999 THEN
        IF (mark > 100) OR (mark <0) THEN flag =
                                              1
           IF flag = 0 THEN
     count = count + 1
           total = total + mark
           ELSE
           PRINT"Out of range"
           ENDIF
  ENDIF
UNTIL mark = -999
IF count = 0 THEN
   average = 0
ELSE average = total/count
  PRINT average
```

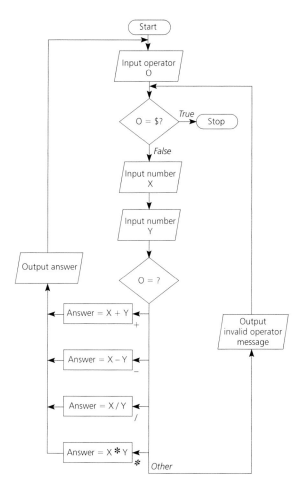

Figure for question 1(e)

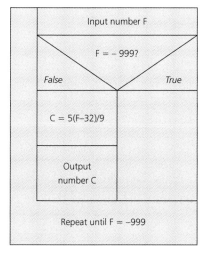

Figure for question 2(a)

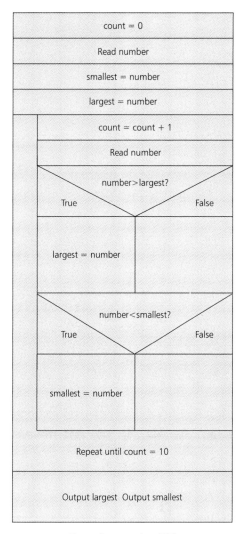

Figure for question 2(b)

4. **(d)**
```
ONERROR PRINT ERL, REPORT$ : END
zero_count =0: pos_count =0: neg_count =0
REPEAT
  flag = 0
  INPUT number
  IF number > 500 THEN flag = 1
  IF number < -500 THEN flag = 1
  IF flag <> 1 THEN
     IF number = 0 THEN zero_count = zero_count
                                            +1
     IF number < 0 THEN neg_count = neg_count
                                            +1
     IF number > 0 THEN pos_count = pos_count
                                            +1
  ELSE
  ENDIF
UNTIL number = -999
PRINT pos_count
PRINT neg_count
PRINT zero_count
```

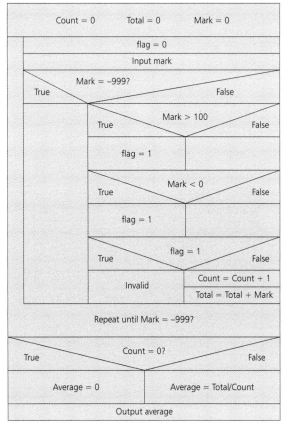

Figure for question 2(c)

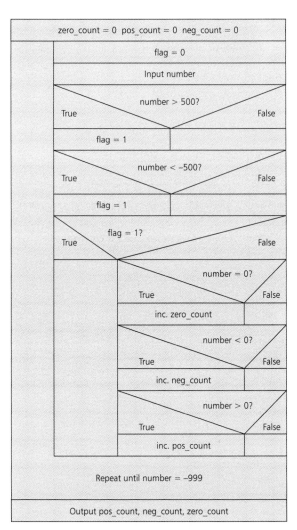

Figure for question 2(d)

4. (e)
```
REPEAT
    INPUT operator$
    IF operator$ <> "$" THEN
      INPUT x
      INPUT y
      CASE operator$ OF
      WHEN "+"
                answer = x + y
      WHEN "−"
      answer = x − y
      WHEN "/"
      answer = x/y
      WHEN "*"
      answer = x * y
      OTHERWISE
                answer = −99999999
      PRINT"Error"
      ENDCASE
      PRINT answer
    ELSE
    ENDIF
    UNTIL operator$ = "$"
```

5. Top down for splitting up the problems into sub-sections ready for coding, bottom up for testing each part before its use with the next stage in the hierarchy of the problem.

6. Objects can be built up independently, then used in a similar way to 'Lego bricks' to build up a larger module. Due to the nature of the objects unforeseen unintentional interaction between the many different modules is unlikely if programmers obey all the appropriate rules.

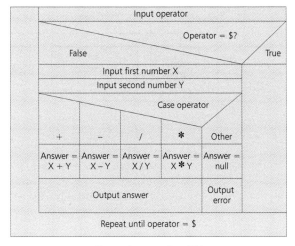

Figure for question 2(e)

Answers to exercise 14.2

1. JSP is particularly suited to structured programming because good structured code production is a natural consequence of following the JSP diagram.

2. Sequence, selection and iteration making use of JSP are shown in the following three diagrams.

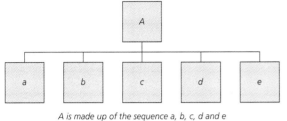

A is made up of the sequence a, b, c, d and e
SEQUENCE STRUCTURE

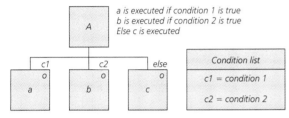

SELECTION STRUCTURE

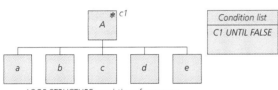

LOOP STRUCTURE consisting of sequence
a, b, c, d and e repeated until condition c1 is FALSE

3. One possible JSP structure is shown in the diagram below.

4. Relationships between elements of a system may be more easily emphasised.

5. The data-flow diagram for your teacher-marked assignments could be as overleaf.

6. In general, problems where cycling through set sequences is necessary. Typical problems involve defining states of any electronic hardware, but more importantly, from a software-analysis point of view, different problems might include the analysis of possible moves in a game, defining rules for computer languages and expressing control-system algorithms (i.e. what can and can't be done when the system is in a particular state.) See diagram overleaf.

7. Decision table for the delivery charges is as follows.

Conditions	1	2	3	4
Price > = £1,000	Y	N	Y	N
Delivery > 100 miles	Y	Y	N	N
Actions				
Free delivery			X	
5% delivery charge	X			X
10% delivery charge		X		

8. A chart showing horizontal bars in which project activity is plotted against weeks, days or months etc. according to the overall schedule of the project. They give an instant visual indication as to the nature of the schedule, but aren't very versatile if situations change rapidly on a day-to-day basis.

9. Time-critical management problems involving 'latest start' and 'earliest finishing times' for whole or parts of projects. An example could be undertaking construction work on a building. Materials need to be delivered such as glass for the windows, tiles for the roof, bricks for the walls and paint for

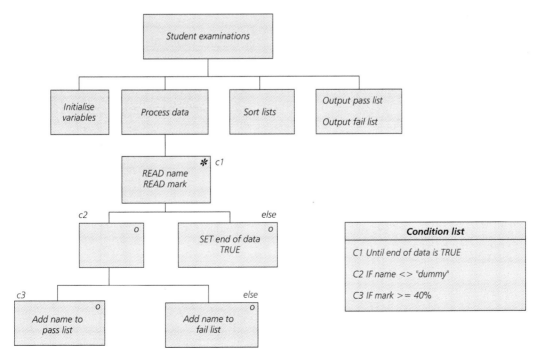

Figure for question 3

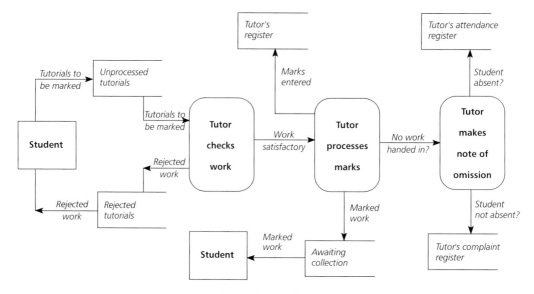

Figure for question 5

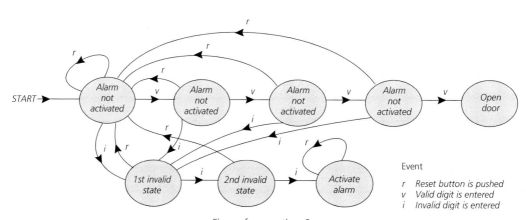

Figure for question 6

the decorations etc. All these resources have to be scheduled and a hold up in any one resource such as bricks for the walls will obviously delay the roof being started etc. The critical path through the project is the path which effectively dictates the completion time, any critical activity within this path may have extra resources allocated to it to cut completion time if this is thought to be important.

Chapter 15 student activities
FORTRAN 90 Programs

(1) Calculation of the average

```
PROGRAM Average
REAL::x,total=0.0
INTEGER::number=0
WRITE(*,*) "Please type in positive numbers
                        terminating with -999"
DO
  READ(*,*) x
  IF(number= - 999) EXIT
     total = total + x
     number = number + 1
END DO
ave = total/number
WRITE(*,*) "The average is ,ave
END PROGRAM Average
```

(2) Matrix multiplication

Sum being carried out is

$$
\begin{array}{ccccc}
x & * & y & = & z \\
\begin{vmatrix} 1 & 2 & 3 \\ 4 & 5 & 6 \\ 7 & 8 & 9 \end{vmatrix} & * & \begin{vmatrix} 9 & 8 & 7 \\ 6 & 5 & 4 \\ 3 & 2 & 1 \end{vmatrix} & = & \begin{vmatrix} 30 & 24 & 18 \\ 84 & 69 & 54 \\ 138 & 114 & 90 \end{vmatrix}
\end{array}
$$

```
PROGRAM MATRIX
REAL, DIMENSION(3,3)::x,y,z
x=RESHAPE( SOURCE=(/1,2,3,4,5,6,7,8,9/),
                                  SHAPE=(/3,3/)
y=RESHAPE( SOURCE=(/9,8,7,6,5,4,3,2,1/),
                                  SHAPE=(/3,3/)
z = MATMUL(MATRIX_x,MATRIX_y)
DO count = 1,3
  WRITE(*,*) z(1,count),(2,count),(3,count)
END DO
END PROGRAM MATRIX
```

Chapter 15 student activities
COBOL 97 Programs

(1) VAT at 17.5%

```
IDENTIFICATION DIVISION.
PROGRAM - ID. VAT - CALCULATION
```

```
DATA DIVISION.
   WORKING STORAGE SECTION.
77 PRICE                 PIC 999V99.
77 INCLUSIVE – PRICE     PIC 9999V99.
PROCEDURE DIVISION.
VAT – CALCULATION.
ACCEPT PRICE.
MULTIPLY PRICE BY VAT GIVING INCLUSIVE-PRICE.
DISPLAY "Without VAT " PRICE "With VAT" INCLUSIVE-
                                            PRICE.
STOP RUN.
```

(2) Compound interest program.

The following program makes use of the standard compound interest formula as follows

Final capital = (Initial amount of money) × ((1 + Interest Rate))$^{\text{Number of Years}}$

```
IDENTIFICATION DIVISION.
PROGRAM-ID. COMPOUND-INTEREST.
DATA DIVISION.
WORKING STORAGE SECTION.
77 INITIAL-AMOUNT     PIC 9999V99.
77 INTEREST-RATE      PIC 99V99.
77 NUMBER-OF-YEARS    PIC 99.
77 CAPITAL            PIC 99999.99.
PROCEDURE DIVISION.
COMPOUND-INTEREST-CALCULATION.
DISPLAY "Please type in the initial amount of money
                                            ".
ACCEPT INITIAL-AMOUNT.
DISPLAY "Please type in the rate of interest".
ACCEPT INTEREST-RATE.
DISPLAY "Please type in the number of years".
ACCEPT NUMBER-OF-YEARS.
COMPUTE CAPITAL = INITIAL-AMOUNT*(1 + INTEREST-
                      RATE/100)**NUMBER-OF-YEARS.
DISPLAY "At the end of your term you will have"
                                        CAPITAL.
STOP RUN.
```

Chapter 15 student activities
Pascal programs

(1) Insertion sort

```
PROGRAM insert_sort(input,output);
VAR current_position, pointer_position, maximum,
                        temp, count :INTEGER;
VAR n : ARRAY[0..20] of INTEGER;
BEGIN
  maximum :=20;
  FOR count :=1 TO maximum DO
    BEGIN
      WRITELN('Please type in number');
      READLN(n[count]);
    END;
  WRITELN('Original list is');
  FOR count :=1 TO maximum DO
    BEGIN
      WRITELN(n[count]);
    END;
  current_position :=1;
  REPEAT
    current_position := current_position + 1;
    pointer_position :=1;
    WHILE pointer_position <= current_position DO
      BEGIN
        IF n[pointer_position] >
  n[current_position] THEN
            BEGIN
              temp := n[current_position];
              FOR count:= current_position DOWNTO
                        pointer_position + 1 DO
```

```
          BEGIN
            n[count] := n[count  – 1]
          END;
        END;
        pointer_position := pointer_position +
                                              1
      END;
  UNTIL current_position = maximum;
  WRITELN('Sorted list');
  FOR count := 1 TO maximum DO
    BEGIN
      WRITELN(n[count])
    END;
END.
```

(2) Factorials based on recursion

```
PROGRAM factorial(input,output);
VAR n, answer, actual_time, start_time, stop_time :
                                        INTEGER;
  FUNCTION factorial(n: INTEGER) : INTEGER;
    BEGIN
      IF n <=1 THEN
        BEGIN
          factorial :=1
        END
      ELSE
        BEGIN
          factorial := n*factorial(n – 1)
        END
  END;
  BEGIN
    WRITELN('Please type in a number');
    READLN(n);
    start_time := time;
    answer := factorial(n);
    stop_time := time;
    actual_time := stop_time – start_time;
    WRITELN(answer);
    WRITELN('It took just',
    actual_time,'centiseconds');
  END.
```

Note: On fast computers the above routine might take less than a few msec for the computer to evaluate the highest possible factorial before arithmetic overflow occurs.

Chapter 15 student activities
BASIC programs

(1) The following makes use of BBC BASIC .

```
INPUT"Please type in a sentence using lower-case
                        letters";sentence$
consonants = 0:vowels = 0:words = 1
FOR count = 1 TO LEN(sentence$)
  Flag = FALSE
  Letter$ = MID$(sentence$,count,1)
  CASE Letter$ OF
    WHEN "a","e","i","o","u" : vowels = vowels +
                            1:Flag = TRUE
  ENDCASE
  IF (Flag = FALSE) AND Letter$<>" " THEN
  consonants = consonants + 1
  IF Letter$ = " " THEN words = words + 1
NEXT count
PRINT"There are ";vowels;" vowels"
PRINT"There are ";consonants;" consonants"
PRINT"The are ";words;" words"
```

(2) The following makes use of BBC BASIC .

```
MODE 116:REM Very high resolution mode
GCOL 0,1
side = 80:x_offset =50:y_offset = 50
x = −1*(side + x_offset):y= −1*(side +y_offset)
FOR vertical_loop = 1 TO 17
  y = y + side + y_offset
  x = −1*(side + y_offset)
  FOR horizontal_loop = 1 TO 22
    x = x + side + x_offset
    RECTANGLE FILL x,y,side,side
  NEXT horizontal_loop
NEXT vertical_loop
```

Chapter 15 student activities C++ Programs

(1) The following is written using Microsoft's C++ compiler.

```
//Square Root evaluation program making use of a
                              library function
#include <iostream.h>
#include <math.h>
void main()
{
double number, root;
cout << "Please type in a number";
cin >> number;
root = sqrt(number);
cout >> "The square root of your number is"
     << root << endl;
}
```

(2) The following is written using Microsoft's C++ compiler.

```
//Generate a given number of specified characters
                          on a single line
#include <iostream.h>
void repeatchar(char, int);//Declare function
    repeatchar
    void main()
    {
    char inputchar:
    int inputnum;
    cout << "Please enter character to be repeated";
    cin >> inputchar;
    cout << "How many times to repeat?";
    cin >> inputnum;
    repeatchar(inputchar,inputnum);          //Call
                              function repeatchar
    }
    void repeatchar(char chin, int numin);   //Define
                              function repeatchar
    for(int x=0; x<numin; x++);
      cout << chin;
    cout << endl;
    }
```

Answers to exercise 15.1

1. Each language has particular strengths and weaknesses because it's not yet possible or efficient to design a language which copes with all requirements. Special languages such as COBOL are ideal for business-type data processing, FORTRAN for mathematical and scientific work, and C++ for application and systems development etc.

2. Historically FORTRAN has been taught on scientific and engineering degree courses – therefore a huge range of experience at this level has been built up. A massive library of pre-written functions exists – if any other language is used then this vast amount of effort would need to be re-coded.

3. True parallel processing means having the hardware to do more than one thing at the same time – usually by using multiple processors. Without appropriate hardware support concurrent algorithms would not run on some machines – until all machines with compilers can support parallel processing there would be an incompatibility problem and the code may not run on single-processor machines.

4. C++ naturally splits up programs into parts, which are protected from influencing other parts – this is ideal for parallel processing operations.

5. BBC BASIC Coin-Tossing program

```
FOR toss = 1 TO 100
  coin_1 = RND(2)
  coin_2 = RND(2)
  IF coin_1 = 1 AND coin_2 = 1 THEN TT = TT + 1
  IF coin_1 = 1 AND coin_2 = 2 THEN TH = TH + 1
  IF coin_1 = 2 AND coin_2 = 1 THEN HT = HT + 1
  IF coin_1 = 2 AND coin_2 = 2 THEN HH = HH + 1
NEXT toss
Combined = TH + HT
PRINT"There were ";TT;"pairs of tails"
PRINT"There were ";Combined;"combined pairs"
PRINT"There were ";HH;"pairs of heads"
```

6. BBC BASIC – very simple spelling checker. The ten dummy words are the numbers one to ten in lower case only. If you have time, expand the ideas to deal with upper and lower case, and accept strings of text. Perhaps you can find a better checking method too!

```
REM Spell checker
DIM word$(10)
REM Read dictionary
FOR count = 1 TO 10
  READ word$(count)
NEXT count
DATA one,two,three,four,five,six,seven,eight,
                                    nine,ten
FOR count = 1 TO 10
  PRINT word$(count)
NEXT count
REM User input
INPUT"Word to be checked";check$
Flag = FALSE
FOR count = 1 TO 10
  IF check$ = word$(count) THEN Flag = TRUE
NEXT count
IF Flag = TRUE THEN PRINT "Correct" ELSE PRINT
                                    "Incorrect"
```

7. The following FORTRAN program has very rudimentary output – it can be considerably improved. You could also program the system to generate a distance-time graph – have a go if you have the time and appropriate facilities on your computer system.

```
PROGRAM Missile
REAL::U,time,S
U = 3
time = 0
WRITE(*.*)"Time     Distance"
Loop: DO WHILE S>0
         time = time + 0.1
         S = U*time − (1*9.81/2)*time**2+10
         WRITE(*,*) time, S
       END DO Loop
END PROGRAM Missile
```

8. Pascal Fibbonacci numbers

```
PROGRAM Fibbonacci(input,output);
VAR sum, number, next, current, count :INTEGER;
BEGIN
  number:= 0;
```

```
  next:= 1;
  sum := 0;
  FOR count :=1 TO 25 DO
    BEGIN
      WRITELN(number);
      sum := sum + number;
      current := number + next;
      number := next;
      next := current;
    END;
END.
```

9. Pascal date conversion – only a simple layout and simple validation techniques have been used.

```
PROGRAM Date_conversion(input,output);
VAR day, month, year : INTEGER;
BEGIN
  WRITELN('Please type in the date in the form dd,
                                      mm, yyyy');
  READLN(day,month,year);
  IF (day < 0) OR (day > 31) THEN WRITELN('Invalid
                                           date')
    ELSE WRITE(day,' ');
  IF (month <0) OR (month > 12) THEN
                      WRITELN('Invalid date');
  CASE month OF
    1: WRITE('January');
    2: WRITE('February');
    3: WRITE('March');
    4: WRITE('April');
    5: WRITE('May');
    6: WRITE('June');
    7: WRITE('July');
    8: WRITE('August');
    9: WRITE('September');
   10: WRITE('October');
   11: WRITE('November');
   12: WRITE('December');
  END;
  IF (year < 0) THEN WRITELN('Invalid date')
      ELSE WRITE(year);
END.
```

10. This question is dependent on the chosen language.

Answers to exercise 16.1

1. A set of rules, which have proved to be very useful in making sure that development of a project is steered through to a successful conclusion. As modern software and techniques have become available, other strategies such as prototyping and altering of the original spec. are now generally acceptable. (See page 341.)

2. Customers often don't know what they want as they are not computer specialists. Prototyping helps to point the way or to develop systems in more heuristic ways.

3. Program flowcharts are too detailed – use systems flowcharts for describing more-complex systems.

4. (a) Below
   (b) Overleaf
   (c) Overleaf
   (d) Overleaf

5. (a) List is not exhaustive – some general pointers are shown.
   1. More efficient 'patient care' and better statistics about the operation of the surgery.
   2. Less waiting time than with a manual system.
   3. Automatic production of prescriptions.
   4. Better management of medical records.
   5. Better accounting in terms of drug purchase and distribution.

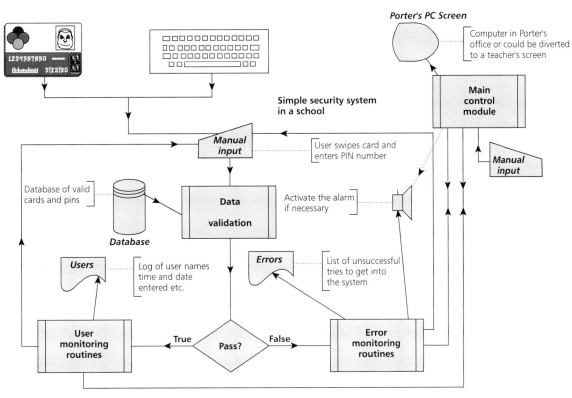

Figure for question 4(a)

Electronic registration system

Figure for question 4(b)

6. Better information dissemination and communication between doctors.

7. etc. etc.

(b) List is not exhaustive – some general pointers are shown.

1. Types of software available.
2. Key word search such as DTP, CAD or PERT etc.
3. Location of appropriate manuals.
4. Where to get expert help.
5. Hardware and OS platform for software.
6. Any extra special peripherals needed such as scanners or graphics tablets etc.
7. etc. etc.

(c) List is not exhaustive – some general pointers are shown.

1. Achieve a reduction in running costs compared to manual operation of the system.
2. Determine most efficient zone in terms of usage – e.g. daytime and evening use, for example.
3. Determine the best places for automatic monitoring of temperature.
4. Automatic shutdown in the event of a system or power failure.
5. Manual override to alter setting if necessary.

6. Summer and winter timetables – special timetables for weekends etc.

7. etc. etc.

(d) List is not exhaustive – some general pointers are shown.

1. Achieve greater efficiency in terms of information distribution to pupils and staff.
2. Allow for instant emergency distribution of notices.
3. Allow automatic cycling through screens.
4. Allow some degree of user choice of screen from each display terminal.
5. Only staff with appropriate authority should alter text and pictures.
6. Multiple levels of user gaining access to a hierarchy of information.
7. etc. etc.

6. (a) List is not exhaustive – some general pointers are shown.

1. Awkward transition from the manual to the automatic system.
2. Staff need to be trained on how to use the system.
3. What happens in the event of a power cut?
4. Patients might need to be reassured about privacy of information. See Data Protection Act.

Theatre booking office

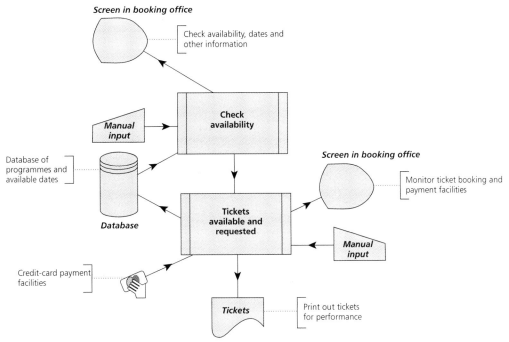

Figure for question 16(c)

Local newsagent shop (delivery processing)

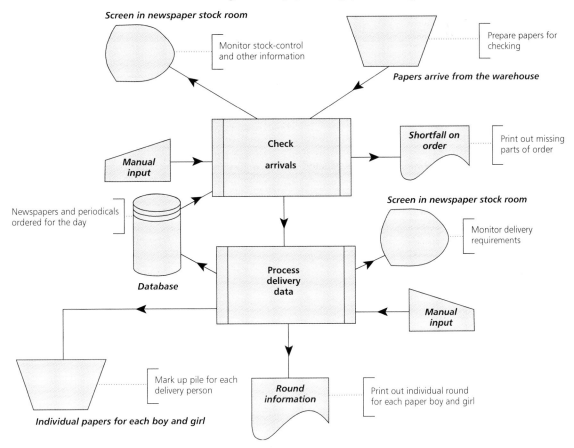

Figure for question 4(d)

5. How is the information in the computer transferred to another surgery when a patient moves?

6. etc. etc.

(b) List is not exhaustive – not so many here as the system is less critical.

1. Database needs to be available on all software platforms!

2. Staff and pupil training will be needed to make full use of the system.

3. etc. etc.

(c) List is not exhaustive – some general pointers are shown.

1. Staff training needed – system will be more complex to use than manual system.

2. Change over to automatic system will have to be done in the summer.

3. Extensive trials will be needed to make sure it operates effectively and safely.

4. etc. etc.

(d) List is not exhaustive – some general pointers are shown.

1. Staff training – people will have to get used to finding a computer to distribute a notice.

2. Cycling through the system on screen might be annoying if too many pages are used.

3. Pupils might find it a novelty to keep changing the screen while others are looking at it.

4. etc. etc.

7. (a) List is not exhaustive – some general pointers are shown.

1. Data protection act must be observed – build this into system.

2. Levels of password protection will be needed if info. is to be viewed by different staff.

3. Possible to encrypt sensitive data.

(b) List is not exhaustive – some general pointers are shown.

1. No problems in security here – database will probably be read-only.

(c) List is not exhaustive – some general pointers are shown.

1. Ensure that no unauthorised person has access to the programmable part of the system.

2. Ensure that appropriate personnel may activate manual override if appropriate.

(d) List is not exhaustive – some general pointers are shown.

1. Password protection to make sure staff have access only to their particular parts of the system.

2. Make sure power and monitors etc. can't be switched off at notice board end.

8. (a) Many purpose-built systems exist – these need investigation and would probably be more cost effective than writing your own software.

(b) Use database package – not much point re-inventing the wheel for a standard application.

(c) Probably need to write customised software – however, market should be investigated.

(d) Probably best to use a multi-media package, but if teletext type system is required then a teletext editor and some sort of carousel-type communications package would be useful.

9. (a) Check on patients appointments and booking system – after extensive stand-alone testing, run in parallel with existing manual system until you are satisfied that the manual system is no longer needed.

(b) Check that many of the key-word searches find the expected items of software. Check that unusual input does not crash the system. Check validation routines when inputting standard queries.

(c) Check that the software recovers from a power failure by removing the power from the system – check that the battery back-up system has kept real time, and that the boot system has restarted properly.

(d) Check that carousel system continues to function for several cycles. Check that any page being displayed can be interrupted by appropriate controls at the monitors – check security by attempting to break into files.

10. Gantt charts and PERT charts to keep project on schedule – CASE aids such modelling and simulation, debuggers and trace routines to help check program modules etc.

Answers to exercise 17.1

1. Verification checks to see if data is the same by reference to an alternative, e.g. 'Stephen' has not be entered as 'Steven'. Validation checks to see if it's sensible, e.g. a person is not 784 years old etc. Integrity means that the data is correct.

2. Any bug after the modules have been tested is likely to be due to an interaction between modules.

3. Single stepping through a program, lists of variables, break points inserted at salient points in the program etc.

4. (a) Choose dates like 31/2 etc. See page 310 for algorithm.

(b) Limit to 2 decimal places, round up, and limit to acceptable range for the application, e.g. private electricity bill unlikely to be £1,000,000.

(c) Limit to sensible maxima given the application, e.g. secondary school pupils between 11 and 20.

(d) Use current registration system – see page 622 for typical examples.

5. (a) Iron out any bugs which have become apparent. Make sure the training manuals are suitable. Make any modifications to methods in the light of six-month experience.

(b) Iron out any minor bugs that might still be left. See if the system needs any major overhaul to meet the changing needs of the business.

6. (a) How to start up the system. Software and hardware needed. How to use the help files, how to get technical support. How to get out of common simple errors.

(b) More technical aspects of the system applicable to more advanced users. How to set up the system for optimum use. How to modify parts of the system to do different things. How to recover from disasters etc.

7. Detailed definitions of the technical solution to the problem. Systems analysis, program development and testing. Detailed comments to accompany the program code. Details of variables and procedures used etc.

8. CASE looks at the project as a whole including development in terms of personnel, time, and other resources. It integrates the software environment into a system similar in principle to the engineering CAD/CAM environment, which added much more onto technical drawing.

9. Black-box testing splits up the software into modules each having one or more input and one output. A table is drawn up to show how variables are tested under appropriate conditions.
White-box testing is carried out by constructing a directed graph for the module under test. The unique paths are identified from the graph, and black-box testing is applied to each path.

Answers to exercise 18.1

1. Using BBC BASIC

```
REM Estimation of root 5
N = 5
xn=2
WHILE ABS((xn*xn) − 5)>0.000005
  xn=0.5*(xn + 5/xn)
  PRINT xn
ENDWHILE
PRINT xn
```

2. From the following diagram you can see that

$$\frac{\pi r^2}{2r \times 2r} = \frac{\textit{Number of points within circle}}{\textit{Total number of points}}$$

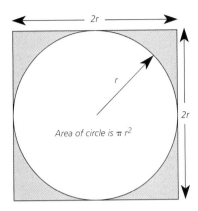

Area of circle is πr^2

Therefore, $\pi = 4\times$(Number of points within circle)/Total number of points. BBC BASIC program to evaluate Pi is as follows.

```
REM Generate approximation for Pi
REM Assume square with a side of 1
INPUT "How many random numbers";number
FOR count = 1 TO number
   x = RND(1):y=RND(1)
   IF SQR(x^2+y^2)<1 THEN hit = hit +1
NEXT count
Pi=4*hit/number
PRINT Pi
```

3. Iteration is a simple idea, but recursion usually leads to elegant and more efficient solutions. Recursion may place heavy demands on storage as each call to a recursive procedure usually involves placing data on a stack.

4. BBC BASIC implementation or recursive function.

```
REM Count down from integer n
INPUT "Please type in an integer";n
PRINT "All integers preceding this number"
PROCcountdown(n)
END
DEF PROCcountdown(n)
   IF n > 0 THEN
      PRINT n;
      PROCcountdown(n - 1)
   ENDIF
ENDPROC
```

5. BBC BASIC implementation of recursive function.

```
REM Summing all positive integers <= n
INPUT "Please type in an integer";n
PRINT "The sum of all positive integers up to and
                        including this number are";
PROCsum(n)
PRINT sum
END
DEF PROCsum(n)
   IF n > 0 THEN
      sum = sum + n
      PROCsum(n - 1)
   ENDIF
ENDPROC
```

6. BBC BASIC implementation of recursive algorithm.

```
REM Recursive reverse string
INPUT "Please type in a string";test$
PROCreverse(test$)
END
DEF PROCreverse(test$)
   IF LEN(test$) > 0 THEN
      PRINT RIGHT$(test$);
      PROCreverse(LEFT$(test$))
   ENDIF
ENDPROC
```

7. BBC BASIC implementation of chip-shop simulation.

```
PROCinitialise
FOR minute = 1 TO 120
 PROCinitialise
 PROCcust_arrive
 PROCcust_serve
 PROCanalyse
NEXT minute
END
DEF PROCinitialise
   customers = 0
ENDPROC
DEF PROCcust_arrive
   Arrive = RND(1)
   IF Arrive < 0.2 THEN new_customers = 0
   IF (Arrive >= 0.20) AND (Arrive < 0.45) THEN
                             new_customers = 1
   IF (Arrive >= 0.45) AND (Arrive < 0.70) THEN
                             new_customers = 2
   IF (Arrive >= 0.70) AND (Arrive < 0.85) THEN
                             new_customers = 3
   IF (Arrive >= 0.85) AND (Arrive < 0.95) THEN
                             new_customers = 4
   IF Arrive >=0.95 THEN new_customers = 5
ENDPROC
DEF PROCcust_serve
   Serve = RND(1)
   IF Serve < 0.35 THEN customers_served = 1
   IF (Serve >= 0.35) AND (Serve < 0.60) THEN
                         customers_served = 2
   IF (Serve >= 0.60) AND (Serve < 0.80) THEN
                         customers_served = 3
   IF (Serve >= 0.80) AND (Serve < 0.95) THEN
                         customers_served = 4
   IF Serve > 0.95 THEN customers = 5
ENDPROC
DEF PROCanalyse
   customers = customers + new_customers
   PRINT"In minute number ";minute;"
      ";new_customers;" have arrived"
   IF customers - customers_served > 0 THEN
      customers = customers - customers_served
   PRINT"At the end of minute number ";minute;"
      There are "; customers;" waiting"
ENDPROC
```

After running the above analysis several times, it is very rare indeed to get 6 or more customers waiting. Therefore, Barry Ramsden does appear to have enough staff.

8. Different mathematical relationships with long sequences can be used to generate pseudo-random numbers. There is no known algorithmic method to generate truly random numbers. See page 395.

Answers to exercise 19.1

1. To make processing more efficient e.g. external merge sort. See page 541.

2. (a) See page 402.

(b) See page 403. (c) No answer needed.

3. (a) See page 402. (b) See page 404. (c) See page 405. (d) See page 408.

4.

7, 3, 9, 1. (7 and 3 compared and swapped.)
3, 7, 9, 1. (7 and 9 compared no swap.)
3, 7, 9, 1. (9 and 1 compared and swapped.)
3, 7, 1, 9. (Swaps were necessary, start again.)
3, 7, 1, 9. (3 and 7 compared no swap.)
3, 7, 1, 9. (7 and 1 compared and swapped.)
3, 1, 7, 9. (7 and 9 compared no swap.)
3, 1, 7, 9. (Swap necessary, start again.)
3, 1, 7, 9. (3 and 1 compared and swapped.)
1, 3, 7, 9. (3 and 7 compared no swap.)
1, 3, 7, 9. (7 and 9 compared no swap.)
1, 3, 7, 9. (Swap necessary, start again.)
1, 3, 7, 9. (1 and 3 compared no swap.)
1, 3, 7, 9. (3 and 7 compared no swap.)
1, 3, 7, 9. (7 and 9 compared no swap.)
1, 3, 7, 9. (No swaps necessary. List is in order.)

5. Data that covers the entire range and multiple values.

6. Split files up into smaller parts. Sort the smaller parts and store on disk. Then do merge sort. See page 541.

7. Depends on your chosen sort of algorithm.

Answers to exercise 19.2

1. (a) See the following tree:

```
                                              1000
1st search                          500     500
2nd search                       250     250
3rd search                   125     125
4th search               63     62
5th search           31     32
6th search         15    16
7th search       7     8
8th search     3     4
9th search 1     2   N.B. Only part of subtree shown
Final sch.1   1
```

2. See page 419.

Answers to exercise 20.1

1. (a) The chip at the heart of a micro system that executes the m/c code instructions. (See pages 424 and 425.)

(b) M/c instructions are fetched from memory, decoded and then executed (carried out) (see page 424).

(c) The Central Processing Unit. (Often the same as the microprocessor in a small micro.)

(d) The Arithmetic Logic Unit. That part of the CPU which carries out arithmetical and logic operations.

(e) A register inside the CPU that keeps track of which instruction is currently being executed.

(f) An electronic circuit that acts as a temporary store for binary data.

(g) A parallel group of wires along which binary data can be sent. (See pages 426 and 242.)

(h) The main place inside the computer in which binary data is temporarily stored. (See pages 425 and 240.)

2. To generate timing signals and to instruct the microprocessor to get on with the next part of the cycle. The output from the clock is an electronic periodic signal consisting of a train of pulses. (See page 425.)

3. Stored as binary data but often accessed as hex data. (See pages 425 and 597.)

4. Address bus – to generate memory and other device addresses. Data bus to carry the data from one part of the computer to another. Control bus to generate control signals such as read/write etc. (See page 240.)

5. Each device is mapped onto the system making use of a unique address – data can be shared using the same data bus – in this way data can be sent to or got from different devices on the system.

6. A memory map is needed so that everybody can agree as to where in memory programs can be run, or where in memory special routines can live safely without being inadvertently disrupted. (See pages 426 and 476.)

7. (a) Acts as the electronic control inside the CPU which routes and controls movements of data.

(b) A register for the Accumulation (temporary storage) of results. (See page 428.)

(c) A register to store the contents of the memory location which was last accessed. (See page 429.)

(d) The Current Instruction Register holds the op code for the current instruction. (See page 429.)

(e) The bus or busses actually inside the microprocessor chip itself. They are the highways inside the chip.

(f) A register, which is used to hold the current address of the memory location currently being accessed.

8. A special code is chosen by the microprocessor manufacturers, which can be decoded by the microprocessor so that appropriate action is taken. These codes are called operation (op) codes.

9. It does not! It's up to the programmer to get the program arranged and interpreted correctly.

10. Assume numbers are in memory locations 100 to 104 inclusive. Assume answer to be put into loc. 105.

The figure at the bottom of the page shows the five original numbers before execution of program – zeros have been assumed in loc. 105. Program shown is typical, result is shown on R.H.S. of the diagram.

A refers to Accumulator, therefore LOAD,A (100) means load the Acc with the contents of memory location 100. ADD,A (101) means add to the Acc, the contents of memory location

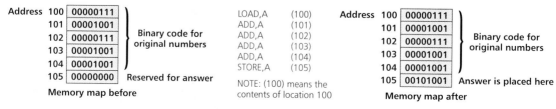

Typical assembly-language mnemonics

Memory map before — Address 100: 00000111, 101: 00001001, 102: 00000111, 103: 00001001, 104: 00001001 (Binary code for original numbers), 105: 00000000 (Reserved for answer)

LOAD,A (100), ADD,A (101), ADD,A (102), ADD,A (103), ADD,A (104), STORE,A (105)

NOTE: (100) means the contents of location 100

Memory map after — Address 100: 00000111, 101: 00001001, 102: 00000111, 103: 00001001, 104: 00001001 (Binary code for original numbers), 105: 00101001 (Answer is placed here)

Figure for question 10

101, and place the result into the Acc. Finally, STORE,A puts the contents of the Acc into memory location 105.

Answers to exercise 20.2

1. Parallel processing is the ability to do more than one thing simultaneously. It is not the same as multitasking (see page 485), and needs special hardware consisting of either a special CPU, or more than one CPU. If software is written to take advantage of parallel processing then a significant increase in speed is possible. (See page 435.)

2. Pipelining can fetch, decode and execute different instructions at the same time. (See page 435.)

3. Some results needed for future processing may not be ready yet. Special software, which splits up the processes into separate tasks, is necessary. (See page 437.)

4. It is the maximum rate at which data can be transferred along the bus measured in bits/sec. Physical limitations of the bus construction and electronics determine the maximum rate. (See page 437 and 438.)

5. Fast cache memory acts as an interface to the faster processors. (See page 436.)

6. Increase the width or upgrade the electronics and increase the clock rate.

7. Independent parts of the problem can be passed over to different processors. If problem is not coded in this way one or more of the processors could be idle for significant periods of time. (See page 437.)

8. (a) Holds number of m/c code instructions in memory to cut down on fetch–execute times.
   (b) Holds chunks of data in this area of cache to save fetch–execute times.
   (c) Wide data bus for higher bandwidth.
   (d) Pipeline architecture can be operating on different instructions simultaneously.
   (e) Hardware to speed up the maths. (Saves accessing software routines in memory.)
   (f) Fast clock rate makes processor work extremely fast.
   (g) A benchmark indicating that 1000 million instructions can be processed each second.

Answers to exercise 21.1

1. M/c is the binary or hex code, assembly language is the mnemonics. (See page 445.)

2. The m/c code is different for each type of machine. It's possible if emulation is used. (Software to make a program appear to be running on the target machine.)

3. These aids to the memory make life very much easier and less tedious for the programmer. The four parts of the instruction are LABEL OPCODE OPERAND and COMMENT. (See page 447.)

4. Op code is the mnemonic representing the operation like ADD or SUB etc. The operand is the data to be operated on, and a comment is for documentation purposes.

5. Different modes of addressing allow programmers to code different data structures more effectively, e.g. the implementation of an array. (See pages 447, 448 and 449.)

6. Put *very* simply, general-purpose registers allow the programmer to have more freedom; however, specific registers are helpful for implementation of many standard operations. (See page 445.)

7. A flag register is used to flag (i.e. bring to the attention of the programmer) certain conditions such as arithmetic overflow and underflow, carry set, or the fact that an interrupt has occurred. (See pages 456 and 489.)

8. Using 80x86 Assembler: MOV   DL,05H
                              ADD   DL,0AH

The method used here is called immediate addition because the constant numbers 5 and 10 (in hex in the above program) appear immediately after the register. 5 is MOVed into the DL register and 10 is ADDed to it so that the result is held in the DL register. Flags indicate if the result is too big – positive or negative etc.

9. Suppose original byte is 10101011. Use 10101011 AND 11100011 + 000111000. Use mask 111000111 to reset the middle digits so that 00011100 can be added without altering other digits – try it and see!

10. Arithmetic shift preserves sign, logical shifts don't (see page 452).

Original number	1 1 1 1 0 0 0 0 1 1 1 1 0 0 0 0
(a) LSL 3	1 0 0 0 0 1 1 1 1 0 0 0 0 0 0 0
(b) ASL 3	1 0 0 0 0 1 1 1 1 0 0 0 0 0 0 0
(c) LSR 3	0 0 0 1 1 1 1 0 0 0 0 1 1 1 1 0
(d) ASR 3	1 0 0 1 1 1 1 0 0 0 0 1 1 1 1 0

11. Carried out in bitwise mode, e.g. 11 AND 10 = 10, and 11 OR 10 = 11 etc. (See pages 451 and 452.)

12. Using 80x86,
    An unconditional jump is   JMP NEXT
    Jump to label next unconditionally
    A conditional jumps is   JNO NEXT
    Jump to label next if NO overflow

13. It is used to point to an area of memory called a stack. Helps the programmer to implement a stack data structure. (See pages 455 and 501.)

14. An assembler is software which converts assembly language mnemonics into m/c code. It has many advantages over hand assembly or writing directly in m/c code. (See page 459.)

15. Different types of assembler support different facilities, e.g. a cross assembler produces object code for a different target m/c etc. Other types – macro assemblers and meta assemblers etc. (See page 459.)

16. Loads the assembled program into memory and links to libraries etc. (See page 459.)

17. Macro assembler supports macros (generation of code from a single instruction) (see page 459). Library routines are code, which can be called up by name (often written by others) and inserted into your programs.

18. Printing out the contents of registers to compare with manually-calculated values.

19. You can use pre-written operating-system routines to perform common but useful tasks like 'get a character from the keyboard' or 'save a block of data to disk', for example.

20. This answer depends on your particular assembler.

Answers to exercise 22.1

1. More powerful chips have led to user-friendly operating systems based on the WIMP environment.

2. To run different software packages at apparently the same time. Useful for transfer of data between CAD and DTP, for example.

3. Enables different software platforms to be run on the same micro. Linux and Windows 2000 are examples.

4. OS written using an OOP language such as C++. Large systems can be developed with more chance of working properly.

5. A Basic Input-Output System, that part of the operating system, which controls Input and Output and tests the hardware on startup etc.

6. Boot files are used to load other parts of the operating system or customise the computer. OS is often not committed to ROM because of frequent updates and bug fixes etc.

7. See the FAT explanation on page 474.

8. It maps out the function of all the blocks of memory, e.g. graphics, I/O etc.

9. A peripheral device may request some processor time to perform a special function. This is usually achieved by means of an interrupt. See page 447 and page 489.

10. Cache memory is usually 'fast SRAM'; it can be used in preference to ordinary DRAM for most-frequently-needed parts of the current program.

11. Long sequences of esoteric commands do not have to be remembered, you can point at an icon instead.

12. Using a special boot file created by the user to load certain programs and utilities etc. It saves the user having to manually go through a large number of operations to set the machine up to individual spec.

13. An error such as disk full, for example, can be detected by the part of the operating system which determines if there is sufficient space to save the data. If not, an error message is produced.

14. A network interface card and network operating system.

15. Most software is written for these particular platforms – it gives a degree of standardisation, which helps to share information. RISC PC, PowerPC and PowerMac have all attempted to change this mould but Linux is succeeding.

16. Making sure users do not have access to other people's work.

17. The operating system is transparent because it's often quite simple to use.

18. Incompatible physical and logical data formats. The network could provide a common communication protocol and ASCII data can be transferred via the network interface.

19. There is no method to guarantee correctness of programs because of the enormous number of different paths through the system. Send patches, which can be added on to the existing operating system.

20. Virtual-reality OS, increase in the use of Java, International information superhighway as a delivery mechanism, speech input and output will be commonplace, possibly thought control in the far future – your guess is as good as mine!

Answers to exercise 23.1

1. Without an OS the computer would be far too complex and tedious to use. The OS carries out most of the fundamental things we take for granted.

2. MVS, Unix or Ultrix.

3. See onion diagrams on page 472.

4. The OS simulates the interface with the user, and thus the picture that the end-users see is not that of hardware, but of the virtual world produced by the OS.

5. Usually by information entered at a terminal in terms of sequences of job-control commands or other commands to perform specific actions such as terminating a series of events etc. (See page 484.)

6. A batch of jobs is automatically run one after the other during the same session.

7. On a micro, both terms mean the same thing! However, on a mini and mainframe, multiprogramming means two or more different programs running at the same time, but multitasking means two or more users making use of the same program at the same time, e.g. ten users may be using the same COBOL compiler.

8. Look at the scheduling diagram on page 487, but think of your own specific example.

9. Interrupts are constantly being executed so that the processor can move between one task and another that requires attention. More important tasks have higher-priority interrupts, peripherals operate extensively using interrupts.

10. Hardware interrupts – e.g. key pressed on keyboard or disk drive not ready etc. Software interrupts – program suspends operation and causes another routine to be run – program times out etc.

11. Important events may be missed if lower-priority things get done instead.

12. Fixed – far less complicated, but less versatile. Variable – more efficient but extremely complex to run. Both systems have many advantages and disadvantages. (See page 492.)

13. Virtual memory makes use of disk space as an effective extension of semiconductor RAM. With efficient memory management, virtual-memory systems can be very effective. (See page 492.)

14. Tasks being continually taken out of and brought back into memory which leads to gross inefficiency.

15. Each user is allocated a small time slice – if it's managed properly the service for each user comes round quickly enough such that they do not notice any gap in processing ability of the computer being used. Multiprogramming may be implemented by allocating each program a separate time slice.

16. More than one processor is needed to share the enormous load, especially with the communication problems for many users accessing the same CPU. Reliability can be increased if more than one main processor is used as a larger amount of redundancy is built in.

17. Buffers and communications controllers or front-end processors.

18. Direct-Memory Access. Releases the processor from managing block-memory transfers.

19. To cope with the horrendous processor-intensive activity that would have been taken up with handling the communication between all the users and the main machine.

20. Distributed – many computers with shared network resources. Centralised – one main machine with many terminals.

21. Some micros now have more power than some of the mainframes used to have in the 1970s and 1980s.

22. Passwords, data encryption. (See page 167.)

23. Thin client technology promises lower maintenance by removing the burden of administering local disk drives. Diskless workstations may act as terminals to powerful servers which undertake most of the processing.

Answers to exercise 24.1

1. (a) A one-dimensional array – there is usually no regard to the order of the data.

   (b) A system in which the end of the list is automatically linked to the beginning of the list by pointers.

   (c) Stack – a list set up and accessed by pointers such that there is a 'top' and a 'bottom' – LIFO, Last In First Out – FIFO, First In Last Out. Stack pointers are used to identify the position of data within the stack.

   (d) Queue – a FIFO stack.

   (e) Array – ordered set of data elements accessed either by row-by-row or column-by-column. Any number of dimensions is possible.

2. This is a project-type question. The pseudocode algorithms in the chapter should provide you with an excellent starting point.

3. This is a project-type question. The pseudocode algorithms in the chapter should provide you with an excellent starting point.

4. These are project-type questions. The pseudocode algorithms in the chapter should provide you with an excellent starting point.

Answers to exercise 25.1

1. A hierarchical data structure based on the idea of a family tree – most data can be expressed in the form of a tree structure.

   (a) A sub-ordinate part of the tree which consists of parents and children.

   (b) A specific data item which may also contain one or more pointers.

   (c) Terminal node – most sub-ordinate node in the tree structure. Child node – one which has a parent node. Parent node – one that has one or more children nodes. Sister node – one in which other nodes have the same parent. Root node – the node at the top of the tree structure.

   (d) Virtually anything can be expressed in this way, but typical examples include parts for a component or pupils in a school.

2. Parent can have a maximum of only two children. Alphabetical names (see page 518).

3. (a) Preorder   a, b, d, h, i, e, j, k, c, f, 1, m, g, n, o.

   (b) Inorder   h, d, i, b, j, e. k, a, l, f, m, c, n, g, o.

   (c) Postorder   h. i, d, j, k, e, b, 1, m, f, n, o, g, c, a.

4. Tree is hierarchical, network is complex. See chapters 28 and 29.

5. (a) See page 524. (b) See page 525.

6. Hierarchical structure making use of pointers (forward, or forward and backward if you need to make sure that you can go up as well as down in the directory).

7. Depends on your chosen high-level language.

8. Depends on your chosen high-level language.

Answers to exercise 26.1

1. (a) The smallest possible element of a file.

   (b) The smallest self-contained subsection of a record.

   (c) A set of fields treated as a single unit of a file, e.g. info. on one particular customer.

   (d) A set of related information, split up into records and fields.

2. (a) Organised with no attention to order of records.

   (b) Organised with regard to some pre-determined order, e.g. alphabetical.

   (c) A record may be accessed without going through all previous records.

   (d) One or more indexes added to a sequentially organised file.

3. (a) Creation of the appropriate structure in memory or on a secondary storage device, ready to accept data.

   (b) Altering records in the file structure, but can also cover addition and deletion of records.

   (c) Combining two files into one, usually in some pre-determined order.

   (d) A special marker that is used to denote the end of a computer file.

4. A number used to point to a specific record within a file in memory or on disk etc.

5. A field by which the record is usually identified, e.g. customer account number.

6. (a) A system of pointers establishing links which enable parts of the file to be accessed quickly.

   (b) An area in memory or on disk used to enable new data to be inserted into an indexed sequential file without completely rewriting the file, i.e. a useful method of updating.

   (c) A set of pointers which enables special paths to be followed through the file data structure.

7. A new master file is produced from a sequentially arranged old master file and a sequentially arranged transaction file. (See page 541.)

8. An address (or pointer) is generated from some key item of data and used to define the address at which the data is stored. If identical addresses are generated then some form of overflow table will be needed (see pages 525 and 548).

Answers to exercise 27.1

1. (a) A copy of a file for purposes of data security in the event of an accident or disaster.

   (b) A file which is accessed by means of a suitable hashing algorithm (see page 525).

   (c) A file structure based on a hierarchical structure such as a binary tree, for example. (See page 549.)

   (d) A file containing temporary data which can be erased after use.

2. A logical record is based on a suitable data structure whereas a physical record is based on a unit of physical storage used on devices such as disk or tape. It's often the case that several logical records fit into a single physical record, and this number represents what's called the blocking factor.

3. Making sure that files are kept up to date, that backup copies are made and general housekeeping etc.

4. Buffers allow for the transfer of larger chunks of data from the secondary storage medium than would normally be the case. Thus processing of the records kept in the buffer is very quick.

5. Pascal code is as follows. (**For simplicity temporary files (i.e. not saved to disk) have been used.**)

```
PROGRAM createfiles(input,output,integer,
                                positive,negative);
VAR integer,positive,negative : FILE OF real;
   item : real;
   count,total : 1..maxint;
(*CREATE FILE OF INTEGERS*)
BEGIN
  write('How many integers will be entered? ');
  readln(total);
  rewrite(integer);    (*Creates integer file*)
  FOR count := 1 TO total DO
    BEGIN
       readln(item);
       integer^ := item;
       put(integer);
    END;
 (*READ FILE OF INTEGERS and CREATE positive and
                                negative files*)
  reset(integer);       (*Reset pointer to
                                beginning*)
  rewrite(positive);    (*Creates positive file*)
  rewrite(negative);
  WHILE NOT EOF(integer) DO
    BEGIN
       read(integer, item); (*Creates negative
                                        file*)
       IF item > 0 THEN
       BEGIN
          positive^ := item;
          put(positive);    (*Puts positive numbers
                                 in pos. file*)
       END
       ELSE
       BEGIN
          negative^ := item;
          put(negative);   (*Puts negative numbers
                                 in neg. file*)
       END
    END;
 (*READ and print out positive and negative*)
    writeln('Here are the positive numbers in the
                            integer file');
```

```
writeln;
reset(positive);
WHILE NOT EOF(positive) DO
  BEGIN
    item := positive^;
    write(item);
    get(positive);
  END;
  writeln('Here are the negative numbers in the
                                integer file');
  writeln;
  reset(negative);
  WHILE NOT EOF(negative) DO
    BEGIN
      item := negative^;
      write(item);
      get(negative);
    END;
END.
```

6. The algorithm required is described in detail on page 540 – it is the same algorithm that reads the sorted master and transaction files to produce a new master file, although the file names will obviously change.

7. Pascal code is as follows. (**For simplicity temporary files (i.e. not saved to disk) have been used.**)

```
PROGRAM Hamburgers(input,output,data);
VAR data : FILE OF integer;
    code, quantity, Hamburger, Cheese_burger,
                      Egg_burger : integer;
    count,total : 1..maxint;
(* CREATE the code and quantity file*)
BEGIN
  write('How many values will be entered? ');
  readln(total);
  rewrite(data);
  FOR count := 1 TO total DO
    BEGIN
      write('Please type in code followed by
    quantity ');
      readln(code,quantity);
      data^ := code;
      put(data);
      data^ := quantity;
      put(data);
    END;
  Hamburger := 0;
  Cheese_burger := 0;
  Egg_burger := 0;
  reset(data);
  WHILE NOT EOF(data) DO
    BEGIN
      read(data,code);
      read(data,quantity);
      CASE code OF
        1 : Hamburger := Hamburger + quantity;
        2 : Cheese_burger := Cheese_burger +
                                    quantity;
        3 : Egg_burger := Egg_burger + quantity;
      END;
    END;
  writeln('Hamburgers', Hamburger);
  writeln('Cheese Burgers', Cheese_burger);
  writeln('Egg Burgers', Egg_burger);
END.
```

8. Pascal code is as follows. (**For simplicity temporary files (i.e. not saved to disk) have been used.**)

```
PROGRAM checkfiles(input,output,fileA,fileB);
VAR fileA,fileB : TEXT;  (*Special text file in
                                    Pascal*)
    word, wordA, wordB : char;
    count, total : 1..maxint;
    flag : boolean;
BEGIN
(*Create first simple text file*);
```

```
write('How many words?');
  readln(total);
  rewrite(fileA);
  FOR count := 1 TO total DO
    BEGIN
      readln(word);
      writeln(fileA,word);(*Write word to text
                                    fileA*)
    END;
(*Create second identical text file*);
  write('type in the data again');
  writeln;
  rewrite(fileB);
  FOR count := 1 TO total DO
    BEGIN
      readln(word);
      writeln(fileB,word);(*Write word to text
                                    fileB*)
    END;
(*Compare both files and flag if in error*);
  RESET(fileA);
  RESET(fileB);
  count := 0;
  flag := FALSE;
  WHILE NOT EOF(fileA) OR NOT EOF(fileB) DO
    BEGIN
      readln(fileA,wordA);(*Read word from fileA*)
      readln(fileB,wordB);(*Read word from fileB*)
      count := count + 1;
      IF wordA <> wordB THEN
      BEGIN
        writeln('Entry',count, 'is not the
                                    same');
        flag := TRUE;
      END;
    END;
  IF flag = FALSE THEN writeln('Both files are
                                identical');
END.
```

Answers to exercise 28.1

1. A database is a purpose built application package, which has an enormous range of facilities as can be seen from page 562. It would be difficult to implement a similar system with unrelated sets of files.

2. A database where all the information is held in a single file. Compare with a relational database.

3. DDL is a Data Description Language; it's a language for describing the relationships between the data. DML is a Data Manipulation Language; it's a language, which is used for manipulations such as updating and deleting data etc. The DBMS is the DataBase Management System; it's a large piece of software, which helps you to design, build and run the database. The data dictionary holds data about data, for example, the structures used for the files in the database.

4. The DBA is the person who has the responsibility for setting up, running and maintaining the database. He or she is not usually the same as the person who simply enters the day-to-day data.

5. The database must be designed in terms of the record-card structure. This involves the field definitions, validation rules, and the layout of the records. If the database is relational then the relations must be set up between the tables (record-card structures), and normalisation may be carried out if necessary (see page 584). Next, typical views of the database might need to be constructed, queries and reports defined, tested, and saved, and all the standard database functions should be tested using dummy data.

6. SQL involves writing code using a query language. QBE means query by example, and often involves the use of pictorial methods to help build up queries. It's easier for inexperienced users.

7. (a) 11yrs to 19yrs for secondary education.

(b) Between £0 and £1000, more allowed if flags are set to indicate some special activity.

8. Make up different views of the database, each having its own security code. Therefore, low security users, for example, would not see the sensitive data displayed on their view of the system.

9. The ability to 'query and alter any erroneous data' that might be stored about you. Firms holding data about you must not misuse the data, hold the data for longer than is necessary or divulge the data to third parties (see page 573).

Answers to exercise 29.1

1. (a) Many to many. (b) One to one. (c) Many to one, but occasional many to many (joint accounts). (d) One to many. (e) Many to many.

2. Possibly arrange on Dewey as shown but network implementation is more versatile – see below.

3. See diagram below

4. It's based on a mathematical relation expressed as a 2D-table, and not on a structure diagram like the hierarchical and network databases.

5. (a) An entry in a cell on a relational table – equivalent to a field in a record.

(b) A tuple or row in a relational table – equivalent to a record in a file.

(c) A 2-D table in a relational database – it's *not* the same as a relationship.

(d) The key (attribute) by which a relational table is best known.

(e) A row from a 2-D relational table.

(f) Altering the relations to conform to the set of Codd's rules.

6. Functional dependency – a one-to-one relationship only exists between the attributes, which are to be functionally or fully dependent. Transitive dependency – if one attribute is functionally dependent on another, which is also functionally dependent on a third, then the first is also functionally dependent on the third.

7. A record in which multiple-field entries are allowed so that the overall length of the record can grow. Eventually the

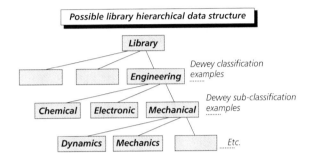

Figure for question 2 (first part)

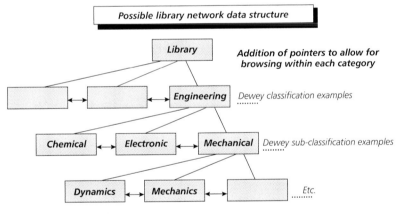

Figure for question 2 (second part)

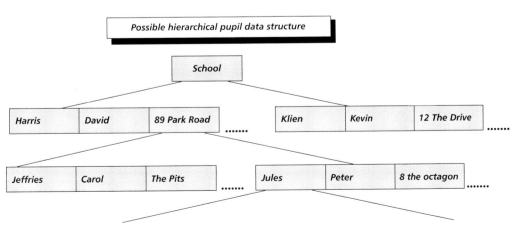

Etc. – Pupils entered as binary tree for fast search on Surname

Figure for question 3

record would not be able to get bigger than (say) the buffer size – also does not conform to the first normal form.

8. Possible arrangement of data in first normal form (i.e. no attribute in either table can have multiple values). Therefore, all records in each table are of the same length.

Student (Student Name, <u>Student ID</u>, Address, Home phone, Company, Company phone)

Subject (<u>Subject code</u>, Subject name, Student ID, Grade, Teacher, Department)

Possible arrangement of data in second normal form. Just using the primary key can uniquely identify (i.e. all attributes in each table.) Note that a composite primary key is needed for Subject grade, as 'Student ID' or 'Subject code' alone could not uniquely identify the grade.

Students (Student Name, <u>Student ID</u>, Address, Home phone, Company)

Company (<u>Company</u>, Company phone)

Subject (<u>Subject code</u>, Subject name, Teacher, Department)

Subject Grade (<u>Student ID</u>, <u>Subject code</u>, Grade)

Third normal form (i.e. no functional dependency on attributes that could *not* act as alternative primary keys).

Student – 'Student name', 'Address' and 'Home phone' could all act as alternatives to the primary key due to strong relationship with student ID. However, 'Company' could *not* be used as a primary key, but as it's the only non-identifying attribute there can't possibly be a relationship between company and another non-identifying attribute.

Company – obviously no problems.

Subject – 'Teacher' and 'Department' are both non-identifying attributes; a teacher uniquely identifies a Department, and therefore a functional dependency exists between these two non-identifying attributes. This will have to be altered to get the data in third normal form. Change to the following.

Subject (<u>Subject code</u>, Subject name, Teacher)

Teacher (<u>Teacher</u>, Department)

Subject grade – again obviously no problems.

The complete set of relations for the database in third normal form is, therefore, given by the following.

Students (Student Name, <u>Student ID</u>, Address, Home phone, Company)

Company (<u>Company</u>, Company phone)

Subject (<u>Subject code</u>, Subject name, Teacher)

Teacher (<u>Teacher</u>, Department)

Subject Grade (<u>Student ID</u>, <u>Subject code</u>, Grade)

Possible problem – Teacher may not be unique – therefore, invent a teacher ID.

9. Declarative query makes use of non-procedural SQL commands, user friendly HCI uses a graphical interface or pre-set queries structured by the DBA.

10. Physical and software security measures must be taken – see page 571.

11. Depends on the database which you have at your school or college.

Answers to exercise 30.1

1. (a) (i) 10 (ii) 40 (iii) 127 (iv) 1339
   (b) (i) 11011 (ii) 10000000 (iii) 1100010101
       (iv) 101011001011111011

2. See page 594 for the method of repeated division. Note: no marks would be awarded in an examination if these sums were worked out any other way.
   (a) 1101 (b) 1111111 (c) 101100101

3. (a) 1101 (b) 11001 (c) 1010001 (d) 10111000 (e) 1010 (f) 101
   (g) 110100

4. (a) 1111 (b) 11110010 (c) 110010 (d) 100011110 (e) 1001
   (f) 1111 (g) 101011

5. (a) 208 (b) C3B2 (c) 13A (d) 131 (e) 8B6F (f) 8C13C9 (g) 17

6. (a) 253 (b) 2554 (c) 60752 (d) 3

7. (a) AB (b) B2 (c) F0 (d) 9954 (e) 16 (f) 55

8. (a) 101100000 (b) 1001111001 (c) 1111111101100000
   (d) 1111101111111111

9. (a) 1110000 (b) 10111101 (c) 1010011100 (d) 111101011001

10. (a) 1201 (b) 173673 (c) 125715 (d) 10000

11. (a) 1D9 (b) 40 (c) DB1 (d) E38

12. Note: convert each number into decimal first.
    (a) 0100/0010 (42decimal)
    (b) 0100/1000/0110 (486 decimal)
    (c) 0010/0110/0011/1001 (2639decimal)

Answers to exercise 30.2

1. (a) 0.01 (b) 0.00001 (c) 1.1 (d) 1111.011 (e) 1101.1001
   (f) 1000011.000011

2. (a) 11111100 (b) 11110011 (c) 10111011 (d) 10000101

3. (a) (i) 1111110110 (ii) 1111001000 (iii) 1001110110
   (b) (i) 1111110111 (ii) 1111001001 (iii) 1001110111

4. (a) 000010000000 (b) 100000110010 (c) 100011000100

5. (a) 11000000.1100 (b) 11101110.0110 (c) 10001110.1101

Answers to exercise 31.1

1. (a) See pages 601 and 605. (b) See page 605. (c) See page 606.

2. (a) 2047 (b) 1 (c) –1 (d) –2048

3. (a) $1 – 1/2^9 = 1 – 0.001953125 = 0.998046875$
   (b) $1/2^9 = 0.001953125$
   (c) 0.001953125
   (d) –0.998046875

4. (a) 0.1000000 0001 (b) 0.1001000 0100
   (c) 1.0100000 0010 (d) 1.0001000 0101
   (e) 0.1000000 1110 (f) 1.0000000 1010

5. *.********/******
   (a) Max positive 0.111111111/011111 i.e. $(1 – 1/2^9)$ x 2^{31}
   (b) Min positive 0.100000000/100000 i.e. $(1/2$ x $2^{-32})$
   (c) Smallest mag neg.1.011111111/100000
       (two's comp of mantissa is 0.100000001)
       i.e. $-(1/2 + 1/2^9)$ x 2^{-32}
   (d) Largest mag neg. 1.000000000/011111 i.e. 1 x (2^{31})

6. See pages 608 and 609.

7. sign
    bit

```
(a)     0 1 1 0 0 0 0    (+48)
      + 1 1 0 0 0        (twos comp of 8)

bit(1) 0 0 1 0 0 0 0    Worked, set bit(1)=1
lost+  1 1 0 0 0        shift right 1 place

bit(1) 0 0 0 0 0 0 0    Worked, set bit(2)=1
lost+  1 1 1 0 0 0      shift right 1 place

       1 1 1 1 0 0 0    Not worked, set
                          bit(3)= 0

Hence answer    1 1 0
```

7. (b)
```
  0  1  1  0  0  1  1   (+51)
+ 1  0  1  0            (twos comp of 6)
─────────────────────
  0  0  0  0  0  1  1   Worked, set bit(1) = 1
+ 1  1  0  1  0         shift right 1 place
─────────────────────
  1  1  0  1  0  1  1   Not worked, set bit(2)= 0
+ 0  0  1  1  0         Restore
─────────────────────
  0  0  0  0  0  1  1
+ 1  1  1  0  1  0      shift right 1 place
─────────────────────
  1  1  1  0  1  1  1   Not worked, set bit(3)= 0
+ 0  0  0  1  1  0      Restore
─────────────────────
  0  0  0  0  0  1  1
+ 1  1  1  1  0  1  0   shift right 1 place
─────────────────────
  1  1  1  1  1  0  1   Not worked, set bit(4)= 0
+ 0  0  0  0  1  1  0   Restore
─────────────────────
  0  0  0  0  0  1  1 . 0  shift right 1 place
+ 1  1  1  1  1  0  1 .
─────────────────────
(1)0  0  0  0  0  0 . 0   Worked, set bit(5) = 1
Lost
```
Hence answer 1 0 0 0 . 1 (i.e. 5116 = 8.5).

Answers to exercise 31.2

1. (a) Any deviation from the theoretically correct value.
   (b) See page 613.
   (c) See page 614.
   (d) $5/7 = 0.714286$ (6 decimal places) $= 0.714$ (3 decimal places).
      Relative error $= (5/7 - 714/1000)/(5/7) = 0.0004$.
   (e) Actual error $= 13.4442 - 13.44 = 0.042$.
      Relative error $= 0.042/13.4442 = 0.00312$ (3 sig fig.)
   (f) 0.0005

2. $0.05/108.3 - 0.05/29.1 = -1.26 \times 10^{-3}$

3. Max absolute error in 31.8 is 0.05, max abs error in 2.16 is 0.005.
   Therefore max abs error in answer will be 0.055.
   Therefore, answer will lie between $33.96 + $ or $- 0.055$,
   i.e. between 33.905 and 34.015.

4. Actual value $3.2 \times 3.2 - 2.8 \times 2.8 = 2.4$ (exactly). m/c works to 2 sig. fig.
   First method: $3.2 \times 3.2 - 2.8 \times 2.8 = 10 - 7.8 = 2.2$.
   rel % error $= (2.2 - 2.4)/2.4 \times 100\% = 8.3\%$
   Second method: $3.2 + 2.8 \times 3.2 - 2.8 = 6 \times 0.4 = 2.4$.
   rel % error $= (2.4 - 2.4)/2.4 \times 100\% = 0\%$. i.e. exact.

Answers to exercise 32.1

1. (a) To change the code into machine-code form that will run on the target machine.
   (b) Compilers, interpreters and assemblers.
   (c) Compiler – translation of a high-level language into machine code with all code being processed at the same time.
      Interpreter – translation of high-level language into machine code just one line at a time – runs in an interactive environment.
      Assembler – changing assembly-language mnemonics into machine code (see chapter 21).

2. (a) Lexical analysis – split up the source code into smaller chunks with individual meaning such as PRINT, for example.
   (b) Syntax analysis – determine whether the string of input code forms valid sentences etc.

   (c) Code generation – necessary for generating the final code on the target machine.

3. Object program – the final code suitable for execution.
   Source program – the program ready to be input to the translation process (usually a text editor).
   Tokens – a representation of part of the source code, which has some individual meaning.
   Parsing – the syntax analysis phase of the translation process.
   Dictionary – a list kept by the compiler of variables etc. in the program.
   Terminal symbols – the final characters that must make up the source code like '1' or 'X' etc.
   Optimisation – carrying out further processing on the code so that it is more efficient in terms of speed of execution or size etc.

4. (a) Identifier (using Pascal).

```
<identifier>::=<letter>|<combination>
<combination>::=<letters><digits>|<digits>
                 <letters>|<combination<letters>
<letters>::=<letter>|<letter><letters>
<digits>::=<digit>|<digit> <digits>
<letter>::=A|B|C|D|E|F|G|H|I|J|K|L|M|N|O|P|Q|R|
                                    S|T|U|V|W|X|Y|Z
<digit>::=0|1|2|3|4|5|6|7|8|9
```

   (b) String (using BASIC)

```
<string>::= ""|"<any character except " >"
```

   (c) Unsigned real number (using Pascal).

```
<unsigned real>::=<decimal number>|<decimal
                 number><exponent>|<digits><exponent>
       <exponent>::= E<digits>|E<sign><digits>
<decimal number>::=<digits>.<digits>
       <digits>::=<digit>|<digit><digits>
          <sign>::= +|-
          <digit>::= 0|1|2|3|4|5|6|7|8|9
```

5.

Using Pascal
(a) Identifier

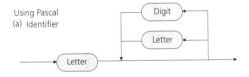

(b) String

(c) Unsigned real number

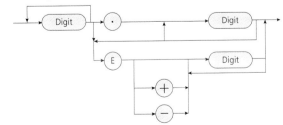

6.

```
<directory entry>::= <surname><title><initials>,
                     <number><street><street/town>
                     <town><telephone no.>
                     |<surname> <title> <initials>,
                     <street><street/town><town>
                     <telephone no.>
                     |<surname> <initials>,
                     <number> <street>
                     <street/town>
                     <town> <telephone no.>
                     |<surname> <initials>, <street>
                     <street/town> <town>
                     <telephone no.>
          <surname>::=<letters>
             <title>::=<DR.>|<REV>                        1
          <initials>::=<group>                            2
             <group>::=<letter>|<letter>,<group>          3
            <street>::=<letters>|<part>,<street>          4
              <part>::=<letters><space>                   5
             <space::=< >                                 6
              <town>::=<letters>                          7
           <letters>::=<letter>|<letters><ietter>         8
      <telephone no.>::=<number>                          9
            <number>::=<digit>i<digit><number>           10
            <letter>::= A|B|C|D|E|F|G|H|I|J|K|L|M|N|
                        O|PQ|R|S|T|U|V|W|X|Y|Z           11
             <digit>::= 0|1|2|3|4|5|6|7|8|9              12
       <street/town>::=.|.<street/town>
                       (Separates street from town)      13
```

Note: position is vitally important (or town and surname definitions could easily be confused).

Note also that some of the very obvious sub-stages, such as a group of single letters becoming a group of multiple letters, have not been shown.

```
  Brown       Y.,      271   Kingsway  Exeter 736442
<letters>     Y.,      271   Kingsway  Exeter 736442
<surname>     Y.,      271   Kingsway  Exeter 736442
<surname> <letter>     271   Kingsway  Exeter 736442
<surname> <group>,     271   Kingsway  Exeter 736442
<surname><initials> 271    Kingsway  Exeter 736442
<surname><initials><number>Kingsway  Exeter 736442
<surname><initials><number><letters> Exeter 736442
<surname><initials><number> <street> Exeter 736442
<surname><initials><number><street><town/street>
                                     Exeter 736442
<surname><initials><number><street><town/street>
                                     <letters> 736442
<surname><initials><number><street><town/street>
                                     <town> 736442
<surname><initials><number><street><town/street>
                                     <town><number>
<surname><initials><number><street><town/street>
                                     <town><telephone no.>
         <Directory entry>
  Zoe       PJ.,         274   Bognor 817325
<letters>   PJ.,         274   Bognor 817325
<surname>   PJ.,         274   Bognor 817325
<surname><letter>.<letter>., 274   Bognor 817325
<surname>    <group>,    274   Bognor 817325
<surname>    <initials>  274   Bognor 817325
<surname>    <initials>  <number>  Bognor 817325
<surname><initials><number><street/town>
                              Bognor 817325
```

7. See pages 621 and 626.

Answers to exercise 32.2

1. (a) P Q * R S – T + .
   (b) M N + 0 P – *.
   (c) A B C D / x + .
   (d) x y z / + u v – /.

2. (a) (A + B) x C.
   (b) X – (Y / Z x S) + T.
   (c) (x + y)*(r – s) * x / t.
   (d) A + B – 3 * (F – G) / H – K * (F – G).

3. (a)

9	placed on stack	9	
3	placed on stack	3 9	
–	sign encountered	6	(9 – 3)
2	placed on stack	2 6	
/	sign encountered	2	Answer 3

(b)

12	placed on stack	12	
9	placed on stack	9 12	
–	sign encountered	3	(12 – 9)
16	placed on stack	16 3	
20	placed on stack	20 16 3	
–	sign encountered	– 4 3	(16 – 20)
*	sign encountered	–12	(3 * –4)
			Answer –12

(c)

11	placed on stack	11	
3	placed on stack	3 11	
2	placed on stack	2 3 11	
↑	sign encountered	9 11	(3 ↑ 2)
+	sign encountered	20	(9 + 11)
7	placed on stack	7 20	
6	placed on stack	6 7 20	
3	placed on stack	3 6 7 20	
/	sign encountered	2 7 20	(6/3)
–	sign encountered	5 20	(7 – 2)
/	sign encountered	4	(20/4)
			Answer 5

Index

Page numbers in bold indicate the most significant reference for that heading.